SOCIOLOGY

ROBERT HAGEDORN

UNIVERSITY OF VICTORIA

SOCIOLOGY

fifth edition

HARCOURT
BRACE
CANADA

Harcourt Brace & Company, Canada

Toronto   Montreal   Fort Worth   New York   Orlando
Philadelphia   San Diego   London   Sydney   Tokyo

Canadian Cataloguing in Publication Data

Main entry under title:
Sociology

5th ed.
Includes bibliographical references and index.
ISBN 0-7747-3284-9

1. Sociology. I. Hagedorn, Robert, 1925-

HM51.S63 1994   301   C93-094260-4

Publisher: Heather McWhinney
Editorial and Marketing Manager: Daniel J. Brooks
Developmental Editor: Dianne Horton
Editorial Assistant: Susan Fisher
Photo Research: Laura Paterson-Pratt
                Joanne Close / Baillie & Holm
Director of Publishing Services: Jean Davies
Editorial Manager: Marcel Chiera
Supervising Editor: Semareh Al-Hillal
Production Editor: Celène S. Adams
Production Manager: Sue-Ann Becker
Manufacturing Co-ordinator: Denise Wake
Copy Editor: John Eerkes
Cover Design: Tracy Walker
Interior Design: John Zehethofer
Typesetting and Assembly: Bookman Typesetting Co.
Printing and Binding: Edwards Brothers Incorporated

Cover Art: *Hats of South America*, by Canadian artist, Irene Klar. Water-
colour. Reproduced with the permission of the artist.

2 3 4 5   98 97 96 95

Preface

This book presents in clear and simple prose an overview of the discipline of sociology using the best data available. Its purpose is to describe how sociologists view the social world, to pose some questions about it, and to explore some of our understandings of it.

There is, however, a major problem in accomplishing this purpose. Sociology, like other physical and social sciences, is faced with growing specialization. As the amount of information in each area of sociology increases, it becomes impossible to know everything about all the areas. Increasingly, there is specialization even within single areas — formal organizations, the family, political sociology, for example. This means that no one person is an expert in "sociology." Some idea of the diversity can be seen in the fact that more than 40 different courses are listed in guides to graduate departments of sociology. Along with these courses and sections there has been a tremendous increase in the number of journals related to subareas.

A simple solution to the problem of specialization is to use specialists to write the various chapters. This is the approach taken here. A question arises as to why such a solution is rarely used in writing introductory sociology textbooks. The answer lies in the problem of presenting writing that is always clear, interesting, and consistent in style. Our solution to this problem was twofold. First, all authors were asked to approach their subareas by using three main theoretical perspectives, which helped to tie the chapters together. Second, each chapter was carefully edited for style, clarity, and interest. Whether we have achieved our goals will be determined by you.

Consistent with these goals are the book's organization and features. The text's nineteen chapters are divided into five units. These units represent very general but distinct sociological categories that unite the individual chapters. The chapters present an overview of the major sociological areas. Many of these areas (for example, deviance and the family) can be studied in more detail in upper-division and graduate courses. In this sense, each chapter represents an introduction to an area of specialization in sociology.

This edition differs from previous editions in three important respects. To begin with, new authors have contributed chapters on population, social inequality, polity, and education. Second, the orientation of the book has changed significantly. Whereas previous editions focused solely on Canadian society, this edition takes a comparative approach. Comparisons are made not only between French Canada and English Canada, but also with the United States and, where possible, Mexico. The North American Free Trade Agreement makes the comparisons timely, but, more than that, comparing a developed and a developing country enables us to have a clearer picture of our own society as well as a better understanding of other societies. This approach takes us back to the beginning of sociology: the early sociologists Max Weber, Emile Durkheim, and Karl Marx employed comparative analysis as the self-evident way of doing sociological research. Third, a new chapter discusses the issue of whether or not sociology is a science and briefly describes current sociological "theories." This chapter was written primarily for the instructor who wishes to pursue these topics.

Features of this book are designed to make learning and remembering easier. They include the use of cross-references between chapters to integrate important ideas and information; pictures to reinforce the written text; boldface type to identify important terms; and boxed readings to illustrate major points. At the end of each chapter you will find a summary of the major points, a glossary that simplifies looking up definitions, and an annotated list of further readings.

The instructor's manual contains a new test bank of objective questions constructed by Dr. Norman R. Okihiro, Mount St. Vincent University, as well as study questions, research projects, and, in many cases, suggestions for films to supplement the text. The test-bank questions are also available on disks for use on microcomputers.

lisher have devoted considerable time to the careful development of this book. We appreciate your recognition of this effort and accomplishment.

We want to hear what you think about *Sociology*, 5th ed. Please take a few minutes to fill in the stamped reply card at the back of the book. Your comments and suggestions will be valuable to us as we prepare new editions and other books.

Acknowledgements

I would like to express my appreciation to the reviewers of the fourth edition: Peter Butler, Dalhousie University; John Fleming, College of New Caledonia; Douglas Keleher, University of Guelph; Murray Knuttila, University of Regina; William Meloff, University of Alberta; Zoran Pejovic, Ryerson Polytechnical Institute; Peter Suschnigg, Laurentian University; and Terry Wotherspoon, University of Saskatchewan. I would also like to offer a special note of gratitude to Leo Driedger, University of Manitoba; Jane Gaskell, University of British Columbia; Murray Knuttila, University of Regina; Kevin McQuillan, University of Western Ontario; and Stephen Richer, Carleton University. Their very detailed comments on the fourth edition and on teaching introductory sociology helped in substantial ways to shape the fifth edition. Finally, I would like to thank all the students and teachers who have provided ideas for improvements in the text, and encourage them to continue letting us know how to improve *Sociology*.

A Note from the Publisher

Thank you for selecting *Sociology*, 5th ed., edited by Robert Hagedorn. The contributors and pub-

CONTRIBUTORS

Reginald W. Bibby
University of Lethbridge

James E. Curtis
University of Waterloo

Leo Driedger
University of Manitoba

Patricia Fitzsimmons-LeCavalier
Carleton University

Jane Gaskell
University of British Columbia

Ellen M. Gee
Simon Fraser University

A.R. Gillis
University of Toronto

John Hagan
University of Toronto

Robert Hagedorn
University of Victoria

R. Alan Hedley
University of Victoria

Alfred A. Hunter
McMaster University

Ronald D. Lambert
University of Waterloo

Guy LeCavalier
Concordia University

Marlene Mackie
University of Calgary

Antonia Maioni
University of Ottawa

Victor W. Marshall
University of Toronto

Pierre Martin
Université de Montréal

Kevin McQuillan
University of Western Ontario

Charles C. Ragin
Northwestern University

Carolyn J. Rosenthal
University of Toronto

Terrence H. White
Brock University

Contents in Brief

Contents

UNIT IV
Social Institutions

UNIT I

The Field of Sociology

The first unit of this book provides an overview of what is generally called theory. Chapter 1 examines the nature of sociology, paying particular attention to current perspectives in sociology and their historical development. The theoretical perspectives of sociology are the lenses through which sociologists see. The answers you get depend on the questions you ask, and the questions you ask depend on the perspective you use. Perspectives determine what you look at and how you see it. Perspectives, therefore, define sociology.

Is a group of people a collection of individuals, or does it have properties of its own? Is society stable, or changing? Do we share basic values, or are we essentially in conflict? The answers to these questions define sociological perspectives, which in turn determine what you will measure and what you will look for, which then determine what you find and what answers you get.

Throughout this book you will read about surveys, participant observation, interviews, rates, averages, standard deviations, correlations, and significant findings. This first unit is concerned with what these terms mean.

Chapter 2 describes how sociologists conduct their research. The approach here is to see the reader as a consumer of information. Divorce rates, crime rates, life expectancy, percentage employed, average income — such statistics are the stuff of life, the content of the daily news. The impact of oil pipelines on the environment, the effect of television violence on children, the legalization of marijuana — our response to such issues determines our future. When presented with research findings, we need to ask several questions. How was this research done? Is it good research? What do all these averages, rates, and percentages mean? Are the findings rational? Are they relevant? Are they true?

The intention in Chapter 2 is to help you evaluate for yourself the vast amounts of information concerning society that are reported in the new media — and in this book.

CHAPTER 1

What Is Sociology?

ROBERT HAGEDORN

Right now you are probably asking yourself, What am I getting into? What is this book about? What is sociology?

To many people, sociology is the most exciting subject on earth, a fresh, lively, coherent, and valuable way of understanding people and the world in which we live. For some people, sociology is so compelling that they invest their entire professional careers in learning it, teaching it, and doing it. People trained in sociology work in a wide variety of jobs in which their knowledge and research influence many decisions that affect our everyday lives.

Sociology is a young science, only about a hundred years old. Like all youngsters, sociology ripples with energy, with promise, with insights, and with the sure sense that what it is doing is *important*.

Sociology is important because it deals with the stuff of everyday life, but in a new way. What we tend to see as almost boringly familiar — the smallest details of human interaction and the largest events on the evening news — take on new meaning and make more sense in light of the basic sociological insight that our behaviour is affected by social forces beyond our control. Not only do we, as individuals, influence society; society also influences us.

This may surprise you. In this country, individuals are important. So is individual effort. People work hard to get what they want — money, power, a better life for their children, a college education, a flashy car, a house of their own. But most of this individual effort takes place in social groups such as businesses, classrooms, and organizations. These social groups affect our behaviour and can significantly determine how successful we are in achieving our goals. Look around, at the students in your class. Most of them had to work hard all through school for good grades. Some have probably worked at a part-time job to help meet expenses. But hard work is only part of the story. Look around again. Are there more women or men? Are there more blacks or whites? How many Native people are in the class? Are these students rich or poor? Social forces influence us and our lives in profound ways, many of which are not at all obvious. For example, the best indicator of who goes to university is not the individual's ability but his or her parents' occupations.

This may seem trivial. Of course society influences us. In many ways the essential insights of sociology, as well as many of its discoveries, seem deceptively like common sense. After all, we are dealing with the stuff of everyday life. Everyone knows about it; it's common sense. Common sense tells you that the more severely you punish people, the less likely they are to repeat the forbidden act. Common sense tells you that reading pornography increases the likelihood of sex crimes. Common sense tells you that capital punishment will reduce crime. Common sense tells you that happy workers are productive workers. Common sense tells you that these statements are obvious. What is not obvious is that each of these statements is false. Far from being trivial, the sociological perspective, with its emphasis on groups and social interaction, increases human knowledge, extends our awareness of ourselves as human beings, and can expand our power over our own destinies.

Each of the following chapters will add to your awareness of the social forces that affect you. In them you will encounter a broad panorama of important social issues — power and the political process, the quality of education, the changing nature of work, life in the city, the growth of large organizations, crime, discrimination, poverty and wealth, and class conflict, to name only a few. More important, you will see how these issues affect your life.

Most sociologists agree on the importance of their work and the basic sociological insight that groups shape behaviour. But many disagree among themselves as to precisely what they study and how they should study it. This is not unusual. Most of the social sciences contain within themselves similar disagreements and debates. In fact, it might be convincingly argued that the social sciences get the spark for many of their most important discoveries and ideas directly from the interaction of conflicting factions within the disciplines themselves. Fortunately for a new student of sociology, most of the internal disagreements within sociology divide the discipline, more or less, into a few basic perspectives.

Beginning to Define Sociology

Before discussing the sociological perspectives and the early theorists whose work underlies these perspectives, we need a definition of sociology. The usual textbook solution is to give a short definition, with a cautionary note that this definition is not really sufficient. Here are some examples. Sociology is: "the scientific study of man's social life" (Horton and Hunt 1972); "the scientific study of human relationships and their consequences" (Caplow 1971); "the scientific study of human society and social behaviour" (Robertson 1981).

Our definition is that **sociology** is the description and explanation of social behaviour, social structures, and social interaction in terms of the social environment (structures) and/or in terms of people's perceptions of the social environment. This definition is longer and more complex than the textbook definitions cited above, but we believe it to be more complete and accurate. In the balance of this chapter, you will study the basic sociological perspectives, the early theorists whose ideas underlie the perspectives, and some examples of how the different perspectives contribute to the sociological fund of knowledge. Then we will return to our definition of sociology. At that time it should make more sense to you and give you a more complete and accurate idea of what sociology is all about.

What is sociology? A brief history of the attempts to answer this question will both help clarify the above definition and set the stage for a further discussion of the problems of defining sociology.

Auguste Comte, 1798–1857

Auguste Comte coined the term "sociology," which first appeared in print in 1838. According to Comte, every branch of human knowledge must pass through three stages of development: the theological, the metaphysical, and the positive or scientific stages. Positive knowledge is based on observation, experiments, and comparison. Comte felt that the comparative method, in which coexisting or consecutive states are compared, was the most appropriate method for this new science. As the last phenomena to fall under invariant natural laws, social phenomena were the ones that would give meaning to all the other sciences. Besides claiming that social phenomena could be studied scientifically, however, Comte did not advance substantively beyond a prophecy of a positivist age.

Early Viewpoints

Shortly after Comte launched the new discipline of sociology, three men writing at roughly the same time tried to answer the question, "What is sociology?" by offering definitions that specified the subject matter of this new discipline as well as the methods to be used in it. The three are Emile Durkheim, Max Weber, and Georg Simmel.

Emile Durkheim, 1858–1917

Emile Durkheim's main concern was to make sociology a separate and unique science. His solution was to define sociology as the scientific study of **social facts** — things that are external to, but constraining upon, the individual.

Most of you would agree with the following statements: North Americans wear clothes in public; rich people are different from poor people; priests behave differently from football players; and large classes are different from small classes. If your reasons or explanations for these statements are: because it is the custom or the law to wear clothes in public; or, income, occupation, and class size make a difference, you are talking about social facts. For Durkheim, the key charac-

Born in France to middle-class Jewish parents, Emile Durkheim spent most of his life as an academic and is considered by many to be the father of modern scientific sociology as well as the originator of the functionalist approach in that field (it had other forerunners in anthropology). He is probably best known for *Suicide* (1897), which is a model of empirical research and statistical/probabilistic reasoning. Durkheim's other major works include his doctoral dissertation, *On the Division of Labor in Society* (1883), *The Rules of Sociological Method* (1895), and *The Elementary Forms of the Religious Life* (1912). One of Durkheim's major goals in life was to establish sociology as a scientific discipline in his country. While he did not succeed during his lifetime (though he held the first professorship in sociology ever to be established in France), his influence on modern Canadian sociology is extensive.

teristics of social facts are that they are *external* to individuals and *coercive* upon them.

These facts that are external to and coercive upon individuals are seen as a separate and distinct variety of phenomena, "and it is to them the term 'social' is to be applied." Because they represent a new order of phenomena that is distinctly social, Durkheim argued bluntly that they could not be explained psychologically: "Consequently, every time that a social phenomenon is directly explained by a psychological phenomenon, we may be sure that the explanation is false" (Durkheim 1964c, originally published in 1895).

Durkheim's classic analysis of suicide is a good example of his view of sociology. He had observed that certain rates of suicide were stable over time and across countries. He found that rates for married persons were lower than rates for divorced persons, and that Catholics had lower rates of suicide than Protestants had. He argued that since the rates were stable — that is, since Protestants everywhere and at different times committed more suicides than Catholics did — one could not explain the rates by relying on the motivations of individual Protestants and Catholics. Durkheim argued that social facts provide the explanation of suicide rates. Specifically, Durkheim argued that the more individuals are integrated into their society, the less likely they are to commit suicide. What explained these rates was the social fact of integration. Both married people and Catholics were more integrated into society than divorced people or Protestants were. Durkheim's study of suicide was a bold attempt to look at a problem that had been seen as uniquely psychological and to treat it instead as uniquely sociological.

Durkheim's crucial suggestion was that **social structure**, that is, social facts external to the individual, can offer an explanation for social behaviour and other social facts. He isolated what he saw as unique to sociology, a science that studies social facts independently of individuals. Society is not only more than the sum of its parts, it is coercive or constraining on the parts.

One example of a social fact is the presidency of your university. The office exists independently of a specific individual, and in a real sense is external to any individual. Further, it is coercive or constraining upon any individual who is elected to the position. Whoever is president is greatly affected by this social fact.

Another example of a social fact is the prestige of a department in a university. Certain sociology departments, such as those at the University of California at Berkeley, the University of Chi-

cago, and Harvard University, consistently have ranked high in prestige. In 1981, 76 percent of the full-time faculty of the department of sociology at Berkeley came from these three universities. Apparently, the prestige of the department from which a person graduates is an important social fact in determining which department will hire that person.

As with all three theorists we shall discuss, it is not the correctness of the particular explanation that is crucial, but rather the general approach and the possibilities it suggests. What is important in Durkheim's case, and therefore worth repeating, is the suggestion that social structure, or social facts, can offer an explanation for social behaviour and other social facts.

Durkheim's approach is evident in a contemporary study by Blau and Schoenherr (1971), who comment:

The formal structure of organizations exhibits regularities of its own. Although organizations are made up of people, of course, and what happens to them is the result of decisions of human beings, regularities are observable in their structure that seem to be independent of the personalities and psychological dispositions of individual members. ... In short ... organizations are not people.

Durkheim's answer to the question What is sociology? was "Sociology is the scientific study of 'social facts'" or, as currently stated, social structures.

Max Weber, 1864–1920

Max Weber (1964) defined sociology as "a science which attempts the interpretive understanding of social action in order thereby to arrive at a causal explanation of its course and effects." "Action" refers to all human behaviour to which an actor attaches **subjective meaning.** For example, a traveller visiting a museum in Spain wanted to find a painting that he thought was in another building. He asked the guard for directions. The guard put his arm out, palm down, and moved his hand up and down. The traveller took this to mean, "go away from me and toward the other building." But as he walked to the other building, the guard moved his hand up and down more violently. When the traveller got to the door, he saw that the other building was completely dark.

Though he suffered from ill health most of his life, the German academic Max Weber exercised a profound influence over European and North American sociology as a consequence of the work he accomplished during productive periods. Often said to have been engaged in a lifelong dialogue with Marx, Weber directed the thrust of many of his major works to the criticism or elaboration of what he regarded as simplistic elements in Marxian thought. He is probably best known for his classic work *The Protestant Ethic and the Spirit of Capitalism* (translated in 1930). But the thesis of this book — and influence of ideology on social structure — is also carried forward in *Ancient Judaism* (translated 1952), *The Religion of China* (translated 1951), and *The Religion of India* (translated 1958). His major work, still incompletely translated into English, is *Wirtschaft und Gesellschaft* (*Economy and Society*, 1922).

He looked back at the guard, who kept moving his hand wildly up and down. Then he remembered that in Spain this motion means, not "Go away" but "Come forward." The guard and the traveller attached different meanings to the symbols being used for communication. The only way to understand this social action would be to know what these subjective meanings were. As Weber (1964) noted:

Action is social in so far as, by virtue of the subjective meaning attached to it by the individual (or individuals), it takes account of the behaviour of others and is thereby oriented in its course.

A **social action** occurs between two individuals when each person takes into account the actions of the other. For Weber, sociology was concerned with the subjective meanings by which people are guided in their social conduct. The purpose of sociology for him, then, was to achieve an objective understanding of how people evaluate, use, create, and destroy their social relationships.

In this view, the individual is the basic unit of analysis. For Weber, sociologists studying a nation should concern themselves with the subjective meaning the nation has for its members, because it is in terms of what the nation means to its members that it is a reality. Contrast this with Durkheim's view that a nation is a reality in and of itself — it is a social fact — and therefore it cannot be explained by its parts, that is, the subjective meanings of individuals.

For Weber, the individual is the sole carrier of meaningful conduct because only the individual can attach subjective meaning or motives to behaviour. The social scientist can impute motives to individuals and thereby go beyond predicting human behaviour to understanding it. This kind of "understanding" is not part of the physical sciences, in which the subjective states of the things investigated are irrelevant. Weber's answer to the question "What is sociology" was, "Sociology is the scientific study of social action," that is, the subjective meanings individuals have.

It is important to note that although both Durkheim and Weber defined sociology by stating what is unique to it, and therefore what separates it from other social sciences, their definitions are diametrically opposed. This opposition is important because it is still with us.

Georg Simmel, 1858–1918

For Georg Simmel, sociology could be defined as the scientific study of "forms-of-sociation." The essence of Simmel's view is that sociology, as distinct from other social sciences, has as its

Simmel accurately described his legacy to sociology: "I know that I shall die without spiritual heirs (and that is good). The estate I leave is like cash distributed among many heirs, each of whom puts his share to use in some trade that is compatible with *his* nature but which can no longer be recognized as coming from that estate."

Consequently, social psychologists cite his work on dyads and triads, symbolic interactionists his methods, and conflict theorists his articles on conflict. Only some network and exchange theorists refer to Simmel's view that sociology is a separate discipline whose subject matter is forms of social interaction.

subject matter the forms of social interaction that occur in all spheres of social life and constitute society.

Simmel argued that the same pattern of interaction occurs with quite different purposes, and the same purposes can result in quite different forms of interaction. Interest, purpose, or a motive represent the content of interaction; the manner or pattern of reciprocity between individuals through which this content attains social actuality is the form. Society is the reciprocal activity of the individuals that comprise it.

For Simmel, the contents of interaction, such as economics, politics, or religion, were already treated by other social sciences. However, the forms or patterns of social relationships were the unique subject matter of sociology and, according to Simmel, could not be reduced to psychological elements. In brief, for Simmel sociology is the study of "forms-of-sociation," or patterns of interaction. Treating them as abstractions, Simmel felt that interaction patterns could be determined in all aspects of social life, for example, in the political, religious, and economic institutions of society. In attempting to establish patterns of interaction, Simmel wrote extensively on such subjects as the stranger, social conflict (which he saw as a "form of association"), city life, superordination and subordination, and the characterization of dyads and triads.

In all these subjects he searched for the form of sociation, those uniformities of human interaction that occur in social groupings of widely varied natures and in conjunction with diverse purposes.

Of the three theorists Simmel is largely forgotten, a fate he foresaw for himself. He is seldom mentioned in introductory texts and is never considered one of the founding fathers of sociology. However, he offered a definition and a distinct subject matter that is the focus of study of current theories.

Durkheim, Weber, and Simmel were explicitly concerned with demonstrating that sociology was a new discipline with a unique subject matter. Each one told us what sociologists study, what sociologists should look at, and the kinds of questions to ask. Each one offered a different answer to the question "What is sociology?" and sociologists today tend to stress one of these definitions. This is the reason for the rather convoluted definition previously given. In this definition, sociology was defined as a science, and it should be noted that all three men saw sociology as a science. However, it is clear that the three theorists did not mean the same thing by "science" and disagreed on the possibility of developing general laws in sociology. In the final chapter of this book, you will find further arguments on the question of whether sociology is a science.

Some Implications of the Three Viewpoints

The three definitions are very general. Substantively, all they have in common is their requirement that sociologists should study social phenomena. "Social," however, can refer to the interaction between two people, two nations, and institutions like the family, as well as the motives and meanings these interactions have for the individuals involved. For example, some of Durkheim's research was concerned with the causes and consequences of the division of labour, suicide, and religion. Weber explored the causes and consequences of authority and power, bureaucracy, and religion. Simmel analyzed the role of the stranger, dyads and triads, and the consequences of urbanization and money. From Comte to the present, this view of sociology as a general science of groups or society has persisted and is reflected in these definitions.

One consequence of this general viewpoint is reflected in the chapters of this book. The authors of each chapter are specialists in their areas, and several of them have joint appointments in other sociology departments and in departments other than sociology. Because sociologists look at any and all social phenomena, this comes as no surprise. In the United States, over 50 specialties in sociology are listed in the guide to graduate schools. There are approximately 40 specialty associations and more than 200 journals that are primarily sociological in content (Turner and Turner 1990:158–159). Further, from 1970 to 1983 more than 40 percent of the professors with sociology degrees in Quebec universities were working in departments other than sociology (Juteau and Maheu 1989:371). Clearly, students with degrees in sociology find work in a variety of areas.

Another very different consequence of this general view of the social world is that it leads to looking at society or a group as a whole. That is, rather than looking at just the family, or religion, or the economy, or the government, sociologists look at how these factors are related to each other and how changes in one effect changes in the other. This has been a distinguishing feature of sociology.

Durkheim, Weber, and Simmel were trying to understand the causes and consequences of changes brought about by the enlightenment and the industrial revolution. The enlightenment was a philosophical movement of the eighteenth century that not only questioned traditional values but also stressed "science" and "reason." The western world's rural, agrarian society was rapidly transformed into an urban industrial society with the onset of the industrial revolution. Part of this upheaval was the creation of this new science called sociology. Given the great changes taking place at this time, it is not surprising that others were also trying to explain the causes and consequences of the enlightenment and the industrial revolution. One such individual, not a sociologist, has had such a profound effect on sociology that he, along with Weber and Durkheim, is frequently referred to as one of the founding fathers of sociology. The man is Karl Marx.

Karl Marx, 1818–1883

Karl Marx stands alone among the theorists we have considered, because of his impact on the world. He wrote many books, articles, and speeches; his theories changed over time; he was both a scientist and a revolutionary. A man of his stature becomes all things to all people. He called himself a philosopher, but some members of every social science claim him as one of their own.

One of the main difficulties in clearly summarizing Marx is that he not only wanted a science of society, but he also wanted to change society. Therefore, his theory of society is also a revolutionary program. It is mainly since the 1960s that sociologists have openly paid their debt to Marx. For a long time, particularly in North America, his work was largely ignored and avoided for political reasons. For these same reasons some members of every social science disclaim him, sometimes bitterly. But no one ignores him.

Essentially, Marx argued, everything that happens in society is caused by economic relationships. Capitalist society is divided into two basic economic classes, each having interests that are fundamentally antagonistic. The class that owns the wealth is the *bourgeoisie,* and the class that produces it is the *proletariat,* or working class. The masses of workers are exploited by a small, privileged elite who manage to control most of the wealth without actually producing it themselves. Society, therefore, consists of classes of people

Born and educated in Germany, Marx went to England after the failure of the 1848 socialist revolution and spent the remainder of his life there, much of it pursuing his studies in the British Museum. He collaborated with Friedrich Engels in writing *The Communist Manifesto* in 1848. The writing of his major work, *Das Kapital*, stretched over the years 1867 to 1894; Engels edited and completed the last two volumes after Marx's death. With V.I. Lenin, Marx is generally considered the father of modern communism.

with unequal power. The inequality of power is the result of the differences in their relationships to the means of production, such as land and factories. The antagonism between these classes is **class conflict**. Periodically, the exploited class revolts and in turn becomes the exploiting class. As Marx put it, "The history of all hitherto existing society is the history of the class struggle" (Feuer 1959).

Marx saw revolution as usually necessary for social change, since the "haves" will not voluntarily give up their power. In capitalist societies the haves are the bourgeoisie, the people who own the land and the factories, and therefore the people who employ labourers in exchange for wages. The "have-nots" are the proletarians or working class, who, because they do not own the means of production, are forced to sell their labour in order to survive. In this stage, the working class revolts against the bourgeoisie and socializes the means of production. In other words, through the revolution, the workers become the owners of the means of production. Since classes are based on ownership of the means of production, and since, after the revolution, the workers own the means, the result theoretically is a classless society.

Marx also saw the economic system as a major force in determining the other elements that make up the *superstructure* of society. Examples of such elements are law, politics, religion, art, and philosophy. The elements of the superstructure are also to be understood in their relationship to the means of production. However, once developed, the elements can play an independent role and can affect each other. For example, Marx referred to religion as "the opium of the people," because religion urged workers to forgo rewards in this life and strive to build up rewards in an afterlife. Religion, therefore, justifies the current economic system (Bottomore 1964).

Marxist concepts that have influenced present-day sociology include the following.

1. Society is constantly changing, and change is inevitable (in contrast to the view that society is stable).
2. Social change is a result of conflict among parts of the social system. Specifically, conflict is an attempt by subordinate classes to change the balance of power in order to gain a greater share of the benefits of the means of production.
3. Economic structures are important in determining other structures in society, as well as in determining an individual's economic standing, life chances, values, and behaviour.
4. The interrelations among the parts of a superstructure must be considered. Any one part, to be understood, must be seen in relation to the others, especially economic institutions.

Furthermore, as an analyst of the class content of historical movements, Marx is unique. He is one of the major contributors to the study of revolutions. It is remarkable that so few sociologists have concerned themselves with the study of revolutions, in light of the importance of revolutions both throughout history and today. In more general terms, Marx has contributed to our understanding of conflict and power as major elements of society.

Four Current Perspectives

Theoretical perspectives are more than attempts to define the subject of sociology. In a sense, a perspective is a pair of glasses for viewing a part of the world. The world is not just there, but is seen and interpreted through the perspective used. A high rate of suicide, for example, can be considered the result of rainy weather or a chemical imbalance, a product of capitalist society, the result of an individual's lack of integration into society, or the result of larger numbers of people defining their situation as hopeless. Each perspective, by stating what sociology is, is also suggesting what questions to ask, what type of independent variable will be used, and what type of explanation is acceptable.

Attempts to classify all of the research done by sociologists into a few major perspectives are somewhat misleading. In their attempts to explain the social world, sociologists freely use their imagination to find explanations for the problems that interest them. However, most sociological research can be realistically classified under a few perspectives that can be traced back to the four theorists previously discussed. At the most general level, sociological work can be classified either as structural, or macro, sociology or as social psychological, or micro, sociology. In order to know which of the two approaches is being used, one needs to look at the explanation offered or what is seen as the cause, that is, the independent variable (see the boxed insert on page 12).

Macrosociology

Generally, **macrosociology** refers to a set of factors, characteristics, dimensions, or variables that exist in society independently of individuals and that are believed to constrain them to behave and think in particular ways. That is, it is assumed that individuals experiencing the same "structure" will behave in the same way and that certain parts of the structure affect other parts.

This approach is not unique to sociology. Structural statements are used often by people in their everyday lives. Young people who contend that you should never trust anyone over 30 are assuming that regardless of individual characteristics (such as personality or conviction), there is something about passing this age that constrains people to behave in a certain way. In fact, a structural argument may be used to support this lack of trust. By age 30, most people are well integrated into society. They are out of school and have been working in an occupation for a few years. Most are married, are in or are supporting a family, and have accumulated some material goods. In short, they are closely tied to the established society and have something to lose by criticizing it or changing it. They are, moreover, entrenched in a web of relationships that further constrain them to behave in respectable and predictable ways.

This example was a statement frequently heard from the baby boomers in the 1960s. Two of these baby boomers were elected president and vice-president of the United States in 1992. A recurrent theme in the election was change, energy, and the end of leaders who had served in World War II. All of these comments reflect the notion that people living through different social conditions think differently. This is a structural explanation.

Another illustration of a structural statement is found in the question, "What do you do?" Literally, this is a ridiculous question (people brush their teeth, dress themselves, go to movies, take showers, sleep), but nobody understands it literally. The question asks about a person's occupation; and the person asking it is imputing to occupation a dominant influence on lifestyle. When we find out a person's occupation, we adjust our behaviour accordingly. We are not likely to tell "dirty" jokes to a priest, and we may feel uneasy in the presence of a powerful figure like a queen or a prime minister.

Macrosociology may be used in two rather distinct ways that can be stated as basic sociological assumptions. The first assumption is that *a specific structure of society determines its other structural characteristics*. For example, Karl Marx was using

Independent and Dependent Variables

To better understand the four theorists — Marx, Durkheim, Weber, and Simmel — as well as current sociological perspectives, it is convenient to introduce the terms *independent variable* and *dependent variable*.

A **variable** is a measurable dimension of a concept that can take on two or more values; for example, sex, education, and income are commonly used variables. Two types of variables — independent and dependent — are important. The nature of the independent variable indicates which sociological perspective is being used.

A *dependent variable* is the phenomenon you are trying to explain or the question you are seeking to answer. For example, if you ask "What causes alcoholism?" alcoholism is the dependent variable. An *independent variable* is the variable that you think explains or causes the differences in the dependent variable. You can think of the independent variable as the cause and the dependent variable as the effect. Or, you can think that what happens to the dependent variable *depends* on changes in the independent variable.

In order to know what sociological perspective is being used, it is necessary to know what the independent variable is, since in many instances the dependent variable is the same. This is demonstrated in the writings of Durkheim, Marx, and Weber. They were all concerned with explaining the same dependent variable: the changes in society and the changing relation of individuals to society.

Durkheim argued that the independent variable — the cause of these changes — was the division of labour.

The occupational specialization that occurred during industrialization resulted in a new type of social cohesion. For Marx, the independent variable was the relationship of individuals to the means of production. In capitalist societies, this would result in the development of two classes and, eventually, in class conflict. The means of production is seen as affecting the relation of the individual to society, the dependent variable.

Weber suggested that the values people have, especially about authority, are independent variables. He suggested, for example, that religious values could affect the type of economic system found in a society. Here he treated religious values as an independent variable and the economic system as the dependent variable. Marx, on the other hand, considered economics — the relationship of individuals to the means of production — as the independent variable and religion as the dependent variable. Durkheim, to simplify, explained rates of suicide, the dependent variable, by the degree of social integration of certain categories of people — for example, married, divorced, or single. Simmel, however, specified only the dependent variable; that is, sociology is the study of patterns of interaction.

What is crucial is that sociology can be defined by the independent variable, by the dependent variable, or by both. The importance of these distinctions can be seen when one asks how sociology is different from other social sciences. Using Simmel's definition, the only problem lies in distinguishing sociology from social psychology.

Using Durkheim's definition, by considering both independent and dependent variables, sociology seems to be different from all other social sciences. If one considers only the independent variable — that is, the explanation must be a "social fact" but the independent variable could be interaction or individual behaviour — sociology is very similar to social anthropology. From a Marxist view, there is little or no difference between sociology and other Marxist analyses of social phenomena. In fact, it has been argued from this view that sociology is not a separate discipline. Further, it is likely that Marxist sociologists have more in common with other Marxist social scientists than they do with non-Marxist sociologists.

Although Marx, Simmel, Weber, and Durkheim saw themselves as "scientists," they meant very different things by the term. On the topic of science, they posed a number of important questions: Can general laws of social behaviour and society be established? Can the general methods of the natural sciences be used to study social behaviour and social structure? If so, are these methods sufficient? Can and should scientists use their knowledge for the betterment of humanity? Is science value-free? These questions are still with us, and sociologists are still divided in their answers. They will be discussed in detail in the last chapter of this book. For now, we assume that sociology is a science and that objective data can be gathered to answer some of the important questions that concern sociologists.

a structural approach when he suggested that capitalist countries are likely to experience one economic crisis after another. Capitalist countries, he argued, are characterized by the profit motive, and as a result, workers receive only a subsistence wage. Profits are plowed back into the corporation and production increases rapidly. But workers, he argued, are not paid enough to buy the product. This situation leads to an economic crisis like financial depression.

The second assumption is that *social structures constrain individual behaviour*. People from cities, for example, behave differently from those in rural areas; and individuals in certain occupations, like physicians or lawyers, are likely to wield greater personal power than are postal carriers or bus drivers. Occupation is often cited by sociologists as an important determinant of behaviour. In its extreme form, this view may be summed up in statements such as "The office makes the person" and "Bank presidents are conservative." Another example of a structural or macrosociological approach is the study of the effects of technology on societies and their institutions, such as religion and the family. Also, population characteristics such as population size and density, family size, fertility rates, death rates, and migration patterns are macro variables. By combining the last two examples of macro variables, one can make such statements as "People in highly industrialized countries have lower fertility rates than do people in less industrialized countries."

Among the macrosociological approaches, and more specific than the above examples, are the structural-functional, or consensus, perspective and the conflict perspective. These two perspectives have dominated sociological thinking at the macro level.

The Consensus, or Structural-Functional, Perspective. Certain assumptions are common to most sociologists who work from the **consensus perspective**.

1. A society or group is a system of integrated parts.
2. Social systems tend to be relatively stable and persistent, and change is usually gradual.
3. A society or group cannot survive unless its members share at least some common beliefs, norms, and values.
4. Social integration is produced by the consensus of most members of the society on some norms and values.

The consensus, or **structural-functional, perspective** is directly related to Durkheim, and the concept of social system is central to it.

Think of your body as a system. The system has certain needs or requirements to maintain its existence (for example, a certain temperature range). When the system maintains a proper temperature, it is in a state of equilibrium, or balance. When your body gets too hot, the equilibrium is threatened and the system adjusts or adapts by perspiring, which returns it to a state of equilibrium. Perspiring is functional in that it helps the

body adjust. In this example, the concept of system is *integral*. In the consensus perspective, the social system is also seen as being composed of integral parts.

The **social system** can be defined by four characteristics: boundaries; interdependence of parts; needs or requirements; and equilibrium.

A system must have *boundaries*. This means you can identify what parts are in the system and what parts are outside it. An example would be your university: what it owns, the buildings, and the people who are members are parts of the university system. Nonmembers are not part of the system.

The parts of the university system are interrelated, or *interdependent*. What happens to one part in the system affects the other parts. If student membership declines, all parts of the system (the number of faculty, the number of programs, standards, the budget) are affected.

The university system has *needs or requirements* if it is to survive (for example, no students, no university). The university needs students, funds for its programs, and salaries for its teachers and other personnel. And it must have some control over its members to ensure that they perform at an acceptable level.

When the university has adequate funds and adequate numbers of students, faculty, and staff, it is in a state of **equilibrium**. If this equilibrium is threatened (if, for example, the number of students increases very rapidly), then the university system will be obliged to adapt itself to a new set of circumstances. It is in the use of equilibrium that social systems differ from human systems. In the case of the human body, the only change that takes place is a return to the original state. In our example, 37°C is the equilibrium state; if the body is hot, perspiring will cool it to 37°C. Social systems, however, change over time. The university grows, and as it grows, a balance or equilibrium — more money, more faculty, more students — is maintained. To describe this condition, the structural functionalist uses the term **dynamic equilibrium.**

It is the concept of social system that makes this analysis structural. What makes it functionalist is the interpretation of the parts in terms of the system. The parts of a system can be functional, dysfunctional, or nonfunctional. Usually, a functional analysis of structures stresses the functional aspects of a part for the system. A part is **functional** if it helps meet the needs of the system, if it helps contribute to the adjustment of the system. A part of the system that is harmful to the rest of the system is **dysfunctional**. A part that is irrelevant to the system is *nonfunctional*. Gans (1972), for example, in his functional analysis of poverty, concluded that poverty persists when it is functional for the rich and dysfunctional for the poor, and that it will persist as long as the elimination of poverty would create dysfunctions for the rich. In the same way, job discrimination against women is dysfunctional for women, but functional for men and nonfunctional for the retired.

In a functional analysis the system is seen as being in a state of equilibrium, or balance, when the needs of the system are being met. But the social systems that structural functionalism analyzes are made up of individuals. For the system to be integrated and stable, the assumption is usually made that the individuals making up the system are committed to the general values of the system. In other words, the structural functionalist assumes that societies have value systems that are shared by their members. If most of the people in a society did not agree on the values of that society, the society would fall apart. In the structural-functional perspective, consensus on the major values, such as laws, is considered a requirement of a social system.

Thus, the structural-functional perspective, as a consensus perspective, stresses order and stability in a society. Institutions like the family, education, and religion are analyzed according to the role they play in maintaining society's stability. Education, for example, teaches the basic values and skills necessary in an industrial society and helps people fit into the appropriate societal positions. As you will see in Chapter 15, the educational system accomplishes this by sorting people on the basis of their achievements and their ability.

In this way individuals are matched with various positions or jobs, and society gets the doctors, lawyers, teachers, machinists, and engineers it needs. Not everyone can be a doctor, and the educational system identifies those who can and want to be, as well as those who can't and don't have the desire. The general view is, therefore, that modern education serves positive functions for society. The maintenance of social order is one outcome of education. Other social institutions and their functions include the economic system, which operates to produce and distribute goods; the family, which performs the functions of early socialization, sexual regulation and satisfaction, and child-rearing; and the political system, which organizes and legitimates power.

The Conflict Perspective. The **conflict perspective** is macrosociological because it assumes that social structure affects human behaviour. But where structural functionalism emphasizes integration, shared values, and social stability, the conflict perspective stresses conflict, power differences, and social change. While conflict theorists do not necessarily follow Marx's class-conflict assumptions, they do follow his general orientation.

The basic elements (adapted from Dahrendorf 1959) of the conflict perspective are as follows:

1. Societies are always changing.
2. Conflict and *dissensus* (lack of general agreement) are always present in every social system.
3. There are elements or parts of every social system that contribute to change.
4. Coercion is always present in society; that is, in every society some people have more power than others.

In this perspective, society is seen as ever-changing, as a precarious balance of groups trying to maintain or improve their power positions. Structural functionalists tend to view institutions and groups as integrated and complementary. Conflict theorists, by contrast, suggest that such groups usually work at cross-purposes, that the goals of one group are frequently at odds with the goals of another. Conflict is seen as pervasive, with each group attempting to improve or maintain its position. These continuous power struggles between groups result in a constantly changing society. What stability there is occurs during (usually brief) periods in which there is domination by one group or a balance of power between groups.

Another characteristic of the conflict perspective is that it tends to view values, ideas, and morality as rationalizations for existing power groups. The basic causes of change are thus to be found not in the values of individuals but in the structure of society. Similarly, power is seen not as a result of individual characteristics, but as owing to position in society. The prime minister, for example, has power because of the nature of the office, not because of any individual characteristics. Others are seen as having power because they control resources, such as money or the means of production. This view also stresses that social facts are part of society and are external to and constraining upon the individual.

A conflict theorist studying education would likely view modern mass education in the following manner. First, it teaches the values and skills of the dominant groups in society in the hope that their values will be accepted and that they themselves will not be challenged. Second, it selects individuals so that the power structure of society will be maintained. As was pointed out at the beginning of this chapter, the best predictor of who goes to university is not the individual's ability but the parents' occupations, suggesting that to a certain extent higher education perpetuates the status structure.

As a general perspective, the conflict model stresses that power and scarce resources are distributed unequally in social systems. Consequently, some groups benefit at the expense of other groups. This in turn leads to conflict and struggles over the distribution of scarce resources and rewards, which results in change being ever-present in social systems.

In summary, macrosociologists assume the existence of variables that are independent of individuals but that constrain or affect the behaviour of individuals. If a variable ignores the particular individuals and/or extends beyond the life of any one individual, for example to parliament or university, it is a macro, or structural, variable. A basic concern of the conflict perspective is social change; from the consensus, or structural-functional, viewpoint the major concern is with social order. If social change is the focus of study, sociologists tend to stress the tensions, strains, and conflicts in society that produce change. If social order is the focus of study, sociologists generally stress those factors that integrate and stabilize a society or group. Durkheim, for example, saw the increase in the division of labour as a new source of social cohesion, whereas Marx saw the increase in the division of labour as increasing alienation from work and creating strain and conflict in society.

Regardless of the differences between some macro perspectives, common to all macro perspectives are the following assumptions:

1. Humans are organized into social systems.
2. Human behaviour and society cannot be understood without attention to the properties of social systems.
3. Social change, deviance, and other social processes develop in the context of relationships among parts in systems.

Microsociology

The basic assumption of **microsociology** is that the explanations of social life are to be found at the individual level and/or in social interaction. Like macrosociology, microsociology has two main subperspectives: symbolic interaction and social-exchange theory. To introduce these two perspectives, to clarify the distinction between macro- and microsociology, and to see how the current perspectives are related to the past, let us return to Weber and Simmel and the conflict perspective.

Weber insisted that conflict is an integral part of social life. However, the objective discrepancies in power and income will not necessarily lead to conflict. It is the way that people define a situation, rather than the objective features of the situation, that must be the focus of analysis, because that will likely determine whether or not conflict occurs. This is the focus of symbolic interaction.

For Simmel, social conflict is a pattern of interaction that is inherent in social life. Simmel gave what is considered a classical analysis of the forms of conflict. His focus on patterns of interaction between individuals, between individuals and groups, and between groups is related to exchange theory. For both Simmel and exchange theorists, the basic unit of analysis is not the individual, but the interaction patterns between individuals.

Symbolic-Interaction Perspective. Suppose you and a friend are walking down a garden path, turn a corner, and suddenly see a large snake on the path. You say, "Hey, that snake will be a great addition to my dance act," while your friend responds, "Get back! It may bite." While you both agree that this is a snake — a fact — your responses to it depend on the meaning you attach to it. A snake may mean good or bad luck, may seem beautiful or ugly, may cause joy or fear. **Symbolic-interaction** theorists maintain that social facts are relevant only to the extent that people attach meaning and significance to them.

Symbolic interaction is the third of the four main contemporary sociological perspectives. Everyday statements that typify symbolic interaction include "I know how she feels, because I have gone through it"; "I understand his depression, because I too have worked on an assembly line"; and "I once lost my job, so I can understand the feelings of those who are forced to retire." That you can know how other people feel in dif-

ferent situations is implicit in such statements as "Anyone who really tries can succeed"; "A good teacher cares about students"; "You're only as old as you feel"; and "He's a good sales rep because he's aggressive." (Contrast this last statement with "He's aggressive because he's a sales rep," which is a structural argument; it implies that there is something about being in sales that makes people aggressive.) These examples express the theme that knowledge of individuals' subjective states is a basic requirement for understanding their acts.

A large percentage of sociological research on delinquency, attitudes, company morale, job satisfaction, and social values stems from Weber's notion of social action. (Recall the story about the tourist in Spain.) Herbert Blumer (1962) has explained symbolic interaction in terms that are

Basic Assumptions of the Symbolic-Interaction Perspective

Assumption 1. People live in a symbolic environment as well as a physical environment and can be stimulated to act by symbols as well as by physical stimuli.

Example: Watching a movie or reading a book can bring laughter, tears, anger, or joy. The words used in these media are only symbols, but they have the capacity to provoke reactions in readers or viewers.

Assumption 2. Through symbols, people have the capacity to stimulate others.

Example: Frowns, smiles, body posture, fists, or changes in the tone of voice are stimuli to other people. They express anger, love, or pleasure, and cause a reaction in others.

Assumption 3. Through the communication of symbols, people can learn huge numbers of meanings and values — and hence ways of acting — from other people.

Example: It is unnecessary for each generation to reinvent the

wheel, or to re-establish social order or most patterns of social life, such as families, churches, or schools.

Assumption 4. Through the learning of culture and subcultures, people are able to predict each other's behaviour most of the time and gauge their own behaviour to the predicted behaviour of others.

Example: When driving a car, drivers expect that other drivers will stop for a red light and proceed on a green. If such behaviour could not be predicted, auto traffic would cause enormous problems for drivers and pedestrians.

Assumption 5. The symbols — and the meanings to which they refer — occur not only in isolated bits, but often in clusters, sometimes large and complex.

Example: None of the symbols of space-age travel would have meaning to our seventeenth-century ancestors or to pre-industrial peoples; only when we understand the entire complex of mod-

ern technical language do any of these symbols make sense.

Assumption 6. Thinking is the process by which possible symbolic solutions and other future courses of action are examined and assessed for their relative advantages and disadvantages in terms of the values of the individual, and by which one of them is chosen for action.

Example: Decisions about which course of study to take or which word to use in conversation, as well as how to act in class, with a date, or at a game, involve the use of symbols.

Source:

Adapted from Arnold M. Rose, "A systematic summary of symbolic interaction theory," in *Human Behaviour and Social Processes: An Interactionist Approach*, Arnold M. Rose, ed. (Boston: Houghton Mifflin, 1962), pp. 3–19. Copyright © 1962 by Houghton Mifflin Company. Used with permission.

directly related to Weber's social action theory. Blumer's ideas may be summarized as follows: Symbolic interaction focuses on people. To the symbolic interactionist, social facts are not things that control, coerce, or constrain people; they are little more than the framework for the real subject of sociology. The symbolic interactionist is not inclined to treat society as a set of real structures distinct from people (Blumer 1962).

Humans are feeling, thinking beings who attach meaning to the situations they are in and behave in accordance with that interpretation. In this perspective, people are considered to be far more than passive recipients of society's norms and values: instead, they are viewed as actively *creating* society. Not only are they capable of learning the norms and values of their society, but they also discover, invent, and initiate new norms and values. They create, interpret, plan, and control their environment. People not only react, but act. Blumer (1962) writes,

The term symbolic interaction refers to, of course, the peculiar and distinctive character of interaction as it takes place between human beings. The peculiarity consists in the fact that human beings interpret or "define" each other's actions instead of merely reacting to each other's actions. Their response is not made directly to the actions of one another but instead is based on the meaning which they attach to such actions. Thus, human interaction is mediated by the use of symbols, by interpretation, or by ascertaining the meaning of one another's actions.

The similarity between Blumer and Weber should be apparent. Both stress individuals' subjective meanings as the fundamental concern of sociology. A basic difference, however, is the symbolic interactionist's emphasis on symbols: on signs, gestures, and, most importantly, language.

A **symbol** is something that stands for something else. A word, for instance, can stand for a thing. Language, gestures, and flags are symbols. The meanings of symbols are arbitrarily determined by the people who create them. For the symbolic interactionist, it is the use of words, or language, that makes human beings unique among all other forms of life. It is our capacity to symbolically represent ourselves, each other, ideas, and objects that makes us human. To a great degree, humans are free from instincts and must rely on symbols to adapt and survive. Human social organization, therefore, is created, maintained, and changed largely because of our capacity to create symbols.

Because humans can agree on the meanings of symbols and share these meanings, they can communicate effectively. Furthermore, because the meanings of symbols are learned through interaction, symbols are necessarily social. Humans communicate and interact by interpreting the symbols that other humans convey. In this process of interaction, they learn to anticipate each other's responses and to adjust to each other. This ability to anticipate the responses of others, or to imagine the viewpoint of others, Mead (1934) calls **role-taking**, or "taking the role of the other." For symbolic interactionists, role-taking is the basic process by which interaction occurs; humans take into account the attitudes, feelings, and subjective intentions of others. In a sense, they can see themselves from the outside, from the viewpoint of another. Role-taking is the process by which they develop self-awareness and a self-concept. This process is examined at length in Chapter 4.

If the symbolic interactionists are correct, the self-awareness of individuals — whether they see themselves as popular or unpopular, good or bad, bright or dull — depends on their perception of how others think about and treat them. Symbolic interactionists also believe that people are generally correct in their judgement of how they are perceived and treated by others. This development of the self through the process of role-taking is a central concept of the interactionist perspective and shows how our very humanness and distinctiveness as individuals are a result of interaction in society. Closely related to this capacity for self-development is the assumption that we are capable of examining and finding symbolic solutions to future problems. In short, humans are capable of planning.

Consider W.I. Thomas's (1928) notion of the "definition of the situation." He claimed that if people "define the situation as real, it is real in its consequences." This again stresses the notion of people as active; it is not the structure that determines this behaviour, but their definition of that structure. By interpreting and defining the situation, an individual is making and remaking the environment. This emphasis on the meanings that the situation and interaction have for the individuals involved has led symbolic interactionists to focus on social behaviour in everyday life, to try to understand how people create and define the situations they experience. For example, street gangs, communes, and work groups have been studied by using this perspective.

A useful way to summarize the symbolic-interaction perspective is to look at the basic assumptions that most symbolic interactionists accept.

1. Humans at birth are capable of response to others, but they are neither social nor anti-social.
2. Humans are acting, thinking, feeling beings who make choices about how to act.
3. Humans respond to others, and their responses to the acts of others depend on the situation in which the act occurs and on the motives that are perceived to underlie the actions.
4. Humans create and use symbols. Human interaction is greatly influenced by the symbols with which people conceptualize the "real world."
5. Through symbolic interaction with others, each human develops a conception of a self, including a conception of a self that is acceptable in the community. It is the self that selects from the continuing activity in the environment to which it will respond.
6. Society is a process in which human beings construct or negotiate social order.

To illustrate these various sociological perspectives, we can ask ourselves how each might be used in studying the students in a classroom. A structural functionalist, focusing on what is common to classrooms, might analyze the functions of tests. A conflict theorist could look at the effects of the power differences between teacher and students. A symbolic interactionist might want to determine how the individual students interpret the class, or the effect of the teacher on the development of the students' self-images.

Social Exchange Perspective. In Ann Landers's advice column, a woman who has been married for eighteen years asks if her husband is a "gem" or "an emotional cripple." She describes her husband as having a violent temper, but he has never hit her. He has had several affairs, never wanted

their children, and reminds her often that "her" kids are "a disappointment." He thinks her family is a "bunch of creeps"; he has never given her a Christmas gift or remembered her birthday; and they have "zero communication." On the "plus side" he is a "good provider," generous with money, neat and clean, well dressed, and "takes wonderful care of the lawn and garden." Most of us would probably agree with Landers that this "appears to be a sad and unrewarding relationship."

It seems worthwhile to ask why this relationship has lasted eighteen years. It is very likely that the wife has remained "stuck" in the relationship because she has had no acceptable alternative: she is not economically self-supporting and there is apparently no one else she loves or who will support her. Given the lack of alternatives, one can interpret the plus side as being more rewarding than the negative side is punishing. Or, as social-exchange theorists might put it, the outcome is positive: the rewards are greater than the cost. The **social-exchange perspective** focuses on the benefits and losses people obtain from and contribute to social interaction. The interaction is considered social in that the satisfaction or dissatisfaction that each person in a dyad receives depends on what both people do. The focus is on the flow of benefits through social interaction.

The past two decades have seen a remarkable increase in the number and complexity of social-exchange theories as well as in empirical research based on these theories (Ekeh 1974; Gergen and Worchel 1980; Emerson 1981). Contributions to these theories come mainly from anthropology, psychology, and sociology. The cross-disciplinary approaches to social exchange and the number of related "theories" make this perspective difficult to describe and at the same time important to understand.

Most social-exchange theorists would subscribe to the following assumptions:

1. People seek others who will satisfy their needs to help them obtain goals. In other words, people act in ways that produce benefits to them.
2. The basic unit of analysis is the form of interaction between individuals or groups. The basic concepts, then, involve social relations, rather than psychological or individual factors.

3. What is exchanged are resources. These resources can be tangible or intangible. Examples of resources commonly studied are love, goods, money, information, and status.
4. All interaction involves costs, which include alternatives forgone.
5. New relations are begun and old ones continue because they are rewarding.
6. People will try to keep their costs equal to or less than their benefits.
7. An important element in any social exchange is power.

Social exchange in sociology and social psychology has been predominantly a microsociological perspective that focuses on two individuals interacting. There have been recent attempts to extend this theory to the macro level, but it is too early to tell how successful this attempt will be.

These four perspectives are based on different sets of assumptions, and so far each has provided a useful way of viewing parts of the social world. Several attempts to combine these perspectives have so far been unsuccessful. This leads to selecting one of them for any particular problem. The three dominant perspectives — structural functionalism, conflict, and symbolic interaction — are recurring themes throughout most of the chapters in this book. Although perspectives do not explain anything, they do indicate the questions that should be asked and, in a general way, the types of variables, macro or micro, that might serve as explanations.

Theories, on the other hand, attempt to answer or explain a particular question. For this reason most research sociologists develop or use theories that are specific to a given field. In some cases, these specific "theories" do not fall under any of the four perspectives. The last chapter of this book deals with this problem. For now, these four perspectives give a unifying theme to all the chapters in this text.

Another unifying theme throughout this book is the use of a comparative approach. Comte suggested that the comparative method was most appropriate for the new discipline of sociology, and it has been a part of sociology since his time. Durkheim, Weber, and Marx used the comparative method. An attempt has been made in this book to make comparisons within Canada, between Quebec and the rest of Canada. Where data are available, comparisons are also made with Mexico and the United States. In light of the 1992 referendum in Canada and recent free-trade negotiations among the three countries, it is especially important to understand the similarities and differences among these political units.

In some of the chapters, a lack of data meant that it was not possible to include Mexico. Partly, this results from some of the characteristics of Mexico; for example, in a country where, in 1982, 42 percent of the population was under 15 years of age, there is not the concern with an aging population that is found in the industrialized nations, which have low fertility rates. Also, Mexico is relatively homogeneous with respect to ethnicity and language, whereas ethnicity is a major area of investigation in Canada, as are race and ethnicity in the United States. The lack of Mexican data affects most of those areas dependent on sociological research. Generally, where we rely on census data, comparisons can be made.

This chapter has presented an overview of the discipline of sociology and a brief introduction to the following chapters. Much has been omitted and simplified. However, these problems are dealt with in more detail in the final chapter. In the final analysis, it is what sociologists do that is the most exciting part of sociology; this "doing" is what you will find in the following chapters.

SUMMARY

1. Durkheim and Weber defined sociology in diametrically opposed ways. For Durkheim, sociology was concerned with social facts, which are external to individuals and which constrain their behaviour. Social behaviour and social facts must themselves be explained by other social facts. Weber, on the other hand, believed that what was uniquely sociological was the human ability to understand the subjective states of individuals. The subject of sociology is the individual's subjective meanings, motives, or definitions of the situation.
2. Simmel defined sociology as the scientific study of forms or patterns of interaction usually behavioural patterns.
3. Marx did not define sociology, but his influence has been direct and profound. For Marx,

society is seen largely in terms of the relationships people have to the means of production and the class conflict that results. Change and conflict, in his view, are fundamental characteristics of society.

4. The four major current perspectives are closely related to these four classical thinkers: consensus theory or structural functionalism is traced to Durkheim; conflict theory stems from Marx; symbolic interaction is clearly related to Weber; and social exchange is similar to Simmel's forms of association.

5. The consensus perspective or structural functionalism, stresses order and stability in society. This perspective emphasizes that a society cannot survive unless its members share some common values, attitudes, and perceptions; that each part of the society contributes to the whole; that the various parts are integrated with each other; and that this interdependence keeps societies relatively stable.

6. The conflict perspective emphasizes that societies are always changing, that conflict and dissensus are always present in society, that parts of every society contribute to change, and that coercion is always present in society because some people have more power than others.

7. Symbolic interaction focuses on people and how they create, use, and communicate with symbols, especially language.

8. Exchange theory focuses on the benefits and cost people obtain in interaction with each other. Power is an important part of exchange relationships.

GLOSSARY

Class conflict. Antagonism between social classes, especially between the class that owns the means of production and the classes that do not.
Conflict perspective. A macrosociological view emphasizing that conflict, power, and change are permanent features of society.
Consensus perspective. A macrosociological perspective that stresses the integration of society through shared values and norms.
Dynamic equilibrium. Parsons's term for the orderly change that constantly occurs among the interrelated parts of a social system.

Dysfunctional. Adjective applied to parts of a social system that disrupt or are harmful to the system.
Equilibrium. In consensus theory, or structural functionalism, the overall balance that exists among the elements in a system.
Functional. Adjective applied to parts of a social system that contribute to the overall stability of the system.
Macrosociology. Study of large-scale structures and processes of society.
Microsociology. Study of small-scale structures and processes of society.
Role-taking. Process of imaginatively putting yourself in the role of another and seeing the world from that person's perspective.
Social action. Occurs between two individuals when each person takes into account the other's actions.
Social-exchange perspective. Set of propositions that relates people's interactions to the level of satisfying outcomes they experience and that specifies the consequences of these outcomes.
Social facts. Durkheim's term to indicate things that are external to, and constraining upon, the individual.
Social structure. Factors that are persistent over time, are external to the individual, and are assumed to influence behaviour and thought.
Social system. Within the consensus, or structural-functionalist, perspective, a series of interrelated parts in a state of equilibrium, with each part contributing to the maintenance of other parts.
Sociology. The description and explanation of social behaviour, social structures, and social interaction in terms of these social structures, and/or in terms of people's perceptions of the social environment.
Structural-functional perspective. A perspective that stresses what parts of the system do for the system. This perspective is usually classified with the consensus perspective.
Subjective meaning. The meaning an individual attaches to a situation, action, or object. For example, a dog may be seen as a source of food, a predator, or a person's best friend.
Symbol. Anything that can stand for or represent something else, such as a word or gesture.
Symbolic interaction. A microsociological perspective that emphasizes the interactions between people that take place through symbols, especially language.
Variable. Measurable characteristic that can take on two or more values (such as age, gender, or violent behaviour).

FURTHER READING

Churchill, Lindsey. "Ethnomethodology and measurement." *Social Forces* 50(1971):182–91. A clear statement of the basic assumptions of this perspective.
Gouldner, Alvin W. "The sociologist as partisan: Sociology and the welfare state." *American Sociologist*

3(1963):103–17. One of the best statements on why science cannot be value-free.

Hagedorn, Robert, and Sanford Labovitz. *Sociological Orientations*. New York: John Wiley, 1973. A slightly different view of the major perspectives or schools of sociological thought.

Juteau, Danielle, and Louise Maheu. "Sociology and Sociologist in Francophone Quebec: Science and Politics." *The Canadian Review of Sociology and Anthropology* 26(1989):363–93. This issue is devoted to sociology in Quebec. See also Raymond Bretan's article in the same issue pp. 557–70.

Merton, Robert K. *Social Theory and Social Structure*. Glencoe, IL: Free Press, 1968. A clear statement of what functionalism is and is not; see especially pp. 19–84.

Mills, C. Wright. *The Sociological Imagination*. New York: Oxford University Press, 1967. A classic introduction to sociology from the conflict perspective.

Ritzer, George. *Sociology: Multiple Paradigm Science*. Boston: Allyn and Bacon, 1975. A more advanced discussion of theories in sociology, which is compatible with this chapter.

Rudner, Richard S. *Philosophy of Social Science*. Englewood Cliffs, NJ: Prentice-Hall, 1966. Chapter 4 is a clear statement on why social science can be value-free.

Stryker, Sheldon. *Symbolic Interactions*. Menlo Park, CA: Benjamin/Cummings, 1980. Excellent statement of this approach and the differences among symbolic interactionists.

Turner, Johnathan H. *The Emergence of Social Theory*. Second edition. Chicago: The Dorsey Press, 1989. A clear and thorough analysis of early theories on which the current theories are built.

CHAPTER 2

Social Research

ROBERT HAGEDORN
R. ALAN HEDLEY

One way to answer the question "What is sociology?" is to look at what sociologists *do*. They do research, which can be the most exciting and interesting part of their job. Research allows sociologists to answer questions they have posed and to discover new things about the social world. An understanding of the process of social research is necessary if you plan to become a professional researcher, and extremely useful even if you do not. You are constantly being called upon to evaluate the results of research. Reading your daily newspaper, buying a car, writing or evaluating reports at work, even buying a bottle of vitamins: all these things require that you reach some interpretation or conclusion. A knowledgeable understanding of how facts are arrived at — that is, of the research process — is essential to a sound interpretation of what they mean.

It is the purpose of this chapter to provide you with enough information to begin to evaluate critically not only the results of scientific research found in the library but also the mass of information with which you are bombarded daily. Academics are not the only ones who do research. Whenever questions are posed, observations made, and conclusions drawn, research is done. In our daily lives, we are continually involved in the research process. The rest of this chapter describes the various stages of social research and some of the obstacles we must avoid in order to arrive at clear answers to the questions we address.

Planning and Doing Research

Robert Burns observed that the best-laid plans of mice and men often go astray. His observation applies with particular force to social research: we should plan and design our research as carefully as possible, but when we come to doing it, we should realize that *inevitably* there will be problems — some we may have expected and some not. There is no such thing as an absolutely perfect piece of research that answers once and for all the particular questions asked. Competing alternative explanations will always be possible for two reasons. First, snags, difficulties, and obstacles are inherent in the research process. Second, even if it were possible to anticipate and thus avoid these snags, it is impossible to design a research project that will produce findings that simultaneously are unambiguous, have general applicability, and pertain directly to the real world.

It is extremely important to realize these inherent limitations at the outset, and they are addressed throughout the chapter. Because of them, every single research result can be accepted only tentatively. We can never know with absolute certainty. However, if we are careful in designing and conducting research and if the same result is repeated on several occasions, we can have confidence in that result.

The research process by its very nature involves uncertainty. We can't get around this, but we can suggest ways to reduce the uncertainty and thus increase our confidence in the results (see Figure 2-1). Think of the research process as an obstacle course and a series of decision points. Researchers have learned a great deal about these obstacles and the kinds of decisions possible. Furthermore, they can estimate the kinds of difficulties you will confront or the uncertainty you will face should you not make or not be able to make the appropriate decision. This is the kind of information you will need when you are assessing research results.

The Research Problem

It is a beautiful Sunday afternoon. You are sitting on a beach in Mexico, taking in the scene. It is easy to distinguish "the locals" from the tourists. Many of the Mexicans have brought picnics with them. You watch more closely as the (mostly) family groups settle in to enjoy themselves. You find yourself making comparisons with similar gatherings at home in Canada. It strikes you that the size of the family groups is much larger here than in Canada. While several generations appear to be represented, it is the children that impress you. They abound everywhere.

You might conclude on the basis of your casual observations that there is something about being Mexican and Canadian that causes this difference. However, before you proceed with this hunch — for at this stage that is all it is — you would first have to find out if the "facts" you observed also occur more generally. (Remember that you have been comparing one isolated beach scene in Mexico with your personal experience in Canada.) Are family units in Mexico actually larger on average than they are in Canada? Are there more children per household? If so, what explains this difference?

Back in Canada, the beautiful Sunday afternoon beach scene returns to you when you are assigned a term project in the research methods course in which you have just registered:

Comparative Research Project

Using Canada as one country and selecting another country of your own choice, identify a dependent variable (something you want to explain) that reveals significant differences between the two countries. Provide two empirical indicators or measures of your

---

FIGURE 2-1   The Stages of Social Research

1. Select the problem.
2. Review previous research on the problem.
3. State the hypothesis (predict what you will find).
4. Construct empirical indicators for all variables in the hypothesis.
5. Set up the research design.
6. Select appropriate sample or population.
7. Decide on data collection method(s).
8. Collect the data.
9. Analyze the data.
10. Interpret the data (write the research report).

---

dependent variable that will allow you to demonstrate these differences.

A **variable** is a factor that can differ or vary from one situation to another or from one individual or group to another. In the example we have been discussing, the variable is "family size." Is there a difference or variation in family size between Canada and Mexico? It is also a **dependent variable** because in this case if there is a difference, we want to explain what accounts for or causes this difference. The variation in this factor depends on or is caused by some other factor(s). The dependent variable is the focal point of a research problem.

How do you find out if there is a difference in family size between Canada and Mexico? Were your impressions on the beach correct? Ideally, in order to answer these questions, you would have to take a count of every household in Canada and Mexico to determine if there is an overall difference. In fact, this is exactly what national censuses do. They enumerate entire populations to obtain information on various key issues. These data are then summarized and made available in published form.

Accordingly, one measure or indicator of family size is the average number of persons per household. **Indicators** are measures of theoretical variables in the same way that a thermometer is a measure of temperature. For any one variable, there are potentially a variety of indicators to measure it. The construction or selection of appropriate indicators of variables is crucial to the research process. The indicators you choose can influence your results dramatically and cause you to draw wrong conclusions. For example, although there are on average 5.3 persons per household in Mexico and only 2.8 in Canada (Kurian 1991:37–38), do all people living in one household necessarily constitute a family? What about family members who are living apart from the household? While "number of persons per household" is a reasonable indicator of family size, it is not perfect.

Another indicator of family size that is readily available is "total fertility rate" (TFR). This is a measure demographers use to estimate "the average number of children a woman will have, assuming that current age-specific birth rates will remain constant throughout her childbearing years" (Population Reference Bureau 1991). For example, according to the *1991 World Population Data Sheet*, a Canadian woman is expected to bear on average 1.7 children during her lifetime, while a Mexican woman will more than double this figure (3.8) (Population Reference Bureau 1991). Although these are very precise measures, they are *projections* based upon *current* age-specific fertility rates. To the extent that the rates change, they become less than perfect indicators of family size.

By now you will begin to appreciate how difficult it is to come up with indicators that truly measure what you want them to measure, and, depending upon what indicator you use, you will produce somewhat different results. Figure 2-2 demonstrates this graphically. The solid circles represent the theoretical variable or concept you are attempting to measure; the broken circles are empirical indicators. In Case 1, the indicator measures only one part or dimension of the variable; in Case 2, the indicator measures part of the variable, but also includes extraneous aspects; and in Case 3, while the indicator includes the variable in question, it is also measuring something else. Case 4 is the ideal. Here the indicator overlaps or corresponds perfectly with the variable it is intended to reflect (so that it is impossible to see the broken circle fitted over the solid circle).

Let's go back to the term project you have been assigned:

Comparative Research Project *(cont'd)*

Conduct a thorough search of the research literature pertaining to your dependent variable. What are the major independent or causal variables that have been found to explain the variation in your dependent variable? Provide a literature review citing at least twenty studies.

In all serious research undertakings, a review of the research literature relevant to the problem is a necessary first step. Because science is a cumulative process, you first want to find out how your research problem relates to other studies in the same area. Because the dependent variable is the focal point of a research problem, it is relatively easy to search the literature on this basis. (For example, most research studies contain reference to the dependent variable[s] in their titles.)

FIGURE 2-2   Achieving Correspondence between Theoretical Variables and Empirical Indicatiors

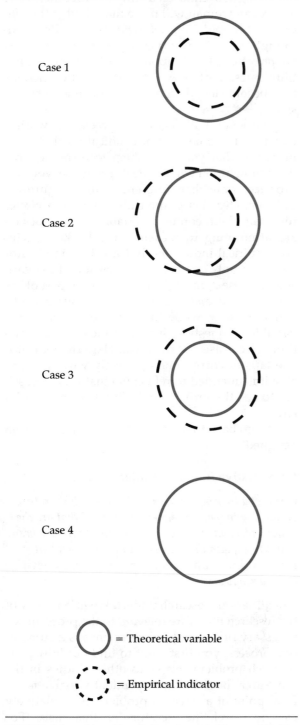

Case 1

Case 2

Case 3

Case 4

◯ = Theoretical variable

◌ = Empirical indicator

SOURCE: Adapted from Hans L. Zetterberg, *On Theory and Verification in Sociology* (Totowa, NJ: Bedminster, 1966), pp. 114–20.

Independent variables, also known as causal or explanatory variables, produce variation in dependent variables. For example, individual values are related to family size; some people are more motivated to have children than others. According to Scanzoni and Scanzoni (1981:505–507), people who believe that children provide social identity, a sense of personal accomplishment, a means for vicarious achievement, and a feeling of power and influence are more likely to have children than those who do not hold these views. Consequently, personal values are one important set of independent variables that explain or account for variations in family size.

While these values are important in the decision of whether to have children, it is unlikely that they account for the difference in family size between Canada and Mexico (unless it could be shown that a greater preponderance of Mexicans hold these values than do Canadians). They explain differences *within* but not *between* the two countries. To address the question of why there are certain differences *between* nations, it is necessary to focus on other variables that distinguish on a national basis.

Religion is one such variable. It is estimated that Roman Catholics constitute almost the entire population in Mexico (93 percent), while in Canada they make up less than half (47 percent) (*The World in Figures* 1987:118, 137). In light of this difference between the two countries, as well as some of the precepts of the Roman Catholic Church regarding birth control, religion could be an important independent variable accounting for at least part of the difference in family size.

Another variable on which there is substantial difference between the two countries is level of economic development (as measured by per capita gross national product [GNP] or the total value of all goods and services produced by the residents of a country). For example, in 1989 the average resident of Mexico produced U.S. $1990, while the average Canadian produced almost ten times that amount (U.S. $19 020) (Population Reference Bureau 1991). Because research has demonstrated that higher levels of economic development are associated with smaller families (see Hedley 1992b:52–55), economic development is also an independent variable that partially explains family size.

We have presented just three independent variables that have been used in the explanation of family size; there are many more (for example, social class, education, government policy, availability of contraception). Some of these are suitable for study *within* countries, while others apply to differences *between* countries. In either case, researchers must examine many independent variables to explain successfully such a complex phenomenon as family size.

Let us return one final time to the term project:

Comparative Research Project *(cont'd)*

Formulate a hypothesis stating how one of the independent variables you have listed is related to your dependent variable.

A **hypothesis** is a prediction of what you expect to find as a result of your research; it is a statement of relationship between one or more independent variables and a dependent variable. In attempting to predict differences between countries, two possible hypotheses have been examined:

1. The greater the proportion of Catholics in a population, the greater will be the number of children per family.
2. The higher the level of national economic development, the fewer will be the number of children per family.

Hypothesis 1 is stating a **direct** or **positive relationship**; that is, a unit change in the independent variable is followed by a unit change in the *same* direction in the dependent variable. This means that *more* Catholics produce *more* children. Alternatively, it also means that *fewer* Catholics produce *fewer* children. (Incidentally, because we have not examined the effect of non-Christian religions on family size, we must limit this hypothesis to predominantly Christian countries.)

Hypothesis 2 is stating an **inverse** or **negative relationship**; that is, a unit change in the independent variable is followed by a unit change in the *opposite* direction in the dependent variable. This means that in countries with *high* levels of economic development, there will be relatively *few* children; conversely, in countries with *low* levels of development, there will be *more* children per family.

To find out whether hypotheses are *good* predictions, we must test them empirically by conducting research. Using Hypothesis 2 as an example, one way to determine how accurate it is would be to rank-order all the world's countries according to their GNP per capita (their level of economic development). (Of all nations for which there are data, Switzerland has the highest per capita GNP [U.S. $32 790] and Mozambique has the lowest [U.S. $80] [*World Bank Atlas 1991*:6–9].) Next to these values we would then insert either the average number of persons per household for each country or the total fertility rate, both of which are indicators of family size. If the indicators of family size range more or less perfectly from low (Switzerland) to high (Mozambique), we will have made a highly accurate hypothesis: it is possible to predict relative family size if the level of economic development is known. The rankings of GNP per capita and total fertility rate are strongly correlated (see the section "Data Analysis" later in this chapter for a further discussion of correlation). On the other hand, if there is very little relation between the two rankings, then we do not have a good hypothesis. The independent variable does not explain variation in the dependent variable.

Figure 2-3 presents in graph form the economic development–family size relationship we have been discussing. The bar chart reveals how all countries in the world (N = 129) are ranked according to GNP per capita. Superimposed on this chart are the total fertility rates for each nation. While there are some anomalies — some countries' fertility rates are either too high or too low for their position in the GNP ranking — generally Figure 2-3 reveals a relatively strong *inverse* relationship between economic development and projected family size. This is indicated by the straight line that runs through the fertility rates. The conclusion to be drawn from Figure 2-3 is that the lower the GNP, the higher the fertility rate; alternatively, the higher the GNP, the lower the fertility rate.

Figure 2-4 summarizes our discussion of the research problem. In the top part of the diagram are the independent and dependent variables. The arrows refer to the direction and type of the expected relationship between these variables; they graphically represent the hypothesis: we expect to find an inverse or negative relationship

FIGURE 2-3   World Nations Ranked by GNP per Capita in Relation to Total Fertility Rates, 1990

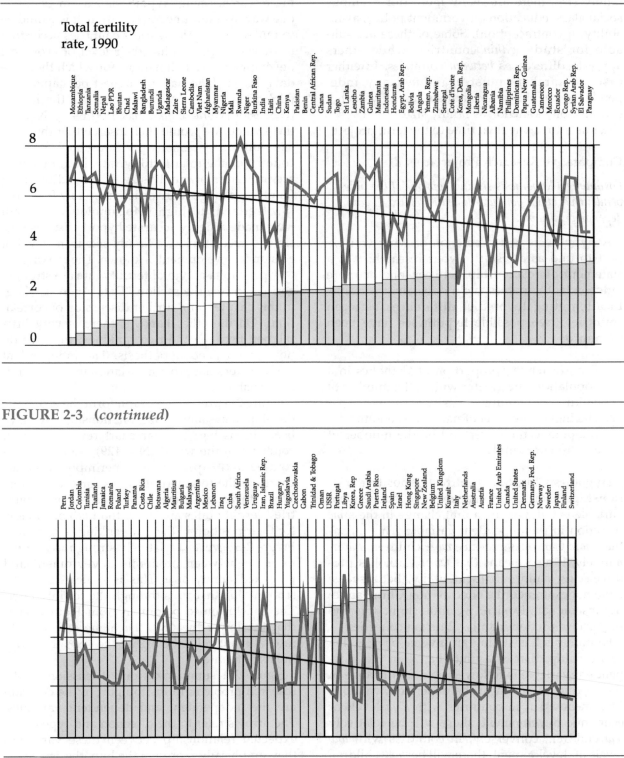

FIGURE 2-3 *(continued)*

SOURCE: World Bank, *World Bank Atlas 1991* (Washington, DC: World Bank, 1991), pp. 22–23.

FIGURE 2-4   The Research Problem: Variables, Indicators, and Hypothesis

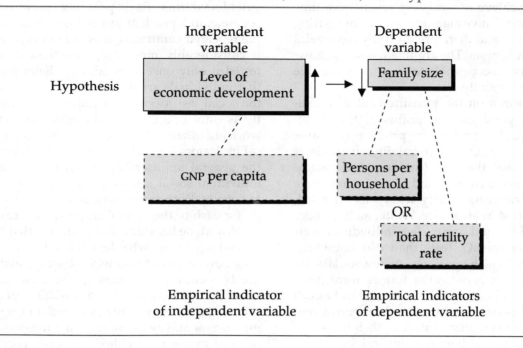

between national economic development and family size. In the lower portion of the diagram are the empirical indicators of both the independent and dependent variables.

The hypothesized relationship between economic development and family size can be tested in a variety of ways. Unfortunately, we may also obtain a variety of answers, depending upon what indicators we use and how we actually do the research. Clearly, if we encounter these kinds of difficulties in systematic, rigorous research, we should certainly be wary of accepting casual observations at face value.

Problems in Measurement

So far, we have indicated some of the difficulties involved in measuring variables and testing hypotheses. We now address this issue directly, because measurement is the weakest part of the research process. A chain is only as strong as its

weakest link; so too are research results only as good as the measurements used to produce them.

Achieving valid results is a major goal of all research. **Validity** is the result of having measured what you intend to measure. This sounds simple enough, but it is one of the most elusive goals in research because we can never be certain that we are indeed measuring what we want. Earlier, for example, we considered the process of constructing empirical indicators of variables. We can never know with absolute certainty whether we have achieved a valid measurement of variables (as illustrated by Case 4 in Figure 2-2), but there are indirect ways of estimating validity and at the same time increasing our confidence in research findings. It is to these strategies we now turn.

Reliability

Reliability is the stability of results over time produced by using the same measuring instrument, or the equivalence of results at one time when more than one investigator uses the same instrument. The argument for reliability is that if we can achieve a consistent result over time or with several investigators, we are measuring what we want and therefore probably have valid empirical indicators. The argument is weak, however, because it is possible to measure a variable reliably but invalidly.

Early research on the measurement of intelligence is a good case in point. Although researchers could consistently produce the same result with their I.Q. tests (reliability), it was later discovered that the tests (the empirical indicators) contained a cultural and class bias and were thus not measuring exactly what was intended, which resulted in invalidity. White, native anglophone, middle- and upper-class individuals averaged higher on I.Q. tests than did nonwhite, non–native-English-speaking, or lower-class individuals — not because the former were more intelligent but because the use of written English (paper and pencil tests) was a more central, and therefore more familiar, feature of their lives.

Consequently, although empirical indicators are routinely evaluated to establish their reliability, and reliability checks constitute an important aspect of the research process, a reliable measure is not necessarily a valid measure. We can, however, be more confident in a consistent result than in one that fluctuates randomly.

Replication

Replication, the systematically repeated measurement of a given relationship, is one of the bywords of science, and it suggests that any single finding by itself is or should be unconvincing. Only with repeated corroboration and confirmation should researchers express confidence in the validity of their findings.

In his classic study, *Suicide* (1964b, originally published in 1897), Emile Durkheim employed two types of replication. His hypothesis was that the more individuals are integrated into their society, the less likely they are to kill themselves. He argued that being married is an indicator of social integration, a bond that links individuals to the larger society. Therefore, married people should have a lower suicide rate than single people.

First, Durkheim tested his hypothesis in all the provinces of his native France for which he could obtain official statistics on the marital status of suicide victims. Each province represented a separate, independent test of his hypothesis, and the repeated confirmation of the hypothesis gave it considerably more credence than if he had tested it only once. Second, Durkheim reasoned that individuals are linked to society through all the social institutions that constitute it. The family is only one social institution; religion and work are others. He constructed separate empirical indicators for each of these institutions to test the general applicability of his hypothesis that individual social integration is inversely related to suicide. With the confirmation of his hypothesis for each of the several empirical indicators he employed, he became more confident that he was indeed measuring what he intended.

By now, many of you will recognize that there are two common themes in the measurement strategies we have discussed: variation and repetition. The key to validity is varied and repeated measurement. The use of several indicators measured by a variety of methods on several occasions should produce a common core of findings in which we can be confident.

Research Design

After a research problem has been selected, previous studies examined, hypotheses formulated, and empirical indicators constructed, it becomes necessary to plan how the research will be undertaken. This is called **research design**, and it is the next stage of social research (see Figure 2-1). We must draw up a deliberate plan or design before doing the actual research in order to eliminate competing alternative explanations for the results we obtain. Research design forces us to anticipate systematically the difficulties we will confront, the decisions we will have to make, and the explanations possible for the results we achieve.

Classical Experimental Design

In science, the ideal type of research design has for many years been the **classical experimental**

"They Rushed Tumultuously to the Cathedral"

What are the dangers of drawing conclusions from limited observations? The following humorous description demonstrates some of the dangers.

I constructed four miniature houses of worship — a Mohammedan mosque, a Hindu temple, a Jewish synagogue, a Christian cathedral — and placed them in a row. I then marked 15 ants with red paint and turned them loose. They made several trips to and fro, glancing in at the places of worship, but not entering.

I then turned loose 15 more painted blue; they acted just as the red ones had done. I now gilded 15 and turned them loose. No change in the result; the 45 traveled back and forth in a hurry persistently and continuously visiting each fane, but never entering. This satisfied me that these ants were without religious prejudices — just what I wished; for under no other conditions would my next and greater experiment be valuable. I now placed a small square of white paper within

the door of each fane; and upon the mosque paper I put a pinch of putty, upon the temple paper a dab of tar, upon the synagogue paper a trifle of turpentine, and upon the cathedral paper a small cube of sugar.

First I liberated the red ants. They examined and rejected the putty, the tar and the turpentine, and then took to the sugar with zeal and apparent sincere conviction. I next liberated the blue ants, and they did exactly as the red ones had done. The gilded ants followed. The preceding results were precisely repeated. This seemed to prove that ants destitute of religious prejudice will always prefer Christianity to any other creed.

However, to make sure, I removed the ants and put putty in the cathedral and sugar in the mosque. I now liberated the ants in a body, and they rushed tumultuously to the cathedral. I was very much touched and gratified, and went back in the room to write down the event; but when I came back the ants had all apostatized and had gone over to the Mohammedan communion.

I saw that I had been too hasty in my conclusions, and naturally felt rebuked and humbled. With diminished confidence I went on with the test to the finish. I placed the sugar first in one house of worship, then in another, till I had tried them all.

With this result: whatever Church I put the sugar in, that was the one the ants straightway joined. This was true beyond a shadow of a doubt, that in religious matters the ant is the opposite of man, for man cares for but one thing: to find the only true Church; whereas the ant hunts for the one with the sugar in it.

Source:

Mark Twain, "On experimental design," reprinted in *Readings in Organizational Behavior and Human Performance*, L.L. Cummings and W.E. Scott, Jr., eds. (Homewood, IL: Irwin and Dorsey, 1969).

---

design. It allows researchers to obtain relatively clear, unequivocal results that are largely attributable to the design's following features:

1. Two equivalent groups are selected. Equivalence is judged in terms of the dependent variable. The most common method for obtaining equivalence is to randomly assign individuals to one or the other group. (Random assignment is explained in the following section, "Sampling.")
2. One group, called the **experimental group**, is subjected to the independent variable. The other group, the **control group**, is treated identically to the experimental group, except it is not subjected to the independent variable.
3. Both the experimental and control groups are measured on the dependent variable twice.

The first measurement (Time 1) occurs *before* the introduction of the independent variable to the experimental group. The second measurement (Time 2) takes place *after* the experimental group has received the effects of the independent variable.

4. The difference between Time 1 and Time 2 for each group is computed (Time 2 minus Time 1). Then any difference in outcome between the experimental and control groups can be attributed directly to the effect of the independent variable. Provided that the groups are equivalent at the outset (which can be demonstrated by the Time 1 measurement) and that they are treated identically in every respect, except for the introduction of the independent variable to the experimental group, any difference in result between the

two groups can only be due to the independent variable.

All of these features of the classical experimental design are illustrated in Figure 2-5. Together they permit researchers to eliminate competing alternative explanations for the results they achieve. Of all research designs employed, it is the strongest with respect to determining causality. Not only can researchers demonstrate that there is a relationship between their independent and dependent variables, the design allows them to state categorically that this relationship is *causal*. This is its most important advantage.

For decades, the classical experimental design has been the norm against which social scientists have judged the adequacy of their research designs. However, it is not perfect. Three problems can arise in generalizing from experimental results. One is that people in an experiment may be *sensitized* and therefore respond differently from people not in the experiment. For example, people who see a violent movie (the independent variable) in an experimental situation are aware that they are participating in an experiment and therefore may respond differently to the dependent variable — for example, aggressive behaviour — from similar people who see the same movie on a Friday night.

The second problem is that in the social sciences experimental subjects are necessarily volunteers and often students. Because of this, they are not representative of the general population. Consequently, the results of the experiment may be quite biased and therefore not generalizable.

The third problem with the classical experimental design concerns its usual setting. Most research employing this type of design takes place in a laboratory, where investigators arrange the environment to conform to the experiment. This setting allows researchers to treat both the experimental and control groups in identical fashion. However, a price is paid for this control. Many of the results obtained from lab experiments are criticized for not reflecting what goes on in the real world. To the extent that this charge is valid, the results also are not generalizable to social behaviour occurring in "natural" settings.

Finally, there is one further problem with the classical experimental design. In many research situations, particularly in sociology, it is simply not possible to design research with equivalent experimental and control groups. In these cases, it is necessary to use deviations from the classical design while recognizing the limitations inherent in them.

Cross-Sectional Design

The most used research design in sociological research is the **cross-sectional design**. Two or more groups with varying degrees of an independent

FIGURE 2-5   Classical Experimental Design

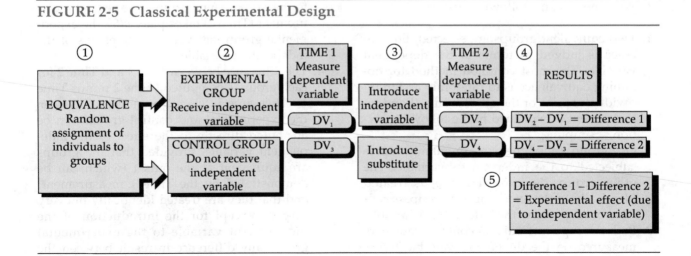

variable are measured at one time to determine how they compare with respect to a dependent variable. The research described in Figure 2-3 is typical of studies that employ this type of design. Countries arranged according to their per capita GNP (independent variable) are also measured on total fertility rate (dependent variable). If the relationship between the two variables is inverse as hypothesized, we can say only that they are correlated. We cannot state that the relationship is *causal* because we do not know whether the countries are equivalent in every respect, except for their level of economic development. (Achieving equivalence is an explicit feature of the classical experimental design.) In fact, we know that they are *not* equivalent in many respects. Therefore, it could be some unknown variable (nevertheless related to economic development) that is *causing* the inverse relationship.

Because equivalence cannot be assumed in the cross-sectional design, researchers employing it are restricted in their ability to make causal assertions. Competing alternative explanations cannot be ruled out as they can in the classical design. For example, one perfectly reasonable alternative explanation for the inverse relationship between national economic development and family size is that the level of education, not the economy, is responsible for or causes the decline in family size. Because there is a strong direct relation between level of education in a country and level of economic development (World Bank 1991:260–261), and an inverse relation between level of education and family size (World Bank 1991:55–61), perhaps education and not economics causes families to limit the number of children they have. Because levels of education and economic development vary in the same direction among countries, it is extremely difficult to disentangle their independent effects. Researchers must be very sensitive to the issue of causality when they use cross-sectional designs.

One important advantage of the cross-sectional design is that it may be used to survey large groups of people. (Imagine conducting a laboratory experiment comparing Canadians and Mexicans.) Either directly through interview and questionnaire or indirectly through access to official statistics and records, it is possible for researchers to study representative samples of the various groups (including nations) in which they are interested. (The section "Sampling" describes how representative samples are obtained, and the section "Data Collection" discusses actual methods of acquiring data.) Consequently, one of the strengths of the cross-sectional design is that it permits researchers to generalize beyond the data they actually collect, a desirable feature when conducting cross-national research. Depending upon how investigators draw their samples, they can generalize about entire populations.

Longitudinal Design

Another popular research design is the **longitudinal design**. It involves measuring a similarly constituted group on at least two separate occasions and can therefore reveal trends where the cross-sectional design cannot. Government censuses are an example of this type of design; they are a decade-by-decade progress chart of a country's development on a wide variety of dimensions. Like the cross-sectional design, the longitudinal design is weak with respect to making causal assertions (there is no control group) but strong in generalizing beyond the data collected.

Some researchers have combined the features of the cross-sectional and longitudinal designs by engaging in comparative studies of two or more groups over time. This kind of combined research design is well suited to the comparative study of nations. For example, in a comprehensive worldwide study of 124 countries, Richard Estes (1984, 1988) examined the relationship between national economic development and the "capacity of nations to provide for the basic social and material needs of their populations." From 1970 to 1983, he measured the progress of these nations using 36 indicators grouped into ten dimensions of national well-being. Thus, he was able to plot the degree to which some nations progressed and others declined in the progress they had initially achieved.

A specific type of longitudinal design is called a **panel study**. It involves studying the *same* group over time and identifying individuals during successive measurement so that it is possible to record not only group change but also *individual* change over time. This is a very demanding kind of design because it involves maintaining meticulous track of people and trying to ensure that they do not leave the study before it is completed. However, in some research projects it may be the only way to acquire this additional information.

Longitudinal designs are not used as much as cross-sectional designs in sociological research. The main reasons for this are added costs of taking two or more measurements instead of one and prolonged time in the field. However, to the extent that the research problem involves the study of change, this kind of design is imperative.

Case Study

The final research design that we will consider is the **case study**. It usually involves an intensive, in-depth, and often prolonged study of one or a small number of cases. Cases can refer to individuals, groups, or situations. The main advantage of the case study is that it "places researchers in the midst of whatever it is they study. From this vantage, researchers can examine various phenomena as perceived by participants and represent these observations as accounts" (Berg 1989:52).

Novelists and journalists, as well as social science researchers, have used the case study method to make their reports more true to the life they are attempting to represent. For example, the novelist John Steinbeck actually lived in the camps of the migratory workers he described in *The Grapes of Wrath*, and John Howard Griffin (1961) chemically altered his skin pigmentation so that he could enter and experience the world of black society. Some of the classics of sociology are richly textured case studies in which the researchers themselves have participated in the lives they are describing (see, for example, Lewis 1961; Whyte 1943).

While case studies are often realistic accounts of life as it is experienced by those involved, the research design itself is flawed. What is reported is heavily dependent on the lens through which it is viewed — the eyes and personal values of usually a lone investigator. It is impossible to replicate a case study to corroborate independently the research results. In this circumstance, the researcher is the measuring instrument. Consequently, this kind of design is open to charges of bias and subjectivity.

Also, similar to the cross-sectional and longitudinal designs, the case study is weak in being able to establish causality. Although many case studies contain causal assertions, there are competing alternative explanations that simply cannot be ignored. It is a matter of conjecture on the part of researchers to attribute causality to factors that occurred *before* the research began or to sort through various motives why people did what they did.

Finally, the case study is weak with respect to generalization. Because the design involves the study of a single or few cases, there is no assurance that they are representative cases. They could be idiosyncratic in a variety of ways.

Figure 2-6 summarizes the advantages and disadvantages of the four research designs we have discussed. Because no design is perfect, we must choose from among them on the basis of what we most want to achieve in a particular study. The goals of social research are to achieve causal explanations that are relevant to daily life and that can be broadly generalized. Unfortunately, none of these designs can attain these three goals simultaneously. This is another reason why we must be tentative in accepting the results of any one research study. Only by the cumulation of consistent results through a variety of designs can we begin to be confident that we are measuring what we intend to measure.

Sampling

At the same time that the research design is being planned, thought must be given to the appropriate sample or population of groups, individuals, or behaviours on which to test the hypothesis. A **population** (or universe) is that body of individuals (or other social units) in which you are interested and to which you will generalize your findings. A **sample** is a smaller representation of this whole, the group that is actually studied. Providing that the sample has been carefully selected, according to well-defined sampling procedures, reliable and valid inferences can be drawn about the larger population.

Taking a sample is not something we do independently of the research we are undertaking. It is an integral part of the research process, and how we do it can greatly influence the kinds of

FIGURE 2-6 Research Designs: Advantages and Disadvantages

Type of Design	Advantages	Disadvantages
Classical experimental design	Causal relationships Experimental control	Obtrusive measurement (sensitization) Representativeness Generalizability Artificial setting Limited applicability
Cross-sectional design	Representativeness Generalizability Easy to administer	Causal relationships Obtrusive measurement
Longitudinal design (Panel study)	Reveal trends Representativeness Generalizability (Individual differences)	Causal relationships Obtrusive measurement Cost and time (Difficult to administer)
Case study	Realism In-depth study Unobtrusive measurement	Subjectivity Replicatibility Causality Representativeness Generalizability Time

results we achieve. For example, 30 or 40 years ago many hypotheses concerning general social behaviour were tested on samples of university students. The researchers were university professors, and their students were convenient guinea pigs. University students, however, are not typically representative of society, and consequently the findings could not properly be generalized to the larger population. University students are on average younger, more educated, of a higher social class, and more homogeneous in their values than the larger society of which they are a part. Any or all of these characteristics could systematically affect the results, so that the conclusions drawn would not be appropriate to society in general.

Consider the popular advertising ploy "Four out of five doctors surveyed recommend. ..." At first glance, this statement appears to suggest that 80 percent of all doctors solidly support Brand X. In order to interpret it accurately, however, we must ascertain the sampling process involved. Were the surveyed doctors a representative sample of the Canadian Medical Association? Were they employees of the company selling Brand X?

A "yes" answer to either of these questions would evoke different levels of confidence in Brand X. Consequently, as with the other stages of research we have discussed, it is necessary to know the method used — in this case, how individuals or groups were selected — in order to assess the findings properly.

Why We Sample

You might think that taking a sample is not as accurate as enumerating an entire population. In many cases, however, it can be more accurate, and here is why:

Destruction of the Universe. This ominous phrase is intended simply to suggest that absolute certainty can be too dearly bought. For example, suppose your doctor asks, "What is your blood type?" Would you prefer the doctor to take a sample of your blood or test the entire population, that is, take *all* of your blood? This example is not unique. In some cases, it is necessary to take a sample rather than a complete enumeration because to do otherwise would destroy the entire universe.

Consider the claim by a light bulb company that its product burns an average of *x* hours. What is the factual basis of this claim? Sampling is necessary. If the company tested its entire population of products, it would have no light bulbs to sell. It would have destroyed the entire universe. We have heard that a fool-proof method of distinguishing real pearls from fakes is to immerse all specimens of both categories in vinegar. But those that dissolve will be the genuine pearls!

Cost. In most research, cost considerations are extremely important. Obviously, if we can obtain essentially the same information at a lower cost, we will do so. Sampling allows such savings, and provided that it is done according to accepted procedures, the data obtained are no less accurate than those from a complete enumeration.

Accessibility to All Elements Within the Universe. In very large populations, such as those of Canada, Mexico, and the United States, it is difficult, costly, and time-consuming simply to locate all the people. Criminals actively avoid being located, many indigents have no fixed address, and occupationally mobile people are constantly relocating. Because of this, even government-conducted national censuses are not completely accurate, even though the attempt is made to count everyone. In Canada, it is estimated that approximately 2 percent of the population are not counted (Kalbach and McVey 1979).

A sample can actually be a more accurate representation of a population than are attempts at a complete enumeration because more time and money *per unit* can be spent in locating relatively inaccessible cases. Consequently, inferences drawn from a sample to a population can be more valid than those drawn from an enumeration — again, provided that proper sampling procedure is observed.

Types of Samples

First and foremost, a sample should be *representative* of the particular population or universe from which it is drawn. There are many dimensions along which a sample may be representative; the researcher, whenever possible, should attempt to represent those characteristics that pertain directly to the problem being studied. For

example, in the economic development–family size problem discussed earlier, if a sample of countries is contemplated, it should mirror the distribution of economic development present within the world population of nations.

If a population is relatively *homogeneous* — if each element of the universe is similar with respect to the problem being studied — sampling is much easier, and any sample is likely to be representative. For example, whether your doctor samples your blood from your finger or your toe is unlikely to make a difference. If the population is *heterogeneous*, however, great care must be taken in selecting a sample that reflects this heterogeneity. For this reason, samples of heterogeneous populations should generally be larger than those drawn from homogeneous universes.

There are two main categories of samples. **Random samples** (also known as *probability samples*) are designed to be representative, and the degree to which they are can be estimated very accurately. **Nonrandom samples** (sometimes known as *nonprobability samples*) are also drawn to be representative, but the extent of representativeness cannot be determined. Nonrandom samples are, however, easier and less costly to take.

Random Samples. The defining characteristic of a simple random sample is that each element within the universe has an equal chance (probability) of being included in the sample. There are several varieties of random samples, but this feature is central to all of them. Because of it, random samples are likely to be representative of the populations from which they are drawn.

An essential aspect of random samples is that the population must be explicitly defined or identified. In order for each element to have an equal probability of selection, all elements must be listed. Suppose that you wish to take a random sample of your class, your university, or your town. It is first necessary to make a list of all the people who make up these populations. In many cases, lists already exist in class lists, student directories, registrar records, voter enumeration lists, city directories, telephone books, and tax records. But you must ensure that these lists correspond to your target population, the group to which you want to generalize your findings. Voter enumeration lists contain only adult citizens; telephone books contain only those people with listed telephones and so probably exclude the very poor, the highly mobile, and those who desire privacy.

The major argument for all random samples is that they are representative of the populations from which they were drawn. Although this point is extremely important to any researcher, there are other factors to consider. Sometimes a case can be made for nonrandom sampling.

Nonrandom Samples. Nonrandom samples are usually considerably cheaper than random ones. In a random sample, it is necessary to locate specifically selected respondents who may not always be immediately accessible. Because of this feature, costs increase. For example, randomly selected people who are not at home must be recontacted at a later date. In a nonrandom sample, by contrast, particular individuals are not chosen. If someone is not at home, the next-door neighbour can be substituted. Also, randomly chosen respondents may not all live in the same geographical area. Consequently, greater expense is involved in reaching these individuals than occurs in nonrandom samples, which are usually geographically clustered in order to cut costs. Thus, although random samples may be more representative than nonrandom ones, they are also more costly.

Another argument for nonrandom sampling is the difficulty encountered in obtaining a random sample. Suppose you are interested in determining the factors responsible for the apathy about student affairs on your campus. To obtain a representative cross-section, you take a random sample from some available lists of students. Questionnaires are mailed out, but only 30 percent respond (perhaps because of the very apathy you are studying). How representative is your sample now, particularly in relation to the problem being researched? The point is that there are often serious and sizable discrepancies between the sampling *plan* and its actual *execution*. The greater these discrepancies, the less preferred is the random over the nonrandom sample.

Finally, in some cases it is simply impossible to take a random sample, and if knowledge is to be gained, a nonrandom sample must be used. For example, in a well-known study comparing the job satisfaction of people from various countries, Soviet refugees were used to form the sample from the USSR. For a variety of reasons, refugees cannot be considered representative of the Soviet labour force. However, at the time no other sampling options existed if Soviets were to be included in the comparisons. Similarly, if a researcher is interested in various aspects of crime and deviance, it is impossible to take a random sample of criminals and deviants. The population is not known, so a nonrandom sample is the only alternative.

Figure 2-7 lists and briefly describes some of the most common random and nonrandom samples

FIGURE 2-7 Commonly Used Random and Nonrandom Samples

Type of Sample	Description
Random	
Simple	Sample in which each element within a population has an equal chance of being selected.
Systematic	Sample in which the first element from a population is selected at random, followed by every succeeding nth element.
Stratified	Series of random samples designed to represent some characteristic in proportion to its distribution within a population. For example, a random sample stratified by gender would comprise two simple random samples of males and females in proportion to the male–female ratio of the population.
Nonrandom	
Convenience	Sample in which elements are selected on the basis of availability (e.g., person-on-the-street interviews).
Judgement	Sample in which the researcher selects elements thought to be representative of a population on one or more dimensions.
Quota	Nonrandom equivalent of a stratified random sample. Sample with the same proportion of certain characteristics as found in the population.

used by social researchers. More detailed descriptions are contained in any standard sampling text (see, for example, Sudman 1976). In addition to using these basic samples, researchers often employ combinations of samples in order to be representative of large populations and yet be able to deal with the individual level. For example, in a comparative survey of Canadian, American, and Mexican university students, the researcher might first take a quota sample of universities in proportion to their regional representation within each country. After having selected particular universities, it would then be possible to contact actual students, either by means of a series of systematic or stratified samples (see Figure 2-7). By carefully combining random and nonrandom sampling techniques in a number of stages, it is thus possible not only to represent the target population (university students in the three countries) but to reduce costs at the same time.

Data Collection

Once you decide what problem you are interested in, the basic research design you plan to use, and the sample or population you plan to study, you gather the data needed to solve your problem. Since, these decisions are not made sequentially, you will already have thought of how to gather the data. It is a fact of life that your decision will likely be a compromise between the best way to collect data and what time and money will allow.

There are two general ways of gathering data: asking people for the information you want, and observing their behaviour or the products (**physical trace evidence**) of their behaviour. To illustrate these ways: if you are interested in the drinking patterns of a community, you could ask a sample of the residents how much and how often they drink; you could attempt to learn their actual drinking behaviour by observing them in bars, homes, and liquor stores; or you could gather physical trace evidence by counting bottles in their garbage cans.

Let us consider the first of our data-gathering methods: asking questions. There are two general ways of asking people for information: by questionnaire and by interview. The questions can be highly structured, with fixed response categories, or they can be open-ended, allowing more flexibility of response.

Questionnaires

A questionnaire is a series of questions to be answered by the *respondent*. It may be handed out at work or school or mailed directly to a person's home. If you sample the general population of an area, the respondents are spread out over a fairly large geographical area, so considerations of time and money may make a mail questionnaire your only choice. The questionnaire includes a letter informing the person of the purpose of the questionnaire, how she or he was chosen, reasons encouraging the person to respond, and, usually, assurance of anonymity. A stamped, addressed return envelope is included, and follow-up letters may be sent out to increase the rate of response.

The importance of constructing a good questionnaire cannot be overemphasized. Following is the preferred procedure for making a structured questionnaire. You first formulate the questions (indicators) that you believe measure the variables of interest. Once you have constructed the items composing the measures of your concepts and the response categories, you pre-test them. Ideally, this involves sampling a group similar to the group you intend to survey. You then analyze the results of the pre-test, to see if they make sense, and interview the pre-test subjects, to see if the questions mean the same thing to them as they do to you. You can also partly determine if any of the items, as well as the whole set of items, is biasing the results. That is, are the questions worded in such a way that they are forcing a certain answer or indicating to the respondents how they should answer? For example, you ask, "How old are you?" The respondent answers, "20." And you ask, "Are you really 20 right now?" and the reply is "No, I'm 19 now, but I'm closer to 20 than 19." Consequently, you rephrase your question and ask, "How old are you, to your nearest birthday?"

Interviews

The procedures used to construct questionnaires are essentially the same as those used to construct interview schedules. Since interviewing involves

The characteristics of the interviewer must not interfere with the results of the study.

human interaction, however, the potential for problems is greater than with questionnaires, mainly because the personal characteristics of re- searchers and respondents must be considered. Research using face-to-face interviews must be designed so that the results of the study are not the consequence of the interviewer's charac- teristics. Age, gender, race, behaviour (a raised eyebrow, a vocal inflection), dress, and general appearance — all can influence the respondents' answers. The chances of this occurring are so great that many books have been written about the interviewing process and techniques for mini- mizing such influence.

The interview itself may vary from a brief, structured session to a lengthy, complicated, un- structured one lasting several hours. The struc- tured interview uses a schedule, which is essentially a questionnaire that is read to the re- spondents in a specified order. A schedule that specifies only some questions is called semistruc- tured; a schedule that simply indicates the gen- eral area to be explored is called unstructured.

There are both advantages and disadvantages to structured interviews. The structured inter- view is easy to score, reduces interviewer bias, is more easily replicated, and is more reliable than an unstructured interview. The major advantage of the unstructured interview over the structured one is that the interviewer can explore the re- spondents' answers. The success of this type of interview, however, depends on the skill of the researcher in winning the respondent's confi- dence and in asking the appropriate questions. It presents serious problems of interpretation; it is also low in reliability and difficult to replicate. Consequently, the tendency is to use structured interviews. However, if the problem being re- searched is very sensitive (for example, human sexual behaviour), or if little is known about the topic being researched, an unstructured interview may be the best technique to use.

Interviews have several advantages over questionnaires:

1. Interviews generally can be longer.
2. The populations are less restricted because the respondents need not be able to read or write; they merely have to understand the language of the interviewer.
3. The response rate is usually higher. Therefore there is less self-selection. For example, the response rates for mail questionnaires are often quite low (a 30 percent return rate is not uncommon).
4. The identity of the respondents is known, which is very useful in determining differences between respondents and nonrespondents.

But interviews have some major disadvantages when compared with questionnaires:

1. Interviews can be expensive to conduct. This problem is becoming so severe that large interview surveys are mainly undertaken now only by large public and private research institutes (such as Gallup and Roper), and structured telephone interviewing is becoming increasingly popular as a means of avoiding some of the expense involved in face-to-face interviews.
2. Interview data can be, to varying degrees, affected by the characteristics of the interviewer.

Doing research in other countries vividly points out these problems. In countries with low literacy rates, questionnaires may be useless. Where they can be used, the problem of assuring that the question you have written in English is the same question when translated into other languages is a serious one. The latter problem also affects the interpretation of interview data.

Observation

Both questionnaires and interviews measure opinions, attitudes, and perceived behaviour. But they do not measure actual behaviour, and actual behaviour may be crucial for certain prob-

lems. Because of this drawback — nonmeasurement of actual behaviour — and because of the problems associated with questionnaires and interviews, some studies employ various types of observation. *Observation* is the term applied to methods of gathering data without direct questioning. There are two different types of observational techniques: one is highly structured and is called nonparticipant observation or, simply, observation; the second type is participant observation.

Nonparticipant Observation. Like other structured techniques, **nonparticipant observation** is based on developing explicit categories in order to increase reliability and replicability and to reduce observer bias. This is much easier said than done. It is extremely difficult to obtain accurate and objective observations. If, for example, several of us observed aggression among children in a playground and we did not carefully arrive at a common definition of aggression, our observations would be quite different. Some of us might see very little aggression; others would witness a great deal, depending on our understanding of the term. If a child picks up a toy and looks as if she is going to throw it at another child, some would record this as an aggressive act; others would not. So, to ensure that we observe the same things in the same way, careful operational definitions of categories are required.

An example of the problems involved in constructing good operational definitions or empirical indicators is provided in an observational study of military leadership (Davis and Hagedorn 1954). The researchers were interested in "ways of giving orders," seen as varying on a democratic–authoritarian continuum. Originally, they assumed they would simply record whether or not an order was democratic or authoritarian. They soon discovered, however, that in many instances they could not even be sure whether an order had been given. For example, a sergeant in a car pool says, "Is there a wrench?" and a private stops what he is doing and brings the sergeant a wrench. Was an order given? The researchers solved the problem by writing down anything a noncommissioned officer said that could in any way be interpreted as an order; then, three people classified the notations into "orders" and "nonorders." Where at least two of the three coders agreed that the statement was an order, it was included in the analysis.

Participant Observation. Systematic nonparticipant observation, using two or more observers to study the same interaction with predefined categories, has not been widely used in sociological research, probably because of the time and expense involved. **Participant observation**, on the other hand, has been widely used and has resulted in some of the classics of sociological research.

Participant observers are part of the social setting in which they observe events. There is wide variation in the degree of participation by the observer. In an extreme form, the observer is a member of the group being observed, and the group is unaware of the observer's role.

A less intense form of participant observation occurs when the researcher stays with a particular small group or lives in a community. In this case, the researcher usually participates in some of the group's activities while observing them. The members of the group or community are aware that they are being observed. This technique was used by Whyte (1943) in his classic study of a street-corner gang in an Italian slum in the Boston area. Whyte lived in Cornerville for three and a half years and participated in most of the group's activities. They knew he was engaged in research, but presumably they did not care.

The third type of participant observation involves the least participation of the researcher in the activities of the group. In this type of observation, the researcher takes on the role of the objective, neutral observer. The group members know they are being observed, and the observer does not usually participate in the group's activities while observing the group. A person observing a classroom, for example, might spend several hours a day for several weeks recording the various behaviours of the class members; a sociologist might observe a work group over a similarly long period of time. There are two basic differences between this type of participant observation and nonparticipant observation. First, the observers do not have preconceived categories for scoring their observations, and second, they tend to spend a much longer time in the field.

There are several advantages to participant observation.

1. The observations take place in a natural setting. An observational study of workers at their place of work, in contrast to an experimental study of students in a laboratory doing the same kind of work, is more natural and for this reason may be more easily generalized. That is, the findings are more likely to be true of workers in general than only of the experimental subjects.

2. By observing over a long period of time, the researcher gathers a great deal of information on many variables. Also, the dynamics of changes that occur in the situation can be explored. Other methods are rarely this adaptable.

3. The observer can record the context, including the emotional reactions of the subjects, in which the behaviour occurs.

4. First-hand experience enables the observer to acquire some sense of the subjective meanings that events have for their subjects.

5. An observer who has established good relations (rapport) with the people being observed may be able to ask sensitive questions that would otherwise not be allowed.

There are, however, at least five major problems associated with participant observation:

1. There is a lack of reliability, which stems from the selective perception of the lone observer. (In this type of research there is nearly always just one observer.) The observer has a particular theoretical orientation, interest, and training — all of which are likely to affect the perception, recording, memory, and interpretation of the events observed.

2. Observers who are not complete participants may sensitize their subjects by their presence. **Sensitization** concerns the alteration of subject behaviour by the presence of the observer. If, when children are being observed, their behaviour in a classroom is different from their normal behaviour, the observer is not getting a true picture of children's classroom behaviour.

3. If an observer is a member of the group, his or her role in the group greatly restricts the observations that can be made. For example, one participant observer who took the role of a machine operator could not observe other

work groups, his foreman, or other superiors. He was restricted to one room in one building with one group (Roy 1959).

4. It is difficult to participate in any continuing group without becoming involved in it. If involvement occurs, loss of objectivity results and the possibility of bias increases. Also, even if the other members of the group are not sensitized by the observer, the behaviour of the group itself changes as a result of the observer's participation.

5. Most observers must wait for occurrences of the behaviour in which they are interested (for example, playground aggression); it is possible that this behaviour may not occur during their time of observation.

Furthermore, with the exception of complete participant observation, all these data-gathering methods — questionnaires, interviews, and observation — have one disadvantage in common: the people being researched know they are being studied, and they may therefore behave differently from the way they otherwise would. This in turn means the results may be biased.

Unobtrusive Data-Gathering. The disadvantage of subjects' awareness of being studied is not inevitable; there are unobtrusive data-gathering methods. Any type of research procedure conducted in such a way that the subjects do not know they are being studied is called unobtrusive. Such measures are rarely reactive — that is, they do not sensitize subjects (or, to put it another way, subjects do not react to being studied). One type of widely discussed unobtrusive measure is the use of **physical trace evidence** (Webb et al. 1981), which can be classified as either erosion or accretion. *Erosion measurements* include any type of data occurring from human behaviour that results in the wearing away of some physical object. Examples of erosion indicators are the wearing away of tiles at an art or museum exhibit (popularity), the wear on library books (use), and the wear on children's shoes (activity). *Accretion measurements* include any type of data resulting from human behaviour that leaves some physical trace. Examples of accretion indicators include garbage, archaeological evidence such as pottery and tools, and graffiti. Although seldom used as a major basis of social research, unobtru-

sive measures can be extremely important for ascertaining the degree to which the other techniques may have sensitized subjects, as well as being used as direct and indirect measures in their own right.

Secondary Sources of Data

Data can be classified into primary sources (data gathered and analyzed by the researcher) and secondary sources (data analyzed by the researcher but gathered by someone else).

An increasingly common source of secondary data is surveys by other social scientists. This has been facilitated by the development of data archives, or data banks. Data archives are depositories where data produced by a number of investigators are available to members for secondary analysis (Parcel 1992).

The advantage of using survey data gathered by other social scientists is the usually high quality of data based on national or regional random samples, a large number of cases, and gathered by experts of large survey organizations. The disadvantage is that the data are seldom a perfect fit with the secondary researcher's needs. The researcher's problem is matching theoretical interest with the available data.

A second major source of secondary data is official statistics. This refers to all data gathered by governments, which includes federal, provincial or state, and municipal governments. The censuses of population for Canada, the United States, and Mexico are frequently cited in this book.

The major advantages of using official statistics are measuring changes and trends over time and making comparisons within and between nations. For example, most of the comparative data in this book are based on official sources.

One major disadvantage of official statistics is changes in the definition of terms, which makes comparisons over time difficult or even impossible. The labour-force concept employed by the U.S. Census Bureau has gone through serious changes in definition, negating the use of labour-force statistics for some problems and making the conclusions from others highly tenuous. A second major problem is that different countries measure or define the same concept differently (see the box "What Is an Urban Area?" in Chapter 17). Lack of standardization of statistical concepts across nations creates serious problems in comparative research.

When using official sources it is easy to forget that someone collected, coded, and computed the various statistics and tables. Consequently, the advantages and disadvantages of interviews and questionnaire surveys also apply to secondary sources. For example, in Canada and the United States, census information used to be collected by interviews. Currently it is collected by questionnaires that have higher rates of error and omission.

A third source of secondary data is statistics gathered by organizations. Every organization keeps records; records of sales, revenue, employment, wages, turnover, absenteeism, promotions, and measures of productivity are common examples. Many official statistics are based on information received from other organizations, such as police departments, schools, hospitals, and businesses. These data are easily available and widely used. When you read in U.S. newspapers about an increase or decrease in crime for the nation, based on the Uniform Crime Reports, these data have been collated from reports sent to the Federal Bureau of Investigation by police departments throughout the nation.

The major disadvantage of data reported by organizations is that they may not be impartial and may follow their own interest in what they count and report. "When the people who report events have clear motives for inflating or deflating the numbers and the people who receive the reports have no authority to demand verification, inaccuracy is guaranteed" (Caplow 1991:5).

A fourth source of secondary data is anything written, filmed, recorded, or televised. The most frequently analyzed materials are textbooks, newspapers, journals, magazines, films and television programs, and advertisements. A particular method for analyzing such secondary sources that has proved increasingly useful to social scientist is content analysis.

Content analysis is "any technique for making inferences by objectively and systematically identifying specified characteristics of messages" (Holsti 1969) — examining the speeches of political candidates, for example, or searching newspaper ads for sexist bias. Content analysis is, then, a systematic procedure for examining the content of recorded information. It renders objective the usually casual and superficial judgements we make of communication content.

There are special problems with content analysis. First is the problem of coding the data or determining the categories. For example, if you want to study changes in gender-role presentation in women's magazines, what categories do you count, what characteristics of women's roles do you look at, and how can you construct exhaustive and reliable categories? You might count the number of fictional heroines who are single and the number married, the number who work, the types of jobs they hold, and the number with and without children. It should be pointed out, however, that even determining who is a heroine is sometimes difficult.

The second special problem is selecting a sample. In the above example, which magazines do you look at, and what time periods do you choose? Virtually any content analysis of mass media involves both a sample of the media (specific books, television shows, or newspapers) and a sample of time. For instance, you might look at a random sample of two women's magazines for a ten-year period. The following example of a content analysis will clarify the problems.

As part of a general study to determine sociologists' ability to make valid social generalizations based on their research, Hedley (1984) did a content analysis of major sociology journals. His first problem was to decide which of the many journals to choose. After seriously considering all the alternatives, he chose the official journals of the national sociological associations in the United States, Canada, and Great Britain. Because he was concerned with the discipline of sociology as a whole, he wished to avoid selecting journals in only one country. Although it would have been ideal to examine official journals from other countries as well, the time-consuming aspect of content analysis simply prohibited this course.

The next problem was selecting a time period. Hedley hypothesized that the methods of recent sociological research are superior to those of the past and, because of this improvement, sociologists can now make more valid social generalizations. He decided to do a content analysis of journals at a ten-year interval, which would constitute a rigorous test of the hypothesis. This decision resulted in his reading close to 7000 pages of sociological research.

The next task was to operationalize the particular methodological features in which he was interested. With regard to research design, Hedley decided that data collected on at least two separate occasions (*longitudinal designs*) are to be preferred over cross-sectional designs because measurement over time tends to reduce the impact of unique historical and social events that can by themselves affect the sociological relationships being studied. He also examined sampling procedures and concluded that representative national or cross-national samples permit greater generalizability than do nonrandom samples and samples of particular groups or regions. Finally, concerning data collection methods, he noted sociologists' very heavy reliance on interviews and questionnaires. To the extent that researchers use other data sources (for example, nonparticipant and participant observation, physical trace evidence, and already available data from the census, newspapers, or institutional records), there is a balance, and thus less likelihood of attributing social generalizations to a particular method of data collection.

Table 2-1 presents part of the results of this content analysis, showing the changes occurring from the beginning to the end of the ten-year period. Hedley's hypothesis is substantiated in the United States and Canada but rejected in Great Britain. At least in North America, then, sociologists' ability to produce valid social generalizations has definitely improved, according to these criteria.

If this example illustrates the difficulties in doing content analysis, it also demonstrates the advantages of such research:

1. The data are accessible and inexpensive.
2. The data cover a long time period; this makes content analysis very useful for studying trends.
3. The data are gathered unobtrusively; that is, the data collection methods are not reactive.
4. Content analysis can be used to study the larger society and macrosociological problems.

Content analysis also has several main disadvantages. First, almost all the material used is screened or processed and the researcher does not know what selection processes have occurred. Clearly, a government-censored newspa-

TABLE 2-1   Percentage Change in Selected Methodological Features of Journal Articles, 1968–1978

Percentage Change in Articles Reporting	Countries in Which Journals Appear		
	United States	Canada	Great Britain
Longitudinal designs	+21%	+9%	–7%
Representative national and foreign samples	+13%	+6%	–6%
Data collection methods other than interviews and questionnaires	+15%	+4%	–5%
Total number of research articles examined	(143)	(61)	(79)

SOURCE: Adapted from R. Alan Hedley, "Social generalizations: Biases and solutions," *International Journal of Comparative Sociology* 25(1984):168. E.J. Brill Leiden, The Netherlands.

per is not a good source of unbiased data. But to some extent all material used in content analysis has been selected by someone for some purpose, and therefore an objective picture may not be possible. Second, content analysis is a very laborious and time-consuming process; this may be one of the reasons it is not used more frequently.

The third disadvantage is that it is very difficult to avoid a great deal of judgement and subjectivity in the coding process and in making inferences. This, of course, introduces bias. The amount of bias can be reduced, but for many types of content analysis it probably cannot be eliminated. The fourth and final disadvantage is that content analysis has historically been mostly used for descriptive and comparative purposes and not for the study of relationships or causal analysis, although there seems to be no inherent reason why it cannot be used for the latter kind of studies.

Which Is Best?

This brings to an end our discussion of the main ways in which social scientists collect their data, and the advantages and disadvantages of each method. It is important to remember that there is no reason to consider any particular method as better than or in competition with the others. Social reality should look the same no matter what technique is used to observe it. Sample surveys using questionnaire or interview schedules are the most common method employed by sociologists to collect data. This reliance on one method implies the disadvantages of that method, as previously discussed. The best approach is to use as many techniques as you can. Then, if the same relationship is observed with a variety of methods, more confidence can be placed in the validity of the findings.

Data Analysis

Analyzing data is a complicated and difficult process. Our concern here is not that you learn how to analyze data; rather, we want to stress the interpretation of the major statistics used in sociological analysis. We hope to make you more competent as consumers of social research. To accomplish this, we will briefly discuss first the processing of data and second the statistics used to describe those data. Because most data in sociology are still gathered by questionnaires or interview-surveys, we will restrict our description to this form of data collection.

Processing the Data

If you do an honours thesis based on a 30-item questionnaire given to 200 students, you end up with 6000 pieces of information—a relatively small number. Even so, it is impossible to analyze the data by flipping through the pages of the questionnaires. Most questionnaire results are analyzed by computers. The first step in this process is to code the data. This involves making up a code book in which each variable is assigned a column number(s). A *column number* refers to one of a given number of columns on a computer file. For example, gender may be recorded in column 3, with row 1 equalling male, row 2 equalling female, and row 3 equalling all other responses, including nonresponses. When this has been done, the next usual step is to go

through each questionnaire and transfer the data to a code sheet. Alternatively, one can transfer the precoded responses directly into the computer.

Coding, then, is reducing the information to a standardized form and always involves a loss of data. For example, in coding census occupations, thousands of occupations must be lumped together. Sociologists, for example, are pooled with people in several other occupations, including penologists and social ecologists. Demographers are coded with statisticians and actuaries. This basic coding is irreversible; you cannot, after the fact, combine demographers with sociologists (Pineo et al. 1977). In the coding process, therefore, you have to be concerned with validity and reliability. A code is valid if it puts similar phenomena in the same category or assigns the same values to similar phenomena. A code is reliable if different coders obtain identical or similar results when coding the same data. Both of these should be checked carefully.

After the data are transferred to code sheets, the common procedure is to have them keyed into a computer for analysis. An increasingly popular technique to use for questionnaires is answer sheets like those students use for taking objective tests. These data can be read by machine and entered directly into a computer. If you decide to do the analysis by hand, using a calculator, however, you will still find it more convenient to put the data on code sheets and work from them.

Quantitative Data Analysis

The enormous amount of information usually gathered in survey research is incomprehensible in raw form. The data are useful only when reduced to some relevant statistic. **Statistics** has two basic definitions. First, statistics mean numbers—the actual data gathered. When someone says, "Statistics show the Tories will win," he or she is using the word in this sense. Average age at marriage, average income, percentage Liberal, and so on are examples of statistics defined as numbers. Second, statistics refer to the theories and techniques that have been developed to manipulate data. Percentages, rates, averages, and measures of relation are statistics in this sense. In either sense, statistics concern the manipulation of numbers.

Certain questionnaire answer sheets can be read by machine and entered directly into a computer.

Some of the first statistics you might use to make sense of your data are percentages, rates, and ratios. For most problems there is little sense in comparing, for example, Canada and the United States on the total number of births, deaths, suicides, or crimes. The United States is going to have more of all of these because of its larger population. Even if the United States has a low crime rate and Canada a high one, the United States will have more crimes. If we want to compare these two or any two units that differ greatly in size, we must control for this factor. This can be done by computing percentages, ratios, or rates.

Instead of computing births, deaths, suicides, and crimes, we compute birth rates, death rates, suicide rates, and crime rates. For example, the crude birth rate is the number of births divided by the population of a given community and multiplied by 1000. This mathematical operation eliminates population size as a factor and thus makes possible meaningful comparisons between groups of different sizes. Percentages provide the same kind of control. The point is that it is not meaningful to compare groups without knowing the size of both groups. For example, 50 people in group A are alcoholics and 100 people in group B are alcoholics, but there are 100 people in group A and 400 in group B. Thus, 50 percent of the people in group A are alcoholics, compared with 25 percent for group B.

Such statistics are usually easy to compute, are necessary for comparing groups of different sizes, and are easy to interpret. Nevertheless, certain questions can be asked to help interpret these statistics:

1. What is (are) the empirical indicator(s) of the variables?

Which Headline Is Correct?

1. *"White Incomes Increase More Than Black!"*
2. *"Black Incomes Increase More Than White!"*
3. *"Little Change Between White and Black Incomes!"*

Many statistics in the mass media — and certainly income statistics should be included — are too important to be handled or read carelessly. The consumer of these statistics needs knowledge to interpret them correctly.

In 1969, white per capita income in the United States was $6522; by 1979 it was $7808, for an increase of $1286. Black per capita income was $3566 in 1969 and $4545 in 1979, an increase of only $979. On the basis of the dollar amounts or the raw numbers, Headline 1 is an accurate statement.

For whites, the increase of $1286 represents 19.7 percent of their 1969 income; for blacks, their increase of $979 is 27.5 percent of the 1969 figure. On the basis of percentage change in per capita incomes, Headline 2 is also accurate.

Now, look at black income as a proportion of white income for the two periods: in 1969 it is 3566/6522, or 0.55; in 1979 it is 4545/7808, or 0.58. On the basis of proportions or ratios, Headline 3 is accurate as well.

Based on the same data, we have three very different conclusions. All are correct, depending on how you analyze the data. Just as you prefer one of these conclusions over the others, so too may the person presenting these data. This suggests that we should add another question to our list of aids in interpreting statistics: what possible biases may the author have?

Which headline is correct?

Source:

Adapted from John G. Keane, "Questionable statistics," *Population Today* 13(December 1985):9.

2. What is the sample or population?
3. What can the specific statistic be compared with?
4. What is the reverse conclusion?

The following example deals with each of these four questions. Consider the following newspaper headline:

30% Failures in Forces' Fitness Test
(Victoria Times Colonist)

The headline alone suggests that the Canadian armed forces are falling apart.

1. What is the empirical indicator or measure of fitness? In this case, fitness meant that a male under 30 years of age had to be able to run 2400 metres in less than 14 minutes.
2. What is the sample or population? In this case the sample was 67 000 military personnel. There was no statement about what the population was, how this sample of 67 000 was drawn, or what portion of the population it represented. This lack of information made it very difficult to interpret what the 30 percent failure rate meant. If all 67 000 were combat troops, who presumably should be in good physical condition, a 30 percent failure would seem to be more serious than if the group included deskbound officers and enlisted men. Also, since the fitness test was defined in terms of males, one might presume that none of the 67 000 was female. But this is only a presumption.
3. With what can we compare this 30 percent failure? No data were given as to the failure rate for the general population, but a major was quoted as saying, "I would suggest the fitness level is slightly above that of the general population but not a great deal better." No evidence was given to support that statement. The article did point out that five years previously, 50 percent had failed. If the tests were comparable, this would suggest considerable improvement in fitness of military personnel. So, is the military falling apart or upgrading itself?
4. What is the reverse conclusion? If the headline had said "70% Pass Forces' Fitness Test," would you have interpreted the statement differently? The meaning behind headlines is often elusive. The next time you read that one in four marriages ends in divorce, remember that three out of four do not.

Measures of Central Tendency

It is frequently necessary to use summary statistics that describe group characteristics. Among the most common of these statistics are measures of **averages**. An average is an important measure because it reduces the data to one meaningful value that is readily understood and easily communicated. We often refer to averages — the average person, average weight, average height, average income, average grade point — and the typical person on the street.

Briefly, there are three types of averages: the mode, median, and mean. The **mode** is the most frequently occurring score or category in a distribution. The **median** is the category or point above and below which half the total frequency lies (it is the middle category that divides the frequency in half). The **mean** is what we usually think of when we use the word *average*. It is the value obtained by adding all values in the distribution and dividing by the number in the distribution. Another way of thinking of the mean is that it is the amount of something that everyone would have if each person had the same. In a group of five people, if two have $1, one has $3, one has $5, and one has $40 dollars, the mode is $1 — the most common category. The median is $3; it divides the frequency in half, two persons having more than $3 and two less than $3. The mean is $10; add up the five amounts and divide by the total number of persons ($50 ÷ 5 = $10).

In describing the central tendency or typical value of the group, the researcher must select the average that best reflects this typical value. The mode is very unstable. In our example, if one member who had $1 finds $4 more, the mode is now $5. Should that member be lucky enough to find $39, the mode would be $40. So one score can drastically change the mode.

The mean is by far the most widely used measure, because it is used to compute many other statistics and because it is relatively stable across samples. Its major disadvantage is that it is unduly affected by extreme scores. This should be clear from the example, where the mean of $10 is not very descriptive of the typical value of the group because of the one person with $40 and the two with only $1 each. If the distribution had been two with $5, one with $10, and two with $15, the mean would still be $10, but it would be a more accurate description of the average amount of money in this group.

The median is not as useful as the mean for computing other statistics and can itself be difficult to compute. If the data are only rank-ordered, or if there are extreme scores, however, the median will likely be the most accurate description. Consequently, if you have reason to believe that there are extreme scores or values, usually true of income data, be wary of the mean and tend to prefer the median.

It is probably obvious at this point that you can have distributions that look very different but have the same mean. This fact suggests that to interpret an average, to know how accurately it describes the population, you need to know what the distribution is like. More specifically, you need to know how far group members depart from the mean. Another way of saying the same thing is that you need to know how the scores are dispersed, or spread, around the mean. In the previous example of five people, if each has $10, there is no dispersion, and the mean tells you exactly what each member has. In the case where four people have $1 and one has $46, however, there is great dispersion around the mean, and it is therefore an inaccurate description of the typical value of the group. It simply does not contain much meaningful information. Averages can be misleading and uninformative, and that is why an accompanying dispersion measure can be helpful.

In order to inform readers of the accuracy of the average, a measure of **dispersion** is usually given. Almost all the dispersion measures you will encounter are based on deviations from average scores, either the median or the mean. The statistic you will most frequently encounter is called the **standard deviation** (SD). The larger the SD, the greater the spread of values around the mean or the less the group members are alike. In our example, the SD for the first distribution where all five have $10 is 0 and for the second distribution is 18. (Eighteen is obtained by subtracting the mean from each score, squaring the results, and summing the squares, then dividing the sum of the squares by the number of people and taking the square root of the result.) A measure of dispersion, then, helps you determine the degree to which an average is an accurate description of the typical values of the group. If you ever go swimming in a strange lake and are told the average depth is 7 metres, find out the standard deviation *before* you dive in.

Measures of Association

The measures we have been discussing are used to describe a single variable, such as income, births, or crime. Sociologists are seldom interested, however, in collecting facts for the sake of facts. Usually they want to know how these facts are related to one another. If they calculate a crime rate, it is to see if it is related to some other variable, such as gender or income. It is relationships that sociologists try to explain. This means that they must determine the degree to which the variables they are interested in are related.

There are many ways to measure **association**, and each one may be interpreted in ways different from the others. However, some general comments will aid you in interpreting these measures. The measures most often used in sociology are *gamma, tau, rho, lambda*, and *r* (the Pearson correlation coefficient). Most measures of association, including all of the ones just mentioned, have values between zero and one. Values close to zero indicate a low relationship; those near one indicate a high relationship. In other words, the higher the value, the greater the relationship between any two variables.

The direction of the relationship is also included in these statistics: positive or negative. A **positive (direct) relation** occurs when one variable increases as the other variable increases, or when one decreases as the other decreases. The two variables move or change in the same direction. For example, many students attend university because of a belief in a positive relationship between education and income. That is, as education increases, income increases. A perfect positive relationship equals +1.00. On the other hand, a **negative (inverse) relation** occurs when one variable increases as the other decreases. For example, as age increases, athletic prowess decreases. A perfect negative relationship equals −1.00.

As we stated previously, there is no one simple interpretation for the various statistics. However, for the most commonly used measure, *r*, the simplest interpretation is in terms of r^2, which is the variance explained. If our $r = 0.70$, $r^2 = 0.49$, which

is the proportion of the variance explained by one variable on the other. In the education–income example, 49 percent of the variance in income is explained by education. This also means that 51 percent of the variance in income is not accounted for by education. With other measures of association, it is necessary to rely on the magnitude of the relationship in order to interpret it; the closer to 1 the particular measure is, the greater the relationship between them.

As an example of measuring the relation between variables, let us return to the hypothesis of the negative relation between level of economic development and family size. One of the ways mentioned to measure relations is "rho," a measure of rank-order correlation. This statistic reveals the difference between the ranks of two variables — in this case, GNP as our indicator of economic development and total fertility rate (TFR) as our indicator of family size.

To illustrate how a rho is computed, we selected seventeen countries from Figure 2-3 that were equidistantly placed with respect to their rank on the GNP scale. (We also included Canada, the United States, and Mexico.) Beside each country's GNP, we inserted the TFR and then computed the rho, that is, the degree to which these two rankings (GNP and TFR) are similar. The rho or rank order correlation is −.81. This is a strong negative relation, which supports the hypothesis that high economic development is associated with relatively small family size (and vice versa).

However, because this is a cross-sectional research design, as previously discussed, other explanations cannot be ruled out. We mentioned that an alternative explanation is the level of education in a country. In order to determine what this relation is, we ranked the same countries in terms of illiteracy rates (a measure of educational level) and again matched them to TFR. The rho between illiteracy and TFR is .77. (Because illiteracy is a measure of the *absence* of education, the rho is positive.) Consequently, there is also a strong negative relation between level of education and family size. Although the relation between GNP and TFR is stronger than that between illiteracy and TFR, nevertheless the results indicate that *both* independent variables (economic development and education) explain a substantial part of the variation in family size. As mentioned earlier, this is because the two independent variables themselves are highly related (the rho between GNP and illiteracy = –.86).

Throughout this example of measuring the relationship between variables, all of the problems discussed previously apply. These include imperfect indicators, the cross-sectional design, sampling problems, and secondary data sources. However, regardless of these problems (which you should constantly be aware of), social scientists continue to try to find answers, because what they are investigating is a serious social concern. These problems, however, lead to serious disagreements about how to reduce the fertility rate in the less developed countries. Some researchers suggest raising the level of education; some suggest changing attitudes and values and providing access to birth control; others support economic aid to increase the level of economic development; and still others state that a more equitable distribution of income will reduce fertility. Most of the arguments used to support these alternative solutions are based on the kinds of evidence and measures of relationship used in this example.

In order to interpret these measures (percentages, rates, and measures of association), sociologists frequently report a "P value." Generally, at the bottom of a table you will see an equation such as $P = 0.05$ (or some other value), or a statement such as "Correlation significant at 0.05 level." This statistic is telling you that the correlation is not a result of chance. To put the point another way, if the study was done again, you would find approximately the same correlation.

In the social sciences, if a relation occurs at the 0.05 level, or 0.01, or 0.001, it is considered statistically significant. To say that the finding is statistically significant is only to say that the finding is very unlikely to be a result of chance. To say that a finding is not a chance finding, however, is not to say what it is. And it should not be confused with saying something is theoretically or practically significant. It does mean, however, that whatever was found is likely what is there; that is, if you do the study again, you will likely find the same thing.

We hope that this brief review of data analysis will give you a sense of how data are processed and analyzed. Furthermore, we hope that the discussion of the major statistics used in the analysis of data will enable you to read with heightened understanding the tables and charts in this book and to interpret the statistics for yourself.

The Value of Research Methods

Knowledge and understanding of what is involved in the research process enables consumers of research findings to assess the results independently and to arrive at their own conclusions. Depending on how the research was undertaken, what kind of design was used, the sample taken, and the data collection methods employed, the results may be more or less valid. The informed consumer can evaluate results in light of these considerations.

As a fruitful exercise in critical evaluation, you can use the information in this chapter to assess the research reported in other chapters of this book. Questions that should constantly come to mind include: How do you know? How good are the empirical indicators? Can any other factors explain this result? Under what conditions does this assertion hold? To the extent that you develop this critical appreciation of research, you will not be obliged to accept the claims of others on faith. Even if you never undertake a single piece of research in your lifetime, it is essential to know what is involved in social research.

SUMMARY

1. Hunches, personal problems, observations, conversations, and theory are all sources of research problems. Whatever the source, the steps in researching a problem are familiarizing yourself with previous research and writing on the problem, stating the relationship you expect to find between the independent and dependent variables, and constructing empirical indicators of the variables.

2. The basic problem in measurement is achieving validity — measuring what you intend to measure. Reliability checks and replication are ways of solving the problem of validity. The key to validity is varied and repeated measurement.

3. The purpose of a research design is to eliminate alternative explanations for the results. The ideal, although not perfect, design is the classical experimental design. A much-used deviation from the classical design is the cross-sectional design. Other research designs include the longitudinal design and the case study.

4. In sociology, most research involves a sample rather than a total population. The major concern in sampling is attempting to make the sample representative of the population. To achieve a representative sample, random sampling procedures are usually employed. Sometimes it is impossible or too costly to use random samples. In these cases, nonrandom samples are drawn.

5. All data collection is based on asking or observing; it can be structured or unstructured. The most commonly used techniques in sociology are structured questionnaires, structured interviews, and participant observation. A particularly useful method for already recorded information is content analysis. All these techniques have advantages and disadvantages that determine their usefulness for a particular research problem.

6. After quantitative data have been collected, they are submitted to analysis. This frequently involves coding the data and keying them into a computer for analysis. Various statistics are used to describe the data and to tell how important findings and relationships are. The emphasis in this section is on how to interpret the major statistics used in sociological research.

GLOSSARY

Association. Statistical relation between two or more variables. The most common measures of association are *gamma, tau, rho, lambda*, and *r*.
Averages. Measures that reduce a set of data to one meaningful value; for example, **the mean**, **the median**, or **the mode**.
Case study. A type of research design in which one or a few individuals (cases) are studied intensively, usually over a long period of time.
Classical experimental design. Research design that involves the comparison of two equivalent groups at two points in time to determine the effects of an independent variable on a dependent variable.

Coding. Process of transforming answers in a questionnaire into usable data.
Content analysis. Any systematic procedure for examining the content of recorded information; usually applied to the mass media.
Control group. The comparison group that is denied the effects of the independent variable in the classical experimental design.
Cross-sectional design. Research design in which two or more groups with varying degrees of an independent variable are measured at one point in time to determine how they compare with respect to a dependent variable.
Dependent variable. The variable that research attempts to explain according to how it is affected by some other variable(s).
Dispersion. Statistics that describe the spread in the scores of a distribution.
Experimental group. The comparison group that is subjected to the independent variable in the classical experimental design.
Hypothesis. Prediction of what you expect to find as a result of research; a statement of the relation between two or more variables.
Independent variables. Causal or explanatory variables.
Indicators. Empirical measures of variables.
Longitudinal design. Research design in which either the same group or similar groups are measured on two or more occasions to determine the extent of change in a dependent variable.
Mean. Sum of all of the scores divided by the number of scores; the score each case would have if the variable were distributed equally.
Median. Score that divides a distribution into two equal parts.
Mode. Score that occurs most frequently in a distribution.
Negative (inverse) relation. Relation in which two variables change in opposite directions; as one increases, the other decreases.
Nonparticipant observation. Systematic, objective observation of social behaviour using explicit predefined categories.
Nonrandom samples. Samples in which the probability of elements within the population being selected cannot be known; easier and less costly than random samples.
Panel study. A type of longitudinal research design in which individuals are identified such that it is possible to measure both individual and group change over time.
Participant observation. Situation in which the researchers take an active part, in varying degrees, in the situation they are directly observing.
Physical trace evidence. Observational data based on accretion or erosion.
Population. Largest number of individuals or units of interest to a researcher; also called a *universe*.
Positive (direct) relation. Relation in which two variables change in the same direction; as one increases so

does the other, or as one decreases the other decreases.

Random samples. Samples in which each element within the population has an equal chance of being selected; also called *probability samples*.

Reliability. Consistency of results over time or with several investigators.

Replication. Systematic repeated measurement of a given relationship.

Research design. A plan for conducting research in order to reduce measurement error and eliminate competing alternative explanations.

Sample. Smaller representation of a population or universe; properties of the sample are studied to gain information about the whole.

Sensitization. Process by which subjects become aware that they are being studied.

Standard deviation (SD). Measure of dispersion based on deviations from the mean.

Statistics. Actual numbers; and the theories and techniques used to manipulate data.

Validity. Property of measurement whereby what is measured is what was intended to be measured.

Variable. Factor that can differ or vary from one situation to another, or from one individual or group to another; a concept that has more than one value.

FURTHER READING

Hammond, Phillip E. (ed.). *Sociologists at Work.* New York: Basic Books, 1964. A collection of essays by sociologists on how they conducted their own research and the problems they encountered.

Kaplan, Abraham. *The Conduct of Inquiry.* San Francisco: Chandler, 1964. An exploration of how we know something is true and how we explain the social world in a clear way.

Katzer, Jeffrey, Kenneth H. Cook, and Wayne W. Crouch. *Evaluating Information: A Guide for Users of Social Science Research.* New York: McGraw-Hill, 1991. A research-methods textbook written from the point of view of consumers of social research.

Labovitz, Sanford, and Robert Hagedorn. *Introduction to Social Research.* New York: McGraw-Hill, 1981. A small, highly readable book that treats in slightly more detail the issues raised in this chapter.

Parcel, Toby L. "Secondary data analysis and data archives." In *Encyclopedia of Sociology*, (Vol. 4). Edgar F. and Marie L. Borgatta, eds. New York: Macmillan, 1992. A clear, brief statement on secondary data, including a good bibliography.

Ragin, Charles C. (ed.) *Issues and Alternatives in Comparative Social Research.* Leiden, Netherlands: E.J. Brill, 1991. Ten recent articles on some of the problems and proposed solutions involving comparative research.

UNIT II

The Individual in Society

At birth we are colour-coded, blue or pink. We are tagged with names, usually according to gender. We are fed the types of food that society deems best. Sooner or later we are toilet-trained, introduced to eating schedules, and taught the proper way to eat. We learn to be polite. We learn whom and what to love, and whom and what to fear. Thus we are born into, and adapt to, a social and (more or less) orderly world.

Our world is ordered by the beliefs, norms, and values of the group into which we are born. Every society has rules governing who is responsible for taking care of children, who is an eligible marriage partner, how to behave when one's father dies, what to eat and how often. Chapter 3 discusses culture: the variations and uniformities in these rules and values.

Implied here is the notion that human beings are systematically taught how to behave, feel, and think. This process of learning to become a member of society continues throughout life. What we learn is part of our culture; how we learn it is called socialization, and is discussed in Chapter 4.

Chapter 5 talks about gender: how sex has been used to categorize people, what this means, what the consequences of gender roles are, and how gender roles are changing.

Chapter 6 examines age and aging. All societies expect different behaviours from the young, mature, and old. As with gender roles, the expectations may vary greatly from society to society, but within each society the expectations are usually very clear. While people in different societies have very different life expectancies, everyone gets older and nobody gets out alive.

Every society has deviants — people who break the rules. Law-breakers are deviants, but so are people who break unwritten rules. The question of what is deviant, the puzzle of who becomes deviant, and the attempts of various sociological perspectives to explain deviance are the topics of Chapter 7.

Wherever possible, data on Mexico have been included in this unit. You should keep in mind, however, that largely because the age structure of Mexico is characterized by a very young population, there is little information available. Also, Mexico has data on crime, but these are not published. Furthermore, there is very little comparative research on values in Mexico.

CHAPTER 3

Culture

JAMES E. CURTIS
RONALD D. LAMBERT

In ordinary language, we may describe people as cultured, meaning that they speak a second language, are well versed in history and philosophy, and appreciate literature and art. It is in this sense that universities are sometimes thought of as places where one goes to "get culture." There is also the related distinction between "high" and "low" cultures, with the implication that the former is superior to the latter.

Sociologists do not ordinarily use the concept of culture in this value-laden fashion. As far as sociologists are concerned, everybody possesses culture as a member of society. To be human is to be cultured. **Culture** refers to shared symbols and their meanings prevailing in any society or part of society. These symbols and their meanings include ideas about facts, ideas about desirable goals, and ideas about how people should or should not act.

The effects of culture can be witnessed in the most mundane situations. Imagine people waiting for a bus, for example. They stand close together but do not speak, apparently oblivious of one another's existence. As the bus approaches, a woman steps back to permit an obviously elderly person to board first. This act is just one indication that the people have, in fact, taken account of each other while waiting. In stepping back, the woman has acknowledged the unwritten rule that one should defer to the elderly in such circumstances. By contrast, an apparently less generous person chooses to protect her position in the queue, adhering to the rule of "first come, first served." She has decided that this rule supersedes rules having to do with age. These rules — indeed, all rules of behaviour — are part of culture.

Social interaction is typically patterned and or- dered because people share in a culture. Consider automobile traffic on city streets, for example. Drivers know what to expect of other drivers, as well as of pedestrians, on the basis of commonly understood rules of the road. Drivers can make reasonably accurate predictions about others' be- haviour on the basis of what others *should* do. As drivers and pedestrians, we routinely stake our lives on the assumption that other people's be- haviour is governed by rules.

Activities as simple as boarding a bus or driv- ing a car, or as complex as sending a rocket to the moon, are possible because people can depend on others to behave in more or less predictable ways. Without this dependability, of course, society would be impossible. No wonder, then, that peo- ple have devised rules to ensure that we act and interact in a predictable and acceptable manner. The sociologist's task is to identify the origins, characteristics, and consequences of these rules, and of people's understandings of them.

Having people do what is expected is only pos- sible when the individuals involved possess re- ciprocal, or shared, understandings, with each person knowledgeable about and motivated to abide by the same rules. All regularly occurring or repetitive social relationships involve a shared understandings. Spouses respond to each other in more or less regular ways over time because of shared understandings. The same is true of the relationships between customers and sales clerks, between parents and children, between the police and criminals, between ministers and members of the congregation, and between people waiting in a queue. These shared understandings of how to behave are not always to our liking. We some- times violate them; but when we do, we often ex- perience feelings of guilt and remorse, or make efforts to keep the violations secret. These re- sponses testify to the power these understandings hold for us, even when we oppose or violate them.

Defining Culture

Shared Symbols and Meanings

Culture, then, involves *shared meanings*. In other words, what is important is the *idea* content of culture. In contrast, some social scientists — especially some anthropologists — emphasize that culture also possesses a *material* side. **Mate- rial culture** consists of all manner of material ob- jects that people create and use, ranging from simple tools to advanced machinery (such as computer) to works of art. For anthropologists, material artifacts often contain the only remain- ing evidence of past cultures.

To fully describe a culture, however, requires more than examining some of the material objects left by its people. This task demands that we draw on the meanings attached to objects by their producers and users; that is, it requires looking at objects as symbols. Crossed sticks may mean fire- wood in one culture and Christ's crucifixion in another. Automobiles, part of our material cul- ture, may be taken as a symbol of social standing, as a practical or impractical means of transpor- tation, as a social problem involving energy de- pletion, or as some combination of these three definitions, depending on the social group doing the defining. Material artifacts embody a culture and communicate their meanings to those versed in that culture, but they do not in themselves constitute the whole of culture.

Let's consider symbols and meanings in more detail. A **symbol** is anything taken by people, as a matter of convention, to stand for something else. It may be any object, sound, word, gesture, or action useful for communicating with others. In other words, symbols achieve much of their sig- nificance because they are the means of commu- nication. Any society or group within a society is a community of interaction — that is, of commu- nication — within which culture is affirmed and modified in varying degrees.

One such community of interaction is sociolo- gists (thought of as a professional group). It is the purpose of a textbook such as this, or of a course in sociology, to introduce the student to the cul- ture of sociologists — that is, to the shared sym- bols that have meaning for sociologists.

Most of the symbols presented here, as you will see, are common to speakers in the larger society, although the meanings attached to them by soci- ologists are more circumscribed and precise. Other symbols are more or less peculiar to soci- ologists, who have fashioned words to refer to specific meanings for which the existing language did not seem adequate. To the unsympathetic

Material culture consists of all manner of material objects that people create and use, ranging from simple tools to advanced machinery to works of art.

traffic; in another it may stand for the availability of sexual services. In other words, when we respond to symbols, we react to the meaning commonly attached to them in particular situations.

The meanings assigned to symbols, at least originally, are often quite arbitrary. Shakespeare's poetic lines "a rose / By any other name would smell as sweet" suggest the arbitrary way we attach words to things. The difference between defining a distance, or the speed of a car, in miles and defining it in kilometres is another example of this. It is historically arbitrary. Having agreed which definition of distance we will use, however, we respond and think in those terms.

We have indicated that the symbols and meanings making up culture are shared. Some aspects of culture are shared by almost all members of a society. Examples from Canadian society include ideas about the monetary value of different coins and paper bills; the rules of traffic governing drivers and pedestrians; and the meaning of parents, police, and teachers. No individual knows or needs all the culture of a society, however. Some aspects of culture — such as the specialized knowledge of medicine, engineering, or law — are shared by only a few people. Culture is like an idea bank on which all members of the society draw, though different groups may use different sections of the bank more than other groups. How much sharing takes place, by which groups and for what aspects of culture, is a research question of special interest to the sociologist.

Loyalty to Culture

If culture is as important and as pervasive as our discussion has implied, then we should expect people to develop intense loyalties to it. And, indeed, they do: witness the loyalty many older Canadians feel for the Imperial system of weights and measures, and their hostility toward metrication. Culture is external to individuals, in the sense that they learn about it, but it is also internal — it becomes part of them and bestows meaning on their lives. So people's loyalty to their culture is an intensely personal matter.

Table 3-1 illustrates cultural loyalty by showing the percentages of English-speaking Canadians, French-speaking Canadians, Americans, and Mexicans who said, in national surveys, that they were proud to be from *their* society. The data in

outsider or to the novice, these words have the appearance of jargon. As you become familiar with them and begin to share their meanings with sociologists, however, you will see these symbols as useful tools for communicating sociological ideas.

It should be emphasized that a symbol, while referring to something else, is not itself the thing that is symbolized. A flag bearing a maple leaf symbolizes the nation, but it is not the nation itself. The word *freedom* symbolizes a certain type of relationship between humans; it is not the relationship itself.

It follows, then, that the same object or concept may mean different things in different contexts. In one context a red light is a symbol for stopping

A Subtle Meaning of "the Umbrella"? *or* Are "Real Men" All Wet?

The meaning of symbols may vary greatly across social groups, even within the same society. Strange as it may seem, something as simple as the umbrella illustrates this. On first consideration this object would seem to have a common meaning for all North Americans — it is something with which to protect oneself in a rainstorm. The following newspaper story, however, tells us that for some people an umbrella symbolizes something about its bearer's manliness. It appeared under the title "Real Men May Use Umbrellas in Navy."

WASHINGTON — After almost two decades of debate, the Navy has decided that its men may carry umbrellas while in uniform.

The decision by Adm. Carlisle A.H. Trost, the Chief of Naval Operations, might not appear to be the stuff of controversy. But his authorization makes the Navy the second military service to allow its men to carry umbrellas. The decision also defies an old military sentiment that a military man protecting himself from the rain with an umbrella looks too effete.

Comdr. Tom Jurkowsky, a spokesman, said Monday that Admiral Trost recently received a recommendation from the Navy's Uniform Board to make the change and decided to authorize the move "as a common-sense approach to the climatic conditions that Navy men have to face."

Previously, only the Air Force allowed its men to carry umbrellas. All four services have allowed women to carry umbrellas for years.

The Navy's Uniform Board and top brass have debated the issue off and on since 1969, always rejecting the change with such explanations as the contention that it would hamper saluting.

Two years ago, when the Army's Uniform Board recommended the same step, Army Secretary John O. Marsh and Gen. John A. Wickham Jr., then the Army Chief of Staff, blocked the recommendation and vowed that no soldier would ever carry an umbrella while they were still in office.

General Wickham has since retired, but Mr. Marsh remains in his post.

A source said at the time that Mr. Marsh and General Wickham considered umbrellas an "artificial affectation" that was "intrinsically unmilitary."

Admiral Trost, while finally breaking with such arguments for the Navy, is issuing some ground rules just to be safe.

Commander Jurkowsky says the Navy is requiring that umbrellas be plain black, that they cannot be carried in formations, that they must not be used as walking sticks and that they must be carried in the left hand to leave the right hand free for saluting.

Admiral Trost's decision does not affect the Marine Corps, a branch of the Navy.

A Marine officer who asked not to be named said he expected his service to continue resisting the move along with the Army.

Source:

New York Times, November 11, 1987. Reprinted by permission of Associated Press.

TABLE 3-1   Percentages Expressing Pride in Their National Origin: Responses by Samples of English Canadians, French Canadians, Americans, and Mexicans

Pride in the Nation*	English Canadians	French Canadians	Americans	Mexicans
Very proud	65.5	51.6	74.8	66.0
Quite proud	28.7	36.6	18.7	22.2
Not very proud	2.9	7.3	2.6	9.7
Not at all proud	0.8	3.1	0.8	1.0
Don't know	2.0	1.4	3.1	1.1

*The question asked was, "How proud are you to be Canadian [American, Mexican]?" It was followed by the five answer options.
SOURCE: Ronald Inglehart et al., *World Values Survey, 1981–1983: Computer File and Codebook*. 3rd ed. (Ann Arbor, MI: Institute for Social Research [producer], 1989. Ann Arbor, MI: Inter-University Consortium for Political and Social Research, University of Michigan [distributor], 1991).

the table are taken from interviews that were conducted with national samples of over 1000 adults in each of the three North American societies between 1981 and 1983 (Inglehart et al. 1990). We will present various results from these surveys in this chapter to set the views of English Canadians and French Canadians in a comparative North American context.

As Table 3-1 shows, loyalty to one's own culture is very common in Canada and the other two societies. Over 85 percent of each sample said they were either "very proud" or "quite proud" to be from their society. However, the proportion of French Canadians who reported being "very proud" was lower than that for the other three samples. This is to be expected in light of the social unrest in French Quebec over recent years and because the label used in the Canadian survey was "Canadian," not "French Canadian" or "Québécois." French Canadians would be more likely to express pride in their "French Canadian" or "Québécois" origins, if these terms had been used.

Loyalty to one's culture is an intensely personal matter.

Since we tend to have such an emotional investment in our own culture, we are often sceptical about the worth of ideas and practices in other groups and societies. Would it not be best for everybody, we may think, if others' beliefs and values corresponded to our own? Anglophones, for example, may believe that francophones would be better off if they simply abandoned their language and adopted a more vital and progressive language — English. This kind of loyalty to one's own culture and belittling of others' cultures is called **ethnocentrism**.

Ethnocentrism reveals itself in judgements about all kinds of beliefs and practices. We may wonder, for instance, how any culture could think that filed teeth are attractive, or how another group could possibly find country music interesting and enjoyable. Until recently many Westerners questioned the "misguided" notion that acupuncture has significant medical benefits, since our own doctors did not practise it. We can detect similar processes between townspeople and students in university communities, between civilians and members of the military, between young and old, between religious groups, between sociologists and psychologists, and so on. Ethnocentrism is involved, then, in our judgements of other cultures, or of other subcultures within our own society. Some social scientists regard this very human tendency as the seed from which most intergroup prejudice grows (LeVine and Campbell 1972).

William Sumner (1960), writing in 1906, was one of the first social scientists to emphasize the pervasiveness of ethnocentric thinking. He argued that it seemed to be a universal phenomenon that people see the world in terms of "us versus them," and disapprove of the ways "they" see and do things.

Why do people think ethnocentrically? There are a number of reasons, including the previously mentioned preference for predictability. Confronting significantly different ideas about how to do things implicitly challenges the judgements inherent in one's own culture. It is easier to simply reject differences out-of-hand than to systematically and repeatedly embark on a major re-evaluation of one's beliefs.

In addition, families, schools, churches, peer groups, and so on, do more than simply teach specific beliefs and values. The culture they transmit is linked to self-images so that acting in culturally approved ways affirms people's self-worth. Acting in culturally disapproved ways, on the other hand, arouses feelings of shame and guilt. Much of what is transmitted is further justified by invidious comparisons that are made with "out-groups" and their cultures. Consider, for example, how religious culture is transmitted in some groups in our society. Beliefs having to do with sin, damnation, and salvation may be taught as catechism and as sacred duty to young children well before they can exercise critical and independent judgement. Children learn to judge their own worth, as well as the worth of people outside the faith, in terms of these emotionally charged beliefs.

The personal disorientation experienced when one is immersed in a foreign culture has been labelled *culture shock*. The experience is shocking in the sense that the things one has taken for granted are profoundly challenged. This happens, for example, when people travel to, or through, other countries for the first time. It may even occur within our own society — for instance, when moving from English to French Canada, from a farm to a large city, from high school to university. The point is less dramatically made when we interact with people from different cultures on our home turf. These contacts may prove awkward, even if they do not produce shock. Hall (1962) offers the following example of a situation where different cultural assumptions about interpersonal space are seen to collide:

A conversation I once observed between a Latin and a North American began at one end of a 4-foot [12-metre] hall. I watched the two conversationalists until they finally reached the other end of the hall. This manœuvre had been effected by a continual series of small backward steps on the part of the North American as he unconsciously retreated, searching for a comfortable talking distance. Each time, there was an accompanying closing of the gap as his Latin friend attempted to re-establish his own accustomed conversation distance.

Many sociologists have cultivated an approach of **cultural relativism** to counteract ethnocentrism when their work involves contact with different cultures. Under this approach sociologists should only describe and explain the workings of a culture; they should not judge it against the morality of their own culture. It is proper to assess the internal consistency of a culture or how successfully it deals with a society's problems, but it is inadmissible to moralize about the culture's goodness or badness. A behaviour that is condemned as immoral in one society may be acceptable in another society. However, in the absence of absolute standards of judgement, it is said to be arbitrary and unscientific to evaluate the moral worth of the behaviour. All cultures are valid when judged on their own terms. In other words, according to cultural relativists, the only way to judge a culture is according to its own standards. To do otherwise is ethnocentric.

The idea that culture is relative to societies is reinforced in the results of cross-cultural studies. Research comparing activities defined as immoral in different societies, past and present, has shown few rules that are universal across all societies. There is evidence that all societies oppose incest and violence within the community, although the specific types of behaviour prohibited (what specific sex-partners are taboo, for example) vary markedly across cultures. Beyond this there are few moral universals. However, ideas about what is moral are present in all societies. Despite the differences among societies in what is thought to be good or bad, all have some ideas about good and bad behaviour. Cultures differ only in their detailed contents.

Culture and Social Behaviour

We have noted that people's behaviour is oriented to their culture and its rules. However, there is no mechanical one-to-one relationship between the culture associated with a particular situation and the behaviour of a set of individuals in the situation. Therefore, we cannot predict all behaviour from knowing the culture of the group.

What we are warning against is a *blueprint theory* of culture, which supposes that culture is always closely followed or that it is overwhelming and absolute in its impact on individuals' actions. We prefer to say that culture frames people's behaviour, rather than rigidly determining it. By *framing*, we mean that people draw on cultural meanings to define the choices available to them and to make sense of their experiences.

Sometimes culture is a poor predictor of people's behaviour simply because the rules have been poorly communicated, or because they are uninformed. It is difficult to abide by rules of which you are ignorant, even if you are otherwise disposed to do so. At other times there is inconsistency in the culture communicated — for instance, when following the rules taught in one situation means contradicting what has been learned in other situations. Conflicting expectations about premarital sex may exist in a person's peer group and in his or her family, for example. Where the different rules learned are not absolutely situation-specific, then following the rules of one group can mean acting contrary to the rules of another group. The ideas and rules taught within a given situation may even be inconsistent among themselves.

Rules also vary in the vigour with which infractions are monitored and sanctions administered. This affects the likelihood that the rules will be obeyed. In a given situation, different activities may be required, preferred, permitted, tolerated, disapproved, or prohibited. For behaviours in the middle of this continuum, predictions based on the rules may be less clear than for behaviours near the ends. Other things being equal, behaviour can be more confidently predicted from strongly enforced rules.

Concepts for Describing Culture

We have emphasized in our definition that symbols and their meanings are essential elements of culture. These provide the basis for different types of shared ideas: beliefs, norms, values, statuses, and ideologies. We will discuss these in turn.

Beliefs

We can distinguish two broad categories of beliefs: descriptive and normative beliefs. **Descriptive beliefs** are ideas or claims about what is, was, or will be, including opinions about cause-and-effect relations. All of the following are de-

scriptive beliefs: politicians are dishonest, God created the universe; cigarette smoking causes cancer; Soviets are superior hockey players. Descriptive beliefs may be mistaken and inaccurate, as judged by scientific rules of proof. But even factually incorrect beliefs can shape the perceptions and behaviour of people who hold them. To a considerable extent our thoughts and actions are shaped by what we are convinced does, will, or did exist. An example is Christians' belief in the existence and meanings of God and Jesus, and the ways these meanings shape and justify the believers' actions.

Table 3-2 gives details on the distribution of several religious beliefs in English Canada, French Canada, the United States, and Mexico. Again, the table is based on responses by the people interviewed in the international surveys discussed above. Table 3-2 shows that there is great consensus across the four samples concerning the existence of God; 90 percent or more of each cultural group agreed with this idea. There is also high consensus (80 percent or more) across the societies concerning the existence of souls. There is less widespread agreement that there is life after death, a devil, hell, heaven, or sin. Also, Canadians, whether English or French, are less likely to hold these beliefs than Americans and Mexicans, and Americans are most likely to believe in these things (compare Reavis 1990). This is consistent with Bibby's (1987a:218–220) theory that Americans are more religious than Canadians because the United States has a more competitive religious "marketplace." By this, Bibby means that the United States has far more churches and sects competing for the sentiments, participation, and financial contributions of members than does Canada. The greater competition for members in the United States is said to place religious beliefs in the media more often (e.g., religious programs on TV), and to lead to more religious teaching, in that country. (Compare Bibby's analysis in Chapter 13 of this book.)

A recent survey of a national sample of 1500 Canadians conducted for *Maclean's* magazine provides other good examples of descriptive beliefs. This poll showed what people in this country believe about themselves compared with Americans. As Table 3-3 indicates, Canadians believe they are less violent and competitive, but

TABLE 3-2 Percentages Holding Particular Religious Beliefs: Responses by Samples of English Canadians, French Canadians, Americans, and Mexicans

Do Believe In*	English Canadians	French Canadians	Americans	Mexicans
God	90.1	94.8	95.3	96.8
Life after death	61.2	62.4	71.0	64.5
A soul	80.1	80.1	88.0	79.6
The devil	44.8	26.2	65.6	51.9
Hell	41.8	27.2	66.7	50.9
Heaven	69.3	64.5	84.6	75.9
Sin	75.4	58.9	88.0	81.8
Reincarnation	27.3	34.5	23.2	46.6

*The question asked was, "Which, if any, of the following do you believe in?" Then the eight-item list above was read to the respondent.
SOURCE: Ronald Inglehart et al.

more hard-working, informed, and honest, and more likely to be concerned about the poor and the environment than Americans are (Phillips and Barrett 1988).

Descriptive beliefs can change markedly over time, as people come to believe new and different things. Examples abound in medicine and science: for instance, it was once thought that draining blood from those who were ill — using

TABLE 3-3 Canadians' Beliefs about Themselves Compared with Americans

Compared with Americans, Canadians Are	Percentage Who Said		
	"More"	"Less"	"The Same"
Violent	8	67	24
Competitive	19	53	27
Hard-working	33	14	52
Informed/sophisticated	34	26	39
Honest and fair	42	6	52
Concerned about the poor	56	10	33
Environmentally concerned	69	11	20

SOURCE: Adapted from Andrew Phillips and Cindy Barrett, "Defining identity," *Maclean's*, January 4, 1988, p. 45.

leeches and such — would cure many diseases. Another interesting example is emphasized in the recent work of Nancy Theberge (1989). She describes how people have come to revise their belief in women's "frailty." She points out that women's increased participation, and success, in such endurance sports as marathons has helped break down the frailty image. In the past, "a vicious circle of illogic and discrimination" existed, in which "women were excluded from sport and their exclusion was interpreted as evidence of their weakness" (Theberge 1989).

Normative beliefs are beliefs about what should or ought to be. They refer to the goodness or badness of things, actions, or events; to their virtuousness or wickedness; or to their propriety or impropriety.

We have referred to several examples having to do with rules governing queues. Other examples are the convictions of some Mennonites that they are morally obliged to wear dark clothing in public and to use the horse and buggy as transportation. Religious doctrines generally involve normative beliefs designed to guide behaviour in various situations. Many economic and political beliefs are of this sort. Some people think that Canada should have a more equitable distribution of income and wealth than exists now; they argue that we should pursue policies aimed at greatly improving the incomes of our poorest citizens, while containing, through more taxes, the incomes of the highest earners. Others think the status quo should be preserved and defended at all costs. Some believe that the traditional family is the cornerstone of society and that divorce and the erosion of family ties should be resisted. Still others believe that family life can effectively take many forms — and, indeed, that it should.

Norms

The rules regulating people's behaviour in particular situations are called **norms**. Norms may or may not correspond to our normative beliefs. People may prefer that there be different rules in a given situation (their normative beliefs), but they may nonetheless choose to honour the prevailing norms, at least for the moment.

Norms are said to be *institutionalized* when they are supported by people's normative beliefs. Sociologists, therefore, have an interest in assessing the degree of correspondence between normative beliefs and established norms. An example of a norm that is not well institutionalized is the current prohibition against capital punishment in Canada. Judging from public opinion polls, there is little support for the legislation. Yet the prohibition legislation persists, governing the behaviour of judges and jurors in our courtrooms. These people follow the rules prohibiting capital punishment despite the public's views — and sometimes despite their own conflicting views.

Sociologists also attempt to explain how normative beliefs may contribute in time to the modification of norms — and, conversely, how the existence of norms may lead people to adopt new normative beliefs. In the former case, for example, the use of a referendum on capital punishment would be one avenue by which people's wishes might be translated into legal norms. As this example suggests, whether normative preferences become norms or not is broadly speaking a political process. In the latter case, human rights codes are premised on the idea that rules forbidding certain kinds of discrimination will lead people to think differently about appropriate and inappropriate behaviour. This is also the subject matter of socialization, the process by which people learn and acquire respect for group norms (see Chapter 4).

Norms are situation-specific. Behaviour prohibited in one situation may be permitted, even required, in another situation. While norms of modesty generally forbid nudity, it is permitted in such specific situations as bedrooms, medical examination rooms, nudist camps, and striptease joints. The general prohibition against taking human life also has a number of well-understood exceptions, including warfare and self-defence. The significance of these distinctions is conveyed in our choice of words: murder, execution, abortion, suicide, assassination, self-defence. The word chosen conveys something about the situation involved, the people in it, and the permissibility of the act.

Norms are of different types. Some norms take the form of written rules, as in the Highway Traffic Act, while others are merely conveyed informally, as when a parent instructs a child how to behave in a restaurant. Some norms, such as rules of etiquette, are advisory in nature, compared with norms against theft and homicide, which are more punitive in their intent. Norms differ in their enforcement, too, some depending on community opinion and others on designated officers of the law. Furthermore, the origins of some norms can be traced, while the history of other norms is a mystery.

These are the kinds of distinctions that Sumner (1960) sought to capture in his well-known classification of folkways, mores, and laws. **Folkways** are rules about customary ways of behaving. Their beginnings lie in tradition, so their precise point of origin is often unknown. The violation of folkways usually results in only minor inconvenience. Since folkways deal with matters of little consequence, members of a society do not have strong feelings about them and their enforcement is informal. Table etiquette is an example of folkways in our society. Eating food with the wrong fork is greeted by little more than stares and the occasional comment from nearby diners.

Mores are "must" rules, referring to "must behaviours" or "must-not behaviours," that are strictly enforced. The norms here are thought to touch on things held dear or sacred. Like folkways, mores are also traditional in origin. An example would be norms against showing contempt for the symbols of one's country, such as booing the national anthem.

Laws take two forms — common and enacted. *Common law* is based on custom and precedent, reflecting the past practice of the courts. *Enacted*

Two Kinds of Values: Instrumental and Terminal

Social psychologist Milton Rokeach has developed two classifications of values based on cross-cultural research, some of which was conducted in Canada while he taught at the University of Western Ontario. He has argued that values can take the form of terminal values, *which are goals, and* instrumental values, *which are standards for judging the means to achieve goals. In his research, people are given a descriptive statement for each value and are asked to rank the terminal values in terms of their personal importance. They are then asked to rank the instrumental values in terms of their importance. Rokeach's two lists of values are presented here.*

Terminal Values

A comfortable life
  (a prosperous life)
An exciting life
  (a stimulating, active life)
A sense of accomplishment
  (lasting contribution)
A world at peace
  (free of war and conflict)

A world of beauty
  (beauty of nature, arts)
Equality
  (brotherhood, equal opportunity
  for all)
Family security
  (taking care of loved ones)
Freedom
  (independence, free choice)
Happiness
  (contentedness)
Inner harmony
  (freedom from inner conflict)
Mature love
  (sexual and spiritual intimacy)
National security
  (protection from attack)
Pleasure
  (enjoyable, leisurely life)
Salvation
  (saved, eternal life)
Self-respect
  (self-esteem)
Social recognition
  (respect, admiration)
True friendship
  (close companionship)
Wisdom
  (mature understanding of life)

Instrumental Values

Ambitious
  (hard-working, aspiring)
Broadminded
  (open-minded)
Capable
  (competent, effective)
Cheerful
  (lighthearted, joyful)
Clean
  (neat, tidy)

Courageous
  (standing up for your beliefs)
Forgiving
  (willing to pardon others)
Helpful
  (working for the welfare of others)
Honest
  (sincere, truthful)
Imaginative
  (daring, creative)
Independent
  (self-reliant, self-sufficient)
Intellectual
  (intelligent, reflective)
Logical
  (consistent, rational)
Loving
  (affectionate, tender)
Obedient
  (dutiful, respectful)
Polite
  (courteous, well-mannered)
Responsible
  (dependable, reliable)
Self-controlled
  (restrained, self-disciplined)

Source:

Adapted from Milton Rokeach, "Some reflections about the place of values in Canadian social science," in *Perspectives on the Social Sciences in Canada*, T.N. Guinsburg and G.L. Reuber, eds. (Toronto: University of Toronto Press, 1974), p. 180.

laws are formally codified and enacted by legislative bodies. Both types of laws are sustained by police and court actions. They are, of course, laws about which people feel strongly, such as those against treason, and others about which they feel mildly or indifferently, such as some traffic laws. The degree of feeling is generally reflected in the severity of the penalty for violations.

Values

In every culture there are general conceptions of the desirable goals, or ends, that people should strive to attain and criteria by which actions should be evaluated. Rokeach (1974) calls these two types of **values** "terminal" and "instrumental," respectively (see the accompanying boxed insert). Values are more general in their application than either norms or normative beliefs. They constitute standards by which people evaluate goals and actions. For this reason, people attach a great deal of emotional importance to them.

Sociologists study the basis for values within a culture, as well as the kinds of trade-offs worked among values in specific situations. We consider the former matter in the second half of this chapter. As far as the latter question is concerned, we should anticipate complex interactions among values because there will generally be at least several values relevant to any given situation. Canadians, for example, are said to value efficiency, meaning that they wish to economize on the use of time, money, and other resources in their activities. They also place a high value on democratic decision-making, with the result that values of democracy and efficiency periodically collide. In some situations, democratic decision-making may prove to be expensive in both time and money, while in other situations what is efficient may lose the support of the people affected. *Value analysis* involves identifying and explaining the kinds of trade-offs among values that cultures tolerate or require.

Statuses

The aspects of culture, statuses, to which we turn next are built on the distinctions just described, but are more complex, in the sense that they combine the cultural elements already defined.

Status defines a position in society according to its rights and obligations. *Status rights* consist of ideas about what you may properly expect from others when you occupy a particular status. *Status obligations* are ideas about what others have a right to expect from you when you are in a given status. Statuses locate people in groups, organizations, and, more generally, in society at large. Certain statuses are relative to the relationships contained in particular groups or organizations. Other statuses, however, such as those based on age, gender, and race, are not specific to any particular group or organization. Nonetheless, they presuppose or imply interaction; men are defined relative to women, and so on.

The most important consequence of statuses is their effect in shaping interactions among people.

The shared understanding of rights and obligations among individuals in different statuses make for predictable and ordered social behaviour. Statuses are generally highly interrelated in the sense that their rights and obligations are defined in terms of one another. A mother, for example, cannot have that status unless and until she has a child. There are no wives without husbands, no teachers without students, no leaders without followers, no bosses without subordinates.

Statuses can be *ascribed* or *achieved*. Entry into an achieved status depends on a person's satisfactory performance of some relevant requirement. Movement into or out of an achieved status, in other words, is based on personal accomplishment or failure. The relevant accomplishments are typically prescribed by the rules of the situation. An example is passing bar examinations and being called to the bar in order to practise law. An ascribed status, by contrast, is assigned to an individual regardless of personal merit. This assignment typically occurs at birth. Examples of ascribed statuses in our society include racial and ethnic status, gender status, and age status. Occasionally, normally ascribed statuses may be changed, as when a person undergoes a sex change operation or when a member of a racial minority passes as a member of the racially dominant group. But these are rare instances.

In a complex society such as Canada, each person possesses several statuses simultaneously by virtue of membership in various social categories, groups, and organizations, and the statuses defining participation in each. All of a person's statuses taken together, at any given time in her or his life, are called a *status set*. The existence of status sets makes for the possibility of *status conflict*, a situation in which fulfilling the obligations associated with one status interferes with the fulfilment of obligations associated with another status. For example, a working mother with young children is often placed in a situation of status conflict. She assumes the status of worker and must perform her duties as, say, an accountant. She must put in long hours at her place of work, thus intruding on her other obligations as mother (and possibly as wife, too). Another example is provided by the status of lead hand in a factory. This person is caught between management and workers, with competing obligations toward each. And young people often find themselves having to reconcile conflicting demands from their parents and from their peer group.

Ideologies

Sociologists define **ideologies** as emotionally charged sets of descriptive and normative beliefs and values that explain and justify how society is or should be organized (Mannheim 1936; Parkin 1972; Lambert and Curtis 1979).

Three types of ideologies can be identified. *Reformist* and *radical ideologies* rally the forces of change, while *conservative ideologies* support existing social arrangements. Reformist ideologies seek changes without challenging the basic rules and regulations — as when medicare, welfare, and unemployment insurance are established without eliminating either the unequal distribution of wealth between workers and the owners of capital, or the principle of private property that underlies our economic order. Radical ideologies call for a fundamental restructuring of society or of one of its institutions, as the Co-operative Commonwealth Federation (predecessor of today's New Democratic Party) did at the time of its founding in the 1930s. The independence movement in Quebec also seeks to restructure the Canadian state. But reformist and radical ideologies may also call for a restoration of former ways of doing things in society. An example would be a proposal to eliminate social welfare measures on the grounds that welfare programs are too costly for taxpayers and that people should take care of themselves as they (allegedly) once did.

Conservative ideologies are sometimes called **dominant ideologies** to emphasize their prevailing and ruling character. Private property and capitalism currently prevail in our society. In the context of a socialist state, however, the dominant or "conservative" ideology would be socialist. Reformist and radical ideologies in any society are called **counter-ideologies** to emphasize their competing, but not prevailing, character (Parkin 1972).

According to Marchak (1975), "ideologies are screens through which we perceive the world .... They are seldom taught explicitly and systematically. They are rather transmitted through example, conversation, and casual observation." The following example suggests how a dominant economic ideology is conveyed in an otherwise innocent exchange between parent and child:

The child asks the parent "Why is that family poorer than us?" and receives an answer such as "Because their father is unemployed." The accumulation of such responses provides a ready index to the organization of the society in occupational terms, and with reference to age and gender roles. The child is informed by such responses that some occupations provide higher material rewards than others, that an occupation is essential, and that fathers, not mothers, earn family incomes. The child is not provided with an explanation for the differential between postmen and sales managers, between the employed and unemployed, between families in one income group and families in the other, but some children think to ask. There are, then, additional responses such as "If you work hard at school, you can go to the top," or "Sales managers are more important than postmen," or "Well, if people don't work, they can't expect to get along in the world." (Marchak 1975)

Counter-ideologies challenge the assumptions and beliefs of dominant ideologies. For example, one might ask (Marchak 1975), Why is education related to occupations? What is meant by "the top," and why should people strive for it? Why is status associated with material wealth? What do sales managers do that makes them important, and to whom is their work important? Why would anyone not work when the penalties for unemployment are so severe? It is the point of counter-ideology to expose ideological inconsistencies and hypocrisies and to offer an alternative vision.

Returning to the data from the comparative surveys of English Canadians, French Canadians, Americans, and Mexicans, we find that a large majority of each society are "reformist" in their orientation, at least in terms of answers to one set of questions asked in the cross-national interviews (see Table 3-4). From 65 to 70 percent of each sample wanted to see gradual reform in their society, as opposed to no change or radical change. The Mexican sample was less likely than the other three samples (9% versus about 20%) to say that the society should stay as it is. The latter is perhaps understandable in light of the poorer economic conditions and quality of life in Mexico as compared with Canada and the United States (see, for example, *Maclean's* 1992).

TABLE 3-4 **Percentages with Different Views about Social Change: Responses by Samples of English Canadians, French Canadians, Americans, and Mexicans**

Society Should Be*	English Canadians	French Canadians	Americans	Mexicans
Radically changed by revolution	3.6	4.9	4.4	9.5
Gradually improved by reform	65.9	69.3	65.1	67.8
Valiantly defended against change	20.0	20.2	20.9	9.3
Don't know	10.5	5.6	9.6	13.5

*The question asked was, "On this card are three basic kinds of attitudes ... [about] the society we live in. Please choose the one which best describes your own opinion."
SOURCE: Ronald Inglehart et al.

Subcultures

In a large and differentiated society such as our own, there is considerable cultural variation among the groups that make it up. Any group that has a great deal of interaction within itself and whose experiences set it apart from the rest of society will tend to develop local cultures, or what sociologists call **subcultures**. These are distinctive sets of beliefs, norms, and values that are possessed by particular groups in society and that set these groups off from others. While a subculture contains culture common to members of the wider society, it also has elements more or less unique to it.

Limited interaction with outsiders makes the development of unique beliefs, norms, and values both possible and probable. Occupational groups, such as medical doctors; ethnic populations, such as Italian Canadians; religious groups, such as Orthodox Jews; people living in small, isolated communities like those in the Canadian North: all such groups will develop sets of beliefs, norms, and values that make sense especially to them. Such differences guarantee that none of us acquires all the culture of a society. There are too many groups for us to be able to learn everything. And none of us can experience all groups; for example, very few of us are Jewish, Lutheran, and Catholic — only three of many religious statuses possible in Canada — within a lifetime.

One thing that often helps to maintain subcultural groups is the ways they distinguish themselves to outsiders through characteristic dress, lifestyles, and vocabularies. These distinctions

sometimes create barriers to interaction between outsiders and group members. At the same time, they make participants in a subculture aware of their discreteness, thus providing a basis for group loyalty. The specialized vocabulary of a group is a particularly obvious badge of subcultural group membership.

The Hutterites provide an example of religious subculture. They are an Anabaptist sect closely related to the Amish and Mennonites who live on farms in the western regions of Canada and the United States. They are the largest family-type communal grouping in the Western world, with over 20 000 members living in approximately 200 settlements (Hostetler and Huntington 1967). Among their beliefs is the idea that communal living is necessary for people to be trained in proper obedience to God. No private property is allowed; no member of the group may individually own so much as a pair of shoes. The Hutterites are set off from the wider society by a distinctive mode of dress — dark clothing for males and long, patterned dresses for females, whether adults or children. Social interaction with outsiders is further restricted by the belief that formal education beyond the primary level should not be pursued; religious services are conducted in German. The Hutterites do not attempt to achieve full social isolation from the wider society and its culture, though. They are successful farmers who trade with people in the surrounding area, and they buy modern farm machinery from outsiders. They also read newspapers, use telephones, and patronize non-Hutterite professionals (such as physicians and attorneys).

Subcultures distinguish themselves through characteristic dress, lifestyle, and vocabularies.

English Canadian and French Canadian Culture

There are no better examples of subcultures than English Canadians and French Canadians. Indeed, some would argue that these two groups are so distinct in some respects that they approximate separate "societies." They have distinct languages, considerable geographic and social isolation, separate political, educational, and religious organizations, and distinct legal and other traditions. Also, a number of writers have reported on differences in cultural values, historically, between English Canadians and the French-speaking people of Quebec (for example, Hughes 1943; Taylor 1964). English Canadians have been depicted as more individualistic, materialistic, and achievement-oriented in their outlook than the Québécois. The Québécois have been described as giving more priority to the

family and the kinship system as well as to religious and spiritual values. In other words, the picture of French Quebec that has emerged from some of the literature is that of a "folk society," compared with the modern, cosmopolitan society of English Canada. More recent studies, however (Baer and Curtis 1984, 1988), have shown that such value differences are now small or negligible where they exist at all. Indeed, some data show results in the opposite direction for achievement orientation, with French Canadians placing higher priority on this (see the accompanying boxed insert). French Canadians have also been said to be more xenophobic — more negative toward immigrants and other outsiders — because they are likely to see their French-language culture as "under seige" by a dominant anglo North American culture and the influx of immigrants and are in need of protection from them (Curtis and Lambert 1975, 1976; Lambert and Curtis 1982, 1983).

Do French Canadians Place Higher Value on Achievement than English Canadians Do?

Contrary to the traditional view of English–French Canadian differences, Baer and Curtis (1984) found that francophones emphasized achievement *more* than their anglophone counterparts. They used the 1977 Canadian Quality of Life survey data from a national sample of 2277 randomly selected anglophones and 896 francophones. When given a set of eleven value items on cards and asked to rank them in piles of "utmost importance," "very important," "fairly important," or "not important at all," francophones gave higher rankings to economic stability, self-development, excitement, love, and helping others than did their anglophone counterparts. There were no significant differences for family security, prosperity, independence, spiritual understanding, and achievement (francophones gave higher ratings to achievement, but this difference was not statistically significant). When responses to the individual items were later combined into factors, francophones were found to have higher scores on an achievement factor (consisting of the items on achievement, self-development, and excitement), a spiritual/helping others factor, and a social participation factor. No significant differences were found for a materialism factor, and anglophones rated family values (family security, economic stability, and love) higher than did francophones. There was no support from these data, then, for the idea that francophones were less achievement-oriented than their anglophone counterparts, or for the view that French Canadian culture restrains francophones from developing interests in economic achievement.

The 1981 version of the Canadian Quality of Life survey contained additional questionnaire items dealing with achievement orientation, and these provided the basis for a second study intended to replicate the pattern of results in the first study (Baer and Curtis 1988). The value items in the 1981 survey were introduced with the following statement:

We would like your opinion about life in general. Please tell me whether you agree or disagree with the following statements using one of the statements on this card [strongly agree; agree; disagree; strongly disagree].

The questions themselves were: (1) "Life is most enjoyable when you are trying to achieve some new goal"; (2) "You should always try to improve your position in life rather than accept what you have now"; (3) "A person ought to set goals for themselves [sic] which are difficult to achieve"; (4) "Unless one learns how to reduce one's desires, life will be full of disappointment and bitterness"; (5) "Those who are always trying to get ahead of life will never be happy"; and (6) "When you come down to it, the best thing to do is be contented with what you have since

you never know what the future will bring."

The accompanying table shows the responses to these items by French Canadians and English Canadians. Francophones were higher in achievement orientation and lower in responses of contentment with what they had achieved. Thus, the earlier findings on differences, the opposite of that predicted on the basis of the previous literature, were upheld in the second study.

A plausible interpretation of these results is that, because of francophones' relatively greater exclusion from economic success in the past, their culture has come to hold the pursuit of achievement in higher regard (Baer and Curtis 1984:422–424). Because economic security and attainment in the world of work was scarcer, it was valued more.

Whatever the differences between English and French Canadian culture today, it is clear that they *do not* include lesser achievement orientation among the French.

Scores in Responses to Six Achievement Questions for the Two Canadian Language Groups

Value Items*	French Canadian Subsample	English Canadian Subsample
Should reduce one's desires	2.53	2.65
Not happy trying to get ahead	2.27	2.46
Life enjoyable when trying to achieve	3.12	3.02
Should try to improve	3.10	2.85
Ought to set difficult goals	2.62	2.41
Better to be content	2.45	2.69

*The responses to these items were scored on a 4-point scale, with 1 = "strongly disagree"; 2 = somewhat disagree; 3 = somewhat agree; and 4 = "strongly agree."
SOURCE: Douglas E. Baer and James E. Curtis, "Differences in achievement values of French Canadians and English Canadians," in *Social Inequality in Canada*, J.E. Curtis et al., eds. (Scarborough, ON: Prentice-Hall).

We can distinguish between two broad theories on French Canadian–English Canadian differences (Lambert 1981). According to the first view, differences between French and English Canadians result from value differences. For example, the historical dominance of English Canadians in business has been said to result from their greater interest in worldly success. The Québécois were scarce in business pursuits because of their greater loyalties to religious and family-oriented values. If the Roman Catholic Church was prominent in Quebec life, this reflected the wishes of the people. Differences in cultural beliefs and values determined the behaviour differences between French and English Canadians.

In more recent years, French–English differences have been interpreted by many as responses to fundamental changes in the organization of Quebec society brought about by the conquest of 1759–62. In this view, Quebec was effectively "decapitated" by the conquest, because much of its secular elite — in the economy, the military, and government — was removed and returned to France. One consequence of this decapitation was that the leadership of Quebec society was left, by default, in the hands of the Roman Catholic Church. Then, with the economy firmly tied into the British system of colonial trade and with English established as the language of commerce, the Québécois were compelled to look elsewhere for valued goals, in the family and the church. In other words, the emergent French Canadian culture was one of accommodations made by the Québécois to their new economic, political, and social circumstances. This theory leads us to expect that the cultural preoccupations of the Québécois will continue to change, reflecting shifts in their economic and political power.

The choice between these two theories is a matter of some political as well as scholarly significance. If behavioural differences between the two language groups are attributable simply to differences in cultural values, then it is tempting to conclude that the people of French Canada simply get what they want or value. If, however, cultural differences are the product of who won or lost a war and the ways in which the winners have organized society, then we are more likely to question the justice of the situation and to entertain the redress of historical grievances.

Canadian and American Culture

Another example of how historical conflicts are thought to have shaped Canadian culture is found in theories on the cultural differences between English Canadians and Americans. One view traces these differences to the quite different reactions of Americans and English Canadians to the American Revolution, while another focuses on the different laws and norms that were transplanted at particular periods in European history to what became Canada and the United States.

Lipset (1963, 1965, 1985, 1990), an American sociologist, best exemplifies the first line of thought. His theory is that the American Revolution was a traumatic event that left its imprint not only on the victorious Americans but also on the defeated British North Americans, who, with the French Canadians, went on to create Canada. Traces of our ancestors' rejection of the American Revolution may be found, it is argued, even today in the culture of English Canadians. Thus, according to Lipset, Canadians show greater deference to authority, are more conservative, are less achievement-oriented and more elitist, and are more likely to put the welfare of the community ahead of their personal interests. It was these values that the losing side, the Tory United Empire Loyalists, carried to the Canadian colonies. Once established in Canada, these values were reinforced by our British, monarchical, and religious traditions. Americans, who rejected Britain and the British values, are more rejecting of authority, more liberal, less elitist, and more self-oriented, it is argued.

It was obviously impossible for Lipset to test the specific link between reactions to the American Revolution and contemporary culture. His approach, therefore, was to test the claim that the two countries differ in their values in the predicted direction. This he did using statistics on divorce, crime, levels of educational attainment, and government-spending patterns and data on public opinion. If Canadians put the common good ahead of self-interest, then they should be less likely to divorce; if they were deferential to authority and more attached to the common good, they should be less likely to commit a variety of criminal offences; if they placed less value on personal achievement, they should spend less money on higher education; and so on. In general,

Lipset argued, the data tended to support his picture of Canada.

Lipset's interpretations of his findings have been criticized on a number of grounds. For example, divorce rates reflect more than people's values and their readiness to say "I quit." Divorce laws affect how easy it is to obtain a divorce. Thus, it is difficult to say how much of the difference between the two countries in divorce was owing to values and how much to legal hurdles for divorce. To correct for this ambiguity, a number of studies have looked at data on respondents' beliefs and opinions about a variety of issues as measures of value orientations (compare Baer et al. 1990; Curtis et al. 1989, 1992; Lipset 1990). Suffice it to say that the results of these studies are equivocal in their support of Lipset's predictions on Canadian–American differences.

The second kind of historical explanation of Canadian culture is called the Hartzian thesis, after its originator, Louis Hartz (1964). Its basic premise is that ideologies develop out of conflict waged by their respective proponents. Compared with the variety of contending ideologies to be found in Europe, however, the debate in North America has been exceedingly truncated. According to Hartz, immigrants to the new North American societies did not carry with them the full spectrum of ideological opinion that prevailed in the countries from which they had come. Only parts of the spectrum made the journey, with the result that these parts were free to flourish unchecked by the ideological adversaries they had known at home. The institutions founded in the new societies, therefore, bore the ideological imprint of their founders. In the case of the United States and English Canada, the English-speaking peoples carried with them the assumptions of liberal individualism. The assumptions of conservatism and socialism were missing or under-represented among the English-speaking settlers of North America, thus permitting liberalism to develop virtually without impediment. But Quebec was another matter. Because this society was founded prior to the French Revolution, it developed as a corporatist and authoritarian extrusion from France.

This theory was later revised by Horowitz (1968) to account for cultural differences between Canada and the United States. While the United States can fairly be described as a liberal society,

Horowitz argued, the appearance of a "Tory touch" complicates the Canadian case. The United Empire Loyalists and our British traditions introduced distinctly nonliberal elements into English Canadian culture. This Tory presence meant that Canadian conservatism would not be like its American cousin, and it provided the fertile ideological soil out of which an indigenous Canadian social democratic party would emerge.

In the accompanying three tables we can assess some of the predictions from the above theories of cultural differences. We again use the data on the four cultures from the international surveys. First, Table 3-5 presents answers to a question on what types of people the respondents would *not* like to see as their neighbours. Included on the list of potential neighbours were "left-wing extremists." On the basis of Lipset's views we might expect the more "conservative" Canadians, particularly English Canadians, to be less inclined to accept left-wing neighbours. Beyond this, we might expect Canadians to be more accepting of others (more collectivity-oriented) than Americans. That is, Canadians should be more accepting of the potentially disruptive neighbours mentioned on the list in the table. In fact, English Canadians, French Canadians, and Mexicans tended to be more accepting of different kinds of neighbours than were the Americans, where these were cross-cultural differences. Only for "large families" and "religious sect or cult members" were English Canadians somewhat less tolerant of the types of neighbours than Americans were. There were no English Canadian–American differences for attitudes toward left-wingers, but French Canadians and Mexicans were less rejecting of this group. Americans were much more fearful of "the emotionally unstable" than were people in the other three samples.

French Canadians were less rejecting of the potential neighbours than English Canadians for all types except "people of other races" and "immigrant or foreign workers," where the levels of rejection, though low, were slightly higher than for English Canadians.

Table 3-6 shows what qualities from a list of seventeen, people in the four North American cultures regarded as desirable in children. Looking at the highest-ranked qualities, again there is much similarity across the four national groups.

TABLE 3-5 Percentages Who Would NOT Like Particular People as Neighbours: Responses by Samples of English Canadians, French Canadians, Americans, and Mexicans

People Not Liked as Neighbours*	English Canadians	French Canadians	Americans	Mexicans
Criminals	38.2	32.1	47.6	49.3
People of another race	3.0	4.9	8.0	6.5
Students	2.4	2.4	2.8	5.1
Left-wing extremists	31.7	19.5	31.0	20.4
Unmarried mothers	2.8	0.0	4.4	6.3
Heavy drinkers	57.7	57.1	56.4	41.0
Right-wing extremists	24.2	16.0	24.5	10.5
Large families	16.4	7.0	7.6	13.8
Emotionally unstable	31.8	15.3	45.6	29.0
Religious sect or cult members	27.7	10.3	22.4	16.8
Immigrant/foreign workers	5.9	6.6	8.5	0.0

*The question asked was, "On this list of various groups of people, could you please sort out any that you would *not* like to have as neighbours."
SOURCE: Ronald Inglehart et al.

High value is placed on "good manners," "honesty," responsibility," and "respect for others." "Religious faith," though, is higher in the values of Americans than of the other groups. In keeping with the stereotype about Canadians that one sometimes hear, both French and English Canadians gave a higher rank to "politeness" than did people in the other two national samples. French Canadians rated "thrift" and "determination" higher than the other samples, and they rated "independence" and "hard work" lower than did English Canadians and Americans. "Obedience" was more important to the Mexican subsample than to the others.

If the rank orders of the top ten rated values are correlated for pairs of cultures, we find much more similarity for English Canadians and Americans than for the other possible pairs. This probably occurs because of the common European cultural origins of the people who established these cultures and the use of the same main language, and, consequently, the easier diffusion of ideas and values from one culture to the other.

Finally, Table 3-7 indicates the extent to which people living in the four cultures had practised each of seven forms of civil protest and civil dis-

obedience. Lipset's theory leads us to expect more civil disobedience, or less obedience to authority, from Americans than from English Canadians, and perhaps from French Canadians. Again, there are more cross-cultural similarities than differences in the data. English Canadians and Americans, followed by French Canadians, were most likely to have signed a petition. Beyond this, the only difference of note was that the Mexicans were less likely to have protested by joining a boycott, attending a demonstration, or participating in an unofficial strike. These forms of political protest are apparently more readily practised by citizens in the three more northerly cultures. There is either a more repressive political environment in Mexico or more deference to authority, or both.

Tables 3-5 to 3-7, taken together, suggest, as do other recent studies (Baer et al. 1990; Curtis et al. 1989, 1992), that Lipset's theory of Canada–U.S. differences in culture should be viewed with caution when applied to the contemporary situation. There is much similarity across the English Canadian and American cultures in particular. Also, while there are many cultural differences across the four North American cultures — languages

TABLE 3-6 Qualities Considered to Be Very Important in Children: Responses by Samples of English Canadians, French Canadians, Americans, and Mexicans

Important Qualities*	English Canadians		French Canadians		Americans		Mexicans	
	%	Rank	%	Rank	%	Rank	%	Rank
Good manners	57.3	(2)	49.9	(2)	61.8	(2)	80.2	(1)
Politeness	37.8	(5)	49.5	(4)	36.0	(6)	27.6	(7)
Independence	27.8	(6)	16.4	(13.5)	32.3	(8)	15.7	(13)
Hard work	21.3	(10)	17.8	(12)	26.8	(10)	19.0	(12)
Honesty	76.0	(1)	82.2	(1)	78.8	(1)	47.3	(3)
Feel responsibility	38.4	(4)	48.8	(5)	43.7	(4)	56.9	(2)
Patience	13.7	(14)	16.0	(15)	14.1	(14)	22.3	(11)
Imagination	10.8	(16)	9.4	(16)	9.4	(17)	12.4	(14.5)
Respect others	55.2	(3)	49.8	(3)	53.2	(3)	39.1	(5)
Leadership	3.1	(17)	4.2	(17)	10.1	(15.5)	5.0	(17)
Self-control	27.6	(7)	32.1	(6)	32.6	(7)	24.9	(8)
Thrift	11.9	(15)	19.5	(10)	10.1	(15.5)	12.4	(14.5)
Determination	18.8	(13)	28.2	(7)	14.8	(13)	10.3	(16)
Religious faith	25.4	(8)	20.6	(9)	39.1	(5)	36.0	(6)
Unselfishness	20.8	(11)	18.8	(11)	18.7	(11)	24.2	(8)
Obedience	22.0	(9)	16.4	(13.5)	27.9	(9)	43.2	(4)
Loyalty	19.5	(12)	26.8	(8)	17.0	(12)	24.0	(10)

*The question asked was, "Here is a list of qualities which children can be encouraged to learn at home. Which, if any, do you consider to be especially important (please choose up to five)?"
SOURCE: Ronald Inglehart et al.

spoken, levels of economic development, various laws, currency used, and so on — several close similarities in beliefs and values are evident.

Cultural Persistence and Change

Having labelled and defined the contents of culture, we are now prepared to consider some of the ways culture is maintained and changed. The related question of how culture is transmitted to new members of society — the problem of socialization — is dealt with in Chapter 4.

Our discussion illustrates the major explanations of how culture develops. These explanations convey the kind of processes thought to be oper-

ating in the creation and change of symbolic meaning within society. We have also grouped these ideas according to three broad sociological perspectives from which they are drawn: symbolic interaction, structural functionalism, and conflict.

The Symbolic-Interaction Perspective

The symbolic-interaction approach focuses on the facts that the use of symbols by people, and the shared meanings of symbols, are basic to a clear understanding of social life. Symbolic-interaction ideas have guided our definition and descriptions of culture.

When we turn to the matter of how the symbolic interactionists view culture's change and persistence, it is important to emphasize that cul-

TABLE 3-7   Percentages of People Who Have Taken Particular Political Actions: Responses by Samples of English Canadians, French Canadians, Americans, and Mexicans

Political Action Taken*	English Canadians	French Canadians	Americans	Mexicans
Signed a petition	65.9	51.2	62.6	9.7
Joined a boycott	14.9	14.6	15.1	0.8
Attended a demonstration	13.4	15.0	12.3	7.6
Joined unofficial strike	4.5	5.2	3.5	1.2
Occupied buildings/factories	1.9	3.8	1.4	1.2
Damaged property	0.0	0.0	0.1	0.7
Fought with demonstrators or police	1.3	1.0	1.9	1.0

*The question asked was, "Now I'd like you to look at this card. I'm going to read out some different forms of political action that people can take, and I'd like you to tell me, for each one, whether you have actually done any of these things .... Have you ...?"
SOURCE: Ronald Inglehart et al.

ture is the product of interaction between people in their everyday social relationships. In these relationships, the culture from the larger society is adapted to daily life, and sometimes new ways of doing things are developed. Culture is fluid rather than static; it is always open to revision. It is especially situated in specific relationships and occasions for interpersonal interaction (Lauer and Handel 1977).

One of the types of shared meanings emphasized in the symbolic-interaction approach is the definition of the situation; it is this that guides the course of interaction in social relationships. A **definition of the situation** is contained in a package of norms governing and regulating a recognizable situation, such as a classroom, a hockey game, or a bathroom; it includes norms defining the appropriate reasons for people's participation in the situation and the goals they may properly pursue within it. It also spells out how these goals may be achieved, as well as regulating the relationships among the various participants. Because definitions are shared, they permit people to co-ordinate their actions in pursuing their goals. Seen this way, a definition of a situation is a source of meaning for participants and observers alike, because it permits them to make sense of the situation.

Culture is seen by symbolic interactionists as the product of interpersonal negotiations. Negotiations may be formal and explicit (for example, when a contract is drafted between a union and an employer). However, most agreements are less dramatic and tangible, as people informally and tacitly communicate with each other about the situations in which they find themselves. Communication is often verbal, of course, but it may also consist of gestures, body language, and people's attire. One way people communicate involves the impressions they create, sometimes intentionally and other times unintentionally, when they first encounter each other. Wearing a clerical collar, highly polished shoes, jeans, or one's hair in a bun, or introducing oneself as "Doctor" — all have consequences for how people regard one another. Impression management and first impressions foster understandings about the meaning people attach to their relationships, their goals, and what actions are acceptable and unacceptable to them. In the words of Erving Goffman (1959),

[When] an individual projects a definition of the situation and thereby makes an implicit or explicit claim to be a person of a particular kind, he automatically exerts a moral demand upon ... others, obliging them to value and treat him in the manner that persons of his kind have a right to expect. He also implicitly forgoes all claims to be things he does not appear to be and hence forgoes the treatment that would be appropriate for such individuals.

People have many motives governing how they present themselves and the kinds of interpretations they invite. They may or may not be conscious of these motives, and they may or may not be sensitive to the cues they convey to others. For this reason, counsellors advise job applicants to dress carefully for interviews with potential employers, lest they create the wrong impression. On the other hand, members of the clergy are often mindful of the stultifying effects their clerical attire has on conversation and on the jokes people tell at parties.

To say that culture for symbolic interactionists is fluid and dynamic does not mean that it is unlicensed, except for the whims of the people involved. Situations physically and socially constrain what can reasonably be done in them and therefore limit the kinds of definitions that are effectively available. It is difficult to play ice hockey, for example, where there is no ice. And what we do in the classroom is surely constrained by the facts of organizational life outside the classroom. Sexual harassment policies, for instance, remind those who are forgetful that the larger community has a continuing interest in what transpires within the classroom, as well as the workplace.

A definition of the situation constrains interaction, but it is not rigid. Relationships between fellow workers or between customers and clerks sometimes turn into romantic relationships, which is to say that the relationships have been redefined. Symbolic interactionists are therefore interested in the subterranean tactics used to reconstruct relationships. Seduction, for example, refers to a class of interpersonal manoeuvres, impressively labelled "realigning actions" by Goffman (1959), that bring about a redefinition of the relationship between a man and a woman. The possibility of realignment underscores the fact that people are actively involved in exploiting and modifying culture, and are not merely its puppets.

The structural-functional and conflict perspectives, to which we turn next, do not necessarily contradict the symbolic-interaction approach. For one thing, much of the cultural content talked about by symbolic interactionists is not at all unique or original to a relationship. Much of it has its origins in the larger culture and is simply reworked for the more immediate requirements of a relationship. We can also easily imagine interpersonal negotiations being studied by sociologists working within the structural-functional and conflict perspectives, even though this would

not be a priority for them. Structural functionalists might analyze what is functional in such negotiations, while conflict theorists might consider the different forms of conflict in such negotiations. The structural-functional and conflict viewpoints emphasize, though, that there are important shared meanings beyond those found in small groups. In addition, these meanings are seen as less transitory and localized than the symbolic-interaction view might lead us to expect.

The Structural-Functional Perspective

Strictly speaking, the structural-functional perspective does not explain why some feature of culture, such as a particular norm, is created (Johnson 1960). Rather, structural functionalism deals more with the reasons for the persistence of cultural elements in a society or group once they are available. This persistence is explained by the *functions* — the positive consequences — of these elements for the society or group. A norm, or some other element of culture, is said to persist because it "works" or is "useful," in some sense. This approach is applied by structural functionalists both to the culture as a whole and to subcultures. For example, structural functionalists may study the persistence of dress codes among motorcycle gangs and their consequences for gangs. A related concern of the structural functionalist is **cultural diffusion**, the way elements of culture are often borrowed by one society (and culture) from another society (and culture) when individuals and groups from the two societies interact. Here, too, the emphasis is on the fact that the borrowed element is adopted because it is useful to people in the borrowing society.

We will first describe three explanations that structural functionalists have offered for the persistence of cultural elements within a society or group. Then we will make some observations on cultural borrowing. It should be noted that these structural-functional explanations, in spite of their different emphases, are complementary rather than contradictory. The processes they describe can each — simultaneously or at different times — affect cultural persistence and change. We reiterate, though, that even if a specific norm, value, or the like is functional for a society or group, this is not necessarily the reason it was originally established.

Culture Mirrors Society. The first (and the most all-inclusive) structural-functional explanation emphasizes that value systems mirror the economic, political, and social organization of the societies in which they appear. As the structure changes, so will its values. This is said to occur because similarities of values and social organization are functional for the smooth working of the society. There are different versions of this view, but we have selected Inglehart's (1977, 1981) for purposes of illustration. In his opinion, ours is a postindustrial society, increasingly characterized by "postmaterialist" concerns and values. Postmaterialist values are largely intellectual, aesthetic, and social in nature. In surveys conducted in ten nations, Inglehart measured these values by people's support for freedom of speech and the importance of ideas in society, as well as their desire for a greater say on the job and in government, for a less impersonal society, and for more beautiful cities. He concluded that these values are becoming important and that materialist values, with their emphasis on social control and economic matters, are losing ground. What Inglehart (1977) calls a "silent revolution" has brought about a "shift from overwhelming emphasis on material consumption and security toward greater concern with the quality of life."

The major transformation in values described by Inglehart is the product of a number of profound changes in the way society is organized that are occurring simultaneously. These social changes include major technological innovations, such as computer-chip technology and miniaturization; changes in the occupational structure, most notably the growth of the service sector of the economy at the expense of manufacturing; the rise in real income since World War II; the immense expansion of higher education and the rising levels of education among the population; the wiring of the world by sophisticated mass communications into what has been called a "global village"; and the appearance of a fortunate generation that has personally known neither total war nor widespread economic depression. Inglehart believes, following psychologist Abraham Maslow (1970), that people's mental and spiritual needs become important once their more basic physical needs have been satisfied. Given these psychological assumptions, he expects and finds that the same factors that produce differences be-

tween societies also engender differences within societies (Inglehart 1977, 1981). Postmaterialist values are most prevalent among those groups in society, such as the young and the well educated, that have benefited most from the social changes taking place.

Of course, history is more complex than any theory admits. Inglehart's description of modern societies sounds strangely dated now, not a decade later. Maybe he anticipated the economic and military malaise of the 1980s when he wrote of possible counter-trends. However, he believed that "the principal evolutionary drift ... is unlikely to be changed unless there are major alterations in the very nature of these societies" (Inglehart 1977).

Cultural Adaptations to Technological Change. New tools increase people's capacity to exploit their environment, with far-reaching consequences for their relationships with each other and thus for the meanings with which they invest their lives.

Three different patterns can be discerned in the effects of technology on culture and social behaviour (Ogburn and Nimkoff 1964). The first is a *dispersion* or *multiple-effects pattern.* The invention of the birth control pill, for example, might have had the following effects, some of them cultural in nature: new ideas about independence on the part of women; a sense that the arrival of children can be effectively planned and can be weighed against alternative investments; smaller families; new notions about the nature of sexual morality.

The second way technology shapes culture involves a *succession of effects* or *derivative effects,* where one effect leads to another, and so on. For example, we have probably not seen the end of the stream of effects produced by the invention of the computer. The ability to process large amounts of information in very short periods of time leads to computer networks and information sharing. This, in time, provokes questions about the privacy of individual citizens, national sovereignty, and the need for laws to regulate access to information.

In the case of *convergence,* the third pattern, the effects of a number of technological innovations come together and produce a common effect. The development of birth control technology, new techniques for building high-density housing with limited space per living unit, and the proliferation of innovations in mass communication (especially satellite transmissions) jointly threaten the survival of minority language groups, such as francophones in Canada.

The Cultural Marketplace and Culture Production. According to another interpretation, an important source of a society's culture lies in the strength and autonomy of its **cultural infrastructure.** This term refers to groups and organizations having a specific interest, often economic, in the creation and conservation of culture. It also includes the ground rules or laws governing the activities of these groups and organizations. The institutions of religion, politics, and education, of course, play an important role in creating and disseminating symbols. But beyond these institutions, we have in mind the various business enterprises, especially in the mass and specialized media, whose economic interests entail some amount of culture production. At various times, the federal and some of the provincial governments have concluded that the private sector needed encouragement or direction in meeting its cultural obligations (see, for example, Crean 1976; Ostry 1978). In the absence of an effective indigenous cultural infrastructure, we know that we will be served by the American infrastructure. We also know that one of the effects of this kind of dependency will be that the culture we consume reflects American preoccupations rather than our own.

It is a useful exercise to think about what aspects of life in Canada would escape our attention were we to depend on other societies to tell us about ourselves. Many of the symbols and shared meanings that make up our culture would be borrowed from other people's experiences and would only accidentally reflect our own. On the other hand, creating an economic base for Canadian literature, from writing through publication to sales, means that our thinking about French–English relations, for example, is enriched. In a similar fashion, Canadian nationalists argued for a long time that there was a relationship between producing Canadian doctorate-holders and hiring them in Canadian universities, on the one hand, and producing new knowledge about Canadian society, on the other. These observations extend no less to the production of scientific and technological knowledge, for these are dynamic ingredients of contemporary culture (see, for example, the Gray Report 1972; Britton and Gilmour 1978).

The Canadian infrastructure includes

- *government bodies* (for example, the Canadian Radio-television and Telecommunications Commission; the Canada Council; the Social Sciences and Humanities Research Council of Canada; and Telefilm Canada);

- *publishers* (for example, Harcourt Brace & Company, a Canadian subsidiary of an American publisher; and James Lorimer, a wholly owned Canadian publisher);

- *periodicals and newspapers* (for example, *Maclean's* magazine and *The Globe and Mail*);

- *electronic media* (that is, privately owned television and radio stations and networks);

- *Crown corporations* (such as the Canadian Broadcasting Corporation); and

- *regulations* (for example, the Canadian-content rules for TV programming and for popular music on radio, the Canadian-quota rule in the Canadian Football League, and the preferential hiring of Canadian faculty in our universities).

The usefulness of this idea for explaining national differences in culture is shown in a study by Griswold (cited in Peterson 1979). She wished to explain the apparent differences in literary taste between British and American novelists writing in the nineteenth century. Americans wrote about "isolated male protagonists combatting nature, the supernatural, or an evil society," while the British wrote about "love, marriage, and domestic bourgeois life" (Peterson 1979). One might try to explain these differences in literary culture in terms of national character and civilization, but Griswold preferred a much more direct explanation. Before 1891, the United States was not a party to the prevailing international conventions respecting copyright. It was cheaper for American publishers to pirate British novels on love and marriage than to pay their own authors. This compelled American authors to turn to topics that were relatively neglected by British authors — hence the peculiar division of literary labour between the two nations. Griswold reports that these national divisions eroded after 1891, when the United States decided to respect literary property rights.

Cultural Diffusion. While the new technology or social inventions that are added to a particular culture sometimes originate from within it, most elements of modern culture appear not to be of this sort. Most of the contents of modern cultures have been gained through diffusion from other cultures, past and present. As noted earlier, cultural diffusion refers to the borrowing of cultural elements from another society in contrast to their independent development within the society. The borrowing takes place, structural functionalists emphasize, because individuals or groups from one society see a way of doing things that seems to work well in another society and they adopt this practice for their own situation. Then the borrowed way is transmitted from generation to generation within the borrowing society.

Cultural borrowing has been a common occurrence for Canadian society. We can easily take for granted our society's cultural borrowing because much of it occurred before our lifetimes and without our direct knowledge. For the same reason,

Cultures Are Heavily Borrowed: An Illustration

Probably no culture is purely indigenous. Each culture involves elements taken over from other cultures from the current period and from earlier times. Indeed, most modern cultures are, like Canada's, largely composed of borrowed elements. In a classic study, the anthropologist Ralph Linton provided a good illustration of this point by caricaturing the beginning of the day for a typical North American male.

Our ... citizen awakens in a bed built on a pattern which originated in the Near East but which was modified in Northern Europe before it was transmitted to America. He throws back the covers made from cotton, domesticated in India, or linen, domesticated in the Near East, or silk, the use of which was discovered in China. All of these materials have been spun and woven by processes invented in the Near East. He slips into his moccasins, invented by the Indians of the Eastern woodlands, and goes to the bathroom, whose fixtures are a mixture of European and American inventions, both of recent date. He takes off his pajamas, a garment invented in India, and washes with soap, invented by the ancient Gauls. He then shaves, a masochistic rite which seems to have been derived from either Sumer or ancient Egypt.

Returning to the bedroom, he removes his clothes from a chair of southern European type and proceeds to dress. He puts on garments whose form originally derived from the skin clothing of the nomads of the Asiatic steppes, puts on shoes made from skins tanned by a process invented in ancient Egypt and cut to a pattern derived from the classical civilization of the Mediterranean, and ties around his neck a strip of bright-colored cloth which is a vestigial survival of the shoulder shawls worn by the seventeenth century Croatians. Before going out for breakfast he glances through the window, made of glass invented in Egypt, and if it is raining, puts on overshoes made of rubber discovered by the Central American Indians and takes an umbrella, invented in southeastern Asia....

On his way to breakfast he stops to buy a paper, paying for it with coins, an ancient Lydian invention. At the restaurant a whole new series of borrowed elements confronts him. His plate is made of a form of pottery invented in China. His knife is of steel, an alloy first made in southern India, his fork a medieval Italian invention, and his spoon a derivative of a Roman original. He begins his breakfast with an orange, from the eastern Mediterranean, a cantaloupe from Persia, or perhaps a piece of African watermelon. With this he has coffee, an Abyssinian plant, with cream and sugar. Both the domestication of cows and the idea of milking them originated in the Near East, while sugar was first made in India. After his fruit and first coffee, he goes on to waffles, cakes made by a Scandinavian technique from wheat domesticated in Asia Minor. Over these he pours maple syrup, invented by the Indians of the Eastern woodlands. As a side dish he may have the eggs of a species of bird domesticated in Indo-China, or thin strips of flesh of an animal domesticated in Eastern Asia which have been salted and smoked by a process developed in northern Europe.

Source:

Ralph Linton, *The Study of Man* (New York: Appleton-Century, 1936), pp. 326–27.

few of us know the exact origins of many of the cultural elements that we employ. Indeed, experts on culture can often only guess at the origin of a word, a type of food, or an item of etiquette. Their roots are lost in antiquity.

When a new item of culture is borrowed from another society, it is useful to distinguish between the separate effects on the borrowing society of two things: the new item of culture and the relationship between the societies that provided for the borrowing. Each can have its own consequences. An example of this difference is provided by Ray's (1974) study of the introduction of new hunting technology into the Native societies of colonial Canada. He showed, on the one hand, that these societies gained an improved capacity to exploit the environment after the cultural borrowing. Guns were clearly more efficient and deadly than arrows, and horses increased hunters' territories. On the other hand, the Native peoples' trading relationships with Europeans created new economic and political dependencies. Both sets of factors exerted an influence on the composition of Native culture. A more contemporary example is Canada's well-known reliance on the United States for much of its technological innovation. This means that technology and economic dependency are intertwined in their cumulative impact on Canadian culture.

The Conflict Perspective

All the structural-functional explanations share the idea that some factor, A (perhaps technological change), leads to Z, a change in some feature of culture. Conflict interpretations, on the other hand, are more complicated. They posit a conflict relationship between at least two factors, A and B, and hold that Z arises from this relationship. Sometimes the A–B relationship is referred to as *dialectical*, implying that there is a productive tension between the two.

The conflict perspective has a certain kinship to the symbolic-interaction approach. Both assume that interaction between A and B leads to Z. They differ in that A and B are individuals in the case of symbolic interaction, but subgroups in society or different societies in the case of conflict theory. A second difference is that interactionists do not start from the assumption that A and B are in conflict; in fact, they generally assume co-opera-

tion between people to find a working consensus. Conflict theorists, alternatively, start from the assumption that A's and B's interests are opposed rather than mutual. Then, out of the clash between their respective ambitions, culture is produced.

The conflict perspective assumes, as do the structural-functional and the symbolic-interaction perspectives, that a minimum level of shared culture exists in a society, even between parties in conflict. That is, there is some mutual understanding between conflicting parties on the character of their differing interests and the fact that their relationship is a conflictual one. Often, conflicting groups share more than this — for instance, a common language and similar goals.

Conflict theorists, however, are more likely to emphasize the cultural differences than the similarities between groups. They also tend to focus on the relationship between the groups: how it is defined; and to what degree, why, and with what consequences it is conflictual. As we will show, the conflict approach also emphasizes how cultural elements emerge from conflict and how they may even come to be shared across the groups involved. What is important to recognize is that conflict, too, is a form of interaction. And it is from interaction, both conflictual and nonconflictual, that culture emerges.

Culture can be seen as an accommodation to conflict, as when groups learn to live symbolically with the ruptures that have occurred in their society and with the resulting unequal distribution of power. As ideology, culture is a weapon used by either side to buttress its position and perhaps even to alter the relationship to its advantage, in time. In the latter case, ideology is a way of asserting the symbolic superiority of one group.

Conflict and Cultural Change. Continued strain toward cultural change is produced by contemporary points of conflict within society. We can illustrate this by referring to Hershel Hardin's (1974) description of culture as a product of structural contradictions. He argues that the basic contradictions or points of conflict in Canada are French Canada against English Canada, the regions against the centre, and Canada against the United States: "To get at the Canadian circumstance ... is above all to see the country in terms of its contradictions — the contending forces that underlie the character of the people" (Hardin 1974). So long as one remains in this country, he argues, it is impossible to escape these sources of creative tension, for they are "the forcing ground of our identity" (Hardin 1974). Canadians interacting with one another around these points of division produce symbols, norms, ideology, and other elements of culture as a means of coming to terms with their society and with each other. Hardin (1974) offers the following illuminating example of the impact of one such Canadian contradiction on a new Canadian:

One poignant case sticks in my mind, because it illustrates the leading Canadian contradiction at work on a man whose identity as a Canadian was still in the process of formation. It was during the St. Leonard controversy over whether all schools should be French-language, or whether there should be English-language instruction available as well. An ethnic spokesman caught in the crossfire protested with quiet emotion to CBC radio that his group was an innocent victim ... because they had no ingrained hostility against French Canadians. "We're not against the French Canadians," he said. "And we're not against the English Canadians. We just want to be Canadian." It never occurred to him that having to explore this linguistic conflict and cope with it, and in intensely passionate, practical circumstances, would give him more insight into what it meant to be a Canadian than most Canadians would gather from a lifetime. Even while he was protesting, he probably had already realized there was no total escape from the contradiction other than by leaving the country. Wasn't that why he was protesting in the first place? And after going through that experience, would he ever agree that being a Canadian and an American involved more or less the same thing?

The origins of this society's culture in conflict, as sketched by Hardin, are vastly more complex than the Lipset and Hartzian theses would have us believe. The central historical conflicts were not settled centuries ago but have persisted through the generations and into the present. Paradoxically, the forces on either side of each contradiction have strengthened their opposites while flexing their own muscles.

The "thick continuity" (Hardin's expression) of our history has created a people for those with the eyes and the patience to see. It is a commonplace for visitors from Britain or the United States to miss what is Canadian, because their sensibilities have been shaped elsewhere. Closer to home, sociology textbooks that treat Canada as a cultural extension of the United States, Hardin would argue, display this same insensitivity. Nor is it uncommon for Canadians to miss what is Canadian, because their ideology is American and borrowed. This is especially the case, he believes, when Canadians persist in seeing Canada as a free-enterprise economy, either forgetting or blind to the fact that this country has a history rich in public enterprise.

Dominant Ideology and the Preservation of the Status Quo. Another conflict-oriented aspect of culture can be observed in the actions of dominant social classes or groups in society, a topic to be discussed more fully in Chapter 9. These classes develop ideologies that are self-justifying and hence help unify the dominant groups themselves. There is great debate among sociologists about how extensively dominant ideology is disseminated in society and how important it is in maintaining the status quo. If people in the subordinate classes are not persuaded by dominant ideology, it may nonetheless intimidate them and impede their development of counter-ideologies (Abercrombie, Hill, and Turner 1980).

If dominant ideology is disseminated, then it makes sense to look at the institutions assigned this task — as conflict theorists have done. Education, religion, and the mass media have been the subject of much research and speculation in this thesis. We will limit our comments to some studies of education.

A good example of research testing the dominant ideology thesis is a study by McDonald (1978) on the establishment of the Ontario public school system by Egerton Ryerson in the nineteenth century. Ryerson believed that the educational system should be firmly under government control, rather than locally controlled. It should be highly regulated and uniform throughout the province, staffed by local and professional teachers, and open to all children. Its mission was to produce loyal citizens who would reject the ideas of republican democracy emanating from the United States. Properly indoctrinated citizens would never again participate in a rebellion like the one crushed in Upper Canada in 1837. The

Ancient Traditions vs. the Law

Prosecutions of two immigrants for "female circumcision" in France highlight an increasingly common cultural clash. Customs in one part of the world are viewed as repulsive in another.

PARIS — The issue unfolding in a Paris criminal courtroom was not whether the two frightened African women cowering in the defendants' box, neither of whom knew enough French to follow the proceedings, were guilty of mutilating their daughters.

Taky Traore and Oura Dacoure, both 31-year-old immigrants from the West African state of Mali, admitted paying another woman $30 each to cut genital parts from their 3-year-old daughters in 1989. On the stand, with the help of a Malian translator, they said they were only conforming to the ancient tradition of their homeland; that the act of "female circumcision" was something they had undergone, as had their mothers and grandmothers before them.

But the real issue before the French jury of seven women and five men was whether sentencing the women to prison would serve as a deterrent, not only here in France but in the parts of Africa where ritual female genital excision — usually cutting off the clitoris and labia minora — is primarily practiced.

"The action that you take today," Prosecutor Jean-Claude Thin told the jury in his closing argument, "will be a message to the community at large."...

At least one African country, Burkina Faso in West Africa, has a law on the books banning female genital excision. But France, which finds itself confronted with the practice in its large African immigrant population, is the only country in the world to have prosecuted mothers and fathers for submitting their daughters to it.

In two separate cases here in Paris recently, the father of one girl and the mother of another were ordered jailed by a French jury for allowing their daughters to be excised. Leaders in French organizations opposed to the practice of female genital excision hoped for more jail terms in the case against Taky Traore and Oura Dacoure, who went to trial last week in the ornate marble and gilt-ceilinged main criminal courtroom of the Palais de Justice.

However, after the two-day proceeding charged with emotional debate about cultural and ethnic relativism in a modern European state, the jury chose to be lenient, giving each of the women a five-year suspended sentence.

No issue of cultural relativism versus Western legal tradition has aroused as much furor as the French prosecution and jailing of mothers and fathers in the excision cases.

"Prison should be the last resort," said Daniel Jacoby, part of the father-daughter team representing Taky Traore. "You would think that in a country like France, we could come up with a solution other than prison."

French authorities, meanwhile, defend their stand against excision on the grounds that ethnic heritage is no valid defense for those who maim children on French soil.

Kofi Yamgnane, France's minister of state for social and racial integration, is a naturalized French citizen who emigrated from his native Togo 30 years ago, when he was a teenager. In a recent interview in the European edition of *Newsweek* magazine, Yamgnane supported the government stand.

"People have to understand that if they are going to live in a country," he said, "they must respect the rules of that country. When we say 'liberty' in France, that means you don't mutilate people. You don't have that right. It may be one thing to do it in Africa, but not here."

International human rights organizations involved in the growing movement to ban the practice of female genital excision look to the relatively tough French stand for support of indigenous women's movements in Africa.

"These mutilations are all the same," Weil-Curiel said. "They hold the girl by force. She screams and calls for her mother, and the blood flows. It is thanks to these trials that the taboo is finally lifting."

Contacted in Gambia, where she is producing a documentary on female genital mutilation, American novelist Alice Walker said she hopes the French cases will have a "ripple effect" in Africa.

Walker's 1992 best-selling novel, *Possessing the Secret of Joy,* delved into the violence and horrors of female genital mutilation as it is practiced in Africa and immigrant communities in Europe.

"Africans have always traveled," Walker commented in response to a reporter's telephone questions. "And of course news of the prosecutions and the sentences will reach Africans and will inevitably have ripple effects. Hopefully, in time, these movements of resistance to female genital mutilation in the West will help African sisters in Africa who are campaigning against this harmful tradition."

Walker has little patience for those who defend the practice of female genital excision on cultural grounds and who oppose prosecution of parents in European courts.

"For African children living in Paris," Walker said, "France is their home, and the government has a duty to protect all children from torture. Torture is not culture."

Source:

Adapted from Rone Tempest, *Los Angeles Times*, February 18, 1993, pp. A1, A10. Copyright © 1993, *Los Angeles Times*. Reprinted by permission.

schools should also promote harmony among the social classes. This meant persuading the working classes that "their interests were also those of the middle and upper classes, and that, as a collectivity, there was a 'common' or 'public good' towards which all must work" (McDonald 1978).

The relationship between people's level of education and their belief in dominant ideology among Canadians was studied by Baer and Lambert (1982). Dominant ideology was signified by support for the kind of economic inequality that prevails in Canadian society and rejection of the idea that government has a responsibility for creating employment. Support for dominant ideology was greatest among the most educated respondents. Belief in dominant ideology was also greatest among people who felt that their income matched their qualifications. Doubts were most frequently expressed by the less educated and by those who felt underpaid (see also Curtis and Lambert 1976).

The findings of the Baer and Lambert study, however, suggest that the aspirations of the founders of our educational system to indoctrinate children from all social classes have not been fully realized. If the point of dominant ideology is social control, then its effects seem to be limited to the most educated members of society. Mann (1970) has claimed that this is all that is really necessary, for there are other ways of controlling people with less education. For one thing, the prominence given to dominant ideology in our mass media and in the educational system may simply undermine the emergence of counter-ideologies. In other words, they disorient more than they persuade. Cynicism bred by our political system, the absence of significant political options, and the control exercised by work and the fear of unemployment may lead to a sense of resignation on the part of citizens. It is less a matter of belief in the status quo, Mann argues, than a matter of "pragmatic acquiescence" on the part of subordinate groups in society to what appears inevitable.

Toward a Unified Perspective

Our treatment of the three perspectives and the explanations generated from them has implied that they are mutually exclusive. This may be a useful device for purposes of exposition, but social reality is not so simply constructed. In fact, the sensitive observer can probably detect all three processes intertwined in the creation of most cultural phenomena. We pointed out earlier that interpersonal interactions are subsumed by the two macro perspectives, structural functionalism and conflict. The problem is inherent in these two perspectives, because they have often been defended as though they were theoretically irreconcilable.

We can find evidence for both processes at work in specific cases, although their mix may well differ among cases. The development of regional and provincial cultures in Canada is a case in point. On the one hand, provincially based economies and cultural infrastructures operate to produce provincial or regional cultures. On the latter point, the British North America Act and its successors, the Constitution Acts, assign to the provinces clear responsibilities in such fields as education. This means that some of the factors that shape culture, as discussed above in connection with the structural-functional perspective, have a provincial presence. On the other hand, there are enduring rivalries and conflicts between regions and between the provinces and the federal government, as Hardin (1974) has emphasized, and these contribute to cultural variations across the country. In fact, political scientist Alan Cairns (1977) has argued that key instruments in the development of the "societies [and cultures] of Canadian federalism" are the governments of Canada themselves. In asserting this proposition, Cairns objects to the traditional view that sees politics and government as mere products of society; once created, they react on society, changing it in the process. Who would deny, for example, the significance of the struggle between the Ottawa and Quebec governments in producing the stuff of culture in this country?

SUMMARY

1. The most useful view of culture is that it is a shared set of symbols and their meanings. The effects of these shared meanings can be seen in people's actions and their relation-

ships with one another, as well as in their manufactured world.

2. Beliefs, norms, and values are the building blocks for more complex components of culture — statuses, ideologies, and subcultures.

3. The fact that culture is defined in terms of some minimum level of sharing or consensus is common across the three basic theoretical perspectives in sociology. However, the three approaches differ in whether they emphasize the functional or conflicting origins and consequences of culture, as well as micro- versus macro-level interests.

4. The symbolic-interaction approach locates culture in specific relationships and situations. Culture is seen as fluid and dynamic rather than static. The principal cultural concept is the definition of the situation, which is a product of people's negotiations with each other. Symbolic interactionists emphasize the initiative and activity of individual actors in the process.

5. According to the structural-functional perspective, culture mirrors the society as a whole or some part of society; culture is also exchanged between societies, in cultural diffusion.

6. The conflict perspective is represented by three explanations. Culture can be interpreted as an accommodation to historical conflict, as a product of social contradictions, or as a weapon used by dominant groups to justify their privileged status and to unify themselves.

7. Each of these three perspectives is sensitive to particular themes in the creation, maintenance, and change of culture. Because the relationship between society and culture is multifaceted, it should be theoretically possible to adopt a unified approach.

8. Although some sociologists emphasize either culture or the organization of society in their explanations of social life, it should not be necessary to choose one over the other. Social process and social change within a society are best understood as products of the interplay between a society's structure and its culture. The sociologist's task is to make sense of this interplay for the research question at hand.

GLOSSARY

Counter-ideologies. Reformist and radical ideologies that call for changes in the status quo.

Cultural diffusion. The process whereby cultural elements are borrowed by one society from another (as opposed to independent development of these elements in each society).

Cultural infrastructure. Specialized groups with an interest, often economic, in the production and preservation of cultural symbols and the supporting ground rules.

Cultural relativism. The view that all cultures are equally valid and valuable and that each culture must be judged by its own standards.

Culture. Shared set of symbols and their definitions or meanings prevailing in a society.

Definition of the situation. Beliefs and norms about an interaction setting.

Descriptive beliefs. Statements or claims about what is, was, or will be, including ideas about cause and effect.

Dominant ideologies. Ruling ideologies that explain and justify the existing ways of doing things.

Ethnocentrism. Tendency to use one's own culture as the only valid standard for evaluating other cultures, societies, and peoples.

Folkways. Traditional rules about customary ways of behaving that are informally enforced and of mild concern to society members.

Ideologies. Emotionally charged sets of descriptive and normative beliefs and values that either explain and justify the status quo or, in the case of counter-ideologies, call for and justify alternative arrangements.

Laws. Norms that have been formally promulgated by a legislative body and are enforced by an executive body of government.

Material culture. Physical artifacts or products of a society embodying cultural meanings.

Mores. Traditional rules about how the individual must or must not behave, invested with strong feelings and informally enforced.

Normative beliefs. Ideas about what should or should not be, referring especially to goodness, virtuousness, or propriety.

Norms. Formal or informal rules stating how categories of people are expected to act in particular situations, violations of which are subject to sanction.

Status. Culturally defined position in society, consisting of ideas about rights and obligations.

Subcultures. More or less distinctive beliefs, norms, symbols, values, and ideologies shared by groups within a larger population.

Symbol. Anything, such as a word, gesture, or object, taken by people as a matter of convention to stand for something else, to have a meaning.

Values. Cultural conceptions about what are desirable goals and what are appropriate standards for judging actions.

FURTHER READING

Audley, Paul. *Canada's Cultural Industries: Broadcasting, Publishing, Records and Films.* Toronto: CIEP/Lorimer, 1983. A study of Canada's cultural infrastructure — performances, problems, prospects, and policies.

Bell, D.V.J., and L. Tepperman. *The Roots of Disunity.* Toronto: McClelland and Stewart, 1979. Describes the contours of Canada's culture and shows the differences across regions, social classes, and linguistic groups.

Crean, S.M. *Who's Afraid of Canadian Culture?* Don Mills, ON.: General Publishing, 1976. A detailed description and interpretation of the personnel, groups, practices, policies, and "facts of life" affecting the arts in Canada.

Hardin, H. *A Nation Unaware: The Canadian Economic Culture.* Vancouver: J.J. Douglas, 1974. This book argues that Canada has a history of public enterprise that Canadians fail to appreciate when they perceive it through the ideological categories of American business.

Hiller, Harry H. *Canadian Society: A Macro Analysis.* Scarborough, ON.: Prentice-Hall, 1986. Discusses Canadian culture and society from the point of view of seven research questions. Chapter 7, "The Question of Identity," is especially relevant.

Lakoff, G., and M. Johnson. *Metaphors We Live By.* Chicago: University of Chicago Press, 1980. Metaphors are sources of meaning. Metaphors taken from areas of life that we understand are applied to areas that we cannot understand on their own terms. Differences in cultures can be found in their prevalent metaphors.

Lipset, S.M. *The Continental Divide: The Values and Institutions of Canada and the United States.* New York: Routledge, 1990. A highly informative sweeping comparison of behaviour rates, survey data on beliefs and attitudes, and information on laws and customs for the two countries.

Marchak, M.P. *Ideological Perspectives on Canada.* 3rd edition. Toronto: McGraw-Hill Ryerson, 1988. An analysis of major political ideologies in Canada and their shifting currents over time. Liberalism, socialism, conservatism, and a new "corporatism" are discussed.

CHAPTER 4

Socialization

MARLENE MACKIE

Human beings must eat to stay alive. For babies, the matter is quite straightforward. They experience abdominal discomfort; they cry; a parent responds; they suck. Adult satisfaction of this basic physiological need is more complicated. Canadians consider some things proper food (steak, hamburgers), but gag at the thought of eating equally nutritious alternatives (caterpillars, horsemeat). Food preferences also mark ethnic group boundaries (Anderson and Alleyne 1979). Italian Canadians are often partial to pasta, German Canadians to sauerkraut, and French Canadians to sugar pie. Eating is surrounded by rules (Goffman 1963a). Even when people are ravenous, they are not supposed to attack the apple pie before the spinach. Adults who jam food into their mouths until their cheeks bulge seem disgusting, especially if they try to talk while they stuff. Plucking an interesting item from a neighbour's plate will result in raised eyebrows. So will scratching one's tonsils with a fork.

How, then, does the carefree infant become transformed into the disciplined adult? There is a one-word answer to this question — socialization. The whole story, of course, is not quite that simple.

Socialization is the complex learning process through which individuals develop selfhood and acquire the knowledge, skills, and motivations required for participation in social life. This process is the link between individual and society and may be viewed from each of these two perspectives.

From the point of view of the individual, interaction with other people is the means by which human potentialities are actualized. The newborn infant is almost completely helpless. Although more is happening in infant heads than scientists previously guessed, the newborn's abilities are limited to crying, sucking, eliminating wastes, yawning, and a few other reflexes. It has no self-awareness. Though it has the potential for becoming human, it is not yet human. The physical care, emotional response, and training provided by the family transform this noisy, wet, demanding bundle of matter into a functioning member of society. It learns language, impulse control, and skills. It develops a self. Knowledge is acquired of both the physical world and the social world. The child becomes capable of taking on social roles with some commitment. It learns whether it is female or male. It internalizes (accepts as its own), the norms and values of, first, the family and, later, the wider society.

Effective socialization is as essential for the society as it is for the individual. Untrained members disturb the social order. For example, physically handicapped people report that children often stare and ask blunt questions about their conditions (Goffman 1963b). Furthermore, Canadian society could not continue to exist unless the thousands of new members born each year eventually learned to think, believe, and behave as Canadians. Each new generation must learn the society's culture. Social order demands self-discipline and impulse control. The continuity of our society requires that children come to embrace societal values as their own. Citizens must adhere to cultural norms because they themselves view those norms as right and proper. Cultural breakdown occurs when the socialization process no longer provides the new generation with valid reasons to be enthusiastic about becoming members of that society (Flacks 1979). However, individuals may redefine social roles and obligations, as well as accepting them as they stand. Social change thus occurs over time (Bush and Simmons 1981).

The heterogeneous nature of Canadian society complicates the socialization process. Although many values and norms are shared by all Canadians, differences are found by language, by region, by ethnicity, by religion, by social class, by urban/rural residence. These variations in social environment bring with them variations in the content of socialization. The perpetuation of these distinctive Canadian groups depends on children learning the relevant subcultural norms and val-

ues. For example, the French Canadian community cannot continue in any meaningful fashion unless children of this ethnic background learn to view themselves as French Canadians, and learn the language and traditions of that group. Similarly, the continuation of the unique features of the Maritime region requires that Canadians who live there acquire, by means of specialized socialization, the identity of Maritimers and the special norms, values, and history of that region.

Historical events — such as the Great Depression, World War II, the protest era of the late 1960s, and the outbreak of AIDS in the 1980s — mean that successive generations of Canadians are socialized differently (Mannheim 1953). For example, Baby Boomers (born just after World War II) and the Generation X (now in their twenties) have had sharply contrasting educational, work, and leisure experiences.

The socialization process explains how commitment to the social order is maintained. Paradoxically, most people find their own fulfilment as individuals while simultaneously becoming social beings. However, it is important to note that socialization for deviance also occurs. Some folks learn to forge cheques, to crack safes, and to snort cocaine.

Types of Socialization

We have defined socialization as the lifelong learning process through which individuals develop selfhood and acquire the knowledge, skills, and motivations required to participate in social life. Incidentally, these various socialization lessons are intertwined. Before we go on, we should make some further definitional distinctions.

Primary socialization is the basic socialization that occurs in childhood. It involves developing language and individual identity, learning cognitive skills and self-control, internalizing moral standards and appropriate attitudes and motivations, and gaining some understanding of societal roles.

Adult socialization occurs beyond the childhood years. Although primary socialization lays the foundation for later learning, it cannot completely prepare people for adulthood. For one

New lessons are learned beyond the family through adult socialization.

thing, our age-graded society confronts individuals with new role expectations as they move through life. Moving beyond the family or day-care centre into the neighbourhood, entering school, becoming an adolescent, choosing an occupation, marrying, bearing children, encountering middle age, retiring, and dying all involve new lessons to be learned.

Also, society changes, and people must therefore equip themselves to cope with new situations — for example, technological job obsolescence brought about by computers, and changes in sexual norms produced by the threat of AIDS.

Finally, some individuals must deal with specialized situations. Geographical and social mobility, marital breakdown, physical handicaps,

and so on all require further socialization (Brim 1966).

Anticipatory socialization occurs in advance of the actual playing of roles. This rehearsal for the future involves learning something about role requirements, both behaviours and attitudes, and visualizing oneself in the role. Children begin to practise being pupils before they ever enter school. Law students mentally try on the role of practising lawyer. We think about being married, being parents, being elderly, before we actually assume these statuses.

Resocialization occurs when a new role or a new situation requires a person to replace established patterns of behaviour and thought with new patterns (Campbell 1975). Old behaviour must be unlearned because it is incompatible in some way with new role demands. Usually, resocialization is more difficult than the original socialization; the established habits interfere with new learning. Fortunately, though, human beings retain the capacity for change across the entire lifespan. Indeed, thousands of organizations, from Alcoholics Anonymous to Zen, are designed to help individuals change (Costa and McCrae 1989).

Resocialization is more characteristic of adult socialization than of primary socialization. However, as youngsters mature, they too are expected to discard former behaviour. Block printing is fine for a first-grade pupil, but a fourth-grade pupil must learn to write. A two-year-old boy can cry when he is frightened, but a twelve-year-old boy who climbs into his mother's lap and whimpers may be considered odd.

Resocialization necessarily confronts the individual with contradictions between old and new behaviour that are sometimes confusing and sometimes painful. A new immigrant to Canada describes learning about this country's food: "If they gave me hot dog, I wouldn't eat it! I thought it was a dog meat! Well, I translated, you see, hot dog. You know, if no one tells you. ..." (Disman 1983). The fact that the nonresponsible, submissive, asexual child must become the dominant, sexually active adult (Mortimer and Simmons 1978) illustrates one contradiction between childhood and adulthood. The resocialization involved in new situations also entails contradictions for adults. For example, the women's movement has resulted in redefinitions of the ways men and women relate to each other. When a woman and a man go out together, who drives the car? Should husbands help with the housework or sit back and watch their wives do it? More dramatic discontinuities between old and new selves are experienced by individuals who get caught up in extreme instances of resocialization such as brainwashing, religious conversion, and "therapeutic" programs in prisons and mental hospitals.

The Lifelong Process

We have noted that socialization is a lifelong process. Despite some anticipatory socialization during childhood, primary socialization simply cannot prepare people for roles and situations that either are unforeseeable at the moment, or lie far ahead in the future. Young adults everywhere are expected to marry, become economically responsible for themselves, and raise children. Later, their offspring leave home, their parents die, and they face grandparenting, retirement, and perhaps widowhood.

Although socialization continues throughout life, the social science literature has emphasized childhood socialization. The main reason for this somewhat distorted focus is that primary socialization provides the groundwork for all later learning. The major structures of personality are formed in childhood. In addition, the lessons learned during this impressionable period are the first lessons, and learning comes easily. We have already pointed out that resocialization is difficult because old behaviour must be unlearned before new behaviour can be acquired. Finally, it should be noted that, even when new expectations do not conflict with previous expectations, primary socialization channels and sets limits for adult socialization. For example, a person who emerges from childhood without a strong motivation to achieve is unlikely to excel in medical school.

A number of fundamental differences exist between primary socialization and adult socialization (Brim 1966), in addition to those just considered.

1. With some exceptions, adult socialization concentrates on overt behaviour, rather than on values and motives. Society assumes that adults already hold the values appropriate for a given role and that they are motivated to pursue that role. All that remains is to teach the incumbents how to behave. Universities, for example, do not attempt to convince students of the value of higher education or to motivate them to work hard at their studies. Prisons, on the other hand, are resocialization agencies, but their high rates of recidivism (individuals relapsing into crime after release from imprisonment) illustrate the impracticality of wholesale attempts to alter basic values and motives.
2. While primary socialization tends to be idealistic, adult socialization tends to be realistic.

Children are taught how society ideally operates and how people ideally behave. They are shielded from knowledge of how society actually operates and how people actually behave. At the same time that parents exhort children to be honest, they protect children from awareness of corruption in government and their own "fudging" of the truth. Part of growing up, then, involves the substitution of sophistication for naïvete.

3. The content of adult socialization is more specific than the content of primary socialization. Although there are exceptions, children learn general knowledge, skills, and behaviour relevant to many roles. Adults, on the other hand, acquire information specific to particular roles. For example, children learn to read and to write. This knowledge is useful in a wide range of roles and situations. By contrast, adults learn to diaper a baby or to wire a circuit board. Such information pertains to the parent and the electronic-technician roles, respectively, and not elsewhere.

4. As a general rule, adults are socialized by formal organizations (schools, corporations), while children are socialized in informal contexts (the family, babysitters, peer groups). This distinction, however, reflects a general tendency rather than a rule. Although the school, for example, is a formal organization, it is an important primary socialization agency. Also, the actual socializing of adults within organizations is often done through primary relationships. For example, the impact of the inmate subculture on prisoners' experience of being incarcerated and on their responses to treatment programs is well documented (Ekstedt and Griffiths 1984). Throughout life, people remain sensitive to the opinions and examples of their family and friends.

5. The nature of the relationships between socializer and socializee differs in primary and adult socialization. The family is the major socializer of the child. Familial relationships are marked by high levels of both feeling and power. Because of the emotionally charged familial context and the power of the parents to mete out rewards and punishments, parents have a tremendous impact on children. In contrast, the relationship between adult socializer and socializee is usually more emo-

tionally neutral and more equal in terms of power. However, this does not mean that the adult socialization experience is devoid of emotion. For example, students at an Ontario medical school are plagued by anxiety and uncertainty (Haas and Shaffir 1992). Moreover, the adult socializee is often in that position voluntarily: one *chooses* to be an apprentice welder or a college student. The volunteer has rights that the conscript lacks in defining what will be learned and how the learning will occur. The youngest child in the Jones family, however, did not choose his or her fate.

Nature versus Nurture

Since the beginning of this century, social scientists have been preoccupied with the relative contributions of biology and environment to human development. Those who have emphasized the role of biology in this nature/nurture debate argued that the individual's psychological characteristics and social behaviour result from the unfolding of inherited factors, such as instincts. On the other hand, sociologists on the nurture side of the argument believed that environmental influences are all-important.

Recent discoveries in biology and genetics have resulted in the problem becoming increasingly complex. Although the nature/nurture debate has not yet been resolved, modern scientists have abandoned the simplistic approach of nature versus nurture. Biology and environment interact to transform the infant into a functioning member of society (Collins and Gunnar 1990). (See Chapter 5 for a discussion of the nature/nurture issue as it applies to gender patterns.)

Socialization provides the link between biology and culture. Biology gives human beings the capacity to learn and the ability to use language. In addition, the human infant's relatively long period of helplessness (compared with that of the lower animals) enforces dependence on adult caretakers. The resulting emotional bonds forged between parents and children are necessary for normal childhood development. This deep emotional attachment gives parents the power needed to socialize children. In other words, children are responsive to parental influence partly because they are dependent on the parents' love and approval.

Effects of Social Deprivation

What happens when parental love and approval are not forthcoming? Two specific cases impressively demonstrate the importance of socialization. Both illustrate clearly that the infant's biological potential cannot be actualized without close emotional attachments to at least one adult. The first case concerns two American children who were deliberately reared in isolation. (Davis 1940, 1947). The second case involves experiments by Harlow and his colleagues on the effects of isolation on rhesus monkeys (Harlow 1959; Harlow and Harlow 1962).

Children Reared in Isolation

Anna was an illegitimate child born in 1921. At the insistence of her grandfather, she was hidden away in an attic-like room until she was nearly six years old. During this period, her mother had given her only enough care to keep her alive. When Anna was discovered, her clothing and bedding were filthy. She was extremely emaciated; her stomach was bloated. There were no signs of intelligence; she was unable to talk, walk, feed herself, or respond to people. At first, it was believed that she was blind and deaf. Four years later, she finally began to develop speech. By the time of her death (a year later), she was operating at the level of the normal child aged two-and-a-half. Although the possibility that Anna was born

Street Children of Juarez

Among Latin America's pressing social problems is the growing number of street children. Freddy is a street child of Juarez, a Mexican border town.

Freddy is sixteen years old. He is the oldest sibling in a family of four brothers and three sisters. His father is an agricultural worker in Culiacan where Freddy was born. His mother takes care of the other children.

Freddy has been living alone on the streets of Juarez for two years. He left home because of the problems there, including his father's drinking and his beatings. The oldest sibling, Freddy was abused regularly as was his mother. He completed only the first grade of school because he was expelled for fighting with other boys. After he left school, he worked in the fields for a while before becoming a street vendor of fruit in Sinaloa. In

Sinaloa he was arrested twice, once for stealing and another time for breaking a window. At the age of eleven he left home and started living on the streets of Mazatlan. He would occasionally stay with relatives there, but he never returned to visit his family. At thirteen he moved to Ciudad Chihuahua and lived on the streets with other boys. In Chihuahua he began to drink and use inhalants and other drugs. He was arrested several times and he was sent to a juvenile home. There he met some boys who were planning to move to Ciudad Juarez. He joined them and has been living and sleeping on the streets there ever since.

He supports himself in Juarez by helping merchants set up and clean during the day and also by doing yard work in El Paso. He has been arrested in El Paso six times for stealing, drug use, and immigration violations. Each time he was taken to the bridge

and released. He has been arrested in Juarez over twenty times and has spent time in an orphanage, a juvenile home, and an adult jail.

Due to lung problems from inhalant abuse, Freddy has been hospitalized several times. He lives with a gang of other boys who also use inhalants.

In each of three interviews with Freddy, he was visibly intoxicated on inhalants or drunk. He appears malnourished and seemingly has mental impairments due to substance abuse. Freddy has been stabbed twice and was shot once. He has not heard from his family in almost four years.

Source:

Mark W. Lusk, Felipe Peralta, and Gerald W. Vest, "Street children of Juarez: A field study," *International Social Work* 32(1989): 289–302.

mentally deficient cannot be ruled out, Davis thinks that "Anna might have had a normal or near-normal capacity, genetically speaking."

Isabelle was also an illegitimate child kept in seclusion. She and Anna were discovered at about the same time, at about the same age. Isabelle had lived with her deaf-mute mother in a dark room shut off from the rest of her mother's family. As a result, she had had no chance to develop speech. Instead, she made only a strange croaking noise. An inadequate diet and lack of sunshine had produced a severe case of rickets. When Isabelle was confronted with strangers, especially men, she behaved like a frightened wild animal. The child appeared to be hopelessly feeble-minded. However, her caretakers began a long, systematic training program. Isabelle went very rapidly through the usual stages of learning characteristic of the years one to six. Within a week, she made her first attempt at vocalization. In less than a year, she could identify written words, and could also write and add. By the time she was eight-and-a-half years old, she had reached a normal level. Davis reported that she was a bright, cheerful, energetic little girl.

Isabelle had two advantages that Anna did not. She received prolonged, expert attention. Also, she had had the constant companionship of her deaf-mute mother. The story of these neglected children points up the primary importance of contact with reasonably intelligent, articulate people in the early years of child development.

Monkeys Reared in Isolation

Monkeys need this early contact too. The experiments by Harlow and his associates on the effects of isolation on rhesus monkeys show that the animals' infantile social experience has crucial effects on their behaviour in later life.

In one of this series of studies (Harlow and Harlow 1962), young monkeys were separated from their mothers a few hours after birth. They were caged in such a way that each little monkey could see and hear other monkeys, although it could make no direct physical contact with them. These socially deprived infants matured into emotionally disturbed adults. The monkeys sat in their cages and stared fixedly into space or clasped

their heads in their arms and rocked for hours. They developed compulsive habits, such as chewing and tearing at their own bodies until they bled. They did not know how to relate to other monkeys, and were either passive and withdrawn or extremely aggressive. Harlow's work showed that there was a critical period of development during which social experience was absolutely necessary. Isolation for the first six months of life rendered animals permanently inadequate. The effects of shorter periods of isolation (60 to 90 days) were, however, reversible.

Another phase of Harlow's (1959) research involved comparing the importance of the act of nursing with the importance of bodily contact in engendering the infant monkey's attachment to its mother. Two surrogate "mother" monkeys were constructed. Both were wire cylinders surmounted by wooden heads. One was bare. The wire of the other was cushioned by a terry-cloth sheath. Each "mother" had a nipple of a feeding bottle protruding from its "breast." Eight newborn monkeys were separated from their natural mothers and placed in individual cages. Each was given access to both types of surrogate "mothers." Four monkeys were fed from the wire "mother" and four from the cloth-covered "mother." All the infants developed a strong attachment to the cloth-covered "mother" and little or none to the wire "mother," regardless of which one provided the milk. Both groups spent much more time clinging to the cloth-covered "mothers" than to the wire "mothers." Moreover, the soft "mother" was sought out for security. Experimenters confronted the monkey infants with a mechanical teddy bear, which moved toward them beating a drum. When frightened by this device, the infants sought comfort from the cloth-covered "mother," whether they had nursed from a wire mother or from a cloth-covered one. These results showed the importance of bodily contact in developing the infant/mother affectional bond.

The cloth-covered surrogate "mother" provided tactile comfort; however, it could not supply communication or training. Therefore, the social development of all the infant monkeys was severely and permanently impaired. Both the rhesus monkey experiments and the case histories of Anna and Isabelle show the fundamental need for childhood social experience. In addition, both show us how futile the nature/nurture controversy really is when nature and nurture are viewed as mutually exclusive alternatives.

Socialization Theories

Although socialization — learning norms, attitudes, values, knowledge, skills, and self-concepts — occurs throughout life, the learning that takes place during the formative years of childhood has been of special concern to psychologists and sociologists. The family, which bears the major responsibility here, has therefore received considerable attention from these social scientists. This section considers the principal ideas involved in four theoretical approaches to childhood socialization: learning theory, Piaget's cognitive developmental approach to moral thought, Freud's psychoanalytic theory, and symbolic-interaction views on development of the self. These theoretical perspectives vary in their emphases on how learning occurs and what socialization comprises, but for the most part, they are complementary rather than opposed sets of ideas. All of them can contribute to our understanding of childhood socialization.

Learning Theory

Very little human behaviour is directly determined by the individual's genetic makeup. For this reason, the precise mechanisms involved in learning are well worth knowing.

Three Main Types of Learning. We are concerned here with three main types of learning: classical conditioning, operant conditioning, and observation. In the first two types, learning occurs as a result of practice or the repetition of association (Yussen and Santrock 1978). However, since much of what children learn is through observation rather than extensive practice, the last type is the most important for socialization.

Classical conditioning was first discovered by Russian physiologist Ivan Pavlov in his famous experiments with a salivating dog. The basic idea is quite simple (Deutsch and Krauss 1965).

Meat powder, an "unconditioned stimulus" (UCS), is placed in a dog's mouth, automatically eliciting salivation, an "unconditioned response" (UCR). A neutral stimulus that does not elicit salivation, such as the sound of a bell, is presented just before the presentation of the food. The neutral stimulus is called a "conditioned stimulus" (CS). Soon the CS by itself elicits the flow of saliva without the meat or UCS. This learned response to the bell is the "conditioned response" (CR).

The classical conditioning paradigm explains some learning children do that is unintended by their parents. For example, a child may munch cookies while watching "Sesame Street." Before long, television becomes a signal to eat. This type of learning also represents one established source of phobias, or irrational fears. Many social attitudes are acquired in exactly the same fashion. If, for example, a little boy has an unpleasant experience with a red-haired girl, he may (unlike Charlie Brown) go through life disliking red-haired girls.

Operant conditioning, a second type of learning, is associated with American psychologists E.L. Thorndike (1898, 1913) and B.F. Skinner (1953). In this case, the organism must first make a specific response. If that response is followed by a reward or a punishment, it then becomes a conditioned, or learned, response. In a typical experiment, a hungry pigeon is placed in a cage equipped with four differently coloured keys. It goes through a trial-and-error procedure of pecking at the keys, eventually pecking the red key. The red key, when depressed, releases food. Because this particular response was rewarded, the pigeon will, after a few trials, go directly to the red key when hungry. In avoidance learning, an animal would be exposed to a noxious stimulus, such as an electric shock. In that case, it would learn to prevent punishment by pressing a certain key. In general, though, punishment is not a very reliable way of shaping future behaviour. It stops unwanted behaviour for the moment, but for various reasons its effects on future behaviour tend to be somewhat uncertain.

Children learn many of their socialization lessons through operant conditioning. Parents positively reinforce desired verbal responses, such as "please" and "thank you." Parents punish unwanted behaviour, such as rude talk, selfishness, or taking candy from stores without paying for it.

One sociologist (Cahill 1987) observed what happens when a small boy attempts to recycle a wad of gum:

While a woman is inspecting cans on a supermarket shelf, an approximately four-year-old boy leaves her side, walks over to a shelf on the opposite side of the aisle, picks up a piece of previously used chewing gum, and starts to put it in his mouth. The woman glances over her shoulder and loudly commands the boy to "STOP." Still holding the gum in his hand, the boy points to the shelf from which he removed the gum and objects that "it was there." The woman responds: "I don't care where you found it. It's been in someone else's mouth."

Although children do learn by operant conditioning, complications inevitably arise whenever results from pigeon and rat experiments are extrapolated to human beings. For one thing, experimenters consciously decide what they want the animals to learn; much human learning, however, is accidental. In addition, human beings find a much broader range of responses rewarding or punishing than do animals. Imagine this scene. A mother and her three-year-old daughter are in the kitchen. The child is bored and wants attention. Because the mother is busy, she is ignoring the child's chatter. Eventually, the little girl repeats the word she heard her father say that morning when he cut himself shaving. The mother, shocked by the profanity, scolds the child — unwittingly reinforcing the vulgar response by giving the bored child attention. Guess what the little girl learns that day?

Observational learning, the third type of learning, was discovered through research on the social behaviour of human beings. Bandura and Walters (1963) have shown that children can learn novel response patterns through observing another's behaviour. No reinforcement or reward is required for such learning to occur. Observational learning does not involve the gradual building up of responses required by operant conditioning.

Language appears to be learned mainly through observation. If children had to learn speech through operant conditioning, they would be senior citizens before they mastered their native language. Each sound, syllable, word, and sentence would have to be uttered spontaneously, then systematically reinforced by the care-takers. Instead, children copy the language behaviour of their adult models (and learn the meaning behind the language forms), just as they imitate other forms of behaviour. Children are especially likely to imitate adult models who are warm, nurturant, and powerful. In families that are functioning effectively, the child's parents provide extremely influential models. Models are also provided when trial-and-error learning is likely to have dangerous consequences; parents *show* their children how to cross streets and how to drive automobiles. During adolescence, the peer group is influential as a model in the use of verbal expressions, hairstyles, clothing, and entertainment preferences (Muuss 1988).

Unintentional learning often occurs through observation, as well as through classical and operant conditioning. Although a father may deliberately demonstrate to his son the movements involved in tying shoelaces, he does not set out to teach the boy his vocal inflections or facial expressions. Similarly, parents often tell children one thing and model quite another. For example, parents may preach that reading books is worthwhile but never read books themselves. Their child is more likely to copy parental deeds than parental words.

Piaget's Cognitive Developmental Approach to Moral Thought

The career of Swiss psychologist Jean Piaget began early. At age ten, he published an article on a rare albino sparrow in a natural history journal. Four years later, he was considered for a position as a curator in a Geneva museum. When this creative child's age was discovered, the offer was hastily withdrawn (Hetherington and Parke 1979).

Piaget's general theory (1928) considers how children think, reason, and remember. The development of moral thought — a sense of right and wrong, an understanding of societal values — is a particularly important dimension of his theory (Piaget 1932). Piaget observed children playing marbles and asked them to explain the game to him. He in turn talked to them about such ethical concepts as stealing, cheating, and justice. In many respects, childhood games are small-scale analogues of society. When children learn about the rules of the game, they are learning, at their level, about the norms of society. Similarly, when they learn to play game roles, they are also learning something about playing societal roles.

From his observations and discussions, Piaget concluded that two stages of moral thought exist. Children from four to seven years old display the more primitive level of morality, **moral realism**. The second stage, **moral autonomy**, develops around the age of eight. Several characteristics are associated with each stage.

The moral realist judges wrongdoing in terms of the outcome of the act. Extenuating circumstances and the intentions of the wrongdoer are disregarded. For example, Piaget told his subjects stories about two boys, John and Henry, and asked them to decide which boy deserved the more severe punishment. John was summoned to the dinner table. He came immediately. As he entered the dining room, he knocked over a teacart that, unknown to him, had been left behind the door. John's collision with the teacart resulted in fifteen broken cups. The other boy, Henry, had been forbidden by his mother to eat jam. When his mother left the room, Henry climbed up to the cupboard in search of the jam and knocked a cup to the floor.

Children under seven years, in the moral realism stage, believed that John should be punished more severely. After all, John had broken fifteen cups while Henry had broken only one. However, the older children, the moral autonomists, were more concerned with the fictitious boys' *reasons* for acting than with the consequences of the acts.

These older children felt that Henry deserved the greater punishment, because his offence had been committed while disobeying his mother's order. John's offence, on the other hand, had been accidental.

The moral realist believes that all rules are sacred and unchangeable absolutes. Rules are handed down by adult authority, and not the slightest deviation from them should be tolerated. The moral autonomist, in contrast, views rules as somewhat arbitrary social conventions. Older children involved in a game agree that certain rules are appropriate or inappropriate to that particular game situation. When the players consent to change, new rules can be adopted.

For example, the moral realist would agree that the child able to knock the most marbles out of a circle drawn in the dirt should have the first turn. Asked why, the moral realist would answer, "That's the rule. That's the way things are done." The moral autonomist would also agree that turns are decided by this preliminary trial. However, the older child would explain the procedure this way: "Well, the first turn has to be decided somehow. There are probably other ways to do it, but we decided to do it this way, and it works fine."

Piaget believes that maturation of cognitive capacities is the primary determinant of moral thought. This cognitive development results from the interaction of genetic capacities and social experiences. According to Piaget, it is the child's

The First Hockey Game

Games teach youngsters about social life. When they learn the rules of the game, they are also learning something about the rules of society. Here, a father describes taking his five-year-old son to see his first hockey game.

"After the face-off both teams skated hard, the lead changed back and forth, and — well, it turned out to be a pretty good game ... , with no ugly stuff and, as pro hockey goes, relatively few penalties. I think this must have been a disappointment for my son, for, aside from eating, the aspect of hockey that seemed to appeal to him most was the penalty box. I decided that it must answer powerfully to something basic in a five-year-old's ideal of justice: immediate, *brief* punishment, and then return to one's peers without shame or guilt. Anyway, he leaned forward expectantly each time the ref blew his whistle, and whenever a player was sent off he appeared to take a stern, Calvinist pleasure in making certain that the offender didn't attempt to return to the ice an instant before his sentence had expired."

Source:

"The Talk of the Town," *The New Yorker*, December 27, 1982.

interaction with peers, rather than with parents, that provides the social experiences crucial for the development of morality. For one thing, free-wheeling games with other children show that rules are conventional products that arise out of co-operation. Parents, on the other hand, are often reluctant to debate the reasons for their rules and regulations. This authoritarian stance promotes the younger child's view of rules as arbitrary and immutable. That, briefly, is Piaget's approach. Many studies have borne him out, showing that children from different cultures and social class backgrounds do go through a stage of moral realism before they reach moral autonomy.

Lawrence Kohlberg (1976) continued to study moral development in the Piaget tradition. In his procedure, those being interviewed were asked to respond to moral dilemmas such as the following:

In Europe, a woman was near death from cancer. One drug might save her, a form of radium that a druggist in the same town had recently discovered. The druggist was charging $2000, ten times what the drug cost him to make. The sick woman's husband, Heinz, went to everyone he knew to borrow the money, but he could only get together about half of what it cost. He told the druggist that his wife was dying and asked him to sell it cheaper or let him pay later. But the druggist said, "No." The husband got desperate and broke into the man's store to steal the drug for his wife. Should the husband have done that? (Kohlberg 1969)

From his analysis of boys' responses to these dilemmas, Kohlberg concluded that moral thought develops through six stages rather than the two hypothesized by Piaget.

Gilligan (1982) discovered that both Piaget and Kohlberg had based their ideas about moral development on research conducted almost exclusively with male samples. From her own observations of people of both sexes, Gilligan maintains that females and males speak with different "moral voices." The male **justice orientation** is concerned with preserving rights, upholding principles, and obeying rules, while the female **care orientation** speaks of concern for, connectedness with, and sensitivity to other people. For example, 11-year-old Jake was clear that Heinz should steal the drug. Jake saw the moral dilemma as "sort of a math problem with humans." He reasoned that while laws are neces-

sary to maintain social order, a judge would give Heinz the lightest possible sentence. By contrast, Amy, also a sixth-grader, argued that Heinz should not steal the drug. Her reasoning was grounded not in law but rather on the effect that the theft would have on the relationship between Heinz and his wife.

If he stole the drug, he might save his wife then, but if he did, he might have to go to jail, and then his wife might get sicker again, and he couldn't get more of the drug. ... So, they should really just talk it out and find some other way to make the money. (Gilligan 1982)

Psychoanalytic Theory

Psychoanalytic theory, as formulated by the Viennese physician Sigmund Freud (1856–1939), is both a theory of personality and a system of therapy (see Brill 1938). In practice, Freud was not an orthodox Freudian. He insisted that his psychoanalytic disciples be passive listeners and never respond emotionally to their patients. However, Freud himself gossiped, cracked jokes, offered advice, and often surprised his patients by handing them photographs of himself (*Time*, March 8, 1982).

Freud's theory views socialization as society's attempt to tame the child's inborn animal-like nature. He believed that the roots of human behaviour lie in the mind's irrational, unconscious dimensions. He assumed that the adult personality is the product of the child's early experiences within the family.

Freud saw the personality as composed of three energy systems: the Id, the Ego, and the Super-ego. The **Id** is the biological basis of personality, the **Ego** is the psychological basis of personality, and the **Super-ego** is the social basis of personality (Shaw and Costanzo 1970).

The Id is the reservoir of inborn, biological instincts. This "seething cauldron of sex and hostility" is wholly unconscious. It seeks immediate gratification: it operates according to the *pleasure principle*. The selfish, impulsive Id is not in contact with the reality of the external world.

Unlike the Id, the Ego develops out of the child's learning experiences with the environment. If all the Id's desires were gratified, the Ego would never emerge. The Ego encompasses the cognitive functions of thinking, perceiving, and memory. It also contains the defence mechanisms (such as rationalization, repression, projection) that have emerged from the Ego's previous encounters with reality. Part of the Ego is conscious and part is unconscious. The Ego's primary purpose is to direct the personality toward realistic, goals: it is oriented toward the *reality principle.* Therefore, the Ego mediates among the demands of the Id, the Super-ego, and the external world.

The Super-ego, or conscience, emerges as a result of the child's identification with her or his parents. Through reward, punishment, and example, the parents communicate society's rules to the child. When these social values and behavioural standards have been "introjected" (adopted as the child's own standards), the Super-ego censors the Id's impulses. This internal authority also guides the Ego's activities.

Freud held that every child goes through a series of personality development stages, each stage marked by sexual preoccupation with a different part of the body — the mouth, the anus, the genital area. Personality development, according to psychoanalytic theory, is essentially complete by five years of age.

Erikson's Revisions. Freud's ideas have been revised by his many disciples, especially Erik Erikson. Though Erikson entered Freud's Viennese circle as a 25-year-old itinerant artist, with no university degree at all, he emerged as a prominent child psychoanalyst. As well, he contributed the term "identity crisis" to our everyday language (Ewen 1980).

Erikson's (1963, 1968) ideas about socialization differ from Freud's in four ways:

1. Erikson is convinced that the rational Ego has an important independent role in personality development. The irrational Id is played down in his thinking.
2. One function of the autonomous Ego, according to Erikson, is to preserve a sense of identity and to avoid identity confusion. While patients in Freud's time suffered from sexual inhibitions, contemporary patients are plagued with questions of who they are or what they should believe in.
3. Freud's biological theory holds that "anatomy is destiny." By contrast, Erikson's theory emphasizes society's role in moulding personality. What is really involved here is a matter of degree.
4. According to Erikson, personality development continues throughout the life cycle, from infancy to old age. It does not stop at five years of age. Adolescents have the problem of establishing their identity. Young adults must establish intimacy with others in deep friendships and marriage, without sacrificing this sense of identity. Middle-aged adults are preoccupied with productivity and generativity (providing guidance for the next generation). Mature adults are concerned with ego integrity, a conviction that the life they have lived has meaning (Ewen 1980). Growth continues through all of these developmental crises.

Contemporary psychologists (Costa and McCrae 1989) agree with Erikson that Freud was mistaken in his belief that personality development ends with childhood. However, they disagree with Erikson's assertion that adults experience significant personality changes throughout life. Rather, the rule is considerable personality stability after the decade of the twenties. The "continuity of personality allows us to use the current self as a reliable indicator of the future self," so that "planning for a career, marriage, or retirement should be based on realistic projections of our needs, abilities, and styles" (Costa and McCrae 1989:68).

Symbolic-Interaction Views

Symbolic interaction, as a theoretical perspective on primary socialization, is more sociological than any of the approaches discussed so far. Like learning theory, it emphasizes the environmental influences that impinge on the child, rather than the unfolding of the child's biological capacities. (Both Piaget and Freud stressed the latter.) However, symbolic interaction directs particular attention to the impact of the social environment. The term "interaction" emphasizes the importance of group influences. These theorists also take issue with the Freudian position that a fundamental conflict exists between individual and society. Symbolic interactionists view the individual and society as two sides of the same coin. One cannot exist without the other.

Interactionists and learning theorists differ on two other major assumptions. Interactionists believe that human behaviour is qualitatively different from animal behaviour, because humans use much more complex language. This assumption is the reason for the word "symbolic" in these theorists' title. A *symbol* is something that stands for something else. A red light means stop. A five-dollar bill symbolizes buying power. Although there is some physical reality "out there," people respond not directly to this "objective reality," but to a symbolic interpretation of it (Charon 1979). These interpretations are called *definitions of the situation*. Definitions of the situation may be personal (idiosyncratic) or cultural (standard meanings embedded in a community's culture and learned through socialization) (Stebbins 1967). Symbolic interactionists are especially interested in how human beings attach meanings to the actions of other people as they attempt to make sense of both themselves and their social worlds.

Finally, symbolic interactionists emphasize the importance of the child's active involvement in role-learning processes, such as role-taking (discussed under "Genesis of the Self," below) and altercasting, as opposed to the more passive processes of modelling or conditioning. **Altercasting** involves casting the other person in a role we choose for him or her in order to manipulate the situation (Charon 1979). For instance, a child may say, "Toby, you're supposed to let me use your bike, because friends are supposed to share" (Weinstein 1969).

Although the symbolic interactionists are interested in many facets of socialization, we will concentrate here on the question of how the child acquires a self. We will consider the pertinent work of two pioneer theorists — Charles H. Cooley and George Herbert Mead.

Cooley's Looking-Glass Self. Cooley was an American sociologist who derived many of his ideas about socialization from observing and recording the behaviour of his own children. He used the metaphor of the looking glass to illustrate his point that children acquire a self through adopting other people's attitudes toward them. The self is social in that it emerges out of interaction with primary group members. Its content reflects the child's interpretation of others' appraisals of what kind of person that child is.

The **looking-glass self** has three elements: "the imagination of our appearance to the other person, the imagination of his judgment of that appearance, and some sort of self-feeling, such as pride or mortification" (Cooley 1902).

Notice that what is important here is the child's *interpretation* of other people's attitudes. This interpretation may or may not be accurate. A little boy may pick up messages from his parents that they think he is short, fat, and clumsy, and that they think being short, fat, and clumsy is deplorable. If the assessment of his extremely authoritative parents is not countered by other sources of opinion, the boy has little choice but to define himself as short, fat, and clumsy. In all likelihood, therefore, he will feel ashamed of himself. Cooley was arguing, as we would put it today, that both self-imagery and self-esteem are social products.

Mead's Theory of the Self. In formulating his ideas about the child's acquisition of a self, Mead elaborated on many of the insights of Cooley, his symbolic-interaction contemporary. Mead's ideas on the subject are, however, much more sophisticated than Cooley's. Mead's major work on the self is contained in *Mind, Self, and Society* (1934), a series of social philosophy lectures given at the University of Chicago, assembled after Mead's death. Although in his own lifetime Mead's impact was through ideas presented in lectures rather than through published works, he was not a charismatic teacher. In fact, he was boring. Schellenberg (1978) tells us that "his lectures were not very dramatic occasions. He seldom looked at his students, and he spoke with little expression. Looking at the ceiling or out a window, he sat and calmly lectured on the subject of the day."

The word "self" has rather mystical connotations. In order to specify what he meant by the "self," Mead made three fundamental assumptions:

1. The newborn infant does not come equipped with a self. Although the infant is born with the physiological potential to reach this goal eventually, the self is acquired, not innate.
2. Mead defined "self" as that which is an object to oneself. At first glance, this definition does not seem very enlightening. However, Mead meant that the self is reflexive. To have a self

You and Your Self

The acquisition of personal identity, or a sense of self, is one of the major goals of socialization. Therefore, researchers often have occasion to measure this concept. Despite its centrality, the "self" remains elusive. One of the most frequently used measures of the self-concept is Kuhn and McPartland's (1954) Twenty Statements Test.

Before you complete this test, remember these three things.

First, the self is difficult to define. Although we know intuitively what we mean when we say we have a self, this label implies a number of related components. It can refer to the stream of consciousness, the self as experiencer of thoughts, emotions, physical sensations. As well, it implies the conviction of continuity over time. (This self who thinks, experiences, and acts today is essentially the same self as the one who thought, experienced, and acted five and ten years ago.) Sometimes, the "self" means the director of action, the planner, and the doer. Sometimes, it means the cognitive picture of who I am, the self-concept. In addition, the sense of self encompasses an ideal self, the self that I wish I were. Related to the latter component is self-esteem, or my evaluation of myself. Finally, the material self, which includes my body and, perhaps, my possessions, seems to be involved.

The first task of researchers is to specify exactly which component of the self they wish to measure. Below, we will focus on the self-concept (Mead's "Me"), and define it as a "set of attitudes toward the self."

Second, techniques to measure the self are often vulnerable to the "social desirability effect," which is the tendency for research subjects to present a flattering view of themselves. For example, people who really regard themselves as neurotic and overweight may not care to reveal these thoughts to a researcher.

Third, measures of the self are sometimes affected by the context in which they are administered. If you complete the measure described below at university, those aspects of your self-concept related to being a student will probably be uppermost in your mind. If you complete it at home, however, family identities may supersede the student dimension of your self-concept.

The Twenty Statements Test
1. Write the numbers one to twenty on a page. The standard instructions for the test read as follows: "There are 20 numbered blanks on the page below. Please write 20 answers to the simple question 'Who Am I?' in the blanks. Just give 20 different answers to the question. Answer as if you were giving the answers to yourself, not to somebody else. Write the answers in the order that they occur to you. Don't worry about logic or importance. Go along fairly quickly, for time is limited. Give yourself about 10 minutes to complete the answers."

is to have the ability to think about oneself and to act socially toward oneself. For most of us, the self is the most fascinating object in the world. We devote considerable time to self-contemplation. When we congratulate ourselves for an honest act or chastise ourselves for a piece of stupidity, we are acting toward ourselves.
3. The self is a communicative process, not a "thing." The self is analogous to a verb rather than a noun; it consists of the processes of thinking and acting toward oneself. The self is not a substantive entity that dwells behind the eyes or under the heart.

Genesis of the Self. Mead's complex explanation of how the child acquires a self can be summarized in a small number of central ideas.

The development of the self depends on development of the capacity to use language. According to Mead, language and self develop concurrently. As a first step in developing self-awareness, the child must differentiate himself or herself as a separate "thing" from the myriad other "things" in the environment. Through language, the child learns the names of things. This object is called a "chair"; that one is called "Mommy." The child learns his or her name along with other object names: there is an object called "George." The child also learns the characteristics of objects. Fire is hot and dangerous. Chairs have four legs and are intended for sitting. Similarly, George learns what sort of object he is — a boy, little, someone who likes cookies. (See Chapter 5 for an application of this theory to gender socialization in particular.)

2. Next, the researcher classifies each of the 20 answers as either "consensual" or "nonconsensual" references. By "consensual references," Kuhn and McPartland meant groups and classes whose limits and conditions of membership are matters of common knowledge (for example, student, male, wife, Baptist, youngest child). By "nonconsensual references," they meant groups, classes, attributes, or traits that require interpretation by the individual. These statements are either ones without positional reference (happy, tall) or consensual references whose meaning is obscured by ambiguous modifiers (good student, ungrateful daughter).

   Go through your 20 answers and write "consensual" or "nonconsensual" beside each of them.

3. The final step is to compute your "locus score." The "locus score" is the total number of consensual references made. The TST was designed to measure Mead's "Me," the self as a social entity. The locus score is intended to provide an indicator of the social anchorage of the self, because it measures citations of social positions.

Some Comparative TST Results

You might find it interesting to compare your own TST results with some of its developers' findings. Differences do not mean that you are abnormal in any way.

1. Most people tend to exhaust all the consensual responses first, before going on to nonconsensual responses. For example, a person might describe himself as "male," "a university student," "a son," "22 years old," and then as "athletic," "skinny," and so on. However, the actual locus score may vary from none to twenty. Kuhn and McPartland argued that the self-descriptions given early are the most important ones. Therefore, they felt that the fact that the consensual responses come first provided evidence for the social nature of the self.

2. The locus score increases with age as people acquire an increasing number of social statuses. The average locus score for 7-year-olds is 5.8, and for 24-year-olds, 11.0.

3. Females mention their gender earlier than do males. Of those university undergraduates mentioning gender at all, the mean rank for females was 1.7, and for males, 2.5.

4. Respondents 19 to 22 years old mention their age in average rank order of 5.6.

5. Most TST responses fall into five general categories: social groups and classifications (such as age, gender, occupation, marital status, kinship relations, ethnicity); ideological beliefs (statements of a religious, philosophical, or moral nature); interests; ambitions; self-evaluations. The fifth category can be analyzed as an indicator of self-esteem.

Source:

Manford H. Kuhn, "Self-attitudes by age, sex and professional training," *Sociological Quarterly* 9(1960):39–55; Manford H. Kuhn and Thomas S. McPartland, "An empirical investigation of self-attitudes," *American Sociological Review* 19(1954):68–76; Marlene Mackie, "The domestication of self: Gender comparisons of self-imagery and self-esteem," *Social Psychology Quarterly* 46(1983):343–350.

Both language and the development of the self require "taking the role of the other." In order to communicate with another person, it is necessary to take the role of the other — that is, to adopt the other's point of view about what is being said. Suppose you greet me Monday morning by asking, "How are you?" Before I can properly reply, I have to put myself in your shoes and decide whether you really want to hear all about my physical and psychological well-being or whether you are merely being polite. In the first case, I will tell you at great length how I am feeling. In the second, I will answer, "Fine, thank you."

The development of the self requires this ability to take the role of the other, which is a fundamental aspect of language use. Because the self is social, the child must be able to adopt the perspective of other people toward himself or herself. Having a self means viewing yourself through the eyes of other people.

Stages of Development of the Self. According to Mead, the ability to role-play and the consequent genesis of the self occur through the two main stages (Meltzer 1978) described below:

1. During the *play stage*, the child begins role-playing. The little girl pretends she is a mother or a doctor or a store clerk. What is important here is that the child is demonstrating the ability to adopt, for example, the mother's role, and to act back on herself from the perspective of this role. In pretending that she is the mother scolding her imaginary child for lying, the little girl is placing herself in her own mother's shoes and reacting to her own

behaviour. This type of play indicates that the self is forming. However, the self at this stage is fragmentary because the child is taking the role of only one person at a time. The self lacks unity because the reflected view of the self is a series of fragmented views, not a coherent whole.

2. A coherent self develops during the *game stage*, when the child becomes capable of taking a number of roles simultaneously. Mead used the game of baseball to explain this process. Playing baseball requires the ability to adopt several different roles at the same time. Being a catcher involves understanding the roles of pitcher, shortstop, umpire, opposing team member up to bat, and so on. The events in a particular game must be understood from all of these various perspectives. The child manages this task by forming a composite role out of all the particularized roles. Mead called this generalized standpoint from which the child views himself or herself the **generalized other**. He called the corresponding standpoint involved in the earlier play stage the **significant other.** During the play stage, the child might think, "Dad says I'm bad when I tell lies." During the game stage, the child would instead think, "*They* say lying is wrong." Behaviour thus comes increasingly to be guided by an abstract moral code rather than the opinion of one individual. Because parents (and other central caretakers) interpret the social order for the child, significant others are the source of the generalized other (Acock 1984).

Mead's ideas imply that self-development does not stop in childhood. As the person adopts new roles and encounters new situations, the self will continue to evolve (Bush and Simmons 1981).

The "I" and the "Me." Mead's formulation of the self makes room for both a socially defined aspect of the self (which was stressed above) and a spontaneous, creative aspect of the self. The **Me** represents the self-concept, especially internalized societal attitudes and expectations. The **I**, on the other hand, is the acting, unique, unfettered self.

Unlike the Freudian Id, Ego, and Super-ego, the "I" and the "Me" collaborate. The "I" provides individuality and initiative for behaviour, while the "Me" provides direction for that behaviour according to the dictates of society. Remember, though, that the self is a process and that the "I" and "Me" are phases of that process, not concrete entities.

Theoretical Overview

The ideas of the learning theorists and of Piaget, Freud, and the symbolic interactionists all contribute to our understanding of childhood socialization. The learning theorists focus on the specific mechanisms involved in socialization. They tell us *how* the child learns the lessons of socialization. Piaget's work, on the other hand, analyzes the development of morality. Both Freud and Mead are also concerned with the question of how society's notions about proper behaviour are internalized by the child. However, their theories also address other questions. Freud emphasizes emotions, sexuality, and the unconscious. In addition, his theory provides many ideas concerning the role played by specific family members in socializing the child. Finally, Mead and Cooley emphasize the social context of child development. The link they isolated between the emergence of self-awareness and the acquisition of language is extremely insightful. The work of these people, then, should be seen as complementary rather than competing systems of thought.

Socialization: The Contemporary Context

What does it mean to grow up in the 1990s? As mentioned above, individuals who were born about the same time and who have similar experiences during their formative years share characteristics throughout their lives that distinguish them from other generations. In other words, the larger society provides a complex and changing socialization context. In this section, we discuss major factors affecting the experiences of Canadians currently 5 to 20 years old.

Effects of Demography

Each generation is somewhat distinctly influenced by *demographic*, or population, characteristics (see Chapter 8). Consider generation size. Members of the present generation in their late teens generally find themselves in overcrowded college and university classrooms. This is partly because they are "echo-boomers," daughters and sons of the huge baby boomer generation born after World War II. Another reason is because they share classrooms with older students who, frustrated in their search for satisfying work, return for more educational credentials.

Demography influences socialization in another important way. The lower birthrate (1.7 per 1000 in Canada generally, 1.43 in Quebec [Gregg and Posner 1990]) means that youngsters have fewer siblings or none at all. Previously viewed as "zealous, egotistical, selfish, spoiled little brats who grew into lonely, neurotic adults" (Pappert 1983), only children have now become commonplace and, hence, respectable. Also, small families translate into socialization advantages for at least some children. Large families can depress the educational attainment and subsequent occupational status of their children (Rossi and Rossi 1990). However, children today are less likely "to have a brother or sister who is five or more years older and who might give them guidance in life" (Beaujot 1990:33). Finally, because parents have fewer children, the potential exists for their relationships with the offspring they do have to increase in intensity.

Declining death rates also involve changes in socialization. The probability of a child's being orphaned or of growing up without grandparents has diminished (Sullivan 1983). Since Canada is an "aging society," children will be increasingly familiar with the elderly. However, death is no longer the commonplace family event it was through most of history. Living in a low-mortality society that isolates the dying in hospitals and nursing homes leaves young people inadequately prepared to cope with death when it does touch their lives.

Population migration into Canada represents an important contextual aspect of socialization. In the 1960s and 1970s, large numbers of people began arriving from Asian, Latin American, and Caribbean countries. These newcomers face the dual challenges of conveying something of their culture of origin to their children while they and their offspring learn to fit into their new society. Often, the new immigrant family protects its members from stress by developing a "creative schizophrenia" that allows its members to be "modern" at work and school, and "traditional" at home (Berger and Berger 1984). As the "first wave of visible-minority immigration in Canadian history" (Gregg and Posner 1990:174), they frequently encounter prejudice and discrimination.

Economic Trends

National economic circumstances during the past fifteen years or so — recession, massive layoffs and plant shutdowns resulting from corporate restructuring strategies, technological innovations, and heightened international competition (Story 1991) — have also affected the socialization experiences of Canadians. Many families are deeply affected by unemployment and poverty.

Economic trends have an especially severe impact on adolescents and young adults. The transition between work and labour force is very difficult for this generation of young people. "In the job-scarce 1990s, many are bouncing between dead-end positions, spending long periods on unemployment insurance, and waking up at age 30 no further ahead than where they were at 18 or 20" (*Globe and Mail*, 1993a). As economic opportunities for young adults dwindle, many older children, instead of becoming independent, return repeatedly to the parental home (Boyd and Pryor 1989). This "crowded nest" phenomenon produces difficulties for both generations. Also, because the work ethic has long been a central motivation in Canadians' lives (Burstein et al. 1984), and teenagers have high occupational aspirations (Empson-Warner and Krahn 1992), youth unemployment and the prospect of the permanent unavailability of preferred jobs are serious concerns for both adults and young people.

Technological developments also affect socialization. Children are experiencing computerized learning and computerized play. In this high-tech era, "for the first time, many youngsters know more than their elders and are ... teaching their elders in ways that parents have traditionally encultured children" (Williams 1983). Young people spend hours immersed with video games. Listening to music is a top leisure activity for Canadian teenagers (Bibby and Posterski 1992). They cocoon themselves in portable stereo headsets. At home, they live in a constant bombardment of noise from radios, stereos, and rock videos. "For more than 10 years MTV has virtually handcuffed young people to their television sets" (Bibby and Posterski 1992:278).

These high-tech leisure pursuits have created a great deal of controversy. Some authorities (Provenzo 1991) worry about the "violence, destruction, xenophobia, racism, and sexism" that characterize Nintendo. Others fret that TV robs kids of their innocence (Postman 1982) and turns them into materialistic, mindless, sedentary "couch potatoes." Many parents worry about rock music's approval of drugs, misogyny, and violence. For example, in 1992, rap singer Ice-T provoked a storm of protest with his song "Cop Killer" ("Die, pig, die ...").

Family Life

As Chapter 12 points out, the Canadian family today is no longer the "classical family of Western nostalgia" (Goode 1963). Many of these changes have serious implications for socialization. Divorce produces inevitable social and economic changes in children's lives. For example, many learn that when marriages break up, "money is tight for winter coats, babysitters, running shoes and penicillin" (Maynard 1984). Moves to new neighbourhoods or communities, which often occur in the wake of a divorce, mean the loss of friendships and the challenge of establishing new ones. Relations with both custodial and noncustodial parents deviate from traditional nuclear-family scripts. Children are likely to find these changes stressful, at least initially. One beloved parent may now be labelled a villain and enemy by the other. A small proportion of fathers become *Mr. Mom*s in custodial-father households. Many more join the legion of indulgent "Uncle Dads" (C.W. Smith 1985), playing limited meaningful roles in their children's lives beyond visiting privileges. Many noncustodial parents eventually disappear altogether. Parents' boyfriends or girlfriends may come and go, exercising temporary authority over children of divorce.

Because of the emotionally charged familial context and the power of the parents to mete out rewards and punishments, parents have tremendous impact on children.

Despite all this, it is important to acknowledge that divorce frequently involves positive consequences for children. Many youngsters benefit by escaping the stressful family environment produced by a conflict-ridden marriage, and by establishing closer relations with their custodial parent. Though divorce can make children cynical about marriage, they do develop a broader vision of "normal" social arrangements (Whitehurst 1984). Children's responses depend on such considerations as their age at the time of divorce, and the level of pre-existing conflict in the home.

As a result of divorce and births to never-married mothers who keep their offspring, many Canadian children are growing up in one-parent families. Single parenthood typically means single motherhood. Families headed by women

Parent–Child Interaction

In her observation of 78 parent–child dyads in Mexican families, Phyllis Bronstein discovered a number of differences between maternal and paternal behaviours. Some of the patterns observed run counter to the traditionally held views of Mexican parental roles: that fathers are more aloof and authoritarian, whereas mothers are more warm and nurturant. The findings, when compared cross-culturally, proved to be similar to findings obtained in observational studies of parents' interactions with infants and young children in the United States.

What emerges from this study of naturally occurring parent–child interaction in Mexican families are findings that are remarkably similar to those obtained in recent observational research on parents and their infants and preschoolers in this country. Mothers spent a greater proportion of their interactions in caretaking activities than fathers did, and fathers spent a greater proportion of their interactions in playful, participatory activities than mothers did. Further, fathers were no less warm or affectionate than mothers, and in fact (relevant perhaps to the kinds of activities they engaged in), they were somewhat higher than mothers on showing friendly affect. In addition, fathers' interactions, more than mothers', involved explaining or giving information to children. Finally, fathers did differ significantly in their interactions with girls and boys, whereas mothers did not. As was found by Kotelchuck (1976), Lamb (1977b, 1977c), Parke and O'Leary (1976), and others, fathers paid more interested attention to sons than to daughters, and as found by Block et al. (1974), they

showed more cognitive/achievement orientation with them. In addition, their low relative frequency of dominant, restrictive, and punitive behaviors to daughters suggests that, as found by Tauber (1979) and Block et al. (1974), fathers may have interacted in a more sociable manner with daughters than with sons.

What these findings reveal within their own cultural context is that fathers in these Mexican families played a distinct and salient role of their own, different from mothers, and very different from the traditional view of the aloof Mexican patriarch. Although there is no measure of the hours per day each father in the present sample spent at home, most did seem to spend most of their nonworking hours and their days off there or in recreational pursuits with their families. Furthermore, when they were with their children, many of the fathers seemed genuinely involved with them, in friendly, nonauthoritarian interaction. They joked and talked with them, showed them how to shoot a marble or polish their shoes, and in the homes where there were sufficient money and space for toys and hobbies, they played dominoes with them or looked at a coin or rock collection together. ...

The other main finding, that fathers but not mothers differed in their behaviors toward girls and boys, suggests that Mexican fathers may play an important role in the socialization of their children for traditional sex roles. Boys were listened to and shown how to do things, which would seem to convey the message that what they have to say is important and that they are capable of mastering new skills. Girls, on the other hand, were treated especially gently, and at the same time, with a lack of full attention and an imposing of opinions and values. The gentle treatment would seem to convey the message that they are fragile and docile — a paternal viewpoint that emerged in this country in earlier self-report studies of fathers' perceptions of children (e.g., Rubin. Provenzano, & Luria

1974; Tasch 1952, 1955). The inattention and imposing of opinion would seem to communicate the view that what females have to say is less valuable than what males have to say, so that females need to be told more what to think and do, and can more readily be interrupted or ignored. Thus in this sample of Mexican families, very different messages were being transmitted to girls and boys — about their roles, their temperaments, their thinking, and their expected behavior — and fathers were the main transmitters of those messages. The findings are also similar to ones emerging from U.S. observational studies of parent–child interaction, in which "adults, particularly fathers, act in more instrumental, task-oriented, mastery-emphasizing ways with their sons and in more expressive, less intellectually rigorous ways with their daughters" (Block 1979). In addition, it should be mentioned that fathers' greater tendency to give information, explanations, and directions to children presents a knowledgeable and mastery-oriented image as a male role model.

What is striking about the findings of the present study is the consistency of fathers' behavior patterns, across different methodologies, cultures, and ages of children. The findings do not match very well with *reports* of fathers' behaviors by children, mothers, and fathers themselves (e.g., Bronfenbrenner 1961; Devereux et al. 1974; Kagan, Hosken, & Watson 1961), in which fathers were generally described as being less warm and more strictive and punitive than mothers. Instead, they support those findings of recent observational studies of parents and very young children, which show that whereas fathers did significantly less caretaking than mothers, they were nonetheless involved, participatory parents who had positive, companionable, and instructive relationships with their children. In addition, the findings support those self-report and observational measures that found fathers but not mothers to differ in their attitudes and behaviors toward girls and boys, particularly with regard to gender-related areas. How widespread these patterns may be across cultures and across different family structures and ages of children are questions worthy of further investigation.

Source:

Adapted from Phyllis Bronstein, "Differences in mothers' and fathers' behaviors toward children," *Developmental Psychology* 20(6) (1984):995–1003. Copyright © 1984. Reprinted with the permission of the American Psychological Association, Inc.
The references in this article are to: M. Kotelchuck, (1976). The infant's relationship to the father: Experimental evidence. In M.E. Lamb (Ed.), *The role of the father in child development* (pp. 329–344). New York: Wiley; M.E. Lamb, (1977b). The development of mother-infant and father-infant attachment in the second year of life. *Devel-*

opmental Psychology, 13:637–648; M.E. Lamb, (1977c). The development of parental preferences in the first two years of life. *Sex Roles*, 3, 495–497; R.O. Parke, & S.E. O'Leary, (1976). Father-mother-infant interaction in the newborn period: Some findings, some observations, and some unresolved issues. In K. Riegel & J. Meacham (Eds.), The developing individual in a changing world: Vol. 2. *Social and environmental issues* (pp. 653–663). The Hague. The Netherlands: Mouton; J.H. Block, J. Block, & D. Harrington, (1974). *The relationship of parental teaching strategies to ego-resiliency in preschool children*. Paper presented at the annual meeting of the Western Psychological Association, San Francisco; M.A. Tauber, (1979). Sex differences in parent-child interaction styles during a free-play session. *Child Development*, 50, 981–988; J.Z. Rubin, F.J. Provenzano, & Z. Luria, (1974). The eye of the beholder: Parents' views on sex of newborns. *American Journal of Orthopsychiatry*, 44, 512–519; R.J.

Tasch, (1952). The role of the father in the family. *Journal of Experimental Education*, 20, 319–361; R.J. Tasch, (1955). Interpersonal perceptions of fathers and mothers. *Journal of Genetic Psychology*, 87, 59–65; J.H. Block, (1979). *Socialization influences on personality development in males and females*. Invited address presented at the annual meeting of the American Psychological Association. New York; U. Bronfenbrenner, (1961). Some familial antecedents of responsibility and leadership in adolescents. In L. Petrullo & B.M. Bass (Eds.), *Leadership and interpersonal behaviour* (pp. 239–271). New York: Holt, Rinehart & Winston; E.C. Devereux, R. Shouval, U. Bronfenbrenner, R.R. Rogers, S. Kav-Venaki, & E. Kiely, (1974). Socialization practices of parents, teachers, and peers in Israel: The Kibbutz versus the city. *Child Development*, 45, 269–281; J. Kagan, B. Hosken, & S. Watson, (1961). Child's symbolic conceptualization of parents. *Child Development*, 32, 625–636.

often experience poverty (Moore 1990). The custodial parent is frequently overwhelmed with responsibility for earning a living, child care, and housework (Michelson 1985). In such homes, the single parent may treat the child as a pseudo-adult equal, loading the child with many of the responsibilities of the missing parent: for example, serving as a listening post for the parent, discussing sex, cooking, cleaning, and caring for younger siblings (Schlesinger 1983).

In addition, many children are growing up in "blended families," with stepparents and siblings unrelated to them by blood. Sociologists are just beginning to understand the nature of socialization in such reconstituted families. Discipline frequently becomes a thorny issue. For example, during courtship of the children's mother, the stepfather often tries to be popular with the youngsters, an "easygoing pal." With marriage, his perceptions of his role tend to change. Now he strives to exercise firm control, as well as love, over the children. The children are apt to resent this discipline, especially if it differs from that of their mother or biological father (Spanier and

Furstenberg 1987). Because they often live elsewhere, a father's children from former marriages tend to be marginal to his newly constituted family (Hobart 1988).

By 1987, more than 60 percent of mothers of preschoolers were in the labour force (Labour Canada 1990). As a result, a majority of Canadian children are now cared for by someone other than a parent (Eichler 1983). Children are increasingly involved with babysitters, peers, television, and secondary socialization agencies such as schools and day-care centres. Fathers are now more actively involved in their children's upbringing (Lamb 1987). Nevertheless, fathers' contributions to the work of child care still tends to be less than mothers' (LaRossa and LaRossa 1989). For example, many fathers view themselves as "babysitting" their own children, as "helping out" by playing with them. Mothers take overall responsibility for the youngsters and perform less pleasant child-rearing tasks.

Finally, the dark side of the family must also be acknowledged. Family members often treat one another with love, support, and warmth. Paradoxically, "the most likely place for a person to be murdered or seriously assaulted is at home, by family members" (Van Stolk 1983). Sadly, adult caretakers frequently misuse their power over children (Lenton 1990).

Novelist Sylvia Fraser (1987) has written poignantly about her own childhood experience of incest: "Thus for me the usual childhood reality was reversed. Inside my own house, among people I knew, was where danger lay. The familiar had proven to be treacherous, whereas the unfamiliar, the public, the unknown, the foreign, still contained the seeds of hope." Obviously, the socialization of battered and sexually abused children, for whom home is not a safe place, is seriously affected (Guberman and Wolfe 1985).

Agents of Socialization

The socialization process involves many types of influences that impinge on people throughout their lives. This part of our discussion will concentrate on four major socialization agents: the family, the peer group, the school, and the mass media. The agents singled out here are important because they affect almost every Canadian. In addition, they all exert a powerful influence during the impressionable childhood years.

Society has charged two of these agents, the family and the school, with the socialization of children. Although much of the impact they have on children is unintentional, both the family and the school also deliberately set out to equip children with the knowledge required to fit into adult society. The influence of the peer group and the media is frequently unintentional.

Family

Although the contemporary family now shares aspects of its function with other agents, the family's impact on the child transcends that of all other agents of socialization. In Clausen's words (1968), "the 'widening world of childhood' spirals out from the parental home." Learning occurs rapidly during these crucial years of early childhood when the family has almost exclusive control and no relearning or contradictory lessons

are involved. Moreover, learning takes place in the context of close emotional bonds. The family touches every sphere of the child's existence. The early immersion of the child within the family guarantees that this institution lays the foundation for the later and lesser influences of the other socialization agents, which are considerably more segmented. Chapter 12 offers more details about the nature and content of socialization by the family.

There is a second reason that sociologists assign primacy to the family. Various family characteristics orient the child to specific configurations of experiences, values, and opportunities. Growing up in a one-parent or blended family is different from growing up in an "intact" family. Also, by being born into a particular family, the child automatically becomes part of a larger family — grandparents, aunts, uncles, cousins. Moreover, the family's social class position means that the child will learn one set of values, rather than another. The opportunities of a child born into an upper-middle-class family are considerably different from those of a child born into the working class. Social class, as we will see below, is the most studied demographic variation in socialization (Wright and Wright 1976). The family's racial or ethnic background is another important determinant of the content of socialization.

Finally, the family's geographical location is also the child's. Growing up in Toronto and growing up in Newfoundland (Firestone 1978) are quite different experiences.

Child as Socializer of the Parents. The socialization that occurs within the family is a two-way process (Ambert 1992). The child is not just a passive recipient of parental influence; youngsters are "at the very least participants in their own development and even co-producers in this enterprise" (Ambert 1992:13). Just as the parents socialize the child, the child also socializes the parents. This mutual influence extends from infancy, where the effect of an infant's cry on the mother is "all out of proportion to his age, size, and accomplishments" (Rheingold 1966), through adolescence and into adulthood.

In infancy, the child's demands and responses serve to teach the mother and father how to behave as parents. A couple looking forward to raising a family have, of course, many abstract ideas of what parenthood entails, which they have gleaned from observation, reading, and so on. Nevertheless, many young adults are very ignorant about babies. (A brand-new mother wrote a newspaper medical columnist to ask whether it was true that her baby could split the seam of its head open by crying.) Interaction with their first-born, however, teaches them the actual behaviours involved in the role of parents. For example, it is one thing to know that parents are responsible for their children when they are ill, and quite another to cope with a sick baby who cannot breathe properly at two in the morning.

Children's multifaceted influence upon their parents continues as they develop from infancy through adolescence. For example, Coltrane's (1989) study of twenty dual-earner American couples with school-aged children reported that for most, parenting was their primary topic of conversation. One father said, "That's what we mostly discuss when we're not with our kids ... is how we feel about how we're taking care of them." Immigrant families provide many examples of children socializing parents. North Americanized adolescents often have great impact on their parents, whose Old World ways they often resent and question (Ambert 1992:139). Mutual parent–child influence in immigrant and non-immigrant families alike frequently continues until the death of the parent.

Social Class. Canadian society, like all other large societies, is socially stratified. (For a detailed discussion of the nature of stratification in Canada, see Chapter 9.) When sociologists discuss *social stratification*, they are referring to the arrangement of a "group or society into a hierarchy of positions that are unequal with regard to power, property, social evaluation, and/or psychic gratification" (Tumin 1967). The occupations of the parents provide the best indicator of the Canadian family's social class position, and this position influences the child's socialization experiences and consequent opportunities.

Statistics Canada reports that in 1990, 17 percent of Canadian children lived in poverty (*Globe and Mail*, 1992). Economic recession, high unemployment, and increasing numbers of women-headed, lone-parent families have exacerbated the economic problems of families at the lower end of the socioeconomic scale (Duncan and

Just as the parents socialize the child, the child also socializes the parents.

Rodgers 1991). As a result, the satisfaction of such basic needs as housing, diet, medical and dental care, and clothing becomes precarious. The amount of income at the family's disposal also determines the less tangible aspects of socialization. Middle-class children enjoy opportunities to read a wide variety of books, to visit museums, to travel, to attend camp, and so forth. By contrast, poorer children are denied experiences like these that widen intellectual horizons. Indeed, hunger, illness, and home conditions not conducive to studying make it difficult for them to get a basic education.

Members of different social classes, by virtue of experiencing different conditions of life, come to see the world differently and develop different conceptions of social reality (Gecas 1976; Kohn 1977). The class origins of a child remain impor-

Poverty in Canada

As poverty rises to strike more than one in seven Canadians, more single mothers fall farther behind, according to a new federal report.

After six years of declining poverty, the proportion of poor Canadians started to climb again in 1990, hitting 14.6 per cent, compared to the 50-year peak of 18.2 per cent in 1983. Once they are calculated, the numbers are expected to be worse for 1991.

The Poverty Profile, released ... by the National Council of Welfare, shows that as poverty climbs in Canada, so does the gap between groups of impoverished people.

On average, the report says, single mothers with children under 18 lived $8,232 below the poverty line in 1990, the worst of any group. Single mothers are also the most frequently poor of all household heads, with 255,000 or six out of 10 living in poverty. That number jumps to eight in 10 for single mothers who did not finish high school.

The report showed 16.9 per cent, or 1.1 million children live in poverty. In 1980, 33 per cent of them came from one-parent families, rising to 40 per cent by 1990.

"Is this the kind of country ... Canadians want?" NDP finance critic Steven Langdon asked in the House of Commons Monday, demanding that the government announce new day-care spaces in Wednesday's economic statement. "These children are poor because their mothers can't work."

The council, a citizens' advisory group to Health and Welfare Canada, defines poverty as having to pay more than 56 per cent of household income for such basic necessities as food, shelter and clothing.

In a city with more than 500,000 people, for instance, the poverty line for an individual is $14,155, and $24,839 for a family of three. In a city of fewer than 30,000, the individual line is $11,072, and $19,076 for a family of three.

Although the lot of seniors in general has improved with better pension plans, individual women over age 65, many of them widows, remain among the worst off. After single mothers, they are the next most likely to be poor, with 330,000, or virtually half living an average $2,486 below the poverty line.

The least likely to be poor were childless couples under 65, where one couple in 12 is poor. In general, the report showed that while no group is immune to poverty, a full-time job, a spouse, a diploma and a small family were the best guarantees against it.

The report found the highest poverty rates in Quebec (18 per cent), Manitoba (17.8 per cent) and Saskatchewan (16.6 per cent). The lowest poverty rate was in Ontario (11.7 per cent), based on a 1991 Statistics Canada survey of consumer finances.

"It's a stark reminder that the fight against poverty is far from over," said Ann Gagnon, chairperson of the Alberta Welfare Council.

The report showed, among many things, that 124,000 Alberta children are from single-parent and two-parent homes living below the poverty line.

About 3.8 million Canadians, or 14.6 per cent of the population, were living in poverty in 1990, according to Statistics Canada. In Alberta, 375,000 people, or 15.4 per cent of the population, were living in poverty.

Source:

Wade Hemsworth, "Poverty rate climbing again," *The Calgary Herald*, December 1, 1992, p. A3. Reprinted by permission of Southam News.

---

tant throughout his or her life. They are a significant influence on educational attainment and eventual occupation (Eggenbeen and Lichter 1991).

Race and Ethnicity. Because Canada is not a "melting pot" that culturally homogenizes its people, ethnicity exerts a major influence on many families. Although most Canadians share a common core of experiences and values, their socialization may also reflect ethnic differences in values, norms, and identity. The matter is further complicated by the fact that ethnic background and social class position are frequently related. For example, as we will see in Chapter 10, in comparison with most other ethnic groups, the British are over-represented in the higher-status occupations.

The role of ethnicity in primary socialization varies enormously. The experiences of the non–English-speaking recent immigrant from Latin America differ from those of the fourth-generation Ukrainian Canadian raised in this country. Ethnicity means something different to the visible-minority child from Jamaica than to the child from Germany, who is physically indistinguishable from Caucasian Canadians. It matters whether a child's mother and father come from the same or from different ethnic backgrounds (Elkin 1983). Ethnicity is a different proposition for aboriginal Canadians than for more recent arrivals (Peters 1984). Clearly, then, the term "the Canadian family" represents an abstract oversimplification (Ishwaran 1976).

Canada is an officially multicultural society that encourages groups to retain their ethnic heritage. Consequently, racial and ethnic background is a major socialization influence. One illustration of the complex socialization effects of ethnicity is educational achievement. When Shamai (1992) examined the mean years of schooling achieved by Canadian ethnic groups between 1941 and 1981, he discovered that almost all groups had remained in the same *relative* position. Although the average amount of schooling of all groups increased over time, the British and the Jews remained "overachievers," while the Scandinavian and German achievement levels remained very close to the overall Canadian average. The "underachiever" groups included the French, Italian, Polish, Ukrainian, and Native Canadians. The only group that broke this pattern was the Asians, who moved from underachievers to overachievers.

Finally, research shows that socialization can be especially difficult for newcomers to Canada. For example, Indian-born parents worry that Westernization will "corrupt" their children, while their Canadian-born children view their parents as "too strict" (Kurian 1991). Clashes occur over such issues as teenagers' dating and career choices. Immigrant parents perceived that Canadian practices such as dating and courtship weakened their authority and threatened basic values of their ethnic group (Wakil, Siddique, and Wakil 1981).

Guiding and protecting a younger brother or sister helps the child internalize his or her parents' perspective.

Socialization by Siblings. Brothers and sisters play an important role in socializing one another. An older sibling can provide a role model. The learning theorists tell us that children learn many of their socialization lessons through imitation. Also, a younger sibling gives the older child the opportunity to try out some portion of the parental role. Guiding and protecting a younger brother or sister helps the child internalize his or her parents' perspective. Much of the older child's influence is, of course, quite unintentional.

Sibling interaction provides practice in cooperation and competition. As Freud observed, sibling rivalry is one of the more emotional experiences encountered in growing up. Humorist Erma Bombeck wonders why a child will "eat yellow snow" but won't drink from his brother's

glass (Blount 1984). Sibling comparisons have an impact on the child's developing self-image (Yussen and Santrock 1978). All children are concerned about how smart, how big, how worthwhile they are. Children with siblings close to their own age arrive at some of these answers by comparing themselves with brothers or sisters. One dimension in this rivalry is sibling concern for equally fair treatment by parents. But at times, brothers and sisters also provide useful allies against parents. Siblings appear to organize themselves into twosomes, bound together by love or hate; these sibling pairs result from such situations as being close in age or sharing a bedroom (Bank and Kahn 1982). The fact that the Canadian birth rate has dropped to 1.7 births per woman (Statistics Canada 1987) means that many youngsters now grow up without siblings. The more adult-oriented only child benefits from the exclusive attention of the parents but, lacking siblings, may be somewhat unskilled in social relations with peers.

According to Connidis (1989), siblings provide support for one another in later life. This tie is especially important for sisters (rather than brothers), and for the never-married, the divorced, and the childless.

Peers

After the family, peers (other children approximately the same age) constitute the second most potent socialization agent. The importance of peer relations is not confined to human beings. Harlow and Harlow (1962) found that interaction with other infant monkeys compensated for most of the negative effects of the maternal deprivation undergone by the experimental groups of monkeys. The age-grading of Canadian society increases the impact of peer socialization; people in similar age categories tend to be segregated in schools, neighbourhoods, and various recreational settings. Propinquity (simply being in the same place at the same time) tends to facilitate friendship.

Although children do not consciously set out to socialize one another, their need for companionship and approval results in mutual learning of a variety of information. Interaction with friends provides the first major social experiences outside the family circle. Peer relations allow children to begin to separate themselves from the family's influence and to develop other facets of their identity. One of the goals of socialization, remember, is the eventual ability to function independently of the family. Another point worth stressing is that peers share relatively equal power. This equality contrasts sharply with the power position of the child vis-à-vis the parents and other caretakers. Some things can be learned only from equal-status peers, for example, what clothing is fashionable.

"Children's attempts to challenge adult authority and gain control over their lives are a major aspect of peer culture from the earliest years" (Corsaro and Eder 1990). For example, children in American and Italian nursery schools were prohibited from bringing personal objects from

An important aspect of peer socialization is that peers share relatively equal power.

home because teachers spent too much time settling ownership disputes. In both American and Italian schools studied, the children evaded this rule by bringing small objects such as Matchbox toys and candy that could be easily concealed in pockets. Candies were a preferred choice "because the child and peers could share the forbidden objects and then go on to consume the evidence, often with teachers close at hand" (Corsaro and Eder 1990:205).

However, peer and family influences are not necessarily in opposition. Peers sometimes reinforce family socialization. For example, Davies and Kandel (1981) found that when the issues concern teenagers' life goals and educational aspirations, rather than current lifestyle matters such as fashions and music, parents are a more important influence than peers.

Canadian Teenagers' Views of Sex and Family

In 1992, sociologist Reginald Bibby and his colleague Donald Posterski surveyed 4000 Canadian teenagers about their attitudes and values. The similarities and differences between Quebec youth and their counterparts elsewhere in Canada make interesting reading.

Source:

Reginald W. Bibby and Donald C. Posterski, *Teen Trends: A Nation in Motion* (Toronto: Stoddart, 1992). Reprinted with the permission of Stoddart Publishing Co. Limited, Don Mills, Ontario.

Percentage Approving

	Quebec Franco	Anglo	Rest of Canada
Premarital sex: love	94	91	85
Premarital sex: like	91	66	56
Homosexual rights	83	83	68
Homosexual relations	55	49	33
Extramarital sex	12	9	9
Abortion: rape involved	94	92	86
Abortion: for any reason	40	45	41
Unmarried couple living together	95	90	87
Children without being married	88	71	65

From early childhood through to old age, people attach a great deal of importance to peer relationships (Matthews 1986). Even young infants stare at each other with fascination. By the age of two, children play alongside each other. By the time they are three of four years old, this parallel play becomes shared play. Most parents know that companionship with other children is a necessity, not a luxury. They take pains to find little companions for their children and worry if their offspring do not seem to make friends. Within a few years, children are able to relate to groups of children. (Recall the emphasis both Piaget and Mead placed on games for the child's social development.) By the age of eight or nine years, most children are concerned with having one special friend. Many of us may remember being rejected by a best friend as one of the poignant tragedies of childhood.

Adolescence marks the peak of peer-group influence. Bibby and Posterski's (1992) survey of Canadian teenagers reported that young people value friendship more than anything else. The teenager's orientation to the companionship, opinions, and tastes of age-mates helps to bridge the gulf between childish dependence on the family and adulthood. However, peer pressure can be painful. Teenage girls told researchers Holmes and Silverman (1992:36), "If you're not nice-looking, you are left out" and "If you don't speak English well, you won't have many friends." One reason so many high-school students have part-time jobs is to provide the name-brand clothing their peers demand (Tanner and Krahn 1991). Although adults have more inner resources than children, they remain sensitive to the opinions of their friends.

School

Industrialized nations such as Canada assign to the school a major role in preparing children for adulthood. The knowledge and skills required to function effectively in urbanized, industrialized societies are too extensive and too complex for parents to convey to their offspring. The educational system performs two major functions for society (Parsons 1959). The *socialization function* involves the internalization of commitment both to broad societal values and to doing the tasks that the society requires done. The *allocation function* refers to the channelling of people through programs of occupational preparation into positions in the socioeconomic structure. (See Chapter 15 for details about how these functions are carried out.)

Most children are eager to begin school. For the majority, enrolling in school is their first encounter with a formal institution. This significant step beyond the family or day-care centre represents "being grown up." In school, the child is treated not as a unique individual but as a member of a cohort (see Chapter 6). If Suzy is feeling grumpy and does not want to go out to play, her parents may abandon their plan to have a quiet house all to themselves. At recess, however, regardless of her mood, Suzy will march out to the school playground with the other pupils. As a lone child at home, she gets her own way. But at school Suzy is "processed" as one of a "batch." Experiences like this prepare children for adulthood, where the demands of organizations often take priority over the individual's own wishes.

Some of the content of socialization is consciously planned; some is incidental to the school's stated goals. For example, the curriculum taught in the classroom is intended socialization. The reinforcement of gender norms ("boys matter more than girls") in the playground is not.

In addition, no two children have precisely the same school experiences. A variety of factors — such as the child's ability and temperament, the parents' social class position and their attitudes toward academic success, the teachers, and relations with the peer group — all influence what happens there. For example, to children from some ethnic minorities or from very poor environments, the school may be an alien place (a resocialization context) that devalues what they have learned in their families (Gecas 1981).

Mass Media

The mass media — television, videotapes, radio, newspapers, magazines, books, movies, and compact discs — are impersonal communication sources, and they reach large audiences. If you try to imagine what a week spent without any of the media would be like, you will gain some idea of the important part they play in the lives of most Canadians.

TABLE 4-1 Average Years of Schooling by Canadians of Different Ethnic Backgrounds, 1941–1981

	1941	1951	1961	1971	1981
British	7.49	8.77	7.73	9.35	10.95
French	5.52	7.03	6.42	7.52	9.85
German	6.10	7.50	7.20	8.65	10.44
Italian	5.34	6.65	5.70	6.04	8.54
Jewish	7.00	8.41	8.31	10.19	12.29
Polish	4.81	6.58	6.70	8.03	10.20
Scandinavian	6.55	8.02	7.53	9.19	10.94
Ukrainian	4.59	6.15	6.49	7.85	9.92
Asians	5.35	6.18	6.83	10.10	11.76
Native people	2.51	3.22	3.72	5.55	7.89
Average	6.49	7.90	7.11	8.53	10.52

SOURCE: Shmuel Shamai, "Ethnicity and Educational Achievement: Canada — 1941–1981," *Canadian Ethnic Studies* 24 (1992): 43–57.

The media act as direct agents of socialization. Television, the "universal curriculum" (Gerbner and Gross 1976), is a major transmitter of culture and information. For this reason, psychologist Gregory Fouts (1980) regards the deliberate elimination of television from the home as a "misinformed and unwitting example of [parental] irresponsibility."

The media reflect nearly every aspect of society, but these reflections are, of course, not necessarily accurate. Children see or hear world news. Their country is presented visually, along with its political leaders, diverse cultures, arts, and sports. Situation comedies ("sitcoms") picture what happens in other people's families. "Cops and robbers" programs present children with an astonishing number of violent crimes each evening. Media advertisements show children all the paraphernalia supposedly required for them to be happy, healthy, and accepted by their peers.

In providing children with common interests and experiences, the media also function as indirect socialization agents. Being part of this "community of discourse" (Tuchman 1979) constitutes a vital dimension of peer socialization.

Television and rock music are especially critical components of young people's subculture. Being television-wise brings prestige on the playground (Ellis 1983). Children discuss what they have seen on television and enact the roles of TV characters in their fantasy play (Fouts 1980).

Who produces the media content that feeds into the youth subculture? Television, radio, and books are packaged by adults in the mainstream of society. However, "much of the music youth listen to is created by individuals close to their own age who stand apart [from] and may be at odds with adult society" (Larson and Kubey 1983).

Child development experts have been particularly concerned about television as a socialization agent. Television has been called the "plug-in drug" (Winn 1977), the Phantom Babysitter, and the Great Leveller, "mowing down all the bright young minds to the same stunted level" (Landsberg 1982). Many children are "zombie" viewers, who watch anything and everything, "silent, immobile, mesmerized" (Goldsen 1979). Television has also been labelled the Total Disclosure Medium because information and imagery intended for adults are readily accessible to children. Youngsters tune in to "incest, promiscuity, homosexuality, sadomasochism, terminal illness, and other secrets of adult life" (Postman 1982).

Television "crowds out" other uses of time (Condry and Keith 1983). Television time is replacing hours of playtime — and, as we have seen, children learn both social norms and social skills through their games.

Considerable attention is being given to the significance of television advertising for children. On a Saturday morning, the typical Canadian child is exposed to approximately 75 commercials. Research shows that although children as young as four can distinguish commercials from programming (through cues such as the use of jingles, faster pacing of material, and adult voice-overs), the majority of first-graders cannot explain the selling intent of commercials (Singer 1986). The situation is confused further by cartoons that feature toys as characters.

The ability of television to influence children has become an extremely important issue. If children are acquiring stereotyped images of women, old people, and ethnic groups; if they regard fictional TV families as more significant than their own extended families; if they pressure parents to buy heavily advertised toys and breakfast cere-

als; and, worse, if they learn to solve problems through violent means from watching crime shows, then this medium constitutes a socialization agent whose power is almost beyond imagination.

Unfortunately, tracing the direct effects of the media is a very difficult research task. When the media operate in the natural environment, their influence is one among many other factors. For example, if Peter behaves aggressively, is the cause the type of television programs he watches, or his family, or his nasty temperament? On the other hand, experimental studies that attempt to control for variables besides media content become so artificial that their conclusions may not hold beyond the experimental situation. However, persuasive data from natural experiments are becoming available. For example, University of British Columbia researchers had an unusual opportunity to study the effects of television when they heard about a town whose location in a valley had prevented it from receiving television until the mid-1970s. By studying this community before and two years after television arrived, they learned a great deal about the impact of TV on children's aggressive behaviour, creativity, leisure activities, and gender attitudes (Williams 1986). More important than any single piece of research, however, are an accumulation of consensual findings from many studies employing a variety of research methods.

In general, research on specific media effects shows that children are indeed influenced by their media consumption. Despite an occasional apparently negative finding, the bulk of the evidence leads to the conclusion that there is a causal relationship between heavy television viewing and overt aggressive behaviour in children and adolescents (Liebert and Sprafkin 1988; Singer and Singer 1988). Social scientists conclude that although other variables — for example, parent/child relations, socioeconomic status — are certainly involved, televised violence is a significant factor in the production and maintenance of violence in our society (Roberts and Maccoby 1985). Put another way, TV is *a* cause, not *the* cause, of aggressiveness and criminality (Liebert and Sprafkin 1988).

However, it is important to remember that children are exposed to media content in a social context. What they see and hear is monitored, at least to some extent, by parents. Similarly, their interpretation of media content is moulded by the opinions of parents, teachers, and friends. Parents may forbid watching violent television series or may recommend an educational series. They often offer their own opinions on fighting as a way of solving differences of opinion, or the advisability of spending the contents of one's piggy bank on a heavily advertised toy. "When parents encourage their youngsters to think about and evaluate content and to consider alternative actions, the impact of negative or antisocial contents [is] considerably reduced" (Fouts 1980). In other contexts, children are exposed to the points of view of the other socialization agents. These may or may not agree with the media's perspectives. In short, the media have an impact on children, but this impact is just one of the influences that shape a child's attitudes and behaviour.

Television's Beneficial Effects. Researchers have also been interested in assessing the mass media's positive socialization functions for children. For example, television has been studied as an agent of anticipatory socialization for work roles. The main conclusion is that "television's representation of occupational roles ... is both a wider perspective than everyday experience and a caricature of the actual world of work" (Peterson and Peters 1983). While television exposes young people to career models beyond their own experiences, the portrayal of occupations has definite limitations. High-prestige professional occupations occur much more frequently and low-prestige occupations much less frequently than in the actual job market.

The discussion of television's contribution to occupational socialization illustrates its unintentional influence on children: children go to television to be entertained but, while being entertained, they absorb much incidental information about their society. Attempts have been made to deliberately harness television's potential to benefit children. Because educators recognize the importance of youngsters' preschool experiences for their later educational development, programs such as "Sesame Street" have been developed to provide preschool experiences at home. CBC's "Street Cents" teaches preteens to be wise consumers. The program compares and criticizes products aimed at kids and tosses "those deemed unworthy into 'The Pit,' a kind of retailers' purga-tory" (*Globe and Mail* 1993b). Furthermore, we can hypothesize that TV programs featuring single-parent or blended families, adopted children, or youngsters with physical handicaps may help children with similar experiences feel comfortable with their situation.

An Overview

This section has dealt with the influence of major socialization agents: the family, the peer group, the schools, the mass media. Children are, of course, also socialized by babysitters and day-care workers; by such institutions as Sunday school and the church; or by community organizations such as the YMCA and the Boy Scouts, with their athletic and camping activities.

As children mature into adults, they encounter an increasing diversity of socialization agents that help them to learn relatively more specialized roles. For example, a considerable amount of occupational socialization occurs on the job. Young interns learn how to be effective doctors partly by attending medical school and partly by practising on hospitalized patients. Newly divorced adults are often socialized into the single role through self-help groups. Many universities offer noncredit courses on topics such as effective parenting, coping with divorce and widowhood, and blended families. On the whole, adult socialization agents tend to be impersonal — formal organizations such as universities, technical colleges, corporations, social welfare agencies, and the like. Nonetheless, family and peers continue to be important influences throughout life.

Oversocialization

Throughout this chapter, we have contended that the socialization process serves both society and the individual. Societal order and continuity depend on members learning to share values, norms, and language. Interaction and role-playing rest on these common understandings. On the other hand, socialization allows individuals to realize their potential as human beings.

Because socialization is such a powerful process, there is a danger that those who read about it may end up with what Wrong (1961) called the "oversocialized conception of man." By this phrase, Wrong meant the erroneous idea that people are completely moulded by the norms and values of their society. Such thoroughgoing indoctrination would, of course, destroy individuality and render nonsensical free will and responsibility for one's actions.

But this does not happen. It is quite true that people brought up in a particular society speak the same language, value much the same things, and behave in a similar fashion. Fortunately, however, they are not all identical products turned out by an omnipotent socialization factory. There are many reasons why absolute conformity just does not occur.

To begin with, each person is biologically unique. The raw material of temperament and inborn aptitudes leaves considerable room for individuality. In addition, human beings possess the ability to question norms and values and to innovate. Socialization theorists have also allowed for some measure of independence. Mead acknowledged the spontaneous, creative "I," as well as the socialized "Me." Similarly, Freud's personality-structure theory contained the impulsive, selfish Id, as well as the conventionalized Super-ego. Individuals make roles as well as take roles, by modifying situations to suit themselves.

Furthermore, although nearly everyone is socialized within the family, the actual content of children's socialization varies from family to family. Even brothers and sisters brought up in the same home experience growing up somewhat differently. Also, the fact that parents and children represent two different generations ensures two different perspectives on the lessons of socialization (Yoels and Karp 1978). And though we can speak of societal norms and values, these are really abstractions that must be interpreted by specific agents of socialization; the people responsible for teaching the child to fit into society have differing interpretations of these norms and values. Finally, because socialization is carried out by multiple agents, the person being socialized is exposed to diverse perspectives.

All of this means that although we can speak about Canadians in general, and in so doing distinguish them from Japanese or Mexicans, we are talking about characteristics that make Canadians similar, not identical. The existence of at least

some deviant behaviour within every society, including our own, testifies to the fact that no system of socialization is perfectly efficient.

SUMMARY

1. Through socialization, individuals develop selfhood and acquire the knowledge, skills, and motivations required for them to participate in social life. This symbiotic learning process is functional for both the individual and the society. From the individual's point of view, intense interaction with adult caretakers allows the infant to realize its human potentialities. Later socialization equips the person to handle societal roles. In addition, socialization ensures that commitment to the social order is maintained over time.

2. Sociologists have distinguished four types of socialization. "Primary socialization" refers to the learning that occurs in childhood. It lays the foundation for all later learning. "Adult socialization" describes the socialization that takes place beyond the childhood years. "Anticipatory socialization" is the role-learning that occurs in advance of the actual playing of roles. "Resocialization" occurs when a new role or situation requires that a person replace established patterns of behaviour with new patterns.

3. Since the turn of the century, social scientists have been perplexed about the relative contributions of biology and environment to human development. More recently, however, evidence that both factors interact to transform the infant into a functioning member of society has resulted in the abandonment of the overly simplistic nature/nurture debate.

4. There are four major theoretical approaches to childhood socialization: learning theory, the cognitive developmental approach, psychoanalytic theory, and symbolic interaction. Learning theory explains the precise mechanisms involved in socialization. Piaget's work focuses on the development of morality. The psychoanalytic approach analyzes the development of personality structure. The symbolic interactionists emphasize the child's acquisition of language and self. These ap-

proaches are complementary, rather than competing, systems of thought.

5. There are four major agents of childhood socialization: the family, the school, the peer group, and the mass media. Because society has given the family and the school a mandate to socialize youngsters, both these agents deliberately attempt to equip their charges with the knowledge and values required to fit into adult society. The influence of the peer group and the media is, for the most part, unintentional.

6. Socialization is a lifelong process. Primary socialization cannot possibly equip individuals for all the roles and situations they will encounter throughout their lives. Compared with primary socialization, adult socialization tends to concentrate on overt behaviour (as opposed to values and motives). It tends to be realistic, rather than idealistic; to be more specific in content; and to occur in formal organizations, rather than informal contexts. In addition, the relationship between socializer and socializee in the adult situation is marked by lower levels of feeling and power than in the childhood situation.

7. The "oversocialized conception of human beings" is a viewpoint that exaggerates the effectiveness of the socialization process. Socialization does not mould members of society into identical products. Fortunately, there is considerable room for spontaneity and individuality.

GLOSSARY

Adult socialization. Socialization that takes place after childhood to prepare people for adult roles (for example, husband, mother, computer technician).
Altercasting. Casting the other person in a role we choose for him or her in order to manipulate the situation.
Anticipatory socialization. Role-learning that occurs in advance of the actual playing of roles.
Care orientation. Gilligan's feminine orientation to morality, which emphasizes concern for and connectedness with others.
Classical conditioning. Type of learning that involves the near-simultaneous presentation of an unconditioned stimulus (UCS) and a conditioned stimulus (CS) to an organism in a drive state (that is, a state during which needs such as hunger or thirst require satisfaction). After several trials, the previously neutral

stimulus (CS) alone produces the response normally associated with the UCS.
Ego. The director of the Freudian personality. The Ego attempts to mediate among the demands of the Id, the Super-ego, and the external world. The Ego, which encompasses the cognitive functions and the defence mechanisms, is governed by the reality principle.
Generalized other. Mead's "organized community or social group [that] gives to the individual his unity of self." Although the equivalence of terms is not exact, "reference group" is the more modern way of referring to this notion of the organized attitudes of social groups.
I. The dimension of Mead's notion of self that is active, spontaneous, creative, and unpredictable. The "I" is a component of a process, not a concrete entity.
Id. The reservoir of inborn, biological propensities in the Freudian personality structure. The selfish, impulsive Id operates according to the pleasure principle.
Justice orientation. Gilligan's masculine orientation to morality, which emphasizes preserving rights and upholding principles.
Looking-glass self. Cooley's formulation of the self as the interpreted reflection of others' attitudes. It consists of "the imagination of our appearance to the other person, the imagination of his judgment of that appearance, and some sort of self-feeling, such as pride or mortification."
Me. The dimension of Mead's notion of self that represents internalized societal attitudes and expectations. The "Me" is an aspect of a process, not a concrete entity.
Moral autonomy. Piaget's later stage of moral thought, in which children over age eight judge wrongdoing in terms of intentions and extenuating circumstances, as well as consequences, and view rules as social conventions that can be changed.
Moral realism. Piaget's early stage of moral development, in which children from four to seven years old judge wrongdoing strictly in terms of its consequences, and believe all rules are immutable absolutes.
Observational learning. No reinforcement or reward is required for the initial learning to occur. However, reinforcements do influence where and when learned responses that are in the individual's repertoire (for example, swearing) will be performed.
Operant conditioning. Type of learning whereby the organism gives a number of trial-and-error responses. Those responses followed by reward (positive reinforcement) tend to be repeated on future occasions. Those responses followed by negative reinforcement, or by no reinforcement, tend to be extinguished.
Primary socialization. Socialization that occurs during childhood.
Resocialization. Replacement of established attitudes and behaviour patterns.
Significant other. The particular individual whose standpoint the child adopts in responding to himself or herself during Mead's play stage.
Socialization. Complex learning process through which individuals develop selfhood and acquire the

knowledge, skills, and motivations required to participate in social life.

Super-ego. The Freudian conscience, or internalization of societal values and behavioural standards.

FURTHER READING

Amert, Anne-Marie. *The Effect of Children on Parents.*
New York: Haworth Press, 1992. An interesting discussion of the many ways children socialize parents.

Bibby, Reginald W., and Donald C. Posterski. *Teen
Trends: A Nation in Motion.* Toronto: Stoddart Publishing, 1992. Attitudes and values of 1984 and 1992 national samples of Canadian teenagers are compared.

Cahill, Spencer E. (ed.). *Sociological Studies of Child
Developing: A Research Annual.* Volume 4: *Perspectives on and of Children.* Greenwich, CT: JAI Press,
1991. Many worthwhile articles on the sociology of
childhood.

Corsaro, William A., and Donna Eder. "Children's
peer cultures." *Annual Review of Sociology* 16(1990):
197–220. An analysis of recent literature on peer
socialization.

McCarrey, Michael. "Work and personal values of
Canadian anglophones and francophones." *Canadian
Psychology* 29(1988):69–83. Reports high value agree-
ment between the two groups.

Rossi, Alice S., and Peter H. Rossi. *Of Human Bonding: Parent–Child Relations across the Life Course.* New
York: Aldine de Gruyter, 1990. Addresses intergenerational family development.

Storandt, Martha, and Gary R. VandenBos (eds.). *The
Adult Years: Continuity and Change.* Washington, DC:
American Psychological Association, 1989. Several
empirical articles on adult socialization.

Thorne, Barrie. "Re-visioning women and social
change: Where are the children?" *Gender & Society*
1(1987):85–109. Argues that the adult-centred discipline of sociology needs to pay more attention to
children.

Whiting B.B., and C.P. Edwards. *Children of Different
Worlds: The Formation of Social Behavior.* Cambridge,
MA: Harvard University Press, 1988. A cross-cultural
discussion of socialization.

CHAPTER 5

Gender Relations

MARLENE MACKIE

Female. Male. The difference that makes a difference. She menstruates, gestates, lactates. He ejaculates and impregnates (Armstrong and Armstrong 1978). She can identify 25 colours, including taupe and magenta. He can identify 25 makes of automobiles, including Aston Martin and Lamborghini. Except for anger, she expresses more feelings (Basow 1992). He thinks sexual humour is funny; she relishes jokes that satirize the status quo between the sexes (Mackie 1990).

Consider courtship. It is women who show primary (though not exclusive) interest in makeup, cosmetic surgery for wrinkles and jowls, and Weight Watchers' meetings. Men, on the other hand, still take more responsibility for initiating contact with women (and the risk of rejection). Surprisingly, males are more romantic, more likely to believe "that true romantic love comes once and lasts forever, conquers all barriers and social customs, is essentially strange and incomprehensive, and must be basic to marriage." Females are more pragmatic. They are convinced that "they can be in love many times, that it may not last, that it inevitably fades into some disillusionment when the honeymoon ends" (Alcock et al. 1988).

As far as marriage is concerned, both sexes are ambivalent. In addition to some common goals, each seeks somewhat different benefits from legal unions: women look at marriage for security, while men seek intimacy and emotional support (Greenglass 1985). The burdens of marriage also differ. Women still assume primary responsibility for housework and children, often as a "second shift" in addition to labour force employment (Hochschild 1989). Women usually head single-parent families. On the other hand, the responsibility for economic support of two-parent families is carried disproportionately by men, whose jobs are better paid.

Gender affects the economic situation of women all over the world. "When the United Nations proclaimed International Women's Year, the data it released showed that women were performing two-thirds of the world's work and receiving only 10 percent of all income, while owning only 1 percent of the means of production" (Acosta-Belen and Bose 1990). These income disparities are especially great in Third World nations. Nevertheless, in Canada and the United States, women tend to be disadvantaged in comparison with men of their class and racial/ethnic group.

Men and women experience physical and mental health differently. The average woman outlives the average man by 7.0 years in Canada, 7.1 years in the United States, and 6.6 years in Mexico (United Nations 1991). Though childbearing puts women at special risk, more men die from serious illnesses, for example, cardiovascular disorders and cancer, and from accidents and violence (Verbrugge 1989). Women are more prone to depression and to phobias; men to personality disorders, such as alcoholism and drug addiction (Al-Issa 1982). In Canada, males are more likely than females to die violently through homicide, suicide, and motor vehicle accidents (Maxim and Keane 1992). However, women are much more likely than men to be killed by spouses, ex-spouses, or partners (Kurz 1989).

Men command a disproportionate share of power, prestige, and resources. As a result, the sexes are socialized differently, play different roles, and have different thoughts and experiences (Bernard 1981). They live out their lives in social worlds that are separate at some points and overlapping at others. "Men and women march to different drummers"; in some respects, "they are not even in the same parade" (Bernard 1975).

The Sociology of Gender Relations

This chapter explores femininity and masculinity in contemporary society. Human social life always and everywhere has been built around the

relationships between the sexes. Changes in these relationships thus affect the entire social structure. In McDaniel's (1991) words, "Pink and blue threads run through everything."

The sociology of gender relations developed in the early 1970s in response to the feminist movement. Until then, with a few exceptions (Hacker 1951; Komarovsky 1946), the social behaviour of females had been ignored by sociologists (Daniels 1975). Sociology was a science of male society (Bernard 1973b) that emphasized those social institutions and settings in which males predominate, such as the occupational, political, and legal systems. Where women were noticed at all, as in the sociology of the family (Parsons and Bales 1955), it was their connection with men that counted. Because work is a core area of sociology, it provides a good illustration of what the discipline looked like before and after the second wave of the women's movement. Earlier books often have titles such as *Man and His Work* (Ritzer 1972) and concentrated on masculine occupations and work problems. For example, analyses of complex organizations overlooked the roles played by female clerks and secretaries. Little was known about nurses, kindergarten teachers, waitresses, typists, or beauticians. Neither housework nor volunteer work were regarded as real work.

Since the 1970s, an explosion of research has attempted to take into account the role of gender in such traditional areas as work, social stratification, politics, deviance, sports, and race/ethnic relations. Also of great significance are the many new areas of special import to women that have emerged. Until the women's movement came along, such topics as the following were, for the most part, unstudied: motherhood, fatherhood, voluntary childlessness, the emotions, violence against women, pornography, gender and language, eating disorders and obesity, and the ecology of gender.

The sociology of gender relations attempts both to remedy the discipline's previous exclusion of the feminine perspective and to encompass the masculine side of the equation (Lipman-Blumen and Tickamyer 1975). Note that the term *gender relations* is not a code-word for women. The women's movement stimulated remedial sociology to analyze previously ignored female behaviour, but sociologists soon realized the futility of attempting to study one sex in isolation from the other. Masculinity and femininity derive their meaning from the relation of one to the other. The roles most influenced by gender (for example, husband, wife) are reciprocal roles. Moreover, the role of power in the perpetuation of gender makes it essential that both sexes be studied.

Although the bulk of the social science literature has been written by men on topics of interest to men, consideration of the implications of cultural beliefs about maleness per se is a recent phenomenon. The literature of the 1970s that attempted to bring masculinity into focus concentrated on the restrictions and penalties attached to being born male. The "essential feminist insight that the overall relationship between men and women is one involving domination or oppression" (Carrigan, Connell, and Lee 1985) was evaded. In books such as Goldberg's *The Hazards of Being Male: Surviving the Myth of Masculine Privilege* (1976), the source of the "masculine dilemma" was seen as primarily psychological. In contrast, many recent discussions of gender from the masculine perspective (for example, Connell 1987; Doyle 1989) have appreciated its basis in the social structure. An important influence in this regard has been gay liberation politics, which have called into question traditional definitions of masculinity and femininity.

Finally, sociologists specializing in gender relations have begun to appreciate the important ways in which race/ethnicity and social class influence the experience of being female or male. The obstacles to equality "white middle-class women face are compounded many times over for women of colour and working-class women" (Zinn et al. 1986). Contemporary sociologists struggle with the challenge of understanding the interplay of gender, race/ethnicity, social class, and sexual orientation in people's lives.

Some Definitions

Before proceeding further, let us define *gender* and distinguish it from the closely related word *sex*. According to the "Humpty Dumpty Theorem," this definition, like all definitions, is a matter of conventional usage:

Humpty Dumpty: When I use a word it means just what I choose it to mean, neither more nor less.

Alice: The question is whether you can make words mean so many different things.

Humpty Dumpty: The question is, who is to be master, that's all. (Carroll 1986).

Sex refers to the biology of maleness and femaleness. The term indicates sexual anatomy (penises, vaginas), sex hormones and chromosomes, secondary sex characteristics (beards, breasts), and coital and reproductive behaviour. **Gender**, on the other hand, is what is socially recognized as femininity or masculinity (Gould and Kern-Daniels 1977). By "exaggerating both real and imagined aspects of biological sex" (Lipman-Blumen 1984), the cultural norms of a particular society, at a particular time, identify some ways of behaving, feeling, and thinking as appropriate for females, and other ways of behaving, feeling, and thinking as appropriate for males. Below we differentiate biologically based and culturally based role behaviours vis-à-vis offspring (Gould and Kern-Daniels 1977).

	Sex Role	Gender Role
Women	Childbearer	Mother
Men	Sperm Donor	Father

Gender is socially constructed and socially alterable. That is, gender is a set of social attitudes that vary greatly from culture to culture and that change over time. Gender is *not* an attribute of the individual, always there, like a nose (Thorne 1983). In other words, gender is an aspect of social organization that matters more in some social situations than in others. For example, gender would be irrelevant for university students concentrating on a chemistry lecture. However, a sociology lecture that focuses on men's and women's contrasting labour-force experience would make gender highly salient for the students. Similarly, gender would be more salient for students on a date than those at home studying.

The Importance of Gender

Our argument for the importance of gender rests on two major points. First, in all human societies, the genders are *differentiated*. A great fuss is made

Gender is a set of social attitudes that vary greatly from culture to culture and that change over time.

over the biological distinctions between female and male. Elaborate sets of meanings are built on them. The impact of gender on the individual begins at the moment of birth and continues until the moment of death. The parents of a newborn infant ask, "Is it a boy or a girl?" Although at this stage the infant is little more than a bundle of tissue with potentiality, members of society immediately begin to react to it in terms of its gender. It will usually be given a name that signals its sex. It may be wrapped in a pink or blue blanket. This initial gender assignment is the beginning of a process that sorts people into different socialization streams (Goffman 1977).

Sex-typing begins even before birth. Lewis (1972) reported that pregnant women responded to the activity of fetuses in a sex-differentiated fashion. If the fetus kicked and moved a great deal, this behaviour was often interpreted as a sign that the baby was male. There is a great deal of folk wisdom on this subject. For example, a child's prenatal position supposedly indicates its sex, boys being carried high and girls low.

Parents' perceptions of their infants after birth continue to be sex-typed. Rubin, Provenzano, and Luria (1974) interviewed 30 pairs of parents at a Boston hospital within 24 hours of the birth of their first child. Fifteen of the couples had daughters and fifteen had sons. Infant girls were described by the parents as "softer," "finer-featured," "littler," and "prettier," while boys were described as "bigger," "stronger," "firmer," and "more alert." Although boys are generally slightly longer and heavier at birth (Barfield 1976), the hospital records showed that these particular male and female infants did not differ in birth length, weight, or health.

Gender touches every social relationship and every sphere of human activity. Although things are slowly changing, there are girls' games and boys' games, women's work and men's work. Being a male university student is not the same as being a female university student. Being a wife, mother, divorcée, widow, or elderly woman is not the same as being a husband, father, divorced male, widower, or elderly man. The male–female distinction serves as a basic organizing principle for every human society (Bem 1981). Family, work, religion, politics, and sports have traditionally employed divisions of labour that cleave along gender lines.

A second reason for gender's importance is that society values men's characteristics and activities more than women's (Lipman-Blumen 1984). The sexes are ranked. As a category, males have more status, power, influence, and resources than do females. The cultural devaluation of females is easily illustrated. In parts of the world such as India, Pakistan, and Bangladesh, where the preference for boys is especially pronounced, "a million girls die each year because they are born female" (UNICEF 1992). In Canada and the United States, where a company, Gametrics Ltd., operates some 50 clinics to offer preselection of offspring sex through artificial insemination, women's groups feared the technique would be used to choose males (*Globe and Mail*, September 3, 1992:A1).

What sex would you yourself prefer to be? Chances are that if you are female, you sometimes wish you were male and, if you are male, you are quite satisfied to remain that way. Why do people condone — even admire — masculine behaviour in a 12-year-old girl and abhor feminine behaviour in a 12-year-old boy? Even the labels for these children, "tomboy" and "sissy," communicate societal sentiments. The answer to this question, and many more just like it, is clear: society values males more highly than females.

Female–Male Similarities and Differences

Society emphasizes both sex and gender. People tend to view these physiological distinctions and the cultural elaborations on them as equally natural. It makes sense to determine just what these differences really are. Possible origins of such differences are explored in later sections.

Misleading Female–Male Comparison. Because so much emotion and mystery surround male–female relations, it is not surprising that many notions about sex differences have been biased

(Tresemer 1975). We dwell on the differences between males and females and ignore their similarities. Men and women are seen as *either* this *or* that, not both. We are fascinated with anatomical differences and reproductive capacities. However, we tend to overlook the fact that males and females really share much the same body blueprint. Psychological traits provide another example. Deaux (1984) analyzed a decade's research on gender in the field of psychology and concluded that gender differences are "surprisingly small." We assume — correctly, as it happens (Hyde 1990) — that males are more aggressive than females. However, this does not mean that *all* males are aggressive, while *all* females are passive. Research shows that this gender difference, as well as others, can be represented as a pair of overlapping normal curves, as in Figure 5.1. The trait appears to be distributed normally within each category, but the two group means differ. Both males and females range from highly aggressive to very unaggressive. The group average for males is somewhat higher, but a substantial number of females will be as aggressive as, or more aggressive than, a substantial number of males.

FIGURE 5-1 Overlapping Normal Curves of Aggressiveness

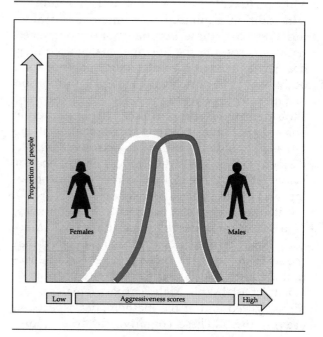

The following classroom exercise makes the point that females and males are not diametrically opposite beings. Ask a number of males and females to answer "yes" to the following questions by raising their hands: Do you have blue eyes? Are you 180 cm or taller? Ever consider growing a beard? Do you like mathematics? Do you know the meaning of "sauté," "puce," and "placket"? Have you cried at least once this month? Ever had a fist fight? Are you a Roman Catholic? Do you like kittens? If people answer honestly — social desirability might influence some responses — you would probably find no gender difference on some questions (eye colour, religion); overlapping, but gender-related responses on others (height, mathematics); and completely dichotomous responses on still others (beard, definition of words).

Gender Differences and Their Sources. "What," asks the nursery rhyme, "are little girls made of? / What are little boys made of?" The answers given by scientists do not mention sugar and spice or snips and snails and puppy-dog tails. Instead, they tell us that, physiologically, females carry two X chromosomes and males an X and a Y chromosome. Female endocrine glands secrete estrogen into the bloodstream, while the primary male sex hormone is testosterone. A female is equipped with ovaries, a clitoris, and a vagina, and a male with testes, a penis, and a scrotum.

In addition, a number of secondary sex characteristics exist; these become more pronounced with puberty. On the average, males are taller, heavier, and have a greater percentage of total body weight in muscle and a smaller proportion of fat. Females have lighter skeletons, different shoulder–pelvis proportions, different pelvic bone shapes, and different socket shapes at the hip and shoulder. These differences contribute to women having less strength, less endurance for heavy labour, more difficulty in overarm throwing, and a better ability to float.

With regard to psychological characteristics, "the sexes are more alike than different" (Maccoby 1980). To date, research has established that the sexes do not differ on tests of general intellectual abilities. Males tend to do better on tests of visual/spatial skills. Males surpass females at the highly gifted end of the mathematical spectrum (Tavris 1992). These cognitive differences are,

however, slight and the performance of females can be significantly altered by training (Deaux 1985). As mentioned earlier, males tend to be more aggressive than females (Hyde 1990). Finally, some evidence suggests that females are more likely than males to conform to group pressure (Eagly 1987).

Researchers' inventory of female/male distinctions grows longer when consideration is given to fashion (trousers and hair length are no longer reliable guides); etiquette and demeanour (who drives the car on dates? who sits sprawling with legs apart?); language (which gender speaks more circumspectly?); nonverbal communication (women are more adept than men in sending and decoding nonverbal signals, especially via the face (Henley et al. 1985); social roles (nurses versus soldiers, mothers versus fathers); and spheres of existence (the domestic world of women versus the public world of men). All of these are tendencies, rather than all-or-nothing differences.

Up to this point, we have concentrated on enumerating gender differences rather than explaining them. The following sections will consider the causes of these differences.

Biological Explanations of Gender

To what extent are men masculine and women feminine because they were born that way? In particular, is women's social subordination a reflection of their biological inferiority? These questions have concerned practitioners of many academic disciplines.

Animal Research

Studies have been made of our evolutionary cousins the monkeys and apes in an attempt to determine whether human sex/gender differences are innate or learned (Tavris and Wade 1984). The logic here rests on the assumption that primates are like human beings but do not undergo the intensive social learning that humans do. Primate sex differences that parallel human sex differences therefore constitute evidence for biological causation of human sex differences.

This type of argument-by-analogy (Tavris and Wade 1984) presents at least three problems. First, the conclusion reached depends greatly on the particular species chosen (Rosenberg 1976). The male baboon is much more aggressive than the female baboon; both male and female gibbons are highly aggressive (Lancaster 1976). As far as human differences are concerned, do baboons support biological causation and gibbons social learning? Second, extrapolation from lower-animal behaviour to human behaviour is risky "for the simple reason that humans are not nonhumans" (Weisstein 1971). As the evolutionary ladder is ascended, the effects of physiology on behaviour become less dramatic and the role of learning more important (Frieze et al. 1978). Third, even when the same label is used for human and animal behaviour, the behaviours may not be at all comparable. Consider, for example, sex differences in aggression. The animal findings refer to such measures as threat displays, the latency of initial attack, and the outcome of fights, whereas the human studies refer to quite different measures, such as verbal aggression, teachers' ratings of assertiveness, questionnaire responses, and so on (Archer 1976).

Do criticisms like these mean that animal studies are worthless to students of human sex/gender differences? Not at all. But research into animal differences is best viewed as a source of hypotheses, rather than definitive answers concerning differences in *Homo sapiens* (Sperling 1991).

The Anthropological Approach

Anthropologists have provided yet another perspective on the question "To what extent do gender questions stem from essential human nature?" Put another way, are the division of labour and male superiority that characterize contemporary Western societies biologically based? See Rosaldo and Lamphere (1974); Friedl (1975); Martin and Voorhies (1975); Ortner and Whitehead (1981); Sanday (1981); Leacock (1983); Liebowitz (1983); and di Leonardi (1991).

The presence or absence of **cultural universals** in the anthropological record is taken to be evidence for or against a biological explanation. If a certain type of behaviour is found in many cultures, despite other variations in cultural patterns, that behaviour is assumed to be biologically determined, or at least linked in some way to physiology. According to this conservative position, existing gender arrangements being "essentially natural, they *should* stay about what they are: major change would be unsuccessful, or would exact too high a price in emotional strain" (Friedl 1975). If, however, cultural comparisons show inconsistency, if social arrangements are sometimes this way and sometimes that, this cross-cultural inconsistency is interpreted as evidence that gender differences are socially caused.

Debate has centred on two interrelated and apparently universal aspects of the anthropological record: male dominance and the division of labour between the sexes. The first cultural universal refers to the fact that although women sometimes have a good deal of informal influence, "societies in which women are consistently dominant do not exist and have never existed" (Friedl 1978).

The second cultural universal summarizes anthropological evidence that all societies distinguish between tasks usually performed by men and tasks usually performed by women. These arrangements appear to have had their original source in women's reproductive capacities, the long helplessness of the human infant, and the generally greater size and strength of men. Since women were tied down with pregnancy and breastfeeding, their activities were restricted to a home base. They were responsible for feeding and nurturing family members of all ages, and for gathering food available near home. Men, by necessity, filled the more public roles of hunter, political leader, soldier, and religious official (Rosaldo 1974).

Most feminist anthropologists acknowledge the near-universality of male dominance and sexually based divisions of labour. However, they challenge the biological inevitability of these gender arrangements. According to them, the cultural meanings given these "natural" facts merit special attention. They point out that considerable cross-cultural variability exists in determining which sex performs which tasks. Feminist anthropologists argue that women's status and the way work is organized have a lot to do with a society's level of technology (Friedl 1975). In hunting and gathering societies, which prevailed for 98 percent of human history, the sexes are generally full economic partners. In horticultural societies, in which food is cultivated by hoe, relations between the sexes tend to be relatively egalitarian (Basow 1992). However, women's status varies with the existence of other customs, such as polygamy. Men's monopoly over large game and warfare gave them advantages over women.

With the rise of agrarian societies some 5000 to 6000 years ago, women's status declined. Sociologist Rae Blumberg (1978) warns: If you believe in reincarnation, hope that you will never come back as a woman in a traditional agrarian society! Because plough cultivation requires few workers at sites farther from the home base, men dominate the economy. As land became property to be owned, defended, and inherited, concern for paternity increased men's desire to control women's sexuality. When class societies developed and goods were produced for exchange rather than for sharing, women's child-care responsibilities rendered them economically dependent on men (Sayers 1982).

Every one of today's industrialized societies emerged from an agrarian base (Basow 1992). Women's status worsened with the Industrial Revolution, which began in England and northwest Europe in the 1800s. Tasks formerly performed in the home were transferred to the factory and taken over by men. Women from the poorer classes also worked in the factories. However, their presence in the workplace was defined as merely temporary diversion from females' primary responsibility to children and home. These women entered the labour force either when factories were especially short of workers or when extra wages were badly needed at home. The dead-end, poorly paid, low-level jobs they filled did little to improve women's status. At the same time, women in the higher social classes were discouraged from working outside the home.

As Basow (1992) points out, the above pattern of viewing women as cheap temporary labour when a society begins industrializing is strikingly evident in many developing countries today, such as Mexico. Manufacturing industries, especially electronics and textiles, have transferred production to export-processing zones in the Third World. "These industries have shown an overwhelming preference for female workers, who are viewed as a cheap, abundant, and politically docile labour force."

As a result of these developments, men increasingly assumed dominance in the public sphere. Men's public activities gave them privileged access to resources and symbols that enhanced their power and provided disproportionate rewards. As dominant groups usually do, males propagated definitions of the situation that aggrandized themselves and their work. There is considerable pressure on subordinate groups, such as women, to accept the dominant groups' definitions.

The real issue then is cultural meanings, not reproductive capabilities. As human products, ideas are subject to revision (Richardson 1981). The notion of male superiority is therefore open to question; moreover, "technology permits humans to transcend biology — people can fly although no one was born with wings" (Huber 1976). Technology has made it possible for the average woman in industrialized nations to be pregnant only a few months of her life. Inventions such as bottle feeding and day-care centres have made the child-bearing function separable from the child-rearing function. The allocation of domestic tasks to women and public tasks to men can no longer be justified on biological grounds. In short, male dominance is universal but not inevitable (Richardson 1981).

Psychosexual Deviations

Gender identity (a person's conviction of being male or female) and genitals usually match. Children born with penises believe themselves to be males and display masculine personalities and behaviour. Similarly, children born with vaginas develop female gender identities and feminine characteristics. Occasionally, ambiguous genitals occur through birth defects or accidents. People with psychosexual abnormalities function, to a certain extent, as natural experiments that provide some insight into the question of the relative weight of biological and social causation in the development of gender. Evidence on both sides has been reported. However, the case described below suggests that **gender assignment** is socially caused.

In the 1960s, the parents of perfectly normal seven-month-old twin boys took their children to a hospital to be circumcised:

The physician elected to use an electric cauterizing needle instead of a scalpel to remove the foreskin of the one who chanced to be brought to the operating room first. When this baby's foreskin didn't give on the first try, or on the second, the doctor stepped up the current. On the third try, the surge of heat from the electricity literally cooked the baby's penis. Unable to heal, the penis dried up, and in a few days sloughed off completely, like the stub of an umbilical cord. (Money and Tucker 1975)

Doctors recommended that the boy's sex be reassigned and that female external genitals be surgically constructed. The child's name, clothes, and hairstyle were feminized as the parents made every effort to rear twins, one male and one female. As the following anecdotes concerning the twins at age four-and-a-half show, both parents and children successfully developed gender-appropriate attitudes and behaviour. The mother, talking about the boy, reported, "In the summer time, one time I caught him — he went out and took a leak in the flower garden in the front yard, you know. He was quite happy with himself. And I just didn't say anything. I just couldn't. I started laughing and I told daddy about it." The corresponding comments about the girl went this way: "I've never had a problem with her. She did once when she was little, she took off her panties and threw them over the fence. And she didn't have no panties on. But I just gave her a little swat on the rear, and I told her that nice little girls didn't do that, and she should keep her pants on" (Money and Ehrhardt 1972). For Christmas, the girl wanted dolls, a doll house, and a doll carriage. The boy wanted a toy garage with cars, gas pumps, and tools. We are told that the feminized twin grew up to be a healthy young "woman" (Schulz 1984).

This case and others suggest that sex by assignment outweighs biological factors in determining gender identity. For example, of 44 cases of individuals with female XX chromosomes, ovaries, excessive male hormones, and ambiguous external genitals, 39 were assigned as female at birth. Thirty-seven of them developed a female identity. In contrast, all five assigned and reared as males developed male gender identity (Green 1974). However, gender reassignment is usually unsuccessful after the age of 18 months (Money and Ehrhardt 1972). By then, the child has the ability to understand verbal labels for gender and to view the world from a "female" or "male" perspective. Finally, we must point out that the conclusions of psychosexual abnormality research have been criticized because gender reassignment has been supplemented by appropriate surgery and hormone treatment. That is, the individual's biology has been modified to correspond to the assigned gender (Hyde 1979).

Hormonal Explanations of Sex/Gender Differences

Humans' growth, reproduction, aging, reaction to attack, as well as the experience of moods that range from elation to depression are all governed by some 45 hormones. These chemical substances also influence sexuality. When hormones flood into the bloodstream at puberty, boys get erections, girls get menstrual periods, and everyone gets acne (Clark et al. 1987). Moreover, the prenatal development of female and male forms of internal reproductive structures and external genitalia is controlled by the secretion of male hormones. Without these hormones, the fetus will differentiate as female, regardless of genetic sex (Williams 1987). Given the significance of hormones and their connection with sexuality, it is understandable why some scientists have posited hormones as the key to gender.

The spectacular growth of endocrinology (the study of hormones) stimulated these and other questions: Do very aggressive men have extraordinarily high levels of testosterone coursing through their bloodstream? Do hormones equip women for lives of baby-tending and sweeping the hearth, and make men natural leaders? Does the volatility of moods associated with premenstrual syndrome disqualify women of childbearing age from responsible positions (Parlee 1973, 1982)? Taking the argument one step further, they ask: Do biochemical variations among people of the same sex account for variations in sex-typed behaviour? Are macho men loaded with testosterone and dainty women with estrogen? Did homosexuals get that way because of hormone imbalances?

Although testosterone administered to animals enhances levels of aggression and produces masculinized behaviour in females, authorities disagree about the connection in humans between testosterone and behaviour (Doyle 1989). Although many studies have found little or no relationship between testosterone levels and various measures of aggression (Lowe 1983), other researchers continue to pursue a link. The dramatic psychological changes, including hostility or "raid rage," in athletes who have used anabolic steroids (Taylor 1985) encourages this line of research.

Are women incapacitated by emotional instability during the premenstrual period? Despite the embarrassment in our culture that surrounds menstruation, premenstrual syndrome (PMS) has recently become a topic for magazine advice columns and TV talk shows. Courts in France now recognize PMS as a legal insanity defence (Tavris 1992). Nevertheless, "half a century's work on the premenstrual syndrome has been flawed by faulty methodology and unfounded interpretations" (Tavris and Wade 1984). Available studies, most clinical and lacking control groups, do *not* establish that mood changes are strongly correlated with phases of menstrual cycle (Tavris and Wade 1984). Although this does not mean that all menstrual distress is in women's heads, "it would be a mistake to assume that menstruating women are more anxious, tense, or antisocial than the average man" (Tavris and Wade 1984). Women have much lower rates of crime and accidents than do men, whether or not these rates are associated with menstrual periods (Epstein 1988).

So what if premenstrual women are moody and men get more aggressive as their testosterone level rises? Although reliable research fails to underwrite these conclusions, "the question relevant to the genders in society is the *meaning* of differences in hormonal levels" (Epstein 1988). While raging female hormones are widely believed to be detrimental to women's participation in public affairs, no similar hormonal barriers disqualify testosterone-maddened males from sensitive decision-making posts. Having the "right" hormones does not explain masculine advantage; having the "wrong" hormones cannot account for women's lower status. Neither sex can use its hormones as an excuse for antisocial behaviour. Since society "expects people to manage their moods and assume responsibility for harming others," feminists worry about criminal court decisions that let "women get away with murder — literally — because it's their 'time of the month'" (Tavris and Wade 1984).

All human fetuses begin by being female; inputs of male hormones are required to differentiate male characteristics in those fetuses having an XY genetic structure. Various sorts of sex/gender nonconformity (cross-dressing, homosexuality, transsexualism) appear to be more common in males than females. These two factors, taken together, make provocative the hypothesis that prenatal hormone imbalances are linked with postnatal departures from masculinity (Green 1974). Because research techniques of the future might reveal hormonal influences, we should remain open-minded about this possibility (Bell, Weinberg, and Hammersmith 1981; Ross 1986). Nevertheless, at the present time, there is very little evidence for hormonal (or genetic) abnormality in homosexuals or transvestites (Baker 1980; Geer et al. 1984; Huston 1983) or transsexuals (Bolin 1987; Ross 1986).

Conclusions. Every approach to the problem of the biological foundation of female/male differences raises more questions than it answers. Biology may be directly involved in social-psychological traits such as aggressiveness, and indirectly involved in the gender division of labour. The secondary sex characteristics of male size and strength may also contribute indirectly to gender differences. In American and Canadian cultures, which value "sheer bigness," the generally greater male body size may translate into status (Garn 1966). The gender-role implications of strength are more obvious. Superior male strength is an ingredient in the traditional gender division of labour. More important, however, is the implicit or actual physical threat that males present to females. As Goffman (1977) points out, "Selective mating ensures that with almost no exceptions husbands are bigger than wives and boyfriends are bigger than girlfriends."

The biological differences between females and males are really very slight in comparison with the immense gender differences erected on this substructure. However, to search for either biological *or* environmental causation of gender patterns, to pose the issue as nature versus nurture, is a misleading and simplistic formulation of a complex question. In gender patterns, as in social behaviour in general (remember the discussion in Chapter 4), both biology and environment are implicated. Biochemical and genetic factors set the stage, but culture and history provide the script for social life (Kunkel 1977). The fact that socialization often emphasizes "natural" sex differences further complicates the situation. For example, our society provides more athletic facilities and opportunities for the physically stronger males. However, because most of the psychosocial differences between the sexes involve learning in one way or another, let us look at socialization as an explanation of gender.

Socialization Explanations of Gender

Chapter 4 defined *socialization* as the lifelong learning process through which individuals develop selfhood and acquire the knowledge, skills, and motivations required for participation in social life. **Gender socialization** involves the particular processes through which people learn to be masculine and feminine according to the expectations current in their society. As we have already seen, there are a number of theoretical approaches to socialization: the learning, Freudian, cognitive developmental, and symbolic-interaction perspectives. Symbolic interaction will be emphasized here.

Each society has its scripts (Laws 1979) for femininity and masculinity. The emotions, thoughts, and behaviour of children are shaped in approximate conformity with these **gender scripts.** However, the content of gender socialization is not uniform for all citizens of a country. Gender scripts are differently interpreted in different social classes, racial/ethnic groups, and regions of a country. In addition, these scripts are age-graded: the gender norms that pertain to given individuals change as they move through the life cycle. Gender stereotypes and gender-role attitudes tell us something about society's scripts for gender socialization.

Gender Stereotypes

Imagine yourself talking with a friend who describes two people whom you have never met. One person is said to be independent, adventurous, and dominant, while the other is described

as sentimental, submissive, emotional, and affectionate. Would it be easier to picture one of these persons as male and the other as female? If you visualize the first person as male and the second as female, you have demonstrated your knowledge of gender stereotypes. What is more, you could be Canadian, American, Nigerian, Pakistani, or Japanese. Cross-cultural research shows that citizens of 30 nations share similar general beliefs about the sexes (Williams and Best 1982).

A **stereotype** refers to those folk beliefs about the attributes characterizing a social category on which there is substantial agreement (Mackie 1973). The term refers to consensual beliefs about the traits people choose to describe categories of people, such as ethnic groups, old people, or university students. In themselves, stereotypes are not good or bad; they simply are. Some stereotype traits are false — for example, that women are illogical. Other traits may be generally fitting but, like all generalizations, fail to take into account individual differences within the sexes or the degree of overlap between the sexes (Williams and Best 1982). For example, the male stereotype contains the trait aggressiveness. Our previous discussion noted both the accuracy of this sex difference and the female/male overlap. In short, "stereotypes both represent and distort reality" (Eagly and Steffen 1984).

Gender stereotypes capture folk beliefs about the nature of females and males generally. Many studies show that, despite the activities of the women's movement, gender stereotypes are "widely held, persistent, and highly traditional in content" (Ward and Balswick 1978). When researchers (Broverman et al. 1972) ask respondents to describe the average man and the average woman, the gender traits fall into a feminine *warmth–expressiveness* cluster and a masculine *competency* cluster. The latter cluster includes such characteristics as being independent, active, competitive, and ambitious. A relative absence of these traits supposedly characterizes women. In other words, relative to men, women are seen to be dependent, passive, noncompetitive, and not ambitious. The warmth–expressiveness cluster, on the other hand, consists of such attributes as being gentle, quiet, and sensitive to the feelings of others. Relative to women, men are perceived as lacking these traits. Gender-stereotype studies (Broverman et al. 1972) also report that many

The Popularity of U.S. Elementary School Children

Between 1987 and 1991, sociologists Adler, Kless, and Adler (1992) carried out participant observation at two Western region American middle-class public schools in a mostly white community. They found the children to have developed stratified social orders, with different bases of popularity for boys and girls.

Boys' Popularity

The major factor that affected boys' popularity was *athletic ability*. BEN: "Everybody wants to be friends with Gabe, even though he makes fun of most of them all the time. But they still all want to pick him on their team and have him be friends with them because he's a good athlete, even though he brags a lot about it. He's popular." *Being cool* also influenced popularity. SIXTH-GRADE TEACHER: "The popular group is what society might term 'cool.' You know they're skaters, they skateboard, they wear more cool clothes, you know the 'in' things you'd see in ads right now in magazines." In the upper grades, popular boys were *tough*, in other words, defiant of adult authority. MARK: "[Members of the popular group] always have to show off to each other that they aren't afraid to say anything they want to the teacher, that they aren't teachers' pets…. One day Josh and Allen got in trouble in music 'cause they told the teacher the Disney movie she wanted to show sucked. They got pink [disciplinary] slips." Popular boys have *savoir-faire*. These children have sophisticated social and interpersonal skills according to peer norms. Travis and Nikko describe

Wren, a boy whose lack of *savoir-faire* earned him labels of "nerd," "fag," "sissy," and "homo."

TRAVIS: *Wren is such a nerd. He's short and his ears stick out.*
NIKKO: *And when he sits in his chair, he crosses one leg over the other and curls the toe around under his calf, so it's double-crossed, like this [shows]. It looks so faggy with his "girly" shoes. And he always sits up erect with perfect posture, like this [shows].*
TRAVIS: *And he's always raising his hand to get the teacher to call on him.*
NIKKO: *Yeah. Wren is the kind of kid, when the teacher has to go out for a minute, she says, "I'm leaving Wren in charge while I'm gone."*

Finally, *academic performance* entered into the popularity equation in complex ways. Boys with serious academic problems were labelled "dummies." Exceedingly smart boys who lacked coolness, toughness, or athletic ability were stigmatized as "nerdy."

MARK: *One of the reasons they're so mean to Seth is because he's got glasses and he's really smart. They think he's a brainy-brain and a nerd.*
SETH: *You're smart, too, Mark.*
MARK: *Yeah, but I don't wear glasses, and I play football.*

Girls' Popularity

Different factors conferred popularity on girls than on boys. *Parents' socioeconomic status* was an important influence. ALISSA: "If your Mom has a good job, you're popular, but if your Mom has a bad job, then you're unpopular." BETTY: "And, if, like you're on welfare, then you're unpopular because it shows that you don't have a lot of money." *Physical appearance* is another powerful determinant of girls' popularity. RESEARCHER: "I walked into the fifth-grade coat closet

and saw Diane applying hairspray and mousse to Paula's and Mary's hair …. It seemed that Diane, who was the most popular girl in the class, was socializing them to use the proper beauty supplies that were socially accepted by the popular clique." *Precocity* was associated with popularity. For example, the most precocious girls showed an early interest in boys. FOURTH-GRADE GIRL describing what it meant to "go" with a boy: "You talk. You hold hands at school. You pass notes in class. You go out with them, and go to movies …" *Exclusivity*, which referred to girls' desire and ability to form elite groups, was also important. BETTY: "If you're not popular, you mostly get treated like you're really stupid. They stare at you and go, "Uhh." In contrast to the boys, the girls did not disdain *academic performance*. Although not all popular girls were academic achievers, they suffered no stigma from high scholastic performance.

In sum, middle-class elementary school girls derived social status from physical appearance, grooming, material possessions, success with boys. By comparison, boys were accorded popularity for distancing themselves from authority and investing in academic effort. Being athletic, displaying toughness, trouble, coolness, and interpersonal bragging and sparring skills earned them esteem from their peers.

Source:

Patricia A. Adler, Steven J. Kless, and Peter Adler, "Socialization to gender roles: Popularity among elementary school boys and girls," *Sociology of Education* 65(1992):169–187.

more of the characteristics valued in Western societies are seen as masculine rather than feminine traits.

Gender stereotypes embody the edicts of societal scripts regarding appropriate major time and energy investments for women and men. According to this "ideal" division of labour, men are expected to work outside the home, marry, and support their families, while women are expected to marry, carry the major responsibility for child-rearing, and rely on men for financial support and social status. Increasingly, it is expected that Canadian and American women will also work outside the home. Nevertheless, attracting a suitable mate and looking after his interests (and eventually those of their children) still take priority over serious occupational commitment. The two clusters of traits reflect this division of labour.

It appears that beliefs about gender develop, at least in part, from people's observations of women and men playing these traditional social roles. For example, children are more likely to encounter women taking care of babies and men wielding authority in the workplace than the other way around, and they come to believe that the characteristics thought to be necessary for child care (nurturance, warmth) and for success in the labour force (dominance, objectivity) are typical of women and men, respectively. It is likely that fundamental changes in the "pictures in people's heads" (Lippman 1922) about men and women reflect social change. In other words, "Gender stereotypes ... will not disappear until people divide social roles equally, that is, until child care and household responsibilities are shared equally by women and men and the responsibility to be employed outside the home is borne equally" (Eagly and Steffen 1984).

The gender stereotypes themselves, since they function as self-fulfilling prophecies, constitute an important impediment to social change. If women are assumed to be less competent, their performance may be judged less successful than it actually is. In addition, if women are assumed to be less competent, they may be given fewer opportunities to assert themselves.

Gender-Role Attitudes

A second component of societal scripts that are learned through socialization are gender-role attitudes. While gender stereotypes refer to shared beliefs about feminine and masculine psychological makeup, **gender-role attitudes** point to people's beliefs about the status of the sexes and the appropriate gender division of labour in the home and workplace. They range from traditional to egalitarian, "from the view that women belong in the home and are responsible for child-rearing, to the view that women and men should have equal access to identical positions and rewards" (Boyd 1984).

Table 5-1 lists six questions that were asked of Canadian national probability samples by researchers Gibbins, Ponting, and Symons (1978) and Ponting (1986). Since four of the six questions from the earlier survey were asked again in 1986, we can draw some conclusions about changes over time. First of all, Canadians' attitudes concerning gender arrangements in the domestic sphere are more traditional than their public-sphere attitudes. In 1986, 64 percent felt that a mother with young children belongs in the home. Moreover, 40 percent believed that a wife should give her husband's career higher priority than her own.

When questions focus exclusively on the woman in the workplace — that is, the implications of her work for her family are left unmentioned — Canadians' attitudes become more egalitarian. Seventy-seven percent said more women should be promoted into senior management positions. Three-quarters of the sample expressed verbal support for the women's movement (questions #5 and #6). Finally, two-thirds said women should have the right to decide whether or not to have an abortion (question #4).

Another important conclusion that can be derived from Table 5-1 is that Canadians' gender-role attitudes have become more egalitarian. The sensitive domestic issues show especially large shifts over time (questions #1 and #2). Ponting's findings agree with several American studies (Cherlin and Walter 1981; Thornton, Alwin, and Camburn 1983). This historical change may be attributed to such factors as the growing labour-force participation of women, public debate and media attention to gender, higher education, and the declining birth rate.

Some categories of Canadians are more liberal than others. Francophones were significantly more liberal than anglophones on questions #3 to

TABLE 5-1   Canadian Gender-Role Attitudes

Attitudinal Item		% Agree	% Disagree	% Undecided/ Neutral**
1. When children are young, a mother's place is in the home.	TOTAL (1986)	64	20	16
	TOTAL (1976)	81	10	9
	Male*	62	19	18
	Female*	65	20	13
	Anglophone*	63	20	16
	Francophone*	62	22	16
2. Although a wife's career may be important, she should give priority to helping her husband advance in his career.	TOTAL (1986)	40	47	13
	TOTAL (1976)	74	21	5
	Male	35	51	13
	Female	44	42	12
	Anglophone	40	47	14
	Francophone	41	47	11
3. In the business world more women should be promoted into senior management positions	TOTAL (1986)	77	8	14
	TOTAL (1976)	72	14	13
	Male	72	10	18
	Female	82	6	11
	Anglophone	73	9	17
	Francophone	87	4	8
4. A woman should have the sole right to decide whether or not to have an abortion.	TOTAL (1986)	66	26	7
	TOTAL (1976)	56	34	9
	Male	67	24	8
	Female	65	27	6
	Anglophone	65	27	6
	Francophone	70	22	8
5. Overall, the women's movement has had more of a positive effect than a negative effect on Canadian society.	TOTAL (1986)***	73	11	12
	Male	71	12	14
	Female	75	11	10
	Anglophone	73	13	10
	Francophone	71	8	15
6. There should be more laws to get rid of differences in the way women are treated, compared to men.	TOTAL (1986)***	74	13	11
	Male	68	18	13
	Female	80	9	9
	Anglophone	72	15	12
	Francophone	80	9	9

SOURCES: Roger Gibbins, J. Rick Ponting, Gladys L. Symons, "Attitudes and ideology: Correlates of liberal attitudes towards the role of women," *Journal of Comparative Family Studies* 9(1978):19–40; and J. Rick Ponting (unpublished 1986 data).
*All sex and language group results refer to 1986 data.
**Because of rounding and "don't know" answers or refusals, some totals do not equal 100%.
***Questions 5 and 6 were not asked in 1976.

#6; no language group differences emerged for the family-related questions (#1 and #2). There is a slight tendency for women to be more liberal than men (questions #3, #5, and #6). However, significantly more men gave the egalitarian response to question #2; sex differences in replies to questions #1 and #4 were not statistically significant. Finally, according to data not shown on Table 5-1, people with more formal education tend to hold more egalitarian attitudes.

The impact of the women's movement on Canadians' (and Americans') thinking about the sexes

The Shame Attached to Being Gay

A close friend of mine has just died of AIDS. He was 34, and his family didn't even know he was ill. "Jim" was too embarrassed to tell them he was suffering from the disease. In the end, I think he just gave up and decided to take matters into his own hands. As a playwright, his only remaining chance for dignity was to time his last curtain.

Jim's story is not that uncommon. There is a deep shame attached to AIDS, and its effects are as painful as the opportunistic infections that despoil the sufferers' bodies. What could be more humiliating than leaving this world with the idea that you have disgraced your family? Or that you have become a non-person who doesn't deserve to live?

This isn't the story I really intended to write. I wanted to discuss what it's like to be 30 years old and gay in the nineties. An older acquaintance challenged me to publish something about this. He wondered whether people in my age group took the freedoms they have just a little too much for granted.

After some reflection, I wondered whether the challenges his generation faced have merely been replaced with different ones, and a lot of other difficulties haven't changed at all.

Some facts of gay life have clearly changed. Gay relationships used to be a criminal offence, and gay people could meet only clandestinely in dark bars or at private parties, often with the fear of police harassment. Now there are more than 20 bars in Toronto that cater to a gay clientele, and a few bookstores. There are glossy magazines, gay publishing houses, Gay Pride Day and a special police patrol that cruises gay districts in the city.

Gays can now legally request limited spousal benefits and (if the government stops dragging its feet) be open about their sexuality in the armed forces. Not so long ago, this list of rights would have been unthinkable. To some people, usually religious homophobes, it still is.

But one thing that hasn't really altered is the shame attached to being gay. This isn't something the government can legislate, although having been listed in Canada's Criminal Code certainly hasn't made the experience any easier.

This shame expresses itself in the gay world as "coming out." If someone is "out," he or she has openly identified himself or herself as a gay person.

Many people who are not gay may not understand the significance of this step. They may think that sexuality is a very private matter and, really, whose business is it? In theory, it's no one's but your own.

In fact, being gay is a lot more complicated than being left-handed or having blue eyes, because it fundamentally changes your relationship to the family structure and challenges socially sanctioned gender roles.

Although experiences vary, "coming out" is usually a painful and heart-wrenching process for your family. Some parents support their children; others can't bear to deal with the news and may become violent, or guilt-ridden. I know of one case where the parents told their friends their son had died, and they have carried on the façade to this day.

I don't think this aspect of the gay experience has changed much. Parents still expect — or hope — that their sons and daughters will marry and have children. The news that this might not be in the cards is still, I think, difficult to accept.

Some gay people do produce families, from a genuine desire to have children, or because they want to appease their parents. We may have spousal benefits and Gay Pride Day, but I'd say most gay people are not "out" to their families and their friends — and they worry that disclosing the truth might imperil these friendships.

A related challenge gay people still face is discrimination. If we don't want to settle down like Ward and June and the Beaver, what are we?

Freaks? Society has expectations, too. Being gay threatens them.

Gay "families" can consist of same-sex spouses with children, or no children, or even a group of close-knit friends, male and female. Some gay men like cross-dressing. So do some straight men, but they usually have to hide the need; the gay community is a little more accepting of unconventional gender behaviour.

And a new challenge our generation faces is the AIDS epidemic, although arguably this is everyone's problem, not just ours.

So much has been written about AIDS and what it means and doesn't mean. Is it a metaphor for a diseased lifestyle? Bigots who believe this tend, conveniently, to forget the other risk groups the disease affects. Certainly, AIDS has heightened the public's distrust and fear of gay people, and deepened the perception that our lifestyle is "unnatural." However, the fastest-growing risk group in industrialized countries now is heterosexuals.

But the disease has also led to a lot of troubling developments in the gay community. There's a subtle discrimination against people who are seropositive.

You see it in the personal ads. A lot of the classified advertisements state whether the person is HIV– or HIV+. Twenty years ago, this was a nonissue. Now, "safer sex" and one's serostatus are facts of life — and death.

I hope Jim's family is reading this today. Their son was unable to share the most basic facts about his illness with them. They had to find out in the worst way possible: after he died. As for you, Jim, this is your final bow, compliments of a friend who cared.

Source:

Steven Minuk, *The Globe and Mail*, December 7, 1992, p. A22. Reprinted by permission of Steven Minuk.

has been significant. However, after analyzing 30 years of Gallup poll data, Boyd (1984) concluded that while enormous changes have occurred with respect to gender issues, Canadians' gender-role attitudes "also reveal a residue of earlier norms and practices."

The Role of the Mass Media in Gender Socialization

A mother writes:

The scene is my backyard.

A bunch of neighbourhood toddlers are taking apart my then four-year-old daughter's new doctor kit. I'm eavesdropping.

"You be the doctor," she says, handing the stethoscope to Jimmy, "and I'll be the nurse."

I blow my cover.

"Why don't you be the doctor and let Jimmy be the nurse?" She looks at me as though I've just dropped in from the Planet Zondar.

"Girls can't be doctors," my daughter says.

I can't believe what I'm hearing. For four years, I've dragged her across town just so she will have a female pediatrician as a role model.

"What about your doctor?"

She looks me straight in the eye.

"On television," she says archly, "doctors are men."
(Airhart 1992).

The mass media are impersonal communication sources that reach large audiences. As such, they function as symbolic socialization agents. Because the media keep people in touch with what is happening in the world and co-ordinate other societal institutions, they have been described as the "cement of modern social life" (Tuchman 1978).

Concerns about the effects on children of violence depicted in the mass media led to the studies described in Chapter 4. Since the advent of the women's movement, a parallel concern has been voiced over the impact of the media on the development of gender attitudes and behaviour. Although exceptions certainly exist within and among media, mass-communication sources convey traditional, often sexist, messages about gender relations. As a quick survey of magazine ads or newspaper comic strips will illustrate, the media exaggerate the dividing lines between females and males. Their caricatured portraits often

The media often exaggerate the dividing lines between females and males.

rely on gender stereotypes. Women (and to some extent, men) are objectified as sexual beings.

Two main factors explain why the media often depict gender stereotypes and devalue females' status. First, despite some improvement over the past two decades, relatively few women hold positions of authority in media industries. Indeed, feminist critics have accused both Canadian and American media of "widespread discrimination against women in broadcast industry employment practices" (Cantor 1988). Moreover, it is hard for those few women who are employed in the media to resist ideas and attitudes that disparage women. Consider the press. Only 6 percent of publishers in Canada are women; 9 percent of editors-in-chief and 6 percent of managing editors are women (Smith 1990:D8). Yet more than half the students in North American journalism classes are now women. "However, change has come hard in a traditionally male-

Hate Slaying of Gay Man Stuns Montreal

MONTREAL — Four youths, described by police as neo-Nazi skinheads, were charged with first-degree murder yesterday in the stalking and killing of a gay man in a Montreal park on Sunday.

Civil-rights and gay leaders expressed profound shock and horror, particularly in light of international events.

"This is a very grave hate crime," said Alain Dufour, leader of the World Anti-Fascist League, a national anti-racism group. "This is a murder with an ideological underpinning..."

Constable Joanne Rivest of the Montreal Urban Community Police said only that four boys, aged 15 to 17, were charged yesterday with first-degree, or premeditated murder. Homicide investigators, who were not available for comment yesterday, told other media that the four were neo-Nazi skinheads.

The body of engineer Yves Lalonde, 51, was found near a path in Angrignon Park, a popular meeting place for gay men, on Monday morning. He had been savagely beaten and robbed of $92.

Steve Pépin, a spokesman for the Montreal Lesbian and Gay Community Centre, said there have been dozens of assaults on gay men in the park in recent months, most by jack-booted teen-aged boys spewing anti-gay invective.

Michael Crelinsten, president of the Canadian Jewish Congress Quebec, said the gravity of the attack cannot be overstated.

"If the reported facts are accurate ... this has to be viewed as one of the most serious incidents of its kind ever in Canada," he said.

"This murder raises the most horrible echoes of the Nazi régime and it's particularly sobering and devastating to see at a time when horrible events of this sort are unfolding in Europe," Mr. Crelinsten said.

(During the Holocaust, the Nazis targeted Jews, gay men, Gypsies and other minorities for extermination.)

Sunday's attack was the worst to date in Montreal, but assaults on gays are commonplace. On the night of the murder, a number of men were assaulted in another downtown Montreal park that is popular with gay men.

And, earlier this year, six men were severely beaten in the Gay Village. Six neo-Nazi youths were arrested in those incidents.

Mr. Pépin of the Lesbian and Gay Community Centre said many of the attacks are believed to be part of an initiation ritual of the white supremacist group White Power Canada, which demands that aspiring members attack at least 10 gays and lesbians. It is difficult to get a handle on the extent of the problem, he said,

because many victims are reluctant to go to police, whom they consider unsympathetic.

Mr. Dufour of the World Anti-Fascist League said racist, homophobic and anti-Semitic views all go hand-in-hand in the teachings of white supremacists and neo-Nazis.

He said lawyers for the anti-racist group will try to intervene in the case against the four youths and attempt to have them tried in adult court. Under the provisions of the Young Offenders Act, offenders under the age of 18 convicted of first- or second-degree murder spend no more than five years in custody.

Sunday's murder rekindled memories of the killing of Montreal gay-rights activist Joe Rose. He was stabbed to death by four teen-aged boys on a city bus on March 20, 1989, after an argument. That case sparked severe criticism of the Young Offenders Act.

Mr. Lalonde's death also serves as a reminder that at least a half-dozen gay men have been killed in Montreal during the past year, and all those cases remain unsolved.

Source:

André Picard, *The Globe and Mail*, December 4, 1992, pp. A1–A2.

---

dominated workplace. Women have had to do all the pushing so far and the pace of change has been glacial" (Smith 1990:D8). A professor at an American school of journalism agrees: "Women are creeping ever so slowly toward the year 2055 when projections indicate they will attain levels in newspaper editorships on a par with their level in the population [53 percent]" (Beasely 1989).

Second, the media are sexist because they mirror cultural notions about gender — they take and accentuate societal images of gender and sexuality — and, in turn, they shape and strengthen these views. To be acceptable, media content must contain dominant social beliefs and images. Mass media represent conservative interests. Large audiences are needed to make profits. These mass audiences respond to contemporary, but familiar images. Therefore "content cannot 'move ahead of' public opinion" (Wilson 1981). There is cause for feminist critics to remain troubled about the impressions of masculinity and femininity conveyed by these powerful, ubiquitous symbolic socialization agencies.

Music provides a good example of the gender imagery conveyed by popular culture. Music is an important source of enjoyment for 89 percent of Canadian teenagers (Bibby and Posterski 1992). "Golden oldies" often idealize women ("Earth An-gel, Earth An-gel, will you be mine?"); country ballads sing about strong cowboys and their unrequited love for bad women. Rock music has been criticized for its misogyny (Harding and Nett 1984). For example, a member of Kiss ("Burn Bitch Burn") boasts about having "bedded down" 3000 women during his rock-band travels (*Herald Sunday Magazine*, September 4, 1988). The message of the rap group 2 Live Crew album "As Nasty As They Wanna Be" also glorifies male studs and submissive women. Bibby and Posterski (1992) quote a study by the Quebec Status of Women Council of 338 rock videos: "More than half the rock videos broadcast on television are blatantly sexist, and the most flagrant offenders tend to get the most air time."

Considerable variation exists in the content of the media. For example, movies vary from *Slumber Party Massacre*, which featured female victims of slashing, to *The Accused*, which tried to convince audiences that no woman, regardless of provocative dress, suggestive behaviour, or unsavoury reputation, deserves to be raped. Nevertheless, traditional gender imagery predominates. It is important to note psychologists' conclusion that "there is solid evidence that the way sex roles are portrayed in the mass media can affect children's and adolescents' attitudes and perceptions of what is and is not appropriate for the two sexes" (Roberts and Maccoby 1985).

The Symbolic-Interaction Perspective on Gender Socialization

Symbolic interactionists, such as Cooley and Mead, view "reality" as a matter of social definition. Socialization involves the acquisition of a self, which is also socially defined. The "looking-glass self" notion described in Chapter 4 holds that children learn who they are by adopting other people's attitudes toward themselves. The roles played by language and significant others in the socialization process are emphasized in this perspective. In this section, we want to apply some of these themes to gender socialization. Because gender consists of social constructions built on female/male physiological differences, symbolic interaction seems a particularly appropriate

theoretical approach to the questions we have been asking in this chapter (Mackie 1987).

Development of Gender Identity. As a first step to self-awareness, the child differentiates herself or himself from other objects in the environment. As you learned in Chapter 4, Mead hypothesizes that the capacity to use language allows the child to learn the meaning of many things, including himself or herself. Names form a basis, then, for the development of the self. A given name individualizes the infant and usually classifies it by gender. That is, baptizing a child "Barbara" simultaneously separates this infant from other infants and signifies its femaleness. Often, parents dress youngsters to advertise their gender. They may be colour-coded in traditional masculine blue and feminine pink, or dressed in miniature versions of adult genderized clothing (baseball caps for infant boys and bows taped to female infants' hairless heads) (Cahill 1989).

Gender classification influences caregivers to treat the infant as a boy or as a girl. For example, for the first six months or so, male infants are touched more, while female infants are talked to more (Lewis 1972). Later, the male toddler is tossed into the air ("How's my big boy?"), while the female child is tickled under the chin ("How's my sweet little girl?") (Richmond-Abbott 1983). In other words, when we attach gender-designating labels we invite gender-specific interactional experiences based on stereotypes (Cahill 1989). The child with a bow taped on her head is regarded as delicate; when she cries she is seen to be frightened rather than angry. In contrast, adults are likely to view the baby wearing a baseball cap as hardy, and to interpret his crying as anger rather than fear (Cahill 1989).

Although the adults who socialize a child place it in a gender class at birth, some time must pass before the child responds to its own self in terms of gender. As noted above, gender reassignment becomes less successful after eighteen months. One reason may be that by that age the child is labelling itself "male" or "female." By the age of three, a child can accurately and consistently answer the question "Are you a girl or a boy?" At the same age, children show preferences for either "girl" or "boy" toys and activities (Kessler and McKenna 1978). This self-categorization as male or female becomes a major axis of identity. However, young children do not necessarily interpret gender in the same way that adults do. For instance, they use facial hair and clothing, not genitals, as gender cues (Cahill 1989). Lindesmith, Strauss, and Denzin (1977) tell the story of the five-year-old acquaintance of theirs who attended a party at which children of both sexes bathed in the nude. When asked how many boys and how many girls were at the party, she answered, "I couldn't tell because they all had their clothes off." This misconception is understandable in a society such as ours, where the naked body is usually covered.

Socialization agents such as the family, peers, mass media, and schools teach children what sorts of traits and behaviours go along with the female/male distinction. Parents admonish that "Boys don't cry" and "Girls don't sit with their legs apart." In the past, children's storybooks were sex-typed. Pyke's (1975) survey of Canadian children's books found few women in jobs outside the home. Women's trademark was the "perennial apron," worn "even by female squirrels." Storybook characters who had interesting adventures were most often male. A recent survey of American children's books discovered that girls are increasingly the active central characters who are having fun. However, the women in these stories are still portrayed as homebound mothers without extrafamilial roles (Grauerholz and Pescosolido 1989). Let us turn now to some examples of how language reinforces the ranking of the sexes.

Language and the Ranking of the Sexes. In many ways, female inferiority is conveyed through language forms and usage. For instance, women's speech is viewed as frivolous and unimportant:

In the English language, we talk and we chat, we jabber and we chatter while men speak, proclaim and express concerns. In the French language, "elle parlote, babille, bavarde, jase, cause" while men "parlent, discourent, discutent." (Martel and Peterat 1984:43)

Moreover, words label. Speaking of women as "the opposite sex" exaggerates male–female differences. In addition to naming, these labels often imply hidden messages about their referents (a father nicknames his small son "Tiger" and his daughter "Dolly"). Emotionally charged verbal labels also serve to control behaviour. Male children are effectively chastised by being called "fags" or "girls." (A basketball coach yells at a boy who isn't playing well, "Where's your purse, Mrs. — ?"). Similarly, the expletive "bitch" carries the connotation that the woman has failed to observe traditional gender standards.

Terms of address also convey gender messages. For one thing, people feel free to be more familiar semantically with women. In the 1990 Liberal Party leadership contest, the frontrunners were "Chrétien," "Martin," and "Sheila." Observations of males and females in parallel positions in various companies and public places showed that women were more often addressed by first names or nicknames, while men were generally dealt with more formally, by title or last name (Eakins and Eakins 1978). Usually men are at the top of work hierarchies and women are at the bottom. Men call the women by their first names, and the women more often address the men by last name plus title (Thorne and Henley 1975).

Despite innovations such as hyphenated surnames, most women continue to lose their surname upon marriage. Men, however, not only keep their last name for life, but pass it on intact to sons. In general, women are labelled in terms of the men with whom they are associated — "Mrs. Jones," "Harvey Hart's daughter." The significance of the now widely accepted neologism "Ms." has been described as follows: "The new privacy regarding marital status symbolically elevated women to personhood from their previous commodity status in the marriage market where "Miss" meant "for sale," and "Mrs." meant "sold" (Davy 1978).

Clearly, language evaluates the sexes. For example, masculine connotations tend to be strong and positive, while feminine connotations tend to be negative, weak, or trivial. All references to God are masculine: Father, Lord, King. The negative connotations attached to the word "woman" become obvious when we compare taking defeat "like a man" and taking defeat "like a woman." The order of word usage also communicates differential evaluation: "men and women," "boys and girls," "husbands and wives." As Spender (1985) points out, it is appropriate "to call a mixed sex group 'guys' or 'men' but it is a mistake —

and an insult — to refer to a group which contains even one male as 'gals' or 'women'."

While individual examples of sexism in language may seem trivial, their combined impact is profound when we remember that people's perceptions of the world are linked closely to their language. As children learn a language, they also learn gender lessons about women's and men's places in society.

Parents as Significant Others. The provocative ideas of David Lynn (1959, 1969) emphasize the significance of parents in gender socialization. Lynn postulates that, because of the greater availability of the mother and the relative absence of the father during early childhood, little girls easily develop their gender identity through imitation and positive reinforcement. However, little boys must shift from their initial identification with the mother to identification with the father. Because male models are scarce, they have greater difficulty than females in achieving gender identity. According to Lynn, males must learn through abstractly piecing together the intellectual problem of what it means to be male. Some of this learning comes from peers and from media presentations of gender stereotypes. Some results from punishment for displays of feminine behaviour. Masculine behaviour is rarely defined positively as something the boy *should* do. One reason is that the male gender role is "so strongly defined in terms of work and sexuality, both of which are usually hidden from the eyes of children" (Colwill 1982). Instead, undesirable feminine behaviour is indicated negatively as something he should *not* do. Consequently, males remain anxious about gender. Females freely imitate males (in fashion, for example), but not vice versa. As adults, men are more hostile than women toward both the opposite sex and homosexuals. Nevertheless, the boy learns to prefer the masculine role to the feminine because being male implies countless privileges.

During childhood, the male role is the more inflexible. More pressure is placed on boys to act like boys than on girls to act like girls. Girls' problems start with adolescence:

Since girls are less likely to masturbate, run away from home, or bite and draw blood, their lives are relatively free from crisis until puberty. Before that, girls do not have to conform to threatening new criteria of acceptability to anywhere near the extent that boys do. (Bardwick and Douvan 1971)

As children of both sexes reach the teenage years, they are exposed to more complex and more precisely defined norms of gender-appropriate behaviour. According to Gilligan (1982), girls' socialization makes connectedness to others all-important to females throughout the life cycle; ruptured relationships, power, and aggression all deeply threaten them. Males, on the other hand, see the world in terms of autonomy, hierarchy, and conflict; it is intimacy that threatens them.

Peers as Significant Others. Children's experience with age-mates is also important in learning masculine or feminine behaviour. Boys and girls have different friendship patterns and different forms of play. Consequently, they acquire different sorts of social skills that may well have implications for their later adult behaviour. Peer activities also reinforce the notion that males are more important than females.

Engaging in what sociologist Fine (1986) has labelled "dirty play" seems important in the gender socialization of little boys. Pre-adolescent pranks such as "mooning" cars (pulling down one's trousers while facing away from the traffic), "egging" cars, and ringing doorbells and running away are thoroughly disapproved of by adults. However, these activities serve as anticipatory socialization for manhood. Males are supposed to be tough, cool, and aggressive. "There is risk involved in throwing eggs at houses or at moving cars; one could get caught, beaten, grounded, or even arrested" (Fine 1986). Boys gain status within their peer group for behaviour adults regard as troublesome. Boys' identity as males is enhanced by engaging in "dirty play," partly because it is "dirty" play (that is, it defies adult, especially female, authority), and partly because it is not *girls'* play.

After formal schooling begins, children's play becomes increasingly sex-segregated. The rare cross-sex play that does occur tends to be courtship activity at an unsophisticated level. According to one study (Richer 1984), the most common type is a chasing game in which girls chase boys and kiss them when they are caught. When boys do bother to chase girls, they pull their hair or push them. Both courtship games (where the desirable males are chased) and the general tendency of both sexes to evaluate boys' activities and boys more positively than girls' activities and girls tend to perpetuate traditional gender arrangements (Richer 1984).

A gender difference exists in the size of children's sex-segregated play groups (Eder and Hallinan 1978). Girls tend to play in small groups, especially dyads (two-person groups). Boys prefer to congregate in larger groups. Thus girls tend to learn the type of interpersonal skills required by small, intimate groups, such as sensitivity to others' feelings, the ability to disclose information about themselves, and the ability to show affection. Boys learn other sorts of skills; in general they learn something about group leadership and decision-making. In addition, girls protect their exclusive groups against the advances of newcomers, while boys tend to welcome new members. Little girls probably blame themselves for the greater trouble they have in making friends.

The type of play preferred by boys versus that enjoyed by girls partly explains the size difference of their friendship groups (Lever 1978). Although such differences seem to be diminishing somewhat, boys tend to play competitive games requiring teams of interdependent players with definite roles. Such games are played according to specific rules (hockey is a good example). In comparison, girls prefer to converse or to engage in physically undemanding activities in an indoor setting that require few participants. Playing dolls or board games does not demand the co-ordination of effort that hockey or baseball does. One result is the learning of different types of skills — and, again, these very likely carry over into adulthood.

Boys acquire the ability to co-ordinate their actions, to cope with impersonal rules, to work for collective as well as individual goals, to deal with competition and criticism. Girls learn to be imaginative, to converse, and to be empathetic. All these social experiences would be valuable for both sexes. While sex differences in play are lessening (many girls now play hockey, soccer, and baseball), the data suggest that the female differ-

entiation and impression of male superiority conveyed by peer socialization are still very strong (Best 1983; Richer 1984).

Conclusions. Symbolic interactionists view gender as a matter of social definition and social behaviour learned through interaction during the socialization process. Other theoretical viewpoints on gender socialization are also useful. For example, Lynn's (1959, 1969) ideas incorporate psychoanalytic ideas that are developed more fully in Chodorow's (1978) analysis of mothering. Learning by imitation is very important in gender socialization. Children growing up in a home organized according to traditional gender patterns regard this organization as perfectly normal and readily accept gender stereotypes (Lambert 1971).

Many social scientists are convinced that the traditional gender stereotypes are arbitrary and even damaging gender scripts for socialization. During the 1970s, some became intrigued with the possibility of making androgyny rather than sex-typing the goal of socialization. The term **androgyny** combines the Greek words for male (*andros*) and female (*gyne*), and refers to the presence of both feminine and masculine elements within individuals of both sexes (Laws 1979). Allowing people to have both instrumental and expressive capabilities within their repertoires may help to free the human personality from the restricting prison of stereotyping (Bem 1976). An androgynous person might characterize himself or herself as understanding and compassionate, *and* assertive, self-reliant, and ambitious. A sex-typed person, on the other hand, might use either the first two *or* the last three traits in self-description. In recent years, the ideal of androgyny has been criticized on the grounds that it does not eliminate gender stereotypes; it just combines them in new ways (Lott 1981).

The current ideal of **gender transcendence** looks to a state where femininity and masculinity are superseded as ways of labelling and experiencing psychological traits (Garnets and Pleck 1979). In a utopian society where gender has been transcended, each child would be taught that the distinctions of girl/boy and female/male are exclusively biological. The multitude of sociocultural elaborations on sex would disappear. Personality traits, interests, hobbies, toys, clothing, occupations, domestic division of labour — none would any longer be a function of sex (Bem 1983).

Social-Structural Explanations of Gender

A structural explanation of gender involves seeing what can be learned about gender by assuming that people's behaviour is influenced by external social factors or patterns of social relationships, such as norms, roles, statuses, social classes, institutions. According to this perspective, gender is the result of societal, not individual, characteristics. The structural-functional and conflict perspectives on gender are reviewed below.

The Structural-Functional Explanation of Gender

Structural-functional theorists like Parsons and Bales (1955) ask how societal arrangements, such as gender differences, contribute to the stability and survival of the social system. The family, as a social institution, is seen as functional for the society because it performs such crucial tasks as satisfaction of sexual needs, procreation, child care, and socialization.

Role specialization of adult family members enhances the ability of the family to perform these functions. The father/husband assumes the instrumental role, meaning that he connects the family to the wider society. In our society, this implies bringing home income from an outside job. The mother/wife, on the other hand, assumes the expressive role. She looks after the relationships within the family.

According to Parsons and Bales (1955), these structural patterns developed from a biological base. The female bears and nurses children. Pregnancy, lactation, and the human child's long period of helplessness restrict women's activities outside the home. Therefore, it is convenient for women to carry out the family's expressive functions. Men perform the instrumental tasks almost by default. Someone has to perform the instrumental role, and men's biology does not restrict their movements in the outside world.

As noted above, feminist anthropologists (Rosaldo 1980) agree that the structural functionalists' distinction between women's domestic orientation and men's public orientation is an extremely important point. Moreover, that distinction goes a long way toward explaining female subordination. Women's dependence on men for food and physical protection makes men seem their natural superiors. Men's public activities (work in the labour market, hunting, military activities, religion) have traditionally given them privileged access to resources and symbols that enhance their power and provide disproportionate rewards. The corollary, according to Rosaldo, is that women would gain power either by entering the men's public world or by encouraging male participation in domestic life. Her solution assumes that males would lack sufficient interest in the domestic sphere to usurp women's authority there.

However, structural functionalists have been severely criticized for putting forth sociological arguments that serve to justify the traditional view that women's place is in the home. Although it is not entirely the fault of structural-functional theorists, "the function is" translates too easily into "the function should be" (Friedan 1963). Just because it is functional for women to stay home does not mean that women *must* stay home. Arrangements that were convenient in preliterate societies do not necessarily make sense in modern societies. For one thing, women need no longer be constantly pregnant to ensure survival of the species. For another, social inventions, such as day-care facilities, free women from these biological imperatives. Furthermore, male physical strength matters much less in our society than it did in earlier societies; anyone can "man" a computer.

Recent research shows that the role segregation hypothesized by the structural functionalists is not a universal feature of family life. For example, motherhood as a full-time occupation held only for middle-class North American women in the 1940s and 1950s (Epstein 1988). The pattern of stay-at-home wives, playing expressive, domestic roles, and breadwinner husbands, solely responsible for instrumental tasks in the public sphere, did not apply in the past to working-class families or those from racial and ethnic minorities. The fact that it characterizes only a small minority of contemporary families explains the lack of enthusiasm for structural functionalism among sociologists of gender relations.

The Conflict Perspective

The analysis of the inequality of the sexes in *The Origins of the Family, Private Property, and the State* (1884), by Karl Marx's associate, Friedrich Engels, provides the starting-point for a conflict theory of gender (Smith 1977; Fox 1982). The main idea here is that females and males are tied to the economic structure in different ways, and this difference explains why males are the more powerful gender (Nielsen 1978).

In capitalist societies, men and women constitute two separate classes. The reason: classes are defined by their relation to the means of production, and the sexes have different relations to these means. The difference flows from the distinction in capitalist societies between **commodity production** (products created for exchange in the marketplace) and the **production of use-values** (all things produced in the home). In a society based on commodity production, such as Canada and the United States, household labour, including child care, is not considered real work because it is done outside the marketplace. Men have primary responsibility for commodity production, women for the production of use-values. Herein lies women's inferior status.

In a society in which money determines value, women are a group who work outside the money economy. Their work is not worth money, is therefore valueless, is therefore not even real work. (Benston 1969)

Nevertheless, women's unpaid work in the home does serve the capitalist system. To pay women for their work would entail a massive redistribution of wealth.

Women who are employed outside the home also have a different relation to the economic structure than do men. For one thing, women's position in the family facilitates the use of women as a **reserve army of labour** (Morton 1972). They are called into the labour force when they are needed (during wartime, for example) and sent home when the need disappears. The cultural prescription that women really belong in the home assures that the women will return to the home (Glazer 1977).

Women's primary allegiance to the family is used by the capitalist system as an excuse for deploying them in menial, underpaid jobs. A large pool of unqualified women in competition for jobs depresses wages. Women are untrained, unreliable workers because their families come first. They require less money than men because they are secondary workers anyway — or so the argument goes.

Women's unpaid labour directly and indirectly subsidizes men's paid labour (Eichler 1978). Women entertain husbands' business acquaintances, type, and help with husbands' small businesses and farms, all without compensation. All these services cost money when someone outside the family performs them. This sort of work allows husbands to devote their efforts to their full-time paid work. However, women's domestic labour limits their ability to commit themselves fully and continuously to their own paid employment. Their traditional double burden constitutes part of the explanation why many women remain stuck in dull, repetitive, low-paid, unattractive jobs (Armstrong and Armstrong 1984).

In general, the conflict perspective explains women's inequality in these structural terms:

[I]t is men who own and control the essential resources. ... Ownership of the most important resource, the means of production, is mainly in the hands of a few men who have power over almost all women as well as other men. ... Men also have control of the next most important resource, access to the occupational structure and control of policy making in the major areas of social life. (Connelly and Christiansen-Ruffman 1977)

The concept of **patriarchy** emphasizes that this domination of women by men is a pervasive feature of the social organization of all kinds of societies (Smith 1983). Women are consistently located in strata below men of their own social group (Lipman-Blumen 1984). Men predominate in the highest strata of every social institution — the economic system, the political and legal systems, the family, the military, the educational and religious systems.

The conflict perspective links the position of women in developing countries with global capitalism-patriarchy (Acosta-Belen and Bose 1990). Colonialism, first in the New World, and centuries later in Africa and Asia, provided the raw materials, precious metals, and labour to support the economic development of what are today's industrialized nations. The First World nations that constitute only one-fourth of the world's population receive four-fifths of the world's income. Almost without exception, "women *everywhere* in the world are worse off than men" (Acosta-Belen and Bose 1990). This means that although women and men living in the contemporary Third World share the colonial experience, gender compounds the oppression of Third World women, just as race does for First World women of colour.

Nevertheless, according to recent elaborations on Marxian theorizing, men's power over women is not the only power differential at issue. Pleck (1981) argues that "patriarchy is a *dual* system, a system in which men oppress women, and in which men oppress themselves and each other." According to this view, the nature of men's relationships with women must be understood contextually as only a part of this more significant masculine "game." Men create hierarchies among themselves, according to such criteria of masculinity as physical strength, athletic capabilities, ability to make money. Men see women as having various uses in their competition among themselves — for example, beautiful women have traditionally been used as trophies of success.

The division between homosexual and heterosexual is a critical aspect of male–male ranking. According to Pleck (1981), "Our society uses the male heterosexual–homosexual dichotomy as a central symbol for *all* the rankings of masculinity, for the division in any groups between males who are 'real men' and have power and males who are not. Any kind of powerlessness or refusal to compete becomes imbued with the imagery of homosexuality."

Despite the foregoing, it would be a mistake to assume that women do not wield any significant social power (Lips 1991). For one thing, women often manage to resist or subvert masculine power. The distinction between **macromanipulation** and **micromanipulation** is useful here:

When the dominant group controls the major institutions of a society, it relies on macromanipulation through law, social policy, and military might, when necessary, to impose its will and ensure its rule. The less powerful become adept at micromanipulation,

using intelligence, canniness, intuition, interpersonal skill, charm, sexuality, deception, and avoidance to offset the control of the powerful. (Lipman-Blumen 1984)

Moreover, some women do have access to power beyond personal, face-to-face situations. For example, upper-class women have exercised considerable power on the boards of cultural and social welfare organizations and social reform groups (Duffy 1986).

Finally, a major point registered by conflict theorists is that traditional gender arrangements are extremely useful to the capitalist system. For example, the ideological position that women really belong in the home, that they are only temporarily in the labour force as secondary earners, obviates payment of fair wages to female workers. One reason why the multinational assembly plants along the Mexican border prefer female employees is the

fact that they are viewed as temporary workers who will accept the lowest possible wages. This is important because these labor-intensive industries are intensely competitive, quick to lay off workers if demand for their products weakens, and subject to collapse during U.S. recessions. (Warren and Bourque 1991).

Similarly, the ideology that links the breadwinner role to masculinity motivates many men to devote their lives to the performance of intrinsically unsatisfying jobs in order to take care of their families. "By training men to accept payment for their work in feelings of masculinity rather than in feelings of satisfaction, men will not demand that their jobs be made more meaningful" (Pleck 1981).

Nevertheless, as the end of the twentieth century approaches, the breadwinner ideology is weakening and the advantages for capitalism (outlined in the previous paragraph) are fading. Women's massive labour-force involvement, their educational achievements, the growth in numbers of lone-parent families headed by women, the continuing high unemployment rates for men, and the decline in real wages mitigate against capitalistic expectations that employed women will return soon to their kitchens, where they really belong (Armstrong and Armstrong 1990). And, as Marx predicted in the case of men, women brought together into the labour force develop consciousness of themselves as workers. Their increasing unionization in Canada (White 1980, 1990) and the U.S. (Blau and Ferber, 1986) is evidence of this. (Compared with men, women in unions are still underrepresented.) For another, the new economic realities discussed above are making it more difficult for men to pin their masculinity on being their families' sole breadwinners (Livingstone and Luxton 1989). We will return to these topics in the following sections.

This discussion completes the trilogy of theoretical perspectives on gender: the biological, social-psychological (or socialization), and structural explanations. These should be regarded as complementary approaches. Focusing on all three increases our understanding of the phenomenon beyond what it would be through appreciation of any one alone. Nevertheless, the various theories of gender remain incomplete. Like any new subdiscipline, the sociology of gender relations (in existence for less than 25 years) must be given time to develop fully.

Gender and Families

The feminist social movement in the wider society stimulated sociologists to think critically about the family, the primary institution for organizing gender relations in society. The insights from the women's movement led them to see the family with new eyes. Feminist revisioning of the family involves these four interrelated themes.

Rejection of Biological Determination of the Family

With some exceptions (Rossi 1984), feminist sociologists reject the assumption that family arrangements are biological in any direct or immutable way. Whether all "real" women want to be mothers, whether the inequality between traditional husbands and wives is "natural," are questioned (Duffy 1988). Luxton and Rosenberg (1986:9) remark:

The myth that all women should be wives and mothers is used over and over to justify paying women low wages in the labour force, to exclude them from many jobs, and to discourage their participation in politics. The myth of natural maternity and domesticity is used to defend the systematic exclusion of women from power.

Although the part played by biology is not denied, the social organization of reproduction, parenting, and the gender division of labour is stressed.

Important indications exist that many members of society also regard the family differently. For example, the increasing numbers of fathers pushing babies in strollers may be diminishing the impact of gender stereotypes that label child care as women's work. Though fathers' participation is not equal to mothers', they are becoming more actively involved in their children's upbringing. Indeed, the new reproductive technologies have irrevocably altered the meaning of motherhood and fatherhood. What does parenthood mean when artificial wombs are being developed by which men can be pregnant through the implantation of an embryo in the male abdomen? When women are impregnated from semen that combines donations from their husbands and strangers? When babies conceived through artificial insemination from the husband are carried by surrogate mothers? When lesbian couples become parents through artificial insemination? (McDaniel 1989).

Criticism of the Monolithic Family

Feminist scholars object to the idealization of the family with a male breadwinner and stay-at-home wife and children as "the normal, most healthy household arrangement" (Thorne 1982). First, romanticizing this traditional form makes little sense when the overwhelming majority of families in First World nations are otherwise. Second, focusing on the traditional form means ignoring or denigrating the diversity of family life experienced by lone-parent families, commuter couples, gay/lesbian families, and so on. These alternative ways of living are characterized as "sad, crazy or unnatural or perhaps even dangerous" (Luxton and Rosenberg 1986). Third, the ideology of the monolithic family reinforces the economic exploitation of women (Thorne 1982). If it is assumed that most people live in a nuclear family and that adult women have husbands to support them, then women's lower wages and disadvantaged position in the labour force are justified by the assumption that their paid work is secondary to that of men. Consequently, policy-makers overlook the problems of other sorts of families, such as the poverty of families headed by women and elderly women living alone, and the need for publicly supported child-care facilities (Eichler 1981).

Feminist scholars (Zinn 1990) also challenge a related monolithic image of the North American family as white Anglo-Saxon. Canada and the United States are, in reality, ethnically and racially diverse societies. To dismiss the family patterns of francophones, Asians, blacks, aboriginals, Hispanics, and so on, as cultural exceptions to the rule is to denigrate the rich experiences of growing numbers of Canadians and Americans.

Scepticism Concerning the Harmonious Family

Before the second wave of the feminist movement, the family was viewed as a harmonious institution, the site of love, intimacy, and protection from the strains of the outside world. Now we realize that the family has a dark side for many people. Although many families do provide the love and protection needed for children to survive and thrive and for adults to actualize their potential, a shocking number expose children, spouses (especially wives), and the elderly to violence. It is paradoxical that while the family can serve as a refuge, a place of affection, comfort, and protection, it also has the potential for being a crucible of conflict and violence (Lupri 1990).

Feminist theorizing locates the etiology of wife battering and rape in the everyday fabric of the relations between the sexes in patriarchal societies. Therefore, family violence is not viewed as a set of isolated events, confined to atypical families. Rather, abuse of family members emerges from the context of a gendered society in which male power dominates and women are "appropriate" victims of abuse (Kurz 1989). Individual men frequently use violence to maintain their power and privilege in the family (Dobash and Dobash 1979). Although research shows that women are also capable of violence against their partners (Brinkerhoff and Lupri 1988), men's

superior strength results in far greater injury to women. Wives' lesser financial resources often explain why battered women cannot easily leave abusive relationships. According to Statistics Canada, more than half the assaults against women reported to police are committed by spouses or former spouses. Men, by contrast, are assaulted by wives or former wives in only 3 percent of the cases (*The Globe and Mail*, November 19, 1992:A5).

Differentiation of Family Experiences

Feminist scholars emphasize that family is not experienced in the same way by women, men, or by female and male children (Thorne 1982). Although this observation seems self-evident in view of what we have just said about family violence, prefeminist sociology assumed otherwise. This newer view recognizes that hierarchical divisions within families produce different and conflicting interests among members (Glenn 1987), of which family violence is an extreme example. It has made possible the realization that resources (such as money and food on the table) are not necessarily shared fairly by household members (Brannen and Wilson 1987). Husbands' earnings, wives' "pin money," children's allowances — the allocation of domestic money is determined, in part, by gender, age, and family power relationships (Zelizer 1989).

The Latin American gender ideology of **machismo** and **marianismo** provide a good illustration of the differing interests of husbands and wives (Stevens 1973). *Machismo*, which means virile, fearless masculinity, "stipulates male superiority and authority, sexual freedom regardless of marital status, and physical dominance over women" (Lips 1991:150). Macho men must be strong, aggressive, physically powerful, arrogant, and devoted to the conquest of women. *Marianismo*, based on the cult of the Virgin Mary, depicts women as spiritually and morally superior to men. Women are exhorted to endure all the suffering inflicted by men's macho behaviour. The woman is to be obedient and submissive to her husband's demands and wishes. "If she is unhappy, she suffers in silence" (Whiteford 1978). Considerable controversy surrounds the actual influence of the Latin American *machismo* ideology (Ingoldsby 1991). Studies of rural Mexico indicate both the importance of male dominance and divergence from it. Husbands and wives assert that the husband has the last word in decision-making. However, in actual practice, power is more evenly divided in household decisions, major purchases, and upbringing of the children (Wiest 1983). Women's increased involvement in wage labour is a threat to *machismo*, which holds men to be economic providers.

Gender and Work

Domestic Labour

Whether or not they also work for pay, most adult women shoulder the primary responsibility for domestic labour. In Canada and the United States, and even more so in developing nations such as Mexico, women spend more of their time working than do men (United Nations 1991). The second wave of the women's movement called attention to the hidden work performed in the home. If life is to proceed smoothly, someone must buy and prepare food, clean, care for the children, maintain contact with kinfolk, and so on. That "someone" is usually the female partner in relationships. For instance, a study of the lives of Mexico City women doing industrial piecework in their homes reported that domestic work is *never* reallocated to men (Beneria and Roldan 1987). Regardless of individual variation in talent and inclination, society consigns "a large segment of the population to the role of homemaker solely on the basis of sex [gender]" (Bem and Bem 1971).

Feminist scholars urged that these hereto invisible domestic activities be defined as productive *work*, and counted as labour in the economies of families and societies. For example, the value of household work in Canada for 1981 was estimated at between $121 and $139 billion. These estimates represented 35.7 percent and 41 per-

Most adult women shoulder the primary responsibility for domestic labour.

cent, respectively, of Canada's gross national product that year (Swinamer 1990). There are several reasons why the women's movement sought to gain societal acknowledgement that domestic labour constitutes legitimate work with economic value. First, failure to recognize and measure women's contributions led to distortions in economic decision-making at the international level. The World Plan of Action of the Objectives of the International Women's Year, adopted in Mexico City in 1975, stated that such failure disparages and devalues women's work and perpetuates the exploitation of women (United Nations 1991).

Second, such acknowledgement was a prerequisite for securing legal recognition of wives' contributions to the family enterprise. Until the late 1970s, most Canadian provinces had family property laws that ignored wives' contributions to farms and other businesses. Second, feminists argued that women's traditional responsibility for most child care and household chores has severely disadvantaged their labour-force participation. Because cultural scripts direct young girls' attention to marriage and family, their career plans are too often "short-term, itinerant, contingent and vague" (Duffy et al. 1989). After marriage, the domestic responsibilities carried by women in addition to their outside employment amount to a second full-time job for many women. As mentioned earlier, this double burden makes it difficult for women to commit themselves as fully as men to paid employment.

Work done in the home will continue to be important to partners of both sexes. Because it "is essential to daily functioning, the allocation of household chores often is a subject of difficult negotiation and conflict among household members" (Coverman 1989). As more and more women have outside employment, male partners are experiencing increasing pressure to assume a more equitable share of household work.

Paid Work

For various reasons, including stereotypical views of male and female abilities, societal scripts that instruct women to give priority to their families, and the higher value placed on males, the labour-force experiences of women and men differ. These distinctions are detailed opposite.

The experiences of men and women in the labour force are very different.

Labour-Force Participation. Since World War II, Canadian society has witnessed an astonishing change in labour-force participation. As wages failed to keep pace with prices, as more money was required to pay for things like mortgages, as technology made housework lighter, as more women obtained higher education, and as birth rates fell, married women in massive numbers moved into the labour force (Armstrong 1987). The increasing number of single-parent families headed by females is another important reason why women need jobs. The year 1980 marked the

TABLE 5-2   Women's Labour-Force Participation

Region	Year	Women's Percentage of Total Labour Force
Canada	1989[a]	44.3
Quebec	1989[a]	43.0
United States	1989[b]	44.8
Mexico	1988[b]	30.0

SOURCE: [a]Labour Canada, *Women in the Labour Force* (Ottawa: Supply and Services Canada, 1990); [b]Jean Stockard and Miriam M. Johnson, *Sex and Gender in Society*, 2nd edition (Englewood Cliffs, NJ: Prentice-Hall, 1992).

TABLE 5-3 Percentage of Female Graduates in Various Disciplines in Canada, 1975 and 1990

Female Graduates	1975	1990
All disciplines	44.4	55.7
Male-dominated disciplines	16.8	36.1
Veterinary medicine	21.0	63.1
Zoology	28.2	54.1
Law	20.8	47.2
Medicine	23.9	45.9
Business management and commerce	13.3	45.8
Political science	25.4	43.7
Agriculture	22.0	41.3
Mathematics	30.8	39.7
Chemistry	19.3	36.7
Dentistry	9.6	35.8
Economics	16.6	32.5
Architecture	10.7	32.5
Engineering	1.8	11.7
Physics	8.9	15.1

SOURCE: Statistics Canada, and adapted from *The Globe and Mail*, December 4, 1992, p. B1.

first time in Canadian history that a majority of women were in the labour force. It also marked the year that 51 percent of American women were in the labour force (England and Browne 1992). By 1989, the participation rate for women was 57.9 percent. Only 43 percent of Quebec women were labour-force participants in that year (Labour Canada 1990). The comparable figures for American and Mexican women are 56.6 percent and 35.3 percent, respectively (Stockard and Johnson 1992).

The above figures underestimate the true situation. Many women do work that remains invisible to the government authorities who compile statistics. The indispensable contribution of women to family farms often goes unappreciated (Ghorayshi 1989). The same is true for North American women who clean houses, babysit, type essays, do alterations and repairs on clothing, and so on. In developing countries, such as Mexico, much of the economic activity of women, especially poor women, also goes uncounted. For example, urban women are involved in domestic service, street vending, and doing sewing or crafts in their homes (Stockard and Johnson 1992).

In comparison with the unprecedented numbers of women entering paid employment, the Canadian male labour-force participation rate has shown a slow decline over the years. Between 1911 and 1979, the male rate dropped from 91 percent to 78.4 percent (Statistics Canada 1974). By 1989, the participation rate was 76.7 percent (Labour Canada 1990). The decline in the male labour force is concentrated at both ends of the male age distribution, as more young men aged 15–19 years remain in school and as more men aged 65 and older retire. Also, economic recessions have had a greater impact on men's than on women's employment (Parliament 1990).

More Canadians now have part-time jobs because of complex changes in the economy. This is especially true for young people. However, in 1989, 24.5 percent of women's employment, compared with 15.1 percent of men's employment, was part-time. This greater involvement of females in part-time work points to the priority of women's home responsibilities. Although domestic and child-care responsibilities explain the involvement of many women in part-time work, part-time work is generally poorly paid, offers few benefits, and is dead-end work (Duffy and Pupo 1992). Also, "it is primarily as part-time workers that many women constitute a flexible pool of labor, a floating reserve" (Armstrong and Armstrong 1990).

Despite the sharp increase in women's labour-force participation and the publicity given to female pioneers in nontraditional occupations ranging from astronauts to truck drivers, work continues to be gender-segregated. "The division of many occupations and employments into 'male' and 'female' is a common phenomenon in all countries, regardless of political systems, levels of economic development, and social structures" (Peitchinis 1989). The concentration of one sex in a relatively few occupations in which its members greatly outnumber those of the other sex is called **occupational gender segregation**. Occupations filled mostly with women include clerks in retail stores, assembly-line workers in

Equity Law's First Report Card

It has been described as having a "tremendous impact" or being "less than useless."

Canada's first employment-equity law for the private sector, which aims to increase the hiring and promotion of women and minorities, has completed its five-year test run. Now the federal government must decide if it is working.

The statistical score card for 1991, released recently by Employment and Immigration Canada, shows that the wage gap between visible minorities and other employees has grown over the five years; that women received more than half of all promotions every year under the law, and in the final year reached their targeted numbers in the work force — though the target itself may be outdated; and that disabled and aboriginal employees, though their numbers have grown each year, are still being hired and promoted in numbers far short of their availability in the work force.

The main question for Ottawa is whether to switch the law's emphasis. Currently, it's on reporting — employers face fines of up to $50,000 for failing to count minorities in their work force. But a House of Commons committee and minority groups want the focus to change to meeting targets — employers would be obliged to meet goals they set themselves, based on the number of positions open each year, and to explain why they fell short, with substantial fines for persistent failure.

"We recommended [fines] but that's after a process which is not just straight prosecution if you don't meet your target," said Alan Redway, the chairman of the House of Commons employment-equity committee, in a recent interview.

Instead, the committee seeks a co-operative approach to avoid long legal battles. The Employment Department and the employer would first discuss whether targets have to be adjusted, based on the employer's circumstances, and how to improve the employer's record.

"If there was a decision not to comply come high water or whatever, the report does call for prosecution," Mr. Redway said.

The law applies only to companies of 100 or more employees in the federally regulated work force, which includes banks, transportation and communications companies and Crown corporations. About 620,000 people working for 350 employers are covered by the law.

It changed the focus from traditional human-rights laws, where it is up to the employee who feels wronged to complain; under employment equity the onus is on the employer to show progress. The law was a softer approach than that of many U.S. jurisdictions — even the name, employment equity, was an effort to avoid the antagonisms of U.S.-style affirmative action.

For the targeted minorities, the progress has been far from adequate. They see much of the apparent progress as illusory — for example, disabled people say their higher numbers reflect a broader definition of disability that includes more people.

"The progress for women is glacial and for other groups it's minimal or even negative," Judy Rebick, president of the National Action Committee on the Status of Women, said in an interview.

To business, the progress is noteworthy. They say the government's year-by-year statistical compilations of their hiring and promotion records may obscure how much work they are doing to make their work forces more diverse and equitable.

"A lot of people make assumptions about how rapidly you can change the nature of a work force," said Bruce Anderson, executive vice-president of Omnibus Consulting Inc., a Toronto-based firm that helps businesses develop employment-equity plans. "They think it can be done much more quickly than it can. There just aren't that many opportunities, particularly in a recession."

Under the 1986 law, a review of its effectiveness was required after five years. That review, completed earlier this year by a special House of Commons committee, has been in the gov-

ernment's hands since mid-May. The government had been expected to introduce amendments to the law, but now says it will issue a response to the committee report without putting amendments forward at the same time. The response is expected this winter.

"My sense is it's not [a priority], quite frankly, which is extremely disappointing to me," said Mr. Redway, a Progressive Conservative from Don Valley East, a central neighbourhood in multicultural Toronto.

His committee found little progress on the whole, though he said not all employers should be painted with the same brush. He said he had expected legislation to be brought forward quickly and he is not quite sure why it won't be.

"I know that just as in the beginning when there were two points of view as to whether we should have this legislation, there are certainly two points of view as to whether we should bring in substantial amendments at this time."

Monique Vézina, Minister of State for Employment and Immigration, which oversees employment equity, did not respond to a request for an interview. An employee in the minister's office said the department's leading spokespersons on the subject are on holiday until next week.

A review of five years of reports from the Minister of State for Employment and Immigration found a mixed bag of results:

Women: Made up 44 percent of the general work force in the 1986 census, the benchmark figure for setting goals. In 1987, they made up 41.2 per cent of the federally regulated work force; in 1991, they made up 44.1 per cent, largely because more men left their jobs than women. They were about 5 per cent of upper-level management in 1987, and 8.38 per cent in 1991; about 32 per cent of middle and other managers in 1987 and 40.8 per cent in 1991. Their earnings, measured against men's average full-time salaries, equalled 70.7 cents for every dollar in 1987, and 72.7 cents in 1991.

Natives: Made up 2.1 per cent of the general work force in the 1986 census. In 1987, they made up .70 per cent of the federally regulated work force; that rose to .96 per cent in 1991. They earned about 9 cents less on the dollar than non-native workers in 1987, and about 12 cents less in 1991. Ten per cent of native male workers were managers or professionals in 1991, compared to 24 per cent of non-native men.

Disabled: Made up 5.4 [percent] of the general work force in the 1986 census. In 1987, they made up 1.6 per cent of the federally regulated work force; in 1991 they made up 2.5 per cent. Representation was highest in Regina (4.09 per cent) and lowest in Montreal (1.65 per cent) in 1991. They were 1.13 per cent of full-time hirings in 1991, up from .7 per cent in 1987 but slightly lower than in 1990.

Visible minorities: Made up 6.3 per cent of the general work force in the 1986 census. In 1987, they made up about 6 per cent of the federally regulated work force; in 1991, 7.55 per cent. In 1987 visible-minority women earned the same as all women, and visible-minority men earned 96 per cent of what all men earned; in 1991, the minority women earned 95.5 cents for every dollar earned by all women, and the men earned 92.15 cents for each dollar paid to all men. They made up 8.02 per cent of hirings in 1991, up from 5.5 per cent in 1987 but down from 10.87 in 1990.

Ms. Rebick says women's higher numbers in the work force reflect demographic changes since 1986 and a worsening economy that has forced more women to seek jobs. Gains have been made largely by white women. The increase of women in middle and other management means little because these managers are paid from $20,000 to $70,000, and women are concentrated in the lower levels, she said.

David Baker, spokesman for a Toronto legal-aid clinic for handicapped people, said some employers are using a broader definition of disability to include people who wear eyeglasses, for example, whether their poor vision affects them at work or not. Employers argue that many disabled people do not identify themselves as such, making the numbers look smaller than they really are.

The First 5 Years

A look back at employment equity, which covers the federally regulated workforce of about 600 000 employees of banks, communications and transportation firms, and Crown corporations*

		Employees (%)	Full-Time Hirings (%)	Full-Time Promotions (%)
Women	1987	41.20	36.80	51.05
	1988	42.12	40.51	55.42
	1989	42.53	41.31	54.65
	1990	43.74	42.68	58.09
	1991	44.11	38.52	55.75
Aboriginal	1987	0.70	0.61	0.59
	1988	0.73	0.86	0.61
	1989	0.79	1.17	0.79
	1990	0.85	1.44	0.83
	1991	0.96	1.66	1.05
Disabled	1987	1.60	0.65	1.40
	1988	1.71	0.81	1.43
	1989	2.34	1.32	2.44
	1990	2.39	1.33	2.84
	1991	2.50	1.13	2.75
Visible minorities	1987	6.00	5.24	6.92
	1988	5.69	7.85	7.66
	1989	6.67	10.90	9.52
	1990	7.09	10.87	11.09
	1991	7.55	8.02	10.92

*Available in workforce: women (44%); aboriginals (2.1%); disabled (5.4%); and visible minorities (6.3%).

"For severely disabled people, there are going to be accommodations required which cost real money and employers are not voluntarily going to spend that money. It may be that we need to look at stronger actions [by government] in relation to disability than for other groups," Mr. Baker said.

Anna Chiappa, executive director of the Canadian Ethnocultural Council, which represents 37 organizations, said the 1986 benchmark figure for visible minorities is outdated — they probably make up 8 per cent of the available work force. (Statistics Canada expects the 1991 census figures to be ready by March or April.)

Her group doesn't support the setting of rigid quotas, but does want an independent agency to monitor employers' progress. "Quotas would just be counter-productive from the point of view of the kind of reaction we would get from employers."

Nancy Leamen, director of human resources policy for the Canadian Bankers Association, said the early years of the law were a time for the banks to create a framework for collecting information. More recently the banks have focused on special measures, such as targeted recruiting of minorities or specialized training and support for natives and disabled employees, she said.

"It's had a tremendous impact," she said of the law. "A lot of people might misunderstand that because it hasn't had a tremendous impact on the figures. It has required those regulated by it to undertake special measures, pro-active programs."

Source:

Sean Fine, *The Globe and Mail*, December 30, 1992, p. A1.

the electronics industry, secretaries, teachers, nurses, and social workers. Men predominate in the highest-status professions (such as doctor, dentist, architect), in higher levels of management, in crafts (plumbing, carpentry, electrical), in assembly-line jobs in durable manufacturing (such as autos), and in jobs involving outdoor labour (England and Brown 1992). Even in newly emerging computer-related occupations, men tend to be managers, directors, systems analysts, and programmers, while women are data-entry operators, tape librarians, and accounts clerks (Peitchinis 1989).

Work in developing societies such as Mexico is also gender-segregated. In the Latin American countries, men predominate in agriculture and industry, and women in service occupations. Women are increasingly involved in the informal economic sector of home-based industries and petty trading (United Nations 1991).

Gender-segregation of work is declining slowly in developed nations such as Canada and the United States. Most of the decrease is coming from women entering "men's" jobs, rather than men entering "women's" jobs. For example, increasing numbers of women are enrolling in university degree programs in law, medicine, business administration, engineering, and so on. Men show less interest than women in challenging gender-stereotyped notions about work (for example, very few men enter nursing programs) because women's work tends to be lower paid and stigmatized by its association with femininity.

Earnings are probably the single most important indicator of women's labour-market progress (Calzavara 1985). On average, Canadian and American women earn about two-thirds the income of their male counterparts (Labour Canada 1990; England and Browne 1992). The difference between the earnings of Canadian women and men persists at all educational levels. Women with a university degree, the highest-paid group, made only 70 percent of the average earnings of male graduates (Parliament 1990).

When worldwide averages are calculated, women receive 30 to 40 percent less than men for doing the same work. Moreover, much of women's work is not recognized as economically productive and not remunerated at all (United Nations 1991). In developed nations, gender differences in income are largely attributable to the gender segregation of work, that is, the clustering of women in lower-paying "female" occupations, and to the hampering effect of women's domestic obligations. However, discrimination is responsible for an estimated five to ten percent of the earnings gap (Peitchinis 1989).

The global transformation of work at the end of the twentieth century is having profound effects on both developed and developing nations (Acker 1992). Gender relations are at the heart of these economic changes. This global transformation involves accelerated international competition, and technological innovations, as well as new ways of organizing work. Employers' search for lower labour costs leads to a shifting global division of labour that is, at the same time, a shifting gender division of labour. Increasing proportions of women are being caught up in the world's wage economy. At the same time, "good male" jobs that guarantee lifetime employment with adequate wages are declining. In the United States, for example, industrial plant closings and a decline in blue-collar employment is linked to the emergence of a new, cheaper industrial force in the Third World (Acosta-Belen and Bose 1990). This means more unemployment and more people surviving in the informal economy. Women's paid work is everywhere becoming increasingly necessary for family survival. Although some people are able to take advantage of newly created job opportunities, groups that are already vulnerable, such as women, and minorities tend to suffer (Acker 1992).

International investment in Latin America has drawn more Mexican women into the labour force, especially in urban areas (Nash and Safa 1986). For example, the *maquiladoras* (subsidiaries of multinational corporations) on the United States–Mexico border prefer women workers in their plants because of women's supposedly "greater docility, manual dexterity, and the fact that they are viewed as temporary workers who will accept the lowest possible wages" (Warren and Bourque 1991). What were "comparatively well-paid manual jobs held by men in the developed regions have become low-paid, exploitative jobs for women in developing regions" (United Nations 1991). Enhanced contribution to family resources enhances women's sense of autonomy in the domestic situation (Beneria and Roldan 1987). However, as mentioned earlier, many

Mexican women are experiencing a double burden of domestic and wage work. According to United Nations figures (1991), until 1975, Latin American women worked almost three hours a week less than men. Now, women are working, on the average, 5.6 more hours a week than men. Also, the fact that women's involvement in wage work occurs in the context of high male unemployment often makes family relations difficult.

Social scientists have much to learn about the complex effects of the global transformation of work on the lives of men and women (Tiano 1987).

Feminist Movements

When people feel neglected, frustrated, or mistreated by the existing social order, they sometimes band together in a social movement to seek a collective solution to their problems. Despite the worldwide historical prevalence of female disadvantage relative to that of males, women's collective revolt against this disadvantage has occurred only in the last century (Chafetz and Dworkin 1986). The first wave of feminism, the Suffrage Movement, developed in the closing decades of the nineteenth and the beginning decades of the twentieth centuries. It took place in North American, European, and other Commonwealth societies.

The end of the 1960s saw women, first in the United States, and then in many other parts of the world, once again collectively organize to protest and improve their lot. For instance, in Montreal:

In November 1969, close to two hundred women, activists from socialist and nationalist groups as well as women who advocated social change, staged a nighttime demonstration in which they paraded in chains. They thought police officers would not dare interfere with them; but the police packed the demonstrators into vans and took them to the police station, where they spent the night. (Clio Collective 1987)

The second wave of feminism, which continues to this day, is one of the most profound political and cultural phenomena of this century. This social movement was itself, in part, a reaction to various structural developments that took place during and after the Second World War. In Canada and the United States, these inter-related societal changes included the disappearance of single-paycheque jobs capable of supporting entire families; the expansion of industries such as personal services, which drew heavily upon female workers; the massive influx of women in the labour force and the consequent decline of the male breadwinner role (Armstrong and Armstrong 1984); more liberal divorce laws; and new reproductive technology. In addition, both men and women were affected by the liberating cultural currents of the 1960s and 1970s: the civil rights, anti-war, student, and gay liberation movements. Francophone feminists were also influenced signicantly by events in Quebec, such as secularism and the revival of nationalism and in the Quiet Revolution following the Duplessis era (Pestieau 1976). In summary, much of the upheaval in people's lives that is frequently attributed to the women's movement in reality has other and prior causes to which the feminist movement was responding.

Feminism in Canada and the United States articulated many sources of women's discontent (Adamson et al. 1988). This movement challenges gender stereotypes and the division of labour in home and marketplace based on these outdated images. It seeks fair treatment of females and males in legislation and courtrooms. It fights for equal access of the sexes to education, training in the male-dominated trades, and executive promotion ladders. It has uncovered and named violence against women, including sexual harassment, incest, date rape, and wife abuse. It seeks to enhance women's political representation. Feminism "has exposed the heterosexism and racism that pervade the entire social system and contribute to the double and triple oppression of lesbians, immigrants, and women of colour" (Adamson et al. 1988). In short, feminists struggle to secure greater power in their personal relationships, families, places of work, and indeed in the running of society as a whole.

The United Nations Conference on Women, held in Mexico City in 1975, was an important catalyst for Latin American feminism (Chinchilla 1991). Although the Latin and North American movements all seek to enhance women's status, feminism varies from country to country (Sternbach et al. 1992). To take an extreme example, patriarchal oppression assumes a different meaning in countries ruled by military dictatorships:

Women in Argentina used their "moral force" as mothers, grandmothers, and sisters of the disappeared to demand an accounting of relatives who had been victims of political repression, while in Chile women converted homes and neighborhoods into centers of collective resistance and survival after the emergence of the Pinochet dictatorship. (Chinchilla 1991)

Contemporary Latin American feminism is "a powerful, vibrant, energetic, creative, and exuberant political force" (Sternbach et al. 1992). Mexican feminism, in particular, concerns itself with a variety of issues, including poverty, economic development, women's health and reproductive rights, and violence against women. Though the challenges in developing countries are enormous, the following example illustrates that progress is slowly being made.

Mexico City has set an interesting precedent: During rush hours, when women are likely to be sexually harassed on crowded subway trains, there are some trains reserved just for women and children. Women may ride on the same trains as the men, but if they do not want to, they have a choice. This is not an ideal solution; it would be preferable to find a way of stopping sexual harassment so that everyone could ride on the same train without worrying. (Lips 1991).

Nevertheless, Mexico City authorities acknowledge that women should not be exposed to sexual harassment.

The Agenda of the Feminist Movement

Despite significant gains made during the second wave of feminism, formidable obstacles to the goal of gender equality remain (Mackie 1991). The struggles ahead concern both national and global arenas as Canadian and American feminists acknowledge their sisterhood with women around the globe. Four compelling, inter-related issues that women struggled with in the 1970s and 1980s remain paramount in the 1990s.

The first issue is the feminism of poverty. In Canada and throughout the world, the poor are disproportionately women and children. The second issue concerns work in the labour force and the home. Until women have fair access to job training, employment opportunities, equal pay for work of equal value, and affordable day care of decent quality, they remain financially dependent on men and subject to their authority. Many women without male financial support, especially single mothers and elderly widows, experience poverty. As discussed above, women's status outside the home depends upon equitable division of work within the home.

Third, in the 1990s, women in many countries must continue the struggle for their own reproductive freedom. "Reproductive freedom" means control over the timing and number of children to be brought into the world. Included in this are the sensitive issues of contraception, abortion, and new reproductive technologies.

Finally, there is the dreadful problem of violence against women. Women throughout the world are disproportionately victims of sexual assault, domestic battering, date rape, child abuse, ritual mutilation, and sexual harassment at work. Feminists understand violence against women to be an inevitable consequence of gendered societies in which male power predominates.

The contemporary gender-stratification system favours men as a group. Not many men would willingly forfeit the power, privileges, and resources that accrue to those at the top of the gender hierarchy. However, masculinity exacts high costs, as well as high rewards. For example, the traditional linkage between masculinity and work fails to satisfy the needs of many men. "Each day men sell little pieces of themselves in order to try to buy them back each night and weekend with the coin of 'fun'" (Mills 1951). Insistence that males achieve, be aggressve and competitive, and resist emotional expression has been described as the "lethal aspect" of the male role (Jourard 1964). The higher male suicide rates and earlier death rates appear, in large part, to be consequences of the masculine role.

Despite the foregoing, social definitions of masculinity are changing. Gay liberation politics continue to call into question the conventional understanding of maleness (Carrigan, Connell, and Lee 1987). In the 1980s and 1990s, small numbers of men belong to groups seeking equality for men who have lost custody of their children, self-help for their violent behaviour, or intellectual understanding of "the new man." The flavour of these groups has been therapeutic or concerned with self-improvement. Although their numbers are as yet relatively small, some men are seriously considering how society must be restructured to achieve gender equality. "Nothing is more certain than that such a goal will never be reached if women are the only ones who change" (Lips 1991).

Traditional gender arrangements continue because they are based on power differences. The ideology that sustains these arrangements is instilled through the socialization process and buttressed by most societal institutions.

SUMMARY

1. The sociology of gender relations examines masculinity and femininity across cultures and historical periods. This subdiscipline, inspired by the feminist movement, attempts to remedy sociology's previous exclusion of women.
2. Human social life is based on the relationships between the sexes. The sexes are both differentiated and ranked.
3. According to the study of animals, the anthropological record, psychosexual abnormalities, and research on hormones, biology seems to be directly involved in cognitive gender differences and aggressiveness and indirectly involved in the female–male division of labour. However, in gender patterns, as in social behaviour in general, both nature *and* nurture are implicated.
4. Theories based on biology, socialization, and social structure provide complementary explanations of gender.
5. The socialization process teaches children society's gender scripts, which include gender stereotypes and gender-role attitudes. As well, children acquire their gender identity through this process.
6. The social-structural approach assumes that gender results from external social factors, not individual characteristics. The structural-functional and conflict perspectives are examples of these macrosociological theories.
7. Feminist revisioning of the family resulted in rejection of previous assumptions that family arrangements are biologically determined

and monolithic. Also, families are not always harmonious. Women, children, and men have somewhat different experiences of family life.
8. Women are increasingly involved in wage labour. Nevertheless, they tend to do more than their fair share of work in the home.
9. The women's and men's liberation movements have pressed for more egalitarian social arrangements and healthier definitions of gender.

GLOSSARY

Androgyny. Presence of both masculine and feminine characteristics within individuals of both sexes.

Commodity production. Goods and services created for exchange in the marketplace.

Cultural universals. Behaviour patterns found in many cultures.

Gender. Societal definition of appropriate female and male traits and behaviours.

Gender assignment. The designation of a person as female or male.

Gender identity. The individual's conviction of being male or female.

Gender-role attitudes. People's beliefs about the status of the genders and appropriate gender division of labour in the home and workplace.

Gender scripts. The details of a society's ideas about masculinity and femininity contained, for example, in gender stereotypes and gender-role attitudes.

Gender socialization. The lifelong processes through which people learn to be feminine or masculine according to the expectations current in their society.

Gender transcendence. Ideal socialization goal in which masculinity and femininity are superseded as ways of labelling and experiencing psychological traits. Boy/girl and male/female would then refer exclusively to biological distinctions.

Machismo. A Latin American gender ideology that depicts men as strong, aggressive, physically powerful, arrogant, and devoted to the conquest of women.

Macromanipulation. Use by the dominant group of the major societal institutions — such as law, religion, and the military — to regulate thinking and behaviour.

Marianismo. A Latin American gender ideology that portrays women as spiritually and morally superior to men.

Micromanipulation. Use by the less powerful of intelligence, interpersonal skill, charm, sexuality, deception, and so on to offset the control of the powerful.

Occupational gender segregation. The concentration of one sex in a relatively few occupations in which its members greatly outnumber those of the other sex.

Patriarchy. A society oriented toward and dominated by males.

Production of use-values. Goods and services produced in the home.

Reserve army of labour. According to conflict theorists, women constitute a flexible labour supply, drawn into the labour market when needed and sent home when the need is past.

Sex. The biology of femaleness and maleness.

Stereotype. Folk beliefs about the attributes characterizing a social category (such as the genders or ethnic groups) on which there is substantial agreement.

FURTHER READING

Beneria, Lourdes, and Martha Roldan. *The Crossroads of Class and Gender: Industrial Homework, Subcontracting, and Household Dynamics in Mexico City.* Chicago: University of Chicago Press, 1987. Interviews with 140 industrial homeworkers show the connections between changing labour-market conditions and the household.

DeKeseredy, Walter S., and Ronald Hinch. *Woman Abuse: Sociological Perspectives.* Toronto: Thompson Educational Publishing, 1991. Discusses date rape, spousal abuse, sexual assault, and corporate violence against women.

Ferree, Myra Marx. "Beyond separate spheres: Feminism and family research." *Journal of Marriage and the Family* 52(1990):866–884. Analyzes the ways gender is constructed in families through symbolic and structural dimensions of labour, paid and unpaid.

Kaufman, Michael (ed.). *Beyond Patriarchy.* Toronto: Oxford University Press, 1987. A collection of articles exploring the links between masculinity and social structure.

Lakoff, Robin. *Talking Power: The Politics of Language.* New York: Basic Books, 1990. Gender is discussed sociolinguistically in Chapter 11.

Mackie, Marlene. *Gender Relations in Canada: Further Explorations.* Toronto: Butterworths, 1991. A comprehensive study of gender in Canadian society.

Martin, Emily. "The egg and the sperm: How science has constructed a romance based on stereotypical male–female roles." *Signs* 16(1991):485–501. An account of how science's views are shaped by its sexist cultural context.

Vorst, Jesse, et al. *Race, Class, Gender: Bonds and Barriers.* Society for Socialist Studies. Toronto: Between the Lines, 1989. Eleven Canadian scholars analyze the combined impact of race, class, and gender.

West, Candace, and Don. H. Zimmerman. "Doing gender." *Gender & Society* 1(1987):125–151. Views gender as a routine accomplishment of everyday life.

CHAPTER 6

Aging and Later Life

VICTOR W. MARSHALL
CAROLYN J. ROSENTHAL

From the early years of sociology, scholars have been interested in the ways aging affects social life. Today, unlike earlier times, almost every Canadian can expect to grow old and, because of the aging of the "baby boom," an ever-increasing number will do so (see Chapter 8). Even in Third World societies, for the first time, large proportions of the population can expect to live into their later years.

Mannheim (1952) suggested a mental experiment in which we should try to imagine "what the social life of man would be like if one generation lived forever and none followed to replace it." Mannheim's experiment, like much contemporary science fiction, directs attention to the ways in which the organization of society has taken into account human aging and mortality. Moore (1966) has described the paradox that human beings are mortal while, in a sense, societies are immortal. To him, as to Mannheim, aging is a key aspect of society as well as an opportunity for social change to occur.

The growing proportion and number of older Canadians, as well as the decreasing proportion and number of young people, affect every aspect of social life. Because of population aging, changes will continue to be made in the way we allocate work and leisure at various points of the life course. On the whole, young adults enter the labour force at a later age than they did 85 years ago, and there are proportionately fewer of them because of continuing low fertility. Retirement, now a taken-for-granted stage of life, was quite rare at the beginning of this century. Our ideas about education are now less tied to the early years and include the concepts of "life-long learning" and "continuing education." Family life is also changing, as people find their parents and grandparents reaching ages thought highly unlikely by Canadians at the time of Confederation. With increasing numbers and proportions of older people in our society, new concerns arise about the ability of social welfare and health care systems to meet the needs of this growing segment of our population.

The sociology of aging is the scientific study of the way in which age is relevant or "makes a difference" in social life and social structure. Age and changes in age make a difference for both individual life and social organization. Our approach therefore encompasses both the experiences of aging individuals and the dynamics of social institutions as they are affected by that age structure. The sociology of aging is therefore not just about "the aged" but about the entire society.

Because of population aging, changes will continue to be made in the way we allocate work and leisure at various points of the life course.

Population Aging

Let us begin with a basic reference point at the beginning of this century. In 1901, of about 5.5 million Canadians, just 5.2 percent were aged 65 or more. In 1991, 11.6 percent of our 27 million people were age 65 or over. The percentage will rise in ensuing years, with the extent of that increase depending primarily on the fertility rate. The rate at which people who are already born will die is changing, but this has less impact on population aging than the numbers to be born, which can change significantly over time with changes in the fertility rate. According to one projection, if Canadian fertility rates increase to 2.1 from their current level of 1.7, then the percentage

of the population aged 65 and older will be 12.8 by 2001 and 19.5 by 2051. However, if fertility rates decline to 1.4 — a level close to that currently experienced in some European countries — the percentage of the population aged 65 and older would rise to 13.6 by 2001 and 29.1 by 2051 (Denton, Feaver, and Spencer 1987).

All population projections rely on assumptions about fertility, mortality, immigration, and emigration. Table 6-1 is based on a continuance of the low fertility and immigration rates that now characterize Canadian society but modest increases in life expectancy. By these assumptions, the percentage increases, together with increases in the total size of the population, translate into very large increases in the *number* of old persons. Assuming continuing low fertility, the number of older Canadians is projected to reach 7.1 million by 2031, compared with about 2.5 million now (Messinger and Powell 1987). Of these, a large

TABLE 6-1 Population Breakdown and Projections for Selected Age Groups, Canada (Thousands)

Year	0–17		18–64		65+		Total
1991	5 692	20.8	18 434	69.5	3 169	11.6	27 296
2001	6 464	22.7	18 181	63.7	3 884	13.6	28 529
2011	5 927	20.1	19 055	64.5	4 544	15.4	29 526
2021	5 780	19.2	18 374	61.2	5 871	19.6	30 025
2031	5 537	18.6	17 114	57.5	7 128	23.9	29 779

NOTE: The 1991 figures are actual population breakdowns rather than projections. The age groups for the 1991 figures are 0–14, 15–64, 65+. The age groups for all other years are those listed at the top of the table columns. Projection for the year 2001 assumes a fertility rate of 1.66 children per woman, net immigration of 50 000, and life expectancy at birth to increase to 74.9 for males and 81.6 for females by the year 1996.
SOURCE: 1991 figures are taken from Statistics Canada, 1992, *Age, Sex and Marital Status, The Nation* (Ottawa: Minister of Industry, Science and Technology, Cat. 93-310), p. 6. Projections for other years are from Hans Messinger and Brian J. Powell, "The implications of Canada's aging society on social expenditures," *Aging In Canada: Social Perspectives*, 2nd edition, Victor W. Marshall, ed. (Toronto: Fitzhenry and Whiteside, 1987), pp. 569–585.

proportion will be very old people in their late seventies and eighties, because of increases in life expectancy at later ages (Dumas 1987:13). Over the same period the numbers of persons aged less than eighteen, after an initial rise, actually declines to a point below the current level.

The age structure of the population is characterized not only by the numbers and proportions in different age groups but also by the median age. The current median age of the Canadian population is about 33.5 and is projected to increase to 42 by the year 2051 (Statistics Canada 1992).

Changes in the age structure of the population vary greatly by gender. Women live about seven years longer than men and currently outnumber men in every age category after age 50–59 (Gee and Kimball 1987:18). In 1991, women were 58 percent of those aged 65 or older, and 69.5 percent of those aged 85 and older (Statistics Canada 1992). By the year 2031, there will be 148 women for every 100 men aged 65 or older, and in the aged 80 and older category, there are projected to be 229 women for every 100 men, compared with a ratio of 192/100 today (Denton, Feaver, and Spencer 1987:22). Not only is the gap in life expectancy between men and women large, it is widening. For example, female life expectancy in the past fifteen years has increased by about two years for women but only about a quarter of a year for men.

Income, Health, and Gender Differentiation among the Aged

Just as the lives of young Canadians differ greatly depending on factors such as their class of origin and their gender, the same factors differentiate people in the later years. In the later years, as well, health becomes an important differentiating feature among people.

Income Differences

Probably the most critical personal dilemma facing the aging individual is difficulty in maintaining an adequate income. At the same time, the provision of income security is an important policy issue facing the society as a whole. In our society, the basic sources of income for most people are tied to their participation in the labour force or to their connection to a labour-force participant. The problem for older people stems from their almost total exclusion from the labour market by the social institution of retirement. As recently as half a century ago, about half of Canadian males over the age of 65 were still in the labour force. In 1991, only 11.3 percent of males and 3.5 percent of females aged 65 or older were still in the labour force, and most people retire before age 65 (Gibson and Foot 1993). In addition, the majority of older women have been prevented by social custom and gender discrimination in the workplace from having the experience of regular, consistent labour-force participation. This diminishes their ability to secure pension entitlements for their later years.

Public transfer payments are the major source of income in retirement. Canada has a three-tiered retirement income system (Powell and Martin 1980). The first tier consists of the federal Old Age Security Program (OAS). All persons aged 65 or older who meet residence requirements receive OAS payments ($379 per month in January 1993) regardless of their work history. Also in the first tier is the Guaranteed Income Supplement (GIS) and the Spouse's Allowance program. The GIS currently provides maximum payments of about $450 per month for a single person and $300 for a married person (these levels are adjusted to inflation). The spouse's allowance is income-tested and provides benefits to people aged 60–64 who are spouses of old-age pensioners. Various provinces add additional support, some of it income-tested, ranging from about $220 to about $1200, depending on province. Currently, about one-third of the total income received by Canada's older population comes from the first tier (Messinger and Powell 1987:572).

The second tier consists of the Canada Pension Plan (CPP) or, in Quebec, the Quebec Pension Plan (QPP). These plans cover almost everyone in the labour force. Both the employee and the employer contribute to these plans, which are portable (that is, their accrued benefits carry over from job to job). About 9 percent of total old-age income stems from the second tier.

The third tier in Canada's income security system for the aged, accounting for about 45 percent of the total income received by the elderly (Messinger and Powell 1987:572), is private income from wages and salaries, investments, private pension plans, life insurance, and other sources. In 1988, seniors received only 16 percent of their retirement income from private pensions and about 21 percent from investments (Marshall and Wigdor, in press). In that year, only 41.6 percent of men and 31.0 percent of women in the paid labour force were covered by a private pension plan (Gee and McDaniel 1991).

The proportion of income received from these various tiers by the aged varies by gender and marital status. Unattached women receive relatively more from the first tier and less from the third tier than do unattached men. The income of married couples is similar to that of unattached men (Gee and Kimball 1987:57).

Over half of all old-age pensioners currently receive at least partial GIS benefits, and 15 percent receive provincial or territorial benefits (Marshall and Wigdor, in press). These are received if income from the second and third tiers is insufficient to bring them to a point near the poverty level.

Even if an employee is enrolled in a private pension plan, there is no guarantee that he or she will collect anything from it (Ascah 1984:425; Messinger and Powell 1987:573). In most private pension plans, employees who leave a company with less than ten years of service or before the age of 45 receive only their personal contributions. Insofar as the company's contribution is viewed as deferred wages, this represents a loss to the employee. Most Canadians change jobs frequently, and women especially have irregular work histories; yet there is very poor portability of pensions. Employees who change jobs must start afresh with a new pension plan, losing the accrued benefits of their previous plans.

Adequate understanding of the economic position of the aged also requires an appreciation of their assets. Home ownership is high, with 72 percent of families with a head aged 65 or older owning their home without a mortgage and another 8 percent owning with a mortgage. For unattached individuals, the figure is 38 percent mortgage-free and another 3 percent owning with a mortgage (NACA 1991:45). Housing is a significant asset for the aged, but their houses are generally older, have a lower market value, and are more expensive to repair, keep up, and heat. Other assets, such as investments, do not play a large part in providing economic security for the aged.

In general, wealth or "net worth" (assets minus liabilities) varies greatly by age and marital status, but seniors, compared with "all ages," report higher mean and median wealth, regardless of marital status. The greater home ownership of seniors is a factor here, but so too is their greater likelihood of being debt-free. For example, in 1984, 29 percent of families headed by a senior and 14 percent of unattached seniors reported a consumer debt (such as a charge-card balance, bank loan, or instalment debt), but for all families, the percentage was 61 percent (NACA 1991:46).

Poverty in Later Life

The result of these financial arrangements is that, although some older Canadians are quite comfortable financially, and many of the wealthiest people in the country are old, the majority of older Canadians are poor or near-poor. Great differences in degree of economic security are found among the older population (NACA 1991).

The economic situation of older Canadians has improved over the past decade. In 1990, 35 percent of unattached seniors and just 4 percent of elderly couples had income below the official government poverty line. This compares with 62 percent of unattached elderly and 13 percent of elderly couples below the poverty line in 1980. Elderly women, however, are still more likely to be poor than men. In 1990, unattached elderly women had a 38 percent chance of being in poverty, compared with just 26 percent of unattached elderly men (Ng 1992). The economic situation of older men and women might improve in the future for a number of reasons. The CPP/QPP was

Although some older Canadians are quite comfortable financially, and many of the wealthiest people in the country are old, the majority of older Canadians are poor or near-poor.

initiated only in 1966 and was not fully effective until 1976. Some very old people had ceased employment prior to the full introduction of the plan. Rising labour-force participation rates for women and reform in private pension plans should enhance their ability to provide economic security. However, the impact of these improvements is limited, particularly for women. They frequently work in industrial sectors with poor or nonexistent private pension arrangements. In general, persistent high unemployment rates in the late 1980s and the early 1990s act to reduce the percentages covered by private pension coverage. Finally, as the Canadian economy shifts toward service-sector jobs, which offer lower wages and less pension coverage, the private pension system cannot be expected to play a significant role in the income security of future generations of older Canadians.

Although most old people are poor, we should not lose sight of the fact that many young people are also poor. The highest poverty group in Canada is currently lone parents with children under age 18, headed by a female parent. Fully 57 percent of such families had poverty-level incomes in 1990, up from 55 percent in 1980. Since 1983, the percentage of such families in poverty has exceeded the percentage of unattached elderly people in poverty (Ng 1992). With declining rates of old-age poverty but continuing high rates of youth and young-adult poverty in lone-parent families, Canadian income-security policy has recently shifted away from an earlier emphasis on income security for the elderly, to focus on children (Marshall, Cook, and Marshall 1993). While this general trend to improve the income security of the elderly may be applauded, several subgroups of the elderly — very old women, widows, and renters (rather than owners) in high-cost communities — remain at considerable risk and can be considered near-poor if not actually poor.

Health

A second major difference among older people is health. Contrary to commonly held beliefs, most people over the age of 65 are quite healthy. However, aging leads to an increased likelihood of a person experiencing chronic health problems, such as heart and circulatory diseases, cancer, arthritis, rheumatism, or diabetes, and experiencing greater severity in the effects of acute health problems (Marshall 1987a; NACA 1989). For example, an older person may take longer to recover from a simple ailment. Older people are also more likely than younger people to have multiple or compounded health problems (Chappell, Strain, and Blandford 1986:35).

From a sociological point of view, one important way to describe how healthy people are is to ascertain whether or not they need help with such everyday activities as preparing meals. These are referred to as **activities of daily living (ADL)**. One study (Tilquin and Associates 1980) asked if respondents in Quebec required help with the following five activities: rising and going to bed, daily personal hygiene, walking around inside the house, bathing, and shopping in summer. The proportion reporting no disability was 84 percent for those aged 65 to 69, but just 67 percent for those aged 75 and over. The results of several Canadian community studies and national surveys are remarkably similar (Marshall 1987a; Statistics Canada 1987b) and suggest that most older people remain quite healthy until their late seventies or their eighties.

Gender differences in health are apparent in the mortality and life expectancy data noted above and in Chapter 8 but appear as well in the ADL data from community studies. There is a significant upward shift in the proportion of people requiring assistance with the activities of daily living at the mid- to late seventies for men, and about the late seventies to mid-eighties for women (Marshall, Rosenthal, and Synge 1983). In this and in other areas such as economic status, it is imperative to consider older men and older women separately.

Most older people, even the very old, live in their own homes. About 7–8 percent of Canadians aged 65+, and 36 percent of those aged 85+, live in institutions such as nursing homes and homes for the aged (Forbes, Jackson, and Kraus 1987:37–40). Most of the institutionalized older people are women. The major factors leading to the institutionalization of the aged are advanced age itself, decreasing health, and the nonavailability of a spouse to provide care with such things as medication, bathing, preparation of meals, shopping, and housekeeping (Shapiro and Roos 1987).

Despite comprising only about 11 percent of the population, older people account for about half of all hospital-bed occupancy in Canada (Auer 1987:29) and about twice as much consumption of physicians' services as their percentage of the population would suggest.

A careful study of health care costs projected into the future (Denton, Li, and Spencer 1987) leads to the conclusion that a quality of health care comparable to that currently provided can be realized without a major shift in the allocation of societal resources. Nonetheless, health-care costs are rising. Major changes in the costs of health care do not result from the changing age structure of the population, but rather from changes in the organization of health-care delivery and in the decisions made about the level of care we wish to provide. For example, in a study for the Economic Council of Canada, Auer (1987:20) notes that increased costs for hospital care in Canada associated with the increase in the proportion of the aged have been offset by cost reductions due to declines in the birth rate. Auer argues that "most of the growth in per capita hospital expenditures did not come from higher hospital admission rates but from higher costs per admission. It is therefore necessary to look at utilization-based factors to determine why the cost per hospital admission (or per patient) increased so much." As but one example, it is currently estimated that in Canada over 10 percent of acute care hospital beds are occupied by inappropriately placed older patients. Most of them could be discharged to more appropriate care settings such as chronic-care hospitals or nursing homes (Aronson, Marshall, and Sulman 1987; Marshall 1987b). The point that health-care costs cannot be blamed on population aging is important in light of frequent allegations, particularly in the popular press, that increased health-care costs are attributable to population aging alone (Marshall 1993).

In a Quebec study, Béland (1989) used a statistical technique called cluster analysis to group older respondents from Hull and Trois-Rivières according to the patterns of use of twelve health and social services. This technique identified five groups that differed in their utilization of services. Two of these were low in utilization, two were intermediate, and one was high. This latter group, heavy users of all services, accounted for only 1.6 percent of the sample, while the low-utilization groups accounted for 14.2 percent. The study thus confirms that all aged are not alike in terms of service utilization. Physical health status was the strongest predictor of use of service, indicating that services were provided to those who need them. For the sociologist of aging, health is as essential a factor to consider in the examination of social life as social class, because it differentiates the life experiences of the aging individual.

Gender

It should be apparent that many concerns about aging and the aged are concerns about women and gender-role differentiation. Not only are most older people female, but the older female is much more likely to be economically deprived than is the older male. The health of older people, as it varies by gender, has profound implications for their day-to-day experiences of physical limitation, dependency on other people, and the discomfort and pain of illness. In addition, as we will describe below in discussing family life, the all-important tasks of providing nursing care and daily assistance to the ill elderly fall mainly to wives and daughters.

Gender is a major differentiator of social status across the life course. In our society, the status of women is, on the whole, lower than that of men. Women, in general, are more likely to be identified with child-rearing statuses, which, judged by the economic rewards associated with them, are not highly valued. Status emanating from occupation is higher for men than women for several reasons. Older men are more likely than older women to have been in the paid labour force. This situation is changing, with over half of women currently of working age in the paid labour force. However, as pointed out in Chapter 5, women continue to be located primarily in jobs of lower status and lower income than those of men. This decreases their accumulated economic worth and deprives them of the deference and prestige that are so important in a society such as ours, in which social worth is closely tied to occupation.

Being old and female places a person in what has been referred to as "double jeopardy" (Chappell and Havens 1980). Our culture values youthful, feminine beauty, but the low economic status and financial dependency of the older woman may be a more important cause of her low social status than is her loss of youthful attractiveness. However, these cultural standards should not be underestimated as a factor influencing the self-esteem of older women, many of whom were strongly socialized to define their worth in these terms. Their male age-peers may also strongly adhere to these standards.

Having considered the demographic aspects of population aging and three important bases of social differentiation among the aged — health, income, and gender — it is important to acknowledge the existence of other important factors affecting the aging experience. The research literature on aging in First Nations peoples is very scarce, but available data describe the disadvantages of older Natives in terms of housing and the accessibility of health services, their greater reliance on informal rather than formal services (Bienvenue and Havens 1986), and their lower life satisfaction (in turn accounted for largely by their socioeconomic disadvantages) (Blandford and Chappell 1990). In the Canadian context, ethnicity is an additional factor of great importance (Driedger and Chappell 1987; Payne and Strain 1990; Ujimoto 1987). While less important than frequently thought (Cape 1987), the rural–urban context has been found to be related to such factors as the social network intensity of the aged (Corin 1987), and the availability of services (Joseph and Martin Matthews 1993). We turn now to an examination of some theoretical approaches that aid our understanding of aging.

Macro-Level Theories of Aging

Macro-level theories of aging deal with the way in which aging individuals are tied to the society and the social status or deference accorded them. We find it useful to view these theories in relation to one very important strand of thought that can be conveniently referred to as the **modernization thesis** of aging.

The Modernization Thesis

One of the founders of the sociology of aging, Burgess, argued that as a result of "modern economic trends" the aged "lost their former favoured position in the extended family." In addition to citing the move from the extended to the nuclear family, he listed urbanization, industrialization, bureaucratization, increased leisure time, and enhanced life expectancy as factors that combine to leave the aged with little of any consequence to do in and for their society (Burgess 1960).

This argument assumes that older people once had a more important place in society and in the family than they currently occupy. These arguments rest on a structural-functionalist view of society as consisting of a number of status positions to which role expectations are attached, all of which contribute in some way to the maintenance and survival of the society.

Cowgill and Holmes (1972) developed a systematic theory of how modernization led to a decline in the status of the aged, illustrated in Figure 6-1. The theory describes four dimensions of modernization. First, modern economic technology creates new urban occupations and leaves older occupations to become obsolete. As obsolete occupations are predominantly held by older people, their status declines relative to that of younger people in the newer, high-technology occupations. Second, urbanization leads the young to establish new families geographically distant from their parents. This creates both residential and social segregation of the old from the young. Third, the progressively higher educational attainment of younger people provides them with more societally relevant knowledge than the old have. Because such knowledge is itself a valued commodity, it enhances the status of the young relative to the old; in addition, educational differences segregate the generations both intellectually and morally. Fourth, advances in health technology increase life expectancy. People are able to remain in the labour force for longer periods of time. This blocks the upward career mobility of younger generations, leading to increased intergenerational conflict. The social institution of retirement, in this theoretical framework, may be seen as an attempt to resolve such conflict at a macro-social level.

The theory is much more complicated than we have described. As originally formulated (Cowgill and Holmes 1972), it included 22 propositions. For example, one of them states: "The status of the aged is highest when they constitute a low proportion of the population and tends to decline as their numbers and proportions increase." This rests on a notion of scarcity based on supply-and-demand thinking from economics. The refined version of the theory relies on chains

of linked hypotheses that you can create by following the diagram in Figure 6-1.

Sociologists argue vehemently about the best ways to describe modernization and how to describe the status of the elderly. For a start, modernization does not progress uniformly across all four dimensions (economic technology, urbanization, educational attainment, and health technology) in any particular society. For example, many societies that today are not well-developed technologically have large urban population concentrations. Nor can it be assumed that any society will progress uniformly along a single dimension from "nonmodernized" to "modernized," or that modernization is an indigenous process.

A second set of problems stems from the conceptualization of social status. If social status were taken to be accurately measured by the proportion of GNP allocated to the aged for health care and pensions, then the status of the elderly has never been higher. It is apparent then, that how one views the relationship between modernization and social status of the aged depends on just what is taken to be an indicator of modernization or of social status.

A third set of problems with the modernization thesis stems from the relative timing of changes in modernization and changes in the social status of the elderly. For example, Cowgill and Holmes, as can be seen from the model in Figure 6-1, argued that retirement followed modernization and contributed to devaluing the status of the aged. However, Quadagno (1980) has shown that "in England and Wales, a substantial portion of the population was retired prior to any demographic aging of the population and well before the application of modern health technology." This finding directly contradicts two of the four major postulated links between modernization and the status of the aged.

A fourth set of problems concerns the assumption of modernization theorists that the status of the aged was high in early historical periods. This assumption rests on a somewhat romanticized vision of the past. Laslett (1976, 1977) has shown that, in England at least, the family and household status of the old was probably never very high and that older people were not as highly integrated into their families as is often assumed in contemporary aging research and in general studies in the sociology of the family.

FIGURE 6-1 Aging and Modernization

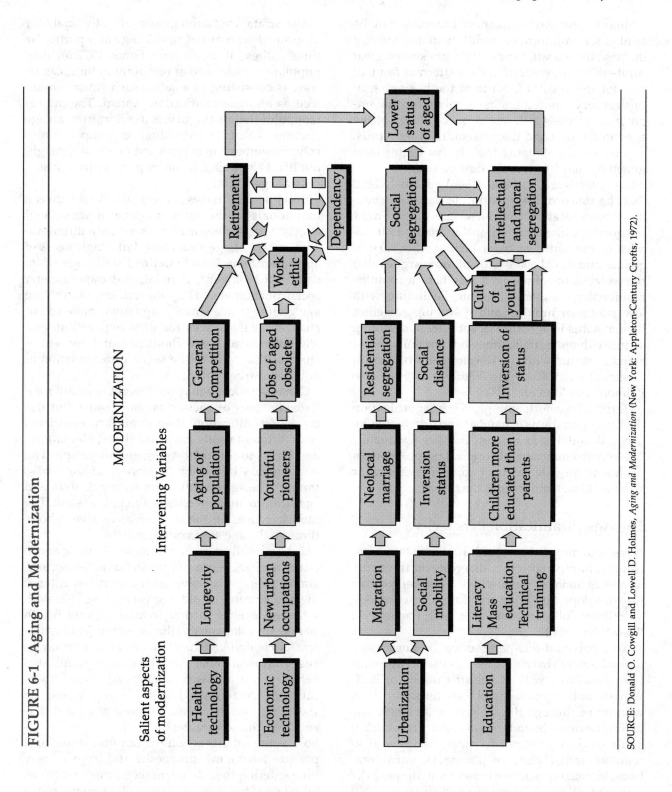

SOURCE: Donald O. Cowgill and Lowell D. Holmes, *Aging and Modernization* (New York: Appleton-Century Crofts, 1972).

Finally, the modernization theorists can be faulted for a uniform or undifferentiated view of the past. In contrast, Synge (1980) has shown great rural–urban differences in the pattern of familial care for the aged in Ontario at the beginning of this century, and others have pointed to the importance of class differences in the status of the aged in the past and the present. In other words, a person's social status has always been determined by many factors in addition to age.

In a later work, Cowgill (1986) acknowledged that the status of the aged in the past has sometimes been idealized and he recognized the need for greater differentiation of the theory as it applies to the status of older people who vary in gender and social class. Cowgill now argues that the social status of the aged may have a complex relationship to modernization, beginning with low status in hunting and gathering societies, higher status in agricultural societies, a declining status with industrialization and, possibly, recent gains in status with the development of postindustrial society (Cowgill 1986:192–193; see also Palmore and Manton 1974).

Despite its shortcomings, the modernization theory, especially as expanded and articulated by Cowgill and his associates, has been valuable. The clearly enunciated theoretical propositions of the theory provided a major point of reference for scholars to test and modify the theory.

The Age-Stratification Perspective

A second major theoretical approach, the age-stratification perspective, also rests on the structural-functionalist perspective. This perspective was developed by Riley and a number of associates (Riley, Johnson, and Foner 1972; Foner 1974; Riley 1976, 1980).

To understand this perspective, it is necessary to understand two concepts: cohort and age stratum (Marshall 1983). A **cohort** consists of individuals born approximately at the same time, who move through the life course together. The definition of the boundaries of cohorts is arbitrary and based on practical decisions made by a researcher rather than on theoretical considerations. For example, a researcher may compare the cohort of all people born in Canada between 1900 and 1905 with that of people born between 1950 and 1955.

Age strata are "aggregate[s] of individuals (or of groups) who are of similar age at a particular time" (Riley, Johnson, and Foner 1972:6). Any population, examined at one point in time, can be seen as consisting of a set of such strata, organized as an age-stratification system. The important point that distinguishes a cohort from an age stratum is that an individual or group assumes cohort membership at birth and retains it throughout life. With aging, a cohort passes through successive age strata.

Every society makes some distinctions between individuals on the basis of age or of age-related events. Our society uses both a finely differentiated system of age strata based on single years of age and a more loosely defined set of age strata based on biological, familial, and more general social phenomena. The arbitrariness underlying age grades or age strata is apparent in the recent changes in legal ages for drinking, voting, and eligibility to marry without parental consent — changes that refer to the social differentiation of adulthood from youth.

Canadian society may be thought of as differentiated not only by social class and gender, but also by age stratification. Age strata are associated with different rights, responsibilities, obligations, and access to rewards. Aging, in this perspective, is a process by which successive cohorts pass through the age-stratification system. Cohort and age stratum are viewed as a dynamic system. The model focuses on the flow of successive cohorts through the age strata of the society.

Cohorts will vary in a number of their social characteristics. For example, in Canadian society, almost every successive birth cohort has entered the age stratum of old age (say, at age 65) with a higher level of income, education, and health status. Simultaneously, the age-stratification system is changing. Expectations for behaviour of age-stratum members, as well as opportunities to behave in certain ways, change from one historical period to another. The school system that the 1900–1910 cohort passed through was far different from that encountered by the 1960–1970 cohort. Some cohorts encounter adulthood during a period of economic prosperity and have an easy time entering the labour market; others reach the initial working years in a time of economic recession or depression. Such accidents of birth are fateful for individuals and for whole cohorts and may affect their life chances, political attitudes, and values in different ways.

Focusing on cohort differences poses an alternative explanation to one based on age. Are people of a certain age politically conservative because aging leads to conservatism or because their formative years were lived during a general societal climate of conservatism? In this view, age differences are hypothesized to result not so much from the aging or maturation of the individuals as from the different experiences that individuals have as a result of their cohort membership.

Such differences may lead to conflict. One example of conflict based on age groups is given by Foner and Kertzer (1978) and concerns the timing of transitions. Because progression through the age strata of a society is normally associated with the increasing access to power and rewards (with the occasional exception of transitions at the very end of the life course, such as retirement), cohorts occupying higher age strata may seek to delay the transitions of younger cohorts, while younger cohorts may wish to accelerate their passage into a higher age stratum. Younger cohorts may wish to lower the age of legal drinking or voting. In the case of the progression into retirement, which decreases power and rewards, older workers may seek to elevate the age of retirement. However, the potential for conflict surrounding process of cohort flow is reduced by the relative flexibility of the age-stratification system in our society and by such adaptive mechanisms as skipping grades in elementary school, early or mature entry into university, and flexible retirement.

When the supply of people provided by an age cohort is either too small or too large in relation to the number of available role positions, then we have a situation of *disordered cohort flow*. The societal response to this is often to change age-related role expectations and the timing of the transitions between age strata. In response to the increasing size of cohorts entering the retirement years, and because of concern about providing economic security to this large cohort in retirement, suggestions have been made to raise the age of retirement or eliminate involuntary retirement. As another example, one reaction to the large baby-boom cohort was to expand the post-secondary educational system. This led in Canada to massive expansion of the university system during the 1970s, thereby delaying entry of many baby-boom cohort members into the labour force. As Waring (1976) points out, many nations have sought to rectify disorders of cohort flow by relying on large-scale immigration or emigration. However, as immigration policies become more restrictive, attempts to maintain an orderly flow of cohorts increasingly rely on adjusting the age-stratification system, such as by modifying age at retirement.

The **age-stratification perspective** and the aging and modernization thesis constitute the major focusses of research interest in the macrosociology of aging. It is noteworthy that both approaches exemplify the structural-functional perspective. While both attempt to deal with fundamental processes of social change, in their different ways they view such change as orderly or smooth and as functional for the society.

The age-stratification approach generated a reaction based primarily on the conflict perspective. Tindale and Marshall (1980; see also Marshall 1983; Tindale 1987) have attempted to go beyond the age-stratification approach by using the concept of generation. In contrast to a cohort, a generation's boundaries are not arbitrary, but depend on characteristics and social experiences shared by cohort members. A **generation** is a cohort, large proportions of whose members have experienced significant sociohistorical changes, such as depressions or wars.

Not all single-year birth cohorts will experience such profound historical and social events in the same way. A difference of a year or two, for example, may mean being too old or too young to serve in the armed forces during a major war. Generational experiences are usually thought of as cataclysmic and shaped by such major changes as depressions or wars. However, as Ryder (1965) has pointed out, "cohorts can also be pulled apart gradually by the slow grind of evolutionary change." Similarly, not all members of any generation will necessarily respond to significant historical events in the same way. For example, some youth in Canada, Germany, and the United States responded to the Vietnam War by becoming doves, while others became hawks (Levitt 1984).

Generational consciousness developed early in life may persist, probably with some modification, throughout life (Dowd 1986). The politically active, antiwar generation of youth and young adults formed from people born on the leading edge of the baby-boom cohort still retains its generational membership as its members pass into their mid-thirties, while its age-group relationship changes. The consciousness of the baby-boom generation of itself as a generation has been nourished by mass marketing and the media.

Tindale and Marshall emphasized that generation, age strata, and class interact to affect people's life chances. That is, one's fate may be influenced by his or her life experiences as historically conditioned by year of birth, by being at a particular place in the age-stratification system, or by one's social class position; and these three factors interact. Class differences influence the encounter of cohort members with important historical events and therefore influence generational experiences. For example, the children of the upper class who reach prime military service age during a major war are less likely to live or die in active service than are the children of the lower class, despite shared cohort membership. Similar class differentiation occurs in response to fluctuations in the economy and the job market (Tindale 1987).

As noted earlier, Cowgill's theory of aging and modernization argued that the growing proportions of older people in the population will lead to increased age group conflict over job scarcity (Cowgill 1986). This conflict may be affected to some degree by differences based on the shared historical experiences of a generation. However, the potential for conflict is probably even greater because of age-group differences in the present. Just as a group of people may form a distinctive consciousness of themselves as different from others on the basis of generational experiences, they may also form such a distinctive consciousness based on age itself. This takes us to the matter of subculture or minority-group formation among the aged, or indeed among groups of any age.

The Aged as a Minority Group versus the Age-Irrelevance Perspective

Two contrasting approaches have been taken to the question of age-group formation in later life. Some scholars argue that the aged are increasingly taking on the characteristics of a group. Others contend that age is of decreasing importance as a basis for group formation. Rose (1965) argued that increasingly the aged were coming to constitute a subculture because of their large numbers, increased vigour and health, collective concerns in fighting for adequate health care, and growing geographical segregation in such areas as small towns or age-segregated housing. He also stressed the exclusion of older people from integration with the society through employment, but he felt that the good health and economic security of most older people would facilitate their interaction and thereby allow them to develop a shared consciousness of themselves as older people.

Older people are discriminated against in the labour markets (Nishio and Lank 1987) and treated legally as a distinct category for many purposes, such as pensions. The extent to which these factors lead to a shared consciousness based on age is, however, open to dispute.

Abu-Laban and Abu-Laban (1980) argue that minority status should be viewed as multidimensional and as a matter of degree, rather than as a uniform attribute of the older person. Different individuals of the same age may vary greatly in their physical characteristics, in the extent of their active participation in the society, in the esteem they are accorded by others, in their power and privileges, and in their ability to resist or be exempt from the disadvantages of age.

At macro levels, the arguments against the formation of an aged minority group or subculture have been clearly articulated by Neugarten (1970). In her view, each successive cohort entering the later years is more like young and middle-aged cohorts with regard to health, educational attainment, income security, and shared social values. Therefore the objective basis for conflict between age groups should diminish.

From the age-stratification perspective, Foner (1974) adds additional support to Neugarten's thesis. Foner argues that the potential for age-based consciousness is diminished by generational consciousness. In other words, because each successive cohort entering the old-age stratum brings with it its unique encounter with history, its values and interests will be different from those of previous cohorts already in the old-age stratum, thereby weakening the unanimity or consensus of shared values. Foner also suggests that membership in associations that are not age-graded provides opportunities for a better understanding and greater tolerance of opposing views.

Recognition by the young that they will eventually grow older, together with tolerance by the old of the frustrations of the young, combine to reduce the potential for age-based conflict. Finally, Foner also argues that material disputes tend to cut across generational cohort boundaries. For example, class interests might unite workers of all ages (see Kernaghan 1982).

On the other hand, it is clear that the past two decades have seen a tremendous increase in concerns about age. The rise of interest in aging is itself an indication of the growing importance of age, as is the increase in volume of potential rhetoric and public policy discussion concerning pensions, health care for the aged, and related issues. An American political scientist, Cutler (1981), has argued that age consciousness is itself a generational cohort phenomenon. The boxed insert (on pp. 174–75) briefly describes one form of age-based conflict as it did, or did not, occur in Canada and the United States.

The Political Sociology of Aging

Other developments in the macrosociology of aging that draw on the conflict perspective, and in particular the political-economy form of the conflict perspective, focus on the political and economic impact of population aging on the old and on the entire society. Guillemard (1977, 1980) offers yet another reason why the apparent strains toward conflict between age groups and generations have not led to much open conflict. She argues that the state actively fosters an ideology that discourages older people from recognizing their common interests and their distinctive and disadvantaged position in society. She describes the promulgation of a positive view of retirement in which retirement is seen as a time for leisure and self-expression. Failure to attain satisfaction in retirement is attributed to inadequate preparation for it by the individual. Such an individualistic ideology directs the attention of many older people away from the structural formations of age-related poverty and leads them instead to blame themselves for their misfortune. As with many other deprived groups, an ideology is provided that contributes to their pacification by "blaming the victim" (Ryan 1971).

Estes (1979) calls attention to the ways in which old age has been defined as a social problem of crisis proportions. Drawing on the symbolic-interactionist approach and on conflict sociology, she argues that

to define old age as a social problem of crisis proportions is politically useful, because such a crisis may be portrayed as not the fault of prior social inaction or economic policy, but as the result of increased longevity, retirement, declining birth rates, and so forth. In addition, the aging crisis label serves to advance the interests of those seeking expansion of government resources to deal with the crisis.

In a similar vein, Robertson (1990) has examined the "social construction" of Alzheimer's disease, showing how, as a political process, the definition of Alzheimer's disease, uncertainty over its diagnostic boundaries, and exaggerated claims as to its "epidemic" prevalence contributed to a "biomedicalization of old age," which served the purposes of a government research agency trying to expand its mandate and funding base. Robertson introduces the term "apocalyptic demography" to describe this "social construction of catastrophe," which describes "an increasing aging population, with its multitude of health problems" that "will place major demands on health care resources" (Robertson 1990:437).

In the area of debate over income security pension policy, Myles (1980, 1984) argues that the rhetoric masks concerns over the control over massive pools of capital. The scope and significance of private pension plans is evident from the following: the assets of trustee pension plans in Canada rose from $21.2 billion in 1975 to $82.7 billion by 1983 (Messinger and Powell 1987:574), and about $130 billion by 1987 (Gee and McDaniel 1991). During the 1975–83 period, life insurance company assets, which also related to the provision of later-life income security, rose from $23.6 billion to $63.4 billion. RRSP savings rose from $14.5 billion to $27.5 billion over the 1975–83 period (Messinger and Powell 1987:574) and were estimated to reach $43.0 billion by 1990 (Deaton 1989:439).

The private pension industry, together with the other components of the third-tier, private income security system, is clearly massive in scope and in its implications for the control and direction of the Canadian economy. Assuming a continuing low growth rate in the population, the value of trusteed pension assets may rise from its

The Intergenerational Equity Debate

In the mid-1980s, a policy issue arose in the United States, but not in Canada, concerning issues of fairness in the allocation of resources to various age groups. The "intergenerational equity" debate arose when claims were made that government policies treat the old more favorably than the young, and that in doing so, the young are being deprived of opportunities for their own well-being. In 1984, Americans for Generational Equity (AGE) was formed by a U.S. senator. It spearheaded attempts in Congress and in the media to reduce government spending on the aged. Newspaper and magazine stories appeared with headlines such as "U.S. Coddles Elderly but Ignores Plight of Children" and "Older Voters Drive Budget." Congressional and media attention spurred academics to get involved, and "intergenerational relations" became a prominent theme at academic conferences in the United States. A counter-group to AGE, "Generations United," was established to work for solidarity among age groups and to fight against the divisiveness fostered by AGE.

In Canada, nothing like this happened, suggesting that there must be something different about Canada and the United States on this age-related issue. To document that the two countries did actually differ in the attention given to the intergenerational equity debate, on-line bibliographical searching was done of newspapers and magazines, to index public concern, and of academic journals to index concern in the scholarly community. Over the eleven years from 1980 to 1990, 30 articles on intergenerational equity were found in the U.S. media, but none in Canada. Stories that dealt with the young and the old in the same story dealt not with the possibility that the old were receiving an inordinate share of resources at the expense of the young, but rather with examples of intergenerational solidarity. They had headlines such as "Young and Young at Heart Give Education a New Twist: Children, Seniors, Learning from Each Other" and "Age Barriers Knocked Down as Youngsters Mix with Elderly." The academic literature gave even more attention to intergenerational equity in the United

States, with 82 citations on that topic over the eleven-year period; no Canadian citations were found in the academic literature of that period. Using a variety of sources, it was also found that while intergenerational equity became a live policy issue in the U.S. government, it was quietly acknowledged as an issue to be contained by Canadian bureaucrats and did not enter parliamentary debate.

Why did the two countries, so similar in so many respects, differ on this point? One possibility is that the objective circumstances in Canada do not warrant a concern about intergenerational equity. However, the more relevant objective circumstance is poverty rates of the young and the old, and these on inspection were found to have followed the same pattern. Poverty rates for the aged in Canada have dropped significantly in recent years, while rates for children have risen slightly and are now higher than rates for the old. The same "crossover" effect occurred in the United States. Objective similarities, then, could not explain differences in the issue.

1991 level of 25 percent of GNP to 66 percent by 2031 (Deaton 1989:236). Nonetheless, many observers charge that the private pension system has failed almost completely to meet the income-security needs of older Canadians. Among recommended changes to the private pension system are better pensions for women, earlier "vesting" (in which the pension credits legally belong to the employee and are not lost with a change of employment), pensions that continue to be paid to a surviving spouse after widowhood, and the splitting of pensions upon marital breakdown.

Myles (1980) notes that "pension policy, then, is not primarily an issue of individual welfare, but rather an issue of power, power to control and allocate the capital generated through the savings put aside by workers for their old age."

Over several years, John Myles has developed analyses of Canadian social policy concerning ag-

ing that are based on a theoretical approach from political economy and done in a comparative context (Myles 1984, 1991). He notes, for example (Myles and Teichrow 1991), that Canada has differed from the United States in that it has not experienced an all-out assault on the welfare state. The "great pension debate" in Canada in the late 1970s and early 1980s was, he argues, not about how to dismantle the welfare state but how to expand it; at the same time, rhetoric in the United States invoked a "crisis of social security" and suggestions that it would have to be abolished or slashed (Myles and Teichrow 1991:84).

Myles characterizes Canada as a "dualistic" welfare state with both public and semiprivate components. In terms of old-age income security, the fully public component, the OAS, is not large in comparison with other economically developed countries, but there is extensive subsidiza-

A second possibility is that Canada is simply a more generous society, a "kinder, gentler" society, than the United States. Many Canadians like to think this is so, but when public-opinion data were examined, support for public-assistance, health, and income-security programs for the aged was found to be remarkably high in both Canada and the United States. Again, similarities cannot be used to explain differences.

A third possibility is that differences in resource-allocation mechanisms in the two countries make the provision of support for the aged less of a flashpoint in Canada. Here, the fact that Canada has universal medicare for persons of all ages but that the United States has medicare only for the aged may lead to a greater recognition on the part of the media and the public, as well as on politicians and bureaucrats, of the large health-related resource allocations to just one age group. The combination of public and private income-security provision in Canada, coupled with the fact that one major component of income security, the OAS, is not tied to labour-force participation in Canada (there is no similar provision in the U.S.), may

also make resource allocation to the aged less visible than it is in the United States, where the Social Security benefits are paid for by pay deductions.

Yet another possible explanation for the differential attention to intergenerational equity relates to important differences in political structure and process. Political parties in Canada meet in caucuses, and party loyalty is a basic principle. This results in a weaker emphasis on lobbying in Canada than is found in the United States. It is more difficult in Canada to make a difference by lobbying an individual member of Parliament than it is to make a difference in the United States by lobbying a congressman. As the personal political fortune of the congressman who founded AGE declined, so has AGE, and it is now not considered to be a powerful lobby group. The issue of "intergenerational equity" remains for discussion and debate, but it is no longer of central policy concern in the United States, and it may never be in Canada.

The social situations of the elderly in Canada and the United States are quite similar in many respects. Both countries have about the same percent-

age of the population over the age of 65, and income security and health care are quite good, by international standards, for the aged in both countries. Widely shared values in both countries are supportive of the aged. Yet a different "politics" of age arose in the two countries. This example is a reminder that social issues, and social problems, are socially constructed and that the relationship between objective circumstances and definitions of the situation is inherently problematic and often political.

Source:

Adapted from Victor W. Marshall et al., "Conflict over inter-generational equity: Rhetoric and reality in a comparative context," in *The New Contract Between the Generations*, edited by V.L. Bengtson and W.A. Achenbaum (New York: Aldine DeGruyter, 1993; John F. Myles and Les Teichrow, "The politics of dualism: Pension policy in Canada," in *States, Labor Markets, and the Fugure of Old-Age Policy*, edited by J. Myles and J. Quadagno (Philadelphia: Temple University Press, 1991).

tion through the tax structure of income-security mechanisms thought, erroneously, by most people to be private: registered pension plans and registered retirement savings plans. This division corresponds roughly to the "dual labour market" (see Chapter 16), in which those in the primary labour market (the public service, large manufacturing industries, and financial institutions) receive both public and semiprivate support for later-life income security, but those in the secondary labour market (retail and consumer services, part-time employees, and employees in small, labour-intensive firms) receive only the public subsidization. Women, he points out, are strongly, and increasingly, found in the secondary labour market, which has the less adequate retirement-income support provisions (Myles and Teichrow 1991:92). An expansion of the public component of the pension system has been resisted by the

Canadian business sector because this would lessen the money available for venture-capital investment by the private sector. Myles (Myles and Teichrow 1991) has documented the process through which the class interests of Canadian corporate capital prevailed to block significant pension reform in Canada.

Many policy issues relating to aging and the aged cannot, therefore, be attributed to demographic causes (Marshall 1993). McDaniel (1987) argues that attributing such problems as maintaining adequate pensions to demographic pressures can lead to political inaction because of a belief that population structure cannot be manipulated by policy thrusts.

Although this chapter so far has focused on social-structural and macro-social theoretical and practical issues, the great bulk of research in the sociology of aging until very recently has been social-psychological. Most of this research has been within the structural-functionalist perspective. More recently, a number of sociologists, including many Canadians, have worked within the symbolic-interactionist perspective. Most of them view conflict as inherent both in the interaction among individuals and in the character of macrosocial relations. Many feel the conflict and symbolic-interactionist approaches provide compatible theoretical perspectives that enable the sociologist to take this broader view — considering the aging individual in an aging society (Marshall 1987c).

The Focus on Individual Adjustment and Life Satisfaction

From the beginning, the sociology of aging has focused unduly on the adjustment of the aging individual to his or her fate in the society. This emphasis on individual adjustment reflects the overall individualistic bias of North American sociology.

Underlying this preoccupation with happiness in later life, there appears to be an assumption by social scientists that this time of life is a problem for those who pass through it, a time when people find it difficult to be happy or satisfied with life.

Three variants of structural-functionalist role theory have been concerned with attempts to predict morale. These are *activity theory, disengagement theory*, and *continuity theory*. While these theories guided voluminous work in the earlier stages of the sociology of aging, their findings can be briefly summarized. The factors that most strongly predict morale or life satisfaction are, in order of importance: health status, income security, and — a distant third — levels of social activity or role involvement.

Theoretical debate among these approaches focused on a structural-functionalist concern with the integration of the individual in society. Individuals were considered to be tied to their society through role occupancy. **Activity theory** hypothesized that the adaptation of the individual to society was threatened by age-related declines in role occupancy. Activity theorists argued that, in order to be happy in later life, people should remain as active in their role-relationships as possi-

ble (Palmore 1969; Maddox 1970; Palmore and Luikart 1972).

This theoretical approach is consistent with both Durkheim's structural-functionalism and a symbolic-interactionist approach. Durkheim argues that few social ties lead to anomie and sometimes to suicide. According to Lemon, Bengtson, and Peterson (1972), the major argument of activity theory "is that there is a positive relationship between activity and life satisfaction and that the greater the role loss, the lower the life satisfaction." Interaction, in symbolic-interactionist terms, is capable of maintaining stable self-concepts or identities and these, Lemon, Bengtson, and Peterson argue, would be the link to self-esteem and, ultimately, life satisfaction. High morale results from activity through the intermediate variable of confirming feedback from others.

Disengagement theory was explicitly formulated in structural-functionalist terms (Cumming and Henry 1961; Hochschild 1975) and argued against the activity theory. Disengagement theory viewed the decline of activity as an inevitable and natural severing of the ties between the individual and the society that was functional to both. The society "granted permission" to the individual to disengage from active participation in social roles. This was seen as functional to the society because it allowed a smooth passing of people through the positions that make up the society, maintaining society as a *dynamic equilibrium*.

Disengagement was also viewed as functional for the individual needing to conserve energy because of failing health. Moreover, the process of disengagement from the point of view of the individual was thought to be initiated by a heightened recognition of mortality. Reduction of activity allowed more time for the individual to prepare for death.

The debate between activity and disengagement theorists dominated the sociology of aging for many years. For the most part, disengagement theory was discredited. Major withdrawal from role relationships such as widowhood and retirement is not voluntary. In general, as noted above, levels of activity do lead to higher life satisfaction, even though this is not a strong relationship. Psychologists (for example, Neugarten, Crotty, and Tobin 1964) found that psychological and sociological disengagement did not always occur simultaneously, as postulated by the theory, and they stressed that there were many styles of successful aging, depending on personality characteristics.

Translated into sociology, the idea that there are many successful ways of aging led to the **continuity theory** (Atchley 1977). Sociologists such as Atchley (1971) and Rosow (1974, 1976) argued, with supporting data, that rather than the actual level of role involvement or activity, changes in role involvement or activity were the important determinants of adaptation in later life. Some people are lifelong loners and happy to be so; others have always been happy only when busy and active with other people. Change in either direction can lead to low morale in later life. These three approaches have produced a wealth of empirical studies. It should be noted, however, that these approaches are more similar to than dissimilar from one another. Unlike other approaches, to be reviewed in sections that follow, they share structural-functionalist assumptions of dynamic equilibrium and the conception of role as the major link between the individual and the society.

Related to this general attitude is the assumption that middle-aged people have to be socialized to old age. Rosow (1974) views socialization as important but inadequate in the later years because of low motivation to learn the devalued role of older person. Symbolic interactionists, focusing on the individual as the active creator of roles, question both the existence of a role of aged person and the importance of this problem (Marshall 1980b). They argue that other more important aspects of aging are completely ignored by these theoretical approaches. The issues discussed in the next section, for example, stand in vivid contrast to structural-functionalism and its stress on the life satisfaction and adjustment area of inquiry.

Identity and Identity Management

Age is a somewhat ambiguous identity marker in our society. Physical appearance usually gives only a very rough clue to a person's age, and in any case, we are not terribly clear as to how expected behaviour should differ by age.

The anthropologist Fry (1976; see also Keith 1982) asked a sample of adult Americans to sort into piles a deck of cards depicting people in typical life situations "based on their decisions regarding the appropriate age or similarity in age bracket" of the people depicted. Respondents could create as many piles as they wished to describe appropriate ages or age brackets. The average number of categories identified was five or six, depending on age, gender, marital status, education, and other variables. Some respondents identified as many as fifteen age categories, but others identified only two; and more than 100 terms were used to describe the categories.

Such lack of agreement as to the age categories used in our society creates some of the flexibility but also some of the points of tension that we discussed in relation to age-stratification theory. Our society does not have a single system of age categories that encompasses all spheres of life and receives wide agreement. To the extent that such agreement is lacking, age-stratification theory — which suggests that there is considerable agreement on a system of age strata — may be considered somewhat unrealistic as a way of understanding the importance of age in our society.

Attitudes toward Being Old

People are not entirely sure just what it means to be old, but they have a vague feeling that it is not such a good thing. It is commonly acknowledged that ours is an "ageist" society, in which people share negative stereotypes of the old and are likely to discriminate against them in various ways. A number of studies suggest that negative stereotypes about later life are held by young, middle-aged, and even old people; a careful review is found in McTavish (1982). However, such studies also identify some positive stereotypes about the aged.

Based on interviews with a representative sample of older persons living in London, Ontario, Connidis (1987, 1989) has shown that community-dwelling older people tend to have a positive view of old age that is coupled with a realistic assessment of its limitations. She asked respondents what they liked about being their age, and what they disliked. Likes were more frequently mentioned than dislikes (90 percent vs. 66 percent). Cross-classifying respondents, 229 of 393 reported both likes and dislikes, suggesting a balanced or realistic view. Asked if, looking ahead, they had any worries about growing older, 62 percent reported no worries. There were gender differences: men were more likely to report no worries than women (72 percent vs. 56 percent) and marginally less likely to report either likes or dislikes about being their age (Connidis 1989). Connidis urges researchers not to exaggerate the negative aspects of aging, thereby contributing to a "social problems" perspective.

Reviewing the research on attitudes toward old age, Kalish (1982) concludes:

Older people consistently view themselves much more optimistically than they are viewed by the non-elderly. However, when older people are asked about "older people in general" they use very much the same stereotypes that the non-elderly use. Once again, we have evidence of the syndrome "I'm fine, but look at those poor old people over there."

We should expect that, to the extent that stereotypes about old age are negative, people will seek to exempt themselves from the status of old. This tendency for people to view themselves as young for their age, or as younger than others might think them, is frequently found in studies on this topic. Yet many people do not appear to dissociate themselves from the status of being old; nor do all older people, or younger people, view old age in highly negative terms. This suggests a more situational interpretation of the relationship between socially shared attitudes and self-identity. That is, people are free to draw from a number of different, and often conflicting, values and meanings in order to make sense of age-related phenomena in any specific situation.

Some social environments provide conditions that make it easier to create or use available meanings (culture) to fashion or sustain one's identity. Marshall (1975a, 1975b) and Hochschild (1973) have shown how older people living congregatively creatively fashion ways to sustain identity to the end, as they deal with impending death. The individual's own stance toward his or her impending death is socially constructed in interaction with others who are all facing the same situation. Rosow (1967) has found that many older people prefer congregate living because it enhances their ability to form new friendships; a finding that no doubt applies to people

at many stages of the life course (for example, students in residence, co-ops, adult-only apartments), and which in all cases enhances the ability to develop shared meanings to interpret experience.

Identity Maintenance in Older Women

A symbolic interactionist approach to identity maintenance is employed by Mac Rae (1990) in her study of older women in a Nova Scotia town. She used participant observation and interviews with 142 women aged 65–98 years (mean age 76.8), of whom 101 lived in their own homes or private apartments and 41 in seniors' apartments or a nursing home. Mac Rae's goal was to examine identity maintenance processes, and she explicitly contrasted her theoretical approach to structural functionalism:

In contrast to an identity crisis view, which emphasizes role as the link between individual and society and roles as the primary components of identity, this study assumes self to be the important connecting link and self-identity is conceptualized as complex and multi-dimensional ... identity emerges and is sustained through social interaction. (Mac Rae 1990:248)

This view leads Mac Rae to examine the social network involvements of these older women. Most did not view themselves as elderly or old, and most retained a positive self-identity based on their informal role involvements and social network ties. There was no evidence of any "identity crisis" in old age, and 98.6 percent of the women said they never worried about who they are. While a structural functionalist might focus on "social identity," the definition of a person by others and based largely on formal role occupancy, Mac Rae focuses on self-identity, or what Goffman calls "felt identity": "the subjective sense of his own situation and his own continuity and character that an individual comes to obtain as a result of his various social experiences" (Goffman 1963b:105; in Mac Rae 1990:254). Identity is built not just on formal role occupancy but on meaningful relationships to others as persons and on a sense of continuity in one's personal attributes over time.

Aronson (1990) also used a methodology that allowed her to describe the experiences of older women from their point of view. She interviewed in depth fourteen women aged 59 to 85 about their views concerning their need for care. This is an area of intense research concern in social gerontology, but one in which the perspective of older people themselves has rarely been assessed. Aronson found a general adherence to widely shared views that adult children should be counted on to provide help to their aged parents if needed. However, these older women experienced difficulty applying such cultural prescriptions to their own lives because they simultaneously held strong views that the old "should not be a burden" to their children and that their children should be free "to live their own lives." As Aronson notes,

They confronted the dilemma of trying to balance real insecurities and needs for assistance with cultural injunctions to be self-possessed and independent. Their efforts to balance these contradictory forces took the form of setting limits on their conduct and their feelings, so that the underlying dilemma was contained, evaded or managed in some fashion. (Aronson 1990:239).

Aronson also found her respondents' experiences "exacerbated by their marginal and precarious social status.... Respondents often experienced their age as a negative characteristic and reported feeling disadvantaged in such public contexts as the work world and in such routine processes as shopping and securing goods and services" (Aronson 1990:241). This leads us to yet another area of identity management in later life.

Stigma and Identity Management among the Aged

People of the same chronological age may be more likely to see themselves as "old" in some kinds of situations than in others. For example, they may be more aware of being "old" when receiving a pension cheque in the mail than when receiving a love letter. They may be less aware of their age when attending a symphony concert with their children than when attending a rock concert with their grandchildren. The extent to which people think about age as a description of themselves, and even the value they place on this description, is therefore variable and situational (Matthews 1979).

A number of studies describe the situational variation of the stigma of being old. According to Tindale (1980), old, poor men in Hamilton, Ontario, do not feel stigmatized when among themselves but, when dealing with outsiders, they feel stigmatized and go to great lengths to attempt to manage their stigma. One method of stigma management used in encounters with strangers is information control, a selectivity of topics open to discussion with others. In addition, the men maintain differentiation among themselves. They stigmatize as "mission stiffs" those of their peers whom they see as adopting without reservation the identity imputed to them by the public.

Whether a person accepts the label "old" will determine the extent to which old people become a reference group, a source of comparison, a scale against which the person measures his or her own abilities, well-being, and indeed all aspects of personal identity. Evaluations of old people and of the self are most likely to be interdependent in the later years and serve self-protective purposes. As Keith (1982) says: "Old people ... think more highly of themselves than they do of old people on the whole. The old, in other words, share many stereotypes of old age, and feel good as individuals because they don't fit them."

All these ways of managing identity are also employed by a group of older women studied by Matthews (1979). In addition, Matthews characterizes many old people as adopting a strategic approach to organizing everyday activities so as to avoid situations that threaten their identity. This may affect such things as the timing of shopping excursions and the choice of restaurants and other public places in order to avoid contact with young people, from whom they fear disrespect.

Exchange and Dependency

One of the greatest fears of older people is that they might become dependent upon others. Some sociologists of aging draw on exchange-theory principles (see Chapter 1) to explain identity management and social interaction patterns of the aged. **Exchange theory** views the individual as strategic and voluntaristic; Dowd (1980) and Mutran and Reitzes (1984) explicitly link the exchange-theory approach to the symbolic-interactionist perspective.

In exchange-theory terms, people are assumed to interact with others in order to obtain rewards, and stable social relationships develop if both parties receive roughly equal rewards in return for roughly equal costs, or if the balance of rewards and costs is roughly equal. With aging, many people lose resources that could be exchanged, increasing their risk of dependency (Marshall, Matthews, and Rosenthal 1992).

The exchange-theory perspective should be viewed as one of the most promising social-psychological approaches to understanding aging (Wellman and Hall 1986). What might otherwise appear to be confusing and irrational behaviour by individuals may be interpreted in exchange-theory terms as rational or strategic behaviour designed to protect autonomy or independence. Some of the older women studied by Matthews (1979) withdrew their participation in a seniors' centre. Matthews argues that this was a calculated decision taken to avoid the costs of having to interact with the centre's middle-aged staff, who viewed the women as old and therefore dependent. Withdrawal was a way for these older women to eliminate the psychological costs of dependency. Examining social exchange within the networks of older residents of East York, Ontario, Wellman and Hall (1986:223) describe efforts to maintain reciprocity at the network level: "Network members do unto others as they would have their networks do unto them."

Life-Course Transitions

In recent years, a number of sociologists, demographers, historians, psychologists, and other scholars, have systematically sought to characterize aging in terms of a sequence of life-course transitions (see, for example, Gee 1987; Norris 1987; Ryff 1986). This work draws on the structural-functionalist approach and relates closely to work on age stratification. However, it also draws heavily on symbolic interactionism (Marshall 1986a). The life course, according to Rossi (1980: 7), may be defined as "the pathways through the age-differentiated structure in the major role domains of life." A conceptual model based on the life-course perspective is presented in the accom-

panying boxed insert. The most important feature of the life-course perspective is a commitment to the belief that, if one is to understand the situation of the older individual, it is necessary to place her or him in a temporal context including the historical biography and the anticipated future.

Hughes's concept of career (1971) and the derivative notion of status passage (Glaser and Strauss 1971) are helpful in understanding life-course transitions. Hughes distinguished between *objective career* (a series of social statuses and clearly defined offices) and *subjective career* ("the moving perspective in which the person sees his life as a whole and interprets the meaning of his various attributes, actions, and the things which happen to him"). Marshall (1980a, 1987b) has applied the career perspective to aging "to point to a person negotiating a passage from one age-linked status to another, and then to others, finally coming to the end of the passage through life at death."

Objective Careers

A number of investigators have noted that the events marking the early stages of objective careers in our society have become more compressed in time and more predictable (Hogan 1981; Hagestad 1982). For example, the average timing of school completion fell significantly during the first half of this century, while the variability around the average age of completing school decreased. In statistical terms, the mean age decreased and the dispersion around the mean also decreased (see "Measures of Central Tendency" in Chapter 2). Similar patterns showing a greater standardization of life events, and an earlier timing of such events, have been observed for age of entry into the labour force, age of first marriage, birth of first child, birth of last child, and marriage of last child. In a similar way, the timing of widowhood has also become more predictable but has moved to a point later in the life course (Gee 1987; Gee and Kimball 1987:83; Martin Matthews 1987). Some of these patterns are visible in Table 6-2.

Only in this century has the empty-nest stage (the period of life from the departure of the youngest child until the first parent dies) of the family life course emerged. Gee (1987) estimates

Factors Contributing to Independence in Later Life

Health and Welfare Canada has had a major policy thrust to promote the independent living of older Canadians. To better understand factors promoting independence, it commissioned the Survey of Aging and Independence, which interviewed about 10 000 Canadians aged 45–64, and another 10 000 aged 65 and older, in September 1992. The conceptual model governing this survey, and the interview schedule were developed by CARNET: The Canadian Aging Research Network. CARNET links 23 social and behavioural scientists as principal investigators across Canada, and well over 100 staff and associated students, to conduct a program of research to promote "productivity and independence in an aging society."

The conceptual model for the Survey of Aging and Independence, shown here, is based on the life-course perspective and can be used to summarize much of the information presented in this chapter. Independent living is a measure of well-being and refers to the perception of being able to carry out life's activities and to have choices about those activities. Gerontological research has established that there are three major determinants of well-being in later life: health, wealth or income security, and social integration. The latter, including social ties and social support, is important, but less so than health and wealth. In a life-course perspective, the sociologist is interested in why it is that some people enter the later years healthier than others, some enter them wealthier than others, and some enter them more securely embedded in social relationships than others. These three major determinants of well-being are themselves viewed as determined or shaped by life-course experiences. In particular, the sector of the economy in which one spends the adult years, one's labour-force history, and one's family history all affect health, income

Factors Leading to Independence in Later Life

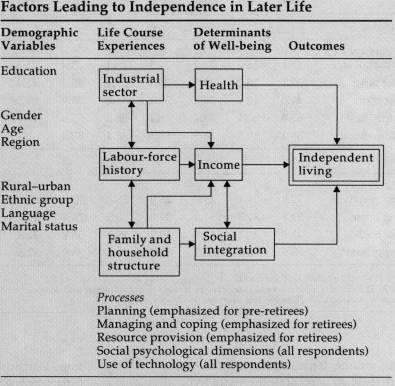

Demographic Variables

Education

Gender
Age
Region

Rural–urban
Ethnic group
Language
Marital status

Processes
Planning (emphasized for pre-retirees)
Managing and coping (emphasized for retirees)
Resource provision (emphasized for retirees)
Social psychological dimensions (all respondents)
Use of technology (all respondents)

SOURCE: CARNET: The Canadian Aging Research Network, Centre for Studies of Aging, University of Toronto, 1992.

security, and social integration. For example, whether one has private pension income after retirement may be influenced by job loss or the industrial sector in which one chose, or was able, to work. Finally, these major life course experiences are shaped as well by such demographic factors as gender, ethnicity and language, rural–urban background, region, and education.

The conceptual model is not a fully deterministic one. Following the principles of interpretive sociology and symbolic interactionism, it is assumed that the individual actively attempts

to cope with present circumstances and plan for the future. Nonetheless, individual lives are highly constrained by structural features such as social class, as emphasized by the political economy and conflict theorists.

While the Survey of Aging and Independence is cross-sectional, the model underlying it is longitudinal. To understand the life chances and fate of the older person, it is important to understand his or her past as well as the future. Where one is depends to some extent on where one has been, and in turn this shapes where one is likely to be in the future.

TABLE 6-2   Median Ages at Family-Life-Course Events

	Approximate Birth Cohorts											
	1831–1840	1841–1850	1851–1860	1861–1870	1881–1890	1891–1900	1901–1910	1911–1920	1921–1930	1931–1940	1941–1950	1951–1960
Females												
Median age at:												
First marriage	25.1	26.0	24.9	24.3	25.1	23.4	23.3	23.0	22.0	21.1	21.3	22.5
First birth	27.1	28.0	26.9	26.3	27.1	25.4	25.0	25.4	23.5	22.9	23.3	24.5
Last birth	41.0	40.0	38.2	36.2	36.2	33.9	29.1	28.8	29.5	29.1	26.7	26.3
Empty nest*	61.0	60.1	58.2	56.2	56.2	53.9	49.1	48.8	49.5	49.1	46.7	46.3
Widowhood	58.2	59.5	58.9	58.3	60.1	59.4	61.3	63.0	67.0	67.2	68.8	69.9
Males												
Median age at:												
First marriage	27.9	29.1	29.2	28.0	28.5	28.4	27.0	26.3	24.3	24.0	23.5	24.6
First birth	29.9	31.3	31.2	30.0	30.5	30.4	28.7	28.7	25.8	25.8	25.5	26.6
Last birth	43.8	43.1	42.5	39.9	39.6	38.9	32.8	32.1	31.8	32.0	28.9	28.4
Empty nest*	63.8	63.1	62.5	59.9	59.6	58.9	52.8	52.1	51.8	52.0	48.9	48.4

*Age at which last child is 20 years old.
SOURCE: Ellen M. Gee, "Historical change in the family life course of men and women," in *Aging in Canada: Social Perspectives*, 2nd edition, Victor W. Marshall, ed. (Toronto: Fitzhenry and Whiteside, 1987), p. 278.

that, among female cohorts born between 1831 and 1840, 90 percent of the years lived after marriage were spent rearing dependent children. In contrast, cohorts born between 1951 and 1960 are expected to spend 40 percent of the years following marriage in child-rearing.

Family life factors such as age at marriage and the timing of child-bearing are consequential for intergenerational relations and for the social character of later life. They affect the average number of children, grandchildren, siblings, and other relatives who will be available to the individual in old age.

Subjective Careers

People have their own ideas about the timing of life-course transitions, and they have some sense of the appropriate timing of such events. This sense has been called the **social clock** (Hagestad and Neugarten 1985). In relation to these social clocks, people see themselves as "on time" or "off time" — early, late, or "just right" — in getting married, forming a family, obtaining a promo-

tion, becoming a grandparent, or retiring. Very little research has actually been done on the extent to which conceptions of life-course timing, or social clocks, are associated with sanctioning in order to keep people roughly "on time" in the life course (Hagestad 1982), but most of us have experienced pressures (sometimes not so subtle) in this regard. One study of cohort differences in the preferred timing of female life events (Fallo-Mitchell and Ryff 1982; Ryff 1986) found that young adult women preferred later ages for family career events, such as having their first child, but earlier events for general life events, such as settling on a career choice, than did middle-aged or older women. The different cohorts attributed their own timing preferences to women of the other cohorts. Such differences in actual preferences, coupled with misperception, create grounds for potential conflict among different generations in families.

In Canada, Gee (1990) found evidence of a "social clock" phenomenon and found that the effect is greater for family than nonfamily transitions. An example, from her study of women in Vancouver and Victoria, is evidence of a "social clock" phenomenon influencing the timing of entry to the grandmother status (Gee 1991). For those who did become grandmothers, the mean age was 50.4 years, making becoming a grandmother a mid-life, rather than a later-life, transition. About half the women at that time were still engaged in parenting young children; the other half were in the "empty nest" stage of life, in which all children had left home. The number of years a woman worked in the paid labour force following the birth of her first child had an effect on the timing of grandparenthood. More years of employment were associated with a delay in onset of grandparenthood. This suggests a possible socialization effect, in which nonfamilial values were transmitted from one generation to the next. In terms of "social clocks," Gee found that grandmothers were more likely than women who were not grandmothers to state a preferred age for becoming a grandmother, and that this age is lower (48.2 vs. 55.2 years). Higher educational levels are associated with higher ideal age for becoming a grandmother, as is a Canadian place of birth. There is a strong association between preferred and actual age of becoming a grandmother. Because this is a cross-sectional study, it is not possible to ascertain whether adherence to age norms influences the timing of these women's daughters' childbearing (a socialization effect) or is a response to it (an accommodation effect). However, the study does demonstrate that a sense of appropriate timing of life events, or "social clocks," is relevant in the lives of older women in Canada.

An aspect of subjective careers that has been neglected in the sociology of aging is the increasing awareness of impending death as age increases. That is, as people grow older, and typically when they see themselves as having about ten years to live, the fact that they are mortal becomes very important to them (Marshall 1980a, 1987b). This recognition is heightened by self-perceived changes in health and by the deaths of parents, siblings, and friends (Marshall and Rosenthal 1982). An awareness of impending death normally leads individuals to focus on their past lives in order to make sense of any past-life events that lack meaning or coherence. In addition, highly aware individuals frequently focus on the meaning of death and engage in con-

crete preparations for it, such as the making of wills and the making of peace in their personal relationships.

Two life-course transitions have been of particular interest to sociologists of aging: retirement and widowhood, which too frequently have been viewed as the problems of the male elderly and the female elderly, respectively. Large numbers of both men and women experience both of these transitions, though in somewhat different ways, and are affected by the transitions of their spouses and those they love. An example of another life-course transition, experienced by only some older Canadians, is given in the accompanying boxed insert.

From Working to Retirement

In an earlier section, retirement was discussed as a socioeconomic institution. Our concern here is with the retirement experiences of individuals. Retirement should be seen as occurring within the context of age discrimination in employment that can either accelerate departure from the labour force or make retirement more palatable for the worker. With increasing age, men and women in the work force frequently encounter pressure from younger employees who feel that their older co-workers are blocking advancement opportunities (Stryckman 1987). Contrary to popular belief, for almost all tasks, skill at industrial work increases with age and older workers are generally as competent and often more accurate, punctual, and committed to the employer than are younger workers (Koyl 1977).

To some extent, seniority provisions provide job security for older workers, giving them advantages over the young (Stryckman 1987; Tindale 1987). Nonetheless, older workers are more harmed by plant shutdowns and layoffs than are younger workers. A shutdown places young and old on the labour market, and the older worker is disadvantaged in that market. A hypothesis of "selective retention" suggests that those older workers who are able to remain in the labour force despite the economic pressures affecting employment opportunities are more highly skilled and educated (Nishio and Lank 1987).

Many Canadians retire before reaching a formal, compulsory retirement age. McDonald and Wanner (1984) report that, by age 63, 75 percent

Snowbirds: Older Canadians at Leisure

Each year, thousands of older Canadians flee the cold winter and head south. They are typically retired and remain in Florida, Arizona, or another warm state, for just under six months each year. Florida "snowbirds" have been studied in a collaborative research program between Canadian and American social scientists interested in migration of the elderly, health, and social policy. In 1986, English-speaking readers of a Florida-based newspaper, *Canada News*, completed a mailed questionnaire, and in 1988 francophone snowbirds were studied.

The decision to begin snow-birding usually follows a period of shorter vacations prior to retirement. Most snowbirds are married (83 percent of francophones and 90 percent of anglophones). More than 70 percent of the respondents owned homes both in Canada and in Florida. This indicates a socioeconomic status higher than the average for their age. Their pattern of seasonal migration is so stable that 21 percent of francophone, and 15 percent of anglophone snowbirds say they think of home as both Florida and Canada equally.

Because they spend almost half their lives in the United States, the health-care utilization of Canadian snowbirds is of policy interest. Before going to Florida, most snowbirds take medical precautions: they get a check-up, stock up on medications from their free-pharmaceutical plans, take out extra health insurance, and leave instructions with children as to how to respond to a medical emergency. Most snowbirds report satisfaction with the health-care system in Florida, but they state that in the event of a serious illness they will cease their pattern of seasonal migration.

In fact, Canadian snowbirds report very low utilization of health services in Florida and almost no utilization of social services. They are thus an economic boon to the Florida economy, reporting spending an average of U.S. $1200 per month in Florida.

On most factors, anglophone and francophone snowbirds did not differ, but francophones tended to settle in a different part of Florida (along the East Coast), they tended to be more youthful, to be less well educated, and to be from lower socioeconomic backgrounds than the anglophones. They also had much larger families, contributing to larger social-support networks.

Snowbirds are of interest because their migratory pattern may disrupt supportive social networks. Francophones, with larger families, have greater kin support from family visits from children and siblings; but anglophones report more friends living near their Florida home. This may relate to the fact that the anglophones have a longer history of seasonal migration. While support networks in Canada may be somewhat weakened by seasonal migration, vacation visits from children and grandchildren, and the fact that snowbirds often migrate "in flocks" of friends, helps to maintain the viability of support networks.

Snowbirding is a lifestyle choice to pursue leisure and to avoid the limitations of the Canadian winter. In particular, the fear of falling is very strong, and somewhat realistic, among older Canadians, and ice conditions leave many Canadian seniors homebound during the winter. Snowbirding represents a choice for an active, leisure-oriented later life for those who can afford it.

Source:

Joanne Daciuk and Victor W. Marshall, "Health concerns as a deterrent to seasonal migration of elderly Canadians," *Social Indicators Research* 22 (1990):181–197; Victor W. Marshall and Richard D. Tucker, "Canadian seasonal migrants to the sunbelt: Boon or burden?" *Journal of Applied Gerontology* 9(4)(1990):420–432; Richard D. Tucker et al., "Older Canadians in Florida: A comparison of anglophone and francophone seasonal migrants," *Canadian Journal on Aging* 11(3)(1992): 281–297.

of Canadian women and 30 percent of men are retired. A national survey of adult Canadians in 1989 (Lowe 1991) found that 63 percent of retirees retired before age 65, only 17 percent at age 65, and 16 percent after age 65. Women were more likely to retire early than were men. Those taking early retirement are disproportionately from higher socioeconomic levels. While the reasons for and implications of retirement in Canada are a major unresearched area, available American and Canadian data lead McDonald and Wanner (1990:79) to conclude that health and potential retirement income are the two most important factors leading to early retirement. Poor health is a cause rather than a consequence of retirement, and retirement may even produce health benefits (Adams and Lefevre 1980; Foner and Schwab 1981). In general, most retirements can be viewed as voluntary (Frenken 1991; McDonald and Wanner 1990:79). Early retirement in the future is likely to reflect fulfilment of earlier life goals. Almost half of Canadian baby boomers plan to retire before they reach age 65 (Lowe 1991). Of all adult Canadians, those with higher incomes are more likely to anticipate early retirement (Lowe 1991).

Every year, thousands of older Canadians flee the cold winter and head south.

Contrary to popular belief, retirement does not appear to be a major crisis for most people (McDonald and Wanner 1990:72–74). In a sample of 300 recently retired men and women in southern Ontario, Martin Matthews and associates asked respondents to indicate the extent to which 34 "life events" affected them. Experiencing the death of a spouse was rated as having the strongest effects, followed by birth of children and marriage. Retirement ranked twenty-seventh. There was some evidence to suggest that retirement was more consequential for men than for women, but the differences were not great (Martin Matthews et al. 1982). In some respects, on the other hand, retirement may be a more consequential life-course transition for women than for men. In many instances, women have had to struggle harder to fashion any stable career in paid employment, and they may therefore value it more (Connidis 1982).

There is no retirement from domestic labour — that form of unpaid work that is essential to the maintenance of our socioeconomic order and still largely the domain of women, even if they are also in paid employment (Luxton 1980). Whether or not the wife has also been in paid employment, the retirement of her husband might produce a profound and, at times, adverse life transition for her. Her home is no longer her castle, and she may find new difficulties with her husband around the house, not quite knowing what to do with himself. Her loss of autonomy may, however, be offset by other aspects of the relationship, such as increased opportunity to express nurturance (Keating and Cole 1980) and to enjoy leisure time with her husband (McPherson and Guppy 1979). Sometimes women and men retire together. For example, farm couples in Alberta were found to plan ahead together for their retirement, a gradual and mutually supportive experience in most instances (Keating and Marshall 1980).

Not enough attention has been paid to the ways in which retirement is affected by social class and type of occupation (McDonald and Wanner 1982, 1990:14). As with most aspects of aging, income security and good health are the critical factors influencing morale and satisfaction with life. Seeing retirement as a negative experience rests on the assumption that work is a positive experience. This assumption is clearly untrue for many individuals and may reflect the middle-class bias of many researchers.

From Marriage to Widowhood

Until quite recently, little was known about the experience of widowhood in later life. However, Martin Matthews (1991) has recently synthesized the Canadian and broader literature in this area. Most men have the bad fortune not to experience this life-course transition because most men predecease their wives: the alleged disadvantages of widowhood for women should be weighed against this alternative. Widowhood is both a social status and a process. The process involves changes in identity and feelings toward the self and the deceased spouse. This process is affected by the social characteristics of the deceased and the survivor, by the nature of the death, and by the social relations that the widowed person maintains.

Many deaths of older people can be thought of as appropriately timed according to the life-course social clock. There is time for the dying person and the spouse to prepare for the death. In general, grief is more intense in the case of a younger death and when death is relatively unexpected (Marshall 1980a; Vachon 1979; Martin Matthews 1991: 17-23).

There is increased mortality among the recently bereaved. Because about three-quarters of the increased death rate among the bereaved is a result of various types of heart disease, the term *broken-heart syndrome* has been applied to this phenomenon (Parkes, Benjamin, and Fitzgerald 1969). Although the dynamics of this syndrome are not clearly understood, they undoubtedly go beyond the stress implied in the folk dictum "She died of a broken heart" to include the stresses of care-giv-

ing that the surviving spouse may have experienced in caring for the other while he or she was dying. Canadian research (Martin Matthews 1987, 1991; Martin Matthews et al. 1982; McFarlane et al. 1980) shows that widowhood is the single most disruptive transition of the life course.

Women, as noted earlier, are much more likely to occupy the social status of widowhood than are men. If they do remarry, this is likely to be after a longer period of widowhood than is the case for men (Northcott 1984). Comparing a Quebec sample of widowed persons who did and did not remarry, Stryckman (1981) found that half the males had remarried within a year and a half of bereavement, while half the females remarried within four and a half years. Although men are more likely than women to remarry, Berardo (1970) has suggested that the transition to widowhood may be more serious for men than for women, partly because it is "off time" in relation to social clocks. However, a Canadian study (Wister and Strain 1986) found no difference in the well-being of elderly widows and widowers.

Much research on widowhood focuses on social support. Lopata (1979) found children to be the most prominent category of kin providing support to elderly female widows in Chicago. A Canadian study conducted in Guelph, Ontario, also found children to be important sources of support. But siblings, especially sisters, were also actively involved in the widow's support system. Half of these widows named a sister as one of the three people to whom they felt closest. Moreover, two-thirds of the widows listed an extended kin member — sibling-in-law, cousin, and/or niece — as part of their emotional support system (Martin Matthews 1987). Wister and Strain (1986) found that widows were more strongly embedded than widowers in interaction patterns with family and neighbours.

Martin Matthews, applying a symbolic-interactionist perspective, stresses the active part that widows play in reconstructing their lives and their identities and in attributing meaning to widowhood. For example, she notes that diminished social ties in widowhood may mean rejection to one widow, loneliness to another, but independence to a third (Martin Matthews 1987, 1991: 17–34). Like retirement and other life-course transitions, widowhood brings changes in identity and in social relationships. Like these other transitions, it is no doubt influenced by social class, cohort, and other bases of social differentiation.

The ramifications of widowhood extend beyond the widow to other family members. If a widow is receiving support from a sibling or from a child, then we should also look at the child who is providing such support. Considerations such as these lead us to a general discussion of the inter-generational family.

Family and Intergenerational Relations

One of our society's most persistent myths about the family is that the elderly are isolated from and abandoned by their children. This is related to a view that our family system consists of self-sufficient nuclear family units composed of parents and young, dependent children isolated from one another geographically, socially, and emotionally. When children mature and leave home, they are thought to sever ties with their parents. If this characterization were entirely accurate, the elderly would be cut off from intergenerational family life. Sociologists have, therefore, been very interested in investigating the family relationships of older people. Three decades of research have led sociologists to suggest that we have a *modified extended-family system* consisting of many nuclear family units maintaining separate households but bound together in ongoing relationships.

The Changing Structure of the Family

Changes in mortality and fertility have made the multigenerational family more common. In one Canadian study (Rosenthal 1987a), 78 percent of a random sample of community-dwelling respondents aged 70 and older were members of three- or four-generation families — a figure comparable to national American data (Shanas with Heinemann 1982). We may expect a substantial increase in the number of four-generation families between now and the end of this century. People now have greatly increased opportunities to have ongoing relationships in adult life with their parents and grandparents and with their adult children and grandchildren. At the same time, families are more and more likely to have some members who are old and frail, placing burdens of responsibility for care on other family members, especially those of the younger generation.

While families now have more generations alive than they did in the past, declines in fertility mean that there are fewer people in each generational level. This also means that people have fewer brothers and sisters. Thus we conceive of the contemporary family structure as being long and thin; it is also somewhat fragile, in the sense that death or geographical mobility may have a greater impact than it has in multigenerational families with more members.

Much research on the family life of older people has focused on their relationships with adult children. To describe this research, the following discussion is organized around certain dimensions of family life.

The Proximity and Availability of Kin

On the whole, most people at age 65 have a spouse. The percentage declines as the years go by, very sharply for women. About four out of five people over 65 years of age have at least one child and at least one sibling. Further, about three-quarters of older people have grandchildren and one-third have great-grandchildren (Rosenthal 1987a).

Clearly, most older people have kin. However, a very small but important minority have no living spouse, children, or sibling (Rosenthal 1987a). These people find it extremely difficult to remain in the community should they suffer health losses in later life (Shapiro and Roos 1987).

Like people of all ages, married old people usually live with their spouses, and those who are widowed or never married are likely to live alone (Connidis and Rempel 1983; Stone and Fletcher 1987). In the Hamilton study, of women aged 70 and over, 23 percent lived with a spouse and 60 percent lived alone. Most older people prefer this living arrangement, striving to retain autonomy from their children (Béland 1987; Connidis 1983; Wister 1985) and for a relationship with their children that has been called "intimacy at a distance" (Rosenmayr 1977). For people over the age of 80, living with a son or daughter is some-what more common, partly because of age-related health problems.

Although most older people do not live with a child, they usually live near at least one of their children. We may assume that this is related, in part, to the concern of children to keep a watchful eye on their parents' condition (Marshall, Rosenthal, and Synge 1983; Rosenthal 1987a) and to the health-care needs of aging parents.

Interaction, Exchange, and Helping Patterns

Contrary to popular belief, most older people interact frequently with their children. For example, studies in the United States, England, Denmark, and Canada of people who do have children suggest that about four out of five older people see a child at least once a week. About half of older people have daily telephone contact with a child, and the vast majority have at least weekly contact (Marshall and Bengtson 1983; Rosenthal 1987a). One of the reasons for such contact is that it allows the exchange of help.

A variety of studies point to high levels of exchange among generations of a broad range of goods and services, including assistance with home repairs, child care, grocery shopping, transportation, health care, and financial assistance and support (Chappell 1983, 1992; Marshall and Bengtson 1983; Rosenthal 1987a). Contrary to popular images of older people as dependent, these studies suggest a more appropriate image of interdependence. Help flows across the generations in both directions, with older people both giving and receiving. Certainly, the amount and type of help given and received varies by the socioeconomic status of the parent and child but, except for the extremely poor, most elderly people are more likely to give financial help to their children than they are to receive it (Cheal 1983; Rosenthal 1987a).

The familial provision of health care is becoming increasingly prevalent as parents live into very old age and experience health losses. If a spouse is present, he or she is generally the primary caregiver (Aronson 1985). If there is no spouse, caregiving responsibilities generally fall to persons in the second-oldest generational level in a family, who may themselves be getting on in

years. Marcil-Gratton and Légaré (1992) report that spouseless older Canadians with few children tend to find the support they need elsewhere, and that future generations of the elderly, with even fewer children, will also likely do so. Women are more likely to be caregivers to the elderly than men. In a patriarchal society, gender roles place caregiving demands on women throughout their adult lives — for children, spouses, and their aging parents. In addition, since men typically predecease their wives, spousal caregiving is predominantly provided by women. In the case of widows, and also widowers, sons do provide considerable care, but not generally as much as daughters.

Familial Norms and Consensus between the Generations

Most people feel some obligation to provide emotional support to other family members and to assist them financially and in times of health crises. However, there are great differences in the strength of adherence to what are referred to as norms of **filial obligation**. In a Prince Edward Island study, younger people expressed stronger adherence to such norms than did elderly people (Storm et al. 1985). In the Hamilton study, few age differences were found. When respondents aged 70 and older were asked to report on their expectations for the help their children should provide to them, their answers were not related to the parental reports of assistance actually received. This lack of relationship is due in part to the abstract nature of the normative statements put to respondents. In symbolic-interactionist terms, filial expectations and their fulfilment are highly "situated": they are realized in concrete circumstances of parental need, familial bonds, and resources (Marshall, Rosenthal, and Daciuk 1987).

Disagreement between parents and children concerning norms of filial obligation or other issues creates the potential for intergenerational conflict. Some research (Bengtson and Kuypers 1971; Marshall and Bengtson 1983) suggests that both parents and children think they are in greater agreement on a number of issues than they really are. Bengtson and Kuypers found that the parents of the college students saw themselves as closer in political ideology to their children than the children considered to be the case. The researchers interpreted this as an example of the *developmental stake* that parents invest in the parent–child relationship. Parents devote many years to building this relationship and want it to be close and successful.

Children, too, want this kind of relationship, but they also have a stake in developing their own autonomy and independence. These differential investments of the two generations contribute to somewhat different perceptions of the characteristics of the relationship. The *developmental* in developmental stake refers to changing perceptions and motivations of both child and parent as they proceed through the life course.

Affective Bonds

A number of investigations focus on such qualitative aspects of intergenerational relationships as closeness, warmth, trust, and concern.

Research in the Netherlands (Knipscheer and Bevers 1985) inquired of older people and their adult children whether the parent–child relationship had become better or worse, compared with the situation in the past. Parents viewed the relationship as stable and thought their children would agree, but children were more likely to see changes for the better. In contrast to the discussion in the previous section, here the developmental-stake principle seems to be weighted toward the younger generation taking the more positive view of the relationship. This may be a reflection of the aging parents' desire to deny growing dependency and of the satisfaction gained by the child in contributing more to the parents' welfare as a representation of increasing equality.

In the Hamilton study (Marshall 1987a), adult children showed a high level of concern about health and health changes in their parents. Daughters, in keeping with traditional gender-role stereotyping, showed more concern than did sons; and fathers were worried about more than were mothers. Greater concern was evident among adult children who were providing more care to parents.

Collateral rather than intergenerational relationships may provide a major basis of support for the elderly now and in the future (Connidis 1989:71–86; Marcil-Gratton and Légaré 1992). As Connidis points out (1989:71), sibling ties are for many the most enduring intimate ties, beginning at birth and outlasting the death of one's parents. With fertility decreasing, siblings constitute an important source of support for those with few children and for those with many. Strain and Payne (1992) have shown that ever-single older Canadians have higher sibling contact than those who have married.

Maintaining the Family

Family relationships do not develop inexorably because of functional requirements of the society. Instead, they are an achievement worked out by family members in response to social and historical conditions. Among these conditions are the demographic changes affecting the family context of older people and their middle-aged children.

On the various dimensions of family life that we have discussed, most families may be aptly characterized as having high cohesion. Not only does this refute myths of the abandonment of the elderly, but it occurs despite the pressures on contemporary families. Economic constraints, geographical mobility, and demographic changes pose threats to the family. Additional tensions arise out of the normal course of intergenerational life. The quest for autonomy and independence by both young and old represents one such source of tension. New members must be absorbed into families. Family relations are disrupted by death. Family members work at maintaining the family through a variety of accommodations and negotiations, including mutual tolerance, self-deception, and role segregation (Marshall and Bengtson 1983; Rosenthal 1987a).

Looking at the extended family, there are changes in its organization that are related to the family life course transitions of its members. Research on "kinkeeping" indicates that many families have one person who takes on the task of keeping the family together and that this is considered especially important in times of family crisis, such as the death of a parent (Rosenthal 1985). Most families have a person who is considered to be the "head of the family" (Rosenthal and Marshall 1986). Such people provide leadership and advice for the extended family. When one "head" dies, another usually takes his or her place (Rosenthal 1987b). Yet another family position is the "comforter" (Rosenthal 1987c), the person to whom other family members turn for emotional support. The presence in most families of such specialized roles suggests that the family is valued and that, because it is valued, its members work to preserve it (Marshall and Rosenthal 1982; Rosenthal 1987a).

In summary, the ramifications of population aging at the level of the family have not demonstrated a failure of the family or the end of the family; rather, these ramifications have shown that people have transformed the family to meet new challenges.

SUMMARY

1. The sociology of aging deals with the changes experienced over the life course, with social relationships of older people, and with the implications, both micro and macro, of individual and population aging for the entire society.

2. Canada has experienced, and will continue to experience, a significant increase in the number and proportion of older people and in the average of the population. The great majority of very old people are women.

3. It is essential to differentiate among the aged by health status, economic characteristics, gender, age itself, and other social characteristics such as ethnicity.

4. Political and social concern about population aging results in large measure from increased societal allocation of resources for the health care and income security of the aged; but economic and service-delivery problems are frequently incorrectly blamed on the aging of the population.

5. Modernization has been associated with a decline in the status of the aged. However, it cannot be assumed that old people had high status in pre-modern societies, nor that age is a more important criterion for assigning status than are other factors.

6. Society is differentiated by age, rights, obligations, and rewards. The age-stratification system itself changes as cohorts with varying social characteristics flow through it.

7. A number of factors, including cross-cutting allegiances and differences within generations, decrease the potential for conflict based on age, while the growth of the proportion of aged people in the population and economic implications of population aging increase the likelihood of age-group conflict.

8. Much of the sociology of aging has focused on happiness. The major predictors of happiness in later life are good health, income security, and, to a lesser but still important extent, supportive interaction with other people.

9. Being old carries mild stigmas. As a result, many people resist identifying themselves as old and adopt various interaction strategies, such as controlling information and selective interaction, to protect their self-esteem.

10. Old age is associated with a decrease in the resources people can exchange in interaction. This may partially explain the decreased role involvements of older people and the kinds of involvements they have.

11. Over the past century, major life-course transitions have become more predictable. Retirement is less a crisis than is usually thought, while widowhood is undoubtedly the most significant transition of later life. Also people develop subjective views of the timing of their own transitions over the life course.

12. Relationships between older people and their adult children are characterized by high levels of interaction, exchange, and solidarity.

13. Structural-functionalist sociology has dominated the sociology of aging at both macro and micro levels. It provides the theoretical foundations for both the modernization and the age-stratification theories, and for the activity, disengagement, and role theories of later life-adjustment.

14. Conflict theorists have developed a political economy of aging. They emphasize that the economic issues underlying provisions for income security for old people are primarily resolved in relation to decisions about the balance between public and private sectors over the control of capital. Other conflict theorists have examined the ways in which age and historical generations have become bases for conflict.

15. Symbolic interactionists have rejected the equilibrium assumptions of the sociology of

later-life happiness and have stressed the strategic interaction of older people as they seek to maximize personal autonomy and self-esteem and to maintain identity.

GLOSSARY

Activities of daily living (ADL). Everyday activities, such as rising and going to bed, personal hygiene, and shopping.

Activity theory. A theory that emphasizes that continuing activity through social roles is required in order to attain high life satisfaction in the later years.

Age strata. Socially recognized divisions ordered over the life course, with which are associated rights, responsibilities, obligations, and access to rewards.

Age-stratification perspective. A theoretical approach that focuses on the progression of birth cohorts through the age strata of a society and, in addition, views the age-stratification system as changing in response to cohort characteristics and other social phenomena.

Cohort. A set of individuals born at approximately the same time, who move through the life course together.

Continuity theory. A loosely defined theoretical approach that argues that life satisfaction in the later years is enhanced by a continuation of lifelong patterns of activity and role involvement, whether high or low.

Disengagement theory. A theory that argues that successful aging involves a mutual withdrawal of the aging individual and society. This is seen as functional for the society and beneficial for the individual. Such disengagement is viewed as normal and, ideally, voluntary on the part of the individual.

Exchange theory. A view of social interaction as an exchange of rewards. Individuals are assumed to seek to maximize rewards and minimize costs.

Generation. When used in other than the kinship or family sense, the term refers to a cohort, large proportions of whose members have experienced significant sociohistorical experiences. Such generational experiences frequently lead to the development of shared generational consciousness.

Modernization thesis. An argument that maintains that as societies modernize, aspects of modernization — such as industrialization, urbanization, increased emphasis on technology, and improved health and longevity — contribute to a decline in the social status of the aged.

Social clock. Socially shared expectations about the normal or appropriate timing and sequence of events over the life course. For example, people may see themselves as making slow or rapid career progress compared with general expectations, or they may see themselves as "delaying" marriage or parenthood.

FURTHER READING

Canadian Journal on Aging. A quarterly journal of scholarly, research-based papers on aging. Many articles reflect a sociology and social science perspective.

Connidis, Ingrid A. *Family Ties and Aging.* Toronto: Butterworths, 1989. An exploration of the family life of the aged, including parent–child and sibling ties, and the situations of single, divorced, widowed, remarried, and childless older people. Family and aging policy is also considered.

Driedger, Leo, and Neena L. Chappell. *Aging and Ethnicity: Toward an Interface.* Toronto: Butterworths, 1987. A critical review of the research and policy literature on aging and ethnicity in Canada, by two sociologists.

Gee, Ellen M., and Meredith M. Kimball. *Women and Aging.* Toronto: Butterworths, 1987. An exploration of aging as a women's issue, by a sociologist and psychologist.

Marshall, Victor W. (ed.). *Aging in Canada: Social Perspectives.* 2nd edition. Markham, ON: Fitzhenry and Whiteside, 1987. Thirty chapters by leading Canadian sociologists of aging, and other social and health scientists, presenting demographic data and information about aging in relation to work and retirement, the family, the health-care system, and other social institutions.

Marshall, Victor W. (ed.). *Aging and Later Life: The Social Psychology of Aging.* Beverly Hills, CA: Sage, 1986. Ten chapters focusing on theory in the symbolic-interaction and interpretive perspectives, as applied to aging and later life.

Novak, Mark. *Aging and Society: A Canadian Perspective.* Scarborough, ON: Nelson Canada, 1988. This introductory-level textbook is written by a sociologist but provides a comprehensive review of aging from the social science perspective.

Rathbone-McCuan, Eloise, and Betty Havens (eds.). *North American Elders: United States and Canadian Perspectives.* New York: Greenwood Press, 1988. Contains chapters by a number of Canadian sociologists of aging exploring social policy, the demography of aging, long-term care, the family, rural aging, and multicultural issues.

CHAPTER 7

Crime and Deviance

JOHN HAGAN

Deviance involves variation from a norm: to be different is to be deviant. But there is more to deviance than this. If there were not, our topic would be considerably less interesting than it is; we would simply be talking about the human diversity that surrounds us. What makes deviance a matter of great interest and importance is the reaction it provokes. Through the reactions of others, diverse human beings may be singled out as both different *and* disreputable.

Kinds of Crime and Deviance

Deviance, then, is variation from a norm and the societal reaction involved. With this definition in mind, let us begin to identify several characteristics that help distinguish among kinds of deviance (Hagan 1977). Table 7-1 illustrates these characteristics for easy comparison.

The first of these characteristics is the *severity of the societal response*. Historically, we have responded to our most serious deviants, including first-degree murderers, by making them liable to capital punishment. We may do so again. At the other end of the spectrum, some deviants, particularly those who are badly disturbed or disabled, are simply ignored. If they are slightly more disturbing, they are ostracized. Between the two ends of this societal-response continuum, there are other types of institutional and community responses, including imprisonment, mental hospitalization, probation, fines, and outpatient treatment. The point is that these many societal responses vary in the degree to which they limit a

TABLE 7-1 Kinds of Deviance

Kind of Deviance	Severity of Societal Response	Perceived Harmfulness	Degree of Agreement	Examples
Consensus crimes	Severe	Extremely harmful	Consensus	Premediated murder
Conflict crimes	Punitive	Somewhat harmful	Conflict	Victimless crimes (e.g., prostitution, narcotics)
Social deviations	Indeterminate	Potentially harmful	Uncertainty	Mental illness, juvenile delinquency
Social diversions	Mild	Relatively harmless	Apathy	Fads and fashions

citizen's freedom. Generally speaking, the more seriously the act of deviance is regarded, the more the freedom of the alleged deviant will be curtailed.

A second characteristic of deviance is the *perceived harmfulness* of the behaviour in question. Some deviant behaviours, like aggravated assault and aggravated sexual assault, are regarded as serious because of the harm they are perceived to cause. Other forms of deviance, including some sexual predilections of consenting adults, are regarded as inconsequential because they are perceived as causing little or no harm. Between the extremely harmful and the relatively harmless are a number of behavioural deviations from the norm that are thought to be only mildly harmful or whose degree of harm is uncertain. Included here are activities like marijuana use. Governments have spent millions of dollars assessing the presumed harmfulness of this drug, while the public has seemed to grow steadily less interested in, even sceptical of, government findings.

In general, however, where a form of deviant behaviour is perceived to be more harmful, it will be seen as more serious. The key word here is *perceived*: the point is not so much what harm these deviant acts do, but what harm they are perceived to do. As Shakespeare observed, "There is nothing either good or bad, but thinking makes it so."

A third characteristic of deviance is the *degree of agreement* among the public about whether an act should be considered deviant. Across nations and generations there is a high degree of consensus that some forms of behaviour are indeed seriously deviant (for example, armed robbery, aggravated sexual assault, and premeditated homicide). Yet there are also many forms of behaviour about which there is considerable disagreement. Included among these debated subjects, called **conflict crimes** because of conflicting opinions regarding them, are most types of drug use and many forms of sexual activity. Finally, there are those forms of behaviour about which most of us are disinterested. Among the more intriguing subjects of our apathy are many fads and fashions. As bizarre as these styles can become, most of us have no strong interest in calling them deviant.

We have briefly considered three related characteristics of deviance: the severity of the societal response to the deviant activity, the perceived harmfulness of the behaviour, and the degree of agreement among the public that the acts involved should be considered deviant. Taken together, these characteristics provide a measure of how seriously a particular form of deviance is taken. In other words, the most serious forms provoke a severe societal response, are perceived as extremely harmful, and are defined as deviant with a high degree of consensus. Less serious forms of deviance result in more moderate or indeterminate forms of societal response, are perceived as less harmful, and may be the subjects of uncertainty or conflict. Finally, the least serious forms of deviance call forth only mild responses, are perceived as relatively harmless, and are subjects of widespread apathy.

Deviance is determined by the reactions of others to certain behaviours. Conflict crimes are often a matter of debate.

Consensus Crimes

With these points in mind, we can now attach names to the kinds of deviance we have begun to identify. The first of these categories comprises the **consensus crimes** (Toby 1974), which are defined by law as crimes. The Criminal Code of Canada specifies a large number of criminal acts, yet only a few are widely regarded as extremely harmful, are severely punished, and are consensually identified as deviant. One such act is premeditated murder. In many nations and for many centuries, laws of a similar form have designated this type of behaviour as a crime. The consistency of these statutes has led some legal philosophers to call such acts *mala en se*, or "bad in themselves." A quick examination of our criminal codes, however, will convince most readers that

the number of *mala en se* criminal and deviant acts is few. History and anthropology demonstrate that most conceptions of crime and deviance are subject to change. What is called criminal at one time or place is frequently seen quite differently at another. This being so, many people find the notion of inherent and universal evil somewhat dubious. This changeable character of crime and deviance is a salient feature of the kind of deviance we consider next.

Conflict Crimes

Our second category of deviance is what we earlier defined as conflict crimes. Although people convicted of conflict crimes may receive punitive treatment from the courts, acts of this type are usually regarded as only marginally harmful and, at that, are typically subjects of conflict and debate. Legal philosophers refer to such crimes as *mala prohibita*, or "wrong by definition." It is significant that many conflict crimes were once consensus crimes, and that some of what were once conflict crimes have now achieved considerable consensus. Into the former category fall many of the "victimless" crimes, including prostitution, drug use, and many sexual acts between consenting adults. For example, during much of this century marijuana use was regarded as a serious form of narcotics abuse requiring strict legal control (Bonnie and Whitebread 1974). Today marijuana use is subject to much milder penalties. Significantly, however, this change did not begin until marijuana use became a part of middle- and upper-class youth cultures in the 1960s. What was once a consensus crime is now a subject of some conflict.

In contrast to marijuana use, sexual assault seems to be a crime whose roots involved conflict; its legal definition has only recently become a focus of debate. It can be argued that historically, rape laws emerged out of men's efforts to protect women — not because these women were women, but because these women were "theirs." From this viewpoint, rape consisted of one man taking the property of another. Consistent with this view is the fact that, prior to 1982, a husband could not be charged with raping his wife. Indeed, Lorenne Clark (1976) demonstrated that rape usually resulted in sentences quite similar to those handed down for robbery (a crime that involves taking property). For most of our Canadian experience these facts have been the subject of apparent consensus, and only recently has the conflict underlying this law become a topic of public concern.

Social Deviations

Our next category consists of **social deviations**. Many of the behaviours included in this category are not criminal but are nonetheless subject to official control. Some are dealt with under statutes defining mental illness, others under juvenile-delinquency legislation, and still others under numerous civil laws that attempt to control various forms of business and professional activities. This vagueness may reflect an attempt to protect the powerful from public harassment; in the cases of juvenile delinquency and mental illness, however, it may be that we simply do not have clear notions of what these official categories include.

The concern in all of this is that while business and professional people may escape official control of their social deviations under such statutes, people with fewer resources may not. Furthermore, those defined as delinquent or mentally ill may be designated as such on the basis of their perceived potential for harm, rather than on the basis of actual harm done. Finally, their assigned treatments may be of indeterminate duration, rather than for a fixed term of punishment. All of this comes from the announced desire to help rather than penalize people who commit social deviations. But such help is all too often perceived by those on the receiving end as punishment and usually constitutes some form of official control. The troubled history of official and unofficial responses to homosexuality is an unhappy example of the latter point.

Social Diversions

Our last deviance category is made up of **social diversions**. All of us personally or vicariously experience these. They are the lifestyle variations that help make our lives more interesting and at times exciting: the fads and fashions of speech, appearance, and play. Constant among these diversions is the pursuit of pleasure, though there is, of course, extreme variation in what is regarded as pleasurable. Joggers brave exhaustion and subzero temperatures in search of the "runner's high," while surfers circle the world and endure the ravages of weather and water in their quest for "the perfect wave." As odd as some of these activities seem to many of us, however, we typically react with no more than a mixture of amusement and apathy to the time, energy, and resources expended by their enthusiasts. Other societies would regard our tolerance of the diverse and the bizarre as indulgent, and indeed it is. We do not consider the behaviours involved good or bad, but simply different, diverse, and, to their participants, enjoyable.

So far we have given an extended definition of deviance, seeking to answer the question "What

Social diversions are the lifestyle variations that help make our lives more interesting, although there is variation in what is considered interesting.

is it?" Let us now turn our attention to the question "Where do we find it?"

Using several alternative approaches (considered later in this chapter) to measuring crime and deviance, sociologists have attempted to collect valid and reliable information about how these behaviours are socially distributed. One way of beginning this task involves comparing the official statistics of crime and deviance with those gathered through one or more alternative methods. Where the findings generated by alternative methods agree with the official measures, we can have some confidence in our conclusions. Where disagreement occurs, we can examine possible explanations for the disparities. Often these alternative explanations can tell us a good deal, not only about the social distribution of deviance, but

also about the official agencies that control deviance. In the next section, we use the strategy just described to consider the distribution of crime and deviant behaviour by gender and social class in Canada.

Social Distribution of Crime and Deviance

Are criminal and noncriminal forms of deviant behaviour randomly distributed in Canadian society? Or do these behaviours occur at different rates among identifiable social groups in our society? Accurately identifying the social distribution of crime and deviance is an important first step toward explaining these behaviours.

Gender Distribution of Crime and Deviance

It is clear that criminal and noncriminal forms of deviant behaviour are not distributed randomly by gender. Regardless of the mode of measurement, men are significantly more likely to be alcoholic (Cahalan 1970), addicted to illegal drugs (Terry and Pellens 1970), and involved in the more serious forms of crime (Hindelang 1979). This does not mean, however, that men in all ways or at all times are necessarily more deviant than women. We know that women tend to take more legally prescribed psychoactive drugs than men (Manheimer et al. 1969) and that they report higher rates of mental illness (Gove and Tudor 1973). It is in criminal forms of deviance that males clearly exceed females. But the relationship between gender and crime is not a simple one. The disparity between the sexes fluctuates with the type of crime, the time, and the social setting. For example, while it has been estimated from official statistics in North America that males exceed females in crimes against the person on the order of more than eight to one, males exceed females on the order of four to one for crimes against property (Nettler 1973).

The most fascinating aspect of this deviance-by-gender situation is the possibility that it may be changing, along with attitudes toward gender roles. It has been argued that women are increasing their involvement in all types of offences, and more specifically that a new breed of violent, aggressive, female offenders may be arising (Adler 1975). On the other hand, it has also been suggested that the new female criminal is more a social myth than an empirical reality (Steffensmeir 1978; Chesney-Lind and Shelden 1992). Both these arguments could have some validity. For example, it may be that the new female criminal is to be found in some areas of crime more frequently than in others. In other words, some convincing evidence suggests that certain areas of crime may be changing faster than others.

For example, a review (Smith and Visher 1980) of official data and **self-report surveys** (anonymously answered by adolescents and adults) on crime and deviance indicates that behavioural differences between the sexes are diminishing (see also Hagan, Gillis, and Simpson 1985, 1987). Interestingly, the gap is narrowing faster for minor deviant acts than for more serious crimes. Similarly, while the relationship of gender to deviance is declining for both youths and adults, the data indicate that this trend is stronger for youths. This latter finding is particularly interesting, because it is consistent with the expected effects of changing gender roles. That is, it seems likely that current shifts in gender roles would have a greater effect on the behaviour of younger women, and this is exactly what the data indicate. These patterns of change deserve to be closely watched in the future.

Class Distribution of Crime and Deviance

The relationship between deviant behaviour and class position is a matter of considerable controversy. At the centre of the debate sits a pair of assumptions that are often viewed as incompatible. The first holds that being a member of the lower class implies a denial of opportunities and a harshness of circumstances to which deviant behaviour is a predictable response. The second maintains that the prejudice and discrimination of official control agents and agencies result in members of the lower class being disproportionately targeted for control. These contrasting assumptions are not necessarily mutually exclusive; the argument will be made in this and in a later section that both assumptions are correct.

The official statistics of crime and delinquency make one point rather clearly: persons *prosecuted* for criminal and delinquent offences are disproportionately members of the lower class (Braithwaite 1981). The issue is whether this official sampling of criminals and delinquents is representative of the population from which it is drawn, or whether it is biased by, for example, selection from one class more than another. The answer to this question seems to depend in part on the type of deviance we are considering.

Self-report data have often been compared with official records to examine the class distribution of crime and delinquency. The most serious forms of crime and delinquency are seldom encountered in self-reports, however, and these comparisons therefore tend to concentrate on the less serious and most frequent types of deviant activity (Hindelang et al. 1981). Self-report studies show a wide range of results (Tittle and Meier 1990). In some, the relationship between self-reported deviant behaviours and class position is weak (Braithwaite 1981); in some, inconsistent (Tittle, Villemez, and Smith 1978); and in some — depending on the measure of class — even positive (Hagan, Gillis, and Simpson 1985). Braithwaite (1981) summarizes 47 of these studies, 25 of which found some evidence that lower-class people more often report deviant behaviours, and 22 of which found no relationship at all between reports of deviant behaviour and class position. Official statistics have traditionally shown such a relationship.

Comparisons with self-report data imply that some class bias exists in the official reports of the most frequent forms of crime and delinquency. One Canadian study (Hagan, Gillis, and Chan 1978) reinforces this conclusion, noting that the police in particular tend to believe that the densely populated lower-class areas of the city most need police patrols. Because more telephone complaints come from these areas, for example, the police may develop an exaggerated idea of such areas' relative incidence of crime and delinquency being recorded, since more police are looking for and finding deviance.

Recently more serious forms of crime have been studied by surveying victims. In the United States, victimization surveys have been used nationwide to examine racial involvement in personal crimes of the common law (crimes against persons that have long been considered serious). These studies reveal a substantially greater involvement of blacks in the crimes of rape, robbery, and assault (Hindelang 1978). There is also some evidence of police bias in this research, but evidence of bias is far outweighed by evidence of real behavioural differences. Insofar as race and class are strongly related in the United States, this American research suggests that there is a relationship between social class and criminal behaviour for serious forms of crime (Reiss and Roth 1993).

It bears repeating, however, that our conception of what constitutes a serious form of deviance is

subject to change. We saw this earlier with regard to marijuana use. Within one generation, marijuana use changed, in the assessment of many, from allegedly causing "reefer madness" to symbolizing radical-chic status. Self-report surveys sometimes reflected this change, documenting higher levels of marijuana use in the middle and upper classes than in the lower (Suchman 1968; Barter, Mizner, and Werme 1970). Significant class changes have occurred in the use of cocaine, but changes in the use of hard drugs like heroin, however, have been less substantial (Blackwell 1988). Self-report and official statistics are in agreement that these hard drugs have been and continue to be used more extensively in the lower class, and their use is still generally regarded as a serious matter.

Official and alternative types of statistics have also been compared in the areas of alcohol abuse and mental illness. Official statistics in these areas, as in others, show a higher representation of the lower class. Self-report studies parallel these findings. For example, household surveys have contained the following question: "Have you or any member of your household ever had difficulty because of too much drinking?" Many of these studies report both higher incidence and higher prevalence of such problems in the lower class than in other classes (for example, Bailey, Haberman, and Alksne 1965; Cahalan 1970). Similar conclusions are found in the area of mental illness. Dohrenwend and Dohrenwend (1969) report that "the highest overall rates of psychiatric disorder have been found in the lowest social class in 28 out of 33 studies that report data according to indicators of social class."

We can thus draw some conclusions. Serious crimes, hard-drug use, alcohol abuse, and mental illness are more prevalent in the lower class, while less serious and more common forms of crime, delinquency, and drug use are more evenly distributed across the social classes. It is in the latter areas that official statistics appear most dubious, because members of the lower class are here disproportionately selected for official attention. To some extent, doubt or confidence in a given deviance statistic depends on how such deviance is measured. Let us turn then from our consideration of the social distribution of deviance to a consideration of how to measure it.

Measuring Crime and Deviance

Because many forms of deviance are controlled officially, they are also counted officially. These enumerations constitute the official statistics of deviance found in the reports of police, of criminal and civil courts, of correctional institutions, of mental health centres, and of various agencies dealing with alcohol and drug abuse. A myriad of statistics exist, therefore; if these were as credible as they are accessible, the sociologist's task would be an easier one. Unfortunately, the same biases that can affect the legislation of crime and deviance (considered below) can also affect the counting of criminal and deviant behaviours. That is, organizations involved in controlling these behaviours may not be strictly impartial, and may instead follow their own interests in the types and amounts of crime and deviance they count.

Giffen (1966), for example, suggests that one latent function of processing skid-row alcoholics in a "revolving-door" fashion is that it makes the criminal justice system look both busy and efficient, and the budgets of control agencies often depend heavily on how busy and efficient these agencies appear. Thus, some statistics produced by official control agencies may tell us more about the agencies themselves than about the persons and events counted. The challenge for scholars, then is to make sociological sense of the statistics official agencies collect.

Analysts of deviance have responded to this challenge by developing alternatives to the use of official records, such as collecting data from nonofficial agencies: insurance companies dealing with theft; hospitals, private physicians, and public health agencies, whose records reflect much alcoholism and drug abuse; and business accounting and consulting firms, which encounter much internal theft and fraud.

A second alternative is to collect and record first-person accounts generated through the anonymous self-report surveys of adolescents and adults and personal face-to-face interviews with subjects in their natural settings. The self-report approach, as seen earlier, has been used to study crime, delinquency, alcohol and drug abuse, and the symptoms of mental illness. Personal interviews are most often used to study *career deviants*, those individuals who persist in deviant lifestyles.

A third approach involves surveys of the victims of crime. Done by telephone or in a door-to-door, census-like fashion, victimization surveys provide a unique measure of deviant behaviour that includes crimes committed against people and property.

A fourth and final approach involves actual observations of deviant behaviour (in which the observer may or may not be a participant). Consensus crimes such as homicide do not, of course, readily lend themselves to being studied in this way. So this method has been used primarily in the study of conflict crimes and other controversial forms of deviance, like homosexuality and marijuana use.

These, then, are four alternatives to reliance on official statistics, which may reflect official control and official preoccupation with certain kinds of deviance.

But why are some forms of difference and diversity subject to official control while others are not? Scholars have been particularly concerned that this discrepancy reflects part of the activities of certain self-interested groups and individuals, who may lobby for the official control of some types of deviant behaviour. Let us therefore turn our attention to the issue of crime and deviance legislation.

Legislation against Crime and Deviance

Moral entrepreneurs is the term Becker (1963) uses for those individuals most active in striving for official control of deviance. These are the people whose initiative and enterprise are essential in getting the legal rules passed that are necessary to "do something" about a particular type of deviant behaviour. Often these individuals seem to be undertaking a moral crusade — they perceive some activity as an evil in need of legal reform, and they pursue this task with missionary zeal (Gusfield 1963). Moral entrepreneurs and crusaders assume that enforcement of the wished-for legal rules will improve the lives of those who are ruled. We will see that this is often a very dubious assumption as we consider two moral crusades that brought legal control of two different types of deviant behaviour in North America.

Narcotics and Alcohol

The moral entrepreneur most responsible for the passage of Canada's first narcotics laws was none other than Mackenzie King (Cook 1969). King became aware of Canada's "opium problem" when he discovered — by accident — that opium could be bought over the counter in Vancouver. As the federal deputy minister of labour, he had been sent to Vancouver to supervise the payment of compensation to Chinese and Japanese Canadian businesspeople who had suffered losses during the anti-Asiatic riots of 1907.

Along the route to becoming prime minister, King made a modest career out of this particular crusade. He was selected as part of a five-person British delegation to attend the Shanghai Opium Commission in 1909. In 1911, as a member of Laurier's cabinet, he introduced a more stringent Opium and Drug Act. By 1920, calls for still more stringent legislation were coming in the form of sensational articles in such periodicals as *Maclean's* magazine. Several of these articles were written by Emily Murphy (1920, 1922), an Edmonton juvenile-court judge who ultimately went on to expand her views in a book titled *The Black Candle*. The background of these efforts tells us much about the way in which moral crusades can be generated.

During the period leading up to our first narcotics legislation, Canadian doctors were probably just as responsible for addiction as were the Chinese opium merchants. Medications containing opiates were indiscriminately prescribed by physicians and used by patients of all classes. In fact, syrups containing opiates, particularly paregoric, were frequently used by mothers for their infants. So it was not only fear of the drug itself, but also hostility toward Asian immigrants, that stimulated much of the narcotics legislation. Many Asian labourers had immigrated to this country, arousing antagonism among whites, who probably feared that their own jobs would be threatened. Much of the parliamentary debate that had preceded the passing of the first Opium Act had involved a proposed trade treaty with Japan that was to allow Japanese immigration.

A dramatic example of how the logically separate and distinct issues of opium and Asian immigration could be tied together occurred in the 1922 narcotics debate, when the following remarks by the secretary of the Anti-Asiatic Exclusion League were read:

Here we have a disease, one of many directly traceable to the Asiatic. Do away with the Asiatic and you have more than saved the souls and bodies of thousands of young men and women who are yearly being sent to a living hell and to the grave through their presence in Canada. (House of Commons Debates 1922; quoted in Cook 1969)

Others, like Murphy (1922), spoke of "Chinese peddlers" bringing about the "downfall of the white race." Thus, hostile attitudes toward a minority group were an important part of the crusading efforts that resulted in Canada's first narcotics legislation.

The moral entrepreneur best known for his role in the passage of American narcotics legislation is H.J. Anslinger, the first Director of the U.S. Federal Bureau of Narcotics (Lindesmith 1947; Becker 1963). Anslinger used his office to arouse American public and congressional concern about what he regarded as a growing "drug menace." For example, in 1937 Anslinger published a widely circulated magazine article, "Marihuana: Assassin of Youth." As in Canada, much of this attention combined hostile attitudes toward minority groups with discussions of the drug problem (Musto 1973). In media accounts, for example, the Chinese were associated with opium (Reasons 1974), southern blacks with cocaine (Musto 1973), and Mexicans with marijuana (Bonnie and Whitebread 1974). The fear was fostered that drug use by minorities posed a particularly dangerous threat to American society.

It made little difference, Duster (1970) reports, that in Canada and the United States, most narcotics addicts were upper and middle class well into the second decade of this century. Not until after the passage of America's first narcotics legislation, the Harrison Act of 1914, did this picture seem to change. By 1920, medical journals were referring to the "overwhelming majority [of drug addicts who came] from the 'unrespectable parts' of society" (Duster 1970). The technique used is often called guilt by association; by persuading the public to associate narcotics use with disenfranchised minorities, moral entrepreneurs were able to lay a foundation for legislation prohibiting the nonmedical use of drugs.

The prohibition against alcohol offers an interesting comparison with drug legislation because, while the latter endured, the former failed. Alcohol prohibition in the United States was a result of the well-organized lobbying activities of the Women's Christian Temperance Union and the Anti-Saloon League. These efforts constituted a moral crusade reflecting an apparent effort to protect an established way of life that was perceived as threatened during the early part of this century by the immigration of new Americans into the nation's cities. Gusfield (1963) argues that alcohol prohibition was a response to the fears of native-born, middle-class Protestants that their established positions in society, and their style of life itself, were endangered by the alcohol use they saw as increasing among the urban immigrants around them. As with drugs, a concerted effort was made to link alcohol with poverty, minorities, crime, and insanity.

Alcohol prohibition was only partly successful, however. Early resistance to it emerged in the ranks of organized labour. When alcohol prohibition attempted to criminalize the mass of the poor, it ran into the opposition of unions and urban political machines.

Timberlake (1963) observes that, although wage earners were unable to thwart the enactment of temperance legislation, they were strong enough to ensure its ultimate failure. He notes that many workers opposed prohibition because it smacked of paternalism and class exploitation. To them it was a hypocritical and insulting attempt to control their personal lives in order to exact greater profits for their employers. The employers themselves had no intention of abstaining. Indeed, it is estimated that as much as 81 percent of the American Federation of Labor was "wet," a figure consistent with Samuel Gompers's claim that the great majority of AFL members opposed prohibition. In sum, alcohol prohibition seems to have failed because it attempted to define as criminal what too large and well-organized a part

Cannabis Criminals

The law is an imperfect social invention. Indeed, the law produces many social embarrassments that most of us successfully ignore. One of these embarrassments is the role our laws have played in creating what Patricia Erickson [1980] calls "cannabis criminals." Erickson has documented the details of this embarrassment in terms it may no longer be possible to ignore.

Did you know that by 1976 more than 100 000 Canadians had been designated "criminal" for simple possession of cannabis? While many of us assume that our attitudes, and therefore our laws, dealing with cannabis have changed, to date changes have not occurred. Erickson reports that the great majority of "cannabis criminals" receive absolute or conditional discharges or fines. Many citizens may wonder why we bother, and Erickson's findings should raise this feeling from curiosity to dismay.

Adopting the sensible standard of the Le Dain Commission, Erickson examines how the costs of criminalizing cannabis offenders compare with the presumed beneficial deterrent effects of cannabis prohibition. To this end, 95 Canadians sentenced for possession of cannabis were interviewed and their responses analyzed.

The implication of Erickson's findings is a stark indictment of the logic of our cannabis laws. What she finds is that being criminalized for cannabis possession has negative consequences of other aspects of the individuals' lives, but no demonstrable deterrent effect in the individuals' cannabis use. Why, then, have these laws been enforced with such apparent enthusiasm?

Erickson's argument here is provocative, providing a more general and important insight into how good legislative intentions can produce bad

law enforcement. The problem is that in Canada special police powers of search, the widespread availability of cannabis to users, rewards to police for generating large numbers of arrests, and few restrictions on the admissibility of illegally obtained evidence in court all seem to encourage an aggressive seeking out of cannabis offenders. Unfortunately, the burden of the evidence reported in Erickson's research is that more problems have been created than solved by this type of law and its enforcement.

Source:

John Hagan, from "Preface" to Patricia Erickson, *Cannabis Criminals: The Social Effects of Punishment of Drug Users* (Toronto: ARF Books, 1980).

of the poor, as well as the rich, were doing. By contrast, narcotics legislation focused more narrowly, and more successfully, on minorities among the poor, who, as such, could be more easily defined as criminal without arousing organized opposition.

Juvenile Delinquency

The work of moral entrepreneurs is often associated with the growth of professional organizations that have their own bureaucratic interests to develop and protect. One example of this is the development of juvenile delinquency legislation and a resulting juvenile-court bureaucracy staffed in large part by probation officers trained in the emerging profession of social work. The efforts that led to the separate designation of juvenile delinquency and to the development of the juvenile courts were often called "child-saving" (Platt 1969). Parker (1976) points out that contrary to common-sense understanding,

the history of child-saving in the twentieth century is not the history of improving the general conditions of child-life (because most of the battles have been won), or the history of juvenile institutions (which changed very little after the initial efforts of the founders of the House of Refuge and their imitators). It is not even the history of the juvenile court itself, because it provided, as legal institutions tend to do, a purely symbolic quality to child work. The real history of the period is a history of probation.

Probation was a new idea at the beginning of this century. Its attraction was the prospect of keeping young offenders in their homes and out of institutions. The emphasis of probation within the juvenile-court movement reflected a concern for the family that pervaded the early part of this century. Known as the Progressive Era, this was a time of extensive social, political, and legal reform work. From this ferment emerged a system of social control that was intended to be less formal and less coercive than institutionalization. The use of probation actually extended the range of control efforts, however, and this new control was imposed largely on the families of the urban poor, often outside the courts (thus limiting or eliminating the possibility of appealing decisions through the legal system). The results of these

Within the juvenile court, probation was designed to keep young offenders home and out of institutions.

activities can be seen in Canada and the United States.

J.J. Kelso, for instance, was a moral entrepreneur who guided the passage of Canada's first juvenile-court legislation. This legislation allowed the development of an entire bureaucracy, staffed primarily by probation officers (Hagan and Leon 1977).

Kelso began as a crusading Toronto newspaper reporter and went on to serve as Ontario's first superintendent of neglected and dependent children. Possibly the most important step toward juvenile-delinquency legislation in Canada came in 1893, when Kelso and others convinced the Ontario legislature to enact a comprehensive Children's Protection Act that gave explicit recognition and authority to the Children's Aid Society (CAS). It became the duty of the court to notify the CAS before initiating proceedings against a boy under the age of 12 or a girl under 13; a CAS officer would then investigate the charges, inquire into the child's family environment, and report back to the court. These procedures were extended the following year to federal law, and a federal Juvenile Delinquents Act was passed in 1908, incorporating and expanding upon the earlier procedures for juveniles. Kelso was prominent in all these efforts; he promoted his beliefs frequently and well.

It is widely believed that the juvenile-court movement just described represented an effort to get children out of criminal courts and prisons. Although this effort does seem to have been one of the purposes of juvenile-delinquency legislation, it was in fact less than successful. Juveniles continued to be sent to institutions. The most dramatic consequence of the new legislation was a rapid expansion of the number of probation officers and of the number of juveniles with whom they dealt. In this sense, control over juvenile behaviour was actually increased by the new legislation. Moreover, in 1924 the federal Juvenile Delinquents Act was amended to include control over adolescents "guilty of sexual immorality or any similar form of vice," effectively making most of the fun of adolescence illegal. The suspicion inevitably arises that one purpose behind much of this moral-reform effort was to increase the "need" for probation officers and spur the growth of this bureaucracy.

A diminished reliance on institutions, combined with increased control (particularly through probation personnel), is apparent in other fragmentary data. The prominent reformer Frederic Almy (1902) wrote from Buffalo that "the ... Juvenile Court has not quite completed its first year, and no definite records have been compiled, but two results are already notable — the decrease in the number of commitments to the truant school and to reformatories, and the increase in the number of children arrested." Between 1913 and 1914 in Chicago, the number of delinquents referred to court rose from 1956 to 2916, an increase of nearly 50 percent in the delinquency rate for Cook County. Haller (1970) notes that the reason for this was that 23 additional probation officers were hired in 1914. Similar points have been made by

Schlossman (1977) regarding the development of the juvenile court in Milwaukee.

A general picture begins to emerge from these reports. The Progressive Era was characterized by a widely shared view that rehabilitation should be family-centred. Advocates of legal reform therefore focused on the offender's home as the locus of treatment and on the probation officer as the key remedial agent. Among the most vigorous proponents were members of groups who eventually became the "professionals" charged with responsibility for probation. Again, one suspects that a purpose of much of this moral-reform effort was to increase both the need for probation officers and the growth of this bureaucracy.

To say that the legislation of deviance is influenced by individual and group interests, however, is not to say that legislation of this kind is unnecessary. But not all such laws can be taken at face value: individual and group interests can determine the form that various laws take. The line that separates those forms of deviance that are socially controlled from those that are controlled officially and by legislation is a fine one.

Theories of Crime and Deviance

We have discussed what deviance is, where it is found, how it is measured, and how and why legislation is introduced against it. Our chief remaining question is, how do we account for the actual phenomenon? How do we explain deviance? We will now turn to theoretical explanations of the class differences in criminal and deviant behaviour discussed above. We will examine these explanations according to the three basic sociological perspectives: structural-functionalism, symbolic interaction, and conflict.

Structural Functionalism and Deviance

Structural-functional theories regard deviant behaviour as the consequence of a strain or breakdown in the social processes that produce conformity. The focus here is on agents (such as the family and school) that socialize individuals to conform to the values of the existing society, and on the ways in which this process can go wrong. This approach assumes wide agreement, or consensus, about what the prime values of our society are. Structural-functional theories try to explain why some individuals, through their deviant behaviour, come to challenge this consensus. In other words, why do individuals violate the conforming values that nearly all of us are assumed to hold in common?

Anomie. The roots of functional theory can be found in Durkheim's notion of **anomie** (1956, originally published 1897). To Durkheim, this term meant an absence of social regulation, or normlessness. Merton (1938, 1957) revived the concept to describe the consequences of a faulty relationship between goals and the legitimate means of attaining them. Merton emphasized two features of social and cultural structure: culturally defined goals (such as monetary success) and the acceptable means (such as education) to their achievement. The problem for Merton was that in our society success goals are widely shared, while the means of attaining them are not.

Merton's theory is intended to explain not only why people deviate but why some types of people deviate more than others. Members of the lower class are most affected by the disparity between shared success goals and the scarcity of means to attain them. The result of this structural inconsistency is a high rate of deviant behaviour.

Merton outlined a number of ways individuals can adapt when faced with inadequate means of attaining their goals. These methods of adapting include *innovation*, comprising various forms of economically motivated crimes; *ritualism*, involving various forms of overconformity; *retreatism*, consisting of escapist activities such as drug abuse; and *rebellion*, involving revolutionary efforts to change the structural system of goals and means. The common feature of these separate patterns is that they all represent adaptations to failure, a failure to achieve goals through legitimate means.

Delinquent Subculture. The adaptations to failure described above occur for groups as well as for individuals. One form of social adaptation is represented by the **delinquent subculture.** Cohen (1955) suggests that members of the lower

class, and potential members of a delinquent subculture, first experience a failure to achieve when they enter school. When assessed against a "middle-class measuring rod," working-class children are often found lacking. The result for these students is a growing sense of "status frustration." Working-class children are simply not prepared by their earliest experiences to satisfy middle-class expectations. The delinquent subculture therefore emerges as an alternative set of criteria, or values, that working-class adolescents *can* meet.

Subcultural values represent a complete repudiation of middle-class standards; the delinquent subculture expresses contempt for a middle-class lifestyle by making its opposite a criterion of prestige, as if to say, "We're everything you say we are and worse." The result, according to Cohen (1955), is a delinquent subculture that is "non-utilitarian, malicious, and negativistic" — an inversion of middle-class values. Yet this is only one possible type of subcultural reaction to the frustration of failure (see Hagan 1991). The theories we consider next suggest three other potential responses to the denial of opportunity.

Differential Opportunity. When legitimate opportunities are denied, illegitimate opportunities may be the only game in town. Cloward and Ohlin (1960) argue that to understand the different forms that criminal and delinquent behaviour can take, we must consider the different types of illegitimate opportunities available to those seeking a way out of the working class. Different types of community settings produce different subcultural responses. Cloward and Ohlin suggest that three types of responses predominate: a stable criminal subculture, a conflict subculture, and a retreatist subculture.

The **stable criminal subculture**, as its name suggests, is the best-organized of the three. According to Cloward and Ohlin, this subculture can emerge only when there is some co-ordination between those in legitimate and in illegitimate roles — for example, between politicians or police and the underworld. One pictures the old-style political machine, with protection provided for preferred types of illegal enterprise. Only in such circumstances can stable patterns be established allowing opportunities for advancement from the lower to the upper levels of the criminal underworld. The legitimate and illegitimate opportunity structures are linked in this way, the streets become safe *for* crime, and reliable upward-mobility routes can emerge for criminals. Interesting relationships are observable among opportunity structures, crime, and ethnicity.

Violence and conflict, on the other hand, are disruptive of both legitimate and illegitimate enterprise. When both types of enterprise co-exist, violence is restrained. In the "disorganized slum," however, where these spheres of activity are not linked, violence can reign uncontrolled. Cloward and Ohlin see these types of communities as producing a **conflict subculture.** A result of this disorganization is the prevalence of street gangs and violent crime, making the streets unsafe for profitable crime.

The final type of subculture posited by Cloward and Ohlin, the **retreatist subculture,** comprises those individuals who fail in their efforts in both the legitimate and illegitimate opportunity structures. These "double failures" are destined for drug abuse and other forms of escape.

So far we have focused on a strain between goals and means as the source of deviant behaviour in structural-functional theory. It is this strain that theoretically produces the subcultural responses we have discussed. Before moving on, however, we should note a final form of structural-functional theory that also takes into account those individuals who are relatively unimpressed by the goals, values, or commitments that our society emphasizes.

Control and Commitment. To have goals and means is to be committed to conformity and to be controlled by this commitment; to have neither goals nor means, however, is to be uncommitted and thus *uncontrolled.* Hirschi (1969) has argued that the absence of control is really all that is required to explain much deviant behaviour. There are other types of controls (beside *commitment to conformity*) that may also operate: *involvement,* in school and other activities; *attachments,* to friends and family; and *belief,* in various types of values and principles. Hirschi argues that deviant behaviour is inversely related to the presence of these controls. Alternatively, as these controls accumulate, so too does conformity. Again, Hirschi's point is that no special strain between goals and

means is necessarily required to produce deviant behaviour; all that is required is the elimination of constraint.

In all the approaches we have considered, values or beliefs play some role in the causation of deviance. The presence of success goals or values without means to obtain them can produce deviant behaviour, as can the absence of these goals or values in the first place. It is an emphasis on these values, and the role of the school and family in transmitting them, that ties the structural-functional theories together.

Symbolic Interaction and Deviance

The symbolic-interaction theories of deviance are concerned less with values than with the way that social meanings and definitions help produce deviant behaviour. The assumption, of course, is that these meanings and definitions, these symbolic variations, affect behaviour. Early versions of symbolic-interaction theory focused on how these meanings and definitions were *acquired* by individuals *from* others; more recently, theorists have focused on the role of official control agencies in *imposing* these meanings and definitions on individuals. The significance of this difference in focus will become apparent as we consider the development of the symbolic-interaction approach.

Differential Association. One of the fathers of North American criminology, Edwin Sutherland (1924), anticipated an emphasis of the symbolic-interaction perspective with his early use of the concept of **differential association.** This concept referred not only to associations among people but also, and even more importantly, to associations among ideas. Sutherland argued that people behave criminally only when they define such behaviour as acceptable. The connection postulated between people and their ideas (that is, definitions) is as follows:

The hypothesis of differential association is that criminal behavior is learned in association with those who define such behavior favorably and in isolation from those who define it unfavorably, and that a person in an appropriate situation engages in such criminal behavior if, and only if, the weight of the favorable definition exceeds the weight of the unfavorable definitions. (Sutherland 1949)

Sutherland (1949) applied his hypothesis in a famous study of white-collar crime, arguing that individuals become white-collar criminals because they are immersed with their colleagues in a business ideology that defines illegal business practices as acceptable.

A student of Sutherland's, Donald Cressey (1971), applied a form of this hypothesis to the specific crime of embezzlement. Cressey interviewed more than 100 imprisoned embezzlers and concluded that they had committed their crimes after they had rationalized, or redefined, these activities using statements like these:

"Some of our most respectable citizens got their start in life by using other people's money temporarily."

"All people steal when they get in a tight spot."

"My interest was only to use this money temporarily, so I was 'borrowing' it, not 'stealing.' "

"I have been trying to live an honest life, but I have had nothing but trouble so 'to hell with it.' "

Techniques of Neutralization. Symbolic-interaction theory is not exclusively concerned with lower-class deviance; it gives considerable attention to crimes of the upper and middle classes as well. But when attention is turned to the underworld, the explanatory framework remains essentially the same. The key to this consistency is Sykes and Matza's (1957) observation that lower-class delinquents, like white-collar criminals, usually exhibit guilt or shame when detected violating the law. Thus the delinquent, like the white-collar criminal, is regarded as an "apologetic failure," who drifts into a deviant lifestyle through a subtle process of justification. "We call these justifications of deviant behavior techniques of neutralization," write Sykes and Matza, "and we believe these techniques make up a crucial component of Sutherland's definitions favorable to the violation of the law" (1957).

Sykes and Matza list four of these **neutralization techniques:** *denial of responsibility* (for example, blaming a bad upbringing), *denial of injury* (for example, claiming that the victim deserved it), *condemnation of the condemners* (for example, calling their condemnation discriminatory), and *an appeal to higher loyalties* (for example, citing loyalty to friends or family as the cause of the behaviour). Sykes and Matza's point is that crime in the underworld, like crime in society at large,

is facilitated by this type of thinking. A question remains, however: Why are underworld crimes more frequently made the subjects of official condemnation?

Dramatization of Evil. The beginning of an answer to this question appears in the early work of Franklin Tannenbaum (1938). Tannenbaum points out that some forms of juvenile delinquency are a normal part of adolescent street life — aspects of the play, adventure, and excitement that many nostalgically identify later as an important part of this period. But others see such activities as a nuisance or as threatening, so they summon the police.

Tannenbaum's concern is that police intervention begins a process of change in the way the individuals and their activities are perceived. He suggests that there is a gradual shift from defining specific *acts* as evil to defining the *individual* as evil. Tannenbaum sees the individual's first contact with the law as the most consequential, referring to this event as a "dramatization of evil" that separates the child from his or her peers for specialized treatment. Tannenbaum goes on to argue that this "dramatization" may play a greater role in creating the criminal than does any other experience. The problem is that individuals thus singled out may begin to think of themselves as the type of people who do such things — that is, as delinquents. From this viewpoint, efforts to reform or deter deviant behaviour create more problems than they solve. "The way out," Tannenbaum argues, "is through a refusal to dramatize the evil." He suggests instead that the less said about it the better.

Primary and Secondary Deviance. Sociologists have expanded on Tannenbaum's version of the interactionist perspective. For example, Lemert (1967) suggests the terms primary and secondary deviance to distinguish between acts that occur before and after the societal response. Acts of **primary deviance** are those that precede a social or legal response. They may be incidental or even random aspects of an individual's general behaviour. The important point is that these initial acts have little impact on the individual's self-concept. **Secondary deviance**, on the other hand, follows the societal response and involves a transformation of the individual's self-concept,

Crime as Work: An Example of the Interaction Approach

The symbolic-interaction theories of deviance place a heavy emphasis on the role of meanings and definitions in the explanation of deviant behaviour. Even when these theories have been applied in the study of very different kinds of behaviour, it has been emphasized that these meanings and definitions can play a quite similar role. Letkemann [1973] illustrated this point in a unique Canadian study of career criminals. His thesis is that crime can be a form of work, incorporating all the elements of a profession. But to understand this contention we must see the world of crime in the same terms — that is, with the same meaning and definitions — as the persons who participate in it. To do this, Letkemann conducted detailed interviews with a sample of skilled and experienced property offenders.

One of the most striking results of these interviews is the awareness of how different the official and criminal classification of offenders can be. The problem is that legal categorizations of offenders according to criminal-code designations often constitute distorted descriptions of offenders' career patterns. For example, while safecracking has been a lively and venerable criminal career in Canada, it is not a term found in the Criminal Code. Instead, offenders involved in this form of criminal work are often convicted of breaking and entering. This example illustrates the need to appreciate the meanings and definitions offenders attach to their own activities.

Pursuing this theme, Letkemann found that his subjects defined not only their own activities, but those of their colleagues in crime, in terms of several important distinctions. The first of these distinctions is between a group referred to as "rounders" and a larger group referred to as "alkies," "dope fiends," and "normals." The first of these groups, the rounders, is distinguished by its commitment to an illegitimate lifestyle, a commitment that is demonstrated in a consistent and reliable, albeit criminal, pattern of behaviour. The sense here is of a concern for "honesty among thieves," in which the emphasis is on a record of consistency and integrity among peers. In sum, the rounder seems to hold and apply work standards that are not so different from those of the more orthodox professions. James Caan, the safe-cracker *par excellence* in the movie *Thief*, was a man's man and a rounder's rounder.

In contrast, the second group is characterized by its use of psychoactive chemicals and involvement in small-scale illegal activities, primarily theft. The alkies, dope fiends, and normals share the dedication of the rounder, but in this case their dedication is to their drug, rather than to their own illegal activities. Property crime for these offenders is a "means to an end" (drugs, alcohol), rather than an end in itself. The importance of this difference is that the dependence of the members of this group on drugs and alcohol makes them unreliable partners in criminal undertakings.

Another important distinction that Letkemann's respondents made is between "amateur" and "experienced" criminals. One identifying feature of amateur criminals is that they are primarily concerned with avoiding conviction. The point here is that experienced criminals have technical skills that make them rather easily identifiable by police. Their concern, then, is less with being detected as the culprits than with making certain that they leave no evidence. Without evidence, of course, there can be no conviction.

Skilled and experienced property offenders also distinguish themselves according to the specializations they pursue. These offenders speak of "having a line" — that is, a generalized work preference and a related repertoire of skills. We will come back to this point in a moment; for now, let us simply note again that the defining features of a criminal occupation are seen to parallel the more conventional world of work.

"altering the psychic structure, producing specialized organization of social roles and self-regarding attitudes" (Lemert 1967). From this point on, the individual takes on more and more of the "deviant" aspects of his or her new role. The societal response has, from this point of view, succeeded only in confirming the individual in a deviant role (Becker 1963, 1964; Hagan and Palloni 1990; Arnold and Hagan 1992).

The Labelling Process. As we have developed our discussion of the interaction perspective, we have focused more and more on the official societal reactions to deviant behaviour, on what many analysts of deviance call "the labelling process." Attention to societal labelling and its effects has involved examinations of not only conventional topics — crime, delinquency, and drugs — but also the much-neglected topic of mental illness. Scheff (1966), for example, has suggested that our society uses the concept of "mental illness" in much the same way as other societies use the concepts of "witchcraft" and "spirit possession." That is, this label provides a catch-all category

A final distinction is drawn in terms of prison experience. This distinction gives new meaning to the common concern shared by labelling theorists that "prisons are schools for crime." Letkemann points out that prison experience can operate much like college or university experience: as a prerequisite to status. Furthermore, some prisons are known for the specialized contacts they allow. For example, since provincial institutions in Canada can hold an offender for no more than two years less one day, they offer little exposure to more experienced criminals. Thus, to obtain full standing as a rounder may require experience in a federal penitentiary, where the more seasoned professionals are often to be found.

Letkemann goes on to describe two kinds of skills that characterize two very different criminal career paths. This description is central to his main argument that crime *is* work, often of a highly skilled form. Therefore, the argument is concerned with defining features that make it explainable, using the same principles applied to understanding legitimate behaviour. The first of these career paths involves surreptitious crimes; the second, overt crimes.

Surreptitious crimes include burglary, and, more specifically, safecracking. These crimes emphasize mechanical skills and victim-avoidance. Persons involved in this kind of criminal work must develop a set of techni-

cal skills: working with explosives and learning how to use them to blow a safe. At the same time, they must acquire a set of techniques for gaining entry to sites where safes are used and for minimizing the chances of being observed in the course of their work. While this set of activities may be defined by law as anti-social, its more interesting feature in sociological terms is that it is so *non*-social: the emphasis here is on avoiding others while engaging in criminal activity.

By contrast, overt crimes, like bank robbery, can involve a highly developed set of social, as opposed to mechanical, skills. In overt crimes, the victims are confronted and skill must be applied to handle this social event in a way that does not lead to violence. While it may often be thought that because a weapon is used an armed robbery involves no skills, the skill required is to avoid the use of a weapon. The film *Dog Day Afternoon* illustrated, at times comically, how in inexperienced hands this type of situation can escalate beyond control. As well, very basic decisions must be made. Does the getaway driver stay in the car or enter the bank? The problem is whether the waiting driver will actually wait, or panic and take off prematurely. Also, who should lead the exit from the bank? While on the one hand it might be wise for the most experienced person to lead the way, the first one out may also be the person most likely to get shot. These and

other factors must be taken into account, and decisions must be made. The point is that a successful robbery is a complex accomplishment, demanding considerable social and planning skills. To the extent that these skills are conscientiously developed and applied, the criminal career will have much in common with other more conventional careers (but see also Katz 1988).

Symbolic interactionists remind us that criminals, like the rest of us, define their worlds and act accordingly. Often, these meanings and definitions are developed with skill and experience. The importance of this different but sophisticated world-view is well summarized by Letkemann: "The model of a criminal as one who takes a craftsman's pride in his work, and who applies his skills in the most profitable way he thinks possible, is very different from the model of the criminal as one who gets kicks out of beating the system and doing evil."

Source:

The references are to Peter Letkemann, *Crime as Work* (Englewood Cliffs, NJ: Prentice-Hall, 1973); and Jack Katz, *Seductions of Crime: Moral and Sensual Attractions in Doing Evil* (New York: Basic, 1988).

wherein we can place a variety of forms of **residual rule-breaking** for which our society provides no other explicit labels.

Scheff (1966) observes that in childhood we all learn the stereotyped role behaviour that is labelled insanity. On the basis of this knowledge, Scheff (1966) suggests that

when societal agents and persons around the deviant react to him uniformly in terms of the traditional stereotypes of insanity, his amorphous and unstructured rule-breaking tends to crystallize in conformity

to these expectations, thus becoming similar to the behavior of other deviants classified as mentally ill, and stable over time.

In other words, the process of labelling mental illness may help create secondary deviance — deviance indistinguishable from the sort that the control agents are attempting to cure.

In the end, symbolic interactionists do not insist that all, or even most, deviant behaviour is caused by officially imposed labels. Official labels are thought, rather, to create special problems for the individuals to whom they are applied, often increasing the chances that additional deviant behaviour will follow. The point is that not only the actor but also the reactors participate in creating the meanings and definitions that generate deviant behaviour. The symbolic interactionists note that the poor are more likely than the rich to get caught up in this process. This point is further emphasized in conflict theory, the approach we consider next.

Conflict Theory and Deviance

The most distinctive feature of the **conflict theories of deviance** is their focus on the role of dominant societal groups in imposing legal labels on members of subordinate societal groups. The issues are how and why this happens. We will see that attention to these issues focuses as much or more on the groups imposing labels as on the individuals receiving them.

Crime as Status. For conflict theorists, crime is a status that is imposed by one group on the behaviour of another. Turk (1969) suggests that "criminality is not a biological, psychological, or even behavioral phenomenon, but a social status defined by the way in which an individual is perceived, evaluated, and treated by legal authorities." The task, then, is to identify the group or groups involved in creating and applying this status.

Turk (1969) responds by observing that there are two types of people in society: "There are those ... who constitute the dominant, decision-making category — the authorities — and those who make up the subordinate category, who are affected by but scarcely affect law — the subjects." In short, authorities make laws that in turn make criminals out of subjects. The difference is a matter of relative power. Authorities have sufficient power to define some subjects' behaviour as criminal. Because the poor have the least power, we can expect the poor to have the highest rate of "criminalization." The process by which groups are differentially criminalized is the subject of much of the following discussion.

Legal Bureaucracy. Determining which groups in society will be more criminal than others is largely a matter of determining which laws will be enforced. Chambliss and Seidman (1971) observe that in modern, complex, stratified societies such as our own, we assign the task of resolving such issues to bureaucratically structured agencies. The result is to mobilize what we call "the primary principle of legal bureaucracy." According to this principle, laws will be enforced when enforcement serves the interests of social-control agencies and their officials; laws will not be enforced when enforcement is likely to cause organizational strain. In other words, the primary principle of legal bureaucracy involves maximizing organizational gains while minimizing organizational strains.

Chambliss and Seidman (1971) conclude that a consequence of this principle is to bring into operation a "rule of law," whereby "discretion at every level ... will be so exercised as to bring mainly those who are politically powerless (i.e., the poor) into the purview of the law." Because the poor are least likely to have the power and resources necessary to create organizational strains, they become the most rewarding targets for organizational activities. In sum, according to the conflict theorists, the poor appear disproportionately in our crime statistics more because of class bias in our society and the realities of our bureaucratic legal system than because of their actual behaviour.

A New Criminology. Arguments such as those expounded in the preceding paragraphs culminated in a call — first sounded in the early 1970s — by a group of British researchers for a "new" or "critical criminology" (Taylor, Walton, and Young 1973, 1975). This group argues that the roots of modern crime problems are intertwined with those of Western capitalism. Capitalist ideology, they suggest, has conditioned the very way we conceive of crime.

For example, the New Criminologists observe that we think about crime largely in terms of "an ethic of individualism." This ethic holds individuals responsible for their acts, thus diverting attention from the social and political structure in which these acts take place. Moreover, this individualist ethic focuses primarily on one group of individuals — the poor — making them the chief targets of criminal law and penal sanctions. In contrast, the New Criminologists argue that employers and other advantaged persons will be bound only by a civil law that seeks to regulate their competition with one another. The New Criminologists maintain that such an arrangement creates two kinds of citizenship and responsibility, the more advantaged of which tends to be "beyond incrimination" and therefore above the law (see also Hagan, Nagel, and Albonetti 1980).

A Marxian Theory of Crime and Deviance. The New Criminology represents the re-emergence of a Marxian theory of crime and deviance. Until recently, early forms of this theory (Bonger 1916; Rusche and Kirchmeimer 1939) were neglected, and the theory consequently remained underdeveloped. Spitzer (1975) is among those who have helped revive and expand it.

Spitzer begins by arguing that we must account for criminal and deviant acts as well as for the status of those labelled as deviants. Thus, "we must not only ask why specific members of the underclass are selected for official processing, but also why they behave as they do." Spitzer's answer draws on the structural characteristics of capitalism. More specifically, Spitzer suggests that what he calls "problem populations" (such as "social junk" and "social dynamite," discussed below) in capitalist societies consist of those whose behaviours threaten the social relation of production. These threats may take various forms as they disturb, hinder, or call into question any of five key components of capitalist society:

1. capitalist modes of appropriating the product of human labour (for example, when the poor "steal" from the rich);
2. the social conditions under which capitalist production takes place (for example, those who refuse or are unable to perform wage labour);
3. patterns of distribution and consumption in capitalist society (for example, those who use drugs for escape and transcendence rather than for sociability and adjustment);
4. the process of socialization for productive and nonproductive roles (for example, youths who refuse to be schooled);
5. the ideology that supports the functioning of capitalist society (for example, proponents of alternative forms of social organization).

All such threats are thought to derive from one of two sources: directly, from fundamental contradictions in the capitalist mode of production; and indirectly, from disturbances in the system of class rule. An example of the first source involves the emergence of "surplus populations" — what Marx called the class of the chronically unemployed — and the problems of unemployment. An example of the second source involves the critical attitudes that educational institutions may produce, resulting in school dropouts and sometimes in student radicals.

Spitzer goes on to suggest that the processes he outlines create two distinct kinds of problem populations. On the one hand, there is *social junk*, which, for the dominant class, represents a costly but relatively harmless burden to society. Examples of this category include the officially administered aged, the physically and developmentally handicapped, the mentally ill, and some kinds of alcohol and drug offenders. In contrast to "social junk," there is also a category described as *social dynamite*. The distinctive feature of people in this category is their "potential actively to call into question established relationships, especially relations of production and domination" (Spitzer 1975). Correspondingly, Spitzer notes that "social dynamite" tends to be more alienated and politically volatile than "social junk." Listed by Spitzer as among the groups with the potential to become "social dynamite" are the welfare poor, homosexuals, and "problem children."

Finally, Spitzer suggests that two basic strategies are used by capitalist societies in controlling criminals and deviants. The first strategy is referred to as *integrative*, the second as *segregative*. The first approach involves control measures applied in the community, such as probation and parole, while the second relies more on the use of institutions. Spitzer notes that integrative controls are becoming increasingly common in capitalist societies as we embrace diversion, decarceration, and deinstitutionalization programs designed to divert or remove designated deviants from prisons and other places of official detainment. Spitzer and others (for example, Scull 1977) have argued that this trend arose due to the spiralling costs of institutionalization and that this treatment is reserved for "social junk." This perspective may well prompt us to think

Suite Crime

When asked whether they are concerned about levels of crime in their city, province, or country, almost half of all Canadians respond in the affirmative. Many also fear that they themselves might become victims of a serious crime such as burglary, armed robbery, rape, assault, or even murder. While a few Canadians do fall prey to these crimes every year, many more become the victims of equally if not more serious forms of socially injurious activity. The cost of street crime pales in comparison with the losses incurred through embezzlement, computer crime, business fraud, professional misconduct and malpractice, false advertising, the marketing of unsafe products, the exposure of employees to dangerous working conditions, income tax evasion, price fixing, illegal mergers, industrial espionage, political corruption, and environmental pollution. ... The principal victims of "suite crime" include businesses, consumers, employees, the public at large, and governments. ...

A single corporate violation can adversely affect the well-being of a staggering number of people. Moreover,

the wrongdoing of higher-status workers and the business organizations for which they work is frequent and the recidivism rate for those convicted is high. Despite these unsettling facts, Canadians barely notice the stealing, maiming, and killing carried out by the hands of professional and business elites. Indeed, many of the injurious acts classified as white-collar, corporate, or "suite" crimes are not prohibited by the Criminal Code of Canada. ...

While accurate estimates of dollar losses attributable to business crimes are extremely difficult to determine, most projections underestimate the magnitude of the figures. Economic analysts put the annual Canadian losses due to embezzlement, computer crime, commercial fraud, unnecessary auto repairs, unneeded home improvements, price fixing, illegal corporate mergers, false advertising, and other business crimes at something in excess of $4 billion. ... By comparison, a predatory street crime such as bank robbery cost Canadian financial institutions only $2.8 million in 1985. Indeed, while the average "take" for a

bank robbery in Canada in 1986 was $3953 ... a single embezzler relieved the Canadian Imperial Bank of Commerce of over $10 million in a 2-year period in the early 1980s. ...

There are several other indications that business crime is both financially costly and on the increase in Canada. According to the Uniform Crime Reports, fraud increased by 42 percent between 1976 and 1984. In 1984, the commercial crime unit of the RCMP investigated 8400 offences involving the misuse of $336 million. Some recent estimates peg the amount of money illegitimately billed by medical personnel to federally and provincially funded health-insurance plans at about $400 million. ...

Not only are Canadians directly preyed upon by unscrupulous white-collar workers and businesses, they are also indirectly victimized in at least two ways. First, losses from illegal acts such as fraud, embezzlement, and corporate espionage are invariably passed on to consumers in the form of higher prices and to the public in the form of higher taxes. Furthermore, the costs associated with the

---

critically about what has usually been considered a humane set of developments, including proposals for halfway houses, group homes, and so on. Scull (1977) writes that deviants are increasingly dealt with "as if they are industrial wastes which can without risk be left to decompose in some well-contained dump." This is quite a different picture of the movement to keep deviants out of institutions than has previously been common.

The Processing of Crime and Deviance

One of the most important consequences of the emergence of the symbolic-interaction and conflict theories of crime and deviance has been a

heightened awareness of the role official agencies play in determining who or what we label criminal or deviant. This increased awareness has stimulated research that focuses on decision-making in official agencies — for example, decisions made about mental-hospital admissions, police arrests, plea bargaining, and judicial sentencing. The often-provocative results have been suggestive of biases in official decision-making.

Processing Mental Illness

Doubting the accuracy with which psychiatrists distinguish the sane from the insane, Rosenhan (1973) designed a unique study to test the diagnostic skills of those who control mental-hospital admission and release. In this study, Rosenhan and eight other individuals with histories free from mental disorders sought admission to twelve

Canadian government's efforts to catch, convict, and chastise business wrongdoers are also borne by Canadian taxpayers. Second, businesses often write off their legal defence costs as tax losses. The result is diminished revenue to the Government of Canada that, as a rule, is compensated for by individual taxpayers. Few Canadians realize the extent to which they are paying for white-collar and corporate crime.

Many Canadians perceive business crime solely as property crime and see its costs entirely in economic terms. The result is an inclination to view commercial crime as a less serious problem than street crime. Street crime raises images of interpersonal violence, while suite crime does not. This is a grave misperception — business crime is frequently violent. The volume of assaults and murders in Canada pales in comparison with the number of injuries, debilitating and life-threatening diseases, and deaths attributable to business enterprises and professions engaging in unsafe practices, marketing dangerous products, violating workplace safety regulations, and polluting the air, the water, and the land.

A cursory examination of some data on deaths related to work drives home the point that business wrongdoing can be considered violent. Death in the workplace ranks third, after heart disease and cancer, as a major killer of Canadians. Canadian criminologists Charles Reasons and his colleagues ... point out that people are killed on the job at a rate ten times the Canadian murder rate. They estimate that almost 40 percent of industrial "accidents" are a result of working conditions that are both unsafe and prohibited under existing law. About 25 percent, they argue, are attributable to conditions that, while not illegal, are dangerous nonetheless.

It is not only workers who become the victims of business violence. People who buy defective merchandise and who use unneeded and potentially dangerous services are also at risk. Estimates of traffic fatalities due to unsafe vehicles range up to 50 percent. Many operations performed by doctors in this country are unnecessary. Nevertheless, all surgery carries some risk, and some patients do develop complications and suffer unduly. A small percentage dies. ...

While the violence perpetrated by businesses and professionals is both real and potentially devastating, it differs from the violence of street crime. In a common violent crime such as an assault, the illegal act is separated from its result by a relatively short period of time — perhaps seconds. In suite crime, the result may occur years after the initial illegal act. For example, pulp and paper companies dump mercury into river systems. Fish ingest the mercury, and people consume the tainted fish. Gradually poisoned, victims increasingly lose control of their muscles and those who are seriously contaminated eventually die. The process takes years. Furthermore, the time span may now extend to centuries. Scientists note that the wastes created by weapons manufacture and nuclear energy production may not just haunt future generations but perhaps kill them as well. The expanding time gap separating act and outcome has given rise to new terms in the study of violence, such as "postponed violence" and "intergenerational crime."

Source:

Ian M. Gomme, *The Shadow Line: Deviance and Crime in Canada* (Toronto: Harcourt Brace Jovanovich Canada, 1993), pp. 393–394, 398–400.

psychiatric hospitals. Each person complained of fictional symptoms (hearing voices saying "empty, hollow, thud") resembling no known form of mental illness. Despite the fictitious symptoms, all the pseudopatients were diagnosed as schizophrenics. Immediately following admission, the pseudopatients ceased to report symptoms and resumed what they regarded as a normal pattern of behaviour. After an average period of more than two weeks, all the pseudopatients were released as "schizophrenics in remission." None of the individuals, in other words, was discovered to be *sane*. These results do not indicate, of course, that there are no differences between the sane and insane; but they do suggest that mental-hospital personnel may often overlook or mistake these differences.

It is important to note that in the above experiment the pseudopatients were seeking admission voluntarily. Gove (1975) has observed that most people who receive psychiatric treatment do so voluntarily and that concerned friends and relatives do not frivolously seek hospitalization for others. Indeed, there is evidence (Smith, Pumphrey, and Hall 1963) that the typical psychiatric patient performs three or more "critical acts," each of which might justify hospitalization, before commitment procedures are initiated. Hospitalization is sought earlier for economically more important family members than for those less consequential to family life (Hammer 1963–64).

Beyond this, Gove (1975) reviews a variety of studies leading to the observation that "officials do not assume illness but, in fact, proceed rather cautiously, screening out a substantial number of persons." Significantly, this results in a situation where (for disorders of equivalent severity) hospitalization is more readily obtained by members of the upper class (Gove 1975). One explanation for this situation, as it relates to courts, is offered by Rock (1968): "The more important problem today is not the filing of petitions [for institutionalization] that are without cause, but rather finding a person willing to petition." Apparently, there are class differences in the willingness to assume the role of petitioner for another person. A second explanation is that some forms of treatment for mental illness may be preferable to other possible fates, particularly when the other forms of response carry the stigma of criminal disrepute. This point will become clear as we turn next to the problems of alcoholism.

Processing Alcoholism

The treatment of alcoholism is perhaps the area where the connection between class background and societal response is most apparent. The descending social rank of the persons typically receiving treatment in private sanitoriums, from Alcoholics Anonymous, and from the Salvation Army will be obvious to anyone who has passed through the doors of each. The underlying issue is, how do members of various classes find their way into these widely divergent treatment situations?

One approach to this problem involves studying the admission and treatment practices of an institution that deliberately tries to attend to people of varying class backgrounds. This type of study seeks to determine whether patterns within such an organization can suggest more general principles for alcoholism treatment.

Schmidt, Smart, and Moss (1968) carried out a study of this sort in the Toronto clinic of the Alcoholism and Drug Addiction Research Foundation. Although this study deals entirely with voluntary admissions, it carries important implications for our concern with the courts. One of its major findings is that lower-class alcoholics in the Toronto clinic were more likely to receive treatment involving drugs administered by physicians, while upper-class alcoholics were more likely to receive "talk" therapies from psychiatrists. These apparently class-related treatment differences could not be traced to differences in diagnosis or age. Differences in verbal skills (also usually related to class) prove to be an intermediate explanatory variable.

Even more interesting than these treatment differences, however, are variations by social class in the sources of referrals to the clinic. Upper-class patients are more likely to find their way to the clinic through the intermediary services of private physicians, middle-class persons by way of Alcoholics Anonymous, and lower-class persons through general hospital and welfare agency referrals. Schmidt, Smart, and Moss conclude that these class patterns are attributable largely to differences among given social settings in tolerating behaviours that result from alcohol excess and to differences in the modal drinking patterns of the classes. Here we are interested in the role the courts play in responding to these class differences.

To understand the role of the courts in the societal response to alcoholism we can use the findings of voluntary-clinic studies as indications of what may be happening in the whole range of agencies, especially in the involuntary sector. Lowe and Hodges (1972) took this route in studying the treatment of black alcoholics in the southern United States. They began by studying a single voluntary clinic but soon found that "any variation in amount of services given to patients within the clinic was insignificant beside the overwhelming fact that so few black alcoholics entered into service at all." Eventually they observed that black alcoholics were less likely to view admission to the clinic as offering treatment and were therefore unlikely to admit themselves voluntarily into any program. Black alcoholics thus frequently found themselves the involuntary subjects of law-enforcement operations that started with the police, took further form in the courts, and ended up in prison. Lowe and Hodges note that the courts rarely attempted to reverse this pattern by making referrals to alternative treatment programs. This pattern holds for Native peoples in Canada.

Hagan (1947b) followed up the treatment received by Native and white offenders in Alberta following incarceration. On the basis of either judicial recommendation or inmate request, offenders in Alberta were considered for transfer to an open institutional setting offering a program particularly designed for alcoholic offenders. However, Hagan found that although the target population of problem drinkers was almost twice as large (proportionately) among Native offenders as among white, more white than Native offenders received treatment in the open institutional setting. Thus, although only a minority of alcoholic offenders from either ethnic group experienced the open institution, white offenders were more than twice as likely as Native offenders to find their way to this treatment setting. There are three plausible explanations for this situation. First, judges might recommend referrals of Native offenders to the open institution less often. Second, Native offenders might seek and accept such referrals less frequently. Third, correctional personnel might consent to the transfer of Native offenders less often. It is important to note, however, that the three possibilities described were certainly not mutually exclusive, and were likely to be mutually supportive. In other words, there may be general agreement that in its present form the open institutional setting is less beneficial for Native than for white offenders.

Policing Crime and Delinquency

Winding up in a correctional institution can be seen as the end-result of a series of decisions whose effect has been likened to using a sieve or a leaky funnel. Most of those whose cases enter the first stages of a criminal- or juvenile-justice system are eventually diverted or deflected from the stream that leads to institutionalization. For example, an offence may go undetected or unsolved in the first place. If an offender is identified, the police may decide against arrest. If an arrest occurs, the prosecutor may decide to dismiss the charges. If a case results in conviction, the judge may decide to suspend sentence. That is, any number of things may happen along the way to prevent the offender from being institutionalized. The issue is the extent to which these outcomes are random, legally determined, or socially biased.

Starting with police decisions made early in this process, some of the most important research has been done by Black and Reiss (1970; Reiss 1971), who distinguish between two basic ways in which police can be mobilized. *Reactive mobilizations* are citizen-initiated (for example, by a telephoned complaint), while *proactive mobilizations* are police-initiated (for example, in response to an observed incident). In the Black and Reiss re-

search, 87 percent of the mobilizations were reactive. This figure implies that the police usually did not seek out deviant behaviour, but rather responded to citizens' complaints about such behaviour. As Black and Reiss note, when a complainant in search of justice makes demands, police officers may feel compelled to comply. Differences in the number of complaints received — between, for example, different neighbourhoods — may therefore help explain differential rates of arrest.

However, Ericson (1982), studying a suburban Toronto jurisdiction, raises some important questions about the applicability of these findings in Canada. Of 1323 encounters observed between citizens and police officers in Ericson's study, 47.4 percent were characterized as proactive mobilizations and only 52.6 percent as reactive mobilizations. "On the surface," Ericson (1982) notes, "our data reveal that patrol officers are much more assertive in producing encounters with citizens than the figures provided by Reiss, Black, and others would lead us to believe." Still, when considering only "major incidents," Ericson reports that more than 82 percent resulted from reactive mobilizations. In serious cases, complainants may still loom large in the decision-making process.

Another study — this one by Smith (1982), who examined 742 contacts between suspects and officers in 24 American police departments — confirms the influence of complainants but also points to the impact of suspect characteristics. According to this study, antagonistic suspects were much more likely to be taken into custody than were suspects who displayed deference (see also Piliavin and Briar 1964). Furthermore, black suspects were more likely to be arrested. Smith suggests that this difference can partly be accounted for by the fact that black suspects were significantly more likely to act toward the police in a hostile or antagonistic manner. Nonetheless, even taking suspect behaviour and victim demands into account, black suspects remained somewhat more likely to be arrested than white suspects.

Prosecuting Crime and Delinquency

Once an individual has been arrested and charged, the media image of the court process is that of a trial by jury, with prosecution and defence attorneys assuming adversarial roles in a battle for justice. In fact, however, few criminal cases follow this adversarial pattern. The typical sequence, followed in up to 90 percent of the cases in some jurisdictions, is for the defendant to plead guilty and forfeit trial. Grossman (1969) observed, on the basis of interviews with prosecutors in York County, Ontario, that guilty pleas were an important way of avoiding the time, expense, and uncertainty of trials. Plea bargaining was seen as an effective way of increasing court efficiency (Blumberg 1967). It is important, therefore, to take a close look at plea bargaining.

Sudnow (1965) has attempted to spell out in sociological terms the procedures involved in bargaining for reduced charges (see also Hagan 1974a; Wynne and Hartnagel 1975a, 1975b). Sudnow notes first that the reduction of charges focuses on two types of offences: "necessarily included" offences and "situationally included" offences. Necessarily included offences are those that occur together by legal definition; for example, "homicide" cannot occur without "intent to commit a murder." In contrast, situationally included offences are those that occur together by convention; "public drunkenness" usually, but not necessarily, occurs in association with "creating a public disturbance." Plea bargaining involves reducing the initial charge to a lesser charge — either a necessarily or situationally included offence.

As Sudnow points out, however, the procedural rules followed in deciding what sort of reduction is appropriate are not entirely defined by law. Rather, lawyers and prosecutors develop working conceptions of what they regard as "normal crimes": "the typical manner in which offences of given classes are committed, the social characteristics of the persons who regularly commit them, the features of the settings in which they occur, the types of victims often involved, and the like" (Sudnow 1965). According to Sudnow, these conceptions of "normal crimes" are used to create an initial legal categorization; attention is then directed to determining which (necessarily or situationally included) lesser offence may constitute the appropriate reduction. As an example, Sudnow notes that in the jurisdiction he studied, a burglary charge was routinely reduced to petty theft; however, "the propriety of proposing petty theft as a reduction does not derive from its ... existence in the present case, but is warranted ... instead by the relation of the present burglary to 'burglaries,' [as] normally conceived." Finally, Sudnow notes that a balance must be established between the sentence the defendant might have received for the original charge, and the probable sentencing outcome for the lesser charge. This brings us to the issue of sentencing.

Judging Crime and Delinquency

Legislation outlining the sentencing responsibilities of the criminal courts in Canada entrusts presiding judges with extensive freedom to determine minimum sentences. A wide range of discretion is also allowed in determining maximum penalties. The problem, however, extends beyond the simple absence of statutory guides to minimum and maximum sentences. There is also confusion as to what basic principles should be used in determining sentences. Decore (1964) notes that even the use of precedents in sentencing is a matter full of contradictions and doubt. Consequently, the criminal justice system relies heavily on the discretion of the sentencing judge, and variation and disparity predictably follow. An important attempt to explain variation in criminal sentences is found in the research of Hogarth (1971).

Hogarth begins by noting that judges in the lower provincial courts in Canada have broader jurisdiction (that is, 94 percent of all indictable cases are tried in these courts) and wider sentencing powers (for example, to life imprisonment) than any comparable set of courts in the Western world. Hogarth then provides data suggesting that Canada in the mid-1960s also had one of the highest rates of imprisonment in the Western world (see also Cousineau and Veevers 1972; Matthews 1972). However, Hogarth also presents evidence of a shift in this pattern, with the heavy reliance on prison sentences giving way to an increasing reliance on fines.

Further evidence of Canada's use of imprisonment is provided in an exceptionally careful analysis by Waller and Chan (1975). This analysis found Canada's overall imprisonment rate no higher than that of the United States and several other countries, with only the Yukon and the

Northwest Territories remaining high in comparison with most American states. Waller and Chan are careful to emphasize the difficulties of drawing any final inferences from the data they present, and to their cautions we will add several additional comments. First, it is not surprising to find that Canada's imprisonment rate per 100 000 population is low relative to that of some other countries, particularly the United States, because Canada's serious crime rate is also relatively low. Considering ratios of incarcerations to occurrences and convictions would allow more useful comparisons. Waller and Chan appropriately point out the complications in accurately computing these ratios using current official data. Second, it should be noted that, where imprisonment rates are highest in Canada (that is, in the north), Native people are most likely to be experiencing the consequences. Finally, we can observe that while efforts to avoid incarceration through the increased use of fines may be successful on the whole in Canada, economic and ethnic minorities unable to pay these fines remain at a disadvantage. These comments should discourage any sense of complacency about the conditions in our courts, a complacency that Waller and Chan clearly disavow (see also Waller 1974).

The research by Hogarth (1971) described above, probably because it concentrated primarily on the large urban areas of Ontario, paid little attention to the social consequences of sentencing for ethnic and economic minorities, particularly Native people. Yet Native people are present in Canadian courts and prison populations far beyond their representation in the general population. To understand the influence of race and other offender characteristics on judicial sentencing, we will need to consider briefly a large body of American research.

A variety of American studies focus on the effects of the offender's race, gender, age, and socioeconomic status on sentencing decisions (for example, Bullock 1961; Green 1961; Nagel 1969; Wolfgang and Riedel 1973). A review of such studies concludes that generally there *is* a small relationship between the extralegal attributes of offenders and sentencing decisions (Hagan 1974a; see also Hagan and Bumiller 1983). However, because the authors of many of these studies have failed to take into account either the seriousness

of offences or the prior records of offenders, it is sometimes difficult to know whether the reported relationships can be taken as evidence of discrimination. For example, do blacks in the United States receive longer sentences because they are discriminated against, or because they commit more serious offences and more frequently have prior convictions?

When these factors *are* controlled for, relationships reported between extralegal-offender characteristics and sentences are sometimes reduced or eliminated (for example, Chiricos and Waldo 1974). However, there continues to be compelling evidence that in certain areas — such as sexual assault (see, for example, LaFree 1980) and white-collar crime (Hagan, Nagel, and Albonetti 1980; Hagan and Parker 1985) — race and class position can make a difference in the severity of sentence received. To this extent the symbolic-interaction and conflict theorists are clearly correct: there is more to criminal and delinquent labels than the behaviours presumed to have provoked them. There is evidence (Hagan and Albonetti 1982) that public perceptions mirror this reality.

Interestingly, judges in Canada are frequently accused of being differentially lenient, as well as punitive, with Native offenders. The apparent leniency may reflect an attempt on the part of some Canadian judges to take cultural differences into account when sentencing Native offenders. However, evidence on this issue suggests that most judges do sentence primarily on the basis of offence seriousness and prior-conviction records. Hagan (1975) divided a sample of Alberta judges into two groups, according to whether they scored high or low on a "law and order" scale. He predicted that judges who scored high would sentence Native offenders punitively, while those who scored low would sentence leniently. Perhaps surprisingly, the results showed that "law and order" judges sentence almost exclusively on offence seriousness, while judges less concerned about such issues provided Native persons with only minimal leniency. More generally, this study suggests that most judges sentence most offenders mechanically, without taking the time to consider their social backgrounds. This is particularly the case, and becomes particularly problematic, for people charged with minor offences.

We noted earlier that the police typically apprehend Native offenders for minor alcohol-related charges. In turn, judges typically sentence such offenders to "so many dollars or so many days." The outcome of this approach is predictable, given the economically disadvantaged position of many Native people: Hagan (1974b) reports that nearly 66 percent of all Native people who go to jail are incarcerated in default of fine payments. This is nearly twice the rate for whites. One result is that in Hagan's Alberta sample, Native people's representation in the prison population is four times that of the general population.

One final point is worth noting: there is evidence that corporate entities are playing an increasingly important role as complainants in Canadian courts — for example, in cases of shoplifting. A study in a suburban Ontario jurisdiction (Hagan 1982) revealed that nearly two-thirds of the victims in cases where an offender was charged were corporations (mostly retail stores). The corporations in this study were better able than individuals to get convictions against the accused. The implication, again, is that the courts may serve some interests better than they do others in our society.

Crime, Race, and Violence in Canada and the United States

We turn now to a topic most Canadians at some time think about, but less often discuss: crime, race, and violence in Canada and the United States. There is no doubt that officially recorded rates of violent crime and many other kinds of deviance are higher in the United States than in Canada. In fact, the disparity between the rates of violent crime in the two countries is clearly growing.

There are differences in kind as well as in the amount of criminal violence in the two countries. In the United States, for example, about half of all homicides involve handguns, while in Canada the figure is approximately 10 percent. Friedland (1981) illustrates this point with some graphic comparisons from the 1970s:

In 1971 there were fewer than 60 homicides committed with handguns in all of Canada. Metropolitan Toronto, with more than 2 000 000 persons, had only four handgun homicides that year. In contrast, in 1979, handguns were used in almost 900 killings in New york City, and 300 in Metropolltan Detroit, and 75 in Metropolitan Boston. ... The six New Eng-

---

FIGURE 7-1   Crime Statistics for Canada and the United States, 1991

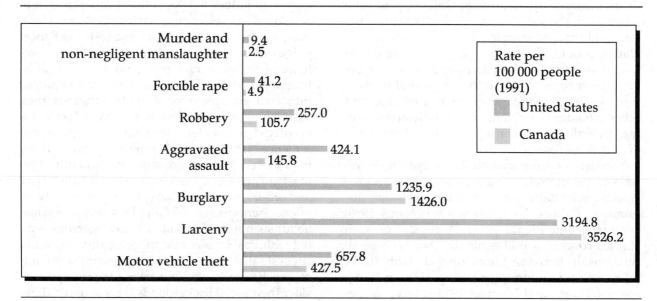

*Rape is not a recognized crime in Canada, where it is termed "sexual assault."
SOURCE: Canadian Centre for Justice Statistics; Federal Bureau of Investigation, *Uniform Crime Reports* Comparison of Canadian and American Crime Statistics, 1990.

land states had over 200 handgun homicides in 1979; the four Canadian Maritime provinces did not have a single handgun homicide in 1979. There were over 10 000 handgun homicides in the U.S. in 1979, almost 20 times the Canadian per capita rate.

The racial character of American criminal violence also differentiates the two national experiences. While blacks constitute about 12 percent of the American population, they are arrested for as much as 40–50 percent of all homicides, forcible rapes, armed robberies, and aggravated assaults (Freeman 1989; Flowers 1988). While there is some evidence that Native people in Canada and the United States also have high rates of assault and alcohol-related crimes (Jensen, Strauss, and Harris 1977; Hagan 1985), there is no indication that the connection between race–ethnicity and serious crimes of violence is nearly as strong in Canada as it is, particularly for blacks, in the United States. There do seem to be real differences between the countries and by race, at least for serious crimes of violence, that are not the exclusive product of the kind of deficiencies in official data discussed earlier in this chapter.

Why, then, are patterns of criminal violence so different in the United States and Canada? And how are these differences connected to issues of race? With regard to violence generally, these national differences are often thought to have a base in the way the American and Canadian West were settled. Quinney (1970) observes that on the American frontier, local authorities were free to develop their own law-enforcement policies or to ignore the problem of crime altogether. Similarly, Inciardi (1975) observes that "the American frontier was Elizabethan in its quality, simple, childlike, and savage. ... It was a land of riches where swift and easy fortunes were sought by the crude, the lawless, and the aggressive, and where written law lacked form and cohesion." Put simply, the American frontier was also a violent frontier — a model in some ways for the city life that followed (Bell 1953).

Canada intended to be different. This is one of the reasons Canada chose to have a federal criminal code, with John A. Macdonald arguing in the Confederation debates that "this is one of the most marked instances in which we take advantage of the experience derived from our observations of the defects in the constitution of the

neighbouring Republic" (cited in Friedland 1981). The Canadian approach initially involved firmer, but necessarily more strategically focused, control (McNaught 1975). MacLeod (1976) notes that by the 1870s, the American government was spending over $20 million a year just fighting the Plains Indians. At the same time, the total Canadian budget (of which defence was only a part) was just over $19 million. According to MacLeod (1976), "it is not a exaggeration to say ... that the only possible Canadian west was a peaceful one." The North West Mounted Police (NWMP), with powers unparalleled by any other police force in a democratic country, were given responsibility for establishing "peace and order." Kelly and Kelly (1976) contend that the RCMP of the 1890s "attended to the health and welfare problems of Indians and Eskimoes," while Brown and Brown (1973) write that "the NWMP were established as a semimilitary force designed to keep order on the prairies and to facilitate the transfer of most of the territory of the region from the Indian tribes to the federal government with a minimum of expense and bloodshed."

Whichever of the above accounts of the role of the NWMP is the more accurate, it is clear that Canada's Native peoples were treated in a significantly different way than were the Native peoples of the United States. America's treatment of both its black and Native minorities was extraordinarily violent. Canada treated its Native peoples — and may still treat them — badly, both socially and economically, but with not nearly as much actual violence. It is plausible that this difference in the form of mistreatment could have had behavioural consequences — for example, in rates of violent crime (on the assumption that violence begets violence).

A more general point can be made before we end this necessarily speculative discussion of national differences. Once again, this point involves the very different policies the two countries have adopted to accomplish quite similar goals. These alternative policies are reflected in what have been called the "due process" and "crime control" models of law enforcement (Packer 1964). Societies vary in their commitment to these models, and it can be argued that, *at least in symbolic terms,* Americans give considerable deference to the due process model, while Canadians have a more explicit commitment to a crime control model.

A Tale of Two Countries: Crime in Canada and the United States

By a variety of crime measures, Canada is only a moderately violent nation, at least as compared with the United States. As noted earlier in this chapter, much violent crime is consensual crime: that is, it involves infrequent and severely sanctioned violations of widely shared, and strongly held, values. Although some differences exist in the collection and categorization of offences in Canada and the United States, the findings suggest an interesting, enduring pattern: over the past ten to twenty years, even with population differences taken into account, violent offences have remained much more frequent in the United States than in Canada.

For example, in 1990 the incidence of the most serious types of violent crime (for example, homicide, attempted murder, rape and aggravated sexual assault, wounding and aggravated assault) was four to five times higher in the United States than in Canada. While there were fewer than 200 violent crimes per 100 000 population in the United States in the early 1960s and fewer than 50 in Canada, the respective numbers increased to more than 500 in the 1980s in the United States, compared with more than 100 in Canada.

A more specific comparison can be made between the two countries in terms of homicide rates. Since bodies are difficult to hide and because homicides are more likely to be reported and solved, homicide statistics are among the most reliable and valid crime statistics. For many years Canada's homicide rate has been between one-third and one-quarter of that in the United states. For example, in 1990 the murder and non-negligent manslaughter rate in Canada was 2.5,

compared with 9.4 in the United States. Compared with other countries, Canada seems to occupy something of a middle ground. In 1985, the Canadian homicide rate was more than two-and-a-half times higher than that of Scotland (1.1) or England and Wales (1.2), but lower than sixteen countries indicated in Figure 7-2.

There are some notable exceptions with regard to comparisons between Canada and the United States. For example, one highly criminalized activity, burglary, is now reported more often per capita in Canada. While in 1962 Canada had about 100 fewer burglaries per 100 000 population than did the United States, 20 years later the rates had increased more than tenfold in both countries, and Canada's rate for the first time exceeded that of the United States. Figure 7-1 reveals that this is still the case as of 1991, and that larcenies are also reported more often in Canada. This pattern is of considerable interest, although it may in small or large part derive from differences in reporting and recording practices between countries, with smaller burglaries no longer even being reported, especially in larger U.S. cities.

One of the most dramatic reflections of national differences in crime and its control in the United States and Canada involves the use of imprisonment. The number of people in prison has increased dramatically in recent years in the United States, while the Canadian prison population has alternated between periods of slow growth and decline. For example, between 1982 and 1985, during a period in which the Canadian prison population remained largely unchanged in size, the sentenced prison population in the United States grew by 22 percent. One

result is that in 1985 about 201 of every 100 000 Americans was in prison, compared with about 95 of every 100 000 Canadians. Another result is that in some U.S. jurisdictions the overcrowding of prison facilities has reached crisis proportions, while in Canada there are few reports of overcrowding. Perhaps partly because of resulting differences in economies of scale, Canada continues to spend more per capita on crime control than the United states, and there are signs that this difference is also growing.

For example, it is estimated that in 1980–81 the average cost per inmate was about $45 000 in Canada, compared with about $8100 in the United States. The difference seems to derive from differences in policy as well as scale. While U.S. prisons often house 3000 to 4000 inmates, the largest Canadian institution houses 500; U.S. prisons commonly house inmates two to a cell, while Canadian inmates are usually housed individually; and Canadian institutions have higher staff-to-inmate ratios. These two countries experience and respond to crime in quite different ways.

Source:

Craig McKie, "Canada's prison population," *Canadian Social Trends*, Summer 1987:2–7; Holly Johnson, "Homicide in Canada," *Canadian Social Trends*, Winter 1987:2–6; Holly Johnson, "Violent crime," *Canadian Social Trends*, Summer 1988:24–29; Robert Cormier, "Corrections costs," *Impact: Costs of Criminal Justice* 2(1984):23–35.

The **due process model** has its roots in the British Enlightenment and in English philosopher John Locke's notion that the law can be used effectively in the defence of "natural" and "inalienable" rights. Accordingly, the due process model is greatly concerned with procedural safeguards thought useful in protecting accused persons from unjust applications of criminal penalties. Because errors can always be made in law enforcement, advocates of the due process model would

FIGURE 7-2 Homicide Rates for Selected Countries (Most Recent Year for Which Data Are Available)

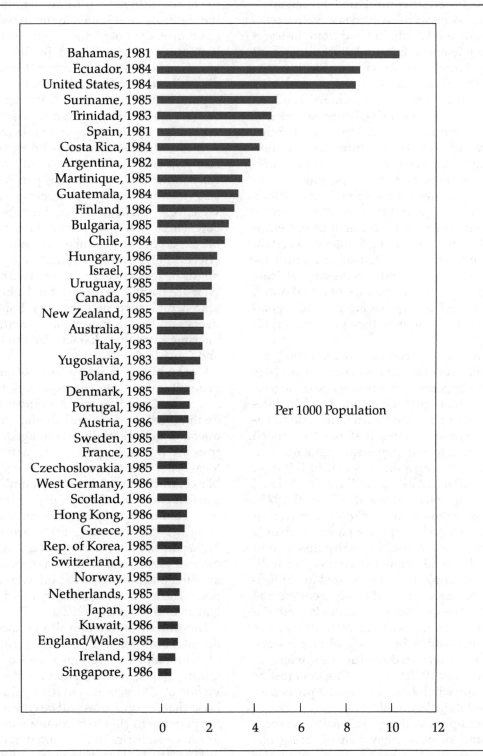

SOURCE: *Understanding and Preventing Violence*, National Academy of Sciences, 1993:52.

prefer to see a guilty person go free before an innocent person is punished.

In contrast, the **crime control model** received its philosophical support from the conservative reaction to Enlightenment thought and from the arguments of Englishman Edmund Burke that civil liberties can have meaning only in orderly societies. Thus, the crime control model places heavy emphasis on the repression of criminal conduct, holding that only by ensuring order can society guarantee individuals' personal freedom. For this reason, advocates of crime control are less anxious than the proponents of due process to presume the innocence of accused persons and to protect such persons against sometimes-dubious findings of guilt. It is not that the crime control model favours the unfair treatment of individuals, but rather that it is willing to tolerate a certain amount of mistreatment when the measures involved are seen as generally necessary, at least symbolically for the maintenance of social order. Under this model, authorities are granted a good deal of discretion as to how they protect individual "rights."

The distinction between the Lockean due process and the Burkean crime control models is clear, but the difference in intent is one of degree. Both have as their goal the creation and maintenance of legal order. With this in mind, one Canadian social scientist notes that the "approach which is truest to our experience and most in keeping with our capabilities is that of Edmund Burke, not John Locke. Canadians ... are [not] creatures of the Enlightenment" (Russell 1975). Some might argue that Canada's Charter of Rights and Freedoms will dramatically change our approach. By constitutionally enshrining Lockean-style "fundamental freedoms" for individuals and limiting the power vested in authorities, the Charter could reduce or remove the national differences between Canada and the United States. But the roots of these differences are deeply embedded in our social and historical fabric, so we remain doubtful. Meanwhile, as Margaret Atwood (1972) noted, "Canada must be the only country in the world where a policeman is used as a national symbol."

A final example, involving national differences in the control of guns, may help to bring our discussion together. Canada has long had tighter and more effective gun-control legislation than has the United States. This distinction, too, reflects the different attitude maintained toward the rights of individuals in the two countries. We have already noted the contrasting records of handgun homicide found in the United States and Canada. We have also noted the historical dissimilarities in the treatment of racial and ethnic minorities in the two countries. The United States violently suppressed its black and Native minorities within a society that makes handguns — a rather democratic instrument of violence — freely available. Canada socially and economically suppressed its Native peoples, but much less violently, and makes access to instruments of violence — particularly handguns — rather difficult. These divergent national experiences could be expected to produce different behavioural effects. For example, Canada's Native peoples might be less violent in their criminal behaviour than are Native peoples in the United States. Research into such matters may hold a key to a deeper understanding of the dramatic differences in crime rates that characterize the United States and Canada.

Meanwhile, it is interesting to speculate more generally about the consequences that may follow from Canadian and American strategies for dealing with crime and deviance. The consequences for the socially advantaged of both countries are much the same: both nations possess a legal order that allows the relatively safe and stable conduct of social and economic affairs. The consequences for the socially disadvantaged in each country are, however, somewhat different. Overall, violent crime rates are significantly higher in the United States than in Canada. Because it is the poor who are far more likely to be arrested and convicted in both countries, it is the poor who are most affected by this difference (see Hagan and Albonetti 1982).

The American situation allows some freedom to deviate, but there is also a heightened likelihood of criminalization for members of subordinate groups. The Canadian situation discourages deviation at all levels; this in turn reduces the likelihood that subordinates will be criminalized. Thus, the poor are likelier to become a part of crime and deviance statistics in the United States than they are in Canada. This difference may reflect an important part of what is unique about the Canadian experience.

SUMMARY

1. Deviation consists of variation from a norm and is made socially significant through the reactions of others.
2. There are several kinds of deviance: consensus crimes, conflict crimes, social deviations, and social diversions. These can be distinguished according to their socially determined seriousness.
3. Whether or not different kinds of deviant behaviour come under official control is influenced by the activities of moral entrepreneurs and various interest groups.
4. There are a variety of means used to count deviant behaviour, including data gathered by official agencies and nonofficial agencies, through first-person accounts, through surveys of crime victims, and through observations of deviant behaviour. A comparison of these measures leads to the conclusion that serious crimes, hard-drug use, alcohol abuse, and mental illness are found more frequently in the working class, while less serious and more frequent forms of crime, delinquency, and drug use are more evenly distributed across the social classes.
5. The structural-functional theories of deviance argue that the presence of success goals or values without the means to attain them can produce deviant behaviour, as can the absence of these goals or values in the first place.
6. The symbolic-interaction theories of deviance are concerned with the role of social meanings and definitions in the production of deviant behaviour.
7. The conflict theories of deviance have focused on the role of dominant societal groups in imposing legal labels on members of subordinate societal groups.
8. Consideration of the processing of various kinds of crime and deviance indicates that social as well as legal factors influence when, where, and on whom deviant labels are imposed.
9. Two societal strategies for maintaining legal order are the due process and crime control models of law enforcement. Although the differences involved are often a matter of ideology and emphasis, at a formal and symbolic level Canada tends more toward a crime control model than does the United States.
10. Serious forms of crime and deviance are more common in the United States than in Canada. The social and historical roots of this difference may reflect an important part of what is unique about the Canadian experience.

GLOSSARY

Anomie. Term originally used by Durkheim to refer to an absence of social regulation, or normlessness. Merton revived the concept to refer to the consequences of a faulty relationship between goals and the legitimate means of attaining them.

Conflict crimes. Acts that are defined by law as criminal and are often severely punished, but are usually regarded as only marginally harmful; typically they are subjects of conflict and debate.

Conflict subculture. Illegal group activity that is prone to violence and is common in settings (for example, "disorganized slums") where legitimate and illegitimate spheres are not integrated.

Conflict theories of deviance. Theories that focus particularly on the way dominant societal groups impose their legal controls on members of subordinate societal groups.

Consensus crimes. Acts defined by law as criminal that are widely regarded as extremely harmful, are severely punished, and are consensually identified as deviant.

Crime control model. Model of law enforcement that places heavy emphasis on the repression of criminal conduct, because ensuring order is seen as the only way to guarantee individual freedom.

Delinquent subculture. Collective response of working-class adolescents to their failure to satisfy middle-class expectations; the result is an inversion of middle-class values.

Deviance. Variation from a norm, made socially significant through the reaction of others.

Differential association. Process by which criminal behaviour is learned in conjunction with people who define such behaviour favourably and in isolation from those who define it unfavourably.

Due process model. Model of law enforcement that emphasizes procedural safeguards thought useful in protecting accused persons from unjust applications of criminal penalties.

Neutralization techniques. Linguistic expressions that, through a subtle process of justification, allow individuals to drift into deviant lifestyles.

Primary deviance. Deviant behaviours that precede a societal or legal response and have little impact on the individual's self-concept.

Residual rule-breaking. Category conventionally called "mental illness" that includes forms of rule-breaking for which society has no specific labels.

Retreatist subculture. Group-supported forms of escapist behaviour, particularly drug abuse, that result from failure in both legitimate and illegitimate spheres of activity.

Secondary deviance. Deviant behaviours that follow a societal or legal response and involve a transformation of the individual's self-concept.

Self-report surveys. Paper-and-pencil questionnaires used with adolescents and adults to obtain first-person accounts of amounts and types of deviant behaviour.

Social deviations. Noncriminal variations from social norms that are nonetheless subject to frequent official control.

Social diversions. Variations of lifestyle, including fads and fashions of appearance and behaviour.

Stable criminal subculture. Illegal group enterprises made more persistent by the protection they receive from persons in legitimate social roles (for example, politicians and police).

FURTHER READING

Black, Donald. *The Behaviour of Law.* New York: Academic Press, 1976. One of the most widely read of recent theoretical works on the way criminal and other kinds of law actually operate in real legal settings.

Boydell, Craig L., and Ingrid Arnet Connidis. *The Canadian Criminal Justice System.* Toronto: Holt, Rinehart and Winston, 1982. An up-to-date and comprehensive collection of readings.

Brannigan, Augustine. *Crimes, Courts and Corrections: An Introduction to Crime and Social Control in Canada.* Toronto: Holt, Rinehart and Winston, 1984. This book focuses on the criminal justice system, giving particular attention to the police, courts, and corrections. New perspectives on these institutions are offered, while common assumptions of the past are questioned.

Chambliss, William, and Robert Seidman. *Law, Order and Power.* Reading, MA: Addison Wesley, 1982. A conflict perspective on criminal law and its enforcement. This book deals with all aspects of the criminal justice system and with the development of criminal law.

Durkheim, Emile. *Suicide.* John A. Spalding and George Simpson (trans.). Glencoe, IL: Free Press, 1964. The classic work on this form of deviant behaviour. Durkheim anticipated much of what is thought modern in sociological theorizing about crime and deviance, including anomie theory and the labelling perspective.

Ericson, Richard. *Reproducing Order: A Study of Police Patrol Work.* Toronto: University of Toronto Press, 1982. This volume presents the results of the most comprehensive field study of policing done in Canada.

Gomme, Ian. *The Shadow Line.* Toronto, ON: Harcourt Brace and Company Canada Inc., 1993. This book provides an analysis of the major theoretical approaches in the sociology of deviance and crime.

Gottfredson, Michael, and Travis Hirschi. *A General Theory of Crime.* Stanford, CA: Stanford University Press, 1990. One of the best-known explanations of crime is called control theory. This book offers the most recent statement of this theory and expands its application to a broad range of behaviours usually designated as deviant.

Griffiths, Curt T., John F. Klein, and Simon N. Verdun-Jones. *Criminal Justice in Canada.* Vancouver: Butterworths, 1980. This volume provides a concise yet comprehensive introduction to the Canadian criminal justice system, with particular attention to the police, courts, and correctional subsystems.

Hagan, John. *The Disreputable Pleasures: Crime and Deviance in Canada.* 3rd edition. Toronto: McGraw-Hill Ryerson, 1991. An integrated textbook treatment of crime and deviance with a twist: it is argued that crime and deviance can be pleasurable, albeit disreputable, pursuits.

Sharing, Clifford. *Organizational Police Deviance.* Toronto: Butterworths, 1982. This book brings together a collection of articles that broadens the subject of police misbehaviour from simple corruption, which can be dismissed as a private moral failing, to pervasive patterns of official action — referred to as "structural deviance" — such as arresting, charging, harassing, and warning, which can have organizational roots.

UNIT III

The Social Base

The fabric of life in every society is largely determined by its social base. The density and distribution of the population, the ways in which society is stratified, the size and distribution of various ethnic groups, and the number and nature of formal organizations all play a part in shaping society.

Consider that Mexico has 85 million people on a total land area of about 2 million square kilometres and that its population will double in 30 years. In comparison, Canada has 26.5 million people on a total land area of over 10 million square kilometres and that its population will double in 96 years. Chapter 8 examines the causes and consequences of the population characteristics of societies.

Every society is stratified or ranked in some way: some people are rich, and some are poor; some lead, and some follow. The ways in which societies are stratified, the amount of inequality, and the degree of mobility between levels are examined in Chapter 9.

The number and distribution of ethnic groups and the interaction between them is very important in most societies, certainly in the three considered here. Chapter 10 discusses the concepts of ethnicity and race, and their importance in understanding society.

Modern societies are increasingly arranged into large, formal organizations. Today, most of us are born, educated, work, and die in formal organizations. Chapter 11 examines some of the causes and consequences of this type of social organization.

CHAPTER 8

Population

KEVIN MCQUILLAN

When we hear the word population, we are likely to think first of countries such as China or India, countries with large populations that appear to us as overcrowded. In these countries, the question of population seems to be of obvious importance. When we think of Canada, on the other hand, the significance of population questions is less apparent. After all, Canada is a large country with a relatively small population. Our everyday life does not seem to be affected by population in the way it might be if we lived in a densely populated country. Yet, when we begin to examine a number of questions that are important to us — finding a job, buying a home, or finding an appropriate partner — we discover that population questions are of considerable importance. That is why many sociologists, economists, geographers, and other social scientists pay considerable attention to the study of population, or demography. **Demography** attempts to understand how the size, rate of growth, and structure of a population are affected by rates of fertility, mortality, and migration. Demographic patterns have far-reaching effects on almost all aspects of social life. These effects are seldom dramatic and usually are not readily observable, but they are important nevertheless. Like a slow-moving current in a stream, they relentlessly move us in certain directions. Demographic factors do not, of course, operate on their own. Their influence often comes about through their interaction with other social and economic factors. But their impact, though often neglected, should not be underestimated.

In this chapter, we will briefly examine how population affects social life and how, in turn, social factors influence our population. In doing so, we will look at how the population of Canada, the United States, and a number of other societies has been changing, and how these changes have influenced the evolution of these societies.

Perspectives on Population

Classical Views of Population

Scholars have paid attention to population issues since the earliest times. Plato and Aristotle both offered suggestions regarding the best ways for society to regulate population (Overbeek 1974:25). But the beginnings of a modern approach to demography date from one man and one piece of writing: *An Essay on the Principle of Population* by Thomas Malthus (1970, originally published in 1798). The first edition of the essay, unlike most sociological essays, attracted considerable public interest. Malthus had wanted to create a stir and produced a provocative account of the role of population in human society. He saw himself responding to the optimistic ideas about the future of society that had come to prominence in the period of the Enlightenment. In contrast to these views, he painted a deliberately bleak picture of humanity's future. Societies may experience considerable technological and social progress, he allowed, but they would nevertheless have to contend with the impact of population growth.

In Malthus's view, human nature was marked by two basic needs or drives: the need to eat and what he termed "the passion between the sexes." As a result, he argued, an increase in the supply of food might produce a temporary improvement in the standard of living, but it would also produce an increase in population size. The growth of population would only be stopped by what he termed "the positive checks" to population: war, famine, and disease. In this grim vision, societies would remain forever trapped at a standard of living close to the minimum needed to survive.

Not surprisingly, Malthus's essay was the target of considerable critical attention almost as soon as it was published. Provoked by these criticisms, Malthus greatly expanded the book in its later editions, changing it from a polemical piece

into a scholarly work (Petersen 1979). In doing so, he introduced one important idea that softened his vision of the future. Human society could avoid the punishing effects of the positive checks to population growth by taking steps to limit the growth of population. For Malthus, who was an Anglican minister as well as a scholar, this did not mean using contraception. Malthus roundly condemned contraceptive practices, referring to them as "improper arts." Instead, he advised people to postpone marriage until such time as they felt sure they could adequately provide for the children that would be born to them. Indeed, he suggested that ministers read a warning to couples during the wedding ceremony alerting them to this situation. Only by using this "preventive check," as he called it, could society avoid going through an endless cycle of population growth followed by rising mortality. Malthus, we might add, followed his own advice. He married in 1804 at the age of 38, and he and his wife had three children (James 1979).

Malthus's ideas on population and society seem rather quaint today. Clearly, developments Malthus could not foresee (and would not have approved of) have radically changed our situation. Technological progress has allowed us to expand food supplies far beyond the levels Malthus could have imagined. And the spread of modern means of birth control has meant that some modern societies now experience not population growth, but population decline. This combination of higher productivity and slower population growth has produced, at least in the industrialized world, a tremendous increase in the standard of living. Yet, while Malthus may have been wrong on the specifics, some writers feel he identified a central dilemma facing human societies. For many countries in the developing world, rapid population growth poses a major challenge to their ability to increase their standard of living. Moreover, Malthus's contention that the resources of the world are finite and that human beings must learn to live within these limits has been taken up by many in the environmental movement today. In language that might have been borrowed from Malthus, they claim that continuous economic growth leads to more rapid exhaustion of irreplaceable natural resources. Like Malthus, they argue that we must restrain our use of resources before nature intervenes through a new series of positive checks to growth.

Among the earliest and most forceful critics of Malthusian ideas was Karl Marx. Never known for his generosity to his intellectual opponents, Marx saved some of his harshest criticism for Malthus, calling his essay "schoolboyish" and "a superficial plagiary" (Marx 1906:675). Why did Malthus's work so upset Marx? No doubt because he felt Malthus was inclined to blame the poor for their own desperate state. The poor are poor, Malthus could be seen to say, because they recklessly produce children they cannot afford to care for. For Marx, the source of poverty lay not with the poor themselves but with the inherently oppressive character of pre-capitalist and capitalist societies.

Although Marx strongly disagreed with Malthus's theory of population, this did not lead him to develop a theory of his own (McQuillan 1979). For the most part, he was content to point out what he saw to be the errors in Malthus's work. Yet, in doing so, he produced some important ideas concerning the role of population in capitalist society. Why, Marx asked, do people like Malthus see societies as overpopulated? The answer, he suggested, was the poverty people saw around them. This led them to the conclusion that if the population were smaller, society's resources would be divided among fewer people and thus poverty would be eliminated. But this was to draw a false conclusion. The real problem, he suggested, was not the size of the population but the economic organization of capitalist society.

In sketching his own response to this problem, he distinguished between "absolute overpopulation" and "relative overpopulation." Absolute overpopulation implied that there simply were not enough resources to provide the necessities of life to everyone. This was a theoretical possibility, but not one societies were likely to face in the near future. Rather, the societies of his day faced the problem of relative overpopulation, the symptoms of which were unemployment and poverty. Capitalist societies needed a surplus population, or what Marx called "a reserve army of labour," to restrain the wage demands of workers. If workers banded together to seek higher wages,

capitalists could threaten to replace them with new employees drawn from the ranks of the unemployed. But what would happen if workers followed the advice of Malthus and strictly limited the size of their families? Would not the resulting shortage of workers eliminate unemployment and increase wages? No, Marx answered. Capitalists would respond by replacing workers with machines, creating a new class of unemployed workers. So long as capitalism existed, Marx believed, so would unemployment and thus the appearance of overpopulation. Only the transition to an economy built on socialist principles would eliminate unemployment and make clear that nature could provide for all people.

As was the case with Malthus, some of Marx's ideas appear odd to readers in the late twentieth century. Yet Marx's ideas have had considerable influence on contemporary analysts of population questions. Some observers of less developed societies argue that their problems lie less in the size of their populations than in the unequal relations between rich and poor countries (Amin 1976). The solution to poverty in the countries of Africa, Asia, and Latin America is not population control (though this may sometimes be helpful) but rather a fundamental change in the economic relations between rich and poor countries. Fairer prices for the exports of developing societies and greater access to investment capital and modern technology will bring greater benefits than will population control to the developing world (Walsh 1974).

The Course of World Population Growth

Before examining further the ideas of social scientists about population growth, let us stop to look at the actual path of world population growth. When we examine the growth of the global population, only two factors are relevant: the number of births and the number of deaths. Demographers have invented a few simple measures to help us understand how these factors determine the rate of population growth. These measures are known as the **crude birth rate** (CBR) and the **crude death rate** (CDR) (further discussion of measurement questions appears in this chapter's sections on fertility and mortality). The CBR is arrived at by dividing the number of births occurring in a population in a given period of time (usually one year) by the total size of the population (best measured at the midpoint of the year). In the same way, the CDR is calculated by dividing the number of deaths by the total midyear population. Both rates are usually expressed per 1000 population — a CBR of 0.016 will be described as 16 births per 1000. The CBR in the world today is approximately 26 per 1000, while the CDR is only 9 per 1000 (World Bank 1992:271). The difference between these two rates is a measure of how fast the population is growing and is known as the **rate of natural increase.** The world population is now growing each year at the rate of 17 persons per 1000 population, or 1.7 percent.

As the data in Figure 8-1 make clear, the growth of world population we are now experiencing is without precedent in world history. Prior to the nineteenth century, human populations tended to grow very slowly or not at all. While societies may well have enjoyed times of prosperity when their population increased significantly, these times were usually offset by periods of decline brought about by what Malthus would have labelled the positive checks to population growth — famine, disease, and war (Coale 1974). The result was that for many centuries the size of the human population remained remarkably stable (see Figure 8-1). But the eighteenth century saw the beginnings of a change in this pattern of stability. As European societies began to apply human knowledge to a variety of economic and technological problems, the conditions were created for a period of sustained population growth.

Most historical demographers would agree that the last half of the eighteenth century — the generations before Malthus wrote his famous essay — saw significant population growth in a number of European countries. With the further development of industry and technology in the nineteenth century, the pace of demographic growth began to quicken. From the 1 billion figure of 1800, the human population grew to some 2 billion in 1920. Rapid as it was in comparison with earlier periods, the pace of world population growth in the nineteenth century pales in comparison with twentieth-century rates. The 2 bil-

---

FIGURE 8-1   Schematic Representation of the Increase in the Human Species

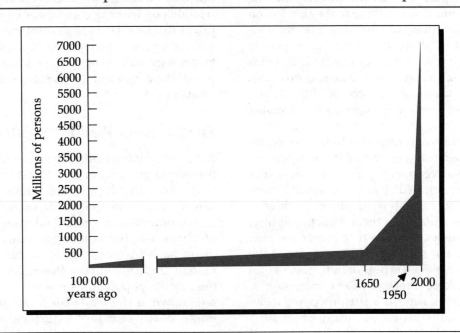

SOURCE: W. Peterson, *Population*, 3rd edition (New York: Macmillan, 1975), p. 9. Reprinted with the permission of Macmillan College Publishing Company. Copyright © 1975 by Macmillan College Publishing Company, Inc.

lion of 1920 became 3 billion in 1960, 4 billion in 1975, 5 billion sometime in the 1980s, and will likely reach 6 billion by the year 2000. These numbers are hard for us to visualize in any meaningful way. But to understand the current pace of growth, you might note that the world population will grow in the next two weeks by an amount roughly equal to the population of metropolitan Toronto.

Although tracking the size of the world population is important, it is equally important to note that any discussion of the rate of growth of the human population obscures as much as it clarifies. In effect, when we examine the question more closely, we find tremendous variation in population growth rates in different parts of the world. On the one hand, in countries like Canada the rate of growth is low, particularly if we exclude the effects of immigration and focus only on natural increase. The rate of natural increase in Canada today is only 0.7 percent. In some countries of Western Europe the rate is negative — there are more people dying than being born and, in the absence of immigration, the total population would decline. By contrast, in some countries of Asia and Africa, population is growing very rapidly. In Kenya, for example, the rate of natural increase is 3.5 percent, a rate that will cause the population to double in size in just 20 years. (World Bank 1992:270).

Demographic Transition Theory

Why do we find such large differences in population patterns? One answer comes from the **demographic transition theory** (Notestein 1945). Developed in light of the experience of the currently developed societies, the theory suggests that societies pass through a three-stage process of change (see Figure 8-2). In the first stage, population grows slowly because high birth rates are balanced by high and fluctuating death rates. In this stage, which was typical of Western societies before the Industrial Revolution, the average woman gives birth to a large number of children in her lifetime, perhaps five or six on average. This high rate of child-bearing is offset, however, by a high level of mortality. As many as one in four babies do not live to see their first birthday, and many of those who do die in childhood. In such circumstances, it is not unusual to find that

FIGURE 8-2 Model of Demographic Transition

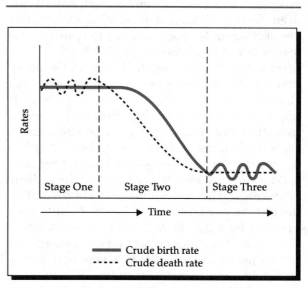

only half of the children born survive to adulthood. The result for society is a slow rate of population growth.

According to transition theorists, this high rate of mortality is an inevitable result of the poor conditions of life that characterize premodern societies. A low level of economic and technological development leaves populations with little protection against the ravages of famine and disease. If these societies are to survive, a high level of fertility is essential. This is not to imply that couples have large numbers of children because of a sense of duty to society. On the contrary, individual families see good reasons for having a large number of children. In premodern societies, children are a valuable resource. From an early age they contribute to the family by doing various household chores, and as they age their value increases. They can be particularly important as a source of support for their parents in old age. Moreover, children in such societies are far less costly to raise than are children in modern, industrial societies. Schooling, if it exists at all, is limited to several years of basic training and is often confined to parts of the year when children's labour is not needed by the family. As a result, children's economic contribution to the family quickly comes to outweigh their cost. To the average couple, then, having children makes good economic sense, and, given the high risk of children dying in childhood, producing a large number of children is a good strategy to ensure that at least a few of them survive to adulthood.

Transition theorists argue that, with the development of a modern economy and the enormous change in living conditions that comes with it, populations move into the second stage of the transition, which is based on a combination of high birth rates and declining death rates. A higher standard of living and improvements in sanitation and health gradually reduce death rates, especially for infants and children. This decline in mortality rates is not immediately matched by a decline in the birth rate, however. Transition theorists suggest that individuals take some time to adapt to this new situation. Strong traditions exist in many societies in support of large families, and even for women for whom child-bearing could be a dangerous and onerous process, producing a large number of children is often seen as a mark of social status. Moreover, religious beliefs and customs frequently forbid the use of birth control to limit child-bearing. As a result, birth rates often remain high for a generation or so after mortality rates begin to decline, and societies thus experience a period of rapid population growth.

Eventually, however, societies pass into the third stage of the transition, in which birth rates begin to decline significantly. The persistence of low mortality gradually convinces couples that they do not need to have a large number of births to produce several surviving children. Moreover, continuing economic and technological change greatly reduce the economic value of children while simultaneously increasing their costs. Childhood in modern societies is no longer spent at work but in school, and the period of schooling has been constantly increasing. During this ever-lengthening period of development, parents are expected to supply a wide array of consumer goods and services to their beloved offspring — music lessons, leather jackets, and a limousine ride to the high-school prom. Not surprisingly, most young couples today continue to want children but conclude that one or two will be just fine. What this means for society as a whole, of course, is a new balance between birth and death rates, and a population that grows slowly or not at all.

Returning to the question of why currently developing countries experience much faster population growth than do countries like Canada, transition theorists would respond that these countries are simply further behind us in the transition process. While Western countries have now entered the final stage of the transition, less developed societies are still in the second stage. This analysis leads them to conclude that as these societies continue to develop, they too will pass into the third stage of the transition, and the population problem will be solved. When this occurs, the world population will once again grow slowly as countries around the world experience low birth and death rates.

Is their view of the future justified? Do populations naturally tend toward a position of zero population growth? Whether this view turns out to be true depends on two questions. First, is their interpretation of the past experience of Western societies correct? Second, is it reasonable to expect that the Western experience can be applied to currently developing countries?

Let's begin with the experience of Western countries. In general, there is little question that societies like Canada have passed through some form of transition. It is undeniable that women in the past gave birth to far more children than is true of women today; similarly, death rates have plunged dramatically over the last two centuries. There is some question, however, about the mechanisms that transition theorists identify as being responsible for this transition. Some critics, for example, question the role of industrialization in bringing about population change. They point out that some countries such as France experienced significant change in birth and death rates before the beginning of widespread industrialization (Knodel and van de Walle 1986). On the other hand, in countries like England, widely agreed to be the first nation to experience an industrial revolution, birth rates did not fall until much later.

Furthermore, some critics claim that a decline in infant and child mortality may not be necessary to bring about a decrease in fertility. They point out that in countries like England, fertility and infant mortality appear to have declined more or less in unison, while in parts of Germany the birth rate actually began to decline *before* the infant

The Course of Canadian Population Growth

The British North America Act, Canada's basic constitutional document, contains a provision requiring that a census of the country be taken every ten years. In 1966, it was decided that a decennial census was not sufficient to keep track of Canada's rapidly changing population, and the federal government decided to hold a census every five years. The information in these censuses allows us to draw a detailed portrait of our national population because the census does not simply count the number of people in the country but also gathers data on a wide variety of characteristics, including ethnicity, occupation, education, and income. Canada's most recent census was conducted on June 4, 1991, and data from that census are now available. As we can see from the accompanying figure, the most recent intercensal period (1986–1991) saw an increase in the rate of growth after six successive periods of decline. From a total population of 25 309 331 in 1986, the Canadian population grew by 7.9 percent to 27 296 859 in 1991 (Statistics Canada 1991).

Not surprisingly, the rate of growth varied significantly across the country. British Columbia, with a growth rate of 13.8 percent, was the fastest-growing province, while Ontario was in second place with an increase of 10.8 percent. With that, Ontario's population surpassed 10 million for the first time. Saskatchewan was the only province to lose population during the five-year period, and its population dropped below the 1 million

Population, Canada, Showing Total Population and Growth Rate, 1956–1991

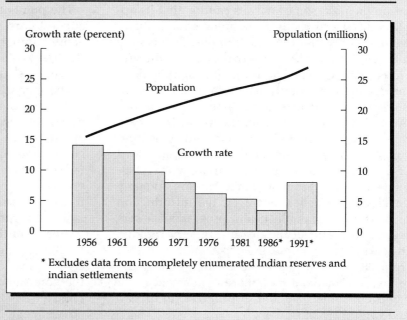

* Excludes data from incompletely enumerated Indian reserves and indian settlements

*Excludes data from incompletely enumerated Indian reserves and Indian settlements.

mark. Manitoba and the Atlantic region grew slowly, while Quebec and Alberta experienced growth a little below the national average. These trends reflect a long-term pattern of movement toward the West. While the Atlantic provinces' share of Canada's population declined from 11.6 percent in 1951 to 8.6 percent in 1991, the proportion of the population in Alberta and British Columbia rose from 15 percent in 1951 to 21.3 percent in 1991.

Source:

Statistics Canada, "Getting Bigger Faster," insert in *Canadian Social Trends,* 25 (Summer 1992).

mortality rate. This discovery has led some analysts to suggest that a decline in the birth rate may actually pave the way for a decrease in the death rate (Knodel and van de Walle 1986). When women have fewer children, they argue, they are able to provide them with a better standard of care, and this may result in lower risks of infant and childhood death.

To many students this may seem like one more academic squabble, something only their professors could get excited about. It is important to note, however, that such theories have important consequences for social policy. If, as transition theorists claim, industrialization is a necessary condition for a decline in the birth rate, then policies designed to encourage the use of family planning methods in Third World societies are doomed to failure. On the other hand, if couples are already motivated to limit the size of their families, as some critics have suggested, they may enthusiastically adopt such methods when they become available, and this in turn may bring about a fall in the birth rate even before the beginning of widespread economic development.

Even if the transition theory provides a good explanation of the experiences of Western societies in the past, some analysts caution that its applicability to currently developing societies may be limited because the situation they face is very different from that of Western societies in the previous century (Teitelbaum 1975). First, they note, the decline in mortality has been much faster in these countries than was true for societies like our own. In Canada's case, for example, the death rate fell gradually over the past century as a result of general improvements in the standard of living and, more recently, important developments in public health and medical care. In many developing societies, however, the introduction of Western-style public health programs has succeeded in reducing the death rate very rapidly. In Mexico, for example, life expectancy increased from 39 years around 1940 to almost 66 years today; in Canada, it took more than a century to achieve a similar amount of progress (Bourbeau and Légaré 1982).

Second, birth rates tend to be much higher in many developing societies (particularly in sub-Saharan Africa) than was true in Western societies in the past. This in turn reflects the fact that in many developing societies marriage is nearly universal and often occurs at a much younger age than was true in the Western experience, allowing women more time to produce children. As a consequence, while the rate of natural increase in Canada probably never surpassed 2.5 percent, in some developing societies today, the rate of natural increase is close to 4 percent per year. At this pace, their populations will double in less than 20 years.

Finally, the population of many developing societies is already much larger than was true of Western societies. For countries like Canada and the United States or even many European societies, a doubling of the population while birth rates gradually adjusted to lower death rates posed no insurmountable problems. Land and resources were abundant, and the spur of population growth probably encouraged more rapid development. Some critics question whether the same can be said of some present-day developing

countries. Can Bangladesh, for example, with a population of 111 million living in an area less than half of the size of Newfoundland, deal with a doubling of its population over the next generation while birth rates gradually fall into line with reduced death rates?

The points raised in the preceding paragraphs suggest currently developing societies face more acute population problems than did currently industrialized societies. It needs to be pointed out, however, than the resources available to devote to these problems are greater as well (Teitelbaum 1975). The most remarkable aspect of the decline of fertility in Western societies is that it came about before the development of modern, efficient means of contraception, and usually in the face of opposition from major institutions in society such as government and religion. By contrast, in countries such as China, Singapore, and Thailand, governments have been enthusiastic supporters of birth control. The most striking example is China, where the government has used coercive means to try to bring about the spread of the "one-child family" (Hardee-Cleaveland and Banister 1988). In many other countries, however, governments have adopted more subtle policies to encourage the spread of contraception. And just as death rates frequently have declined more rapidly in developing societies, in several cases birth rates have fallen dramatically as well. In Thailand, for example, women in the 1960s had, on average, more than six children (see Table 8-2). Today, they average just over two.

In sum, then, transition theory cannot be taken as a fool-proof explanation of population trends. Neither should it be dismissed entirely, however. It can best be seen as a guide to the factors that must be considered when examining long-term changes in population patterns.

Fertility

Social and Biological Factors Affecting Fertility

In our discussion of transition theory, we have already begun to look at the topic of fertility. Here we will examine the question in more detail. We will first introduce some essential terms for analyzing the question and then briefly discuss the crucial issue of fertility measurement.

When demographers speak of human fertility they are simply discussing the question of having children. In doing so, however, they assign a specific meaning to the term fertility, one we need to be aware of to understand the results of their research. Despite its "biological" sound, demographers use the term fertility to refer to the actual child-bearing record of a woman or a group of women. By contrast, they use the term "fecundity" to refer to the biological potential of a woman or a group of women to bear children. Thus, a woman may be fecund (able to give birth to a child) but not fertile (she has not yet given birth to a child). Needless to say, if women made full use of their biological potential to bear children, birth rates in human societies would be very high indeed (Bongaarts and Potter 1983). And, of course, there are examples of women who have borne a great many children. Prime minister Jean Chrétien, for example, is the eighteenth child in a family of nineteen children.

On the whole, however, fertility rates tend to fall well below the biological maximum, and not only in modern, industrialized societies. There are a variety of reasons for this. First, most societies have developed a series of practices and customs that, often unintentionally, tend to limit fertility (Coale 1986). In Western societies, the most important illustration of this is the influence of marriage patterns on child-bearing. Until recently, it was widely accepted that only married couples should have children, and hence child-bearing outside of marriage was uncommon. But since marriage usually occurs well after the beginning of a woman's child-bearing years, many years of potential child-bearing were thus "lost." It is unlikely that people deliberately delayed marriage in order to avoid having children. There are a wide variety of reasons that lead people to marry in their mid-twenties rather than in their teenage years, but from a biological viewpoint, the effect has been to limit fertility. Other practices as well can unintentionally reduce fertility levels well below their biological maximum. Much recent research has shown that breastfeeding acts as a kind of natural contraceptive and reduces the likelihood of the mother becoming pregnant. In societies where it is common to breastfeed children for a lengthy period of time after birth — and in some developing societies this may extend up to two years — the effect is to increase the length of time between births and thus reduce fertility (Bongaarts and Potter 1983). Again, it seems unlikely that the majority of women continue to breastfeed in the hopes of delaying another pregnancy. It is more likely that they simply accept lengthy breastfeeding as the normal and proper way to care for their children. The fertility-reducing effect of this practice is therefore an unintended side-effect of a particular cultural practice.

In our society, of course, the most important fertility-reducing practice is contraception, and it is consciously used by couples to prevent child-bearing. The use of contraception is now almost universal among married couples in Canada. A recent survey of Canadian women found that among married women not pregnant or attempting to become pregnant, 93.3 percent were using some form of contraception (Balakrishnan et al. 1985). While past research had pointed to significant differences among women from different religious and ethnic backgrounds in their willingness to use contraception, recent evidence suggests these differences have largely disappeared. Moreover, the same survey shows that sterilization was the most popular method of contraception among married couples, while unmarried women were most likely to use the pill. The data on sterilization are especially striking and suggest that sterilization rates in Canada are significantly higher than in other modern societies with similar population structures.

Fertility Measurement

How many children does the average woman have? This may seem a straightforward question, but it is a remarkably difficult one to answer. If you go on to study population questions in more detail, you will find that demographers have developed a number of ways to answer this question. For our purposes, however, we need examine only a few. We have already discussed the crude birth rate, which provides a general measure of the rate of child-bearing in a population. Useful as it is, the CBR has one major limitation. It considers child-bearing in relation to the entire population, not in relation to those capable of having children — women of child-bearing age. If women of child-bearing age decline as a proportion of the total population, the crude birth rate will decline even if the average woman continues to have exactly the same number of children.

To avoid this problem, demographers have developed some simple alternatives to the CBR. One is to examine **age-specific fertility rates**. These rates are obtained by dividing the number of births to women of a given age by the total number of women of that age in the population. Since only women of child-bearing age are included, the problem of changes in the makeup of the total population is avoided. These rates have two additional benefits. One is that we can observe changes in the age pattern of fertility. Although the overall level of fertility may not be changing, we may find that fertility rates are decreasing among younger women but increasing among older women. Second, if we add up the age-specific rates for women across the child-bearing years, we arrive at an estimate of the average number of children a woman will bear in her lifetime if she experiences the current age-specific rates of fertility. This measure, which is of great importance in demography, is called the **total fertility rate** (TFR), and it may be expressed per woman (for example, 1.7 children per woman) or per 1000 women (1000 women will bear 1700 children).

Before leaving the question of measurement, one further distinction is worth introducing. The measures discussed so far — the CBR, age-specific fertility rates, and the TFR — are all based on information gathered at one point in time. For example, the TFR for 1992 is computed by relating the number of births in 1992 to the number of women of child-bearing age at that point in time. Such measures are referred to as **period measures** because they refer to a particular period of time. But what if, for some reason 1992 produces an unusually small crop of babies? Perhaps because of hard economic times, a significant number of couples decide to delay having a child until the situation improves. If this occurs, the birth rate will correctly inform us of this slowdown in births, but if we attempt to use it as an indicator of how many children couples will ultimately have, we will be misled. The drop in the TFR for that year may be a purely temporary occurrence

and not a sign of any underlying change in the size of families.

To deal with this problem, demographers have developed a second approach to measuring behaviour, known as the cohort approach (Ryder 1965). The basic principle is very simple. All people who share a common starting point belong to a particular cohort; if you were born in 1970, you are a member of the 1970 birth cohort. The members of these cohorts can then be observed over time, and their behaviour can be recorded. For example, women born in 1950 are now approaching the end of their child-bearing years. We could then record the total number of children born to women who were themselves born in 1950. The result would be a cohort total fertility rate. Unlike the period total fertility rate discussed above, there is nothing hypothetical about this rate — it refers to the actual behaviour of a real group of women. Moreover, unlike the period measure, it is unaffected by year-to-year fluctuations in births. Since the cohort measure shows the number of children women of a particular cohort ultimately produce, it makes no difference whether they have those children early in life or delay them until later. In that sense, it is a truer picture of the fertility behaviour of women. This does not mean that **cohort measures** are necessarily better than period measures, however. For some purposes, it is more important to know about year-to-year changes in behaviour. Thus it is best to see period and cohort measures as complementary, providing information about behaviour from two different perspectives.

Fertility in Developed Societies

Having learned something about how to measure fertility, we can now use that knowledge to examine fertility behaviour in various societies. Table 8-1 shows period total fertility rates for a number of advanced, industrial societies. Not surprisingly, the data indicate that fertility rates in all these countries are relatively low. Since a total fertility rate of slightly more than two children per woman is necessary to avoid population decline, we can see that most advanced societies now face the prospect of a natural decrease of population and, in the absence of immigration, a decline in their total population. Although transi-

TABLE 8-1 Total Fertility Rates for Selected Industrialized Nations, 1950–1989

Country	1950	1960	1970	1980	1989
Canada	3.46	3.90	2.33	1.75	1.77
Quebec	3.81	3.76	1.97	1.70	1.61
U.S.A.	3.09	3.65	2.48	1.84	2.01
Sweden	2.28	2.20	1.92	1.68	2.01
Italy	2.49	2.41	2.43	1.64	1.29
Germany	2.10	2.37	1.99	1.45	1.39
France	2.93	2.73	2.47	1.95	1.62

SOURCE: *Canada and Quebec:* 1950–1970, Statistics Canada, 1975, pp. 56, 60; 1980, Statistics Canada, 1982, p. 9; 1989, Statistics Canada, 1991, pp. 25, 28. *United States:* 1950–1970, U.S. Bureau of the Census, 1975, p. 50; 1980, U.S. Bureau of the Census, 1983, p. 63; 1989, National Center for Health Statistics, 1991, p. 20. *European Nations:* All years, J-P. Sardon, "Le remplacement des générations en Europe depuis le début de siècle," *Population* 45:947–967.

tion theory assumed that fertility decline would stop when birth rates approached two children per woman, there is no necessary reason for them to do so.

If we compare the evolution of birth rates in the various societies, we see that while all now experience relatively low fertility, there are nevertheless important differences among them. Some countries, such as Italy, Germany, and France, have been experiencing a fairly steady downward drift of their fertility rate. All three of these countries now have fertility levels significantly below replacement level. In other cases — Sweden, for example — the fertility rate has begun to climb in recent years after having reached a low level during the 1980s. The situation in North America has been even more complex. In Quebec, which historically had had a very high level of fertility, the TFR is now lower than in English Canada or the United States. Indeed, fertility rates in the United States and English Canada have followed a kind of roller-coaster pattern in the decades since the end of World War II. In both cases, fertility rates rose sharply in the 1950s, creating the phenomenon known as the Baby Boom. Rates then plunged dramatically, reaching their lowest points in the early 1980s. Since then, there has been a gradual movement upward and, in the

United States, the TFR surpassed two children per woman in 1989, the first time that has occurred since 1972.

Among the factors that have influenced recent fertility patterns is the changing timing of child-bearing. The postwar period saw a shift toward younger child-bearing. Couples were marrying younger, and this usually meant an earlier start on child-bearing. One effect of this was to increase the total fertility rate during the 1950s. Recently, however, we have been witnessing an important shift in the other direction. Women are delaying the start of the family-building process. Age at marriage has been rising, and there is often a long delay between marriage and the birth of the first child. As a result, we are seeing an increasing number of women past age 30 (and even a small number past age 40) becoming first-time mothers (Wadhera and Miller 1991).

The increasing presence of women in higher education and the growing involvement of women in the labour force no doubt lie behind this shift to later child-bearing. Many women probably feel it is better to establish themselves in a career before taking on the commitments involved in having children. Furthermore, many couples feel the need to acquire greater financial stability before becoming parents. This delay in child-bearing served to decrease fertility rates during the 1970s and 1980s. The recent increase in fertility in countries like Sweden, the United States, and Canada may reflect the births occurring to those women who had postponed having children. When we are able to examine the cohort rates for these women, we may discover that they too had approximately two children on average, and that their decision to shift child-bearing until a later age caused the temporary decline in fertility rates during the 1980s.

One other significant trend that deserves mention is the weakening of the link between marriage and child-bearing (Rindfuss and Parnell 1989). Until very recently, having children was seen as something that should take place only within the confines of marriage. The proportion of babies born to unmarried women was traditionally very low in Western societies. In Canada, for example, as late as 1960, only 4.3 percent of children were born to unmarried mothers. Moreover, in the past, a large proportion of these children would be given up for adoption shortly after birth. In recent decades, however, the proportion of children born to nonmarried women has been rising sharply. In 1990, 24.4 percent of births in Canada and 37.9 percent of births in Quebec occurred to unmarried women (Statistics Canada 1992). In the United States, 25.7 percent of births and 63.5 percent of births to black women occurred outside of marriage (U.S. Bureau of the Census 1991). The circumstances surrounding these births may vary greatly, of course. In some cases, the child may be born to a couple in a relatively stable relationship, while in others the birth may occur to a woman on her own, with no financial or other support from the father. Frequently, particularly when the mother is young, the birth occasions considerable hardship for mother and child. One recent study indicated that two-thirds of families headed by a never-married mother live below the poverty line (McQuillan 1990).

One of the best-researched topics in demography is what is called differential fertility. This issue simply involves examining the association between certain traits of couples having children — their income and level of education or ethnicity, for example — and the size of their family. In Canada, we find that the traits affecting child-bearing today are rather different from those that played a leading role in the past (Beaujot and McQuillan 1982). For older generations of Canadians, characteristics such as ethnicity and religion were very important. If we examine the experience of women born between 1917 and 1921, we find that Catholic women had an average of 3.8 children while Protestant women had an average of only 2.7 children. One important consequence of this religious effect was the high rate of fertility observed in Quebec, a province with an overwhelmingly Catholic population. When we turn to more recent generations, however, we find that the effect of factors like religion has decreased drastically. For women born in the post–World War II era, we now find almost no significant difference between Catholics and Protestants. Members of some smaller religious groups, such as Mormons and Pentecostals, still have significantly larger families, but given the small proportion of the population belonging to these denominations the effect on overall fertility levels is small (Beaujot and McQuillan 1982).

While the effect of characteristics like religion is now limited, other characteristics such as education continue to exert an important influence. Virtually all Canadian women today are likely to produce a relatively small number of children, and the further women go in their schooling, the smaller the number of children they are likely to have. According to the 1991 census, women over 45 years of age with less than nine years of completed schooling had had an average of 3.8 children, while those who had completed university had had only 2.2 children (Statistics Canada 1993). Although these differences may be reduced among younger generations of Canadian women, it seems unlikely they will disappear entirely.

Fertility in Developing Societies

Few topics have attracted as much attention from demographers as fertility patterns in developing societies. Much of this research has centred on finding ways to bring about declining fertility in these parts of the world. No magic solution has been discovered, but in the process of searching, these observers have greatly increased our knowledge and understanding of child-bearing in different social contexts.

In reviewing this work, the first thing that becomes apparent is the great variability in behaviour among developing countries. As the data in Table 8-2 make clear, while it may have made sense to speak of a Third World fertility pattern in the 1960s, that pattern no longer exists. All the countries listed in the table had fertility rates in 1965 that were high by Western standards. But over the last generation, these countries have followed a variety of paths. Let us look at a few of them to gain some clues as to the sources of declining fertility in the developing world.

South Korea is perhaps the most outstanding example of a society that has experienced both rapid economic growth and rapid fertility decline. Indeed, it makes little sense now to speak of Korea as being a developing country. A rising standard of living, growing urbanization, and industrialization have transformed the country and brought about a shift to a fertility pattern similar to that of Canada or other Western countries. It is a near-perfect example of the kind of change predicted by demographic transition theory.

TABLE 8-2 Total Fertility Rates for Selected Developing Countries, 1965 and 1990

Country	1965	1990
South Korea	4.9	1.8
Singapore	4.7	1.9
Thailand	6.3	2.5
China	6.4	2.5
India	6.2	4.0
Mexico	6.7	3.3
Peru	6.7	3.8
Uganda	7.0	7.3
Pakistan	7.0	5.8
Iran	7.1	6.2

SOURCE: World Bank, *World Development Report 1992* (New York: Oxford University Press, 1992), pp. 270–271.

Thailand provides a somewhat different example, one favoured by those who emphasize the importance of cultural factors in producing fertility decline. Thailand has experienced rapid economic growth in recent years; by some accounts, it had one of the fastest-growing economies in the world during the 1980s (World Bank 1992). Yet, fertility decline has seemed to leap ahead of economic development. Although income levels are still low by Western standards and much of the population remains in rural areas, the total fertility rate now stands not far above Western levels. Clearly the growing economy has influenced this process, but some analysts argue that particular features of the Thai culture have played an important role as well. The majority of the population is Buddhist, a religion that has raised no objections to the use of contraceptives. Moreover, women in Thai culture have a considerable degree of autonomy, particularly in comparison with those in many developing societies (Knodel et al. 1987). Although some of these features may not be easily transferable to other societies, many observers believe the importance of the Thai case is that it demonstrates that where the culture is open to the practice of fertility control, birth rates may decline significantly before the society achieves a high level of development.

The third example of large-scale fertility decline, China, again presents a strikingly different pattern. In this case, the impetus to fertility decline has come from one source — the government. Since the early 1970s, the Chinese government has introduced a series of ever-more-stringent fertility policies, culminating in the introduction of the one-child-family policy in 1979 (Goodstadt 1982). This policy uses a series of rewards and punishments to induce couples to have only one child. There is little doubt that the policy has been effective, but it also raises important ethical as well as practical questions. The ethical questions touch on the lengths to which governments may go to influence people to behave in certain ways. Well-verified reports from China suggest government officials have gone as far as forcing women in the later stages of pregnancy to undergo abortions (Greenhalgh 1986).

Few societies are likely to accept such constraints on individual behaviour or have the bureaucratic apparatus to enforce them. As such, the relevance of the Chinese example for other developing countries is probably limited. But the Chinese case raises a second, more practical question. As noted in our discussion of the demographic transition, once fertility decline begins, there are no examples of this process reversing. Yet, in all the cases studied so far, fertility decline has occurred in a context in which couples were free to decide on the size of their family. This has not been the case in China, and many observers believe that if the government were to relax its fertility policy, many Chinese couples would decide to have additional children. If true, it suggests that coercive government policies are unlikely to bring about a lasting decline in fertility.

A second group of countries demonstrate a pattern of more moderate fertility decline. As the figures in Table 8-2 show, countries like Mexico, Peru, and even India have experienced important decreases in fertility. Yet those rates still remain well above the level that would halt population growth. Indeed, because of the relatively low mortality rates in many of these nations and their young populations, their populations continue to grow rapidly. For example, during the 1980s, the rate of natural increase in Mexico was 2.1 percent.

The remaining nations in Table 8-2 reflect a pattern of continuing high fertility. Although there is considerable diversity in the group of high-fertility countries, most nations with very high fertility are found in Africa and the Islamic world. These rates are not the simple result of ignorance or lack of access to contraception. In surveys conducted in these countries, women demonstrate knowledge of contraception and often indicate they have at times used various contraceptive methods. At the same time, they express a desire to have what we would consider a large number of children. Analysts point to a combination of economic and sociocultural factors as leading to this pattern of high fertility. In many parts of Africa where families are engaged in subsistence farming, children continue to be economically useful to their parents, as they were in Western societies in the past. They participate in aspects of agricultural work from an early age, as well as performing household tasks and services to their elders such as running errands (Caldwell 1976). Even in urban areas, children can contribute to family income from an early age by doing unskilled work or begging in the streets. Where family loyalties remain strong, the ability of one child to do well at school and land a well-paying job may bring important benefits to the whole family.

Cultural factors appear to contribute to the persistence of high fertility as well. In many societies, particularly where women's roles centre largely on the family, producing a large number of children adds to a woman's stature within her family and community. For men as well, being the father of a large family may be seen as both adding to their prestige and augmenting the power of their family or lineage within the community. Often this is reinforced by religious values that either support high fertility or oppose the use of fertility control. Where such a powerful combination of economic and social supports for high fertility exists, birth rates may remain high despite the influx of Western ideas and official attempts to lower the birth rate.

Given this diversity of experience among Third World countries, can any definite conclusions be drawn about the course of fertility? Many analysts would suggest two. First, while the link between economic development and fertility decline is not a simple one, it does appear that once a society achieves a high level of economic development, birth rates decline to near or below replacement level (Watkins 1986). Second, on an individual level, there appears to be a strong connection between education for women and lower fertility (Caldwell 1980). A variety of studies have shown that women in developing countries who succeed in attaining at least a high-school education go on to have significantly smaller families. Extending this to the majority of women in society is, of course, a difficult task for poor societies and points again to the significance of economic development for population change.

Mortality

Mortality Measurement

There is one certainty in the study of mortality: all of us will die some time. What demographers are interested in is when. In considering the question of mortality change, our first response may be to focus on what demographers call longevity — the maximum length of years a human being might expect to live. In fact, however, longevity has probably changed very little over the centuries. Although the very elderly are always rare, we can find people in high-mortality societies who lived to a ripe old age. Mortality change has come about not because human beings can now live to older ages but because a far greater proportion of our population can now expect to survive to what we consider to be old age. Dufour and Peron (1979) note, for example, that between 1931 and 1971 the proportion of women in Quebec who could expect to reach their sixty-fifth birthday increased from 62 percent to 87 percent. In countries like Canada, reaching retirement age is now the norm.

As we did with fertility, we will briefly consider the problem of measuring mortality before discussing the factors associated with mortality change. Since death, unlike childbirth, is a certainty for all of us, one might think that measuring mortality would be an easier task. But this is not so, and here we can introduce only some important aspects of the problem. We have already discussed the crude death rate (CDR), which relates the total number of deaths to the total size of the population. Clearly, however, the risk of dying varies greatly by age: the likelihood of a death occurring among a group of nursing-home resi-

Family Life and Child Mortality in Past Times

Demographic transition theory emphasizes the effect of high rates of infant and child mortality on fertility. Faced with the prospect of one or more of their children dying, families opt to have a large number of children to increase the chances of having at least a few who survive to adulthood. Mortality rates are, of course, averages based on the experience of the population as a whole. As the following two examples show, the experiences of individual families can differ widely with respect to child survival. It may well have been this uncertainty about the survival chances of children that encouraged couples to continue having large families.

Example 1

Husband: HESS, Sebastien

Birth date: January 4, 1732   Death date: October 10, 1792

Wife: MULLER, Anne Marie

Birth date: July 3, 1729   Death date: January 27, 1801

Marriage Date: January 19, 1751

Children	*Birth date*	*Death date*
Anne Marie	April 2, 1755	January 6, 1761
Sebastien	April 17, 1759	February 20, 1761
Marie Marguerithe	November 22, 1761	March 26, 1762
Anne Marie	June 6, 1763	June 29, 1791
Sebastien	May 29, 1768	June 13, 1768
Catherine Marguerithe	April 20, 1770	December 23, 1845

In this example, drawn from the church records of a village in northeastern France, the couple had six children, four of whom died in infancy or early childhood. A fifth died at age 28, and as a result only one child was alive at the time the parents died. Note also the interesting pattern of names. It was the custom to have a child named after each parent. When the child carrying that name died in childhood, the name was "reused" for subsequent children — a practice many in modern societies might consider unacceptable.

Example 2

Husband: BOEGLER, Jean Georges

Birth date: February 11, 1730   Death date: November 16, 1791

Wife: BICKEL, Anne Marie

Birth date: October 26, 1729   Death date: February 23, 1792

Marriage date: January 9, 1753

Children	*Birth date*	*Death date*
Jean Georges	January 1, 1754	September 17, 1816
Jean Jacques	December 9, 1755	August 27, 1817
Anne Marie	August 2, 1758	December 18, 1812
Chretien	March 25, 1762	May 22, 1833
Jean	November 23, 1764	November 29, 1832
Jean Martin	March 3, 1770	March 19, 1776

In this happier example, only the last child died in childhood. The parents, both of whom lived to be more than 60 years of age, had five of their children still with them when they died. The five surviving children all married and produced a total of 37 grandchildren.

Source:

Examples are based on the parish registers of baptisms, marriages, and burials contained in the Archives départementales du Bas-Rhin, Strasbourg, France.

dents at a given time is far greater than is the likelihood among a group of university students. The proportion of Canada's population in the older, high-risk age categories is growing, and this will have the effect of raising the crude death rate. This does not mean, of course, that health conditions are deteriorating or that people are dying younger. Paradoxically, the length of life for the average person can be increasing while the crude death rate is rising. As a result, other measures are needed to help us understand the changes occurring in the risk of mortality at various ages.

As was true with fertility, the first step in doing this consists of computing **age-specific death rates**. This is done by relating the number of deaths to persons of a given age to the total number of persons of that age in our population. These rates can be used to examine the varying risk of dying throughout the life cycle. More importantly, they can be used to construct what demographers call a **life table**, a statistical model that estimates the number of years persons of a given age can expect to live. In most discussions

of mortality, demographers refer to a product of the life table called the **expectation of life at birth**. While computing this statistic is complicated, its meaning can be simply described. Expectation of life at birth refers to the average number of years a group of new-borns can expect to live if current mortality risks prevail throughout their lifetime.

Table 8-3 provides some data on expectation of life at birth for a number of developed and developing societies. It shows that in all developed societies, life expectancy is now well above 70 years and, for women, occasionally surpasses 80 years. Developing countries too have experienced considerable progress in recent years. For many (though by no means all) countries in Asia and Latin America, expectation of life at birth now is more than 60 years. The lowest levels tend to be found in the less developed societies of sub-Saharan Africa, where life expectancies below 50 years are not uncommon. High rates of HIV infection in a number of these countries will make the task of raising life expectancy even more difficult in the years ahead (Bongaarts 1988).

Mortality Change

As we saw earlier, Western societies in the past experienced very high mortality rates. In some cases, expectation of life at birth was as low as 25 years. Remember that this is an average figure; it certainly does not imply that the majority of the population died in their early adult years. On the contrary, then as now, the early adult years were among the safest in life. If we examine mortality risks by age in a high-mortality population, we find the rates are U-shaped. That is, the risk of death is highest in infancy and early childhood, declines throughout later childhood and adolescence, and then gradually rises throughout the adult years to again reach high levels in older age. As life expectancy increases, the risk of death declines for all age groups, but the biggest declines occur among infants and young children. Saved from death in their first years of life, these children then stand a good chance of leading a full life.

Having described the changes that occur as mortality declines, we can now inquire as to the reasons for mortality decline. Probably the first reason that comes to mind is the growth of qual-

TABLE 8-3 Expectation of Years of Life at Birth for Males and Females, Selected Countries, 1985–1990

Country	Males	Females
Canada	73.0	79.8
United States	71.5	78.3
France	72.3	80.5
Italy	72.0	78.6
Switzerland	73.9	80.7
Mexico	62.1	66.0
Chile	68.0	75.0
Bolivia	50.9	55.4
China	68.0	70.9
South Korea	66.9	75.0
Bangladesh	56.9	56.0
Nigeria	48.8	52.2
Ethiopia	44.4	47.6
Tanzania	51.3	54.7

NOTE: Data for Mexico refer to 1979.
SOURCE: United Nations, *1990 Demographic Yearbook* (New York: United Nations, 1992), table 22.

ity medical care. As is often true in demography, however, the obvious response is not the right one. The problem with this answer, at least as far as countries like Canada are concerned, is that medical advances came along well after mortality rates had begun to decline. Mortality rates were already falling in most Western countries in the last half of the nineteenth century when medical knowledge was modest (to say the least) and when only a small proportion of the population had any contact with doctors or hospitals (McKeown 1976). What then caused the initial fall of mortality in Western societies? Most observers point to a variety of causes, but chief among them are an improving standard of living and the growth of effective public health and sanitation measures.

Thomas McKeown, an English physician, has argued that a rising standard of living led to better nutrition among populations in the past and brought with it greater resistance to disease (McKeown 1976). As evidence, he points to diseases such as tuberculosis. The death rate from tuberculosis declined steadily throughout the late nineteenth and early twentieth century, although no effective medical treatment was devised until the 1930s. With this disease and many others, he argues, better nutrition allowed people to survive once-fatal diseases, and, in the process, they often developed immunity to further outbreaks of the same disease. Improved public health and sanitation also helped to lower death rates. As cities developed effective ways of delivering clean water to households and of ridding cities of garbage and human waste, death rates from diseases such as cholera and typhoid fever declined sharply. In recent generations, medical advances have produced further progress in the fight against mortality, but, in most Western societies, life expectancy had already reached 60 or higher before medical care began to exert a real influence.

We must note, however, that while medicine's contribution to lower mortality in Western countries has been modest, this is not true in the case of developing countries. What is striking about the data in Table 8-3 is that the figures are relatively high even for countries that remain very poor. In Bangladesh, for example, where gross national product per capita is only $210 (compared with $20 470 in Canada) (World Bank

1992), life expectancy is more than 56 years, a figure attained in Canada only in the 1920s. One reason for this is that many developing countries have been able to import advances in medical care and public health that occurred over a long period of time. As a result, death rates have often fallen very rapidly, even in the absence of widespread economic development. There are, however, limits as to how far this process can go. Palloni (1981) has argued that mortality decline in some Latin American countries has stopped or even reversed in recent years. In his view, only real socioeconomic development will permit these countries to proceed further toward Western levels of mortality.

Differential Mortality

As we saw in the section on fertility, differences in fertility levels among groups in Canada's population have declined over time. We might have expected to discover the same situation when studying mortality. Yet, recent research on mortality patterns in Canada and other industrial countries show not only the persistence of differences in life expectancy between social groups, but, in some cases, an expansion of those differences. Three of the most significant differences are discussed below.

Undoubtedly the most significant is the difference in life expectancy between males and females (Verbrugge 1985). As the data in Table 8-3 demonstrate, in all industrialized societies (and in most developing ones as well) women outlive men, often by a significant amount. In Canada, the advantage held by women has increased markedly in recent generations, moving from just three years in 1931 to just under seven years today. A variety of factors have been proposed to account for the difference. In one way or another, most centre on the different social roles and behaviours of men and women. Some touch on differences in exposure to risk — women have historically been employed (inside or outside the home) in situations that entail lower risks of mortality, whether through accident, stress, or environmental factors. Other explanations focus on coping strategies; studies in Canada and elsewhere have noted a greater tendency for women to respond effectively to illness by seeking medical help.

The importance of social factors in explaining this difference leads to an important question regarding the future: as women's roles change and become more similar to traditionally male roles, will the advantage held by women in life expectancy shrink or even disappear? The most recent data available suggest that for the first time this century, life expectancy for men has been growing faster than for women, though a gap of 6.7 years still remains (Dumas 1991). Only the future will tell whether this is the beginning of a shift toward greater equality in the risk of dying.

A second and puzzling difference concerns variation in life expectancy by marital status. Again, studies from a variety of nations have shown that married persons enjoy a significant advantage over single, divorced, or widowed persons (Gove 1973; Adams 1990). The difference is larger for males, but marriage provides some advantage to women as well. One possible explanation for this situation centres on what is called a "selection hypothesis." What this means is that the difference we see between the married and unmarried may not be a result of differences in their situation, but rather is the result of differences in the characteristics of those who marry and stay married versus those who do not. To cite an obvious example, alcoholics may be more likely to divorce than nonalcoholics and also more likely to die younger as a result of alcohol abuse. The difference we would see in life expectancy between the married and divorced would reflect the influence of this factor. In this case, it is not so much divorce itself, but the behaviour that led to divorce that is associated with the higher risk of mortality. In general, though, while selection factors cannot be ruled out as contributing to the advantage enjoyed by the married, most research seems to point toward lifestyle differences between the married and nonmarried as carrying the most weight. The married state is considered to be a more orderly, stable style of living that entails fewer health risks and perhaps better care when problems occur.

A third important category of differences involves class and ethnic variations in mortality. It is distressing to find that even in Canada, which boasts universal medical insurance, important differences in life expectancy by social class remain. One recent study suggests that while class

Native people in Canada continue to suffer significantly higher death rates than other groups, despite some progress in recent years.

differences have declined in recent years, the difference in life expectancy between the highest and lowest income groups is still 3.7 years (Wilkins et al. 1990). Similarly, ethnic-group membership also is associated with differences in life expectancy. French–English differences, once marked, have largely disappeared (Dumas 1991), but Native people in Canada continue to suffer significantly higher death rates despite some progress in recent years (Rowe and Norris 1985). In the United States, the differences between blacks and whites are striking and have been growing during the 1980s. Between 1984 and 1989, life expectancy for white males grew by almost a full year, moving from 71.8 to 72.7. During the same period, however, the life expectancy of black males fell from 65.6 to 64.8, increasing the black–white differential to almost eight years (National Center for Health Statistics 1992).

As in all these situations, no one factor can be identified as being responsible for these differences. Most research on the problem identifies two groups of factors that lead to the observed differences. One group reflects the economic and social deprivation these groups experience: poorer-quality housing and nutrition, greater environmental risks of disease and accidents, and poorer-quality medical care. A second group focuses on behavioural differences by social class or ethnicity, noting that members of disadvantaged groups are more likely to engage in behaviour patterns that carry high health risks. A number of studies have shown that rates of smoking and drug use tend to be higher among persons from lower-class backgrounds (Health and Welfare 1990; Health and Welfare 1992). Taken together, these sets of factors have created an enduring pattern of difference in the health and mortality experiences of different segments of our population.

Mortality by Cause of Death

As death rates have declined and life expectancy increased, the leading causes of death in industrialized societies have changed significantly as well. Communicable diseases, the leading cause of death in preindustrial societies, have gradually been replaced by a new set of factors. Table 8-4 provides information on the leading sources of death in two societies, Canada and Mexico. The Canadian pattern is fairly typical of that experienced by industrialized countries in North America and Europe. For both men and women, heart disease and cancer are by far the leading causes of mortality. Indeed, over two-thirds of Canadians now die as a result of these two sets of diseases (Brancken 1991). When we look beyond these two, however, we find some interesting differences between men and women. For males, accidental and violent death is the third-leading cause of death, while among women respiratory diseases hold third position. As the data indicate, the death rate from accidents and violence for men is more than double the rate for women, and for some specific causes of death in this category, such as suicide, the male rate is more than three times

TABLE 8-4 Leading Causes of Death for Males and Females, Canada, 1989, and Mexico, 1981

Cause of death	Canada		Mexico	
	Males	Females	Males	Females
Heart disease	296.9	266.0	93.8	91.9
Cancer	219.2	172.7	34.9	32.4
Respiratory disease	71.5	52.0	69.3	58.0
Accidental and violent causes	73.6	32.3	156.4	36.9
All other causes	144.0	130.4	325.8	268.7
Total	805.2	653.4	680.2	503.4

NOTE: Rates are expressed per 100 000 persons.
SOURCE: Statistics Canada, "Mortality — Summary List of Causes 1989," *Health Reports* 2(1) (Supplement 12):6–9; United Nations, *Demographic Year 1985* (New York: United Nations, 1987) table 32, p. 851.

the female rate. Men thus not only face higher rates of mortality overall but fall victim to a rather different set of causes than do Canadian women.

The data for Mexico are illustrative of the mortality experience of many developing nations. Note that the death rate from all causes is actually lower than in Canada, despite the fact that life expectancy in Canada is almost ten years longer. Although a fifteen-year-old Canadian faces a lower risk of death than a fifteen-year-old Mexican, the risk of dying for a sixty-year-old Canadian is higher than for a fifteen-year-old Mexican. And since a much larger proportion of Mexicans are in the younger age groups, the death rate for the population as a whole is lower than in Canada, where a relatively large proportion of our population is in the older, high-risk age groups.

A second fact to note is the lower death rates from heart disease and cancer — diseases most likely to affect older persons. In countries like Mexico, other causes of death, such as infectious diseases, continue to play a significant role, while in Canada their impact has been greatly reduced. In 1981, for example, the death rate for infectious intestinal diseases was 49.2 per 100 000 in Mexico but only 0.2 per 100 000 in Canada (United Na-

The Demographic Impact of AIDS

AIDS, or Acquired Immune Deficiency Syndrome, is a disease that "results in a gradual impairment of the human immune system and the consequent emergence and recurrence of a variety of infections and neoplasms" (Palloni and Glicklich 1991:21). The disease is a result of infection with the HIV or Human Immunodeficiency Virus, a virus that is most commonly transmitted through sexual intercourse or through an exchange of blood products, such as transfusion or the use of contaminated syringes. Although the word has already become a part of the popular vocabulary, the virus that causes AIDS was identified by scientists only in 1983. As a result, our knowledge of the disease is limited, as is our understanding of its likely demographic effects.

One major difficulty demographers face in predicting the impact of the AIDS epidemic on mortality levels is the poor quality of data available. This, in turn, results from a number of problems. HIV infection does not immediately produce AIDS, and the infected person may not show any symptoms of illness for quite some time. Unless the person is tested for the presence of the virus, diagnosis and reporting of the case are unlikely to occur. Moreover, medical knowledge of the disease and its consequences is still limited, especially in the developing areas of the world. This, combined with the fear that has become associated with the disease, undoubtedly leads to significant under-reporting.

Nevertheless, despite the uncertainty involved, recent research suggests the numbers affected by the

infection and subsequent disease are rising rapidly. In the United States, for example, which has reported the largest number of AIDS-related deaths, over 22 000 deaths were recorded in 1989, making it the eleventh-leading cause of death (National Center for Health Statistics 1992). In Canada the numbers have been lower, though the total for 1989 reached 851, an increase of 62 percent from the 1987 figure (Dumas 1991). Significant numbers of deaths have been reported in Western Europe and Africa as well. Indeed, officials fear that the number of cases reported in the developing countries may fall significantly below the actual number experienced.

Studies of the epidemic to date identify two patterns of prevalence. In North America and Western Europe, the disease has been heavily concentrated among young males, and the major methods of transmission have been homosexual intercourse and intravenous drug use. In Canada, for example, 94 percent of the deaths from AIDS recorded in 1989 involved males. In Africa and the Caribbean, on the other hand, deaths have been roughly equally divided between males and females. Heterosexual intercourse and transmission from mother to child appear to be the leading methods of transmission.

Given the relatively long time between HIV infection and the onset of AIDS (the average incubation period may be as long as eight to ten years), judging the future impact of AIDS on mortality levels is difficult. Information about the prevalence of HIV infection is essential for making accurate predictions, but this is, under-

standably, hard to come by. Most surveys have focused on high-risk groups in the population. The high levels of infection revealed are not a good basis for estimating the impact on the population as a whole. Nevertheless, using the best available information, the World Health Organization estimates there are currently 8 to 10 million persons worldwide who carry the infection. For countries currently recording high rates of infection, the demographic consequences could be severe. In his analysis of the African situation, John Bongaarts has concluded that "in the most severely affected countries the death rate could double, with disastrous effects on the health care system, the economy, and the fabric of society" (Bongaarts 1988:93).

Source:

References are to A. Palloni and M. Glicklich, "Review of approaches to modelling the demographic impact of the AIDS epidemic," in *The AIDS Epidemic and Its Demographic Consequences* (New York: United Nations, 1991), p. 21; National Center for Health Statistics, *Health, United States, 1991* (Hyattsville, MD: Public Health Service, 1992); Jean Dumas, *Report on the Demographic Situation in Canada 1991* (Ottawa: Statistics Canada, 1991); and John Bongaarts, "Modeling the demographic impact of AIDS in Africa," in *AIDS 1988*, in R. Kulsted, ed. (Washington, DC: America Association for the Advancement of Science, 1988), p. 93.

---

tions 1985:752–757). Finally, it is interesting to note that the gap in death rates from accidents and violence between men and women is even larger in Mexico than in Canada. Indeed, for Mexican males the death rate for accidental and violent causes is greater than for any other broad category of causes.

Migration

Defining Migration

When we consider the growth of the global population, we need consider only fertility and mortality rates. When we begin to examine national or regional patterns of population growth, however, we need to consider the movement of people into or out of these regions. Demographers refer to this type of movement across legally defined boundaries as migration. Internal migration refers to movement across boundaries within countries. A young person from Nova Scotia who takes a job in British Columbia and establishes permanent residence there is an internal migrant. Although there are exceptions, most nations allow people to move about freely within the borders of the country. This makes studying internal migration more difficult because very often there is no legal record documenting the move.

By contrast, international migration, which involves crossing a national boundary, is almost always regulated by law, and governments typically collect statistics of the number of persons entering (and sometimes the number leaving) the country. It should be noted, however, that some countries experience a significant amount of illegal or undocumented immigration. This is true, for example, in the United States, where large numbers of immigrants from Mexico and Central America enter the country each year without legal authorization to do so. As with many issues in sociology, then, we need to remind ourselves that official statistics present only a partial view of the problem under study.

International Migration

Canada, the United States, and indeed all nations in the Western Hemisphere are lands formed by immigration. Since the seventeenth century immigrants from Europe and elsewhere have poured into the Americas, transforming forever the character of these lands long inhabited by a variety of Native peoples. The period from roughly 1840 to 1914 marked the high point of

Since the seventeenth century, immigrants from Europe and elsewhere have poured into the Americas, transforming forever the character of these lands long inhabited by a variety of Native peoples.

immigration to the Americas and turned the United States, in particular, from a thinly populated, agricultural nation into an economic giant. Canada, too, benefited from the burning desire of millions of Europeans to establish themselves in the New World. Relative to the small size of the nation's population at the time, the numbers arriving were huge. Canada's population totalled just over 7 million people in 1911, but in the years 1911–1913 more than 1 million immigrants arrived (Beaujot 1991:105). Many of these quickly moved on, most to the United States, but the many who stayed helped develop Canada's natural resources and swelled the populations of its still-small cities.

The period between World Wars I and II was marked by much lower levels of immigration, but after 1945 immigration to Canada and the United States again increased. Thousands of Europeans, uprooted by war and the economic chaos that accompanied it, looked to the Americas for the chance to start a new life. And though the origins of the immigrants have changed, Canada continues today to be a country open to immigration. In no year since World War II has Canada accepted fewer than 70 000 immigrants, and in 1991 231 000 new immigrants arrived (Employment and Immigration Canada 1993). In proportion to the size of its population, Canada continues to be one of the world's leading recipients of immigration.

Given Canada's colonial links, first to France and later to Great Britain, it is not surprising that the earliest immigrants to Canada came from these nations. As political and economic changes

---

FIGURE 8-3   Major Source Countries of Canadian Immigrants, 1989

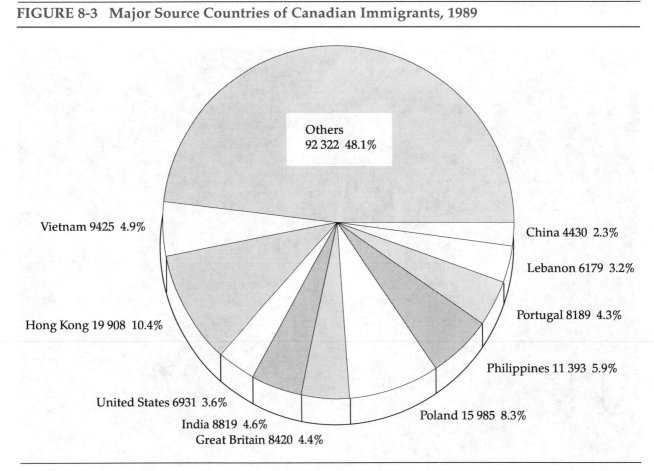

SOURCE: Employment and Immigration Canada, *Immigration Statistics 1989* (Ottawa: Minister of Supply and Services, 1991).

occurred, however, the origins of immigrants to Canada have constantly changed. Very often, these changes have been met by a degree of hostility from the native-born population. When thousands of Irish immigrants fled to Canada in the nineteenth century, many were met with open hostility. Later, as the number of immigrants from the British Isles declined, Canada began to turn to Central Europe as a new source of people. Again, there was a reaction against people who spoke a different language and were seen as too different to fit into Canadian society. In recent years, the sources of immigration to Canada have once again changed. As the data in Figure 8-3 indicate, while significant numbers still arrive from various European lands, Canada's newest immigrants are increasingly likely to come from countries in the developing world. Surveys indicate that today, as in the past, the numbers and origins of immigrants are provoking a negative reaction among some segments of the population (Angus Reid Group 1989). Hopefully, as in the past, this phenomenon will be short-lived as immigrants adapt to Canadian society and the native-born come to accept them as part of the Canadian nation.

Many countries in the world suffer from poverty and political conflict, and as a result the number of potential immigrants to Western countries is very high. Canada, like most other industrialized nations, has set up an elaborate screening process to determine who qualifies for admission to the country. Those accepted fall into three broad categories:

1. *Family class immigrants:* Persons admitted to Canada on the basis of their relationship to persons already living in the country. In these cases, their relatives living in Canada undertake to provide support to them once they are admitted as residents.
2. *Independent immigrants:* Persons who are admitted to Canada on the basis of their ability to meet the formal selection criteria established by the federal government. This system gives an advantage to those with higher levels of education, occupations currently in demand within Canada, and knowledge of English and French. In recent years, a special program has been created to attract migrants

willing to invest a significant amount of capital in the country.
3. *Refugees and designated classes:* Persons who request entry because of a fear of persecution within their own country or because of political turmoil or war in their country of origin. In the past, the majority of refugees came from the formerly communist nations of Eastern Europe. More recently, large numbers have come from nations in the developing world as well, such as Lebanon and Vietnam.

One consequence of the selective immigration system Canada has established is that immigrants admitted in recent years have tended to adapt to Canadian society very quickly. In terms of income and employment patterns, immigrants differ very little from native-born Canadians (Beaujot 1991).

An important, if sometimes unspoken, concern of Canadian immigration policy is the settlement of Canada's "open spaces." Despite the huge size of Canada, its population is concentrated in a small portion of its territory. Governments have often hoped to use immigration to bring people to underpopulated parts of the nation. On the whole, such policies have failed. Immigration did help to settle the fertile lands of the West in the early part of the century, when land-hungry immigrants from central Europe settled in Manitoba, Saskatchewan, and Alberta. In recent years, however, the majority of immigrants have been drawn to the economic and commercial centres of the country, more than 60 percent saying they hoped to settle in Toronto, Vancouver, or Montreal (Beaujot 1991). In the post–World War II period, immigration has had the effect of widening rather than reducing the differences in population growth among different regions of the country.

As Canadians, our interest in international migration tends to concentrate on the inflow of people to our country. But for the developing countries that send us immigrants, migration is also a source of concern. In the nineteenth century, the outflow of migrants from Europe to the Americas was almost certainly a benefit for both the sending and receiving countries. Emigration helped to ease the population pressures felt by European countries experiencing rapid growth and industrialization, which was already draw-

Population and Resources: Are There Too Many People?

Any discussion of population growth in recent years is usually linked to the issues of overpopulation, starvation, and the depletion of the world's scarce resources. The rapid growth of the world's population over the last few decades is usually seen as an important factor in a coming environmental crisis. This perspective, which constitutes the conventional wisdom on population, has been articulated by many writers, none more convincing than American ecologist Paul Ehrlich. In 1968, he wrote *The Population Bomb*, probably the most widely discussed book on population since Malthus's original essay. In Malthusian terms, he predicted a global crisis involving starvation, rising mortality levels, and environmental disaster as a result of the unprecedented population growth that characterized the late 1960s (Ehrlich 1968).

Recently, he and his wife Anne have released a new book entitled *The Population Explosion*, which argues that the catastrophic events earlier predicted have already arrived (Ehrlich and Ehrlich 1990). Hundreds of millions have already perished through starvation and malnutrition, world grain production is falling, and quality agricultural land and water supplies are diminishing. Underlying these problems, according to the Ehrlichs, is rapid population growth. Growing numbers of people place a burden on the ecosystem that is unsustainable. This is clearly true in the world's poorer societies, where the basic necessities of life are scarce and expensive, but it is just as true in the developed world. Given the very high level of consumption in rich countries, even the slow rate of population growth in recent years contributes substantially to a coming environmental disaster. The world needs not only a halt to growth but, in their view, population decline. Each of us can contribute by having only one or at most two children. If this does not come about voluntarily, they suggest, governments will eventually move toward the kind of coercive population policy that exists in China.

The Ehrlichs present a somewhat more extreme and popularized version of what most demographers would support. Indeed, finding someone on the other side of the issue was not easy until the appearance in 1981 of a book entitled *The Ultimate Resource*, by an American economist, Julian Simon. Is there a population crisis? Are there too many people? Are resources being used up? Is pollution getting worse? Simon's answer to all these questions is no. For Simon, scarcity can be measured in only one way — by looking at the price of goods. If the world's scarce resources are being exhausted, their prices will go up. But, he argues, the real price of most resources has been going steadily down. In relation to our salaries, items such as food, oil and other energy supplies, and the minerals needed to produce consumer goods are cheaper now than ever before. What about pollution? For Simon, things have never been better. Cities today are far cleaner than the cities of the past, and the environment of the industrialized societies is cleaner than that of the developing societies. Indeed, it is our higher standard of living that makes us more sensitive to pollution and leads us to demand stronger action on the environment. Are there not too many people, and does not population growth make things worse? No, Simon says; people are the "ultimate resource," the source of new ideas that have led to the steady improvement in the human condition. Necessity is the mother of invention, and population pressure leads people to develop new and more efficient ways of doing things. (Simon 1981).

Can we say which side of this debate is right? Not really, but the two protagonists did engage in an interesting contest (Tierney 1990). In 1980, Simon offered to bet that resources would be more plentiful in 1990, and thus their real price would decline during the 1980s. He challenged any opponent to select resources he or she felt would become scarcer and thus more expensive. Ehrlich and his associates couldn't resist, saying they would "accept Simon's astonishing offer before other greedy people jumped in." They chose five resources — copper, chrome, nickel, tin and tungsten — which they felt would appreciate in value over the decade. They "purchased" $200 of each element (in 1980 prices). If the resources went up in value, Simon would pay them the difference between the 1990 price and the $1000 they paid in 1980. If they went down in price, Ehrlich and friends would pay Simon the difference. Who was the winner? Simon, by a clear margin. The real price of all five materials fell during the 1980s, and the same quantities that Ehrlich paid $1000 for in 1980 could have been purchased in 1990 for only $618. Simon offered the same wager to Ehrlich for the decade of the 1990s, but Ehrlich and his friends declined the wager. Ehrlich, however, failed to acknowledge defeat. Commenting on Simon's position, he claimed that Simon was like a man who had just jumped off the roof of the Empire State Building. Asked how he felt as he passed the tenth floor, the man replied, "Just fine so far."

Source:

References are to Paul Ehrlich, *The Population Bomb* (New York: Ballantine, 1968); Paul Ehrlich and Anne Ehrlich, *The Population Explosion* (New York: Simon and Schuster, 1990); John Simon, *The Ultimate Resource* (Princeton, NJ: Princeton University Press, 1981); and J. Tierney, "Betting the Planet," *New York Times Magazine,* Dec. 2, 1990, p. 52.

ing larger numbers of migrants to the cities. For the developing world today, however, the benefits of international migration are not so clear. Given the rate of population growth in the developing world, the number of migrants who leave is too small to make much of a difference. The population of India alone grows by about 15 million people per year, or roughly 20 times the number of immigrants admitted by Canada and the United States in recent years. Moreover, the tendency of industrialized countries to admit only those with a high level of skill and education often means that the developing countries are robbed of the skilled persons they need to aid in their own development. The balance, of course, is not completely negative. Immigrants often send money to help relatives back home, and this inflow of funds can be valuable for the economy of the home countries. Nevertheless, it is not surprising that developing countries have often raised the question of international migration when arguing for better treatment in their dealings with the industrialized world.

Internal Migration

Canada, like all highly developed societies, has a very mobile population. Census data suggest that almost half of Canadians will change their residence at least once during the five-year period between censuses, though only about 5 percent will change their province of residence (Statistics Canada 1989). Although individuals move for a variety of reasons, migration research makes clear that economic factors play a primary role. In Canada, this has most often meant that Ontario

Much of Canada's internal migration has been the movement of people from rural to urban settings.

and British Columbia have been the greatest recipients of internal migrants. Examining migration data for the four decades from 1951 to 1990, Dumas (1991) has shown that British Columbia has been a consistent gainer of population through internal migration, while Ontario gained more people than it lost in all decades except the 1970s. For the other Canadian provinces, the balance of movement has been mostly negative, although Alberta did gain a large number of migrants during the oil boom of the 1970s. Quebec, on the other hand, has lost an estimated 400 000 residents over the last two decades, many of them anglophones who have left in the wake of political changes (Dumas 1991:64). This emigration, combined with the lower fertility rate in Quebec, has resulted in the province's share of the national population total declining from 28.9 percent in 1951 to 25.3 percent in 1991.

Although internal migration and urbanization have been important in Canada, the numbers involved seem small when compared with the masses of people moving toward the cities of the developing world. The sheer size of the population in many developing countries and the rapid rate of growth they are experiencing creates a huge pool of potential migrants. The poverty and lack of opportunity in the rural regions eventually convince many to take their chances in the big cities, despite the appalling conditions of life many experience once there. Mexico provides an outstanding example of this process. Continuing rural–urban migration, combined with a high level of natural increase, has pushed the population of Mexico City over the 20 million mark, making it the largest urban area in the world (United Nations 1992).

Age–Sex Structure

Populations differ not only in terms of size and growth rates, but also in terms of their age–sex structure. The rates of fertility, mortality, and migration experienced by a population combine to shape the age–sex structure of that population. Demographers have worked out several useful tools to help us examine this issue. The simplest and most commonly used is the **population pyra-mid** (see Figure 8-4). Population pyramids are simply pictures or graphic representations of the make-up of a population at a particular time. By simply drawing to scale bars representing the number of persons in each population category (for example, males 30–34 years of age), we get an image of the overall distribution of a population. Once we understand the nature of these graphs, we can tell at a glance the important characteristics of a population.

In populations with a high rate of fertility, the graph will look like a real pyramid. That is, it will have a broad base and will narrow gradually as it moves up to the older age categories. Such populations are said to be young populations, since a large proportion of the population is in the childhood and adolescent years. In some African countries today, for example, 50 percent of the population is under age 15. In many Western societies, which have been aging rapidly in recent years, less than 20 percent of the population will be under age 15. These countries' population pyramids resemble blocks more than pyramids. They have a narrow base, and the width of the bars representing some of the older age categories may actually be wider than those representing the number of children.

When asked to consider the reasons for population aging, most students immediately respond that declining mortality leads to population aging. It seems obvious that increased life expectancy will produce larger numbers of old people and thus population aging. In fact, this is not true. The fertility rate is the primary determinant of a population's age structure. So long as the fertility rate remains high, each generation of women on reaching the child-bearing period will produce more than enough children to replace themselves and their spouses. The result will be an ever-widening base of the population pyramid, and thus a young society. And this will remain true whether life expectancy is 30 or 80.

Figure 8-4 shows population pyramids for Canada and Mexico. The Canadian pyramid does not neatly fit the image of a young or old population. The reason for that is that Canada's population has been passing through a period of dramatic change. Look at the size of the bars representing the age groups 25–44. These groups represent those born during the Baby Boom and constitute

FIGURE 8-4   Age-Sex Pyramid of the Populations of Mexico, 1990 and Canada, 1991

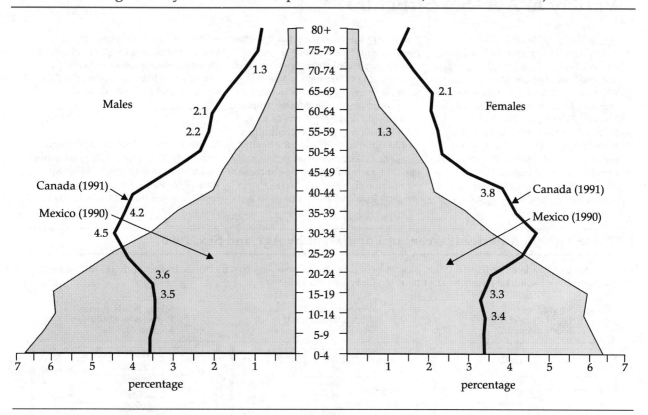

SOURCE: *Mexico*: United Nations, *The Sex and Age Distributions of Population* (New York: United Nations, 1991), p. 266. Canada: Statistics Canada, *The Nation: Age, Sex and Marital Status*, catalogue no. 93-310 (Ottawa: Minister of Industry, Science and Technology, 1992), pp. 108–115.

a bulge in the age distribution. As we move down to the base of the pyramid, we see the results of the falling birth rate in Canada over the last few decades. These groups are smaller than those in the middle adult years and give the pyramid a relatively narrow base. If low fertility continues in Canada, the pyramid will gradually take on a block-like appearance and the population will continue to age. As Chapter 6 points out, this raises a number of important issues for society and government to deal with.

The Mexican situation is rather different. As the data in Table 8-2 indicate, fertility decline in Mexico has only begun. Thus the top part of the figure follows a classic pyramid shape. From the age group 15–19 up to the oldest groups, the pyramid narrows considerably and only a tiny proportion of the population is in the oldest age categories

(United Nations 1991). The bottom of the pyramid reflects the recent decline in fertility, however. The size of the bars for the age groups under 20 are very similar. If fertility rates continue to decline, Mexico will experience a radical change in its population structure and the prospect of even more rapid population aging than has occurred in Canada.

Another tool demographers have developed to help us understand the effects of population age structures is the **dependency ratio**, which relates the number of persons in what are considered the dependent age categories to the number in the independent or working-age categories. Conventionally, the dependent age categories comprise those under the ages of 15 and over 65, while the working population consists of those between 15 and 64. Developed for making international com-

Variety in Age–Sex Structure

Age–sex pyramids are most commonly used to examine national populations. Yet, as the accompanying figures indicate, age–sex pyramids can often be more revealing when used to consider local or regional populations. The three city pyramids examined here show markedly different patterns. Sandy, Utah, is clearly a young, family-oriented community with lots of children. Washington, D.C., is dominated by young and middle-aged adults, many working for government or agencies associated with government. Miami Beach is, of course, especially attractive to retired persons. Its population reflects this with the large proportions in the older age groups, especially among women. Examine these three pyramids and ask yourself how these communities would differ in their need for health care, education, and other public services. How would knowledge of these population characteristics affect your strategy if you owned a fast-food outlet or a video-rental store? What if you were running for political office? Demographics play an increasingly important role in marketing goods, services, and even politicians.

Source:

Judith Waldrop, "Secrets of the age pyramid," Reprinted with permission © *American Demographics*, 14(8)(August 1992):46–53. For subscription information, please call (800) 828-1133.

Three Ages in America (Percent of Population by Age and Sex, 1990)

The age pyramids of youthful cities have a broad base. Baby-boom towns bulge in the middle. Retirement communities look like columns that lean to the women's side.

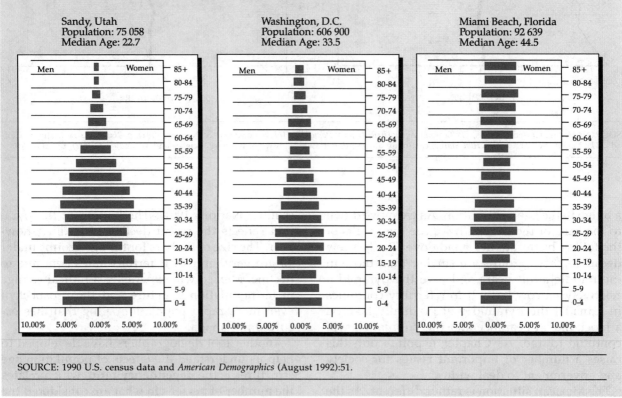

Sandy, Utah
Population: 75 058
Median Age: 22.7

Washington, D.C.
Population: 606 900
Median Age: 33.5

Miami Beach, Florida
Population: 92 639
Median Age: 44.5

SOURCE: 1990 U.S. census data and *American Demographics* (August 1992):51.

parisons, the dividing lines for the age categories do not fit very well with contemporary Canadian reality. Moreover, it treats children and the elderly as being equivalent, although the direct cost to government is much higher when the dependant is an elderly person rather than a child. Nevertheless, the measure provides a reasonable indicator of how population change has been shifting the balance between the independent and dependent parts of Canada's population.

Figure 8-5 shows how the dependency ratio in Canada has been evolving in recent years and how it is projected to change in the years to come. The data show that the burden of dependency is now relatively low in Canada (Chawla 1991). High fertility rates during the Baby Boom pushed the dependency ratio up during the 1950s and 1960s, but since then it has declined and will remain relatively low until the large Baby Boom cohorts begin to swell the ranks of the elderly around the year 2011. At the same time, the number of persons in the working-age categories will be reduced by the low fertility rates of recent decades. It is the combination of these trends that will put great pressure to bear on governments charged with providing services to the elderly population and paying for them with the taxes collected from those in the labour force.

When the changing age structure of society is discussed, the focus is, understandably, on the growth of the elderly and the challenges this poses for society. But it is also true that other age groups are affected by changes in the population's age structure. Indeed, one economist be-lieves that the changing age structure is the key to understanding societal change in recent years. Although his theory is complex, Richard Easter-lin's basic message regarding age-structure changes can be summarized simply (Easterlin 1987). He argues that it is an advantage to be born into a small cohort — that is, during a period of low fertility — and a disadvantage to be born into a large cohort. Being a member of a smaller co-hort, he reasons, means less competition and thus greater opportunity. By contrast, those born when fertility is high — members of the Baby Boom cohorts, for example — face intense com-petition throughout the life cycle and reduced chances of success. This occurs because many ac-tivities in our society are age-graded. Most peo-ple enter university after high school, marry and look for their first house in their late twenties or early thirties, and expect to retire in their sixties. If we are born into a large cohort, there will al-ways be a large number of people wanting to do the same thing we want to do. As a result, it may be harder to get accepted into university or a professional school and harder to find our first

---

FIGURE 8-5 Canada's Dependency Ratio,* Actual and Projected, 1965–2050

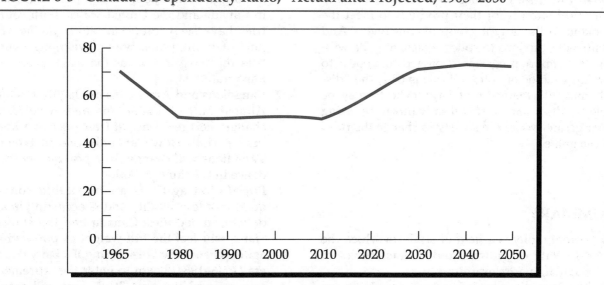

*People under age 15 and aged 65 and over per 100 people aged 15–64.
SOURCE: R. Chawla "An Aging Society: Another Viewpoint," *Canadian Social Trends*, (1991), *20*. p. 3. Reproduced with the permission of the Minister of Industry, Science and Technology, 1993.
Readers wishing further information on data provided through the co-operation of Statistics Canada may obtain copies of related publications by mail from: Publications Sales, Statistics Canada, Ottawa, Ontario, Canada K1A 0T6, by calling 1-613-951-7277 or toll-free 1-800-267-6677. Readers may also facsimile their order by dialling 1-613-951-1584.

job. When we look to buy a house, we find that houses are in demand and prices have risen. When we and our peers retire, we place a strain on pension systems and may have to get by with a lower pension.

Members of smaller cohorts benefit from the opposite situation. Easterlin believes that members of smaller cohorts, faced with less competition, benefit from higher incomes and lower unemployment throughout their lives. This leads him to be optimistic about the near future, since the small cohorts born in the 1970s are now reaching the early adult years. As they begin entering the labour force, he feels that they will encounter less difficulty in finding employment and will be able to command relatively high salaries. Lower unemployment for young workers and rising incomes will benefit not only young people themselves but, he argues, will have beneficial effects for society as a whole.

Although many believe that Easterlin pushes his argument too far, it is undoubtedly true that cohort size does influence the life chances of its members. At the same time, other observers have noted that cohort size can also work to a group's advantage by giving its members more political and economic weight within society (Preston 1984). Businesses anxious to achieve maximum sales will often tailor their products to meet the demand of the largest group of consumers. And politicians, anxious to collect votes, may be willing to support programs designed to appeal to the largest bloc of voters. If this is true, the "disadvantaged" members of large cohorts may be able to offset part of this disadvantage by using their greater weight in society to change the rules of the game.

SUMMARY

1. Demography is a field of study in which the size, rate of growth, and characteristics of populations are examined.
2. The world's population now stands at approximately 5.3 billion and is growing at the rate of 1.7 percent per year. Most of this growth is occurring in the developing countries of Africa, Asia, and Latin America.
3. Demographic transition theory remains the most influential explanation of population change. This theory argues that societies pass through a three-stage process of change, from a state of slow population growth based on high rates of fertility and mortality to a new equilibrium in modern societies based on low fertility and low mortality.
4. Fertility refers to the rate of child-bearing in a population. Current data indicate that all developed societies experience fertility rates at or below the level required to replace the current population. While many developing societies have experienced significant declines in fertility in recent years, most still experience relatively high levels of fertility.
5. The study of mortality is primarily concerned with variation in the average length of life. Expectation of life at birth is over 70 years in all developed societies, though important differences by sex, ethnicity, and social class remain. Many countries in the developing world have experienced rapid improvements in mortality levels, though a number of African countries continue to experience relatively high rates of mortality.
6. International migration continues to be an important component of population growth in Canada and the United States. Both countries have seen important shifts in the origins of immigrants, with developing countries replacing Europe as the major source of immigration.
7. Canadians and Americans are highly mobile. Almost half of Canadians and Americans change their residence at least once in a five-year period. However, only one in twenty Canadians will change their province of residence in the same period.
8. Population aging is an inevitable consequence of low fertility and is occurring in all developed societies. Canada and the United States will feel the full weight of population aging when those born during the Baby Boom era (1946–1964) begin to enter the retirement ages around the year 2010. This will result in a significant increase in the dependency ratio and considerable pressure on governments to provide funding for pensions and health care.

GLOSSARY

Age-specific death rates. Measures of mortality for specific age groups. They are computed by dividing the total number of deaths occurring to persons in a given age group by the total number of persons in that age group.

Age-specific fertility rates. Measures of the rate of child-bearing for specific age groups of women. They are computed by dividing the number of births occurring to women of a given age group by the total number of women in that age group.

Cohort measures. Any indicator that measures the behaviour over time of a group of persons sharing a common starting point, such as their year of birth or year of marriage.

Crude birth rate. A measure of fertility or child-bearing computed by dividing the total number of births in a given period of time by the total population.

Crude death rate. A measure of mortality computed by dividing the total number of deaths in a given period of time by the total population.

Demographic transition theory. A theory that states that populations pass through a three-stage process of change from high to low rates of fertility and mortality.

Demography. A word of Greek origin used to describe the discipline that studies population processes.

Dependency ratio. A measure based on the ratio of persons in what are thought to be the dependent age categories (those under 15 and those over 65) to those in the working-age groups (those aged 15 to 64).

Expectation of life at birth. A measure derived from a life table that estimates the average length of life for persons exposed to a given set of age-specific death rates.

Life table. A statistical model that uses information on the probability of dying at given ages to estimate the average number of years of life remaining for persons of various ages.

Period measures. Any indicator that measures demographic behaviour during a particular time period, such as a year or decade.

Population pyramid. A graphic illustration showing the numbers or proportions of the population in each age–sex category.

Rate of natural increase. A measure of population growth based on the difference between the birth rate and death rate. The measure can be computed by subtracting the crude death rate from the crude birth rate.

Total fertility rate. A measure of fertility that indicates the average number of children a group of women will have in their lifetime if they experience a particular set of age-specific fertility rates.

FURTHER READING

Beaujot, Roderic P. *Population Change in Canada.* Toronto: McClelland and Stewart, 1991. A remarkably complete review of our knowledge of Canadian population issues that contains a discussion of the relationship between demography and social policy.

Caldwell, J.C. *Theory of Fertility Decline.* New York: Academic Press, 1982. An excellent though difficult collection of essays by one of the leading scholars of demographic change in the developing world.

Canadian Social Trends. A quarterly publication of Statistics Canada, this social science magazine presents short, readable analyses of current topics of interest, with a special focus on social policy issues.

Dumas, Jean. *Report on the Demographic Situation in Canada 1991.* Ottawa: Statistics Canada, 1991. Now appearing on a yearly basis, this series provides up-to-the-minute information on population trends in Canada.

Easterlin, R.A. *Birth and Fortune.* 2nd edition. Chicago: University of Chicago Press, 1987. A provocative analysis of the impact of fluctuating birth rates on the fortunes of different age groups in the population.

Ehrlich, P., and A. Ehrlich. *The Population Explosion.* New York: Simon and Schuster, 1990. A strongly written argument in favour of population control in both the developing and developed world by two leading environmentalists.

Population and Development Review. The leading demographic journal, which regularly presents original and provocative analyses of population issues.

Simon, J. *The Ultimate Resource.* Princeton, NJ: Princeton University Press, 1981. An original work that goes against the conventional wisdom by arguing that continued population growth is a benefit to the human species.

Weeks, John R. *Population: An Introduction to Concepts and Issues.* 5th edition. Belmont, CA: Wadsworth, 1992. A readable text that provides a good introduction to the field of demography and presents current data on American population trends.

CHAPTER 9

Social Inequality

ALFRED A. HUNTER

Sadly, Alfred Hunter died after he wrote the first draft of this chapter. I have tried to write the final draft as well as he would have. Given Alf's intelligence, skills, and knowledge, this is unlikely. I suspect he would have said "Nice try Bob."

Bob Hagedorn

"It's become fashionable to have Burger King, Domino's, and Taco Bell right on the high school campus. This is not for lunch. This is for career day" (Jay Leno on "The Tonight Show," September 14, 1992).

For thousands of years, thoughtful observers have noted that some individuals and groups command more of life's scarce and valued resources than do others. These people enjoy additional privileges and exercise greater power. Such social inequalities seem to have characterized every civilization and historical period, although they have differed greatly in degree and type from place to place and over time. They affect every aspect of our lives, even if we are not always conscious of it. Why do some defer voluntarily to others' wishes, as commoners to the queen or as workers to their supervisors? Is this necessary? Is it just? What, finally, are the consequences of these social inequalities for individuals, groups, and the larger society? This chapter addresses these and a number of related questions in a comparative analysis of the three North American societies: Canada, the United States, and Mexico.

Some Theories of Social Inequality

The questions posed above are ancient. Sociology, though, is new, having emerged as a discipline only in the second half of the nineteenth century. The questions are, however, no less sociological for that. Some sociologists even argue that they are the fundamental questions of the discipline. Certainly they are among the principal questions that the major social thinkers have asked. How have some of these thinkers answered these questions? How do their answers help us understand the organization of societies and the principles according to which societies change?

The history of social thought is too long to permit a detailed discussion of theories of inequality here. Fortunately, however, most modern theories are variations on a relatively small number of common themes. This allows us to identify a few major schools of inequality theory and to offer a brief summary of their central ideas.

With some oversimplification, there are three contending camps of inequality theory today: the Marxist one originates in the writings of Karl Marx and Friedrich Engels, the Weberian builds upon the works of Max Weber, and the functionalist theory is by Kingsley Davis and Wilbert E. Moore. There also is a postindustrial society theory, which, in the arguments of different authors, can be Marxist, Weberian, or functionalist.

From Marx

Karl Marx (1818–1883) and his long-time collaborator Friedrich Engels (1820–1895), two German social thinkers, proposed a theory of how societies are constituted and reconstituted that is still very much with us after 150 years. In the Marxian scheme, societies are organized around people's relationships to the means of production. These relationships define people's memberships in different social **classes**. In capitalism, there are essentially three classes: those who own the means of production — the mines, mills, and factories — and who employ others; those who work for themselves only, and those who are employed for a salary or a wage. The owners are the capitalist or bourgeois class, called collectively the **bour-**geoisie. The self-employed are the petit bourgeois class, or the *petite bourgeoisie*. The employees are the working or proletarian class.

According to Marxist theory, the bourgeoisie is the dominant class in capitalism, and the major social institutions, including government, operate more or less on its behalf. The relations among the classes in capitalism provide the basis for a contradiction that is the major motor of social change. Specifically, the bourgeoisie seeks to increase its profits through such practices as reducing employees' wages and increasing the length of the working day. The proletariat resists these attempts at exploitation in various ways, including absenteeism, quitting, strikes, and mass support for anti-capitalist, revolutionary political parties. This class conflict typically envelops more and more people in increasingly organized forms of protest, which end in the overthrow of the bourgeoisie by the proletariat and the economic, political, and social reorganization of society.

In the time since Marx and Engels wrote, capitalism has evolved considerably. Consequently, many modern-day Marxist scholars have tackled the task of adapting Marx and Engels' analyses to the conditions of contemporary capitalism. One important aspect of the evolution of capitalism that modern Marxists have addressed is the transformation of the labour process. The development of the factory system in the nineteenth century, Marglin (1974) has suggested, gave capitalists increased control over workers by bringing them together under one roof to be supervised directly by management. Braverman (1974) has argued that this facilitated the application of scientific management. Scientific management, or "Taylorism" (after its author, Frederick W. Taylor), includes a set of principles for reorganizing work in which owners and managers possess the secrets of production. Each worker then performs a small number of repetitive tasks requiring little or no knowledge or skill (see Chapter 11).

Another important aspect of the evolution of capitalism over the past century that many neo-Marxists have addressed is the differentiation of the class structure. At the time of Marx and Engels, those who owned the means of production controlled the means of production. With the emergence of the joint-stock corporation, however, came the new phenomenon of the separation of ownership and control. This created two new categories of people: owners without function (stockholders) and functionaries without ownership (managers). Partly as a result of this, it is no longer possible to describe the class structures of contemporary capitalist societies adequately in terms of the "big three" classes of bourgeoisie, petite bourgeoisie, and proletariat.

Although neo-Marxists generally agree that capitalist class structure has become more complex over time, they do not all agree on how best to depict these complexities today. Eric Olin Wright (1985:88) distinguishes first between owners and nonowners of capital. Among the owners, he identifies three groups. These groups include the bourgeoisie, who are those with enough capital to hire workers and not work themselves. Among the non-owners, he locates additional groups: those who exploit through control of organizational resources, those who exploit through credentials, and the proletariat, who control no organizational assets and possess no credentials. For Wright, the principal class division in capitalism is between the bourgeoisie and the proletariat. Managers occupy what he refers to as the

"principal contradictory location" in the class structure. Their position is "contradictory" because the bourgeoisie use their capital to exploit them and they use their control over organizational assets to exploit others. For Wright, finally, exploitation is possible because some people control productive private property or have certified knowledge or skills in production, while others command no property or knowledge. Figure 9-1 shows a simplified version of Wright's scheme of classes in capitalism.

From Weber

Another German social thinker, Max Weber (1864–1920), was a critic of Marxism, although he took more issue with what Marx and Engels left out of their theory than with what they put in it. Class and class conflict are important in understanding social organization and social change, as Marx and Engels argued. But so, too, are status groups and status group conflict. Where classes are aggregates of individuals with like material circumstances or life chances, status groups are

FIGURE 9-1   A Typology of Social Classes in Capitalism

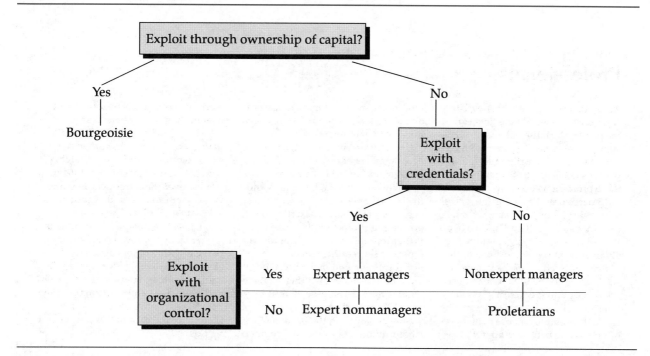

SOURCE: Adapted from Eric Olin Wright, *Classes* (London: Verso, 1985), p. 88.

collections of people who share similar levels of honour or **prestige** and a particular subculture or style of life. That is, classes are phenomena of the production of goods and services. Status groups are expressions of the consumption of goods and services. Both classes and status groups, however, can organize and contend for political power. Status groups are often defined along occupational, racial–ethnic, or religious lines. The police are an example of a status group, as are francophone Canadians and fundamentalist Christians.

For Weber, the master trend of history was in the direction of increasingly strong connections between people's professional training and their occupational responsibilities and rewards. Societies and organizations that assign their members to positions and compensate them in relation to their technical qualifications are better able to cope with the changing demands of their environments than are those that do not operate according to these principles. In a word, they are more efficient. This is why government, business, and many other social institutions are increasingly organized along bureaucratic lines. In contrast to other organizational forms, such as gerontocracy (which rewards the elderly) and pa-

triarchy (which rewards men), bureaucracy rewards certified expertise.

New generations of Weberian theorists have also developed, at least partly in response to new generations of Marxist thought. Among the most prominent neo-Weberians is the British sociologist Frank Parkin. For Parkin (1979), neo-Marxism is fundamentally flawed. First, in what he styles as a "bourgeois" critique, Parkin contends that definitions of many key concepts (for example, social class) are inconsistent from one neo-Marxist writer to another. Second, neo-Marxist theory does not explain racial–ethnic, religious, or other nonclass divisions and conflicts very well. Finally, the Marxist dichotomy of bourgeoisie versus proletariat is too simplistic. A rejuvenated version of Weberian theory, he concludes, makes better sense of contemporary capitalism.

Parkin begins his analysis by extending and refining Weber's concept of social closure. For him, social closure is the process by which members of one group systematically exclude and subordinate others and, perhaps, usurp others' resources as well. The bourgeoisie in capitalism is the group of entrepreneurs and professionals that has excluded, subordinated, and usurped the resources of other groups. They have done this by using the

Professionals

Accountancy, architecture, dentistry, engineering, law, and medicine are the principal traditional or self-regulating professions. Together with certain other highly qualified technical workers (such as MBAS), members of these professions make up perhaps 12 to 15 percent of the labour force north of the Rio Grande and somewhat less than that south of it. In Parkin's neo-Weberian scheme, they comprise, along with entrepreneurs, one of the two major fractions of the bourgeoisie. In Wright's neo-Marxist analysis, they occupy contradictory class locations as experts — "contradictory" because their employers use ownership of productive private property to ex-

ploit them and they, in turn, use academic credentials or professional certificates to exploit others.

Usually self-employed 100 years ago, members of the self-regulating professions are today commonly salaried workers, at least in Canada and the United States. They remain, however, very influential, asserting their power and protecting their prestige through professional associations that typically set requirements for educational training and maintain standards for ethical conduct (hence, "self-regulating"). These associations may even bargain collectively on their members' behalf in the fashion of a labour union. For example, provincial

medical associations negotiate with provincial governments over fee schedules. Some of these associations have on occasion even authorized strike actions, as did the Saskatchewan Medical Association in 1964 in protest over the introduction of universal medical care in that province.

Whether employed or self-employed, self-regulating professionals are typically very well paid in comparison with workers generally. For example, the average earnings of Canadian dentists, lawyers and notaries, and physicians and surgeons over the past 50 years have never been less than twice the earnings of the average worker.

laws controlling private property and credentials. This group includes the bourgeoisie, expert managers, and expert nonmanagers in Figure 9-1. Exclusion and subordination define the general category of exploitation. Marx's concept of the exploitation of the proletariat by the bourgeoisie is a particular case of this. In capitalism, the bourgeoisie is the dominant class that commands the apparatus of the state in its own interest. As well as the bourgeoisie, finally, there are in capitalism also various intermediate groups (such as teachers and nurses) and subordinate groups (such as industrial workers) that employ legal or not-so-legal tactics to exploit the members of other groups, for example, clients, racial–ethnic minorities, and women.

Functional Theory of Stratification

Functional theory, which has a long history in anthropology and sociology, begins with the analogy of human society as a living thing, an organism. It is based on the assumption that social practices endure if they contribute to societal survival. Two mid-twentieth-century American sociologists, Kingsley Davis and Wilbert E. Moore, co-authored the functional theory of stratification, which is an application of functionalist principles to the study of **social inequality** (Davis and Moore 1945).

The functional theory of stratification begins with the observation that there is social inequality, or "social stratification," in every society. This exists because, in any society, the work necessary to maintain individuals and the group is divided among various positions, some of which are more important than others for societal survival and more demanding in their skill requirements. It matters, therefore, who performs which tasks. Conscientious people must do the important jobs; competent people must do the high-skill ones. If this is to happen, however, these jobs must offer extra income, prestige, leisure time, or other rewards. Otherwise, there would be little reason for people to perform well in important positions or to undertake the extended training necessary for high-skill ones. In every society, then, some positions are filled by those who have the most talent or who put out the most effort. This is the process of achievement. In every society, too, some positions are filled through arbitrary assignment on the basis of such attributes as age, race–ethnicity, and sex. This is ascription. No society, though, can rely entirely on either achievement or ascription in filling positions (Kemper 1974). Some achievement is necessary for societal survival.

Politicians

For neo-Marxists and neo-Weberians, politicians govern more or less at the pleasure of the bourgeoisie; for functionalists, they govern with the consent of the people whom they represent. In contrast to the financial rewards of billionaires and top executives and managers in the private sector, those for politicians are limited. Still, top federal and provincial government politicians live very well by the standards of most Canadians. In the 1991–92 fiscal year, capital and operating expenses for Rideau Hall, the governor general's 175-room residence, amounted to over $3 million, including $25 000 spent on "lightning protection." This was up slightly from the amount for 1990–91. In 1991, the governor general's salary was $87 600 per year. For the prime minister's official residence at 24 Sussex Drive in that same year, expenses came to $248 505 (versus $350 000 in 1990–91). The prime minister earned $64 400 per year in salary in 1991 as a member of Parliament, plus $73 600 extra salary as the prime minister, plus a tax-free expense allowance of $21 300, plus 64 first-class return air fares for trips anywhere in Canada. For the leader of the opposition's residence, Stornoway, expenses came to $71 081 (versus $235 000 in 1990–91). The leader of the opposition earned the $64 400 M.P.'s salary in 1991, plus $49 100 extra salary as leader of the opposition, plus the tax-free expense allowance of $21 300, plus the 64 air-flight credits, plus a $2000 motor vehicle allowance. Ordinary members of Parliament, finally, received the standard salary, plus the standard tax-free expense allowance, plus the 64 air-flight credits.

Source:

Business Week, April 19, 1993. Reprinted by special permission. Copyright © 1993 by McGraw-Hill Inc.

Some ascription is a cheap way of filling unimportant, low-skill positions.

According to this theory, governments exist to maintain law and order and to mobilize the resources necessary to achieve larger social goals. These are their main functions. In societies with governments, therefore, political office-holders are an important group. They are, however, always relatively few in number, and ultimately they hold office at the sufferance of others whom they represent, rather than by virtue of any special talents or training. So, their powers are more limited than one would think, simply taking into account the rights that attach to their offices. In every society, experts contribute to societal survival by producing, applying, and passing on knowledge. Technical knowledge, however, deals only with selecting the most efficient means to achieve goals. It does not involve setting the goals themselves. As a result, experts generally serve economic, political, or other masters; they rarely rule themselves. In capitalism, finally, private business anchors the economy, and those who own productive private property can accumulate considerable wealth. Consequently, in a capitalist society, politicians, experts, and business leaders are more highly rewarded than are garbage collectors, street cleaners, and clerks.

Postindustrial Society Theory

Postindustrial society theory cuts across the three schools described above. Daniel Bell (1973) is a neo-Weberian and functionalist proponent of postindustrial society theory and the person who seems to have coined this term. Alain Touraine (1971) is a Marxist advocate of the theory. Briefly, these theorists argue that advanced capitalism is in transition to a new form of society in which the provision of services replaces the production of goods as the foundation of the economy. In the postindustrial society of the future, the university will be the centrepiece, and the powerful will be those who command advanced theoretical knowledge. For Bell, postindustrial society will be essentially harmonious, based on a broad value consensus, and presided over by experts. For Touraine, however, it will be basically fractious, wracked by conflicts between the elite group of professionals and technicians and the larger public subordinated to them.

Some Theoretical Issues

It is useful to distinguish among different kinds of social inequalities, since not all inequalities may have the same explanation. In particular, there are relational and distributive inequalities (Coser 1975). **Relational inequalities** are those in which one individual or group yields to the demands of or voluntarily acquiesces to the wishes of another. **Distributive inequalities** are those in which some people or groups possess more of some scarce and valued resource than others do. Examples of such resources are education, wealth, and income. Following Kemper (1974), relational inequalities can be grouped into two categories. First, there are inequalities in power; that is, some people can impose their wills upon others. Second, there are inequalities in prestige, as when some receive admiration and respect from others. Distributive inequalities also can be grouped into two categories: inequalities in privileges, such as the leisure or discretionary time people have; and inequalities in possessions, such as the income people earn from their jobs and the wealth they accumulate over time.

When two theories answer different questions, both may be useful. Marxist and Weberian theories of social classes and prestige groups are primarily accounts of relational inequalities. The functional theory of stratification is largely an explanation of distributive inequalities. Consequently, some combination of Marxist or Weberian theories and functional theory may be necessary to explain social inequalities. Marxist and Weberian theories, however, sometimes disagree and do not, therefore, simply complement one another. It is important to evaluate theories relative to one another, looking especially at points on which they disagree. Some important points on which these theories seem to disagree include:

1. Are high-skill jobs being replaced by low-skill ones? (Marxism suggests "Yes.")
2. Are existing jobs being deskilled? (Marxism argues "Yes.")
3. Are rewards increasingly linked to merit? (Weberian and functionalist theories imply "Yes.")
4. Are experts becoming more powerful? (Postindustrial society theory contends "Yes.")

Achieved and Ascribed Status

There are two ways people can be assigned to positions in the stratification hierarchy of a society. One way is being assigned a position based on inherited characteristics such as sex, race–ethnicity, age, and the strata of one's parents. The latter case is illustrated by nineteenth-century India, where one's position was determined by the position, or caste, of one's parents. Being assigned a status based on these characteristics is called an **ascribed status**, characteristics over which we have no control.

The second way of being assigned a status is through personal effort. By working hard, getting an education, and improving skills and talents, an individual can move up the social ladder. This is **achieved status**, and a person has control over his or her destiny.

A society based solely on achievement, and in which rewards are based solely on merit, is called an open society. A society based solely on ascribed status, in which position in the social hierarchy is determined by inherited characteristics, is called a closed society. The degree of **social mobility** within a society is a measure of how open or closed it is. The more mobility there is, the more movement up and down the social ladder, the more open the society. It will be apparent in the following discussion of relational and distributive inequalities that both ascribed and achieved statuses are involved in the inequalities found in Canada, Mexico, and the United States.

The various measures of "class" are apparent from the above discussion of theories of social inequality. In the numerous studies of stratification, or class structure, class may be measured by the objective criteria of income, occupation, education, and combinations of these three. It may also be measured subjectively, by researchers asking people which of the following class(es) they belong to or by using occupational prestige scores, which are based on an average rating of occupations by various samples. Occupational prestige ratings appear to be very similar in almost all countries and all time periods. The class structure of any given society will vary considerably, depending on the measure used. In cross-societal studies, the objective measures of income, occupation, and/or education are the most widely used.

It is important to note that objective measures tell us nothing directly about **class consciousness**. It would be a gross mistake to assume that everyone classed as working class or lower class on the basis of income or occupation identified with that class. For example, an overwhelming majority of people in the United States and Canada, when asked to classify themselves in terms of class position with no further guidance, consider themselves "middle class." When respondents are given a choice of lower, middle, and upper categories, typically three-fourths or more choose "middle class." When given a choice between lower, working, middle, and upper, approximately an equal number (38–45 percent) select working- and middle-class categories. The number and names of the class choices affects the self-placements of respondents. This simply means that subjective measures, like objective measures, should be interpreted with caution.

Relational Inequalities (Power, Authority, and Prestige)

Whether Marxist or Weberian, most theorists agree that the two poles of the capitalist class system are big employers and workers with nothing to sell but their labour power (bourgeoisie and proletarians in Figure 9-1). Top managers (largely expert managers in Figure 9-1), the most contentious category, is considered a separate group.

The Bourgeoisie

The bourgeoisie "are different from you and me" (with apologies to F. Scott Fitzgerald). In Canada and the United States, big employers make up less than 1 percent of the labour force. In Mexico, they are fewer still. Big employers are rich by definition, and most rich people are big employers. According to *Forbes* magazine (July 20, 1992), there were 291 billionaires in the world in 1992, almost all of them major entrepreneurs. Of these, 10 were Canadians, 101 were Americans, and 7 were Mexicans. On a per capita basis, Canada and the United States have about the same number of billionaires; Mexico has far fewer. In Can-

TABLE 9-1 Major Canadian Entrepreneurs: Their Principal Businesses and Estimated Wealth

Name	Principal Business	Wealth ($billion)
Kenneth Roy Thomson	Newspapers, Hudson's Bay Co.	7.5
K.C. Irving and three sons[a]	Gas stations, oil refineries	6.0
Garry Weston	Baking, grain trade, packaged foods	2.7
Charles Bronfman	Seagram, Cineplex Odeon	2.7
Four Eaton brothers[b]	T. Eaton	1.4
Edward S. (Ted) Rogers	Rogers Communications	1.3
Galen Weston	Grocery stores, packaged foods	1.3

[a]Counted as four, since their combined wealth exceeds $1 billion each.
[b]Counted as one, since their combined wealth is about $250 million each.
SOURCE: Adapted from Harold Seneker, (ed.) "The World's Billionaires," *Forbes*, July 20, 1992, pp. 158, 160.

ada and the United States, the chance of earning or inheriting possessions worth $1 billion or more is about 1 in 2.5 million; in Mexico, it is about 1 in 12.3 million. Table 9-1 shows the ten Canadian billionaire entrepreneurs, their principal businesses, and the amounts of their wealth.

How do people become major entrepreneurs? At least two factors are very important. First, a great many of them have come into large inheritances. For example, of those listed in Table 9-1, this is true of Thomson, the three Irving sons (father only recently deceased), the two Westons, Bronfman, and the four Eaton brothers. People who become major entrepreneurs, then, are seldom "self made," "rags-to-riches" successes.

Second, most of them have been unusually lucky in investing their money. This is well illustrated in cases where they lose their great wealth. Consider, for example, the three Reichmann brothers and Nelson Skalbania. In 1991, *Forbes* estimated the Reichmann brothers' net worth at $6.3 billion; in 1992, information filed with an Ontario court suggested that the Reichmanns were as much as $2 billion in debt (*Forbes*, July 20, 1992, p. 160). In the 1970s and early 1980s, Nelson Skalbania was a rich real-estate and sports entrepreneur from Vancouver. At various times, he owned the Indiana Pacers of the (now defunct) World Hockey League, the Atlanta Flames of the National Hockey League, and the (now defunct) Montreal Alouettes of the Canadian Football League. In 1980, he bought the Major Junior A

New Westminster Bruins of the Western Hockey League for his 20-year-old daughter to run. Shortly thereafter, Skalbania declared bankruptcy. Although he has continued to be active in business, he has since enjoyed only modest success. It appears as if the Reichmanns and Skalbania were first very lucky and then very unlucky. The Reichmanns invested heavily in commercial real estate (such as London's Canary Wharf) just before a global recession. Skalbania invested heavily in real estate just before a western Canadian recession.

People who become major entrepreneurs do not appear to have special gifts for commerce. Rather, some people come into substantial inheritances. Of these, some make business investments (for example, in video cassette recorders). Of these, some make fortunes (having invested in VHS format) and others lose their inheritances (having invested in Beta) for reasons unpredictable beforehand.

Who are the biggest entrepreneurs in the United States and Mexico? How did they acquire their holdings? As with their Canadian counterparts, they are typically luckier-than-average people from wealthier-than-average families. According to *Forbes* magazine, the wealthiest American entrepreneur is William Henry Gates III, with a net worth estimated at $7.7 billion (*Forbes*, Oct. 19, 1992, p. 92). Gates, who began his business life with a $1 million trust fund set up for him by his grandparents, is the co-founder, president, and principal stockholder of Microsoft Corporation, producer of DOS, Windows, and many other computer software packages. He translated considerable wealth into a fortune through a stroke of luck (Wallace and Erickson 1992). When IBM contacted Microsoft to write some programs for its secretly planned personal computer in the late 1970s, Gates found out that IBM needed an operating system for the new machine. He then purchased the rights to an existing operating system, named 86-QDOS, from another company for $50 000, revised it for IBM, and renamed it DOS. Currently in version 6.0, DOS resides in almost every IBM-compatible personal computer in the world, with annual sales in the hundreds of millions of dollars.

Forbes estimates the wealthiest Mexican to be Emilio Azcarraga ("El Tigre") Milmo. El Tigre is a U.S.-born military-college dropout who has parlayed his father's communications conglomerate into a $3.4 billion radio, television, satellite, and newspaper empire that he owns and controls.

If they acted only as isolated individuals, big employers would be very influential. Sometimes, however, they act in concert with others, which makes them even more influential. How does this happen? Being capitalists, typically from very similar social backgrounds, they share certain interests in common. As well, they often either know one another or have mutual friends and acquaintances. For example, they may have attended the same exclusive private schools (such as Upper Canada College) and elite universities (such as McGill and Queen's). They frequently serve on the boards of directors of one another's companies. They also often live near one another. Table 9-2 shows the wealthiest neighbourhoods in Canada. Notice that only one is not in central Canada (Calgary) and that only two others are not within easy commuting distance of downtown Toronto (Montreal and Sudbury).

Top Executives

Upper-level executives in private enterprises (largely expert managers; see Figure 9-1) make up no more than about 10 percent of the labour force in Canada and the United States. They probably make up less than that in Mexico.

How do people become top managers? First, those who do are almost always people who have

TABLE 9-2 Postal Code, City, and Percentage of Families with Annual Incomes above $100 000, 1991

Postal Code	City/Area	Percentage of Families with Annual Incomes above $100 000
H3Y	Montreal, Quebec Westmount	18
L4G 3G8	Aurora, Ontario	18
M4W	Toronto, Ontario/ Rosedale	16
P3E 4S8	Sudbury, Ontario	15
M4T	Toronto, Ontario/ north of Rosedale	14
N4N and M2L	Toronto, Ontario/ northeast of Rosedale	14
L3R 2L6	Markham, Ontario	14
T3E 6W3	Calgary, Alberta/ Springbank	14

SOURCE: Statistics Canada.

had careers in corporations. They are wise in the culture of large-scale business enterprise and experienced in making decisions that involve people and property. Second, they are typically university-educated professionals, most often accountants, engineers, lawyers, or MBAs; they are certified "experts" of one kind or another. Third, they tend disproportionately to be from well-to-do families. This is true of well-educated people generally, including professionals. Fourth, they are almost all men. For women, there is at best a "glass ceiling" that intersects the corporate ladder; there is at worst a manned barricade (Cunningham 1984).

Upper-level executives in large corporations in Canada and the United States are well paid. Table 9-3 shows the average annual compensation, including salaries plus bonuses, stock options, and other benefits, for the best-paid executives in the 50 largest Canadian public corporations in 1991. As these data show, top managers in major companies earn a great deal of money — an average of well over $1 million a year for those working for Seagram and Thomson and an overall average

of $315 000 a year for those in the 50 largest Cana-
dian public companies. This is about ten times the
average earnings of employed men in Canada.
Upper-level executives in large corporations are
well paid in Mexico, too. Because university-educated professionals with corporate experience are
very rare in that country, they tend to be relatively better paid in Mexico than in Canada or the
United States.

Are upper-level executives who work for large
corporations paid in relation to their merit? In
55 percent of the cases considered here, the executives' earnings rose or fell between 1990 and 1991
as the value of their companies' stocks also rose
or fell. From this, the *Financial Times of Canada*
concluded, "Forget the business bashers: executives earn their dollars" (*Financial Times* May 11–
17, 1992, p. 4). The value of a company's stock,
however, can increase or decrease for many reasons. If it goes up, there will generally be more
money available for executives' incomes; if it goes
down, there will usually be less money for this.
Consequently, executives' incomes can rise and
fall with stock values even when their performance has little or nothing to do with determining
these values.

TABLE 9-3 Average Annual Compensation of Best-Paid Top Executives in Largest Canadian Public Corporations, 1991

Corporation	Number of Top Executives	Average Top Executive Salary Plus Bonuses
Seagram Company	17	$1 243 932
Thomson Corporation	8	1 217 584
Imperial Oil	6	702 167
Hudson's Bay Company	6	621 534
Canadian Pacific	6	551 840
George Weston	20	500 035
Average, 50 largest		315 000

SOURCE: Adapted from Richard Anstett and Mark Stevenson,
"The Myth of the Overpaid Executive," *Financial Times of Canada,*
May 11–17, 1992, p. 4

The Working Class

Narrowly defined, the working class includes
only proletarians (Figure 9-1). Broadly defined, it
includes all those who are employed. This means
that the working class makes up between about
40 and 85 percent of the labour force in Canada
and the United States and 95 percent or more in
Mexico.

In Canada and the United States, over three-
quarters of the men and more than half of the
women either have jobs or are looking for them.
What kinds of jobs are these? Currently, over
70 percent of the working class are employed in
service jobs, which includes business, personal,
and social service jobs, along with wholesale and
retail trade. Only a minority work in manufacturing (about 23 percent in Canada, 25 percent in
the United States), and fewer still in agriculture
(about 5 percent in Canada, 3 percent in the
United States). In both countries, manufacturing
and agricultural jobs both have declined in relative importance over time, from about one in
three jobs 30 years ago to one in four today. Well-
paid managerial and professional jobs prolifer-
ated in the 1960s and 1970s (Hunter 1988; Myles
1988), and the average skill level of jobs rose. This
is consistent with Bell's argument and contrary to
Braverman's. More and more, service jobs (especially those in business and social services) are
either fairly high-skill and well-paid or (particularly those in retail and wholesale trade and personal services) quite low-skill and low-paid.
Manufacturing jobs, finally, tend to have intermediate skill requirements. As a result of these
several developments, both "good" and "bad"
working-class jobs have become increasingly
common, and working-class jobs in the middle
are increasingly rare (Myles and Fawcett 1990).

Most Mexican men either have or are looking
for jobs. Only about a third of Mexican women,
however, are in the labour force. The complexion
of working-class jobs in Mexico is also quite different from that in Canada and the United States.
These jobs are about equally divided among service, agriculture, and manufacturing, which represents a big change from the recent past. Prior to
the 1970s, the Mexican labour force was largely
made up of unskilled agricultural workers. Increases in managerial and professional, office,

and skilled and semi-skilled production jobs have made up most of the difference.

Labour unions are the principal organizations representing the interests of the working class. Today, about 31 percent of the labour force in Canada, 18 percent in the United States, and 35 percent in Mexico belong to unions. These figures are quite low relative to many other countries. In Finland, for example, over 90 percent of the labour force are union members, as are about 85 percent of workers in Denmark and Sweden. Union membership in Canada has risen about 30 percent since World War II, although it has fallen slightly in the past eight years. Union membership in the United States, however, has dropped almost 50 percent in the postwar period and very sharply in the past fifteen years.

The Canadian Labour Congress (CLC) is an affiliation of many labour unions. It has been formally aligned with the New Democratic Party (NDP) since the early 1960s, although it has never been very successful in rallying workers to vote for the NDP. The American Federation of Labor–Congress of Industrial Organizations (AFL–CIO) is the American counterpart of the CLC. In contrast to the CLC, the AFL–CIO has been wary of formal political alliances. The Confederation of Mexican Workers (CTM), a large collection of unions, has long dominated the Mexican labour movement. The Institutional Revolutionary Party (PRI), in power since 1929 and effectively Mexico's only political party, tolerated corruption among the CTM leadership from the 1930s to the 1980s and favoured CTM unions for wage and other benefits "in exchange for political loyalty" (Riding 1989:84). As one would expect from their diverse political connections, unions in Canada have generally been more militant than those in the United States, and more militant in the United States than in Mexico. From 1987 to 1990, for example, an average of 90 working days per 1000 people per year were lost in Canada in industrial disputes; in the United States, the corresponding figure was 25 days; in Mexico, it was 7 days.

The largest and most effective unions in Canada and the United States tend to be in the public sector of the economy — the three levels of government — and in the monopoly sector, which includes small numbers of large firms, such as the automobile industry. The smallest and least effective unions tend to be in the competitive sector of the economy, that is, in large numbers of small firms. As well, labour unions have been more successful in organizing public- and monopoly-sector workers than they have in signing up competitive-sector workers.

Distributive Inequalities (Possession of Scarce and Valued Resources)

Distributive inequalities are those in which some groups or individuals have claims on greater privileges or more possessions than others do.

One distributive inequality in society is a difference in privileges, such as the leisure or discretionary time people have.

The usual measures of distributive inequalities are wealth, income, education, and occupation. How unequally are possessions distributed in Canada, the United States, and Mexico?

Income

In 1991, the per capita gross domestic product — the average value in U.S. dollars of the goods and services generated in a country by each man, woman, and child who lives there — was $25 350 for Canada, $25 863 for the United States, and $3163 (1990) for Mexico. These figures put Canada and the United States among the top five or ten (of 120 or so) countries in the world. They put Mexico about forty-fifth. In relative terms, Canada and the United States are very rich countries. Mexico is neither very rich nor very poor. How, then, does the affluence of each of these countries translate into material rewards for those who live in them?

FIGURE 9-2 Number of Minutes at Job to Pay for Big Mac and Large Fries, Toronto, New York City, and Mexico City

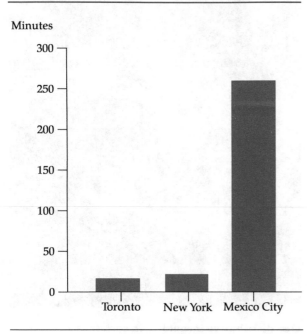

SOURCE: Diana Clifford, "Quizzes and Quantums: An Eclectic Grab Bag of the New North America," *The Globe and Mail*, September 24, 1992, p. C10.

There are many for whom the consequence of inequality is the lack of basic needs such as housing.

In capitalist systems, it is possible to earn large amounts of money as an entertainment or sports celebrity. Bill Cosby is at the top of the international list. *Forbes* magazine estimated Cosby's annual earnings for 1991–92 at $98 million. Oprah Winfrey was next at $88 million, followed by Kevin Costner at $71 million and New Kids on the Block at $62 million. Janet Jackson was fortieth on *Forbes*'s list at $22 million. Although there were no Canadians or Mexicans in the top 40, some do quite well. For example, Raghib "Rocket" Ismail, an American, is Canada's "$18 million man" (over a four-year contract), playing for the Toronto Argonauts of the Canadian Football League; another athlete, Mario Lemieux, a Canadian, is on a seven-year, $42 million contract with the Pittsburgh Penguins of the National Hockey League (*Forbes*, September 28, 1992, pp. 87–91).

Celebrities, of course, represent the unusual. What, then, of the usual? In the past 40 years, Canadians' and Americans' average incomes have risen a great deal. In 1951, Canadian men earned an average of $2575; in 1989, they earned $27 628. Most of this increase, however, was due to inflation. In real terms, Canadians' and Americans' incomes have about doubled since the early 1950s (Hunter 1993; Karoly, forthcoming). Moreover, these increases have not been continuous. Between 1977 and 1983, Canadian men's real in-

comes actually fell, as did women's between 1981 and 1983. American men's incomes fell in the early 1970s, and have changed little since the mid-1970s; American women's incomes also fell in the early 1970s, but have risen more or less continuously since the mid-1970s. As for Mexico, "during the period 1974–76, real wages ... declined by 25%; during the period 1976–79, a 20% decline was registered. The trend continued ... through the early 1980s, with real wages' falling over 30% between 1982 and 1985" (Gentleman

FIGURE 9-3 Percentages of People Reporting Frequent or Very Frequent Depression or Stress, Classified by Annual Earnings

On average, the more people earn, the more likely they are to report stress and the less likely they are to report depression.

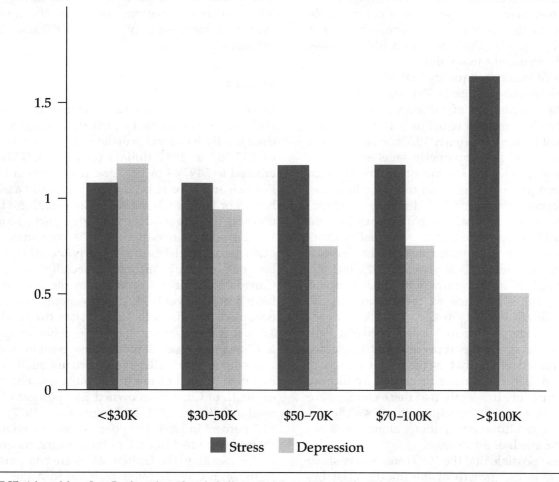

SOURCE: Adapted from Joan Breckenridge, "Canada Suffering Bad Case of Blues," *The Globe and Mail*, October 1, 1992, p. A10.

1987:55). The decline in real wages in Mexico has been such that the average Mexican worker had about half the purchasing power in 1991 that he or she had in the late 1930s.

The concept of "average income" treats everybody as if they were equal, whereas some people get more than others. It also deals with people as isolated individuals, whereas many people live in families that pool the financial resources of two or more individuals. In Canada in 1951, 42.5 percent of families had two or more income recipients; by 1989, this had risen to 86.3 percent. In the period since World War II, households in the top fifth of the income distribution have received about nine times as much income, on average, as those in the bottom fifth. In 1951, the top fifth of households earned 42.8 percent of the total income and the bottom fifth earned 4.4 percent. In 1989, the top fifth earned 43.2 percent of the total income and the bottom fifth earned 4.8 percent (Hunter 1993). Over time, then, there has been a considerable increase in the number of income earners per family in Canada. There has been little change, however, in income inequality.

Levels of income inequality in the United States are quite similar to those in Canada. At the same time, the distribution of incomes in the United States has become less equal over time. This is a trend that began in the early 1970s, accelerated in the 1980s, and has apparently levelled off. "In other words, over the last twenty years, the rich have been getting richer, and the poor have become poorer" (Karoly 1992:vi). In the case of Mexico, "since international comparisons of income distribution began, the extreme inequality characterizing Latin American countries has been a source of commentary" (Berry 1987:202). In 1977, the top fifth of income earners in Mexico earned about 20 times as much on the average as the bottom fifth (Roniger 1990:42).

Table 9-4 shows that in Mexico, between 1950 and 1980, the size of the upper and middle classes has increased while that of the lower class has decreased. Because class is measured by income and occupation, it is likely that these changes are largely the result of structural changes. The decline in agricultural occupations alone could account for much of the change.

It is also possible that the 1990 census may show a decline in the growth of the middle class be-

TABLE 9-4   The Class Structure of Mexico, 1950–1980* (Percent)

Social Class	1950	1960	1970	1980
Upper	1.7	3.8	5.7	6.2
Middle	18.0	21.0	27.9	31.1
Lower	80.3	75.2	66.4	63.7

SOURCE: Adapted from Stephanie Granato and Aida Mostkoff, "The class structure of Mexico, 1895–1980," in J.W. Wilkes, ed., *Society and Economy in Mexico* (Los Angeles: UCLA Latin American Centre Publications, 1990), p. 111. The classes are based on a combination of income and occupation.

cause of a lack of economic growth between 1980 and 1990. On the other hand, if the North American Free Trade Agreement (NAFTA) becomes a reality and the number of manufacturing and white-collar occupations increases, the middle class will increase between the 1990 and 2000 censuses.

Wealth

Over time, Canadians have accumulated more and more possessions. In 1970, the average Canadian family had a net worth (assets minus debts) of $32 382 in 1992 dollars (Oja 1987). This increased to $49 744 in 1977 and to $62 295 in 1984. For rich and poor alike, the single greatest asset is homes or vacation homes. For the wealthiest one-quarter, the largest debt is mortgages in homes; for the poorest one-quarter, it is consumer and other personal debts. Buying a home takes a big bite out of family income, especially in central Canada and British Columbia, as the data in Table 9-5 show. Over time, the percentage of owner-occupied dwellings in Canada has dropped. In 1956, it was 67.6 percent; by 1976, it had dropped to 62 percent, where it more or less remains today.

Wealth is distributed even more unequally than earnings in each of the three countries. The richest tenth of Canadians owned 53.3 percent of the total wealth in 1970, 50.7 percent in 1977, and 51.3 percent in 1984. The poorest tenth owed more than they owned in each of these years. Inequalities in wealth in the United States are comparable to those in Canada (*New York Times*, August 16,

TABLE 9-5 Family Income and Housing Costs, Selected Canadian Cities, 1992

City	Average Family Income	Average House Price	Total Payments as Percentage of Income[a]
Vancouver	$62 628	$251 916	34.7
Toronto	64 548	214 181	29.6
Victoria	55 339	187 920	29.2
St. Catharines	53 515	132 245	23.1
Montreal	54 187	119 370	21.1
Calgary	57 568	131 534	20.7
Ottawa	68 021	145 951	20.3
Edmonton	57 157	109 989	18.1
Quebec City	48 001	83 410	18.1
Halifax	55 555	99 842	17.4
Winnipeg	53 463	83 637	17.1
St. John's	49 623	91 065	16.4
Saint John	52 931	82 025	14.3

[a]Assumes a 25% down payment and a 9.63% mortgage for 25 years.
SOURCE: Adapted from Clayton Sinclair, "Home-Price Index at 20-year low," *Financial Times of Canada*, August 10–16, 1992, p. 4.

1992, p. 3E). Since the mid-1970s, tax cuts for the rich and small increases in workers' wages have lowered rates of home ownership and pension-plan participation and, thus, increased inequalities in wealth. In Mexico, wealth inequalities are probably much greater than in Canada or the United States. The Revolution of 1910 was initiated under the peasant leader Emiliano Zapata's slogan of "Land and Liberty" (Riding 1989:181). The major goal of the revolution was to redistribute land from the small number of very wealthy landowners to the millions of landless, rural poor. Land reform, however, never really happened. In a country whose dry climate, great mountain ranges, and thin, sandy topsoil are ill suited to agriculture, the most fertile, irrigated land is still largely owned by the few.

The Poor. Governments often use the concept of poverty to classify certain people as having an acceptably low standard of living for reasons not entirely of their own making. The government,

then, assists these "deserving poor" with lower taxes and welfare to help raise them out of their condition.

There are two ways to define poverty: relative and absolute. In a **relative** definition, the poor have fewer resources than others do. The Government of Canada uses a relative definition of poverty in which any individual or family spending more than 58.5 percent of its income on food, clothing, and shelter is poor. As Canadians have become increasingly affluent, this percentage has been revised progressively downward over time. For example, in the 1950s, 70 percent was the figure used. According to the current criterion, 14 percent (or 3 800 000) of Canadians were poor in 1991; this is up from 11.8 percent in 1986 and 12 percent in 1981. Had the 70 percent cutoff been retained, the percentage of Canadians defined as poor today would, of course, be lower than 14. The Government of the United States also uses a relative definition of poverty that resembles the Canadian one. Because the two countries are similar in affluence, the results of applying this definition are also similar. In the United States in 1991, 14.2 percent of the population was classified as poor. As for Mexico, because it is much poorer than either Canada or the United States, almost everybody would be poor if Canadian or American criteria were used.

In an **absolute** definition of poverty, the poor cannot provide for the essential requirements of life. Recently, a Canadian economist revived the debate on relative versus absolute definitions of poverty. "Poverty means not being able to acquire all basic physical needs," by which criterion about 1 million Canadians are poor, argues Christopher Sarlo in a study published by the Fraser Institute, a conservative think tank (*Hamilton Spectator*, July 15, 1992, p. 1A). This is about one-quarter of the number who are poor according to the official definition.

One difficulty with a relative definition of poverty is that it is subject to revision whenever the average living standard rises or falls. Then, whenever the criterion is revised, the classification of who is poor changes. This makes strict comparisons over time and from place to place problematic. Another difficulty with a relative definition is that poverty may be impossible to eliminate, no matter how affluent people become,

---

FIGURE 9-4   Persons per Motor Vehicle, per Television Set, and per Habitable Room, Canada, United States, and Mexico

---

Luxuries, conveniences, and necessities are much scarcer in Mexico than in either Canada or the United States.

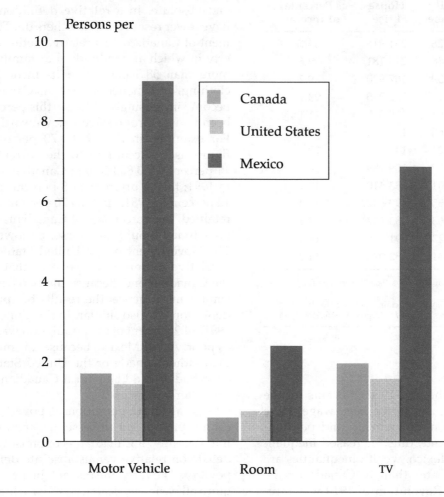

---

simply because it is defined relatively. One difficulty with an absolute definition of poverty is that there is probably no such thing as minimally adequate food, clothing, or shelter. Another difficulty is that, even if there were such things, cultural standards of what is and what is not edible (or wearable or habitable) would often prevent people from realizing them. Who, for example, would eat any kind of beef, including a bull's testicles ("prairie oysters")? Who would eat insects?

Redistributing Wealth. One of the goals of taxation is the redistribution of income from the wealthy to the poor. How effective is it in achieving this end?

Taxes. When most Canadians think of taxes, they probably think of income taxes, provincial sales taxes, and the recently introduced goods and services tax (GST). There are, however, other major taxes as well, including municipal property taxes. In 1991, the average Canadian family paid out just under 40 percent of its cash income on federal, provincial, municipal, and other taxes. For 1992, the Fraser Institute estimated that the average family paid out about 44 percent of its

The inability of the poor to provide for the essential requirements of life is an absolute definition of poverty.

income on taxes (*Globe and Mail*, July 22, 1992, p. A14). Table 9-6 gives these figures for each province. They range from $27 784 for Ontario to $14 360 for Prince Edward Island.

It is difficult to compare the overall tax systems of different countries, since the services provided in each are different. Overall, however, taxes are considerably higher in Canada than in the United States. While Canadian taxes amount to over 40 percent of the gross domestic product (up from about 32 percent in 1980), American taxes come to just over 30 percent (about the same as in 1980). Canadian government expenditures on education and health, however, are considerably higher than American government expenditures on these services. When this is taken into account, the tax bills in the two countries are quite similar.

Some taxes are progressive, taking relatively more from high-income people. Income taxes, for example, are progressive. Some taxes, however,

TABLE 9-6 Estimated Average Family Total of Federal, Provincial, Municipal, and Other Taxes by Province, 1992

Province	Total Taxes ($)
Ontario	27 784
British Columbia	24 133
Quebec	21 808
Alberta	21 664
Manitoba	21 450
Saskatchewan	20 542
Nova Scotia	17 944
Newfoundland	17 870
New Brunswick	17 294
Prince Edward Island	14 360

SOURCE: Adapted from Michael Kesterton, "Social Studies," *The Globe and Mail*, July 22, 1992, p. A14.

are regressive, taking relatively more from low-income people. Municipal property taxes are regressive, as are sales taxes and the GST. The tax system in Canada is not particularly progressive for most people, and it is actually regressive for the very poor. That is, the poorest Canadians pay out relatively more in taxes than they earn. This is possible only because of the government benefits they receive. Overall, taxes in Canada redistribute little income from the rich to the poor. Taxes in the United States appear to redistribute even less, and taxes in Mexico even less again.

Transfer Payments. Transfer payments ensure that certain categories of people, often including the very young and the very old, have some minimal standard of living. In Canada, they include unemployment insurance, workers' compensation, and the Canada Pension Plan. Sometimes these payments go to individuals or families regardless of economic circumstance. This was true of the recently discontinued family allowance, Canada's first universal social program, begun in 1945. Sometimes they are directed particularly at the needy. In Canada's new program of monthly pay-

The United States: The Rise and Rise of Child Poverty

"First call for children" should not be a problem for rich nations. But in the most prosperous nation of all, child deprivation has increased even as wealth has risen and poverty among other age groups has fallen.

In the 1960s, the proportion of US children living in poverty was halved from 27% to 14%. In the 1970s, it crept back to 17%. Then, in the 1980s, it rose again to 22% — even in a decade of almost uninterrupted economic growth and a near 25% increase in America's GNP.

Over the same 30 year period, overall poverty in the United States, and especially among the elderly, has declined. Driven mainly by government action, the proportion of older citizens (65+) living in poverty fell by more than two thirds.

So why has a nation with the demonstrated capacity to reduce poverty failed to do so for its children? *Child Poverty in America*, a report from the Washington-based Children's Defense Fund (CDF), clears the way for its answer by exploding some myths.

The stock image of the black child born to an unmarried, unemployed mother living on welfare in a big city is a description which fits fewer than one in ten of America's poor children. Inner-city blacks and Hispanics are certainly over-represented, but a majority of America's 12 million poor children are white. Most live outside big cities. Most live in families with

only one or two children. And most belong to households where at least one parent works.

The main reasons for rising child poverty are, first, the erosion of benefits provided by government to poor families with children and, second, the steady fall in real wages among America's unskilled.

The average weekly wage of non-supervisory workers fell by approximately 20% between 1973 and 1990. At the same time, the government's commitment to a minimum "family wage" appears to have faded; even after recent increases, the real minimum wage in 1990 is 20% less than it was in 1980. For a full-time, year-round worker, the minimum wage still leaves a family with one child almost $2000 below the poverty line.

As falling incomes have increased the need, government support for children has been gradually withdrawn. The real value of Aid for Families with Dependent Children (AFDC) has dropped by approximately 40% over 20 years. Today, less than 10% of all cash benefits go to poor families with children. Other groups have fared much better: over half of all people in poor families without children receive enough help to pull them above the poverty line — as opposed to only 14% of people in poor families with children.

Attempting to weight these factors, the report attributes just over 40% of

the rise in child poverty to the decline of government support, just over 30% to falling real wages among the poor, and just under 30% to the rise of mother-only families.

Calling on the United States to use its resources to end child poverty by the year 2000, the CDF argues that "our high poverty rate is interfering with the healthy development and education of millions of our children and threatens the nation's economic and social future."

"Eliminating child poverty," on the other hand, "would give the nation a huge running start on tackling the educational, health, substance abuse, crime, and other problems that seem so daunting."

And the cost? Money is by no means the only answer, but the CDF puts the bill at $28 billion a year (for raising every poor family with children up to the poverty line). This is less than 1% of America's GNP; it is also less than the amount received each year by the richest 1% of Americans as a result of additional tax breaks approved in the last 15 years.

Source:

The State of the World's Children, 1992 (New York: Published for UNICEF by Oxford University Press, 1992), 22.

ments to selected low-income families, for example, the major winners are "working poor" families. Families on welfare or unemployment insurance get the minimum payments, and families with annual incomes of $50 000 or more are the major losers. In the United States, these payments include Aid to Families with Dependent Children, food stamps, medical care and pensions for the elderly, and various benefits for military veterans. In Mexico, the federal and state governments operate hundreds of social welfare programs.

In Canada, the United States, and Mexico, transfer payments redistribute little income. They also do not guarantee a life above the poverty line. In the United States, for example, welfare benefits for a family of three range from $412 per month in Mississippi to $1184 per month in Alaska (*New York Times*, July 5, 1992, p. 16L). The United States government's poverty line for such a family, however, is $940 per month. Although there are hundreds of social welfare programs in Mexico, they are often ineffective because they are poorly planned or underfunded. As well, they may favour certain already advantaged groups (such as unionized workers or state employees), or the officials administering may require bribes or siphon off the benefits for themselves.

Achievement

In every society, people move into positions in the economic division of labour at least partly through competition on the basis of ability and training. Then, in meeting the obligations of these positions, they provide for themselves and their families. This is the process of achievement. In industrializing or industrialized societies, the achievement process ordinarily begins with people attending school in order to qualify for an occupation. Then, they enter the labour market to compete for vacant jobs. Finally, they work in occupations to earn a living.

Educational Attainment. In Canada, the United States, and Mexico, people have stayed in school longer and longer. In 1961, Canadians had completed about 8.5 years of schooling on average, and about 5.5 percent had earned university degrees. Today, they have completed just over twelve years of schooling, and about 10 percent have degrees. Americans have just under thirteen years of schooling, and some 20 percent have degrees. Mexicans have less than five years of schooling, and perhaps fewer than 1 percent have degrees.

These three countries have also invested more and more of their resources in formal education. Currently, Canada spends 7.2 percent of its gross domestic product on education, which is the highest proportion in the world. The United States spends 5.7 percent, which is still high by international standards. Mexico spends 3.5 percent. The increasing emphasis on education can be seen in the transformation of educational institutions in each of the three countries since World War II. For example, at the primary school level, there are 16 pupils per teacher on the average in Canadian schools (versus 26, thirty years ago), 20 in American schools (versus 29), and 32 in Mexican schools (versus 47).

Starving Artists

In Canada, very few people earn a living wage working as artists. In 1989, dancers earned an average of $13 000, authors earned $11 079, and visual artists earned $11 444 (EKOS Research Associates, cited in *The Globe and Mail*, August 1, 1992). Consequently, most artists supplement their incomes through other kinds of employment. So, for example, an Ontario study found that authors earned an average of $27 267 per year from all sources, which is about the same as the average worker in that province (Ontario 1991). Not all fared so well, however. Ontario musicians and singers earned an average of $15 927 from all sources; painters, sculptors and related visual artists earned $16 332; dancers and choreographers earned $16 997; and actors and actresses earned $18 872.

Source:

Godfrey, Stephen. "Artists deserve a hand," *The Globe and Mail*, August 1, 1992, p. C7.

Education and Opportunity

Martin Lambert left school at 16 because "it was no use sticking around — school was just stupid and boring."

He is not alone: only half the students who entered secondary schools run by the Montreal Catholic School Commission in 1984 had emerged with a diploma by 1991.

But, unlike many dropouts, Mr. Lambert, now 19, is back in class — thanks to EPOC Montreal, a project underwritten by the Bank of Montreal. The project's initials stand for education, placement, orientation and communication.

"I was tired of the dead-end, minimum-wage jobs." Mr. Lambert said. "And I realized that no matter how bad classes could be, life could be a lot worse, a way more scary."

Mr. Lambert is not exactly bubbling over with youthful enthusiasm, but he is at least trying to break free from the lost generation of dropouts that threatens the province's and the country's competitive and economic viability.

Quebec's dropout rate stands at 36 per cent, the worst in Canada and many times greater than Japan's 2 per cent.

Given the statistics, it is ironic that one of the most popular academic theses today is that the main reason students are skipping out of class is the economy itself.

"To counter the virtually uncontested classical theme that schools are to blame for dropouts, I offer the bold view that we wouldn't have so many dropouts if the economy and the job market were not so screwed up, so anemic and so damaged," François Baby, a professor of education at Laval University, told a recent conference examining the problem.

When the Quebec government launched a $42-million program called *Chacun ses devoirs* (loosely translated: Everyone Has Homework To Do) last year, it focused on the traditional methods of trying to entice potential secondary-school dropouts to stick it out to the end.

No matter how imaginative these programs are, critics argue, young people know that as long as the economy is stagnant their chances of employment after graduation are slim.

Further, they argue that the groundwork for failure is set early in a child's schooling, and that rigid, old-fashioned methods of teaching are not suitable for children who need nurturing and nursing as much as learning.

One innovative aspect of the provincial plan, however, was to set aside $10-million to establish a primary-school breakfast and lunch program.

The theory, said former education minister Michel Pagé (who resigned last month), was that hungry children cannot learn.

Studies by the provincial Education Ministry found that children from poor backgrounds are 2½ times more likely than middle-class children to drop out before graduating from secondary school.

Another difficulty in dealing with the dropout epidemic is that the problem is far from monolithic. There are significant differences seemingly based on sex, language, religion and culture.

For example, two boys drop out of school for every girl, a statistic "too striking to ignore," said Jocelyn Berthelot of the teachers' union *Centrale de l'enseignment du Québec.*

Traditionally, boys have dropped out in larger numbers than girls to take blue-collar jobs. Today those jobs no longer exist but the trend continues. A newer theory points to socialization, suggesting that because girls are more group-oriented, peer pressure keeps them in school.

Quebec government statistics also show the dropout rate for francophones is about 7 per cent higher than for anglophones. A slightly larger gap exists between students in Roman Catholic and Protestant schools, the Catholic rate being higher. In aboriginal schools — the Crees and Inuit have their own school systems — the dropout rate is as high as 82 per cent.

The high dropout rate for natives is tied directly to poor economic prospects. This, in large part, also explains the higher rate for francophones: poor neighbourhoods are predominantly francophone.

The "religious" gap is more complex. Although school boards are denominational, the labels are deceptive. A large percentage of "Catholic" students are not Roman Catholic and there is no religious instruction at all in "Protestant" schools, whose students are often Jewish, Muslim or of other faiths. The biggest factor seems to be that private schools tend to skim off the best students, in large part from the Catholic school system.

A Statistics Canada study found that more than 50 per cent of children who repeat an elementary grade do not get a high-school diploma.

Yet, the much-talked-about $42-million plan to counter the dropout problem offers little to offset those fundamental issues. Students who fail early still get tagged as failures and rarely shake the label.

The Pagé plan, as it came to be known, consists of some goals and general recommendations, but left the nuts-and-bolts to individual school boards.

The main goal set out by the province was to halve the dropout rate within five years. In general, the minister's advisers recommended that high-school students have more stability (fewer teacher changes and less choice of subjects) and increased access to technical programs, and that students be encouraged to become more involved in extracurricular activities.

The plan won the backing of virtually every sector of the education field, from teachers to administrators, largely because it offended no one: the powerful teachers' union supported the plan because it did not decree programs centrally, exactly what administrators were looking for (along with the necessary funds to implement the plans.)

The decentralized approach has spawned all sorts of programs, whose success will probably not be known for years. But a Laval University study of 232 projects on dropouts is a sobering counterbalance to the aura of hope.

"The impression is that positive results will flow from noble objectives," said Laval researcher Lynda Gosselin, who concluded that the vast majority of programs were useless.

But not every program has failed. Among those that were successful at preventing potential dropouts from leaving school there were common elements, she said. They were simple, straightforward and gave students a lot of individual attention.

For example, Jean Dolbeau Secondary School in the Lac St-Jean region red-flagged all students with poor exam results (40 per cent of the 225 students) and gave them a second chance, in addition to 20 hours of tutoring. The Chutes Montmorency School Board near Quebec City set up an educational SWAT team (consisting of a learning specialist, a social worker and teachers) that held individual meetings with poorly performing students, offering counselling and tutoring. And the Outaouais-Hull School Board offered free literacy courses to parents, making learning a family affair.

The problem with most programs aimed at bringing dropouts back is that they target middle-class students, rather than those from poor backgrounds, said Yvon Lefebvre, an education professor at the University of Quebec in Montreal. (Generally, middle-class students leave school because they are bored, while the poor students leave because their families need the money.) They also tend to assume dropouts are intellectually inferior, rather than acknowledge they are bored or have social problems.

An exception is provided by Pierre Brazeau, a former school dropout who now heads St-Antoine Secondary School in St-Hyacinthe. He created a

Quebec Quandary

Secondary school begins at Grade 7 in Quebec. For every hundred students who enter it:

- *Three drop out by the end of the first year;*
- *Six drop out in Secondary II (Grade 8);*
- *Eight drop out in Secondary III (Grade 9);*
- *Nine drop out in Secondary IV (Grade 10);*
- *Ten drop out in Secondary V (Grade 11);*
- *Only 64 leave with a diploma. Of the 36 dropouts, 24 are girls.*

Of the 64 graduates:
- *Four enroll in trade schools;*
- *Twenty-six enroll in a college "career" program*
- *Thirty-four enroll in an academic college program or other post-secondary studies.*

Source:

Statistics Canada

program that has an 80-per cent success rate in getting dropouts to finish their diploma. (Most programs are happy to reach 50 per cent.)

In Mr. Brazeau's "dream school for dropouts" most work is done in groups, and classroom participation is mandatory. A typical school week also consists of 13 hours of "social and personal development workshops" in addition to 21 hours of class in small groups.

Mr. Lefebvre said the school system needs to change fundamentally, to become more practical and less driven by the "dictée de Pivot" (a popular television dictation competition) syndrome.

Sylvain Bélisle, co-author of a study looking at the Quebec job market in the year 2000, said 90 per cent of new jobs created in the coming decade will be in electronics, health care, computers and engineering. Not only are the fields of study not stressed in the traditional secondary-school format, but the need for recycling and retraining will make learning habits an important asset for workers, one that will leave dropouts even further behind.

A federal study by a Senate committee found investing time and money to eliminate the dropouts who leave school for economic reasons would result in paybacks of $33 billion over 20 years in improved work, taxes and transfer payments.

But the fact remains that most programs operate on a shoestring and depend on the personal dedication of teachers involved.

And much-talked-about efforts such as Quebec's anti-dropout initiative have to be examined in a larger context. The same year it was launched, the province slashed $100-million from the education budget, including $25-million from adult-education programs, to which many dropouts turn for help and which have long waiting lists.

Source:

André Picard, "$42-million project struggles to keep teens in school," *The Globe and Mail*, December 30, 1992, p. A5.

Occupational Attainment. Why the concern for education? First, people generally believe that a better-educated person is more likely to have a job and, therefore, to earn a living. While this holds true in Canada and the United States, it does not do so in Mexico. Second, most people also believe that a better education improves access to desirable occupations. In Canada, the United States, and Mexico, this belief is true although, in industrializing countries such as Mexico, people are often unemployed because they have too much education for the jobs available. Table 9-7 presents levels of educational attainment and earnings for males, along with Pineo–Porter status scores (Pineo and Porter 1967), for a selected set of occupations in Canada. The status

TABLE 9-7   Education and Earnings (1986) and Prestige Rankings (1967) for Ten Occupations

Occupation	Percentage with University Degree	Average Annual Earnings ($)	Prestige
University professor	99.3	37 456	84.6
Physician	99.2	78 663	87.2
Civil engineer	68.1	37 057	73.1
Architect	59.6	32 072	78.1
Insurance agent	16.2	26 557	43.7
Travelling salesperson	14.2	28 150	40.2
Bartender	4.2	5 331	20.2
Funeral director	3.2	23 772	54.9
Cook	1.6	8 790	29.7
Bus driver	0.7	17 857	35.9

SOURCE: *1986 Census of Canada*; Peter C. Pineo and John Porter, "Occupational Prestige in Canada," *Canadian Review of Sociology and Anthropology* 4(1967):24–40.

scores measure people's evaluations of the "social standing" of various occupations. These data illustrate the fact that the higher the educational attainment of persons in an occupation, the higher that occupation's earnings and status. Third, most governments assume that a better-educated population creates a wealther country, although, at least to some extent, a wealthier country could also create a better-educated population. That is, it is not clear which (education or wealth?) is the chicken and which is the egg.

Why do better-educated people have more desirable occupations? There are at least two kinds of reasons. First, in order for people to be productive in them, some jobs require more general abilities and specific skills and greater self-discipline than other jobs do. Formal education (as signified in the number of years successfully completed, the number of diplomas or degrees earned, and so on) certifies these skills and work habits. Some people, then, have both the inclination and the resources to stay in school longer than others and, because they become more highly trained, they also become better paid. This

is Davis and Moore's argument. Second, certain occupations, such as the self-regulating professions of law and medicine, control the licensing or training requirements that newcomers must satisfy to become members. These groups sometimes raise these requirements to restrict new entrants to an elite few with the appropriate accents, manners, and tastes. Then, these groups may capitalize on their newly elevated status or simply take advantage of the law of supply and demand to exact more rewards from clients or other subordinate groups. This is Weber's and, later, Parkin's argument (Hunter and Leiper, forthcoming).

Why do wealthier countries tend to have better-educated populations? The usual answer is that better-educated people are more productive economically. This may be true, but probably only to a point. First, people who are very well educated for their jobs may produce less than people who are less well educated, perhaps because they are less highly motivated (Berg 1970). Second, wealth may cause education, as well as the other way around; for example, a good education may be something that rich people can better afford than poor people. Third, some countries with very high proportions of certain kinds of highly educated people (such as lawyers and stock analysts) may produce less than countries with lower pro-

TABLE 9-8   Occupational Distributions, Canada (1989), Mexico (1988), and the United States (1990) (Percent)

Occupation	Canada (1989)	Mexico (1988)	United States (1990)
Professional, technical	17	9	16
Administrative, managerial	13	2	12
Clerical and related	18	8	17
Sales	9	14	11
Service	13	15	14
Production, transport	27	29	28
Primary	3	23	2
Total	100	100	100

SOURCE: *Year Book of Labour Statistics* (Geneva: International Labour Office, 1991).

portions of them, possibly as a result of talented people's energies being spent in occupations that create little or no value. "The Magee curve" (see Figure 9-5) illustrates this possibility for lawyers. As for people whose job it is to predict whether particular stocks will rise or fall in value, repeated studies have failed to show that stock analysts do any better at this than ordinary people do throwing darts randomly at the names of stocks on a board or tossing dice (for example, American Broadcasting Corporation's, "20/20": "Who Needs Experts?" Friday, November 14, 1992). Whatever the connection between national wealth and the education of the population, politicians and policy-makers in Canada and the United States increasingly doubt that additional expenditures on education will add much to the national wealth. As a result, real investments in

education have slowed or fallen in many provinces and states over the past ten or twenty years.

Ascription

In every society, people move into certain occupations on the basis of attributes not directly related, if related at all, to their capacities to carry out the duties that come with those occupations. These attributes include gender, socioeconomic background, and race–ethnicity. This is the process of ascription.

Socioeconomic Background. An important element in how successful a person is socially and economically is how successful her or his parents were. In modern industrial societies such as Canada and the United States, better-educated, well-

---

FIGURE 9-5   The Magee Curve: "How Many Lawyers Ruin an Economy?"

Once a country has more than 23 lawyers per 1000 white-collar workers, Stephen Magee's research suggests, its productivity begins to decline.

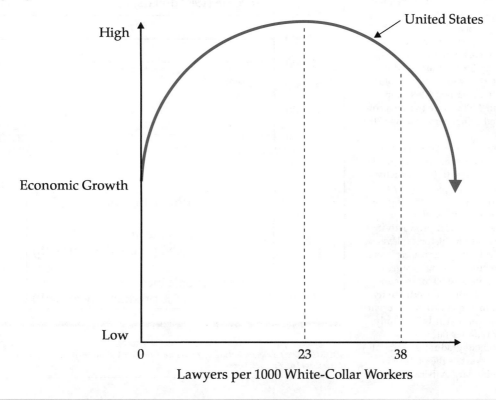

SOURCE: Stephen P. Magee, "How Many Lawyers Ruin an Economy?" *The New York Times*, September 24, 1992.

Father Does Best?

All of the Democratic presidential candidates warn that this generation could be the first to face downward mobility.

"We are the first generation in the history of the United States that's going to give less to our children," former Massachusetts Sen. Paul E. Tsongas says.

"I refuse to stand by and let our children become part of the first generation to do worse than their parents," Arkansas Gov. Bill Clinton says.

Polls and casual conversations show that many Americans share the fear that their children will face declining living standards.

But are those fears justified?

Frank G. Levy, an economist at the University of Maryland, has made probably the most comprehensive attempts to measure generational progress. In a new book co-written with Richard C. Michel, Levy plots the lifetime earnings of a typical young worker today against the lifetime earnings of his father.

For young men and women with a college degree — still only about one-fourth of the work force — the prognosis is fairly optimistic. Measured in 1987 dollars, the typical 30-year-old college graduate earned $26 000 in 1986 — about $4000 more than his college-educated father earned at age 30 in 1961.

But whether today's young college graduate maintains that lead depends on whether the growth in productivity continues its sluggish pace of the last decade or rises to a higher figure closer to the long-term trend.

As the chart shows, if productivity growth returns to its historical level, today's typical college graduate is projected to top out at average wages of $51 200 — about $10 000 more than his father's peak. But, if productivity continues to inch forward at its recent pace, the son's best year will be only $1700 better than his father's.

For high school graduates — about 55% of all workers — the picture is much gloomier, largely because of the

Father–Son Income Comparison

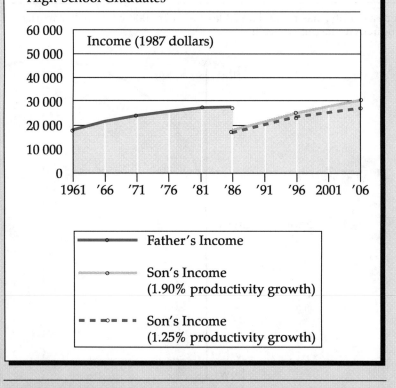

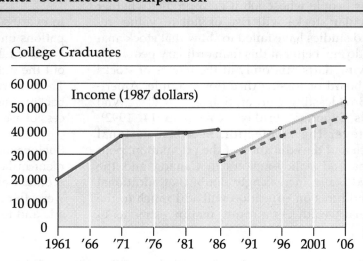

SOURCE: *The Economic Future of American Families*, Urban Institute Press, 1991. Paul Gonzales/*Los Angeles Times*

decline in high-paying manufacturing jobs. Even at a high rate of productivity growth, Levy and Michel estimate that today's 30-year-old high school graduate — though slightly ahead at this point in his life — will just about equal his father's best wages. But, if productivity growth continues at its recent rate, he will fall 20% short of his father's peak.

Which future seems more likely? Lawrence Mishel, research director of the Economic Policy Institute in Washington, citing continued pressure from imports and the decline of unions, concludes that "any way you look at it, the vast majority of workers are going to see their opportunities erode."

Even increasing the number of college graduates would not help much, Mishel argues, "because at most 30% of the jobs by the year 2000 will require a college education. If we educated three-fourths of the work force with a college degree, they wouldn't all see their wages rise."

But Levy is cautiously optimistic that the restructuring of American business — hastened by the pressure of the recession — may seed the ground for greater productivity, and earnings, gains in the 1990s. At least that is what he hopes.

"The definition of the American dream is mass upward mobility," Levy says. "To my mind, when you have people who have a set of aspirations that are not totally out of whack and they fail to reach them year after year, that gives rise to a search for scapegoats."

Source:

Ronald Brownstein. Copyright, 1991, *Los Angeles Times*, January 27, 1991, p. A16. Reprinted by permission.

---

to-do parents tend to have better-educated children, and better-educated people are more likely to find desirable jobs (Boyd et al. 1985a). Research shows that about one-third of the differences in educational attainment among Canadians and Americans are attributable to differences in their socioeconomic backgrounds. This happens because, among other things, well-placed parents have intellectual and material resources that benefit their sons and daughters, and they instil high educational and occupational aspirations in their children. That they live in neighbourhoods populated with others of their kind, and that their children grow up and go to school with other advantaged children with high aspirations, reinforce this. In more traditional societies such as Mexico, affluent parents often marry their daughters off to the sons of other affluent parents and bequeath their own wealth directly to their sons when they die. Even though the mechanisms are different in each case, however, the results are the same: inequalities in one generation are to some extent reproduced in succeeding generations. At the same time, the reproduction of inequalities over time is always far from complete. In every society, some among the low-born rise and some among the high-born fall. That is, there is always some upward and downward intergenerational **social mobility**.

Intergenerational social mobility takes two forms: structural and exchange. **Structural mobility** occurs when good jobs increase in number more quickly than bad jobs do (creating upward mobility) or vice versa (leading to downward mobility). Exchange mobility happens when, changes in job opportunities aside, some people for a variety of different reasons rise above or fall below their parents' social positions. Given that Canada and the United States are mature industrial cum postindustrial societies and that Mexico is a rapidly industrializing one, there may be greater upward mobility of a structural kind in Mexico today than in either Canada or the United States. At the same time, the new industrial jobs being created in Mexico are largely unskilled, low paying, and perhaps only marginally preferable to the agricultural labouring jobs that they have replaced.

Gender. Men and women in Canada and the United States have about the same number of years of schooling. The women, though, are somewhat more likely to have completed high school, while the men are slightly more likely to have earned university degrees. The men in Mexico, however, appear to be better educated on average than are the women. In particular, Mexican men are about four times as likely as Mexican women to have university degrees. Today, approximately half of all new university graduates in Canada and the United States each year are women. Soon, many more than half will be women. In the late 1980s, there were 113 women for every 100 men enrolled in postsecondary educational institutions in Canada (United Nations 1991). The ratio was 110 women to every 100 men in the United States. By contrast, there were 66 women for every 100 men enrolled in postsecondary educational institutions in Mexico.

Beyond elementary school, females and males study quite different subjects. Specifically, males are much more likely to take mathematics or science courses in secondary school and to enter postsecondary programs that require math or science. In Canada, for example, between 45 and 50 percent of new graduates in law (compared with 21 percent in 1975) and medicine (compared with 24 percent in 1975) are women. Only about 13 percent of new graduates in engineering, however, are women.

Over time, the labour-force participation of women has increased considerably in Canada, the United States, and Mexico, although it remains lower than that of men. In Canada and the United States today, approximately 40 percent of the labour force is female; 25 years ago it was closer to 30 percent in Canada and 35 percent in the United States. In Mexico, some 30 percent of the labour force is female; 25 years ago it was about 17 percent.

Working at a job for pay contributes value to the economy. So does working in the home for no pay. Being a homemaker involves helping to maintain others who work for pay and helping to raise the next generation of workers. This is why homemaker should be considered an occupation along with other occupations. In Canada, the total number of hours per year spent in working at a job for pay is about the same as the total number spent in working at home for no pay — about 21 billion hours, in each case — according to a Statistics Canada study (*Globe and Mail*, June 19, 1992). Economists estimate that the contribution of unpaid housework, child care, and other home-maintenance activities to the economy amounts to between 32 and 39 percent of the gross domestic product, or between $216 billion and $263 billion in 1991. About two-thirds of this work is done by women.

In Canada, the United States, and Mexico, men are more evenly distributed among occupations than women. Table 9-9 shows this for Canada. Over 30 percent of employed women are in cleri-

TABLE 9-9 Occupations of Men and Women, Canada, 1989 (Percent)

Occupation	Men	Women
Managerial, administrative	13.7	10.7
Other professionals		
Social science	1.3	2.3
Natural science, engineering, mathematics	5.3	1.6
Diagnostic/treatment health	0.7	0.5
Others	2.8	2.5
Teaching	2.2	5.6
Nursing, related health	1.2	8.6
Clerical	5.9	30.5
Service	10.3	17.0
Sales	9.0	9.9
Primary	6.7	2.2
Processing/machining	7.7	1.8
Product fabricating, assembly, repair	11.7	4.2
Construction	10.4	0.3
Transportation	6.1	0.7
Material handling/crafts	4.9	1.8
Total*	100.0	100.0

*Variances from 100 are the result of rounding.
SOURCE: Catharine Shea, "Changes in Women's Occupations," Statistics Canada. *Canadian Social Trends*. Autumn, 1990, p. 23.

cal occupations, working as secretaries, typists, file clerks, and the like. A further 17 percent are in personal-service occupations. There are no occupational categories with such large percentages for men. Although the profile of women's occupations in each of the three countries is becoming more similar to that of men's occupations over time, changes have occurred very slowly.

In each of the three countries, some occupations are almost entirely filled by women and others by men. Occupational categories largely populated by women in Canada include nursing and related health (85.4 percent) and clerical (80.4 percent). Those largely populated by men include construction (97.8 percent), transportation (91.4 percent), processing/machining (84.1 percent), and natural science/engineering/mathematics (80.8 percent).

"... In the Home"

Nomura Securities Co. of Japan, the world's largest brokerage firm, announced plans in 1992 to cut 2000 jobs in the following five years. The company intends to eliminate women workers especially, on grounds that women tend to quit sooner than men, typically leaving when they get married.

Canadian women employed full-time and year-round earn on the average about 66 percent of what comparable men do. This has changed very little in recent years. American women's wages are about 70 percent of men's; this is up from less than 60 percent twenty years ago. In the United States, real earnings for men have fallen since the early 1970s and real earnings for women have risen; one consequence is a shrinking gender-earnings gap (Karoly 1992:35). In Mexico, real wages have fallen for both men and women over time, but government data gathering and processing in that country shows little of the art, science, or rigorous attention to detail required for such tasks as precise comparisons between men's and women's earnings.

How is it that women's socioeconomic experiences are so different from men's? First, from early childhood, females do better than males in verbal tasks. Males show no more quantitative skills overall than females. Males may be superior in mathematical problem solving, but females seem to excel in computation, and neither sex has an advantage in understanding concepts (Felson and Trudeau 1991). Beyond the middle grades in school, however, boys become more likely than girls to take mathematics and natural (but not necessarily life) sciences courses. These differences presage a complex and still little-understood process that culminates in women concentrating in clerical occupations and men dominating mathematical and natural scientific ones. These occupational differences, in turn, help to account for women's lower earnings. Occupations that require advanced mathematics or natural science training, such as engineering, also tend to pay well.

Second, men's and women's different roles in the care and nurture of childen is certainly a strong factor in women's lower rates of labour-force participation and more frequent employment interruptions, although it affects most women for only a few short intervals in their lives. That women have historically been much less likely to work for pay is probably one reason why they have fewer advanced university degrees: there was less motivation to acquire them. Because employers often pay a premium for employees with advanced degrees, this also helps to explain women's lower earnings (Hunter and Leiper 1993). Employment interruptions are a major element in women's lower earnings as well. In addition to the earnings that women lose while out of the labour force, employment interruptions cause losses in earnings when people return to the labour force because of experience, pay raises, and promotion opportunities missed. A recent Canadian study estimates, for example, that "a 40-year-old teacher who re-enters her profession after a 10-year absence will forego $159 000 in earning potential for the remainder of her career" (*Globe and Mail*, July 7, 1992, p. A6). Finally, employers, who are mainly men, prefer to hire men for full-time, year-round, high-paying jobs, other things being equal (Denton and Hunter 1991).

If women's socioeconomic experiences are often very different from men's, there is nevertheless a clear convergence of the sexes in these matters in all three countries. In particular, the educational, labour-force participation, occupational, and pay gaps have all progressively narrowed over time. What might account for this? One possible factor is that women have increasingly entered the labour force to maintain or improve the standards of living of their families. This increases the motivation for women to stay in school longer. And better-educated women tend to get higher-paying jobs. Another factor might be that men are generally bigger and stronger than women, but physique is less and less relevant in the labour market today, save for a small number of professional sports. A final possible factor might be that, in profit-driven economies, private-sector employers lose money in the long run if they prefer to hire men and pay them more than they pay women. The reason is that, if an employer does this, others will hire women and pay them appropriately, and the employer will be left with an overpriced male workforce.

Some female–male differences, such as size and strength, are obviously biological in origin; others, such as tastes in automobiles, are just as obviously learned in social interaction. Yet others are more likely to be grounded in some combination of biology and learning. Some researchers point out, for example, that females' and males' brains are not the same and that the sexes do not always use their brains in exactly the same way. Although the significance of this is the subject of debate, the right hemisphere of the brain (from which come creativity and the emotions) and the left hemisphere (where analytical thought originates) seem to be more closely connected, physically and functionally, in females than in males. Females and males are also typically brought up to take on very different gender roles. As a result, the effects of biology and social learning cannot always be separated. At the same time, it is important to appreciate in all of this that, while the behavioural differences between the sexes may sometimes be large, the physiological differences are almost always small.

Race–Ethnicity. Prior to the sixteenth century, aboriginal peoples occupied the territory now divided among Canada, the United States, and Mexico. Since that time, however, the three countries have acquired quite different racial–ethnic complexions. Both Canada and the United States are largely societies of the descendants of European immigrants. Observers (for example, Porter 1965) often characterize Canada as a "mosaic" of racial–ethnic groups that have managed to retain important elements of their cultures. Over 200 years after the defeat of the French by the British, for example, about one in three Canadians is a native French-speaker. By contrast, commentators commonly describe the United States as a "melting pot." Regardless of their ancestry, for example, most Americans are native English-speakers. At the same time, approximately 8 in 100 Americans are Hispanics or Latinos — native Spanish speakers (mainly Cuban and Mexican immigrants and Puerto Ricans) or people with Spanish surnames. And about one in ten Americans is an Afro-American or black. In Mexico, it is customary to distinguish among those of Spanish origin, Indians, and mestizos (Indian and Spanish), although the lines that divide these groups (Indians and mestizos, especially) are not clear. Fewer than one Mexican in ten is biologically, culturally, or socially identified as Spanish, about one in ten is identified as Indian, and the remainder are identified as mestizos.

In Canada up to World War II, Quebec lagged well behind Ontario economically. Quebec was a rural, agricultural society, served by a classical educational system producing the traditional class of lawyers, physicians, and priests, but ill-equipped to train educated labour for an industrial society. Over the past 40 years, however, much has changed. Quebec has emerged as an affluent, modern society with an educational system at least comparable to the currently much-criticized one in Ontario. Today, anglophone (native English-speaking) Canadians are still on average slightly better-educated than francophone (native French-speaking) Canadians, although the differences between the two groups are now small, closing quickly, and confined to older persons. In 1986, some 10 percent of anglophones had university degrees, for example, as compared with 8 percent of francophones and 11 percent of "allophones" (neither native English- nor native French-speakers). As well, anglophones and francophones now fare about the same in terms of labour-force participation, occupational attainment, and earnings.

The history of anglophone–francophone conflict has gone ahead since the conquest, sometimes openly and other times not, but generally by means other than armed combat. It has accelerated rapidly since World War II, a period of rapid economic development for both Quebec and the rest of Canada, continuing in its most active and mass forms in the 1970s (with the Quebec crisis and the subsequent election of the Parti Québécois), the 1980s (with the failed Quebec referendum on sovereignty association and the failed Meech Lake Accord), and the 1990s (with the failed Charlottetown constitutional agreement). Since Quebec is now, on the whole, as wealthy a society as the rest of Canada and has its own complete set of government, business, labour, and other fully functioning elites, aspira-

Teachers and Talk

In Westfield, Massachusetts, in 1992, 403 residents signed a petition to the school board that teachers with "pronounced foreign accents" not be permitted to teach the first and second grades (*New York Times*, July 5, 1992). "The petition called for no teacher to be assigned to first or second grade 'who is not thoroughly proficient in the English language in terms of grammar, syntax and — most important —

the accepted and standardized use of pronunciation.' " The mayor, a Greek immigrant with a Greek accent and a master's degree in education, agreed. The state education secretary, a Cuban native and former kindergarten teacher, thought the petition fostered bigotry. The office of the state attorney general offered the judgement that the petition, if successful, would violate state antidiscrimination

laws and threatened to sue the Westfield board if it acted favourably on it. On a vote of 3 to 0, the board's curriculum subcommittee finally rejected the petition.

Source:

National Report. *The New York Times*, July 5, 1992, p. 12L.

---

tions for independence arising within that province are not illuminated very much by a Marxian class analysis. These aspirations are, however, made clearer by a Weberian analysis in which francophones are a status group exerting closure over its own membership and usurping others' resources in an attempt to create a country for themselves whose powers will never be subordinate to those of the federal government of Canada.

If the grand racial–ethnic divide in Canada is between anglophones and francophones, in the United States the principal divisions are among whites, Hispanics, and blacks. In the United States, whites have about 12.7 years of schooling on average, blacks have about 12.4 years, and Hispanics have about 12 years. Whites, however, are much more likely to have four years of university or more (20.9 percent) than blacks (11.3 percent) or Hispanics (10 percent). Whites are less likely than Hispanics to be unemployed, and Hispanics less likely than blacks to be unemployed. Whites also tend to have more desirable jobs, and they earn more on the average than do Hispanics or blacks. Hispanic families earn about 65 percent of what white families earn annually; black families earn less than 60 percent of what white families earn. There is, of course, a long history of bad race relations involving whites and blacks in the United States, beginning with blacks being brought over to North America as slaves in the fifteenth century. Slavery ended with the Civil War, but the economic exploitation and political suppression of blacks changed only slowly over the next 100 years, until the civil rights movement

in the 1950s and 1960s, when blacks caught the favourable eye of the Democratic Party. The assassinations of John and Robert Kennedy and Martin Luther King, along with the one-term presidency of Lyndon Johnson brought about by his failure to end the Vietnam War, however, left the movement without effective leadership or powerful sponsors.

As you will see in Chapter 10, the history of Mexico since 1521, when Cortés led the Spanish in conquest, is a tale of continuing Spanish domination, the dispossession and disappearance of the Indians, and the emergence and growth of mestizo culture and society. Today, typically well-educated and well-travelled Mexicans of Spanish origin, living largely in Mexico City and other large northern cities, dominate the country's economic and political elites. Illiterate Mexicans of Indian descent, concentrated in southern rural communities, inhabit the opposite end of the socioeconomic scale. The mestizo majority settles the vast regions in between.

Among racial and ethnic groups in North America, clearly the most disadvantaged economically are the aboriginal peoples. In the United States, for example, the Native peoples are less than half as likely to have university degrees as Americans generally; they earn on the average only about two-thirds as much per year; and they are over twice as likely to be poor. In fact, the poorest county in the United States is where the Pine Ridge Reservation of the Oglala Sioux is located. In 1989, 63.1 percent of Pine Ridge residents lived below the poverty line (compared with about 14 percent for the country

TABLE 9-10   Treading Water

After adjusting for inflation, U.S. household income has crested and subsided in several distinct waves over the past 25 years; 1991's average of $30 126, measured in constant 1991 dollars, was slightly lower than the $30 333 recorded in 1973.

Median Household Income

Year	Income	Year	Income
1991	$30 126	1978	$30 396
1990	31 203	1977	29 249
1989	31 750	1976	29 088
1988	31 344	1975	28 597
1987	31 246	1974	29 384
1986	30 940	1973	30 333
1985	29 896	1972	29 746
1984	29 383	1971	28 529
1983	28 741	1970	28 803
1982	28 737	1969	29 000
1981	28 833	1968	27 973
1980	29 309	1967	26 801
1979	30 297		

1991 Household Income by Race

Asian/Pacific Islander	$36 449
Anglo	$31 569
Latino	$22 691
Black	$18 807

SOURCE: U.S. Census Bureau, cited in *Los Angeles Times*, September 4, 1992, p. A27.

as a whole). In both Canada and the United States, the rates of educational participation among the aboriginal peoples are rising rapidly. This has not led to comparable gains in employment, occupations, or earnings, however. An important reason for this is that most Native peoples' reserves, along with Alaska, Yukon, and the Northwest Territories, where the aboriginal peoples are concentrated, are remote from centres of economic activity, poor in natural resources, and ill-suited to agriculture. Therefore, they offer few economic opportunities for those who live there, whether well educated or not.

The Foreign and the Native Born. Canada has had a continuing flow of immigrants in the twentieth century. Today, just under 1 in 7 Canadians are foreign-born. Of these, about 7 in 10 are European or American in origin. About 2 in 10 are from Asia or the Caribbean. Most of the European and American immigrants are white ("nonvisible") and came before 1967. By contrast, most of the Asian and Caribbean immigrants are nonwhite ("visible") and arrived in the 1970s or 1980s.

Overall, the foreign-born in Canada have about the same amounts of formal education and employment experience as the native-born. They also work about the same number of hours per week and weeks per year, and their occupations are similar. And, when certain statistical adjustment between the two populations are taken into account, the two groups earn about the same on the average. In Canada, therefore, there seems to be "no significant discrimination against immigrants in general" (deSilva 1992:36) (although it is likely that this is a consequence of an immigration policy that admits primarily the wealthy and the highly educated). Recent immigrants are more likely to be unemployed, however, than either not-so-recent ones or the native-born. As well, immigrants with foreign education certificates and experience earn less than either the native-born or immigrants with Canadian education and experience. Also, "it takes all but the youngest immigrants up to 20 years to catch up to the earnings of Canadians, though catch up they nearly always do" (deSilva 1992:36). Why might this be? DeSilva notes that immigrants, especially recent ones, are much less likely than native-born Canadians to speak English or French in the home. This suggests to him that there may be economic discrimination against the foreign-born, if they speak heavily accented English or French.

The United States stopped large-scale immigration in 1924 and started it again in the 1970s. The result is that about 1 in 15 Americans today is foreign-born. Just under 1 in 3 of the foreign-born is European in origin. About 1 in 5 is from Asia, an additional 1 in 5 is from Central America, and 1 in 10 is from the Caribbean. The European immigrants are nonvisible and not especially recent; the Asian, Central American, and Caribbean immigrants are typically quite visible and relatively recent. Especially in the major cities since World War II, conflicts between the native (both blacks and whites) and the foreign-born (Latinos and, more recently, South Asians) have waxed and waned but never really disappeared. These conflicts have taken distinctly economic tones in recent years, as in the boycotts of Korean variety-store owners by blacks in New York and Los Angeles. Mexico has no recent history of substantial immigration. It has, however, a continuing history of large-scale, illegal emigration, mainly to the United States.

Continental Economic Integration

In 1988 Canada, under the government of Prime Minister Brian Mulroney and the Conservative Party, signed a free-trade agreement with the United States. Yet, in his campaigns for the party leadership in 1984 and in the 1984 federal election, Mulroney either opposed such an agreement or said nothing about it. This remarkable sequence of events came about, Richardson (1992) argues, because of the unusual dominance of the capitalist class at that time. Under these conditions, the state typically enjoys little autonomy, and its policies closely reflect those of the dominant class. Business organizations in Canada predicted that the free-trade agreement would increase Canadian access to American markets, allow competitive companies to expand, and force noncompetitive ones to be more efficient or to go bankrupt. It would also provide cheaper products for Canadians. Organized labour anticipated that it would cause workers' wages and other benefits to drop and under- mine occupational health and safety measures. It would degrade environmental standards, and it would result in many American branch plants in Canada relocating to the United States or shutting down altogether. A worldwide economic recession began at about the same time as the free-trade agreement, however, making it difficult to determine what the effects of the agreement have actually been.

In 1990, Mexico persuaded the United States to enter into negotiations for a free-trade agreement. Traditionally, the Mexican government has been very protectionist. This changed in the early 1980s, however, when a sudden drop in oil export prices contributed to Mexico's defaulting on its international loan payments. Not long after, the Mexican government launched an economic reform program to make Mexican business more profitable. The government sold off many state-owned companies worth many billions of dollars, removed the privileges of corrupt union bosses, relaxed laws restricting foreign investment, and dismantled many trade barriers. For Mexico, a free-trade agreement with the United States would be an obvious next step. Although Mexico took the initiative, the United States became interested in more open economic relations with Mexico when the Mexican government eased export restrictions for the *maquiladoras*. The *maquiladoras* are approximately 2100 (mainly) United States–owned plants, employing some half a million Mexicans. They import parts and raw materials to Mexico for processing and export them duty-free back to (mainly) the United States. The Canadian government, concerned that foreign investors would avoid Canada if it were not part of a larger free-trade area, joined the discussions. In 1992, the three governments concluded negotiations on

Need Only Whites Apply?

In 1992, the Canadian Civil Liberties Association conducted a study of employment agencies in Canada in which, posing as U.S.-based employers, investigators inquired as to whether the agencies would refer only white people for job interviews. "One agency representative at first said her agency would not discriminate, but added, 'We will be selective.' When asked if the agency would screen out members of visible minority groups, she said: 'I got you, I got you ... screen out people ... Oh yeah, yeah. I don't think that would be a problem.'

"Another agency representative, noting that discriminatory hiring practices are illegal, said: 'You just don't do it over the phone ... but we can still satisfy the customer. ... We will do exactly what the customer wants, but just do it around the corner.'"

Source:

Galt, Virginia. "Agencies still prefer whites only" *The Globe and Mail*, September 8, 1992, p. A8.

what is likely to become a North American Free Trade Agreement (NAFTA).

In Canada and the United States, business and labour organizations hypothesize both advantages and disadvantages for NAFTA. On the one hand, it would open up opportunities for Canadian and American firms to sell capital goods of all kinds (for example, airplanes, electrical generating equipment, and resource extraction machinery) and to participate in major infrastructure construction projects (such as subway and telephone systems). The small but growing Mexican middle class offers new markets for Canadian and American consumer goods and services. Canadian and American companies would be made more efficient by having to compete in a larger market, and Canadians and Americans would have access to cheaper goods. Also, high-paying, high-skill jobs would stay in Canada and the United States, and low-paying, low-skill jobs would move to Mexico. On the other hand, workers' welfare would suffer. Standards of environmental protection would fall, and jobs would disappear as manufacturing operations were relocated to Mexico. At the same time, trade between Mexico and Canada is small. Ironically, we buy computers and television sets from Mexico; they buy newsprint, sulphur, and wheat from us. While trade between Mexico and the United States is large by comparison, Mexico is a minor United States trading partner. Also, the attractions of investment in Mexico may often be exaggerated. Labour turnover there is high, communication and transportation systems are underdeveloped, and worker skills are low. As a consequence, the real cost of Mexican labour may be much more than it first seems to be, and the real savings of relocating to Mexico may be small. So, the effects of NAFTA in Canada and the United States are likely to be modest, except in particular sectors of the economy.

The probable consequences of NAFTA for Mexico, however, are considerable. In particular, many new (mainly low-wage, relatively low-tech) industrial jobs will be relocated from Canada and the United States to that country. At the same time, many small Mexican businesses, such as the thousands of "mom-and-pop" lunch counters, are not likely to survive competition from large American corporations, such as fast-food outlets, leaving many workers unemployed. Also,

Mexican corn producers cannot compete successfully with their American counterparts, which will send many unskilled Mexican farm labourers to seek jobs in the cities. In addition, the big Mexican corporations will have to abandon their traditional practice of providing housing, social services, and other benefits to workers and their families. To make adjustments for displaced workers easier and to increase the benefits of free trade, the Mexican government has begun a $3 billion National Solidarity Program of public works projects to improve the country's infrastructure.

Conclusion

Nothing in nature, including human society, is ever predetermined. The major reason for this is that no individual person, social group, or other system is ever so isolated from influences outside itself that it can develop undisturbed. Events that cannot be anticipated beforehand always intervene to move a system in one unexpected direction or another. Consequently, although the best guide to what will happen in the future is what has occurred in the past, we can only project past trends into a likely future — we cannot accurately predict the future from knowledge of the past.

We are all witnesses to history. But we are all participants in history, too. That is, we observe social life and how it changes; we also influence how social life changes. So, not only is nothing ever predetermined in human society, we are active agents in charting the course that the societies in which we live take. As responsible members of society, we should be well informed of social trends and actively involved in the political decisions that might turn them toward the greater good. In the domain of social inequality, what are the major social trends? What are some of the directions that social change might take in the future?

The transformations of Canada and the United States from manufacturing to service economies are now largely complete. Overall, one consequence of the changing occupational mix involved in this seems to be that job skills have been upgraded over time (Hunter 1988). What this does not show and what none of the theories consid-

Some Possible Consequences of Nafta

BIG AZUL. Mexican workers are also doing jobs that were once exclusive to America's high-tech corridors. Mireya Ruíz, 27, is developing software for IBM in Guadalajara. Her husband, Jorge Ramos, also a programmer, works there, too. Jobs like hers pay high wages for Mexico, up to $1,600 a month. And despite IBM's turmoil in the U.S., its Mexico operation saw a 10% hike in sales last year and added 7% more jobs to the payroll. The head office even decided to move a big software project from Rochester, N.Y., to Guadalajara, where software engineers are as proficient as they are in the U.S. — and half as cheap. The plant is one of IBM's bright spots worldwide. It manufactures 140,000 PS/2 personal computers and 4,400 AS-400 intermediate computers each year — nearly all for export.

More typical, though, are Mexicans like Arturo Arriaga, the Monterrey steelworker. Two years ago, the high school graduate passed a battery of psychological and aptitude tests and was placed in an elite "multiskills program" at steelmaker Galvak. He and 129 others attended night classes and learned how to work in Japanese-style groups. Since then, productivity has jumped, and Arriaga's pay has risen from $47.75 to $67 per week, plus overtime. While that still doesn't give Arriaga a lot of money, he's not even thinking of joining his mother, a legal immigrant in the U.S. Screwing a bulb into a dangling light socket, he explains: "It's rare for companies to invest so much in training."

They sure don't along the 2,000-mile border with the U.S., where multinationals operate in a sort of no-man's land, with one foot on each side of the border. Originally, no one in Mexico City or Washington paid much attention. Since the *maquiladoras* bought and sold next to nothing in Mexico, government economists didn't even consider them a part of domestic industry. But while Mexico was preoccupied with its debt crisis in the 1980s, the *maquiladoras* quietly developed from simple, labor-intensive assembly into sophisticated, world-class manufacturing.

Mexico's junior-high-school dropouts are now learning the skills of plastic injection, manufacturing TV sets, and assembling refrigerators. Companies benchmark the *maquiladoras* against competitors in Malaysia, Taiwan, and Korea. "Now, we run our Mexican factories with basically the same premise as in the U.S.," says James Meyer, senior vice-president at Thomson Consumer Electronics Inc. in Indianapolis. "They use state-of-the-art, expensive, very, very modern equipment. These are not high-volume sweatshops."

MORALE BOOSTS. These days, Thomson doesn't hesitate to haul down the latest machinery to make its GE- and RCA-label TVs. But unlike the auto and appliance plants in Mexico's interior, the *maquiladoras* don't do as much training, pointing to the high turnover rate — reaching 10% a month. Instead, they keep wages low and can afford to add extra layers of quality control.

Plant managers go to great lengths to boost morale at *maquiladoras*. In many ways, they turn the plants into industrial high schools, giving their young drop-outs a version of high school life. They bus the workers to and from work and give them free lunch. They plaster walls with booster slogans and urge workers to play on the plant's soccer and baseball teams.

Still, workers desert the *maquiladoras* in droves, some quitting to take care of a child, others changing just to switch baseball teams. There's no loss in pay, since *maquiladora* associations fix salaries to avoid costly bidding. But after trying out two or three *maquiladoras*, many workers return home — or cross the U.S. border. Others take more lucrative work. "If you have to support yourself, the *maquila*'s impossible," says Virginia Segura, a 25-year-old prostitute in Tijuana who solicits business on a corner near the cathedral.

While the *maquiladoras* can boast of high growth and quality manufacturing, they're a public-relations disaster for NAFTA. Americans looking for a preview of North American free trade look first to the border, where they see industries that prevent their low-wage workers from organizing, while Mexico City looks the other way.

NAFTA opponents argue that this imbalance keeps Mexican wages low, hastening the southward migration of jobs and dragging salaries downward throughout the region. They point to workers such as Eligio Rodríguez, a 33-year-old industrial engineer in Ciudad Juárez. Rodríguez says he was fired last summer from his $123-a-week job at a components factory called Electrónica Dale, which belongs to Vishay Intertechnology Inc. in Malvern Pa. Now he's charging they fired and blackballed him for trying to organize a union. Dale's personnel chief, Robert Schmitt, won't answer questions about Rodríguez' case, saying only that Rodríguez is a member of the leftist Party of the Democratic Revolution, the PRI's main opposition.

That small conflict in Juarez is merely one signpost pointing to the battles that lie ahead. But in the long run, the turmoil certain to accompany union — on both sides of the border — could be worth it. After all, a democratic, productive, and prosperous Mexico could help power North American growth well into the 21st century. But it's a relationship that needs careful handling. Says Xerox Corp. CEO Paul A. Allaire: "The key challenge of NAFTA is assuring that the harmonization of U.S. and Mexican standards is upward, not downward."

Meanwhile, workers at the GE-Mabe plant in Queretaro are soaking up everything they can from an English-language video on refrigerator assembly. Asked if they understand English, one answers *Claro que si* — of course. The others nod, keeping their eyes on the TV.

These are new North American workers, ambitious and hardworking, the first foreigners ever to pursue the American dream without pulling up stakes. Without leaving home, these Mexican workers are changing the face of North America.

By Stephen Baker in Mexico City, Geri Smith in Monterrey, and Elizabeth Weiner in Ciudad Juárez.

Source:

Business Week, April 19, 1993, pp. 91–92.

ered here predicted, however, is that service jobs have become increasingly divided into the high-skill, high-paying jobs (such as systems engineer) and the low-skill, low-paying jobs (such as fast-food cashier), with fewer and fewer jobs in the middle (Myles and Fawcett 1990). One consequence of this, in turn, is probably the increasing levels of income inequality that can be observed in both countries in recent times. As for Mexico, the movement from an agricultural to a manufacturing economy clearly changes the kinds of skills that jobs require, but does not so obviously change the levels of occupational skill requirements — for example, is a farmhand more or less skilled than a factory worker? In all three cases, it should be noted, there is nothing inevitable in the changes that have taken place. Some affluent Western countries (Sweden, for example) have adopted policies to maintain their manufacturing sectors and inhibit the development of a "hamburger economy." And Mexico probably could have remained largely agricultural or taken some other course altogether.

In all three countries, there are at best only loose connections between merit and rewards and no clear trends over time. The very rich are usually lucky people from well-to-do families or individuals with unusual skills in areas of popular culture that, for reasons of historical accident, just happen to command a high price. The better educated do tend to get more desirable jobs and earn more. This is probably due in part to their being more productive workers. It is probably also due in part to their being able to exact a premium in pay because of the extra status that their diplomas and degrees carry (Hunter and Leiper 1993). And it is probably also due in part to their tending to come from economically and socially advantaged families to begin with. Women in Canada, the United States, and Mexico are less likely than men to be employed and, when they do work for pay, they earn less on the average than men with similar qualifications and equivalent jobs. Over time, the gender-earnings gap has narrowed considerably in the United States. It has narrowed relatively little, however, in Canada, and it is not clear what has happened to it in Mexico. Finally, if some ethnic or racial inequalities may have decreased in recent years (for example, Asians in Canada and the United States),

others have not (aboriginal peoples in Canada and the United States).

Governments can deal with inequalities in wealth in many ways, including taxes. Steeply progressive income taxes can redistribute wealth. Wealth and inheritance taxes (Canada has neither) can redistribute wealth in the current generation and reduce inequalities in affluence inherited from the previous generation. Affirmative action and pay- or employment-equity legislation can address inequalities originating in workplace discrimination.

Affirmative-action programs, in which members of a disadvantaged group are accepted for education or employment under a set of rules different from those applying to other people, have a fairly long history in the United States. They are more recent in Canada. In Canada, Ontario has been quite active among political jurisdictions in North America in attempting to identify and deal with discrimination on the job. This began with a pay-equity plan for men and women and, to be implemented shortly, an employment-equity plan for certain designated groups. Briefly, Ontario's planned employment-equity scheme would target four groups: aboriginals, people with disabilities, members of visible minorities, and women. Under it, employers would be obliged to employ and promote people in each of these groups in proportion to their representation in the community and in various occupations.

Finally, solutions to one social problem can create new social problems. The rich sometimes flee high income, wealth, or inheritance taxes by moving to other countries. This at once preserves their possessions and denies the home country tax revenues to redistribute. Affirmative-action programs, at issue in 1992 for women and visible-minority-group firefighters in Kitchener and Toronto, are often controversial because they aim to eliminate discrimination against a disadvantaged group by creating discrimination against an advantaged one. When implemented, such programs frequently leave members of the disadvantaged group feeling that they are not worthy, despite their success, and members of the advantaged one feeling that they are failures, despite their worth. Finally, pay- and employment-equity schemes generally require that substantial government bureaucracies be established if they are to succeed. Thus, they can be quite expensive to put into place and administer. This directs resources away from other places where they may be needed.

SUMMARY

1. There are three main contending theories of inequality: the Marxist model, the Weberian model, and the functionalist Davis–Moore model. Postindustrial theory, in the arguments of different authors, may be Marxist, Weberian, or functionalist.

2. According to Marxist theory, the bourgeoisie is the dominant class in capitalism, and the major social institutions, including government, operate mainly on its behalf. The self-employed comprise the petite bourgeoisie. The employees are the working or proletarian class.

3. According to Weber, class and class conflict are important in understanding social organization and social change, but so, too, are status groups and status-group conflict. Status groups are collections of people who share similar levels of honour or prestige and a particular subculture or style of life. Status groups are often defined along occupational, racial–ethnic, or religious lines.

4. According to the functional theory of stratification, there is social inequality or "social stratification" because, in any society, the work necessary to maintain individuals and the group is divided among various positions, some of which are more important than others for societal survival and more demanding in their skill requirements. It matters, therefore, who performs which tasks; thus, these jobs must offer extra income, prestige, leisure time, or other rewards.

5. Postindustrial society theory argues that advanced capitalism is in transition to a new form of society in which the provision of services replaces the production of goods as the foundation of the economy.

6. Relational inequalities are those in which one individual or group yields to the demands of or voluntarily acquiesces to the wishes of an-

other. Distributive inequalities are those in which some people or groups possess more of some scarce and valued resource, such as education, income, or wealth, than others do.

7. The two definitions of poverty — absolute and relative — are discussed. Relative poverty is defined in terms of the poor having fewer resources than the non-poor (less income to spend on such items as food, clothing, or shelter). Absolute poverty refers to the poor as those not able to provide the essential requirements of life.

8. The goal of taxation policies and transfer payments is to redistribute income from the wealthy to the poor; in reality, little income is redistributed.

9. The structure of occupational prestige in Canada parallels that of other developed countries. The various religious, ethnic, and racial groups in Canada have different levels of social prestige.

10. There is substantial inequality in the distribution of authority in Canada.

GLOSSARY

Absolute poverty. The inability to provide for the essential requirements of life.

Achieved status. A position in a status hierarchy attained by individual effort, such as educational or occupational attainment.

Ascribed status. A position in a status hierarchy into which an individual is born or assigned on the basis of inherited characteristics, such as sex or race.

Authority. The ability of an individual or group to have their commands obeyed because their commands are perceived as legitimate.

Bourgeoisie. Karl Marx's term for people who own and control the means of production.

Class. A set of individuals sharing similar economic conditions.

Class consciousness. Groups of people sharing the same economic position who are aware of their common class position and identify with it.

Class, status, party. For Max Weber, class is economic, status is prestige, and party is political power. All three are measures of inequality and can vary independently.

Closed class-caste. A society characterized by maximum inequalities of opportunity. There is little or no upward mobility, and positions are assigned by ascription.

Distributive inequalities. Inequalities in privileges and possessions.

Objective class analysis. A measurement of social classes based on such factors as occupation, income, and education.

Open-class society. A society in which opportunities for social mobility are maximized.

Prestige. Social honour, reputation, or respect.

Relational inequalities. Relational inequalities are those in which one individual or group yields to the demands of or voluntarily acquiesces to the wishes of another.

Relative poverty. Economic deprivation compared with the resources other individuals or groups.

Social inequality. A situation in which the members of society have unequal amounts of valued resources, such as money or power, and unequal opportunities to obtain them.

Social mobility. Upward or downward movement of individuals or groups into different positions in the social hierarchy.

Structural mobility. Social mobility that occurs as a result of occupational changes.

Subjective class analysis. The definition and measurement of social class based on respondents' perceptions of their own position in the class hierarchy.

FURTHER READING

Boyd, Monica, et al. *Ascription and Achievement.* Ottawa: Carleton University Press, 1985. The best source on opportunity and mobility in Canada.

Breton, Raymond, et al. *Ethnic Identity and Equality.* Toronto: University of Toronto Press, 1990. An analysis of the relationship between ethnicity and inequality for eight ethnic groups in Toronto.

Canadian Social Trends. An invaluable resource for sociologists.

Curtis, James, et al. *Social Inequality in Canada.* Scarborough, ON: Prentice-Hall, 1988. A collection of readings about the Canadian case.

Grabb, Edward G. *Theories of Social Inequality: Classical and Contemporary Perspectives.* 2nd edition. Toronto: Holt, Rinehart and Winston, 1990. A lucid introduction to the major theoretical perspectives on inequality.

Hunter, Alfred A. *Class Tells: On Social Inequality in Canada.* 2nd edition. Toronto: Butterworths, 1986. An informative Canadian text.

CHAPTER 10

Ethnic and Minority Relations

LEO DRIEDGER

"Ethnic" comes from the Greek word *ethnos*, meaning a group bound together and identified by ties and traits of nationality, culture, and race. French Québécois, for example, promote a national and cultural ethos that originated in France. Aboriginals, too, have subcultural and racial ties and traits. Canadians whose origin was British identify with their heritage as well. Each of these three groups constitutes *ethnos*.

An **ethnic group**, according to Shibutani and Kwan (1965), "consists of those who perceive ... themselves as being alike by virtue of their common ancestry, real or fictitious, and who are so regarded by others." An ethnic group includes a sense of belonging and particular ways of acting, thinking, and feeling.

Gordon's (1964) definition differs somewhat in emphasis from Shibutani and Kwan's: "An ethnic group is a group of individuals with a shared sense of peoplehood based on presumed shared sociocultural experiences and/or similar characteristics." This sense of sharing includes all di-

299

mensions of language, nationality, culture, religion, and race. This is the group's **ethnic identity**. Ethnicity is thus a very broad term, which recognizes that all people have basic historical origins, but that the form and importance of this heritage may vary from group to group. Their sense of belonging and loyalty may also vary.

When people of many different nations, cultures, religions, and races come into contact with each other, some are bound to be more numerous, or influential, or both. Thus, minority/majority relations are inevitable. A group can be considered a minority if it either has fewer members than another group or has less influence than another group. In Canada, the Hutterites are considered a minority on both these counts: their numbers are relatively few, and they also lack political power. The Jews are also considered a minority group, but largely because their numbers are relatively small; they have more influence than their numbers might suggest. French Canadians are a minority, too — everywhere except Quebec, where they are the numerical and political majority. While Canadians of British origin constitute the majority in the Atlantic provinces and Ontario, they constitute a minority in Quebec, due solely to their relatively small numbers in that province. In Canada, much of the economic — as well as political — power is concentrated in the hands of British Canadians.

Wagley and Harris (1958) summarize five important characteristics of minorities:

1. Minorities are subordinate segments of complex societies.
2. They have special physical or cultural traits that are usually held in low esteem by the dominant society.
3. They are self-conscious units bound together by special traits.
4. Membership is transmitted by descent, capable of affiliating succeeding generations.
5. By choice or necessity members usually marry within the group.

According to these general characteristics, Hutterites, aboriginals, blacks, and Jews will almost always be seen as minorities in Canada. Germans, Ukrainians, Scandinavians, and Italians will also constitute minorities most of the time. The basic difference between an ethnic group and a minor-

ity group is that each of us belongs to an ethnic group or groups, while not everyone belongs to a **minority group**. Minority status has to do with either the size or the lack of power of a group.

Europeans in a New World

When the year 1992 arrived, North Americans could not decide whether to celebrate or mourn Columbus's arrival in the Americas 500 years ago. New technology in the late sixteenth century propelled the Spanish, the British, the French, and other Europeans across the Atlantic, but they did not soon learn to live with the original inhabitants of the Americas. They sailed west to bring home the spices they valued from the Asian east, but found the Americas blocking their way. The search for a northwest passage to the Orient continued for centuries. Meanwhile, European diseases like smallpox devastated the aboriginal populations, and those who survived were sometimes befriended but too often slaughtered, robbed, enslaved, and segregated on reserves within their own lands. Race and ethnic relations must be discussed in the context of these tragedies. That is why many could not celebrate the coming of Columbus to the Americas.

The Spanish in Mexico

Columbus's expedition was sponsored by the Spanish crown. He landed in the Caribbean and began exploring the islands in the Gulf of Mexico. Soon, the Spaniards found the three great civilizations of the Maya (already in decline) in Central America, the Inca in Peru, and the Aztecs in central Mexico (now Mexico City). Today, the Plaza of Three Cultures venerates the Aztec, Spanish, and mixed-blood (*mestizaje*) cultures that have emerged. In front of the church a plaque carries these words: "On August 13, 1521, heroically defended by Cuauhtémoc, Tlatelolco fell into the hands of Hernán Cortés. It was neither a triumph nor a defeat: it was the painful birth of the *mestizo* nation that is Mexico today" (Riding 1989:3). Ethnically, 90 percent of Mexicans today are mixed bloods called *mestizos*.

Hardly 30 years after Columbus first landed in America, Hernán Cortés and his small band of

Spanish conquistadors found the beautiful city-state of Tenochtitlan, with a population estimated at 80 000, on an island in the centre of Lake Texcoco, now the site of Mexico City. The inhabitants of the city-state were ruled by Moctezuma and later Cuauhtémoc, who had subjugated the surrounding peoples. When Cortés first saw the city's pyramids, palaces, markets, and the imperial power of the Aztecs in 1519, he marvelled at its splendour. There was also much gold, which the Spaniards craved. After several battles, the city and the Aztec empire fell to the Spaniards in 1521.

After Tenochtitlan fell, the Spaniards destroyed the capital, built Roman Catholic churches from the ruins of Aztec temples, and as new masters enslaved many to work gold and silver mines and fields (Riding 1989:29). The Spanish came mostly as conquering males without their families, so rape and intermarriage were common. The conquistadors struck out from Mexico City, spreading death through destruction, massacres, and European diseases. Perhaps two-thirds of the victims died from smallpox and other European diseases. Some Indians fled to the mountains, deserts, and jungles, but most were dominated by the Spanish conquistadors. Their religion became a blend of Roman Catholic and Aztec rituals. Very few settlers came from Spain as families, so the meeting of peoples resulted in European–aboriginal mixes of culture and race.

The British American Colonies

In 1607, the British established their first colony at Williamsburg, Virginia, on the east coast of what is now the United States. The families came to settle permanently to work the land as agriculturalists, not to dominate and exploit. Many European settlers were themselves fleeing persecution. They settled on lands inhabited by aboriginals who were food-gatherers and producers, not city and empire builders like the Maya, Aztecs, and Incas. Aboriginals and Europeans often lived together peaceably, but conflict inevitably grew as more and more British, German, Dutch, and other European immigrants increasingly occupied the aboriginal lands. The pressures for more land often drove the aboriginals farther west, where they were followed by European invaders.

Here too, European diseases decimated aboriginal populations. While these people were not usually enslaved, they were pushed westward increasingly, until Europeans also wanted their hunting grounds in the nineteenth century. As western territories became new states, they joined the union of states in the east. To make room, reservations were formed, onto which the aboriginals were gathered, often by force and with much bloodshed. Many aboriginals did not sit by idly without fights while the buffalo were slaughtered and their livelihoods destroyed. By now, the European population was mushrooming through the influx of immigrants from Europe. The food-gathering peoples could not effectively resist the coming of the more numerous immigrants.

While Europeans increasingly invaded aboriginal territories, they prospered as agriculturalists, especially in the southeast, by raising cotton, which was raw material for British clothing factories. Ships carrying cargoes of cotton to Europe began stopping along the African cost on the return trip to pick up cargoes of black slaves. European capitalists soon developed a lucrative slave trade by buying and selling humans to work the cotton fields of America, with escalating profits both ways across the Atlantic. A slave class emerged in America, over which the free North and slave South fought a bloody civil war in the 1860s. Some 125 years later, white–black racism has become a major means of stratification in the United States, even after schools, jobs, and institutions were allegedly racially integrated.

Although the United States took half of Mexico's territory from Florida to California and up the West Coast in the 1800s, even today the Mexican American population, too, is not well integrated. Today, large numbers of legal and illegal Mexican immigrants are entering the southern United States, seeking work in the orchards and gardens of the southwest. While European groups may have increasingly become a "melting pot," these whites have been careful to resist racial intermarriage. The United States is experiencing a new type of ethnic relations, quite different from that in Mexico (Lieberson and Waters 1990).

New France and Acadia

While many European countries fished on the Grand Banks of Newfoundland before 1500, it was not until 100 years later that the French first

The British royal family is a symbol of British ancestry shared by many descendants of British immigrants.

settled at Port Royal (now Nova Scotia) in 1605 and Quebec in 1608, the same time Williamsburg was founded (Vallieres 1988). These French settlements, started by Samuel de Champlain, brought settlers to create a New France in Acadia and along the St. Lawrence River. Like the settlers along the U.S. East coast, these newcomers were agriculturalists and fishing people. Farther north along the St. Lawrence, French settlers had generally good relations with aboriginals, quite unlike the European fishermen who hunted Newfoundland's aboriginal Beothuks to extinction.

While gold in Mexico and cotton in the United States drove European entrepreneurs, in Canada it was the fur trade. Rather than enslaving aborig-

inals and blacks, French and British fur traders developed trading routes via the *coureurs de bois* between Montreal and the West and Hudson's Bay and the West. The aboriginals became important suppliers of furs, in exchange for European goods. The aboriginal–European trade networks resulted in mutual benefits, including intermarriage and the formation of a Métis nation on the Prairies.

The competition and wars between European colonial powers to gain control of raw materials in the colonies were often fought on Canadian soil. Acadia and parts of the Atlantic territories changed hands many times between the British and French, until in 1759 New France (now Quebec) became part of the British empire. During these colonial struggles, Native peoples found themselves siding either with the French or the British in many battles. Early Canadian aboriginals became part of the European colonial agenda in the struggles of these capitalist enterprises. In the 1990s, never-ending constitutional talks are part of the heritage of unjust wars in the past. According to some, New France should have remained a free, independent nation like English Canada, the United States, and Mexico, maintaining the French language, culture, and sovereignty. That is what the Québécois nationalist movement is trying to recover.

Power Relations of Peoples

The European invasions and occupation of North America in the past 500 years is clearly a history of European colonial dominance over nonindustrialized aboriginals who were forced into subservience. Unquestionably, the power has been with the Spanish in Mexico, the northern Europeans in the United States, and the British and French in Canada. The patterns of dominance, however, have varied demographically. In Canada the two colonial (British and French) powers have always dominated; in the United States, the British and Germans have been dominant demographically; and in Mexico a small minority of Spanish have dominated.

These patterns of power relations continue to affect contemporary ethnic and racial power relations in the three countries (see Table 10-1). In Mexico, less than one in ten of the population is of only Spanish origin. This small minority of whites is looked up to, however, while the nearly one-third who are aboriginal are at the bottom of the stratification system. The vast majority (90 percent) are *mestizos*. Skin colour and wealth are important markers of status. Even among *mestizos* light-coloured skin is highly valued (Riding 1989:30). Clearly race, culture, and social status are three means of stratification.

The British, the first European arrivals in the United States, still make up the largest segment of the American population. The Germans are in second place. The 27 million blacks in the United States represent one out of eight Americans, more than the total population of Canada. It is estimated that roughly one-third of the population

TABLE 10-1 Percentages of Selected Ethnic Groups in Mexico, Canada, and the United States

Ethnic Groups	Mexico (1990)[a]	USA (1980)[b]	Canada (1981)[c]
British		45	40
French		6	27
German		22	5
Spanish	9	2	
Mixed	60		7
Black		12	
Aboriginal	29	3	2
Other	2	10	19

SOURCE: [a]World Almanac and Book of Facts, New York: Harper, 1992; [b]Stanley Lieberson and Mary C. Waters, *From Many Strands: Ethnic and Racial Groups in Contemporary America* (New York: Russell Sage Foundation, 1990), p. 34. U.S. Bureau of the Census, 1980 Census of Population, Supplementary Report. "Ancestry of the Population by State, PC 80-S1-10 (Washington, DC: U.S. Government Printing Office, 1983), table 1; [c]Statistics Canada 1981 Catalogue 92-910, 1981 Census and catalogue number 92-912, 1981 Census. Ottawa: Minister of Supply and Services Canada.

are of mixed origins and that only 3 percent are of aboriginal heritage. The dominance of the two European groups is clearly evident demographically, and they are also heavily represented among the higher classes.

In Canada, English and French Canadians make up roughly two-thirds of the population. Canada's multicultural policy is also evident; only 7 percent of Canadians declare a mixed heritage (Fleras and Elliot 1992a). Aboriginals represent only 2 percent of the population. Historically, then, as the British and French have been the most important ethnic demographic factor in Canada and the British and Germans in the United States, the *mestizos* have been the greatest factor in Mexico.

Canadian Immigration

To understand the patterns of ethnic relations in Canada, we must first analyze the demographic and ecological macrostructures. (The term *ecological* is used here in the sociologists' sense of having

Being *Mestizo*: Ethnicity in Mexico

Mexico calls itself a *mestizo* nation, as do most countries in Latin America. But racially, Mexico is more like Colombia or Venezuela than like Argentina or Paraguay, and the word *mestizo* has a double meaning. In general use, *mestizo* means "born of parents of different race," and in that sense, Mexico is a *mestizo* nation, but the term tells us little, because it does not specify the parent races. *Mestizo* historically meant "born to a Spanish and an Indian parent," and in that sense — a sense that Mexicans still adopt to describe themselves today — it is more often wishful than real.

Indo-America suffered a holocaust when the Spaniards came, but most of the decimation was bloodless. Plagues killed people by the millions. The Spanish brought measles, chicken pox, smallpox, and probably malaria, diseases that had been unknown before, and for which Indians had not developed resistance. The indigenous population was reduced in the span of a century from some 15 million to 25 million — nobody knows for sure — to about three-quarters of a million. Even the most conservative estimates place the death rate at six-sevenths of the total population. Every family had members to mourn.

As the indigenous population sank, mines and plantations faced labor shortages. Spaniards brought African slaves to cover the labor shortfall. Census figures for the colonial era show that from 1570 to about 1650, blacks outnumbered whites in New Spain by a ratio of three to one. Even afterward, when the balance shifted, the black population remained half as great as the population of Caucasian descent. What these ratios mean is that Africans probably contributed as much to Mexico's gene pool as Spaniards ever did. But Mexico remained a predominantly Indian country. Even at their peak, Europeans and *criollos*, or native-born persons of European descent, accounted for no more than eight one-thousandths of the total population. The country's indigenous or Indian population was always 60 percent or more of the total, but as the decades passed, a mixed-race population came to life. By 1810, it constituted New Spain's second-biggest population block, of nearly 40 percent. With independence in 1821, both immigration and the keeping of racial records waned, but most scholars believe that today Mexico's majority is of mixed race. But it is not necessarily *mestizo*....

During the colonial years, one's status at law depended upon pedigree, and the Spaniards developed a dizzying set of codes to keep track. An Indian who had a European grandparent, for example, was termed a *mestindio*, an Indian with an African grandparent, a *mulato lobo*, etcetera. Ultimately, all these codes proved unworkable, because the number of possible racial permutations is infinite. But those codes shed light on the word *mestizo*, and on the way that Mexico works today.

According to the codes, colonial authorities could grant or deny certain obligations, immunities, and privileges, based on findings of race. For example, Spaniards and *criollos* had access to the professions. Nonwhites were barred. Indians could not own guns or horses, but they were entitled to communal lands, and were at times exempted from taxes that Spaniards and *criollos* had to pay. As in the United States, it was illegal to hold whites in slavery. The enslavement of Indians or of persons of mixed ancestry was sometimes restricted and sometimes banned outright, depending upon changing historical circumstances. But African slavery was always legal. A *mulato pardo*, as a child

---

to do with the spacing of people and institutions, and their resulting interdependency.) When did the many peoples first come to the land we now call Canada, and where have they settled? Did Canadians of various racial, ethnic, cultural, and religious origins cluster more in one region than another? If so, why? What are the implications of such varied enclaves and patterns for ethnic relations?

A Demographic History

To document the coming of *Homo sapiens* to Canada, we begin with the earliest Native peoples. They were followed much later by the French and British, who traded in and settled this vast territory. Later still, many other Europeans came — and, more recently, Third World immigrants. A short history will help us gain some perspective on who came when and to whom Canada belongs.

The Earliest Inhabitants. Anthropologists tell us that the earliest *Homo sapiens* came to the two American continents at least 12 000 years ago, probably via the Bering Strait. (The aboriginals were here, therefore, when the Europeans were barbarians roaming the European continent.) In the sixteenth century, the French and British immigrants encountered aboriginals on the central plains and northlands who were food gatherers. The Hurons and Iroquois had begun farming

born to an African and an Indian parent was called, could not be legally enslaved, but could also not partake of the landed status accorded the Indian population by Spanish law. Most of the mixed-race population lived in a legal netherworld, more at liberty than the Africans, but not as protected as the Indians or as privileged as the Spaniards.

A mistaken theory about "dominant blood" led the Spaniards to design codes in which Negritude or African ancestry was always a negative factor. For example, most of the codes permitted the Spanish entitlement of persons whose great-grandmothers had been of the indigenous race if their parents and grandparents were all of Spanish lineage. But some of the codes denied European status to anyone who admitted African ancestry of any kind. Liberalization of the codes allowed for the European entitlement of ostensible Spaniards who could show an absence of African ancestry back to the generation of their great-grandparents, i.e., a generation later than those whose ancestry was measured on the Euro-Indian scale. Because the Europeanizing provisions of the codes were not realistic — thousands of legal non-whites were accepted as white in everyday life — their chief effect may have been to encourage evasion of the law. The codes left modern Mexico a legacy of contempt, and also a discon-

certing phrase, "*mejorar la raza*," or "to improve the race." Improvement, in the context of the phrase, means whitening or Europeanization.

The term *mestizo* designated a category in the old racial codes. An ostensible Spaniard was called a *cuarterón* under the codes if he had a black grandparent, and a *castizo* if his non-white grandparent had been Indian. The child of a black and a white parent was called a *mulato*, as under the racial codes once in effect in the United States. The child of a white and an Indian was called a *mestizo*: The term that Mexico uses to describe itself means not only "born to parents of different race," but something much more precise. The grandchildren of *mestizos* were eligible for European privileges if their parents were both white, but the grandchildren of *mulatos* were not. *Mestizo* was an official term that implied an absence of African ancestry in a country where blacks were nearly as numerous as whites. As a term to describe the Mexican nation as a whole, it greatly exaggerated Spanish lineage. It also associated Mexicanhood with an economic strata, that of the overseers' class. *Mestizos* were the foremen of the mixed-race and Indian populations. A recent study of 145 ranches and plantations near Córdoba, Veracruz, in 1788, for example, shows that "the Spaniards registered, in their majority, were

owners of ranches.... The *mestizos* many times appear registered as foremen of a ranch owned by a Spaniard.... In respect to the 145 ranches, we found only three of them as property of indigenes. No Indian was foreman on any ranch in which the owner was a Spaniard." The term *mestizo*, when it originally came into Mexican use, implicitly depicted Mexico as a nation that had been somehow denied the privileges of first rank, but as one that, in the span of two generations, could almost magically acquire European (and therefore improved) standing. It made the same sort of claim that Mexico's modernizers have been making in political life ever since.

The legacy of African slavery in Mexico is strongest in two coastal states where plantations were vast, Veracruz and Guerrero. Both states are home to towns whose populations are largely black, and the traits of African ancestry are widely distributed across their general or *mestizo* populations.

Source:

Dick J. Reavis, *Conversations with Montezuma: Ancient Shadows over Modern Life in Mexico* (New York: Morrow, 1990), pp. 248–251. Copyright © 1990. By permission of William Morrow & Company, Inc.

(Trigger 1969), however, and the Natives of the West Coast were engaged in large-scale fishing (Rohner and Rohner 1970).

Canadians tend to see a very small part of the great variety of aboriginal groupings who live throughout the two Americas. We also often forget that the aboriginals have lived in what is now Canada 25 times longer than have any Europeans. This fact gives rise to interesting questions: Whose land is Canada, and what are the land rights of Native peoples who have not yet signed treaties with white immigrants?

The Charter Europeans. The French and British settlers in Canada are considered by Porter (1965) as Canada's two **charter groups.**

In 1871, when the first census after Confederation was taken, almost all (92 percent) of the 3.5 million people who lived in Canada were either of British (61 percent) or French (31 percent) origin. Except for a small number of Germans (6 percent), early eastern Canada was two-thirds British and one-third French. Table 10-2 lists immigrants to Canada by nationality. The 1871 census did not include the estimated half million or more aboriginals scattered over the northern territories, because the census included only the four original eastern provinces — only a fraction of the territory that is now Canada.

The British North American Act, 1867, legalized the claims of the two original European immigrant groups for such historically established

TABLE 10-2   Country of Origin of the Canadian Population,[a] 1871–1991

Ethnic Group	1871[b]	1901	1921	1941	1961	1981	1991[f]
Total[c]	3 486	5 371	8 788	11 507	18 238	24 084	26 994
Charter Europeans							
British	2 111	3 063	4 869	5 716	7 997	9 674	7 712
French	1 083	1 649	2 453	3 483	5 540	6 439	6 179
Other Europeans	240	458	1 247	2 044	4 117	4 625	4 146
Austrian, n.o.s.	—	11	108	38	107	41	27
Belgian	—	3	20	30	61	43	31
Czech & Slovak	—	—	9	43	93	68	59
Finnish[d]	—	3	21	42	59	52	39
German	203	311	295	465	1 050	1 142	912
Greek	—	—	6	12	56	154	151
Hungarian[e]	—	2	13	55	126	116	101
Italian	1	11	67	113	450	748	750
Jewish	—	16	126	170	173	264	246
Dutch	30	34	118	213	430	408	358
Polish	—	6	53	167	324	254	273
Portuguese	—	—	—	—	—	188	247
Russian	1	20	100	84	119	49	38
Scandinavian	2	31	167	245	387	283	174
Ukrainian	—	6	107	306	473	530	407
Other European	4	5	37	61	102	285	333
Asiatics	—	24	66	74	122	742	1 353
Chinese	—	17	40	35	58	289	587
Indo-Pakistani	—	—	—	—	—	121	420
Indochinese	—	—	—	—	—	44	116
Japanese	—	5	16	23	29	41	49
Other	—	2	10	16	34	247	181
American Aboriginals	—	—	—	—	—	632	556
Indian	—	93	110	117	208	413	365
Inuit	—	—	—	9	12	23	30
Métis	—	—	—	—	—	78	75
Hispanic American	—	—	—	—	—	118	86
Multiple Origins	—	—	—	—	—	1 761	7 048
Other	52	84	53	64	242	191	—
Black	—	—	—	—	—	—	225

[a]Numbers rounded to the nearest 1000.
[b]Four original provinces only.
[c]Excludes Newfoundland prior to 1941.
[d]Includes Estonia prior to 1941.
[e]Includes Lithuania and Moravia in 1901.
[f]Statistics Canada, *Ethnic Origin, The Nation*, catalogue no. 93-315, 1993, pp. 12–26.
SOURCE: Dominion Bureau of Statistics, *1961 Census of Canada*, Bulletin 7:1–6, 1966, Table 1; Statistics Canada, *1971 Census of Canada*, Bulletin 1:3–2, 1973, Table 1; D. Kubat and D. Thornton, *A Statistical Profile of Canadian Society* (Toronto: McGraw-Hill Ryerson, 1974), Table 1-10; Statistics Canada, *1981 Census of Canada*, catalogue no. 91-911 (Ottawa: Minister of Supply and Services, February 1984).

privileges as the perpetuation of their separate languages and cultures. The Royal Commission on Bilingualism and Biculturalism (1965) continued to support and encourage the charter-group status of the French — even though, by 1981, immigrants of other ethnic origins composed one-third of the Canadian population. By 1991, they composed one-half.

Since so much of the history of Canada has been dominated by the presence of these two charter

The first immigrants came to Canada at least 12 000 years ago, probably via the Bering Strait.

(European-origin) groups, Canadian literature in every field tends to reflect French–English relations. Both Britain and France explored various regions of North America, and numerous skirmishes and wars were fought: the most famous in 1759, when Canada became British. However, the Acadians had already lived in the St. Lawrence region for 150 years; their roots and traditions were well entrenched. So it was necessary to recognize distinctive English and French regions of influence on the Canadian upper and lower shores of the St. Lawrence River. Since then, the francophones in Quebec and the anglophones in the rest of Canada have tended to see each other across the Ottawa and St. Lawrence rivers as distinctive cultural and linguistic solitudes. Some scholars have called these solitudes "two na-

tions" residing in one (Crean and Rioux 1983; Fleras and Elliott 1992a).

Much research has evolved dealing with English–French relations. Breton, Reitz, and Valentine (1980) address the problem of cultural boundaries and how this affects the cohesion of Canada; Richmond and Kalbach (1980) are concerned with the proportions of populations and their adjustments; deVries and Vallee (1980) focus on languages; Crean and Rioux (1983) are interested in politics and power relations; Berry, Kalin, and Taylor (1977) studied the attitudes of Canadians with respect to this duality and the potential for pluralism. Although the history of Canada has been influenced mostly by these two charter groups, a shift is taking place that will modify the original dominance of the early Europeans.

The Multi-European Entrance. Although European settlers other than the French and British represented only about 7 percent of the Canadian population in 1871, many more have since immigrated to join the two charter groups. Table 10-3 shows that in 1901 the charter groups constituted a great majority; but by 1991 this majority had dwindled to roughly half, and the others represented the other half of the Canadian population. While the French-origin population held more steady, the proportion of British origin had dropped drastically. The British and French ranked first and second, followed by the Germans, Italians, and Ukrainians.

Most of these other European groups entered Canada well after the charter groups. Many of the Germans came to Ontario as early as 150 years ago, but the majority of the others arrived in a country where the charter groups had already established the political and economic patterns. In other words, the rules were made and the terms of admission were set down. Some of the earlier European immigrants, such as the Germans, Scandinavians, and Jews, had a relatively high status and have been upwardly mobile, but more recent immigrants, with some notable exceptions, have remained largely in the lower strata of Canadian society.

Recent Third World Immigrants. Table 10-4 shows that in 1951, shortly after World War II, the leading immigrant source countries were predominantly northern European; in 1990, a prominent

TABLE 10-3 Composition of the Population of Canada by Ethnic Origin, 1901 and 1991 (Percent)

Ethnic Origin	Total	B.C.	Alta.	Sask.	Man.	Ont.	Que.	NB	NS	PEI	Nfld.
1901											
British	57.0	59.6	47.8	43.9	64.4	79.3	17.6	71.1	78.1	85.1	
French	30.7	2.6	6.2	2.9	6.3	7.3	80.2	24.2	9.8	13.4	
Other	12.3	37.9	46.0	53.2	29.4	13.4	2.2	4.1	12.0	1.5	
Total	100.0	100.0	100.0	100.0	100.0	100.0	100.0	100.0	100.0	100.0	
1991											
British	28.6	35.5	28.1	23.7	25.0	35.7	5.1	44.3	58.4	65.6	88.4
French	22.9	2.1	3.0	3.1	5.0	5.3	74.6	32.8	6.2	9.2	1.7
Other	19.6	33.0	35.0	37.7	40.0	36.5	12.3	4.5	9.6	3.7	2.4
Multiple	28.9	29.4	33.9	35.5	30.0	22.5	8.0	18.4	25.8	21.5	7.5
Total	100.0	100.0	100.0	100.0	100.0	100.0	100.0	100.0	100.0	100.0	100.0

SOURCE: Dominion Bureau of Statistics, *1921 Census of Canada*, Vol. 1, 1924, Table 23; Statistics Canada, *Ethnic Origin, The Nation*, catalogue no. 93-315, 1993.

number of the ten leading source countries were Third World countries. This change in immigration trends to some extent reflects the change in Canadian immigration procedure from a discriminatory to a point system, which was introduced to provide immigrants of all countries with a more equitable chance to enter Canada.

The new regulations for selection of immigrants, established in 1967 and modified from time to time, set forth nine criteria for entrance.

"Independent" applicants are assessed by and awarded points according to these nine criteria; those able to score 50 or more points out of 100 are given permission to enter Canada, from any part of the world. Canadian citizens may also sponsor close relatives by agreeing to support them if necessary for the first year. "Sponsored" close relatives do not need to meet the requirements of the point system. The "nominated" applicant (intermediate between "independent"

TABLE 10-4 The Leading Source Countries of Immigrants, Selected Years

1951	1960	1968	1976	1984	1990
Britain	Italy	Britain	Britain	Vietnam	Hong Kong
Germany	Britain	United States	United States	Hong Kong	Poland
Italy	United States	Italy	Hong Kong	United States	Lebanon
Netherlands	Germany	Germany	Jamaica	India	Philippines
Poland	Netherlands	Hong Kong	Lebanon	Britain	India
France	Portugal	France	India	Poland	Vietnam
United States	Greece	Austria	Philippines	Philippines	Portugal
Belgium	France	Greece	Portugal	El Salvador	China
Yugoslavia	Poland	Portugal	Italy	Jamaica	Britain
Denmark	Austria	Yugoslavia	Guyana	China	United States

SOURCE: Department of Manpower and Immigration, *The Immigration Program*, Vol. 2, *A Report of the Canadian Immigration and Population Study* (Ottawa: Information Canada, 1974) p. 84; *1976 Immigration Statistics*, Table 3; and Employment and Immigration Canada, *Annual Report to Parliament on Future Immigration Levels*, 1985. Ottawa: Minister of Supply and Services Canada, 1985. Statistical Appendix; Immigration Statistics, Employment and Immigration Canada, 1986-90.

and "sponsored") is subject to the point system, but can gain extra points by means of short-term arrangements with relatives. This new policy is designed to facilitate entry of next-of-kin, but it gives more non-Europeans a chance to compete for immigration as well. Thus, in the last 25 years many more immigrants from non-European countries have entered Canada than previously, adding more racial, religious, and ethnic heterogeneity to our population (Balakrishnan and Kralt 1987).

Regional Ethnic Mosaic

Our discussion so far of population patterns over time illustrates that the aboriginals inhabited the land first, followed by the French, the British, other European groups, and Third World immigrants. Table 10-2 shows that the various groups increased at different times. Table 10-3 indicates that the many groups were unevenly distributed throughout Canada. It is obvious that the various Canadian regions are very different ethnically, and we need to examine these differences.

Culturally and linguistically, Canada can be regarded as six regions: the Northlands, the West, Upper Canada, Lower Canada, New Brunswick, and the Atlantic region. Today, the regions vary from multicultural and multilingual in the northwest to unicultural and monolingual in the east. High concentrations of Native people in the north, other ethnic groups in the west, French Canadians in Quebec, and British in the east constitute an interesting mix of cultural values and social organizations.

The Northlands. The Northlands include all of the Yukon, the Northwest Territories, Labrador, and roughly the upper three-quarters of the six western and central provinces (British Columbia, Alberta, Saskatchewan, Manitoba, Ontario, and Quebec). This area constitutes about 80 percent of the Canadian land mass, though it includes a relatively small proportion of the Canadian population. Demographically, it is the area where 69 percent of the population is of native origin, and 56 percent uses its native tongue at home. Vallee and deVries (1975) illustrate that these northern Indian and Inuit peoples perpetuate multilingual and multicultural societies, where European influences are increasing but not yet dominant.

The aboriginals lived here first, and they occupy the majority of our land area. However, they constitute a very small percentage of our population, and are, economically and politically, virtually powerless. The trend, however, seems to be for aboriginal people to come south, into more urban settings. There is strong evidence that, having moved, they quickly adopt either English or (in Quebec) French; only 33 percent of Native people in urban areas use their mother tongues (Vallee and deVries 1975). The Northlands are multicultural and multilingual.

The West. The West, which includes the southern portions of British Columbia, Alberta, Saskatchewan, and Manitoba, was the domain of food-gathering peoples, and was settled most recently by immigrants of many European origins. The region is highly rural and agricultural; it includes a multitude of substantial British, German, Ukrainian, French, and smaller ethnic settlements. A diversity of European ethnic groups settled the region and established social institutions.

Aboriginals constitute a significant proportion of the population on the Prairies. Asiatics represent an important part of British Columbia's population. Although many western ethnic groups seek to retain their language, the language used at home by the majority — 85 percent — is English. The West is multicultural and anglophone.

Upper Canada. Until recently, Upper Canada, now southern Ontario, was English linguistically and British culturally. It was the stronghold of the British, a charter group whose large population promoted urban industrial growth while maintaining a strong economic and financial base.

But lately this urban industrial area has attracted many newcomers to its labour market, especially immigrants to Toronto. These immigrants represent many cultures from northern and southern Europe, as well as the Third World. Therefore, the urban areas of Ontario are changing from being very British to being highly multicultural and multilingual. These new immigrants, however, are competing for jobs, and are therefore learning English. So, although British culture and the English language are not threatened in Upper Canada, multiculturalism is on the rise. Some 75 percent of Ontarians use English at home (Vallee and deVries 1975). Only about

5 percent speak French at home. Although Ontario has made some efforts to become bilingual (French and English), it appears that English is dominant and other languages subordinate. This region could best be described as anglophone with strong multicultural trends.

Although the linguistic and cultural conditions of the West and Upper Canada may seem similar, they are very different historically. The West has been strongly multicultural and multilingual throughout its short history. But since it is less industrialized, new immigrants do not seem to be streaming into the area in large numbers. Consequently, it is not as culturally diverse as southern Ontario.

Quebec. In Quebec, 82 percent of the population speak French at home (Statistics Canada 1981). Speaking English in the home is declining, from 13 percent in 1971 to 10 percent in 1981. One reason for the persistence of English in Quebec is that the economic elite tended to be English and were influential because of their industrial connections with the rest of North America. Toronto is now Canada's dominant financial and industrial base, which means that business headquarters and offices are slowly shifting to Ontario. Therefore, the power of the English business elite in Quebec will continue to decline and the use of French will increase.

A second reason for greater French linguistic and cultural influence in Quebec involves provincial legislation favouring that language. The influence of the Québécois nationalists resulted in some English interests leaving Quebec, redoubling the emphasis on French language and culture.

The more than 5 million French Canadians living in Quebec constitute the largest regional ethnic block in Canada. With their long Canadian history, their drive for French identity, federal efforts to promote French in Canada, and provincial legislation to protect French language and culture, it is likely that southern Quebec will remain the strongest single ethnic region. Quebec is francophone and francocultural.

New Brunswick. In New Brunswick, about 25 percent of the residents speak French at home; about 66 percent speak English at home. Other languages are spoken in the home by fewer than 10 percent of the population. This area supports only 2 or 3 percent of Canada's population. The French in New Brunswick will in all likelihood retain their language, because they are part of the bilingual belt adjacent to francophone Quebec. French–English bilingualism is therefore both a current fact and the pattern for the future. Cultures other than French and English are not represented in large numbers in New Brunswick. New Brunswick is Canada's only bilingual and bicultural region.

The Atlantic Region. The most easterly Atlantic region (Nova Scotia, Prince Edward Island, and the island of Newfoundland) is unilingual and unicultural. Of the residents in this area, 95 percent speak English at home (Vallee and deVries 1975). Their long history is largely British, and demographically they are British. Very few immigrants enter these provinces. This area supports only 6 or 7 percent of the Canadian population, and it is highly unlikely that residents of this region will push for heterogeneity. Their Native population is very small, their black population is anglophone and small, and other ethnic groups are hardly represented.

This discussion of our country's cultural and linguistic composition suggests that Canada is indeed a **regional mosaic**. The differences between the multicultural and multilingual northwest and the unicultural and unilingual east are great. Indeed, New Brunswick is the only region that approaches a bilingual and bicultural condition, and it is a very small part of Canada. The recommendations of the Royal Commission on Bilingualism and Biculturalism (1965), whose first report advocated a bilingual and bicultural nation, have been promoted by the federal government of Canada. Diversity, however, seems to be more in line with the cultural, linguistic, demographic, and ecological realities of the nation. Canada is a mosaic of many ethnic cultures and languages. Such diversity is a source of problems — but a source, too, of opportunities for expanding our personal and national horizons, by experiencing and appreciating the rich variety that is the hallmark of Canadian society.

Ethnic Stratification

A regional mosaic indicates the ecological distribution of ethnic groups. A "vertical mosaic" (Porter 1965) indicates strata of status and prestige. Some ethnic groups are heavily represented in the upper strata of the power elite; other groups are heavily represented in the lower strata. Let us start our examination of **ethnic stratification** with a discussion of the legal status of three ethnic categories — *charter groups, entrance groups,* and *treaty status groups* — and follow this with a discussion of the social class groupings of ethnic categories by education, income, and occupation.

Legal Ethnic Status

Charter Groups. We noted earlier that the British North America Act, 1867 (now known as the Constitution Act, 1867), gave the British and French charter-group status. Though the Canadian charter-group status of the French is legally secure, the French have always been "junior partners" with the British, and they have had difficulty matching the numerical, economic, and political strength of the British. The French came to rely on regional segregation and on institutional and cultural development as a means of counteracting British dominance (Crean and Rioux 1983).

The collective dominance of the charter groups has never been seriously challenged, because of the high levels of British immigration and the high rate of natural increase in the French population that were experienced in the past (the latter rate is now among the lowest in Canada). Also, the ethnic structure of a country, in terms of its charter and noncharter groups, is determined early and tends to be self-perpetuating. The French have held at about 30 percent of the Canadian population (although that has declined recently); the British have always been the largest ethnic group (although their proportion, too, has been dropping steadily).

At the time of Confederation, the British and French in Upper and Lower Canada and the Atlantic Region (other than Newfoundland) formed a bilingual and bicultural nation, with few representatives from other countries. It is these other immigrants who are in the process of slowly changing Canada from a bicultural to a multicultural and plural society, and it is to them and their statuses that we now turn.

Entrance Groups. Many ethnic groups are not founders of the country; they enter as immigrants and are called **entrance groups.** Porter (1965) calls the position to which ethnic groups are admitted and at which they are (at least initially) allowed to function in the power structure of a society *entrance status.* For most entrance groups in Canada, this position is characterized by low-status occupational roles and a subjection to processes of assimilation laid down by the charter groups. This situation held and holds for immigrants generally. Less "preferred" immigrants, moreover, although allowed to enter Canada, were channelled into even lower-status jobs than the norm. Because of their later entrance, they were often left with marginally productive farmlands.

Some immigrants of German, Dutch, Jewish, Chinese, and Scandinavian origin entered Canada earlier than many of the others; they can be considered older entrance-status groups. Many Germans, such as the ones who settled in the Berlin (now Kitchener–Waterloo) area, have been here more than 150 years; in Manitoba many have been here for more than a century. Many of these older immigrants have moved out of entrance status into higher educational, financial, and occupational statuses. The Jews, for example, placed great value on education, and have entered higher-status occupations — higher, on the average, than those of any other groups, including the charter groups.

Immigrants from eastern Europe, however, came in large numbers in the early twentieth century; southern Europeans came later still. Ukrainians, for example, were left with relatively less fertile rural areas to settle, and urban Italians, many of them unskilled, were left with the relatively more menial jobs. Third World immigrants who arrived during the 1970s were better educated and more highly skilled than were the eastern Europeans, and often entered the higher occupational strata; but since many were different by race, culture, and religion, they often found competition difficult.

Treaty Status Groups. According to Frideres (1974),

Until 1755 the English followed a policy of expediency. At first they chose to ignore the Indians, but when this was no longer feasible (because of westward expansion), they chose to isolate them (through the reserve system), or to annihilate them (as in the case of the Beothuk Indians of Newfoundland).

By 1830, Indian Affairs, initially a branch of the military, had become a part of the public service (Surtees 1969). The Indian Act was first passed in 1876, and has been revised a number of times since then. The general policy at first was to isolate aboriginals on segregated reserves, thus freeing most of the land for use by Europeans.

The first treaties were made in 1850: these included the Douglas Treaty in British Columbia, and the Robinson Superior and Huron Treaties in Ontario. As Europeans increasingly moved westward, Treaties 1 to 11 were begun in southern Manitoba in 1871, a year after Manitoba became the first western province. By the terms of these agreements, aboriginals ceded most of their land to the Europeans, and received in return reserved land claims; annuities of $3 per person; and various gifts of clothing, medals, and equipment. Thus the **treaty** groups were created.

At present there are about 240 000 treaty aboriginals, who belong to 592 bands located on more than 2200 reserves west of the province of Quebec (Canadian Almanac 1988). Treaties with aboriginals have generally not been made in the five easterly provinces, most of British Columbia, large parts of the Yukon, and the Northwest Territories. There may be as many non-treaty aboriginals as there are aboriginals under treaty; in addition, there are large numbers of Métis (offspring of unions involving nonaboriginals and aboriginals).

Although Native peoples were the original inhabitants of the land Canada now occupies, status Indians are currently designated "wards" of the federal government. This lowly legal status was originally intended to restrict them to small groups, so that white Europeans could more freely occupy the land. This legal **segregation** has had the additional effect of creating many islands of inertia and poverty, with little hope of improvement. Many aboriginals and nonaboriginals are very unhappy about the subordinate legal

status of the aboriginal people. Some of them question whether any of the treaties, made between literate Europeans and illiterate Native peoples, are valid. To return to our initial question: Whose land is Canada, especially the vast areas where no treaties have been signed as yet?

Socioeconomic Status

There are forms of status other than legal. The amount of income people earn, the years of education they have obtained, and the occupation in which they are engaged are all indicators of socioeconomic status. Most Canadians desire more money; those who attain it thereby gain prestige. Similarly, education is often seen as a means of obtaining well-paying occupations; education is therefore also valued by many. Blishen (1967) used the combined indicators of income and education to develop a socioeconomic occupational index that ranks occupations. Pineo and Porter (1967) also ranked occupations, by asking respondents to order the occupations according to prestige. Thus, various populations can be ranked by socioeconomic status, or strictly by occupational prestige. Ethnic groups can be ranked in this way as well.

In his classic study of Canadian ethnic stratification, John Porter (1965), using census data prior to 1961, suggested that Canada was highly stratified into four major categories. The charter groups (British and French) were on top, followed by other northern Europeans, eastern and southern Europeans, and last, visible minorities. In his early studies, Porter (1965) suggested that these strata might remain solidified, with limited opportunities for mobility, especially for visible minorities and others who were unwilling to give up their ethnic identities. By 1985, Porter modified these predictions because later census data showed more mobility, since immigration policies changed in the 1970s.

Edward Grabb (1992:220), using 1986 census data, showed that Jewish Canadians ranked first on all three indicators of education, income, and occupation, while the British had slipped to fifth in income, seventh in occupational status, and twelfth in education (Grabb 1992). Japanese Canadians ranked second in income and occupational status, and third in education, taking overall second position after Jewish Canadians. Recent immigrants, such as the Portuguese, ranked last (twentieth) on all three indicators, lower than Canadian aboriginals who ranked sixteenth on income, seventeenth on occupational status, and nineteenth on education. Visible minorities were found at all levels, with the Japanese highest, followed by the Chinese and East Indians in the middle, and blacks and aboriginals near the bottom. A considerable reordering had occurred.

Edward Herberg (1990) illustrated by using recent census data that Porter's early rigid hierarchy has changed greatly. "Of the top one-third of groups in 1981 post-education, five out of the six highest are visible minority groups," so that "these data patently depict a near reversal from Canada's pattern of ethno–racial education stratification in 1921–31, and even in 1951" (Herberg 1990:212). Herberg's findings support Gordon Darroch's (1979) earlier contention that ethnic mobility and stratification are changing.

Aboriginals are especially heavily represented in the lower-status occupations, and many are unemployed. Many Native peoples have emerged only recently from the food-gathering state, and their special status as wards of the federal government has made it very difficult for them to compete socioeconomically. The middle-class curriculum in schools has not served many Natives well, and they have been reluctant to enter unfamiliar industrial occupations. Thus, Canadian aboriginals find themselves in the lowest socioeconomic stratum. Some writers, such as Cardinal (1969), have referred to them as the "niggers" of Canada, the disadvantaged targets of discrimination by Canadian whites.

Racial Differentiations

If this were a chapter in an American sociology text, race would likely be the central theme. A full 12 percent of the American population is black; America has as many blacks as Canada has people, plus some 6 million Hispanics. By comparison, Canada is predominantly Caucasian; only about 5 percent of Canadians are nonwhite. Canadian aboriginals (2 percent) and Asiatics (3 percent) represent the largest of the nonwhite groups. Some might therefore contend that race is

not a significant factor in Canada, and does not need special treatment. They would be wrong.

There are at least three important reasons for including race as an influential factor in Canadian stratification. First, aboriginals, although only 2 percent of our population, were the first inhabitants, have special legal status, and are perceived by many as belonging to another race. Second, new immigration laws now permit many more immigrants from the Third World to enter Canada than previously, and many of these are neither of European racial stock nor of Judeo-Christian religious background. Third, Canadians are greatly influenced by their neighbour to the south, and the preoccupation of Americans with racial questions also tends to affect Canadian attitudes and thinking. A brief discussion of race is therefore necessary (Ramcharan 1982; Li and Bolaria 1983).

Anthropologists tell us that **race** is an arbitrary biological grouping; estimates of the racial component of large populations are still based on subjective opinions (Hughes and Kallen 1974). Physical features, genetics (including blood types), and theories about racial origins have given rise to various classifications. Although there are many such classifications, "Caucasoid," "Mongoloid," and "Negroid" are the most common. Head form; face form; nose form; eye, lip, and ear form; hair, skin, and eye colour; hair texture and amount of hair on the body; and stature and body build have all been used as criteria for racial classifications. Skin colour (Caucasians, white; Mongoloids, yellow; Negroids, black) is the most common criterion. However, large groupings of the world's people, such as the aboriginals of the Americas, the East Indians, and the Pacific Polynesians, do not fit any of these three categories. Many scholars, especially in the United States, also find that differences between races (such as intelligence levels) tend to disappear in controlled situations. Then why have whites of European origin made so much of race, and of skin colour especially?

Although we cannot delve deeply into the origins of racial differentiation here, it would appear that European explorers found that most of the people they encountered were of darker skin colour, and were also less technologically advanced, than the Europeans themselves were. "Technologically advanced" and "superior" tended to be equivalent in the European mind. Europeans thus developed an image of "white superiority" (Driedger, 1989).

Northern Europeans in particular, the dominant population in Canada, tend to be very conscious of skin colour and often classify people accordingly. Certainly, the aboriginal people — who are segregated on reserves, and who are also racially classified as Mongoloid — are accorded low status in Canada. There is already evidence that, as more Third World immigrants, racially classified Negroid and Mongoloid, enter our larger cities, racial incidents tend to erupt more frequently.

Porter (1965) suggests that the idea of an ethnic mosaic, as opposed to a **melting pot**, impedes the process of social mobility: "The melting pot with its radical breakdown of national ties and old forms of stratification would have endangered the conservative tradition of Canadian life, a tradition which gives ideological support to the continued high status of the British charter group." As you saw in Chapter 9, however, this situation seems to be changing; many entrance groups are gaining status educationally, occupationally, and economically, but are retaining many of their ethnic characteristics. The Jews are an excellent example of high upward mobility coupled with high maintenance of ethnic identity.

Any theory of Canadian ethnic relations must make provision for these multidimensional regional, economic, and political status structures in order to account for the factors that influence the composition of the Canadian mosaic, and also the identity of individual ethnic and racial groups.

Theories of Persistence and Change

What happens to the multitudes who enter Canada? How do they adjust to their new environment (Richmond and Kalbach 1980)? Do some immigrants fare better in one region than in another? Do they simply wish to retain a separate identity, or are they determined to maintain geographic/ethnic boundaries that will keep them separate? Various theories have been developed

to explain what will happen to ethnic groups in an industrial/technological society. The first two theories, *assimilation* and *amalgamation*, assume that the urban industrial forces of technology will result in vanishing ethnicity. The third and fourth theories, *multivariate assimilation* and *modified pluralism*, admit that the technological forces will change the ethnic minority, but predict that groups will retain ethnic characteristics in part, or in a changed form. The remaining two theories, *ethnic conflict* and *pluralism*, posit the maintenance of ethnic identity in both rural and urban environments (Driedger 1989). A discussion of the six theories follows.

Assimilation: Majority-Conformity

The theory of assimilation has influenced North American thinking greatly since the 1920s. It is the product of an evolutionary perspective, which assumes that ethnic groups are constantly becoming more like the majority culture, represented in Canada and the United States by the British. This theory tends to be deterministic; **assimilation** assumes that the power of the majority will be too much for any minority group to resist, and therefore the group will assimilate into the majority.

A chief advocate of this concept was Robert Park, who contended that immigrants, when they came into contact with the new American society, either followed the course of least resistance (contact, accommodation, assimilation) or took a more circuitous route (contact, conflict, competition, accommodation, fusion) (Driedger 1989). (These two possibilities are designated Route A and Route B, respectively, in Figure 10-1.) Whereas the latter route would take longer and entail considerable resistance on the part of the immigrant, the end results would be the same: assimilation and a consequent loss of distinctive ethnic identity.

Enough minorities did assimilate as Park predicted to keep American researchers occupied with documenting this process. For 50 years these scholars tended to ignore groups that retained a separate identity and tended to regard their separateness as a relatively insignificant and temporary factor in the total pattern of minority–majority relations. The assimilation theory was so influential, combined with the evolutionary thinking of the day, that evidence to the contrary often made little headway.

FIGURE 10-1 Parkean Assimilation Alternative

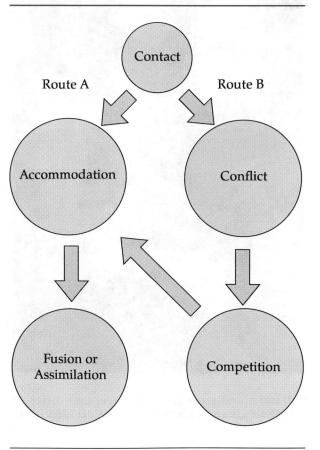

The theory of assimilation was and is attractive because it is dynamic. It takes into account the distinctiveness and enormous technological changes visible in North American societies. Furthermore, numerous studies show that many northern European groups, such as the Dutch, the Scandinavians, and the Germans, do lose many of their distinguishing cultural traits, such as original-language use, fairly quickly. However, in the eyes of some, assimilation theory is too deterministic. That is, as a macro theory it may explain a general process for some groups, but it does not take into account the many aspects of cultural change that may not all be moving in the same direction. Further, it does not sufficiently account for the possibility of nonassimilation by some groups. Finally, it does not address the idea that when assimilation is complete, the end result may

not resemble the majority culture (that is, Anglo-Saxons), but may turn out to be something quite different.

We learn from Canadian history that many British leaders had the Anglo model in mind for Native peoples, the French, and everyone else. Lord Durham, for example, assumed that others would assimilate into the dominant British legal, political, economic, and cultural system. And many seem to have hoped that somehow even the French would finally so assimilate, although via Park's more circuitous route of conflict and competition. These leaders assumed the pre-eminent desirability of British social institutions.

Amalgamation: Melting Pot

Amalgamation theories differ from assimilation theories by suggesting that immigrant groups will be synthesized into a new group. The evolutionary process is the same as that of assimilation, but the end result is a melting pot — an amalgam, different from any of the groups involved. This concept is frequently taken by Americans to be typical of their society. They broke free of British dominance 200 years ago and created a nation ostensibly dominated by no one group. All contributed to the American dream, with its new constitution, a multitude of cultures from many parts of the world, and a system of free enterprise. Independence and freedom were popular watchwords. It was a new nation, a new culture, a new continent, a pot to which all might contribute.

Herberg (1955) contends, however, that in America the Protestants, Catholics, and Jews have never "melted." Nor have they in Canada. People of minority races — well represented in Canada by the aboriginal peoples and in America by 27 million blacks — seem not to be melting very noticeably either. To what extent other ethnic groups, such as the French, Chinese, and Italians, are melting is the subject of much research, and it is perhaps somewhat early to tell. But certainly the French in Quebec remain a bulwark against amalgamation. The prophesied synthesis is slow in coming in Canada, and even in the United States, where the melting-pot theory is often applied, more and more scholars are having doubts about its usefulness (Newman 1973).

Canada's relatively open immigration policy has provided the potential opportunity for many peoples to contribute to a melting pot. At the time of Confederation, however, the two founding peoples represented most of the population, and as we have seen, their historical influence has been much stronger than any of the other groups that followed. Early British and French influences have tended to dominate early Canadian history and the lives of more recent immigrants. The two charter groups have fought hard not to amalgamate either culturally or linguistically, so that from the beginning our pot has contained ingredients that do not melt.

The synthesis of British, French, Germans, Ukrainians, Italians, Canadian Indians, and others into a recognizable national character has been a long time coming. Perhaps it is this "melting" process, more than any other, that is needed to develop a spirited Canadian nationalism. The Americans, on the other hand, have stressed amalgamation more and have evolved a stronger feeling of nationalism than Canadians have been able to manage. Could this be why Canada is seriously discussing the possibility of Quebec's separation? Perhaps too many Canadians feel that some parts of Canada are not really so much a part of them. Speculation aside, amalgamation seems not to explain the Canadian scene as well as some other theoretical perspectives. Perhaps in the future amalgamation may apply to a greater extent than it does now.

Cultural pluralism suggests that over time different ethnic groups maintain their distinct identities.

Pluralism: Ethnic Mosaic

The metaphor of the mosaic to describe the plural Canadian society is useful in answering such questions as the following: How are the tiles in the mosaic distributed? Are the tiles equal, or can some be seen as more important than others because of their size or the way in which they cluster in the total design? What would be missing if particular tiles no longer remained distinctive? The first question corresponds to the regional and spatial distribution of various ethnic groups in Canada; the second, to the status and power of the various ethnic groups within the total society; and the third, to the cultural and institutional contributions of the groups.

Cultural **pluralism** suggests that, over time, different ethnic groups maintain their unique identities. Cultural pluralism is often viewed as an arrangement whereby distinct groups live side by side in relative harmony. One proponent of this view was Horace Kallen, who did so for three main reasons (Newman 1973). He argued that, first, while there are many kinds of social relationships and identities that can be chosen voluntarily, people cannot choose their ancestry. Second, each of the minority groups has something of value to contribute to a country. And third, the American constitution carried with it an assumption that all were created equal, even though there might be many distinct differences. Kallen wishes to refute the reigning notions of assimilation and the melting pot.

Assimilationists and amalgamationists emphasize the overwhelming influence of social phenomena like technology and urbanization as constituting the master trend that would sweep all forms of ethnic differentiation before it. Cultural pluralism, on the other hand, tends to focus on countervailing ideological forces, such as democracy and human justice, fundamental to which are the beliefs that all people are of equal worth and all may live as they choose, provided that they respect the rights of others. Whereas the preceding theories call for the disappearance of immigrant and racial groups, pluralism holds that there may be greater resistance to assimilation and amalgamation than had formerly been thought, and that the trend toward permissive differentiation already seems to be set. In Canada, we have accepted pluralist religious expressions and a diversity of political parties and ideologies. **Multiculturalism** in Canada is now also increasingly promoted — although not without some resistance, as Burnet's (1978) review and the support for the Reform Party clearly show.

In 1971, the government of Canada announced a policy of multiculturalism within the bilingual framework. The government sought to encourage and assist Canadian cultural groups who so desired to continue to develop their cultural heritage, while seeking also to acquire one of the two official languages and thus increase their integration into the Canadian society. Berry, Kalin, and Taylor (1977) and Bibby (1987b) show in their national studies that people in Quebec (predominantly French Canadians) and the Atlantic provinces (predominantly British) are not sold on multiculturalism, while people in Ontario and the West, where more of the noncharter groups reside, are more in favour of multiculturalism.

Our large French Canadian population has always made up a very substantial, very distinct tile in the mosaic. Pluralists would say, too, that the aboriginal people of Canada's Northlands represent several more, quite durable tiles in the mosaic, and that, to a lesser extent, so do Canada's blacks, Jews, Hutterites, Doukhobors, Italians, Asiatics, and many other groups (such as the Ukrainians and Germans in block settlements on the Prairies). Canada's aboriginal peoples, dominant charter groups, and relatively open immigration policy seem to have contributed toward the creation of a differentiated country, more like Belgium or Switzerland than like either of our most influential allies, Britain and the United States.

Multivariate Assimilation

The central theme of Milton Gordon's (1964) *Assimilation in American Life* is **multivariate assimi-**lation, the theory that assimilation is not a single social process but a number of subprocesses, which he classifies under the headings "cultural" and "structural." Cultural assimilation includes acceptance by the incoming group of the modes of dress, language, and other cultural characteristics of the host society. Structural assimilation concerns the degree to which immigrants enter the social institutions of the society and the degree to which they are accepted into these institutions by the majority. Gordon suggests that assimilation may occur more in the economic, political, and educational institutions, while it may be resisted more in the areas of religion, family, and recreation. It would seem, therefore, that the opposing processes of assimilation and pluralism may occur simultaneously, depending on the dimension of ethnic activity examined. But as Newman (1973) points out, "Gordon contends [that] once structural assimilation is far advanced, all other types of assimilation will naturally follow."

Gordon's multivariate approach forced scholars out of their unilinear rut. But each of the seven stages or types of assimilation he established (listed in Table 10-5) tended to be oriented toward either an assimilation or an amalgamation target.

Gordon's major contribution is his complex, multilinear, multidimensional view of the assimilation process. It has been seen as a considerable improvement on Park's assimilation cycle. Although Gordon was mainly concerned with assimilation as such, and did not dwell on pluralism, he did not negate plural expressions in the areas of religion, the family, and recreation. The Hutterites emphasize religion, for example, and the Jews the family.

Modified Pluralism

Glazer and Moynihan (1963) are able to distinguish four major events in New York history that they think structured a series of ethnic patterns in that city. The first was the shaping of the Jewish community under the impact of the Nazi persecution of Jews in Europe and the establishment of the state of Israel. The second was a parallel, if less marked, shaping of a Catholic community by the re-emergence of the Catholic school controversy. The third was the migration of southern blacks to New York following World War I and

TABLE 10-5   Gordon's Seven Assimilation Variables

Subprocess or Condition	Types or Stages of Assimilation
Changes of cultural patterns to those of host society	Cultural or behavioural assimilation
Large-scale entrance into cliques, clubs, and institutions of host society, on primary group level	Structural assimilation
Large-scale intermarriage	Marital assimilation
Development of sense of peoplehood based exclusively on host society	Identificational assimilation
Absence of prejudice	Attitude receptional assimilation
Absence of discrimination	Behaviour receptional assimilation
Absence of value and power conflict	Civic assimilation

SOURCE: Milton M. Gordon, *Assimilation in American Life* (New York: Oxford University Press, 1964).

continuing through the 1950s. The fourth was the influx of Puerto Ricans during the fifteen years following World War II.

Their implicit point is that the melting pot did not function in New York. They claim further that throughout America's history the merging of the various streams of population that remained differentiated from one another by origin, religion, and outlook seemed always to lie just ahead, but the looked-for commingling was always deferred.

Glazer and Moynihan suggest that the blacks are often discriminated against, and their assimilation is not tolerated by the majority. The Jews, with their distinct religion, do not wish to assimilate, but rather are proud of their identity. The Puerto Ricans and Irish Catholics represent combinations of these variations: over time they change, but they remain distinct ethnic groups.

Perhaps the Hutterites best represent pluralism with controlled change. Most other groups, however, change a great deal more over time, yet many retain a distinctive identity. This would

seem to suggest **modified pluralism**. The francophones in Quebec are a good example of change from a predominantly rural, religious population, to an increasingly urban, industrial one. But this enormous shift in value orientations seems not to have affected their determination to survive as a distinct people in North America. Modified pluralism takes account of change, as do the assimilation and amalgamation theories, but it also provides for the degrees of pluralism often demonstrated in Canadian groups such as aboriginal peoples, Italians, French Canadians, Jews, Asiatics, and many others.

Glazer and Moynihan hold that all groups change, but those able to shift from traditional cultural identities to new interest foci may maintain their identities in a modified form. This view recognizes change, maintains that identification can be shifted, suggests that some groups may change more than others, and implies that the outcome may be a pluralist mixture with a non–Anglo-conformity target. Indeed, Glazer and Moynihan contend that traumatic experiences, such as conflict, encourage the development of a sense of identity among minorities. And that brings us to our sixth and last theory of ethnic change and persistence: conflict.

Conflict: Dialectical Change

The theories of assimilation and amalgamation suggest an ordered society, one for the most part in a state of equilibrium, within which social change and group conflict are but temporary dislocations. In contrast, the theories of pluralism, multivariate assimilation, and modified pluralism allow for a greater measure of inherent conflict in the social system. But Georg Simmel (1950a) contends that conflict is the crux of the matter, and that both conflict and consensus are ever-present in society. His general assumption is that all social phenomena reflect a combination of opposed tendencies.

The conflict focus, although concerned with structure and institutions, emphasizes the processes of ethnic-group relations. Since conflict implies the meeting of people with dissimilar or opposite values and norms, it includes processes of competition, confrontation, and argumentation. Consequently, we will define *social conflict* as "all relations between sets of individuals that involve an incompatible difference of objectives (with regard to positions, resources, or values)."

One way to view conflict is as Marx did in *The Communist Manifesto*: "The history of all hitherto existing society is the history of class struggles." As was described in Chapter 1 and elaborated on in Chapter 9, Marx saw the relationship between the bourgeoisie and the proletariat as a class struggle between opposites, as a macro power struggle for control over the economic and political institutions of a society, and as pervasive conflict that would inevitably lead to revolution.

Marx viewed this struggle as much more serious than ethnic territorial squabbles; changes in Eastern Europe illustrate how bitter conflict can become. Most ethnic groups in Canada do not aspire to such an extensive power struggle, although the FLQ movement in Quebec might be a good example of one that did. And the Parti Québécois can be seen as a milder form of conflict institution, since it would seek to gain sovereign control of Quebec's economic, political, and social institutions.

While conflict may occasionally take the form of revolution and secession, it is also present in lesser forms. When many subgroups and a multitude of cultures exist side by side they will maintain distinct identities, thus providing a potential for conflict of values, territorial interests, and power relationships. Jackson (1975) studied French–English relations in the Windsor, Ontario, area and found considerable competition and conflict, which he viewed as a normal outcome of the processes of power-position and boundary maintenance by these groups. By the same token, Quebec's "Quiet Revolution," the aboriginal peoples' quest for equal rights, and the relations between adjacent ethnic Prairie communities all demonstrate a constant potential for dissension. Hutterite expansion into more of the Alberta farmlands (and subsequent restrictive legislation); the conflict of ethnic groups over language rights and education during the Manitoba Schools Question; and Bill 22 and the conflicts of Italians and recent immigrants with the Quebec government over English education in Montreal are all examples of such ethnic counter-cultural conflicts.

These theories — assimilation, amalgamation, and the rest — have been introduced to illustrate attempts by various scholars in a variety of situations to explain how immigrants in our society change, adjust, and persist in their ethnic identities. While the first three may be important ideal descriptions, few, if any, societies conform to any of them. And while ideal, general theories are much too broad and sweeping to explain the many specific changes undergone by scores of particular ethnic groups in a variety of definite regions in Canada. The more precise multivariate, modified pluralist, and conflict versions are therefore needed to account for many more changes and to explain in much more detail the enormous diversity of our country.

Ethnic Identity

In our discussion of Canadian ethnicity we noted that the two charter groups, the British and the French, are by far the two largest ethnic groups in Canada.

The British have from the outset been dominant demographically; English-language use is dominant outside Quebec; and British economic, political, and legal influence on the nation is strong. The French are highly segregated. In the province of Quebec they can maintain some of their linguistic, cultural, and legal distinctiveness by provincial government control. So much we have already determined.

The Anglo-dominant industrial and political environment acts as a magnet on ethnic minorities. Access to jobs, economic enterprise, and influence are appealing. But how do the Hutterites, the Jews, the native Indians, the French, and others retain a separate identity when they wish neither to assimilate nor to amalgamate? On the other hand, are there racial and ethnic groups who may wish to assimilate into Canadian society, but who are not permitted to compete equally? In this section, we explore ethnic identity maintenance, and in the next section, ethnic prejudice and discrimination. These are the two sides of the identity coin: voluntary and involuntary maintenance of ethnic identity.

In our discussion of ethnic identity in this section, we consider *group identification*. To what extent do various ethnic groups in Canada adhere to distinctive cultures that differentiate them

Louis Riel: Traitor or Hero?

Métis leader Louis Riel vividly illustrates this chapter's sociological emphases. As European immigrants invaded the Native Indian lands, they disrupted a food-gathering way of life. Rich farmlands for the immigrants meant eviction for the Natives. Conflict was inevitable and continued until the Europeans prevailed. The Indians were herded into reserves, and to this day they remain in the lower strata of Canadian society. Many lost their former identity, and only a few are now beginning to make a new life. Prejudice and discrimination against Indians and Métis are common. People of Indian ancestry are shunted to the margins of Canadian society. Very few know what to do about it, and still fewer care.

Brilliant, eloquent, compelling, moody, sensitive, argumentative — all these words applied to Louis Riel. He was born in St. Boniface, where his French father owned a flour mill, but he was educated in Montreal, where he first studied for the priesthood, then, after his father died, turned to law. When Marie-Julie Guernon's father refused Riel's request to marry his daughter, Riel packed his bags and set out for the United States ... Chicago ... Minnesota ... finally back to the Red River settlement — places he had last seen when he was just a boy.

By 1868, more easterners were entering the area — settlers from Ontario and the Maritimes who wanted farmland; Americans selling union with the United States; members of the Canadian Party plugging union with Canada. Sir John A. Macdonald wanted farmland. The Métis were apprehensive.

The next year Macdonald bought the Métis homeland from the Hudson's Bay Company and appointed William McDougall governor of the vast new territory. Riel was enraged. When McDougall tried to reach Fort Garry, he was turned back by the Métis. Riel took over Fort Garry, set up a provisional government, took several prisoners (including a man named Thomas Scott), and demanded a Bill of Rights for his people. His provisional government persisted, and Manitoba became Canada's fifth province in 1870.

Riel's fatal error was executing Thomas Scott. Scott had escaped and made a vain attempt to liberate Fort Garry with his supporters. Scott was a troublesome, defiant Ontario Orangeman. He was tried by Métis court-martial, found guilty of insubordination, and executed. As news of his death spread, Ontario Orangemen demanded quick revenge. Riel was forced to flee to the United States.

Fifteen years later, in 1885, Riel was invited by the Métis in Batoche, Saskatchewan, to plead their cause with the federal government. The buffalo were now gone. Big Bear and his Cree, who had refused to sign Treaty 6 in 1876, were becoming increasingly restless. Poundmaker, one of the foremost chiefs to sign the treaty, had become bitter. In the south there was Piapot; in Alberta, Crowfoot, chief of the Blackfoot. There was rebellion in the air.

The final drama unfolded in Batoche in 1885, when Riel and his Métis fought against the Second Army sent from eastern Canada. The Métis were greatly outnumbered, as well as short on ammunition and supplies, and the hoped-for native Indian allies did not join the final battle. It was Riel's last fight, and it was all over in a few days.

On September 18, 1885, in a crowded Regina courtroom, six English-speaking jurors pronounced Louis Riel guilty of treason. Two months later he was hanged.

Less than 100 years later, commemorative monuments to Louis Riel stood on the legislative grounds in both Regina and Winnipeg. Hindsight had led to second thoughts. More and more the Regina execution seemed unjust, and Manitobans increasingly consider Riel the father of their province. His grave occupies a place of honour in front of the oldest Roman Catholic basilica in the west, located in St. Boniface, which is now part of metropolitan Winnipeg. It is surrounded by the La Verendrye monument, the French St. Boniface college, the French Catholic archdiocese, the museum and first Grey Nuns hospital, the CBC French radio and television station, and the recently built French cultural centre. Louis Riel's grave is the hub of an important Franco-Manitoba centre.

The CBC film *Riel* documents the sequence of events in this western drama. Rudy Wiebe's novel *The Scorched-Wood People* (McClelland and Stewart, 1977) portrays the life and aspirations of the Métis on the South Saskatchewan River.

Source:

Thomas R. Berger, *Fragile Freedoms* (Toronto: Clarke, Irwin & Co., 1981).

from the rest? Dashefsky (1976) defines group identification as

a personal attachment to the group and a positive orientation toward being a member of the group. Ethnic identification takes place when the group in question

is one with whom the individual believes he has a common ancestry based on shared individual characteristics and/or shared sociocultural experiences.

Dashefsky (1976) has reviewed some of the literature on identity and identification, which illustrates the many dimensions attributed to this concept:

Rosen [1965] has ... argued that an individual may identify ... with others on three levels: First, one may identify oneself with some important person in one's life, e.g., parent or a friend (i.e., significant other). Second, one may identify oneself with a group from which one draws one's values, e.g., family or coworkers (i.e., reference group). Last, one may identify oneself with a broad category of persons, e.g., an ethnic group or occupational group (i.e., a social category). It is on the third level that ethnic identification occurs.

That, very briefly, is what constitutes identification. We turn now to the various kinds. In our discussion of ethnic identification we shall touch on six identification factors: ecological territory, ethnic institutions, ethnic culture, historical symbols, ideology, and charismatic leadership. These factors are some of the basic components of an ethnic community, and taken together they constitute what Gordon (1964) refers to as a group of individuals with "a shared sense of peoplehood."

Territory

Maintaining a separate language and culture is difficult and unlikely without a sufficiently large ethnic concentration in a given area. Minorities need territory that is within their control — territory within which their offspring may then perpetuate their heritage (Breton and Savard 1982). This can be best done in a tightly knit community. Community space thus becomes an arena in which ethnic activities occur and are shared.

In Quebec, French Québécois retain control of the provincial territory, where they perpetuate their language and culture through religious, educational, and political institutions. French scholars such as Rioux (1971) have shown how, historically, the French were the first Europeans to settle along the St. Lawrence River, where they set up a seigneurial (manorial) system, with the long, narrow tracts of land still in evidence today. Miner (1939) describes beautifully the community life of the 1930s in St-Denis, a typical rural French-Catholic parish: everyone spoke French, attended Roman Catholic churches, and generally lived as depicted in the 1971 Claude Jutra film *Mon Oncle Antoine*. Gold (1975), who studied

St-Pascal, the adjacent community, describes how the modern rural French Canadian parish has changed, but how territory remains very important in maintaining rural Quebec culture.

The Hutterites constitute a good example of a rural ethnic community characterized by extensive boundary maintenance and controlled exposure to outsiders. Indian reserves also demonstrate ethnic territorial segregation. Chinatowns are urban examples (Lai 1988; Li 1988). Most minorities cannot maintain such exclusive control over a territory; it is a goal, however, to which many minority groups seem to aspire.

Ethnic block settlements are common, especially in the West. The Germans are heavily concentrated in the Kitchener–Waterloo area of Ontario; and the Ukrainians settled in the Aspen Belt, which stretches from Manitoba's Inter-Lake region to Edmonton. Rural hinterlands often supplied migrants to the city who tended to perpetuate the "urban villager" way of life — as illustrated by the north end of Winnipeg, until recently the stronghold of Ukrainians, Poles, and Jews (Driedger and Church 1974). Richmond (1972) also found extensive residential segregation in Toronto. Kalbach (1980) found historical Jewish and Italian settlement patterns in Toronto and traced how they shifted over time.

Individuals, then, can identify with a territory; it is the bounded area within which ethnic activity can take place. Territory is essential.

Ethnic Institutions

Forces of attraction are generated by the social organization of ethnic communities within their established social boundaries. Integration into one's own ethnic community, supported by the "institutional completeness" of the group, reinforces solidarity (Breton 1964).

The importance of institutional completeness is that the extent to which a minority can develop its own social system, with control over its own institutions, is the extent to which the group's social actions will take place within the system. Religious, educational, and welfare institutions are therefore crucial. Driedger and Church (1974) found that in Winnipeg, for example, the French and the Jews maintained the most complete set of religious, educational, and welfare institutions of all ethnic groups. These two groups were also the most segregated — in St. Boniface and the north end, respectively, where they had established their institutions. The French and the Jews identified with both territory and ethnic institutions. Residential segregation and institutional completeness thus tend to reinforce each other.

Ethnic Culture

Kurt Lewin (1948) proposed that the individual needs to achieve a firm, clear sense of identification with the heritage and culture of the group in order to find a secure ground for a sense of well-being. The territory becomes a crucible within which solid ethnic institutions can be built and within which ethnic culture can be protected.

Ethnic culture identification factors have been studied by numerous scholars (Breton, Reitz, and Valentine 1980; Ishwaran 1980). Driedger (1975), for example, found at least six factors that tended to influence group adherence to culture: language

use, endogamy (marriage within the group); choice of friends; and participation in religion, parochial schools, and voluntary organizations. The French and the Jews in Winnipeg, who were more residentially segregated and who maintained their ethnic institutions to a greater degree than some other comparable ethnic groups, also ranked high on attendance at parochial schools (79 and 74 percent, respectively), endogamy (65 and 91 percent), and choice of in-group friends (49 and 63 percent). Use of the French language at home was significantly widespread (61 percent), as was church attendance (54 percent). Research on the importance of language is quite extensive — as shown by deVries and Vallee's (1980) work, as well as many Statistics Canada (1985b) studies. Other ethnic groups (such as Canadians of German, Ukrainian, Polish, Scandinavian, and British origin) supported their in-group cultures less actively.

Examination of territorial, institutional, and cultural identification factors suggests that they

Community space becomes an arena in which ethnic activities occur and are shared.

tend to reinforce each other; when individuals of a given ethnic group identify with their group along these lines, they then tend to remain relatively more ethnically distinct and proportionately less prone to assimilation. Such maintenance of distinctive ethnic features is necessary to the integrity of the Canadian ethnic mosaic.

Historical Symbols

Villagers may perpetuate their ethnic social structure and community as an end in itself, without much reference to their past or future. Among ethnic urbanites, however, a knowledge of their origins and pride in their heritage would seem to be essential for a sense of purpose and direction. Without such pride and knowledge, the desire to perpetuate tradition rapidly diminishes. The Jews expose their children to a ritualized ethnic history expressed in the form of symbols: special days, fasts, candles, food habits, and other commemorative observances. Such historical symbols can create a sense of belonging, of purpose, and of continuing tradition that is important and worth perpetuating.

A comparison of identity among seven ethnic groups in Winnipeg indicated strong in-group affirmation and low in-group denial among the French and the Jews (Driedger 1976). Jewish students and French students were proud of their in-groups, felt strongly bound to them, wished to remember them, and contributed to them. The French indicated particularly low in-group denial; they did not try to hide, nor did they feel inferior about, their ethnicity; they seldom felt annoyed or restricted by their identity. The Ukrainians, Polish, and Germans felt less positively about themselves as ethnic groups, and at the same time were more inclined to deny their ethnicity. Ethnic heritage can therefore be a strong or weak, positive or negative, influence on personal identity.

Ideology

For certain individuals, a religious or political ideology can relegate cultural and institutional values to second place. For many in the younger generation, territory, culture, and ethnic institutions seem less intrinsically valuable than for their elders. As urban ethnic youth become more sophisticated, they tend to value their ethnicity less. A political or religious ideology, however, supplies purpose and impetus; it promotes values considered more important than cultural and institutional ones.

Often, there is a very strong correlation between religion and ethnicity. Almost all French Canadians are Roman Catholic, and the parish system in rural Quebec has been studied thoroughly (Miner 1939; Gold 1975). Of course, Catholics have also founded many essentially ethnic urban parishes: in Quebec City, in Montreal, and in Winnipeg. Similarly, most Canadians of Polish origin are Roman Catholic, and, consequently, urban Polish parishes abound.

By the same token, Jewish religion and culture are so interdependent as to seem identical; they are so unified that the distinction between "religious" and "ethnic" tends to blur. Indeed, Zionism has been and is so strong that Jews from all over the world have migrated to Israel. Closer to home, Mennonites and Hutterites also integrate and thus mutually strengthen their cultures and religious ideologies.

Ideology can help unite a people, but it can also divide them. The Ukrainians are a good example of divided loyalties. The Ukrainian Catholic and the Greek Orthodox faiths are and have long been opposed. This opposition has led to conflict among Ukrainians themselves, illustrating both the importance of ideology and its potentially divisive power.

Identification with religious beliefs or a political philosophy adds force and point to the question "What is the meaning of this territory, these institutions, and this ethnic culture, and why should it be perpetuated or changed?"

Charismatic Leadership

Charismatic leaders have played important roles in a variety of minority movements: Martin Luther King and Malcolm X among American blacks; and Harold Cardinal among Alberta Indians, to name a few. Individuals with a sense of mission often adapt an ideology to a current situation, linking it symbolically with the past, and using the media effectively to transform the present into a vision of the future.

Such charismatic leaders ordinarily use social-psychological means to gain a following. Designed to create trust, these methods forge a cohesive loyalty to both leader and in-group. The leader's commitment is passed on to the followers, resulting in new potential for change. In the beginning, the group may not be particularly oriented to territory, institutions, culture, and heritage. But slowly, as the movement ages, such structural features become more important.

Although there may be many more ethnic dimensions with which minorities identify, we have noted that territory, institutions, culture, heritage, ideology, and charismatic leaders are crucial. Different ethnic groups identify more with some of these dimensions than with others, and some groups are more successful than other groups in maintaining a distinct community. The Hutterites have successfully survived in a rural setting, for example, and the Jews have for centuries done so effectively in the city. Any study of ethnic identity needs to explore such dimensions and foci of ethnic identification.

In many ways this discussion of ethnic identity can be capped by introducing the concept of ethnocentrism. Identity and ethnocentrism are closely linked. Sumner (1906) coined the term **ethnocentrism** to describe the tendency of ethnic groups to view other people and groups in such a way that "one's own group is the center of everything and all others are scaled and rated with reference to it. ... Each group nourishes its own pride and vanity, boasts itself superior, exalts its own divinities, and looks with contempt on outsiders." Although Sumner seems to emphasize the negative aspects of ethnocentrism, the concept does have its positive side. Murdock (1931) thought that "positive ethnocentrism" would include a belief in the unique value of the in-group; satisfaction, solidarity, loyalty, and co-operation with it; and preferences for association with members of it. Positive ethnocentrism is akin to positive ethnic identity. Murdock also recognized negative ethnocentrism: believing in the superiority of one's own group and judging others strictly by that group's standards; ignorance of, and lack of interest in, other groups; and potential hostility toward out-groups. Ethnic identity and ethnocentrism can provide security and support for minority individuals and groups. However, if taken too far, these loyalties can also create problems of hostility toward out-groups, including

prejudice and discrimination. It is to these negative features that we turn next.

Prejudice and Discrimination

In our discussion of ethnic identity we illustrated positive features of ethnicity. There can also be many negative variations, including social distance, stereotypes, prejudice, and discrimination.

Social Distance

When Simmel (1950a) introduced the concept of **social distance**, he proposed, among other relationships, the existence of an inversely varying association between in-group solidarity and social distance from out-groups. The closer you feel to the group, the further you feel from others. Simmel's discussion of "the stranger" shows both social nearness and social distance. Consider these minority Canadians: immigrants coming as strangers to a new land; French Canadians visiting other parts of Canada and feeling like strangers; aboriginal peoples segregated in reserves away from the urban industrial mainstream; Jewish Canadians who feel they are practising their religion among a strange and seemingly alien majority. How can these strangers, who strongly identify with their in-group culture and tradition, retain their own social world — or "ground of identification," as Lewin (1948) would put it — and at the same time relate securely to others? We would expect minority strangers entering the environment of others to be secure only if grounded in an ethnic reference group, or if socially and psychologically motivated by the norms of such an in-group. Hence "distance" and "security" are linked concepts.

Levine, Carter, and Miller Gorman (1976) contend that "Simmel's utilization of the metaphor 'distance' was by no means restricted to his pages on the 'stranger,' [but] constitutes a pervasive and distinctive feature of his sociology as a whole." They summarize the meanings Simmel attached to distance as follows:

1. ecological attachment and mobility;
2. emotional involvement and detachment; and

3. the extent to which persons share similar qualities and sentiments.

Simmel himself also thought that distance could be expressed many ways. While recent work has attempted to sort out these meanings, Bogardus (1959), famous for his "social distance scale," chose to use "the degree of sympathetic understanding that functions between person and person, between person and group, and between group and group" as his measure of social distance. The Bogardus scale has been widely used, although not extensively in Canada.

Driedger and Mezoff (1980) studied a random sample of 2520 high-school students to determine students' feelings about different degrees of closeness in their contacts with members of various ethnic groups. Students were asked about people they would be willing to marry, have as a close friend, have as a neighbour, work with, or be acquainted with. They were also asked whether they would be willing to ban members of these ethnic groups from Canada, or to impose "visitor only" status on them — that is, not allow them as immigrants. The students (almost all of whom were Caucasian) were much more willing to marry those of European origin than those of non-European origin (for the most part these latter were non-Caucasian). Willingness to marry, which Bogardus considered a measure of "nearness," seems therefore to indicate less nearness toward non-Europeans. The study also showed that as students identified more strongly with their in-group, they tended also to prefer more distance from others, possibly in order to maintain their identities. Although many of the high-school students indicated a willingness to be close friends with most non-Europeans, most suggested an unwillingness to marry a non-European. This does seem to indicate a desire for identity maintenance. Relatively few students wished to bar these groups from Canada or to receive them only as visitors, although 11 percent preferred such a distance from the Jews. Such extreme desire for distance is in this instance most likely evidence of prejudice.

Stereotypes

A **stereotype** is an exaggerated belief associated with a category. It differs from a category in that it is a fixed idea that accompanies a category and carries additional judgements or "pictures" about a category or group. A stereotype may be either positive or negative and is often used to justify behaviour toward a specific group. Negative stereotypes of racial and ethnic groups have been and are widespread. Jews are supposed to be shrewd and ambitious, Italians heavily involved in crime, Irish men drunkards, aboriginal people lazy and undependable, Germans aggressive and boorish: all stereotypes, all negative. Positive stereotypes are also numerous: Asiatics are supposed to stress family loyalty, Hutterites to be very religious, the British to be efficient.

Mackie (1974) found that her group of 590 adults selected from organizations in Edmonton had an overwhelmingly negative image of Canadian aboriginal peoples as sharing neither the work nor the success values of the surrounding society. The stereotype of Hutterites was mostly positive (clean-living, religious, hard-working, thrifty, rural, law-abiding, pacifistic, sexually moral, sober) but also contained negative elements (exclusive, opposed to higher education, old-fashioned, disliked). Mackie's sample also reported a flattering image of Ukrainians. On the other hand, Berry, Kalin, and Taylor (1977) found that in Quebec images of Ukrainians were not nearly as positive as those in Edmonton, which illustrates how stereotypes may vary by region. Mackie, of course, tried to determine how far these stereotypes conformed to fact and to what extent they did not. She found some correlations and some exaggerations.

Prejudice

The word "prejudice" derives from the Latin *praejudicium*, which means precedent, a judgement based on previous decisions and experiences (Allport 1954). Words change over time, and **prejudice** has come to mean thinking ill of others without sufficient warrant. One dictionary defines it as "a feeling favorable or unfavorable toward a person or thing, prior to, or not based on, actual experience." These definitions suggest that prejudice is unfounded judgement and that emotions are heavily involved. While biases can be both positive and negative, we tend to think of ethnic prejudice today as mostly negative, although Allport suggests that such prejudgements

Democracy Betrayed

In 1988, Prime Minister Brian Mulroney and Art Miki of the National Association of Japanese Canadians signed a historic redress agreement in which Canada acknowledged having treated the Japanese unjustly and agreed to make symbolic redress payments to Japanese individuals and the community. The following is from a submission by the National Association of Japanese Canadians to the federal government.

In February 1942, the government of Canada ordered the expulsion of all Canadians of Japanese ethnic origin from the West Coast of British Columbia. By its action, the government perpetrated the view that ethnicity and not individual merit was the basis of citizenship. The seven years that followed witnessed the violation of human and civil rights on a scale that is without precedent in Canadian history (Sunahara 1981).

Armed with the unlimited powers of the War Measures Act, RCMP officers entered homes without warrant, day and night, giving people only hours to move. Fishing boats, automobiles, and radios were confiscated. A dawn-to-dusk curfew was imposed on "every person of the Japanese race" (Adachi 1976). Husbands and wives were forcibly separated, the men interned in road camps in such places as Rainbow, Jasper, and Yellowhead. Those who refused to abandon their families were sent to prisoner-of-war camps at Petawawa and Angler in Ontario.

The government's first measure, which was to intern only "male enemy aliens," rapidly escalated to the removal and incarceration of each and every Japanese Canadian. Families were ejected from their homes and placed in animal pens in Hastings Park, Vancouver, which became the clearing house for removal to the interior of British Columbia. On March 28, 1942, the British Columbia Security Commission, the civilian body established to carry out the uprooting, announced the sugar beet program. Families were allowed to stay together on the condition that they leave British Columbia to work in the beet fields of Alberta and Manitoba, where there was an acute labour shortage. The first to go were families from Steveston and Fraser Valley. On arrival, they were inspected and chosen for labour like slaves at a public auction (*A Dream of Riches* 1978).

Having been branded "enemy aliens" by the highest authority in the land, Japanese Canadians were met with suspicion and distrust in their forced migrations. Alberta accepted them only on the condition that the federal government guarantee their removal after the war was over. They were prohibited from buying or leasing land and could not grow crops except by special permission from the minister of justice; businesses and residential leases were strictly controlled; and municipalities such as Chatham, St. Catharines, and Toronto banned Japanese Canadians from their city limits.

The Security Commission began its work on March 4, 1942, and, by October, its mandate had been accomplished: 21 000 people of Japanese ethnic origin had been displaced from their homes and torn from their livelihood without recourse to legal appeal. Yet these deprivations merely presaged what was to come.

constitute prejudice only if they are not reversible in the light of new facts.

Allport further suggests that prejudgement is normal and necessary, because the human mind can think only with the aid of categories or generalizations. A human being is continuously bombarded with millions of stimuli, and it is impossible to react to them all. As a result, we tend to select for attention and memory only a relative few of the many experiences available to us. Our minds form clusters of previous experiences for guiding daily adjustments. As we have new experiences, we tend to assimilate them as much as possible within the clusters already formed. This enables us to identify related objects quickly.

These categories are also more or less emotional, depending on what the experiences of a particular individual may have been. Thus, a person may feel more negative about some experiences (and the people related to those experiences) than about others. Some categories are more rational than others, but the clustering process permits human beings to slip easily into ethnic prejudice. Erroneous generalizations can be made, with the result that some categories of people may evoke not merely feelings of dislike, but feelings of actual hostility.

Such tendencies toward bias are present in the media, books, and everyday conversations that mould our impressions. Depending on prejudicial

Once Japanese Canadians were uprooted from their communities on the west coast, the Custodian of Enemy Property, who was solemnly charged with holding homes, businesses, and property *in trust*, proceeded to liquidate these belongings *without the owners' consent*. Possessions that had taken lifetimes to accumulate were disposed of in fleeting moments. Furniture, appliances, sewing machines, pianos, and household goods were snapped up at fire-sale prices by the general public. Unopened and unvalued boxes and trunks of china, silver, clothing, and irreplaceable family heirlooms were auctioned off for $2 per bid. Homes and businesses were sold by public tender to eager buyers. In the Fraser Valley alone, 769 farms comprising 13 000 acres [5260 ha] of the finest agricultural land in British Columbia were disposed of for $64 per acre (Berger 1981; Sunahara 1981). The 1200 fishing boats impounded on December 8, 1941, were disposed of under Orders-in-Council P.C. 288 and P.C. 251, which were passed on January 13, 1942. Any capital from property sales was wiped out by realtors' and auctioneers' fees, storage and handling charges, and deductions for welfare while interned. Japanese Canadians, unlike prisoners of war or enemy nationals under the Geneva Convention, were forced to pay for their own internment.

In August, 1944, Prime Minister William Lyon Mackenzie King declared, "It is a fact no person of Japanese race born in Canada has been charged with any act of sabotage or disloyalty during the years of war" (King 1944). Nevertheless, in 1945, when World War II was clearly over, the government once again invoked the spurious issue of loyalty to deal with the "problem" of Japanese Canadians still remaining in British Columbia.

A "loyalty survey" was conducted throughout the detention camps of British Columbia during April and May of 1945. Proof of loyalty consisted of "volunteering" to remove oneself east of the Rocky Mountains. Those unwilling or unable to make such a move were to be classified as disloyal, divested of citizenship and nationality, and banished to Japan. The original orders authorized the deportation of 10 000 Japanese Canadians. A groundswell of public opinion, reinforced by a declaration from the United Nations that the act of deporting citizens was a crime, stopped this action by the government, but not before 4000 Japanese Canadians, half of whom were Canadian-born, had departed for Japan. Those who escaped exile to Japan were forced to disperse across Canada.

Once outside British Columbia, however, restrictions continued. In 1944, the House of Commons passed a special order to ensure that Japanese Canadians expelled from British Columbia would be unable to vote in federal elections; lack of franchise in British Columbia had prevented Japanese Canadians from voting in federal elections as long as they remained in British Columbia.

Source:

Adapted from National Association of Japanese Canadians, *Democracy Betrayed: The Case for Redress* (a submission to the government of Canada on the violation of rights and freedoms of Japanese Canadians during and after World War II), 1984. Winnipeg: National Association of Japanese Canadians, 1984. Ken Adachi, *The Enemy That Never Was: A History of the Japanese Canadians*. Toronto: McClelland and Stewart, 1976; Thomas R. Berger, *Fragile Freedoms: Human Rights and Dissent in Canada*. Toronto: Clarke, Irwin and Co., 1981; Japanese Canadian Centennial Project. *A Dream of Riches: The Japanese Canadians, 1877–1977*. Vancouver: Japanese Canadian Centennial Project, 1978; Ann Gomer Sunahara, *The Politics of Racism: The Uprooting of Japanese Canadians During the Second World War*. Toronto: James Lorimer, 1981.

---

bias, young people can be referred to as "youthful" or "immature"; people who are cautious may be regarded as "discreet" or "cowardly"; someone who is bold may be considered "courageous" or "foolhardy."

While social distance from others may be the result of a desire to maintain a separate ethnic identity, it can also, as we have observed, stem from negative attitudes. Berry, Kalin, and Taylor (1977) found that those who favoured multiculturalism in Canada also tended to have more positive attitudes toward others. Canadians of British and French origin, however, although they tended to have fairly positive attitudes toward each other, wished to identify less with others.

Those who were more ethnocentric still, such as Quebec francophones and British Maritimers, tended to be more negative toward new immigrants and multiculturalism. Similarly, Cardinal (1969) claims that prejudice against Canadian Indians is common and occasionally reflected in the media.

Tienhaara (1974) found in her analysis of postwar Canadian Gallup polls that historical situations created varied responses. Polls taken in 1943, during the war, showed that a majority of Canadians thought that Japanese people living in Canada should be sent back to Japan, although the respondents made distinctions between those Japanese who were Canadian citizens and those who were not. After the war, Canadians became more tolerant, but many still favoured deportation. In fact, most Japanese people living on the Pacific Coast of Canada during World War II were sent inland involuntarily.

A 1955 poll taken in Canada showed that more than one-third of the respondents did not wish to have "a few families from Europe come to [their] neighbourhood to live" for a variety of reasons. A national poll in 1961 showed that over half the Canadians questioned thought we should continue to restrict nonwhites. A poll in 1963 showed that almost two-thirds would not move if "coloured people" came into their neighbourhood, but over one-third — 38 percent — said they would or might (Tienhaara 1974). These polls seem to indicate that, depending on historical situations and social events, there are latent or potential attitudes of prejudice among many Canadians.

Discrimination

Prejudice is an attitude; **discrimination** is action that is usually based on prejudiced attitudes. Allport (1954) argues that "discrimination comes about only when we deny to individuals or groups of people the equality of treatment which they wish." Hagan (1977) suggests that in this connection four distinctions are important: differential treatment, prejudicial treatment, denial of

desire, and disadvantaging treatment. Obviously, we cannot treat everyone equally; distinctions must be made. This constitutes *differential treatment*. Although this may not be discrimination as such, it can be a predisposition to discrimination. *Prejudicial treatment* will likely lead to unfair treatment. *Denial of desire* involves placing restrictions on the aspirations of some members of society, such as their desire to live in any part of the city, or their desire to belong to any club, if they can afford it. (In some cities of the United States, for example, despite widespread official desegregation, blacks still cannot buy houses in strictly white neighbourhoods. Jews often claim that they are denied membership in select clubs.) *Disadvantageous treatment* is a clear form of discrimination that may take a variety of forms.

Allport (1954) outlines several forms of disadvantageous treatment. *Anti-locution* (verbal expressions such as jokes and name-calling) would be the mildest form. *Avoidance* is more severe: prejudiced people restrict their own movements so that they do not come into contact with undesirables. *Discrimination* is still more intense in that now acts of inequality, of disadvantage, extend to the ethnic or minority victim, including disadvantages in citizenship, employment, education, housing, or public accommodation. It gets worse. *Physical attack* (ejection from a community, lynchings, massacres, and genocide) would be the severest form. Until recently blacks were still

The 1992 Los Angeles Race Riots

Few will forget the scores of TV reruns of the beating of Rodney King by four police officers in Los Angeles in 1992. All who saw the beatings, filmed by an amateur photographer, agreed that the beatings were brutal, indiscriminate, and inhumane. Officers beat a helpless victim lying on the ground while other police watched. Most expected justice to be done in the courts.

When the officers were freed without charge, the largest riot in American history erupted. Anger was unrestrained: Los Angeles County became an inferno of riots, looting, and mayhem. Police were nowhere in sight,

and the law of the streets ruled. When the riots quieted down, most businesses in the area had been looted and burned and jobs of hundreds had been lost. Property damage was in the tens of millions of dollars and included schools, community centres, and churches. An urban community lay in ruins.

A 1992 UCLA survey showed that these cataclysmic events did very little to change the attitudes of residents about economic, ethnic, political, and social life (reported in the *Los Angeles Times*, December 22, 1992). Surveys before and after the riots showed that

fear, alienation, hostility, and despair were rampant both before and after. There were however, some changes. When asked, "Does America owe your group a better chance?" more Asians (37 compared with 44 percent) and blacks (55 compared with 75 percent) said yes after the riots, but Latinos (64 and 64 percent) and Anglo (17 and 15 percent) attitudes were unchanged (Bobo 1992). However, Anglo attitudes about living with neighbours such as Asians (22 and 40 percent), blacks (15 and 28 percent), and Latinos (21 and 39 percent) had become more favourable after the riots.

lynched in the United States; massacres of aboriginal people occurred in Canada; and the Jewish holocaust is still fresh in our memories, as Glickman and Bardicoff (1982) clearly show. Religious and political persecution remain constants in Northern Ireland, the Middle East, Eastern Europe, and elsewhere.

Driedger and Mezoff (1980), in their sample of 2520 high-school students in Winnipeg, found that perception of discrimination varied among ethnic groups (see Table 10-6). About one-third of the students reported discrimination. Jews, Italians, and Poles perceived the greatest discrimination in the classroom and in textbooks. The Jews, especially, reported discrimination in clubs, and denial of access that was free to others. While verbal abuse was reported most often, the Jews reported vandalism and physical attack as well. Blacks and Asians often report discrimination — and such reports seem to be growing more frequent every week, especially in large urban centres like Toronto.

One of the things sociologists do is study the way society is structured for discrimination. Canadian immigration laws permit quotas and restrictions on immigrants considered undesirable. Agencies and institutions restrict the opportunities of treaty Indians, nontreaty Indians, and Métis. The cycle of poverty is too often nourished rather than eliminated. During World War II, as noted earlier, the Canadian government forcibly evacuated Japanese Canadians from the West Coast and sent them inland because of a perceived threat to national security. (Not until 1988 did the Canadian government make restitution for these wrongdoings by agreeing to make payments to survivors — and to the Japanese Canadian community — and by issuing a formal apology for the unjust treatment they received from the government 40 years previously.) The Chinese were legally restricted from voting and denied access to public places, especially in British Columbia. Laws were passed in Alberta to restrict the expansion of Hutterite colonies. While English and French languages were once legally used in Manitoba, and other ethnic groups were permitted to educate their children in their own mother tongues, these rights were later changed and English alone was forced on minorities. Racism is increasingly raising its head in urban cen-

---

TABLE 10-6   Type of Discrimination Reported by High-School Students, by Ethnic Groups (Percent)

Type of Discrimination	Discrimination reported by								
	Jews (N = 290)	Poles (227)	Italians (65)	French (396)	Ukrainians (517)	Germans (333)	Scandinavians (78)	British (502)	Total (N = 2408)
Total[a]	68	51	46	45	36	33	19	18	35.5 (856)
Ethnic jokes	50	45	37	33	30	23	9	8	27.5 (662)
Verbal abuse	53	17	19	21	13	19	8	4	18.3 (440)
Language ridicule	27	15	30	29	13	13	4	8	15.7 (377)
Hate literature	19	2	6	4	3	5	0	2	5.0 (121)
Physical attack	21	2	3	4	3	3	1	2	4.7 (114)
Vandalism	13	1	2	1	2	3	1	0	2.7 (64)

[a]The percentages in this row represent the proportion of students in each category who reported at least one type of discrimination or reported discrimination in a given place.
SOURCE: Leo Driedger and Richard Mezoff, "Ethnic prejudice and discrimination in Winnipeg high schools," *Canadian Journal of Sociology* 6 (1980):13.

tres such as Toronto and Montreal. Nova Scotia has discriminated against blacks. In most societies, including Canada, there are powerful attempts to control and sometimes repress minorities. Those who control the political and economic institutions often use such power to their own advantage, forgetting about the rights and aspirations of the weak. This frequently leads to conflict, because many minorities feel that Canada is theirs as well — it does not belong only to those who have power.

Although studies of discrimination in Canada are few, discrimination clearly does exist, as native Indians, Jews, and non-Caucasian immigrants can well attest.

Three Ethnic Strategies

Much has changed since the Europeans encountered aboriginals in North America 500 years ago. In Mexico the aboriginals have declined to less than one-third of the total population; almost two-thirds are of mixed origins, and only one in ten is of Spanish European origin. Nevertheless, white skin and European status are highly valued. What changes will a North American free-trade agreement bring to Mexico, the poorest of the North American nations? How will Mexicans' identities and status change?

It is more than 200 years since Americans declared their independence from Britain. Since then the aboriginal population of the United States has declined to 3 percent of the total population, while the Europeans dominate. One out of eight Americans are black, who first came as slaves and now find themselves at the bottom of the socioeconomic hierarchy. The United States sought to become a melting pot, where all might be assimilated into a common American dream. However, one-fourth of the population are visible minorities (blacks, Hispanics, aboriginals), and they have not "melted" easily. The more fortunate whites often have not let them become free and equal.

The colonial presence has also lingered long in Canada, where the British and French Canadians who represent half of the population still look across the Ottawa River with much distrust. Constitutional talks have continued, on and off, for 125 years. Canada still struggles to integrate its colonial past, both with the aboriginals who were here first and the multicultural one-half who have come later. Will Canadians be able to live together in their diversity? Can just solutions be found so that fragile freedoms prevail (Berger 1981)? Each country has found quite different ways to deal with ethnic diversity. Now we want to try greater economic co-operation. Have we learned anything in 500 years since Columbus?

SUMMARY

1. An ethnic group is a group of people with shared sociocultural experience and/or similar characteristics. Its members perceive themselves as alike by virtue of their common ancestry. An ethnic group that is subordinate to any other group is called a minority group.

2. Canada is a land of immigrants. The Native peoples arrived first, followed much later by the Europeans. The French originally settled in what is now Quebec, followed by the British, and other northern, eastern, and southern Europeans. Today, the British constitute the largest ethnic group (40 percent), followed by the French (27 percent).

3. Only New Brunswick approximates a bilingual and bicultural area. The rest of Canada is highly diversified ethnically and marked regionally by the various native, French, British, and other European cultures. Thus, multiculturalism in a bilingual framework seems to reflect the demographic and regional facts of Canadian life.

4. Most urban industrial societies are highly stratified, and in Canada the ethnic groups are differentially located in the various strata. The British and the French, the two character groups, have special language status legally enshrined in the Canadian Constitution. This legal advantage, together with their early arrival and large populations, make them the two most powerful groups. But the French have always been junior partners. The treaty status groups, the Native peoples, were relegated to reserves by treaties that made and kept them subordinate. The entrance groups came later.

5. With the increase of the Canadian Indian population, as well as a large influx of new

immigrants, Canada has increasingly been faced with ethnic diversity. Various changes have occurred, and conflicts have arisen. Whose land is Canada? The question is on the minds of many. Official bilingualism and multiculturalism are hotly debated. No one theory seems best to explain Canadian ethnic change, though many — such as assimilation, amalgamation, pluralism, multivariate assimilation, modified pluralism, and conflict — have been suggested and studied.

6. Early in Canadian history many groups actively sought to maintain their ethnic identities by territorial segregation in rural communities; others were forced into reserves and ghettos. Some believe that language is the most important means of preserving ethnic identity; others value religion most highly; still others seek to foster heritage, endogamy, and choice of in-group friends. Ethnic identity can be maintained through identification with an ecological territory, with ethnic institutions, with an ethnic culture, with historical symbols, with an ideology, or with charismatic leadership.

7. Amidst the Canadian ethnic diversity, some groups are valued more highly than others. In many cases, distances between groups simply maintain identity, but sometimes they emerge as either prejudice (a prejudgement, usually negative and not based on actual experience, of a group of people) or discrimination (an action toward a group of people based on prejudiced attitudes).

GLOSSARY

Amalgamation. Process by which groups are blended into a melting pot where none remains distinctive.

Assimilation. Process by which a group becomes like the dominant group, and no longer remains distinctive. Also referred to in North America as "Anglo-conformity."

Charter groups. The two original European migration groups (British and French) whose legalized claims for such historically established privileges as the perpetuation of their separate languages and cultures are enshrined in the Canadian Constitution.

Discrimination. Process by which a person is deprived of equal access to privileges and opportunities available to others.

Entrance groups. Ethnic groups that are not founders of the country and whose members enter as immigrants after the national framework has been established.

Ethnic group. Group of individuals with a shared sense of peoplehood based on presumed shared sociocultural experiences and/or similar characteristics. They perceive themselves as alike by virtue of their common ancestry.

Ethnic identity. Attitude of being united in spirit, outlook, or principle with an ethnic heritage. An attachment and positive orientation toward a group with whom individuals believe they have a common ancestry and interest.

Ethnic stratification. Order in which ethnic groups form a hierarchy of dominance and socioeconomic status in a society.

Ethnocentrism. Tendency to see one's in-group as being in the centre of everything and to judge other ways of life by the standards of one's own group.

Melting pot. Situation in which the amalgamation and blending of groups have left none distinctive.

Minority group. Ethnic group that is subordinate to another group.

Modified pluralism. Glazer and Moynihan's modification of pluralism theory, describing a situation in which numerous groups maintain distinctly different cultures, ideologies, or interests; although they will be changed and modified somewhat, they will not be transformed entirely.

Multiculturalism. A policy relating to or designed for a combination of several distinct cultures.

Multivariate assimilation. Gordon's modification of assimilation theory, which maintains that assimilation is not a single social process but a number of cultural, structural, marital, identificational, attitudinal, behavioural, and civic subprocesses.

Pluralism. Social situation in which numerous ethnic, racial, religious, and/or social groups maintain distinctly different cultures, ideologies, or interests.

Prejudice. A feeling (usually negative) toward a person, group, or thing prior to, or not based on, actual experience. Prejudging others without sufficient warrant.

Race. Arbitrary biological grouping of people on the basis of physical traits.

Regional mosaic. Distinctive ethnic patterns formed by the various regions of a country that have different combinations of linguistic and cultural groups.

Segregation. Separation or isolation of a race, class, or ethnic group by forced or voluntary residence.

Social distance. In contrast to social nearness, Simmel defines social distance as ecological, emotional, and social detachment from others.

Stereotype. Opinions and judgements of others that create an exaggerated view of a type of person or group.

Treaty status. Certain privileges and obligations passed on to Canada's aboriginals from their ancestors, who signed treaties with the Canadian government.

FURTHER READING

Berger, Thomas R. *Fragile Freedoms: Human Rights and Dissent in Canada.* Toronto: Clarke, Irwin, 1981. Berger deals with the loss of freedoms by the Acadians, the Métis, Japanese Canadians, and religious and aboriginal minorities.

Bolaria, B. Singh, and Peter S. Li. *Racial Oppression in Canada.* 2nd edition. Toronto: Garamond Press, 1988. Deals with race and racism toward aboriginals, Chinese, Japanese, East Indians, and blacks in Canada.

Breton, Raymond, Wsevolod W. Isajiw, Warren E. Kalbach, and Jeffrey G. Reitz. *Ethnic Identity and Inequality: Varieties of Experience in a Canadian City.* Toronto: University of Toronto Press, 1990. A major study of eight ethnic groups in Toronto and their identity retention, segregation, class inequalities, and political organization.

Dickason, Olive Patricia. *Canada's First Nations: A History of Founding Peoples from Earliest Times.* Toronto: McClelland and Stewart, 1992. A history of Canada's 55 aboriginal peoples, colonial pressures, resistance, co-operation, and the revitalization of Native communities.

Driedger, Leo. *Ethnic Canada: Identities and Inequalities.* Toronto: Copp Clark Pitman, 1987. A collection of 22 readings on ethnic theory, demography, ecology, identity, conflict, and the need for human rights and social equality.

Driedger, Leo. *The Ethnic Factor: Identity in Diversity.* Toronto: McGraw-Hill Ryerson, 1989. An integrated volume on ethnic relations in Canada, dealing with the effects of industrialization on ethnic identity, stratification, and human rights.

Elliott, Jean Leonard, and Augie Fleras. *Unequal Relations: An Introduction to Race and Ethnic Dynamics in Canada.* Scarborough, ON: Prentice-Hall, 1992. Ethnic identities, race relations, multiculturalism, and inequalities are the focus of this textbook on ethnicity.

Fleras, Augie, and Jean Leonard Elliott. *Multiculturalism in Canada: The Challenge of Diversity.* Scarborough, ON: Nelson Canada, 1992. A discussion of the dimensions of multiculturalism, linguistic and cultural perspectives, "mainstreaming," and prospects for the future.

Fleras, Augie, and Jean Leonard Elliott. *The Nations Within: Aboriginal–State Relations in Canada, the United States and New Zealand.* Don Mills, ON: Oxford University Press, 1992. This comparative study of aboriginal peoples in three countries deals with self-determination, social status, government policies, and Native aspirations.

Frideres, James S. *Native People in Canada: Contemporary Conflict.* Scarborough, ON: Prentice-Hall, 1983. 2nd edition. A comprehensive sociological study of aboriginal peoples in Canada.

Halli, Shiva S., Frank Trovato, and Leo Driedger (eds.). *Ethnic Demography: Canadian Immigrant, Racial and Cultural Variations.* Ottawa: Carleton University Press, 1990. Contributions of 25 of Canada's top demographers describe ethnic cohesion, fertility, mortality, migration, and class.

Herberg, Edward N. *Ethnic Groups in Canada: Adaptations and Transitions.* Toronto: Nelson, 1989. Herberg reviews ethnic groups in Canada, considering immigration, changing cultures, new adaptations, and changing transitions.

Kallen, Evelyn. *Ethnicity and Human Rights in Canada.* Toronto: Gage, 1982. A discussion of Canadian human rights and the 1981 Charter and new Constitution.

Li, Peter S. (ed.). *Race and Ethnic Relations in Canada.* Don Mills, ON: Oxford University Press, 1990. A collection of new essays on ethnicity, including a demographic overview, immigration policy, multiculturalism, human rights, the politics of language, governmental policies, class differentials, and pluralism.

Samuda, Ronald J., John W. Berry, and Michel Laferrière (eds.). *Multiculturalism in Canada.* Toronto: Allyn and Bacon, 1984. A collection of writings on multicultural policies, attitudes, and adaptation.

CHAPTER 11

Formal Organizations

TERRENCE H. WHITE

In developed societies, organizations are everywhere. Governments, stores, hospitals, schools, universities, churches, restaurants, railways, airlines, funeral homes, and massage parlours are but a few pieces in the vast organizational mosaic of Canadian society.

Ask a group of people what *organization* means, and you will receive a wide array of answers. For some, the term is synonymous with bureaucracy. For others, it suggests the dull routine of work, or the fun of membership in a ski club. Or it may have more sinister connotations, evoking thoughts of organized crime and the Mafia. Ask sociologists for their views on the subject, and they are likely to respond guardedly: "Well, that depends. Are you talking about voluntary associations, or formal organizations, or complex organizations, or institutions, or what?"

Such a wide range of responses is understandable because *organization* is a very general term with many possible meanings. So it is necessary to narrow the focus on the term. This chapter examines the nature of organizations and their effects on our lives. Our main attention will be on formal organizations. But lest we narrow our focus too quickly, let us begin by looking at the role of organizations in the broader social spectrum.

Social Organization

Organizations are a universal attribute and a natural consequence of the social behaviour of human beings. People are *social* in that they do not live in isolation from other people. There are, of course, always a few people who do live most of their adult lives in isolation — hermits, for example. But even they find themselves in social settings from time to time in order to get essential supplies, emergency health treatment, perhaps a bath, or whatever. Generally, no functioning human is ever totally asocial — or not for long.

The reasons for this social tendency in human beings are many. At the most basic level, the biological necessities of human procreation require social behaviour if the species is to survive. Human sexual intercourse, the usual prerequisite activity to children — test-tube babies notwithstanding — presupposes co-operative social action. And offspring are dependent on adults for many years. In the absence of provisions for reproduction and child care, the species would disappear. At the most fundamental level, therefore, human social behaviour is necessary to ensure human survival.

Furthermore, when people interact with others, they may find themselves developing dependencies other than those associated with mere survival. If, for example, I am a farmer and you are a blacksmith, I may find that ploughing is easier and more effective using a metal plough that you have made. In return for the plough, I provide you with fresh vegetables and grain for your family. And later, if my horse needs shoeing, I bring that work to you. And so it goes.

What happens is that, in the process of our social interaction with each other, certain mutual dependencies develop. You need the food I grow, and I need your blacksmithing skills. Unable to do everything for ourselves, we divide most of the work so that we tend to do those things at which we are good and for which we have special facilities. As a consequence, we come to rely on others for additional skills, goods, or services. A basic division of labour results. **Division of labour** refers to the tendency for general tasks and roles to become increasingly specialized.

These three concepts — social behaviour, division of labour, and dependencies on others — are interrelated (see Figure 11-1). Human intelligence, skills, and abilities are not evenly distributed, so social behaviour eventually results in a very rudimentary division of labour. This division may be along gender and age lines, as in primitive tribes

FIGURE 11-1   Relationships among Social Behaviour, Division of Labour, and Dependencies on Others

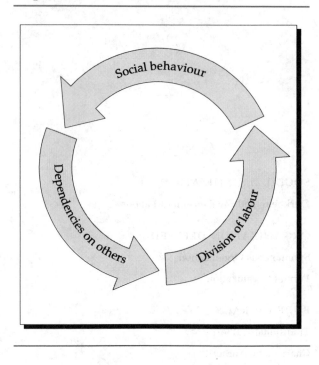

in which the males are usually the hunters and women and the elderly tend to family and household duties. Or it may be more of an occupational division of labour, as in the example of the farmer and the blacksmith.

The division of labour, no matter how simple or basic, leads to increasing dependencies among people that, in turn, reinforce social behaviour. As industrialization or development advances in a society, the cycle of interrelationships among these three components (gender, age, and occupation) becomes even more intense, with greater specialization in work resulting in a more complex division of labour, and so on. As a consequence, most people become bound into a web of dependency; they need others in order to survive or at least to live in the manner to which they are accustomed. The intricacy of these developments creates an expanding need for the co-ordination and control of the various elements in society. As this cycle of relationships develops and intensifies, the necessity for organization increases.

Durkheim and the Division of Labour

An early scholar who pointed to the link between the division of labour and the necessity for social organization was Emile Durkheim. He was interested in the impact on societies of the increasing division of labour. In *The Division of Labour in Society* (1964a, originally published in 1893), he focused on the question of *social solidarity* — What is it that binds people together in larger social networks? — and the mechanisms that create social solidarity. He identified two types of social solidarity: mechanical and organic.

In primitive societies, Durkheim suggested that the links between people take the form of **mechanical solidarity**. Based on strong systems of common beliefs, the division of labour is rudimentary, with people engaged in similar tasks and having relatively high degrees of self-sufficiency. Because people are able to supply most of their own basic needs, their dependencies on others through the division of labour are not great. As a result, their social bonds are kinship and neighbourliness. Outside the basic family unit, they get together with other people because they want to, rather than because they have to in order to survive.

The division of labour leads to increasing dependencies among people. Greater specialization in work results in a more complex division of labour.

But as societies evolve and become more complex, the division of labour increases, and specialization results in greater differentiation among people. No longer is everyone doing relatively similar fundamental tasks. Consequently, individual self-sufficiency decreases and greater dependencies on others develop. Greater dependency means that people must maintain social relations in order to survive at a desired standard. This basis for solidarity Durkheim termed **organic solidarity.**

The state of the division of labour is a critical element in Durkheim's analysis. Social behaviour mediated through the division of labour, as we saw above, determines the development of organization. As societies evolve from mechanical to organic solidarity, the specialization in the division of labour and the complex interdependencies generate needs for co-ordination and control. That is, they generate the need for organization.

Durkheim's focus on society as a system and his analysis of the impacts on human behaviour as an aspect of social structure are good examples of the elements in the structural-functional approach.

Organization Defined

Organization is a general term encompassing many interrelated elements. In order to identify the basics of organization, let us employ an imagined set of circumstances. You are driving in the country when you happen upon a farm where the barn is burning. Wanting to help, you join the farmer and a group of neighbours standing before the blaze. The necessity for action is obvious if damage to the barn is to be contained and the fire's spread to adjacent buildings averted. Fortunately, there is a water well in the yard, some buckets are lying around, and a ladder sits close at hand.

Given these particulars, you can easily imagine the next step. Those at the fire start a bucket brigade, moving water from the well to the barn and up the ladder onto the fire. Each individual performs a specific task, and probably some attempt is made to match people to appropriate tasks. The heavy chore of drawing water from the well, for instance, is assigned to a well-muscled individual, and people afraid of heights are on the ground rather than at the top of the ladder, facing the blaze.

Let us step back for a moment and analyze some of the components of this situation — for example, the group's goals. The burning barn presents a very clear challenge or goal for the people on the site: to put out the fire. And as it happens, a necessary prerequisite for an organization is a goal or series of goals whose achievement serves as a motivation for concerted action.

In our imaginary farmyard, the means for achieving the goal are clear: to move the water from the well onto the fire. The men and women could each fill their own buckets and run with them individually to the fire. These disorganized and independent actions may be successful if the fire is small and our firefighters are all fairly strong and hardy. On the other hand, such unrelated individual actions may result in failure if the fire is big. Imagine people crowded at the well waiting to fill their buckets, people bumping into each other and spilling their water en route to the fire, and so on. Clearly, the bucket-brigade organization is much more likely to realize the group's goals.

Our bucket brigade illustrates some important concepts besides the achievement of goals. First, it exemplifies the use of a technology in goal achievement. **Technology** is the application of a body of knowledge through the use of tools and processes in the production of goods and/or services. In this case, the technology is based on the knowledge that water can be used to extinguish certain types of fires. The tools in this instance are simply the buckets and the ladder, while the process involves filling the buckets and passing them along a human chain to the fire. Certain additional resources are required if the technology is to function; here they are the supply of water and people to fill the various roles or jobs in doing the work. Thus, in our elementary organization, the bucket brigade, the resources of water and volunteers are utilized in a division of labour employing a simple technology to achieve the goal of putting out the fire.

Back to the scene of the blaze. Good progress is being made in getting water to the fire, but a problem has developed, one requiring co-ordination: the buckets, once emptied on the fire, are not being returned to the well so that the process

Technology is the application of a body of knowledge through the use of tools and processes in the production of goods or services.

can be repeated. Several uninvolved children are commissioned to return the empty buckets regularly to the well, thus completing the circuit.

An observer of the scene would be impressed not only with the need to solve problems in pursuit of the goal but also with the communication between members of the organization as suggestions pass among them and as they give each other encouragement or reprimands for ups and downs in performance. In addition, one person has emerged as a leader, whose concern it is to co-ordinate the activities of the group, as well as take the lead in identifying and resolving problems. The reader will be relieved to learn the happy ending of this scene: the fire is speedily doused and only minor damage to the barn has resulted.

To sum up, our organization, the bucket brigade, although not as complex as a metropolitan fire department or a large business, does contain the basic elements of an organization:

1. goal(s)
2. resources (for example, water, buckets)
3. technology
4. division of labour

5. co-ordination
6. communication
7. leadership

An **organization**, therefore, is an entity in which people and resources are co-ordinated through a division of labour in the use of a technology to achieve a goal. Co-ordination, control, and problem-solving are facilitated through communication and leadership.

Spontaneous Organization

Our bucket brigade has disbanded; all the stalwart men, women, and children are enjoying a well-deserved rest. While it was in operation, though, the brigade constituted a good example of an organization. Furthermore, it was an example of a **spontaneous organization.** The fire was a one-time event. The people who were at the scene of the fire linked themselves in a co-ordinated activity to achieve a specific goal at a particular time. The goal achieved, the organization resolved itself into individuals, who went their separate ways.

Spontaneous organizations are often generated in crisis or emergency situations. For instance, volunteers may band together to fill sandbags and build dikes during a flood. Or the first people to arrive at a car accident may organize to extricate victims, provide first aid, and direct traffic. Once people and other regular service personnel arrive, this temporary organization scatters.

Spontaneous organizations do not always occur, however, even though a worthwhile goal or goals may be clear. One reason for nonoccurrence may be that the technology to achieve the goals is not known or readily available. Consider the events one evening in a mountain campground overflowing with campers and their children. In the middle of the site was a large dumpster container full of compacted garbage. After supper, a black bear and her two cubs strolled through the campground to the container, and the mother climbed inside and began throwing out leftovers for her hungry cubs.

Everyone in camp pressed forward to watch the proceedings; oblivious to the onlookers, the three bears ripped open garbage bags and consumed practically everything but the cans. One of the cubs climbed up and into the high-walled container to join the mother. After a while, the mother clambered out and waited for her cub to join her. But the cub could not get out. The mother's concern mounted and she began bellowing and tentatively charging the crowd. The longer this behaviour went on, the more it became a threat, especially in view of the many children nearby.

Adults in the crowd began to look for some solution to the problem of getting the cub out of the garbage container. But no ready solutions were apparent. In this instance, participants in a possible organized action to achieve a goal were unable to proceed because no suitable technology was known to them; the situation was compounded further by their fear.

A bit later, a park warden drove up in his truck, surveyed the scene, and left. He quickly returned with a fence post, drove alongside the container, rolled down his window, and leaned the post against the inside wall of the container so that the cub could climb out. Mother and cubs reunited and scrambled into the bush, while the campers glanced sheepishly at one another with why-didn't-we-think-of-that looks.

So spontaneous organizations may not form because the appropriate technology is either unknown or unavailable to those at the scene. Also, of course, the goal may not be clear, as in unfamiliar circumstances such as an earthquake or tornado. Another possibility is that people on the scene are not prepared to make a commitment to co-operative action for reasons of fear. For example, bystanders may watch motionless on a dock while someone is drowning or ignore the pleas for help from an assault or mugging victim. Such people do not want to get involved.

Formal Organization

Many organizations are more enduring than the spontaneous ones we have considered so far. Earlier we referred to the circular nature of the interrelationships among social behaviour, division of labour, and social dependencies. We observed that as these links intensify, societies move, in Durkheim's phrasing, from mechanical to organic solidarity. Along with these developments, we suggested that people tend increasingly to be enmeshed in a dependency web whereby the specialized division of labour makes them more

reliant on others for survival at a desired standard of living. To manage the complexity of these links, societies come to be increasingly formalized. **Formalization** is a process by which the informality of relationships in earlier social situations is gradually replaced by varying degrees of rules, codes of conduct, laws, and other means of regulation.

Formalization is a way of guiding and regularizing human interactions; it is an attempt to avoid the chaos that would result if every human contact was completely spontaneous. Most cities, for instance, have a network of stoplights to regulate, guide, and control traffic flow in areas of congestion.

The intent of formalization is to achieve social order and a degree of stability through the patterned conduct of individuals and social units. As a co-ordination mechanism, formalization is an attempt to anticipate possible variations and to reduce them to an acceptable range of desired behaviour through the use of guidelines, rules, and regulations. Formalization begets formalization, and in time the resulting volume necessitates that the rules be codified in written form to ensure that they are consistent and enduring.

Few areas of Canadians' lives are not subject to the incursions of formalization. Governments have laws and bylaws governing everything from traffic to trash. They certify our births and deaths and collect taxes in between. We sign contracts, arrange mortgages and loans, and make wills for our heirs. Our clubs and associations require commitments and dues from members; students comply with course requirements to accumulate degree credits. Social contact relies on varying degrees of formalization to provide acceptable conduct and to ensure stability and continuity. Formalization may also be a co-ordination and control technique in organizations.

In our earlier example of the bucket brigade a spontaneous organization developed in response to particular circumstances of the moment and disbanded when the task was completed. Others elsewhere may decide that fire protection is not something that can be left to the chance that each time people will happen to appear at the fire scene and successfully organize to battle the blaze. Instead, they elect to have in place a continuing capability to answer fire alarms and to provide a ready-made organization to deal with emergencies. Fire departments, volunteer or full-time, are examples of formal organizations. Unlike the spontaneous organization — our bucket brigade — the fire department is an organization of relatively enduring character that normally outlives individual members.

You may recall from earlier chapters that a role is the behaviour expected of the incumbent of a particular position. In a formal organization, the roles necessary in its division of labour are specified in its documents, and the requirements of each role are written out in job descriptions. When the fire chief retires, the department usually does not disintegrate; instead, a new individual is recruited to fill the vacant role and the department continues to meet its goals.

Continuity and formalized procedures are the main characteristics that distinguish a formal organization from a spontaneous organization. We are now in a position to complete our definition. A **formal organization** is a relatively enduring or continuing social entity in which roles and resources are co-ordinated through a division of labour in the use of a technology to achieve a goal or goals. Co-ordination, control, and problem solving are facilitated through communication and leadership and are formalized through written rules and procedures.

Spontaneous organization is encountered at different times throughout our lives, but formal organizations have more profound and frequent effects on us. These will be our focus for the remainder of the chapter. One of the first scholars to stress the importance of formalization was Max Weber.

Bureaucracy

There are many possible ways of structuring and administering an organization. From societies to universities, one of the great problems in survival and success is how to co-ordinate social behaviour so that a reasonable degree of social order is maintained and desired communal goals are attained. Central to any consideration of social order are the means of control. How does a society or organization get people to co-operate? What power does it have over its members to ensure conformity to established norms? Who is to wield this power?

Weber was much intrigued by questions of social order and power. Why, he wondered, do people obey commands from persons in authority? Is it because the person issuing the command has *power* and is able to achieve her or his objectives in spite of resistance? Or is it a question of *discipline* — is it because people, as a condition of their membership in the group, are expected to obey?

His further analyses led him to conclude that one factor people assess before deciding whether or not to obey is the legitimacy of the authority issuing the command. From this perspective, Weber argued that there are three major bases of legitimate authority: traditional, charismatic, and legal-rational. Table 11-1 outlines these three types of authority and some of their characteristics.

Traditional Authority

Traditional authority rests on "an established belief in the sanctity of immemorial traditions and the legitimacy of the status of those exercising authority under them" (Weber 1947). In monarchies, for example, people may believe in the divine right of their king or queen to rule. People accept the authority as legitimate because they believe that it is a God-given right transferred down through eligible descendants and delegated under certain conditions to members of the official court. Likewise, people may accept that, in families, the parents exercise authority over their children by virtue of the early dependence of children on them for survival. Traditional authority is something we see in a limited way in Canada with the monarch and her or his representatives, the governor general, and the various provincial lieutenant-governors.

Charismatic Authority

Charismatic authority, by contrast, depends "on devotion to the specific and exceptional sanctity, heroism or exemplary character of an individual person, and of the normative patterns of order revealed or ordained by him" (Weber 1947). The authority of charismatic figures derives from the belief that they are special, that they possess some exceptional ability or magic that inspires the loy-

TABLE 11-1   Characteristics of Ideal Types of Authority

	Rational	Traditional	Charismatic
Source of leadership	Leader has special training or expertise to occupy the position	Leader traces origin to a traditional status or was born into the position	Leader has special personal qualities: e.g., magical powers, exemplary character, heroism, etc.
Name of rank and file	Members, citizens	Subjects, comrades	Followers, disciples
Grounds for obedience	Owed to a set of rules, laws, and precedents, to an office rather than the individual who fills the office	Owed to leader out of personal loyalty because of leader's personal wisdom	Owed out of duty to recognize a charismatic quality and act accordingly
Form of administration	Highly trained personnel who are appointed and dismissed, whose task it is to keep written records and implement leader's policy	Personal retainers of the leader chosen on basis of social privilege or the favouritism in which leader holds them	Persons who are called to serve on the basis of the charismatic qualities they themselves possess
Relationship to property	Strict legal separation between property of leaders and community	Leader often legally possesses all property in the realm and others own only what leader gives them	Leaders are not expected to own much but are supported through the devotion of their followers
Form of opposition	Directed against the system	Directed against the person of the leader	If leader does not continue to show charismatic qualities, he or she loses authority and followers leave

SOURCE: Adapted with the permission of The Free Press, a Division of Macmillan, Inc. from *The Theory of Social and Economic Organization* by Max Weber, translated by A.M. Henderson and Talcott Parsons. Ed. by Talcott Parsons. Copyright © 1947, renewed 1975 by Talcott Parsons.

alty of their followers. Such is the pervasive character of leaders of various religious cults, such as the "Moonies" or the Doukhobors. Although infrequently used to describe contemporary politicians, political charisma has been attributed to Winston Churchill in Great Britain, Mohandas Gandhi and Jawaharlal Nehru in India, Mao Zedong in China, Kwame Nkrumah in Ghana, John F. Kennedy in the United States, Pierre Trudeau in Canada, and Nelson Mandela in South Africa.

Legal–Rational Authority, or Bureaucracy

We occasionally witness charismatic leadership, but by far the most frequent authority pattern we experience is Weber's third type. **Legal–rational authority** is based "on a belief in the 'legality' of patterns of normative rules and the right of those elevated to authority under such rules to issue commands" (Weber 1947).

The underlying process of this type of authority is formalization. As a result, legal–rational authority tends to be more systematic and impersonal than either traditional or charismatic authority. Weber argued not only that this was the case but that organizations based on rational authority tend to have similarities. He called the pure form of this authority pattern **bureaucracy.**

Weber was curious about the relationships between an increasingly complex division of labour

The British monarchy is one of the few examples of traditional authority in Canada.

in a society and the nature of the organizations in which that work was done. As we have already noted, his research indicated that as work and the division of labour become more complicated, there is a tendency for the organizational form in which the work is undertaken to resemble what he referred to, in its pure form, as bureaucracy.

Weber identified certain common features of bureaucratic organizations.

1. A bureaucracy is governed by a set of fixed and official rules and regulations. They outline the jurisdictions and responsibilities of each unit and usually each position in the organization. In a large hospital, for instance, the housekeeping department is charged with maintenance and upkeep of the facility, as opposed to the nursing departments, which are charged with patient care. Within the housekeeping department, the tasks of laundry personnel are specified and are quite distinct from those of dishwashers in the kitchen

area. Thus we can see that a bureaucracy has a set of comprehensive rules that govern the division of labour in the organization and clearly fix the duties and jurisdictional areas of each department and each person within it.

2. A bureaucracy has a *pyramid of authority*. That is, there are various levels of authority, and the lower offices are supervised by the higher ones. With so many rules and regulations instructing everyone as to the expected practices and outcomes of their offices, an extensive chain of command is necessary to monitor and oversee operations. A function of the hierarchy is to make certain that people and departments actually do what they are supposed to do, and in the proper manner. A characteristic of bureaucratic authority pyramids is that each supervisor has a limited sphere of authority. His or her span of control is confined to particular subordinates, and, in turn, subordinates are expected to acknowledge and respond to the authority vested in their immediate supervisor.

3. The management of the organization is based on written documents. "Get it in writing" is the key to successful bureaucratic management. These written documents — whether memos, reports, letters, or computer printouts — are all preserved in the files for future reference, guidance, or clarification.

4. The written rules and procedures in a bureaucracy ensure that clients are treated in a consistent fashion without regard to personal considerations. This impersonality of relationships applies not only to client contacts but also to contacts among members of the bureaucracy.

5. Because the rules that govern the operation of a bureaucracy are so specific as to the duties and responsibilities of each unit and position, there tends to be a relatively high degree of specialization in tasks. This high division of labour often means that a prerequisite for assuming a position in the organization is some degree of specialized training.

6. The presence of extensive operating rules and the impersonal nature of many of the interactions in a bureaucracy are means of ensuring that people are recruited into the organization and promoted within it on the basis of their performance, competence, knowledge,

Towards Modernization

Arturo Arriaga closes the sheet of steel he uses for a door, fastens a chain, and snaps shut the padlock. The 23-year-old Monterrey worker can't afford much more than a spare cinder-block house with no phone. Still, he considers himself on the fast track. Since beginning a new training program at Galvak, a specialty steel company, he and his co-workers have seen productivity skyrocket and their pay nearly double, to $13.38 a day. If Arriaga passes his next test, he'll get another promotion. Sure, Arriaga says, Mexican dishwashers and farm workers earn more in the U.S. "But here I have a real career."

As Arriaga and millions of other Mexican workers pursue their careers, few realize how closely their progress is monitored — and controlled — by government officials. Every Thursday morning for the past six years, a cadre of economists, including six Cabinet members and top business leaders and union officials, has gathered around a large table in the Labor Secretariat offices in Mexico City. There they thrash out agreements that control prices and wages and brainstorm on ways to boost productivity. It's the kind of social pact that has been tried in many other Latin American countries. But only in Mexico, with its one-party rule, have such agreements stuck. Mandated by the country's leading economist, President Carlos Salinas de Gortari, the goal is to lift the productivity of Arriaga and his fellow workers to First World levels.

In their drive to modernize Mexico, Salinas and his planners command nearly every variable of the economy. To smother inflation and preserve Mexico's huge labor cost gap with U.S. and other producers, Salinas fixes salaries through a complex business-labor agreement that's known as *el pacto*. He anoints — and boots out — labor union bosses and state governors alike. A few years ago, he quietly banished an obstreperous American president of Chrysler de Mexico, who was quickly replaced by a Mexican. Salinas' technocrats juggle import duties and steer investment from one region to another.

In short, Salinas and his number-crunchers run a near-command economy, much closer to the Asian model than any other country in the West. It has produced an astounding success. Today, Mexican workers are reaching for better and better industrial jobs. But to clinch Mexico's modernization, Salinas wants to link his small, top-down economy to the freewheeling giant to his north through the North American Free Trade Agreement.

It's an unprecedented, politically explosive First World-Third World marriage. As Mexicans climb up the job ladder, they in essence fight, *mano a mano*, for U.S. jobs. As hundreds of thousands of unemployed U.S. workers have discovered, "the jobs in the U.S. that are vulnerable are not the $6-an-hour jobs, but the $18-an-hour ones," says Harley Shaiken, labor economist at University of California, San Diego. "It goes to the core of the U.S. industrial base." And Mexico's overarching government raises the question whether it is possible to integrate work forces managed under such different rules.

Indeed, Northern eyes are opening to the powerful advantage Mexico has in its young, rapidly growing, low-cost labor pool. Nearly four out of ten 18-year-olds entering the continental labor market are Mexicans — this in a country with a mere 5% of U.S. gross national product. Strengthening Mexico's hand are low wages and high productivity. Pay in Mexico remains about one-sixth the U.S. level, while productivity has grown at twice the U.S. rate in the past five years. The most dramatic gains are at corporations such as Ford, General Electric, and IBM, whose Mexican plants match and often surpass their U.S. counterparts in productivity and quality. Since Salinas' term started in 1988, $26 billion has flowed into Mexico in part for new plants and to upgrade existing ones, helping to create 2 million new jobs, as the U.S. has shed them by the thousands.

ONE-WAY FLOW. Salinas has managed Mexico almost too well. Its quick climb is now shaking the philosophical underpinnings of a North America Inc. Traditional free-market thinking, embodied in NAFTA, maintains that job growth in Mexico makes for a more prosperous region while slowing migration to the north. That prosperity will increase the appetite for U.S. exports, thus preserving high-wage jobs in the U.S. But now a growing chorus of NAFTA opponents argues that Mexico's industrial policy creates an unlevel playing field. With the government holding down salaries and keeping a tight grip on unions, critics say, Mexico will suck in the jobs, all right. But with wages held down, Mexicans can afford to buy little of what they make. That could spell delayed gratification for Mexicans and the U.S. exporters who await their prosperity.

The stage is set for a bruising battle over NAFTA in Washington. Debate is focused on two side agreements — on labor rights and environmental regulations. NAFTA foes from Ralph Nader to Lane Kirkland seek to weaken Salinas' grip on the economy, treating Mexican labor as an unfair trade advantage needing to be offset by a "social" tariff in some cases. But Salinas, who chooses a successor this fall and bows out in late 1994, needs to broker a smooth transition. He can be expected to resist, with diplomatic pressure and a lobbying barrage, any side deals that would crimp his power.

Source:

Business Week, April 19, 1993, pp. 85–86. Reprinted by special permission, copyright © 1993 by McGraw Hill Inc.

and ability. Such advancement is based on achievement criteria; that is to say, people in a bureaucracy move ahead because they are best qualified to fill the requirements of the position as outlined in the operating rules and duties of the bureaucracy. Recruitment and advancement involving favouritism or particularism — in which the basis is who you know or being someone's daughter or son or other reasons unrelated to the demands of the job — are regarded as inconsistent with the underlying principles of bureaucracy.

These six components of bureaucracy are seen to be minimum essentials if the organization is to operate efficiently and endure. Highly bureaucratized organizations are most likely to develop in situations in which the tasks essential to the organization's technology are, by nature, routine and repetitive. It is also the view of many observers that, as organizations grow, the necessity for control and co-ordination increases and, therefore, so does the tendency toward bureaucratization. We shall explore this observation more fully later.

Bureaucracies are more likely to persist when their environments are relatively stable. As we shall see, organizations seek to avoid or reduce uncertainty. A bureaucracy, through its formalized rules and authority structures, attempts to anticipate requirements and demands so that it can operate predictably and consistently. Another consequence is to ensure with the greatest probability possible that its members will perform in a predictable and consistent fashion.

Department-Store Bureaucracy: An Example. We have all experienced the standardizing qualities of bureaucracies. Most people who shop at a department store pay for their purchases with cash or a credit card. These are the normal procedures, and customers who follow them are speedily processed through the cashier's line and are on their way.

If you have ever varied from the norm and used a personal cheque as payment, then you have created a special circumstance. The smooth flow of customers grinds to a halt as you write your cheque (often having to inquire as to the date, the exact amount of the purchase, and other neces-

sary bookkeeping details). The cashier asks, "Do you have a valid driver's licence and major credit card?" These documents are carefully scrutinized and appropriate notations are made on the cheque. Furthermore, accepting a cheque is usually outside the specified jurisdiction of cashiers. Therefore, your variation from the norm calls into action a series of carefully orchestrated alternative procedures. The cashier rings a bell or uses the public address system to page a supervisor, who may take some time to appear. The supervisor carefully reviews the documents and makes appropriate notations on the cheque. Some stores have additional procedures, such as further clearance with a central registry and so on. A similar variation from the norm occurs when you make a major purchase using a charge card. Any purchase above a set maximum value must be approved by an authorization centre. A malfunctioning magnetic strip on the card or congested phone lines can make a simple procedure lengthy. Regardless of the specific details, every reader will recognize the basic scenarios.

In order to avoid bad cheques (and encourage use of their charge cards) or unauthorized credit charges, stores and other businesses have highly formalized rules and procedures and clearly specified jurisdictions of responsibilities for dealing with customers in these circumstances. The rules and hierarchy of authority combine to provide a consistent and reliable means of dealing with these variations from the standard expectations. One is treated the same throughout the store, regardless of the clerk or the department.

The rules were made in an attempt to anticipate variations from the norm, and if there are unanticipated difficulties, such as a man offering a live pig as payment, they can be referred up the hierarchy to responsible authorities for a decision. Students in colleges and universities usually become familiar with bureaucratic problem-solving as they attempt to drop or add courses, transfer from one program to another, or cope with student aid procedures.

The more variations an organization regularly experiences, the more difficult it is to anticipate and cover them in the regulations. In other words, in highly changeable and uncertain circumstances, it becomes impossible to incorporate all the exceptions in the rules. If there are too many exceptions, the hierarchy will eventually get bogged down in providing interpretations and directions. So, as we indicated earlier, a bureaucratic form of organization performs best in situations involving a routine technology in a relatively stable environment.

At about the same time Weber was studying bureaucracy, certain developments were occurring in North America that were to have a profound influence on the study and operation of organizations.

The Organization

In the 1860s and 1870s, industrialization was well advanced in the United States and was slowly picking up momentum in Canada. With industrialization had come concentrations of workers in plants and factories and the rise of large-scale industrial organizations. In this context came the development of a movement in North America to see how organizations might be made more efficient and productive.

An industrial engineer, Frederick Winslow Taylor, believed that the full potential of industrial organization was not being realized because of inefficiency and that the answer to this problem lay in more systematic management. He viewed organizations as large mechanical systems (like machines) and suspected that much of their inefficiency was a result of what he thought was a natural tendency of workers to take it easy and not to produce at their optimal capacity.

Scientific Management

Taylor's strategy was to make every worker a specialist responsible for a single, narrowly defined task. The key, he argued, was to find the one best way to do each and every task. The means to achieve this desired perfection in productivity was through what he modestly called **scientific management.**

For Taylor, individual workers were simply instruments of production to be employed by management in the same way as the machines of the plant. The responsibility for finding the one best way of doing a job rested with management be-

cause, Taylor explained, "the science which underlies each workman's act is so great and amounts to so much that the workman is incapable (either through lack of education or through insufficient mental capacity) of understanding this science" (1947, originally published in 1911).

As the first time-and-motion specialists, proponents of scientific management sought to improve organizational productivity through more efficient procedures. To find the one best way of completing a task, they would observe workers who were thought by their supervisors to be the most capable at that job. The work patterns of these superior employees would be analyzed and broken down into their basic components, then rearranged to make them more efficient. The workers were subsequently retrained in the job, doing it in the prescribed best way, and put on an incentive pay scheme so as to encourage continued use of the desired procedures.

Taylor's method became widely used because it increased productivity and workers generally made more money than they had before. His approach was to focus on individual roles in organizations because he believed groups tended to constrain individual productivity.

Scientific management, although successful in many organizations, was not without its critics. The methods were seen to be too employer-oriented; unions felt that the greater efficiency derived would result in fewer jobs. On humanitarian grounds, speeding up work routines was believed to be potentially damaging to health. Highly specialized work was thought to deprive people of meaning in their work. The rapid pace and income geared to exceeding a production minimum put older workers at a considerable disadvantage.

Although Taylor and other scientific management advocates were practically oriented, they tended to have a view of organizations quite similar to Weber's. They saw the organization as an instrument for the co-ordination of human action in the achievement of specified objectives. With the organization viewed as a machine-like instrument, the clear objective of scientific management became to fine-tune the efficiency of highly specialized roles by determining the one best way for each.

The Weberian and scientific management conceptions of organizations tend to be rather narrow and limited; they are concerned mainly with an impersonal focus on internal organizational structure and process. Even though these perceptions came early in the development of our knowledge about organizations, they continue to have a profound influence over many practitioners today. Structure is still an important factor in the study of organizations.

Structure

In our definition of formal organization, we suggested that co-ordination, control, and problem-solving in the organization are facilitated through communication, leadership, and varying degrees of written rules and procedures. Indeed, written rules and regulations are a mechanism of formalization that Weber demonstrated to be a major component of bureaucracy. As we have seen, one function of these formalized regulations is to define the relationships among the various positions that the division of labour comprises and to establish a hierarchy of authority. That is, the rules describe the organizational structure.

The relationships among various roles in a division of labour may be left to chance, as with our bucket brigade. But formalization is a characteristic of formal organizations that ensures a deliberate patterning of behaviour so that good achievement is not left to chance. Instead, the requirements in relationships for the optimal division of labour are specified in advance and serve as a model for the organization's operations.

You may recall from Chapter 3 that a position in a social network is designated as a status. President, vice-president, treasurer, and secretary are common statuses in organizations. What the oc-

cupant of a particular status is required to do is known as a role. A university department may have an unfilled status — for instance, an assistant professor. The people in charge of hiring will be looking for someone to take on the status; his or her likely role will be to teach some junior-level courses, conduct research, and assist with minimal administrative responsibilities.

Formalization usually states how an organization's various statuses are to be arranged into some sort of a structure. **Organizational structure** is the pattern of relationships among the organization's component statuses. The rationale for the particular structure is usually the complementary or interdependent nature of various roles for the completion of specific tasks important to the organization.

As the example in Figure 11-2 shows, a radio station may elect to group its personnel according to specialties, with the advertising and sales people in a department separate from the broadcasters. Furthermore, it may place one person in charge of each of the groups with a title such as "assistant manager — sales" or "assistant manager — broadcasting." At the top of the hierarchy will be a station manager. This structure not only specifies the links among various statuses based on role specializations but also provides for a basic authority hierarchy.

The structure of an organization may be relatively *simple*, such as that of the radio station, or it may be very *complex*, with numerous statuses of various levels in a myriad of specialized departments or units, as in a multibranch bank. Figure 11-3 illustrates several types of complex structures. An organizational structure may specify an authority hierarchy, such as a **centralized struc-**

FIGURE 11-2 Structure of a Radio Station

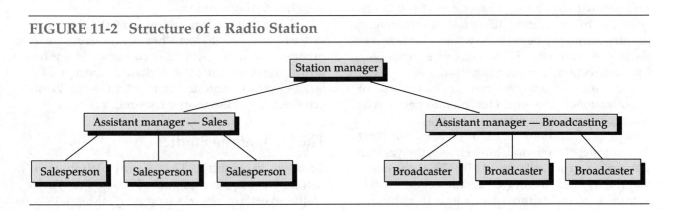

FIGURE 11-3   Structures of Organizations

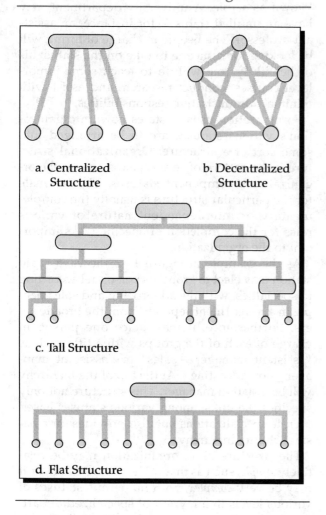

a. Centralized Structure

b. Decentralized Structure

c. Tall Structure

d. Flat Structure

alistic societies like Canada and the United States, for instance, organization charts tend to show specific roles along with detailed job descriptions prescribing formal duties and responsibilities. "By contrast, organization charts in more group-oriented societies such as Hong Kong, Indonesia and Malaysia, tend only to specify sections, departments and divisions except for the top one or two positions. Group-oriented societies describe assignments, responsibilities, and reporting relationships in collective terms" (Adler 1986).

Organizational structure has remained a key variable for researchers since Weber's pioneering work, and later in this chapter we shall review some of the influential structural impacts or constraints. But at this stage in our analysis, there are two key points: that the formal structure of an organization refers to the expected patterns of relationship among its various statuses, and that the formal structure was of primary concern for early organization researchers and theorists.

On a more practical level, organizational structure has been and remains a key concern for managers and employees. For instance, recent slack economic times have caused many companies to "downsize," to reduce unnecessary layers of organization. This flattening process has frequently targeted middle management and its support functions, such as planning and data analysis. In some situations, too many middle managers were dropped and senior managers found it inefficient "managing when there's no middle" (Lorinc 1991). Middle-management functions have sometimes been reinstated but in more appropriate and reduced numbers. Organizational structure over time is not static and changes according to the development of the organization in a manner somewhat similar to the evolution of the human skeleton during a lifetime.

Early understanding of organizations tended, as we have noted, to focus heavily on structure. A broader and more personalized view did not begin to develop until some chance findings at a large electrical manufacturing plant — the Western Electric or Hawthorne research.

The Hawthorne Studies

Between 1924 and 1932, a series of important studies were conducted at the Hawthorne Works of the Western Electric Company (Mayo 1945;

ture, in which subordinates report directly to a supervisor. Or it may be a **decentralized structure**, in which no supervisor is specified. An organizational structure that specifies many levels of hierarchy is referred to as *tall*. Alternatively, the structure may be relatively *flat*, with few levels in the hierarchy. These six terms — simple/complex, centralized/decentralized, and tall/flat — are some of the more common descriptions of organizational structure. They refer to patterns or configurations of the statuses observed.

Most organizations have an *organization chart* that outlines the relationship between the various statuses, or structural roles. Adler (1986) has noted that the composition of organization charts varies according to the culture of a society. In individu-

A radio station is an example of an organization with a relatively simple structure.

Roethlisberger and Dickson 1947). The original research was undertaken, in the scientific management tradition, to test the relationship between the quality of the lighting under which people worked and its effects, if any, on their production. The initial results were inconclusive, and the research continued with a total of seven studies exploring a range of physical conditions of work. Of the seven, four are well known: the Relay Assembly Test Room Experiment, the Second Relay Assembly Group Experiment, the Mica Splitting Test Room Experiment, and the Bank Wiring Room Observation Study (Parsons 1974). The last study is of particular relevance to our considerations.

The work habits of the fourteen men in the Bank Wiring Room were observed over time. These three soldermen, nine wiremen, and two inspectors were engaged in complicated wiring and soldering of banks of wires making up telephone exchanges. The men were paid on a piecework basis, which the company intended as an incentive for groups to produce at a maximum pace. The more they produced, the more they would be paid.

The experimenters found that in this particular group, however, the financial incentives of piecework did not urge workers to ever-increasing levels of production. Instead, the group had informally decided that wiring two exchanges a day was a reasonable output. This constituted for them "a fair day's work," and they produced steadily at that pace with little concern for the piecework incentive.

Managing in the Maquiladora

Working in Mexico demands a different management style. A foreign operation's success here often depends upon the local director's ability to adopt a more personalized management style. "To get anything done here, the manager has to be more of an instructor, teacher, or father figure than a boss," says Robert Hoskins, who manages an assembly plant, or *maquiladora*, for Little Neck, N.Y.-based Leviton Manufacturing Co. in the border city of Ciudad Juárez. Indeed, Ken Franklin, who manages assembly plants in Juárez's giant Bermudez Industrial Park, visits the production line every day at 6 a.m. to greet each worker individually. "In Mexico, everything is a personal matter," he says. "But a lot of managers don't get it."

Foreign companies often make a mistake by selecting managers based upon their skill in production rather than human relations, consultants say.

Source:

Drew Fagan, "Canada wakes up and smells the chili," *The Globe and Mail*, September 24, 1992, p. C1.

Not only did the informal work group keep an eye on how much members produced, but they actively sought to bring everyone into line with group norms. If a man worked above the accepted level, he was labelled a "slave" or "speed king," and if he consistently worked below standard, he was known as a "chiseller" (because he was making others in the group carry him). If sarcasm was ineffectual in enforcing the informal group norm, other group members would give violators a sharp punch on the shoulder in what was called "binging."

These actions were seen as means for workers' groups to control changes in plant routines. It was the workers' belief that if some of them consistently produced at higher levels, the company would expect that of everyone. Also, they had become comfortable in their relationships with other group members and were convinced that changes in rates of production caused by rate busters might put others out of work and lead to the breakup of groups.

Group norms on productivity in the Bank Wiring Room served to neutralize the effects of the company's piecework system. The group held its members in check and produced at a steady two units per day. Another observation was that, in spite of the rules, soldermen and wiremen rotated their jobs from time to time in order to provide some variety in their tasks and to reduce the tedium and boredom of repetitive jobs.

These findings were totally unexpected and provided new and valuable insights into the internal operations of organizations. The Hawthorne studies diverted researchers from the machine-like view of organizations consistent with the perspectives of Weber and Taylor. Instead, researchers discovered that individuals and groups within an organization may act in ways not predicted by formalized rules and structures. This recognition or discovery of informal organization represented a significant advance toward a more adequate and balanced understanding of organizations and their operations.

As indicated earlier, the formal structure of an organization refers to the expected or desired patterns of relationships and behaviours. The Bank Wiring Room Study demonstrated that organizational structure has an important additional dimension — the *social* dimension.

The discovery of the social dimension of organizations led to a rash of studies of so-called informal organization. Many of them confirmed the Hawthorne findings that organized work groups tend to slow production down (Mathewson 1931; Anderson 1944; Roy 1952). A number of researchers detailed how people in organizations cope with the working conditions created by various structural and technological arrangements. Roy (1954), for example, described his participant-observer experiences as a machine operator doing very simple and repetitious work. (See Chapter 2 for a discussion of participant observation as a research method.) Roy and his immediate group of workers spent long hours over a six-day week performing the following role:

Standing all day in one spot beside three old codgers in a dingy room looking out through barred windows at the bare walls of a brick warehouse, leg movements largely restricted to the shifting of body weight from one foot to the other; and arm movements confined, for the most part, to a simple repetitive sequence of place the die, punch the clicker, place the die, punch the clicker; and intellectual activity reduced to computing the hours to quitting time.

How did the machine operators cope with the tedium and meaninglessness of their jobs? Roy (1959) and his work group played little games to pass the time and made the most of social contacts. They also employed trivial rituals to break the routine. For example, each day one of the workers brought a couple of peaches and shared them with the others during a morning break; this was "peach time." The same person also brought a banana in his lunch bucket; each day, one of his co-workers would sneak into the bucket, consume the banana with much flourish, and announce "banana time!" There would be a ritual protest that the banana had been stolen, and so on. But the next day, the worker would bring another banana, and "banana time" would be repeated to the delight of the entire group. "Peach time" and "banana time" were followed throughout the day by "window time," "pickup time," "fish time," and "Coke time." These little devices, not predicted by the structure or rules of the organization, helped these organizational participants to cope with their daily regimen.

The Bank Wiring Room Study and subsequent research kindled an interest in the human side of organizations. They underscored the point that organizations are not merely structures for producing goods or services; they also contain human beings who are capable of acting and reacting. Human relations in organizations, as a result, became a major preoccupation of organization researchers. The organization became a context in which to view people at work. From this changed perspective, subsequent research drew on a number of social-psychological theoretical resources, including those of symbolic interactionists, to explore such questions as worker alienation, job satisfaction, group cohesiveness, and decision-making and change, to name but a few.

Before looking at some of these issues, it is important to stress that although this shift in emphasis from a machine-like view of organizations to a concern with what was happening to people in organizations was a major one, it did not result in the demise of scientific management or concern for organizational efficiency and productivity. That strongly entrenched emphasis continued, and improvements in technology, advancements in automation, and so forth served to keep organizations competitive. But with the addition of the human-relations perspective, the study of organizations was broadened. It had become apparent that, in addition to the technical system of an organization, there is a social system; a broadened sociotechnical perspective is essential to a fuller understanding of organizations (Trist and Bamforth 1951).

Roy's study illustrates some of the ways people devise for coping with the specific conditions of their work within an organization. It also provides a good example of alienation, which we shall explore next.

Alienation

Karl Marx. In the Hawthorne research and in Roy's accounts, we were introduced to the effects that organizations have on their members. This aspect of industrialization and the development of large-scale work organizations had many years earlier interested Marx. It was his view that people distinguish themselves from animals the moment they begin to produce their means of subsistence. Production of goods in order to assist oneself to stay alive was, for Marx, a basic social fact.

Marx believed that people can find self-fulfilment only through productive, or creative, labour. Work is a central feature of people's identities and allows them to develop to their fullest potential. As the industrialization process occurs and a capitalist system develops, however, the process of self-realization for individuals becomes frustrated and **alienation** results. That is, people begin to lose control of their destinies because they no longer possess the major means of production. Instead, they work in organizations on someone else's machines. Expanding on this concept of alienation, Marx (quoted in Bottomore and Rubel 1956) asked,

In what does this alienation consist? First that the work is external to the worker, that it is not a part of his nature, that consequently he does not fulfill himself in his work but denies himself, has a feeling of misery, not of well-being, does not develop freely a physical and mental energy, but is physically exhausted and mentally debased. The worker, therefore, feels himself at home only during his leisure, whereas at work he feels homeless. His work is not voluntary but imposed, forced labour. It is not the satisfaction of a need, but only a means for satisfying other needs.

For Marx, individuals experience alienation as a result of shifts in ownership patterns, changes in technology, and the rise of industrial organization. Alienation, according to Rinehart (1987), "refers to a condition in which individuals have little or no control over (a) the purposes and products of the labour process, (b) the overall organization of the workplace, and (c) the immediate work process itself." We are reminded of Roy and his co-workers looking through barred windows at a brick wall while they placed the die, punched the clicker, placed the die, and punched the clicker.

Technology. Robert Blauner (1964) was interested in the impact that technology has on workers — how what someone does in his or her work (the technology) affects that person. In the early 1960s he performed a secondary analysis on data involving workers in a number of industries in an attempt to answer the following question: Under what conditions are the alienating tendencies of work organizations the strongest, and under what conditions are they the weakest or least noticeable?

Blauner argued that technology is a key factor in an organization's distinctive character. In view of this position, it is not surprising that he turned to differences in technology to see if they might explain differences in alienation levels. As a preliminary step, he identified four basic technologies in the industries he studied: assembly-line, machine-tending, continuous-process, and craft technologies.

The work processes on an *assembly line* are highly particularized, so that each worker has a very small number of routine, specialized tasks to complete. Each worker generally has a fixed work station, and the pace of the line determines the speed at which people work. The manufacture of automobiles was Blauner's example of this type of technology.

In *machine-tending technologies*, work processes are highly routine, and workers' tasks consist of watching or tending to the needs of machines. Blauner saw textile manufacturing as representing this type of technology. In the production of textiles, large machines spin the fibres and automated looms weave materials. The worker's role is paced by the machines; when the machines run out of materials, the worker replaces the spools of fibre, and so on. Simple tasks are completed according to the needs of the machines.

Continuous process is a very advanced form of technology in which a raw material, such as petroleum, enters one end of the operation and undergoes a number of automated conversion steps; finished products are derived at various stages along the way. Blauner used oil refining and chemical production as examples. The complexity of this kind of technology requires workers to be highly knowledgeable about the processes, so that they can monitor operations and make spur-of-the-moment decisions when necessary to ensure continuous operation.

Craft technology is characterized by a considerable amount of handwork. It also tends to be relatively unstandardized because it is difficult to establish routines in a technology in which the products vary considerably. In Blauner's sample, craft technology was represented by printers. Because of the skill involved, printers must use judgement and flexibility in organizing and executing their work.

Blauner arranged these four technologies according to the level of control, meaning, and self-expression they afforded the worker. Assembly-line work provided very little of these features for individual workers, while machine tending contained slightly more of each. Continuous-process technology, he found, provided workers with greater control, more responsibility, and more meaning in their work than did the previous two. The highest levels of control were found in craft technology.

Worker alienation — feelings of powerlessness, meaninglessness, self-estrangement, and social isolation — was highest, he found, for assembly-line workers, and diminished as technologies afforded more control, meaning, and self-expression.

For his sample, therefore, alienation was lowest among printers. Blauner's findings are summarized in Table 11-2; similar results were found by Fullan (1970) in a Canadian study.

Whenever individuals, groups, or organizations interrelate, there is, of course, the potential for conflict. Within organizations, labour and management may have differing objectives or views that lead to conflict. The organization may, from time to time, find some of its elements conflicting with each other. Research on alienation also serves to remind us that factors within the organization, such as its technology, may stimulate conflict. The perspective of conflict theory increases our sensitivity to such possibilities in organizational analysis.

Technology remains a major focus of interest for researchers who examine alienation-producing conditions in organizations. Alienation is likely to be lowest in organizational settings in which members have control, meaning, and opportunities for self-fulfilment in their roles. We saw earlier that Roy and his group of machine-tenders coped with the alienating tendencies of their organizational roles through informal social activity. Many researchers have attempted to explore the dynamics of groups in the social structure of organizations and the impact they have on individuals and the successful attainment of organization goals.

Group Dynamics

We have been considering some of the ways in which the organization acts to influence the interaction of its members. People in organizations find themselves in a variety of circumstances. Some people, for instance, work in isolation, while others work in groups of varying sizes. People working in groups may be dependent on one another to complete a joint task, or they may do their jobs independently but be in close proximity to one another. We have already seen how groups may act to influence the production standards or levels of their members. But, of course, all groups do not influence their members to the same extent. In attempting to account for these differences, the concept of **cohesiveness** has proven useful.

Groups differ according to how much individuals perceive themselves as members, how much interest they have in belonging to the group, and how highly they regard other members of the group. Where individuals identify themselves as members of the group, where group members want the group to remain together, and where group members have a high regard for each other, there will be a group with high cohesiveness.

Groups vary in the degree to which these characteristics are present, and researchers have investigated what difference, if any, this makes. In other words, they have considered what variations in behaviour and attitudes may normally be expected when a person belongs to a highly cohesive group rather than a group with low cohesion.

Seashore (1954) looked at this matter in a study of 228 work groups of different sizes, comprising 5871 individuals working in a machinery factory. He saw group cohesiveness as "an attraction of

TABLE 11-2 Blauner's Findings on the Relationship between Technology and Alienation

Industry	Technology	Control over Work	Meaning in Work	Self-Expression	Alienation
Printing	Craft	Very high	Very high	Very high	Very low
Oil refining	Continuous process	High	High	High	Low
Textiles	Machine tending	Low	Low	Low	High
Automobile assembly	Assembly line	Very low	Very low	Very low	Very high

SOURCE: Robert Blauner, *Alienation and Freedom* (Chicago: University of Chicago Press, 1964). © The University of Chicago. All rights reserved.

group members to the group in terms of the strength of forces on the individual member to remain in the group and to resist leaving the group." Seashore's major findings are summarized here:

1. Members of highly cohesive groups exhibit less anxiety than members of less cohesive groups.
2. Highly cohesive groups have less variation in productivity among members than do less cohesive groups. Highly cohesive groups, such as the group in the Bank Wiring Room, establish and enforce a group standard that is usually missing in less cohesive groups.
3. Highly cohesive groups differ more frequently and significantly from the plant norm of productivity than do less cohesive groups. Highly cohesive groups tend to have productivity levels either noticeably above or noticeably below the plant norm.
4. Whether the productivity of a highly cohesive group is above or below the plant norm is a function of the degree to which its supervisor is perceived by group members to be knowledgeable about the work and to provide a supportive setting for the group. If members of a highly cohesive group feel secure in their setting (feel that the group will be able to continue to exist), they are more likely to have productivity above the plant norm than will members of a highly cohesive group in which the organizational setting is not as supportive of the group.
5. Similarities in members' ages and educational levels are not related to the degree of cohesiveness in a group. Instead, group cohesiveness is positively related to opportunities for interaction by members. Such opportunities are most likely to occur in smaller groups of relatively stable composition.

Seashore's findings on group cohesiveness are entirely consistent with expectations based on some of the studies we have already reviewed. Roy's cohesive group, for instance, provided relief from the alienating tendencies of the members' work through such social diversions as "peach time" and "banana time." White (1977) showed that individuals' opportunities for belonging to cohesive groups and other social networks were factors more important than organization size in explaining workers' attitudes about their jobs. And, of course, we recall the impacts of group standards on productivity as evidenced in the Bank Wiring Room Study.

More recently, Ouchi's (1981) study of the reasons for Japan's success in international trade detailed the way that organizational culture in that country is based on the effective use of teams in production. Many more North American organizations are now emphasizing team-building and empowering teams to undertake increased responsibility in production and quality control, so as to derive the benefits attributed to highly cohesive groups. But individualism is a strong characteristic of Canadian and American traditions, and as a result, not everyone enjoys or can work effectively with others. Getting groups to perform as teams is a challenging undertaking requiring training, commitment, and careful selection of participants.

Alienation — along with its positive counterpart, job satisfaction — and cohesiveness are examples of the types of research interests that have been pursued since the Hawthorne studies. The organization is a setting in which to view and seek improved understandings of human behaviour and the social system. One important final example, which we shall now consider, relates to opportunities for organization members at the lower levels to be involved in decision-making.

Decision-Making in Organizations

Decision-making is a central component in the operation of organizations. Decisions involving the purposes of an organization and the means for their pursuit are a constant matter of concern for organization members. These policy matters are often long-term, but in almost every instance of an organization's activity, there are problems to be solved and decisions of the moment to be made. As we have seen, organizations are structured with an authority hierarchy that is usually charged with assuming the dominant role in decision-making. As a matter of fact, in many organizations this decision-making role becomes an exclusive and jealously guarded right of management.

Not all organizations have such a straightforward designation of exclusive decision-making responsibility to management. In unionized settings, for instance, negotiated collective agreements specify the limits of such authority and detail procedures for resolving grievances, bargaining on wages, working conditions, and so on. As another example, universities have senates responsible for establishing academic policy, boards of trustees oversee financial matters, and administrations implement senate and board decisions and manage day-to-day operations. Jurisdictional disputes are frequent, and as a result, universities tend to be characterized by considerable political activity.

We are also reminded that the technology a person works with may afford very little opportunity for flexibility and decision-making. This was the case for Blauner's assembly-line and machine-tending workers, in contrast to those in continuous-process and craft technologies. There have been many research efforts since the Hawthorne studies to examine the possibly good effects that a more broadly based decision-making structure and process have on participants. But before considering these, we should return to the Hawthorne studies and the Relay Assembly Test Room Experiment.

Relay Assembly Test Room Experiment. The Relay Assembly Test Room Experiment took place at the Hawthorne Works of the Western Electric Company from 1927 to 1932. It involved the study of a small group of women (several members of the group changed at one point) making relay assemblies for telephones. In the tradition of scientific management and industrial psychology, the researchers were attempting to see if changes in conditions affecting worker fatigue would result in increased productivity and morale. The assembly of a telephone relay was completed by a single worker and required about a minute's time. Since each worker produced a large number of relays each day, it was relatively easy to observe the effect on productivity of any changes introduced.

Before the start of the experiment, the women's normal work week was 48 hours long and included Saturday mornings; the only break provided during the day was a brief lunch period. The changes introduced in the Relay Assembly Test Room Experiment centred largely on rest pauses and the length of the work day and work week. One of the first changes introduced was the

introduction of two five-minute rest breaks during the day; after five weeks, this schedule was changed to two ten-minute rest breaks; then after four weeks, six five-minute breaks, and so on.

As these minor changes were introduced, any effects on the women's behaviour and attitudes were noted. During the majority of the changes introduced, the workers' attitudes and morale remained good, their productivity increased, and their absenteeism decreased (Parsons 1974).

Most observers tended to attribute the positive outcomes of the Relay Assembly Test Room Experiment to the cohesive work group. Before the experiment, the women were part of a 100-member department. This large size precluded the opportunities to form cohesive groups that were available in the smaller setting during the test.

Much later, analysts re-examined the data from these experiments and argued that although the cohesive nature of the work group was an important factor, equally important was the fact that the women in the experiment had an opportunity to participate in decisions about matters that affected them, an opportunity that they had not had before in their work. Blumberg (1968) comments on this factor (emphasis is added):

I believe that a major, *although of course not the exclusive, explanation for the remarkable increases in productivity and morale lay in the crucial role which the test room workers played in determining the conditions under which they worked. The operatives, from the very beginning of the experiment, were drawn into the decision-making process and achieved a large measure of direct and active control over their tasks, and working conditions. In other words, a small but* genuine *dose of workers' participation was introduced into the test room.*

It is important to note that the women's participation in decision-making was not contrived or irrelevant to their work; rather, it was, as Blumberg has described, genuine. In addition to cohesiveness, the lesson to be learned from the Relay Assembly Test Room Experiment is put most succinctly by Kahn (1975): "Real participation has real effects. When people take a significant and influential part in decisions that they value, the quality of decisions is likely to be improved and their implementation is almost certain to be improved."

Many organization studies have examined the amount of control individuals have in their work, and, as in Blauner's (1964) study on technology and alienation, there has been remarkable consistency in reporting positive association with job satisfaction. Where control and relevant participation in decision-making are present in organizations, individuals are more likely to have higher job satisfaction and lower alienation. There are fewer studies of the effects of control on productivity, and those that have been undertaken have yielded less clear-cut results. That is, control and participatory decision-making may or may not have direct positive relationships with individual performance levels.

Just as the Hawthorne studies shifted the focus of organization research more than 50 years ago, so did a more recent view of organizations as open systems effect a considerable change.

Organizations as Open Systems and Their Task Environments

Most of the materials we have reviewed so far have tended to reflect a very simple view of organizations as **closed systems.** According to this concept, organizations are relatively self-contained units with particular structural arrangements and individual behaviour patterns that can be accounted for by factors internal to the organization. Max Weber, as we have seen, viewed organizations or bureaucracies as mechanisms for control of participants, and his overriding interest was internal mechanisms and operations of bureaucracies. Similarly, the human-relations researchers we considered were interested in organizations only insofar as they provided a context within which to assess attitudes and to view groups and individual behaviour. Adherents of these essentially closed-system approaches conceive of organizations as autonomous social entities; the analytical approach is largely one of short-range observation and deduction because of a belief that "all consequences of action are contained within the system and all causes of actions stem from within it" (Thompson 1967).

There has been a gradual tendency to regard this closed-system view of organizations as too narrow because organizations are also part of a larger social system (Barnard 1938; Selznick 1949;

Clark 1956; Parsons 1960; Scott 1987). Organizations do not operate in a vacuum; instead, they are located in a multifaceted environment. They are affected by governments and their legislation, by customers and suppliers, by competitors, and by numerous other external bodies and groups. An organization may attempt to insulate its internal operations as much as possible, but its environment will ultimately affect even these. Figure 11-4 depicts, in simplified form, an organization as an **open system**: in this model, the organization is dependent for its viability in part on external inputs and outputs.

An automobile plant, for instance, buys steel, electronics, glass, and component parts from suppliers and hires its workers from the community. These inputs from the outside are necessary for the organization's operation. The organization's internal procedures combine these resources so that vehicles roll off the assembly line. But, once again, without sales of the cars and trucks to outside customers, the organization is unlikely to survive. Information about the success of its products or the availability of various input resources, for instance, provides feedback for the organization that is important in determining its future moves. John Donne's admonition "No man is an island, entire of itself" applies equally well to organizations.

FIGURE 11-4 Organizations as Open Systems

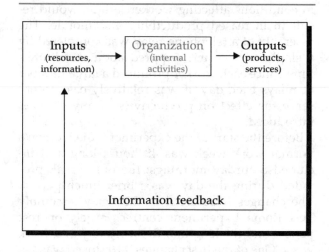

Automakers can be vulnerable to outside forces that are beyond their control. If, for instance, a parts supplier experiences a strike and is unable to provide required parts, then car production can be interrupted. Japanese organizations attempt to control similar uncertainties through linkages known as "keiretsu." Vertical keiretsu are "pyramids of companies that serve a single master. Every large manufacturer, whether it belongs to a horizontal group or not, dictates virtually everything — including prices it will pay — to hundreds of suppliers that are often prohibited from doing business outside the keiretsu. At the pyramid's bottom is a swarm of job shops and family ventures with primitive working conditions and subsistence-level pay and profits" (*Business Week* 1992). Horizontal keiretsu are groupings of major companies from a number of industrial sectors held together by joint shareholding and a common bank. While affording

large Japanese companies with more predictable supplies, stability, reduced uncertainty, and greater competitive advantage, keiretsu would likely be viewed outside of Japan as restrictive trading practices and not be allowed in many countries such as Canada and the United States.

Task Environment

When we regard an organization as an open system, we take a more realistic view of it; in order to comprehend its operation, we must not only understand its internal workings, but also identify those elements in its environment that significantly influence it. We must determine not only how an organization reacts to its environment but also how it acts to influence and control its environment.

Furthermore, if we become concerned with an organization's environment, we are confronted

The physical component of a fish plant's task environment determines its location close to a source of seafood.

with the problems of exactly defining the boundaries of that environment. Is an organization's environment everything external to it? Technically, this is the case, but practically speaking there are some elements in the environment that are more important than other elements to a given organization. A manufacturer of air conditioners, for instance, is likely to be especially concerned with climate, since more air-conditioning customers live in warmer regions than in colder ones. Dill (1958) suggests that in analyzing organizational environments, it is useful to think of a **task environment**, or those elements in an organization's environment that "are relevant or potentially relevant to goal setting and goal attainment."

Figure 11-5 depicts a typical manufacturing organization's task environment. In Canadian society, organizations are influenced by a wide range of government legislation at the federal, provincial, and municipal levels. Legislation governs among other things, hours of work, pollution and noise limits, safety, union activity, health standards for products or services, taxation, competition practices, exports, imports, sexual harassment, pay equity, and building codes. A comprehensive list would be so long that it would save considerable space to list those areas of an organization's existence not affected by government legislation.

O'Toole (1981) provides a chilling example of how legislation and court interpretations in the extreme can pull internal organizational operations away from a reasonable standard of common sense: "A Brooklyn College professor is suing his college on the grounds that he was fired because he is an alcoholic, and the government is arguing that it is illegal for colleges to prefer sober professors to alcoholics because alcoholics are considered handicapped persons under the 1973 [U.S.] Rehabilitation Act."

In most task environments, suppliers and customers are equally important; related to them are an organization's competitors. But to determine accurately the components of a task environment, we should also consider four significant subareas: the political, the physical, the economic, and the sociocultural.

Political Environment. The political component of a task environment, through government legislation and regulation, affects in some way or other virtually all of an organization's activity. The extent of government regulation and intrusions into the operations of Canadian organizations has become so pervasive that many companies now compare the political environments of provinces and even countries to decide where it is most preferable to locate new enterprises or even relocate existing operations. Organizations, of course, may and usually do lobby to influence developments or changes in government legislation. **Lobbying** consists of activities by various interest groups wishing to state their cases to politicians in the hope of influencing the course of legislation.

Physical Environment. The physical component of an organization's task environment is often a major consideration. The weather in Canada is frequently a factor in organizational planning. It may affect the location of organizations, such as fruit or vegetable growers, who need warm summers, water, and moderate winters. It may also affect the scheduling of activities; in oil drilling and logging, for instance, access to isolated locations makes winter months the most desirable period for operations. The most visible and negative feature of the interrelationship between organizations and their physical environments is pollution.

Economic Environment. The impact on organizations of the current unsettled economic envi-

---

FIGURE 11-5   Some Elements in a Typical Task Environment

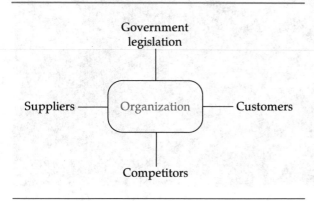

ronment underscores its importance. The bulk of organizational theory and models was generated during the economic boom years after World War II. Continuous growth was, therefore, an underlying assumption. Not surprisingly, managers have generally proven ill-equipped to deal with the consequences of prolonged economic downturns or uncertainties. These circumstances have created opportunities for mergers and takeovers that, in Canada, are leading to increasing concentrations of corporate ownership in a small number of huge conglomerates.

Sociocultural Environment. The sociocultural features of an organization's task environment are increasingly important. The significance of issues relating to language for organizations in Quebec, for instance, is a matter of historical record. Lucas (1971) and Perry (1971) give excellent accounts of the relationship between organizations and their host communities. Of particular interest are the large number of Canadian communities that are dominated by a single industry or company.

Figure 11-6 depicts some of the important elements in these four subareas of the task environment of an organization. The examples given are by no means complete, and their relevance for any specific organization varies. Also, it is important to realize that, although we have dealt with each of the four task environments separately, what happens in one area may have consequences in another. If, for instance, public opinion (a sociocultural element) becomes persuasive about a particular state of pollution (a physical element), then politicians (a political element) may be moved to provide pressure or legislation or even funds to force or encourage organizations to take desired action on the matter. Finally, it is worth re-emphasizing that organizations and environments are in a state of dynamic tension: the organization's role may be proactive or reactive or both.

Complexity and Change in Task Environments

We have identified four major subareas within task environments. Dill (1958) characterizes task environments further as being homogeneous or

FIGURE 11-6 The Task Environment

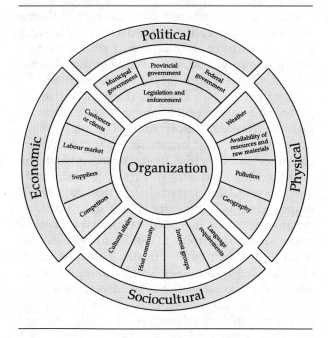

heterogeneous, and stable or rapidly shifting. Homogeneous or heterogeneous refers to the relative complexity in the task environment. Does the organization produce a single product for a single customer? Its task environment would be highly homogeneous. The production of a single product for multiple customers would be less homogeneous. The production of multiple products for multiple customers would create a highly heterogeneous task environment.

The stable or shifting characterization refers to the amount of change in the task environment. Making a single product for the same customer every time would be a very stable task environment in comparison with that of providing a single product for a different customer each time.

Researchers have considered the effects of various task environments on organizations. Lawrence and Lorsch (1967), for example, were interested in combinations of the two characteristics. They concluded that the shifting–heterogeneous task environment contained the greatest degree of uncertainty, and the stable–homogeneous, the least. They wanted to determine those organizational characteristics that are required to deal effectively with different levels of uncertainty. "Such a question," said Lawrence and Lorsch, "is quite different from the central theme of most organizational studies, which have tended to focus on the question of what is the one best way to organize, irrespective of the external environmental conditions facing the business."

These researchers selected three industries to represent various points along a continuum of task-environment uncertainty. The plastics industry was the most uncertain, the standardized-container industry the least uncertain, and the packaged-food industry was roughly in the middle. Lawrence and Lorsch found that, as a result of the changing complexity of task environments, organizations in the plastics industry created many specialized roles to deal with various dimensions of their environments. This role differentiation led to problems of integration; control and co-ordination of the more diverse roles required continual mechanisms of conflict resolution and problem-solving. As a result, the uncertainty generated by the task environment necessitated structures and processes in which "the lower and middle echelons of management had to be involved in reaching joint departmental decisions; these managers were centrally involved in the resolution of conflict. In resolving conflict all the managers relied heavily on open confrontation." In order to be responsive to change, organizations in the plastics industry created specialized roles to deal with specific characteristics of their task environments, and control and co-ordination mechanisms were brought down to the lower level of the organization.

Conflict resolution in a changing environment needs to be based on familiarity with the current situation and to be relatively speedy to ensure appropriate solutions. When the ship is sinking, fast action is required. You cannot wait for a response to the captain's request for action from the general manager at head office, who in turn contacts the vice-president of operations, who must clear his or her directives with the president. A steep hierarchy is not conducive to a fast response time, which is required in uncertain environments such as that of the plastics industry.

By contrast, the low uncertainty in the task environment of the standardized-container industry meant that events could be anticipated in advance in much the same way as we earlier described for bureaucracies. As a result, specialized roles for dealing with the environment were not required, and the formal hierarchy of the organization was suited to the resolution of problems. Middle managers did have some influence, but the real power rested with those at the top.

The packaged-food industry was structured and acted in a manner closer to that of the plastics industry than that of standardized-container operations. Because organizations in packaged foods experienced a fair degree of uncertainty, they had different roles for their environmental contacts and decentralized decision-making. But "the major difference between them was that the plastics organization appeared to be devoting more of its managerial manpower to devices that facilitated the resolution of conflict," according to Lawrence and Lorsch.

The comparative results of Lawrence and Lorsch's research are summarized in Table 11-3. This study is an important one because it clearly shows that successful organizations adopt structures and procedures appropriate to the conditions of their task environments.

Lawrence and Lorsch provided some insights into the dynamics of management required under situations of varying uncertainty. A more explicit statement of the suitability of particular management styles to varying environmental contingencies was contained in an earlier study by Burns and Stalker (1961), who sampled twenty firms in the British electronics industry. In their interviews with managers, Burns and Stalker observed two polarized and idealized styles of management: the mechanistic and the organic.

Mechanistic management is typically bureaucratic in style. Everyone's duties and responsibilities are precisely defined. Communication is filtered upward through a formalized hierarchy of authority and in this way is maintained by those at the top. "This command hierarchy is maintained by the implicit assumption that all knowledge about the situation of the firm and its tasks is, or should be, available only to the head of the firm" (Lawrence and Lorsch 1967).

By contrast, the **organic management** style is much less formalized. Reliance on the formalized hierarchy is less evident. Instead, decisions are based on knowledgeable suggestions, whether

TABLE 11-3 Uncertainty in the Task Environment and Consequent Structures and Procedures

	Plastics Industry	Packaged-Foods Industry	Standardized-Containers Industry
Environmental uncertainty	High	Medium	Low
Role differentiation	High	Considerable	Low
Decentralized decision-making	High	Considerable	Low
Conflict resolution	Heavy management involvement across levels	Some management involvement across levels	Heavy reliance on bureaucratic hierarchy

SOURCE: Paul R. Lawrence and Jay W. Lorsch, *Organization and Environment: Managing Differentiation and Integration* (Cambridge, MA: Harvard University Press, 1967).

they come from the top or bottom of the hierarchy. As a result, communication patterns are much more open and tend to be lateral as well as vertical. Commands give way to consultation, and status differentials are of minor import. Duties and responsibilities are not clearly defined and are subject to change as conditions warrant.

You may have guessed under which conditions each management style was most prevalent. Burns and Stalker observed that the organic style was usual among electronics firms in particularly uncertain or unstable task environments, where new problems seeking new solutions are the norm. The mechanistic style typified managers in electronics firms in relatively stable, unchanging task environments.

In our review of the open-system model of organizations, we noted the importance of task environments to organizations and their operations, and we saw how organizations adapt to the particular demands of their environments by altering their structures and processes. We also argued that organizations are not merely reactive but that they adopt proactive strategies through which they attempt to influence or change parts of their task environments.

In addition, we noted that government legislation provides not only constraints on organization behaviour but opportunities as well. In the next section we shall explore this more fully

when considering incorporation processes and the corporations that result.

Corporations

Canadian federal and provincial governments have large volumes of legislation that relate to organizations within their jurisdictions. This legislation may regulate labour practices, pollution controls, product standards, and a host of other organizational subjects. One segment of these statutes is, however, particularly relevant to organizations as such: it is concerned with corporations. These laws in particular provide both constraints on organizations and some unique opportunities. It is little wonder, then, that the dominant business mode in Canada is the corporation.

The simplest way to conduct business, however, is as a **sole proprietor.** A person purchases the necessary local business operating permits and sets up shop. Little video-rental stores or small word-processing services or corner pizza takeouts will likely be sole proprietorships. These owners use their own resources to establish and develop the businesses. They reap the profits of their efforts, but if they get into financial difficulty, they are in a legal position of unlimited liability. That is, not only may the assets of the business have to be sold to satisfy creditors, but "the owner's personal assets such as house, furniture, car, and stocks, may be seized, if necessary, to pay the outstanding debts of his business. Thus a person's life savings could be wiped out by a business failure" (Amirault and Archer 1976).

Sometimes individuals wish to collaborate in a business venture and establish a **partnership.** A partnership operates in much the same way as a sole proprietorship, but there are additional people and sources of money on which to base the venture. Unlimited liability is generally also a feature of partnerships, and one has to be very careful about selecting partners because all are responsible for partnership debts. If, for instance, one partner cannot meet his or her fair share of the debts, the other partners must assume it. The sole proprietorship and partnership are easy and convenient to start, but the situation of unlimited liability is a risk that could be very costly for participants.

A **corporation**, on the other hand, is a legal entity that interested persons may create if certain criteria are met. The founders incorporate their joint venture with a province or the federal government. Operating capital is provided by the sale of shares, and the affairs of the corporation and the rights of the shareholders are overseen by a board of directors. The major advantage of the corporation is that it affords the shareholders limited liability, in that they stand to lose only to the extent of their investment in the corporation; other personal effects are not liable to claims by creditors. Other advantages for this legal entity, the corporation, include separation of ownership and management, possibly lower income taxes, and enduring existence (Amirault and Archer 1976; Smyth and Soberman 1976).

These advantages have made the corporation the dominant organizational form in developed societies, and most of the organizations we have studied throughout this chapter are corporations. Two questions that have been of considerable interest to organization researchers in Canada concern the sources of power and control in Canadian corporations and the patterns of existence for these corporations.

In his classic work *The Vertical Mosaic,* Porter (1965) examines the locus of power in various sectors of Canadian society. Of particular interest to us is his study of what he refers to as "economic power" — that is, who controls big business. Porter was concerned with how large corporations are administered and how they form links with other corporations. Because many of Canada's biggest corporations are largely or wholly owned subsidiaries of large American, British, Japanese, or other foreign corporations, the power probably rests with the board of directors of the parent companies.

Porter discovered that economic authority in Canada is concentrated in relatively few hands — there is a frequent tendency for a director of one large corporation to sit on the boards of others. This situation of two or more corporate boards having a common director or directors creates an interlock between these boards and their corporations and recalls a mild version of our earlier reference to the Japanese keiretsu. There are striking patterns of interlocking directorships, and key individuals in these networks hold large numbers of such posts. This is particularly true of bank directors.

The central figures identified in this interlocking directorship matrix constitute Porter's "economic elite." In assessing their backgrounds, he found that in many respects they are a very homogeneous group. They attended similar private schools and universities; intermarry; belong to similar clubs, organizations, and churches; and maintain close ties in their social and political activities.

Clement (1975) provides a follow-up analysis and finds similar trends. His picture of the economic elite shows it tending to be even more exclusive than previously, with little evidence of penetration by persons of lower social origins. In another study, Clement extends his view of the corporate elite because "it is no longer possible to provide an adequate understanding of the power structure of Canadian corporations without expanding the horizons of study outside into the United States and, to a limited extent, beyond" (1977).

The works of Porter and Clement, as well as Carroll's (1986) recent study, provide valuable data and insights for readers on the nature of power in large corporations and the extent to which it is controlled by a relatively small elite group.

White (1978) examined a range of variously sized corporations with different patterns of ownership — Canadian versus foreign, private versus public — to determine the locus of control within them. He finds that the size of the corporation is not as important a factor as ownership in explaining the activity of corporate boards of directors. For example, boards of independent or parent corporations are more active in control than those of subsidiaries. The suggestion is not that subsidiary corporations are not closely monitored but that the mechanisms are somewhat different:

Control of subsidiaries by parents is considerable, but it usually tends to be exercised through management links rather than by the subsidiary's directorate. In subsidiary corporations in our sample there is at least one senior manager in the parent who is responsible for subsidiary operations. The chain of command from the parent to the subsidiary is through this responsible authority in the parent to his (or her) subordinate who heads the subsidiary. This link is the control coupling for the parent, a bypass around the subsidiary's board which in most instances is little more than a legally prescribed structural adornment. (White 1978)

The composition of the board, says White, is a second important factor related to board of director control or lack thereof. If the board is made up of some directors who are outsiders, not employees of the corporation, then the board is more active than if it consists solely of inside directors. Corporate directors traditionally delegated day-to-day operations to managers and were expected to exercise reasonable care in overseeing management. Dozens of new laws, however, are making directors personally responsible for their actions. They now need to know more about what the corporation is doing and can no longer delegate most responsibility to management. For instance, they are personally liable if their corporations fail to pay sufficient GST or do not adhere to environmental protection or health and safety standards. The role of director is being transformed, and in a number of situations, the risks are becoming perceived as greater than the benefits.

Corporations and corporate control remain dominant factors in Canadian life, and organization researchers have only begun to systematically explore their impacts.

SUMMARY

1. The need for organization is consistent with the social nature of humans. Basic divisions of labour result in increasing interdependencies, and in order to maintain some degree of social order, preliminary forms of organization are generated.
2. The establishment of an organization centres on goal attainment. Its establishment may be spontaneous, left to chance or circumstance, or it may be established and maintained in a more formalized manner.
3. Early theorists and researchers regarded organizations as closed systems and were mainly concerned with their formal structures and processes. The technical system tended to be a primary focus. Only with the accidental discoveries of the Hawthorne studies did there develop a more balanced view that included the social system as well.
4. In the scientific-management perspective of organizations, individual workers are regarded as instruments of production to be employed by management in the same way as machines. Efficiency is achieved by finding the one best way to do each and every task.
5. Technological or organizational arrangements that fail to give people reasonable control over important aspects of their work and that deprive them of social contacts and meaning in their tasks are likely to result in worker alienation.
6. Every organization interacts with other organizations. Those elements outside the organization that affect its operations or directions constitute its environment.
7. Corporations are legally created entities that allow people to establish organizations while minimizing their personal liabilities. Most organizations in business and industry are corporations.

GLOSSARY

Alienation. Individuals' feelings that, as workers, they are small, meaningless parts of an insensitive production system over which they have little control.
Bureaucracy. A formal organization based on the application of legal–rational principles.

Centralized structure. Structure of an organization in which authority and decision-making are concentrated in a few people at senior levels.

Charismatic authority. Authority that is based on the belief that the individual leader is special and possesses some exceptional ability or magic, which inspires loyalty in the followers.

Closed system. Theoretical perspective of organizations as relatively self-contained units in which particular structural arrangements and individual behaviour patterns can be accounted for by factors internal to the organization.

Cohesiveness. Conditions whereby individuals identify themselves as members of the group, members want the group to remain together, and group members have a high regard for each other.

Corporation. Legal entity created for purposes of conducting business; it has an existence separate from that of its members while providing them with limited liability.

Decentralized structure. Structure of an organization in which authority and decision-making are widely distributed among people at various levels.

Division of labour. Process whereby general tasks and roles become increasingly specialized.

Formal organization. Relatively enduring or continuing social collectivity in which roles and resources are co-ordinated through a division of labour in the use of a technology to achieve a goal or goals. Co-ordination, control, and problem-solving are facilitated through communication, leadership, and varying degrees of written rules and procedures.

Formalization. Process by which the informality of relationships is gradually replaced by varying degrees of rules, codes of conduct, laws, and other means of regulation.

Legal-rational authority. Authority based on belief in the legality of formally specified rules and relationships.

Lobbying. Activities by special interest groups aimed at influencing government legislation.

Mechanical solidarity. Feeling of people in primitive societies that they are held together by kinship, neighbourliness, and friendliness.

Mechanistic management. Management style in which duties and responsibilities are precisely defined, communication is filtered upward through a formalized hierarchy of authority, and control is maintained at the top.

Open system. Theoretical perspective of organizations whereby particular structural arrangements and individual behaviour patterns can be accounted for by a combination of factors internal to the organization and its external environment.

Organic management. Management style in which decisions are based on knowledgeable suggestions, communication patterns tend to be lateral as well as horizontal, duties and responsibilities are not rigidly defined, and status differentials are of minor importance.

Organic solidarity. Dependencies among people in developed societies created as a result of a more specific division of labour.

Organization. A collectivity in which people and resources are co-ordinated through a division of labour in the use of a technology to achieve a goal. Co-ordination, control, and problem-solving are facilitated through communication and leadership.

Organizational structure. Patterns of relationships among organization statuses.

Partnership. Joint business venture in which normally all partners experience unlimited liability equally.

Scientific management. Taylor's term for achieving perfection in productivity by finding the one best way to do each and every task.

Sole proprietorship. Simplest manner in which to establish a business; the sole owner experiences unlimited liability.

Spontaneous organization. Temporary co-ordination of individuals and resources that disbands when its task or mission has been completed.

Task environment. Those elements in an organization's environment that are relevant or potentially relevant to setting goals and attaining them.

Technology. Application of a body of knowledge through the use of tools and processes in the production of goods and/or services.

Traditional authority. Authority that is based on followers' belief that the monarch has a divine right to rule that is transferred down through eligible descendants.

FURTHER READING

Coleman, James S. *Power and the Structure of Society.* New York: W.W. Norton, 1974. Traces the development of corporations as unique legal creations for the transaction of business affairs.

Kiesler, Sara B., *Interpersonal Processes in Groups and Organizations*; **MacKenzie, Kenneth D.**, *Organizational Structures*; **Pfeffer, Jeffrey**, *Organizational Design*; **Tuggle, Francis D.**, *Organizational Processes.* Arlington Heights, IL: AHM Publishing Corporation, 1978. A series of books that examine contemporary directions in the study of organizations.

March, James C., and Herbert A. Simon. *Organizations.* New York: John Wiley, 1958. A good description of the many facets of organizational structure and operation.

Ouchi, William. *Theory Z.* Reading, MA: Addison-Wesley, 1981. Describes the adaptations Japanese organizations have made of conventional organizational designs for their particular needs and culture.

Perrow, Charles. *Complex Organizations: A Critical Essay.* Glenview, IL: Scott, Foresman and Company, 1972. A critical view of major theoretical perspectives on organizations.

Peters, Thomas J., and Robert H. Waterman, Jr. *In Search of Excellence*. New York: Harper and Row, 1982. Examines the internal structure and processes of those corporations most successful in adapting to today's environmental uncertainties.

Thompson, James D. *Organizations in Action*. New York: McGraw-Hill, 1967. Discusses approaches to the study of organizations and development of a framework for their analysis.

Zald, Mayer N. (ed.). *Power in Organizations*. Nashville: Vanderbilt University Press, 1970. A collection of articles exploring the nature of power structures and relationships in a variety of organizational settings.

UNIT IV

Social Institutions

Institutions are defined as relatively stable sets of norms, values, and beliefs developed to resolve the recurring problems faced by all societies. They are a central part of social structure and are major factors defining society.

Family, religion, polity, and education are the social institutions considered in this unit. They are found in every society and are different within and between societies. Each chapter of this unit deals with these institutions as they appear in other societies and discusses how the various sociological perspectives have been used to analyze them.

Marriage and the family are the concerns of Chapter 12. How we are socialized into family roles and the national and ethnic differences among families are discussed. Other topics included in this chapter are getting married, staying married, divorce, and family violence.

Every society defines which religious beliefs are acceptable, the correct way to honour god(s), and the acceptable ways to become a priest or minister. Chapter 13 defines what religion is and why it is important to the individual and society. How do we explain the universality of differences in religion, and what is religion's future? This chapter explores these questions.

How do people govern themselves and maintain order in society? Chapter 14 examines the similarities of, and differences between, the political processes of Quebec, anglophone Canada, the United States, and Mexico.

Every society has some systematic way of educating its members. In the societies mentioned above, this task is accomplished largely by schools, although less so in Mexico. What is the purpose of schools? What difference do they make? How are they organized? Is there equal opportunity for all to be educated? How is the educational system changing? These are some of the issues explored in Chapter 15.

CHAPTER 12

What Is the Family?

ELLEN M. GEE

The family is considered the most basic social institution. Although the form it takes can vary considerably from society to society and has changed over time in many societies (such as in North America), the family always and everywhere plays a pivotal role in meeting basic societal needs. These needs include reproducing and socializing new members, producing and/or distributing goods and services, transmitting wealth, and ensuring social order. At the same time, the family plays an important role in the lives of most individuals: it is the social setting in which we forge a sense of who we are; it usually provides us with a sense of belonging; and it is an arena in which a large part of everyday social interaction occurs.

The importance of the family as a social institution can be illustrated by its relationship to other topics covered in this book. For example, a major part of socialization occurs within the family setting; gender roles are both learned and played out in families; fertility level, an important determinant of population growth, results from decisions and actions taken at the family level; families play an integral role in the lives of elderly persons, often providing care and support; and the particular form of social inequality in a society is experienced at the family level.

In other words, understanding the family is fundamental to understanding society. By studying families, we can better grasp the workings of society. But we must also examine the wider social environment as it influences the family. A useful way of thinking about our task in this chapter is that we look at both *the family in society* and *society in the family*. In the first case, we are concerned with the roles families play in meeting social and individual goals. When families change, the society and the lives of individuals change. In the second case, we are concerned with the ways in which characteristics of the wider society influence the structure, organization, and functioning of families. When society changes, the family is affected.

Given its fundamental role vis-à-vis society, the study of the family is an important part of the sociological enterprise. But when we try to analyze the family from a sociological viewpoint, we encounter a number of difficulties. One problem is that most of us live, or have lived, in family settings; therefore we feel that we are experts on this aspect of social life, at least in our own society. Yet knowledge about the workings of our own family does not help; it may even hinder us from gaining a wider understanding of families. In other words, our "insider" status as family members can blind us to a comprehensive, analytical perspective on families and family diversity. A second difficulty is that in many societies — Canada and the United States among them — family life is played out in a basically private arena. Sociologists cannot observe family behaviour as easily as more public types of behaviour — the kind that occurs in the workplace, in schools, or in clubs, for example. And, since many aspects of family life are "sensitive" or are considered to be "nobody else's business," data gathered by sociologists may contain inaccuracies that are hard to trace and identify.

Another difficulty emerges when we attempt to examine families in a number of different societies and social groups, as we do in this chapter. Data may contain elements of noncomparability, due to different practices in defining and measuring aspects of family life. Or data may be scarce for some dimensions of family life, as is the case for Mexico. When empirical data are lacking, we must be careful not to rely upon stereotypes in our thinking about family life in that society or group.

Also, there are difficulties in defining the family. We will turn to this issue in the next section. After considering the definition of family, we turn to a comparative examination of families in different cultures and focus on a number of dimensions — including family structure, types of marriage, rules of marriage, descent, residence, and authority — with an emphasis on five North

American groups: anglophone Canadians, francophone Canadians, white Americans, black Americans, and Mexicans. We will then look at how the family is viewed in the three major sociological perspectives, as well as in two others that are important in the sociology of the family: the feminist perspective and the family life course perspective. The last part of this chapter examines a number of aspects of contemporary families in five North American groups.

What Is the Family?

While the family is often considered to be an "obvious" concept, it has proven very difficult to define. In everyday life, we use the term in a variety of ways. Consider the following statements:

"My family came from the old country at the turn of the century."
"I grew up in a small family."
"My family is close-knit."
"I would like to start a family."
"I want a son to carry on the family name."

In each of the above statements (adapted from Hayford 1987), the term "family" is used in a different way, but we have no difficulty in understanding what is meant. We use this word to refer to many kinds of relationships, interactions, and identities.

For sociologists, a definition of the family that takes into account its variety of meanings within a society and that has universal applicability has proven elusive. Consider these two often-used definitions of the family:

[The family] finds its origin in marriage; it consists of husband, wife, and children born in their wedlock, although other relatives may find their place close to the nuclear group, and the group is united by moral, economic, religious and social rights and obligations. (Coser 1974)

[The family] is a social arrangement based on marriage and the marriage contract, including recognition of the rights and duties of parenthood, common residence for husband, wife and children, and reciprocal economic obligations between husband and wife. (Stephens 1963)

Both these definitions stress the biological role of the family (the production of children) and emphasize that family members are tied together by a system of rights and duties. However, these definitions fail (as perhaps any definition will) to take account of the various forms the family may take, both in a society and cross-culturally. In North American families, these definitions do not include, for example, families based on a common-law union; cases where a single adult lives with his or her children; situations in which a remarried person sees his or children on a regular basis, but the children live with a former spouse; and families in which one spouse commutes between two households. Also, both definitions imply that a childless couple is not "really" a family. In addition, the Stephens definition does not take into account families that include members beyond the nuclear unit of husband, wife, and children. In other words, these standard definitions of the family exclude too much of the variety of family life.

Eichler (1983) argues that the problem with defining the family lies not so much in the "family" part as in the "the" part. When we assume that there is such a thing as "the" family, we automatically, and arbitrarily, make other groupings non-families. She suggests that we would be better off looking at how families vary along six key dimensions:

The Procreative Dimension. Families are social units responsible for the production of children. Variation along this dimension for a given couple ranges from having children with one another, to rearing various combinations of children from other unions, to having no children. Children may also be raised by one adult who has never, or who is no longer, married.

The Socialization Dimension. Families act as one of the primary agents in the socialization of children. Within the family setting, parents may be the major socializers, or other family members may have a crucial role. Both parents may be involved in the socialization of children; only one parent may be involved, as is the case with deserting fathers; one parent may be the primary parental socializer and the other parent may have visitation rights; or neither parent may be involved — as, for example, when a child is given up for adoption. In some societies and social groups, adult family members other than parents have an important socialization role. For example, in some societies the mother's brother is culturally prescribed to play a role much like that often played by fathers in North America; within many black American families, grandparents play an important part in socialization, but it is not a cultural prescription (that is, it is more voluntary and situational and less clearly defined.)

The Sexual Dimension. Persons married to one another form a unit in which sexual intimacy is permitted and expected. Here, the variations for a married couple could include having sex with each other only; having sex with other persons (either along with each other or not); or being celibate. In Canada and the United States, extramarital sexual intimacy is frowned upon, but premarital sexual activity has become more acceptable (Hobart 1989; Thornton 1989). In many other societies, extramarital sex is permitted. This is the case in Mexico — but for men only. However, sexual relations within marriage have a distinct characteristic in all societies: they carry obligations with them. As Stephens (1963) puts it, sex within marriage is never "free."

The Residential Dimension. Families form the basis of the residential distribution of persons. At one end of the spectrum, all family members (however the society defines family membership) reside together. At the other end, at least theoretically, all live in separate residences. In the United States and Canada, it is expected that a married couple and their dependent children will share a residence, although, as we will see, there are many deviations from this expectation. Rules of residence can be quite different in other societies, as will be discussed in the next section of this chapter.

The Economic Dimension. Family members are tied together economically, in terms of obligations as well as in the actual provision of economic support. One family member may be responsible for supporting all other family members. At the opposite end of the continuum, all family members are totally independent. In fact, neither of these extremes ever occurs. While it may sometimes appear that one member is totally responsible, the contributions of others make the "breadwinner" role possible. And total independence requires economic equality, which is impossible for children and extremely difficult for women. In other words, family members exist in relations of economic interdependence.

The Emotional Dimension. Since families are important primary groups, their members are emotionally involved with one another. The quality of emotional relationships ranges from the highly positive to the highly negative, although detachment is also possible. There is cross-societal variation concerning which particular relationships are most emotionally laden. In Canada and the United States, people place a strong emphasis on the husband–wife relationship (the conjugal bond). In Mexico, the mother–daughter relationship is the most emotionally close (Penalosa 1968).

So we can say that families are units within society whose members interact along these six dimensions in a variety of different ways. This variation, which exists both within a society and across societies, occurs for both *ideal* and *actual* family behaviour. Societies vary in terms of what is considered the "best" (or the normative) way to organize family life, and they differ in the actual ways that family members live out their lives together. But all societies are similar in one respect: no society has even been able to avoid a discrepancy between the ideal and the actual in family matters. To use mainstream North America as

an example, ideal family organization involves a heterosexual man and woman who marry and, in terms of the key dimensions outlined above, (i) have children; (ii) both raise the children into adulthood; (iii) are sexually intimate with each other and no one else; (iv) reside together with their own children, and no one else's, until, and only until, those children reach maturity; (v) cooperate together economically (although there is an unwritten rule that economic contribution is not quite equal); and (vi) have a mutually satisfying emotional relationship. We only have to look around us to see that this socially constructed ideal family situation does not correspond to the reality of family life for many people. Yet, in comparison with this mythical ideal, many families are deemed to be pathological or deviant (Andersen 1991). Inevitable gaps between ideal and actual family life highlight the problem of defining "the" family.

Let us consider the variety of arrangements created by different societies to deal with matters related to the family. We cannot put family arrangements in our society into perspective unless we have comparative information to draw upon.

Cross-Cultural Variation in Family Patterns

In all societies, families consist of persons tied together by marriage (*affinal relations*) and by

Redefining Family

TORONTO — The Ontario government must pay survivor pensions to partners of gay and lesbian civil servants under a "leading edge" human rights decision Tuesday that could trigger similar changes across Canada.

The order will also have far-reaching effects on the private sector in the province because the words "of the opposite sex" when defining marital status have been removed from the Ontario Human Rights Code, officials said.

"The Human Rights Code now applies with its new wording to all employers in Ontario," said Catherine Frazee, chief commissioner of the Ontario Human Rights Commission.

Rulings by the three-member board of inquiry on the application of the Human Rights Code take effect immediately and are legally binding. But they can be appealed through the courts.

"Protection under the Human Rights Code for gays and lesbians

in Ontario extends to protect the relationship as well as the individuals who are gay and lesbian." Frazee. said.

Source:

Adapted from *Vancouver Sun*, September 2, 1992, p. A3. Reprinted by permission of The Canadian Press.

blood (*consanguine relations*). The marriage may not be a legal arrangement; and the blood tie may be fictive (as in adoption), partial (as with half-siblings), or nonexistent (as the case with child-less couples). Nevertheless, marriage and blood ties form the basis of family and of kinship units. Although biology (being related by blood) is an integral component of the family as an institution, different societies have developed a tremendous variety of ways to organize families and family life. This illustrates the predominance of social over biological determinants of human behaviour. Let us now look at these variations in more detail. Much of the cross-cultural information that follows is derived from Murdoch's (1957) sample of 554 societies; however, our focus will be on five major North American social groups.

Family Types

The most basic family type is the **nuclear family**, consisting of a married couple and unmarried children who live apart from other relatives. (Childless couples and lone-parent families are also considered nuclear families). This is the fam-ily type most familiar to Canadians and Americans. The nuclear family is distinguished from the **extended family**, which consists of two or more nuclear families joined together through blood ties, that is, through a parent–child relationship. The classic example consists of a husband and wife, their unmarried children, their married sons, and the wives and children of the married sons. The members of this three-generation unit may reside in one dwelling, in a cluster of adjacent dwellings, or simply nearby. One subtype of the extended family is of historical importance in the francophone Canadian case. The **stem family** is a three-generational family in which only one son, upon marriage, remains in the parental home (along with his wife and children). Other sons move away upon marriage, as do all daughters.

Among Mexicans and black Americans, the extended family plays an important role. The classic extended family is not common, although among rural and poor Mexicans, sons usually reside near their parents after marriage. Also, there is evidence of temporary stem-family arrangements both in past and present-day Mexico (Lomnitz and Lizaur 1978). In black American households,

Biological versus Social Fatherhood

In the latest development in a custody struggle that could break new ground in California family law, a Canoga Park man was awarded custody Monday of a 4-year-old boy whom he has been raising but did not father.

An elated Larry McLinden, 43, won primary custody of Larry McLinden Jr., who was declared his legal son by the same court last month even though he is not the boy's biological father and never married the child's mother.

"I do believe that Larry McLinden will afford Larry Jr. a more stable environment," ruled Los Angeles Superior Court Judge Dana Senit Henry after a day of testimony in the custody dispute between McLinden and the boy's mother, Karen Hamilton Munyer, 34, of Inglewood.

McLinden has maintained that he believed the boy was his biological son until he and Munyer broke off their relationship and she told him that he was not the father.

The judge, who earlier ruled that McLinden should be considered the boy's father because the two are psychologically attached, also granted McLinden's request to terminate any parental rights for Matthew Florence, whom blood tests identified as the child's most likely biological father.

Florence did not appear at Monday's hearing and consented to the suspension of his rights, lawyers for McLinden and the boy's mother said.

McLinden, an investment banker, said he expected to win custody, given his previous court victory.

Munyer will be allowed to have her son on alternate weekends and alter-nate Wednesdays, the judge ruled. Munyer and McLinden, who have equally shared the boy's time for the last two years, should have joint authority in decisions affecting the boy's upbringing, with final say in educational matters resting with McLinden, the ruling said.

The case received widespread attention last month when Henry pronounced McLinden as the boy's "natural" and "psychological" parent even though the two are not biologically connected.

Source:

Adapted from Henry Chu, *Los Angeles Times*, January 28, 1992, pp. B1, B3. Copyright © 1992, Los Angeles Times. Reprinted by permission.

the incidence of extended family arrangements is twice that found in white American households, even when differences in income are controlled (Farley and Allen 1987). The shared residence of women, their daughter(s), and their grandchildren accounts for a substantial proportion of extended families among African Americans (Beck and Beck 1989). The black American extended family system has been variously described as an adaptive response to the situation of blacks in America and as a remnant of West African culture (Hatchett et al. 1991). In both Mexican and black American society, nuclear families are embedded in networks of multigenerational kin, and the boundaries of the nuclear family are flexible. Nuclear families may also be joined through marriage ties. Plural marriage produces **polygamous** families. This leads us to our next topic: types of marriage.

Types of Marriage

Marriage, in the broadest sense, constitutes a commitment or exchange that is recognized by the society in which it takes place. There are four basic types of marriage. **Monogamy** involves the marriage of one man and one woman. It is the only type of marriage legally permissible in North America, although in Mexico some men maintain a mistress and a second set of children (Riding 1989). In societies that practise **polygyny**, one man is allowed to have more than one wife. While this is the preferred marriage type in approximately three-quarters of societies, its occurrence is quite rare because only wealthy men can afford the expense of multiple wives and numerous children. In polyandrous marriage, one woman has more than one husband. Unlike polygyny, **polyandry** is rare as an ideal, as well as in practice. There are only four known polyandrous societies, although a few societies allow polyandry as a variant marriage type. In **group marriage**, more than one man is married to more than one woman. A very uncommon marriage type, it tends to co-occur with polyandry.

Marriage Rules

Societies also have rules about other aspects of marriage. One set of rules concerns whom one is eligible to marry. There are two basic norms in this regard: exogamy and endogamy. With **endogamy**, marriage must occur within a defined social group. An often-cited example is the marriage practices of Hindus in India; one must marry within one's caste. There are elements of endogamy within Canada and the United States, particularly with regard to race. Both countries have had miscegenation laws that prohibited marriage between whites and nonwhites. Now, it is only expected that whites will marry whites, blacks will marry blacks, and so on. In the case of **exogamy**, marriage must occur outside a defined group. Classic examples occur in China and other Asian countries (see the accompanying box). The rule of exogamy may be viewed as an extension of the **incest taboo**. All societies have incest taboos — prohibitions on close relatives marrying and/or having intimate sexual relations — although they vary in stipulating who is "off limits" to whom.

Another set of rules determines who decides whom one will marry. In the case of **arranged marriage**, one's spouse is chosen by one's parents and/or family elders, and financial negotiations between the two sets of families often play an important role in decision-making. While this type of marriage is common worldwide, it is not part of the North American family system. (However, it occurred in the past among various Native groups in Canada, the United States, and Mexico, and continues among some Mexican aboriginal groups). With **self-selected marriage**, individuals choose for themselves whom they will marry.

Kinship Systems

Societies erect rules to determine how kinship will be reckoned. Descent can be traced through both the male and female lines — one is considered to be related to both one's mother's and one's father's relatives (*bilateral descent*). This is the system that exists in North America, although children usually take their father's surname. However, Mexicans follow the Spanish practice of children taking the surname of both parents, a custom that is clearly more bilateral than that of Americans and Canadians. Descent may be traced along the male line only; in this case, one is considered related only to one's father's relatives — they are the only relatives that "count" (*patrilineal descent*). Alternatively, where descent fol-

Illustrating Exogamy

SEOUL — Businessman Kim Eui Kyong and his one-time student, Kim Kyoung Sun, made one basic mistake. They fell in love before checking their family tree.

Sure they had the same surname — but *Kim* in Korea is like *Smith* in the United States, only more so. More than one in five South Koreans are Kims. It turned out that Eui Kyong and Kyoung Sun shared a paternal ancestor who lived about the time that the English poet Geoffrey Chaucer was writing his *Canterbury Tales*, back in the 14th Century. Their common blood amounted to one drop in 14 million or so.

No matter. In South Korea, it is too much.

For here, uniquely, two people with a common ancestor anywhere in their paternal lineage — no matter how far back — are forbidden by both law and custom to marry. China, where the idea of banning intra-clan marriages originated, abandoned the practice at the turn of the century. Communist North Korea abolished a law similar to the south's in the late 1940s, although Koreans there reportedly still frown on clan marriages.

But that was little consolation to the Kims, who risked official sanctions, financial penalties and social ostracism to marry illegally.

"What have two persons in love like us done to disturb society?" the businessman asked rhetorically. "Who could be hurt? Why should a law cause such agony to those who haven't hurt anyone?"

The Kims' story illustrates a continuing struggle here between still-powerful Confucian ideas about the sanctity of the clan and the realities of modern South Korean life. (The issue is sensitive enough that the couple's given names have been changed in this article at their request.)

The standing of the clan is an offshoot of the Confucian emphasis on the family as more important than the individual, and on the senior male member as the head of the family. It is common for Koreans to keep multivolume registers tracing their ancestry back hundreds of years. The major clans — more than half of South Koreans are named Kim, Lee, Park, or Choi — maintain offices and staffs that compile records, build monuments to major clan ancestors and maintain their graves.

Article 809 of South Korea's Family Law bars marriage between any man and woman "with the same family name and the same place or origin" — members, in other words, of the same clan, believed to share a male ancestor. Article 815 bars marriage through four generations if there is a common ancestor in the maternal lineage of one or both of the partners.

Marriages that run afoul of either of those articles cannot be registered, and are therefore not legal. In practical terms, that means that husbands can't claim a tax exemption for their wives, and any children of the union are technically illegitimate.

Parents sometimes disinherit children who marry within the clan, and other social pressures exist. Kim said he fears that a rival at work in one of South Korea's mid-sized conglomerates might use his marriage to discredit him.

The social pressures are so widespread here that some intra-clan couples separate rather than face them. Suicides, too, have occurred.

Source:

Sam Jameson, *Los Angeles Times*, March 17, 1992, p. H4.

---

lows the female line, one is considered to be related only to one's mother's kin (*matrilineal descent*). Within many foreign-born minority groups in the United States and Canada, descent follows one line only; and most Native groups and black Americans were characterized by either patrilineal or matrilineal descent in their traditional family systems.

An aspect of Mexican kinship deserves special note. A Spanish-origin fictive kin relationship system, based on godparents and termed *compadrinazgo*, is an important dimension of family and social life. Godparents are chosen to play a part in the ceremonies (such as baptisms) of godchildren and have other responsibilities toward their godchildren. The relationship between godparents and godchildren is termed *padrinazgo*. However, the most important relationship is between parents and godparents — *compadrazgo*. They call each other "compadre" (co-father) and "comadre" (co-mother) and recognize obligations of mutual assistance and solidarity. The compadrinazgo system is used to reinforce existing ties of social and economic support as well as to create new relationships, often with persons of higher socioeconomic status. Either way, this fictive kinship system creates an extra "buffer" of social resources for dealing with life's problems.

The rules erected to determine how kinship is reckoned are closely related to rules of residence. Most societies have stipulations, conventions, or rules regarding where, once married, a couple will reside. One such rule stipulates that the couple will move away from both sets of parents.

While this is the general rule in Canada and the United States (with occasional exceptions), it is the preferred practice in a minority of societies — about 10 percent of Murdoch's sample. The most common convention involves the couple moving in with, or nearby, the husband's parents (*patrilocal residence*); this arrangement is preferred in approximately 60 percent of societies and is the preferred arrangement in Mexico. Considerably rarer is a rule requiring the couple to live with, or nearby, the wife's parents (*matrilocal residence*).

Many other rules of residence have been adopted at one time or another by smaller numbers of societies. For example, the couple may be expected to reside with the husband's mother's brothers; or the couple may live with the wife's parents for a few years, then move to the husband's parents. Once again, we see that a substantial degree of diversity is involved in matters related to the family.

Family organization varies in terms of power structure. In **patriarchal families**, authority resides with men (particularly older men) and is meted out autocratically. The power men wield in this type of arrangement extends beyond the family and kin setting to the wider society. Patriarchal family arrangements, which tend to occur in conjunction with patrilineal descent and patrilocal residence, have been very common throughout human history, occurring most frequently in pre-industrial, autocratic states such as pre-industrial Japan, China, India, and the Middle East (Stephens 1963). Such arrangements do not, by the strictest definition, occur in Western democracies. In recent years, the term "patriarchy" has become a shorthand descriptor for male domination in Western societies. However, we are not a "true" patriarchy: the degree of gender inequality is less; we do not have patrilineal descent (with power vested in the eldest male in the male line); and we do not have patrilocal residence rules.

In **matriarchal families**, authority is in the hands of women. Unlike the patriarchal case, however, the power that women have within the family and kin setting does not extend to the wider society. It has been argued that black American families are matriarchal (Moynihan 1965), due to a heritage of slavery and discrimination that has rendered families unstable and, thus, controlled by women by default. Others, such as black sociologist Charles Willie (1991) dispute that African American families are matriarchal. In **egalitarian families** (also called "democratic"), authority is shared equally by men and women. While this is an ideal that is realized only sometimes, it is the normative foundation of Canadian and American families.

This section has provided a brief overview of the wide range of family arrangements that exist cross-culturally. It is important to note that type of family pattern has a significant relationship with the wider society and has a major impact on the lives of individuals. To give one example, if descent in a society is traced along the father's line, then kin groups (called *clans*) will be a basic element of social structure. These kin groups will form the basis of economic, political, and religious organization. The society will likely be patriarchal as well, which affects the nature of relations between men and women and the power structure in general. Kin group membership will determine the individual's rights and obligations, will dictate his or her interpersonal behaviour, and will be a major source of his or her sense of "belonging."

We have now placed contemporary North American families within a comparative perspective. Canadian and U.S. families are typically nuclear units based on self-selected monogamous marriage in which descent is traced through both female and male lines. Couples live apart from both sets of parents and have something approaching an egalitarian authority relationship. Historically and cross-culturally, this is quite a rare way of organizing family life. It has been termed the **conjugal family** pattern because of its emphasis on the husband–wife tie and its relative de-emphasis on the wider kin network. Mexican families, although also based on monogamous marriage and bilateral descent, are characterized by a greater degree of kinship embeddedness (which de-emphasizes the husband–wife relationship), patrilocal residence (at least ideally), and more gender inequality in husband–wife relations.

As we end this section, it must be emphasized that although family organization varies substantially, families everywhere manage to accomplish essentially the same tasks. These tasks relate to the six dimensions we examined in the preceding section: procreation, the socialization of children, sexual regulation, the location of persons in residential units, economic co-operation, and the provision of emotional support.

Theoretical Perspectives

As you already know, there is no "correct" theoretical perspective within sociology; the various perspectives represent different ways of looking at the same phenomena. Within the sociology of the family, there are five major theoretical approaches: structural-functionalism; the conflict perspective; the feminist perspective; symbolic interactionism (and other related micro-theories such as social-exchange theory); and the family life course perspective.

The Structural-Functional Perspective

Structural functionalism has dominated the sociological study of the family, particularly in the United States. In terms of the family, structural functionalism has focused on two major issues: the functions the family fulfils for society (that is, the contribution the family makes to maintaining societal equilibrium), and the functions of the subsystems within the family.

A major structural-functional tenet is that, with urbanization and industrialization, the family lost some important social functions. In the past, the family performed numerous functions and, indeed, was the social institution around which all other aspects of society revolved. With industrialization, new social institutions — such as schools — developed, each taking over at least some of the tasks that families used to perform (Ogburn 1933). Also, industrialization required the separation of home and workplace; hence, according to structural-functional theory, the family ceased to be a unit of production and became a mere unit of consumption. As a result, family functions have been reduced to three: the replacement of individuals (reproduction), the socialization of new members of society, and the provision of emotional support. This last function is highlighted when the family is referred to as "a haven in a heartless world" (Lasch 1977). Accompanying this loss in functions has been a change in structure: industrialization led to the demise

of the extended family and the emergence of the nuclear family (Goode 1970). Parsons (1954) referred to the "isolated conjugal family," which he saw as the type of family best suited to meet the economic and social needs of industrial society.

When focusing on the functions of the subsystems with the family, structural functionalists emphasize the division of labour between men and women. In industrialized societies, the roles of husband and wife are differentiated: the husband performs the *instrumental* tasks — the "breadwinner" role — and the wife performs the *expressive* tasks — providing emotional support and nurturance to other family members (Parsons 1955). According to this perspective, this gender-based division of labour is necessary for the integration and stability of families and of modern industrial societies.

According to structural functionalists, women perform the expressive tasks by providing emotional support and nurturance to other family members.

Given the dominance of structural functionalism within sociology, it has come under close scrutiny. In terms of the family, major challenges have come from two fronts: historical demography and feminist sociology. Research done by historical demographers (for example, Anderson 1971; Laslett and Wall 1972) demonstrated that the nuclear form of the family predominated in European-based societies long before industrialization. Indeed, Levy (1965) has shown that the nuclear family was the dominant family form throughout all of human history, because high mortality levels made family extension impossible even in those societies that highly idealized it. Criticisms from feminist sociology will be covered in a later section.

The Conflict Perspective

Marx and Engels were influential proponents of a conflict approach to the family. A fundamental proposition of the Marxist perspective is that the family in capitalist society is an exploitive social institution. In fact, according to this approach, it is the family that is primarily responsible for women's oppression. This is in direct contrast to the structural-functional view of the desirability of a gender-based division of labour.

The conflict perspective focuses on family change and the economic determinants of that change. Like structural functionalism, it views industrialization, particularly the separation of home and work, as a major cause of family change. However, the conflict perspective assesses the consequences of capitalist industrialization differently, holding that the creation of a work–family dichotomy led to the removal of women from the public arenas of life and a subsequent downgrading in their status. This perspective also points out that bourgeois class interests are served by a family system that oppresses women and downplays their economic contribution both to families and to the wider society.

The conflict perspective takes a more complex view of the relationship between economic change and family change than does structural functionalism. The latter holds that industrialization causes the family to change in certain virtually inevitable ways. (However, some structural functionalists, such as Goode [1970], have suggested that the family may change prior to indus-

trialization in ways that make the society more receptive to economic change.) In contrast, the conflict model considers the relationship between economic change and family change to be a dialectical one. That is, inherent tensions and contradictions in the mode of production lead to changes in the structure of economic organization; these in turn affect family life and family arrangements, creating tensions and conflicts within the family arena that have implications for the wider economy.

The idea of conflict as inherent in family life contradicts the notion of family harmony implicit in structural-functional concepts such as the division of labour based on gender. Within the conflict perspective, relationships between husbands and wives and between parents and children are deemed to be continuously confrontational because each has different interests. Thus, the conflict perspective has led to a concern with such phenomena as spouse abuse, battered children, and family violence in general.

Although the conflict model provides a useful way of looking at families, little research or writing on the family exists within traditional Marxist analysis. This is so because domestic labour does not produce "surplus value"; therefore, it does not fit into the standard Marxist conceptualization of economic relations (Porter 1987). Only in the last fifteen years or so has the conflict perspective been applied to the study of the family, with its adoption by some feminist scholars focusing on women's inequality in the family, the economy, and society in general.

The Feminist Perspective

Feminist sociologists have been highly critical of a number of aspects of structural-functional theory as it applies to families. They have challenged the postulate that the family has lost its productive functions and become only a unit of consumption (Cowan 1986). According to the feminist perspective, this way of looking at the family ignores the contributions that women make as wives and as mothers. The feminist perspective is also critical of the idea that the family functions as an emotional refuge (see, for example, Bernard 1973a; Barrett 1980). Instead, it is argued that while family life is structured for the emotional benefit of men, it is (or can be) emotionally crippling for women. In a related vein, feminist sociology has not accepted the Parsonian idea that the conjugal family "fits" well with the needs of modern industrial society, suggesting instead that the conjugal family creates tensions and strains that work to the detriment of wider social stability.

Feminism has challenged the public–private dichotomy that is an element of both structural-functional and conflict perspectives. It is argued that the dichotomy is overly simplistic (Eichler 1980) because social life involves numerous overlapping and interdependent contexts. This perspective has focused attention on the interrelationships between work and family patterns.

The feminist perspective involves more than a critique of other theoretical approaches and their concepts. A major concern of the feminist perspective is the relationship between family and state. It is argued that the state oppresses women in the interests of men, in the interests of capital, and as an outcome of the intersections of both types of interests as played out in varying historical contexts (Barrett 1980). Such oppression is buttressed by two fundamental beliefs in society: that women are nurturant "by nature," and that any earnings of married women are not critical to the economic status of the household (Cheal 1991).

Feminist sociology is action-oriented, with a political agenda. It seeks to change society in ways that will enhance the status of women in society and in families and that will validate the contributions, experiences, and viewpoints of women in all social institutions, including the family.

The three perspectives we have looked at so far represent macro approaches to the study of the family — they focus on the family as an institution in society and on its relationship with other aspects of society. In contrast, the symbolic-interaction perspective is a micro approach; it addresses the dynamics of social relationships within family settings.

The Symbolic-Interaction Perspective

In the examination of family life, symbolic interaction turns our attention to the subjective aspects of family relations, particularly shared meanings and shared expectations in marital and family interaction. A number of concepts related to the major sociological concept of *role* are important in this perspective. In family interaction, individuals are constantly involved in role-taking, which involves imagining oneself in the role of the other person (the *counter-role*) and then perceiving and judging one's acts from that standpoint. This interpretive process occurs in husband–wife interaction, and the "give and take" that results is necessary for marital stability. Role-taking is particularly important in the socialization process. As children, we observe the roles played by family members and incorporate these roles into our own personality structure. Through interactions in the family setting, we come to define the acts of others and, in that way, become aware of our own actions. In other words, we learn everyone else's roles first and then learn to react to ourselves in terms of these other roles.

One may be said to have a self only in relation to other people; the self emerges out of a social — that is, familial — context. Thus the most important process in socialization is learning how to perceive one's acts from the standpoint of other people; much of this learning occurs within family interaction. Note, then, the different approach taken to socialization within this micro perspective as compared with macro approaches. Whereas structural functionalism, for example, looks at socialization in relation to the wider society (that is, as a family function), symbolic interaction focuses on *how* individuals are socialized, on the interactive social processes involved in learning to be a functioning member of society.

Role-taking is closely linked to the set of expectations that guides role performance and the evaluation of role performance. In families, there must be a degree of consensus about what is involved in the roles that each family member plays. If a wife and husband have different expectations about their respective roles, marital stability is threatened. Any family member who feels unable to meet role expectations will experience discomfort, or *role strain*. The classic (and stereotypical) example is the woman who feels overburdened by parental, spousal, and career duties. Note, however, that this perspective focuses on the subjective experiences of individuals. People in positions that look exactly the same from an objective point of view may perceive things quite differently: one person's negatively experienced "stress" may be the next one's positively experienced "exciting challenge."

The symbolic-interaction approach to the family, then, is concerned with the internal workings of families, with the interactive context in which family roles and relationships are subjectively defined, redefined, and played out. Emphasis is placed on the subjective aspects of family interaction and the dynamics of the interactive process. An emphasis on interactive dynamics also occurs in other microsociological theories — for example, social-exchange theory, which explains family behaviour in terms of incentives and disincentives, negotiation, and bargaining (see, for example, Nye 1982; Scanzoni 1982).

Our last approach to the family, the family life course perspective, combines elements of macro- and microsociology. It may be viewed as an attempt to link or integrate the two levels in the understanding of family life.

The Family Life Course Perspective

This new perspective within the sociology of the family focuses on family change in conjunction with wider social change and with individual change (Elder 1985; Hareven 1978; Demos 1986). At the macro level of analysis, this approach examines structural changes in the family in relation to historical factors and wider societal development. At the micro level, it looks at changes in individual families and at individuals in families as they move through time.

According to the family life course perspective, there are two types of time: *social time* and *family time*. **Family time** refers to changes that occur within a family over time. For example, a childless couple becomes a family with young children, then reaches the "empty nest" phase, and eventually widow(er)hood. Of course, not all families go through all family life course transitions, and some families may have very complex patterns due to divorce, death, and remarriage. And some individuals may experience very few, if any, family life course transtions. **Social time** refers to changes occurring in the wider society that influence the family life course. For example, the joint action of changes in fertility and mortality will determine the type and timing of transitions (Gee 1990); changes in the level of female labour-force participation will influence the way the family life course is experienced; and changes in the legal and ideological environment will in-fluence the degree of variation in the family life course (for instance, whether divorce is a likely event).

The family life course perspective takes into account the individual's location in historical time, as well. For example, people born in the Great Depression experienced, in general, a different family life course from those born during the "baby boom." The first group faced a very favourable economic situation due to its small size (less competition for jobs) and an expanding economy when it reached young adulthood. As a result, its family life course was speeded up — persons born in the depression married young, had their children young, and experienced the "empty nest" at relatively young ages. The "baby boomers" faced a very different situation. This cohort's large size created a high degree of job competition, which, coupled with a stagnating economy, has meant that family life course events have occurred at later ages.

A related issue concerns the normative timing of life course events. Elder (1978) has pointed out that a "social timetable" exists, dictating the preferred ages for experiencing family (and other) life events such as getting married, having one's first child, and so on. Depending upon the degree to which this timetable has been internalized, being "off-time" can produce distress for the individual.

The family life course perspective provides a missing link in our understanding of the relationships among individual, familial, and social change (Hareven 1987). It points out the developmental dynamic that is characteristic of family change in the context of wider social and historical factors.

Families in North America

In this section, we examine aspects of family structure, organization, and functioning in five major North American social groupings.

Types of Households

To set the stage for this examination and to introduce topics that will be looked at in more detail later in the chapter, we will first turn our attention to the distribution of household types in Canada and the United States (see Table 12-1; recent and comparable data for Mexico are not available for this table and for other tables and graphs. Data and information that can be obtained for Mexico are interwoven in the text.) We see that about one-third of households are not nuclear, with the majority of these being one-person households. Within the four groups, approximately one-quarter of households are of the one-person type. (In contrast, only 4 percent of Mexican households are one-person households [deVos 1991]). The high proportion of households in the United States and Canada in which persons live alone is due to a number of factors: the aging of the population (widows, and sometimes widowers, living alone), relatively high rates of divorce, and increases in the age at marriage.

Only about one-half of Canadian and American households have children. Although exact data are not available for Mexico, it can safely be assumed that considerably more households there have children, given a total fertility rate that approaches 4 children per woman (compared with rates that range from 1.7 in Canada to 2.2 among black Americans) and that nearly 40 percent of the population is under the age of 15 (almost double the figures for the United States and Canada) (Population Reference Bureau 1992). The distribution of households in terms of "couples with children" and "lone parents" differs across the four groups in Table 12-1; most noticeable is the high percentage of lone-parent households among black Americans. Lone-parent families will be looked at in more detail later in this chapter.

Mate Selection

Despite the high proportion of one-person households, most people legally marry at least one other person. By ages 45 to 54, the percentages never-married are in the range of 5–9 percent in North America, although the figures for black Americans are somewhat higher (approximately 10–15 percent) (see Figure 12-1). Nevertheless, the proportion of people who marry (and live with their spouse) has declined over the last quarter-century, particularly among black Americans. A U.S. analysis of the decline of marriage among white and black Americans indicates that the decline is not due, for the most part, to socioeconomic factors such as the increased education and labour-force participation of women; rather, changing family attitudes and behaviours (such as a higher likelihood of parental divorce, an increased cohabitation, a desire for fewer children, and the greater acceptability of unwed motherhood) have set up a trend that continues by its own momentum (Mare and Winship 1991).

TABLE 12-1 Distribution of Household Types, Canada and United States, 1991

| | Total | Couple | | Lone Parent | One-Person Household | Other |
		With Children	Without Children			
Canada	10 018 267	3 729 795 (37.2%)	2 782 500 (27.8%)	903 745 (9.0%)	2 297 055 (22.9%)	305 172 (3.0%)
Quebec	2 634 300	961 285 (36.5%)	628 325 (23.9%)	260 315 (9.9%)	650 355 (24.7%)	134 020 (5.1%)
U.S. whites	80 968 000	21 893 000 (27.0%)	25 121 000 (31.0%)	6 550 000 (8.1%)	20 319 000 (25.1%)	7 085 000 (8.8%)
U.S. blacks	10 671 000	1 933 000 (18.1%)	1 636 000 (15.3%)	3 240 000 (30.4%)	2 778 000 (26.0%)	1 084 000 (10.2%)

SOURCE: Statistics Canada, *1991 Census — Dwellings and Households*, catalogue no. 93-311 (Ottawa: Minister of Industry, Science and Technology, 1992); U.S. Bureau of the Census, "Household and Family Characteristics: March 1991," in *Current Population Reports*, series P-20, no. 458 (Washington, DC: Government Printing Office, 1992).

FIGURE 12-1   Percentage of People Never Married at Ages 45–54, Canada and United States, 1990–91

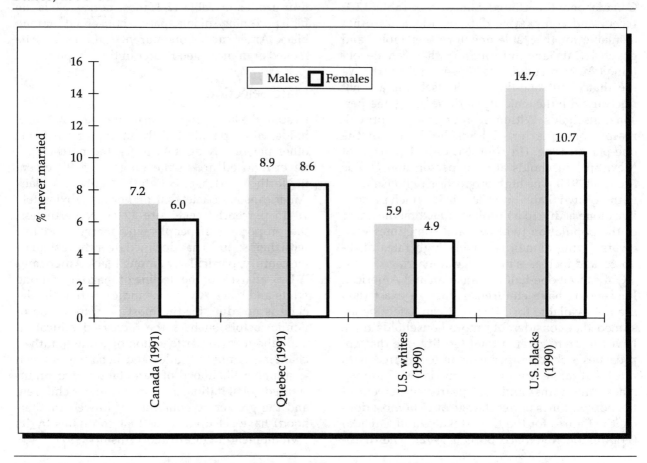

SOURCE: Statistics Canada, *1991 Census — Age, Sex and Marital Status*, catalogue no. 93-310 (Ottawa: Minister of Industry, Science and Technology, 1992); U.S. Bureau of the Census, "The Black Population of the United States: March 1991," *Current Population Reports*, series P-20, no. 448 (Washington, DC: Government Printing Office, 1991).

What are the norms and processes that govern whom we marry? Although some Mexican Native groups, the more isolated rural population in Mexico, and some immigrant groups in Canada and the United States retain their traditional practice of arranged marriage, most North Americans are guided by a norm that stipulates that they should choose whom they marry on the basis of love. Such a norm is rather rare from a cross-cultural perspective: most societies do not leave something as important as who marries whom to the capriciousness of an ill-defined emotion. However, despite our norm, marriages do not occur randomly; clear patterns are observable. This is illustrated by the operation of **homogamy**, or

"like marries like." Homogamy occurs along two dimensions: personal and social. *Personal homogamy* means that people with similar personality characteristics and similar levels of physical attractiveness tend to marry one another. *Social homogamy* means that people with similar social characteristics tend to marry. For example, people usually select spouses with the same racial origin, ethnic origin, religion, and level of schooling. Except for racial origin, homogamy involving ascribed characteristics has decreased in recent years. For example, in Canada approximately 25 percent of anglophone and 15 percent of francophone husbands marry out of their ethnic group. The likelihood of marrying out is associated with the small size of an ethnic group (except for French Canadians), being native-born (except for French Canadians), high occupational status, and high educational status (Kalbach and Richard 1991). Religious out-marriage is even more common than ethnic exogamy. The rate has tripled over the last century, with the largest increases for Protestants and the smallest increases for Jews (Kalbach and Richard 1991). However, marriages between white and black Americans remain quite rare, even though legal prohibitions no longer exist (since the landmark *Loving v. Virginia Supreme Court* decision of 1967). Only 3.6 percent of black American men and 1.2 percent of black American women marry outside their race (Tucker and Mitchell-Kernan 1990). Despite Mexico's heritage of racial mixing, the preference is for persons to marry within their "ethnic group," as it is socially defined (Otero 1992). For example, among the middle classes there is a concern that offspring not be too *"mestizo*-looking" (Riding 1989) — that is, that they apparently have mixed blood. So, generally we can say that the principle "opposites attract" may work for magnets but not for people in choosing their mates.

The nonhomogamous element in North American marriage practices is age at marriage. Wives are about two years younger than their husbands in first marriages. While this may not seem like a big difference (it was larger in the past), it has an important social consequence. It sets up a process by which an economic disadvantage accrues over time. The younger person (the wife) begins the marriage with fewer social assets — less schooling, less job experience, and a lower income. This disadvantage cumulates over the years: the husband's job will usually be given priority because it is more important to the overall economic situation of the family. For example, the husband's job may dictate that the family must move; the wife, if working outside the home, will have to start over whenever they relocate. The wife will usually be the one who quits her job to care for young children (unless her income is sufficiently high to make her job "pay off," given the high cost of child care). Over time, the initially small economic difference between husband and wife becomes a substantial gap — a process termed the *mating gradient.* From a structural-functionalist viewpoint, the mating gradient functions to ensure gendered role differentiation; from a femi-

nist point of view, it reinforces women's subordination; and from a conflict perspective, it operates as a structurally defined source of conflict between husband and wife.

Due to the operation of the principle of homogamy, spouses choose one another from within a socially delimited range of "possibilities," a range rather tightly controlled by parents of high socioeconomic status and much less controlled by lower-class parents (Zinn and Eitzen 1987). This choice-making occurs within the context of the dating process, which functions, at the same time, as a mechanism for us to "practise" for our eventual role as husband or wife. Research on dating interaction, and particularly the process of moving from "just" dating to "serious" courtship, has revealed the importance of variables such as physical attraction, shared values, and role compatibility (Adams 1980). Most research on dating has been concerned with young, single heterosexuals. At present, we do not know about dating among the previously married and among gays and lesbians.

Marriage and Marital Relationships

We already know that most North Americans marry. Let us now look at what marriages are like on this continent.

Division of Household Labour. Since female labour-force participation has increased dramatically over the last few decades within all five North American groups, one would expect that the division of labour within the domestic unit would change as well, that husbands would take on more domestic chores. However, numerous Canadian studies (Lupri and Mills 1987; Luxton 1980; Meissner et al. 1975; Michelson 1985a; Shaw 1988) and U.S. studies (Berk 1985; Dutchin-Eglash 1988; Hochschild 1989) indicate that the husband's share of household tasks remains small. Research data for black Americans is mixed: on the one hand, it is reported that, in general, black American men contribute less than white American men (Goldscheider and Waite 1991); on the other hand, there is evidence that black American men share more in household work than their white counterparts (Broman 1988; Ross 1987), although women continue to do the "lion's share" of it. In Mexican families, there is a rigidly defined division of labour by gender. Even within the urban middle classes, this continues to be the case; while domestic servants do the actual housework, the wife's role is to be responsible for the management of the domestic staff (Riding 1989).

In the United States, there is some evidence that men are increasing their time spent in domestic tasks and that gender differences in housework are *beginning* to erode (Goldscheider and Waite 1991). Nevertheless, the prevailing pattern in North America is that women do "women's work," although their husbands may "help out." Whether or not we accept the ideological underpinnings of structural-functionalist theory, it appears that Parsons was correct in describing modern families as having a high degree of gender-based role differentiation.

This situation carries with it the potential for conflict between the spouses and within the wife, who is, in popular media terms, "overloaded" in her attempts to be "superwoman." The study of family and work conflicts is complex (Armstrong and Armstrong 1987): some research indicates that household work is an area of conflict between spouses (Booth et al. 1984; Suitor 1991), but there also is considerable evidence that most couples are satisfied with their division of labour (Hill and Scanzoni 1982; Pleck 1985). The women facing the most distress (anxiety, depression, and so on) are not overloaded career women, as is so often depicted (they can afford housecleaning services and restaurant meals), but rather working-class homemakers, who work long, arduous hours in socially isolated conditions and receive few social rewards.

Marital Power. Marital power is usually conceptualized (and operationalized) in terms of husband–wife decision-making. In North America, socially structured variation in marital power ranges from the husband making virtually all decisions to joint decision-making. (Although there may be cases in which the wife exercises more power than her husband, they are rare and outside of normative expectations.) At one extreme in North America is the Mexican family; men are expected to rule with absolute power. While there are variations and some couples work out a more egalitarian arrangement (Falicov 1982), male supremacy is buttressed by the ideal of *machismo* — exaggerated masculinity, including aggressive-

ness, strength, courage, hypersexuality, the "conquest" of women, and protectiveness toward women. The female counterpart is *marianismo* or *hembrismo* — a cult of the moral and spiritual superiority of women that gives them the strength to subordinate their own needs and to tolerate the excesses of machismo. Thus, women, through their submissiveness, play a role in shaping the style of marital relations in Mexican society (Ingoldsby 1991). Given this cultural background, changes toward more egalitarian marriages are slow in the making, even in the face of modernization and economic development.

Within anglophone and francophone Canada and in white America, marriages are more egalitarian than in Mexico, but joint decision-making is rare. Black American marriages display the highest degree of power equality (Beckett and Smith 1981; Ross 1987).

It is generally found that wives who are employed outside the home have more power, relative to their husbands, than do homemakers, especially regarding financial matters (Ferber 1982; Rank 1982). However, within black American families, egalitarianism in marital power is maintained even when the wife's employment status and earnings are controlled (Ross 1987). Thus, it might be that, as argued by Ferree (1984), the impact of female employment on marital power depends upon how women choose to use their potential power and on their view of female power as legitimate. Such an argument, which focuses on power from a subjective point of view, is in keeping with a symbolic-interactionist perspective.

Marital Satisfaction. Satisfaction with marriage varies by sex and by stage of the family life course (Lupri and Frideres [1981] for Canadian research; Ade-Ridder and Brubaker [1983] for U.S. research), but not by employment status of wife (D.S. Smith 1985). Men are more satisfied with their marriages than are women. This is perhaps not surprising, given the previous discussion of inequalities in domestic labour contribution and marital power. The stronger predictor of marital satisfaction, however, is stage of family life. Cross-sectional research indicates that both husbands and wives are satisfied in the beginning years of marriage. Satisfaction declines quite substantially, particularly among women, when the couple has preschoolers in the home, and declines even further until all children leave home. After that, there is a marked increase in marital satisfaction. The low levels of satisfaction with marriage during the child-rearing years can be viewed, from a symbolic-interaction perspective, as due to role strain.

This entire pattern of results must be viewed cautiously, given the cross-sectional nature of the research upon which it is based. It is possible that the presence of children may not "really" lower marital quality; rather, it may delay the divorces of dissatisfied couples and thus create an association in cross-sectional data (White and Booth 1985b). Similarly, the high satisfaction in later life may occur because most unsatisfactory marriages have dissolved before this stage of life and would not be included in study samples.

Marital Dissolution. Marriages break up as a result of either divorce or death. Over the years, the percentage of marriages that end in divorce has increased; the percentage dissolving due to death has decreased (Robinson and McVey 1985).

Divorce. Over the last 25 years, divorce has increased among both anglophone and francophone Canadians and among both white and black Americans. However, divorce is more common in the United States than in Canada. It is estimated that approximately 60 percent of first marriages in the United States will end in divorce (Bumpass 1990); in Canada, estimates are in the 30–40 percent range (Adams and Nagnur 1988; Basavarajappa 1979; McKie et al. 1983).

In the United States, black Americans are much more likely to divorce than are white Americans. Within Canada, francophones have experienced a more rapid rate of increase in divorce than have anglophones. (see Table 12-2). In Mexico, divorce is not common, but marital separation and abandonment of wife (and children) occurs frequently (Riding 1989).

Divorce in Canada and the United States has increased as a result of a combination of factors operating in the wider society: declining religious influence; increasing female labour-force participation, which has lessened women's economic dependence; the rise in public-assistance payments, which reduces the dependence of wives on husbands; decreasing mortality, which has

TABLE 12-2 Divorced Persons per 1000 Married Persons (Divorce Ratios), Canada and United States, 1971–1991

	1971*	1981*	1991*
Canada			
Male	15	34	54
Female	21	50	80
Quebec			
Male	8	35	60
Female	11	52	91
U.S. white			
Male	32	74	112
Female	56	110	153
U.S. black			
Male	62	149	208
Female	104	258	358

*1970, 1980, and 1990 for the United States.
SOURCE: Statistics Canada, *1991 Census — Age, Sex and Marital Status*, catalogue no. 93-310 (Ottawa: Minister of Industry, Science and Technology, 1992); Arlene F. Saluter, "Marital Status and Living Arrangements: March 1990," in *Current Population Reports*, series P-20, no. 450 (Washington, DC: Government Printing Office, 1991).

meant that unhappy marriages are less likely to dissolve due to death; changes in divorce laws, which have made it easier to divorce; changing views of what marriage should be like — an increased focus on intimacy, expressiveness, and mutual gratification; and increased individualism and "hedonism" (the "me" generation) (Ambert 1990; Bumpass 1991; Michael 1988). Of these factors, increasing female labour-force participation has received the most research attention. The relationship between divorce and women's employment outside the home has caught the eye of structural functionalists (who use it to show the importance of maintaining traditional spousal roles for marital stability) and conflict theorists (who use it to illustrate the dialectic between changes in the mode of economic organization and family change).

Which marriages have the highest risk of divorce? A Canadian study indicates that the probability of divorce is more than three times greater for people who marry before the age of 20 than for those who marry after age 25 (Balakrishnan et al. 1987). Other important factors include premarital conception (leading to a "shotgun" wedding) or the birth of a child; having no religion; living in an urban area; experiencing an economic crisis such as unemployment; and lack of marital homogamy — the existence of racial, educational, or social class differences between spouses. Also, it has been suggested that extended family households, which impair spousal relationships, may be a factor in the high incidence of divorce among black Americans (McAdoo 1988).

So far, we have looked at the "hard facts" about divorce, but divorce has another important side. As a legal and interpersonal process, divorce is difficult for the couple involved, their children, and other family members. Peters (1987), using a symbolic-interaction perspective, shows how the process of separation and divorce proceeds through stages, with changing definitions of marital roles, other familial roles, and self-identity. These reformulations occur in an interactive social context of interpersonal conflict and negotiation. While divorce is never easy, it is easier for some than for others. Those who have the least difficulty have been married only a short time, have no children, are young and employed, and share few material possessions with the former spouse (Ambert 1990).

Widowhood. In North America, widowhood is largely a women's issue. More than 80 percent of widowed persons are women; among persons aged 65 and over, nearly one-half of women are widows. Women are more likely to experience the life course transition into widowhood for two reasons: they tend to be younger than their husbands, and they live longer than men. Widowhood is the most stressful family role transition that women experience (Martin Matthews 1987). Along with experiencing bereavement and adjustment to loss, widows generally face a sharp drop in income, and a substantial proportion of them fall below the poverty line (see Gee and Kimball [1987] for Canadian data; Zick and Smith [1988] for U.S. data).

Widowhood also carries with it the potential for social isolation, but research findings indicate that most widows, health permitting, are quite involved with age peers, sometimes called "the culture of widows." It has often been assumed that men who are widowed are more likely to be lonely and socially isolated because they lack a peer group of widowers to draw upon. However, both Canadian research (Wister and Strain 1986) and U.S. research (Brubaker 1991) indicate few differences between widows and widowers in well-being. Wister and Strain (1986) suggest that this finding may be due to gender differences in definitions of minimal social support; that is, as a result of their earlier socialization, widowed men may expect, and settle for, less. It is also possible that men who remain widowers (who do not remarry) represent a special group comprising people who are quite satisfied with their marital status. This leads us to our next topic, remarriage.

Remarriage. A relatively high incidence of divorce should not be taken to mean that people reject marriage. Individuals may reject a particular marriage, but they do not give up on the institution itself. As shown in Table 12-3, in Canada nearly one-quarter of marriages are second (or later marriages); in the United States, the figures are higher, particularly for whites.

There are several differences between people who are marrying for the first time and those who are remarrying after a divorce. One major difference often concerns the presence of children (although some people who are marrying for the first time also have children). Remarriages that involve children are called **blended** (or *reconstituted*) **families**. Establishing a workable relationship with stepchildren (who may or may not reside with the remarrying spouse) presents a challenge to remarriages. The difficulty is heightened by the fact that North American society has not yet worked out a set of norms and expectations to guide these relationships. Should the stepparent act as a parent or as a friend? Should the child call the stepparent by a kinship name (which one?) or by his or her given name — should it be "Dad" or "Ryan?" The interactive setting of blended families calls for much definition, redefinition, and negotiation of role performances.

Another difference is that the age difference between spouses in remarriages tends to be larger than the two years typical among those marrying for the first time. Also, remarriages tend to involve less homogamy in social class and ethnicity (Peters 1987). The interactive difficulties that arise in remarriages (in the absence of guiding rules), together with the lower degree of marital homogamy, may account for the fact that remar-

TABLE 12-3 Percentage Distribution of Brides and Grooms, by First or Later-Order Marriage, Canada and United States, 1986 and 1990[a]

	Brides		Grooms	
	First Marriage	Later Marriage	First Marriage	Later Marriage
Canada[b] (1990)	77.4	22.6	76.5	23.5
U.S. whites[c] (1980)	60.0	38.6	60.8	37.9
U.S. blacks[c] (1986)	72.3	26.8	69.7	29.5

[a]May not total 100% due to missing data on previous marital status.
[b]Quebec data not available.
[c]U.S. data exclude eight states and the District of Columbia.
SOURCE: Statistics Canada, *Health Reports*, Supplement No. 16, 1991, vol. 3, no. 4, "Marriages 1990" (Ottawa: Statistics Canada, 1992); *Vital Statistics of the United States, 1986*, Vol. III — *Marriage and Divorce* (Hyattsville, MD: U.S. Department of Health and Human Services, 1990).

riages are more prone to end in divorce than first marriages.

Remarriage following widowhood has received considerably less research attention than has remarriage following divorce. However, we do know that age and duration of widowhood are important determinants of remarriage probability. Persons widowed at younger ages are more likely to remarry, and the likelihood of remarriage rises shortly after widowhood and falls thereafter (Smith et al. 1991). Also, we know that widowers are more likely to remarry than widows, especially among persons widowed at older ages. This is a direct result of the shortage of older men relative to older women — older women have only a small pool of men from which to draw a prospective partner, whereas older men have an excess number of women from whom to choose. Among women widowed at younger ages (that is, during middle age), black Americans and those with dependent children are less likely to remarry (Smith et al. 1991). In Mexico, widows, regardless of age, are expected not to remarry; women should remain faithful to their deceased husband. Men, on the other hand, are free to remarry (Riding 1989).

Common-Law Unions. Everyday observation tells us that common-law unions (also called cohabitation, consensual unions, "living together," and in francophone Canada, *union libre*) have become more prevalent and socially acceptable in recent years in Canada and the United States. Not so long ago, such arrangements were rarer and were disparagingly referred to as "living in sin" or "shacking up." Because of this past stigma, we do not have much information about common-law unions. The Canadian census has collected data on this type of living arrangement only since 1981; in the United States even less data are available. Approximately 8 percent of all Canadians aged 15 and over were living in a common-law union in 1990, with the highest percentage (13) in Quebec (Stout 1991); it is estimated that 4 percent of Americans aged 19 and over were cohabiting in 1987–88 (Bumpass and Sweet 1989). The percentage of persons who have ever cohabited is 28–29 percent in Canada (1990) and estimated to be about 25 percent (1987–88) in the United States, with no significant difference between white and black Americans.

In marked contrast to Canada and the United States, common-law unions (or *free unions*) in Mexico are an aspect of traditional marriage practices. They are most commonly found among the rural, the poor, and the Native populations, who continue to retain conservative attitudes and customs that the middle and upper classes have abandoned (Weil 1975). With general modernization, the incidence of cohabitation has probably decreased somewhat (Otero 1992). Research related to common-law unions in Mexico has yet to be done; the following discussion applies to Canada and the United States only.

"Living together" is usually a one-time-only experience for people who choose this arrangement.

In Canada in 1990, only 7–8 percent of persons have lived in more than one common-law union (although this does represent an increase over the 1981 figure of 2 percent). About two-thirds of first common-law unions result in marriage in Canada; in the United States, the comparable figure is approximately 60 percent (Bumpass and Sweet 1989; Stout 1991). These data suggest that most common-law unions are not casual relationships; they are a prelude to marriage (Burch 1985). It appears that a new family life course stage is emerging, at least among some portions of the U.S. and Canadian population.

Why are increasing numbers of people choosing this alternative? It is generally agreed that factors operative in the wider society — improved methods of birth control, increased availability of abortion, more permissive attitudes toward premarital sexual activity, economic insecurity, and higher divorce rates — have functioned together to facilitate the growing popularity of common-law unions (Hobart 1983). Stout (1991) stresses the economic advantages of cohabitation, such as the economic benefits of sharing costs, the smaller expenses involved in exiting the relationship, and the tax and transfer-payment advantages of not legally marrying. At the individual level of analysis, persons most likely to cohabit are those who did not complete high school (despite the "preppy" stereotype), who were brought up in families that received welfare, and who lived in a single-parent family while growing up (Bumpass and Sweet 1989).

Interest in the consequences of common-law unions has fuelled investigations concerning the relationship between common-law unions and marital stability. Are people who have lived common-law more or less likely to have marriages that end in divorce? It is often assumed that living together before marriage gives marriage a "dry run," resulting in increased stability in marriage. Research findings do not support this everyday belief. DeMaris and Leslie (1984) report no difference in stability between marriages preceded by a common-law union and those not so preceded. Research in both Canada (Balakrishnan et al. 1987) and the United States (DeMaris and Rao 1992) shows that cohabitation is associated with a *higher* risk of marital dissolution. (However, the risk of separation and divorce is not as high among younger cohabitators, for whom "living together" is more common [Schoen 1992].) It is not clear why marriages preceded by cohabitation have a greater risk of dissolving. The risk could relate to cohabitation *per se* or to factors associated with the type of individual who is attracted to a consensual union (or both, in some combination).

Parenting and Parent–Child Relationships

In this section, we move away from a focus on the marital unit and turn our attention to parents and children. Of course, such a distinction is quite arbitrary, since family life for most people involves a complex combination of relationships with spouses, parents, and children. Nevertheless, for analytical purposes, it is useful to separate our topics.

Child-Rearing

Although the number of children born to women in North America is at an all-time low (see Chapter 8 for a discussion of declining fertility and of fertility differentials among North American groups), it is still the case that most adults have children (childlessness is considered later in this section). The transition to parenthood is a major change in an individual's life, particularly for women, who, whether or not they work outside the home, assume most of the duties involved in rearing children. We have already mentioned that marital satisfaction declines during the child-rearing years. In addition, research indicates that, on the whole, parents score lower on well-being than do nonparents (Umberson 1989). However, the impact of parenthood on well-being depends on the social context; greater negative effects are associated with single-parent and stepparent family arrangements (White and Booth 1985a); divorced (compared with widowed) marital status (Umberson and Gove 1989); women (Reskin and Coverman 1985); young children in the home (Umberson 1989); economic hardship (Ross and Huber 1985); and inadequate child-care arrangements (Ross and Mirowsky 1988). Research sup-

Role strain during the child-rearing years is a cause of marital dissatisfaction.

ports the symbolic-interaction idea that the parent role contains role strain and the feminist argument that family arrangements operate to the detriment of women; it does not support the structural-functional argument that children are necessary for successful adjustment in adulthood (Parsons and Bales 1955).

A large amount of sociological research related to children in the past decade focuses on two topics: the mother's employment outside the home in relation to the adjustment and well-being of children, and the effect of lone-parent family arrangements on children. These research foci are not surprising, given significant increases in female labour-force participation (and presumably, changes in the role of women in the wider society, the workplace, and the home) and growth in lone-parent family arrangements. Here, we look at the first topic only; a discussion of lone parents appears in a later section.

Despite expectations — derived both explicitly and implicitly from structural functionalism — that maternal employment will have negative effects on children, numerous studies have found no relationship between maternal employment status and children's adjustment and achievement (for example, Bianchi and Spain 1986; Moore et al. 1984). It is possible that employed mothers actually do not spend much less time with their children than did full-time homemakers in the past, because time now spent working outside the home substitutes for time previously spent doing housework and caring for more children (Hoffman 1987).

As women's labour-force participation has increased, some research has focused on ways that fathering may have changed. Furstenberg (1988) reports that the amount of father–child interaction has increased but, for the most part, fathers remain "bit players" in parenting. Some men have taken on a key role in child care in cases where the mother and father "take turns" looking after children because of the hours of their work — for example, shift work and workdays that are not of the "9 to 5" type (see the accompanying box). These parents may function as sequential single parents; depending upon their resources and stressors, the quality of care provided to their child(ren) will vary (Menaghan and Parcel 1991). If a father's unemployment is the reason for his increased contact with children, the quality of father–child interaction tends to be low (McLoyd 1989).

Who looks after the children when the mother is at work? In the United States, it is reported that the major source of child care for pre-schoolers with employed mothers is relatives (Presser 1989). Among black Americans, grandparents (particularly grandmothers) play an important role in the provision of child care (Cherlin and Furstenberg 1986). In Canada, there is a lower reliance on relatives for child care; fewer than one-quarter of children aged under 6 who have an employed parent(s) are cared for by relatives (Beaujot and Beaujot 1991). This difference may be due to a greater availability of day care in Canada.

Child Care: Work and Family Contradictions

A massive, $3-million child-care survey has found a "startling" 45 per cent of working parents with children under 13 do not work nine-to-five shifts.

The report, published yesterday by Statistics Canada, is the first of 15 to come from the Canadian National Child Care Study, the country's largest look at who is minding the children.

The findings, experts said, show for the first time the huge variety of child-care needs facing Canadian families.

"The needs of parents and children are very diverse," said Dr. Robert Glossop, co-ordinator of programs and research of the Vanier Institute of the Family in Ottawa. "And we're still dealing with a [child-care] system that has a very homogeneous idea of family and a very homogeneous idea of the working world."

And the results are one of the first compelling signs of how mightily the modern family is struggling to meet the demands of children and work.

The study by Dr. Lero, Alan Pence, Hillel Goelman and Lois Brockman, surveyed more than 24 000 Canadians in 1988 about their family lives. The four university professors set out to find out where Canadian children are during what time of the day. Part of their mandate is to determine how many children are in need of child care and to figure out if that care exists.

The survey found:

- almost a quarter of parents who had primary care for their children worked at least one day each weekend;
- more than a quarter worked at least one weekday evening per week;
- almost one in eight worked three or more weekday evenings;
- 10 per cent worked a fixed late shift;
- 28 per cent had irregular work schedules.

"The results clearly indicate child-care programs and services [including school] that are available only on weekdays at fixed times, ending by or before 6 p.m. may not fully meet the child-care needs of as many as 47 per cent of pre-schoolers and 45 per cent of school-age children," the report said.

And the study found almost 17 per cent of dual-earner couples with children under 13 had deliberately arranged their work schedules so children could be cared for by a parent.

The report estimated 60 per cent of families with children under 13 (1.6 million families) needed some child care while parents worked.

"We just don't have an ethos or policy perspective that looks at the harmonization of family and work," said Donna Lero, a professor at the University of Guelph and the study's project director.

Some experts said the difficult picture the report paints of modern fam-

ily life may put the government under pressure to reinstate child care issues on its agenda.

"It will have its influence and impact," Dr. Glossop said. "It may bring the topic of child care back into focus with a sharper lens."

Barbara Kilbride, executive director of the Canadian Day Care Advocacy Association, said the report will stiffen the resolve of her group to make child care an election issue.

"It's been very, very difficult with this government to keep this issue up and running," she said.

The study's preliminary report was issued in February just two days after the federal government announced it had killed long-promised plans to establish a national day-care program.

Child-care experts said the findings of the study show focusing on care only during core working hours is not enough.

"Nine-to-five child care isn't going to necessarily serve all the needs of people in the future," said Dianne Bascombe, assistant executive director of the Canadian Child Day Care Federation. She noted that one care centre in Ottawa is now open for 24 hours a day.

"This child-care issue is not going to go away," she said.

Source:

Allana Mitchell, *The Globe and Mail*, July 28, 1992, p. A6.

Leaving Home

In the normal and normative course of events, children leave their parental home and establish their own independent residence, although black American and, especially, Mexican children are expected to remain near their parents. This transition is considered to be part of becoming an adult in contemporary North America. In the past, leaving home often co-occurred with getting married; now, it is more likely to occur before marriage, although marriage remains an impor-

tant reason for leaving home. Daughters tend to leave home at younger ages than do sons. In the Canadian case, this is attributed to the earlier physiological and psychological maturation of females; the younger age at marriage for women; and the expectation that sons will be main breadwinners and, thus, require more training and socialization (Ravanera et al. 1992). In the case of Mexico, it is because sons are more likely to make an economic contribution to the parental household. A daughter may be allowed to leave home, often to become a household servant, in the hope that she will be able to send back some of her pay to her parents (deVos 1989). Also, stepchildren leave home at younger ages than do natural children (Burch 1985).

Around 1950, the age for leaving home began to decline in Canada and the United States. Parents began to experience an "empty nest" phase of the family life course, a stage when all children have left home. In earlier times, many people did not live long enough to see all their children leave home. With increased longevity, decreased fertility, and a decline in the age at which child-bearing was completed, the empty nest became an important part of the family life course. Research focused on whether the departure of the last child was a trauma for mothers. Studies found that the transition to the empty nest is a neutral or somewhat positive experience (a "relief") for most women; it is a crisis for only a small percentage of women (Gee and Kimball 1987). This finding is perhaps not surprising, given our earlier discussion of the negative impact of children on marital satisfaction and on personal well-being, and given the fact that more women now participate in the labour force, so that their lives are not focused *solely* on child-rearing. Nevertheless, it was assumed that the empty-nest transition was a difficult one for women.

In the last decade or so, the age at which children leave home has increased in both Canada and the United States (Boyd and Pryor 1989; Glick and Lin 1986). A "new" phenomenon is upon us: the *cluttered nest*, a situation in which children are both leaving home at later ages and returning to their parental home, sometimes after marriage breakdown (and with children of their own) and sometimes because of unemployment or underemployment. The reasons for the recent upward trend in age of leaving home may include increased unemployment, the high cost of housing, less pressure to marry (related to looser sexual norms), the high divorce rate, and an increasing number of births to unmarried women (Glick and Lin 1986).

Parents and Adult Children

Relationships between adult children and their parents are diverse and depend on a number of variables, including geographical location, personality factors, sex of child, and ethnicity.

Overall, however, these relationships are quite important in people's lives; it is simply not true that children abandon their parents in old age. Canadian research indicates that approximately 80 percent of the care and support that older people receive comes from informal sources, particularly family members (Chappell et al. 1986). Research in the United States also indicates the key role that children play in caregiving to their elderly parents for both white and black Americans (Cicirelli 1983; Gibson and Jackson 1987; Horowitz 1985). In Mexico, as well, children (and grandchildren) provide care to the aged.

After the spouse (usually the wife), daughters and daughters-in-law are the family members most likely to provide care. Indeed, many families are reluctant to go "outside" for help. Also, sibling relationships are very important to aged Canadians (Connidis 1989), white Americans (Goetting 1986), and especially black Americans (Chatters et al. 1989). Findings such as these deal a severe blow to the structural-functional idea of the modern family as an isolated nuclear unit. They are more in line with the family life course perspective's concept of social time: changes in the wider society (in this case, increased longevity) influence the number, and experience, of family life stages.

It is important not to think of the elderly as only the receivers of care, help, and assistance. Most older people are not frail and do not need care from their children and other relatives. Indeed, reciprocity between adult children and their older parents is key to understanding this relationship. In other words, each helps the other out — financially, instrumentally ("doing things"), and emotionally — until and unless poor health limits the parent(s), which usually does not occur until very advanced ages.

Lone Parents

There have always been lone parents in North America. This was partly due to high mortality (lone parenthood via widowhood) and partly due to black American family practices. Yet, lone parenthood was not considered a social problem in the United States until, in the past 25 years or so, substantial increases occurred in the white population (Hatchett et al. 1991) and, in Canada and the United States, the reasons for it changed from death of a spouse or parent to others of a presumably more voluntary nature.

Figure 12-2 illustrates the trend of increase in lone-parent families since 1970. It is immediately apparent that all four groups in the United States and Canada experienced increases over the period, that the incidence of lone-parent families is lower in Canada and Quebec than in the United States, and that black Americans have a very high percentage of lone-parent families. Exact data for Mexico are not available, but it is suggested that about one-half of children in nuclear families live with one parent only (Riding 1989). It must be remembered that this type of data is cross-sectional and underestimates the likelihood of *ever* living in a lone-parent situation. For example, it is forecast that nearly one-half of white American and 85 percent of black American children born in the 1980s will live in a lone-parent family before reaching the age of 18 (Bumpass 1984).

The major reason for the increase in Canada and the United States, as a whole, is rising divorce rates. For example, in Canada, approximately 60 percent of lone parents are divorced or separated (including broken common-law arrangements) (Ram 1990). However, unmarried motherhood is becoming an important route to lone parenthood. In fact, among black Americans, children in lone-parent families are more likely to be living with an unmarried mother than with a divorced parent (Ellwood 1988). As can be seen in Figure 12-3, the percentage of births to unmarried women is very high (63.5 percent) among black American women but is not low in any of the groups, particularly francophone Canadian women (35.6 percent). (Quebec has the highest fertility rate of single women in the ten Canadian provinces [Ram 1990].)

In Mexico, a somewhat different constellation of factors is at work. As divorce is quite low, it is

---

FIGURE 12-2 Percentage of Lone-Parent Families, Canada and United States, 1970–1991

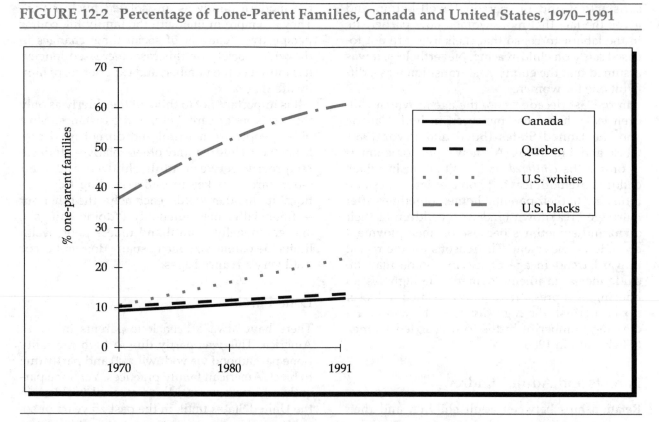

SOURCE: Statistics Canada, *1971 Census — One Parent Families*, catalogue no. 93-721; *1981 Census — Canadian Families in Private Households*, catalogue no. 92-905; *1991 Census — Families: Number, Type and Structure*, catalogue no. 93-312; U.S. Bureau of the Census, "Household and Family Characteristics: March 1991," *Current Population Reports*, series P-20, no. 458 (Washington, DC: Government Printing Office, 1992).

FIGURE 12-3 Percentage of Births to Unmarried Women, Canada and United States, late 1980s

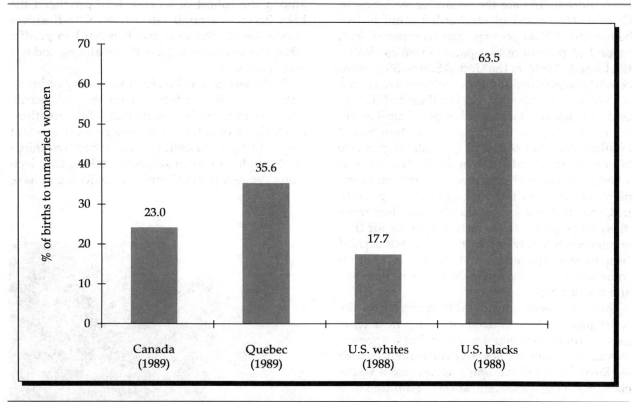

SOURCE: Statistics Canada, *Health Reports*, supplement no. 14, 1991, vol. 3, no. 1, "Births 1989" (Ottawa: Statistics Canada, 1991); *Vital Statistics of the United States, 1986*. Vol. I — *Natality* (Hyattsville, MD: U.S. Department of Health and Human Services, 1990).

not the major reason for the high level of lone parenthood; however, the abandonment of wives and children is not rare, especially in free (consensual) unions (Weil 1975). Men are expected to show their virility through "conquering" women; thus, male adultery is virtually a norm. In addition, it is culturally prescribed that men should have a mistress (Ingoldsby 1991). Both casual affairs and relationships with mistresses drive up the number of births to unmarried women and contribute to an increase in the number of lone-parent households.

Throughout North America, the vast majority of lone-parent families are headed by women. This is related to a number of factors: women are more likely to get custody of children following divorce, men are more likely to remarry, women are more likely to be widowed, and unmarried women have little recourse, except to give their children up for adoption. What underlies the increase in mother-led families? Garfinkel and McLanahan (1986) show that in the United States the increase in women's employment (women's economic independence) is the key factor involved. Other factors that have been examined — men's decreasing employment, increases in public assistance and government transfers, and changing social values — do not appear to be significant. With regard to the last factor, the evidence is that changes in attitudes and values regarding divorced and single mothers followed, rather than preceded, the growth in mother-led families that began in the 1960s.

The increase in female-headed lone-parent families has important economic implications. The income difference between mother-led families and "intact" families is very large. In the United States and Canada, the family income of female-headed households is around 40 percent that of husband–wife families with children. Even more telling are the following statistics. In Canada, 60 percent of mother-led families live below the official poverty line (compared with around 12 percent of two-parent families (Statistics Canada 1991). In the United States, 38 percent of white mother-led families are poor, compared with 6 percent of two-parent families; and 56 percent of black American mother-only families are poor, compared with 13 percent of two-parent families (Bianchi 1990). (The generally higher rate of poverty in Canada than in the United States is a result of national differences in the measurement of poverty, not of more "real" poverty in Canada). Why are mother-led families more likely to be poor? Three factors account for this: women's lower earning capacity, the lack of child support from the father, and the low level of income support provided by the state (McLanahan and Booth 1991).

There has been considerable research on the consequences for children of living in a lone-parent family. Findings are mixed, but it appears, overall, that there are negative consequences such as: lower levels of academic achievement (especially for boys) and educational attainment; a greater risk of creating a lone-parent family (either through divorce or never-marriage) when the children become teenagers or adults; and low income levels. Many of the negative consequences stem from poverty in childhood, rather than from living in a lone-parent family *per se* (McLanahan and Bumpass 1988).

Childlessness

Childlessness has never been rare in either the United States or Canada. Among Canadian and white American women born between 1850 and around 1920, approximately 10–15 percent of the ever-married bore no children (Farley and Allen 1987; Gee 1986). Among black American women, the percentages are even higher, reaching 30 percent for women born around the turn of the century. At least two factors account for this relatively high rate of childlessness: the existence of marriages "in name only" because of the legal difficulties and social stigma attached to divorce, and higher infertility (particularly among black American women, where it was associated with

tuberculosis and venereal diseases). The percentage of childless women dropped substantially among the cohort of women who produced the baby boom to around 7–8 percent. Childlessness is now on the increase, but it is hard to predict what the eventual level will be among today's young women.

Childlessness may be either voluntary or involuntary. Research conducted on the voluntarily childless in Canada reveals that while one-third of childless couples decide before marriage that they will have no children, the other two-thirds go through a series of stages in making this decision (Veevers 1980). Couples who decide to have

Given that family life is played out in a private arena, that we expect family relationships to be emotionally laden, and that family relationships involve power inequalities, it is perhaps not surprising that the family can be a violent environment.

no children must work out strategies to deal with the stigma of childlessness and with pressures from parents, friends, and physicians. The voluntarily childless are more likely to have no religious affiliation, to be raised in a Protestant home, to have few siblings, to be of middle-class origin, and to have high levels of educational attainment.

Involuntary childlessness (sterility) has become increasingly important in recent years. It is generally agreed that about 10–15 percent of couples are involuntarily childless (Miall 1986), thus signalling an increase in sterility since the time of the baby boom. Possible reasons for this increase in infertility include involuntary childlessness associated with waiting too long to try to begin having children, side effects of contraceptives (for example, pelvic inflammatory disease related to IUD use), and decreased sperm counts, possibly related to pesticides and pollutants. Whatever the reasons, the social and economic consequences are significant. Adoption is now very difficult — unmarried mothers are more likely to keep their children, and decreases in mortality have made orphanhood very rare. As a result, many couples find that they must redefine themselves and their relationship in making the transition to (likely permanent) nonparenthood (Martin Matthews and Matthews 1986). Many seek assistance in the new reproductive technologies, but they have a low success rate. Also, these technologies have created confusion and sparked debate in the wider society about their legal and moral implications.

Family Violence

Given that family life, particularly in nuclear families, is played out in a private arena (and thus comes under minimal external social control), that we expect family relationships to be emotionally laden (and emotions can have a negative side), and that family dynamics involve power inequities, it is perhaps not surprising that the family can be a violent environment. Also, Western culture has traditionally approved and sanctioned violence in the family (Drakich and Guberman 1987). An old English saying, "Horses, wives, and chestnut trees; the harder you beat them, the better they be," illustrates the long-standing Western acceptance of violence in the family setting.

Types of Spousal Abusers

In the epidemic of family violence gripping America, it's become painfully clear that men who batter their intimate partners come from all classes and all walks of life.

According to Michigan psychologist Donald B. Saunders, Ph.D., there are three distinct types of men who abuse their partners. They are distinguished most sharply by how they handle their emotions, how they use alcohol, what their attitudes are toward women, and whether they have a childhood history of victimization.

Type 1 men are "family-only" aggressors — not likely to be violent outside the home. The least sexist, they are concerned about their image and try to consider right and wrong. These men, says Saunders, tend to be "doormats until they erupt with alcohol." They overcontrol hostility, and consciously use alcohol to loosen up and express feelings; their violence is linked with alcohol half the time. They are least likely to have been abused as children, and are the least psychologically abusive. Of all the types, they derive the most satisfaction in the relationship.

Type 2 men — the generally violent — use violence outside the home as well as in it. Their violence is severe and tied to alcohol; they have high rates of arrest for drunk driving and violence. Most have been abused as children and have rigid attitudes about sex roles. These men, Saunders explains, "are calculating; they have a history with the criminal justice system and know what they can get away with."

Type 3 men are emotionally volatile, with high levels of anger, depression, and jealousy. They have rigid attitudes about sex roles and fear losing their partners. They are not severely violent as often as Type 2s, but are more psychologically abusive, and the least satisfied in their relationship. They tend to be young, educated, and open about their problems.

Treatment programs apply the same methods with all batterers, but Saunders believes different treatment strategies might work better. "But all need men's groups to learn how to relate equally to their partners and to other men."

Source:

Adapted from *Psychology Today*, Sept.–Oct., 1992, p. 18. Reprinted with permission. Copyright © 1992 (Sussex Publishers, Inc.).

We do not know whether family violence has increased in recent years. However, we are certainly more aware of it and less willing to view it as socially acceptable. We do know that there is a "generational transmission" aspect to domestic violence — children who were abused or who witnessed abuse in their family are more likely to be abusive as adults. People who were themselves the victims of child abuse are more likely than nonvictims to abuse their children, but such a background does not guarantee abusive behaviour to children. Persons who saw their parents engaged in physical violence are more likely to be abusive spouses than are persons who were physically disciplined by their parents. Again, this does not guarantee violent behaviour. Rather, a complex set of social and psychological processes are involved in the perpetuation of domestic violence across generations (Gelles and Conte 1991).

Perpetrators of family violence are almost always men; victims are wives, children, and older people. In other words, the strongest and most powerful tend to victimize the weakest and least powerful. This pattern does not arise by accident; it is the result of male gender-role socialization and gender-related inequalities both in the family and in the wider society.

SUMMARY

1. Defining family is very difficult; there is no such thing as "the" family. Families may be looked at in terms of six key dimensions: procreation, socialization, sexual intimacy, residential location, economic interdependence, and emotional involvement.

2. There is always a discrepancy between ideal and actual family organization and behaviour.

3. Substantial cross-cultural variation exists in both family structure and family organization.

4. The two basic family types are nuclear and extended.

5. There are four types of marriage: monogamy, polygyny, polyandry, and group marriage. Polygyny is the preferred marriage type in three-quarters of societies.

6. All societies have rules about who is eligible to be a marriage partner and how a spouse may be chosen, as well as rules regarding kinship descent, residence, and authority. Fictive kinship plays an important role in the Mexican family system.

7. Structural-functional theory regarding the family focuses on the loss of family functions brought about by industrialization and on gender-based role differentiation within families. The conflict perspective is concerned with the dialectical relationship between family change and economic change. The feminist perspective is critical of a number of concepts regarding the family that are part of the structural-functional and conflict perspectives, is concerned with the relationship between the family and the state, and seeks to raise the status of women and validate women's experiences and viewpoints. Symbolic interactionism looks at the subjective aspects of the interactive setting of family life. The family life course perspective attempts to integrate macro and micro dimensions of family change.

8. In Canada and the United States, approximately one-quarter of households contain one person only.

9. Although the proportion marrying has been decreasing over the last 25 years (especially among black Americans), most people in Canada and the United States marry at least once. Most marriages are characterized by homogamy and by inequality in domestic labour and marital power. Marital satisfaction varies over the family life course.

10. In conjunction with changes in the wider society, the incidence of divorce has increased in the past 25 years in both Canada and the United States, although it is higher in the United States. Age at marriage is an important predictor of divorce.

11. Remarriages are more prone to divorce than are first marriages. Less homogamy and the interactive difficulties involved in blended families may account for the greater risk of divorce in remarriages.

12. The incidence of common-law unions has increased in the last decade in the United States and Canada. In Mexico, where cohabitation is part of traditional marriage practices, the incidence may have declined in recent years. In Canada and the United States, marriages preceded by a common-law union run a higher

risk of divorce or separation than do marriages not so preceded.

13. Parents, on the whole, tend to have lower levels of well-being than nonparents.

14. There is no evidence that maternal employment has negative effects on children.

15. Adult children do not abandon their elderly parents. The aged are not just care-receivers; adult children and their parents are involved in reciprocal exchange relationships.

16. Since 1970, the percentage of lone-parent families has increased; the percentage is very high among black Americans. Most lone-parent families are headed by women and have a high incidence of poverty.

17. Family violence is not a new phenomenon; it is part of the cultural fabric of North America, and reflects male gender-role socialization and socially structured inequalities that are gender-related. There is a "generational transmission" dimension to domestic violence, but children from abusive homes do not necessarily become abusers themselves.

Incest taboo. Rule that prohibits close relatives from marrying and/or having intimate sexual relations with each other.

Marriage. A commitment or exchange, recognized either legally, contractually, or socially, in which reciprocal rights and obligations are carried out.

Matriarchal families. Families in which power is vested in females.

Monogamy. The marriage of two persons only.

Nuclear family. Family type consisting of a married couple and any unmarried children who live apart from other relatives.

Patriarchal families. Families in which power is vested in males; this power extends to the wider society as well.

Polyandry. The marriage of one woman and more than one man.

Polygamous families. Occur when nuclear families are joined together through marriage ties.

Polygyny. The marriage of one man and more than one woman.

Self-selected marriage. Marriage in which individuals choose for themselves whom they will marry.

Social time. Changes occurring in the wider society that have an influence on the family life course.

Stem family. A three-generational family in which one son, upon marriage, remains in the parental home, along with his wife and children.

GLOSSARY

Arranged marriage. Marriage in which the spouses are chosen by parents and/or by other family elders.

Blended family. Type of nuclear family that is based on remarriage and includes children from a previous marriage or marriages; also known as a *reconstituted family*.

Conjugal family. Type of nuclear family characterized by an emphasis on the husband–wife tie and a relative de-emphasis on the wider kin network.

Egalitarian families. Families in which the spouses share equally in power and authority.

Endogamy. Marriage rule stipulating that marriages must occur within a defined social group.

Exogamy. Marriage rule stipulating that marriages must occur outside a defined social group. This rule may be seen as an extension of the incest taboo.

Extended family. Family type consisting of two or more nuclear families joined through blood ties — that is, through a parent–child relationship.

Family time. Changes that occur within a family as it develops over time.

Group marriage. The marriage of more than one man and more than one woman.

Homogamy. Persons with similar characteristics choosing one another for marriage partners. Occurs along two dimensions: personal and social.

FURTHER READING

Baker, Maureen (ed.). *Families: Changing Trends in Canada* (2nd ed). Toronto: McGraw-Hill Ryerson, 1990. A recent book of readings that focuses on contemporary issues such as divorce, aging families, family violence, social policy, and non-traditional living arrangements.

Booth, Alan (ed.). *Contemporary Families: Looking Forward, Looking Back*. Minneapolis: National Council on Family Relations, 1991. Contains 28 essays by leading U.S. family sociologists, each providing a synthesis and analysis of research done in the 1980s on a specific topic, e.g., mother-only families, determinants of divorce, marital communication, parental employment and family life, etc.

Cheal, David. *Family and the State of Theory*. Toronto: University of Toronto Press, 1991. A comprehensive survey and analysis of sociological theories about family written by a Canadian sociologist.

Frances K. Goldscheider and Linda J. Waite. *New Families, No Families? The Transformation of the American Home*. Berkeley: University of California Press, 1991. Based on U.S. longitudinal data, this book provides a description and analysis of changes in American families.

Journal of Marriage and the Family. The leading family journal, it contains articles dealing with all facets of family life. U.S.-based, but contains many articles with an international focus.

Mandell, Nancy and Ann Duffy (eds). *Reconstructing the Canadian Family: Feminist Perspectives*. Toronto: Butterworths, 1988. Eight articles on the family written by leading Canadian feminist scholars.

Ramu, G.N. (ed.). *Marriage and the Family in Canada Today*. Scarborough, ON: Prentice-Hall Canada, 1989. A book of readings covering a wide range of topics relating to Canadian family life.

Ursel, Jane. *Private Lives, Public Policy: 100 Years of State Intervention in the Family*. Toronto: Women's Press, 1992. A feminist analysis of family–state relations in Canada.

Veevers, Jean E. (ed.). *Continuity and Change in Marriage and Family*. Toronto: Holt, Rinehart and Winston of Canada, 1991. A large volume, containing 40 previously published articles on issues related to family change in Canada. Contains a very useful introduction by the editor, examining eight major trends that characterize change in Canadian families.

Willie, Charles V. *A New Look at Black Families* (4th ed.). Dix Hills, NY: General Hall, 1991. Using a case study approach, this book looks at 18 widely differing African American families, focusing on everyday family life in the context of social class and race.

CHAPTER 13

Religion

REGINALD W. BIBBY

Religion has been present in virtually every society since the beginning of time, although its influence has varied from culture to culture and from century to century. In different places and in different eras, religion has known both its dark and golden ages. Moreover, changes such as the rise of rationalism and the advent of modern science and technology have led many observers to predict its demise. Yet religion lives on into the present, embraced by at least a minority in all cultures. Social scientists have, consequently, given it considerable attention.

Sociology and Religion

Sociology uses the scientific method of investigation to study social life. In doing so, it seeks to understand reality by relying on what we perceive through our senses, on perceptions that are empirical and can be verified. Sociologists can thus discover patterns of behaviour and develop theories to explain these patterns. Religion, on the other hand, has traditionally asserted that the world we know through the senses is just part of a greater reality, which — because of the limitations of perception — can be known only through faith. Historian Arnold Toynbee (quoted in Cogley 1968) notes:

[The world] is not limited to that part of it which is accessible to the human senses and which can therefore be studied scientifically. ... The key to a full understanding of this part [may] lie in that other part of [the world] which is not accessible.

401

Science and religion, therefore, are two different approaches to knowledge. In their pure form they are compatible. Science deals with the perceivable, religion with the nonperceivable. Science and sociology are unable to make statements about issues of religious faith — for example, claims that there is a God or that God is the source of events or ideas. These are supernatural claims and therefore cannot be resolved by science. Conversely, as Durkheim (1965) pointed out, religion "can affirm nothing that [science] denies, deny nothing that it affirms." Conflict between the two arises only when they invade each other's territory, such as when "creationists" believing in a literal Biblical account of how the world came into being want equal time in the science classroom with the proponents of evolution.

Sociology focuses on the social component of religion. People hold beliefs, worship together, possess attitudes, relate to others, vary in their mental health, and display a wide variety of lifestyles and social characteristics. While sociology cannot pass judgement on the truth of religious claims, it can explore questions relating to the social aspects of those claims — who believes what, the relationship between individual commitment and group support, the personal and societal factors that influence the inclination to be religious, and the impact of religious commitment on attitudes and behaviour. As Weber (1963) put it: "The essence of religion is not even our concern, as we make it our task to study the conditions and effects of a particular type of social behaviour."

What is important for our purposes is not whether religious beliefs *are* true, but rather that they are *believed* to be true and therefore have potential consequences for individual and social life.

Theoretical Traditions

The sociology of religion has been strongly influenced by three individuals: Karl Marx, Emile Durkheim, and Max Weber.

The Voice of God or Human?

Social scientists cannot address the issue of whether or not God exists. However, they can explore the sources of the claims people make "in God's name." Sometimes human claims attributed to God are contradictory, suggesting that social rather than supernatural factors are involved. An example is the conflicting arguments of the archbishop of Toronto and Dr. Henry Morgentaler concerning abortion.

TORONTO (CP) — The archbishop of Toronto has urged his congregation of more than 1.1 million Roman Catholics to fight laws that "do not sufficiently protect the unborn."

Without referring specifically to the recent acquittal of Dr. Henry Morgentaler and two associates on abortion-related charges, Gerald Emmett Cardinal Carter declared, "Even where partial protection is afforded, the law is being flouted."

Carter's statement was in a letter read or distributed Sunday in the archdiocese's 196 parishes.

"This is not just a church matter," the letter said. "This is the killing of innocents.

"As citizens, as well as believers in God's law, we cannot stand idly by. Our position is without equivocation.

"I urge all Catholics, all Christians and all who respect human life to work together to curb and, if possible, eliminate this abomination."

EDMONTON (CP) — Dr. Henry Morgentaler said Thursday he has come to the conclusion that "God is guiding my hand" during abortion procedures.

"God told me to help women," Morgentaler told a wildly cheering crowd of about 700 at a fund-raising speech in Edmonton Thursday night. Gerard Liston, 25, an anti-abortionist, had asked him why he did not give up performing abortions.

"God is all-powerful," Morgentaler replied. "If He wanted to, He would have stopped me. I have come to the conclusion that God is guiding my hand."

The crowd howled with derision when one anti-abortionist asked, "How do you know you haven't aborted a Messiah?"

Source:

Canadian Press, November 25, 1984 (Carter) and January 17, 1985 (Morgentaler). Reprinted by permission of The Canadian Press.

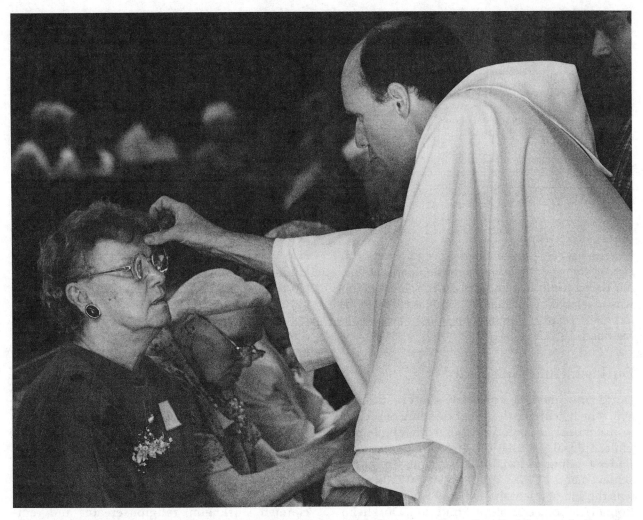

What is important for sociologists is not whether religious beliefs are true, but rather that they are believed to be true, and therefore have potential consequences for individual and social life.

Marx and Conflict

Marx (1970) asserted that "man makes religion; religion does not make man" and argued that man has "found only his own reflection in the fantastic reality of heaven, where he sought a supernatural being." This human creation, Marx felt, compensated the deprived and represented "the self-consciousness and self-esteem of a man who has either not yet gained himself or has lost himself again."

Central to Marx's thought on religion is the belief that religion serves to hold in check the explosive tensions of a society. Aligned with the interests of the dominant few, religion soothes the exploited majority like an anesthetic — "the opium of the people" — binding them to the inequalities at hand and bottling up their creative energies. Consequently, the dominant few encourage religious belief among the masses as a subtle tool in the process of economic exploitation. So intertwined are society and religion, wrote Marx, that attacks on religion are often attacks on society. Attacks on feudalism were above all attacks on the church; revolutionary social and political doctrines were simultaneously theological heresies (Marx 1964).

Marx saw religion as an inadequate salve for a sick society. When the sickness is remedied, there will be no need for the salve. Accordingly, he

"So much for ... Christianity"

The social principles of Christianity justified the slavery of Antiquity, glorified the serfdom of the Middle Ages and equally know, when necessary, how to defend the oppression of the proletariat, although they make a pitiful face over it.

The social principles of Christianity preach the necessity of a ruling and oppressed class, and all they have for

the latter is the pious wish the former will be charitable.

The social principles of Christianity transfer ... all infamies to heaven and thus justify the further existence of those infamies on earth.

The social principles of Christianity declare all vile acts of the oppressors against the oppressed to be either the just punishment of original sin and

other sins or trials that the Lord in his infinite wisdom imposes on those redeemed.

So much for the social principles of Christianity.

Source:

Karl Marx and Friedrich Engels, *On Religion* (New York: Schocken, 1964), p. 83.

viewed his criticism of religion as an attempt to expose the chain that was binding people, in order that it could be removed. To criticize religion was to enable individuals to think, act, and fashion their reality with illusions lost and reason regained.

Durkheim and Collectivity

Durkheim inherited nineteenth-century positivism, which held that the scientific study of society — in contrast to a preoccupation with religious or philosophical speculation — would produce an understanding of social life that would rival the achievements of the natural sciences. Though he was the son of a Jewish rabbi and was raised in a Roman Catholic educational tradition, Durkheim ended as an atheist and anti-cleric. (His work is covered in more detail in Chapter 1.)

In *The Elementary Forms of the Religious Life* (1965), Durkheim argued that religion has a social origin. Through living in community, people come to share common sentiments, with the result that a **collective conscience** is formed. It is experienced by each member, yet is greater than the sum of the individual consciences. When individuals have the religious feeling of standing before a higher power, they *are* in fact in the presence of a greater reality. But this reality is not a supernatural being; it is actually the collective conscience of society. So it is that humans create the idea of "God" out of their experience of society. In actuality, God is no more than a symbol for society.

Having experienced this apparent supernatural force, humans proceed to classify all things into

two groups — the **profane and the sacred**. In Christianity, for example, sacred objects have included the cross, the Bible, and holy water. Religious beliefs articulate the nature of the sacred and its symbols, while religious rites are developed as rules of conduct prescribing how women and men should act in the presence of the sacred.

Since all societies feel the need to uphold and reaffirm their collective sentiments, societal members come together as the church. According to Durkheim (1965), "The idea of religion is inseparable from that of the Church" since it is "an eminently collective thing." Even when religion seems to be entirely a matter of individual conscience, society is still the source that nourishes it. Besides meeting needs at the individual level, claimed Durkheim, religion creates and reinforces social solidarity. Collective life is thus seen as both the source and the product of religion. Accordingly, he defined religion as "a unified system of beliefs and practices relative to sacred things ... which unite into one single moral community called a Church, all those who adhere to them" (Durkheim 1965).

Durkheim saw religious thought and scientific thought as closely related. Religion, like science, tries to take the realities of nature, humanity, and society and translate them into intelligible language. Yet, while both pursue the same end, scientific thought is a more perfect form than religious thought.

In 1922, Durkheim observed that the times were characterized by "moral mediocrity." He readily acknowledged the decline of traditional Christianity. Unlike his teacher, Auguste Comte, however, Durkheim did not see religion as disappear-

According to Durkheim, besides meeting needs at the individual level, religion creates and reinforces social solidarity.

ing. Although the forms of expression might change, Durkheim predicted that the social impetus that gives rise to religion will remain, and with it religion. Likewise, Durkheim contended that there will always be a place for religious explanations. Science is fragmentary and incomplete, he wrote, advancing too slowly for impatient people. Religion will therefore continue to have an important explanatory role.

Weber and Ideas

Weber was trained in law and economics. His interest in the origin and nature of modern capitalism led him into extensive debate with Marx and stimulated much of his work in the sociology of religion. Weber did not concern himself with the question of whether or not religion is ultimately true or false. Rather, he recognized that it has a social dimension that can be studied accord-

ing to its nature and relationship to the rest of life. He maintained that apart from its supernatural emphasis, religion is largely oriented toward *this* world. As a result, he argued that religious behaviour and thought must not be set apart from the range of everyday conduct.

In *The Protestant Ethic and the Spirit of Capitalism* (1958b), for example, Weber examines the possibility that the moral tone that characterizes capitalism in the Western world — particularly the attitudes toward work embodied in the **Protestant ethic** — can be traced back to the influence of the Protestant Reformation. He states in his introduction, "The following study may thus perhaps in a modest way form a contribution to the understanding of the manner in which ideas become effective forces in history."

Like early University of Chicago symbolic interactionists such as W.I. Thomas and George Herbert Mead, Weber maintained that ideas, regardless of whether they are objectively true or false, represent one's definition of reality. Consequently they have the potential to influence behaviour. In Thomas's famous phrase, "If we define things as real, they are real in their consequences." Accordingly, Weber emphasized the need for interpreting action through understanding the motives of the actor ("Verstehen"). Such as awareness is to be sought, he said, through placing oneself in the roles of those being studied.

Weber took religion seriously as a factor that can influence the rest of life. This is not to say that he saw religious ideas as completely independent causal factors. Rather, he recognized that religious ideas are involved in highly complex processes of interaction with many other factors in producing behaviour. Yet, in analyzing the sources of behaviour, Weber insisted that religious ideas need to be considered.

Weber early became aware that he needed to study other societies as well in order to take culture into account in examining the influence of religion (Parsons in Weber 1963). After 1905, therefore, he embarked on a number of comparative studies of religion that unfortunately were left incomplete at his death. In *Sociology of Religion* (1963), which was compiled and translated after Weber's death, he noted that god-conceptions are strongly related to the economic, social, and political conditions under which people live. The birth of the gods of light and warmth, rain and earth have been closely related to practical economic needs; heavenly gods ruling the celestial order have been related to the more abstract problems of death and fate. After political conquest, the gods of the conquered are fused with the gods of the conqueror, reappearing with revised characteristics. Furthermore, the growth of *monotheism* (belief in one god) is related to goals of political unification.

Beyond the social sources of the gods, Weber dealt with such major themes as religious organization and the relationship between religion and social class. He discusses the function of priests and prophets and of *routinization* (the important process whereby a personal following is transformed into a permanent congregation). Weber further noted that different groups within society vary in their inclination to be religious: peasants are religious when they are threatened; the nobility find religion beneath their honour; bureaucrats view religion with personal contempt, while regarding it as a manipulative tool; the solid middle class see it in ethical terms and, to varying degrees, accept it; artisans freely adopt religion; and the working class supplant it with other ideologies.

Freed from concern with the truth or falsity of religion, Weber's work represents a major step forward in the scientific study of religion.

Religion: Its Nature

In defining religion for social scientific study, we might begin by noting that humans develop systems of meaning to interpret the world. As Glock and Stark (1965) point out, some systems — commonly called "religions," and including Christianity, Judaism, and Islam — have a supernatural referent. Others, such as a science-based system ("scientism") and political "isms," do not. These latter systems could be viewed as human-centred or **humanist perspectives.** The two types of system differ on one critical point: religion has a concern for life's meaning, while humanist perspectives have a concern for making life meaningful. Humanist Bertrand Russell stated this difference well: "I do not think that life in general has any purpose. It just happened. But individual human beings have purposes" (quoted in Cogley 1968).

Religious perspectives suggest that our existence has meaning beyond that which we as humans decide to give it. In contrast, humanist perspectives play down the search for the meaning of existence in favour of a concern for making existence meaningful. If life does have meaning beyond what we assign to it, then that meaning lies with some supernatural or transempirical reality; if we dismiss the transempirical referent then we ask a different set of questions. We shall define **religions** as systems with supernatural referents that are used to address the meaning of life. Humanist perspectives, on the other hand, are empirically based systems used to make life meaningful. This chapter focusses on the former.

Personal Religiosity

Individuals vary in their levels of religious commitment. A major issue in the scientific study of religion is how to define and measure **personal religiosity**. The hurdle is a most important one, for until we can first specify what constitutes religiousness, we cannot proceed to examine the characteristics of religious people — namely, the sources and consequences of their commitment. Suppose you set out to learn something about the "religious" people in your sociology class, such as whether or not they have better self-esteem than other students. How would you first determine who those "religious" people are?

Most of the early empirical work in the field used one of three basic indicators to determine religiosity: group identification, membership in a religious organization (such as a church), and service attendance. Following such leads, you could presumably do a survey of your class and ask questions such as, "What is your religious preference?; "Do you belong to a congregation?"; and "How often do you attend religious services?" If you opted for the group identification measure, you might then define as people who are "religious" as those who list a group, and the nonreligious as those who say they have no group preference.

One analysis of the consequences of religious commitment (Lenski 1961) explored differences in areas like economic and educational attainment between "Protestants," "Catholics," and "Jews." It should be apparent, however, that knowing someone is a "Protestant" tells us very little about the person's actual commitment to the Christian faith. Similarly, affiliation with religious cultural groups such as Mennonites and Hutterites does not guarantee that a given individual is highly religious. Likewise, church members may be active or inactive, committed or uncommitted. And church attendance, while indicative of religious group participation, has the disadvantage of excluding people who could — by our definition — be very devout yet not active in religious organizations.

In recent years, therefore, social scientists have been inclined to view religious commitment as being multidimensional. The dimensions proposed by American sociologists Charles Glock and Rodney Stark (1965) may still offer the best scheme for analyzing religiosity without introducing a church involvement or Christian theological bias. Briefly, they contend that while the religions of the world vary greatly in the details of their expression, considerable consensus exists among them as to the more general ways in which their adherents demonstrate religiosity. Glock and Stark cite four such manifestations: belief, practice, experience, and knowledge, referring to them as the core **dimensions of religiosity.** The religiously committed, say Glock and Stark, typically hold certain beliefs (concerning the supernatural and life after death, for example), engage in specific practices (such as prayer and worship), experience the supernatural, and possess a basic knowledge of the content of their faith.

In Canada, the ongoing *Project Canada* national surveys, which originated in 1975, have provided pioneering, comprehensive data on personal religiosity in this country. The surveys have found that Canadians exhibit relatively high levels of belief, practice, experience, and knowledge (see Table 13-1). Indeed, over 8 in 10 say that they believe in God, 7 in 10 think that there is life after death, and 6 in 10 pray privately at least once a month.

On the surface, late twentieth-century Canadians would therefore seem to be a highly religious people. However, important questions can be raised concerning the depth of this apparent religiosity. The surveys have found that only about 40 percent of Canadians claim to be committed to Christianity or some other religion (2 percent), with less than half of them demonstrating the belief, practice, experience, and knowledge characteristics deemed central to commitment by Glock and Stark. Among the other 60 percent of Canadians, some 40 percent indicate that they are interested but not committed to any religion, while the remaining 20 percent simply say that they are not religious (Bibby 1987). In Quebec the committed figure stands at 38 percent; in the rest of the country the level ranges from about 30 percent in British Columbia through some 45 percent on the Prairies and in Ontario to a high of around 65 percent in the Atlantic provinces.

In short, isolated religious beliefs and practices abound. But it appears that the majority of Cana-

TABLE 13-1   Religion Commitment along Four Dimensions, Canada

Dimension		Percentage
Belief		
God	Yes, I definitely do.	56
	Yes, I think so.	26
	No, I don't think so.	10
	No, I definitely do not.	8
Divinity of Jesus	Yes, I definitely do.	47
	Yes, I think so.	27
	No, I don't think so.	13
	No, I definitely do not.	13
Life after death	Yes, I definitely do.	40
	Yes, I think so.	28
	No, I don't think so.	18
	No, I definitely do not.	14
Practice		
Private prayer	Daily.	30
	Several times a week.	12
	About once a week.	8
	About once a month.	9
	Hardly ever/never.	41
Experience		
God	Yes, I definitely have.	21
	Yes, I think I have.	23
	No, I don't think I have.	31
	No, I definitely have not.	25
Knowledge	Who denied Jesus three times? (Peter)	46
	The second book in the Bible? (Exodus)	25

SOURCE: Reginald W. Bibby, *Project Can90.*

dians are not strongly committed to either traditional or nontraditional kinds of religion. However, as we will see shortly, such a pattern is hardly unique to Canada.

Collective Religiosity

It is frequently argued that one can be religious without having anything to do with religious organizations such as churches or synagogues. Most social scientists, however, would maintain that personal religiosity is highly dependent upon **collective religiosity**, group support of some kind. Such dependence is not unique to re-

ligion, but rather stems from a basic fact of life: the ideas we hold tend to come from our interaction with other people. However creative we might like to think we are, the fact of the matter is that most of the notions we have about life and ourselves can fairly easily be traced back to the people with whom we have been in communication, such as family, friends, teachers, and authors. We hold few ideas, religious or otherwise, in isolation from other people. Moreover, if we are to retain ideas, they must be continually endorsed by those around us — not necessarily a lot of people, but at least by a few who think the way we do.

Although it is frequently argued that one can be religious without having anything to do with religious organizations, most social scientists maintain that personal religiosity is highly dependent upon group religiosity.

The point is not that we as individuals are incapable of creativity, but rather that our ideas are for the most part socially imparted and socially sustained. So it was that Durkheim (1965) contended that

it is the Church of which he is a member which teaches the individual what these personal gods are, what their function is, and how he should enter into relations with them ... the idea of religion is inseparable from that of the Church.

In modern societies, where religious orientations compete with nonreligious ones, the existence of social groupings that can transmit and sustain religious ideas is essential to the maintenance of those ideas. Over the centuries, religion has not lacked for such support.

The Church–Sect Typology. Those who have examined religious groups in predominantly Chris-

tian settings have historically found themselves dealing with two major kinds of organizations. One the one hand there have been numerically dominant groupings — for example, the Roman Catholic Church in medieval Europe, the Church of England, and the so-called "mainline" denominations in Canada and the United States (Episcopalian, Anglican, Methodist, Presbyterian, and United Church). On the other hand, smaller groups that have broken away from the dominant bodies have also been common. These smaller groups have ranged from the Waldensians of the twelfth century, through the "protestants" four centuries later, to the Baptist and Pentecostal splinter groups found in virtually every major North American city today. Consequently, sociologists studying religious groups have given considerable attention to a conceptual scheme that features these two major organizational forms. The framework, known as the **church–sect**

typology, is an attempt to describe the central characteristics of the two types and to account for the origin and development of sects.

In perhaps the typology's earliest formulation, Weber differentiated between church and sect primarily on the basis of each group's theology (churches emphasize works, sects stress faith) and relationship to society (for churches, accommodation; for sects, separation). Weber noted the irony in the sect's development: while initially a spin-off from an established church, the sect gradually evolves into a church itself (Gerth and Mills 1958). The sect movement is at first characterized by spontaneity and enthusiasm; in time, however, these traits give way to institutionalization and routinization. Thus Weber saw the sect in dynamic terms, moving along the church–sect continuum. In what has come to be regarded as a classic work, H. Richard Niebuhr (1929) used the dynamic relationship between church and sect to explain the appearance and ultimate absorption of new religious groups in Europe and the United States.

The church–sect typology has been extensively employed in the sociology of religion. It has been the central framework in a number of key studies, both American (for example, Niebuhr 1929; Pope 1942; Demerath 1965), and Canadian (for example, Clark 1948; Mann 1962). The terms "church" and "sect," "church-like" and "sect-like" have, moreover, been household words in the discipline. Further, over the years, modifications in the typology have been numerous, as analysts have sought to deal adequately with diverse forms of religious organization. Howard Becker (1950) and Milton Yinger (1971) have been among those who have sought to expand the simple church–sect dichotomy.

More recently, however, the typology has been discarded by a large number of sociologists because of its apparent limitations as an analytical tool. Its legacy, nonetheless, is apparent in the continuing use of organizational types. Rodney Stark and William Bainbridge (1985), for example, in their important research on new religious movements, have defined sects as deviant religious movements within nondeviant religious traditions; in contrast, they view cults as deviant religious movements within deviant religious traditions.

Organizational Approaches. The result of the increasing dissatisfaction with the church–sect typology has been a growing tendency to study religious groups within the framework provided by the sociology of organizations. The obvious advantage to this approach is that sociologists of religion can draw upon the extensive organizational literature available and have access to well-developed concepts and analytic frameworks.

From an organizational point of view, major groups might be seen as similar to companies — the Roman Catholic Church as "a multinational corporation," the United Church as a company that is "Canadian owned and operated." An individual congregation might be examined along a number of dimensions, including:

1. the nature and the sources of its members;
2. its formal and informal goals;
3. the norms and roles established to accomplish the group's purposes;
4. the controls used to ensure that norms are followed and roles are played; and
5. the success the group experiences in pursuing its goals.

Studies of this kind include Paul Harrison's (1959) pioneering examination of the American Baptist Convention and Kenneth Westhues's (1973, 1978) analyses of the Roman Catholic Church, in which he has viewed that organization as a type of nation-state. Although such case-study types of research are still relatively few, they can provide considerable insight into the nature of religious groups.

Looking, for example, at Protestant churches, one notices that members are typically the children of existing members and that new recruits are frequently church members who are geographically on the move. In following twenty theologically conservative groups in Calgary over 25 years, Bibby and Brinkerhoff (1973, 1983, 1993) found that some 70 percent of new members had come from other conservative churches, while approximately 20 percent were the children of members. Only about 10 percent of the new members had come from outside these conservative groups, and even these people had commonly been fairly active in other, more theologically liberal churches, such as the United Church.

Because new members come primarily from an existing pool, churches are in considerable competition with each other. One area of competition is leadership: here smaller, lower-status congregations are usually at a severe disadvantage in relation to larger and more prestigious groups. As early as the 1960s, ministers within major American denominations were found to have standards comparable to those of secular executives when considering interchurch movement (Mitchell 1966). Comfort and success loomed large, with the result that "attractive" churches in all denominations searched further for their ministers and held them longer than those deemed less attractive. A study of over 500 Southern Baptist ministers about a decade later similarly revealed that the dominant pattern of ministerial movement was from smaller to larger congregations (Wimberley 1971). There is little doubt that such tendencies continue into the 1990s.

Such competition does not stop with ministers and other church workers. Physical attributes and range of services are also significant, with the result that churches tend to build structures as lavish as their resources will permit. In 1985, for example, the Queensway (Pentecostal) Cathedral opened in Toronto. The structure had seating for 4000 people, was serviced by twelve ministers, and had an annual budget of over $3 million. Churches, like secular businesses, also expand their services and personnel in keeping with their economic means. And in this pursuit of members — who have been observed (Berger 1961) to pick their churches as carefully as they pick their golf clubs — congregations run the risk of compromising their "product" to attract the "consumer." Indeed, competition among churches may often be resolved not in favour of the most religious but in favour of the least religious (Demerath and Hammond 1969).

The conscious and unconscious goals of Protestant churches vary by congregation and members. As with those of other social groupings, these goals commonly appear to be in conflict. "Formal goals" (such as spiritual growth) derived from religious doctrine frequently exist in tension with "survival goals" (such as numerical growth) that are related to the need simply to keep the congregation alive (Metz 1967). Glock and his associates (1967) have suggested that churches have

difficulty reconciling the pastoral or "comfort" function with that of the prophetical or "challenge" function. Even apart from comfort issue, efforts to be prophetic can sometimes have unsettling effects. The national leadership of the United Church of Canada has viewed itself as prophetic in calling — since the mid-1980s — for the denomination to allow homosexuals to be eligible for ordination as ministers. In taking such a controversial position, however, the United Church has lost not only a sizable number of individual members but entire congregations who have found "the vision" unacceptable. Prophecy has its organizational costs.

Still other observers (Hadden 1969; Hoge 1976) have noted that North American Protestantism has historically experienced tension between emphases on individual versus social redemption. University of Manitoba sociologist Leo Driedger (1974), for example, in a study involving 130 Winnipeg Protestant clergy, found theologically conservative ministers far less inclined to favour social change than were their theologically liberal counterparts. University of Western Ontario sociologist Ted Hewitt (1992) concluded that, despite its seemingly high-profile identification with justice concerns through its Conference of Catholic Bishops, even a group like the Roman Catholic Church in Canada "has largely failed to marry rhetoric to concrete action." Hewitt argues that it has been much less successful than its Brazilian counterpart, for example, in entrenching social-justice programs into the life of the Church.

Despite this apparent divergence in what people expect their religious groups to do, there is good reason to believe that churches survive and, to varying degrees, thrive precisely because different goals are realized. A rather extreme but informative example is the skid-road mission (Bibby and Mauss 1974). The mission operators, skid roaders, and suburban supporters all appear to have very different informal goals. The operators need employment, the skid roaders need food and lodging, and the suburbanites need an outlet for their talents. Yet the mission nonetheless functions in such a way as to allow these varied goals to be attained. Thus, somewhat ironically, the skid-road mission survives, even though it largely fails to accomplish what it officially claims to do — rehabilitate homeless derelicts, rather than simply provide them with short-term food and lodging.

If groups are to achieve their official or formal goals, they must establish norms for thought and action, and roles for members to play. These norms and roles are in turn facilitated by communication, which co-ordinates the interaction, and by the use of social controls in the form of rewards and punishments.

Many Protestant groups, reliant as they are upon volunteers, have considerable difficulty in executing goals in this norms/roles/communication/social-control pattern of efficient organizations (Brannon 1971; Wood 1981). Congregations compete for volunteer members, and are dependent on them for attendance, financial support, and general participation. While they can establish norms concerning belief and behaviour and assign organizational roles for members to perform, churches have few and weak methods of social control in such a "buyer's market." In short, churches are painfully vulnerable organizations. The clergy receive no exemption from such organizational fragility. On the contrary, they are highly dependent on these volunteer parishioners. Such a reality has important implications for what clergy can do and how they can do it.

The overall result is that congregations are largely "paper organizations." Yet the informal structure of churches is worth watching. One study of small churches found that individuals without formal leadership have considerable influence: longstanding members were observed to have a voice beyond their formal roles; people who gave the most money had to be consulted on key decisions; relatives of official leaders had unofficial input (Chalfant et al. 1981). Another study of churches large and small documented the presence of "inner circles" — groups that tend to control the affairs of local congregations (Houghland and Wood 1979). While the researchers concluded that such groups often arise because of the absence of strong ministerial leadership, it seems equally plausible that inner circles also function to restrict such leadership.

Westhues (1978), a sociologist at the University of Waterloo, has offered a stimulating organizational analysis of the Roman Catholic Church. He points out that the Catholic Church is a multinational religious body that both predates nation-states and, like them, has a high degree of organization. As a result, relations between the Catholic Church and nation-states like Canada and the United States essentially are relations between equals. But not all host countries will so recognize the church, a fact that frequently forces it to make adaptations.

In the United States, the Catholic Church was denied special recognition in the founding of country; it was relegated to a common category with other religious bodies, all of which are given no official public authority. Tax monies could not be used to build churches, pay clergy, or support schools. The church responded by trying to create a self-contained Catholic world, a subsociety within American life that included such institutions as schools, hospitals, welfare agencies, senior citizens' homes, and so on. Nevertheless, the "Catholic church in America remains today what it was defined to be two centuries ago, the voluntary construction of that minority of American citizens whose active commitment permits it to continue to exist" (Westhues 1978:248).

In Canada, writes Westhues, there was no rigid principle of church–state separation. Rather, the creation and evolution of the country has seen the Roman Catholic Church partially institutionalized in Quebec. The church in that province has historically had the right to use tax money to support the church and its related educational and social service institutions. In all provinces except British Columbia and Manitoba — which together account for less than 5 percent of Canadian Catholics — church schools receive legal recognition and public assistance. In general, says Westhues, the "opposition between civil society and the Catholic Church has never been so pointed in Canada as in the United States, fundamentally because the two are less distinct" (Westhues 1978:255). Yet, in Canada, region, language, ethnicity, and legal status have divided Catholics, so that the national church is scarcely more integrated than the nation itself. Westhues summarizes the differences between the Catholic Church in Canada and in the United States as follows:

1. The church is integrated to a partial but significant degree into the legal and constitutional structure of Canada, but not of the United States.

2. The Catholic population has high geographical concentration in Canada, but not in the United States.

3. Catholics account for a larger proportion of the Canadian than the American population.

4. The extent of structural assimilation is greater for American than for Canadian Catholics.

5. A major issue for the church in the United States has been the extent to which it should "Americanize"; "Canadianizing" has never arisen as an issue.

6. The communication links across the Canadian church seem weaker than in the United States, yet the vertical links with the Vatican are somewhat stronger.

7. The Canadian church enjoys marginally higher prestige within international Catholicism than does the American church. (Westhues 1978:256)

The Canadian Situation. Affiliation with religious groups has been widespread in Canada since the founding of this country. Close ties always have been apparent between Canadians of British descent and the Church of England, Methodism, and Presbyterianism; between the French and the Roman Catholic Church; and between other ethnic groups and the churches of their homelands. Such general affiliation continues to be very common in Canada. Indeed, as of the 1981 census, less than 8 percent of Canadians indicated that they had no religious preference (see Table 13-2). Although group preferences differ in various parts of the country, on a national basis Roman Catholics comprised 47 percent of the population and Protestants 41 percent. The remaining 4 percent consisted of those with other religious preferences.

It is therefore an exaggeration to think of Canada as a diversified religious mosaic. The reality is that almost 90 percent of Canadians identify with Christianity. The second-largest category consists of those with no preference but, as we will see shortly, many of these are only temporarily removed from Christian group identification. Only a small minority of about 4 percent of Canadians have ties with other religions. While there obviously is diversity in the way people across the country express Christianity, it is clear that "a Christian monopoly" exists in Canada.

TABLE 13-2 Religious Identification in Canada, the United States, and Mexico, 1900, 1970, and 2000 (Percent)

	1900	1970	2000
Canada			
Roman Catholic	42	50	51
Protestant	57	44	34
None	<1	3	9
Other	1	3	6
Quebec			
Roman Catholic	90	89	87
Protestant	8	8	7
None	<1	1	4
Other	<1	2	2
United States			
Roman Catholic	18	29	38
Protestant	78	62	50
None	1	5	8
Other	3	4	4
Mexico			
Roman Catholic	99	96	92
Protestant	<1	1	2
None	<1	2	5
Other	<1	1	1

SOURCE: David B. Barrett, *World Christian Encyclopedia* (New York: Oxford University Press, 1982) and, for Quebec, estimates based on census and survey data.

Christianity's dominance has been particularly evident in Quebec, where the Roman Catholic Church enjoyed considerable control over the life of the province until the end of the 1950s. Over 90 percent of the population in Quebec have identified themselves as Catholics during this century. The Christian faith has also been pervasive in both Mexico and the United States. Mexico has known a Roman Catholic monopoly proportionately similar to the situation in Quebec. Brought to Mexico in the early sixteenth century, Catholicism continues to be the religion of some 95 percent of the citizenry. Far from being a faith simply imposed from the outside, the church in Mexico now has a clergy comprised primarily of nationals (Barrett 1982:487). In the United States, about 90 percent of Americans continue to identify with Christian groups. The monopoly has taken a somewhat different form from that in Canada and Mexico. Protestants outnumbered Catholics by 4 to 1 in 1900, although the ratio now stands at about 2:1.

When asked about actual *membership* in religious groups, rather than mere affiliation, more Canadians — about 30 percent — claim to belong to churches than to any other single voluntary group. According to various polls, approximately one in four say they attend services weekly, and roughly the same proportion of people with school-age children expose those children to church schools.

At the same time, however, there has been a considerable decline in church attendance in recent years, as indicated by the Gallup poll findings presented in Table 13-3. Gallup asked Canadians if they attended a service "in the last seven days" — consequently adding sporadic attenders

to those who claim they attend every week. Using such a measure, Gallup found that, since approximately the end of World War II, Protestant attendance dropped off from around 60 percent to about 30 percent, levelling off in recent years. For Roman Catholics, the decline appears to have started around 1965, and moved downward from roughly 85 percent to 45 percent through the early 1990s.

This attendance drop is further documented by the *Project Canada* national surveys. While one in four Canadians claim they currently attend services on a weekly basis, almost three in four maintain that they attended weekly when they were growing up. In Quebec, the drop-off between 1965 and 1975 was staggering — from about 70 percent to 35 percent (Bibby 1987a). It now stands at approximately 25 percent. Mexico has also

While one in four Canadians claim they currently attend services on a weekly basis, almost three in four maintain that they were attending weekly when they were growing up.

TABLE 13-3   Church Attendance for Roman Catholics and Protestants, Canada, 1946–1992 (Percent)

"Did you happen to attend church (or synagogue) in the last seven days?"

	1946	1956	1965	1975	1985	1992
Roman Catholics	83	87	83	61	43	43
Protestants	60	43	32	25	29	32
National	67	61	55	41	32	33

SOURCE: Gallup Canada, Inc.

experienced a dramatic decline in church attendance since 1960 — from 70 percent to a level today of about 15 percent (Barrett 1982:487). In the United States, on the other hand, weekly service attendance has remained fairly stable at around 40 percent — virtually unchanged since at least the early 1940s (Greeley 1991).

Given the above-noted dependence of personal religiosity on collective religiosity, this significant decrease in service attendance in Canada and Mexico undoubtedly has been accompanied by a decline in the national levels of personal religious commitment. Research suggests that belief and practice fragments persist. The majority in both countries continue to want "rites of passage" carried out. A major 1988 survey of Canada's 15- to 24-year-olds found that, even though only about 20 percent were regular attenders, some 80 percent anticipated turning to religious groups in the future for birth-related ceremonies, 85 percent for weddings, and 90 percent for funerals (Bibby and Posterski 1992). In Mexico, over 90 percent of the population have been baptized and 80 percent confirmed, and 77 percent of those who are married have had the ceremonies performed by the church (Barrett 1982:488). But there undoubtedly has been a significant erosion in the portion of people in both countries who are committed to religion as a system that gives meaning to their lives.

The downward pattern of involvement in Canada and many other countries may, of course, change. Indeed, some observers contend that it is changing, that there is a renewed interest in religion. Critical to discerning such trends are the individual and societal factors that influence the prevalence of religious commitment.

Religion: Its Sources

Much of the early work in the scientific study of religion focused on primitive or simple cultures in which religion was highly pervasive. Everyone seemed religious, so it is not surprising that observers sought to understand the origin of religion itself, rather than the sources of individual variations in commitment. However, individual differences in religion's importance in modern societies have called for explanations of why some people are religious and others are not. These explanations have tended to focus either on individuals or on the social structure.

Individual-Centred Explanations

At least three dominant "person-centred" explanations of religious commitment have emerged. These explanations are probably as old as the major religions themselves.

Reflection. The desire to comprehend reality is widespread among humans. Anthropologist Clifford Geertz (1968) notes that

it does appear to be a fact that at least some men — in all probability, most men — are unable ... just to look at the stranger features of the world's land-

scape in dumb astonishment or bland apathy without trying to develop ... some notions as to how such features might be reconciled with the more ordinary deliverances of experiences.

While reflecting on the meaning of existence, people have commonly concluded that life has a supernatural or transempirical dimension. As Weber (1963) put it, religion is the product of an "inner compulsion to understand the world as a meaningful cosmos and take up a position toward it." For some, religion appears to be the result of considering one's place in the universe, as the psalmist does in the following passage:

When I consider thy heavens, the work of thy fingers, the moon and the stars, which thou hast ordained; What is man, that thou art mindful of him? (Psalms 8:3–4, King James Version)

Psychologist Abraham Maslow (1963) has written that people have "a cognitive need to understand." As a result, individuals need "a religion or religious surrogate to live by, in about the same sense that [they need] sunlight, calcium, or love."

Canadians who say they often think about questions pertaining to origin, purpose, happiness, suffering, and death are generally somewhat more likely than others to exhibit religious commitment. Yet the tendency is very slight. Fewer than one in three of the people in Canada who often raise these "ultimate questions" give evidence of being religiously committed. At the same time, some of the committed do not appear to be raising the questions. Indeed, some 10 percent of Canadians who exhibit traditional Christian commitment say that they have never thought about life's origin and purpose. This latter group appears to "learn the answers" by uncritically accepting religious teachings — before they consciously ask the questions.

Socialization. A second person-centred explanation of religious commitment considers religious commitment as the product of learning. As noted earlier, ideas for the most part are socially instilled through individuals and institutions. People who are exposed to social environments that are positive toward religion — whether an entire society, a community, an institution, or a reference group — would therefore be expected to be religious. As Freud (1962) put it, many learn religion just as they learn the multiplication table.

Family and friends, so central to socialization generally, are also the key sources of both personal religiosity and group involvement. It is no secret that religious groups grow via relational links, notably friendship, marriage, and, most important, birth (see, for example, Yinger 1971; Roof and McKinney 1987; Iannaccone 1990). The related factors of *association* and *accommodation* also seem to be important.

The inclination for association has often found expression in religious group involvement. For example, in both Canada and the United States, churches and synagogues have played an important role in the social life of both native-born and immigrant people in communities of all sizes. Involvement has undoubtedly fulfilled a variety of functions — among them, helping to satisfy an individual's desire for identity, providing social status, and enhancing group solidarity. Not surprisingly, participation has been observed to follow class and ethnic lines. Hiller (1976), for example, comments that the churches of Canadian immigrants have played a vital role by helping to provide an ethnic anchor in an alien society.

Accommodation to social pressures, notably those of primary groups, seems to be another source of religious group involvement. For example, one marital partner may become more active in response to the hopes and expectations of the other, friends in response to friends, and some parents in response to having young children (see, for example, Roozen et al. 1990; Brady 1991). In tightly knit rural communities, as well as in larger communities where religion is pervasive, accommodation appears to act as an important source of religious involvement. Religiously homogeneous populations, such as those found historically in Quebec and Mexico, as well as the evangelical American South, seem to provide classic examples of accommodation.

The *Project Canada* analyses have documented a noteworthy relationship between the commitment of respondents and that of their parents (Bibby 1987a). Some 90 percent of Canadians with Protestant parents are Protestants themselves today. The same level of identification is also found for people with Roman Catholic parents. Further, close to one in three Canadians with fathers or mothers who attended services weekly are regular attenders themselves, as compared with about one to ten of the respondents with parents who were not attending weekly (see Table 13-4). Those whose parents were highly involved are also more likely than others to indicate that religion is "very important" to them.

However, overall, there has been a significant intergenerational decline in religious participation. Regardless of whether or not their parents were weekly attenders, the majority of adult offspring were *not* attending weekly as of 1990. To the extent that Canadians do attend services, religious socialization through the home appears to be an important source of participation. Today, for example, about 25 percent of school-age children are involved in religious group programs; but over half of their parents are also regular attenders. Such findings are consistent with those

The commitment level of one's spouse is strongly related to personal involvement and the valuing of religion.

TABLE 13-4 Socialization by Current Attendance and Importance of Religion (Percent)

	Current Weekly Attenders	Those Viewing Religion as "Very Important"
In Childhood		
Mother's attendance		
Weekly	32	32
Less than weekly	13	19
Father's attendance		
Weekly	34	33
Less than weekly	15	20
Own attendance		
Weekly	29	31
Less than weekly	12	17
Today		
School-age children		
Weekly	54	48
Less than weekly	15	16
Husband or wife		
Weekly	75	71
Less than weekly	18	12

SOURCE: Reginald W. Bibby, *Project Can90.*

of Bruce Hunsberger (1980, 1984), whose analyses of students at Wilfrid Laurier University and the University of Manitoba led him to conclude that an emphasis on religion in childhood is positively associated with later religiosity.

Table 13-4 also confirms that the commitment level of one's spouse is strongly related to personal involvement and the valuing of religion. In over 70 percent of the cases, if one's partner was a weekly attender, so was the respondent. In less than 20 percent of the instances was one attending weekly if the spouse was not attending regularly. The same pattern held for viewing religion as "very important."

In adulthood, then, two factors — the involvement and commitment level of one's parents and spouse — appear to be important determinants of both participation and the valuing of faith.

Deprivation. A third person-centred explanation, which has long been popular with both scholar and layperson, is that the religious are drawn primarily from society's deprived or disadvantaged. Such people allegedly turn to religion as a means of compensating for their deprivation. The idea is one which has received considerable Judeo-Christian support (for example, "Blessed are the poor in spirit. ... Blessed are the meek ...") and has characterized the thinking of such influential social scientists as Marx and Freud. Glock and Stark (1965) contended that five types of deprivation are predominant in the rise and development of religious and secular movements: economic, social, organismic (that is, physical or mental), psychic, and ethical. The first three types are self-explanatory; psychic deprivation refers to the lack of a meaningful system of values, and ethical deprivation refers to having one's values conflict with society.

Yet if deprivation is measured by using "objective" indicators such as income, health, and social relationships (probing economic, organismic, and social deprivation respectively), deprivation is neither consistently nor strongly related to religious commitment in either the United States (Roof and Hoge 1980) or Canada (Hobart 1974). This is not to say that deprivation is never a significant factor for some individuals and some religious groups. But generally speaking, the committed in North America are not any more or less disadvantaged than others.

Structure-Centred Explanations

So far we have examined what we might call "kinds of people" explanations of religious commitment. What these explanations have in common is their emphasis on individuals, who are said to turn to religion out of reflection, socialization, or deprivation. An adequate understanding of commitment, however, must also take into account the societal context in which people find themselves and its influence on religious inclination. Individual religiosity is not formulated in a vacuum; it is highly dependent on the larger social environment in which individuals and their reference groups are located. Clark (1948), for example, has argued that in Canada's past the tendency of sect-like religious groups to emerge was

tied directly to the existence of unstable conditions produced by factors such as immigration and economic depression. With industrialization and increased prosperity and stability, sects tended to evolve into denominations — a process referred to as **denominationalism.**

The climate that modern societies provide for religion is a subject of considerable controversy. On the one hand, there are those who claim that increasing industrialization and postindustrialization contribute to a decline in the pervasiveness and influence of religion. Such a **secularization argument** dates back at least to Comte, Marx, Freud, and Durkheim. On the other hand, there are a number of observers who claim that religion, traditional or otherwise, persists in such societies. According to such thinking, religion continues to have an important place in modern settings, addressing questions of meaning and purpose, as well as responding to widespread spiritual interest. The precise role of religion in modern cultures is still far from clear. Considerable cross-cultural research is necessary to clarify the picture.

The *Project Canada* findings make it possible to explore how some of the correlates of change in Canada — such as urbanization, greater education, work-force participation, and exposure to mass media, along with the sheer passage of time — are related to religious commitment. To be consistent with the secularization argument, commitment should be low overall, with minor differences explained by social characteristics such as community size and education. Over time, people in rural areas should come to resemble their urban counterparts in being nonreligious; the same should be true of both high-school dropouts and college graduates, the retired and those under the age of 30. The culture should be so secularized that no sector of the population remains untouched.

What do the findings show? Differences continue to exist by age — reflecting the different eras in which Canadians were raised. But as education, work-force participation, and media exposure *increase*, commitment tends to *decrease* only slightly (see Table 13-5). These data suggest that Canada is already a highly secularized society. Significantly, there is a tendency for the modernization–secularization pattern to be reflected

TABLE 13-5 Attendance and Importance of Religion by Industrialization Correlates (Percent)

	Current Weekly Attendance	Those Viewing Religion as "Very Important"
Era (date of birth)		
1935 & earlier	40	44
1936–1955	22	23
1956–1972	12	16
Education		
High school or less	25	29
Some postsecondary	18	21
Degree or more	27	26
*Workforce participation**		
Not employed outside the home	22	25
Employed outside the home	19	20
TV viewing		
15 hours a week or less	26	29
More than 15 hours a week	22	24
Region		
Atlantic	41	42
Quebec	23	25
Ontario	21	23
Prairies	22	25
British Columbia	22	26

*Limited to those 18 to 65 years old.
SOURCE: Reginald W. Bibby, *Project Can90*.

regionally: the somewhat less industrialized Atlantic provinces have a higher level of commitment than do the other regions. It appears that much of the drop-off in Roman Catholic Church attendance between 1965 and 1980 was related not primarily to the changes resulting from Vatican II, but rather to the accelerated modernization of Quebec.

An Assessment

In modern societies, religion frequently finds itself competing with the world of here and now. Emphases upon science, technology, and human progress are accompanied by the expectation that a person's attention, capabilities, and energies will be directed toward the successful living-out of everyday life. Such an orientation toward "this world" is perpetuated quite unconsciously by virtually every major institution and is assimilated with equal unawareness by the average person.

To the extent that people in highly developed countries like Canada are religiously committed, the key sources of their commitment are neither institutions such as the media or education nor the desire for compensation in the face of deprivation. Rather, the Canadians who are religiously committed tend to be those so socialized. Religion, like so many other things, is transmitted through relationships, primarily learned from and supported by family and close friends, with the assistance of one's religious group.

But with the industrialization and "postindustrialization" of Canada, two important developments have occurred that have seriously affected the social transmission of religion. First, the influence of family, friends, and the group has been reduced by the advent of other decisive socializing agents, including secular peer groups, mass media, and the educational system. These agents are typically concerned with everyday life. As a result, however inadvertently, they instil a "this world" outlook with empirical and material emphases.

Second, in addition to the decreasing effectiveness of religious socialization, as personal religious commitment decreases, there simply is less commitment to transmit. As we have seen, almost three in four Canadians had attended religious services when they were growing up. But only one in three school-age children are now receiving the same level of religious exposure.

In short, religious socialization is the key determinant of commitment. But socialization efforts — when they are made — are commonly neutralized by a strongly secular culture. The result is a decrease in the number of people who are even attempting to religiously socialize their children. The implications for the continuing decline in commitment are obvious.

Religion: Its Consequences

From the standpoint of social scientist and layperson alike, one of the most significant questions about religion is its consequences. Does religion have an impact on the way individuals live their lives, or is it largely irrelevant? If such an influence exists, does religion contribute to individual and societal wellbeing, or is it inclined to produce anxiety and guilt, social indifference, and bigotry? And, if religion does have an impact, positive or negative, to what extent is this impact unique to religion, and to what extent is it common to other institutions?

Historically, those who value faith have claimed that religion has consequences for individuals and hence for societies. Christians, for example, are likely to maintain that mature followers of the faith should find that it influences them both personally and in their relations with others. Specifically, the committed experience joy, satisfaction, peace, and hope. Moreover, they would probably point out that, according to their tradition, committed, mature Christians will show compassion in their interpersonal relations and exhibit qualities such as concern for others, acceptance, benevolence, forgiveness, self-control, honesty, and respect. In living out such a norm of love, Christians are expected to follow ethical guidelines such as the Ten Commandments, the Sermon on the Mount, and the teachings of the Apostle Paul. At the same time, religious groups certainly differ on specific norms. If an issue such as abortion is perceived as "religiously relevant," one would expect that the attitudes of the committed would be influenced; if not, their attitudes would simply vary according to other factors such as age and education.

Social scientists exploring the causal effects of Christianity, then, give their attention to two main areas: personal characteristics and relations with others. However, they do not limit the possible outcomes of their research to those predicted by religion. Rather, they also freely explore commitment's possible latent or unintended consequences. One religious counsellor tells of dealing with a distraught young woman who exclaimed, "My troubles began the day I became a Christian!" (Southard 1961). The sociologist keeps an open mind to such a possibility. Similarly, the ideal of Christian love does not stop the researcher from probing the incidence of Christian hostility.

Personal Consequences

It is interesting that Marx and Freud essentially conceded that religion contributed to positive personal characteristics such as happiness, satisfaction, and hope. Their adverse criticism rested in their belief that such qualities were based upon illusion rather than reality. However, their concessions were largely speculative rather than soundly documented.

Actual research on consequences of individual commitment is surprisingly limited and further suffers — as do consequence studies generally — from serious methodological flaws. *Time-order* is often vague, so that one does not know whether religion is the cause, the effect, or simply correlated with something like happiness; the *strength of relationships* is not always specified; and *controls* for other explanatory factors are commonly inadequate (Bouma 1970; Wuthnow 1973; Levin and Markides 1986).

Apart from methodological shortcomings, the research findings on religion and what we might refer to generally as "mental health" are contradictory. Social psychologist Milton Rokeach (1965), summing up a number of his studies, wrote:

We have found that people with formal religious affiliation are more anxious [than others]. Believers, compared with non-believers, complain more often of working under great tension, sleeping fitfully, and similar symptoms.

Yet researchers have consistently found a negative relationship between religious commitment and *anomia* (Lee and Clyde 1974) — a characteristic of valuelessness and rootlessness that Srole (1956) considers related to anxiety. Further, as early as the work of Beynon (1938), Boisen (1939), and Holt (1940), involvement in groups such as sects and cults was seen as providing improved self-images and hope in the face of economic and social deprivation — a theme echoed by Frazier (1964) for American blacks, Whyte (1966) for Canadian rural–urban immigrants, and Hill (1971) for West Indian immigrants in Britain. Yale researchers Jacob Lindenthal and his associates (1970) found in a New Haven, Connecticut, study of some 1000 adults that religious group involvement and mental health were positively related, a finding corroborated by Stark (1971) using a California sample, and — in Canada — by Frankel, Hewitt, and Nixon (1992) using a University of Western Ontario student sample.

Analyses in Canada suggest that people who exhibit religious commitment are slightly more inclined than others to claim a high level of happiness, to find life exciting, to express a high level of satisfaction with family, friends, and leisure activities, and to view death with hope rather than with mystery or even fear (Bibby 1987b). However, when controls are introduced and the impact of other variables like age, education, community size, and region are taken into account, the apparent modest influence of commitment is found to dissolve. A recent analysis by Ellen Gee and Jean Veevers (1990), for example, found that the positive correlation between religious involvement and life satisfaction held nationally, but not in British Columbia.

In short, religious commitment, by itself, appears to have a very limited influence on valued personal characteristics. Moreover, it is often less important than such variables as age, education, or employment in predicting personal wellbeing, even among active church members.

Interpersonal Consequences

One of the first empirical attempts to examine the relationship between religious commitment and compassion was carried out by Clifford Kirkpatrick in 1949. Using a Minnesota sample of students and other adults, Kirkpatrick found that religiously committed people were actually somewhat *less* humanitarian in their outlook than others.

Some 20 years later, two important studies gave support to Kirkpatrick's findings. Stark and Glock (1968), in their classic examination of American religiosity, contended that traditional Christian commitment was negatively associated with social concern. They did note, however, that this was true for Protestants but not for Catholics, where the relationship was slightly positive. In an attempt to explain this difference, they suggested that Protestants are more inclined than Catholics to see social problems as being solved through God's changing of individuals. Catholics — and more theologically liberal Protestant groups — assume that even devout humans are far from perfect and therefore attempt to offer guidance that will enhance human relations.

Rokeach (1969), drawing on a representative American sample of some 1400 adults, similarly observed that, overall, religious commitment was negatively related to social compassion. In the case of Roman Catholics, however, he found that no relationship (positive or negative) existed. He concluded that "the results seem compatible with the hypothesis that religious values serve more as standards for condemning others ... than as standards to judge oneself by or to guide one's own conduct."

These findings, however, have not gone unchallenged. Research conducted on some specific religious group — on Mennonite students, by Rushby and Thrush (1973) — and in certain localities — in a southwestern American city, by Nelson and Dynes (1976) — has found a positive relationship between commitment and compassion.

Considerable research has also been carried out on another facet of interpersonal relations — racial prejudice. Richard Gorsuch and David Aleshire (1974) reviewed all the published empirical studies on the topic through the mid-1970s and concluded that the key to understanding conflicting findings is the way in which religious commitment is measured. If church membership is used as the measurement, members are more prejudiced than those who have never joined a church. If beliefs are used, the theologically conservative are more prejudiced than others. And if church attendance is the measure of commitment, then the marginal church members show more prejudice than either the nonactive or the most active members. Gorsuch and Aleshire (1974) concluded that

the results of the present review are clear: the average church member is more prejudiced than the average nonmember because the casual, nontheologically motivated member is prejudiced. The highly committed religious person is — along with the nonreligious person — one of the least prejudiced members of our society.

These researchers point out, however, that the precise role organized religion plays in the influencing of prejudice is unclear. Sophisticated studies that measure the impact of churches on individuals over time simply have not yet been done.

An analysis of *Project Canada* data has disclosed that the religiously committed in Canada do not differ significantly from others with respect to their interpersonal relationship attitudes (Bibby 1987a). They hold a similar view of people, claim a comparable level of compassion, and appear to be no more or less tolerant of deviants, minority groups, and people of other religious faiths than are other Canadians. Further, in contrast to the findings of Rokeach and Stark and Glock, no noteworthy differences appear in the interpersonal attitudes held by Roman Catholics and by Protestants.

There is, however, one area where the Christian religion still appears to speak with a fairly loud if not unique voice — the area of personal morality, notably sexuality. Here, Christian churches with varying degrees of explicitness tend to function as opponents of "moral innovation." Examples include opposition to the changing of sexual standards, to the increased availability of legal abortion, to the legalized distribution of pornographic material, and to the legalization of prohibited drugs.

Table 13-6 reports findings that support the "opposition to moral innovation" argument. Religiously committed Canadians are more inclined than others to hold negative attitudes toward nonmarital sexuality, homosexuality, abortion, pornography, and the legalization of marijuana. A national study of Canadian Mennonites has similarly found that commitment has consequences for the moral rather than for the social sphere (Driedger, Currie, and Linden 1982). Yet, even here, the influence of religion both nationally and by religious groups, while important, is generally no more significant than the year of

TABLE 13-6 Moral Attitudes by Attendance and Importance of Religion: Percentage Opposed

	Premarital Sex	Extra-Marital Sex	Homo-sexuality	Abortion: Rape	Abortion: Child Unwanted	Distribution of Pornography	Legalization of Marijuana
Attendance							
Weekly	51	94	83	28	79	55	91
<Weekly	11	80	60	4	43	28	71
Religion's importance							
Very important	49	94	83	24	77	55	90
<Very important	10	80	60	5	42	27	71

SOURCE: Reginald W. Bibby, *Project Can90.*

one's birth. What this means is that the era in which a person was born is just as important in determining opposition to moral innovation as is religious commitment; and in Canada's past, resistance to moral change was greater than in recent years or today.

Religious commitment in Canada, then, appears to have relatively little influence in the areas of personal characteristics or interpersonal relations, where secular influences abound; it has its greatest influence in the sphere of personal morality.

Societal Consequences

The influence of religion can be examined not only in terms of individuals and social interaction but also with reference to society as a whole.

Pope Liked but Ignored

Two public opinion polls, one taken before Pope John Paul II's 1984 visit to Canada, and the other after his departure, point to the selective use of Roman Catholicism by Canadian Catholics. While the Pope himself is respected, what he says is not necessarily taken seriously.

September 8, 1984
OTTAWA — A major pastoral goal of Pope John Paul's visit is doomed even before he sets foot in Quebec City Sunday, according to a national opinion poll commissioned by Southam News.

The survey strongly suggests the Pope will be cheered as a media superstar, respected for his goodness, applauded for his engaging personality but ignored as irrelevant when he preaches on individual and public morality.

Preaching to the public on morality and humanity is one main goal of a papal visit, according to Vatican officials. The other is to strengthen the resolve of local bishops and priests.

Yet more than half the 1011 adults interviewed for the poll reject the pope's social thinking as "out of touch" and object to any religious figure taking strong stands on political and economic issues.

Barely one in seven — rising to nearly one in five among Catholics only — consider John Paul's social thinking in line with Canadian society. Only a third of those interviewed even like the idea of religious leaders speaking out on politics and economics.

Such widespread opposition means the Pope will be preaching mostly to people with closed minds, whether restating his traditional views on contraception and abortion or outlining his progressive ideas on social justice and human work.

"He gets it from both sides," agreed a leading Catholic theologian who requested anonymity. "Liberals object to his moral traditionalism and the conservatives balk at his ideas for political and economic reform."

While Canadians may turn off the preaching, they will give a joyous and warm welcome to the "Pope for all Christians" on his 12-day visit.

Three out of four interviewed this July said the papal visit was a good idea, rising to 88 per cent approval among Roman Catholics. Only eight per cent of Canadians think the visit is a bad idea, largely because of the expense, estimated from $50 million upward. Another seven per cent say the visit is a good idea so long as taxpayers don't wind up with a big bill.

January 31, 1985
OTTAWA (CP) — More than three-quarters of Canadians of all denominations approved of Pope John Paul's September visit, but they remember the man more than his message, a Gallup poll released today indicates.

The poll, commissioned by the Canadian Conference of Catholic Bishops, found 77 percent of respondents approved of the visit for a number of reasons, including the spirituality of the event and its unifying effect.

Of the 15 per cent who disapproved of the Pope's presence, 82 per cent cited the cost of the visit as the reason.

Residents of Atlantic Canada and Quebec showed more interest and support for the visit than did the rest of the country, says the survey, conducted in October, a month after the Pope's departure.

The survey estimated 10 per cent of Canadian adults, fewer than two million, attended a papal event or watched motorcades. That number is far lower than was originally planned for by church and security officials.

But 63 per cent of those surveyed said they followed the papal visit through television, newspapers or radio.

Father William Ryan, a general secretary for the conference, said the poll confirms that the visit "helped Canadians to take time out to think about important issues while at the same time enjoying an historic and spiritually renewing event."

It now is up to the church to foster this interest, Ryan said in a statement. "The long-range effects (of the visit) are harder to estimate."

Source:

Peter Calamai, *Southam News*, September 8, 1984, and *Canadian Press*, January 31, 1985.

From at least the time of Marx and Durkheim, observers have argued that religion contributes to solidarity. Marx was particularly critical of what he saw as the fusion of religion with the interests of the powerful, to the point where political and theological heresies were synonymous. Similarly, Durkheim saw the supernatural as both reflecting the nature of a society and functioning to unite it.

Religion, of course, can sometimes also be disruptive. Efforts on the part of Protestant leaders to bring about social change have challenged the Canadian status quo (see, for example, Crysdale 1961; Allen 1971). At the provincial level, Roman Catholicism in Quebec can be seen as having contributed to considerable cultural and regional cohesion. But at the national level, this contribution to solidarity can be seen as having been disruptive to Canadian unity. In the United States, Jerry Falwell's "Moral Majority" became a vocal "Christian Right" committed to altering the nature of American life through influencing the country's major institutions. The disruptive effects of religion can also be seen in the Protestant–Catholic strife in Northern Ireland; in the Islamic resurgence in Iran; in the Hindu–Sikh conflict in India; and in the call of the Roman Catholic clergy for political and economic change in Poland and Latin America. The Canadian Council of Roman Catholic Bishops has been especially vocal in criticizing the profit orientation of the country's economy and in opposing attempts to stymie workers' efforts to organize — even going so far as to indict T. Eaton stores in Toronto in the late 1980s. Disruption is also a consequence of the activities of other religious groups, including Canadian Doukhobors and youth-oriented cults. Conflict occasionally arises over the opposition of Christian Scientists and Jehovah's Witnesses regarding blood transfusions and over the pacifist stance of Quakers and Mennonites.

Nevertheless, Peter Berger's (1961) observation of some 30 years ago still seems generally valid: while an adequate sociological theory of religion must be able to account for the possibility of dysfunctions, Durkheim's assertion that religion integrates societies aptly describes religion in America. Religion, at least the mainline segment of organized Christianity that embraces the largest number of affiliates, appears largely to endorse culture rather than to challenge it, to reinforce North American society as we know it rather than to call for its reformation. As University of Calgary sociologist Harry Hiller (1976) has put it: "There are times then when religion can be a vital force in social change. ... But as a general principle, we can say that in Canada organized religion has generally been a conservative force supporting the solidarity of the society. ..." Historically the Protestant churches have reflected the British position of legitimizing authority through supporting government — for example, offering prayers for its success in securing order and justice (Fallding 1978). Significantly, America's new "Christian Right" is calling not for revolution but for a return to "the values that made America great."

At times, religion has been a central component of cultural domination.

Religion, then, has a strong tendency to mirror culture. To the extent that it does so, it gives supernatural endorsement to culture, and indeed functions as "social cement." Only when certain segments of society develop ideas in opposition to the dominant societal norms and attribute those ideas to a supernatural source is religion potentially divisive. There is good reason to believe that the dominant religious groups exercise considerable social control over the legitimization of ideas proposed by less powerful groups (such as the gay religious community's assertion that "God loves gay people too").

More than a few observers decry this inability of religion to rise above culture. Theologian Paul Tillich (1966) wrote that religion "cannot allow itself to become a special area within culture, or to take a position beside culture." In describing the social roots of denominationalism, Niebuhr (1929) called such division "an unacknowledged hypocrisy, a reflection of the inability of churches to transcend the social conditions." Will Herberg (1960) stated that religion in America seems to possess little capacity for rising above national consciousness. "The God of judgment," he said, "has died." Berger (1961) claimed that American religion is not unlike a nation-serving imperial cult, an unconsciously affirmed state religion.

Nevertheless, religion's inclination to mirror culture rather than to stand apart from it may be inevitable. If humans, however unintentionally, create religion in their own image, it is not at all surprising that religion leans toward personal and societal endorsement rather than toward personal and societal judgement.

Religion: Its Future

Since social scientists first turned their attention to religion, they have been divided on the question of its future. Comte asserted that the world was experiencing an ever-increasing level of rationalism, with religious ideas progressively giving way to metaphysical and then scientific modes of thought. Marx and Freud also saw religion as being replaced by reason, a movement that would usher in a superior quality of life.

Durkheim, on the other hand, was among those who saw religion persisting. Religious explanations, he said, may be forced to retreat, reformulate, and relinquish ground in the face of the steady advance of science. Yet religion will survive, both because of its social sources and because of its social functions. This secularization–persistence debate has not diminished in recent years.

The Secularization Argument

According to the proponents of the secularization argument, traditional religion has experienced a decline that parallels the rise of industrialization. The increase in specialized activities had led to a reduction in the number of areas of life over which religion has authority, including meaning. Such a trend can be seen in the church's loss of influence in Europe since the medieval period, or in the similar loss of authority experienced by the Roman Catholic Church in Quebec since approximately 1960.

Secularization further involves adopting an empirical/material outlook whereby the individual's focus and commitment are given to the reality perceived through the senses. This "secularization of consciousness" is assumed to have correlatives that we noted earlier, including urbanization, higher education, work-force participation, and exposure to mass media.

The Persistence Argument

Other observers, however, have questioned this posited decline of religion, arguing instead for its viability. There are various forms of the **persistence argument**. Kingsley Davis (1949) has contended that because of the functions that religion performs, its future is not in question. Although there is a limit to the extent to which a society can operate guided by illusion, says Davis, there is also a limit to which a society can be guided by sheer rationality. He therefore argues that while religion will certainly experience change, including the birth of new sects, it is unlikely to be replaced by science and technology.

In a similar fashion, Harvard social forecaster Daniel Bell (1977) has argued that a return to the sacred is imminent. After three centuries of emphasis on the rational and the material, we are beginning to experience the limits of modernism and alternatives to religion. "We are now groping for a new vocabulary whose keyword seems to be limits," says Bell. New religions will consequently arise in response to the core questions of existence — death, tragedy, obligation, love.

Talcott Parsons (1964) notes that Christianity continues to flourish in the modern Western world, "most conspicuously in the United States." Specialization, he writes, need not be equated with a loss of significance for religion. On the contrary, religious values have now pervaded society, and religion is currently being sustained with unprecedented efficiency, precisely because religious organizations can concentrate on religion. Parsons further sees "the individualistic principle inherent in Christianity" as contributing to religious autonomy. Individuals are responsible for deciding what to believe and with whom to associate in socially expressing and reinforcing commitment. Far from being in a state of demise, then, Christianity for Parsons is characterized by *institutionalization* and **privatization**.

For Andrew Greeley (1972, 1991), secularization is a myth. Contemporary religion does indeed face secular pressures and is certainly unimportant for some people. But Greeley contends that such pressures and variations in commitment are not unique to our time. He has complete confidence in religion's future.

More recently, Rodney Stark and William Bainbridge (1985) have argued that humans persist in having intense desires that "only the gods can satisfy." The reality of death, for example, calls for answers about what, if anything, happens after we die. Science, relying as it does on empirical means of knowing, is unable to address life-after-death issues. Because such questions persist as part of our efforts to comprehend our existence, a market exists for religion. Consequently, if secularization leads to the demise of some religions and groups, it will also lead to the appearance of new expressions and organizations to service "the religious market." Some will be "sects," breakaway groups from established bodies. Others will take the form of "cults," with origins outside of previous religions. The net result is not the end of religion but the replacement of some faiths and groups with new ones. Religion constitutes an ever-changing marketplace. Rather than de-

stroying religion, say Stark and Bainbridge, secularization stimulates it.

One the one hand, then, a number of social scientists see increasing industrialization and postindustrialization as having a negative effect on religious commitment that is largely irreversible. On the other hand, other observers deny the existence of such a relationship.

The Preliminary Evidence

The debate over modern industrialization's relationship to religion clearly needs to be informed by cross-cultural data if the role of religion in highly developed settings is to be understood apart from specific societal idiosyncrasies.

International Data. In a significant summary of international Gallup Poll data, Lee Sigelman (1977) reported that religious commitment varies significantly between countries. Beliefs and their importance are highest in the developing Third World countries and lowest in the highly developed western European countries such as Scandinavia, West Germany, France, and Britain, along with Japan (see Table 13-7). Consistent with the secularization hypothesis, the commitment level

TABLE 13-7 Religious Beliefs and Their Importance for Selected Countries and Areas (Percent)

	Beliefs: Very Important	God	Life after Death
India	81	98	72
Africa	73	96	69
Far East	71	87	62
Latin America	62	95	54
United States	56	94	69
Canada	36	89	54
Italy	36	88	46
Britain	23	76	43
France	22	72	39
West Germany	17	72	33
Scandinavia	17	65	35
Japan	12	38	18

SOURCE: Compiled from Lee Sigelman, "Multi-nation surveys of religious beliefs," *Journal for the Scientific Study of Religion* 16(1977):290.

of an increasingly postindustrialized Canada lies between these two extremes. The plunge in Roman Catholic service attendance in Quebec in the 1960s and early 1970s would seem to provide a classic modern-day example of industrialization's impact on religion. Similarly, the sharp post-1950s decline in church attendance in Mexico would seem, at least in part, to reflect increasing modernization.

Stark and Bainbridge (1985), however, having carried out extensive research in the United States, Canada, and Europe, provide data confirming their hypothesis that cults will abound where conventional churches are weakest. Yet their evidence for cult viability is based almost exclusively on the presence of cult headquarters and centres, rather than on data indicating that these groups are making noteworthy numerical inroads into national populations. Until new movements embrace the nonreligious, the secularization thesis has not been seriously challenged. While these international findings do not exclude the possibility of a return to religion, as envisioned by Davis and Bell, at this point the data appear to support the secularization thesis. A clear-cut, contrasting "return to religion" pattern is not visible.

There is one important societal exception to this general relationship between industrialization and religion — the United States. In that country, commitment levels remain high. In recent years, Greeley (1989) and Finke and Stark (1992) have made the case that organized religion has known a high level of stability over time. Yet, the argument continues to be made that the United States, far from being exempt from such a pattern, gives considerable evidence of being secularized not only from without but also from within (see, for example, Herberg 1960; Berger 1961; Luckmann 1967, Bellah et al. 1985). While outwardly reasonably alive and well, American religious organizations, it is argued, are being increasingly infiltrated by American culture, with the result that secularization does not stop at the church steps.

But this process works both ways. Religion has historically been strongly embedded in American ideology and continues to play a significant role in powerful nationalistic tendencies, or what Robert Bellah (1967) and others have referred to as **American Civil Religion**. As Herberg (1960) put it:

Americans, by and large, do have their "common religion" and that "religion" is the system familiarly known as the American Way of Life. ... By every realistic criterion the American Way of Life is the operative faith of the American people.

As a result, says Herberg, "To be a Protestant, a Catholic, or a Jew are today the alternative ways of being an American." Consistent with such a position, Armand Mauss and Milton Rokeach (1977) have argued:

Any comparisons between the United States and other countries in religious matters must take into account the unique part that religion has played in the history of the United States. ... In America, a declaration of belief in some kind of deity is little more than an affirmation of the national heritage. {This is why} belief in deity can easily coexist, as it always has in America, with continuing increases in educational levels and in scientific advancements.

Still, mainline Protestant denominations, along with the Roman Catholic Church, have experienced considerable membership losses since the 1960s. Some observers have argued that, prior to that time, institutional religion in America prospered because the values expounded by Protestants, Catholics, and Jews were consistent with conservative political and family values (Nelsen and Potvin 1980). As a result of the post-1960s shift in values, religion is no longer experiencing its previous level of "establishment." Instead, an increasing level of "disestablishment" has been taking place, especially among the affluent young. This shift has so far had the greatest impact on the affluent, educated, culture-affirming mainline denominations. But the trend will eventually spread to the more conservative denominations as well (Hoge and Roozen 1979).

In sum, compared with the situation in other developed countries, religion in the United States continues to flourish. However, that is not to say that it is exempt from the secularizing tendencies found elsewhere.

The Canadian Situation. To varying degrees, Canadians assert belief in God, claim to pray and to experience God, believe in the divinity of Jesus, and maintain that there is life after death. The *Project Canada* surveys have further documented widespread interest in supernatural phenomena more generally. For example:

- Almost one in three Canadians find astrological claims to be credible.

- Some 60 percent think ESP exists; the same proportion say that they have experienced premonition.

- Almost 65 percent believe some people have special psychic powers, while about one in two claim that they have experienced telepathy.

- Only about 30 percent rule out the possibility that people can communicate with the dead.

Supernatural beliefs and practices are alive and well in Canada. Yet, as noted earlier, when asked point-blank, only about 40 percent of Canadians say that they are committed Christians, with just half of these people exhibiting the conventional belief/practice/experience/knowledge kind of commitment conceptualized by Glock and Stark. The precise content of the religion of the other one-half is unclear. A mere 2 percent claim to be committed to religions other than Christianity. The remaining 60 percent of the population is uncommitted (40 percent) or nonreligious (20 percent). And, on a given weekend, only one in three people across the country can be found in churches and synagogues.

It appears on the surface that commitment to established religion is not high and that the religious situation in Canada represents fairly open territory for new competitors. So it is that Irving Hexham and his colleagues (1988) have written that "a market exists for new religious movements in Canada to fulfil needs which many people do not see traditional churches meeting." But looks can be deceiving.

Invariably, the question asked is, "Where are the dropouts going?" Some observers have said that they are joining new religions. Lakehead University sociologist David Nock (1987) has documented that a relationship does indeed exist between a province's "no religion" level and its apparent receptivity to cults — a claim that William Swatos (1991) goes to great lengths to refute. National survey data, however, show that only about 1 percent of Canadians claim to be even

strongly interested in activities and groups such as TM, Hare Krishna, the Moonies, Eckankar, and Scientology. Fewer than half of those expressing strong interest are actually participating in any groups (Bibby 1987a). The possibility that interest and involvement are transitory is suggested by the finding that almost another 3 percent of Canadians say that they had once been strongly interested in one or more of the new religions (see, for example, Bird and Reimer 1982). Toronto psychiatrist Saul Levine (1979) suggests that the large dropout rate associated with new religious movements in part may indicate that cult values that are initially attractive — such as group identification versus individualism, sharing versus competition, and spiritualism versus materialism — are found to be impractical in the long run.

An examination of the claims of Stark and Bainbridge has also uncovered little support for cult inroads (Bibby and Weaver 1985). The analysis focused on people who came from homes in which their parents claimed no religious affiliation. It found that, over their lifetimes, about one in three adopted a religious tie. The affiliation, however, was with Catholic or Protestant groups, rather than with a cult. In addition, panel data involving "religious nones" — referring to people who indicate they have no religious preference — found that one-third who had no tie in 1975 had relinquished their "no affiliation" status by 1980, with the level rising to one-half by 1985. However, as with the parental "nones," they were now claiming Catholic or Protestant, rather than cult, ties.

The "new religion" numbers are small and are expected to remain so in the foreseeable future. As of the late-1980s, this country of 25 million had only about 700 full-time Scientologists, 450 Hare Krishna members, 350 to 600 Moonies, and 250 Children of God.

Other observers have argued that evangelical conservative Protestant groups such as Pentecostals and Baptists are picking up large numbers of people who are dropping out of the mainline groups. There is little evidence to support such an assertion. Nationally, conservative Protestant groups presently comprise about 7 percent of the population; in 1871, that figure stood at 8 percent.

Survey findings also do not support the possibility that many people are substituting television "electronic churches" for service attendance. Only 2 percent of Canadians say that they regularly watch religious services on TV or listen to them on radio — a decline from 29 percent reported in a Gallup poll for 1958. Some seven in ten people who regularly watch religious programs are also weekly service attenders, suggesting that the programs are largely a supplement for those involved in religious groups, rather than a substitute for those who are not involved.

Still others, like Parsons, maintain that religion is now taking a less visible, privatized form. The problem with this assertion is that such personal expressions of religion are very difficult to locate. Perhaps more seriously, with the possible exception of the 20 percent who exhibit nontraditional commitment to Christianity, at least 60 percent of Canadians simply do not claim to be committed, privately or otherwise.

If not the new religions, the evangelicals, or private forms, then the choice of the religiously inactive, say some, must be the obvious remaining option — no religion. At first glance, support for that assertion appears to exist. In 1971, only about 4 percent of Canadians told the census-takers that they had no religious preference. By 1981, the figure had risen to 7 percent. However, the analysis of "religious nones" just mentioned found that most are single and young. As these people marry and have children, many of them leave the "none" category and adopt a Catholic or Protestant affiliation. That affiliation, very significantly, is usually the same one as that of their parents. Most appear to reaffiliate not out of spiritual urgency, but because of the need for rites of passage pertaining to marriage, the baptism of children, and death. The newly affiliated tend to be nominal in their beliefs and practices. The result is that within a short number of years, more than one in three "religious nones" join the 90 percent of Canadians in claiming to have Protestant or Catholic ties.

In short, the research for religious dropouts in Canada yields an intriguing result: few have actually left home. Indeed, as noted earlier, almost 90 percent of Canadians with Catholic parents remain Catholics, as do some 90 percent of those with Protestant parents. Within denominations there is also remarkable stability across generations — about 75 percent for United Church affili-

ates, 70 percent for Anglicans, and 65 percent for conservative Protestants. The figure for other world religions is about 80 percent. Even in the "no religion" category," some 65 percent of offspring reflect their parents' choice in being unaffiliated (Bibby 1987a).

Clearly, religious group identification is valued in Canada. But it is equally clear that Canadians differ considerably in the role they want religion to play in their lives. Some embrace it wholeheartedly, seemingly as a system of meaning that informs much of their lives. Others want some beliefs, some practices, some specialized services. Still others — a small minority — want nothing from religion or religious organizations

It may well be that the significant religious development associated with the industrialization of Canada has not been the abandonment of religion. Rather, it is the tendency of Canadians to reject Christianity as an authoritative system of meaning, in favour of drawing on Judeo–Christian "fragments" — selected beliefs, practices, and organizational offerings — in a highly specialized, consumer-like fashion. In a similar manner, Canadians select fragments of other non-naturalistic systems — astrology, ESP, and so on — without adopting entire systems. In the words of Stark and Bainbridge, they become "consumer cults."

While religious groups might decry such selective consumption, over time they have in fact responded to this consumer mentality. In the face of consumer demand, Canada's main established groups — the Roman Catholics, United Church, Anglicans, and Protestant conservatives — have been offering increasingly varied "religious menus." The charismatic movement, providing people with a pentecostal-style of faith (one that emphasizes spiritual gifts like healing and speaking in tongues), embraces more than one in ten Protestants and 3 percent of Roman Catholics and Anglicans. The United Church Renewal Fellowship, organized nation-wide, represents an effort to change the church spiritually from within and is particularly attractive to those who are evangelically minded. The social activists in the major denominations have not lacked for interest groups that have focused on issues such as nuclear disarmament, human rights, poverty, and equality of the sexes. Canada's religious groups have been patient with the individual who wants minimal involvement. They seldom withhold basic rites of passage from such people, deny them admission to services, or remove them from membership rolls.

Thus it is that the Catholic, Anglican, United, and conservative Protestant of today typically have the option of being detached or involved, agnostic or evangelical, unemotional or charismatic. Switching, even to the "none" category, rarely takes place, because it has become increasingly unnecessary. One can find what one wants — in whatever quantity, ranging from a lot to a little to virtually nothing — in the familiar confines of the tradition in which one was reared. Contrary to the assertion of Stark and Bainbridge, the Canadian "religious market" is in fact very tight. The diversifying of functions by Canada's religious establishment has made it extremely difficult for new rivals to penetrate the country's religion market.

The stability of the religious scene in Canada, along with its prevalent "fragment" style, has been further documented, by a national survey of teenagers between the ages of 15 and 19 (Bibby and Posterski 1985 and 1992). The survey has found that the country's "emerging generation" differs negligibly from adults in terms of religion. Approximately 90 percent of teenagers claim the same group affiliation as their parents, and only about 2 percent indicate any strong interest in the new religions. Their belief, practice, experience, and knowledge levels are similar to those of adults. Interest in other supernatural phenomena is also very high (see Table 13-8).

Yet, when it comes to commitment, only about the same proportion of teens as of adults — some 25 percent — say that religion is "very important" to them. Fewer than one in five attend religious services regularly, and only 15 percent of teens say that they receive a high level of enjoyment from church or synagogue life (including only one in two of the regular attenders). When they are 15, 19 percent are going to services frequently; by the time they are 19, that figure drops to about 13 percent, similar to the attendance level of adults who are 18 to 29 years old.

Like their parents, however, young people are not particularly angry with religious groups. About 40 percent indicate that they have a high level of confidence in religious leaders — a confi-

TABLE 13-8   Religiosity of Canadian Teenagers and Adults (Percent)

	Adults	Teenagers
Belief		
God	83	81
Divinity of Jesus	75	80
Life after death	68	64
Some have psychic powers	59	69
Contact with the spirit world	39	44
Astrology claims are true	34	53
Practice		
Pray privately	59	46
Read horoscope	50	62
Read the Bible	24	17
Attend religious services	23	18
Watch religious programs	18	8
Experience		
God	43	34
Knowledge		
Peter denied Jesus	46	41
Salience		
Religion very important	26	24

SOURCE: Reginald W. Bibby, *Project Can90*; Reginald W. Bibby and Donald C. Posterski, *Project Teen Canada Series*.

dence level lower than that of educational leaders (67 percent), but ahead of politicians (30 percent). Moreover, they seldom make religion a target of humour. But the dominant tendency is to draw selectively from religion, rather than allowing it to become an all-embracing system of meaning. Rather than being religious dropouts, Canadians have become highly selective consumers who, rather than wanting much, want very little from the nation's religious groups.

It may well be that the structural and cultural changes associated with Canada's entry into the postindustrial "information" age have made meaning systems that encompass all of an individual's life incongruent with the varied roles people must play. Expressed another way, fragments are perhaps more functional than all-encompassing religions in a society that requires people to compartmentalize their experiences in order to play a number of diverse roles. Religious systems may also seem frequently at odds with dominant cultural values such as rationalism, consumption, and enjoyment.

If so, then people do not choose belief, practice, and service fragments over systems because there are no system options. Rather, they choose fragments because the fragments are more conducive to present-day life. As Bryan Wilson (1975:80) put it, modern societies offer "a supermarket of faiths; received jazzed-up, homespun, restored, imported and exotic. But all of them co-exist because the wider society is so secular, because they are relatively unimportant consumer items."

Rather than being novel to Canada, such a "fragment" pattern should be typical of other highly developed countries that have also known the historical dominance of one or more major religions. Indeed, this appears to be the position of British sociologists Roy Wallis and Steve Bruce as they view Europe and beyond. They write that people both inside and outside religious groups "synthesize various selections to suit their own tastes. New ideas are simply added to the sum total of legitimate ideas; there is no possibility of producing a neat, coherent set of dogmas" (Wallis and Bruce 1984:22).

As in Canada, the future of other highly industrialized societies should not lack for the presence of religious fragments. Whether fragments will become meaning systems, religious and otherwise, will depend largely on major changes in the structural and cultural makeup of those societies.

SUMMARY

1. Sociology uses the scientific method to study religion; in contrast, religion explores reality beyond what can be known empirically.

2. The sociology of religion has been strongly influenced by the theoretical contributions of Marx, who stressed the compensatory role of religion in the face of economic deprivation; Durkheim, who emphasized both the social origin of religion and its important social cohesive function; and Weber, who gave considerable attention to the relationship between ideas and behaviour.

3. Religion can be defined as a system of meaning with a supernatural referent used to interpret the world. Humanist meaning perspectives make no such use of the supernatural realm and attempt instead to make life meaningful.

4. Personal religious commitment has increasingly come to be seen as having many facets or dimensions, with four being commonly noted: belief, practice, experience, and knowledge.

5. Collective religiosity instils and sustains personal commitment. The theologically centred church–sect typology has been increasingly abandoned in favour of organizational analyses that examine religious collectivities in the same manner as other groups. In Canada, organized religion has experienced a considerable decline in participation in recent years, a trend that has had critical implications for commitment at the individual level.

6. The variations in the levels of individual commitment that characterize complex societies had led to explanations that emphasize individual and structural emphases. Reflection, socialization, and deprivation have been prominent among the individual explanations, while the dominant structural assertion has been the secularization argument.

7. The key source of religious commitment in Canada is socialization. Due to the highly secular milieu in which religious socialization efforts must take place, such efforts are decreasing in both incidence and impact.

8. Religion appears to be at best one of many paths leading to valued characteristics such as personal happiness and compassion.

9. While religion sometimes has a disruptive impact on society, it more commonly seems to contribute to social solidarity, frequently mirroring the characteristics of groups and societies.

10. Historically, observers of religion have been divided on its future, asserting both secularization and persistence hypotheses. Internationally, the secularization argument appears to have substantial support.

11. The search for alleged religious dropouts in Canada reveals that few have turned to new religions, conservative Protestant groups, privatized expressions, or the "religious none" category. Most still identify with the established groups.

12. The apparent paradox of widespread beliefs and practices existing alongside relatively

low commitment suggests that many people in Canada find it functional to draw selectively on religion, rather than embracing it as an all-encompassing system of meaning. Such a pattern is to be anticipated in developed societies more generally.

GLOSSARY

American Civil Religion. Tendency for nationalistic emphases in the United States to have many characteristics similar to religions; established Judaic-Christianity is drawn upon selectively.

Church–sect typology. Framework, dating back to Weber and Troeltsch, that examines religious organizations in terms of ideal-type, church and sect characteristics.

Collective conscience. Durkheim's term, referring to the awareness of the group being more than the sum of its individual members; norms, for example, appear to exist on a level beyond the consciences of the individual group members.

Collective religiosity. Religious commitment as manifested in and through religious groups; key to the creation and sustenance of personal religiosity.

Denominationalism. Tendency for a wide variety of Protestant religious groups to come into being, seemingly reflecting variations not only in theology but also — and perhaps primarily — in social characteristics.

Dimensions of religiosity. Various facets of religious commitment; Glock and Stark, for example, identify four: belief, experience, practice, and knowledge.

Humanist perspectives. Systems of meaning used to interpret the world that do not have a supernatural referent (e.g., communism, scientism).

Persistence argument. Assertion that religion will continue to have a significant place in the modern world, either because it never has actually declined, or because people can absorb only so much rationality and materialism.

Personal religiosity. Religious commitment at the level of the individual.

Privatization. Parsons' term for the alleged tendency of people to work out their own religious beliefs and associations in an individualistic, autonomous manner.

Profane and the sacred. Two categories by which Durkheim claimed all things are classified; the sacred represents those things viewed as warranting profound respect, the profane encompasses everything else.

Protestant Ethic. Term associated with Weber, referring to the Protestant Reformation emphases of Calvin, Luther, and others upon the importance of work performed well as an indication of living one's life "to the glory of God"; key characteristics include diligence, frugality, rational use of time.

Religion. System of meaning used to interpret the world that has a supernatural referent (for example, Christianity, Hinduism, astrology).

Secularization argument. Assertion that religion as it has been traditionally known is declining continuously and irreversibly.

FURTHER READING

Bibby, Reginald W. *Unknown Gods: The Ongoing Story of Religion in Canada.* Toronto: Stoddart, 1993. Draws on the work of the author and others in examining the paradox of organized religion having severe numerical problems at a time of heightened spiritual interest in Canada.

Clark, S.D. *Church and Sect in Canada.* Toronto: University of Toronto Press, 1948. A Canadian classic that examines the social factors contributing to the rise of different types of religious groups in this country.

Hewitt, W.E. (ed.). *Sociology of Religion: A Canadian Focus.* Toronto: Butterworths, 1993. The most up-to-date collection of articles on religion by leading Canadian social scientists. It provides students with a good introduction to the country's religion researchers and the range of their work.

Graham, Ron. *God's Dominion.* Toronto: McClelland and Stewart, 1990. A highly readable, journalistic view of the diversity of religious activity in Canada. An excellent complement to the quantitative research of social scientists.

Niebuhr, H. Richard. *The Social Sources of Denominationalism.* New York: Henry Holt and Company, 1929. A classic attempt to probe the role of social factors (for example, economics, nationality, race, region) in creating denominationalism in Europe and America.

Roof, Wade Clark, and William McKinney. *American Mainline Religion.* New Brunswick, NJ: Rutgers University Press, 1987. An exceptionally fine overview of religion in the United States. Rich in data, analyses, and interpretations.

CHAPTER 14

Polity

CHARLES C. RAGIN
ANTONIA MAIONI
PIERRE MARTIN

The **polity** is the primary arena of **power** in society; it includes all politically oriented actions. The polity exists for the purpose of deciding who gets how much of what, and why. It has changed, is changing, and will continue to change. Any study of modern society must include a study of the polity because the polity includes **government**, and government is everywhere.

The purpose of this chapter is to acquaint you with the polity. Studying the polity includes examining how government — or "the **state**," as social scientists often call it — affects our lives, how we sometimes organize and try to change the state, how political organizations such as **parties** channel the interests of different groups, how individuals influence each other, and how people and organizations pursue their different interests in the political arena. The study of the polity also includes a consideration of how institutional arrangements — for example, elections and decisions about who can vote and who can run for office — may distort or even subvert the link between ordinary citizens and government officials.

Canada is a **democracy**. This means that theoretically all citizens can participate in the political process. This chapter focuses primarily on the Canadian polity, but much of the discussion will be relevant to the polities of other advanced societies, such as those of the United States and Western Europe. Many parallels can be drawn between these polities because modern democratic countries share many political features. For example, all advanced democratic countries have political parties. In societies where democracy is less firmly rooted, such as in Latin America or

Eastern Europe, the polity is also a key institution, but its functioning may be very different. To illustrate these differences, this chapter also focuses on the Mexican polity.

Contenders are political organizations that represent the interests of members of society (Tilly 1978). Most contenders represent the specific interests of large categories of individuals (for example, physicians) or organizations (such as businesses providing similar products or services). The Canadian Association of Retired Persons, for example, represents senior citizens and retired persons and defends their rights to adequate social benefits. The Canadian Manufacturers Association represents the interests of major industrial firms in Canada. Such associations have their counterparts in the United States in the American Association of Retired Persons and the National Association of Manufacturers. These interest organizations are called contenders because they are the groups most active in trying to sway the state and gain advantages for their members. Not all contenders are organized interest groups. Some are simple collectivities that come together and press their demands on the state without the aid of any national, provincial, or local organization. Figure 14-1 shows some of the major contenders in the Canadian, U.S., and Mexican polities. In most modern societies, organized contenders such as interest groups have become increasingly important. Accordingly, this chapter focuses extensively on the actions of these groups.

Power and the Polity

The polity embraces all political aspects of society. It is best thought of as an arena where different groups in society push their interests and compete with each other for advantage. This arena extends from the formal institutions of government, at every level, all the way down to the daily discussion of political issues by individuals in society. Even politically motivated graffiti splashed on a wall by a disgruntled and isolated individual is part of the polity.

The term "polity" is unfamiliar to many; it is rarely used even by journalists who write about political matters. But if you ask most people how they feel about the government, how and why they voted in the last election, or how they think the tax system ought to be changed, you discover very quickly that they are familiar with the polity as an institution. This is because the government of a society is part of its polity. The polity includes all politically oriented behaviour in a society — everything from arguing politics with a friend and cheating on income taxes to overthrowing the government. The term "government" refers only to the formal institutions of society that make, interpret, and enforce laws. Because the polity includes all politically relevant behaviour in a society, anything that is related to the government of a society is relevant to the polity.

The polity is the most powerful institution of modern society. All members of Canadian society are profoundly affected by what happens in Ottawa and in their provincial capitals. This becomes obvious when a major national or international crisis occurs, but it is also true of day-to-day life. For example, the mere suggestion that a major government program such as Old Age Security may be altered in some way can capture the attention of the public and generate widespread debate. Millions of Canadians depend on these government transfers for their food and shelter, and millions more benefit indirectly because they are released from the personal responsibility of providing for those supported by this program, such as elderly parents.

Almost every polity has political parties. Political parties resemble contenders because they represent large groups of individuals, but political parties do not typically represent specific or narrow interests. Parties bring together many interests and combine them into a single voice. In other words, parties try to attract the support of many different contenders (and their followers) by promoting policies consistent with the wishes of a large number of contenders.

At the individual level, power is the ability to impose your will on others. At the level of the polity, it is the ability to exert your will through the state, either directly (for example, as a government minister) or indirectly (through, for example, a political organization). When power is institutionalized, the agent in power is said to have **authority**. When this authority is widely ac-

FIGURE 14-1   Members of the Polity in Canada, United States, and Mexico

Canada	United States	Mexico
Canadian Chamber of Commerce 170 000 institutions	**Chamber of Commerce of the United States** 180 000 companies	**Concanaco; Confederación de Cámaras Nacionales de Comercio** (Confederation of National Chambers of Commerce) More than 400 000 firms
Canadian Manufacturers Association	**National Association of Manufacturers** 12 500 companies and subsidiaries	**Concamin; Confederación Nacionale de Cámaras Industriales** (Confederation of National Chambers of Industry) More than 100 000 firms
Business Council on National Issues Chief Executive Officers of 150 largest corporations	**Business Roundtable** Chief Executive Officers of 200 largest corporations	**Consejo Coordinador Empresarial** (Businessmen's Co-ordinating Council Leaders of seven principal business groups
Canadian Federation of Independent Business 80 000 small and midsize businesses	**National Federation of Independent Business** 560 000 small and midsize businesses	**Canacintra; Cámara Nacional de la Industria de Transformación** (National Chamber of Transformation Industry) 86 000 small manufacturing enterprises
Canadian Petroleum Association 125 institutions	**American Petroleum Institute** Over 200 companies	**Pemex; Petróleos Mexicanos** (Mexican Petroleum Company) The only petroleum company in Mexico, owned and controlled by the government
Canadian Labour Congress 85 institutions	AFL–CIO; **American Federation of Labor and Congress of Industrial Organizations** 14.2 million members	**CTM; Confederación de Trabajadores Mexicanos** (Confederation of Mexican Workers) 5.5 million members
Canadian Federation of Agriculture 18 provincial farm organizations and co-operatives	**American Farm Bureau Federation** Over 3.8 million farm families	**Confederación Nacional Campesinas** (National Peasants' Confederation)
National Council of Women in Canada 750 000 members in affiliated groups	**National Organization of Women** 250 000 members	**Consejo Nacional de Mujeres de Mexico** (National Women's Council of Mexico)
Canadian Association of Retired Persons 55 000 individuals	**American Association of Retired Persons** 32 million, aged 50 and over	
Canadian Wildlife Federation 230 000 individuals	**National Wildlife Federation** 3.5 million individuals	**Pronatura; Associación Mexican Proconservación de la Naturaleza** (Mexican Association for Nature Conservancy) 700 members
National Firearms Association 40 000 members	**National Rifle Association** 3 million members	

FIGURE 14-1 (*continued*)

Canada	United States	Mexico
Canadian Abortion Rights Action League 18 000 members	**National Abortion Rights Action League** 400 000 members	
Campaign Life Coalition 50 000 members	**National Right to Life Committee** 500 000 affiliated members	
Canadian Medical Association 46 000 physicians	**American Medical Association** 271 000 physicians	
	National Association for the Advancement of Colored People 345 000 individuals, mostly black Americans	
Assembly of First Nations 573 aboriginal nations represented by their chiefs		

Selected Interest Groups in North America. This figure lists a number of prominent interest groups that function in similar areas in the three countries of North America, and the people and organizations they represent. Each one is a contender in the political process because it actively tries to influence that process to the advantage of its members.

SOURCE: *Canada*: Micromedia Ltd., *Directory of Associations in Canada*, 1991–1992 (Toronto: Micromedia, 1991). *United States*: Foundation for Public Affairs, *Public Interest Profiles, 1992–1993* (Washington, DC: Congressional Quarterly, 1992); John J. Russell, ed. *National Trade and Professional Associations of the United States* (New York: Columbia Books, 1992). *Mexico*: Sidney Weintraub, *A Marriage of Convenience: Relations between the United States and Mexico* (New York: Oxford University Press, 1990).

cepted throughout society, it is said to be **legitimate authority** (Weber 1947).

Many people use the term "state" as a substitute for "government," but state is broader in meaning than government. State refers to the formal institutions of society that make, interpret, and enforce laws, whereas government is more transitory than state and refers primarily to those occupying positions within these institutions. The term "polity" is even broader because it also includes the major groups in society that strive to influence, control, or dominate the state.

Origins of the State

The state has not always been the most powerful of all institutions in human societies. The earliest societies, known as band and village societies, had very weak states, and some early societies were completely stateless. This is not to say that individuals did not exercise authority in these primitive societies, but this right to tell others what to do probably existed only in families. Early states were simply an extension of the authority of parents and elders. Furthermore, the exercise of this authority was probably necessary only when the band or village was threatened in some way. These early societies had weak states because population densities were low and food plentiful. If an area became too densely populated to provide a good diet, primitive peoples would simply disperse and migrate to less densely populated areas.

The first strong states developed in what are known as impacted areas. Some very fertile areas (like river valleys) are surrounded by areas (like deserts) where it is difficult to sustain life. People are less likely to migrate from an area that is becoming too densely populated if they cannot eke out a living in a nearby area. So they stay, and the population of the fertile area becomes denser and denser. Food becomes more scarce in the im-

When power is institutionalized, the agent of power is said to have authority. When this authority is widely accepted, it is said to be legitimate authority.

pacted area as the population grows, and methods of increasing food production must be devised. This is where the state comes in. Some primitive societies developed strong states to oversee the production and distribution of food and other products. These societies survived, while those that did not develop a strong state became stagnant and sometimes disintegrated, or were conquered by societies that had developed strong states (Harris 1978).

In primitive societies, the state became strong as the need for a disciplined and hard-working labour force increased. The primary means the state used to maintain production was brute force — physical **coercion**. Today, the state still holds a monopoly on the legitimate use of physical coercion, but it does not resort to brute force routinely to get its way. Still, the biggest part of the "order"

that the state ensures is society's economic order — its system of producing and distributing wealth — and the question of who gets how much and why remains ultimately a political question.

In Canada, the polity is involved in the production and distribution of wealth in society in several ways. It protects property rights, for example. Political authorities will stop you from using your neighbours' property without their permission. It also redistributes some wealth through social and welfare programs and through taxation (because some are taxed more than others). It is the biggest spender in our society, and its expenditures can go to the poor through welfare programs, but they often also go to support the very rich owners of large businesses (for example, through government contracts and subsidies). Elected officials and government bureaucrats

State refers to the formal institutions of society that make, interpret, and enforce laws, whereas government is more transitory than state and refers primarily to those occupying positions within these institutions.

Authority

Primitive and modern states exercise power in society because they are seen by the members of society as possessing the authority to do so. It is sometimes hard, however, for a state to win from society this right to exercise power. Many countries in Africa and Asia, for example, were once colonies, and their states lack authority because citizens associate these governments with the domination of the former colonial powers. In Eastern Europe and the former Soviet Union, states that many experts had considered invulnerable revealed themselves as inherently weak because they were not considered legitimate by large numbers of their citizens. In all these countries where states are relatively recent, the polity has not yet been institutionalized to the extent that it has in the more established democracies.

When power is institutionalized, it is seen by members of society as a property of the institution (an agency of the government), not as the

make far-reaching decisions about how to spend vast sums: Will more be spent on education, or will businesses be taxed less? To spend more on education may create greater equality in society; to tax profits less would increase the gap between the richest and poorest members of society but perhaps increase gross domestic product. Do we want a more equal society, or one with more inequality but perhaps greater total production?

All of the functions of the polity — to ensure social order, to provide a way to change society in an orderly manner, and to provide for the welfare of individuals in society — are related in some way to the polity's major function: determining who gets how much and why.

When power is institutionalized, it is seen by members of society as a property of the institution, and not as the property of particular individuals.

property of particular individuals. In other words, the one who exercises power is seen not as an arbitrary ruler but as an office-holder who is exercising power that belongs to that office. Once power is institutionalized it may be seen as legitimate authority, but this result is not always automatic, as the collapse of the communist states of Eastern Europe dramatically demonstrates. Thus, even after power has been institutionalized (and authority created), a citizen may see the institutionalized power as illegitimate in some way. After the American Civil War, for example, Southerners viewed the Reconstruction governments imposed by the North as illegitimate, even though they recognized the authority of these governments. In present-day Quebec, many citizens dispute the legitimacy of the federal state's control over their own society, but they still recognize the authority of the federal government and abide by its laws. When authority is both recognized and respected it can be called legitimate authority.

According to Max Weber (1947), there are three basic types of authority. The first is called **traditional authority**. This type of authority is based on custom. In primitive societies, for example, the extension of the rights of parents led to a governing agency composed of a council of elders. This agency based its authority on the customary rights of parents. A second type of authority is called **charismatic authority**. If an individual's power in society is based on personal qualities, qualities that attract a large number of devoted followers, then that individual's authority is called charismatic. Some argue, for example, that part of the authority of former Prime Minister Pierre Elliott Trudeau was initially based on his personal appeal. The same has been said of former Quebec Premier René Lévesque, whose personal appeal did much to further the nationalist cause of the Parti Québécois, which he founded. The United States also has had a number of charismatic leaders, such as Franklin D. Roosevelt and John F. Kennedy.

Charismatic authority is difficult to perpetuate and institutionalize. To maintain their power, charismatic leaders must routinize their charisma and thereby turn it into the third type of authority, **legal-rational authority**. This third type is based on the authority and presumed correctness of formal rules, not on the authority of customs

or persons. Legal-rational authority is by far the predominant type in modern societies. In well-established democracies such as Canada and the United States, the bureaucracy of the government is organized according to the legal-rational model. The duties of each office are specified in laws, and all government officials are required to do things "according to the book." They must follow the guidelines established in rules and regulations mandated by legislators acting on behalf of the people.

The Political Process

A good way to begin the study of political processes and of political sociology in general is to examine the experiences of political contenders involved in important policy decisions. The actions of political contenders constitute the bulk of day-to-day politics in modern polities, and they shape some of the most important decisions taken by governments. Here we examine the issue of North American free trade. In Canada, contenders battled over a free-trade agreement with the United States in 1988, and the issue has continued to divide these groups ever since. In the United States, free trade with Mexico has been much more politically sensitive than this first agreement with Canada. Similarly, in Mexico trade liberalization represents a very radical change after decades of strictly protectionist policies.

Contenders in the Politics of Free Trade

Before we introduce the contenders jostling over free trade in North America, we must understand why trade is politically important. To do so, we need to answer three questions. First, what are the advantages of trade? Second, why do states protect their national markets? The third question is at the core of the polity as the primary arena of power: Who gets how much of what, when the state makes trade policies, and why?

Adam Smith (1776) claimed that a government could best ensure the wealth of the nation by opening its borders to "free trade" with other nations. To see how this theory works, you can draw a parallel between countries and individuals. In modern societies, individuals do not make all that they need themselves. Rather, they tend to specialize and to exchange the fruits of their labour with each other. Just as no individual can be fully self-sufficient, no country can efficiently produce everything its citizens need or want. Thus, it makes sense for countries to specialize, to some extent, and to trade. According to Adam Smith's theory, the less states interfere with trade, the more their populations can benefit from specialization and competition.

States, however, have generally been reluctant to surrender control over trade. Import duties bring tax revenue, and they can protect a nation's burgeoning industries from foreign competition. A state may also seek to reinforce the unity and independence of its society by favouring economic linkages within its borders rather than across them. Indeed, trade protection played an important part in the political and economic development of the three countries of North America.

After the United States declared its independence in 1776, the new nation erected trade barriers to stimulate its own manufactures, instead of depending upon British imports. In Canada, Prime Minister John A. Macdonald's "National Policy" of 1879 was based on the belief that the east–west integration of the new federation required protection from U.S. manufacturers. After the Great Depression of the 1930s, Mexican leaders sought industrial development through import substitution (producing goods locally that were once imported and protecting local producers from foreign competition) and control over foreign investment, with some success, but Mexico never caught up with its northern neighbours.

Although trade barriers such as import duties may serve valuable national goals, they mostly benefit employers and workers in the protected industries, who, in turn, pressure their government to maintain these barriers. These "defensive contenders" are concentrated, and their interests are specific. However, consumers who may gain from freer trade are diffused and their interests less certain, and they face the usual barriers to collective action that inhibit the political mobilization of unconnected individuals. Lifting trade barriers can cause unemployment and bankruptcies in import-sensitive industries, and even if jobs and business opportunities are available, it may be costly to retool plants and retain workers.

Thus, governments often find it difficult to resist pressures for protection.

Finally, liberalizing trade and investment can alter the distribution of power in society, which ultimately determines "who gets how much of what and why." In an open international economy, large corporations can move operations to other countries, but workers usually are not mobile. The scenario is now familiar in Canada and the United States: If labour refuses to yield to management demands for a wage freeze or cut or for the reduction of benefits, management often has the option to close the plant, lay off production workers, and open another plant in a country where wages are considerably lower, such as Mexico. Products can then be imported into the home market. Governments also may be vulnerable when they face large corporations in a free-trade environment because businesses can threaten to move operations to another jurisdiction when they face government taxes or regulations they consider constraining. For example, a business might move from Canada to Mexico to escape strict environmental standards or from the United States to Mexico to escape employment guidelines that would force changes in the gender or racial composition of the firm's workforce. In day-to-day politics, the relative vulnerability of workers and governments in open, global markets can mean limited power for groups pressing for more social services, greater income redistribution, stricter environmental standards, or regulations favouring unions.

Many specialists blame protectionism for the depression of the 1930s and attribute the rapid growth of industrial countries since World War II to the reduction of trade barriers and the phenomenal expansion of international trade. When governments restrict trade too much, consumers and workers all pay the price of slower growth. Yet, liberalization always takes a toll on some groups and individuals. In short, trade is politically important because it concerns not only the total wealth of society, but also the distribution of that wealth and the degree of control the state may exert over the economy.

Free Trade Politics in Canada

The 1988 Free Trade Agreement (FTA) with the United States was a decision of historic proportions. It was also very complex: the text of the agreement itself is as thick as a phone book, and about as much fun to read. The story of how the agreement came about, however, is fascinating. Bilateral negotiations took more than a year and ended in October 1987, minutes before the deadline. The real political battle came later, when a federal election was called for November 1988. This account of free-trade politics in Canada focuses on four dimensions of the debate: symbols, interests, federal–provincial relations, and party competition.

In this very divisive debate, each side appealed to powerful symbols. For its supporters, the FTA was the key to Canada's prosperity in a competitive world. Its rejection would lead to an economic catastrophe. In the 1984 campaign, Brian Mulroney's Progressive Conservatives did not call for free trade. Mulroney promised economic renewal as Canada emerged from recession, and national reconciliation, because Liberal policies had alienated Quebec and the West. He also wanted better relations with the United States. In 1985, when the Liberal-appointed Macdonald Commission endorsed free trade as a panacea for Canada's ailing economy, Mulroney seized the opportunity. Free trade provided the glue that could hold his goals together. On the one hand, his economic ideology would be secured in a bilateral deal limiting the scope of future government intervention in the economy. On the other hand, because free trade appealed to Quebec and the West, Mulroney might have a chance to solve the constitutional mess inherited from his predecessors.

As we saw above, trade is necessary for economic growth, but unfettered markets can make it more difficult to achieve important social goals. When economic integration takes place between unequal partners, the capacity of the smaller country to achieve such goals may be reduced even more. Thus, critics warned that free trade would be socially and politically disastrous: Canada's sovereignty would be gobbled up by its giant neighbour; Canadians would lose valued social programs, such as medical care; and countless Canadians would lose their jobs.

There was little room in this debate for shades of grey. On both sides, leaders used emotional images to shape public opinion. The debate, as Doern and Tomlin (1991) aptly summed it up,

was about "faith and fear." How could a decision be made amidst such uncertainty and conflicting values? Whereas ordinary Canadians often could not sort out what the FTA meant for them, most contenders knew what their interests were. A contender's success depended on its capacity to convince the public that its own interest corresponded with the general interest.

Opponents of the FTA held a slight lead in public opinion polls at election time. The 1988 Canadian Election Study found that about 42 percent of the public opposed the FTA, 38 percent supported it, and 20 percent were undecided or uncommitted. To make their case, FTA opponents emphasized nationalism, social equity, and the risk of Canadian jobs drifting south. The latter concern made the Canadian Labour Congress (CLC) and other unions the most virulent adversaries of free trade. Union leaders warned about the loss of jobs, but they also feared that market forces would force the Canadian government to make its laws more favourable to employers, which would reduce the power of the unions.

Labour was joined in its opposition by a wide variety of groups representing protected industries, women, churches, poor people, senior citizens, environmentalists, academics, and artists. These groups formed a coalition called the Pro-Canada Network. Although their leaders argued convincingly and passionately against the FTA, the groups could not always mobilize their own members. For example, the survey cited above found only a small difference between opposition to the FTA among union members (44 percent) and other respondents (41 percent). However, while 53 percent of people with family income over $60 000 supported the FTA, only 31 percent of those making less than $40 000 supported the deal. Interestingly, many more men (45 percent) than women (30 percent) supported the FTA.

FTA supporters were led by business groups. The powerful Business Council for National Issues (BCNI), founded in 1976, represents the largest businesses in Canada, including many subsidiaries of U.S. corporations. BCNI led the charge for free trade throughout the 1980s. For the Canadian Manufacturers' Association (CMA), support for the FTA did not come naturally because many members benefited from trade protection. Eventually, the CMA adopted the export-

Corporate Support for the Free-Trade Deal

Canadian electoral regulations impose limits on how much political parties can spend in advertising during a federal election campaign. However, in 1988, there were no limits on the amounts that could be spent by groups campaigning on behalf of the free trade agreement itself. This passage from Graham Fraser's narrative history of the 1988 election shows how the pro–free-trade forces reacted to mid-campaign news that the Liberal Party was moving ahead of the Progressive Conservatives in the polls. Fraser makes a parallel between the mobilization of the business community in 1988 and a similar campaign against the Co-operative Commonwealth Federation (CCF) in 1945.

On Tuesday November 1, the published polls confirmed what the Tories knew from Allan Gregg: the Liberals had risen dramatically. The Environics poll, published in the *Globe and Mail*, showed that the Liberals had moved into a six-point lead, with 37 per cent of decided voters, with the Conservatives at 31 per cent and the NDP at 26. The feeling, which was stimulated even more a week later with the publication of a Gallup poll, provoked in the business community that endorsed free trade something of the same response that the initial Decima polling had stimulated at the centre of the Tory campaign: confusion, followed by a determination to retaliate.

The result was an overwhelming avalanche of advertising and propaganda: full-page newspaper advertisements, folders, brochures, speeches by executives in the lunch-room, employee "information sessions," letters to workers in pay envelopes — a tidal wave of frenetic activity by the corporate community that has been estimated to have cost anywhere from $2 to $3 million (the Liberal estimate — and almost as much as the entire Liberal advertising budget) to $10 million (the thumbnail estimate current in the labour movement) to a whopping $56 million calculated by Nick Fillmore in *This Magazine*, which includes the federal governments' promotions, the Tory election spending, campaigns by provincial governments and the Canadian Alliance for Trade and Job Opportunities, its member organizations and additional corporate donors over the previous two years.

Ingenuously, Hugh Segal [a Tory adviser] would claim that the onslaught of third-party advertising was not helpful, that no one read it, and that it had little impact. This was comparable to a duellist complaining that an AK-47 was inelegant. Inelegant the corporate swarm may have been by the standards of the advertising community; its sheer tonnage was astonishing — 800,000 copies of a four-page brochure on free trade, and full-page advertisements in Sunday newspapers, the day before the election — and they were completely outside the controls and restrictions of the provisions of the Canada Elections Act.

Thus, Crown Life Insurance organized a meeting for four hundred employees, which purported to be an open discussion of the agreement, and consisted of a lecture by a vice-president who was an advocate of the agreement. The Canadian Alliance for Trade and Job Opportunities acknowledged that it had encouraged its 150 member companies to set up employee programs. James Richardson and Sons of Winnipeg distributed the newspaper advertising supplement on

ers' view that safe access to the U.S. market was needed to make Canadian industry competitive.

At the height of the debate, dozens of business groups joined with the Consumers' Association of Canada to form the Canadian Alliance for Trade and Job Opportunities. This coalition was led by two unlikely allies: the former Progressive Conservative Premier of Alberta, Peter Lougheed, and former federal minister Donald Macdonald, a Liberal whose royal commission had launched the debate. For business groups, the government's decision to initiate FTA talks was in itself a victory, but they also needed to convince an electorate that had serious doubts. To overcome these doubts, they had two advantages over opponents: (1) Only one major party pressed their case, rather than two, which meant that a clear, unified message was presented to voters, and (2) they had money — lots of it. In the 1988 campaign, pro-FTA groups spent millions of dollars in advertising, eschewing the limits imposed by Canadian law upon campaign spending (Fraser 1988).

The FTA decision was also influenced by the way the issue played in Quebec, where the Progressive Conservatives won 63 of the 75 seats. Unlike federal parties, both major provincial par-

free trade to its three thousand employees, as did Canfor Corp., a Vancouver forest-product company.

In Toronto, Enfield Corp., a finance management company, distributed ten thousand copies of a free-trade paper to employees and shareholders. The supermarket chain Loblaws inserted a letter endorsing the Free Trade Agreement in the pay envelopes of its employees throughout Ontario. In Sault Ste Marie, the president of Algoma Steel, Peter Nixon, went on television to say that the defeat of the Free Trade Agreement would cost $1 million in jobs. Similarly, Stelco endorsed free trade in a message inserted in employees' pay envelopes, saying that the deal was crucial for the future of the steel industry.

In smaller companies, the pitch was more direct and more brutal. In his study of the business campaign on behalf of the deal, Nick Fillmore recounts how the president of Valley City Manufacturing, a wood-working company employing 150 people in Dundas, Ont., called a special meeting and told his employees that many of them might lose their jobs if the deal did not go through.

Individuals who had not been involved in public life before became heavily involved. Jack Fraser, the president and chief executive officer of Federal Industries in Winnipeg,

became the driving force behind the Manitoba free-trade group. David Culver, the president of Alcan, became active in both the Business Council on National Issues and the Alliance for Trade and Job Opportunities. As one Tory put it later, "There are a lot of business people who got heavily involved — and really enjoyed it. They may not go away now." It was an extraordinary closing of corporate ranks, which created a kind of schism between business and labour, rich and poor, affluent region and poor region, such as the country had rarely, if ever, seen before. But veterans of the NDP, who had either lived through or learned the history of the party, remembered the 1940s. In his memoirs, David Lewis recounts how the Canadian Chamber of Commerce had developed plans to "combat the menace of the CCF" in 1943, and how the Canada Life Insurance Co. sent instructions to their branch managers on how to bring the CCF threat to the attention of customers.

In addition, free-enterprise organizations were established in order to finance crusaders like Gladstone Murray, who waged a constant campaign against the CCF with a $100,000 fund provided for him by many of the same firms (Algoma Steel, Stelco and many others) which, forty-five years later, were funding the Business Council on National Issues, the Canadian

Alliance for Trade and Job Opportunities, and the avalanche of pro-free trade advertising.

"You may vote CCF against my advice as this is your privilege," said J.H. Andres of Lyman House, in a letter to employees during the 1945 election which was remarkably similar in tone to the messages conveyed to thousands of employees by their corporate employers in 1988. "I cannot, however, accept the responsibility of maintaining employment for you and the other members of our organization for any length of time under a CCF-controlled government."

Forty-three years later, the tone of the attacks had changed; no-one accused the opponents of free trade of being Communists or Nazis, a common charge by the coalition of business interests that threw itself into the battle in 1945. But the mobilization of resources by the business community was remarkably similar.

Source:

Graham Fraser, *Playing for Keeps: The Making of the Prime Minister, 1988* (Toronto: McClelland & Stewart, 1989), pp. 325–327. Reprinted by permission.

---

ties in Quebec backed the FTA. Among francophone Quebeckers, 43 percent supported the deal, compared with 36 percent in the rest of Canada. (Only 25 percent of non-francophone Quebeckers were favourable.) For Liberal Premier Robert Bourassa, support for free trade among the emerging elite of francophone entrepreneurs — often called "Québec Inc." — weighed more heavily than the opposition of members of his own party who were close to the federal Liberals. Also, both Bourassa and Mulroney had staked their political future on the Meech Lake constitutional accord, which was popular in Quebec. In

the Parti Québécois, many believed that the FTA would help the cause of Quebec sovereignty, since freer trade with the United States reduces Quebec's economic dependence on Canada.

If given the choice, Brian Mulroney would probably not have called an election on the free-trade issue. But the refusal of the Liberal-controlled Senate to ratify the FTA forced him to cut short his five-year mandate. This election was more dominated by a single issue than any in recent history. The choice was simple: A Progressive Conservative vote was a vote for the FTA; a Liberal or New Democratic Party (NDP) vote was a vote against the deal. On November 21, a majority voted against. Yet, with 43 percent of the vote, the Progressive Conservatives managed to get 169 of the 295 seats in the House of Commons (57 percent), a clear majority, while the Liberals got 83 and the NDP 43. In many ridings, Tories won because anti-FTA votes were split between the Liberals and the NDP. Why did the two parties not co-operate to defeat the Progressive Conservatives if they thought the FTA would be so catastrophic for Canada? Only their former leaders, John Turner and Ed Broadbent, may know for sure. For Turner and Broadbent, however, failure to win this critical election precipitated the end of both their political careers.

Trade Politics in the United States

In the United States, free trade with Canada was not overly divisive, but recently considerable attention has been given to a similar agreement with Mexico. Whereas Canada is rarely seen as a "problem" in the United States, Mexico is a different story, because of issues such as the national debt, drug smuggling, transborder pollution, and illegal immigration. In terms of trade policy, Mexico poses a problem for many U.S. citizens (and for many Canadians) because it is much less developed. The North American Free Trade Agreement (NAFTA) is thus much more politically sensitive in the United States than the FTA was.

In recent years, many U.S. corporations have taken advantage of Mexico's low wages and poorly enforced regulations to set up assembly plants called *maquiladoras*. To accommodate these plants, the Mexican government relaxed restrictions on foreign investment to attract hard currency to pay its large debt to foreign banks, including many U.S. and Canadian ones. These products can be sold for less than goods produced in the United States or Canada because Mexican wages there are dramatically lower than the wages to the north (often less than a dollar per hour), and environmental and work-safety regulations are practically ignored, which again lowers production costs and increases profits. In short, producing goods in Mexico for sale in the United States means big profits for U.S. corporations and low wages (relative to U.S. standards) for Mexicans, along with environmental degradation.

Consequently, NAFTA is strongly opposed by the American Federation of Labor and Congress of Industrial Organizations (AFL–CIO). Although it admits that open trade might help poor Mexican workers, the AFL–CIO fears that this would lead to an irresistible downward pressure on wages and work-safety standards for its own members. Anti-pollution groups are also concerned that the lowest common denominator would prevail in environmental regulation. Similar arguments have been voiced by Canadian opponents of NAFTA. These defensive contenders strike sensitive chords in the U.S. and Canadian publics at a time of high unemployment and unprecedented awareness of environmental issues.

Free trade would benefit large corporations by making it easier to invest in Mexico, and it could benefit banks by helping Mexico to repay its debt. Also, job creation in Mexico might reduce the flow of illegal migrants, which might appeal to those who would like to see less Mexican immigration into their country. A key supporter of free trade with Mexico is the Business Roundtable, which represents the 200 largest U.S. corporations, including banks, manufacturers, and financial companies. It is similar to Canada's BCNI and was active on behalf of the FTA in Canada, as part of the American Coalition for Trade Expansion with Canada (ACTECAN). This coalition was assembled expressly to lobby for the FTA, and the Coalition for North American Trade and Investment (CNATI) does the same for NAFTA.

Pro-NAFTA forces have successfully caught the ear of the pro-business Republican Party, except in areas likely to be hard-hit by jobs lost to Mexico. Democrats are closer to labour and environmental groups, but they nevertheless have been forced to listen to their constituents in Texas and other states who stand to gain from increased exports to Mexico. Power in the U.S. government is divided between the executive branch (the president) and the legislative branch (the Congress), while these two branches are fused together in the Canadian government. Thus, it is hard to predict which way major policy decisions will go, especially when, as was the case between 1981 and 1992, different parties control the two branches. In 1991, the U.S. Congress very narrowly approved the initiation of free-trade talks with Mexico. NAFTA was an important part of the

1992 election campaign and is likely to remain a very contentious issue in U.S. politics.

Trade Politics in Mexico

In Mexico, the move away from protectionism represents perhaps the boldest economic change since the Revolution of 1910. The opening of Mexico to North American trade is part of a broader change toward both economic and political liberalization, but it was also partly prompted by Mexico's need to obtain hard currency to repay its enormous foreign debt.

The Mexican polity is dominated by the Institutional Revolutionary Party (PRI). The combination of one-party rule and state control of the economy has produced a cosy relationship between the PRI and several groups in Mexican society. These groups, who tend to favour the maintenance of trade barriers and investment controls, include owners of protected industries, state-owned corporations, organized labour, small farmers and land owners, and those who work for the government. Many of these contenders, including the Confederation of Mexican Workers (CTM), are affiliated with the PRI, and they have pressed from within the PRI to slow the pace of liberalization. But many others have abandoned the PRI and joined the left coalition of Cuauhtémoc Cárdenas. Cárdenas, capitalizing on his popularity and on the hardship suffered by the disaffected poor, has been able to make inroads in the PRI's political domination.

Many contenders actively seek the opening of the Mexican economy, including large-scale manufacturers and agricultural producers, multinationals operating in Mexico, bankers and owners of financial capital, and some members of the middle class stymied by the political status quo. Large business organizations are very close to the PRI, but they also formed a distinct group, the Businessmen's Co-ordinating Council (CCE), to press for rapid liberalization. Mostly in the north of the country, some of the most dynamic businesses have abandoned the PRI in favour of the National Action Party (PAN), which promotes a pro-business agenda.

Between these contenders and the PRI machine, a key force in the turn to economic openness has been the highly specialized technocrats at the top of the PRI leadership, including the president himself, Carlos Salinas de Gortari, elected in 1988. Like many less developed countries, Mexico had accumulated a huge foreign debt. This foreign debt, in turn, placed serious constraints on the range of economic policy alternatives open to the government. Thus, the decision to push for free trade was very much a top-down decision, and it constituted a dramatic break with the past. Mexico's decision to opt for free trade was forced on it by international conditions — it was a response to the limited options available to a less developed, debtor country in a world economy dominated by a small number of economic superpowers. It was not a decision that evolved from the interests of citizens organized into parties and contenders.

This pattern of political change in response to international forces is common in less developed countries. Also common is the top-down character of decision-making, with contenders and citizens scrambling to make adjustments in a system of limited political contention. Because Mexico is dominated by a single party, much of the debate about free trade and much of the jostling among contenders has been carried on within the PRI.

Lessons from the Contenders

What do these stories about contenders illustrate? First, and perhaps most important, they show what the polity is all about: power. The polity is the realm of power. All the contenders involved in major trade-policy decisions want power. BCNI and the Business Roundtable, for example, want power because they want the government to implement policies that help large corporations thrive in domestic and foreign markets. The CLC and the AFL–CIO want power because they want the government to protect and improve the gains workers in Canada and the United States have made over the last 50 years. In Mexico, contenders for organized labour and business have similar goals, but their relationship with the state is very different because it is largely mediated by the PRI.

The second lesson that these stories illustrate is that the state is a prize, and contenders compete for its control in the arena of power, the polity, by influencing voters and working in and around the major political parties. The 1988 election in Canada shows this most clearly. To win the free-trade battle, contenders had to win the battle for the state, which they fought through the competition between parties.

The third lesson illustrates the diversity of the goals of contenders that may attempt to influence the state. Consider, for example, the very diverse goals defended by opponents of free trade in Canada. The goals of most of these groups were economic, particularly those representing industries seeking to maintain import duties on their products, or the major unions, representing the interests of workers. However, other groups had goals that were more cultural in nature; they wanted to defend the values that they thought make their country distinct from its neighbour. Finally, as is the case for U.S. and Canadian groups opposing NAFTA, political activity on the issue of free trade also can be driven by a concern for the environment.

The fourth lesson is that what matters most in this arena of power are organization and resources. In the Canadian election of 1988, pro–free trade forces were united behind only one party and spent millions of dollars to help elect Progressive Conservative MPs. The anti-FTA forces, by contrast, were divided between two parties and could not convince the leaders of the NDP and Liberal Party to mount a cohesive campaign against free trade. The labour unions and popular groups that composed the Pro-Canada Network could not raise nearly as much money as the FTA supporters, who could tap into the vast resources of the business community. In the arena of power (that is, the polity), the contender that can raise the most cash and motivate the greatest number of people tends to be the most powerful.

Perhaps not as obvious as the above is a fifth lesson: contenders reflect their society. A contender does not succeed simply because of the resources at its disposal. It would not succeed if it did not champion issues considered relevant to many members of society. For example, the proponents of free trade in Canada were able to influence voters to a significant degree because, aside from the intrinsic value of the FTA deal itself, the Canadian public believed that open trade can benefit consumers and that Canada depends on the U.S. market for its exports. To a large ex-

tent, also, support for free trade reflected Canadian society because it was perceived, rightly or wrongly, as a way to assert the power of regions at the expense of the central government. This feeling was conveyed, in the West, by former Alberta Premier Peter Lougheed and, in Quebec, by the pro-sovereignty Parti Québécois and by the autonomist Quebec Liberal Party. In a similar vein, labour unions failed to dominate recent political debates both in Canada and in the United States because they are weak compared with those of many other industrialized countries. In Sweden, for example, the party that champions workers is called the Social Democratic Party, and it is very close to (some would say controlled by) the Swedish labour unions. The Social Democratic Party has been the ruling party in Sweden for most of the post–World War II period. By comparison, Canada has a weak labour movement — labour is allied with the NDP. The United States has an even weaker labour movement. Labour is now a junior partner in the coalition of groups that make up the Democratic Party.

While these stories of contenders illustrate a great deal about the political process, they also provide a glimpse of the structure of the polity. It is the structure of the polity that we consider next.

A Simple Model of the Polity

Figure 14-2 is a simple model of the polity. This figure shows that society has a basic economic and cultural organization that influences and shapes the attitudes and behaviours of individuals. The economic and cultural organization of society is reflected in the existence of diverse economic classes and cultural groups. These different classes and groups provide a basis for the formation of political organizations known as contenders. Contenders attempt to influence political parties, the state, and individuals. People also join and work for political parties. Parties directly influence and participate in the state, in the governing of society. The state has the power to regulate and alter society's economic and cultural organization, and the state may also alter

FIGURE 14-2 A Simple Model of the Canadian Polity

The State			
Political Party	**Political Party**	**Political Party**	**Political Party**
New Democratic Party	Liberal Party	Progressive-Conservative Party	Regional parties, e.g., Reform Party Bloc Québécois
Contender	**Contender**	**Contender**	**Contender**
Offensive	Challenger	Member	Defensive
(e.g., Assembly of First Nations; women's groups)	(e.g., Gay and lesbian groups; minority rights)	(e.g., Canadian Manufacturers Association)	(e.g., Canadian Association of Retired Persons)

Individuals

Shaped by social structure

Social Structure

Economic Aspects (e.g., classes)	Cultural Aspects (e.g., religion or language)

A model of the polity. All the basic units of the polity — state, parties, contenders, individuals, and social structure — influence each other.

the polity. By altering the structure of the polity, the state is able to influence which interests in society will be dominant.

The best way to understand the polity model presented in Figure 14-2 is to consider each of its elements one at a time, starting at the base of the model.

Social Structure

The easiest way to understand social structure is to think of it as having main two parts, economic and cultural. These two major areas of society affect the polity in several ways. They provide a basis for the major conflicts in society, and they are important sources of societal goals.

Societies differ significantly in cultural composition. For example, Canada is culturally diverse: while it is dominated culturally by people of British and French descent, it also includes aboriginal peoples, and almost all the world's major ethnic and national groups are represented in Canadian society. A similar culturally diverse situation ex-

ists in the United States, which is compounded by racial antagonism stemming from its history of slavery. Although we often think of Mexico as a culturally homogeneous society, there are notable differences between descendants of Europeans and indigenous peoples. In each of these societies, such different groups of people have different cultural traditions, which they wish to affirm and protect.

Sometimes, this can lead to conflict between groups. In Quebec, for example, some English-speaking citizens feel threatened by language laws making French the only official language in the province. French-speaking citizens, on the other hand, feel that such policies are justified to safeguard their language and culture in North America. Likewise, they feel strongly that Quebec should be recognized as a distinct society in the Canadian federation, while many people outside of Quebec do not feel that this special status is warranted.

Canadian society is culturally diverse in other ways, besides ethnicity and national origins.

There are groups fighting for sexual freedom (for example, to end discrimination against homosexuals), and there are groups that want to re-establish what they see as "decency." Some groups are trying to improve the status of women, while other groups are trying to protect women's traditional position in society. Another area of cultural conflict concerns life-cycle issues. Many organizations are trying to get recognition from the government of the special rights and needs of the aged, who are among the most vulnerable in modern societies. Others are working to gain greater protection for the young, especially from brutal parents. Still others are trying to protect the "unborn." All these different conflicts are cultural conflicts because they concern visions of what society "ought" to be like, especially with respect to the experiences of those at the most vulnerable stages of the life cycle. These questions involve difficult ethical issues because they concern allocation of scarce resources. To supply the elderly with the best possible health care in their last years of life, for example, might mean that we would have to reduce the quality of health-care services for newborns and young children.

While modern societies differ substantially from each other in cultural composition and value orientations, they are similar in economic composition. All the major industrial countries of the world, for example, have a large working class; a sizable class of technicians and professionals; a large commercial class that distributes, sells, and services the many products of society; and a small class of wealthy individuals who own or control factories, business, banks, and other property and capital.

Similarly, that people who have different economic positions in society also have different political interests is a fact reflected in almost all countries. In most industrialized countries, for example, there are trade unions that strive to protect and promote the interests of workers. These trade unions tend to be politically active and to align themselves with sympathetic political parties (Lipset 1960). In these countries, there are also associations that bring together the owners of the major industrial and financial institutions. These organizations are also politically active, and they generously support parties and politicians who share their views on the economy. In the United

States, these groups are so strong that opposing Democratic and Republican candidates are sometimes supported by the same big-business groups. As a result, no matter which candidate wins, the victor will be indebted to big business. Almost all major economic groups or classes in modern societies are politically active in this way.

Sometimes these groups support contenders that are relatively narrow — for example, the producers of a particular product may form a politically active association. At other times they support broad associations, such as a national chamber of commerce representing business interests. The basic economic issues and economic groups thus tend to be very similar in advanced industrialized countries. Unlike cultural conflicts, these economic conflicts rarely concern what "ought to be" in a moral sense. Most often they concern policy issues that affect the standard of living of different economic classes and groups in society.

So we can say, then, that the position of a person in society's economic and cultural organization shapes the interests he or she is likely to express in the political arena. Cultural interests tend to be shaped as the individual is socialized. Economic interests, in contrast, tend to be shaped by occupation. Individuals carry these different interests with them into the political arena, where contenders and parties compete for their support.

Individuals

Individuals are the raw material of the polity. Individuals influence other individuals; they form and join contenders; they support political parties; and they elect government officials.

At the most microsociological level, individuals affect the political attitudes and behaviours of other individuals. For example, sociologists have learned that most political attitudes are learned at an early age. Therefore, an important part of socialization is **political socialization.** Studies of political behaviour have shown that individuals tend to be strongly influenced by parents, teachers, and their peers. These agents of socialization, together with the mass media, condition the formation of an individual's political preferences, values, and conduct (Landis 1983). At school, for example, children are encouraged to develop pride in a country's political symbols. Canadian children outside of Quebec are taught respect for the queen. Children in the United States pledge allegiance to their flag. In Mexico, the ideals of the 1910 revolution are imparted to children at an early age.

Political socialization is also affected by the context of a person's surroundings. A young person from the Lac Saint-Jean region of Quebec, which has a solid tradition of nationalist politics, might be likely to support Quebec sovereignty. A union member living in an NDP stronghold such as Oshawa, Ontario, will be more likely to support the NDP than the Progressive Conservatives or Liberal Party, but his nonunion neighbour may be just as likely to support the NDP, which he might not do if he lived in a different area. This is a contextual effect, because it is the person's context or social environment that influences his or her political attitudes and behaviour.

Individuals also affect contenders. They can get together and establish an interest organization, or they can donate time or money to an existing organization, from which they can derive a measure of influence and a sense of belonging. In effect, these political organizations provide a sort of buffer between the individual and the state and act as conduit for the flow of interests and information, so both individual and contender benefit. Participation in political parties also provides many of these same benefits for individuals. Political parties also provide a buffer between individuals and the state, and they provide an avenue for direct participation in the governing of society. For many politically active people, participation in the activities of political parties is more rewarding than participation in the activities of issue-oriented political organizations (contenders) because parties are more directly concerned with gaining power as an end in itself. This makes joining parties most attractive to individuals more interested in power itself than in particular issues.

Apart from being able to vote for the candidate of their choice, individuals have relatively little direct influence on the state. Most contact occurs through contenders, such as interest organizations, or through political parties. The most direct contact most people have with the state is paying taxes or receiving services. When government was more local, people had more say in their government. They were more truly self-govern-

The most contact individuals have with the state is through local government.

ing. Over the years, however, local governments have had less and less power. As power has been lost to the federal and provincial governments, people have become less directly self-governing. This is why intermediaries such as political parties and interest organizations have become so important in modern society. It also explains why many have become apathetic — government seems very distant from the average citizen.

Contenders

There are two basic types of contenders: **challengers** and **members**. Challengers are groups that do not have a significant voice in government. Members, on the other hand, are groups that are established contenders; BCNI and the CMA are definitely members. Usually, coalitions of members form governments. These ruling coalitions usually operate through a party (and sometimes through a coalition of parties), dominating the party's policies for extended periods.

The difference between a member and a challenger can be most easily grasped by example: In the past, groups representing Canada's Native peoples did not wield effective power in the Canadian polity. Native leaders felt ostracized and marginalized in Canadian politics. In the past decade, however, Native groups have become more vocal and militant about expressing their political grievances, including land claims and the right to self-government. Now, the Canadian government and all Canadian politicians must pay attention to aboriginal peoples and the issues that affect them. Being recognized by the state is an important sign that a challenger is becoming a member, one who has a voice in the polity.

The most important goal of every challenger is to become a member of the polity. The process of becoming a member is difficult for groups that have interests that strongly conflict with those of established members. In all industrialized countries, for example, working-class organizations such as labour unions had to work very hard to establish membership in the polity. Countless strikes and political demonstrations were necessary before working-class individuals were given the right to form unions or even the right to vote (Bendix 1968).

The process of organizing a new contender (a challenger) and mobilizing people is known as **resource mobilization** (Tilly 1978). In order to challenge an existing power structure, it is necessary for less powerful people to pool their resources (money and time) and to use these resources to gain recognition. When a group engages in a political demonstration, it expends some of its mobilized resources and attempts to attract the attention of government officials and the general public. In a sense, a political demonstration is an "advertisement" of the power of a newly mobilized group, aimed at the state and at the general public.

One problem faced by all contenders, and especially by challengers, is **free riders.** Assume that you are a member of a disadvantaged minority that is now forming an organization to protest the injustices suffered by its members. You have to

decide: Do I want to join this group and participate in its activities? If you are a rational person, you might not join. You will simply hope that the newly mobilized challenger is successful and that the injustices you have been suffering will be remedied. This is a "rational" strategy because you don't lose any of your resources (time, energy, or money). Yet you reap the same benefits as the other members of your minority. You are a free rider. This strategy is rational at the individual level; at the group level, however, it is disastrous. If all members of the disadvantaged minority followed the same logic, the injustices the group has suffered might never be removed. Interest organizations must therefore overcome the free-rider problem. More generally, the free-rider problem is one of the most difficult obstacles that all contenders, but especially challengers, face.

There is another way to distinguish between types of contenders, in addition to the challenger–member distinction (Tilly 1978). Some contenders are primarily defensive contenders, who seek to maintain the status quo, while others are primarily offensive — they want change. Defensive contenders try to protect their positions in society. Contenders who represent major corporations, for example, are primarily defensive. They do not want their favoured position to be challenged in any way. An offensive contender, on the other hand, is one who pushes for change. In Canada, as we saw in the free-trade story, the Business Council for National Issues was an offensive (change-oriented) contender because its members endorsed a very profound transformation of Canada's international economic policy. Some critics have argued, moreover, that the free-trade deal with the United States was a way to lock the Canadian state into the kind of pro-business policies that BCNI favoured.

To some extent, challengers tend to be change oriented, and members status quo oriented, but there are significant exceptions. Contenders representing the interests of Native peoples, for example, are now members, yet they continue to push for changes in Canadian society and reduce tensions in their relationships with other Canadians. Also, to some extent, the business groups that pushed for free trade in Canada were change-oriented contenders, because they sought change beyond a status quo in which they were already advantaged. There are also defensive challengers. Challenging groups sometimes form in response to changes being forced on them by government. For example, protected industries opposed to free trade joined together and organized a response to this threat.

Political Parties

Parties emerged in nineteenth-century Canada out of groups representing opposing interests (or contenders): English-Canadian big-business "Tories" allied with conservative "Bleus" from Quebec versus the reformist "Grits" allied with anticlerical "Rouges." After Confederation, these coalitions developed into national parties, the Conservatives and Liberals, that attempted to represent a broad spectrum of interests. Despite persistent regional and linguistic differences in their bases of support, these two parties still sought to appeal to all regions, classes, and ethnic and religious groups (Thornburn 1985). In the United States, similar broad coalitions of interests and factions emerged around two parties, the Republicans and the Democrats, despite George Washington's concern that parties would corrupt the democratic process. He feared that with the development of parties, political representatives would vote according to the dictates of their parties rather than the dictates of their consciences.

However, the fact that parties have emerged and become a fact of life in virtually all democratic countries indicates that they play a crucial role in the polity. The primary goal of parties is to seek the powers of electoral office, that is, to form the government. But parties, whether in government or opposition, also increase the integration of the polity. Unlike contenders, parties do not generally push one issue or the interests of only one group. Rather, successful parties are those that are able to persuade different groups in society to join together and reconcile their different interests in a common agenda or platform. This encourages compromise and moderation. If the polity consisted only of different contenders trying to get all that they could for their members, it would be in perpetual turmoil. Also, when parties go before the public and seek their votes, candidates for office must defend the party's program. By defending a coherent platform, parties force individual voters to consider the good of the country as a whole rather than their own separate interests. This helps to reduce conflict in the polity and in society.

Some political analysts, however, argue that political parties are in decline and that their role in the polity is being undermined. They point to the increase in the influence of interest groups, bureaucrats, and the electronic media. In Canada, the growing importance and complexity of federal–provincial negotiations also threaten the effectiveness of party politics (Meisel 1985). There has also been a recent surge in single-issue contenders (such as the antinuclear groups) that seem to do a better job than do parties of getting people involved in politics. Another frequently heard criticism is that the major parties, both in Canada and in the United States, are "out of touch" with ordinary people and that the interests and goals of the major parties are so similar that they do not offer effective alternatives to voters. Cynics wonder if parties matter, after all — whether it really makes a difference if "Tweedledum" or "Tweedledee" is in power.

There is some truth to these charges. In some countries, such as those of continental Europe, where proportional representation allows even small parties to win government seats, voters are presented with a variety of parties offering many positions on issues. In Canada and the United States, the major parties attempt to take broad, moderate positions to appeal to as many voters as possible. However, there are some important exceptions to this general pattern. As the 1988 Canadian election showed, a crucial issue like free trade can rivet the attention of voters and polarize support for parties. Likewise, at the provincial level, the election of the Parti Québécois in 1976 served as a potent reminder of a party's power to formulate and promote a distinct agenda for change. In the United States, the two major parties diverge somewhat in their bases of support and the attitudes of their supporters. The Democrats tend to attract working-class and ethnic voters and those that favour government programs to promote economic and social justice. Republicans, on the other hand, tend to draw their support from those who are better off, who have more traditional economic and social views (regardless of their economic well-being), and who oppose further government intervention in the economy.

The Canadian party system may be more effective in representing divergent positions because it includes viable parties as well as the two major parties. The most successful of these has been the NDP, which originally began as the Co-operative Commonwealth Federation (CCF), an agrarian reform coalition in western Canada that later allied itself with the labour movement. The NDP was unequivocal in its opposition to free trade in 1988 because of the perceived threat to Canadian jobs and social programs. The social-democratic NDP espouses a substantial role for the government in the redistribution of wealth and believes that the state is responsible for providing full social protection for its citizens. Although most of the NDP's social programs were implemented by Liberal governments, the NDP was instrumental in focusing the public's attention on the need for such reforms. It has been less successful in obtaining political power, partly because the major parties have been able to cut into its potential support, and also because of the constraints of the Canadian electoral system. We will discuss these constraints more fully later.

The Mexican polity differs from its northern neighbours in that it has been dominated, for much of this century, by a single political party, the Institutional Revolutionary Party (PRI). PRI candidates have repeatedly been elected by wide majorities to the presidency (limited to one term), and the party has consistently dominated the national legislature. The dominance of the PRI has created a situation in which the party and the state are nearly fused into one. Indeed, if the party controls the state bureaucracy, it is also true that the state bureaucrats control the party. For example, the current president, Carlos Salinas de Gortari, is a product of the bureaucracy, in which he rose as a *técnico* (technocrat), before he was elected in 1988 with 51 percent of the vote.

In recent years, despite the recurrence of electoral fraud, alternative parties have come to the fore and captured a significant portion of the electorate. In the 1988 presidential election, the National Democratic Front (a coalition of leftist parties) presented a candidate, Cuauhtémoc Cárdenas, who sought to hold back the market-liberalization efforts of the Salinas government. As the son of the legendary 1930s president, Lázaro Cárdenas, his name lent him much political clout, enough to collect an impressive 31 per-

cent of the "official" votes. The opposition to the PRI is divided, however, because another party, the National Action Party (PAN), which seeks accelerated liberalization of the economy, received 17 percent of the presidential votes.

The 1991 election to the Chamber of Deputies confirmed the PRI's firm grip on state power: it won 290 of the 300 seats open to direct suffrage and 30 of the 200 seats distributed proportionally to all parties. The opposition charged that this victory was due to electoral fraud, which has always been alleged to contribute to PRI victories. Gradually, the Mexican polity is becoming more open, notably in terms of freedom to criticize the government, but much room for reform remains. To remain dominant, the PRI will need to implement its political and economic reforms successfully, while not arousing too much discontent among the beneficiaries of the corruption that so often accompanies the fusion of state and party institutions.

The State

The polity is an arena where contenders compete for the ultimate prize, the state. It is rare that a single contender wins the prize. Usually, contenders hope just to participate in the making of national policy and legislation. In Karl Marx's scenario of the polity in capitalist countries, the contenders representing working-class interests ultimately win possession of the state. Even in the few remaining communist countries, however, many interest groups participate in the formulation of national policy. In modern societies (noncommunist and communist), the production of laws and policies requires input from many groups.

The state is the dominant institution of society because it has a monopoly on the legitimate use of physical coercion. This monopoly is important, because a key function of the state is to maintain order. However, excessive use of physical coercion — through the police, for example — can generate strong opposition to the state and require the use of even more physical coercion. If at all possible, the state tries to accomplish its objectives without using too much direct physical coercion.

While the state has a monopoly on physical coercion, it often allows other actors and institutions in society to use it within set limits. Parents, for example, are allowed to coerce their children. Bouncers are allowed to remove unruly patrons from bars. Religious groups are allowed to sanction members, and members accept sanctions as part of the cost of belonging to the group. Over time, however, the state has placed greater limits on the right of groups and individuals to use coercion. Child abuse has become a major issue, for example, and governments have started to crack down on child abusers.

The state regulates society; it also regulates the polity. The state can legitimize the rights of certain contenders. Since 1982, for example, the Canadian Charter of Rights and Freedoms has guaranteed the rights of linguistic minorities, women, and Native peoples. However, the state can also choose to declare certain contenders illegal. During the "October Crisis" of 1970, the Canadian government invoked the War Measures Act to summarily arrest individuals in Quebec on the basis of their association with pro-independence or leftist organizations, although they had done nothing illegal. The federal government defended its actions by claiming that these individuals were conspiring to overthrow the Quebec government, although no evidence has been shown to this effect. In the United States, the Smith Act made any conspiracy to advocate the violent overthrow of the government a criminal act. Although this clearly limits the freedom of speech guaranteed by the First Amendment to the U.S. Constitution, the Supreme Court has ruled that the state was justified in protecting its position as the ultimate power in society, even if it must violate its own laws to do so. These examples reveal the contradictions inherent in the exercise of power in a democracy.

Beside attempting to regulate contenders, the state also regulates all aspects of the political process. Individual voters are required to meet specific age and citizenship requirements. For a long time, bars were closed during polling time on election day in Canada. The activities of parties are carefully monitored by the state as well. Each party and candidate for office in Canada is required to file a financial report. Financial contributions to parties are regulated, and there are strict controls on how these funds may be raised or spent. The amount spent and the time allocated for campaign advertising are also subject to certain limits. Through these and other measures, the state sets the terms of political competition and restricts the activities of contenders, parties, and individuals in the polity.

State Structures and Political Processes

We have seen that the state regulates the polity — for example, by restricting how much money can be spent in a campaign. Perhaps less obvious is the fact that a country's constitution also sets limits on the polity and how it may change (Bendix 1968). Many countries, for example, have systems of proportional representation (PR). In PR systems, parties receive seats in the national legislature in direct proportion to the number of votes they receive nationwide. For example, if a Marxist–Leninist party won 1 percent of the votes in Canada, in a PR system it would receive 1 percent of the seats in Parliament. In Mexico, 200 of the 500 seats in the Chamber of Deputies are assigned by proportional representation. The Canadian and U.S. polities, however, do not have PR. Instead, a system of **single-member, simple-plurality** electoral districts (SMSP) is used. In SMSP systems, only one candidate per party may run in an electoral district, and the candidate who wins the greatest number of votes wins the seat for that district in the legislature. This is often referred to as the "first past the post" or "winner take all" system, since a candidate need only have a plurality, not a majority, of the votes cast in order to win. This is why, as we saw earlier in the 1988 Canadian federal election, free-trade opponents complained that the Progressive Conservative Party managed to get a majority of seats in the House of Commons with only a minority of the actual votes.

To the extent that democratic institutions are those that express the "will of the people," PR systems are more democratic than SMSP systems because there is a direct connection between the party preferences expressed by voters and the party composition of the national legislature. In SMSP systems, a party could win less than a majority in every electoral district (say, 34 percent of the vote in close three-way races), but win 100 percent of the seats in the national legislature. Thus, two-way races tend to dominate in each electoral district in SMSP systems, and minor parties get shoved aside; there is no point in voting for them. It is clear, however, that there are more than two national agendas possible, and that many voters become disillusioned by the narrow choices they are offered. In this way, SMSP systems not only discourage new parties from forming and small parties from growing, they also discourage disaffected voters from participating.

The United States is a classic case in this regard. It has evolved into a nearly perfect two-party system where minor parties have almost no impact at the federal level. Minor parties do run candidates, but they have a harder time getting recognition or actual votes because their chances of winning are so small. In 1992, even the popular multibillionaire Ross Perot bowed out of an attempt to run for president as an independent because he could not overcome the obstacles to

outsiders built into the American two-party system. However, the Mexican case shows that a PR system does not necessarily translate into a genuine multiparty system, as it does in many European countries. The powerful PRI has dominated both presidential and legislative elections in Mexico for most of this century, even after the 1977 electoral reform that instituted a partial PR system. On the other hand, a SMSP system does not necessarily rule out the presence of effective third parties. In Canada, "third parties" have consistently challenged the two-party system (see Figure 14-3).

The reasons for the success of third parties in Canada despite a SMSP system have to do with other structural aspects of the Canadian polity.

FIGURE 14-3   Political Parties in Canadian Federal Elections

Party Names	Period	Number Contested	Average Percentage of Votes
Liberals	1878–1988	31	43.5
Conservatives	1878–1988	31	43.0
Co-operative Commonwealth Federation/ New Democratic Party	1935–1988	17	14.7
National Progressives	1921–1930	4	10.0
Reconstruction	1935	1	8.7
Social Credit	1935–1988	17	4.5
Créditistes	1962–1968	2	4.5
Bloc Populaire	1945	1	3.6
Patrons of Industry	1891–1896	2	2.2
Reform Party	1988	1	2.1
McCarthyites	1896	1	2.0
Labour Party	1900–1940	11	1.0
Christian Heritage	1988	1	0.8
Parti Nationaliste	1984	1	0.7
Communist Party	1921; 1930–1988	19	0.5
Confederation of Regions	1984–1988	2	0.4
Rhinoceros Party	1979–1988	4	0.3
Greens	1984–1988	2	0.3
Union Populaire	1979–1980	2	0.2
Libertarians	1979–1988	4	0.1
Party for Commonwealth	1984–1988	2	0.1

SOURCE: Thomas Mackie and Richard Rose, *International Almanac of Electoral Politics* (London: Macmillan, 1984); Government of Canada, *Report of the Chief Electoral Officer*, 1984, 1988.

Unlike the United States, Canada is a parliamentary system based on party discipline and responsible government. The head of the government, the prime minister, is the leader of the party that wins the most seats in the House of Commons. When there is no clear majority of seats, the government must depend on the support of a smaller party, which is said to hold the "balance of power." The NDP, for example, has played this balancing role in the past by supporting the Liberal Party. In return, it pressed the Liberals to endorse some aspects of its own program of social reforms. Party discipline holds the parliamentary system together because a governing party requires its members to vote together. This means that groups or individuals in fundamental disagreement with the major parties' platforms will tend to look for representation outside of them. In the United States, where legislators are less bound by such requirements, mainstream parties have been able to more effectively absorb and often neutralize divergent elements.

The other important structural factor that influences political representation is the nature of Canadian federalism. Both Canada and the United States are federal systems, which means that governing powers are divided between the central and the provincial or state governments. The federal system in the United States has evolved into a centralized one dominated by the national government. Canadian federalism is still evolving and is now more decentralized and characterized by power-sharing between the federal and provincial governments. While the federal government still retains important powers, the provinces are increasingly exercising autonomy in many areas of jurisdiction (Landes 1983). Canadian federalism affects political representation because it gives an important voice to regional issues and concerns. The Canadian party system began as a coalition of regional interests, and today regionalism remains an important political factor in elections. Federalism also reinforces the influence of regionally based protest movements. Almost all the third parties that have been influential at the federal level began as regionally based movements. In addition, third parties, such as the Social Credit Party and the NDP, have successfully formed governments in several provinces.

Compared with the United States and Mexico, there is more wide open political competition in Canada, especially at the level of political parties. Despite the constraints of the SMSP system, there are three strong parties in many areas of Canada and a good deal of local variation as well. The United States conforms closely to the dictates of the SMSP model: competition is largely restricted to two parties, and these two parties seek the support of overlapping portions of the mainstream of voters. In Mexico, despite a partial PR system, the PRI remains dominant — a legacy of its association with the Mexican Revolution and the party's continued grip on political spoils. Basically, the PRI is "the best game in town," even if it is not the only game. Figure 14-4, which shows recent election results in the three North American countries, offers a snapshot of the levels and types of political competition.

The best way to understand the impact of political structures on the polity is to consider how national politics might change if, overnight, the SMSP system were swept away and replaced with a PR system. Would allegiance to the three strongest parties in Canada (or the two in the United States, or the PRI in Mexico) crumble? Would more people vote? What kind of small party might attract your support? How would national policy be influenced by a new party that put the environment first in its national agenda (as does the Green Party in Germany) or a new party that put women's issues first (as has occurred in Iceland)?

Theoretical Perspectives

The three major sociological perspectives are all relevant to the study of the polity. Each perspective emphasizes a different part of the polity model presented in Figure 14-2, because each perspective starts with fundamentally different assumptions about people and about society.

Structural Functionalism

The structural-functionalist perspective assumes that the social order is natural and that the purpose of the state is simply to maintain and regulate the natural order that already exists. This natural order exists, according to this perspective, because members of society agree in their

FIGURE 14-4   Election Results, Canada, United States, and Mexico, 1988

Country	Party (leader)	Percentage of Votes
Canada (federal)	Progressive Conservative Party (Brian Mulroney)	43.0
	Liberal Party (John Turner)	31.9
	New Democratic Party (Edward Broadbent)	20.4
	Reform Party (Preston Manning)	2.1
	Others[1]	
United States (presidential)	Republican Party (George Bush)	53.4
	Democratic Party (Michael Dukakis)	45.6
	Libertarian (Ron Paul)	0.5
	New Alliance (Lenora Fulani)	0.2
	Others[2]	
Mexico (presidential)	Institutional Revolutionary Party/Partido Revolucionario Institucional (Carlos Salinas de Gortari)	50.4
	National Democratic Front[3]/Frente Democrático Nacional (Cuauhtémoc Cárdenas)	31.1
	National Action Party/Partido Acción Nacional (Manuel Clouthier)	17.1
	Others[4]	

[1]In order of support: Christian Heritage, Rhinoceros, Greens, Confederation of Regions, Libertarians, Commonwealth, Social Credit.
[2]In order of support: Populist (D. Duke), Consumer (E. McCarthy), American Independent (J. Griffith), Independent (L. LaRouche), Right to Life (W. Marra), and ten other minor candidates.
[3]This was a leftist coalition of three parties: Authentic Party of the Mexican Revolution (PARM); Popular Socialist Party (PPS); and Socialist Workers' Party (PST).
[4]Mexican Democratic Party: 1.0%; Mexican Socialist Party: 0.4%.
SOURCE: Government of Canada, *Report of the Chief Electoral Officer 1988*, appendix A, p. 19; *Congressional Quarterly Weekly Report*, January 21, 1989, p. 139; *The New York Times*, July 15, 1988, p. 3.

basic values. Structural functionalists call this basic agreement value consensus. Among the basic agreements that make up this value consensus, for example, is the agreement that the state has a legitimate monopoly on the use of physical coercion in society.

The state at times must use physical coercion to co-ordinate the different parts of society. While this unequal distribution of power might be seen as something that would disrupt society's natural order, structural functionalists argue that because the state implements societal goals, its use of force is seen as necessary and legitimate. Inequities in the distribution of power are recognized as necessary by members of society because all members benefit from these inequities. In other words, people submit to the authority of the state because they realize that society will benefit from the co-ordination the state supplies.

An important part of the structural-functionalist argument is the notion that the state must be a reflection of society. The state must reflect society because one of its major functions is to implement the values of society — the state achieves society's goals. If, for example, there were substantial agreement in society that all sexual discrimination should be eliminated, then the state would try to accomplish this goal. Similarly, if there were substantial agreement in society that military involvements with other countries should be avoided, then the state would try to avoid situations (such as dependence on the natural resources of potentially hostile countries) that might encourage the use of military force.

If the state is to achieve society's goals, it must have some way of knowing what these goals are. This is, according to the structural functionalists, the function of the polity. They argue that democracy is an especially good system for transmitting the goals of society to the state (Lipset 1960). Democracy allows members of society to participate in the selection of government officials and thereby provides an avenue for the expression of public interests and goals. Democracy, more than any other system, they reason, forces the state to be sensitive to society. Because it is sensitive, it can implement society's goals.

Because structural functionalists see the state and the polity in this way, they are interested in only certain parts of the polity model presented in Figure 14-2. Of paramount importance to them is how individuals communicate their desires to the state and how the state implements the goals of society. Therefore, structural functionalists are most interested in the flow of information from individuals through contenders and political parties to the state, and in the actions taken by the state to implement society's goals. If groups in society feel left out, they reason, it must be because of some communication failure, and the access of these groups to the state must be improved.

Structural functionalists believe that the state will implement policies that provide the greatest good for the greater number if it has sufficient knowledge of people's concerns and needs. They also believe that people will go along with whatever the state does as long as they continue to believe that the state is acting in everyone's best interests.

The Conflict Perspective

The conflict perspective, in contrast, assumes that order is not natural and that it must be imposed by some agency, such as the state, which has the legitimate authority to regulate the use of violence in society (Weber 1947). Structural functionalists assume that value consensus is natural; conflict theorists assume that value and goal conflict is inevitable. When conflict theorists look at society, they see economic classes with incompatible economic interests and cultural groups with incompatible cultural goals. The state, according to this perspective, tries to prevent the seemingly inevitable clash of these very different segments of society by maintaining its authority as the regulator of the use of violence.

Conflict theories do not argue that this difficult task of maintaining order in society is accomplished by the state in an impartial manner. They see the state as necessarily biased in favour of the dominant economic groups in society. The state

sides with these groups because it is the most rational course of action available to the state (Mills 1956). If the state tried to enact policies than ran counter to the interests of these groups, it would have a difficult time enforcing its policies. After all, these groups control resources (such as revenue) that the state needs. A manufacturer can expand overseas, for example, if it is unhappy with the economic climate fostered by the state. The state does not have sufficient resources to combat these groups.

These groups were the focus of John Porter's influential study of economic, political, bureaucratic, and ideological elites in Canadian society (Porter 1965). He found that each elite group fulfilled specific functions in society. They were not fully autonomous from each other, nor were they in constant conflict. Rather, these elites tended to be very homogeneous in terms of their social background and shared values, and they were able to reach accommodation through a "confraternity of power." Porter concluded that this confraternity was dominated by economic elites, especially the "corporate" elite, which consisted of the largest and most important business and financial institutions in Canada.

In the Marxist version of conflict theory, the state is seen as not only dominated by powerful economic elites, it is also considered a tool of these wealthiest members of society: those who own factories, banks, and other businesses (Marx 1967). For example, Wallace Clement (1975) suggested that the corporate elite in Canada is able to impose its capitalist values and interests through its control of the Canadian state. Marxist theory sees the state as an institution that makes capitalism possible. The state attempts to foster favourable economic conditions in which capitalism can flourish. It protects the corporate elite from the potentially rebellious masses by providing police and security services and by offering the masses social services, such as welfare and unemployment benefits, to weather economic downturns.

How can a society with a democratic political system allow the state to favour the interests of the rich and powerful? Conflict theorists have little trouble with this question. From their perspective, the major political parties in Canada and the United States would be considered essentially moderate parties that support the existing distribution of power and wealth. Conflict theorists also contend that the political process is a sham; no matter which party gets into office, it will have to pay attention to the wishes of the rich and powerful. This has been true even for governments formed by parties sympathetic to labour in certain Canadian provinces, for example the NDP in British Columbia and Ontario. Conflict theorists also note that, more often than not, a political party needs powerful and wealthy backers to get elected. Once elected, government officials may be pressured to enact policies consistent with the interests of their backers. Conflict theorists argue, finally, that the political process itself is not only a sham, but also an empty ritual, existing only to give the powerless a feeling of participation. This feeling of having participated in the selection of government officials helps to keep the powerless from rising up and overthrowing the government.

Most conflict theorists have little faith in electoral democracy. They see it as part of a system of oppression, not as a mechanism for transmitting the interests of individuals to the state. Therefore, they are concerned with only certain parts of the polity model in Figure 14-2. Essentially, conflict theorists are interested in how powerful groups control the state and how the state keeps the powerless in line.

Symbolic Interaction

The symbolic-interactionist perspective assumes that order can be natural or unnatural. According to this perspective, social order is "problematic" because different groups in society see the world very differently. The process of socialization is central to the symbolic interactionist perspective. Socialization occurs mostly at the group level, where the individual internalizes organized attitudes; these organized attitudes are called the "generalized other." The generalized other that is internalized varies from one group to the next. The generalized other that an upper-class Yorkville Torontonian internalizes, for example, is very different from that internalized by a fisherman in an Acadian village in New Brunswick. Because of these differences in socialization experiences, different groups in society develop different world views. Social order in society is therefore problematic because society is actually composed of many different societies, each with

its own understanding of the world, of what's fair, of what's right and wrong.

One insight relevant to the polity suggested by the interactionist perspective concerns the relationship between social cohesion and what George Herbert Mead (1934) called "the hostile attitude." Mead noted that groups adopting a hostile attitude toward other groups or individuals are more cohesive than those that do not. He pointed out, for example, that in everyday situations, when the topic of a group's discussion shifts from the admirable qualities of someone whom the group likes to the qualities of someone the group dislikes, a feeling of oneness quickly emerges in the group. Mead was deeply troubled by this phenomenon because its prevalence suggested that society would always be composed of groups held together by their hostility toward other groups. He also used this argument to explain why nations are so easily drawn into war.

Another insight provided by the symbolic-interactionist perspective concerns the use of symbols. Interactionists consider social reality to be a symbolic reality, and they treat communication as "symbolic interaction." The use of powerful symbolic phrases is very important in the political arena. Contenders, parties, and politicians must use such phrases skilfully if they are to survive.

Consider the example of semantic manipulation in the opposition between "pro-life" and "pro-choice" forces in the debate over abortion. The two groups are on opposite sides of the abortion issue, yet both present themselves as being for something that people value — life and choice. An important contender in the debate over the FTA, the Pro-Canada Network, also made intensive use of symbols to rally public opinion against free trade. Of course, it was trying to imply that supporters of free trade with the United States were, somehow, "anti-Canada." Perhaps an even more blatant example of symbolic manipulation is the use of the Mexican Revolution as an enduring symbol by political leaders in Mexico who contend that any reform of the established order betrays the spirit of the revolution that institutionalized the present system. The symbolic manipulation of the revolution by partisans of the status quo has long been evident in the name of the dominant party itself, which simultaneously evokes these two ideas: the Partido Revolucionario Institucional (Institutional Revolutionary Party). Political analysts argue that the successful manipulation of symbols is important to success in politics.

The symbolic-interactionist perspective, like the other two, emphasizes only certain parts of the polity model in Figure 14-2. It emphasizes the effects of social structure on individuals (socialization) and the ways in which the state, parties, and contenders influence individuals by using symbolic phrases and images. What is lacking most in the interactionist perspective is an understanding of the polity as a system of power and domination.

The Modern Polity

Now that we understand what the polity is and does, let us discuss where the modern polity came from and where it is going. There are two basic arguments concerning the development of the modern polity. The first, based on the structural-functionalist perspective, emphasizes political modernization. The second, based on the conflict perspective, emphasizes **modernizing revolutions.**

Political Modernization

The political-modernization view of the development of the modern polity emphasizes the importance of democracy in making possible both economic growth and social stability. Supporters of this argument assert that the two forces, democratization and economic development, build upon each other. If economic development occurs in the absence of democracy, the polity is likely to become unstable because economic changes, such as those associated with industrialization, are seen as disruptive. Only certain kinds of political systems can handle the disruption that these changes bring. Democracy is best suited for this task because it is a resilient system; it can absorb the new groups generated by economic changes, and it provides important channels for the expression of social frustrations. In short, democracy preserves stability by adjusting the polity and making it reflect society (Lipset 1960).

When the supporters of this argument look at the history of the advanced countries of North America and Western Europe over the past several hundred years, they find support for their arguments. Originally, these countries were undemocratic. As they began to experience economic development, they became unstable. New economic groups such as merchants and artisans (and, much later, workers) began to push for social change. These new groups eventually forced the political system to open up and enact democratic measures. This process culminated in universal adult suffrage, the right of all adult citizens to vote in national elections. Even working-class individuals without property were given the opportunity to participate in the polity. By 1900, most adult males in Canada and the United States were eligible to vote. Universal suffrage, however, came later. In Canada, for example, women were not permitted to vote in federal elections until 1918, and Native peoples were not formally extended this right until 1960. Women in the United States were only allowed to vote in national elections after 1919, and Native Americans after 1924. Moreover, effective voting rights for all black Americans were not enforced until 1965.

Some supporters of this argument have suggested that democracy may even promote economic development. Because democracy accompanied the industrialization of Europe and North America, they reason, it may be one of the forces that spurred industrialization in these countries. This leads to the conclusion that contemporary underdeveloped countries should adopt democratic institutions if they hope to achieve significant economic development. Few underdeveloped countries have adopted democracy with great success, however. Generally, the democracies that have been established in underdeveloped countries have not lasted very long. The alternative perspective on the development of the modern polity, which emphasizes modernizing revolutions, offers an explanation of why this is so.

Modernizing Revolutions

Supporters of the modernizing-revolutions view on the development of the modern polity adhere to a conflict model of the polity. That is, they believe that the state is dominated by the most powerful groups in society. It makes little difference, according to this argument, whether a polity is democratic or not. What matters most is which groups control the state.

Groups that control the state are, of course, very reluctant to relinquish any of their control. In fact, because the state is such a prize, those who control the state will fight to maintain their power. According to the modernizing-revolutions argument, therefore, if a new and powerful group in society wants to gain control of the state, it must first overthrow existing power groups by way of a modernizing revolution.

When supporters of this perspective look at the past several hundred years of European and North American history, they too find support for their arguments. Several European countries, as well as the United States, have experienced a modernizing revolution. A modernizing revolution is a special kind of revolution. Most revolutions simply change the individuals in power, and the basic power groups controlling the state remain the same. A modernizing revolution accomplishes much more than this. It removes antimodern power groups and replaces them with a coalition of pro-development groups (Moore 1966).

According to this argument, Great Britain experienced the first of the world's modernizing revolutions. The English Civil War ended royal absolutism in Britain and brought new power to landed aristocrats (who were beginning to produce goods for national and international markets) and to merchants. After commercial interests gained the upper hand in the polity, Britain became economically dominant in the world. The French Revolution brought similar changes to French society, and the French grew strong enough economically and militarily after their revolution in 1789 to challenge the British in the world economy. The United States also had a modernizing revolution, the American Civil War. This war defeated the antimodern slave society of the South, and allowed northern commercial interests to dominate the country after 1865. All of these modernizing revolutions brought to power groups that were committed to economic development. The important point is that it took revolutions to bring them to power. Once in power, they were able to take control of the economy and shape it according to their interests (Moore 1966).

The modernizing-revolutions argument suggests that similar revolutions may be necessary in underdeveloped countries, to the extent that their polities are dominated by groups opposed to economic development, before these countries will experience such development. In some underdeveloped countries, for example, the groups in power are landowners who produce agricultural goods sold internationally. These groups may oppose industrialization because it might bring about changes that would disrupt their power. Supporters of the modernizing-revolutions perspective would argue that countries such as these will not have economic development until revolutions overthrow these power groups and replace them with pro-development groups. Mexico is an interesting case, because its modernizing revolution was, in many ways, incomplete.

In Mexico, the road to modernization has been long. Spanish domination until the Wars of Independence (1810–21) left no democratic tradition, and Mexico was ruled by a succession of *caudillos* (strong men) throughout the nineteenth century. There was an interval of somewhat liberal rule under Benito Juárez (1858–72), but the century ended with the ruthless dictatorship of Porfirio Díaz (1876–1910). Then, modernization was blocked by the political domination of the church and the army, while the economy was dominated by foreign companies. The excesses of the Díaz regime led a coalition of working-class and middle-class groups to seek a violent overthrow of the government and a transformation of the state.

The Mexican Revolution began in 1910 with a violent struggle for the control of the central state that consecrated heroes such as Pancho Villa and Emiliano Zapata. Although the central state had not fully secured power in all regions, the turmoil ended in 1917. The 1917 Constitution nationalized natural resources and gave the modernizing forces — workers, the middle classes, and the local bourgeoisie — a political voice. But the state was not strong enough to fully implement modernizing reforms against the resistance of premodern groups. Rather than open the system to democratic competition, modernizing forces rallied behind a single party, which became the PRI in 1946. The party effectively mobilized and integrated the working class and peasants in its political organizations. However, after the Cárdenas regime of 1928–34, these groups were increasingly left behind by an economic-development strategy that produced growth, but at the expense of increasing inequality and international economic dependence. As the discussion of Mexico's move toward free trade showed, even if parts of the bourgeoisie benefited from this strategy, it became a drag on the development of other sectors of business. Whether the push for economic liberalization will allow Mexico to take the final step toward true democratization and multiparty competition, however, is still an open question (Rueschemeyer, Stephens, and Stephens 1992).

The popular image we have of democracy is that it is the best of all political systems and that it is responsible for prosperity. The conflict perspective challenges this view by suggesting that the revolutionary overthrow of antimodern groups, not democracy, is the key to prosperity. While the conflict perspective is as much a partial view of the world as the structural-functionalist view, it is important to be able to see society from these different points of view.

Conclusion

This chapter presented the polity as the arena of power, where the interests of individuals and groups are channelled and confronted in a contest whose prize is the control of the state. This contest ultimately determines not only who gets what, but also the direction taken by society as a whole. The decision taken by the three national governments of North America to move toward free trade is a good illustration of this. In Canada, free trade will affect both the distribution of wealth and power within society and the overall direction of its future. Some people fear that economic integration with the United States could make Canada vulnerable to the same kinds of problems that ail American society, such as inequality, violence, and a limited access to social services. But others point out that without the sustained growth that free trade can potentially bring, Canadians may not be able to afford the social programs that they have long taken for granted. In the contest to determine the direction taken by society, contenders strive to promote the interests of those whom they represent, while po-

litical parties seek to convince voters that they offer the best solutions and the best people to implement them. As we have seen, the whole "game" is conditioned by rules embedded in the institutions of the state.

The example we have chosen to illustrate the interplay of contenders is also a good illustration of how the three sociological approaches apply to the study of the polity. Structural functionalists would argue that the three governments' decisions to opt for continental free trade is in fact a rational and predictable response to the increasing globalization of the world economy. Even if there is resistance in society, this perspective would maintain that North American continental integration is in the best long-term interest of each society as a whole. As states in Europe and East Asia are also moving in a similar direction, this argument would seem credible. For conflict theorists, however, the same decisions can be understood as the result of the imbalance of power in these societies in favour of those who could benefit most from more open markets. Proponents of this approach would certainly cite the huge amounts of money spent during the 1988 Canadian election campaign by pro–free-trade businesses in support of their argument.

Finally, because it was so difficult for individual Canadians to sort out what free trade meant for their own self-interest, the free-trade debate can also be analyzed from the standpoint of symbolic interaction. Symbols of Canadian nationalism were used (some would say abused) by both sides in the free-trade campaign. Free traders defended their position by projecting an assertive image of firms and workers able to compete with the best in the world. Opponents presented a gloomier image as they warned Canadians that what made their nation distinct from its giant neighbour would be threatened by a "capitulation" to American economic and cultural power. For the Canadian public, these images almost cancelled each other out. Quebec nationalists, however, reacted much differently. Proponents of Quebec sovereignty joined with those who simply sought more power for Quebec within Canada in supporting free trade. Perhaps because they felt more culturally secure, especially given their distinct language, Quebec nationalists felt that free trade would loosen the grip of the federal state on Quebec society.

The mention of Quebec nationalism also reminds us that the Canadian polity is confronted with other challenges, in addition to changes in the world economy. Despite efforts by successive Canadian governments to integrate Canadian society into a cohesive entity, the reconciliation between the structure of the polity and societal differences has remained problematic. Since 1990, the failure to ratify the Meech Lake agreement, which would have recognized officially the distinct status of Quebec in the Canadian federation, has reactivated the fervour of partisans of Quebec sovereignty. Some analysts argue that Quebec nationalism will find a way to express itself within federalism (Dion 1992), but others maintain that the turn toward sovereignty is irreversible (Weaver 1992). In the end, whichever direction Quebec takes, the societies and polities in Quebec and the rest of Canada will still face the challenges of coexisting under some form of political arrangement.

Of course, the Canadian polity is not alone in facing difficult challenges. With the implementation of the Single European Act and the debates on the treaty of Maastricht in 1992, Western European states are opening their markets and societies to an unprecedented degree. This may become problematic for smaller states, whose populations may fear the dominance of the newly reunited Germans. In the United States, the dismantling of the Soviet bloc and the end of the Cold War has left that society in search of a rallying political direction. Americans emerge from their "victory" with a troubled industrial economy, a sense of despair bred by poverty and racial tensions in the inner cities, and the personal insecurity that stems from such problems as the astronomical cost of medical care without affordable insurance. These and other issues have made American society turn inward, and they are testing the ability of its polity to meet domestic challenges. Mexico shares a challenge with many other polities in Latin America and many other less developed countries: to reconcile rapid liberalization in the economic sphere with a still relatively weak democracy that may be ill-equipped to mediate the political conflicts that are inevitable in a market economy.

Although most state institutions tend to be durable, as our discussion of the state has shown, no institution is guaranteed to last forever. Who would have predicted, ten years ago, when the Soviet Union was branded as the "evil empire," that the communist states of Eastern Europe and the Soviet Union would collapse like a house of cards? In the former Yugoslavia, the breakdown of the state precipitated violent social conflicts. Elsewhere in Eastern Europe, even if there has been less violence, the process of building democratic institutions and a market economy also involves the potential for social conflicts to spin out of control.

To understand any society and to have a clear idea of where it is going, the study of the polity is essential. In this chapter, we have used the example of free trade in North America to illustrate how important political decisions are made. But the range of social issues that depend on the interaction of individuals, contenders, parties, and the state in the polity is limitless. The progress of democracy in the world has led some to argue that we are witnessing the "end of history" (Fukuyama 1992). Even if this were true, however, politics will always continue to be marked by changes. Because of these changes, the study of political sociology will remain a challenge, and a necessity.

SUMMARY

1. The polity includes all political aspects of society. It embraces the state, political parties, contenders, and individual citizens. The polity can be thought of as an arena of power where different groups compete for control of the state.

2. The state has a monopoly on the legitimate use of force in society. It does not always exercise this monopoly. Often, it allows other agencies in society to use physical coercion, within limits. The state is the ultimate means to cultural and economic ends.

3. The political process involves four kinds of actors: the state, political parties, contenders, and individuals. But polity contenders play a key role. They are able to generate considerable political activity because they represent the interests of particular groups in society.

4. Structural functionalism emphasizes how individuals communicate their desires to the state and how the state implements the goals

of society. Structural functionalists argue that people submit to the authority of the state because they believe that the state acts in the best interest of the society as a whole. They also believe that democracy is a good system of government because it maximizes the flow of information from society to the state.

5. The conflict perspective emphasizes the control that the powerful and the rich have over the state and the ways in which the state keeps the powerless in line. According to this perspective, the state serves the interests of the rich. The rich control the electoral process and prevent any significant change from occurring.

6. Symbolic interactionism provides insights into how different world views make order problematic, and how symbols are used by politicians, government officials, contenders, and political parties to influence voters.

7. There are two basic views on the development of the modern polity. According to the political-modernization view, democracy promotes economic development, and vice versa. According to the other view, modernizing revolutions were necessary because antimodern groups controlling the state had to be forcefully removed.

8. The polity is a key institution of social change in society, but it also can be a key obstacle to social change. When political institutions are not deeply rooted in a society, the potential for chaos and disorder is great. Even when institutions appear stable and enduring, as they did in Eastern Europe until the late 1980s, they may be swept away if they lose their legitimacy.

GLOSSARY

Authority. Power that has been institutionalized so that it is no longer seen as the property of an individual, but rather as the property of a position or office.

Challenger. In the polity, a contender representing a group that is outside of the power structure.

Charismatic authority. Authority that is based on an individual's special qualities.

Coercion. The use of force to achieve objectives. (The state controls the use of force in society.)

Contender. In the polity, an organization that represents the interests of large numbers of individuals or firms.

Democracy. A system of government that provides for some form of participation of all citizens in the political process.

Free rider. A person who benefits from a collective good, but did not contribute to its attainment.

Government. The part of the state that is concerned with making, enforcing, or interpreting laws.

Legal-rational authority. Authority that is based on the presumed correctness and legitimacy of written rules. It is vested in positions, not specific individuals.

Legitimate authority. Authority that is recognized by members of society.

Member. In the polity, a contender whose interests are recognized by the state.

Modernizing revolution. A type of revolution that involves the overthrow of antimodern groups by prodevelopment groups.

Political party. An organization of individuals that formulates national policies and attempts to win the support of diverse groups of individuals for its program.

Political socialization. The process whereby people are socialized into political values and attitudes.

Polity. Everything connected to government in society, which includes all forms of political behaviour.

Power. The ability of a group or individual to control the behaviour of another group or individual, whether the latter wishes to cooperate or not. At the level of the polity as a whole, power is the ability of a contender to influence the government.

Proportional representation. An electoral system that awards seats in national legislatures based on the proportion of the vote a party wins in the country as a whole.

Resource mobilization. In the polity as a whole, the process whereby individuals pool their time, energy, and money to form a contender and participate in the political process. In social movements, it is the process whereby activists build loyalty and commitment for their cause and assemble followers, funds, and resources, all of which increase the capacity to act collectively.

Single-member-simple-plurality. An electoral system that is based on electoral districts, with each district sending one representative to the national legislature. The candidate with the most votes in an electoral district becomes the district's representative.

State. The institutions which regulate government and society and which have a monopoly on the use of physical coercion.

Traditional authority. Authority that is based on custom.

FURTHER READING

Bendix, Reinhard (ed.). *State and Society.* Boston: Little, Brown, 1968. A good introduction to the field of political sociology for the advanced student. This excellent anthology of articles includes major empirical and theoretical works on the state.

Clement, Wallace. *The Canadian Corporate Elite.* Toronto: McClelland and Stewart, 1975. Incisive analysis of the people who run Canada's top corporations, based on a class analysis of Canadian society as a whole.

Doern, G. Bruce, and Brian W. Tomlin. *Faith and Fear: The Free Trade Story.* Toronto: Stoddard, 1991. A clear, even-handed account of the politics of the free trade agreement in Canada by two political scientists.

Fraser, Graham. *Playing for Keeps: The Making of the Prime Minister, 1988.* Toronto: McClelland & Stewart, 1989. The best narrative history of the 1988 federal election, by one of Canada's best political journalists. This book helps understand how the game of politics is played when it really counts.

Fukuyama, Francis. *The End of History and the Last Man.* New York: Free Press, 1992. A commentary on the historical significance of the fall of Soviet communism.

Landes, Ronald G. *The Canadian Polity: A Comparative Introduction.* Scarborough, ON: Prentice-Hall, 1983.

Lipset, Seymour M. *Political Man.* New York: Doubleday, 1959. A collection of Lipset's essays, presenting the structural-functionalist view of the polity, including the basics of the political modernization arguments.

Meisel, John. "The Decline of Party in Canada." In *Party Politics in Canada* (5th ed.). ed. Hugh G. Thornburn, Scarborough, ON: Prentice-Hall, 1985. An analysis of Canada's party system, especially its recent past and present trajectories.

Mills, C. Wright. *The Power Elite.* New York: Oxford University Press, 1956. An insightful analysis of the U.S. polity, using the conflict perspective. The book discusses links among political, economic, and military elites.

Moore, Barrington, Jr. *Social Origins of Dictatorship and Democracy.* Boston: Beacon, 1966. An examination of modernizing revolutions in Great Britain, France, the United States, Russia, China, Germany, and Japan, with a brilliant explanation of the differences between types of modernizing revolutions.

Porter, John. *The Vertical Mosaic: An Analysis of Social Class and Power in Canada.* Toronto: University of Toronto Press, 1965. A classic study of classes in Canadian society.

Rueschemeyer, Dietrich, Evelyne Huber Stephens, and John D. Stephens. *Capitalist Development and Democracy.* Chicago: University of Chicago Press, 1992. A wide-ranging comparative study of the social origins of democracy in all regions of the world.

Thornburn, Hugh G. (ed.). *Party Politics in Canada* (5th ed.). Scarborough, ON: Prentice-Hall, 1985. Classic collection of analyses of Canada's party system and politics.

Tilly, Charles. *From Mobilization to Revolution.* Menlo Park, CA: Addison-Wesley, 1978. An exhaustive discussion of the political process, including revolutionary overthrow of the state.

Weber, Max. *The Theory of Social and Economic Organization.* New York: Oxford University Press, 1947. The best theoretical treatment of the polity by a classical theorist.

Weintraub, Sidney. *A Marriage of Convenience: Relations between the United States and Mexico.* New York: Oxford University Press, 1990. A wide-ranging analysis of political and economic relations between the United States and Mexico, with special focus on trade and immigration.

CHAPTER 15

Education

JANE GASKELL

Education is something every university student knows well. It is within the framework of an educational institution that you will study this chapter, and your work as a student can be the object of reflection as you work your way through the ideas presented here. How are you studying this text? Why are you studying it? What is included, and what is left out? What do you expect as a result of the study? Who is studying with you? Each of you knows education a little differently from the other. In this chapter, you will draw on your own experience with schools to fill in things not presented here. You will have some set opinions on what schools are like, why they are like that, and what might be done about it. This knowledge is what makes sociology interesting, and it will inform your reading. But you will also be challenged to try to see education through a variety of lenses, to understand it in ways that are different from your usual ways and that challenge your taken-for-granted knowledge of schooling. Rethinking what you already know is as difficult as learning something new.

Consider the classroom. You have experienced it as a student — perhaps as a competition for marks, as a boring performance by a teacher, as an exciting introduction to new ways of thinking, as a place where you felt confident, as a place where you did not know the language or felt discriminated against, or as a place to make friends and engage in romantic adventures. Your teachers also know something about classrooms, from a point of view different from your own. Perhaps they experienced it as a struggle for control, as a place to prove their competence and earn some money, as an intellectual challenge to present ideas clearly, as a drain on their time with their families. And parents, politicians, social workers, employers, taxpayers, and superintendents all have experiences of schooling that frame their questions about it and their understanding of it.

In this chapter, you will encounter a variety of ways of thinking about education, a variety of theories for understanding how it works and why. You will prefer some approaches to others. But try to understand who would be likely to see education that way, why it might make sense, and how you could pursue the analysis. The sociology of education is the study of how education takes the social forms it does, how it is linked to other institutions in the society, and how it affects the people who work in it. There is no one best understanding, but an exciting dialogue among different theorists, models, and bodies of evi-

dence. The multiple perspectives that exist in sociology are mirrored by the multiple experiences people have of education and by the multiple ways they come in contact with it. Keep your own experiences in mind as you read this chapter.

Sociologists have asked many questions about the educational system, but most of them can be related to questions of equality and inequality (who succeeds in school and why), questions of curriculum (what knowledge is transmitted in school and why), and questions of the relation between education and work (how changes in education are related to changes in the economy, and why). There are, of course, many other questions — about parents and teachers, ethnicity and gender, and citizenship and school organization — but most of them can be related to a concern about equality, knowledge, and the economic uses of schooling.

After presenting various theoretical approaches to education, this chapter discusses the history and organization of schooling in Canada, the United States, and Mexico. The descriptions are far from exhaustive, but they provide enough information for you to think more concretely about the organization of equality, curriculum, and linkages to work in three systems.

Schools prepare students for adult society by developing attitudes, knowledge, and skills.

Structural-Functional Approaches: Schools Reflect Society

In 1954, Talcott Parsons wrote an essay on education called "The School Class as a Social System: Some of Its Functions in American Society." He argued that the schools do two things. They "socialize" students, that is, they develop in students the attitudes, knowledge, and skills necessary in the adult society; and they "allocate" students to positions in the adult social order — they grade and sort students for the labour market. In both these ways, schools are integral to the functioning of the larger society: they reflect society, and they allow a new generation to carry it on.

Socialization does not take place only in the school. Families, churches, peers, baseball teams, gangs, and many other institutions and groups teach children many things. But schools are sanctioned by the state to socialize children, to teach them what they need to know. Cognitive learning is important; reading, writing, and arithmetic, as well as Canadian history, algebra, and Shakespeare, are part of what students in Canadian schools are taught. These constitute the **Formal Curriculum**. But Parsons also drew attention to the values, attitudes, and predispositions children learn in school — the moral dimensions of schooling, such as work habits, initiative, and obedience. These are known as the **Informal Curriculum**. A good pupil is one who learns both the cognitive and the moral dimensions of schooling well.

For Parsons, the differentiation of students along axes of achievement is also a necessary part of schooling: "The fundamental American value of equality of opportunity places a value both on initial equality and on differential achievement" (Parsons 1954:210). Students who learn more must be rewarded for it in school. Grades signal their superior relative achievement, and the adult society will then allocate them to adult roles based on their relative performance. Because school reflects what is necessary in the adult society, those who do better in school will do better in adult society. Marks are the exchange system that signal one's level of achievement, so getting an "A" in class suggests someone deserves to take a position of responsibility when she or he leaves school. Those who "drop out" or receive poor marks, on the other hand, deserve less responsible, less demanding, and less financially rewarding jobs.

Parsons's argument rests on the functionalist theory that has been laid out in Chapter 1 and will be returned to in Chapter 19. The schools are part of an organic social system in which each part works in harmony with the others, much as heart, lungs, and pancreas are interrelated and mutually supportive. Though institutions are not always in equilibrium, by and large the schools serve the rest of the society by socializing children for their adult roles and allocating them to those adult roles in which they can make their best contribution. Schools are necessary for a stable, fair, and orderly society.

Drawing on Parsons's argument, Robert Dreeben (1968) set out in a good deal more detail what aspects of the curriculum students need to learn to function in adult society, and how the

structure of schools serves these functions. His argument is a good illustration of the structural-functional analysis of what is learned in school. He calls attention to four norms involved in schooling and necessary for adult society — achievement, independence, universalism, and specificity — and he relates each to the organization of schools. He shows that the structure of schools is "functional" in helping children to move from their families to the larger social structure. Although in their families children are accepted for who they are, in schools they are taught by an adult who knows little about their home life and who changes every year, so that children learn that their value is dependent on what they achieve, not who they are. So schools teach the norm of achievement. Although, in their families, children work with others, in schools they must learn to do their own work. Working together is, interestingly, called "cheating" in most circumstances, so schools teach the norm of independence. Although in families children are treated differently from their siblings, depending on their needs and personalities, in classrooms they learn about being treated alike, as members of an age-graded class where the same work (like spelling lists or a certain page of the math textbook) is expected of all. This means that children learn universalism as a norm. Although at home all aspects of their personalities and relationships can be taken into account, when they are in school they learn to be treated specifically as students. Other aspects of their lives become irrelevant when they walk through the door of the classroom — they learn the "specificity" of roles.

For Dreeben, teaching the ability to accept, understand, and function under norms of universalism, achievement, specificity, and independence is one of schooling's major contributions. You might pick other norms that the schools teach to illustrate the ways they reflect the larger society and socialize students into it. Students learn to be bored politely, a habit that serves them well at work and at home. They learn to deal with social exclusion, competition, and criticism. More positively, they learn the value of hard work, rules of fair play, and discipline. In these ways and many more, schools teach students to function in the adult social world.

The sorting function of schools is also undeniable. Grading practices are sorting practices. In

Foucault on James Millar: Analyzing the School Promoters

Michel Foucault is a sociologist associated with the postmodernist movement and concerned with analyzing the way our everyday discourse reflects and creates power relations. Domination comes not from external coercion, he believes, but from the internalized habits and assumptions we take for granted. He critiques the exercise of power in particular local settings, and his critique can be used in interesting ways to reflect on schooling.

The turn of the century was the time when the forms of schooling we now experience as "natural" were put into place. Bruce Curtis draws on Foucault's theories to analyze the expansion of schooling in this period as a project of the middle classes. In his analysis of James Millar (1842–1901), one of Ontario's school promoters, he points out how students were regulated "through their capacity for pleasure, desire and self control or liberty." "Nineteenth-century educational reformers were not content simply to create students who accepted certain political relations. They sought something more active and more elusive at the same time, something they referred to variously as "cheerful" obedience, "willing" obedience or "implicit and cheerful" obedience. They sought nothing less than the transformation of the selves of students to the point where existing political arrangements were lived as natural."

Read the words of Millar and reflect on his version of schooling in light of Foucault's analysis.

The aim of the school is to make good citizens. Successful citizenship is the highest product of education. ... Education is therefore the formation of character, and this has to do with the entire nature — physical, intellectual, moral and religious. There is perhaps no question which has more importance for the nation than education. In some respects the government of the school is the continuation of the government of the home. The family, as has been noticed, is a little state. The school is also a little state, but larger than the family. The school, like the home, must have certain rules. These rules are such that many generations have found necessary. They must be regularity, punctuality, order and obedience. (Canadian Citizenship 1899:24–25).

Too often, the acquisition of knowledge, rather than the formation of good habits, is assumed to be the end of educational efforts. (School Management 1897:80)

It is a well-understood maxim in teaching that children should be trained to acquire for themselves. The successful teacher wakes up the mind, sets pupils to think, gets them to work, and arouses in them the spirit of enquiry. In the greater part of our acquisitions we are all self-taught. All knowledge, at the outset, must be learned by its discoverer without an instructor. True teaching is not what which gives knowledge, but that which stimulates pupils to gain it. In a sense it may be said he is the best teacher who instructs least. ... Teaching should stimulate study. ... Hard study is beneficial. Children that are "spoon-fed" remain children. For one pupil that is injured by hard study, one hundred will be benefited by increased mental activity. Hard study develops manhood and forms the royal road to success. (School Management 1897:208–209)

Source:

P. Corrigan, B. Curtis, and R. Lanning, "The Political Space of Schooling," in Terry Wotherspoon (ed.), *The Political Economy of Canadian Schooling* (Toronto: Methuen, 1987).

the secondary school, students start to take different courses, at different levels of difficulty, depending on how they have achieved. Some take courses that prepare them for university; some head directly into the labour market. Those who get to university are still competing — some for medical school, business school, or law school; some for places in orchestras, for scholarships, or for recommendations from professors. The educational system makes differences among students, differences that matter outside the school. In functional theory, this is seen as a contribution, both to the larger society, for it ensures the right people get into the right positions, and to young people themselves, who end up in positions suited to their talents and predispositions.

Meritocracy

In functional theory, schools are important because they constitute a **meritocracy** that allocates people to adult positions on the basis of their achievement. Functional theory considers differences among students and among adults as benign if they are based on achievement in school and if they contribute to the more efficient **allocation** of resources in the society as a whole. Differences based on ascription (for example, on place of birth), are differences that block the efficient and fair allocation of people in the social order, so they need to be reduced. An equal society, in this view, would be one in which adult position is based more fully on school achievement and in which more children are helped to achieve in school.

But a great deal of research shows that social class and ethnic background continue to predict how well students will do in school, even while measures of ability or I.Q. also show a relationship to school achievement. Parsons recognized that both ascription and achievement determined occupational status, but he believed that achievement was becoming increasingly important. John Porter, in his classic, *The Vertical Mosaic*, emphasized the problems Canadian schools faced in educating all students equally: "No society in the modern period can afford to ignore the ability which lies in the lower social strata. Whatever may be said about average intelligence and social class, the fact remains that in absolute numbers there is more of the highly intelligent in lower classes than in the higher" (Porter 1965:198).

Porter provided a great deal of evidence that those who stayed in school were from families with higher socioeconomic status and that those who went to university were a particularly class-biased group. He called for much greater effort to ensure the accessibility of higher education to students from lower-income backgrounds. "Without such policies intergenerational continuity of class will remain, mobility deprivation will continue, and external recruitment will still be required to meet the needs of a complex occupational structure" (Porter 1965:198). Still today, the statistics on Native students' dropout and achievement rates are appalling, and poverty holds back the achievement of many. The largest studies of social mobility and education have been done not in Canada, but in the United States and Britain (Jencks 1972; Kerckhoff 1990). Canadian studies, however, continue to show the correlation of social class with school achievement and university enrolment (Guppy 1992; Boyd et al. 1985a; Porter, Porter, and Blishen 1982).

In functionalist theory, the problem becomes one of how to put students from different social class, ethnic, or racial backgrounds on an equal footing to compete. Some come to the school with families that are less supportive, less educated, or less able to speak the language and help their children with schoolwork. This brings elements of ascription back into the system, for these students are held back, not by their abilities, but by the position into which they are born. The problem, then, is to provide the kind of remedial help that will put them on a fair footing and allow them to learn and compete equally.

Many special programs for disadvantaged youngsters have been based on this kind of analysis. They are designed to compensate for the deficiencies of the home environment and help the child adapt to the norms of the school. Since the school reflects the dominant norms and knowledge of the society, it is important that students learn them quickly, before falling behind and being placed in a program that confirms their disadvantage for another generation. Inequalities of social class, ethnicity, language, and race are considered "fixable" through the school, if enough remediation is provided. It is not inequality *per se*, but inequality that prevents children learning and competing equally in the school environment, that is the problem.

This argument did not quite hold in relation to gender, at least for Parsons in the 1950s. He recognized that girls and women competed equally in school, but then did not do the same things as men did when they became adults. Women worked primarily in the family, while men worked in the paid labour force. Why should they get the same schooling for quite different functions in the society? "This basic expectation for the girl stands in a certain tension to the schools curricular coeducation with its relative lack of differentiation by sex" (Parsons 1954:217). But Parsons concluded that schooling was useful for women because it taught them how to deal with their children and encourage them at school. "The educated woman has important functions as wife and mother, particularly as an influence on her children in backing the schools and impressing on them the importance of education." Gender differentiation is taken for granted in this world of benign difference, but educating

Today more people would argue that women should be educated equally with men so that they can compete equally with men in the labour market.

women for a man's world is still considered appropriate.

Today more people would argue that women should be educated equally with men so that they can compete equally in the labour market. The differentiation Parsons accepted as functional for the society, especially for the family and work, sounds very old-fashioned in denying women their right to equality. We assume that if women study the same social and intellectual curriculum as men, it is because they want and deserve access to the same choices. Gender is an ascriptive criterion that should not interfere with judgements based on achievement. Girls in school tend to get higher grades and to drop out less often. They are more likely to go on to higher education today, although this has only happened in the past five years. The problem for women is not educational disadvantage, at least as measured

in the traditional ways of marks and achievement tests, but disadvantage in turning educational achievement into achievement in the larger society.

Status Attainment and Human Capital Theory

A fair amount of research concerning the relationship between achievement in school and achievement in the labour market concludes that schooling is the best predictor of success at work. Again, the largest are U.S. and British studies that correlate success at school with success at work and find a strong relation (Coleman 1966; Blau and Duncan 1967; Kerckhoff 1990). Unemployment rates are lower and incomes higher for better-educated Canadians.

Status attainment models are based on functionalist models of achievement at school and work (Horan 1978; Knotterus 1987). Researchers take a single measure of achievement and relate it to success at work, measured on a single axis of income or status. The researcher searches for the size of the relation between achievement in school and achievement at work and for the ways this relation is affected by social class, some measure of intelligence, and perhaps sex, self-concept measures, or attitudes. Such models tend to find the predicted correlations, although, depending on how the variables are measured and what kind of population is surveyed, the correlation coefficient can be quite low. A great deal of the variance in labour-market success that cannot

The belief that school teaches what people need to know in the society, and that those who learn most and best at the school will contribute most to the society, is expressed in economic terms in "human capital theory."

be accounted for by success in school has been attributed to "luck" or to the problems of measuring these variables accurately and creating appropriate models of the process (Jencks 1972; Boudon 1973).

The belief that school teaches people what they need to know in the society, and that those who learn most and best at school will contribute most to the society, is expressed in economic terms in **human capital theory**. As the name implies, this theory suggests that the economy works on the basis of human, as well as physical, capital. Schools provide the human resources necessary for our economic productivity as a country. People with the most human capital will be paid the highest wages, signalling the greater contribution they make to the economy. There is a good deal of evidence that well-educated people do earn more than less-educated people, as indicated above. There also is evidence that countries with more educated people are wealthier than countries with fewer educated people. Education does seem to pay off economically.

Human capital theory has been very important in arguments for increasing society's investment in education. If educated people are more productive, spending money on education is an excellent investment, not a drain on resources. The other part of this argument is that modern industrial society demands more in the way of skills and knowledge than did previous societies, and that education needs to expand in order to fulfil the need for a more educated workforce. The need for achievement-based criteria for allocating people to positions at work expands in a more complex technological economy. In 1964, the Economic Council of Canada estimated that investments in education were much more likely to pay off than were investments in new buildings, equipment, or small business. The result was higher spending on universities and community colleges across the country and a dramatic increase in enrollments in higher education. The most recent report from the Economic Council of Canada continues to argue that human capital is our most important resource and increasingly necessary in a competitive world economy where technological advances are constant. It is through concepts like these that theoretical understandings of education and how it works have important implications for politics and practice.

Conflict Approaches: A Challenge to Consensus

This functionalist view of how education reflects the society is a fairly happy one, in that it views education as benefiting both the individual and the collective. It fits with many people's experience of schooling, especially those who have done well in school and at work, and it fits with a basically liberal view of the world (Marchak 1975). It is particularly popular with those who are successful in school because it suggests that what they learn is important and that their success justifies their continuing privilege as adults. However, this kind of sociological theory has been challenged in many ways. Conflict theory does not see the individual and the group, and society as a whole, as a cohesive unit that functions for the welfare of all. Instead, society is viewed as a struggle between groups with different kinds of power and resources. Groups with more power are likely to control schooling and to impose their culture on it. Control of the educational agenda will always be a focus of struggle, as many social groups and movements try to affect it.

In 1976, a book by Sam Bowles and Herb Gintis, called *Schooling in Capitalist America*, drew from a Marxist version of conflict theory to challenge the dominant Parsonian functionalist view of schooling. Bowles and Gintis agree that schools reflect what it takes to be successful in the society, but they argue that this is only because the dominant classes control both the schools and the larger society and use them both to perpetuate their own power.

Education plays a dual role in the social process whereby surplus value, i.e. profit, is created and expropriated. On the one hand, by imparting technical and social skills and appropriate motivations, education increases the productive capacity of workers. On the other hand, education helps defuse and depoliticize the potentially explosive class relations of the production process, and thus serves to perpetuate the social, political and economic conditions through which a portion of the product of labor is expropriated in the form of profits. (Bowles and Gintis 1976)

Notice the way Bowles and Gintis agree with Parsons. Schools teach values and knowledge; they sort people out. However, they do it not for the common good, but for the greater profitability of capital, for the greater good of the already privileged. Education does not serve the society as a whole; it serves the privileged few. Their book is an exploration of how this works.

Because the rich control economic power, they can also control the educational system. Through it, they impose their knowledge, their culture, and their desired ways of behaving on everyone else. The less privileged are predictably less successful, as they are less familiar with the culture of the school and less willing and able to conform to its demands. They are soon sorted out into different streams in the high school, where they are taught a curriculum that prepares them to accept their subordinate position and rehearses their docility, obedience, and respect for authority. Just as important, everyone is taught that this system of sorting is fair, because success at school is equated with achievement and merit, and this belief legitimizes the existing social order, preventing anyone from seeing the bias of the system.

Bowles and Gintis's analysis of schooling reflects a less benign experience of classrooms, but one most people can empathize with. Schools do not teach what everyone needs to know to be fully functioning adults; they teach things from the culture of the dominant classes; they teach things that will encourage people to fit into the workplace. The norms of school are not what everyone needs to know as a citizen; they do not include democracy, co-operation, creativity, or autonomy. Instead, schools emphasize norms that will turn students into good workers for others. Students learn about alienated labour, hierarchy, and the fragmentation of knowledge and tasks. Schools do not develop students' intellectual and social competencies; they fit students for a work process that extracts surplus labour from them and that emphasizes obedience and conformity rather than serious thought and initiative. School "corresponds" to work; neither school nor work are good for most people.

Bowles and Gintis point out that schools reproduce the class structure. Schools stream students, and those who are streamed into the lower tracks experience more alienation, more fragmentation of work, and more hierarchy. "Even within a single school, the social relationships of different tracks tend to conform to different behavioral norms. Thus in high school, vocational and general tracks emphasize rule-following and close supervision, while the college [and university] track tends toward a more open atmosphere emphasizing the internalization of norms." And all students learn about the "I.Q. ideology," which says that those who do well in school deserve the better jobs, the better wages, and the greater power. Through teaching this belief, schools legitimate and perpetuate the inequalities they create. They prevent people from seeing equality as a possible ideal; they encourage youth to blame themselves if they end up in low-paying jobs. They provide the ideological underpinnings for an unjust social order.

Bowles and Gintis turn Parsons's analysis on its head. They argue that schools serve the larger social order, but they also argue that that social order benefits only the few who are powerful, who exercise control over the economy. The analytical difference is expressed in their critical account of the content of schooling and its norms. The continuity lies in the close connections posited between schools and the society in which they are located.

Maintaining Dominance through Schooling

A conflict model of schooling assumes no harmony among the groups who make up society. It makes the issue of equality the central problem for schooling. It assumes that some benefit from schools at the expense of others and that those who do well in school benefit at the expense of those who do not. Knowledge is power. Control of knowledge and of the "sorting machine" is control of power.

It is the structure of schooling that becomes the focus of the analysis of equality. To understand why some groups benefit, conflict analysis draws our attention to the question of whose knowledge is reflected in the schools and which groups are served by the norms it fosters. Instead of calling for remedial programs for the disadvantaged, as Parsons would, conflict theorists suggest that we change the structure and organization of schooling so that it more fairly reflects the knowledge and norms of less powerful groups.

Many theorists have made this kind of argument. The work of Pierre Bourdieu on "cultural capital" has been particularly influential in shaping the discussion of how education reproduces the inequalities in society. Bourdieu defines the sociology of education as "the science of the relations between cultural reproduction and social reproduction." It "endeavours to determine the contribution made by the educational system to the reproduction of the structure of relationships between classes, by contributing to the reproduction of the structure of the distinction of cultural capital among these classes" (Bourdieu and Passeron 1977). In other words, education teaches and sorts on the basis of culture. Those with the kind of background or "habitus" to allow them to participate easily in the dominant culture that characterizes educational institutions will reproduce their privilege through education. Bourdieu explores this in his studies of university students in France.

A Canadian study of music classrooms by Shepherd and Vuilliamy (1983) explores how this works in Ontario schools. The distinction between "school music" and "student music," they conclude, is less pronounced in Ontario classrooms than in British classrooms, because in Ontario, music is a marginal subject in the curriculum and a wide scope of music is allowed into the classroom. However, the ways teachers take up the study of music, from within a classical European paradigm, emphasizing formal structure and musical notation, manages to make students' understanding of "their" music irrelevant for the purposes of instruction. It imposes a dominant musical ideology and socializes students into epistemologies that underpin industrial, capitalist society. Instead of encouraging personal, individual statements through music, music classes encourage the impersonal and abstract manipulation of a simple harmonic–rhythmic framework.

Native peoples have similarly argued that the structure and organization of schooling excludes their knowledge, their spirituality, and their understanding of the world. Many Native peoples have struggled to get more control over the schools their children attend, and to change the content and organization of what is taught. Robert Regnier (1987) reports on the "Wandering Spirit" school in Toronto, where "each morning children and staff ritually smudge themselves in sweetgrass smoke." This symbolizes a challenge

Many Native people have struggled to change the content and organization of what their children are taught.

to white ways of knowing and behaving and becomes the cultural and spiritual framework for learning and teaching.

This kind of analysis of the ideology of schooling, of what is taught, and of how it is studied can be pursued in all subject areas. Studies of textbooks have pointed out that school versions of history are the versions held by employers rather than by workers and by English Canadians rather than Native Canadians (Osborne 1980; Anyon 1979). Furthermore, school history usually is the history of powerful male figures moving in the public sphere, rather than of immigrant groups, women, and the dispossessed. The language demanded in school is "standard English," the language of the dominant group, while dialects and perfectly intelligible but nonstandard speech are not allowed (Bernstein 1977). School art and literature is drawn from the classic European tradition, along with Canadian examples that share

in the assumptions of this tradition. Few women artists, musicians, and writers are mentioned. Whose knowledge, whose culture is reflected in schools? Your experience, along with sociological studies, probably will tell you it is most often the knowledge and culture of men with a European heritage and a reasonable standard of living. For this is the dominant culture and the knowledge of the powerful.

The norms of schooling similarly reflect and justify the status quo. Competition involves learning to accept inequality as a legitimate outcome of individual differences, rather than as a structure that perpetuates injustice. Schooling reinforces inequalities in contemporary society and works hard to convince students that inequalities are the result of individual effort and talent.

The conflict tradition, then, tends to examine the inequalities involved in schooling as a function of social inequalities reflected in the structure of the school curriculum. Instead of looking for ways to fit students and their families better for school, it tends to point to ways in which the school could adjust better to students and their families. The school, like the society, is controlled by the relatively powerful. Educational change would entail change in the relations of power outside the school.

Credentialing

Bowles and Gintis argue that schools reflect the needs of employers for a docile labour force. They reanalyze status attainment data to argue that it is schooling, not ability, that accounts for success at work. Randall Collins (1979) takes the argument about school credentials further to demonstrate that credentials act as a signal to employers about the kind of culture students have and thus are a barrier to equality in the labour market. Credentials do not signal the knowledge or skills necessary to perform a job; they indicate instead that someone has been able to get through school and therefore can display the class and ethnic culture, the ways of acting and thinking, that are demanded there. Many individuals could quite adequately perform certain jobs they are disqualified from, but they do not have the right credentials. Educational credentials, then, become a sign of "cultural currency" and an irrational barrier to equality in the labour market.

Collins's argument is based on a critique of the technocratic, industrial model of society espoused by functional theory. Instead of an increasingly complex society that demands more sophisticated skills in the workplace, Collins posits a society where jobs are "deskilled" by technology and access to good jobs is controlled by a **credentialing** system in which credentials bear little relation to skill. He assumes most people can do most jobs and learn them in a short time at work. The chapters of his book, *The Credential Society*, show how professional groups like doctors and lawyers exclude anyone without the "proper" education in order to regulate the labour market and keep wages high. He also documents how the competition for credentials has produced "credential inflation," a highly irrational system that demands far more schooling from people than is necessary for the workplace or good for anyone.

Human capital theory and status attainment models assume that everyone competes with everyone else in the labour market and that employers will hire the person with the best qualifications. But people search for work in specialized labour markets that are set apart by their requirements for credentials and for certain personal characteristics. The existence of "segmented labour markets" has been important in providing an alternative account of why the relation between education and work posited by functional theory is inadequate. The argument can be seen most clearly in relation to women. Women earn much less for each year of education they bring to the labour market than men do. Canadian women who worked for a full year, full time, and had a high-school education earned $18 042 in 1987, while similar men earned $28 444. Women with a university education earned $31 259, while similar men earned $44 891. Women's rate of unemployment was also higher: 8.3 percent, compared with 7.4 percent for men in 1988 (Statistics Canada 1990).

Women have not been able to turn their educational advantage into labour-market success in the way human capital theory or status attainment models would predict, unless one assumes that women's education costs less in foregone income or that women in some other way bring less knowledge and skill to their work. Why? Women have been segregated into a set of jobs where men do not look for work — clerical, secretarial, certain kinds of service occupations, and factory jobs are held almost exclusively by women. These occupations tend to pay less for education than do male-dominated occupations. They also tend to offer less on-the-job education to workers. So, even if women have a great deal of education, unless they move outside these labour markets or change the nature of these jobs, they will not increase their wages. In order to turn their education into income, women must change the value placed on their credentials in the labour markets in which they compete. The problem is not lack of education; it is that education *per se* is not valued across the board by employers and used to allocate people to work in the simple way that status attainment models suggest. The organization of firms, of labour markets, and of hiring practices must be understood as complex institutional pro-cesses that sometimes do and sometimes don't reward education and educational credentials.

Interpretive Approaches: Meaning and Culture

Both structural-functional and conflict perspectives offer a view of education that is painted in broad strokes and that offers a general interpretation of how schools either "correspond to" or serve the larger social structures of the society. Both try to understand the way schools really are, and why. Interpretive approaches to sociology are more interested in elucidating how people understand and therefore respond to schooling than in providing the definitive account of schools. Following the lead of symbolic interactionism, they ask how people define a situation and what meaning it has for them.

Studies in this tradition of the sociology of education tend not to be grand theories of how the system works, but small studies that look in detail at how a particular setting is organized and understood. They take a very close look at the everyday interactions and understandings that constitute schooling. They observe how students, teachers, and parents derive meaning from their experience of school and act on it. While most of them draw in one way or another on some macrosociological theory, they are less concerned with clarifying theory than with elucidating the various meanings participants bring to their experience of schools and with understanding how social context matters. This kind of scholarship is becoming increasingly concerned with reflecting on the role of the sociologist, who after all becomes a participant in the process of producing meaning from observation and writing.

This section describes some studies of school processes that try to explain what school feels like to the people in it, and that work from this explanation to an understanding of how school as an institution should be understood in its social context. These studies look at many of the same questions addressed above — how do schools produce inequality, how is school related to work, how is the curriculum arrived at — because these questions underlie most of what sociologists have

asked about education. But their approach focuses on people as makers of meaning — as interpreters of an ambiguous social world.

The Production of Inequality

One of the most important studies of the production and reproduction of understandings about schooling was Paul Willis's book, *Learning to Labour* (1977). Willis takes a Marxist view of class reproduction in schools. But he starts his book with this observation:

The difficult thing to explain about how middle class kids get middle class jobs is why others let them. The difficult thing to explain about how working class kids get working class jobs is why they let themselves. ... There is no obvious physical coercion and a degree of self-direction. This is despite the inferior rewards for, undesirable social definition, and increasing intrinsic meaninglessness of manual work: in a word, its location at the bottom of a class society. (Willis 1977:1)

Willis questions how the "I.Q. ideology" could possibly convince young people to take working-class jobs and wants to know how young people understand schools and work so that they "choose" working-class jobs. Why do they understand work as an attractive option, when most sociologists have seen it as a terrible option?

Willis "hung around" with a few working-class male adolescents known as "the lads." He interviewed them and followed them to their homes and leisure-time activities. He tried to understand their culture, their understandings of school and work, and the connections between them. He reports that the lads did not accept the I.Q. ideology of the school; they did not believe the well-meant liberal platitudes that school is good for you and will open up opportunities in the class structure. Instead, they rebelled against the school, its teachers, and its promise of upward mobility by vaunting their physical activity in the face of its bookishness, their masculinity in the face of its femininity, their outrageousness in the face of demands for conformity, their rudeness to counter the demand for politeness, and their self-assertion in the face of the demand for docility. Willis explores the ways in which their understanding of the school and of class structure was taken up within the culture of working-class masculinity and the shop floor to produce an understanding of the world that allowed them to rebel, but at the same time confirmed their position at the bottom of society, in the working-class jobs of their fathers.

Willis examines class and school structure in relation to the production of meaning and culture. He sees the reproduction of class society not as a structural necessity, but as a cultural achievement that must be accomplished over and over again in the school. It is not determined by capitalism or any other structure of power but acted out within particular structural conditions and ideologies by particular people. Every time this is done, it is done slightly differently, because each person reworks the culture, recreates it, and gives it new meanings. This is an active creation by inquiring human beings, not a passive reception of a given culture.

Annette Lareau (1991) explores the interaction of parents with the school. Lareau wanted to know how social class differences are given social meaning in the day-to-day interactions parents have with their children and the teachers. She knew that children from working-class homes are less likely to do well in school, but she wanted to know how this is worked out in everyday interactions and understandings. So she chose two different schools, one working-class and one middle-class, and interviewed the teachers, parents, and children. She observed the classroom and attended parent–teacher interviews. She tried to understand what people actually do and why, from their point of view.

Lareau shows how upper-middle-class parents have the competence to help their children in school because they understand the language and the social patterns practised there. Their social status is a resource they can use to get the attention of the teacher and to have their opinions taken seriously. Their self-confidence and status convinces them they have the right, even the responsibility, to intervene. They have the income and material resources, the networks, and the expectation that work and home should be connected, not kept apart. Thus a variety of beliefs, resources, and practices amount to an effective intervention by middle-class parents that is denied to working-class parents.

Both Willis and Lareau examine a question raised by structural-functional and conflict theories: How is sorting accomplished and justified in schools? Both examine it by looking in great detail at the activities and understandings of the people involved. Both give a sense that "the system" is not a static monolith — people and their actions constitute that system, and people change and rebel. They do so within a structure that shapes what is possible and within a set of dominant beliefs that shape the meanings they are able to make.

Classroom Knowledge

The things taught in school can be seen as tightly determined by the social structure and reflecting either what everyone needs to know or the culture of the dominant group. But curriculum can also be seen as a struggle over meaning, as a daily negotiation between people with different conceptions of what is true and important and what it all signifies. The curriculum is constructed in the daily interactions of students and teachers; it is influenced by teachers, school boards, students, parents, and employers and changes over time.

What is learned in school? Linda McNeil (1991) shows that what is taught in schools is no mere reflection of a larger social order; it is the product of teachers' decisions as they try to satisfy the requirements of their jobs within their own understandings of what is possible and desirable. In schools, teachers' primary concern must be to manage, to control students, and to produce the grades for which they are accountable. Teachers take broad curriculum guidelines and turn them into little bits of knowledge, assignments, and tests that can be marked and used to grade and sort students. McNeil looks closely at how and why teachers fragment knowledge and insist on control, as well as how and why, in turn, students respond with disengagement from the knowledge and hierarchy that confront them. Unlike Bowles and Gintis, she attributes the curriculum and the resultant reproduction less to the interest of capital and more to the understandings and requirements of life inside schools. McNeil explores how teachers think about their work. She finds their concerns to be concrete ones that arise in their working conditions, just as the concerns of students do.

Another study of the curriculum that focuses on meaning in classrooms is Peter McLaren's *Cries in the Corridor* (1980). McLaren taught in Toronto's Jane–Finch corridor, an area where many new immigrants with low-paying jobs live and send their children to school. He writes as a teacher, transcribing the talk of the students in his class and reflecting on his practice as he struggles to meet their needs. The book is written as a diary, and although the analysis is not made explicit, a portrait of an inner-city school emerges that explores the complexity of family, school, administrative structure, curriculum, teachers, and values. The effects of poverty and culture, that of the teachers as well as the parents and children, are explored as they interact to produce failure for kids. McLaren's study is much less tied to sociological theory than McNeil's and is much more located in his commonsense understandings as a teacher. It is one of the few close-up portraits of Canadian classrooms. By writing his account as a diary, McLaren makes his perspective part of the account. The analyst, no less than the students, parents, and teachers, creates meaning rather than simply reporting it.

Three sociological approaches to schooling have been set out here: structural functionalism, conflict theory, and interpretive approaches. They are not mutually exclusive; there is overlap between the way Parsons sees schools functionally related to the larger society and the way Bowles and Gintis see schools as a focus of the struggle between groups in the society. Both studies suggest a fairly strong structural relation between the school and other social institutions, while most interpretive studies consider the relation to depend on the generation of meaning and culture. But the interpretive studies need some macrosociological understandings about where schools fit in the social order to make sense of their observations about how teachers understand their students, why students drop out of school, and the extent to which curriculum is a compromise among students, teachers, and the state. Although the approaches are related, they highlight different dimensions of schooling and reflect the various concerns and experiences of the sociologists who do the research and write the books. Within each kind of analysis there is great variation in the themes that the sociologists have chosen to develop. There is much scope for further research and interpretation of schools and the development of an understanding of Canadian education.

Schooling in North America

This section describes and analyzes the Canadian education system, particularly the areas of equality, curriculum, and relation to work. Comparative information about the United States and Mexico is provided in order to outline the Canadian system clearly as a system located in its own history, social structure, and cultural mix. As you read, try to think of studies and ways of understanding that might be suggested by sociologists with a structural-functional, conflict, or interpretive bent.

History and Organization

Canada. When Canadian children are under 5 years of age, their parents, especially their mothers, are expected to care for and educate them. Other forms of child care for young children are paid for privately and barely regulated by the state, although low-income families in which the mother is employed outside the home may be subsidized, and public child-care centres must conform to basic safety and health requirements. When children reach the age of 5 or 6, however, the state requires them to attend an accredited school, allocates public funds, and regulates the schooling. The provinces have constitutional responsibility for education, although the federal government has provided some funding, mostly for postsecondary and vocational schooling. The question of public funding for religous and private schools has been controversial at several points in Canada's history and is handled differently in different provinces. Quebec provides for both Catholic and Protestant schools; Ontario, Saskatchewan, and Alberta provide funding for Catholic schools as a second public system; and Newfoundland has a true denominational system, which allowed for public funding of Pentecostal and Salvation Army schools, among others. British Columbia provides public funding for privately controlled schools of any kind — Jewish, fundamentalist or evangelical Christian, or elite boarding schools — as long as they conform to certain basic provincial requirements for curriculum and teacher certification. Only about 5 percent of children in Canada attend private schools.

The structure of public schooling at the elementary and secondary level varies somewhat from province to province across the country, because the Constitution states that education is a matter of provincial jurisdiction. Junior kindergarten for 4-year-olds is provided at public expense in Ontario, while kindergarten is not compulsory in some other provinces. Some provinces provide junior high schools for grades 6, 7, 8, and/or 9, while others place students in elementary and secondary schools only. Most provinces keep students in secondary school through grade 12 before they are considered eligible for university or community college programs. In Quebec, students attend secondary schools until grade 11, at which point they must attend a CEGEP (college d'enseignment général et professionel) for two years before they are eligible for university. In Ontario, thirteen grades have been required before university, but the extra year is being phased out.

Community colleges and universities are all publicly funded, though they charge student fees. Community colleges are structured differently across the country, from CEGEPs for all in Quebec, to vocational colleges in Ontario, to British Columbia, where vocational and university-equivalent instruction are offered at the college level. Each province has universities of different sizes and complexions, many of which are very competitive in their entrance requirements.

Legally, students must stay in school until they are 15 or 16 years of age. However, a substantial proportion of students stay on well beyond the official leaving age. In 1984, for example, 93 percent of 16-year-olds and 67 percent of 17-year-olds were attending elementary and secondary schools. At the time of the census in 1986, the median level of schooling for the population aged 15 and over was 12.2 years. This level of education is among the highest in the world.

Today we take the organization of our educational system for granted. The period between about 1840 and 1870 marked the transition to compulsory, age-graded schooling, paid for by taxes, controlled by the state, and organized hierarchically from the centre. Dr. Egerton Ryerson, the superintendent of Ontario schools during this period, was like many of the "school promoters" of his time, a religious man who feared chaos in his changing society (Prentice 1975). He saw the schools as a way to impose order on an increasingly volatile social world. He wanted the school system to produce a disciplined workforce and to teach children from every social class about their place in the social whole. Age-graded schools were introduced in the name of rational and efficient organization. The standardization of curriculum and the creation of different streams for different children, depending on their social destination, was also achieved by Ryerson in myriad struggles with local school boards, who often preferred local autonomy and a more flexible organization (Gidney and Millar 1990).

In Quebec, the basic framework of the school system was established in the same period (Wilson, Stamp, and Audet 1970). The two famous superintendents there were Dr. Jean-Baptiste Meilleur, from 1842 to 1855, and Pierre Joseph Oliver Chaveau, from 1855 to 1867. But in 1875, largely because of the substantial debt incurred by the state, responsibility for public instruction was given to the Catholic and Protestant committees of the Council for Public Instruction, signalling the creation of two virtually independent school organizations; the Catholic and the Protestant. Until the "quiet revolution" of the early 1960s, the Roman Catholic Church controlled secondary and higher education in the French Catholic system, although the English Protestant system evolved much like its counterparts in the rest of Canada. Fees were charged by the church for education beyond the elementary grades, the elite were quickly separated from the rest of the students, science was downplayed, and the content of the curriculum had to be acceptable to the church. In the early 1960s the Jean Lesage government set up a royal commission to investigate education in the province. Known as the Parent Commission, it recommended major changes: taking control away from the church except in moral and religious matters, instituting free secondary education, and offering free postsecondary education at the level of the new CEGEPs. The

CEGEPS were an attempt to increase accessibility and to keep vocational and academic students together longer than was the case in any other system of education in Canada.

Many of Canada's old universities and colleges were founded by churches. The oldest is King's College, a denominational college in Nova Scotia founded in 1789. Laval University was founded by the Jesuits in 1852. Some, however, like Dalhousie University (1818) and McGill University (1821), were founded as independent institutions. Some universities have evolved from technical institutes (for example, Memorial and Lakehead Universities), and a few were creations of the provinces (for example, the universities of Saskatchewan and Alberta). Postsecondary education in Canada expanded dramatically after World War II. Enrolments increased, and new institutions, especially community colleges, were opened. Today, all Canada's universities are publicly funded and governed.

The United States. In the United States, the structure of the educational system is very similar to that in Canada. State-funded public schools are compulsory for those aged 5 to 15. The schools are age-graded from kindergarten through grade 12, after which point college and university programs are widely available. The secondary-school curriculum is even more diverse than in Canada and has prompted more than one educational reformer to decry the lack of coherence and rigour in the secondary school system. Universities are state supported and charge fees, although there is also a tradition of privately controlled universities. These universities charge much higher student fees than state universities and tend to have large endowments. World-famous institutions like Harvard, Yale, and Stanford have no equivalent, in prestige or private endowments, in Canada.

The American Constitution enforces the separation of church and state. The view that there should be truly common public schools for all children was based on the fear of denominationalism and the republican sentiment of the thirteen colonies. No religious schools in the United States are publicly funded. Schooling became compulsory during the mid-nineteenth century amid debates similar to those held in Canada. While some of the first histories of American education saw the expansion of public schooling as the dawning of enlightenment, later revisionist histories have considered schools as mechanisms to control the unruly working classes or create a national culture, as successful entrepreneurial activity by educators, or as expressions of local civic pride (Katz 1975a; Tyack 1974).

Mexico. The revolutionary tradition of the Mexican state is reflected in the structure of its educational system. Free and universal education was established in the 1857 Constitution. Many schools had been controlled by the Roman Catholic Church, but in 1917, in an attempt to counter the power of the church over the socialization of children and to more securely establish the new state, the Constitution specifically banned priests and nuns from operating their own schools. Since then, the country has tried to use schools as an instrument of nation-building, aiming to break down the influence of the church over the schools, to promote equality, and to strengthen a sense of national culture and independence.

Elementary schools are officially free and compulsory, although these regulations are frequently ignored. It is estimated that half of Mexico's children fail to complete the required compulsory six years of school. There are not enough classrooms to house all the children who should officially be in school. The World Bank reports that Mexicans on average had 4.7 years of schooling in 1992, while in Canada the average was 12.1 and in the United States it was 12.3.

Mexico had only seven universities in 1940, but by 1966 there were 83 institutions of higher education, of which 33 were universities (25 government-controlled, eight private). The Autonomous National University of Mexico is the largest of the public universities and considered to be the major centre of higher learning and research. It spends about 40 percent of the budget for higher education in Mexico, but as its name suggests, it has defended its autonomy from the state. In Mexico, 15 percent of 20–24-year-olds are enrolled in postsecondary education, while the figure is 66 percent for Canada and 63 percent for the United States.

Equality

Canada. In Canada, students from wealthier backgrounds perform better in schools and stay there longer. Students who leave before completing high school are more likely to come from poorer backgrounds. Aboriginal people have much lower rates of educational attainment than do nonaboriginals. The 1986 census indicated that 45 percent of on-reserve and 24 percent of off-reserve Native adults had less than a grade 9 education, compared with 17 percent of the non-Native population (Economic Council of Canada 1992).

Staying in school beyond the compulsory leaving age and going on to university has always been closely related to class background. Axelrod (1990) notes that from 1920 to 1950, nearly half of the students at Memorial University of Newfoundland came from middle- and upper-class backgrounds, while only 10 percent of Newfoundland society was composed of these groups. Axelrod writes of Canadian universities in the interwar years as "making the middle class" — in other words, instilling in students the understandings and habits of middle-class Canada. Many of these habits and understandings excluded those who were not white males with an Anglo-Saxon heritage. "Overwhelmingly white, Anglo-Celtic Protestant, and to a lesser degree Catholic, English Canadian universities were determined to preserve their cultural mix. Like those administering immigration policy, university officials did this not by banning minority groups, but by rigidly controlling their numbers" (Axelrod 1990:32) The "nonpreferred" students at the University of Manitoba, for example, consisted of women, Jews, Ukrainians, Poles, Dutch, Norwegians, Germans, Italians, and Mennonites. Students in these categories had to have much higher marks than "preferred" students to be admitted.

The expansion of universities since World War II has done little to change this class bias. Robert Pike sums up a variety of sociological studies by concluding that "there was no indication that the university expansion had been accompanied by more than a small increase in the participation rates of students of lower class origins relative to the participation of students from the more privileged classes" (Pike 1981:5). Neil Guppy comes to the same conclusion: "The effects of higher educational expansion in Canada, as this relates to equality of opportunity, would seem to have operated to preserve the place of privilege at the university level" (Guppy 1984:89). In 1985, the Report of the Royal Commission on the Economic Union and Development Prospects for Canada reported that children whose parents hold bachelor's degrees were three times more likely to attend university than were children of parents without degrees. Parents of students at community colleges tend to have lower levels of education than parents of university students.

Until recently, women have been less likely than men to attend university. Between 1920 and 1960, women constituted 20–25 percent of university enrollments. This has increased dramatically in the last 30 years. By 1970, women made up almost 37 percent of university enrollments, and by 1988, women's enrollment surpassed men's. As Bellamy and Guppy put it, "One way of illustrating the trend in enrollment patterns is to note that in the last 35 years, the number of male students has increased by 294%, while female enrollments have increased by an astounding 1420%" (Bellamy and Guppy 1992:169). Gender difference remains clear in enrollment patterns at universities, however: women constitute about 11 percent of engineering students, 42 percent of medical students, 45 percent of commerce students, 59 percent of arts students, 70 percent of education students, and 96 percent of nursing students (Bellamy and Guppy 1992).

The reasons for the differential success and enrollment patterns of various kinds of students can be traced to their own characteristics, but also to the character of the school system within which these differences are translated into differences in academic achievement. School financing varies across the country. The Atlantic provinces spent $4800 per pupil for elementary and secondary schools in 1989–90, while Quebec and Ontario spent $6000. A recent study by the Economic Council of Canada concludes that "this regional spending pattern plays a significant role in explaining the poorer educational achievement of the Atlantic provinces." It also points out, however, that this is far from a complete explanation, because levels of funding do not translate easily into school achievement.

Because children in Canada attend the school in their own neighbourhood, by and large, they attend school with children who share their own social background. Several studies, like the ones by Lareau and McLaren cited above, have shown the dramatic effect that neighbourhood composition has on the curriculum and social relations of even very early schooling. In recent years the introduction of French immersion programs, to which many English-speaking professional middle-class families send their children, has exacerbated the segregation of relatively privileged students in the public schools (Olsen and Burns 1983).

The practice of grouping students within classrooms has also been considered a factor in the differential success of students. Early in the elementary schools, different reading groups — the "robins" and the "swallows" — are separated and subjected to different expectations and different teaching. Stephen Richer (1979) has studied the organization of a kindergarten class by focusing on gender divisions. He shows how a kindergarten classroom continues a process of gender-identity formation through voluntary seating patterns that separate girls and boys, a higher use of physical aggression by boys, and play patterns that reproduce stereotypical "mummy" and "daddy" roles. A more recent study of grade 8 classrooms by Linda Eyre (1991) shows continuing informal separation of girls and boys in class, verbal harassment of girls and ethnic minorities, and gender-specific expectations about who performs technical and domestic tasks.

In secondary schools, a more formal streaming process tends to further separate students, ostensibly by academic ability and interest, but actually also by class, gender, and ethnicity. Until the late 1960s students in secondary schools were clearly streamed into vocational or academic programs, each with its own course requirements, examinations, and diploma. Students from working-class homes were more likely to be in the vocational stream, girls were more likely to be in the typing classes, and children from most ethnic minorities were more likely to be in the lower academic streams.

In the early 1970s, overt streaming, mandated by the school, was replaced by a system in which students streamed themselves through their selection of courses. Today streaming is more disguised in some provinces than in others by the organization of the secondary school curriculum. Ontario has had a clearly streamed system that is defended by the teachers' federation but is increasingly being questioned by the government. Indeed, the elimination of streamed grade 9 classes, scheduled for 1994, has created a great deal of public controversy.

Ontario schools offer courses at different levels, labelled gifted, academic, general, basic, and so on, and numbered hierarchically from one to six. A grade 11 student could choose to take a "level 6" history course, for example. Only levels 5 and 6 provide an "academic" credit that is counted at the university level. Students tend to see themselves as being in one stream or another, although they do not have to take all their courses at the same level.

In British Columbia, the process is more subtle. Few courses are officially streamed; only a few are labelled "modified," signalling a lower level of difficulty. Other courses are offered to all students who decide to enrol at a particular grade level, for example, algebra 11, English 10, and history 12. Differences in students' programs arise through the types of courses they select and the extent to which these courses count toward university admission, rather through the level of difficulty officially attributed to the course. The more academic students planning to continue their education take more mathematics, science, language, and history courses. Those who are not planning or being encouraged to continue take more vocational electives, more business math, home economics, media studies, and human biology, for example (Gaskell 1992).

Some of the studies of the changes in streaming practices in the 1970s stressed how pleased students were to take responsibility for their course choices, instead of having them imposed by the school. Students felt much more in control of their own school careers, and, if they did badly or could not get into university, they would tend to blame themselves for selecting the wrong courses, instead of blaming teachers or the school for inadequate instruction (Fleming 1974). But streaming has merely become more difficult to describe and assess because, under the new system, statistics are hard to collect and rarely reported. The streaming is not hidden from the students, who understand their relative position, nor from postsecondary institutions, who deny entry to students who have not taken appropriate courses.

The United States. Jonathon Kozol (1991) has written a searing indictment of the inequality in U.S. schools. He targets funding policies that allow wealthier neighbourhoods to spend much more money on their local schools than poorer neighbourhoods can afford to spend. He describes the ravaged neighbourhoods of urban America, which spend between $5000 and $8000 per student, compared with the affluent suburbs, where up to $17 000 per student is spent for well-tended buildings, curriculum materials, and teachers' salaries. His book is one of the most recent in a series of impassioned debates in the United States about whether schools provide equality of opportunity.

The question of racial equality has had much greater prominence in the United States than in Canada, reflecting the historical and contemporary importance of the black American community. Schools were finally desegregated legally in 1954, after it was decided by the courts, in the famous case of *Brown versus the Board of Education*, that schools for black and white Americans could not be equal if they were separate. In 1964, during the "war on poverty," a survey of educational opportunity was commissioned by the U.S. Congress. Sociologist James Coleman documented inequalities in school resources, but more importantly in the reading and mathematics achievement of students from different classes and races. He found, most provocatively, that the characteristics of a school, including the money spent per pupil, the qualifications of teachers, and the existence or size of the gym and the library, bore little relation to students' results in tests of achievement. What did seem to matter was the social class of the children's parents and the racial composition of the school. Racially integrated schools were better for students, especially black students.

These findings were extremely controversial. Educators did not like the idea that resources "made little difference," and the survey was reanalyzed and debated for its adequacy in many ways. The finding that home background is the most important predictor of reading and math scores has remained a robust one in many other surveys. The value of racial integration was also hotly contested. Programs for busing white children to black neighbourhoods and black children to white neighbourhoods to produce equality of educational opportunity were implemented, evaluated, applauded, and criticized.

Today the value of allowing families to choose schools for their children has become a major debate in the United States. A variety of proposals exist for increasing parental choice of schools, creating a freer market in education, and reducing the role of the state. Some argue that choice will help to break the hold that social class and race have on neighbourhood schools, school attendance, and achievement. Others argue that choice will only exacerbate existing segregation and inequality (Chubb and Moe 1990). Sociologists are engaged in research on what the effects are, and how reorganization might be accomplished.

Mexico. The state has emphasized the educational system as a route to social mobility and social equality, especially by expanding the availability of primary schooling into rural areas. Literacy campaigns have provided meal and health programs for schoolchildren and provided educational centres to serve both rural and urban areas. Literacy is estimated at a relatively high 87 percent in Mexico, compared with 99 percent in the United States and Canada. But drop-out and illiteracy rates are particularly high in rural areas, and educational attainment is strongly related to region and social class background. According to Medina and Izquierdo (1978:34–35):

About 42 percent of the population lives in the countryside, as we have seen, and there the rate of school attendance in the sixth grade is only 9 percent, compared with 63% in urban areas — an incredible disparity. Furthermore, it is clear that economic factors are decisive in access to education, because 18 percent of school-age children who do not attend school are absent because of insufficient funds. Ninety-three percent of the families whose children do not attend school for economic reasons have monthly incomes under 1,000 pesos and at the other extreme, 91 percent of the student body of the University of Mexico comes from the 15.4 percent of families who are wealthy.

The huge class differences that persist in Mexico are mirrored in the educational system. Expansion of the educational system has benefited the middle- and upper-income sectors. Higher education serves approximately 4 percent of the population but consumes 20 percent of the educational budget. Recently, enrollment has grown much faster at the university level than in the primary schools (Morales-Gomez and Torres 1990).

Knowledge

Canada. Guidelines for what will be taught in Canadian schools are arrived at by provincial ministries of education, through advisory committees that represent government officials, teachers, and often the interested public. Elected school boards can often approve local variations in these guidelines and develop their own courses. Curriculum is translated into practice by teachers in their classrooms, with some supervision from principals, curriculum specialists at the provincial and local levels, and other teachers. The process is a political one in which the public has a clear role. It is also a fairly loose one, especially when, as is almost always the case, testing and reporting to parents is controlled by teachers. Province-wide examinations, which were the norm in Canada in the 1960s, were phased out in the 1970s and then gradually and selectively reintroduced in the 1980s.

The elementary curriculum is based largely on language arts and mathematics, with social studies, science, music, art, and physical education also having their place. Students tend to be taught several subjects by the same teacher, a structure that allows the integration of content from one area to another and encourages a "child-centred" pedagogy. There is virtually no explicitly vocational content in the elementary curriculum, although "relevance" to children's lives is an integral part of what most teachers espouse.

The secondary school curriculum in Canada today has been described as a "smorgasbord" or "cafeteria." A very wide range of courses is available for credit toward a high-school diploma, especially in large urban schools. Students are required to take some core subjects, usually English, mathematics, social studies, and science. Canadian history, social studies, and literature are introduced at some point in the curriculum, reflecting an emphasis on citizenship and nationalism. The wide variety of options includes courses that are vocational in their orientation (such as carpentry, electronics, marketing, accounting, home economics, typing, and work experience), courses that are considered more academic (for example, history, geography, calculus, French, physics, and computer science), to courses in fine arts, personal development, and physical education (including music, painting, drama, community recreation, photography, and guidance). The common requirements for all students are more extensive in the earlier grades and quite minimal in the final two years of secondary school, allowing the streaming described above.

This pattern has evolved over time. At the turn of the century, Canadian secondary schools offered an eclectic mixture of useful subjects for the local bourgeoisie (such as accounting, penmanship, surveying, and navigation) alongside Latin and the more traditional subjects (Gidney and Millar 1990). Most students would pick up a smattering of different kinds of courses. In the early twentieth century, the introduction of subjects of use to the working class occasioned much debate. Typing, manual arts, some technical subjects, and home economics were added to the curriculum at the urging of business and school reformers, but these subjects were clearly labelled vocational and second class and were separated from academic courses. As enrollments increased, these vocational offerings expanded, but they remained firmly segregated and "second class." Many schools through the 1930s and 1940s resisted the incursions of the reformers, and the traditional academic curriculum remained prominent.

Debates about the appropriate divisions and boundaries in the curriculum are never over. The recent Radwanski report in Ontario argued strongly for a common core curriculum that would eliminate the "cafeteria" approach to secondary schooling. The "Year 2000" reforms in British Columbia have attempted to integrate subject areas to a much greater extent than has been the case. However, universities tend to defend the traditional discipline areas, which are the basis of university organization and professional life. Sociologists have looked at university discipline communities as "academic tribes" with distinctive social relations and hierarchies of their

The Framing and Classification of Knowledge

Public Schools, City of Toronto. — Time Table, Male Department, Third Division — Hours of Study, from Nine A.M. to Noon; and from One to Four P.M. — Occupation of Time.

From	To	Monday	Tuesday	Wednesday	Thursday	Friday
9.00	10.00	Reading, Scriptures with Sacred Geography	Reading — Derivations, 5th Book; Dictation, 4th Book.	Reading — Dictation, 5th Book; Science (Natural), 4th Book.	Reading — History, 5th Book; Political Economy, 4th Book.	Repetition and Elocution
10.00	10.50	Writing — Small Hand	Writing — Large Hand	Drawing	Writing and Book-keeping	Writing of Figures; Revision of Euclid
10.50	11.00	Forenoon recess				
11.00	12.00	Arithmetic — Examine Simple Rules	Arithmetic — Compound Rules	Arithmetic — Proportion	Arithmetic — Fractions, &c.	Arithmetic — Repetition
12.00	1.00	Noon Intermission				
1.00	2.00	Grammar — Letter-writing (Composition)	Analysis of Sentences — Comp. of Sim. Nominatives	Grammar — Composition; Des. of Objects; Abstracts	Analysis of Sentences — Written Parsing or Comp.	Repetition of Grammar and Analysis; Composition
2.00	2.50	Geography of America — Map Drawing	History	Geography (General) — Map Drawing	History	Repetition; Geography Object Lesson
2.50	3.00	Afternoon recess				
3.00	3.55	Arithmetic, Algebra, Euclid	Arithmetic, Algebra, Mental Arithmetic	Arithmetic, Euclid, Science (Natural)	Arithmetic, Algebra, Mental Arithmetic	Singing and Recitation of Poetry, &c.

N.B. The School to be opened and closed with Scripture Reading and Prayer. Books from the Library will be given out each Friday afternoon.

In schools, knowledge is divided up among subjects that change somewhat over time and from country to country. But perhaps the most remarkable thing is how constant the school curriculum has been. Examine the accompanying timetable for the Toronto public schools in 1859.

What has changed since 1859? What has remained the same? What accounts for the constancy and the change?

Source:

D. Lawr and R. Gidney. *Educating Canadians: A Documentary History of Public Education* (Toronto: Van Nostrand Reinhold, 1973), p. 111.

own and with power over knowledge production and dissemination (Beecher 1989).

Debates about what belongs within subject areas in the school curriculum continue, as various groups attempt to have their culture and knowledge represented. The debates about heritage language programs illustrate some of the tensions of Canadian society and its commitment to multiculturalism. Various communities that do not speak English as a first language want their children educated in, for example, Greek, Spanish, or Mandarin, in order to pass on their culture and learning to their children. Multiculturalism is an official policy in Canada, so some school boards have tried to accommodate these demands by allowing after-hours instruction in "heritage languages" or integrating it into the school day. Cummins and Danesi report, "During the last decade there has been a rapid expansion of heritage language teaching provision in most parts of Canada. Both federal and provincial funds have contributed to this expansion. However, public opinion is divided on the needs of government support for heritage language teaching, especially in the regular school system" (Cummins and Danes; 1990:49). The debate has been particularly divisive and emotionally charged in Ontario and Quebec because it raises the question of whose culture and whose heritage constitutes Canada. The notion of two founding nations and languages — English and French — is challenged by the notion that other languages should also be taught in the common school.

A look at the content of history courses in Quebec schools and in English Canadian schools provides a second illustration of the way social and historical context shapes curriculum. A study of Canadian civic education in 1968 found that textbooks in English Canada offered a bland consensus interpretation of Canadian society, based on "nice, neat little acts of Parliament." Quebec textbooks discussed quite a different history (Tomkins 1986). In 1977, the Royal Commission on Bilingualism and Biculturalism worried that there were two mutually exclusive historical traditions representing the two different linguistic communities. In the 1992 constitutional debates, it was apparent that this situation had not changed. There is an increased demand for a social history of Canada that includes Native peoples, rural communities, the role of women, and the organization of labour unions, but in many cases history texts continue to represent Canada's history as a political struggle dominated by powerful men of Anglo-Saxon or French background.

The United States. American school curriculum has been shaped by an ongoing series of debates about the nature of knowledge, the needs of children, and the needs of the society. The secondary school curriculum has been the focus of the most public debates. After 1880, schools began to add science, modern languages, and technology to the pre-existing "humanistic" curriculum of Latin, Greek, mathematics, and a smattering of history, English, and geography. With the industrial revolution came the desire to tailor the curriculum to the needs of a new society, to rationalize and streamline and provide different kinds of education for different kinds of students. In the 1890s, a report by the "Committee of Ten," headed by Charles Eliot, president of Harvard University, recommended four programs of study — the classical, the Latin-scientific, the modern languages, and English — all of which focused on broad academic learning and were suitable both for college admission and for "life." But by 1918, another report, this time dominated by educators and called "the Cardinal Principles," defined many more aims of education — health, citizenship, vocation, leisure time, home membership, and so on — and recommended a differentiated curriculum in which different kinds of students appropriately learned different kinds of things. Subject matter in the curriculum became an instrument through which students would learn to function in society, rather than the repository of general knowledge for all. Students destined for different positions in society needed different kinds of knowledge and skill. Vocational courses for those destined for working-class jobs became standard fare.

Debates about the content of curriculum in the United States can be linked closely to the social context in which they arose. After the Russians launched *Sputnik* at the height of the cold war, American curriculum reform centred on science and mathematics teaching. The "new math" resulted from a major national reform effort, launched by university researchers and mathematicians, that was based on beliefs about children "learning by discovery." The new curriculum was aimed at college-bound students and was introduced in the secondary grades. It revolutionized textbooks in the early 1960s as concepts such as sets, nondecimal bases, prime numbers, and factors were introduced for the first time. The reform foundered on the noncomprehension, not just of teachers, but of parents, as it spread through the curriculum to all children and all families. A concept developed by top-flight mathematicians was unable to change the culture of schools and negotiate the institution of schooling (Lazerson et al. 1985)

More recently, attempts to change the social studies curriculum to include the experience of a more diverse school population have brought into the schools the debates about racism and equity that are also going on outside the schools. New York state issued two widely publicized reports, *A Curriculum of Inclusion* in 1989 and *One Nation, Many Peoples* in 1991. Both reports criticized existing curricula for not adequately reflecting the varied experiences of "people of different races, sex, cultural heritage, national origin, religion, and political economic and social background and their values, beliefs and attitudes." Both also evoked a storm of protest from critics who feared that curriculum would become "ethnic cheerleading on the demand of pressure groups," who described the recommendations as a "divisive, far out, liberal sham," and who wondered "Will the center hold?" (Cornbleth 1992).

Mexico. In Mexico also the curriculum has been a point of contention. The curriculum is highly centralized, reflecting the organization of the state and its use of schools in nation-building. In 1960, free and universal textbooks were mandated by the state in an attempt to control the content of the curriculum. As one politician stated at the time, "Mexico is only one country, so it has only one history." The central government still mandates textbooks for the entire country. In 1985–86, 71.7 million textbooks were produced and distributed free of charge by the central government.

The curriculum has been used to try to combat the influence of the church and to promote socialism. In 1934, the Constitution was amended to define education as a socialist enterprise aimed at giving students "a rational and exact concept of the universe and of social life." Angry protests led to the withdrawal of this dictum. Responses to the mandated texts in the 1960s included complaints that they were Marxist in character and too open in sexual matters. Mexican universities have been a particularly strong source of opposition to the state, and have participated in a long history of student activism.

The Mexican curriculum reflects the power of the dominant classes. The language of instruction is Spanish, although in some areas indigenous languages can be used in the first few years of primary school. One study of a Mexican classroom found that the Maya-speaking children of subsistence farmers sat in the back, "learning almost nothing," while the few Spanish-speaking sons and daughters of the "middle class" progressed (Sanders 1979). Textbook discussions of indigenous cultures are limited to brief mentions

Television and Mexican Reality

Children's understanding of the world comes from many places other than schools. This study of the impact of television on knowledge in Mexico points to the critical importance of media in teaching children.

In June 1981, the government's National Consumer Institute tested 1800 primary school children in Mexico City on their comparative knowledge of "television reality" and "national reality" and came up with dramatic results. The children, who were found to spend an average of 1460 hours in front of the television as against 920 hours in school each year, provided correct answers for 73 percent of questions about television and only 38 percent of questions about the country. For example, 92 percent knew that a duckling used to advertise chocolate cakes said "Remember me" and only 64 percent identified Father Miguel Hidalgo as author of the phrase *"Viva la Independencia!"*; 96 percent recognized television cartoon characters, but only 19 percent the last Aztec emperors; 98 percent identified Superman, while only 33 percent knew who Emiliano Zapata was; 96 percent recognized a local television character and only 74 percent could name the then President, López Portillo; and 77 percent identified the trademark of Adams Chiclets and only 17 percent spotted the Monument to the Revolution. More children also knew the times of television programs than the dates of religious festivals, including Christmas.

Source:

Alan Riding, *Distant Neighbours: A Portrait of the Mexicans* (New York: Vintage, 1989), p. 314. Copyright © 1984 by Alan Riding. Reprinted by permission of Alfred A. Knopf, Inc.

of the great pre-Hispanic civilizations and do not acknowledge their continued existence.

Relation to Work

Canada. The belief that investment in education will pay off in the labour market is widely held in Canada. As schooling expanded in the 1950s, human capital theory shaped the thinking of policy-makers. As the Economic Council of Canada (1964) wrote:

An attempt to make an approximate calculation of the contribution which increased education has made to the growth of the real income of Canadians, and a comparison with similar calculations for the United States, has been undertaken in a special study. The essence of this approach is to determine, on the basis of available information and of certain assumptions, what the real income per person would have been in 1961 if the quality of the labour force, as measured by its educational attainment, had not changed since 1911. ... These calculations suggest that in the neighbourhood of one-quarter of the increase in real per capita income over this period is attributable to the increased educational stock in the labour force. Moreover, this should be regarded as a minimum estimate. It is based only on the preceding estimates of increased average years of formal schooling, together with increased average daily school attendance. It takes no account, for example, of increased education and training outside the elementary and secondary schools and universities, or of the increased quality of education over time.

Paul Axelrod traced the expansion of higher education through the 1950s and 1960s and concluded that "the programs themselves reflected and reinforced the utilitarian objects and the ideological corollaries of a free-enterprise society" (Axelrod 1982:29). He showed how the expansion of professional programs was premised on the needs of the economy and was supported by local business elites. Curricula responded to the perceived needs of employers and of students who wanted professional jobs.

The theory that increased education would "pay off" for business lost some of its prominence in the 1970s as the problems of an "overeducated" and underemployed workforce became prominent. However, with the economic challenges of a global economy and the resulting economic restructuring in Canada, more concern has surfaced about the economic imperatives of having a well-educated labour force. In 1992, the Economic Council of Canada reported:

Educational attainment has a strong influence on earnings and employment, and since most Canadian adults participate in the labour market, this link is of vital importance to the economy. Indeed, education is a good investment: after taking account of the direct costs of schooling and of forgone earnings, the additional income from completing secondary school yields a rate of return of some 30 percent for individuals. We know from past Council work that better-educated people tend to hold jobs that are more secure and more satisfying. That study also showed that unemployment rates are higher for persons with lower levels of education and that the risk of unemployment that they face has been increasing substantially over time.

The contribution of skill development to economic performance has special significance today when, quite simply, the Canadian economy is under threat. ... To improve productivity, trade performance, and innovation — to improve the overall competitiveness of a firm, an industry, or an entire economy — one of the critical factors is the enhancement of human skills. Indeed, individually and collectively Canadians face a painful choice: develop skills or accept low wages.

In 1964, the policy conclusion was to invest more money in education in order to expand enrollments, especially in community colleges and universities. In 1992, the conclusion was to spend money on education more effectively by emphasizing linkages between educational institutions and private enterprise, apprenticeships, and partnerships. In both cases, the engine for economic reform is the economy, and the test of educational effectiveness is economic productivity. But exactly how education can better contribute to economic competitiveness is poorly understood. Is it the content or the amount of education that matters? Are close institutional linkages between schools and workplaces desirable? Should schools encourage the development of broad and general skills?

The United States. Recent school-reform efforts in the United States have been driven very explicitly by the rhetoric of economic competition, often with the Japanese. In 1983, the National Commission on Excellence in Education opened its report, *A Nation at Risk*, with the statement: "Our once unchallenged preeminence in commerce, industry, science and technological innovation is being overtaken by competitors throughout the world" as "the educational foundations of our society are presently being eroded by a rising tide of mediocrity." A flurry of reports followed, all arguing for tighter requirements and higher standards for high-school graduation and all linking this to the economic prosperity of the country.

Again the question arises, what kind of education has the most economic payoff? Most school-reform efforts following *A Nation at Risk* called for higher academic standards, fewer curriculum options, and more standardized testing to measure the results of schooling. Another group, however, argued for more vocational curriculum to tie schools more closely to the needs of the workplace. The argument has persisted since the turn of the century. During the Progressive Era, reformers impatient with the "irrelevant" Greek and Latin curriculum argued that students should learn skills that would fit them for jobs in the new industrial economy. More recent arguments for career education and work experience in the secondary schools sound surprisingly similar. A more vocational curriculum is seen as being more useful for both students and employers. But others worry that tying curriculum too closely to the workplace does not produce thoughtful citizens and broadly educated parents, but develops narrow skills that are quickly outmoded in a changing economy.

Although technological progress is usually assumed to increase the complexity of tasks and the need for educated workers, this has been questioned by American sociologists. Rumberger (Burke and Rumberger 1984) pointed out that many of the new jobs spawned by the computer industry in the Silicon Valley were low-level manual jobs that involved the assembly of parts. The introduction of technology into supermarkets and offices has sometimes made jobs only more repetitive, not more skilled. With the export of many of these repetitive jobs to low-wage countries around the world, however, Robert Reich, President Bill Clinton's economic adviser, argues that investing in America's educational infrastructure is the only way to keep America's competitive advantage. This suggests a new world economy in which educational levels are even more strongly tied to jobs.

Mexico. The debate about how much money to invest in increasing the education of the population is a difficult one in Mexico. The state has been strongly committed to investment in education as the vehicle for national development and the preparation of human resources. In 1973, Luis Echeverria, then president of Mexico, stated:

The contribution of education to development is obvious. It shows itself in the formation of qualified individuals; in the ability of a people to absorb and produce technological innovations and raise the level of productivity on the job; and in the accumulation and diffusion of knowledge. Education also has direct effects on socio-economic mobility and contributes to the stimulation of the creative capacity of the population. In other words, education is changing the mental structure of the people which is the first step towards social change. (Quoted in Brooke et al. 1978)

Echeverria summed up the tenets of human capital theory and Parsons's analysis of the contribution of education to society. In Mexico, human capital theory has underlain a dramatic expansion of the educational system. Between 1970 and 1983, the number of students attending high school tripled and the number of university students quadrupled. In 1960, of students entering primary school, one out of 43 graduated from university. Twenty years later, this ratio was one out of nineteen. Teachers constitute almost three-quarters of all central government employees.

Some Mexicans, including some sociologists, wonder whether the effort makes sense. Unemployment has risen among university graduates. The expense of the system is so great that the quality of instruction and curriculum suffers. Classes are overcrowded and qualified teachers are hard to find. Employers may favour educational expansion because it allows them to refuse employment to the lower classes on the basis of credentials, rather than increase productivity. Brooke et al. (1978) found that not one of the company officials they interviewed in Mexico mentioned improved productivity as a reason for hiring the more schooled. The authors conclude that "the tenuousness of such a relationship favours an interpretation that emphasizes the importance to employers of maintaining a socially and culturally homogeneous work force that shares the values of the organization." Collins's version of credentialing, rather than human capital theory, underlies this explanation.

Reform efforts by the government, however, have met stiff resistance from students and faculty. When exams were instituted as a means to control the rate of admissions in 1966, students launched a three-month strike, which led to the rector's resignation. In 1968, the student movement embraced a wide range of political, social, and economic issues. Several students died in the protests and the state faced a crisis of legitimacy. The result was a further expansion of education and some democratic reforms in the state structure.

Toward a Sociological Analysis of Education

Sociologists have approached the analysis of education in various ways. They have drawn different conclusions about the way education is structured and the way it relates to other social institutions. It is clear that education has an impact on the society: people emerge from the educational system with particular ways of understanding the world and behaving in it. It is also clear that education as an institution is shaped by social forces in the economy, in families, in the state and the culture. While everyone has been a student and knows a lot about education, relatively little has been written from this knowledge and analyzed within a sociological framework.

SUMMARY

1. Structural-functional theory analyzes educational institutions as part of a social system in equilibrium and stresses the role of schools in the socialization and allocation of youth.
2. Conflict theory analyzes educational institutions as the outcome of struggles between different groups for control of knowledge and power. Most often, social class groups are considered, but the analysis can be made more broadly to consider how men and women, teachers and parents, groups with different cultural traditions, or special-interest groups try to gain access to schools and to the curriculum.
3. A third tradition emphasizes the way people in schools give meaning to their experience: how they interpret and understand what goes on in schools.
4. Canadian schools reflect in many ways the federal, democratic, and market-economy traditions of the country. The differing traditions of English and French Canada have shaped the organization and content of schools, and the emergence of multiculturalism as the federal policy framework has shaped recent discussions of schooling.
5. The quest for equality has been part of the argument for school expansion, but in Canada social class continues to be strongly associated with school achievement. Women, on average, now surpass men in most measures of school achievement.
6. Schools in the United States have grown from many of the same traditions as Canadian schools, but American race relations and the constitutional separation of church and state have marked U.S. education.
7. Education in Mexico has been a primary instrument of political and economic development. The country's relative poverty and its revolutionary centralized state have shaped the debates about curriculum and educational development. Large differences in wealth are reflected in continuing educational inequality.
8. The contribution of education to economic growth is widely acknowledged by sociologists and politicians. However, the limits to this contribution in the case of a country like Mexico, and the particular mechanisms that translate education into income, are poorly understood.

GLOSSARY

Allocation. Process of matching people to positions in the labour force on the basis of their schooling.

Credentialing. Process of giving diplomas and other formal recognition of school achievement, which in turn make candidates eligible for jobs.

Formal curriculum What is formally prescribed to be taught in schools.

Human capital theory. Economic theory holding that the skill level of the labour force is a prime determinant of economic growth.

Informal curriculum. Things that are learned in school even though they are not part of the formal curriculum.

Meritocracy. Social system based on the principle that those with talent should rise to positions of power and responsibility.

Socialization. Process of teaching children the norms, knowledge, and skills they need to function in the society.

Status attainment models. Models of the determinants of achievement in the labour force based on regression models, which include individual variables such as social class status, schooling, intelligence, aspirations, and achievement.

FURTHER READING

Bernstein, B. *Class, Codes and Control. Vol. 3. Toward a Theory of Educational Transmission*, (2nd ed.). London: Routledge and Kegan Paul, 1977. Analyzes the ways in which the structure and organization of school knowledge reflects relations of power, both in the primary grades, where integration is stressed, and in later grades, where a stricter progression and differentiation of subjects is apparent.

Bowles, S., and H. Gintis. *Schooling in Capitalist America.* New York: Basic Books, 1976. An influential discussion of the ways in which schools correspond to the needs of employers in a capitalist economy.

Collins, R. *The Credential Society.* New York: Academic Press, 1979. A critique of human capital theory's emphasis on education as a place where skills are developed because they are needed by the society.

Gaskell, J., and A. McLaren. *Women and Education* Calgary: Detselig, 1991. A collection of articles looking at the way gender relations shape teaching, access to knowledge, and the forms of curriculum in Canadian schools and universities.

Gidney, B., and W. Millar. *Inventing Secondary Education: The Rise of the High School in Nineteenth Century Ontario.* Kingston and Montreal: McGill–Queen's Press, 1990. Traces the development of schools in Ontario, from their local, voluntary, and ungraded roots to the form they have today.

Guppy, N., and K. Pendakur. "The effects of gender and parental education on participation within postsecondary education in the 1970s and 1980s." *Canadian Journal of Higher Education* 19(1) (1989): 49–62. The article explores the effects of gender and parental education on students' decisions to study part-time or full-time. Part-time study has been particularly important for women and students with less educated parents. While gender differences in participation rates at college and university have disappeared, differences related to parents' education persist.

Kliebard, H.M. *The Struggle for the American Curriculum 1893–1958.* Boston: Routledge and Kegan Paul, 1986. Discusses the competing interest groups and ideologies that have marked the development of the contemporary American curriculum, emphasizing debates about humanism, child-centred curriculum, vocationalism, and social reform.

Lareau, A. *Home Advantage: Social Class and Parental Intervention in Elementary Education.* Philadelphia: Falmer Press, 1991. Based on a research study of parents, teachers, and children in two schools, one working-class and one middle-class, this book traces the way parents deal with the school differently in the two communities.

McNeil, L. *Contradictions of Control, School Structures and School Knowledge.* New York: Routledge, 1986. Based on research in one American high school, this book explores how teachers decide what to teach and how.

Morales-Gomez, D.A., and C.A. Torres. *The State, Corporatist Politics, and Educational Policy Making in Mexico.* New York: Praeger, 1990. A discussion of educational policy in Mexico in the twentieth century, based on an analysis of the state and social conflict theory.

Pike, Robert M. "Sociological research on higher education in English Canada 1970–1980: A thematic review." *Canadian Journal of Higher Education* 11(2) (1981): 1–25. Pike notes that there has been little sociological research on higher education in Canada. The research that has been done looks at how education maintains inequality in the society, as children from middle- and upper-middle-class families are greatly overrepresented in universities. There is also some research on the organization of higher education, and on changes in student attitudes, values, and behaviour.

Tompkins, G.S. *A Common Countenance: Stability and Change in the Canadian Curriculum.* Scarborough: Prentice Hall, 1986. A comprehensive survey of the influences on Canadian schools, beginning with New France in about 1650.

Willis, P. *Learning to Labour.* Farnborough, UK: Saxon House Press, 1977. A study of how and why "the lads" choose to leave school for working-class jobs.

UNIT V

Social Change

For thousands of years, human beings and their ancestors walked, or rode horses, or sailed ships. In 1926, the rocket was invented, and in 1934, the jet engine. In 1969, astronauts walked on the moon. The world is changing, and the rate of change itself is accelerating.

It took more than a million years for the world's human population to reach about a quarter billion, in A.D. 1. It took an additional 1650 years for the population to double, to about half a billion. But it took only 200 years for it to double again; it reached 1 billion in 1850. Less than 100 years later, it was 2 billion. Then it doubled again in 36 years, reaching 4 billion by 1976. By the year 2000, it is expected to double again, to 8 billion. What will your world be like in a decade or two?

For a very long time, the role a person played in youth was not much different from that played in later life: a farmer was a farmer; a parent was a parent. Today, roles change constantly. For example, sociologists estimate that 10 years from today, half the jobs now available to high-school graduates will have faded out of existence. They will have been replaced by jobs that do not yet exist.

Social change is an essential ingredient of our society. Most of the earlier chapters of this book include some discussion of social change in particular areas, such as the family and education. Two fundamental changes that occurred in the Western world were the industrial revolution and urbanization.

It is no accident that sociology developed during the industrial revolution. The changes that this revolution brought about in society were a major concern to Durkheim, Weber, Simmel, and Marx. Chapter 16 makes clear the differences in the degree of industrialization by comparing Canada, the United States, and Mexico. The importance of these differences and their consequences are discussed.

Chapter 17 discusses another of the major social changes of modern times, the population shift from rural to urban areas. Like industrialization, urbanization in developing countries takes a different pattern than it does in developed countries. This chapter examines the causes and consequences of urbanization.

Chapter 18 is a more general and theoretical treatment of social change, paying special attention to groups that promote or resist change.

Chapter 19 discusses the enduring issue of whether or not sociology is a science, and provides analysis of recent developments and changes in sociological theories.

CHAPTER 16

Industrialization and Work

R. ALAN HEDLEY

"What do you do?" This question isn't specific, yet we all know what it means: "What *work* do you do?" This important question is almost always asked a few minutes after strangers meet. Work is such an integral part of our lives that the answer reveals much more about a person than simply what he or she does for a living. It also allows us to estimate the individual's educational level, probable income, prestige, and lifestyle. In other words, because work is so central in our society, it is a major source of personal and social identity.

Work is the driving force in society. It is primarily a means to other ends, although for some people it becomes an end in itself. Work permits us to exist, and the type of work we do determines in large part the quality of that existence. **Work** is any activity that permits individuals a livelihood; it includes conventional paid employment within the labour force, as well as illegal employment outside it and homemaking. (Those people — usually women, because of domestic divisions of labour — who take care of home and family are also workers, even though they are not directly paid for their labour. Their homemaking activity permits others in the family to concentrate their energies more fully on paid employment. However, some homemakers also enter the labour force; their responsibilities for maintaining the household do not diminish, as the chapters on gender relations [Chapter 5] and the family [Chapter 12] indicate.) In this chapter, we examine how the institution of work affects us and how we in turn view the world of work.

The Industrial Revolution

The history of modern work can be traced to the **industrial revolution** at the end of the eighteenth century (see Lenski, Lenski, and Nolan 1991). As a result of a number of technological changes, the whole structure of British and European societies was thrown into radical social change. Beginning in the textile and agricultural-equipment industries, large factories utilizing mechanical power and employing hundreds of workers were built to produce a hitherto unimagined volume of goods. These goods, because they were made more cheaply than was possible by traditional methods, were distributed widely throughout society; thus, their production provided a great stimulus to the European economy.

The new agricultural equipment was responsible for increasing yields per hectare, thereby raising per capita income and freeing people who had worked on the land to serve the new industrial enterprise. It was now possible to produce more food with less labour.

The industrial revolution was revolutionary because it produced changes far beyond those required to implement the new production techniques. The institution of work itself was changed in several important respects. Several interrelated features of this revolution make it stand out as one of the most important turning points in how we do work and how we think about it (see Hedley 1992b:63–97).

1. *Mechanical power.* In the late 1700s, James Watt patented the modern steam engine for practical commercial use (see Mantoux 1961). For the first time in history it became possible to replace the relatively feeble power of people and animals and the often capricious power of wind and water with a strong, constant source of energy. The harnessing of steam meant that people could then accomplish feats formerly not within their grasp.
2. *Large-scale organization.* In order to utilize the power of steam efficiently, it became necessary to build large engines to drive the industrial machinery. Only in this way was mechanical power more cost-effective than human power. Large factories were built in order to achieve economies of scale, or greater volumes of output at a reduced cost per *unit* of output. This marked the beginning of modern bureaucratization and the preponderance of wage- and salary-earners, as opposed to self-employed people in the labour force. (Recall the discussion in Chapter 11 on this topic.)
3. *Market production.* Mechanical power and large-scale organization were responsible for the widespread change from subsistence to market production. People produced goods no longer only for their own needs but for a larger, amorphous market of consumers. In order to take advantage of the increased capacity of mechanized production, industrial entrepreneurs had to create a demand for their great volume of goods. In this way, industrialization resulted in what we have come to call the marketplace. Various goods are produced according to the demand that exists for them. This is one of the essential bases of mass production.
4. *Improved transportation.* The need to obtain raw materials for manufacture and to get goods to market resulted in a great expansion and improvement in transportation. In fact, this was the second stage of the industrial revolution as the steam engine was applied directly to transport. Railways and steam ships fed the increased production, which required ever-increasing access to surrounding areas.
5. *Urbanization.* Because the first factories were large in order to achieve economies of scale and because they had to locate near available sources of energy (such as coal), the people in labouring classes had to go to and live near these factories. Industrialization thus was accompanied by urbanization as large industrial towns and cities sprang up in the vicinity of these factories. (The history of modern urbanization is presented more fully in Chapter 17).
6. *Time metric.* The co-ordination of equipment and labour involved a scheduling problem previously unexperienced. Because steam is powerful only when it is contained under pressure and because that pressure is expensive to maintain, precise work schedules had to be established to accommodate the new

industrial enterprise. Time, hitherto recorded as day and night, was now measured meticulously by the minute.

7. *Division of labour.* Work in the large, steam-powered factories came to be organized differently than it had been. No longer was each individual worker responsible for the manufacture of a completed product. Instead, work was broken down into specialized tasks, so that a group of relatively unskilled workers could complete these tasks with a minimum of training. An integral part of the industrialization process was a division of labour on a scale never before witnessed.

8. *Labour market.* With the introduction of a division of labour came a demand for various categories of specialized labour. In order to match supply with demand, the idea of an industrial labour market was established. Consequently, two modes or sectors of production — the agricultural and the industrial — came to co-exist, each operated by different principles. The older agricultural sector was organized traditionally, with no clear demarcation between work and other social activities; work there was primarily family-based and constituted one of the many functions in which families engaged. On the other hand, work in the industrial sector was strictly defined and was available only for those within the labour market. Individuals not in the labour market were economic liabilities in that they were not earning wages. The principles of an industrial labour market thus influenced the move toward smaller families and increased female labour-force participation.

9. *Ideology.* Because the changes that were introduced were so radical and occurred over a relatively short period, some justifying rationale or ideology was required to explain the new type of society that was emerging. One important legitimating ideology was Protestantism, in which work is held to be of service to God. Particularly in the view of Calvinists, work — and more important, hard work — is a religious duty. According to the **Protestant work ethic**, how successful one is in this endeavour can be measured by how much money and property one acquires.

Therefore, the early industrialists were gratified not only by their labour and the amount of capital they gained, but also by the knowledge that they were being employed in the service of God.

Another important set of beliefs that provided justification for the industrial revolution, a rationale that has become one of the most dominant political ideologies in the world today, came from the work of the Scottish moralist Adam Smith (1937, originally published in 1776). Smith, the father of modern capitalism, advocated "free enterprise." Unfettered by government intervention, the marketplace is governed by the law of supply and demand, which acts in the best interests of all. Industrialists and capitalists therefore felt justified in almost any activity in which they engaged.

All of these features transformed the societies in which they appeared — first in Britain and later in Germany, France, the United States, and Canada. One set of reactions to these changes resulted in the formation and consolidation of the discipline of sociology. Each of the three early theorists discussed in Chapter 1 — Durkheim, Weber, and Marx — wrote major works on what they believed to be the most important issues arising out of the industrial revolution.

Industrialization in the World Today

In 1850, when industrialization was well under way in both Europe and North America, per capita income in the industrialized, developed nations was 70 percent higher than it was in the developing countries of the world (Murdoch 1980). Today, this income gap has increased many times over and is continuing to grow. Industrialization has produced a disparity among the peoples of the world on a scale never before thought possible. According to Prime Minister Pierre Trudeau, who was representing Canada at a Western Economic Summit meeting in 1981, "The gap between them [the 'South'] and us is so wide that we had better manage a change in our economic relations with them before we find it thrust upon us" (cited in Crow and Thomas 1983:71).

Table 16-1 reveals the substance of this gap. It presents the results of a United Nations survey of all countries in the world ($N = 160$) classified according to their industrial status (UNDP 1991). Industrialization not only affects how much income a country and its citizens generate (national output), it also defines the type of work performed (employment), the kind of infrastructure a society is able to maintain (infrastructure), how quickly a population grows (population growth), and, therefore, the quality of life of ordinary citizens (quality of life).

Before examining Table 16-1's figures in detail, it is important to realize that these statistics present a general overall picture of conditions in all countries of the world that is based on the classification of countries as "industrial" or "developing." Does industrialization make a difference? By comparing the columns (which distinguish industrial status) in each of the rows (which specify various conditions), it is possible to "see" the vast differences that industrialization makes in all aspects of life. This is what is meant by "the gap between them and us."

Table 16-1 presents two measures of national output: per capita gross national product (the total value of goods and services each citizen on average produces) and real per capita gross domestic product (what this output means in terms of individual purchasing power). Both measures reveal the huge gap in income between industrial and developing countries, particularly the "least developed" of these countries — 39 nonindustrial nations targeted by the U.N. for priority international development assistance. The figures on comparative purchasing power for 1960 and 1988 document the fact that the income gap between industrial and developing countries is growing. In 1960, per capita purchasing power in the 33 industrial countries was 5.9 times greater than it was in the developing countries (11.2 times greater than in the least developed nations). By 1988, this gap had increased to 6.6 and had almost doubled with respect to the least developed countries (19.9). Clearly, as all studies have shown, industrialization is strongly related to both national and individual income (see Hedley 1992b: 63–97, 127–158).

What people do for a living also changes as a result of industrialization. In developing countries most people are employed in agriculture, while in industrial countries most work in the service and industrial sectors. Other changes in employment involve greater female labour-force participation and a decrease in the dependency ratio (the proportion of the population who are defined as dependent — those under 15 and over 64 years of age).

An important aspect related to industrialization is the development of a societal infrastructure capable of supporting an industrially based economy. The **infrastructure** of a society is the institutionalized response of its people to the central problems faced by the society. In industrialized nations, an infrastructure is responsible for the health and education of citizens so that they can contribute effectively to society as workers. In addition, it regulates and deals with a whole host of problems relating to transportation and communication, economic development, the administration of justice, the protection of national sovereignty, and social welfare, to name only a few.

Table 16-1 reveals how well-developed the infrastructures of the industrial nations are, compared with those of the developing countries. With regard to health, while the number of inhabitants per doctor and per nurse are specific measures, they more generally indicate the extent of the health and medical establishment throughout the various countries surveyed. In industrial countries, each practising physician has on average a caseload of 460 patients, while clearly much of the populace in developing countries does not have access to medical doctors. They continue to care for themselves by using traditional folk customs that they have practised for centuries. Occasionally, in times of widespread famine or pestilence, formal medical practitioners may intervene on their behalf. However, in countries where on average there are 5000 or even 20 000 inhabitants per doctor, it is obvious that the medical infrastructure does not extend to all.

The data on education reveal a similar story. Enrollment in primary and secondary schools is a near-universal requirement for the citizens of industrial societies in order to prepare them more adequately for entry into a complex, industrially based economy. One-third continue their formal

TABLE 16-1 Industrialization in Relation to National Output, Employment, Infrastructure, Population Growth, and Quality of Life

Correlates of Industrialization	Year	Industrial Status[1]		
		Least-Developed Countries	All Developing Countries	Industrial Countries
National Output				
GNP per capita (US$)[2]	1988	230	710	12 510
Real GDP per capita ($)[3]	1960	420	790	4 690
	1988	720	2 170	14 350
Employment				
Percentage of population in labour force	1988–89	38.8	43.9	48.5
Women as percentage of labour force	1988–89	27.1	31.1	39.6
Dependency ratio[4]	1990	90	69	50
Percentage of labour force in:				
Agriculture	1965	83.5	72.1	22.2
	1985–88	73.1	61.2	11.6
Industry	1965	5.8	11.3	36.4
	1985–88	7.0	12.7	28.0
Services	1965	11.0	16.7	41.5
	1985–88	19.9	26.1	60.4
Infrastructure				
Health				
Population per doctor	1984	21 410	4 590	460
Population per nurse	1984	4 910	1 910	150
Education				
Primary/secondary enrollment ratio[5]	1986–88	41	70	97
Tertiary enrolment ratio	1986–88	2.6	6.5	33.8
Mean years of education[6] — total	1980	1.4	3.5	9.1
— male	1980	2.1	4.4	9.4
— female	1980	0.8	2.5	8.8
Primary pupil–teacher ratio	1986–88	47	35	19
Communication				
TVs per 1000 population	1986–88	6	40	480
Newspaper circulation/1000 population	1986–88	5	34	342
Population Growth				
Estimated percentage of world population	1960	7.0	68.5	31.5
	1990	8.3	77.1	22.9
	2000	9.4	79.7	20.3
Percentage of annual population growth rate	1960–90	2.5	2.3	0.8
	1990–2000	3.0	2.0	0.5
Total fertility rate[7]	1990	6.1	3.9	1.9
Quality of Life				
Under-5 mortality rate[8]	1989	199	116	18
Maternal mortality rate[9]	1980–87	530	290	24
Daily calorie supply[10]	1984–86	89	107	132
Persons per habitable room	1979–82	—	2.4	0.8
Years of life expectancy at birth	1990	50.7	62.8	74.5

NOTES
[1]In the United Nations' *Human Development Report 1991* (UNDP, 1991:199), 33 countries (all European nations, Canada, the United States, Japan, Australia, New Zealand, the former USSR, and Israel) are classified "industrial"; the remainder (*N* = 127) are termed "developing." Of this latter group, 39 are categorized "least developed," a U.N. designation for countries with an annual per capita GNP of $300 or less. The vast majority of these least developed countries are in Africa (74%) or Asia (18%).

TABLE 16-1 (*continued*)

[2]Gross national product (GNP) and gross domestic product (GDP) are two slightly different measures of national output. GNP measures the total domestic and foreign output claimed by residents, whereas GDP measures the total final output of goods and services produced by an economy — that is, by residents and nonresidents.

[3]"The United Nations International Comparison Project (ICP) has developed measures of real GDP on an internationally comparable scale using purchasing power parities (PPP) instead of exchange rates as conversion factors, and expressed in international dollars" (UNDP 1991:195).

[4]"The ratio of the population defined as dependent, under 15 and over 64 years, to the working-age population, aged 15–64" (UNDP 1991:193).

[5]"The number enrolled in a level of education, whether or not they belong in the relevant age group for that level, expressed as a percentage of the population in the relevant age group for that level" (UNDP 1991:193).

[6]For adults 25 years and older.

[7]"The average number of children that would be born alive to a woman during her lifetime, if she were to bear children at each age in accordance with prevailing age-specific fertility rates" (UNDP 1991:193–194).

[8]Per 1000 live births.

[9]Per 100 000 live births.

[10]Expressed as a percentage of daily requirements.

SOURCE: Adapted from UNDP (United Nations Development Program), *Human Development Report 1991* (New York: Oxford University Press, 1991), pp. 122–169.

education at the postsecondary level. In developing countries, most adults have completed barely three years of primary school; postsecondary education is a luxury reserved for the scant few. The data on the developing countries also indicate that education is considered to be more important for males than for females. While adult males (25 years and older) have on average completed 4.4 years of formal schooling, adult females have only 2.5 years, that is, close to half of what men have achieved. In the least-developed countries, the differences are even more extreme. In this group of nations, school attendance is not a viable option for the majority of school-aged children, particularly girls.

The final measures of the presence and adequacy of an infrastructure deal with communication — in other words, with how well social systems provide people living and working in different areas with access to the same information. In industrial countries, most households have television sets and access to daily newspapers. However, in developing countries, the exception is the rule. Fewer than four people in 100 own a television set and read the newspaper. This means that for the most part, the citizens of these countries rely on small, informal networks for their information. The data on both education and communication suggest that there is no general body of knowledge and information available to most inhabitants.

The data on population growth reveal that not only is the gap between industrial and developing countries increasing, but the proportion of

people living in developing countries is also growing. In 1960, the developing nations accounted for slightly more than two-thirds of the world population; by the year 2000, it is estimated that they will make up four-fifths. This means that even more people may be subject to the kinds of conditions described above.

In demographic terms, the developing countries have not completed Stage Two of the demographic transition. (Demographic transition theory is described more fully in Chapter 8.) As a consequence, they have relatively low mortality rates in comparison with their fertility rates. This is illustrated in Table 16-1 by the total fertility rate. According to current age-specific fertility rates, it is estimated that, on average, each woman in the developing countries will bear approximately four children during her lifetime. The number rises to six in the least-developed countries.) By contrast, the industrial nations are entering the third and final stage of the demographic transition; their birth and death rates are approximately the same. The total fertility rate of women in industrial countries is 1.9. This is referred to as replacement-level fertility, which in time produces zero population growth.

Finally, as mentioned at the outset, industrialization directly affects the quality of life of ordinary citizens. Table 16-1 presents five indicators that attest to this fact, but there are hundreds more. Most of us do not consider surviving to our fifth birthday to be an amazing feat, but in some developing countries it can be a phenomenal hurdle. For example, in Afghanistan (one of the least-developed countries in Table 16-1), there is a 30 percent chance against it (UNDP 1991:141). For all the developing nations, there is greater than one chance in ten that a child will not live past its fifth birthday; in the industrial countries this risk is reduced to less than two in 100.

Not only are the chances of not reaching one's fifth birthday relatively high in the developing countries, there is a ten-times-greater probability that the child's mother will not be there to share in the celebration. A mother's death during childbirth is still not uncommon in many of these countries. Also, the basic amenities, such as food and shelter, are at more of a premium.

The final indicator in Table 16-1 is a measure of the quantity of life, rather than its quality. Yet, comparative life-expectancy figures disclose the surrounding conditions in which people live their lives. For example, to state that the average Canadian baby born in 1990 may expect to live almost twice as long as one born in Sierra Leone indicates much more than simple longevity; it indicates the life circumstances in the two countries.

All the measures presented in Table 16-1 are highly correlated to national levels of industrialization. Whether they concern national output, employment, infrastructure, population growth, or quality of life, these data show that the level of industrialization explains much of the variation among countries. These factors together provide documentation for the assertion that the growing gap between the industrialized rich countries and the developing poor ones constitutes one of the most pressing social problems in the world today. Two former Canadian prime ministers, Lester B. Pearson and Pierre Elliott Trudeau, spent much of their terms in office attempting to persuade nations to help redress this imbalance, but many complexities are involved and their work failed to produce any concerted efforts.

Differential Paths of Growth and Development

The basis of the problem lies in the different patterns of growth and development in the rich and the poor nations. During the original industrial revolution in Europe, population growth was high, thereby reducing much of the productivity gain achieved through industrialization. One solution to this problem was emigration. From 1840 to 1930, at least 52 million Europeans (double Canada's present population) emigrated (Davis 1974). This emigration was of two types (see Murdoch 1980). One type involved permanent settlement in the temperate regions of the world (Canada, the United States, Australia, New Zealand, and southern South America and Africa) and was an important safety valve in the control of European population growth. The second type of emigration was to the tropical areas; its main purpose was not settlement but the acquisition of valuable raw materials (gold, silver, diamonds, and other goods not indigenous to Europe) that helped to finance the industrialization process in the home countries. Each of these migratory patterns contributed significantly to the development and modernization of the industrializing European nations.

Today, the problems are more complex, and it is not possible for industrialization in the developing nations to occur in the same way. As Table 16-1 indicates, population growth in the developing countries is 2 percent per year. This means that the economies of these nations must grow annual by this amount just to cope with their population growth. Furthermore, even though the present world migration pattern has changed and there is now a general population movement from the poor to the rich nations, this emigration is insufficient to check the poorer nations' population growth. Given the present population of the developing countries — over 4 billion — and their annual rate of growth, the industrial nations would have to accept more than 81 million immigrants per year, or an increase of 6.7 percent. Thus, the safety valve of emigration that existed for the industrializing European countries cannot be used by the developing nations.

Another major obstacle is the financing of the very expensive industrialization process. This was largely achieved in the European industrial revolution through the exploitation of countries in the tropical regions or, as one author put it, the pillage of the Third World (Jalée 1968). Although some academics and politicians in the developed nations have suggested that it is now only fair for the industrial countries to repay their debt to the developing nations and assist financially in their industrialization (Tinbergen 1976), generally this support has not been forthcoming in amounts sufficient to bring about the desired changes.

Since the mid-1980s, the developing nations have been heavily in debt to the developed nations; debt repayment has exceeded official development assistance, causing an overall negative flow of capital to the developing countries. According to the World Bank (1991:125), "At the end of 1989 the debt of the severely indebted low-income countries was equivalent to their combined GNP." Thus, it is impossible for these countries to accumulate independently the capital necessary to achieve industrialization.

These differences in the growth and development patterns of the industrial and developing nations mean that the gap between the rich and the poor probably will continue to increase. It seems inevitable that at some point this gap will be perceived as intolerable by the rapidly growing populations of the developing nations. If the world's resources are not shared more equitably, it is likely that social unrest in all forms will increase dramatically. Already there are signs of discontent: mounting acts of terrorism and civil disobedience, massive illegal migration, rising crime rates, and internal disputes that escalate into international conflicts. Twenty-five years ago, Lester Pearson predicted: "Before long, in our affluent, industrial, computerized jet society, we shall feel the wrath of the wretched people of the world. There will be no peace" (quoted in Tinbergen 1976).

Industrialization in Canada, the United States, and Mexico

Industrialization is a complex process with several interrelated dimensions. Together, these dimensions allow researchers to compare the level of industrialization in one country with that of another and consequently to evaluate the effects of this process.

- *Economic activity and labour.* Predominant emphasis on agricultural and other harvesting activities (such as fishing, hunting, and trapping) is supplanted by industrial activities involving the transformation of raw materials into finished and semifinished manufactured goods.

- *National output.* Proportional increase in the contribution of industrial activity to overall national wealth or income.

- *Organization.* Increasing performance of work in the context of formal, complex organizations.

- *Mechanization.* Systematic replacement of human and animal energy with controlled, inanimate sources of power.

- *Technology.* Increasing reliance on the development of systematic methods and innovative practices in the performance of work.

On the basis of these criteria of industrialization, Canada and the United States are classified as industrial in Table 16-1, while Mexico is assigned developing status. To determine specific differences among these three countries, Table 16-2 presents empirical indicators for each of the above dimensions. On the first measure — percentage of labour force in industry — there is a remarkable similarity among the three countries. Approximately one-fifth of the labour force in each country is classified as industrial. However, the table does not indicate what the other four-fifths do. In Canada and the United States, the overwhelming majority (76 percent and 78 percent respectively) work in the services-producing tertiary sector, while in Mexico only 57 percent are so employed. Even though the table shows similar percentages of workers being employed in industry in Canada, the United States, and Mexico, the workers who are *not* represented in the table reveal differences. Because many more workers are employed in agriculture in Mexico (23 percent) than in either Canada (5 percent) or the United States (3 percent), and because of substantial differences in employment in the tertiary sector, Canada and the United States are more developed industrially than is Mexico.

During industrialization, initially there is a shift in employment from the agricultural **primary sector** to the industrial **secondary sector.** Upon achieving mature industrial status, which includes the introduction of labour-saving equipment and machinery in the primary and secondary sectors, there is another employment shift to the more labour-intensive **tertiary sector.** The secondary sector involves the manufacture of finished and semifinished goods, and the tertiary sector provides services, including transportation, communication, the provision of public utilities, most professional work, and all occupations in commerce, finance, health, education, welfare, and

TABLE 16-2   Measures of Industrialization in Canada, the United States, and Mexico

Measure of Industrialization	Canada	United States	Mexico
Economic Activity/Labour			
Percentage of labour force in industry (1985–88)[1]	19	19	20
National Output			
Manufacturing as a percent of GDP (1989)[2]	13	17	23
Organization			
Percentage of labour force self-employed (1978–86)[3]	9	8	27
Mechanization			
Energy consumption per capita (kilograms of oil equivalent) 1989[4]	9959	7794	1288
Technology			
Percentage of professional and technical workers in labour force (1987)[5]	16	15	7

SOURCE: [1]United Nations Development Program, *Human Development Report 1991* (New York: Oxford University Press, 1991), pp. 150, 183; [2]World Bank, *World Development Report 1991* (New York: Oxford University Press, 1991), pp. 208–209; [3]George Thomas Kurian, *The New Book of World Rankings* (New York: Facts on File, 1991), [4]World Bank, *ibid.*, pp. 212–213; [5]Kurian, *ibid.*, table 150.

recreation or leisure. The emphasis on employment in the tertiary sector has been described as a transformation to **postindustrial society** (Bell 1967). (The history of this process for Canada is presented in Table 16-3.)

Industrialization is not an all-or-nothing phenomenon; it has stages. While Canada and the United States are generally acknowledged to be developed, this does not mean that Mexico is not. Mexico is referred to as a **newly industrializing country (NIC)** (see Hedley 1992a). This means that on some of the dimensions described above it achieves industrial status, while on others it does not. Although cut-off points are used for classification purposes, in fact all countries in the world can be placed somewhere along a multidimensional *continuum* of industrialization.

The second measure of industrialization in Table 16-2 reveals that manufacturing contributes a higher percentage to the gross domestic product of Mexico than it does in either the United States or Canada. Again, this reflects the greater emphasis placed on the tertiary sector in the latter two countries. However, it also points to the fact that manufacturing includes the making of goods and articles by machinery *and* by hand. An examination of the manufacturing industry in Mexico re-

veals that a significant proportion of it is achieved by traditional handcraft methods (for example, in the making of pottery, textiles, metalworks, and woodwork). Consequently, although manufacturing is indeed an essential component of industrialization, there is considerably more involved. It is necessary to examine in detail the context (organization), conditions (mechanization), and methods (technology) under which this process takes place. This underlines the fact that no empirical indicator is an absolutely perfect measure of the concept it is reflecting.

The third measure of industrialization refers to its organizational context. In all highly industrialized countries, including Canada and the United States, the overwhelming majority of workers in the labour force are either wage or salary earners. This reflects the fact that they work in complex organizations that are the custodians of scarce and valuable resources (capital, equipment, plant, and so on) necessary for the performance of work. Relatively few workers are self-employed. Table 16-2 reveals that the proportion of self-employed workers in Mexico is three times greater than in Canada and the United States. Consequently, on this measure there is clear evidence that Mexico is less industrialized.

Most professional work is part of the tertiary employment sector.

The final measure of industrialization, technology, is based on the percentage of professional and technical workers in the labour force. According to Kurian (1991:table 150):

Without at least 10% of the labour force employed in both basic and applied research, no country can hope to become industrialized. The demand for professional and technical workers is so great in postindustrial nations that it has given rise to the phenomenon known as the "brain drain," where professional and technical workers leave their developing countries to work in Western industrialized nations.

Significantly, professional and technical workers only constitute more than 10% of the economically active population (the optimum according to manpower experts) in 25 nation-states.

Consequently, on this measure too, while Canada and the United States achieve industrial status, Mexico does not.

Mexico, like other newly industrializing countries such as Brazil, Venezuela, Taiwan, South Korea, Hong Kong, and Singapore, represents a "mixed case." Although it is the world's eighth-largest producer of commercial vehicles (vans, trucks, buses, tractors, and semitrailer combinations), only 50 percent of its roads are paved. Whereas the percentage of its labour force that is unionized is twice that of the United States, administrators and managers make up just 1 percent of all workers (11 percent in Canada and the United States). While Mexico has more airports

The fourth measure also indicates that Mexico is not as industrialized as its neighbours to the north. Based on energy consumption per capita — the driving force of industrial equipment and machinery — Canada appears to be even more industrialized than the United States. In terms of per capita energy consumption, this is true, but it is also true that all energy consumed does not drive machinery. Canadians, as you well know, live in a cold climate and consume much energy just to keep warm. Also, Canada, the largest country in the world, consumes large amounts of energy for transportation. Consequently, its position in the rank-order of industrialization is inflated when per capita energy consumption is used as the empirical measure. Once again, this highlights the fact that no measure is perfect; we must always be attentive to flaws and anomalies.

The emphasis on employment in the tertiary sector has been described as a transformation to postindustrial society.

TABLE 16-3 Employment in Canada's Occupational Structure, 1881–1988 (Percent)

	Occupational Sector		
	Primary[1]	Secondary[2]	Tertiary[3]
Agricultural Society			
1881	51	29	19
1891	50	26	24
Industrial Society			
1901	44	28	28
1911	40	27	33
1921	37	27	37
1931	32	28	40
1941	31	28	41
1951	23	33	44
Postindustrial Society			
1961	14	32	54
1971	9	28	63
1981	7	25	67
1988	6	23	71

[1]"Primary sector" includes all those working in agriculture, mining, logging, fishing, hunting, and trapping.
[2]"Secondary sector" includes those working in manufacturing and construction.
[3]"Tertiary sector" includes those in transportation, communications, utilities, trade, finance, insurance, real estate, public administration, and other services.
NOTES
• The difference between year percentage sums and 100 is due to rounding.
• The difference in the percentage distribution of sector employment between Tables 16-2 and 16-3 (Canada 1988) is due to the use of slightly different classification procedures.
SOURCE: Data for 1881–1971 adapted from Joseph Smucker, *Industrialization in Canada* (Scarborough, ON: Prentice-Hall, 1980), p. 78; data for 1981 and 1988 adapted from Ross McKitrick, *The Current Industrial Relations Scene in Canada 1989: The Economy and Labour Markets Reference Tables* (Kingston, ON: Industrial Relations Centre, Queen's University, 1989).

Work Values

While there is a great deal of comparative data on the industrial and socioeconomic structures of Canada, the United States, and Mexico, only a few studies have investigated what workers in these three countries think about work — what is important to them in their jobs. One question that has been addressed is the degree to which workers in different countries share the same values and attitudes toward work. Geert Hofstede (1980) conducted a questionnaire survey of approximately 60 000 employees employed by one large American "high-tech" corporation with subsidiaries in 40 countries, including Canada and Mexico. The employees and managers of each subsidiary were indigenous to the host country in which the corporation was located. Given that the organizational structure, production technology, and composition of the labour force were similar in all countries, Hofstede argued that any differences revealed in the survey would very likely be cultural differences.

Part of Hofstede's survey asked workers to indicate the relative importance of fourteen work goals. Responses to each of the goals were recorded on a five-point scale ranging from "of utmost importance to me" to "of very little or no

In highly industrialized societies, the overwhelming majority of workers in the labour force are in complex organizations that are the custodians of scarce and valuable resources.

with scheduled flights than does Canada (72 versus 61), one-quarter of its residential dwellings do not have electricity, one-third have no safe piped water, and over two-fifths have no sanitary facilities (Kurian 1991). In some ways Mexico appears to be industrial, on other ways not. However, according to the criteria presented in Table 16-1 and Table 16-2, it falls somewhat short of what is generally acknowledged to be a fully developed, industrialized nation.

El Pacto: Removing Labour Barriers to Entry

Who are these formidable neighbours [south] of the U.S.? They're some 10 million skilled and semiskilled workers, the top third of Mexico's work force. From Mexico's dusty Silicon Valley outside Guadalajara to the Pacific canyons south of San Diego, they're adapting quickly to the latest Japanese production systems. They're taking the controls of million-dollar machines and are churning out world-class autos, TVs, and computers. "People who live in little villages with dirt roads can handle any job we give them," says Charles Parks, president of Guadalajara circuit-board maker Adelantos de Tecnología, a subsidiary of SCI Systems Inc. in Huntsville, Ala.

And how do they turn out such high-quality work? Mexicans are not only eager for work and cheap to hire but they are also a cinch to train. Paying a rate of $2 to $3 an hour, companies can afford months of training, indoctrinating workers with the latest quality and lean-manufacturing systems. The workers are also young and open to new methods. After a decade of economic crisis and the halving of their buying power, Mexicans are also hungry, willing to work hard and long. Top talents hone their skills at the many branches of Monterrey's Institute of Technology. Below them, a vast fix-it society, born of years of scraping by, is putting its resourcefulness to work on the factory floor.

Still, the bottom tier of workers, some 20 million with little schooling, toil in Mexico's pre-industrial world. They sharpen knives on grindstones attached to bicycles and hitch plows to solitary horses. Salinas knows that he must speed up the monumental job of improving Mexico's public schools and push more children through the system.

This is crucial for all of North America, with its work force graying in the north and growing in the south. With or without NAFTA, a growing share of the region's work force will be coming from youthful Mexico. Already, for some companies, the border is disappearing. In the old silver-mining town of San Luis Potosí, a six-hour drive north from Mexico City, Ken Reynolds, a 52-year-old machinist from Fastoria, Ohio, is helping install a new crankshaft line at a Cummins Engine Co. plant. It was a painful decision for Reynolds to volunteer for Mexican duty. Friends treated him as a turncoat as Cummins laid off 100 workers in Fastoria, "I lost a lot of friends up there, but I gained a lot down here," he says.

The San Luis operation is one of Cummins' best-rated in the world. Its work force is young — the average age is 25 — and highly educated. In fact, the local university pumps out so many engineers that many of them accept work on the factory floor just to get a foot in the door. The company sends workers for training to the U.S., and it organizes them in self-managed teams, where they learn a broad range of jobs. Pay is low, with most workers earning about $80 a week, plus another $50 in government-mandated benefits. But in a country with no unemployment benefits, the union doesn't press hard for higher pay. "They're more interested in job creation," says Norman Brown, the plant manager. And more jobs are coming, thanks to the factory's high quality and low costs. Cummins is everything Salinas is after. It's modern, international, and strongly integrated into Mexico's economy, buying 30% of its parts locally.

Plants such as Cummins' are the culmination of Mexico's long march up from the *maquiladora*, or border assembly plant. A decade ago, when Mexico still ran a protected economy, it rented its excess cheap labor to U.S. companies. The result was clusters of *maquiladoras* along the U.S.-Mexico border. Hundreds of thousands of workers handled piecework for U.S. industry, assembling imported parts and sending them back across the Rio Grande.

It was with that simple exchange of labor that Salinas sold free trade and Americans embraced it. Instead of sending offshore work to Asia, the thinking went, send it to Mexico. But a funny thing happened on the way to North American unity. Far from Salinas' whiz kids in Mexico City, in the vast deserts of Mexico's north, U.S. auto makers uncovered the potential of young, semi-skilled Mexican workers. By the late 1980s, Buick Centuries and Mercury Tracers made in Mexico were winning quality awards; Mercedes-Benz and Nissan Motor Co. were setting up plants; and Salinas' chief asset, his vast labor pool, was suddenly enhanced by the new mantra "quality."

UPGRADE OR ELSE. The carmakers remain the showcases for Mexican quality. But other manufacturers are taking the time to train young Mexicans — and reaping rewards. The turnaround began seven years ago, when Mexico joined the General Agreement on Tariffs & Trade and tore down its trade barriers. Suddenly, companies that were producing overpriced goods for Mexico's closed economy had to upgrade operations to world-quality levels. Otherwise, they would be buried by cheap imports. That spurred an industrial revolution in Mexico. For

importance." Table 16-4 presents the rank-ordering of these fourteen goals by Canadian, American, and Mexican employees. It can be seen that there are both similarities and differences in the rankings. For example, workers in all three countries agree on what is most and least important. "Challenging work" was ranked either first or second, while "employment security," "good fringe benefits," and "good physical working conditions" were generally perceived to be the

the first time ever, companies demanded quality from Mexico's industrial workers. And they delivered.

Now, an industrial elite led by companies such as GE, Kodak, Goodyear, Nissan, and a handful of Mexican blue-chips is doing the heavy lifting for Salinas' modernization. The President personally co-ordinates this investment, wining and dining executives, often bending his schedule to accommodate them. One time, even as he was heading abroad, Salinas squeezed in time for General Electric Chairman John F. Welch Jr., picking up Welch in his limousine and chatting with him on the way to the airport. The personal attention didn't hurt. In the past three years, Welch has invested $400 million to build refrigerators and ranges in Mexico.

To be sure, Mexico still has plenty of problems. Roads are cratered and crowded border cities are chaotic. And Salinas has yet to root out much of the corruption, from traffic cops to customs officials on the take. Plenty of U.S. businesses are happy to stay north.

But for those who head south, Salinas has helped clear the way with industrial policies like *el pacto*, Mexico's national wage and prices contract. First unveiled as an anti-inflation program in 1987, *el pacto* established guidelines on prices and wages endorsed by business and labor. It gave Salinas control over Mexico's transition from a closed to an open economy. Answering critics who complain about squelched wages, Salinas and his team stress the war on inflation. Says Treasury Secretary Pedro Aspe: "Inflation is the cruellest tax on the poor."

Over the years, Salinas shifted the focus from prices to productivity. When the usually submissive unions strike for higher wages, Salinas and his economists look at production. If the workers meet world standards —

as do the Ford Motor Co. workers who struck at Hermosillo earlier this year — Salinas often lets the strike run its course. Ford workers in March won a wage hike that has been hushed up but is widely suspected of surpassing *el pacto's* limits. Ford officials deny this. Indeed, wages could eventually inch up, as they have in Korea and Taiwan, eating into Mexico's advantage. But when workers do not pass muster on productivity, the government can deem the strike "political" and declare it "nonexistent." That forces workers to give up either the strike or their jobs.

Salinas established the new rules for labor last summer in what became a battle for the country's industrial future. While Salinas has never hesitated to hammer union bosses who crossed him politically, the President drew a new economic line with a strike at Volkswagen de Mexico. The battle erupted when the government-controlled union at VW, based in Puebla, signed on to a massive restructuring plan to raise productivity. VW management insisted the new agreement was vital for global competitiveness. This was hardly idle talk, since VW supplies the entire North American market from Puebla. But a group of dissidents, fearing layoffs, opposed the plan. After weeks of a bitter strike, Salinas gave VW permission to rip up the union contract. The company promptly fired 14,000 workers and rehired all of them, minus some 300 dissidents, under a new contract. Within days, VW revamped its entire Mexico operation — the German carmaker's first such experiment anywhere. Out is the old seniority system. Training, lots of it, is a must. Workers are now promoted according to skills and performance.

The dispute redefined the strategic role of Mexican labor. For 50 years, workers have been a pillar of the one-

party system — strikebreakers, precinct leaders, gofers, and above all, Institutional Revolutionary Party (PRI) loyalists. The longtime union leader, 93-year-old Fidel Velázquez, had workers in lockstep behind the PRI for decades. Now the favored union leaders are like Francisco Hernandez Juarez, head of the telephone workers' union, who has jumped on Salinas' productivity bandwagon. Today, workers are economic soldiers marching Mexico into the global economy.

Leading this army of workers behind Salinas is a cadre of internationally minded managers and engineers. Take José Berrondo, a 44-year-old Mexico City native who went to high school in Pittsburgh and later got an MBA from the University of San Francisco. Fifteen years ago, when Berrondo began his career at Mabe, a Mexican appliance manufacturer, his international experience mattered little. But in 1989, with Mexico's economy opening, GE teamed up with Mabe to make gas stoves in San Luis Potosí for North America. Nex, GE bought into Mabe's refrigerator manufacturing in Querétaro. Suddenly, Berrondo, who runs both plants, has a green light to build world-class facilities.

It's a once-in-a-lifetime chance to devise his own manufacturing system. So Berrondo is borrowing pieces from all over the world — some from a trip to Korea, others from his dogeared books on Toyota and Harley-Davidson. In the rapidly expanding Querétaro plant, he has instituted *kanban*, or just-in-time systems, borrowed a year ago from Toyota.

Source:

Reprinted from April 19, 1993 issue of *Business Week* by special permission, copyright © 1990 by McGraw-Hill Inc.

least important of the goals listed. The most pronounced differences in the rankings were for "sufficient time for personal life" (Canadians evaluated this as the fourth most important goal; Mexicans ranked it as the least important); and

"training opportunities to improve or learn new skills" (Mexicans rated this as their most important goal; Americans put it in eleventh place).

The rank-order correlation (the extent to which rankings are similar) between Canada and the

TABLE 16-4   Rank-Order Importance of Work Goals in Canada, the United States, and Mexico

Work Goals	Rank-Order of Goals in		
	Canada	U.S.	Mexico
1. Challenging work and sense of accomplishment	1	1	2
2. Full use of skills and abilities	2	6	3
3. Good working relation with manager	3	8	9
4. Sufficient time for personal life	4	7	14
5. Opportunity for advancement	5	2	4
6. Training opportunities to improve or learn new skills	6	11	1
7. Work with co-operative people	7	5	5
8. Live in desirable area	8	4	8
9. Freedom to adopt own approach to job	9	10	7
10. Getting recognition for good work	10	9	10
11. Opportunity for high earnings	11	3	6
12. Employment security	12	12	11
13. Good fringe benefits	13	13	13
14. Good physical working conditions	14	14	12

SOURCE: Adapted from Geert Hofstede, *Culture's Consequences: International Differences in Work-Related Values* (Beverly Hills, CA: Sage, 1980), pp. 403–404, 415.

In Canada, the United States, and Mexico, challenging work is one of the highest considerations of workers.

United States is .63. While there are many similarities (for example, items 1, 12, 13, 14), there are also some significant differences (items 8, 3, 6). The correlations between Canada and Mexico (.56) and between the United States and Mexico (.55) are lower.

These findings correspond to the data presented on industrialization; that is, there are more similarities between Canada and the United States than between either Canada and Mexico or the United States and Mexico. These results are also consistent with a later study on values, carried out by Nevitte and his colleagues. In this research, the investigators were concerned with two questions: "Do the basic values of Mexicans, Canadians, and Americans differ in significant ways?" and "Are the differences growing larger over time, or are the goals of North Americans converging?" (Nevitte, Basañez, and Inglehart 1992:245). To address these questions, they conducted an interview survey of nationally representative samples from all three countries at two different times — 1981 and 1990. They found that while there are differences between the values held by Mexicans and those held by the other two countries, convergence is taking place. They conclude that "on the basis of these findings, one might surmise that the responses of the Mexican public resemble those of other Western societies but are at an earlier point on the trajectory" (Nevitte, Basañez, and Inglehart 1992:248).

Work and Social Position

While the work we do influences our own attitudes and values, it also has a strong impact on those around us. The jobs we hold largely establish our social standing; other people and organizations evaluate and treat us according to our occupation. Occupation forms a fundamental basis of social ranking:

In all complex societies, industrialized or not, a characteristic division of labor arises that creates intrinsic differences between occupational roles with respect to power; these in turn promote differences in privilege; and power and privilege create prestige. Since the same process operates in all complex societies, the resulting prestige hierarchy is relatively invariant in all such societies, past and present. (Treiman 1977:128)

According to Donald Treiman (1977), not only does the work we do determine our social ranking, but because of the similarity in the division of labour from one society to another and the fact that comparable increments of power and privilege accrue to the same positions cross-culturally, people holding the same job in different societies experience approximately the same relative prestige. Treiman equates prestige with moral worth, esteem, respect, and regard. In other words, much of the respect that we merit in society flows directly from the work we do.

Treiman made a comprehensive investigation of all the studies on **occupational prestige** that had ever been conducted to find out if his hypothesis was correct. Altogether, he found prestige surveys from 60 countries (including the three in North America) in which representative samples were asked to rate a variety of occupations. A total of 509 occupations were evaluated. Treiman then created a correlation matrix in which he computed the degree of convergence of

one country's prestige ranking with that of all other countries. Of 1386 rank-order correlations, the overall mean average correlation was .79. In other words, in spite of cross-cultural variation and differences in the degree of industrialization, most countries had reasonably similar occupational prestige hierarchies.

When Treiman compared the prestige rankings of only industrialized countries, the correlations were even higher. For example, the rank-order correlation of occupational prestige between Canada and the United States is .98 (Treiman 1977:81); the two rankings are virtually interchangeable. However, even the correlations of Canada and the United States to Mexico are higher than the overall average (Canada — Mexico = .88; U.S. — Mexico = .87). Given the fact that Mexico is a newly industrialized country, many of the same criteria are used in evaluating jobs there as in Canada and the United States.

From the national prestige rankings of all 60 countries, Treiman constructed standard prestige scores for each of the 509 occupations originally evaluated. This resulted in the Standard International Occupational Prestige Scale, which ranges from "chief of state" (90 points on the scale) to "gatherer" (–2 points). The mean average score of the scale (43.3) is also the score represented by "office clerk." Table 16-5 presents the standard prestige scores of 50 common occupations that Treiman evaluated. Clearly, not only do power and privilege vary along Treiman's prestige scale, but these two attributes are also highly correlated with income, education and training, authority, autonomy and control, and the substantive complexity of jobs. Thus, we may conclude that the prestige attached to particular occupations is a function of all the dimensions that together define what an occupation is.

Thus, Treiman's scale is an excellent approximation of how the citizens of all these countries apportion the relative worth of one's employment. Consequently, it is safe to say, for example, that in each of these countries, on average, a physician is more highly evaluated than a lawyer (see Table 16-5). Similarly, nonmanual occupations are generally regarded with more esteem than are manual occupations. As Treiman himself concludes, "The Standard Scale scores will provide highly accurate estimates of the prestige of spe-

TABLE 16-5   Rank-Order of Fifty Common Occupations on the Standard International Occupational Prestige Scale

Rank	Occupational Title	Score	Rank	Occupational Title	Score
1	Physician	77.9	26	Garage mechanic	42.9
2	University professor	77.6	27	Mechanic, repairman	42.8
3	Lawyer, trial lawyer	70.6	28	Shopkeeper	42.4
4	Head of large firm	70.4	29	Printer	42.3
5	Engineer, civil engineer	70.3	30	Typist, stenographer	41.6
6	Banker	67.0	31	Police officer	39.8
7	Airline pilot	66.5	32	Tailor	39.5
8	High school teacher	64.2	33	Foreperson	39.3
9	Pharmacist	64.1	34	Soldier	38.7
10	Armed forces officer	63.2	35	Carpenter	37.2
11	Clergyman	59.7	36	Mason	34.1
12	Artist	57.2	37	Plumber	33.9
13	Teacher, primary teacher	57.0	38	Sales clerk	33.6
14	Journalist	54.9	39	Mail carrier	32.8
15	Accountant	54.6	40	Driver, truck driver	32.6
16	Civil servant, minor	53.6	41	Bus, tram driver	32.4
17	Nurse	53.6	42	Miner	31.5
18	Building contractor	53.4	43	Barber	30.4
19	Actor, actress	51.5	44	Shoemaker, repairer	28.1
20	Bookkeeper	49.0	45	Waiter	23.2
21	Traveling salesperson	46.9	46	Farmhand	22.9
22	Farmer	46.8	47	Street vendor, peddler	21.9
23	Electrician	44.5	48	Janitor	21.0
24	Insurance agent	44.5	49	Servant	17.2
25	Office clerk	43.3*	50	Street sweeper	13.4

*This number represents the mean score on the scale.
SOURCE: Donald Treiman, *Occupational Prestige in Comparative Perspective* (New York: Academic, 1978), pp. 155–156.

cific occupations in any nation in the world" (Treiman 1977:179).

Note that Treiman's scale measures relative, not absolute, prestige. For example, we cannot assert that physicians in Canada, the United States, and Mexico receive identical amounts of prestige; it is only legitimate to say that they are accorded more prestige on average than are heads of large firms, engineers, and high-school teachers (see Table 16-5). The standard prestige scale measures the *relative* merit of occupations as perceived by all members of society.

According to Treiman, the similarity of occupational prestige rankings throughout the world is explained by the fact that work is similarly organized from one society to another. Regardless of level of economic development or cultural values, all social systems engage in a division of labour so that their members can survive. Because all societies, past and present, face essentially the same problems in order to survive, the basic structure of the division of labour in each society is similar. This division of labour may be simple or complex, but its fundamental characteristic is that it differentiates people according to function. Virtually anyone can do some tasks, while relatively few are capable of performing other tasks. Also, in order to co-ordinate functions, some people must be placed in positions of authority over others.

The horizontal and vertical differentiation arising out of the division of labour creates differences among people with regard to skill and authority; those with unique skills that are highly prized and those with authority over others have more power than those who do not. With power comes the privileges it commands, and because power and privilege are universally valued, deference is shown to the similarly powerful and privileged few among the world.

In short, occupational groups are able to convert their command of scarce resources — skill and knowledge, economic power, and authority — into material advantage, both by virtue of the superior market position command of these resources provides, and by virtue of the ability to directly manipulate the system that such power creates. For this reason, there is a general consistency in the skill, economic control, authority, and material reward hierarchies of occupations in all societies, and a similarity in these hierarchies across societies. (Treiman 1977:19)

Treiman's research demonstrates the powerful and constant impact of occupation on one's social standing. The spillover of work into nonwork is enormous because it influences not only how we think and behave, but also how others act toward us.

Cultural Convergence

In 1960, Clark Kerr and his colleagues wrote a book in which they set out "the logic or imperatives of industrialization," that is, those uniformities (universals) that appear in social structures and social processes regardless of where in the world or in what cultural context industrialization is introduced (see Kerr et al. 1964). In their words:

Industrialization came into a most varied world; a world with many cultures, at many stages of develop-

ment from the primitiveness of quasi-animal life to high levels of civilization. It was a world marked by great diversity, in terms of the contrast between the least and the most civilized societies; a world more diverse than at any other time during the history of mankind on this planet. In the midst of this disparity of systems there intruded a new and vastly superior technique of production; a technique which by its very nature was bound to spur imitation, since the more modern was always superior. This technique knew no geographical limits; recognized no elites or ideologies. Once unleashed on the world, the new technique kept spreading and kept advancing. (Kerr et al. 1964:223)

Because the results of technology or a technique of production can be precisely measured in terms of its quantity and quality of output, it is possible to determine which technology is superior in accomplishing specific objectives, and consequently the superior technology becomes widely adopted. This was the fate of specialized and mechanized factory production. It was enthusiastically endorsed first in Europe and North America and later in Japan, Russia, India, Latin America, and East Asia.

The central tenet of the **convergence thesis**, as it came to be known, is that upon the introduction of technologically superior factory production, structural adaptations are made that in turn have repercussions on other aspects of society until eventually all industrialized societies, no matter how dissimilar they were initially, converge in certain patterns of social organization, values, and behaviour. Some of the direct or first-order consequences include "an open and mobile society that assigns occupations to workers on universalistic grounds, an educational system that serves the needs of industry, a hierarchically differentiated and disciplined work force, a consensual web of rules regulating industrial social life, and increasing governmental involvement in industrial relations" (Form 1979:4). Other more far-ranging or second-order consequences include the trends toward urbanization, bureaucratization, secularization, smaller nuclear families, greater female labour-force participation, and more societal and international interdependence. In other words, industrialization provokes such immediate and widespread social changes that all nations, North and South, East and West, in adapting to this uniform process, themselves become more standardized.

Not only do social structures and processes adapt to industrialization; there also occurs a manifest change in human personality and behaviour. In an ambitious study of working men in six developing countries (two in Latin America), Inkeles and Smith (1974) attempted to discover whether the nature of the work these men performed (industrial or nonindustrial) influenced what they valued in society. The researchers found in all countries that experienced factory hands — more than traditional urban (nonindustrial) workers, rural–urban migrants, and cultivators of the land — scored high on an "overall modernity" scale. With respect to values, the "modern" worker was more likely to:

- be open to new experience and accept change;

- be oriented toward the present and future rather than the past;

- be concerned with being on time and planning in advance;

- believe in self-determination and reject fatalism;

- be independent of traditional authority figures;

- believe in the efficacy of education, science, and technology;

- be ambitious for self and children;

- be tolerant of social differences; and

- be interested in civic and community affairs and broad social issues.

The data we have reviewed with respect to industrialization in the world today, with particular reference to Canada, the United States, and Mexico, generally support the convergence thesis. Table 16-1 and Table 16-2 document the relationships between industrialization and increasing levels of education, a more comprehensive organizational base, greater female labourforce participation, and smaller family size. Also, the discussion of work values reveals a convergence over time in the direction that Inkeles and Smith found; and certainly the research on occupational prestige supports convergence, particu-

larly among industrialized countries. In the concluding section, we examine evidence that provides even more support for the convergence thesis — greater societal and international interdependence.

Work in a Changing Society

A Canadian university president observed recently that "we cannot escape the generalization that political units are becoming relatively smaller, while economic units are becoming larger. ... Technology has changed the world as profoundly and irreversibly as it did after Pearl Harbor fifty years ago. Modern communication and transportation make political contraction and economic expansion (i.e., political fragmentation and economic integration) inevitable" (Strong 1991:9). Canadians need look no further than their own country to realize the truth of this statement. As this chapter is being written, the daily headlines alternate between constitutional attempts to maintain the political unity of this country and progress on negotiations toward a North American Free Trade Agreement (NAFTA). Since 1989, Canada has had a bilateral **free trade** agreement (FTA) with the United States.

Some 70 years ago, an American sociologist, William F. Ogburn (1922), coined a new term — **cultural lag**: "The failure of one aspect of a cultural complex to keep pace with the changes in some other related aspect, as the failure of social institutions to keep pace with the rapid advances in science" (*Webster's New World Dictionary* 1984). Ogburn conceived the theory of cultural lag by observing the uneven pace of development within society and the corresponding unequal rates of change that produced maladjustment and strain. Through a variety of empirical investigations, he developed the thesis that changes in material culture or "the applications of scientific discovery and the material products of technology" (Ogburn 1964;79) occur at a faster rate than do changes in the nonmaterial, adaptive culture (values, norms, patterns of social organization, and so on), thereby causing maladjustment in the nonmaterial culture, or cultural lag.

One important conclusion that Ogburn drew from his work on cultural lag is that with ever-increasing technological accumulation and change, our major adjustment as a culture is to the technological environment we have created, rather than to the nonhuman environment and biological limitations that have previously served as our major constraints. His words ring with remarkable clarity today:

Unlike the natural environment, the technological environment is a huge mass in rapid motion. It is no wonder then that our society with its numerous institutions and organizations has an almost impossible task in adjusting to this whirling technological environment. It should be no surprise to sociologists that the various forms and shapes which our social institutions take and the many shifts in their function are the result of adjustments — not to a changing natural environment, not to a changing biological heritage — but adaptations to a changing technology. (Ogburn 1964:85)

As a result of technological developments in transportation, telecommunications, microelectronics, and information transfer, we now have what has been termed an integrated **global economy**, in which the **transnational corporation (TNC)** predominates through an **international division of labour.** "In the 1980s the two hundred largest TNCs in the world produced an astounding 30 percent of total world output, substantially improving upon the impressive 19 percent share in 1970. From these figures it is clear that the transnationalization process is far from complete" (Hedley 1992c).

According to Kenichi Ohmae (1991), a Japanese management consultant who works for a large American TNC, we are living in a "borderless world":

On a political map, the boundaries between countries are as clear as ever. But on a competitive map, a map showing the real flows of financial and industrial activity, those boundaries have largely disappeared. (p. 23)
The global economy follows its own logic and develops its own webs of interest, which rarely duplicate the historical borders between nations. As a result, national interest as an economic, as opposed to a political, reality has lost much of its meaning. (p. 228) [See Figure 16-1.]

Trade and Investment in North America

In examining the economic relations between Canada, the United States, and Mexico, some have suggested that the proposed NAFTA will simply formalize production, trade, and investment patterns that already characterize the three economies (see Eden and Molot 1992). In graphic terms, the United States represents the "hub" and Canada and Mexico are two "spokes."

This analogy is well demonstrated in the comparative trade figures for each country (see Table 16-6). Both Canada and Mexico are similarly and overwhelmingly dependent on the large, central market of the United States. More than 60 percent of their exports are destined for the United States; similarly, more than 60 percent of their imports come from that nation. Only one other nation in the world (Somalia) is more dependent on just one country for its exports. In a study of approximately 100 nations for which he could obtain data, Müller (1988:61–62) found that, on average, a nation's largest trading partner accounts for only approximately 30 percent of all its exports. In other words, both Canada and Mexico are extremely vulnerable in their trade relations with the United States. While Canada is also the United States's largest trading partner (Mexico is third, after Japan), it accounts for less than one-quarter of U.S. exports and less than one-fifth of U.S. imports.

As well as trade, **foreign direct investment** by TNCs in other countries has become an increasingly popular economic strategy that blurs political boundaries. It is in this vein that Canada has been referred to as a "branch-plant economy." In 1985, American TNCs invested $63.4 billion in Canada. This represented 75.5 percent of all foreign direct investment in Canada. In terms of total sales, 29 percent of all goods and services produced in Canada were sold by foreign-controlled firms, that is, firms in which at least 50 percent of the stock is owned by non-Canadians. (Actual operating control can be achieved with a good deal less than 50 percent ownership.) In the manufacturing sector, foreign-controlled firms were responsible for 49.2 percent of total sales (*Canada Facts* 1989:41).

In Mexico also, foreign direct investment has become an important aspect of the economy. Since 1965, with the introduction of the Border

FIGURE 16-1   The Shape of North America Inc.

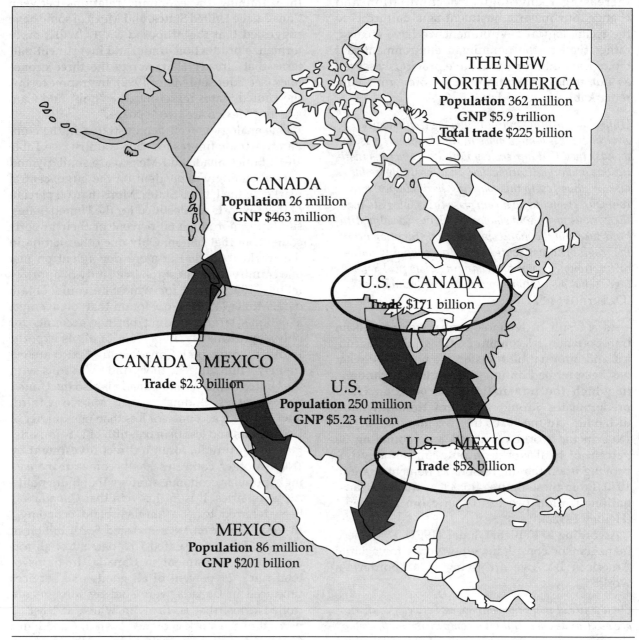

THE NEW
NORTH AMERICA
Population 362 million
GNP $5.9 trillion
Total trade $225 billion

CANADA
Population 26 million
GNP $463 million

U.S. – CANADA
Trade $171 billion

CANADA – MEXICO
Trade $2.3 billion

U.S.
Population 250 million
GNP $5.23 trillion

U.S. – MEXICO
Trade $52 billion

MEXICO
Population 86 million
GNP $201 billion

SOURCE: Reprinted from *Business Week*, November 12, 1990, p. 103 by special permission, copyright © 1990 by McGraw-Hill Inc.; based on data from the U.S. Commerce Department and Mexican Commerce Secretariat.

Industrialization Program (referred to as the **maquiladora program**) TNCs have become an ever-increasing presence in Mexican society. Foreign-controlled (largely American) factories, located mostly on Mexico's northern border, bring in duty-free components that are assembled by low-wage Mexican workers for subsequent export (see Gereffi 1992). The only value added to these products in Mexico is the cost of labour. Because of Mexico's relatively low labour costs,

TABLE 16-6 Percentage Share of Canada, United States, and Mexico in Total Exports and Imports of Each Country, 1970, 1980, and 1987

	1970	1980	1987
Canada			
Exports			
United States	65.4	63.1	75.5
Mexico	0.6	0.6	0.4
Imports			
United States	71.1	70.1	68.0
Mexico	0.3	0.5	0.4
United States			
Exports			
Canada	21.3	15.3	23.9
Mexico	4.0	6.8	6.4
Imports			
Canada	27.9	16.4	16.7
Mexico	3.1	5.0	4.8
Mexico			
Exports			
United States	70.3	65.8	64.7
Canada	0.9	0.8	1.5
Imports			
United States	63.7	61.4	61.9
Canada	2.0	1.9	2.8

SOURCE: Adapted from Dorval Brunelle and Christian Deblock, "Economic blocs and the challenge of the North American free trade agreement," in *North America Without Borders? Integrating Canada, the United States, and Mexico*, Stephen J. Randall, ed. (Calgary: University of Calgary Press, 1992), p. 125.

it is hoped that this government-sponsored program will attract further foreign investment, thus contributing to Mexico's bid for full industrial status and an improved standard of living. According to recent figures, this program is already very successful:

The number of maquiladora *plants in Mexico has grown from 620, in 1980, to nearly 1,900, by 1990. The personnel employed in Mexican* maquiladoras *during this period expanded from 100,000 to 450,000 and, according to forecasts, that figure will grow to 600,000 by the end of the century. Total* maquiladora *exports soared from almost $2.5 billion in 1980 to $10.1 billion in 1988. ... Maquiladoras account for 11 percent of Mexico's total manufacturing employment, with a much higher impact (26 percent) in the six border states.* (Gereffi 1992:138, 139)

In both Canada and Mexico, whether it be trade or foreign direct investment, transnational corporate interests seem to have exerted their will, almost despite government involvement. This is what Ohmae (1991) refers to as the "borderless world" and no doubt is what Ogburn would have referred to as a case of cultural lag. Jacques Ellul reminds us that our political and legal institutions that legislate, govern, and administer the actions of modern corporations (transnational or otherwise), were created in the seventeenth and eighteenth centuries and consequently "are adapted to situations that have nothing to do with what we now know. ... No political action in the normal, strict sense of the term is adequate today" (Ellul 1981:71).

While national governments have been traditionally well-suited to deal with affairs that originate and terminate within their own borders, they are ill-equipped to handle transnational problems. The current world system of nation states does not have appropriate means to effectively deal with international affairs — for example, international relations (consider how many wars and border disputes and conflicts there are at any one time), nonterritorial resources (such as the oceans, the seabed, the airwaves, the sky, and space), and transnational business. Because of this cultural lag, a new system of supranational bodies and agreements is currently being negotiated in a piecemeal, *ad hoc* way in an attempt to deal with some of these problems.

One such (potential) agreement is NAFTA, an attempt by the governments of Canada, the United States, and Mexico to exert some control, in the interests of their citizenry, over a process that has already largely taken place. Through direct negotiation, it is hoped that many future problems, such as job loss, industrial restructuring, and community and regional dislocation, will be minimized. While these are very real concerns, the governments involved do not have the power to satisfy all the competing stakeholders in each country. They are engaged in a co-ordinated, almost impossible effort to maximize gains and minimize losses in the best interests of all. However, as a result of these formal negotiations and the more informal process of transnationalization that preceded them, we may expect even more convergence in the industrial economies of these three countries than exists currently.

FIGURE 16-2

SOURCE: David Anderson/Miller Features Syndicate, *Victoria Times-Colonist*, August 27, 1992, p. A5.

Work in a New Era

All the developments discussed thus far in this chapter have contributed to vast structural changes in society. In turn, these changes affect both how we perceive work and what we actually do at work. Very recent developments may cause us to rethink and redefine what work is. Some observers believe that we are now experiencing a work revolution just as profound and with as

Aging Canadians and Young Mexicans

There is no better picture of what the world will look like as it enters the next century than that of Canada and Mexico. Canada, like the other nations of the rich industrial world, will be an aging society with slowing population growth. It will be increasingly worried about paying for an elderly population and about how to cope with labour shortages. As Canada grows older, it could become less entrepreneurial in business and more conservative in politics; and it will face relentless competition from Mexico — although, if Canada is smart, it will move to capitalize on opportunities in the much faster-growing Mexican economy. Without aggressive policies to create an Information Age economy using ideas and innovation to create wealth and high incomes, Canada could stagnate; but if it upgrades the skills of its people and uses new technology, it could become more productive and better off even while its population ages.

Meanwhile, in Mexico, where there is a young and fast-growing population that is typical of much of the developing world, the emphasis will be on education, investment, jobs, and exports. As a youthful country, Mexico will be highly entrepreneurial, luring young Canadians as well as Mexicans. And as Mexicans gain experience and education, they will move into many of the industrial sectors that once belonged to countries such as Canada. Mexicans will not be content to be a low-cost labour pool for rich countries; they will pursue new technologies and high-value activities. Because of the rising productivity and rapid rates of family formation, Mexico's economy will show strong growth and its people will enjoy a fast-rising standard of living. Within 20 years, Mexico could have an economy about the same size as Canada had in 1990. (Today, Mexico's economy is barely 40 percent that of Canada's.) Forty years from now, Mexico will almost certainly have a bigger economy than that of Canada. But Mexico's rapid growth will cause it to pay more attention to the environment. ...

In many ways, Canada and Mexico are proxies for the world at large. During the next several decades, a major reshaping of the world will take place as developing countries with young populations expand and as their economies accelerate, while the rich industrial nations experience slow population growth or even declining populations and face sweeping changes in the world's economic, technological, and military balance of power. Yet if the situation is properly handled, the industrial countries of the North and the developing countries of the South could both enjoy a new prosperity. Mishandled, the world could face turbulence, environmental chaos, uncontrollable migrations, religious and nationalistic fanaticism, and economic protectionism and decline.

Source:

David Crane, *The Next Canadian Century: Building a Competitive Economy* (Toronto: Stoddard, 1992), pp. 33–34.

many far-reaching implications as the industrial revolution.

Industrialization, when it first occurred in Britain 200 years ago, resulted in a redefinition of the concept of work. Work became an explicit set of contractual obligations physically separated from private life in both time and space. Traditional work did not involve such a contract or such a separation. It took place within the context of the family as and when the need dictated. With the industrial revolution, however, work became a specifically defined activity that occurred at the workplace of the employer according to a prearranged, set schedule.

Today, as a result of the electronic revolution, it is no longer necessary to perform much of what we do within explicitly defined space and time parameters. Although a worker is still contractually responsible for achieving organizational goals, much more flexibility has been introduced into the system. Because most work today involves the manipulation of information rather than materials, former time and space constraints have become redundant. Instead, workers are linked to each other in a freefloating electronic network. The personal, portable computer is "the workplace." Where and, within certain limits, when workers perform their duties has become largely irrelevant (see the box on page 522).

It is important to ask what changes this new work arrangement will produce, and how it will modify our existing attitudes toward work. One potentially far-reaching consequence is that work loses the pre-eminence it once held. It becomes, instead, just one of many activities that can be fitted into a personal time schedule. Although work still must be done, it can be done more at the discretion of the individual worker. Very

The Dawn of Digital Dominance

When you talk to an associate in Japan over a fibre-optic connection your voice reaches him before it reaches your secretary across the room. In the next decade, the secretary may also move around the world with little impairment of her services.

The waves of light that bear her voice will carry her image as well, and the image of any document or the code of any computer program. Your computer will reach across the globe to a printer, an automated machine tool, or a giant screen.

With the collapse of time and space will come a collapse of companies. Between your computer and the things that it will soon be able to get its hands on lie throngs of experts — all shortly for the chop.

Expect also the collapse of schools, bureaucracies, broadcasting systems and traditional corporate structures.

In the past decade, the acceptance of digital technology has been relatively slow because of the high cost of image-processing and the lag in developing communication tools capable of handling digital information. This "slow" start, soon to be a thing of the past, meant that managers could disparage the impact of digital technology; the paperless office, after all, remained as probable as the paperless bathroom.

Productivity experts could deny the significance of the changes; from retailing to banking, the service firms with the most computers seemed to show the least productivity growth.

Teachers could imagine that they competed only with other teachers in the neighborhood. All was cosy in its complacency.

Now the change, the real change, is about to break over us. Nearly all communications in future, whether down wires or through the air, will use the electromagnetic spectrum — where everything moves at the speed of light.

The electromagnetic spectrum will be the engine of economic growth in the next decade. Here are some results. New videos will offer images in three dimensions. Graphics displays will be able to make images into solid plastic models. Computer displays will be donned like a pair of glasses. Pocket phones will be as mobile as a watch and as personal as a wallet. World finance will be a single simultaneous arena of investment and exchange. And in the household, news, hobbies or culture from anywhere on the globe will all be interactively controlled by the viewer.

"Virtual reality," the highest-tech of last year, will become a household appliance.

These breakthroughs will result from a millionfold rise in the cost effectiveness of computing and communications technologies. Early in the next decade, microchip engineers will put the logical power of 16 Cray supercomputers on a single sliver of silicon. Sixteen Crays today would cost some $320 million.

Containing some 1 billion transistors, the "16-Cray chip," by contrast, will be made for under $100. Meanwhile, the four-kilohertz telephone lines to the world's homes and offices will explode into the billions of possible hertz of fibre optics.

The personal computer will collapse into a cellular phone, portable everywhere and accessible by voice and pen for an array of programs, led by electronic mail. The television will become a telecomputer, capable of receiving, transmitting, storing, editing and processing digital video from anywhere reachable by the fibre network.

This new machine will usurp the conventional television, the VCR, the laser disc, the game machine, and nearly all other analog appliances. These changes will also transform the global culture of business.

Ruling this transformation is the physics of the microchip. After just 10 years of personal computer history, virtually all office equipment is smart, digital, and distributed. The change came so fast that many still misunderstand it.

As recently as 1978, nearly 100 per cent of the world's computer power was concentrated in large central-processing units with dumb terminals attached. This was the classic IBM model. By 1990, such machines held less than 1% of the world's computer power. Driven by the power of microelectronic advances, there was a PC microprocessor on every desk as powerful as an early 1970s mainframe.

But the biggest change is yet to come. Fibre-optics technology is doubling its cost effectiveness every 18 months and is now advancing twice as fast as microelectronic technology. As prices drop and computers become indistinguishable from telephones, the potential market will surge from millions of desk tops to billions of living

likely this will result in a diminution of the value attributed to work because it will increasingly have to compete with other important activities. No longer will work occupy its own separate space–time domain.

How extensive will these changes be? What proportion of the labour force will be affected? Farmers still must sow seeds; construction workers still have to work at building sites; and surgeons still have to appear in operating rooms. (See the box on page 524, however, for an explanation of how some surgeons do not need to appear in operating rooms.) According to Cordell (1985:33), "by the mid-1990s, an estimated 15 percent of the workforce may be telecommuting, that is, working away from a central office."

rooms and even more billions of sound and video systems. Just as desk-top PCs overthrew IBM's centralized regime of a few thousand mainframes during the 1980s, so in the 1990s, the PC will overthrow the few thousand broadcasting stations and far fewer networks.

Unlike the mainframe computers, the broadcasting stations do not even have dumb digital terminals attached; they have analog "idiot boxes." Just as desk-top terminals gained computing power greater than early mainframes, passive televisions will soon give way to powerful, all-digital telecomputers that will exceed the image-processing power once wielded by entire broadcast stations. They will be in your living room before the decade is out.

In 1992, the digital movement will be sweeping through the video industry, allowing the complete production of a film on a single computer workstation and its transmission down fibre lines to any suitable display system.

Although European and Japanese companies still imagine there remains a place for analog HDTV, in the United States, by order of the Federal Communications Commission, all high-end television video is likely to be digital. This change will also bring about the collapse of production companies, eliminating hundreds of steps (and experts) between the producer of a film and its viewing, wherever you choose.

1992 will be the pivotal year for all this: the true dawn of digital dominance. The best-selling PCs will begin to come from firms that make digital cellular phones and master the miniaturization and low-power technologies required for mobile computing.

The computerization of office services, which has absorbed 60–80 per cent of computer investment over the past decade, will decline. But similar services will move into homes.

One of the most important of these new markets will be education. The telecomputer will allow any parent or small group of parents to summon the best teachers in the world to their living rooms for interactive courses far superior to anything that can be offered by an existing local school.

In the 1990s, all institutions will have to respond to these new technologies, each of which will spring from an ever-increasing mastery of the electromagnetic spectrum, both in fibre and air.

In particular, a global wavescape, open to all, will affect all cultural activity. Today, video culture is dominated by two forces: localization and vulgarization. Both derive from the technology of broadcasting, a top-down, master-slave system in which a small number of media authorities, in combination with advertisers or government bureaucracies, shape and schedule programming.

Because the programming has to capture a large proportion of the miscellaneous audience at any particular time and place, the shows must target the lowest common denominator of shocks and sensations, prurient interests, and morbid fears and anxieties.

This arrangement is inevitable as long as the receiver — the television — is dumb, an idiot box, and all the "intelligence" is at the stations. But the millionfold rise in computing power will make this system as obsolete as the mainframe with dumb terminals attached.

All will be reversed: the "intelligence" will reside at home, the dumbos will be at the stations.

Broadcast television is a tool for tyrants. Totalitarian systems, such as the former Soviet Union or Eastern Germany, had nearly as many television sets as capitalist systems such as the United States and Western Germany. But totalitarian regimes have only one-tenth as many two-way systems such as telephones and computers.

The breakdown of broadcasting is accelerating the crisis of all authoritarian systems — whether public schools or network television or socialist theories — that treat all people as if they were the same.

As Michael Rothschild put it in his book, *Bionomics*, "Rather than constant combat, the hallmark of intense competition is diversity."

The new era will be one of flourishing individual culture and thus an era of higher and more demanding business management. Managers will have to master a more libertarian organization of business that tolerates the differences between individuals.

By giving each individual in the information age the power of a factory owner in the industrial era, the new generation of computers will hugely enhance economic competition and progress.

Source:

George Gilder, London: Hudson Institute.

Consider briefly the implications of telecommuting for some of our established institutional arrangements. What consequences does it have for the family? Certainly it could ease some of the current problems surrounding day care; at the same time, it could radically alter marital relations and the household division of labour. It is also possible that there will be a slowing of urbanization because it will no longer be necessary for many workers to live near the business core. This, in turn, could have consequences for arterial and transportation systems as well as for communities that surround the major urban centres.

The relationship between employee and organization will also undergo substantial change. For

With the industrial revolution, work became a specifically defined activity that occurred at the workplace of the employer at some prearranged set schedule.

example, what will become of employee identification, commitment, and loyalty to the company when the major linkage is electronic instead of physical? Will informal social interaction, which now occurs face-to-face at the workplace, appear in formally communicated information transfers (already there are signs of this); and what consequences will this have for personal relationships in general? Also, the area of labour relations will experience yet another upheaval as white-

"Reach Out and Touch Someone"

The surgeon was away, but the operation was a success. The world's first experiment in remote surgery took place in Italy and the U.S. recently. Needless to say, the implications for the future of health care are quite staggering.

The surgeon was physically present in the University of Southern California, but the operating room was in Milan, Italy. The patient was a pig. The surgeon wore virtual reality-like "sensory" gloves and a helmet, and

his surgical incisions were transmitted by satellite to Milan where a half-metre high IBM robot carried out his manoeuvres using an arm equipped with a pair of forceps.

Explained Alberto Rovetta, the Italian engineer who conceived of this medical experiment: "The technique we are perfecting will solve a common problem in treating patients — how to save a man who is lying ill in one place when the doctor is somewhere else and time is running out."

Conceivably in the future, long distance operations can be used in obstetrics and tumor removals, according to physicians involved in the experiment.

Source:

Alexander Besher, "California surgeon reaches out to operate in Milan." *Victoria Times-Colonist*, 24 July 1993, p. D1.

collar unions attempt to build computer-driven solidarity.

Herbert Simon, a Nobel prize winner in economics and a leader in research on artificial intelligence, has addressed the issue of the relationship between technical and social change and, to use his words, "what makes technology revolutionary." He maintains that "when technology reshapes society, it is not the result of a single invention, but of a host of additional, completely unanticipated inventions, many of them of the same order of magnitude as the first one in the chain" (Simon 1987:7). Consequently, much like the steam engine in the industrial revolution, the computer by itself was not revolutionary. It was not until hitherto unrelated inventions (such as developments in telecommunications) were combined that the seeds of revolutionary change were sown.

Returning to the relationship between technological and social change, Simon is both optimistic and cautionary. His words are a fitting conclusion to this chapter:

Technological revolutions are not something that "happen" to us. We make them, and we make them for better or for worse. Our task is not to peer into the future to see what computers will bring, but to shape the future that we want to have — a future that will create new possibilities for human learning, including, perhaps most important of all, new possibilities for learning to understand ourselves. (Simon 1987:11)

SUMMARY

1. The industrial revolution, occurring at the end of the eighteenth century, radically altered the organization of work. The factory system of production and the development of the steam engine led to the manufacture of many products for consumer markets.
2. Industrialization has produced great disparity among the nations of the world, and the gap between rich industrial and poor developing countries is increasing enormously. People in industrial nations are employed primarily in services and manufacturing. They have relatively high per capita incomes, fully developed infrastructures, low population growth, and a high standard of living.
3. Industrialization is a multidimensional process. It is measured in terms of economic activity, output, organization, mechanization, and technology. According to these measures, Canada and the United States are fully industrialized nations; Mexico is a newly industrializing country.
4. Canadian, American, and Mexican workers share some basic work goals. Challenging work is perceived to be of utmost importance to the overwhelming majority, regardless of where they live. However, the value structures of Canadians and Americans are more similar to each other than they are to Mexican values.
5. People throughout the world have similar prestige rankings in their evaluation of occupations. This occurs because of the similarity of the division of labour in all societies. Thus, it is possible to create a standard international occupational prestige scale.
6. The similarities in the process of industrialization are thought to produce further similarities in the larger social structure. This perspective is known as the convergence thesis.
7. Canada and Mexico are extremely dependent on the United States for trade and investment. As a result of foreign direct investment by American-based transnational corporations, the economic integration of North America is already largely a fact of life. The proposed North American Free Trade Agreement will simply formalize many existing arrangements.
8. The electronic information revolution is changing popular conceptions of work. Much of the work that is performed need no longer be confined in space and time. Rather, workers can be linked to their employment through interlocking electronic networks.

GLOSSARY

Convergence thesis. Thesis asserting that the process of industrialization produces a common world culture.
Cultural lag. Failure of one aspect of a cultural complex to keep pace with the changes in a related aspect, such as the failure of social institutions to keep pace with advances in science.

Foreign direct investment. Financial investment, usually by a transnational corporation, in the assets of another country.

Free trade. Trade between two or more nations that is unrestricted by tariffs, quotas, or other protectionist policies.

Global economy. Increasing economic interdependence of and integration among all nations, resulting from technological innovations in transportation, communication, and information transfer.

Industrialization. Multidimensional process that involves a shift toward industrial employment in a mechanized and organizational context, which results in a greater contribution of manufacturing to national output.

Industrial revolution. Series of technological and organizational changes in manufacturing that occurred in Britain during the latter part of the eighteenth century; its essential features included machine production, the factory system of manufacturing, and mechanical motive power.

Infrastructure. Social-services support structure of a society, including health, education, welfare, transportation and communication systems, and justice.

International division of labour. Process engaged in by transnational corporations, wherein they conduct various operations and produce particular products throughout the world according to strategic corporate objectives.

Maquiladora program. Border industrialization program instituted by Mexico in which foreign-controlled factories import duty-free components that are assembled by low-wage Mexican workers for subsequent export.

Newly industrializing country (NIC). Country that is industrialized with respect to some indicators but not others. Examples include Mexico, Brazil, Taiwan, South Korea, Hong Kong, and Singapore.

Occupational prestige. Rankings of occupations in terms of their social standing. Indicators of social standing include the power, privilege, income, education, authority, autonomy, and complexity associated with occupational roles.

Postindustrial society. Economy in which emphasis is placed on the services-producing tertiary sector in terms of employment and national output.

Primary sector. Division of the occupational structure in which employment involves either harvesting or extracting goods, for example, agriculture, logging, mining, fishing, hunting, and trapping.

Protestant work ethic. Ideology stating that work is service to God, one's duty is to work hard, and success in work is measured by money and property.

Secondary sector. Division of the occupational structure in which employment involves the transformation of raw material into finished or semifinished manufactured goods.

Tertiary sector. Division of the occupational structure in which employment involves the provision of services.

Transnational corporation (TNC). Enterprise that undertakes foreign direct investment, or owns or controls income-gathering assets in more than one country, or produces goods or services outside its country of origin, or engages in international production.

Work. Activity that permits one a livelihood. Work includes conventional paid employment, illegal employment, and homemaking.

FURTHER READING

Anderson, John, Morley Gunderson, and Allen Ponak (eds.). *Union-Management Relations in Canada.* Don Mills, ON: Addison-Wesley, 1989. A collection of eighteen articles on all aspects of labour–management relations in Canada that includes comparative data.

Hedley, R. Alan. *Making a Living: Technology and Change.* New York: HarperCollins, 1992. An historical and cross-national examination of industrialization and work in Britain, the United States, and Japan.

Inglehart, Ronald, Neil Nevitte, and Miguel Basañez. *North American Dilemmas: Trade, Politics and Values.* Ann Arbor, MI: Institute for Social Research, 1991. Part of the World Values Survey, in which the authors compare the basic values of Canadians, Americans, and Mexicans.

Krahn, Harvey J., and Graham S. Lowe. *Work, Industry, and Canadian Society.* Scarborough, ON: Nelson, 1988. A Canadian text on industrialization, labour force, organizations, workers, and industrial relations.

Kurian, George Thomas. *The New Book of World Rankings.* New York: Facts on File, 1991. A compendium of national rankings on the economy, population, politics, military power, education, crime, energy, health, culture, and so on.

Lenski, Gerhard, Jean Lenski, and Patrick Nolan. *Human Societies: An Introduction to Macrosociology* (6th ed.). New York: McGraw-Hill, 1991. An examination of how societies have evolved over time, with particularly good chapters on industrialization and the industrial revolution.

Randall, Stephen J. (ed.). *North America Without Borders? Integrating Canada, the United States, and Mexico.* Calgary: University of Calgary Press, 1992. A collection of 27 articles, the result of a 1991 University of Calgary conference, "Facing North/Facing South: Contemporary Canada–United States–Mexico Relations."

CHAPTER 17

Urbanization and Urbanism

A.R. GILLIS

Urban sociology is more than simply the study of social phenomena that occur in cities. It frequently emphasizes different viewpoints and focuses on distinct topics. Like other subfields, it includes both structural-functional and conflict viewpoints, as well as historical and contemporary approaches. Symbolic interaction has not been widely popular with urban sociologists (which probably means that their specialty is not popular with symbolic interactionists).

Students of cities routinely include the physical environment and the size of populations as important variables in their research. Because of a concern with "place," urban sociologists are continually faced with the question of whether particular environments cause people to behave in different ways, or whether different people are attracted to certain types of places. (This is known as *selection*). A focus on place not only distinguishes urban sociology from other areas, but also forms the basis for a link with more "applied" fields, including geography, social-policy research, planning, and architecture. (This side of urban sociology pleases utilitarians and sometimes bothers purists.) In any case, a concern with the physical as well as the social environment typically distinguishes sociologists who study cities from those who do not. So urban sociology is more than simply the study of social phenomena that happen to occur in cities.

It is hard to define the word "city" in a way that pleases everyone. Architects, planners, and civil engineers, for example, are mainly interested in planning, design and physical factors, and the way they view and define "city" reflects these

What Is an Urban Area?

Current definitions of the word "urban" vary widely from one country to another. In Greece, for example, municipalities and communities containing fewer than 10 000 people are not classified as urban: but in neighbouring Albania, any towns with 400 or more are.

In Canada the minimum population necessary for a locality to be classified as urban (a "census urban area" or CUA) is 1000, while in the United States and in Mexico the figure is 2500. These different definitions of "urban" make international comparisons difficult. Statistics Canada tells us that approximately three-quarters of the Canadian population live in urban areas. The United States census reports roughly the same figure for that country, while in Mexico two-thirds of the population is urban. However, the levels of urbanization in the United States and Mexico are, from the Canadian standpoint, understated. From our perspective, the proportion of the U.S. and Mexican populations living in towns of 1000 or more are in fact greater than 75 and 66 percent, respectively.

Here is another definitional problem: classifying a village containing 1000 people (or, for that matter, 2500 people) as an urban area has little intuitive appeal. For most of us, the idea of "urban" brings to mind places like Tokyo, New York, Montreal, and Toronto rather than Gimli, Manitoba, or Gibson's Landing, B.C., both of which are classified as urban areas in Canada. In view of this incongruity, in 1931, Statistics Canada (then the Dominion Bureau of Statistics) developed the concept of "census metropolitan area" (CMA) in the hope of offering a more satisfactory description of the number of Canadians who were living under urban conditions, not just in urban areas.

A CMA was defined as a principal city with at least 50 000 inhabitants: an urbanized core with a population density of at least 1000 people per square mile (2.6 km²); or an area outside the central city that either has a labour force of which at least 70 percent are engaged in nonagricultural activities, or has a total population of at least 100 000. This definition was more coincident with the spirit of the term "urban" as embodied in most of the early theories about urban life (nonagricultural) and the minimum size of a city (large). Unfortunately, the definition did not take into account what has recently become an essential element of the modern metropolis: living in one community and commuting to work in another. Most likely in response to this, in 1981 Statistics Canada redefined the CMA as

the main labour market area of an urbanized core (or continuously built up area) having 100,000 or more population. ... CMAs consist of (1) municipalities completely or partly inside the urbanized core; and (2) other municipalities if (1) at least 40% of the employed labour force living in the municipality works in the urbanized core, or (b) at least 25% of the employed labour force working in the municipality lives in the urbanized core. (Statistics Canada 1982)

The United Nations (*Demographic Handbook for Africa* 1968) uses the following classification scheme:

Big City: a locality with 500,000 or more inhabitants.
City: a locality with 100,000 or more inhabitants.
Rural Locality: a locality with fewer than 20,000 inhabitants.

Canada's definition of a CMA is roughly equivalent to the United Nations' "city" classification. There are now 25 CMAs in Canada, all of which have been growing at a faster rate than the total population, indicating that the country is not just urbanizing, but "metropolitanizing." This is particularly apparent in southern Ontario, which seems destined to become one very large metropolitan area (Gillis 1987).

So how urban are Canadians? The fact that Canada is 75 percent urban does not mean that each of us is three-quarters urban and one-quarter rural in orientation. A sociologist would say that this sort of reasoning is an example of an *ecological fallacy*. The characteristics of an aggregation are not necessarily displayed in the same proportions in each of the members that make it up. Urban sociologists, who examine collectives such as cities or neighbourhoods and draw conclusions about the individuals who live in them, must be particularly careful to avoid these pitfalls of aggregation and disaggregation.

What the statistic actually means is that three out of four Canadians live in urban areas, and one does not. Moreover, in 1991 six out of ten lived in a CMA, one out of two lived in a "big city" (a metropolitan area of 500 000 or more), and three out of ten could be found in metropolitan areas of one million or more (Montreal, Toronto, or Vancouver). This suggests that Canada is an urban society. And it is. However, as Lucas (1971) points out, "many people in Canada live nowhere." Because of Canada's position in the world economy as a supplier of resources, many urban Canadians live in small, single-industry towns: Lucas counted 636, few of which were larger than 10 000 in population. When we call Canada an urban society, then, we should keep in mind that a substantial proportion of the population still lives in rural areas and small towns, and that life in these areas is very different than in larger urban centres (Lucas 1971; see also Marsh 1970).

Source:

Demographic Handbook for Africa (Addis Ababa: United Nations Economic Commission for Africa, 1968); A.R. Gillis, *CMAs, Submetro Areas, and Megalopolis: An Examination of Montreal, Toronto, and Vancouver* (unpublished report to Statistics Canada, 1987); Rex Lucas, *Minetown, Milltown, Railtown: Life in Canadian Communities of Single Industry* (Toronto: University of Toronto Press, 1971); Leonard Marsh, *Communities in Canada* (Toronto: McClelland and Stewart, 1970); Statistics Canada, *1981 Census Dictionary* (Ottawa: Supply and Services Canada, 1982).

interests. Since social scientists are concerned with social life, their view of the city and what they regard as its distinct features leads them to a somewhat different definition.

Sociologists define a **city** as "a large concentration of people who work in a wide range of specialized and interdependent occupations that, for the most part, do not involve the primary production of food." Note that this definition does not ignore the physical characteristics of cities. The phase "large concentration of people" implies that the number and density of people are noteworthy urban characteristics. In fact, many urban sociologists suspect that population density and other environmental factors have major effects on social life in cities. However, what matters most to sociologists is how people in rural and urban areas differ in the way they organize their work, their social lives, and their personalities. This, and the costs and benefits of doing so, is the subject matter of urban sociology. For sociologists, then, the city is the physical manifestation of a particular type of social organization.

The sociological definition, or *model*, of the city is also useful because it points to factors (or variables) that allow us to construct explanations of where, when, and why the first cities were built, as well as how they grow, spread, and sometimes decline. These are important questions for sociologists, especially in view of the recent and continuing rural-to-urban shift of the world's population.

The Origin of Cities

Until recently, social scientists thought that the first permanent settlement with enough people to be called a city was built about 5000 years ago in the Middle East. However, recent archaeological evidence suggests that the first walled city may have been built 8000 to 10 000 years ago. (In fact, one of the first cities may have been Jericho, a city far more famous for its destruction than for its construction.) In any case, since *Homo sapiens* has been around for at least 250 000 years, it is clear that the natural history of humanity has occurred almost exclusively in wilderness and rural environments.

The relatively short period that people have lived in cities suggests to some scholars that pastoral living is our natural or preferred way of life. This may be true, but for the most part our ancestors' lives in the wilderness were probably less indicative of preference than of necessity. Until agriculture was invented (about 10 000 B.C.), the land simply would not sustain an urban population.

Agricultural Surplus

According to our definition, a city is a large number of people living in a relatively concentrated area. To feed these people, a great amount of food must either be produced in and around the area or be brought into it from farther away. Moving large amounts of food long distances requires relatively sophisticated technology, and growing a great amount of food in a concentrated area requires high-yield agriculture. Neither of these requirements comes easily to people with primitive skills. To make matters worse, the urban population does not contribute to the production of food, so the rural residents who are growing it must supply not only themselves, but city dwellers as well.

Even if early humans had been inclined to live in cities, they could not have done so. They were too busy producing food for their own consumption. This typically involved following or herding the source of food around as the seasons changed. This nomadic life ruled out the possibility of settlement anywhere, let alone in cities. As people advanced technically, a larger **agricultural surplus** could be taken from a wider range of environments. But important technological innovations did not emerge until recently in the natural history of humans.

In view of this, it is not surprising that the first cities were built in the rich alluvial valleys of the Tigris, Nile, and Indus rivers, and, somewhat later on, in similar environments in Central America. These sites allowed people with simple technology to grow a surplus of food in a relatively concentrated area, and to feed a relatively large number of people who were not themselves contributing to the production of food.

Sociologists point to several factors that may have caused people to produce a surplus of food and to construct cities. Two major types of factors can be distinguished: limiting factors and motivating factors. **Limiting factors** include the natural environment and the technical ability of people to alter it. These factors determined where cities could *not* be built. **Motivating factors** include cultural values and social structure as elements that may have inclined people to build the first cities.

Limiting Factors

The Natural Environment. According to Bronowski (1973), the first cities resulted indirectly from the emergence of a new relationship between people and a specific part of their physical environment: wheat. Modern bread wheat resulted from the accidental cross-fertilization of several kinds of wild grasses. The seeds of the new plant had a low chaff content, and the chaff separated easily from the kernel. This impaired the dispersal of the seed by the wind, which might have caused the extinction of the new hybrid. Because the chaff contains cellulose, it cannot be used for energy by humans, but the kernel is an efficient source of energy. The new hybrid was therefore a good food source for humans, who saw its value and replaced the wind as its principal means of dispersal. In this way, people and wheat became involved in a mutually beneficial or *symbiotic* relationship. The plant provided people with a concentration of calories; in return, people had to refrain from eating the whole harvest and save some portion of it for planting next season's crop, thus ensuring the hybrid's survival.

This symbiotic relationship was the basis for the development of agriculture, which provided an important and desirable alternative to the hunting/gathering and herding economies that had

When people were released from the pressures of the seasonal nomadism of hunting/gathering and herding societies, the economic base of urban life was established.

previously characterized human societies and kept people on the move.

The discovery and domestication of wheat, and of rice in Asia and of corn (maize) and potatoes in America, allowed both plants and people to settle in mutually advantageous locations, such as the Mesopotamian basin. Settlement and the ease of storing wheat greatly helped people to create a surplus of food. The head of a family could support more household members and would need to devote less time and energy to producing food for survival.

Some family heads were released entirely from food production, while others continued to work at full capacity to feed themselves, their families, and all those not engaged in food production. In this way, the presence of ideal growing conditions and a high-yield grain set the stage for the emergence of agriculture, the production of a food surplus, settlement, and the division of labour. People were released from the pressures of the seasonal nomadism of hunting/gathering

and herding societies, and the economic base of urban life was established.

Technology. Ideas and technology have helped humans to construct environments favourable to the production of an agricultural surplus and to build the physical artifacts that contain urban populations. Natural environments, in contrast, often forced people to be nomadic. When game or edible plants disappeared from one region because of overhunting, overgrazing, or the changing seasons, people had to move on to where game and edible plants were more abundant. People who lived under such conditions were hardly in a position to settle down and construct cities. Agricultural technology gave people more control over their natural environment and allowed them to stay put.

The application of human ideas has frequently changed the natural environment, making it a more productive and less aversive place to live. People have discovered and even developed a

Images of the City

The word *city* brings different images to the minds of different people. And different cities, because of their traits, physical symbols, and nicknames, elicit different images — New York, world status; Washington, politics; Chicago, virility (gangsters); and San Francisco, elegance.

Cities' traits tend to be emphasized or exaggerated by nicknames, which are particularly popular in the United States. Here in Canada, we have "the Cradle of Confederation" (Charlottetown), "the Forest City" (London), "the Stampede City" (Calgary), and "the Gateway to the North" (Edmonton). Montreal competes both with San Francisco and with Paris, Ontario, to be known as "the Paris of North America." Nicknames are generally positive, often reflecting boosterism, but as with other stereotypes, this need not always be the case: one of Toronto's nicknames is "Hogtown."

Some cities also have physical symbols, which may or may not be useful.

The Golden Gate Bridge symbolizes San Francisco, while also allowing access to Sausalito; but the St. Louis Arch has no use but to symbolize that city as "the Gateway to the West." A unique natural silhouette, like Montreal's Mount Royal, can also symbolize a city, as can a constructed silhouette, like the New York skyline.

The most distinctive city monument in Canada is probably the CN Tower in Toronto. The tower serves as a communications centre and is gradually gaining worldwide recognition as the symbol for the city. However, it is still unclear what meaning we should attach to this monument. Suggestions range from an exclamation point (or Toronto's finger to the rest of the country) through more Freudian phallic interpretations, characterizing the residents of the city.

Specific cities vary in the nature of their overall ambience or image. In comparing popular images of New York, Paris, and London, Milgram

(1970) found that New York was distinguished primarily on the basis of architecture and "the pace of life." In contrast, London elicited images of its citizens and social quality, while Paris brought to mind both physical and social characteristics equally. As with the concept of "city" itself, then, both physical and social characteristics seem to be important in describing the character of specific cities, with some more physical and others more social (Lynch 1960).

Source:

Selected references to Kevin Lynch, *The Image of the City* (Cambridge, MA: MIT Press, 1960), and Stanley Milgram, "The experience of living in cities," *Science* 167 (1970):1461–1468.

wide variety of high-yield crops (such as wheat), learning how to care for them by improving their natural environments with various devices ranging from fertilizer to irrigation. Technology has vastly improved people's capacity to extract surplus food from the physical environment and greatly expanded the range of environments that will tolerate large numbers of people and cities.

City walls, as well as private and public buildings, are alterations of the natural environment to suit certain human needs. Walls protect those they enclose from external threats, and buildings and cities themselves provide protection from extremes in climate. But concentrating large numbers of people in cities poses numerous challenges involving shelter, transportation, sewage disposal, and so forth. These challenges cannot be met with the methods used in rural areas, where the scale is small and the population is dispersed. New technological solutions must therefore be developed and applied. Thus, a city can be seen as a technical device that alters or controls the effects of the natural environment by substituting for it a *built environment.*

So we can see that humans applied technology to the natural environment in two ways important for the origin of cities: the production of surplus food and the construction of built environments. This combination not only protected people from natural threats but also solved many of the problems associated with large numbers of people living in close quarters. Technology thus made people less vulnerable to the limitations and variability of the natural environment. In an agreeable natural environment, simple technology may suffice to allow the survival of persons or plants. But complex technology enables a disagreeable natural environment to be improved. The absence of a minimal combination of natural environment and technology means that a city cannot be built. We can conclude that certain environmental conditions, whether natural or altered, are necessary for the origin of cities.

The first cities emerged in natural settings that were hospitable to plants and people — necessarily so, because of the low level of technical development 10 000 years ago. After all, the plough was not even invented until the fourth century B.C. (Palen 1987). Later, as people extended their knowledge of and skills for environmental improvement, cities were constructed on a wider range of sites.

Motivating Factors

Although an agreeable environment, whether natural or improved, is *necessary* for the origin of cities, it is not *sufficient*. The fact that people are able to stockpile a surplus of food does not guarantee that they will do so. For example, Tuan (1974) noted that some areas of New Guinea provided inhabitants with more food than they could eat. Yet they had not stockpiled a surplus that would allow a division of labour between food producers and others. As a result, urbanization had not occurred. This example demonstrates that the part played by the environment in the origin of cities is one of limiter, not motivator.

Since the inhabitants of New Guinea had little or no experience with cities, it is had to argue that their failure to stockpile food and to urbanize reflected a preference for rural living. Instead, sociologists suggest that either certain structural or cultural factors, or both, are necessary before a population can urbanize. These characteristics were absent in the New Guinea population. Before there can be cities, people must be organized at the very least into providers and nonproviders of food. Sociologists have several explanations for the development of this division of labour.

Culture. Social scientists who favour a functionalist model of society (for example, Davis 1955) observe that general and widespread economic benefits flow from large-scale operations and a division of labour. They argue that the first cities arose because the original inhabitants somehow discovered these economic benefits and took steps to realize them.

Others believe that the origin of the first cities had less to do with economics than with religion. According to Adams (1960) and Childe (1950), the first public buildings were temples, which often doubled as granaries. Priests may have been the first nonagricultural workers, forming the nucleus of urban society. They gave spiritual sustenance, supported and disseminated a hierarchy of values, and supervised the collection and storage of the agricultural surplus (the first religious donations).

This argument is generally consistent with a structural-functional view of the relationship between culture and social structure; social organization is seen as a manifestation of culture and efficiency. These views emphasize co-operation, consensus, and the importance of values and ideas as the motivation for developing cities. However, what helps some (in this case urbanites) may hurt others, and the founding of the cities may not have been universally beneficial. It is possible (and, according to many sociologists, more likely) that contention and conflict were the social forces that generated the initial cleavage of the populace into providers and consumers of food — the division of labour that resulted in the first cities.

Social Structure. From a conflict perspective, the division of labour into providers and consumers of food resulted from the victimization of the former by the latter. In other words, nonproducers specialized in taking food from farmers, who were then forced to extract still more nourishment from the environment in order to survive and to plant a crop in the next growing season. From this viewpoint, the creation of surplus food accompanied or followed, rather than preceded, the division of labour and the first cities.

The thieves probably began as nomadic hunters and animal herders in central and western Asia who had more luck with livestock than with farming. However, once they domesticated the horse, these nomads became a force to be reckoned with. The horse amplified their expertise as hunters and enabled them to extend organized plundering to a new level: war. Millennia ago, the Scythian riders swept out of the Far East into the rich farmland of eastern Europe and the Middle East to take the food that they could not produce at home (Bronowski 1973). Eventually it made more sense for these raiders to occupy the land they plundered than to leave and then return the following year. Thus, the horse soldiers became a ruling class of warriors who established themselves behind walls — first of fortresses, then of castles, and finally of cities. They created an agricultural surplus by forcing farmers to produce more food to avoid starvation or to maintain their standard of living. This situation also prompted farmers to invent more labour-saving agricultural technology (Polanyi 1957; Sjoberg 1960).

When Cortés arrived in what is now Mexico City, he found an Aztec settlement of about 200 000 people who were sustained through the subjugation of neighbouring tribes. Since the horse was a Spanish import, it is clear that in America it was not necessary to have horses to subdue farmers, take their food, and use it to sustain urban populations. In fact, cities and literate civilizations had come and gone long before the Europeans arrived in the Americas (see, for example, Sharer and Grove 1989 on the Olmecs). The horse, however, was probably a critical factor in the defeat of the Aztecs by the vastly outnumbered conquistadors.

Sociologists vary in their opinion of how much force had to be used to get farmers to give their food to the ruling elite. Outright pillaging, involuntary taxation, and exchanging food for protection and other services each involve different degrees of open coercion, with the last involving less force than fraud (and not even that, if the exchange can be deemed fair by some absolute standard). It is at this point that the conflict argument shades off into a consensus view of the relationship between a city and its **hinterland** (the surrounding area from which a city draws its food and other raw materials).

FIGURE 17-1 The Origin of the First Cities

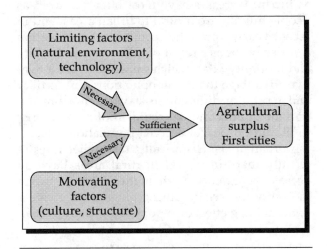

NOTE: Necessity is the state or level that one variable must reach before another can change. Sufficiency is the state or level reached by one variable that *always* produces a change in another.

In any event, culture, social structure, or both in combination (Mumford 1961) can be seen as necessary motivating factors in the development of the first urban settlements. Like the natural environment and technology, however, culture and/or structure are not by themselves sufficient to account for these primal cities. Unless a surplus is possible — and the natural environment and technology may or may not permit this — the motivation to produce surplus food will be fruitless (literally) and disappear, along with the would-be urbanites. So, both limiting and motivating factors are necessary; but neither by themselves are sufficient to produce a city. Not until these factors are considered together is there a satisfactory explanation for the origin of the first urban settlement in Mesopotamia, about 10 000 years ago. At that time, only this location provided the necessary combination of conditions for the genesis of an urban settlement. (For more general discussions of this approach, see Schnore 1958; Duncan 1959; Duncan and Schnore 1959; and Tilly 1974.)

Urbanization

Urbanization refers to an increase in the proportion of a given population living in areas defined as urban. Increases have most often occurred as people migrate from rural to urban areas, and in recent years, from other countries. Urbanization can also occur as a result of differences in fertility and mortality rates, which sometimes give a relative advantage to urban populations. But fertility and mortality differentials have been more important in affecting **deurbanization** — a *decrease* in the proportion of a given population inhabiting urban areas. Historically, the higher rates of fertility that are typical in rural areas have on occasion combined with higher rates of urban mortality (especially during plagues) to create a deurbanizing effect on a population (Tilly 1976a).

Urbanization: The Ancient Period

Ancient cities were small by today's standards and contained only a tiny proportion of the world's population. Athens, the foremost city of classical Greece, peaked with a population of 120 000 to 180 000. Both limiting and motivating factors constrained its size; poor soil and simple agricultural technology combined with a cultural preference for limited growth to keep city populations low (Davis 1955; Palen 1987).

The other great city of the ancient period was Rome. A more generous natural environment, technical advances (especially in the areas of agriculture and the transportation of people, produce, and water), a more complex division of labour, and a cultural interest in expansion combined to push Rome far beyond the size of Athens. Estimates of the size of ancient Rome, whose population peaked around the birth of Jesus, range between 250 000 and 1.6 million (Palen 1987).

Deurbanization: The Middle Ages

Rome was the largest and most powerful city the world had ever seen, but when the Roman Empire declined and fell (or moved its centre to Constantinople), neither the city nor its population could be maintained. When the Vandals cut the city off from its grain-producing areas in Africa, the empire was dealt a serious blow, and the population of Rome ultimately dwindled to less than 50 000 by A.D. 600 (see Yoffee and Cowgill 1991).

The demise of the Roman Empire, like the decline of Greece before it, resulted in the disintegration of an extensive social network with a city at its centre. All roads had indeed led to Rome. They carried raw materials, food, traders, and labourers to the city, and armies from it to collect taxes, maintain order in the provinces, and extend the empire's frontiers. The fall of Rome heralded a period of deurbanization and the return of Europe to rural life. The vast network developed by Rome shrivelled, and outlying localities were forced once again into isolation and self-sufficiency. During urban growth, people flowed into the city on all the roads that led to Rome. In decline, the same roads took those people away. Their return to the land, food production, less complex organization, and to local rather than imperial domination marked the beginning of a 600-year period of economic and cultural stagnation (Pirenne 1939). During this epoch few cities surpassed 100 000 in population, and Arabia succeeded Europe as the regional centre of civilization and cultural innovation.

Cities and Culture

For both Athens and Rome, dramatic developments in the arts, the sciences, and other dimensions of culture coincided with the rise of the city and its empire. Their decline was followed by an extended period of cultural inertia known as the Dark Ages. After the fall of Rome, Europe did not again begin to urbanize until the eleventh century, when innovations in abstract and material cultures were also reborn (Huizinga 1924; Pirenne 1939).

This pattern suggests that there is an important relationship between cities and culture. We already saw that cultural factors affected the origin of cities, but it seems that cities also affected culture and civilization. (Both "civic" and "civilization" are words derived from *civis*, the Latin word for "citizen.") Athens and Rome are exemplary in this respect, having developed and disseminated the classical traditions and served as the bases for Western civilization itself.

One way to understand the cultural contributions of Athens, Rome, and other great cities is by viewing the city as a mechanism for controlling time (Innis 1951) as well as space. Because they did not have to feed themselves and because of the efficiency of a more complex social organization, citizens of cities like Athens and Rome may have had more leisure time than did their rural counterparts (Herskowitz 1952). Inadequate leisure time can be seen as a limiting factor preventing innovation and experimentation. Pushing back the amount of time spent on agricultural work freed people to do other things. (See also Mumford 1963; Landis 1983; and Rifkin 1987 on the importance of time and its measurement.)

More importantly, permanent settlement allowed an *accumulation* of *collective* knowledge and cultural artifacts (nomads do not carry libraries). This released people from the tyranny of memorization and the oral tradition and enabled residents to examine a wider range of lessons from the past. For example, after the demise of Athens as a centre of knowledge, the legacy of the golden age of Greece was contained in the Alexandrian library. It contained hundreds of thousands of papyrus manuscripts, including as many as 500 by Aristotle, from all over the Hellenistic and Semitic worlds. Unfortunately, like civilization itself, the library could not withstand the rising tide of the uncivil. The last works were burned by fanatical Christians in A.D. 391.

In addition to housing accumulated knowledge, cities attracted and sustained resourceful people from a wide range of rural regions and different occupational backgrounds to work in specific occupational roles. (The same factors that caused individuals to break away from traditional ties and migrate to cities may also have inclined them to be innovative in other ways.) The concentration and social interaction of creative people with different cultural backgrounds proved to be fertile ground for the growth of new ideas and cultural change. In fact, "a large concentration of creative people from different cultural backgrounds who do not have their time consumed in food-producing activities" is not only a good description of a city, but of a university, where the objective is the production and dissemination of knowledge and its application: technology.

The motivating factor for many cultural advances may have been the need felt by the urban elite to keep records concerning the taxation of the hinterland and the administration of the empire. Primitive accounting may have led to the development of mathematics and related fields. Astronomy and other advances in the sciences may have resulted from pressure to improve agricultural technology (Childe 1950). However, the greatest of the cultural innovations associated with cities and civilization probably was literacy. The association between it and urbanization endures into the twentieth century (see, for example, Gillis 1993a), and goes back a long way. In fact the relationship between cities, literacy, and civilization may be close to linear. In the Americas, the beginning of classical Mayan civilization was marked by a king writing his name in stone in an early city more than 3000 years ago. When the last king was captured and killed in A.D. 761, it signalled not only his end, but the end of hieroglyphic inscription, cities, and the classical civilization of the Mayans as well. By the end of the millennium the Mayan people had returned to rural life, agriculture, and oral traditions.

The ancient cities illustrate that the causal arrow between urbanization and the development of culture goes both ways. That is, cities are not only the products of people's ideas and values, but also the agents of innovation and cultural change. In this respect, cities are more than repositories of economic and human capital. Whether voluntary or not, they are complex organizations that generate and amplify social and cultural capital, igniting ideas and stimulating specialized interdependent activities that extend far beyond the productive capacity of individuals or collections of individuals working independently (see Gillis 1993a, 1993b, on cities as social capital, and more generally Bourdieu 1984; Coleman 1990).

Reurbanization: The Renaissance

During the Middle Ages, all that remained of the Roman Empire was the Christian church, which maintained an organizational network extending across political boundaries far beyond Rome. There were many political boundaries, because Europe was governed by a large number of local despots who maintained power within their estates or duchies. Populations were predominantly rural, economies were agricultural, and the hierarchy was feudal. Two important changes brought it to an end. One was the use of gunpowder and cannons, first chronicled in 1325, which changed the nature of warfare and enabled monarchs to try to extend their powers. The other was the ascendency of a new social class: the bourgeoisie. These were tradesmen, who were organized in guilds, owners and operators of small businesses. As their name implies, they lived in cities.

In the eleventh century, Europeans began to return to urban areas and to a new kind of social life. Towns were small by today's standards. However, according to Weber (1958a, originally published in 1921), each city had the following features:

1. a fortification;
2. a market;
3. a court of its own and at least partly autonomous law;
4. a related form of association (guilds, professional associations); and

5. at least partial political and administrative autonomy.

Weber thought that cities like this were characteristic of Europe and had an important effect on the economy (see also Chirot 1985).

By the fourteenth century, the economy of Renaissance Europe was becoming a city-centred, trade-oriented version of capitalism. The feudal self-sufficiency of the medieval period was in decline. Cities promised farm workers a place to live, greater freedom, and a better occupational deal than did the feudal manor, to which serfs were tied by law. However, if serfs could avoid capture for a year, they were then considered to be free. Hiding out on another feudal estate made less sense than moving to a city. As a result, enterprising serfs increasingly fled farms for the cities. If they were able to persuade the city leaders and the guilds that their particular skills were worthwhile, they would be admitted. In this way, urbanization in Europe contributed to the destruction of the feudal economy and promoted the concentration of skilled labour and capital in cities (Marx 1965, originally published in 1867–95). Thus, the city affected the structure, as well as the culture, of Western societies.

The development of cities in Europe during the Renaissance was associated with important changes in culture (such as the Protestant Reformation) as well as in the economy (such as the rise of modern capitalism). The major effects on cities during this period were the forces of urbanization, discussed above, and the countervailing force of deurbanization caused by the bubonic plague. In the three-year period from 1348 and 1350, the plague killed about a quarter of the population of Europe. By 1400, a third of Europe's population was dead from the plague, and over half the residents of cities had died (Zinsser 1965; Langer 1973; McNeill 1976). The mortality rate from bubonic plague was higher in the cities than in the rural areas, reflecting the inadequate garbage and sewage disposal in most cities, as well as the greater ease with which communicable diseases spread in high-density settings, where rats, fleas, and people were in close contact. (The fleas fell from rats living in people's attics; see Walter 1988.)

In the short run, then, the plague had a deurbanizing effect on the European population. But in the long run, bubonic plague dealt the final blow to feudalism and actually stimulated urbanization. The death of so many peasants, by totally depleting the already weakened supply of rural farm workers, accelerated the collapse of the feudal economy. Survivors left for the cities, where the plague had created severe labour shortages and capital had become increasingly concentrated through inheritance (McEvedy 1988). By the fifteenth century, the forces of urbanization had countered the forces of deurbanization and labour and capital began to concentrate once again in European cities.

Plagues continued into the seventeenth century, but never again affected the size or distribution of the population the way they did in the latter part of the fourteen century. The descendants of the survivors of the fourteenth-century plague were probably more resistant to the plague, according to McEvedy (1988). Still, the mortality rate from all causes continued to be higher in cities than in the countryside until the end of the nineteenth century, with the advent of formalized medical case provided through hospitals. Hospitals, and the specialized medical care associated with them, are necessarily urban phenomena that continue to reduce the mortality of those who have access to them. Over time, this has given urbanites in general, and the residents of large cities in particular, a definite advantage in delaying death. However, due to urbanites' relatively low levels of fertility (considerably below replacement), migration to cities continues to be necessary to sustain their populations.

The Modern Era: Industrialization

The urbanization of Europe proceeded slowly until late in the eighteenth century, when the entire population began to grow quickly, apparently because of a sudden drop in mortality rates. This drop probably resulted from Jenner's invention of the smallpox vaccine in 1872 and from a general improvement in health. This was attributable to a significant increase in the amount and availability of food, which was in turn made possible by an extended period of good weather and by several important advances in agricultural and transportation technology (McKeown 1976). Extra food not only allowed a larger population to be better nourished, but released more people from agricultural occupations and rural areas. Many migrated to the cities, and for the first time in history, close to 10 percent of the human population inhabited urban localities.

Apart from the natural environment, the most important factor limiting the expansion of cities is a lack of technology. Over the centuries, people have used many kinds of techniques to extract larger and larger food surpluses from an increas-

How Many Farmers Would It Take?

In the first cities, between 50 and 90 farmers were required to produce enough food to sustain themselves and just one other person. This tiny surplus determined that the population of the earliest cities could not be large. However, as technology improved, fewer farmers were required to sustain one nonfarming urbanite. By the beginning of the nineteenth century, the number of farms required to sustain an urban family had been reduced to nine. At this time the largest city in the world was Edo (Tokyo), at one million (Rozman 1975), and the second-largest was London, with a population of 900 000 (Davis 1955).

Industrialization further decreased the number of farmers required to sustain an urbanite, further increasing the potential size of cities.

Today, in industrialized countries, one farmer can sustain him- or herself and approximately 45 other people. In the United States, for example, less than 5 percent of the employed population is engaged in agricultural occupations, and the largest metropolitan area in the country is New York, with more than 16 million people (Palen 1981; Gist and Fava 1974). At present, Tokyo leads the world with just under 26 million (Editors of *Time*, 1993).

Source:

Kingsley Davis, "The origin and growth of urbanization in the world," *American Journal of Sociology* 60 (March 1955):430; Noel P. Gist and Sylvia F. Fava, *Urban Society*, 6th edition (New York: Thomas Y. Crowell, 1974); G. Rozman, "Edo's importance in the changing Tokugawa society," *Journal of Japanese Studies* 1(175):91–112; John Palen, *The Urban World* (New York: McGraw-Hill, 1981); Editors of *Time*, "Megacity," *Time* 141(2)(Jan. 11, 1993):30–40.

ingly wide range of natural environments. Because of this, technologically advanced nations have been able to take labourers from agricultural occupations and reallocate them to other tasks in urban centres. The most important technical advance in this respect was industrialization.

Industrialization replaced animate sources of energy (humans, horses, oxen) with inanimate sources of energy (mainly fossil fuels). This involved substituting machines for tools as energy converters. For example, the horse collar and harness are tools that convert horse power into pulling power, but the tractor is a machine that transforms inanimate energy into pulling power. Industrialization evolved from water wheels in the hills of rural England as steam-powered cottage industries. Under the control of ascetic Protestants like the potter Josiah Wedgwood, this early industrialization ("protoindustrialization") was used to mass-produce consumer goods for wide distribution. In contrast, the mechanization of France and Switzerland, for example, involved the production of watches and mechanical toys for the elites. As usual, there was also an environmental factor enabling England to industrialize — an abundance of coal, which a Scotch distiller turned into a purer, hotter-burning form: coke. So coal, new technology, and Protestantism combined to make England the centre of the industrial revolution and one of the most industrialized nations in the world (Bronowski 1973).

Industrialization had art least three major effects on the city:

1. The application of industrialization to agriculture greatly increased the efficiency of farm workers and the size of the surplus they could produce. This change probably released many workers from farming and created a pool of labourers for work elsewhere (McQuillan 1980).
2. The application of industrialization to transportation greatly extended the hinterland on which an urban area could draw. This increased the incoming amount of food and raw materials and reduced the danger of starvation due to crop failure in a specific region. Such territorial extension had special implications for Canada, because it allowed England to draw on the colony as a supplier of wheat even more than it had done before.
3. The industrialization of factories resulted in a new type of city — the manufacturing city. Ironically, as it replaced human labour in some sectors, especially in agriculture, industrialization also produced a demand for workers in other sectors (for example, a growth in demand for factory workers). So the industrial revolution was also a social revolution that saw the emergence of new relationships between people and machines, and the development of highly specialized jobs and complex hierarchies. Industry moved down from the hills to the towns and cities, where both the labour supply and the demand for its products were located. Thus, people and capital, which had been dispersed throughout rural areas, became concentrated in factories, which were themselves concentrated in industrial cities.

These effects combined to greatly expand the potential for the proliferation and growth of cities. Increased agricultural productivity meant that there was more food to send to cities. More efficient transportation technology and more extensive social organization meant that greater amounts of food could be sent faster and farther than before, and the promise of employment, more consumer goods, and a better life attracted millions of rural migrants to cities.

It is noteworthy that both the housing and working conditions in nineteenth-century industrial cities may have been a clear improvement over rural poverty. Nevertheless, by today's standards the living and working conditions of many factory workers in these cities were dreadful, inspiring both labour unrest and rebukes of industrial capitalism by Marx and many other writers. However, the city also provided indirect relief. The concentration of so many industrial workers enabled workers to seek refuge in unions. This, and the interdependence of urban industrial economies, gave labour a powerful new tool for protest and collective action: the strike (Tilly 1986).

Urban Futures and Postindustrial Economies

The last two centuries have seen a flood of people moving from rural to urban areas around the world. Urbanization has been most intense in industrialized countries, for the reasons outlined above. For example, England was one of the first countries to industrialize and also one of the first to experience a massive movement of people to the cities. As a result, Great Britain is now one of the most urbanized countries in the world, with 80 percent of its population living in urban areas (about 70 percent of the population live in large cities).

The rate of urbanization of the world's population is shown in Table 17-1. Between 1800 and 1950, the urban population of the world doubled every 50 years. After 1950, however, the urban population began to increase at a rate that would see it tripling every 50 years. Projections indicate that, by the year 2000, 61 percent of the world's population will be living in urban areas, with some two-thirds of these living in cities with populations greater than 100 000. As with all projections, this one assumes that current trends will continue. However, there are signs that the rate of urbanization in some industrialized countries, including Canada, is starting to decline and may even reverse (Bourne 1978).

Modern industrial countries are already heavily urbanized. Between 70 and 80 percent of the inhabitants of industrialized countries now live in urban areas, and it is unclear whether a much greater proportion of these populations will be able to do so in the future. Even now, some adjacent cities in industrialized countries have spread so much that their boundaries are beginning to merge. The result of this process is called a **megalopolis** or conurbation. North American examples of this phenomenon include the urban belt that extends from Massachusetts to Virginia along the east coast of the United States, and the "Golden Horseshoe," which stretches from Oshawa to Buffalo around the western shore of Lake Ontario (Gillis 1987a).

It is unclear whether nonindustrialized developing countries will industrialize and urbanize as have Western countries. Some social thinkers believe that capitalist countries are overurbanized and contain too many residents who are not productively employed (see, for example, Szelenyi 1981). Further, industrial growth depends on the consumption of fossil fuels, particularly oil and gas (see Figure 17-2). Whether this consumption can continue indefinitely is uncertain. In fact, if urbanized, industrialized countries do not eventually reduce their dependence on nonrenewable resources, deindustrialization will inevitably begin in Western societies. The natural environment limits the degree to which we can urbanize, and we have developed the technology to extend the limits greatly by converting fossil fuels to energy. In fact, oil, gas, and coal — as part of the natural environment — may well become limiting factors through total depletion. The question is not whether, but when.

Certain types of urban areas face environmental limitations in other ways as well. Cities in desert areas or in mountains (such as Mexico City) may have been viable when populations were small and pollution levels were low. However, such wonderful locations are attractive, and rapid growth can push populations beyond the capacity of technology and the environment to provide water and handle the disposal of sewage and air pollutants. Like many other cities in less industrial countries, Mexico City has gone through a recent growth surge, swelling from 4 million to 15 million in only 40 years, and now has one of the most serious pollution problems in the world. Similarly, some metropolitan areas like Toronto depend on traffic and sewer systems that were designed for the small populations who built them. Unless the technical situation is improved, the quality of life in such cities will decline, won-

TABLE 17-1 Percentage of World Population Living in Urban Areas, Actual and Projected, 1800–2000

Year	Urban (over 20 000)	Large Cities (over 100 000)
1800	2	2
1850	4	2
1900	9	6
1950	21	13
1975	42	26
2000	61	42

NOTE: Percentages are rounded.
SOURCE: Kingsley Davis, "The origin and growth of urbanization in the world," *American Journal of Sociology* 60 (March 1955):430; Kingsley Davis, *World Urbanization 1950–1970*, Vol. 2 (Berkeley, CA: Institute of International Studies, 1972), pp. 126–127.

FIGURE 17-2 World Use of Energy Sources

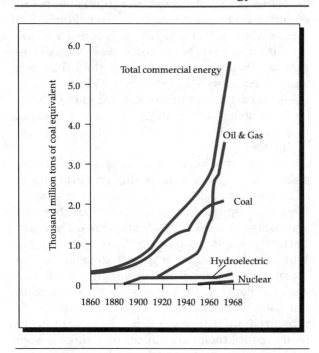

NOTE: World use of coal, oil, and gas has boomed in a single century. The substitution of inanimate sources of energy for the work energy of humans and animals is one of the hallmarks of industrialization. Used to propel machines, these new sources of energy have enormously increased productivity. (*Population Bulletin*, April 1971, p. 10. Based on data from Political and Economic Planning, *World Population and Resources*, London: George Allen and Unwin, 1964; and United Nations, *World Energy Supplies*, 1958 (#1), 1960 (#3), and 1970 (#13)).

SOURCE: Noel P. Gist and Sylvia F. Fava, "World Use of Energy Sources," *Urban Society*, 6th edition (New York: Thomas Y. Crowell, 1974), p. 30. Copyright 1993, 1941, 1948, © 1956, 1964, 1974 by Thomas Y. Crowell Company, Inc. Reprinted by permission of HarperCollins Publishers Inc.

derful locations will become less attractive, and deurbanization will result.

Deurbanization may occur as a result of variation in motivational as well as limiting factors. For instance, some social thinkers (for example, Toffler 1970, 1982) believe that a third major technological innovation has arrived (the first was the invention of agriculture; the second, industrialization) and that it is beginning to affect working life and the nature of cities in postindustrial societies. Toffler's "third wave" is the recent explosion of information services associated with technological innovations such as transistors, fibre optics, and microchips. Satellite dishes, televisions, modems, computers, fax machines, and the like are increasing our capacity to communicate to such an extent that physical proximity is becoming less and less important for the co-ordination of people doing specialized jobs. Conference calls increasingly replace conferences, and people are able to live farther from their workplace, especially in information-service industries. As such industries and work patterns expand, complex organizations and the people who operate them may become less concentrated. So urbanization may decline in postmodern national states.

Although many current projections have suggested that the world will be highly urbanized in the future, deurbanization is a distinct possibility. It happened in ancient Rome, and again, temporarily, with the bubonic plague in fifteenth-century Europe. Huge Mayan settlements in Mexico and Mesoamerica were abandoned by their residents when London and Paris were still villages. Deurbanization has also happen in modern times. In 1970 the Khmer Rouge, an army of activists led by Pol Pot and other disciples of dependency theory, took control of Cambodia (Kampuchea). In a ruthless pursuit of equality, the revolutionary government abolished private property, exterminated the educated elite, and depopulated the major cities of the country. These actions completely wiped out the class of urban professionals (dramatically depicted in the 1984 movie *The Killing Fields*) and eliminated any services that could be offered by the state or the private sector (Ngor and Warner 1988). As a result, more by incompetence than design, one in eight Cambodians died, and the country is now largely rural (Chandler 1991).

Deurbanization may also be occurring more gradually in other nonindustrialized countries (Szelenyi 1981) as well as in some major centres in North America because of technical change and economic relocation (Frey 1987). This is unlikely to result in the devastation that followed the fall of Rome, the bubonic plague, or the carnage in Cambodia. However, evolution toward an urban future is by no means guaranteed.

Urbanization in Canada

Urbanization began in what is now Canada some time after French colonization in the seventeenth century. In the mid-1600s, the outposts of Quebec City, Montreal, and Trois-Rivières each contained fewer than 1000 people; by 1765, Quebec City and Montreal had grown into towns of more than 5000. It is noteworthy that at this time, New France was about 25 percent urban, while less than 10 percent of the population of the thirteen English colonies to the south lived in urban areas. This difference may reflect the fact that, because it was based on the fur trade, New France was more of a commercial centre than its southern neighbour, which was primarily an agricultural colony. It may also reflect a greater antipathy on the part of the English for urban living (Gillis, Richard, and Hagan 1986).

By 1825, Fort York (later Toronto) was a garrison of about 2000 people, while Quebec City and Montreal had each passed 20 000. By the mid-1800s, Montreal was a city of more than 50 000 and both Quebec City and Toronto had populations of more than 30 000. In the Maritimes, Saint John and Halifax competed for regional dominance, each containing more than 20 000 people. In 1850, about 7 percent of the populations of the Maritimes, Lower Canada (Quebec), and Upper Canada (Ontario) lived in cities of 20 000 or more, compared with a world figure at that time of 5 percent (Stone 1967). So, by world standards, Canada was an urbanized country at its birth in 1867.

Stone (1967) notes that "Canadian urban development probably had its 'take-off' toward high levels of urbanization in the 10 to 15 years following Confederation in 1867." In this respect, Canada followed the pattern of urban growth found in northwest Europe and in the United States. In the twentieth century, the urbanization of Canada continued, lagging slightly behind that of the colonial powers of the industrialized Western world, but remaining far ahead of most other colonies and former colonies.

Canada's pattern of urbanization, like that of the United States, moved from east to west. Limiting factors causing this pattern included the physical environment, transportation technology, and the harsh climate of the North. Motivating factors were also important, including increasing population pressure in eastern Canada and the attraction of the natural resources (initially furs, and later wheat and oil) that could be found in the central regions of the continent.

Limiting Factors. The first Europeans landed on the east coast of North America. Given their level of technology, the Europeans found the forests virtually impenetrable. But Native technology, in the form of the canoe, allowed rapid movement along rivers and lakes. So during the European exploration of the continent, water was the principal means of transportation (see the movie *Black Robe*).

As the Europeans pushed their frontier westward, taming the wilderness, towns and cities sprang up behind them as forts and service centres. Most of those on the east coast began as ports: cities such as St. John's, Halifax, Saint John, and Charlottetown were built on natural harbours that gave ships protection from the sea and allowed cargo to be unloaded and transported inland. Quebec City, Montreal, and Trois-Rivières were situated on the St. Lawrence River in key natural locations favouring defence and transportation. As with the seaports, most of these cities were *transportation nodes*. Montreal, for example, was built at a point where the St. Lawrence narrows. There, people and goods were transferred from ocean-going ships to smaller vessels that could proceed westward on the St. Lawrence and Ottawa rivers, while furs and other raw materials travelled eastward on the St. Lawrence. (The importance of transportation modes is reflected on another level by the clustering of offices, shopping centres, and high-density residences around subway stops in cities.)

Generally, the largest cities in Canada and the United States were eastern ports for ocean-going ships. In the United States, such places as Boston, New York, and Philadelphia were and still are among the largest and most influential cities in the country. In Canada, however, the St. Lawrence allowed the penetration of ocean-going vessels farther west. As a result, the east coast of Canada was partly bypassed, curtailing the development of its cities. For general discussions of the importance of the St. Lawrence in Canada's development, see Creighton (1956) and Lower (1939).

The westward movement of settlers in Canada was hampered to the north by climate, muskeg, and blackflies, and to the south by the political boundary with the United States. As a result, settlement was largely confined to a westward expansion along the southern border. Because of these and other limiting factors, then, most Canadian cities are transportation nodes located on waterways and relatively near the United States border. In the twentieth century, especially during the last half, new technology has reduced dependence on waterways as transportation routes. So some newer cities, such as Regina, have been built on railway lines instead of rivers. Similarly, other cities that began as water-transportation nodes have become air-transportation nodes. For example, Edmonton's status as "Gateway to the North" now has less to do with the North Saskatchewan River than with the city's Industrial Airport, from which planes increasingly take off in the search for oil and other raw materials in the North. This has produced increased movement away from the American border.

Because Canada was colonized from its coastal regions inward, and chiefly from east to west, Canadian cities differ greatly in age. As a result, a city like Quebec contains a wider range of old and new buildings than does a city like Calgary. This — along with the tendency for newer cities to be built on grids, with numbered rather than named streets, and with an automobile rather than a pedestrian orientation — gives a very different character to eastern and western cities. Eastern cities are more picturesque, established, and European in atmosphere than the newer western cities, which are more modern, efficient, and American. (British Columbia's coastal cities are older than the western cities of the Prairies.) For these reasons, there is more variability among North American cities than among cities in other new countries, such as Australia, where most cities were founded at the same time, around the coast of the continent. (See Clark 1968; Kerr 1968; Bourne 1975; and Hiller 1976 for discussions of the development of the Canadian urban system.)

Motivating Factors. By 1867, most of the arable land in the eastern provinces was occupied (Stone 1967), so migration flowed west. The scarcity of eastern land and the lure of assorted natural resources probably provided most of the motivation for the drive to the West.

The discovery and settlement of Canada by Europeans was part of a widespread pattern of colonialism, particularly on the part of France and England. Like other colonies, Canada specialized as a supplier of staples and raw materials to European countries. Because of this, European colonial powers were able to divert the energy they would otherwise have spent on primary production (the production of food and other raw materials) to manufacturing and other urban industrial activities (Innis 1930, 1940).

With the decline of the British Empire, Canada became less attached to England but more closely tied to the United States, where it now sends more than three-quarters of its exports (still largely raw materials) in exchange for manufactured goods and services.

Models of Development and Dependency

Development. Social scientists note that the nature of the relationships between countries is often the same as that between a **metropolis** (a large urban area and its suburbs) and its hinterland. Countries, metropolitan regions, and cities send manufactured items, ideas, and technology to nondeveloped and rural areas in exchange for labour and raw materials. The effects of such relationships on the hinterland are a source of continuing debate among social scientists. Sociologists who emphasize culture, consensus, and functional models point to the benefits of the division of labour to both parties and the system as a whole — for example, the great advances in medical care and general standard of living that an association with the United States has brought to developing countries. Just as Athens and Rome developed and disseminated advances in arts, science, and technology to their hinterlands, the United States is considered by functionalists to do the same for its hinterland, which includes Canada as well as less developed areas of the world.

Dependency. Conflict theorists are less persuaded of the mutual benefits and focus more on the political and economic nature of the relationship between metropolitan areas and their hinterlands. They argue that the benefits to the hinterland from this association go largely to a small, local, *indigenous elite* and to the *comprador elite*, the representatives of the metropolis who live in the hinterland and manage the economy. Further, the relationship puts pressure on the economy of the hinterland to become heavily specialized in the production of raw materials needed by the metropolis. Narrow economic diversification, particularly in the manufacturing sector, increases the strength of the relationship between metropolis and hinterland. This increases the dependency of the hinterland on the metropolis for goods and services that might otherwise have been produced locally. Conflict theorists see such economic dependence as leading to political powerlessness, retarded or even reversed industrial development, and the erosion of indigenous culture and its replacement with a mass culture that either justifies or obscures the whole arrangement. The needs of the metropolis, not the interests of the hinterland, prevail. Ultimately, if the resources of the hinterland are non-renewable (for example, oil), the area risks not only underdevelopment but also abandonment by the metropolis when the resources become depleted or obsolete. For detailed discussions see Innis (1930, 1940), Frank (1969), and Bell and Tepperman (1979).

In Canada this model, known as the **dependency theory**, is most often applied by Toronto-based nationalists to the relationship between this country and the United States (see, for example, Laxer 1973; and Warnock 1974). However, it is noteworthy that on the international level "Canada is in the 'semi-periphery' of the world economy" (Beaujot and McQuillan 1982). Some parts of the country, notably southern Ontario and west Montreal, are considerably less peripheral than others. So the relationship between the urban industrial region of Canada and the rest of the nation can also be viewed from the metropolis–hinterland perspective (Davis 1971; House 1985). For example, some historians believe that the Maritimes would have been better off if they had not become a satellite of Upper Canada, thus losing their potential for local industrialization, urbanization, economic and political independence, and cultural integrity (Acheson 1977). Central Canadians protected their own manufacturing interests by imposing tariffs on competing items imported from the United States. So Maritimers had to pay more for manufactured goods than they would have paid if they had remained independent (see also Marsden and Harvey 1979).

From this viewpoint, the development and dissemination of Canadian nationalism reflects the struggle between central Canada and the United States for dominion over the Canadian hinterland (Berger 1969, 1970). Like continentalist perspectives, which overlook differences between Canada and the United States, nationalist arguments may trivialize or ignore regional differences with disparities within Canada. In fact, Clark (1966) suggested that anti-Americanism in Canada has often been used to divert attention from regional disparity within the country by focusing discontent on an external threat. Unlike the continentalist argument, however, the nationalist position implies that ties with the United States foster regionalism and that people in the hinterland would be better off if the country was less dependent on the United States.

This may or may not be true. Since dependency theory argues that metropolitan areas benefit more than do their hinterlands from the association, such benefits wind up disproportionately either in the cities of central Canada or in the metropolitan regions of the United States. So, in either case, without greater industrial decentralization, the Canadian hinterland may remain relatively deprived.

At present, the links between urban centres in Canada are often weaker than the north–south links between Canadian cities and their U.S. counterparts (Lithwick and Pacquet 1968; Caves and Reuber 1969; Bourne 1975). This suggests that, insofar as the Canadian hinterland is indeed dominated by metropolitan regions, these areas are located disproportionately in the United States. (See Garreau 1981 for an interesting elaboration of this theme.)

It is noteworthy that the extent to which metropolitan areas dominate their hinterlands varies, depending in part on how much competition the cities have (see Zipf's 1953 "rank-size" equation and also Christaller 1963 on "central place theory"). Too much competition (many urban areas of comparable size) produces considerable duplication of goods and services and prevents a country from taking advantage of economies of scale. An example of this would be a multitude of small hospitals containing only general practitioners and no specialists. On the other hand, one large metropolitan area may treat its hinterland poorly, keep it dependent by discouraging more widespread urbanization, and generally retard the industrial development of the country. An example of this in health care would be one large metropolitan hospital with many specialists, to which most physicians are attracted, and to whom citizens far from the city have at best limited access. This type of urbanization is characteristic of nonindustrialized countries and extractive economies.

In Mexico, Mexico City, with more than 15 million residents, is by far the largest city in the country, and contains more than 20 percent of the population of the entire country. In contrast, the largest metropolitan area in Canada is about 4 million, representing about 14 percent of the total population. Although the Canadian urban profile is more "industrial" than Mexico's, it is noteworthy that Canada is on the nonindustrial side of Zipf's (1953) "rank-size" equation (and has difficulties keeping physicians from flocking to the higher-paying jobs and superior facilities in the metropolitan centres).

Dependency theory can be applied on a world level to assess relationships between countries, on a national level to describe the relationship between regions within countries, or, as it was originally developed, on a regional level to characterize the relationship between cities and hinterlands. Whether one's locale is best seen as a metropolis or a hinterland typically depends on whether one looks upward to the exploiters or downward to the victims. For example, many Canadians outside Toronto may feel that "Hogtown" is too dominant within the country. But many Torontonians feel threatened by New York or by the United States in general. This suggests that a hierarchical exchange network may be more appropriate than the dependency model for characterizing the relationship between locales (see, for example, Wallerstain 1974). This also suggests that dependency theory functions as a community ideology that is antagonistic to larger, more dominant communities while ignoring the subordination of smaller communities that are lower in the hierarchy.

In addition to its one-sided perspective, dependency theory also has run into some problems of fact. Suppliers of raw materials are not always economically and politically dominated by the metropolitan areas with whom they trade. For example, today the survival of the industrial nations of the West depends on oil from the Middle East, where capital accumulates and has been invested in the industrial West. This would seem more like mutual dependency or symbiosis than dominance, were it not for the fact that the industrial West continues to slip deeper and deeper into debt (to the nations of the Middle East).

A Tale of Two Cities. The drift from the British to the American economic sphere had important effects on the urban structure of Canada. Although the rise of its western cities may yet change things, "Canada's metropolitan development has been a tale of two cities: Montreal and Toronto" (Laxer 1975). Partly because of its location on the St. Lawrence, Montreal was the dominant metropolis during the early years, under the British. As Canada's ties to the Untied States grew, Toronto's links to New York — through the Great Lakes, the Erie Canal, and the railway system — gave the Ontario capital an edge over Montreal as an exporter. This link, along with the richness of southern Ontario farmland, broke the commercial dominance of Montreal in the middle of the nineteenth century, and the ascendancy of Toronto began (Spelt 1955). Montreal's banks, with their links to London, continued to have a strong national influence well into the twentieth century. But after the Great Depression, the construction of American auto plants in southern Ontario greatly extended the economic power of Toronto. By the end of World War II, Montreal's banks and head offices had begun moving to Toronto (Spelt 1973). This trend continued until, in 1976, Metropolitan Toronto's population finally surpassed Montreal's metropolitan population by 554 people. Between 1976 and 1981, Metro Toronto's population grew another 7 percent, crowding 3 million. At the same time, metropolitan Montreal grew only 0.9 percent, to 2 828 349. Since then, the gap between the two major cities of Canada has grown wider. By 1986, the Toronto metropolitan population was larger than Montreal's by half a million; by 1991, the difference was about three-quarters of a million (see Table 17-2).

Although it is tempting for English Canadians to attribute the relative decline of Montreal to Quebec separatism, the latter may be more of a consequence than a cause. Toronto's dominance as *the* Canadian metropolis is probably a much

TABLE 17-2 Population of Canadian Census Metropolitan Areas, 1991, and Percentage Change, 1971–1991

Rank 1991	Census Metropolitan Area	Population 1991	Percentage Change			
			1971–76	1976–81	1981–86	1986–91
1	Toronto	3 893 046	7.7	7.0	9.5	13.4
2	Montreal	3 127 242	2.7	0.9	2.1	7.0
3	Vancouver	1 602 502	7.8	8.7	8.9	16.1
4	Ottawa–Hull	920 857	11.8	3.6	10.1	12.4
5	Edmonton	839 924	11.7	18.1	6.0	8.5
6	Calgary	754 033	16.5	25.7	7.2	12.3
7	Winnipeg	652 354	5.2	1.1	5.6	4.3
8	Quebec City	645 550	8.1	6.3	3.3	7.0
9	Hamilton	599 760	5.2	2.4	2.8	7.6
10	London	381 522	6.9	4.9	4.7	11.5
11	St. Catharines–Niagara	364 552	5.6	0.8	0.2	6.2
12	Kitchener	356 421	14.1	5.7	8.1	14.5
13	Halifax	320 501	7.0	3.6	6.6	8.3
14	Victoria	287 897	11.5	7.0	5.8	12.8
15	Windsor	262 075	–0.5	–0.6	1.2	3.2
16	Oshawa	240 104	12.4	14.1	9.2	18.0
17	Saskatoon	210 083	5.8	15.3	14.6	4.7
18	Regina	191 692	7.4	8.7	7.7	2.8
19	St. John's	171 859	8.8	6.5	4.6	6.1
20	Chicoutimi-Jonquière	160 928	1.8	5.1	0.2	1.6
21	Sudbury	157 613	–0.4	–4.5	–4.6	5.9
22	Sherbrooke	139 194	1.8	6.1	3.8	7.1
23	Trois-Rivières	136 303	0.6	5.1	2.8	5.8
24	Saint John	124 981	5.8	0.9	0.2	3.1
25	Thunder Bay	124 427	4.0	1.8	0.2	1.8

NOTE: For each period, percentage change is calculated by using the boundaries at the end of the period. This table excludes the populations of one or more incompletely enumerated Native reserves or Native settlements.
SOURCE: Statistics Canada, *Census of Canada 1991* (Ottawa: Supply and Services Canada, 1991).

less recent phenomenon than current growth rates imply. Unlike Montreal, Toronto is part of a megalopolis that includes large industrial centres such as Hamilton (Jacobs 1982). This megalopolis, which extends from Oshawa to Buffalo, is known as the "Golden Horseshoe" or the "Mississauga Conurbation" (Baine and McMurray 1984) and has probably been the commercial centre of Canada for years. The relocation of head offices from both Quebec and the Atlantic provinces to the Golden Horseshoe and beyond is more likely a continuation of long-run economic trends than a consequence of short-run politics (*cf.* Jacobs 1982).

World Networks and Modern Cities

Cities are concentrations of people who participate in and maintain local institutions, but modern urbanites are affected in a very real way by circumstances far beyond the boundaries of their immediate community. The world economy affects the nature of North American cities, the interconnections between them, and the lives of their inhabitants. For example, a worldwide energy crisis in the 1970s produced shock waves that devastated some industries and the cities that depended on them, while at the same time creating an economic boom in others. Increasing oil prices and competition from the European and Japanese auto industries combined to stagger the U.S. auto industry as well as its principal city, Detroit. Meanwhile, other cities such as Houston and Dallas, flush with accumulating oil revenues, were able to grow rapidly and diversify their economies by getting involved in the emerging computer industry. At the same time in Canada, the two fastest-growing census metropolitan areas (CMAs) were Calgary and Edmonton, which underwent population increases of 25.7 and 18.1 percent, respectively, between 1976 and 1981. During this period Canada's "Motor City," Windsor, was one of the only CMAs in the country to lose population (the other was Sudbury, which was suffering from a sagging nickel market). The fall of oil prices ended the boom, and the growth rates of the two Alberta cities dropped sharply in the early 1980s. Those CMAs with more diversified economies have shown more stable rates of growth (see Table 17-2); they are like balanced stock portfolios — declines in one sector of the economy can be offset by increases in another.

Between 1986 and 1991 the population in Canada's CMAs grew by 1.5 million, with almost a third of the increase (461 065) in Toronto. The fastest growth rate during this period was recorded by Oshawa (18 percent), followed by Vancouver (16.1 percent) and Kitchener (14.5 percent). By 1991, a clear majority (61 percent) of the Canadian population lived in metropolitan areas. However, whether the metropolitanization of Canada will continue in the face of the severe recession of the early 1990s remains to be seen.

The nature of a city and the lives of its residents, then, depend in part on its *raison d'être* and its position in local, national, and world economies. Some cities — for example, Hamilton and Sudbury in Ontario — are highly specialized industrial centres, containing a large proportion of blue-collar workers, wide fluctuations in times of employment and prosperity, and periods of intense labour–management conflict. Other cities — such as the provincial capitals and Ottawa — are to a large extent administrative centres, with a large proportion of white-collar workers; historic government buildings, parks, monuments, museums, theatres, and other symbols of high culture; and relative socioeconomic stability.

Another way that the world economy has affected the nature of Canadian cities is through migration. Cities depend largely on in-migration and immigration for their growth, and at different times various parts of the world have contributed to the latter. Wars, famines, and other less dramatic events have pushed waves of immigrants to North America, where they hope to find better economic and social circumstances. Many arrive after relatives or friends have established beachheads in the new world: such *chain migration* has helped concentrate people with particular ethnic backgrounds in particular cities at particular times. For example, in the early nineteenth century, the Highland Clearances depopulated Scotland and sent tens of thousands of families to various centres in North America; a little later, the Irish potato famine drove tens of thousands more families to cities in the northeastern United States and what is now Atlantic Canada. As a result, cities such as Boston, Halifax, and others received a strong infusion of Celtic culture, which combined with English institutions to give these cities a distinctive character that each still exhibits. Other centres — for example, Quebec City, Montreal, and New Orleans — reflect architecturally, linguistically, and in many other respects the cultural heritage of their French founders. Onion-shaped domes on Eastern Orthodox churches attest to the arrival of sizable Ukrainian populations in the newer cities of the Canadian West. The nature of some North American cities is shaped by the fact that one particular ethnic group has dominated social and cultural institutions — as in the case of Victoria and Quebec City, which are predominantly English Canadian and French Canadian cities, respectively. In others, such as New York, Montreal, Toronto, and Vancouver, a number of ethnic groups coexist, providing a more cosmopolitan character (and a wider range of restaurants). It is interesting to note that the ethnic combinations can produce an element of similarity. San Francisco, Vancouver, and Toronto, for instance, were all basically British at first, but expanded later with waves of Chinese and Italian immigration.

In some respects, then, like neighbourhoods and the individuals who live in them, different cities can be quite distinct, varying in age, ethnicity, occupation, social class, and associated characteristics.

Urban Ecology

Social scientists have several explanations for the ways in which individual cities grow. The most influential of these was developed by Ernest W. Burgess (1925) at the University of Chicago. His general orientation (developed by Burgess and two of his colleagues, Robert E. Park and Roderick D. McKenzie) is known as **human ecology**. This term refers to the application of ideas from plant and animal ecology to the study of the relationship between humans and their physical habitat (Park, Burgess, and McKenzie 1925; McKenzie 1968).

The Concentric Zone Model. Burgess constructed a **concentric zone model** for cities (see Figure 17-3) and applied to this model the following concepts from natural ecology: segregation, competition, invasion, succession, and natural areas.

Segregation refers to a tendency for certain activity patterns (such as commercial or residential activities) or certain groups of peoples (such as different income or ethnic groups) to cluster and try to segregate themselves by excluding other activities or groups from "their" territory. To the extent that they are successful, they form a *natural area* (a neighbourhood that is relatively homogeneous).

The idea of a natural area is embodied in the notion of *deviance service centre*. Although they can be as large as states (for example, Nevada, with its legalized gambling and prostitution and quick divorces) or metropolitan areas such as Atlantic City, deviance service centres are most often a section of a city, a peripheral neighbourhood, or a suburb. One of the most famous of these centres was Southwark, directly across the Thames from London. In Shakespeare's time (the turn of the seventeenth century) both he and his Globe Theatre were situated in Southwark, providing popular adult entertainment. For additional amusement an abundance of drinking

FIGURE 17-3 Burgess's Concentric Zone Model Applied to Chicago

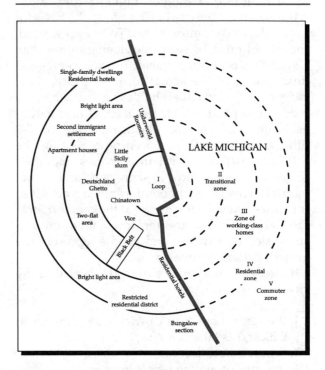

SOURCE: Redrawn from Ernest W. Burgess, "The growth of the city: An introduction to a research project," in *Studies in Human Ecology*, George A. Theodorson, ed. (Evanston, IL: Row, Peterson, 1961), p. 41.

establishments, hotels, brothels, and prostitutes (the latter licensed by the bishop of Winchester) accommodated patrons who were unable or unwilling to make it back to London before curfew. Jails, including the original "Clink," housed more disruptive revellers, and Winchester Cathedral was available for repentance. Thus, without being inside the physical, political, or moral boundaries of the city, Southwark provided both legitimate and illegitimate entertainment for the people of Elizabethan London.

Competition occurs when one activity or group encroaches on the territory of another. To the extent that such an *invasion* is successful and the incumbent activity or group is eliminated or driven out, *succession* occurs. Some people and activities can share the same physical environment by operating at different times of the day.

Areas that are commercial by day are often recreational at night. See Tilly (1974) and Melbin's fascinating 1987 account of "night as frontier."

Burgess used the city of Chicago as the basis for his model of concentric zones. To be appreciated, the model must be seen as dynamic rather than static. The concentric zones are not very good descriptions of the actual form of a city. (Few cities actually look like a bull's eye, and when the model is applied to Chicago itself, almost half of each zone falls into Lake Michigan, as Figure 17-3 illustrates.) Instead, the concentric zones describe different patterns of urban activities and their tendency to concentrate, segregate, and create natural areas. The competition among activities for scarce space (more intense at the centre than at the periphery) and the territorial invasion and succession of activities and people represent the growth pattern of urban areas.

Burgess's zones radiate from the centre of the city:

   I. the central business district (CBD), known in Chicago as "the Loop";
   II. the zone of transition;
   III. the zone of working-class houses;
   IV. the middle-class residential zone; and
   V. the commuter zone.

These five zones form the basis of the Burgess model, although two additional zones have sometimes been included: peripheral agricultural areas and the hinterland (Wilson and Shulz 1978).

Zone I is the central business district (CBD), the commercial as well as the geographic centre of the city. Retail shopping areas, entertainment centres (nightclubs, restaurants, theatres, art galleries, museums, hotels, and the like), and office buildings abound in the inner core of the CBD. The edge of this zone includes wholesale businesses, markets, and warehouses. Because of its centrality, the land in Zone I is the most valuable in the city. In fact, this land is so expensive that only commercial enterprises usually have the combination of motivation and means necessary to buy it. In the competition for the scarce space near the centre of the city, then, commercial activities "win" by completely taking over the territory formerly occupied by residential activities.

Zone II — the zone of transition — is where the real action is. As the name suggests, this region is the combat zone: the main arena for competition between residential and commercial activities, with the latter usually destined to drive out the former. That is, the commercial activities in the CBD expand into a sector that formerly contained houses and related residential activities (child-rearing, house-related work, leisure activities, sleeping, and the like). One important effect of this invasion is the deterioration and devaluation of these areas as residential environments. As homes decline in value, they become a source of cheap rental housing. Speculators hold them for the potential commercial value of the land on which they are situated. In the interest of minimizing the costs of holding such property, they spend little or no money to maintain the buildings, while at the same time attempting to maximize the number of renters they contain. The result is the crowded, deteriorating housing known as slums.

It is likely but not inevitable that the invasion of commercial activities will result in succession, segregation, and a natural commercial area. Slums endure when the expected commercial expansion fails to occur.

The inexpensive housing in the transitional zone lets people with low incomes live in the city: the poor and unemployed, immigrants with little money, the physically and mentally disabled, and marginal people who survive through illegal commercial activities (mugging, theft, and the sale of such illicit commodities and services as drugs and prostitution). Because of this, the transitional zone was viewed as "disorganized" by the Chicago sociologists.

As immigrants arrive in the city, they often locate in the cheap housing of the transitional zone. The arrival of members of alien ethnic groups amounts to the invasion of an area, and can provoke longer-term residents to move out in order to maintain their own ethnic integrity. When the members of ethnic groups become able to afford better housing, the pull of purely residential zones combines with the push from the invasion of more recent arrivals to propel them from Zone II. Just as commercial activities invade, compete with, and succeed the original inhabitants of those neighbourhoods, so do some ethnic groups invade the localities of others, and succeed them in their old neighbourhoods.

Zone III contains inexpensive houses often inhabited by the upwardly mobile children of immigrants who settled in the transitional zone. In Chicago, these houses are typically semidetached. The upwardly mobile children of the residents of Zone III in turn try to move farther out into the suburbs, into the commuter zone.

Zone IV is the zone of better residences, where middle-class people live. Zone V is the commuter zone, where people with cars live in middle-, upper-middle, and upper-class suburbs. Most of the residences in Zones IV and V are single, detached houses.

Like all ideal types, the concentric zone model reflects reality in some times and places better than it does in others. Nevertheless, this model provides some important general insights into the processes and form of urban growth.

For example, Burgess is generally accurate in his observation that activities and groups tend to concentrate within specific areas of North American cities. In fact, recent studies show that over the last few decades socioeconomic and ethnic residential segregation has increased in the cities of both the United States and Canada, especially in the larger ones (Marston and Darroch 1971; Richmond 1972, Balakrishnan 1976, 1979; Kalbach 1980; *cf.* Herberg 1988). Also, Burgess was generally accurate in noting that the socioeconomic status of urbanites increases directly with the distance of their residence from the city centre. In the United States, higher-status people have been more inclined to live farther from the centre of cities than have people in lower socioeconomic strata.

Although these observations seem accurate for many North American cities, it must be emphasized that Canada and the United States are industrial countries containing relatively new cities. In countries where the development of cities preceded industrialization or where industrialization has not occurred, the patterns observed by Burgess are not always found. For example, in pre-industrial cities, slums are more likely to be situated on the outskirts of the city, with the residences of the wealthy located downtown. The general tendency for commercial and residential activities to be segregated, with commerce at the centre of the city, seems also to be a modern industrial phenomenon. In pre-industrial cities, many shopkeepers live in the same building in which they conduct commercial activities (Sjoberg 1960, 1973).

The concentric zone model should be applied with care even in North America. Both cultural constraints and the physical environment have occasionally produced incongruities between the Burgess model and urban realities. For example, cultural constraints in the form of zoning laws have often kept commercial activities from pushing into residential areas. Also, in a number of North American cities, there have been successful attempts by young urban professionals ("yuppies") to reclaim deteriorated sections of both commercial and transitional areas for residential purposes — a process known as *gentrification*. Toronto's "Cabbagetown" area is exemplary in this respect. (See Whyte's 1988 celebration of social life in the centre of cities.) So commerce need not always invade and succeed residential areas.

In other instances the physical environment may prevent the operation of the forces Burgess observed in Chicago. Vancouver, for example, bounded on one side by mountains and on the other by the sea, has developed an outer ring containing both commercial and residential sections. These areas are connected and many of their residents do not work "in town" (Hardwick 1971).

Although the concentric zone model was developed in Chicago in the 1920s, it continues to be relevant. The patterns of segregation, competition, invasion, and succession Burgess described can still be observed in many North American cities. However, as we have seen, application of the model is restricted. It does not fit pre-industrial cities or smaller cities and towns. Moreover, topographic factors and cultural values can produce important deviations from the Burgess model, even in large industrial cities. The concentric zone model should be seen as an ideal type that illustrates the general operation of certain ecological principles in large cities in industrial capitalist societies — in particular, in the midwest United States. Seen this way, the model has value (Guest 1969).

The Sector Model. Social scientists have produced other models of city growth in an attempt to improve on the idea of concentric zones. Hoyt (1939) proposed a **sector model** of urban expansion, which emphasizes transportation arteries rather than concentric rings. Like Burgess, Hoyt believed that activities and groups are segregated into natural areas and that cities expand outward. But Hoyt argued that the commercial and residential areas and different ethnic and income groups expanded from the centre of cities in wedge-shaped sections, along natural boundaries and transportation arteries. Figure 17-4 shows the sector model applied to Calgary in the early 1960s.

The sector model accounts for the existence of high-rent residential areas near the centre of cities (such as Forest Hill in Toronto and Westmount in Montreal) and acknowledges the importance of traffic arteries. In this way the sector model is an improvement over the concentric zone model, which was developed at a time when most people did not have cars and when highways were less important.

The Multiple-Nuclei Model. Like Burgess and Hoyt, Harris and Ullman (1945) believed that activities and groups were segregated within areas of cities. But Harris and Ullman rejected the idea that these natural areas radiated from the centre of the city in either concentric rings or wedge-shaped sectors. Instead, they saw the city as a series of centres, or *nuclei*, that attract similar activity patterns or social groups and repel others. For example, both the University of Western Ontario in northwest London and the University of Alberta in south-central Edmonton act as nuclei for several smaller colleges and schools, a number of research institutes, a university hospital (related to the medical school), and a variety of student-related service centres (such as bookstores, recreational facilities, pubs, and taverns),

FIGURE 17-4   Sector Model Applied to Calgary, 1961

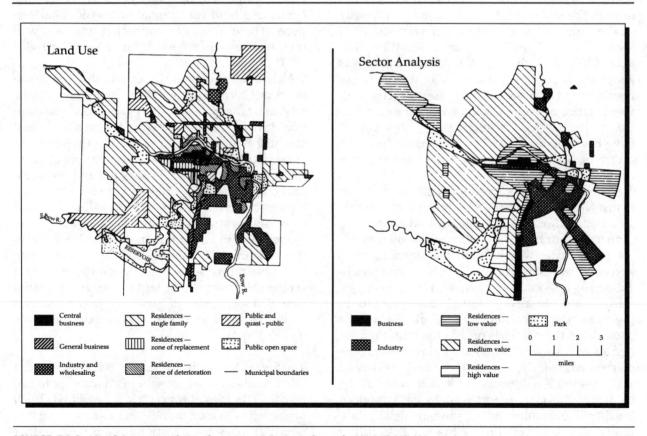

SOURCE: P.J. Smith, "Calgary: A study in urban pattern," *Economic Geography* 38(1962):318–328.

as well as both faculty and student housing. Other nuclei emerge around mutually supporting (or symbiotic) commercial activities (such as law firms, insurance companies, and real estate offices), around industrial activities, and around residences.

The **multiple-nuclei model**, illustrated in Figure 17-5, is most applicable to cities that have developed with the automobile as a major means of transportation; cars have allowed much more decentralization of facilities and city sectors. The concentric zone model, the sector model, and the multiple-nuclei model are ideal types. Each stresses different aspects of city growth. They are alike in portraying competition, segregation, and natural areas as characteristic of urban areas. All three were developed from observations of relatively new cities in industrial capitalist societies. The models differ in the extent to which they emphasize the invasion and succession of economic activities in residential areas and the relation of the different areas to one another. No single model perfectly fits any specific city. However, all models emphasize factors that to varying degrees affect the expansion of all cities, especially in the United States.

Edge Cities

In recent years, a new variant on the multiple-nuclei model has been described by several writers. Garreau (1991), for example, notes that many suburban areas began as residential areas, where people slept and lived on the weekends. These were bedroom communities. However, shopping centres grew to serve the suburbanites, and these, followed by the arrival of industry and jobs, attracted the labour supply. This transformed suburban bedroom communities into "edge cities," where people work as well as live.

Edge cities, then, are self-sufficient suburbs with a shopping centre at their centre. They are relatively safe and homogeneous in terms of education, class, employment, and ethnicity. However, if their residents are living the American dream, those who are left behind in the downtown core are living the American nightmare, deprived of employment opportunities, social services, and safety. They are "the truly disadvantaged" (Wilson 1987).

FIGURE 17-5 Multiple-Nuclei Model of a City

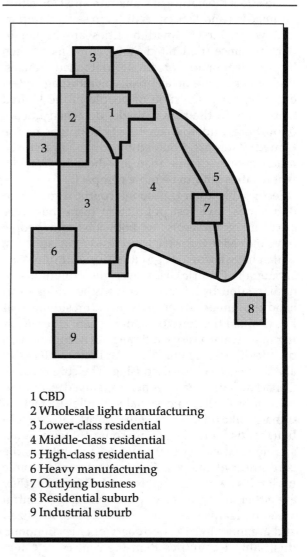

1 CBD
2 Wholesale light manufacturing
3 Lower-class residential
4 Middle-class residential
5 High-class residential
6 Heavy manufacturing
7 Outlying business
8 Residential suburb
9 Industrial suburb

SOURCE: Chauncy D. Harris and Edward L. Ullman, "The nature of cities," *Annals of the American Academy of Political and Social Science* 242(Nov. 1945):7–17.

Canadian and U.S. Cities. Because general rather than specific statements are a goal of social science, sociologists typically generalize from their observations. But urban sociologists must be aware that most of the published observations concern U.S. rather than Canadian cities. Certainly the similarities between the two countries are great — probably much greater than the differences — but there are differences, and some of these affect the nature of Canadian and U.S. cities.

Canadian and U.S. cities differ in several important ways. First, Canadian cities are higher in density, since the United States contains a much higher proportion of single, detached houses. Probably because of tax breaks on mortgage interest, a higher proportion of people in the United States live in their own single, detached houses (Goldberg and Mercer 1986). So cities in the United States are troubled by urban sprawl to a much greater degree than are those in Canada, where cities tend to be more compact.

Second, like their U.S. counterparts, some Canadian cities have lost population from their core areas in recent years, as both jobs and people have moved to industrial and residential suburbs, which have become edge cities (for example, Mississauga in Ontario). However, the growth of Canadian suburbs has not involved the widespread exodus of inner-city employers and residents that has drained the cores of so many U.S. cities, leaving in its wake a restricted range of occupations, a drastically reduced tax base, and entire blocks of abandoned residential housing. The core areas of Canadian cities have generally stayed economically, physically, and socially viable. In fact, in Canada, like other parts of the world, these neighbourhoods typically contain some of the most desirable (and expensive) housing. In contrast, the core areas of many U.S. cities contain a visible underclass who are unable to leave because they are either unemployed or poorly paid. The central areas of many U.S. cities have deindustrialized and are more like the periphery of cities in nonindustrialized countries than the centres of Canadian metropolitan areas. The overall rate of violent crime is six times greater in the United States than in Canada, and much of the criminal activity occurs in the inner-city areas of our neighbour to the south. This situation shows no sign of improving, and it may even be becoming worse (Massey and Denton 1987; Wilson 1987; Lichter 1988). For their part, Canadian cities are relatively safe and are perceived as such by their residents (Bourne 1975). So the differences between the suburbs and cities with respect to socioeconomic factors and crime are much greater with the United States than in Canada.

Third, Canadian city-dwellers use public transit much more often than do U.S. urbanites. The lower rate of crime and the compact form of Canadian cities probably has a lot to do with this. But the United States has also been accused of being "based on the religion of the motor car" (Mumford 1968). There are more cars — and, accordingly, more highways — in and around cities in the United States than in Canada. Dense networks of federally funded freeways are another distinctive feature of U.S. urban areas (Goldberg and Mercer 1986). It is unclear whether this orientation toward the automobile reflects real cultural differences or whether this "car culture" is simply another manifestation of the higher standard of living in the United States.

These differences indicate that the three models of city growth, which were all developed in the United States, probably fit cities in that country better than in Canada. This is not to say that these models are irrelevant for Canadian cities; it merely means that they should be applied with care and modified for the Canadian context. Even within Canada, cities differ dramatically in form, so a particular model fits some better than others. Montreal, for example, constrained by its island site, is an older and more compact city of apartments and renters (Linteau and Robert 1977). In contrast, Toronto is a newer, more sprawling metropolis of single, detached, owner-occupied houses in distinct neighbourhoods and suburbs, all connected by highways.

Urbanism

Besides trying to explain the origin, growth, and proliferation of cities at the macro level, urban sociologists have also examined urban social life at the micro level. Studies of individuals and small groups involve more social-psychological than purely sociological orientation. However, the same variables (environment, technology, structure, and culture) used at the macro level can be used as limiting and motivating factors to explain phenomena at the micro level.

Urbanism refers to the attitudes, beliefs, and behaviours or lifestyles of people who live in cities. Many sociologists think that there is a great difference between the lifestyles of people who live in urban and those who live in rural environments. Furthermore, the changes required of people who move from one environment to the other are said to produce a variety of social and psychological pressures. Some social scientists believe that urbanism itself, rather than the change from a rural lifestyle to city living, causes social disorganization and psychological disorders among urban dwellers.

Community Organization

In 1885, the German sociologist Ferdinand Tönnies produced one of the first analyses of rural/urban differences. He argued that rural social organization involves small populations; close, personal relationships among people, most of whom share common values; a collective orientation or sense of identity; informal social control; intense kinship ties to extended families; and a strong respect for tradition as the basis for these patterns and social obligations (Tönnies 1957, originally published in 1887). Tönnies referred to such systems as **Gemeinschaft** ("community") organizations. On the other hand, urban systems contain many people with different values and more individualistic attitudes. Interpersonal relationships tend to be specific, pragmatic, impersonal, and temporary. Nuclear rather than extended family orientations predominate; social control is formal, with laws, courts, and police. Tönnies called this type of organization **Gesellschaft** ("association") in its orientation.

Because of a relative shortage of people, residents of rural areas and small towns are likely to know one another in a variety of contexts and statuses. Social-network analysts use the term *multiplexity* to describe such an arrangement. For example, your dentist may also be your client or customer, belong to the same clubs or friendship groups as you do, live in the same neighbourhood, and be married to your cousin. So when you go to the dentist, your relationship is more than just that between dentist and patient. You have a number of shared connections and interests. In contrast, in cities, your semi-annual visit is likely to be the only time you see your dentist in a six-month period. You are unlikely to know each other in any other context; thus, apart from

the weather and sports, you probably have little to talk about (if you can talk at all). Harris (1981) suggests that multiplexity of roles may mean that you get better service in small-town settings, where people are more likely to care; a botched extraction or filling may deprive a dentist of a golfing partner as well as a patient. On the other hand, if you become dissatisfied with your dentist's work, all these connections make it difficult to replace him or her. In any case, multiplexity may be an important factor in making community life in rural areas and small towns different from social life in cities.

Cities are highly specialized organizations, and, as we have seen, this specialization has a physical manifestation, especially in larger cities. The extreme segregation of different types of activities from each other can distort the view one has of the nature of the community and of life itself. For example, people who live in rural areas in pre-industrial societies are likely to be familiar with all stages of the life cycle, including death. Meat-eaters not only may have seen their most recent roast on the hoof, but may have assisted in its birth, its raising, its slaughter, and its preparation for the table. In contrast, urban carnivores who order a hamburger are unlikely to have been near, let alone inside, the slaughter-house that provided the meat they intend to consume. Giddens (1982) and others refer to this removal of essential aspects of life from the industrial world as *sequestration*. It preserves the "flow of everyday life" for most urbanites. Sequestration may also produce differences between rural and urban people in their orientation to nonhuman animals. In rural areas, animals are seen more instrumentally — as sources of food, clothing, and energy — while in urban areas, attitudes are more expressive and animals are largely viewed (and used) as pets or zoo curiosities.

Tönnie's work was the basis for a number of similar rural/urban analyses. Durkheim's "mechanical" and "organic" solidarity (see Chapter 11), Miner's "folk-urban continuum," and Parson's pre-industrial and industrial "pattern variables" all parallel Tönnie's views of the differences between rural and urban life. However, the most important intellectual offspring of his work probably is Louis Wirth's (1938) article "Urbanism as a Way of Life."

"Urbanism as a Way of Life"

Wirth (1938) drew heavily on the ideas of Georg Simmel (1950), as well as those of Tönnies, in developing his viewpoint. Simmel argued that urban environments produce a continuous and intense bombardment of stimuli. The sounds, sights, and smells of the city combine with the press of large numbers of people to assault the nervous systems of its residents. According to Simmel, urbanites cope with such high levels of stimulation by developing techniques to filter the onslaught of noise and unnecessary information. People in cities learn to ignore what is not directly relevant to them as they engage in routine work and leisure activities. Thus, urbanites can sleep with the sounds of traffic in the background, ignore intimate conversations occurring between other people within listening distance, and treat most of those they encounter with a minimum of interpersonal involvement.

Most urban dwellers could not cope with the demands of city living in the relaxed and spontaneous way of rural people.

FIGURE 17-6   Wirth's Model and the Selection Model

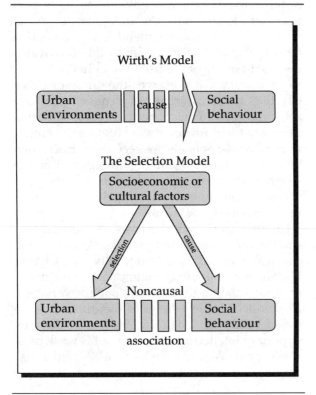

As noted before, cities contain large numbers of people in specialized and interrelated roles. According to Simmel, co-ordination and planning are necessary to bring the right people together in a particular place at a specific time. For example, the removal of your tonsils usually requires the co-ordinated efforts of at least one physician, an anaesthetist, several nurses, and many other technicians and workers to prepare the equipment, the patient, and the room for the event. All must meet at a specific location at the same time. Such co-ordination of specialists and locations produces pressure on urbanites to be punctual: "The clock is not merely a means of keeping track of the hours, but of synchronizing the actions of men (and women)" (Mumford 1963; see also Rifkin 1987). Because of this concern, the residents of urban areas are more often in a hurry than are their country cousins.

If city folks invested emotion and time in every person they met, noticed every sound they heard, and paid attention to every new or different sight they encountered, they would be constantly behind schedule. Both individuals and social systems would break down. So people in cities move and think quickly. They learn to act on little information and avoid becoming bogged down with details, including the personal life of the people they meet. It is because of this that life in the city is sometimes seen as a "rat race," especially by rural people.

According to Simmel, then, the more relaxed, personal, and spontaneous way of living that is possible in rural societies simply would not allow anyone to cope effectively with the demands of the city. People in urban areas think differently and engage in unique lifestyles, and those who migrate from rural to urban areas must learn to do so too. (For an updated elaboration of Simmel's argument, see Milgram 1970.)

Wirth (1938) extended Simmel's argument and focused more on the social than on the psychological side of urban life. He thought that the elements of the urban environment with the greatest impact on social life in cities are the size, density, and social heterogeneity of their populations. Wirth's model of the city is based on these three variables. He argued that extensive exposure to large numbers of socially different people causes urbanites to withdraw psychologically and reduce the *intensity* of social interaction. This leads to superficial, impersonal, and "segmented" social relationships; increased individualism, self-interest, and anomie (normlessness); low morale; and reduced community integration. Wirth's picture of life in the city, then, is relatively asocial (*cf.* Sennet 1970; Gillis and Hagan 1990).

Selection

The views of Simmel and Wirth are examples of environmental determinism (the idea that the physical environment can affect or determine people's attitudes, behaviours, or conditions). The urban environment is seen as causing people who live in it to be different from their rural counterparts. This is not, however, the only way sociologists explain differences in rural and urban lifestyles. Other sociologists believe that differences between people in one environment and those in another reflect cultural or structural factors and "selection," rather than the impact of either environment on inhabitants.

The **selection theory** holds that while situations or behaviours and places may be related, the physical environment need not be the *cause* of the situations or behaviours. Instead, they suggest that people with particular characteristics choose to live in some areas of the city while avoiding others. Additionally, certain people are given access to some areas but denied access to others. This denial may take the form of direct discrimination, but in industrial capitalist societies, the mechanism is typically more indirect, though equally persuasive: wealth.

Earlier we saw that some areas of the city — for instance, the transitional zone in the Burgess model — contain cheap, high-density housing and socially heterogeneous populations. Most people who live in such areas are poor and are plagued with a variety of poverty-related troubles. Few of them would choose to live in these physical or social circumstances, but low income prevents them from moving elsewhere. In contrast, the suburbs are typically homogeneous, low in density, and contain middle- or upper-income populations who face few of the income-related troubles of slum dwellers. Consequently, density and heterogeneity are correlated with such problems. But in this example, income determines both residence (through selection) and income-related problems. If this is true, the conclusion that density or heterogeneity is causing the problems would be a spurious (false) interpretation. From a selection standpoint, then, the physical environment is merely a place where action occurs; it is not important as a cause (see Figure 17-7).

The selection argument can also be used to explain rural/urban differences in behaviour. According to Simmel (1950b) and Wirth (1938), the urban environment causes people to behave in particular ways. A selection argument denies the causal impact of the environment. Instead, demographic, cultural, and socioeconomic variables cause people to behave in specific ways and also determine whether they live in rural areas or migrate to cities.

Most people who migrate from rural to urban areas do so for economic reasons (Fischer 1984). This includes people with highly specialized skills, who are *pulled* to the more lucrative markets in urban areas. It also includes people with

The selection argument holds that people with particular characteristics choose to live in some areas of the city while avoiding others.

low skill levels, who are surplus labour in rural areas. These people are *pushed out* and gravitate to urban areas, where they also find little demand for their limited skills. Clark (1978) calls the latter category the "new urban poor" (see, for example, Don Shebib's classic Canadian film about Nova Scotians *Goin' Down the Road* to Toronto.)

Because urban areas tend to attract migrants from the top and the bottom of the range of marketable skills, rural areas lose a portion of their most talented and ambitious young people. At the same time, rural areas lose a portion of those who are most likely to experience "instability and deviance" (Fischer 1984). This migration pattern has the effect of stabilizing the skill levels, as well as lowering the proportion of young people and misfits, in rural populations. Urban areas, on the other hand, wind up with younger populations who have highly specialized skills, and a higher proportion of unemployables and deviants. To the extent that this selective migration occurs, then, we would expect to find differences between rural and urban areas in rates of crime as well as other forms of deviance. However, it is selection and composition, rather than differences in the nature of the rural and urban environments, that cause the association (see Gordon 1975, 1976; Romanos 1979; Butterworth and Chance 1981; Laub 1983; Fischer 1984).

These are the central questions social scientists have about the effects of the urban environment on people. Some, like Simmel, Wirth, and Milgram, argue that elements of the urban environment actually shape and determine human attitudes and behaviours. Others, like Herbert Gans, argue that rather than the physical environment, only social and cultural factors affect the lives of people.

Environmental Opportunities and Constraints

Michelson (9176) has developed a viewpoint that falls between the environmental determinist and social-selection perspectives. He argues that persons with particular lifestyles are attracted to some environments and repelled by others. Because particular places discourage or inhibit certain kinds of behaviours, people who want to engage in these behaviours will try to avoid these environments. For example, few highrise buildings provide either adequate soundproofing or the space that workshop activities require. As a result, people committed to puttering in a workshop will feel pressure to select residences more appropriate to the pursuit of their hobby.

Similarly, the suburban housing environment is often seen as conducive to home-centred, child-oriented lifestyles. Couples with young children typically prefer to live in single, detached houses in the suburbs rather than in other types of housing in the city. In fact, Clark (1966) discovered that it is more the desire for an affordable single, detached house than the desire to live in the suburban environment that attracts young married people to the suburbs. On the other hand, people with fewer or older children are often less child-oriented and are more likely to enjoy the facilities of a downtown environment as a place to live. (For discussions of the relationship between life cycle and housing environment, see Clark 1966 and Michelson 1976, 1977.)

This view of the relationship between environment and behaviour on the micro level is the same as the macro-level view we took earlier when we looked at the origin of cities. That is, the

FIGURE 17-7 Canadian Crime Rates by City Size Expressed as Ratio of Small-Town Rates, 1978

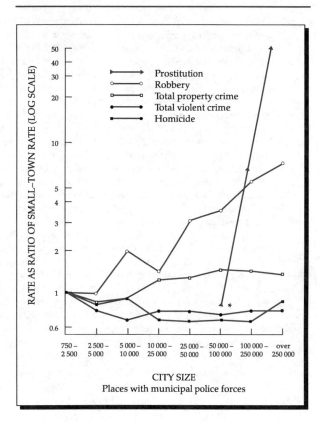

*Too few prostitution crimes in cities below 50 000.
SOURCE: Claude Fischer, *The Urban Experience*, 2nd edition (New York: Harcourt, Brace Jovanovich, 1984), p. 106.

physical environment can act as a limiter, preventing people from doing things. This is the case both for building cities and for workshop activities in the home. The physical environment does not so much motivate human behaviour, as Wirth (1938) suggested, as inhibit some activities and allow others. Some environments are necessary (if not sufficient) for the occurrence of certain behaviours. Warm climates or flat topography prevent the possibility of alpine skiing, and highrise apartments discourage or inhibit boat-building as a hobby. Because of this, significant statistical associations can be found between specific environments and specific behaviours. From this per-

Population Density and Social Pathology

In 1962, John Calhoun found that when rats are exposed to high population densities for long periods of time they change their behaviours. They engage in aberrant activities: rape, aggression, asexuality, careless mothering, infanticide, and cannibalism, among other things. Calhoun attributed these behaviours, which he considered symptoms of "social pathology," to excessive population density.

It seems obvious that extremely high population densities *can* cause all sorts of unpleasant experiences — including death — in rats, humans, and other animals. So the relevant question is not *whether* population density causes discomfort, but *what level* of population density is required to produce symptoms of crowding, what these symptoms are, and what can be done about it.

Research on humans has produced conflicting results, but the general absence of extreme social pathology in areas of the world with relatively high densities (such as Hong Kong and Calcutta) suggests that even higher densities are probably required before people begin to behave like Calhoun's rats (Gillis 1979b).

Unlike rats, people invent techniques enabling them to overcome many unpleasant aspects of their physical environment. Urbanites have developed a variety of ways of "cocooning" — protecting themselves from stimulus overload (Altman 1975). For example, watching television may be a way of psychologically withdrawing from potentially unpleasant surroundings such as those with high population densities (Gillis 1979a).

Population density probably does affect people, and it may affect some cultural groups more than others (Gillis, Richard, and Hagan 1986). But the types and levels of density in the Calhoun experiment have little relevance for understanding what effects density may have on people or why such effects occur. In any case, Canadians apparently need not worry too much about becoming cannibals, at least not because of excessively high population density.

Source:

Irwin Altrman, *The Environment and Social Behavior* (Monterey, CA: Brooks/Cole, 1975); John B. Calhoun, "Population density and social pathology," *Scientific American* 206(1962): 139–148; A.R. Gillis, "Coping with crowding: Television, patterns of activity, and adaptation to high-density environments," *Sociological Quarterly* 20(1979a):257–277; A.R. Gillis, "Household density and human crowding: Unravelling a non-linear relationship," *Journal of Population* 2(1979b): 104–117; A.R. Gillis, M. Richard, and J. Hagan, "Ethnic susceptibility to crowding: An empirical analysis," *Environment and Behavior* 18(1986): 683–706.

spective, then, the physical environment is neither irrelevant, as the selection argument suggests, nor a determinant, as Simmel and Wirth described it. Instead, the physical environment plays an important and complex part in affecting urban life in a variety of ways apart from direct determinism (Gillis 1979a, 1979b).

City Life and Social Networks

Although social scientists have several explanations for rural/urban differences in attitudes, behaviours, and conditions, it remains unclear exactly what actual differences exist between rural and urban lifestyles. For example, the social isolation, psychological withdrawal, and anomie that Wirth (1938) attributed to urbanites is also found in rural populations (Leighton 1959). It is not at all clear that psychological withdrawal or other disorders are more prevalent among urban than among rural populations (Webb and Collette 1977, 1979; Crothers 1979). This probably means that like life in the city, life in rural areas is also not easy for many people. The strain of the factory assembly line and rush-hour traffic may be more than matched by the physical and mental strain associated with farming, fishing, and the limited facilities available in rural areas. The belief that life is somehow better in the countryside may reflect only romantic nostalgia for a rural past, an increasing ignorance of many of the harsher aspects of rural life, and a tendency to take for granted many urban conveniences, such as high pay and access to specialized medical care, dental care, education, and entertainment.

If characterizations of rural life have been too favourable, most descriptions of urban life have been too unfavourable (White and White 1962). Urban life is much less atomized or anomic than Wirth and his colleagues (in what has come to

In urban areas, although social networks are not physically identifiable in the same way as they are in neighbourhoods, small towns, and villages, they nevertheless exist as social entities.

be called "the Chicago school") believed. Gans (1962a, 1962b, 1967), Jacobs (1961), Reiss (1959), and Wellman (1979) note that city folks have friends too and are involved in important social networks that are analogous to communities. These networks may, like Gans's "urban villages," have discrete physical settings. But even when these networks are not physically identifiable in the same way as are neighbourhoods, small towns, and villages, they nevertheless exist as social entities. Social networks flourish in urban areas as "communities without propinquity" (Weber 1963; Gillis and Whitehead 1970). Extended families with frequent and intense interaction are often maintained in cities, although residences may be physically distant (Young and Willmot 1957; Pineo 1971). People in cities may indeed be less likely to be friends with their next-door neighbours. But the reason for this unneighbourly behaviour may have less to do with the

size, density, and social heterogeneity of the urban population than it has to do with the fact that city people frequently change residence (Sorokin and Zimmerman 1929). This results in friends and relations being widely dispersed and also reduces people's time or inclination for getting to know their neighbours. In small rural communities, intimate contacts are more likely to live nearby because people move less often. In any case, people in cities seem to draw their friends more from their place of work or their voluntary associations (recreational clubs) than from their neighbourhoods.

City-dwellers are not as friendly or helpful to strangers as are rural residents (Franck 1980; Fischer 1981). This, along with the fact that urbanites are not very friendly with their neighbours, could lead one to think of the city as socially cold. But it is not. Urbanites draw a sharper distinction between friends and strangers, and have a larger proportion of friends who do not live close to them. But these represent important differences in the *form* of rural and urban friendship ties, rather than differences in their number of strength.

Differences in individual and group life in rural and urban areas may have been more dramatic when Wirth published "Urbanism as a Way of Life" in 1938. At that time, many of the residents of Chicago had been raised in rural areas; the "urbanism" Wirth described may have been their way of adapting to what was, for them, an unfamiliar environment. Most North Americans are now considerably more familiar with urban environments, both from firsthand and secondhand experience. The mass media, especially television and satellite dishes, bring urban values, beliefs, and behaviours to rural regions. Just as many urbanites are now fans of "country" music, many rural residents may adopt urban lifestyles without actually spending much time in cities. As a result, rural and urban belief systems and styles of life may have converged over the last few decades.

Finally, there is evidence that North American cities have changed in theoretically important ways since Wirth's time. More and more people have moved to smaller, socially homogeneous suburbs and edge cities, and until the last few years the centres of cities were declining in popu-

Planning and Progress

When social change is agreeable we call it "progress"; when it is intentional we call it "planning." Urban or town planning is an attempt to improve life by intentionally changing the structure or management of urban environments: it is a "concrete" expression of social policy.

Social scientists contribute to planning on both conceptual and methodological levels. Sociological concepts and research motivate, guide, and justify changes in both the design and management of urban areas. For the most part, however, it is probably in the critical evaluation of planning efforts that sociology makes its most important — albeit not its most appreciated — contribution to the field (Gans 1970; Smith 1979).

Whether a specific plan or design represents progress is not always easy to determine. What seems useful or beautiful to some people may not appeal to others. Planners, architects, and developers may consider a pet project a success for a variety of aesthetic, technical, and economic reasons. But they are rarely affected by the projects they produce, and typically have little in common with the people who are. Planners, architects, and developers are usually highly educated, middle class, cosmopolitan, white, and male. As such, they are not always representative of the majority of urban residents, especially those who live in low-income areas or slums.

Since differences in social class, lifestyle, and gender affect the way people "fit" with the urban environment (Michelson 1976, 1977; Gillis, 1977, 1979), declaring a project successful (or defining a change as progress) on the basis of professionals' reports may be premature. User evaluation studies should be conducted to see how the consumers themselves react.

For example, many attempts to clear slums and relocate residents in modern, efficient, and socially integrated public housing projects have been apparent successes. That is, planners, architects, and other professionals have assumed that slum-dwellers would prefer newer housing to older buildings and disorganized neighbourhoods. While this may be true, professionals often overlook the importance of the informal organizations that flourish in physically deteriorating neighbourhoods (Whyte 1943; Jacobs 1961; Gans 1962). Even when professionals recognize the value of informal social networks, they are often too optimistic in expecting such organizations to emerge immediately in new, socially integrated developments. To residents who value friends and neighbours over modern housing, such developments may be worse to live in than the slums they left behind.

From the viewpoint of nonresidents, clearing slums is aesthetically pleasing and placing former residents in integrated housing projects may be seen as socially valuable. So some people will define a change as progress, while others will not. When such differences of opinion develop, those who are most directly affected by a change do not necessarily prevail. Instead, professional policy-makers and planners are more likely to dictate end results, especially if the opposition is not socially powerful. Clairmont and Magill (1974) showed this clearly in their account of the destruction of Africville, a community of black Canadians in the north end of Halifax.

The poet Robert Frost wrote that, "Home is the place, where, when you have to go there, they have to take you in." His words emphasize the fact that unlike "house," "home" implies a set of social relationships, obligations, and expectations. It means much more than the physical structure that shelters people. In this way the meaning of "community" is similar to that of "home," while "district" corresponds to "house."

Sociologists and other social scientists contribute to both people and planning by conducting evaluative research on the effects of planned change. The results of such studies often place policy-makers, planners, and their products in a bad light, and evaluative research may not provide solutions to the problems it uncovers. Nevertheless, such research is important. Politically, it provides a voice for people who might otherwise be unheard. It also alerts sincere but misguided meliorists to inadequacies in their plans. Without this information, mistakes would continue to be made and more progressive solutions (if they exist) might remain undiscovered.

Source:

Donald Clairmont and Dennis Magill, *Africville: The Life and Death of a Canadian Black Community* (Toronto: McClelland and Stewart, 1974); Robert Frost, "The death of the hired man," in *The Poetry of Robert Frost*, Edward Connery Lathem, ed. (New York: Random House, 1979); Herbert Gans, *The Urban Villagers* (New York: Free Press, 1962); Herbert Gans, "Social planning: A new role for sociology," in *Neighborhood, City and Metropolis*, Robert Gutman and David Popenoe, eds. (New York: Random House, 1970); A.R. Gillis, "High-rise housing and psychological strain," *Journal of Health and Social Behavior* 18(1977):418–431; A.R. Gillis, "Coping with crowding: Television, patterns of activity, and adaptation to high-density environments," *Sociological Quarterly* 20(1979):267–277; Jane Jacobs, *The Death and Life of Great American Cities* (New York: Random House, 1961); William Michelson, *Man and His Urban Environment*, 2nd edition (Reading, MA: Addison-Wesley, 1976); William Michelson, *Environment Choice, Human Behavior, and Residential Satisfaction* (New York: Oxford University Press, 1977); Michael Smith, *The City and Social Theory* (New York: St. Martin's, 1979); William F. Whyte, *Street Corner Society: The Social Structure of an Italian Slum* (Chicago: University of Chicago Press, 1943).

lation size and density. The reduction in the size, density, and heterogeneity of urban (and suburban) populations may have all but eliminated the social and psychological impact of these population variables (Guterman 1969). However, for some city-dwellers, density and heterogeneity may still cause malaise. For example, people who have little money and few housing alternatives often have to live in areas where density and heterogeneity are high. When this happens they are more likely to suffer from psychological strain (Gillis 1983). So the combination of Wirth's factors and an inability to escape may produce in more limited areas the effects he observed in Chicago on a more widespread basis.

Urban Deviance

There are several reasons for the proliferation and distribution of urban crime. One viewpoint, drawn from the arguments of Simmel and Wirth, centres on the freedom and anonymity found on city streets. Urbanites are more tolerant of differences and nonconformity (Stephan and McMullin 1982; Wilson 1985; Tuch 1987). They also draw a sharper distinction between friends and strangers, and are much more likely to treat the latter with indifference. This attitude shows up in the phenomenon of "bystander apathy," which not only allows deviants to get away with their behaviours, but may even *provoke* deviance. Many of the city's strange sights and activities may in fact be expressions of individualism and attempts to gain recognition, to be a "somebody" (Rainwater 1966). Because it is hard to make any impression at all on an audience of blasé urbanites, some efforts go beyond the bizarre and wind up damaging property and shocking or injuring passers-by.

This view suggests that both creativity and expressive crime can come from the same source. In fact, creativity and deviance can be hard to distinguish. The graffiti covering New York City subway cars can be seen as an artistic and stylized form of vandalism. Street musicians often break local laws when they perform, and the once-shocking affectations of punk rockers were in some ways the precursors of current fashions. Even the Hell's Angels can be seen as a sometimes dangerous manifestation of this "Hey, look at me!" phenomenon, falling somewhere between a loose-knit pack of demented thugs and a band of modern knights, cultural symbols that represent individualism, freedom, and romance (Thompson 1968).

If anonymity increases with the size of localities, then the expression argument accounts not only for differences between rural and urban areas, but also for differences between small and large cities. Moreover, once areas become known as centres of expressive deviance, they may attract colourful characters and repel more conservative people. On a broad scale, California can be seen as something of a magnet for both bizarre and creative people. On a more specific level, San Francisco and New York probably attract nonconformists for this reason, and on an even more confined level, particular areas within cities do the same. Greenwich Village in New York has attracted unusual people for many years. In the 1960s, San Francisco's Haight-Ashbury district drew flower children, hippies, and users of psychedelic drugs from all over the continent. The Yorkville area in Toronto attracted beatniks in the 1950s and hippies in the 1960s. The 1970s and 1980s, however, saw Yorkville transformed into the chic domain of yuppies, while the Yonge Street strip has become Toronto's main deviance service centre. Anonymity may combine with selection to produce some of the deviance we see in urban areas: the risk-takers go where the action is. In so doing, they deprive their home area of their creativity, eccentricities, and criminality, which are added to what Tilly (1976b) calls the "chaos of the living city." Adventurous people may also commit crimes when they visit cities, driving up the crime rates in urban areas (Gibbs and Erickson 1976).

Although Thrasher (1927) and, more recently, Katz (1988) argue that deviance can be expressive and even fun, most sociologists in the Chicago school believed that urban deviance was the result of the breakdown of social order. Newman (1972) produced an interesting variant of this argument. He suggested that some types of urban architecture inhibit or prevent surveillance and control in neighbourhoods, as well as within apartment buildings. High walls, underground parking areas, long corridors, and hidden spaces such as stairwells discourage residents from taking responsibility for what happens there. Criminals can lurk behind walls or in stairwells; they can loiter in hallways, where they are bothered by neither the police nor the residents. Because of these design factors, which are typically associated with high-density housing, such areas of the city have higher rates of crime than others have (Gillis 1974).

Newman's view of the effect of the physical environment is similar to Michelson's and to Bronowski's (both discussed earlier). That is, the physical environment — in this case, urban architecture — prevents or permits action, rather than motivating it. Law-abiding people are not driven to thoughts of mayhem by the sight of a stairwell. But someone with mugging or sexual assault in mind may be deterred by the absence of such a secluded space. It is when residents are either unable or unwilling to provide informal surveillance that urban spaces can become attractive crime sites (see also Gillis and Hagan 1983). This situation may be aggravated by the routine activity patterns or urbanites, which frequently leave houses empty, lowering surveillance and providing more appealing targets for thieves (Cohen and Felson 1979; Felson and Cohen 1980).

Although Newman's view accounts for differences in crime rates among different buildings, neighbourhoods, and areas of the city, other explanations also fit the data. One of these is drawn from the symbolic-interaction tradition. By definition, areas of the city with high-density housing contain a lot of people. Consequently, the police pay more attention to these locations as likely trouble spots. It makes little organizational sense to deploy many police in low-density areas, since there are neither as many potential victims nor as many potential offenders in these locations. Thus, high-density areas tend to be overpatrolled, while lower-density areas are underpatrolled. As a result, incidents that take place in high-density areas are more likely to be detected and processed as criminal offences than are those that happen in low-density areas. This outcome occurs independently of the socioeconomic status of the populations involved. So the principle of "seek, and ye shall find," rather than actual differences in rates of criminal behaviour, is the reason that some areas have higher rates of crime than others have (Hagan, Gillis, and Chan 1978).

A similar argument can be used to explain differences between rural and urban crime rates. In rural or smaller urban areas, the police are more informal, and less likely to process minor offences as crimes. Because larger cities have modern, more bureaucratic police forces, minor offences are more likely to be processed "by the book" — as crimes (Wilson 1968). It is interesting to see that both viewpoints — the one suggesting that higher crime rates are the result of "under-control" (inadequate surveillance by residents), and the one attributing higher crime rates to "overcontrol" by the police — produce logical explanations of these differences in crime rates. In fact, recent studies show that both views may be empirically accurate, depending on the nature of the offence (Gillis and Hagan 1982).

It is hard to determine the precise relationship between urbanization and crime. If one focuses on rates of serious crime (such as homicide, sexual assault, and aggravated assault) and long-run trends, there is little doubt that urbanization is related to crime. But the relationship is *negative*. Historical analyses show that in Western countries rates of serious crime have been in decline over the last several centuries (Lane 1980; Gurr 1981; Gillis 1984, 1987b, 1989, 1993c). At the same time, the urbanization of these countries has increased. Moreover, some cross-sectional analyses of serious crimes show that rural areas continue to be more dangerous than urban areas. In some parts of rural Mexico, for example, machismo and alcohol combine to make residents more likely to be murdered than wartime Londoners were to die from the Blitz. In Canada, rates of expressive violence continue to be somewhat higher in rural than urban areas (Nettler 1982; Wilinson 1984). However, as Figure 17-7 shows, rates of more rational crime (for example, robbery) and vice (for example, prostitution) are directly related to the size of Canadian communities (Fischer 1984).

Before deciding that urbanization does not cause crime and rejecting all the theories outlined earlier, we should note two points. First, overall rates of *minor* crimes have been increasing dramatically over the last five centuries, and urbanization may indeed be a causal factor in this shift (Gillis 1984, 1989). The second point concerns very recent trends in violent crime. Historically, serious crimes against persons have most often involved family members and friends. For example, women had more to fear from their husbands and male friends than from anyone else; only a minority of homicides, sexual assaults, and aggravated assaults involved strangers. This continues to be the case in Canada and other Western countries. But recent trends suggest that important changes may be taking place. Over the last several decades, homicide rates have stopped declining and have begun to increase. This change is largely the result of an increased incidence of people killing strangers — people with whom they have had no previous contact (Gillis 1985). Since this shift has only been going on for a few decades, it is hard to decide whether the pattern represents a new trend or only a short-term fluctuation or drift. Brown's (1984) observations of his native Harlem over a 20-year period have led him to believe that social life in cities is deteriorating. Many of the young residents of large cities are frustrated and feel like nobodies. They place little value on themselves or others. Therefore, according to Brown, the action of killing someone, especially a stranger, is simply not as repugnant to these young people as it would have been to their counterparts 20 years ago. In fact, if the killer is caught, the notoriety conferred by peers and the press may be better than no attention at all (Brown 1984). See also Jones (1992) on Mark David Chapman — an "acute nobody" before he murdered a "somebody," John Lennon — and Elliott Leyton's (1986) argument that assassins and multiple murderers are inspired by their downward mobility and the feeling that they had been forsaken by society.

Several of the theories of urban crime fit with Brown's description of the situation in Harlem. But Harlem is not representative of all urban centres, so whether the patterns described by Brown will be observed elsewhere remains to be seen. However, postwar **suburbanization** — the movement of upwardly mobile urbanites toward the suburbs and edge cities — depleted the core areas of many U.S. cities of their most law-abiding citizens as well as of their principal taxpayers. The departure of the former would increase the proportion of criminals in the remaining population of core areas, which would increase the crime rate in cities. The departure of the latter would decrease the money available for social services, including policing, which would further aggravate the situation. This shows that the relationship between social disorganization and crime may go both ways. That is, higher crime may promote out-migration, which results in further disorganization. Since suburbanization has been occurring in both Canada and the United States since World War II, Harlem may simply be an extreme case of a phenomenon that is widespread, particularly in the United States. If this is true, suburbanization may be the cause of the recent reversal of the five-century decline in serious crime that urbanization brought to Western nations. In the meantime, public fear of urban crime continues to grow (Fischer 1984; Sacco 1985), and people continue to move to the suburbs to avoid crime (Fuguitt and Zuiches 1983), a process that depletes the populations of the major cities in the United States and Canada. However, there are signs that this out-migration is subsiding — and, with gentrification, may even be reversing. So reports of the death of the great North American cities may be premature (see Whyte 1988).

New Urban Sociology

Dependency theory and a Marxian conflict orientation are the bases of what has been called the **new urban sociology** (Zukin 1980). For adherents of this view, the term "urbanization" refers not only to the proportion of a given population who live in areas defined as urban, but also — and more importantly — to the localization of labour, the concentration of capital, and the integration of hinterlands into the capitalist world system (see, for example, Harvey 1975, 1976; Castells 1976, 1977, 1983). For the new urban sociologists, "urbanism" refers to "the culture of industrial capitalism" (Zukin 1980).

Historically, the relationship between industrialization and urbanization is strong. Some nonindustrialized countries are not highly urbanized. The new urban sociologists recognize this and argue that patterns of urbanization reflect not only industrialization but the forces of capitalism as well. From their viewpoint, urban sociology has traditionally focused on at least irrelevant and at most intervening variables, rather than the ultimate political and economic causes of urbanization. Structural functionalists are seen as missing the point, because their views do not take account of the industrial capitalist context in which they make their observations.

For example, Lorimer (1978) argues that the proliferation of highrises in Canadian cities occurred because this type of housing gave developers the biggest payoff. Lower-density housing gave developers the biggest payoff. Lower-density housing is actually cheaper to build on a per-unit basis and is also more popular with planners. The majority of consumers still hope to live in low-density housing, viewing it as an important component of their ideal family life. Research in Calgary and Edmonton has even shown that living in highrises is related to psychological strain in women with children at home — and that the higher up they live, the worse the strain gets (Gillis 1977).

According to the new urban sociologists, the combination of industrial technology and the pursuit of profit — rather than construction costs, the preferences of planners, or consumer demand — has structured the physical and social character of urban Canada. Furthermore, because housing demand has outstripped supply, urban residents must now either pay a much higher proportion of their incomes to own a house in the city or leave for the suburbs. The dream of owning a house has pulled many to the suburbs, while others have abandoned the dream and now try to make their lifestyle conform to the available high-density downtown housing.

Rex (1968) argues that this competition among consumers for residences is the most salient manifestation of urban inequality, and that social mobility occurs between "housing classes." Most of the conflict occurs at the borders of these classes, as higher-income earners compete with one another for mortgages and entry into the relatively exclusive home-owner class, while lower-income urbanites compete with one another for access to public housing (Rex 1968; *cf.* Szelenyi 1972).

The new urban sociologists also suggest that the traditional viewpoints serve the state by defining urban social movements as deviance or disorganization and by blaming the urban environment for producing violence and misery. These perspectives, they suggest, deflect attention from the idea that urban social movements — even those that find expression in violence — represent the attempts of exploited people to challenge an oppressive elite. For example, in their study of the effects of urbanization on collective violence, Lodhi and Tilley (1973) found that collective disorders such as riots vary independently of other types of crime. This is not surprising since, unlike other crimes, many "contentious gatherings" seem to be politically, not criminally motivated (Lupsha 1976; Tilly 1976a). The new urban sociologists contend that classifying these activities together as urban violence, disorganization, or deviance not only obscures important differences in their origins, but justifies their repression by the state (Castells 1977).

In some respects, the new urban sociology is neither new nor urban sociology. It is based on Marxian conflict theory and the dependency model, and neither of these is new. It resembles the study of social movements that happen to occur in urban areas (see, for example, Castells 1983). A concern with the physical environment has traditionally characterized urban sociology, yet the new urban sociology either ignores physical factors altogether or reduces their importance from a leading to a supporting role. In spite of these differences, though, new urban sociology contributes to the subfield, drawing it more into the mainstream of sociology and pointing out new directions for students of cities. However, followers should not go too far. The specific emphasis on capitalism and industrialization is of no benefit to sociologists who focus on the origin and growth of cities in nonindustrial, noncapitalist settings. The motivation for constructing the first cities may indeed have been the exploitation of one group by another, but this extends far beyond capitalism. The new urban sociologists' fixation on advanced capitalism is unnecessarily narrow.

Also, "jut as the early urban sociologists treated some urban social groups as maladjusted, so some of the new urban sociologists view these groups as heroic resisters or embryonic revolutionaries — rebels in an urban paradise, an anti-capitalist conscience. To put it mildly, this may be a mistaken appraisal" (Zukin 1980). Lodhi and Tilley (1973) suggest that not all those who engage in urban violence can be seen as politically moti-

Territoriality, Community, and Ideology

"Peace! You never know what peace is until you walk on the shores or in the fields or along the winding red roads of Abegweit on a summer twilight when the dew is falling and the old, old stars are peeping out and the sea keeps its nightly tryst with little land it loves. You find your soul then ... you realize that youth is not a vanished thing but something that dwells forever in the heart. And you look around on the dimming landscape of haunted hill and long white sandbeach and murmuring ocean, on homestead lights and old fields tilled by dead and gone generations who loved them ... [and] you will say, 'Why ... I have come home!' "
–Lucy Maud Montgomery

Many ethologists — scientists who study the behaviour of nonhuman animals — are convinced that people have an innate willingness to defend their home area and the people in it. They call this tendency "territoriality." Whether it is innate or learned, a form of territoriality seems to exist in humans. For example, the closer to home they are, the more likely people are to protect the person and property of others (Gillis and Hagan 1983).

In spite of this, sociologists disagree about the importance of the physical environment as a determinant of **community.** Some, such as Reiss (1959), have placed great emphasis on a territorial factor; others, such as Martindale (1964), have ignored the importance of territory and focused exclusively on the ideas of social interaction, shared values, and group consciousness. Because a specific territory may contain several distinct, and even competing, groups, most sociologists seem now to regard territory as a nonessential component of urban or rural

communities. However, Westhues and Sinclair (1974) note that "while the physical setting is not the only important factor that leads to community formation, it is a basic and important one. Physical boundaries may create an isolated group, hence limiting the social interaction which is necessary for community formation." Once again, then, the physical environment influences through limitation. Moreover, Westhues and Sinclair (1974) also note that the physical environment can help symbolize a community for its members: "When there are real physical boundaries, like mountains or rivers, that delimit a particular geographic area, the people in that area are more likely to develop a sense of social cohesion. When the village limits encompass distinctive scenery, that scenery can come to symbolize in an important way the distinctiveness of the social life that goes on there."

Applying these principles on a broader scale helps us understand how the residents of a place like Prince Edward Island are able to maintain a well-defined collective identity in spite of its small size (129 765 people in 1991) and despite strong political and economic pressures to merge with one or more of the other Atlantic provinces. The 14-kilometre-wide Northumberland Strait symbolically, as well as physically, separates the province and its residents from the mainland, which is probably why some Islanders oppose being joined to the mainland with a "fixed link." Moreover, the outstanding beaches and unusual soil colour of PEI have been used as symbols for the uniqueness of Islanders and their style of life. (For example, listen to Nancy White's song "Red Is the Soil.")

Whether people in specific communities have a distinctive lifestyle — and if it is distinct, whether it is better than life elsewhere — is difficult to determine. However, the accuracy of such an idea may be far less important than the effect of believing it. Such notions are "community ideology," which Westhues and Sinclair (1974) define as "a set of beliefs distinctive to the community which serves to justify its existence, to give residents a sense

of pride in living there, and to unify the residents as a result of that pride." Community ideology is based on historical and geographical individuality, and may be an important component of community survival — particularly in the case of small towns (or provinces), whose young people are constantly tempted to migrate to larger centres.

Community ideology helps small localities resist total depletion through migration by offering intangible rewards to people who stay. "The basic item in community ideology is simply that living in the village is better than living elsewhere" (Westhues and Sinclair 1974). Community ideology and a local history also give meaning and a sense of belonging to a location, and this may have psychic and spiritual benefits. "To inhabit a place physically, but to remain unaware of what it means or how it feels is a deprivation more profound than deafness at a concert or blindness in an art gallery. Humans in this condition belong *nowhere*" (Walter 1988). Clearly this was not the case with L.M. Montgomery.

Source:

The quote at the beginning is from Lucy Maud Montgomery, "Prince Edward Island," in *The Spirit of Canada* (1939), as quoted in Francis W.P. Bolger, Wayne Barrett, and Anne Mackay, *Spirit of Place: Lucy Maud Montgomery and Prince Edward Island* (Toronto: Oxford University Press, 1982). References are to A.R. Gillis and J. Hagan, "Bystander apathy and the territorial imperative," *Sociological Inquiry* 53 (1983):448–460; D.A. Martindale, "The formation and destruction of communities," in *Exploration in Social Change*, G.K. Zollschaun and W. Hirsch, eds. (London: Routledge and Kegan Paul, 1964); Albert J. Reiss, Jr., "The sociological study of communities," *Rural Sociology* 24(1959):118–130; E.V. Walter, *Placeways: A Theory of the Human Environment* (Chapel Hill: University of North Carolina Press, 1988); Kenneth Westhues and Peter R. Sinclair, *Village in Crisis* (Toronto: Holt, Rinhart and Winston, 1974).

vated. Similarly, just as traditional scholars may have overstated the impact of the physical environment, the new urban sociologists may be too inclined to disregard it. Defining urban areas solely in terms of labour, capital, and social structure facilitates and extends Marxian views of social life. But for students of cities the definition is less satisfactory. "Cities are, above all, places whose analysis requires a sense of spatial and physical structure" (Tilly 1981).

It is hard to rely solely on argument to sort out the competing claims of traditional and new urban sociology. Both perspectives are deficient. One ignores the political and economic context of the urban environment; the other makes excessive and strident claims on its behalf. However, although not definitive, data shed important light on the issue.

Cross-sectional and longitudinal analyses of the impact of urbanization, industrialization, and capitalism are hampered by the fact that the three variables are too entangled to enable researchers to sort out their independent effects (Gillis 1984). This situation — where conceptually independent variables are in fact highly correlated with each other — is known as *multicollinearity*, and efforts to estimate such variables' correlations with dependent variables are usually unreliable.

One of the ways of improving this situation is to get more information on urbanization and its correlates and on patterns of city growth in countries with a range of political and economic systems. By so doing, we can determine to what extent the findings of the Chicago school can be generalized beyond capitalist countries. So far, information is scarce, but what we have supports both sides. For example, under their brand of socialism, cities in the Soviet Union were not as highly segregated with respect to the social status of residents as were those in either industrial or pre-industrial capitalist countries. However, instead of living in working-class areas of the city, many urban labourers in eastern-bloc countries lived outside the cities and commuted to work. Also, despite the absence of profit-seeking developers, unpopular highrises still managed to proliferate in the industrial eastern bloc, and parents and children were required to live in them. Finally, although neighbourhoods within cities differed little from one another in socioeconomic status, housing was clearly allocated — in terms of both quantity and quality — on the basis of power and privilege (Bater 1980).

As usual in the social sciences, the available information indicates that it would be worthwhile to get more information. There may indeed be universal patterns and consequences of urbanization, but their expression seems to be greatly affected by the political system, economic structure, level of industrialization, and historical experience of different nations. Thus, rather than replacing traditional perspectives, new urban sociology sparked debate in an old subfield, drew attention to the importance of context, and provoked promising new directions for research.

SUMMARY

1. Sociologists define a city as a large concentration of people engaged in a wide range of interdependent occupations that, for the most part, do not involve the primary production of food.

2. The shift of the world's human population from rural to urban areas has been associated with technical, organizational, and cultural developments that have allowed the development of large agricultural surpluses. Industrialization seems to have had the largest effect on urbanization.

3. The urbanization of Canada temporarily followed the patterns in industrial Europe and the United States, proceeding generally from east to west.

4. At present, about three-quarters of the Canadian population live in urban areas. In recent years, the most obvious change in the Canadian urban population has been within cities; many have stopped growing or are even declining in population, while their suburbs have grown dramatically.

5. One of the most important explanations of the relationship between metropolitan areas and their hinterlands is the dependency theory. This perspective has also been used to explain the relationships among countries and among religions within countries. It is one of the bases for the new urban sociology.

6. Several perspectives have been developed that incorporate ecological principles to explain the growth of an individual city. The

concentric zone, sector, multiple-nuclei, and edge city models are four of these. All have some applicability within the large cities of industrial North America, but less so in Canada than in the United States, where they were developed.

7. Social scientists have provided various explanations for the existence of a distinct urban way of life — that is, urbanism. The most important of these theories is Wirth's. He focused on the size, density, and social heterogeneity of urban populations and argued that these factors cause segmented social relationships, social isolation, and psychological withdrawal. But recent evidence suggests that the impact of these variables may no longer be as great as in the past.

8. A number of arguments have been developed to explain urban deviance. However, except for recent trends, the overall relationship between urbanization and serious crimes is negative. In Canada, people are still safer in the cities than in rural areas.

GLOSSARY

Agricultural surplus. Quantity of food greater than that required to meet the needs of its producers.

City. Large concentration of people engaged in a wide range of specialized and interdependent occupations that, for the most part, do not involve the primary production of food.

Community. Identifiable self-conscious group with shared common interests. Communities may or may not have a territorial base, and they vary in their level of self-sufficiency.

Competition. Action of two or more groups or activities that attempt to occupy the same area.

Concentric zone model. Model of the city in which economic and residential activity patterns and social groups are segregated in concentric zones, with economic activities located at the centre of the city and residential activities located toward the periphery.

Dependency theory. Theory that the economies of hinterland areas become so specialized in primary industries (such as farming, fishing, or the extraction of raw materials) that trade with metropolitan areas for manufactured goods and services is necessary for the hinterland population to maintain a given standard of living. This places the hinterland in a politically disadvantageous position.

Deurbanization. A decrease in the proportion of a given population inhabiting urban areas.

Edge cities. Self-contained, new suburban cities located adjacent to older cities.

Gemeinschaft. Tönnies's term for relatively small organizations characterized by a commitment to tradition, informal social control, intimate interpersonal contact, a collective orientation, and group consciousness.

Gesellschaft. Tönnies's term for relatively large organizations characterized by formal social control, impersonal contact, an orientation to individualism, and little commitment to tradition.

Hinterland. Rural or nonindustrialized region from which a city or metropolitan area extracts labour, food, and other raw materials.

Human ecology. Application of such ecological principles as competition, invasion, and succession to the scientific study of human behaviour.

Limiting factors. Variables that can prevent or inhibit change in other variables.

Megalopolis. Greek term for the most powerful of several cities in a given country or region. The term is now used to describe an unbroken urban region created when the borders of two or more metropolitan areas expand into one another (also known as a *conurbation*).

Metropolis. Relatively large urban area containing a city and its surrounding suburbs. The term has also been used to refer to an industrial region or society that transforms raw materials extracted from its hinterland.

Motivating factors. Variables that can produce or encourage changes in other variables.

Multiple-nuclei model. Model of a city as several specialized areas located along and connected by major traffic arteries, such as highways. Unlike the concentric zone and the sector models, the multiple-nuclei model does not suggest that zones radiate from the centre of the city.

New urban sociology. This perspective, which is based on Marxian conflict theory and the dependency model, emphasizes the impact of industrial capitalism on the form of urban areas and the lives of the people they contain.

Sector model. Model of a city as a series of wedge-shaped sectors radiating from the centre of the city, each containing different activities or land uses and separated from each other by major traffic arteries or natural boundaries.

Segregation. Tendency for specific activities or groups to cluster and exclude other activities or groups from occupying a region or neighbourhood at the same time.

Selection theory. Viewpoint that relationships between the physical environment and behaviour reflect the migration or movement of people with particular characteristics to particular places.

Suburbanization. Increase in the proportion of a given population living on the outer limits of a metropolitan area.

Urbanism. Set of attitudes, beliefs, and behaviours that are thought to be characteristic of city-dwellers.

Urbanization. An increase in the proportion of a given population inhabiting areas designated as urban.

FURTHER READING

Baldassare, Mark (ed.). *Cities in Urban Living.* New York: Columbia University Press, 1983. A good collection of articles on topics in urban sociology that have appeared in sociology journals.

Bronowski, Jacob. *The Ascent of Man.* London: British Broadcasting Corporation, 1976. Chapter 2, "The Harvest of the Seasons"; Chapter 3, "The Grain in the Stone"; and Chapter 8, "The Drive for Power" are particularly relevant to the study of cities. (*The Ascent of Man* is also available on film.)

Clairmont, Donald, and Dennis Magill. *Africville: The Life and Death of a Canadian Black Community.* Toronto: McClelland and Stewart, 1974. A detailed account of the destruction of Africville (a settlement of black Canadians in the north end of Halifax) and the complex motivations behind this "urban renewal."

Clark, S.D. *The Suburban Society.* Toronto: University of Toronto Press, 1966. This monograph discusses the forces affecting the urbanization of Toronto.

Fischer, Claude. *The Urban Experience.* 2nd edition. New York: Harcourt, Brace, Jovanovitch, 1984. A good review of current work in American urban sociology. The author presents his own views on the importance of city size, subcultures, and social networks. This is one of the best-written and most interesting texts in urban sociology.

Goldberg, Michael A., and John Mercer. *The Myth of the North American City: Continentalism Challenged.* Vancouver: University of British Columbia Press, 1986. An analysis of cities in North America that highlights differences between Canada and the United States.

Kennedy, Leslie W. *The Urban Kaleidoscope.* Toronto: McGraw-Hill Ryerson, 1982. An examination of most of the models and theories developed by urban sociologists, with special attention given to Canada.

Lucas, Rex A. *Minetown, Milltown, Railtown: Life in Canadian Communities of Single Industry.* Toronto: University of Toronto Press, 1971. A detailed account of the impact of small, single-industry towns on the institutions and lives of their inhabitants. A classic in the study of Canadian communities.

Lyon, Larry. *The Community in Urban Society.* Chicago: Dorsey, 1987. An excellent urban sociology text that focuses on the community and on different approaches to analyzing it.

McGahan, Peter. *Urban Sociology in Canada.* 2nd edition. Toronto: Butterworths, 1986. Another good examination of urban sociology in the Canadian context.

Palen, John J. *The Urban World.* 3rd edition. New York: McGraw-Hill, 1987. A good general text in urban sociology. Includes sections on urbanization in the Third World.

Westhues, Kenneth, and Peter R. Sinclair. *Village in Crisis.* Toronto: Holt, Rinehart and Winston, 1974. An interesting study of community life and change in a small Ontario town (Elora) on the fringe of larger urban centres.

Whyte, William H. *City: Rediscovering the Center.* New York: Doubleday, 1988. An interesting micro-level analysis of the behaviour of people in urban spaces, by a student of cities who likes them. (See also Whyte's film *The Social Life of Small Urban Spaces.*)

CHAPTER 18

Social Movements and Social Change

PATRICIA FITZSIMMONS-LECAVALIER
GUY LECAVALIER

"The Fury of Oka: After the Showdown, Indian Leaders Promise a Violent Autumn" (Maclean's, September 10, 1990).

"106,000 Chant in Quebec: 'We Want a Country'" (Toronto Star, June 26, 1990).

"Firm to Serve Injunctions on Logging Protesters: Group Planning to Intensify Campaign" (Vancouver Sun, July 19, 1991).

"Anti-Racism Protestors Heckle Rae: 15 Arrested as Youths and Police Clash Again in Toronto" (The Gazette, May 8, 1992).

Many people think that the era of social protest died with the 1960s. As the above headlines suggest, this popular view falls short of reality. The marches, demonstrations, sit-ins, and other protest tactics associated with the 1960s have since been adopted by social movements advocating a wide range of social changes. A diversity of peace, environmental, women's rights, minority rights, and gay rights movements, as well as anti–seal hunt, anti-pornography, anti-cutbacks, anti-smoking, pro- and anti-abortion, and other single-issue movements have engaged in organized shows of discontent. Protest may no longer be the focus of campus and media attention, and a number of the 1960s movements may have disintegrated, but the use of protest has spilled over to many contemporary causes.

What Are Social Movements?

Change-Seekers, Change-Resisters

What are these social movements that are still so much a part of life? **Social movements** are collective attempts to promote, maintain, or resist social change (Wood and Jackson 1982). Frequently, they are associated with demands for a change in the status quo to improve a disadvantaged group's material circumstances — like those of Canada's Native peoples. Other movements demand what they see as improvements in the established social, ideological, or political order. Environmental activists demand that efforts to avert an ecological disaster be made a priority in government policy-making. Gay rights groups ask that their lifestyle be treated as a legitimate alternative, not as a deviant activity. Religious sects claim the same freedom as established churches do to recruit converts. Whether the goals involve changes in the class, social, or political status quo, all such groups are social movements.

The movement demands just listed would be described as **reformist**. Movements are said to be reformist when they seek adjustments in society's way of doing things to include new interests, while keeping the overall existing system. But change-seekers do not always have such limited goals. A discontented group may also aim to replace established elites, institutions, or values to make the movement's interests the main ones in society. Movements claiming such a displacement of the established order would be described as **radical**. They may focus on any social sector or relationship. A workers' movement to replace a capitalist economic system with a socialist one would be a radical movement. The many independence movements attempting to change national boundaries qualify as radical political movements. In a less obvious vein, a religious movement that wants its spiritual values to dictate society's social and political behaviour qualifies as a movement for radical social transformation.

In practice, social movements tend to be rated on a reformist-to-radical scale according to the degree of change they advocate in the status quo. Groups claiming more moderate changes or step-by-step solutions are generally regarded as reformist. Those groups devoted to more extensive or immediate changes are generally regarded as radical.

Social movements are not necessarily change-seekers; they may also be change-resisters. In the 1960s, social movements became strongly identified with demands for liberalizing changes, for greater lifestyle freedom, and for greater government intervention to promote social and economic equality (Freeman 1983; Inglehart 1990). Although some changes were won, new movements have emerged since the 1970s to resist further change or to reverse some of the changes and return to a more traditional social order (Caplow 1991). These efforts to resist or reverse change won by social movements are called **counter-movements.**

This movement and counter-movement phenomenon is a prominent feature of the debate over Canada's abortion laws. Protesters favouring abortion on demand (the pro-choice movement) are opposed by protesters favouring restricted access to abortion (the pro-life movement). The pro-choice movement aims to liberalize abortion laws and access. In response, the counter-movement aims to roll back the liberalized legislation (see the accompanying box). The current blend of movements to advocate change, to maintain recent change, or to resist and reverse change clearly illustrates the diversity of outlooks that social movements may have, even though they are all change-related.

Like change-seekers, change-resisters may also be rated on a moderate-to-radical scale, depending on how far their goals vary from the status quo.

Nonroutine Group Action

At a time when society is bombarded with social changes of many sorts, what distinguishes social movements from other change-related activities? By definition, social movements must have some degree of group action and shared goals. Isolated individual acts that result in change do not qualify as a social movement. For instance, many parents may object to violent television programs and restrict their children's television viewing to nonviolent shows. Such separate, unrelated acts do not constitute a movement against television violence. It would be different if some objectors

The Cost of Dissent

The 1988 Supreme Court of Canada decision to strike down the federal abortion law left the pro-choice movement and the pro-life movement locked in an ongoing struggle to define a new law. Here is an account of the high costs that such a struggle between a movement and a counter-movement can entail.

Laboratory tests today are expected to establish whether a bomb caused the massive explosion and fire that wrecked an abortion clinic in central Toronto [on May 18, 1992].

A spokesman for Consumers' Gas said ... that a natural-gas explosion appeared to have been ruled out.

Dr. Henry Morgentaler, who spent much of the day rescheduling operations at Toronto's other three abortion centres for the 20 to 25 women who normally undergo operations each day at his controversial Harbord Street clinic, said he was certain it was bombed.

"I have no doubt whatsoever. This building has been the target of attacks for a long time. We had lots of security. We had steel doors, we had cameras front and back, we had a roof that was fortified; everything was there to prevent this kind of thing. But it looks like a professional job."

Dr. Morgentaler vowed to rebuild the clinic. But he and other pro-choice advocates also said they feared the incident marks a spillover of violence from the United States, where scores of abortion clinics have been bombed or set afire.

No one was hurt in the 3:30 a.m. blast at the Morgentaler clinic, which is in an area close to the University of Toronto campus that is often busy in the early-morning hours. ...

One clue pointing to sabotage was the way the explosion occurred; although the force tore a hole right through the red-brick, three-storey semi-detached structure, crumpled walls, and showered the street with debris, the only other damage sustained was to the ground-floor section of an adjacent coffee shop. ...

Damage was estimated at about $500,000 — full replacement of the building and most of its contents. In January, a small fire believed to have been set deliberately caused about $5,000 damage at the same clinic.

If a bomb was used this time, it would be the first incident of its kind at the more than 30 abortion clinics operating in Canada — clinics that in 1990 accounted for more than a quarter of the 94,000 abortions performed across the country.

Pro-choice activists greeted the incident with dismay. "I was horrified, stunned. This happening in Canada? I don't believe it," said Kit Holmwood, president of Canadian Abortion Rights Action League. ...

U.S. statistics compiled by the Washington-based National Abortion Federation show that in the past 15 years more than 100 clinics across the United States have been bombed or set on fire, most recently in Helena, Mont., while hundreds of others have been broken into and vandalized.

Carolyn Egan of the Ontario Coalition for Abortion Clinics said security measures at other clinics are being reassessed.

The adjacent premises used to be the home of the Way Inn, a cafe and counselling operation run by anti-abortion activists, notably Rev. Ken Campbell, evangelist president of Choose Life Canada.

A temporary injunction granted to the Morgentaler clinic in December, 1989, forced the activists to move. As part of a bid to make the injunction permanent, the Ontario Court of Justice last week heard what is termed "discovery" — a laying out of the facts.

Mr. Campbell, one of those named in the suit, said yesterday that he had no idea who might have bombed the clinic and that "there is no pro-life organization in Canada that condones violence."

At the same time, he said, "this is only what we warned government agencies would be the consequence of the failure to stop violence against humanity at facilities like this."

Since June, 1991, the Ontario government has approved full financing to abortion clinics in Ontario.

"When we have state-sponsored violence, when as many human lives are terminated daily at this facility as in the explosion at the Nova Scotia mine," Mr. Campbell said, "then violence begets violence."

Source:

Timothy Appleby, *The Globe and Mail*, May 19, 1992, pp. A1, A5.

grouped together to raise people's awareness of the problem and to promote a boycott of violent programs so that networks would change their practices. Then, the shared commitment to change would take on a social movement character. While shifts in individual attitudes and tastes often contribute to social change, the people involved form a social movement only when they consciously support a shared cause.

Another distinguishing social movement feature is that it is a **noninstitutionalized activity**. Social movements are said to be noninstitutional-

The movement and counter-movement phenomenon is a prominent feature of the debate over violence toward women.

ized because their members cannot routinely meet their needs through society's established way of doing things. They do not have ready access to authority or legitimacy in the social sphere that concerns them. Since they do not have routine influence in decision-making, social movements explore ways of advancing their goals that are out of the ordinary. Social-movement action is essentially nonroutine action to promote interests that are not met by society's established institutions and conventions (Tilly 1978; Jenkins 1981; Wood and Jackson 1982).

To say that social movement activity is noninstitutionalized does not mean that it is nonorganized. Some social movements have a high level of formal organization with a distinct hierarchy of authority, well-defined operating procedures, and membership criteria. A movement such as the National Action Committee on the Status of

Women is one such formal organization (Phillips 1991). Other movements are loosely organized, as are consciousness-raising groups. Riots sparked by a particular incident of discrimination are even more loosely organized. Thus, in terms of their internal organization, social movements may range from the highly to the loosely structured. But it is in terms of their external relations with the larger society that social movements are defined as noninstitutionalized. This is because movement goals are not routinely treated as rights by society's established institutions. For instance, until recently, Canadians' right to smoke was taken for granted, and nonsmokers' rights were not institutionally backed. In the past few years, however, many communities and employers have responded to protesters' demands for limits on smoking, and the federal government has introduced legislation that would ban all tobacco advertising. All such moves make the anti-smoking movement's goals more institutionalized than at the time of its formation in the 1970s. But the movement still has a long way to go to institutionalize its main goal of a smoke-free society.

Success and Institutionalization

All social movements begin with noninstitutionalized interests, and their success depends on these interests being institutionalized to some degree. There are several dimensions to **movement success**. A movement attains partial success when society recognizes and accepts its representatives as the defenders of a legitimate set of concerns. Another kind of partial success is attained when a movement achieves some of its stated goals (Gamson 1975). But a movement gains full success only when its interests are fully institutionalized, that is, when society routinely recognizes and enforces the movement's goals as rights.

So many movements achieve partial success that it is often difficult to decide where social movements stop and mainstream interest groups or political parties begin. The Parti Québécois (PQ) provides a good example of the problems partial success can cause a social movement. This political party sprang from a coalition of social movements for Quebec independence in the 1960s. The PQ's twin goals of getting its representatives elected and gaining Quebec independence were clearly noninstitutionalized at its foundation.

In response to low voter support for outright independence in the 1976 election campaign (see Table 18-1), the party had to separate its twin goals. It announced that independence was not an issue in the election and that a vote for the PQ would be taken solely as a vote for good government. The party promised to seek the voters' support for sovereignty-association (a softer form of political independence keeping an economic association with the rest of Canada) in a later referendum. This step-by-step strategy led to electoral success; in November 1976, the PQ formed the Quebec government. But the referendum on sovereignty-association, held in May 1980, was defeated because almost 60 percent of the voters rejected it. In campaigning for the provincial elec-

TABLE 18-1 Average Support for Independence in Quebec, 1962–1991* (Percent)

Period	Number of Polls	For	Against	Undecided
1962–65	2	8	76	17
1968–72	6	11	73	17
1973–74	2	16	69	15
1976	1	18	58	24
1977	10	19	69	13
1978	3	14	75	10
1979	6	19	71	10
1980	9	24	64	12
1981	2	23	65	12
1982	2	22	68	10
1983	2	20	74	7
1984	1	16	76	7
1985	1	15	74	11
1988	1	28	47	25
1989	3	34	53	13
1990	9	46	45	9
1991	8	45	44	11
1990 (Feb.–Apr.)	4	44	46	11
1990 (May–Jun.)	3	43	49	8
1990 (Nov.–Dec.)	2	56	36	9
1991 (Feb.–Jun.)	5	46	43	11
1991 (Sep.–Oct.)	3	43	47	10

*Questions varied from poll to poll, but referred to either the "separation" or the "independence" of Quebec. Respondents were asked whether they were favourable to it or not, or whether or not they would vote for it in a referendum. The averages were unweighted.
SOURCE: Maurice Pinard, "The dramatic reemergence of the Quebec independence movement," *Journal of International Affairs* 45(2)(1992):480. Published by permission of the *Journal of International Affairs* and the Trustees of Columbia University in the City of New York.

tion the next year, the PQ again downplayed and delayed the decision on independence and was re-elected with an even larger majority.

Thus, the PQ gained electoral success for many years, but it failed to institutionalize its original main goal of independence. This contradiction created obvious conflicts for many of the party's activists, who had devoted time, money, and expertise to the PQ because they were committed to the independence cause. While it was in office, the party retained a strong social-movement character that frequently conflicted with its more routine, vote-seeking character. The tensions inherent in this dual character eventually led the PQ to split just before the 1985 election, a low point in Quebec nationalism that saw Robert Bourassa's Liberal Party sweep back to power (see Table 18-1). There followed a two-year struggle for control of the PQ between the soft-core electoralists and the hard-core independentists. In this struggle, René Lévesque's move to soften the party's pro-independence image was met by his replacement as leader by the even more moderate Pierre-Marc Johnson. He, in turn, was replaced by Jacques Parizeau when the hard-core independentists finally took control of the party in 1987.

This renewal of the PQ's focus on independence did not lead to major gains in the 1989 election, which the Liberals won again. But it did put the PQ in a position to push the Liberals and all of the Quebec elites into a harder nationalist stand, as they rode the wave of spectacular growth in Québécois's pro-independence sentiments in the 1988–91 period (Pinard 1992). On average, no more than a quarter of Québécois had ever supported the total independence of Quebec from Canada before 1988 (see Table 18-1). But, at the crest of a new nationalist wave in late 1990, over one-half of Québécois favoured total independence. The rise in support for the softer sovereignty-association option was even more spectacular. When not asked to choose between the two nationalist options, over two-thirds of Québécois favoured sovereignty-association at that time (Pinard 1992).

Why was there such a sudden spurt in sovereigntist support, after Quebec nationalism had seemed to be a dying cause through most of the 1980s? Two major factors cited by Picard (1992) are:

- The widespread feeling that English Canada had insulted and rejected Quebec. This hostility peaked in June 1990, with the death of the Meech Lake Accord, when Bourassa's efforts to gain even the moderate reforms needed for Quebec to sign the Canadian constitution failed.

- The growing sense of Québécois identity and economic self-confidence in the 1980s. This self-confidence grew as the laws to make the French language dominant in Quebec's economy led to a rapid rise in francophones' social status and affluence.

In 1990, it looked like the independence cause had achieved greater success when the PQ was free to act like a social movement than when it was constrained by the need to govern. By 1992, such movement success already seemed out of reach — the nationalist wave seemed to be crashing. Québécois faced both a serious economic recession and the need to make a final choice of nationalist options in a new referendum. In this risky atmosphere, the shrinking support for total independence — already apparent in 1991 (see Table 18-1) — had sunk as low as 34 percent, according to some opinion polls (Lisée 1992). When forced to choose in opinion polls, more Québécois preferred the moderate reforms of renewed federalism than either of the more sovereigntist options, just as they had in the 1980 referendum period (Pinard and Hamilton 1984; Pinard 1992). Whether the reforms the rest of Canada was prepared to offer Quebec went far enough remained a matter for the referendum campaign to resolve.

In another sudden turnaround, the PQ saw support for its independence cause fading while its popularity with the voters was well ahead of the Liberals' (Pinard 1992). With a good chance of winning the next election, the tension between the PQ's twin goals surfaced again in severe criticism of Parizeau's leadership. Since Québécois's volatile political opinions respond both to the rest of Canada's actions and to economic conditions, it is hard to predict where this roller coaster of partial success will leave the PQ.

Traditional Approaches

Classical Theories

Social movements are not a prominent preoccupation of the classical sociological theories. Traditionally, they are treated as exceptional events in the collective behaviour spin-off of the symbolic-interaction approach.

Structural Functionalism and Breakdown Theory. For structural functionalists, the discontent that spawns social movements is caused by a disequilibrium in the social system when society changes too fast. The source of change most frequently cited is too-rapid economic development, but other major dislocations, such as serious economic depressions, massive rural–urban migration, or rapid bureaucratization, might provoke conflict. In this view, not all parts of the social system adapt to change immediately: some lag behind. These lags lead to disorganization since social structures are no longer consistent with the social values that legitimize them. Established social values no longer make sense of the individual's everyday reality. This inconsistency loosens society's hold over the individual's behaviour and encourages unrealistic hopes, fears, and beliefs in utopian solutions for the new social problems. It is a breakdown in the social system that generates the disorganization and unrealistic beliefs that foster social movements in this view.

For structural functionalists, social movements are only transitory phenomena. They disappear once the social system has made a realistic adaptation to change by co-ordinating its social structures and legitimizing values. Such transitory conflict is not a major concern for functionalists. When social movements do receive attention in this tradition, they are attributed to the temporary disorientation and disorganization provoked by changing times, an approach called **breakdown theory.**

Marxism. Classical Marxism does focus on conflict and social change, but concentrates on a very limited range of workers' protests and revolutionary movements. Karl Marx argued that the working class, in capitalist societies, had an inherent interest in revolution because capitalist development led inevitably to the deterioration of the workers' economic position and the gradual destruction of the independent middle class. Thus, society became polarized into two clearly opposed classes of workers and owners. By concentrating the working class in cities and factories, the capitalist system also promoted a consciousness of common class interests and working-class solidarity against oppressive conditions. In this approach, it is not the disorganization but the solidarity of the discontented that leads to movements for revolutionary change. Marxist analysts concentrate mainly on the degree and clarity of class exploitation to explain revolutionary movements or on the sources of "false consciousness" that mask the underlying class conflict to explain the absence of revolutionary action.

Smelser's Synthesis. Smelser (1963) made an effort to overcome the limitations of the structural-functionalist and Marxist approaches in order to develop a comprehensive theory of social movements. Borrowing from a wide range of research and analytical concepts, Smelser attempted a synthesis of the major findings on social movements. He argued that discontent alone is not a sufficient cause of social movements. Before grievances can be translated into a social movement, the discontent must be filtered through other social conditions that encourage a belief in collective solutions and facilitate the organization of collective action and resistance to social control. Combining a functionalist analysis of discontent and generalized beliefs with a Marxist emphasis on the need for shared consciousness and solidarity in the face of repression, Smelser's highly abstract theory has sparked more debate than theoretical application. However, his accounting scheme, stripped of its theoretical underpinnings, has been used by researchers to indicate the list of social conditions to be studied in analyzing social movements (Pinard 1971; Oberschall 1973; Wood and Jackson 1982).

Collective Behaviour Theories

The most widespread traditional approach to the study of social movements treats them as part of collective behaviour, including phenomena as diverse as panics, crazes, fads, fashion, and crowds of all sorts. In the collective behaviour tradition, social movements are associated with all group outbursts, whether change-related or not. What such collective behaviour is supposed to have in common is its distinctive difference from everyday behaviour. Unlike everyday behaviour, collective behaviour is not supposed to have a rational base. In this tradition, a group action that is unconventional is also seen as somewhat irrational.

LeBon's Theory. The collective behaviour tradition was deeply influenced by the work of the nineteenth-century French analyst Gustave Le-Bon (1960, originally published in 1895). LeBon was appalled by the intensity of the riots and the erosion of aristocratic authority during the century encompassing the French Revolution and the subsequent industrial revolution. He branded this era "The Age of the Crowd," as it seemed to him that unruly mobs and the masses had taken over the power to direct society. LeBon attributed to crowds a distinct psychological state — a uniform group mind — a kind of herd instinct that suppresses individual differences and moral judgements. In crowds, he believed, individuals lost their critical faculties. Therefore, people in crowds were suggestible, ideas were spread by contagion, and behaviour was easily manipulated by emotional leaders. LeBon argued that crowds were amoral and dangerous because they acted in unison, directed by this highly contagious group mind. It is worth noting that LeBon not only attributed a crowd psychology to rioting groups but also to juries, parliaments, and other types of groups where decision-making was not controlled by traditional elites. Although LeBon's bias against democratic institutions was dropped by later theorists, his notion that people massed in crowds catch an irrational common psychology became widely applied in sociological research.

Blumer's Theory. LeBon's influence is most clearly visible in the work of Herbert Blumer (1951). Blumer thought that collective behaviour was distinct from normal everyday behaviour because the usual process of symbolic interaction was suspended in crowds. Rather than interpreting one another's actions and responding on the basis of rational thought, people in crowds bypass interpretations and directly copy one another's reactions, in a state of **circular reaction**. Like LeBon's idea of psychological contagion, Blumer's postulated circular reaction rapidly stimulates passions and builds up a common mood of social unrest. As the crowd fixes on shifting targets for this unrest, disorderly episodes of collective action ensue. In Blumer's approach, social movements are the somewhat more organized forms that emerge from this epidemic of social unrest.

Criticisms of Collective Behaviour Theories. Although the collective behaviour approach to social movements was widely accepted for many years, there is little compelling evidence to support its view of collective irrationality (Berk 1974; Jenkins 1981). Collective action at times is violent or disorderly, but that does not mean it is irrational or that a special psychological state is needed to explain crowd dynamics. It is true that everyday rules of behaviour are often inadequate guides in exceptional circumstances, such as a spontaneous protest. However, there is a great deal of evidence to support the alternative **emergent norm** thesis that new norms tend to be generated to guide and contain behaviour in such exceptional circumstances (Turner and Killian 1972). Research about even highly disorderly episodes of collective action, such as riots, has frequently uncovered orderly guidelines controlling behaviour (Rudé 1967; Oberschall 1968). Individuals in a disorderly setting may have difficulty getting the information needed to assess their personal situation fully. But people do the best they can to make rational choices with the information available, just as they do in other aspects of life (Berk 1974).

Much of the initial research challenging the collective irrationality thesis sprang from observations of the race riots that swept through several American cities in the 1960s. The rioters' goals and the targets of these riots were neither chosen at random nor strictly on impulse. The riots focused on longstanding grievances that community representatives had been articulating through more conventional channels for years, with little success. For instance, after persistent community complaints about police practices, one Los Angeles riot was sparked by the arrest of a black youth, for which police were accused of using undue force (Oberschall 1968). The targets of most personal attacks during the 1960s rioting were Los Angeles police officers — those directly linked to the grievance — not other law-enforcement officers attempting to control the riot scene. Targets for burning and looting were also narrowly chosen; residences, government and social service agencies, and black-owned businesses were spared, while white-owned businesses were more likely to be attacked. By far the majority of ghetto residents did not take part in the rioting, contrary to the "swept away" concept of collective behaviour involvement. Most residents did what they could to control the situation and to help bystanders caught in the disorder. Even in such an extraordinarily disorderly bout of collective action, then, there was much evidence of strategic thinking and individual rationality.

This pattern was repeated in the 1992 Los Angeles race riot. It was sparked by the not-guilty verdict favouring the Los Angeles police in their videotaped and highly publicized beating of a black man, Rodney King, during an arrest. The difference in 1992 was that the extensive television airing of that brutal beating led 72 percent of white Americans to find the pro-police verdict unjustified, an opinion shared by 92 percent of black Americans (*Newsweek* 1992). This raised consciousness of racial injustice encouraged more sympathetic media and public reaction to the 1992 riot than to the 1960s ones. Just as in the 1960s, most residents of South Central Los Angeles did not take part in the burning and looting and did what they could to restore order. For instance, when a white truck driver was badly beaten in front of television camera crews, four black residents risked their lives to drag him to safety (*Time* 1992a). Much of the looting and neighbourhood damage was done by outsiders, including whites who were looking for free goods. The severity of the rioting has been blamed on a fatal early retreat by the Los Angeles police when the violence was still containable and on their inept crowd-control tactics in the following days (*Time* 1992b). This lax crowd control gave rioters the signal that they would not have to pay for their violent and illegal acts. The convincing threat that they would be caught and punished, represented by the intervention of the National Guard and the army, brought the rioting under control.

These and other findings give little support to the irrational crowd psychology concept. Crowd bystanders are not automatically swept into participation in protest action. Among those who do participate in collective protest, not all play the same role — most people do not engage in acts they disapprove of and scatter if the action threatens their well-being. Although collective behaviour theorists maintain that social movements evolve from bouts of collective unrest, the evidence shows the opposite. Protest action usually springs from already-existing social movements. Most demonstrations are planned by and recruit participants who are already members of organizations directly or indirectly linked with the cause. For instance, the 1970 Toronto demonstrations against the war in Vietnam and the Kent State killings attracted members from 50 associations with pacifist leanings, ranging from middle-class citizen groups to Yippies and Maoists. Demonstrations that lack the means of co-ordinating such diverse groups' actions are more likely to be marked by disorder, as this demonstration was (Frank 1984). But most demonstrations have organizational means for guiding their participants' actions. For example, most of the demonstrators involved in the Toronto experience were veterans of other quality-of-life and peace protests that were dramatic enough to attract media attention but seldom disorderly. Protest action generally attracts people who already have personal or organizational links or a common outlook on a social problem: it does not often recruit converts at random off the streets.

There is a certain **safety in numbers** factor in large crowds that can promote disorderly acts because it makes them appear to be cost-free. The larger the number of people involved in an action, the less the blame for that action can be attributed to any one individual. The fact that individuals can at times get away with behaviour that would be punished in another setting can encourage disorder, especially in spontaneous collective action like riots, where there are few official leaders to be held responsible for the group. Taking disorderly action that has no personal cost cannot as such be branded irrational, since it could result from a rigorous analysis of the individual's potential payoffs and penalties. In any case, the evidence shows that most collective action is not disorderly, despite the temptation that the safety-in-numbers factor would seem to offer (Berk 1974). This is so because most protesters are already socially linked and not anonymous, or because most suspect that violent protest would hurt their cause.

This was the case of the community leaders who organized a 1992 Toronto demonstration to protest police shootings of blacks. The multiracial march by 500 demonstrators was originally peaceful. Then, 500 uninvited outsiders, mostly youths, swelled the crowd to 1000 — well out of the organizers' capacity to control (*Maclean's* 1992). Some of these youths, attracted by the safety in numbers that the peaceful demonstration created, started to kick in store windows and take cigarettes, clothes, stereo equipment, and other goods (McInnes and MacLeod 1992). This peaceful demonstration quickly degenerated into "the Yonge Street Rampage." As the original demonstrators scattered, the looters were isolated — their actions were no longer cost-free. The organizers felt that they and their cause were unfairly blamed for this violence, which they did their best to control

(Elder 1992). They made moves to assure that their anti-racist message — not a violent image — dominates future protests (see the accompanying box).

There is no compelling research evidence to indicate a fundamentally irrational basis for collective action. With the common thread of irrationality broken, there is also little reason to group the study of social movements with all other kinds of unconventional group behaviour. The change-related dimension, as much as the collective dimension, distinguishes social movements. Current research approaches regard groups with change-related goals — that is, social movements — as a distinct category for analysis.

The Safety-in-Numbers Factor

Experts say that the "Yonge Street Rampage" was the work of students taking advantage of a peaceful demonstration to cover looting and swarming so they would not get caught. Whether rampage or riot, it did wake authorities up to serious race problems that they had long ignored.

It's been called a race riot, a sorry new chapter in police–black relations. But with the dust settled and the attention of politicians and news media starting to drift elsewhere, the people who monitor youth behaviour in Toronto are calling is more of a giant swarming than anything else.

Police specialists, street-youth workers and teachers interviewed yesterday presented a picture of suburban high-school students — black and white — who passed the "word" around Monday afternoon that there was an opportunity for excitement and trouble downtown.

They latched themselves onto a demonstration organized by black community leaders to protest against

the Rodney King case in Los Angeles and the shooting of a black man by a Toronto police officer. Quickly the demonstration was transformed into a rampage of window-smashing and looting along Yonge Street. ...

Youth experts yesterday said the behaviour was identical to that in several incidents in Toronto over the past four years: vandalism at the closing of the annual Canadian National Exhibition, and gangs of young people running — "swarming" — through the downtown Eaton Centre and suburban shopping malls stealing merchandise.

But while this assessment provides a new definition of what happened on Yonge Street on Monday night, the experts also described the participants in the rampage as angry — an anger rooted in part in the feeling of discrimination experienced by growing up black in the city. ...

A Toronto high-school teacher who asked not to be identified said the word was going around his school on Monday that students were going to go to the protest and "swarm and have a good old time."

"They knew because of the political climate they could taunt the police, they could vandalize property and

they could steal with very little chance that they would get caught." ...

Some believe that racial prejudice was a factor. "Growing up black in Toronto is fundamentally a different experience than growing up white," Mr. Worrell said.

"It's almost a rite of passage for a young male to be stopped on the street for just being black. Imagine if that happened to you on a regular basis. ... What perception would that put in your mind about the state and how society views you?"

Lloyd Perry, a black lawyer who has worked with young people, argued that despite the alienation many youths feel, they must have respect for law and order.

"They can't justify criminal acts by saying that 'Well, I'm an alienated youth.'"

Source:

Craig McInnes and Robert MacLeod, *The Globe and Mail*, May 7, 1992, pp. A1, A6.

Sources of Discontent

Current approaches treat social movements as normal reactions to conflicting interests over the distribution of rewards in society's various institutions. Current approaches also treat social movements as rational activities, in which the calculation of group and individual interests is neither more nor less rational than in any other social activity. Analysts who focus on underlying conflicts of interest to explain social movements ask the research questions: Why are these people dissatisfied? What makes them believe that change is needed or must be prevented? Not all analysts agree on the nature or level of the grievances most likely to encourage social movements.

Absolute Deprivation

Many analysts seek the source of social movements in the structures of disadvantage built into society. Among the most common structural sources of discontent they find are economic and occupational inequalities. Even movements that do not have an explicit class character often are rooted in economic deprivation. For instance, the movement to improve the status of women concentrates heavily on the barriers to income equality that women face.

But structural grievances need not be only economic. Scott and El-Assal (1969) have attributed the rise of student unrest in the 1960s to the rapid growth of multi-universities — large, heterogeneous, impersonal universities resembling knowledge factories. They maintain that, in these new structures, students had little direct contact and influence with professors or the university bureaucracy. These blockages produced educational grievances that erupted in protests for student rights and representation in decision-making. Indeed, their research shows that student protest action was much more likely to occur on large multi-university campuses than on smaller campuses. Disadvantages that are structurally maintained in any of society's institutions might be possible sources of discontent.

Among the most studied protest groups in Canada are the prairie farmers' movements that surfaced during the 1920s and 1930s. Prominent explanations for the emergence of the Farmers' Union, the Progressives, the Social Credit League, and the Co-operative Commonwealth Federation (the CCF — the parent of today's New Democratic Party) point to economic and political discontent that originated in the structure of the farm economy. All of these agrarian protest movements appeared during depressed economic times (MacPherson 1953; Irving 1959; Lipset 1968; Skogstad 1980). Compounding the problems of hard times was the farmers' heavy financial dependence on banks and other commercial institutions:

That relationship was one of subordination and dependence, and of extreme vulnerability to the vicissitudes of the market. Dependent on monopolistic banks for credit, subordinate to the railways, elevator companies and the Grain Exchange for the marketing and prices of their farm products, and at the mercy of eastern manufacturing interests for the costs of their agricultural supplies, farmers were almost completely unable to control the prices and sale of their products. (Skogstad 1980)

Given this structure of dependence, western farmers had developed an entrenched distrust of eastern banks, railways, and other commercial institutions, which they felt were exploiting them (Morton 1950). This distrust was transferred to the federal political parties, which seemed to support the eastern interests (Smith 1967; Skogstad 1980). When falling prices for their products forced a drop in farm incomes, the sum of the farmers' grievances incited them to launch local protest parties.

In such an interpretation, social movements are considered to be a direct response to declining material conditions. History is full of revolts, rebellions, and political protests that fit this model. In eighteenth-century France, recurrent food riots were caused by sharp increases in food prices and growing hunger among the urban poor (Rudé 1967). In nineteenth-century Europe, artisans organized attacks on the factory machines that had eliminated their jobs (Jenkins 1981). In the 1960s, citizen groups emerged to defend downtown Canadian neighbourhoods from the freeway, highrise, and commercial development that was destroying the quality of life in these residential areas (Magnusson 1983). More recently, the 1990

Oka crisis was sparked by that town's attempt to expand a golf course onto an ancestral Mohawk burial ground (Hornung 1991; York and Pindera 1991).

While many movements are related to a severe decline in a group's economic or political position, many others are not. For example, the 1960s women's movement surfaced even though women had made educational gains that were beginning to bring them status and income gains. Although their economic conditions were not deteriorating, women's situation was still far from equal to that of men. Whatever the gains they had made, women were deprived of equal opportunities for job advancement and equal returns on their education. We might say that women suffered from limited opportunities or blocked mobility; that is, they faced major barriers to achieving full equality with men whatever their education. Rather than being based on deteriorating conditions, the grievances underlying the women's movement appear to have been based on structurally restricted opportunities. This type of discontent, based on inequality rather than on deteriorating conditions, is also the source of many ethnic and racial movements.

Structural disadvantages rooted in either deteriorating life conditions or unequal opportunities are known as **absolute deprivations.** Analysts who rely on absolute deprivation to explain social movements hold that the greater the actual disadvantage a group faces, the greater the likelihood that a social movement will be formed. Absolute deprivations are concrete and generated by the social structure, in contrast to relative deprivations, which depend heavily on subjective feelings.

Relative Deprivation

The notion of relative deprivation adds a social-psychological dimension to discontent. Some theorists stress that being disadvantaged alone is not sufficient to stir discontent strong enough to incite social movements. They maintain that to provoke protest people must feel that a disadvantage is unfair or unjust. This perception depends on individual experiences and beliefs. People feel deprived relative to their expectation of fair treatment. People who have been led not to expect much do not rebel when they don't get much. It is

feelings of relative, not absolute, deprivation that are thought to stir discontent.

Relative deprivation occurs when people do not get what they think they should get (Gurr 1970). When achievements are low, relative to expectations — when people don't get the rewards they feel entitled to — they are likely to rebel. In this **frustration–aggression approach**, the level of frustration is matched directly by the level of aggressive behaviour. The greater the difference between what people expect and what they get, the more intense the frustration and conflict.

The relative deprivation approach to the study of social movements was proposed by James Davies (1962) to explain the outbreak of revolutions and rebellions. He maintained that revolutions are most likely to occur when a prolonged period of economic growth and wellbeing is followed by a period of sharp decline, like a sudden depression or a serious stock market crash. This rise-and-drop pattern, he said, generates a sense of relative deprivation, because the period of improving fortunes raises expectations that are dashed when a depression, war, or some other crisis brings a sudden downturn in the economy. In contrast, a steady deterioration of the economy would not generate conflict because people's expectations would have had time to deflate gradually. According to Davies, the greater the gap between the original economic success and the later failure, the more violent the ensuing political conflict.

Gurr (1970) expanded on the original rise-and-drop definition of relative deprivation to include any social conditions that make people expect more without increasing their satisfaction. He also included any conditions that reduce satisfaction without making people expect less. Their expectations might rise because they are exposed to new beliefs about the rewards they are entitled to or to new information about the gains that other groups have made. Even if their situation remains stable or is improving, people may feel deprived if other comparable groups begin to pull ahead of them. Any happenings that raise the standards of justice or of fair treatment in a group can provoke relative deprivation. In this view, the less that people get relative to these new expectations, the greater the frustration and more intense the rebellion.

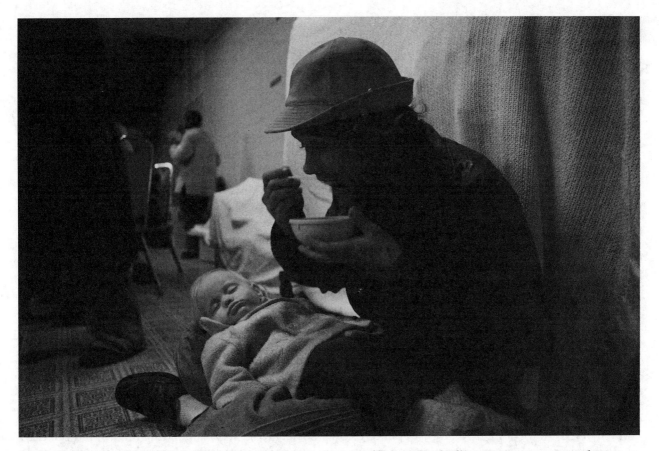

Some theorists stress that being disadvantaged alone is not sufficient to stir discontent strong enough to incite social movements.

The relative deprivation notion is central to an approach that emphasizes perceived institutional deficiencies as the source of social movement discontent (Clark, Grayson, and Grayson 1975). In this approach, a large gap between the way people expect to be treated and the way they are treated provokes dissatisfaction because it makes them feel that institutional practices are unfair. When institutions fail to measure up to people's expectations and standards of fairness, the resulting dissatisfaction provokes feelings of restlessness and the urge to do something to change the offending situation. For instance, the discontent behind the 1960s youth movement has been attributed to the clash between young people's new expectations of personal freedom rooted in liberalized child-rearing practices and the personal restrictions that young people faced in increasingly bureaucratized universities and work settings (Clark et al. 1975; Westhues 1975). The frustration of holding do-your-own-thing ideals in live-by-the-book institutions sparked a sense of relative deprivation and the youth revolt. This frustrating gap may result from a sudden deterioration of treatment or the growth of new ideals, or both at the same time. The greater the gap between ideal and real institutional practices, the greater the perceived unfairness and the likelihood of a social movement.

Absolute versus Relative Deprivation

The debate over the relative or absolute nature of the deprivations most likely to spark social movements has raged on in the research literature for years.

Although the concept of relative deprivation is based on social psychological principles, attempts to measure it have focused on group rather than individual characteristics and on objective rather than subjective measures of treatment. Gurr (1970) uses such indicators as employment rates, drops in production, increased taxes, and loss of income status to approximate subjective evaluations of expectations and achievements. A case could be made for absolute deprivation as much as for relative deprivation in many of the situations studied. For instance, relative deprivation theory has commonly been used to explain the emergence of the civil rights movement and race riots in the United States (Morgan and Clark 1973). Can we say that the source of racial discontent was relative deprivation because blacks' expectation of equality with whites grew much faster than the actual improvements in their life conditions did in the 1960s? Or can we say that the racial discontent was based on real incidences of discrimination and absolute, structurally based inequalities? Data on educational and income levels, housing conditions, and residential segregation have been used to argue both sides of this case (Marx and Wood 1975).

Much of the choice of interpretation depends on whether the analyst sees protest action as a means of releasing pent-up frustrations — the relative deprivation perspective — or as a means of combating real conflicts of interest and structural disadvantages — the absolute deprivation perspective. The tendency among social movement analysts has been to adopt the absolute deprivation interpretation, especially when serious inequalities are involved (Marx and Wood 1975). Many analysts reserve the notion of relative deprivation for the unfulfilled ideals that give rise to social movements not based on obvious material disadvantages, for example, certain lifestyle movements such as the "Moonies" and other religious cults. Whether the interpretation stresses the absolute or relative aspect of discontent, research findings offer little support for the direct frustration–aggression link that the relative deprivation approach has advanced (Marx and Wood 1975).

Currently, those who retain the relative deprivation concept use it to pinpoint sources of dissatisfaction but not to fully explain the form or intensity of rebellions (Clark et al. 1975). This is

the case of another social-psychological approach — the postmaterialist theory of social movements support (Inglehart 1990). Inglehart maintains that the middle-class generation born since 1945 in Western societies has experienced a major shift in values and ideology to a "new politics." In this approach, these children of affluence — especially those who are university educated — have been socialized during a period when they could take economic security for granted. They have surpassed materialism to focus instead on postmaterialist values such as the sense of belonging, self-fulfillment, self-expression, and the importance of aesthetic and intellectual needs. This new value system promotes high ideals and, in turn, lifestyle and quality-of-life dissatisfaction. Postmaterialist ideals give rise to social movements such as environmental, status of women and minorities, and peace movements. As Nevitte, Bakvis, and Gibbins (1989) have shown, the postmaterialist generation's high ideals have created a "new politics" in Canada. But the new generation has not given up its material concerns. Rather, these postmaterialists perform a balancing act between their economic and ideological self-interest that creates different kinds of "new politics" from society to society, depending on the "old politics" and elites already in place. The link between the postmaterialists' ideals and their political action is too indirect to fully predict their social movement behaviour.

Resource Mobilization

Commonplace Conflicts

The currently dominant approach to the study of social movements does not concentrate on absolute, relative, or any other kind of deprivation to explain collective action. Instead, it focuses on the ways in which personal, organizational, and political resources encourage people to take group action for social change. This is not because conflicts over the "good things" in life are not considered central to society. Rather, conflicts and discontent are thought to be so common to society's institutions that knowing why people are dissatisfied cannot tell you what, if anything, they are going to do about it. How can a severe disadvantage directly explain why one group unites to protest for social change, when other equally disadvantaged or dissatisfied groups suffer in silence? As Oberschall (1973) explains:

At any given moment, there exists a certain distribution of scarce resources and of rewards — the good things desired and sought after by most, such as wealth, power, and prestige — among the individuals, groups, and classes in a society. Some are better off, and others are worse off. Those who are favored have a vested interest in conserving and consolidating their existing share; those who are negatively privileged seek to increase theirs, either individually or collectively.

Not only are serious disadvantages not enough to explain the appearance of social movements, they are not even necessary. The dissatisfaction behind movements is based on any group's desire to keep or get more of the good things in life, whether they are privileged or underprivileged. Dissatisfaction is widespread in society because of the conflicts over rewards that drive social life. Since, as Oberschall (1973) says, the good things in life are in short supply, those who have wealth, prestige, and the power to control their life circumstances want to keep those advantages and get more, while the disadvantaged want a greater share. When the privileged fail to get what they want through the well-institutionalized means that usually work for them, they are likely to be dissatisfied and desire a social change that would benefit them. Although the truly disadvantaged are in a position to have a chronic and wide-ranging desire for social change, they are not the only dissatisfied people in society. In an affluent, "have-it-all" society such as ours, any want can become a need, and difficulties in fulfilling that need can be defined as a social problem. The current spate of upper-income movements to achieve the perfect body or the New Age of psychic harmony show that the potential for dissatisfaction is almost infinite, whether based on deprivations or on high ideals.

Although dissatisfaction is commonplace in society, discontented people are likely to form social movements only when it seems likely that they can improve their situation by acting together. Discontent is common, and yet social movements come and go, many grievances are never aired, and the social movements that do surface don't always arise when dissatisfaction is at its worst. If there were a direct link between discontent and social movement formation, wouldn't we have seen a major youth movement in the early 1990s, when expectations of affluence were still high but job opportunities were rapidly shrinking due to the economic recession? It is not likely that young people felt less frustrated or worried about their future in the early 1990s than in the 1960s. Rather, it seems likely that it was riskier for young people to challenge the established order in the 1990s setting of limited opportunities than in the 1960s setting of growing wealth and job opportunities.

Even many severely disadvantaged groups do not rebel because they feel powerless to change their situation through collective action (Tilly 1978). Poverty-stricken peasants may endure the most demeaning living conditions until leaders emerge who can afford the costs of organizing their cause, until outside sympathizers pour resources into their cause, or until some event weakens the authorities' ability to punish them for rebellion. Discontented groups are sensitive to the costs and probable benefits of collective action. If the group does not have the organizational resources needed to mount a collective challenge for change, or if such a challenge stands little chance of success, no social movement is likely to appear — whatever the level of discontent. When collective action is too costly or hopeless a pursuit, individuals look for personal means of coping or escaping their problems; they look for individual rather than collective solutions to their problems.

In the currently dominant resource-based approach, it is not the absence of dissatisfaction or frustration, but the high cost of organizing an effective response to problems that is most likely to discourage social movements.

Discontent or Resources?

There is considerable research evidence to support the idea of an indirect link between discontent and social movement involvement. Pinard (1971) found that, although the poor were the most discontented Quebeckers, they were the least likely dissatisfied group to support Quebec's Social Credit movement. As in many other protest movements, the poor were late joiners, giving support only after the backing of better-off farmers and workers had made the party a viable political force. Likewise, Lipset (1968) found that Saskatchewan's CCF movement was not built on the support of the poorest farmers, even though they were most exposed to the economic reversals of the 1930s depression. The protest action was initiated by the highest-income and highest-status farmers, with the poorest joining in large numbers only after the depression had passed. A review of research findings shows that it is frequently not the most discontented, but those discontented who can best afford the risks of collective action, who tend to launch protest movements (Jenkins 1981). Peasants who have independent land rights are more likely to rebel in defence of their interests than are peasants who are highly dependent on the favour of large landlords (Wolf 1969). Ghetto residents with jobs and strong neighbourhood links were more likely than the unemployed and socially isolated to take part in the 1960s riots (Feagin and Hahn 1973). These are only part of a long list of cases in which it was the dissatisfied having the highest level of resources — not those having the highest degree of absolute or relative deprivation — who initiated collective action.

An even less direct link between discontent and social movement formation has been found in other studies. Comparing the characteristics of cities that did with those that did not experience race riots in the 1960s, Spilerman (1976) found no relationship between levels of black deprivation, either absolute or relative, and the incidence or severity of rioting. The cities with high black unemployment rates, dilapidated housing conditions, and large gaps between black and white income levels did not have more outbreaks of rioting than others. Two factors were highly related to rioting: the riot cities were most likely to be those with the largest black populations and those located outside the South. It was in cities where the black population was large enough to have some political impact that riots to end discriminatory practices were most evident. In the southern United States, rioting was discouraged by the severe punishment that usually met black dissidence — a reflection of blacks' severe lack of political resources. Riots emerged mainly in those cities where disorderly tactics could work — where riots stood a chance of getting results other than all-out repression.

While the American riot studies show the central importance of political resources, other studies have shown the importance of organizational resources to social movements. A review of industrial violence over a 130-year period in France found that growing social ties and organizational links among industrial workers were much more directly related to protest action than were economic downturns or income losses (Snyder and Tilly 1972).

There is, then, much evidence that changing levels of discontent are too indirectly related to episodes of collective action to explain movement formation. Even so, most analysts who find conflicting interests and dissatisfaction too pervasive to be decisive do give discontent at least a secondary role in social movement formation. Many hold that social movements are more likely to be sparked by direct threats to a group's interest than simply by aspirations for a greater share of society's rewards (Oberschall 1973; Tilly 1978). Events, such as changes in policies or practices that threaten a loss of rewards, that create obvious barriers to achievement, or that directly confront ideals, frequently — but not necessarily — give rise to social movements. Other analysts maintain that no widespread sense of grievance or threat need precede a social movement at all (McCarthy and Zald 1973). Rather, the feeling of discontent is often spread by the movement itself, initiated by only a handful of leaders. This was the case of the environmental movement, which started with a few natural scientists and policy researchers who used the media to spread an awareness of pollution as a social problem (Wood 1982; Kamieniecki 1991). Until then, pollution had been of only vague concern to the general public, not a matter of widespread discontent. In a particularly striking example, American environmental movements had used the media to raise public awareness of radon gas as a health risk by the mid-1980s. This forced the government to take a tough stand on measuring and regulating levels of radon gas in American homes. In contrast, no Canadian environmental group had pushed the radon issue onto the public agenda. By 1990, neither the Canadian public nor the government showed much concern for this potential health hazard (Harrison and Hoberg 1991).

Those who downplay the role of discontent stress that sharing an interest in social change is no guarantee that people will act together to bring about change. Wanting social change is not enough. Taking collective action requires a lot of resources. It requires time, money, expertise, leadership, and a host of other resources to mount the kind of challenge that can compel society to accept change. Before an assortment of concerned people can act together, they have to put a lot of effort into getting enough resources under the group's control to challenge their opponents. This process of attracting, co-ordinating, and applying resources for a common goal is called **resource mobilization**. In the resource mobilization approach, a group's capacity to act together and its chances of making gains through group action are the most decisive factors in social movement formation. If the cost of group action for change seems likely to outweigh the benefits, no social movement will emerge. This focus on organizational and political resources affects the choice of research questions that are considered important. Rather than ask why people are dissatisfied, the resource mobilization analyst asks: What chance do these people have of organizing a collective demand for change? What makes them think that a collective challenge can overcome the opposition to change? The answer lies in the group's access to resources that could lower the cost of organizing an effective solution to their problems.

The Obstacles to Mobilization

The very nature of their desire for social change poses a mobilization dilemma for social movements. Demands for change in any of society's institutions are likely to be resisted by those individuals or groups who benefit from existing arrangements. Groups advocating change start with few established means of influence, but they face opponents who have low-cost, institutionalized means of defending their position. Demands for change challenge the position of groups whose interests are recognized as legitimate, who have ready access to decision-makers, and whose rights are enforced by society. For instance, when anti-nuclear activists picket a nuclear plant, the owners and members of the population who favour nuclear power do not have to come out in force to prevent a blockade. Their rights are protected by law, law-enforcement agencies bear the cost of keeping the demonstration under control, and the state bears the cost of prosecuting disorderly protesters. But the movement has to bear the direct costs of its on-going organization, the demonstration, and its activists' legal defence. Since its goals are not institutionally protected as rights, the anti-nuclear movement has to meet the full costs of pursuing its goals. Moreover, the pronuclear interests are recognized by governments and large segments of the population as the legitimate ones. Movement demands that seem illegitimate risk hardening opposition and alienating public opinion, rather than raising the awareness and sympathy needed to build support for the cause. Since movements do not have routine recognition or support, they face serious obstacles to meeting the cost of pursuing change. However, their opponents' resources to resist change are usually formidable and well-institutionalized.

Social movements don't only face the high costs imposed by their opponents. They also face an internal mobilization dilemma, due to the collective nature of the good a movement pursues. Unlike a private good, which benefits only a particular person, a **collective good** benefits all members of a group or social category, whether or not they contribute to gaining it (Olson 1965). If an anti-pollution movement wins an end to acid rain, everyone benefits from the resulting clean environment, not only the people who took part in the movement.

It is difficult to mobilize support for a collective good because it is not always in a person's immediate individual interest to invest in such a group interest. Investing in a social movement entails opportunity costs — committing resources to social change means giving up leisure, career, or other personal opportunities to which the resources could have been devoted. Social movements also entail direct participation costs, such as involvement in numerous meetings or the risk of arrest or of being branded a troublemaker, which few people are anxious to bear. Since the benefits of social change will be shared by everyone anyway, individuals have an interest in letting others take on the major costs of procuring that change. For instance, the concerned student who spends three years getting a degree and a job benefits as much from a clean environment as the dropout who spends most of that time successfully protesting for the clean-up of a hazardous-waste dump. Those who benefit from a collective good without contributing to it are called **free riders.** Free riders get the best of both worlds. Others pay to improve their group position, while they pour all of their own resources into personal advancement. This tension between a person's individual and collective interests leads to the familiar cry: "Why doesn't somebody do something about it? But don't look at me — I'm too busy."

The tension between individual and group interests has another dimension. An individual has no reason to make sacrifices for a collective cause, if that person's effort does not seem to make a noticeable difference in advancing the cause. In a classic example involving economics, Olson (1965) argued that an individual would not be likely to cut personal spending to bring down inflation, since one such effort would not appear to have much impact on the overall economic situation. Still less would an individual be expected to volunteer for a pay cut to fight inflation, for the good of all. People ask: "Why should I be the one to pay? What harm could my little raise do anyway?"

This logic also applies to social movements. No one has an interest in depleting the ozone layer that protects the earth from overexposure to the sun. But individuals have trouble seeing how their dependence on the fluorocarbons in their own air-conditioned cars, homes, and offices contributes to the problem. Giving up their personal air-conditioning would not end pollution. Their single gesture would seem to be an insignificant drop in the bucket. An individual's sacrifice is even less likely to seem worthwhile if people have no reason to expect that enough others would make a similar sacrifice to solve their shared problem. Why should one person pay the cost of pursuing change, if others who would benefit are not going to do likewise? Since one individual can't possibly pay the full cost of a collective good, a personal contribution may seem insignificant or useless.

With the combined effects of the free-rider syndrome, the tendency of individuals to downplay their impact on group problems, and the high costs imposed by opponents, it is not surprising that many deprived groups never overcome mobilization obstacles to form social movements. People can be expected to invest in collective action only when the benefits involved outweigh the personal costs. This cost–benefit reasoning explains why the better-off members of dissatisfied groups are frequently the ones who launch social movements; an investment in collective action is less of a sacrifice for them than for the deprived (Fitzsimmons-LeCavalier 1983). Individuals who have lots of resources — money, free time, organizational experience, and respectability — can afford to take risks for potential gains. The very deprived, on the other hand, have few resources that are not devoted to survival needs. They are not only powerless but nearly resourceless; for them, the costs of collective action are enormous. Benefits have to be tangible and almost assured before the deprived can afford to take risks to gain them.

Selective Incentives

Simply having many resources doesn't guarantee that a person will invest in collective action. The better-off people are, the more they can afford individual solutions to their problems or individual escapes. Well-off people are not likely to be more inclined than anyone else to bear the costs of pursuing collective goods when their personal share of the good may be slight. They are as likely as anyone else to engage in free-rider behaviour and to downplay their personal responsibility for group problems.

Highly institutionalized groups that pursue collective goods have found a solution to attracting such individuals' resources. They provide **selective incentives,** personal rewards that are available only to people who contribute to the collective cause, not to free riders (Olson 1965; McCarthy and Zald 1973; Oberschall 1973). For instance, professional associations that lobby for the interests of a whole occupational group provide such personal benefits as professional journals, conventions at reduced travel rates, certification, and other career enhancements only to those who pay their membership dues. All scientists benefit from their professional association's lobbying, but only paid-up members get to present their research findings at the association's meetings — an important step in career advancement. Political parties hold out the promise of patronage appointments and other political plums to those who contribute heavily to building and maintaining the party, particularly to those who remain loyal during the party's years out of power. Providing such separate, personal incentives is one of the chief means that organizations use to assure that individuals contribute to group efforts. If only a few people are going to pay for the whole group's benefit they want to know "What's in it for me?" The more personal resources they put into the group, the more personal payoffs they will need in return.

While some organizations offer personal inducements for participation, others offer selective sanctions for nonparticipation. These are penalties only for those individuals who do not contribute to the collective cause. Governments do not rely on the population's interest in collective goods, such as top-quality hospitals, to inspire voluntary tax payments; they use compulsory taxation. They apply fines and penalties to individuals who don't contribute their assigned share to collective goals. Discontented groups may have to do the same thing to build a social movement.

Social movements can solve their mobilization problems by giving activists selective incentives. But they are seldom in a position to hand out the material inducements or punishments that institutionalized groups use to assure participation. Their very nature — nonroutine and unconventional — means that movements would have to mobilize a lot of voluntary resources before they could hope to maintain support through material payoffs or coercion. At the same time, their mobilization costs are higher than those of other voluntary groups, because of the opposition provoked by the movements' challenge to the status quo. Luckily for social movements, there are social conditions that can help overcome the serious obstacles to mobilization.

Organizational Resources

Social movements escape heavy mobilization costs if they can avoid building their organizations from scratch. In fact, discontented groups

that manage to mobilize something more than sporadic, short-term protests usually are built on resources transferred from established organizations. Recruiting support for a challenging group on an individual-to-individual basis is extremely costly and forbidding. But **bloc recruitment**, the attraction of groups of people who have already-existing links and means of co-ordinating their actions, makes collective action much more affordable. If people experiencing a new problem already have ways of pooling their resources, there is a strong chance that they will pursue a collective solution to that problem.

Pre-established links reduce the costs of collective action in several ways. If the people facing a threat have a long-lasting shared identity, the individuals involved are more likely to feel that the group problem is their problem and contribute accordingly. Thus, a television show that is seen as an insult to a distinct ethnic community is more likely to elicit strong protest than is a show that insults the random set of viewers opposed to the recreational use of drugs like marijuana. Anonymous viewers have little basis for developing a sense that they share a problem with the random collection of others who are also offended by a program. In many longstanding ethnic communities, however, a person's fate is habitually identified with the group's fate. When people share such a strong group identity, individuals are more inclined to act in a group-oriented way.

People are even more likely to act in a group-oriented way if they are tied together by shared networks of communication and friendship (Tilly 1978). When individuals are already linked by shared beliefs and information networks, these channels of communication offer an easy means of spreading a consciousness of new threats. In addition, when people are already linked by friendship networks of exchanged favours and duties, these channels of cooperation offer a low-cost means of pulling individuals into the fight for group goals. Building on existing channels of communication and co-operation is one of the main means social movements use to overcome the obstacles to mobilization.

Numerous studies have shown the mobilizing effect of established information and friendship networks. Pinard (1971) found that, in Quebec, the discontented farmers and workers who met other similarly discontented individuals socially were highly likely to know about and support the Social Credit movement. The most socially active discontented were early joiners and strong supporters of the cause, while the socially isolated gave little support. In Alberta, Social Credit support rapidly spread through the rural areas among the religious followers of William Aberhart; Aberhart's Calgary-based radio sermons were enormously popular in the 1920s, having an estimated 200 000 to 3000 000 prairie listeners. When he used his radio show to spread the Social Credit solution to economic problems during the depression, Aberhart's religious followers gave their strong support to his political cause (Irving 1959). In both Alberta and Quebec, the new political movement spread along the lines of established social networks — clear instances of bloc recruitment.

But the strongest incentive to collective action comes when a threatened group has existing formal organizational links. If there are already a large number of associations within a group facing a new social problem, there will also be a ready supply of leaders having both the experience and organizational backing needed to defend the group. The presence of community, voluntary, political, and occupational associations means that there are also likely to be many individuals whose personal resources are already openly committed to the group (Oberschall 1973). These associations offer more powerful channels for pooling and applying a diversity of group resources than informal friendship networks do. When pre-established leaders, participants, and associations throw their support behind efforts for social change, a movement's mobilization costs are dramatically reduced. Recruiting five associations with leaders, staff, offices, and 1000 members each can mobilize a social movement much more rapidly than spending the same amount of time recruiting five individuals.

Pinard (1971) found that membership in farmers' groups or labour unions had an even stronger effect than involvement in friendship networks had on support for Quebec's Social Credit movement. While socially active, discontented individuals were more likely to support the movement, participants in farm and labour associations gave strong support to the movement, whether they personally felt discontented or not. The leaders of the local farm and labour associations had

adopted the Social Credit solutions to the widespread economic problems in rural Quebec. In turn, the participants in these committed associations backed and voted for the movement even if they themselves did not suffer from the economic problems — another obvious case of bloc recruitment.

Likewise, Lipset's (1968) study of Saskatchewan shows that the first major backers of the CCF's protest platform were the already-established leaders of the province's many consumer and marketing co-operatives. These co-operatives had been set up to eliminate farmers' dependence on middlemen and unstable prices. It has been estimated that, on average, each Saskatchewan farmer was a member of as many as four or five such co-operatives. In addition, the rural areas had a dense network of voluntary associations offering the social, health, and other community services otherwise only available in distant cities. The active participants in these co-operatives and community associations gave early and strong backing to their leaders' sponsorship of CCF protest. The membership, meeting places, and other physical and social facilities controlled by the associations were turned to building the protest party. The movement's rapid and extensive mobilization depended heavily on the support these existing organizations made available.

Indeed, Brym (1978) argues that the absence of a similar agrarian protest movement among the equally discontented New Brunswick farmers is a direct result of the lack of such pre-established organizational links. In New Brunswick, subsistence rather than commercial farming predominated. Farmers, therefore, remained socially isolated, having little reason to associate in co-operatives, since they were not involved in outside markets. Attempts to mount protest parties in economic hard times were never very successful. The cost of mobilizing such a socially isolated set of individuals was too high to be sustained, and farm protest efforts in that province quickly died out.

Social Incentives

Established networks and associations are such strong mobilizers because they are in a good position to apply **social incentives** — including social pressure, the threat of lost career contacts, and the social pleasure of shared activities with friends — to ensure that individuals recognize their personal interest in supporting the group. In fact, Oberschall (1973) maintains that highly integrated groups, whether held together by informal or associational links, frequently generated social movements because they so thoroughly blend their members' individual and group interests. In a highly integrated collectivity, an individual is not free to pursue purely personal interests with no concern for the group.

Leaders of such groups usually have their personal power and status so closely tied to the group's position that they have built-in selective incentives for group defence. Leaders stand to lose more than others if the group's interests suffer, and to gain more than others if the group's position improves. For instance, being the leader of an ethnic community that is losing rights, members, and social standing is not a very rewarding position, either financially or socially. Being the leader of an ethnic community that stands to gain in wealth, membership, or social and political strength is a distinctly rewarding position. The leaders' personal standing is so tied to the group's standing that they can seldom afford to act like free riders and hope that someone else defends the group against new problems.

Once a group's leaders have thrown their personal and associational resources behind a cause, it is not always easy for the members of a cohesive group to ignore that cause. In a highly integrated social structure, a good part of a person's social life, or even livelihood, may depend on maintaining good relations with other group members. Earning approval in the group means doing your share for group goals — pulling your weight. There can be powerful social pressures for conformity to group ends, as well as sanctions for nonconformity. It's hard to be a free rider when your close friends and colleagues twist your arm to participate in a movement and treat you as disloyal if you do not. For instance, professionals whose clients come mainly from their own ethnic group can feel obliged to donate their skills to that group's causes to avoid a loss of business. But cohesive groups don't only apply such sanctions. They also have strong social incentives to reward participation. It can be a lot of fun to work for a cause you believe in with people you know and like. The threat of lost social and

career contacts, as well as the social pleasure of shared activities with friends, can all be used by cohesive groups to assure that individuals recognize a personal interest in supporting group interests. The ready supply of resources that already-established groups can deliver to a social movement gives such solidary groups a strong mobilization advantage.

Social Segmentation

Every social movement has to have some kind of organizational base. If it can borrow an already-existing base, the movement's mobilization costs will be significantly reduced. But knowing the way a group is organized does not tell us how easily that organization can be transferred to protest. Solidary networks can work either for or against movement formation (Pinard 1971). If group leaders oppose a movement, the same social incentives and sanctions that can be used to encourage movement support can be used to suppress it. There is little incentive in speaking out for a movement you personally believe in, if your group actively resists the cause. To know how available a group's organizations will be for protest, it is important to know if it can afford to make enemies of those who will be challenged by that protest. The more dependent a group's leaders are on its potential opponents, the less likely it is that the group's organizational base will be used for challenging action.

For a group to throw resources behind demands for social change, its leaders and associations must be more alienated from than tied to the movement's opponents. Studies on the American civil rights movement illustrate this point (Von Eschen, Kirk, and Pinard 1971). While active participants in other social movements and dissident political groups were likely to get involved in the civil rights cause, participants in mainstream political parties were not likely to get involved. Active members of established political parties were linked to the reward-and-approval structures of institutions threatened by the movement's demands. This dependence made the risks of civil rights protest unacceptable to mainstream political activists.

Being cut off from any specific institution may encourage a group to challenge that institution. But strong social movements are most likely when a dissatisfied group has little dependence on any outside group or institutions — when the group's social and economic life is almost totally limited to its own members. A society is said to have high levels of **social segmentation** when there is great social distance and few ties of interdependence between at least two of its groups (Oberschall 1973). The level of social segmentation indicates how tied to or cut off from one another groups are. Under conditions of extreme segmentation, social groups may be so segregated that they constitute almost complete minisocieties, each with control of a wide range of institutions, linked only by a few overreaching political and economic structures (Breton 1991). The more segmented a social group, the more cut off its leaders and active participants will be from outside opponents' reward-and-approval structures. Consequently, high segmentation encourages a sense of alienation from outsiders and makes challenging the interests of a powerful outside opponent less risky.

External Breaks, Internal Bonds

It is possible to get a fairly accurate idea of the groups most likely to engage in ongoing protest by examining the nature of the social breaks between groups and the social bonds within them. In Canada, provinces have only weak links to one another and a great deal of independent control over their own institutions. The food- and resource-producing provinces, such as Alberta and Saskatchewan, have few direct co-operative links with the more industrialized regions. Quebec is even more segmented from other provinces and regions. Its extensive set of francophone social networks and institutions add language barriers to the already weak links between provinces. This combination of weak external ties and extensive internal organization gives the provinces, regions, and francophone Quebec a high capacity to mobilize against threats to their separate interests (Clark, Grayson, and Grayson 1975). Not surprisingly, matters of provincial control, regional development, and Quebec autonomy have been the central and recurrent themes of Canada's major political protest movements. These regional tensions were obvious in the conflicts sparked by Canada's recent round of constitutional negotiations, between 1986 and 1992 (Swinton and Rogerson

1988; Behiels 1989a). Manitoba and Newfoundland's opposition to Quebec's bid for a distinct-society clause during the Meech Lake debates was matched by Ontario and Quebec's opposition to Alberta's bid for a "triple-E" Senate in the post–Meech Lake negotiations (Fidler 1991; Granatstein and McNaught 1991). These heightened regional conflicts promoted the rise of the Reform Party in the West. On the other hand, they also encouraged the resurgence of the Quebec independence movement as well as the split of the independentist Bloc Québécois from other federal parties.

Other groups also have weak ties to outsiders; for instance, Canada's Native peoples are highly segmented from non-Natives. However, the Native peoples are divided internally by language and different band identities, cultures, and regional interests. In addition, they have little independent control over the valuable organizational resources needed to mobilize a social movement because their funding is so dependent on the federal government, which is also their frequent adversary. Consequently, for many years Native peoples did not have readily available, low-cost means of maintaining a united movement organization. Because of this organizational difficulty, Native protest from the 1960s through the mid-1980s was sporadic, even though Native grievances have been serious and chronic (Ponting and Gibbins 1980). In the 1980s, Native organizations invested heavily in lobbying tactics. They participated in a round of federal–provincial constitutional conferences on aboriginal affairs with raised expectations that their demands for self-government were finally going to be entrenched as rights. But the Native lobbying groups were divided into various status and non-status Indian, Métis, Inuit, and territorial groups, split further into moderate and radical factions (Behiels 1989b). They could not mount the common front needed to challenge the rising provincial-rights movement among the premiers, who were committed to gaining provincial control over the natural resources under dispute in Native land claims (Hall 1989). By the time the Meech Lake Accord was drawn up, both Native representatives and Native rights had been dropped from the constitutional debates, sacrificed to the stronger provincial-rights movement.

To build strength, Native protesters turned their modest resources to gaining media coverage, a move that raised their profile but not their payoffs to any great extent (Ponting 1986b). Langford and Ponting's (1992) analysis of a national survey shows that by 1986 most Canadians combined a low awareness of Native peoples' problems with a generalized sympathy for their situation. Despite the greater media attention Native peoples' had gained, Canadians' sympathy had actually declined slightly between 1976 and 1986, and a majority opposed granting them special status or Native self-government. By the end of 1991, this picture had changed dramatically. In a national survey on a post–Meech Lake constitutional proposal, slightly more than half of Quebec residents and two-thirds of the rest of Canadians supported Native self-government (Windsor 1991). In fact, Native self-government was the most popular feature of this constitutional proposal, which included distinct-society recognition for Quebec, a new Canadian economic union, and an elected Senate. Only 28 percent of Canadians approved the total package (Windsor 1991).

What had happened between 1986 and 1991 to bring about this stunning rise in public support for the Native cause? Three main factors explain the Native peoples' increasing capacity to push their interests to the top of the public agenda:

- An assembly of Native leaders vowed to stand together to back Native protests in the face of the betrayal of their lobbying efforts, whatever the nature of the demands or the tactics (Behiels 1989).

- Elijah Harper, a Native member of the Manitoba legislature, refused to cast the final "yes" vote needed for unanimous consent to introduce the Meech Lake Accord for debate (Cohen 1991). This standoff in the Manitoba legislature killed the Meech Lake Accord that had killed the Native bid for constitutional reform. It did so by delaying its approval beyond the national deadline for adoption of the accord. This apparent single-handed protest was, in fact, engineered by the Native peoples' common front (Cohen 1991; York and Pindera 1991). Its success forced the provincial and federal leaders to take Native demands seriously.

- The media coverage of Harper's constitutional coup and the ensuing Oka crisis,

backed by the media exposure of the moderate, articulate leaders of the Assembly of First Nations, placed Native issues centre-stage in Canadian households. This raised Canadians' concern and sense of urgency that Native grievances should be solved. This public support of other Canadians gave Native organizations more independence from the state's resources for protest (see the accompanying box).

Only when such a segmented group's independence from its opponents is matched by a capacity to act together will a strong movement for social change emerge.

Driedger's (1986) study of a Saskatchewan Mennonite community's successful movement to block an Eldorado nuclear plant shows that another structural factor can further heighten a segmented group's mobilization potential. The Mennonite leaders were independent from their pro-nuclear opponents and in control of their own group's strong network of traditional ties. In addition, they had developed an extensive network of ties to outside sympathizers such as politicians, academics, and other religious and pacifist group leaders. These resource-rich outsiders could be counted on to defend the Mennonites' cause, saving them considerable organizational costs. When deep external breaks with opponents and strong internal bonds are coupled with such established links to powerful outside allies, the chances that a discontented group will form a social movement are extremely high.

Breton (1978, 1991) maintains that the pattern of links between and within ethnic groups not only affects their capacity to act collectively, it affects the kind of issues that will generate ethnic conflict. When ethnic groups are tightly organized internally and independent from one another, they will make demands for collective rights. This segmented situation will raise conflict over collective representation and the defence of each group's separate set of institutions. On the other hand, when ethnic groups already share a lot of social links and common institutions, conflict will revolve around individual civil rights and equal opportunities for ethnic individuals' advancement in an integrated society. The more separate the groups already are, the more their movement demands will be for even greater separation. This

The Oka Standoff: Success or Setback?

Sometimes it's hard to know what real impact a social movement's tactics had on winning social change. Here, Native leaders give differing views of the success of the Warriors' violent tactics during the Oka standoff.

The gunfight that erupted near Oka last July 11 shattered the silence in the pines and made heard the often silent voice of aboriginal people.

One year later, the issues that sparked the 77-day armed standoff at the home of the Mohawks of Kanesatake remain sadly unresolved. But the voice grew in strength and intensity.

"In retrospect, Oka was probably a good thing for natives and non-natives," said Peter Kulchyski, acting chairman of the native studies department at Trent University.

"Non-natives have gained an appreciation of the seriousness of issues, as well as the level of frustration and anger in aboriginal communities, and aboriginal people have been empowered by being taken seriously," he said.

The advances made by native people during the past year are phenomenal. The federal government has announced a royal commission on native concerns, promised to include aboriginal leaders in constitutional negotiations, initiated a streamlined land-claims process and endeavoured to revamp the reviled Indian Act.

At least two provinces, New Brunswick and Quebec, are considering native-only seats in their legislatures, while British Columbia and Ontario have speeded-up land talks in a bid to avert Oka-like confrontations.

"There is now, in Canada, a hunger for knowledge about aboriginals and a vastly more educated media writing about these issues," Mr. Kulchyski said. "That, along with shrewd and astute native leadership, is forcing the hand of government."

But Saul Terry, president of the Union of B.C. Indians, said the gains are illusory. "Our expectations are more publicly exposed but governments are just paying lip service. They're not doing anything concrete to address land claims and self-government."

He points to the Gitksan and Wetsu'et'en, who lost a major land-claim battle in court, and to the continuing economic and social ills of native communities across the country as proof that there is no serious will to address the issues of social justice for aboriginal people.

"Oka exposed the injustice that we have been experiencing for generations but the government responded with nothing more than public relations announcements. It's despicable manipulation, not progress," Mr. Terry said. ...

Daniel-Paul Bork, the wampum keeper with the Student Assembly of First Nations, said the impression among non-natives that Canada's 500,000 status Indians have become far more militant in the wake of the Oka crisis is largely overblown.

He points to the election of Ovide Mercredi to the presidency of the Assembly of First Nations as proof that "Indians, overall, are still very moderate, not radical or violent like the Warriors."

Mr. Mercredi, a proponent of Gandhian civil disobedience, has taken great pains to distance himself from the heavily-armed Warriors who stole the spotlight at Oka.

"I'm not interested in working with militants whose only interest is to create trouble and who are not interested in the moral authority to create change to bring about better conditions for their people," he said shortly after his election.

In other words, now that natives have the attention of governments and the public, it is important that they act to achieve long-term, reasonable goals, such as resolving land claims to get a territorial base and self-government to secure control over their futures.

The Warriors, who won support by espousing the cause of native sovereignty, are now widely reviled because their links to cigarette smuggling, gambling, arms trading and other questionable activities has been widely reported.

Mr. Bork said the message that peaceful militancy is the path to success has not been lost on the younger generation.

"Oka really made us think about things, and most of us realized that we need territory, we need self-government to survive as First Nations."

He said that it is important to note that it was young people who took to the streets in solidarity with the Mohawks involved in the armed conflicts at Kanesatake and Kahnawake last summer. They are also the ones forging powerful alliances with environmental, civil rights and social justice groups.

"Many of us grew up being humiliated and ashamed but Oka made us proud to be Indians again," Mr. Bork said.

For that reason, academics and native leaders agree that today's manoeuvring is but a political ripple and the real impact of Oka will be felt many years down the road, when the young aboriginal people come of age in native leadership.

Source:

André Picard, *The Globe and Mail*, July 10, 1991, p. A3.

prediction quite accurately reflects the emphasis on demands for individual rights and equal integration made by most of Canada's ethnic groups, and the demands for collective rights and further institutional separation made by the independence movement in highly segmented Quebec (Morris and Lanphier 1977).

Opportunities for Success

As we have noted, the resource mobilization approach holds that social movements will emerge when the costs of pursuing challenging action are lower than the gains to be made through that action. No matter what kind of organizational base it has, a group is not likely to push collective demands for change if those demands provoke nothing but heavy losses. It is important, then, that groups seeking social change have reason to believe that their opponents are vulnerable to collective action. Since the state is the main target and mediator for such demands, this usually means that the polity must be vulnerable to the movement's pressure tactics (Tilly 1978). Before engaging in collective action, people ask: What good will it do? In that sense, social movements are directly dependent on expectations, but not the expectations that relative deprivation theorists think would increase frustration and discontent. Rather, it is the expectation that the movement will be a success — that it really will help solve their problems — that incites group leaders and members to participate in a social movement.

Much of the expectation of success depends on past political and movement experiences. Through their own experiences and those of others who have challenged the system, people build up a repertoire of social-change tactics that worked or were acceptable in the past. Social-movement success breeds other social movements. Social-movement failure breeds hopelessness and demobilization or a major shift in tactics. But expectations of success also depend on the existing balance of power between challengers and their opponents. Social movements have to pursue change through nonroutine tactics precisely because their concerns are not taken seriously by decision-makers in crucial institutions. Movements have to find innovative means of exerting pressure because they do not have easy access

to conventional ways of influencing decision-makers.

Since a movement's demands for social change are likely to be opposed by groups who do have institutionalized power, there is no guarantee that authorities will always be vulnerable to the pressure tactics that worked in the past or that worked elsewhere. For instance, a government slipping in popularity could be very vulnerable to a movement with strong voter appeal. A newly elected government with a strong majority would be much less vulnerable. Different government structures and orientations encourage activists with similar ideals to adopt a different repertoire of tactics in different settings. The American environmental movement mainly targets the federal government for protective laws and regulations. Faced with the conservative Reaganomics of the 1980s, it has evolved as a very loose set of large to small single-issue lobby groups (Caplow 1991). This proliferation of movements seeks solutions to a wide assortment of isolated problems — from the dangers of nuclear power to water and air pollution, to endangered wildlife, to waste disposal and recycling.

Western European environmentalists have taken a more united, confrontational, politicized approach to solving the same problems (Kamieniecki 1991). There, activists have tended to form Green parties that attack the whole range of environmental issues through demonstrations and direct challenges to established political parties (Kitschelt 1987). By the late 1980s, Green parties held elected seats in eight Western European parliaments (Kamieniecki 1991). These very different forms of political pressure have led to mixed results but moderate success for environmentalists in both settings — a record of partial success that neither was likely to achieve using the other's tactics (Kamieniecki 1991). With the 1990s' "globalization" of the most serious environmental problems — like ozone depletion, the greenhouse effect, deforestation, and species extinction — both the American and European movements are searching for new tactics and new decision-makers to target to solve problems that surpass established political boundaries (see the accompanying box).

Turner and Killian (1972) maintain that a social movement can adopt essentially three types of

Environmentalists: An Endangered Species?

Professional social movements avoid heavy mobilization costs by building on the donations of outside sympathizers to support a full-time core of activists. These movements are vulnerable to shifts in their backers' disposable incomes and tend to suffer in bad economic times.

The recession is hitting the environmental movement hard — so hard that many groups are slashing budgets and reducing staff.

The Ottawa-based Friends of the Earth has half the staff it had in the spring. Greenpeace is cutting four or five staffers from its complement of 50. The Western Canada Wilderness Coalition reduced its staff by 30 per cent.

Opinion polling shows that the environment remains near the top of the public's list of worries about the future, but hard economic times have produced a marked decline in donations that few charitable organizations have escaped. ...

While the recession is the immediate cause of the cutbacks, the environmental movement is also going through a fundamental change, organization managers say.

Pollution Probe executive director Janine Ferretti had to lay off staff and suspend publication of a magazine to keep her group's head above water.

She describes the situation as "a testing time."

As she sees it, the movement, like the industrial economy that it so often criticizes, is going through a shakeout period that some organizations will not survive, while others will emerge in a form their original backers may not recognize. "It is not going to be pretty or easy," she says. ...

Groups that simply promote confrontation or do little more than proclaim environmental disaster are losing their appeal, says Colin Isaacs, an environmental consultant and former executive director of Pollution Probe. "They are not providing an intellectual product that the public is as interested in buying as they used to be."

Giving up the black-and-white view they had when they were on the barricades in favour of the shades of grey required at the policy table may make it harder to raise money. The public seems to support those who fight the system more than those who work within it.

"We're not seen in the same way we used to be," says Louise Comeau, who recently left Friends of the Earth to join the Sierra Club's campaign against atmospheric pollution.

"The media is not prepared to cover us sitting at the table negotiating with government and industry. But that is where we are going and so we have lost our profile. ...

"We have not done a very good job of maintaining our relevancy in the public's mind. That takes work."

Ms. Ferretti points out that maintaining relevance with government and industry also takes money. Organizations that were once staffed with low-paid generalists, fuelled by ideals and granola, now find they need the services of lawyers, economists or toxicologists, few of whom are available for the $30,000 to $35,000 a year that most groups have been paying staff members.

There has also been a change in management style. Originally, many groups were run co-operatively, but growing budgets and payrolls have prompted boards of directors to demand more accountability. As a result, organizations have had to hire professional managers and auditors and adopt formal budgets. This has made many long-term employees unhappy and increased the turnover rate.

Some observers feel the various pressures are transforming the environmental movement in Canada, prompting various groups to focus on just which issues they can take up, what approach they should take and which level of government they should try to influence.

Greenpeace, for instance, feels that it is unique in its ability to raise issues internationally, Ms. Mahon says. At the same time, it recently reduced its number of high-priority issues to eight from 38.

Ms. Ferretti and Mr. Isaacs say they expect the Canadian movement will follow in the footsteps of its U.S. counterpart. At the national level, they explain, a small number of very-well-financed, professional organizations employ a battery of experts who in Mr. Isaacs' words have "the qualifications to go eyeball to eyeball with government and industry."

Source:

James Rusk, *The Globe and Mail*, September 2, 1992, pp. A1, A6.

collective tactics: persuasive, bargaining, and coercive. Persuasive tactics rely on the authorities holding certain values that can be activated in favour of the movement's goals. A group whose demands for social change are a major challenge to established interests is not likely to achieve success by persuasion alone. Bargaining tactics rely on having something valuable to trade with authorities, such as votes or a potential impact on their reputations. Bargaining can depend on getting broad public support, or at least the support of some powerful sector that authorities cannot afford to ignore.

Coercive tactics depend on the symbolic or actual disruption of institutional life in order to bring compliance with group demands. Most coercive tactics, such as marches, demonstrations, or sit-ins, are designed to cause only minor, non-violent upsets to routine. They are aimed at gaining public attention and sympathy, or at showing the movement's already considerable support in order to build bargaining power. Other coercive tactics are more directly disruptive: for instance, Greenpeace attempted not only to protest but to stop the seal hunt by chasing seal herds away from the hunt site and putting coloured marks on baby seals to reduce the value of their fur. Highly coercive tactics, such as threatened violence, rioting, or terrorist tactics, depend on directly inflicting damage to force a response from authorities. Highly coercive tactics are extremely risky in terms of both the repression and the backlash they can provoke. In many circumstances, violence raises the risks of movement participation without increasing the likelihood of success; violent protest is not often adopted by social movements. But, as the many hijackings, hostage-takings, and terrorist bombings show, if violent or illegal acts promise to get results with few risks for those involved, they may become attractive means of dissent.

Even though most movements avoid violent protest, most do use some kind of coercive strategy in their challenge to overcome opposition to their demands. In Western democracies, a protocol of protest has evolved that tolerates the orderly, disciplined expression of discontent (Oberschall 1973; Tilly 1978). Demonstrations that follow this protocol inflict mainly symbolic disruption. But the officially tolerated protest tactics are not cheap — they call for a high level of organizational resources, negotiating skills, and "showbiz" skills if the media are to be interested in transmitting the movement message. And even standard protest action can turn to violence, making movement activity much riskier and costlier.

Protest is a dynamic process. Its course depends as much on the authorities' as on the movement's actions, as was illustrated by a study of four Cana-

dian street demonstrations that ended in violence: a Ukrainian Canadian demonstration against the USSR (Toronto, 1971), an anti–Vietnam War demonstration (Toronto, 1970), the Saint-Jean-Baptiste Day demonstration (Montreal, 1968), and a Yorkville sit-in (Toronto, 1967) by hippies, who wanted traffic blocked and youth hostels subsidized to preserve Yorkville as Canada's anti-materialistic, countercultural mecca. Frank (1984) showed that, in each of these four cases, violence was a police response to protest action that the law-enforcement authorities considered deviant. These protests that became violent had three points in common.

- First, the activities did not follow standard protest protocol; the action was either disorganized, chaotic, or spontaneous, and police found the behaviour unpredictable and difficult to control.

- Second, the police judged the protesters to be of low, marginal, or counter-cultural status — not "respectable."

- Third, police officers resorted to beating and other violent acts to break up what they considered to be illegitimate protest.

In three of the four cases, the movement lost credibility and bargaining power because of the violent outcome. The Ukrainian Canadian protesters, however, gained sympathy because of what a later inquiry termed the "police riot" — the obvious loss of police officers' control over their own actions. Sometimes violent outcomes lead to mixed gains for social movements. It took the shock of the violent "Yonge Street Rampage" to force the Ontario government to confront the Toronto police force's longstanding race relations problem. In the wake of the riot, the government appointed a consultative committee to recommend ways of improving race relations, dealing with black youth unemployment problems, and limiting police use of deadly force (Elder 1992). The riot served as a "wake-up call" to governments who had long ignored these serious problems. But the movements that had organized the originally peaceful demonstration were left with the heavy costs of clearing their names and causes of the blame for violence that they had not encouraged (see the box entitled "The Safety-in-Numbers Factor").

Many analysts have found that police perceptions of respectability play an important role in their reaction to protesters (Frank and Kelly 1979; Torrance 1986). Middle-class protesters, whom authorities consider respectable, are allowed a lot of leeway for "letting off steam" during protest activities. The irony is that disadvantaged and marginal groups, who often do not have the organizational resources for anything but spontaneous protest, are the very groups whose protest activities are least likely to be met with a favourable response. The difficulty involved in finding protest strategies that are both affordable and effective has a strong demobilizing effect on social movements.

Affordable Effective Action

In deciding what kind of tactics are most likely to bring results, movements are highly constrained by their own resource base, as well as by their opponents' and the public's likely reactions. The search for social-change tactics that are both affordable and effective creates very different protest situations for social movements.

The Canadian Native Peoples' Protest Situation. Ponting and Gibbins (1981) have shown why the wide range of persuasive, bargaining, and coercive protest tactics adopted by Canadian Native peoples in the 1960s and 1970s were largely ignored by most Canadians. Even the confrontational and violent tactics that many feared would cause a backlash against the Native cause remained irrelevant to the Canadian public. It is not that Canadians felt indifferent to violent protest; the findings in this study show that the majority of Canadians found persuasive and bargaining tactics, as well as protest marches, acceptable. But they found more coercive tactics and, in particular, threatening violence unacceptable. Native protest was ignored because it was so sporadic and regionally isolated that both the protest and the Native problems had not really registered with the non-Native population. Barricading remote logging roads did not hit close enough to home to bother most Canadians. In their choice of strategies, the Native peoples faced a dilemma. They did not have the organizational base to rely

only on the persuasive and bargaining tactics that most Canadians approve of. But the more coercive tactics they could mobilize resources for were not acceptable and threatened to provoke backlash, if they attracted attention at all.

By the 1990s, both Native peoples' bargaining and coercive tactics had become dramatically more relevant to Canadians. The double effect of their bargaining skill in quietly blocking the Meech Lake Accord and their coercive skill in resisting the army in the Oka crisis, in the suburbs of Montreal, had raised the relevance of their cause (York and Pindera 1991). Barricading logging roads in remote areas might not have hit home for most Canadians. Barricading a major commuter bridge to Canada's second-largest city did. But, while these protests have raised the value of Native peoples' political resources, they still face the tactical dilemma of controlling backlash politics. The Native cause has gained public popularity, but it has become a direct threat to important political actors. As we have seen, Québécois were less favourable to Native demands than were other Canadians after the Oka crisis (Winsor 1991). Langford and Ponting (1992) see a link between the rising popularity of the Reform Party's economic conservatism and backlash against Native demands. York and Pindera (1991) maintain that the Oka crisis brought political gains for moderate Native leaders who were left to keep the radical warriors under control, without provoking serious splits in their own communities. These splits between warriors and moderates have already led to a civil-war-like situation on the Ontario–New York Akwesasne reserve (Hornung 1991). This tactical dilemma is very common to resource-poor groups and hurts their chances of winning their demands (see the box entitled "The Oka Standoff: Success or Setback?").

The Quebec Non-Francophones' Protest Situation. Even among resource-rich groups, the difficulty of finding effective collective-action tactics can discourage social-movement formation. A good illustration of this comes from Quebec, where the nonfrancophone minority has adopted mainly individual, rather than collective, solutions to its language grievances. At first glance, Quebec's nonfrancophones would seem to have "textbook-perfect" conditions for mounting a collective challenge. The measures taken by Quebec governments to remove English as an official language, culminating in the mid-1970s in Bill 101, caused great discontent. Furthermore, the non-francophone minority is highly segmented. It is divided from the francophone majority by language, separate social networks, and a set of separate minority institutions — the kind of independence that tends to encourage the mobilization of a collective stand.

But a close look shows that these conditions were not as well structured to promote collective action as they first appeared to be (Fitzsimmons-LeCavalier and LeCavalier 1981, 1984). For one thing, the nonfrancophone population is multicultural. It is made up of many ethnic, racial, language, and religious groups. The nonfrancophone community associations and service institutions are also divided along these culturally diverse lines. Even more limiting, most nonfrancophone institutions depend on the Quebec government for funding and continued survival. A survey of nonfrancophone leaders' opinions showed that the difficulties involved in getting the diverse minority representatives and organizational resources united in a common cause was a major drawback to collective action (Fitzsimmons-LeCavalier and LeCavalier 1984, 1989).

But these heavy organizational costs were magnified by the leaders' belief that acting collectively would not improve the minority situation. When language tensions were very high in Quebec, the defence of nonfrancophones' language rights could have been interpreted as a rejection of the francophones' rights, themselves a threatened minority in the Canadian context. Confronting the Quebec government on language issues could have meant political suicide for the leaders of the government-funded minority institutions. The limited opportunities for success through collective action encouraged nonfrancophones to adopt individual solutions to overcome their minority situation. The main individual solution was to master French — in 1981, nearly two-thirds of the nonfrancophone labour force was bilingual. Another individual solution was to escape the minority situation — almost 15 percent of nonfrancophones left Quebec between 1971 and 1981 in the so-called exodus.

As Quebec's language laws worked to strengthen the position of French, francophones'

langauge grievances eased and a greater openness to minority problems emerged. In response to this greater political openness, nonfrancophones started taking co-ordinated stands to press for changes in the conditions of minority life in the 1980s. As in many other cases, it was at a time of increasing political opportunities, not at the time of the greatest discontent, that the mobilization of a movement for social change surfaced.

Nonfrancophones' collective action peaked in the 1989 provincial election in response to a new language crisis. The Bourassa government had used the "notwithstanding clause" in the Canadian Constitution to overturn a Supreme Court ruling that Quebec's French-only sign law was illegal. Many nonfrancophones considered this a betrayal of Bourassa's earlier election promise to legalize bilingual signs. Their outrage provoked the formation of an English-rights protest party, the Equality Party. In that election, the Equality Party won four seats in the Quebec legislature and used them to push a pro-federalist stand. But this English-rights movement soon ran into the new wave of nationalism in the post–Meech Lake era in French Quebec (Pinard 1992). Faced with the surging support for independence and the Parti Québécois, the political opportunity for a strong pro-English stand was quickly cut off. Membership in the Equality Party dropped from the original 10 000 to only 3000 in 1992 (Bauch 1992). One of its elected representatives deserted the party, and internal disputes led to frequent calls for a leadership review. This rapid demobilization left the English-rights movement in disarray. Given the volatile roller coaster of Québécois nationalist sentiment, most nonfrancophones retreated to a low-profile stand on language rights and to individual solutions for the problems related to their minority situation in Quebec. The climate of closing political opportunities, not less dissatisfaction, was the main factor in the demobilization of this protest movement.

The Mexican Anti-NAFTA Protest Situation. In August 1992, a North American Free Trade Agreement (NAFTA) was struck between the United States, Canada, and Mexico. This continent-wide pact had to win legislative approval in all three countries before finalization — a process widely expected to lead to a war of protest. In the United States, the deal risked falling hostage to

Mexico: Silencing Protest

For last year's [Mexican] state and local elections, two parties — the Party of the Democratic Revolution (PRD) on the left and the National Action Party (PAN) on the right — formed a joint coalition to fight the PRI [Mexico's long-ruling party].

Today, some of the opposition are out of prison on conditional bail and several prominent activists are seeking political asylum in the United States. Jorge Cardenas Gonzalez, the 67-year-old, right-wing, millionaire industrial who "lost" the governor's race to the PRI, has been hounded out of politics.

"He's very depressed," says his son, Jorge Cardenas Gutierrez, who's seeking asylum in Texas. "My father has been in politics all his life. He is a fighter. But this time they would have taken away everything. They made him declare that he would retire from politics."

All face charges:

- Ana Maria Guillen, from the *colonias*, soft-spoken, middle-aged woman whose political anger grew out of seeing her child and others have to walk a footbridge over raw sewage to get to school.
- Gutierrez Vasquez, who says his ribs were broken after he was beaten by prison authorities following his arrest.
- Cardenas Gutierrez, the wealthy, dapper radio station owner and son of the defeated gubernatorial candidate, who faces a possible 120 years in jail.
- Rolando Martinez Calderoni, the defeated Matamoros mayoral candidate from the rightist PAN party, a successful architect and sole owner of an industrial group, who fled to the U.S. to escape jail with what he described as proof of electoral fraud and who is also seeking asylum.
- Francisco Garcia, a radio journalist whose crime was to question the official election results in his commentaries on Cardenas Gutierrez's XEEW station in the days following the vote. He fled to Texas to escape jail. "You are guilty if the government says you are guilty," says Garcia. "I was telling the truth. That is all."

Three days after the election in Tamaulipas, on Nov. 11, returns were being counted in Matamoros. The problem was that electoral officials invited a handful of PRI and PRI-affiliated parties into the state electoral offices while the ballots were being counted. Representatives of both the PAN and the PRD were locked out and riot police were called in to enforce the blockade, with tear gas, truncheons and dogs.

People began to riot outside. Fire-bombs were thrown, the building went up in flames, ballot boxes were hurled into the street and people were left roughed up and bleeding.

Cardenas Gutierrez has hours of videotape of these events. A few critical points, quite clear in the tapes, would appear to prove that the government's charges were a fabrication:

- Only three or four men — always the same ones — threw the fire-bombs that ignited the electoral offices. These men were unidentified and were not arrested. Yet opposition members ended up being charged with arson and the destruction of public property.
- Cardenas Gutierrez, an organizer and scrutineer for his father's campaign, was trying to get into the electoral offices the day of the riot. The video shows him pushing forward in the melee and being pushed back by a man in camouflage. That appears to be the extent of his involvement.
- Juan Gutierrez Vasquez, of the PRD, was on the sidelines, or absent, for most of the rioting. But when the firetrucks finally arrived — two hours after the riots began — he is clearly seen trying to move the crowd aside to let the firetrucks pass. He is the only one doing so. Yet he is charged with arson. Unidentified men are seen trying to stop the trucks.
- Guillen is charged with terrorism, destruction of property and inciting mob violence. In the very first moments of the riots, she was struck in the head and was bleeding. She reeled back dazed, and in subsequent frames, is seen holding her head and staggering. Her participa-

election-year presidential politics, evaluation by advisory groups, debate in Congress, and opposition from strong labour unions (Saunders and Fagan 1992). With only 30 percent of Canadians in favour of NAFTA, the Brian Mulroney government braced for a flashback to the protests against the original Canada–U.S. Free Trade Agreement (FTA) that dominated the 1988 federal election (Mertl 1992). The original deal had prompted pro-FTA business alliances to confront an assortment of anti-FTA union and nationalist movements and NDP provincial governments (Saunders and Fagan 1992). This pitched battle for voter support was waged mainly through the media, and both the pro- and anti-FTA movements mounted multi-million-dollar ad campaigns (Feschuk 1992). In contrast to these tough-sell situations, observers predicted that Mexican President Carlos Salinas

tion appears to have been quite limited.

"The government wants us to be afraid so that we will not participate any more," said Gutierrez Vasquez. "That would be their victory. They would have won. But we are not going to let that happen this time, no matter how difficult. We are going to keep working."

He had time to think in jail. He developed a plan for a new movement, Mexico Despierta (Mexico Awaken) to educate the population about how to vote in advance of next year's national elections.

"We Mexicans have been quiet for a long time," says Cardenas Gutierrez. "No more.

"We have been dealing with governments like this for a long time. And during that time, nobody cared. It makes me just crazy. You see what they do, what they get away with, and you just don't believe it.

"They have exploited our children, our natural resources and the futures of my sons, grandsons and great-grandsons. In 30 or 40 years, we are going to have nothing. If nothing changes, I see a very bad future. Well, I don't want that to happen."

In some ways, elections here in Tamaulipas weren't even the most violent. Last July, the PRI won in the state of Michoacan, west of Mexico City, despite allegations of widespread fraud.

According to several reports, among them the U.S.-based human rights group Americas Watch, four PRD members were gunned down in an ambush in the aftermath of the elec-

tion, and five more were killed in the months that followed.

In a related case, Americas Watch reported: "On Sept. 23, 1992, Michoacan-based researcher and election observer Morelos Marx Madrigal Lachino was kidnapped in Mexico City by two armed men wearing caps like those often used by police. The kidnapping occurred while he was heading for the airport to fly to Ecuador to attend a religious conference. Madrigal was held incommunicado, beaten and interrogated for three days about his ties to the PRD and the non-partisan Convergence of Civil Organizations for Democracy, which had co-ordinated independent election monitoring in Michoacan. He was then dumped, blindfolded, on a Mexico City street."

On Jan. 19, the Montreal-based Human Rights Social Justice Committee reported:

"The municipal elections in Michoacan this year were marked by severe violence and recurrent violations of the most basic human rights. Some of the atrocities which occurred during the months of December, 1992, and January, 1993, include the following:

• The beating of Sergio Figueros Martinez in La Piedad by unknown people, which led to his death on Dec. 2, 1992.
• The assassination of Noe Alejo Morano by eight members of the judicial state police on Dec. 24, 1992, in the community of Hurio, municipality of Parecho.
• The assassination of Miguel Nipita Hernandez on Dec. 25 by a member of the municipal police in Charpan.

• The assassination of Franciso Ayila Reyes on December 16, 1992, at 9 a.m., while on his way to work at the La Florida hacienda in Jungapeo.

All told, 47 people were killed, all of whom were associated with the opposition.

Escalating political violence is the reason so many people are trying to flee to Canada. Ottawa lawyer and human rights activist Patti Strong testified about human rights abuses before the external affairs committee studying the NAFTA last month.

She tabled statistics from the Immigration and Refugee Board showing that, in the first nine months of 1992, 220 Mexican citizens applied for refugee status, a sharp increase over earlier years. Of those who applied, 192 succeeded in establishing a credible basis for their claims during initial hearings. Of the 79 claims for which decisions had been given by Sept. 30, 35 Mexicans were granted refugee status under the Geneva Conventions.

"We raise serious questions about the fact that the Canadian government is entering into a free trade agreement with a country which has become one of the major refugee-producing nations in this hemisphere," Strong told the committee.

"On the subject of human rights, NAFTA is completely silent."

Source:

Linda Diebel, *Toronto Star*, March 13, 1993, p. D4.

---

de Gortari faced an "easy sell" getting NAFTA passed by his legislature (Saunders and Fagan 1992). In Mexico, the political opposition was weak and the government's control over the security forces needed to silence protest strong (Manguel 1992; Saunders and Fagan 1992).

Part of President Salinas's easy-sell situation stemmed from NAFTA's popularity with Mexican voters (*Le Devoir* 1992). This pro-NAFTA feeling

was matched by the popularity and success of the Harvard-trained president's economic reforms (Alm 1992). Under Salinas's economic modernization program, Mexico had pulled out of its debt crisis to establish a steady record of growth that had Mexicans replacing the standard "Yankee Go Home" cry with a "Yankee Come Down" boosterism (Jacot 1992). But the extremely high expectations for affluence that NAFTA raised were clouded by the voters' suspicion of the ruling party's poor honesty-in-government record. Since his election in 1988, Salinas had developed an "iron hand in the velvet glove" style, fitting his position as the crusading economic reformer leading an established governing party used to one-party rule. In that election, a populist left-wing opposition party emerged to form Mexico's first official opposition since 1929. Together with a right-of-centre party, Salinas's opponents reduced his ruling party from total political control to a slight majority of voter support (Rohter 1988a).

This almost-overnight democratization led to charges of vote fraud and large anti-government demonstrations demanding public vote recounts — charges repeated in Mexico's 1992 elections (Rohter 1988b; Golden 1992). These anti-government demonstrations were put down, as Salinas took over his presidential duties by playing up his economic modernization program and playing down his democratic modernization platform. Despite his new-guard image, he kept much of his party's old guard in key positions, particularly those controlling the police and security forces needed to crush anti-government dissent (Rohter 1988c). According to various international observers — including Amnesty International, PEN International (a writers' organization), Americas Watch, and the *New York Times* — there followed a round of arrests, mistreatment, disappearances, and assassinations by security forces of union leaders, opposition party members, journalists, and community leaders that made the right to voice anti-government opinions extremely costly (Treaster 1989; Morely 1992).

Sensitive to international criticism that could hurt the NAFTA deal, President Salinas personally intervened in the most flagrant cases of attacks on his opponents. He also appointed an advisory Human Rights Commission and drafted laws limiting the use of torture and physical force by government officials (Manguel 1992). But as the honesty-in-government crises in neighbouring Latin American countries showed, ending entrenched corruption, influence-peddling, and intimidation tactics in political systems where government officials at all levels have long had a "licence to steal" is not that simple (Brooke 1992). Traditionally, tax evasion has been a national sport, leaving state services underfunded and elites of

all types open to blackmail and harassment. Government officials have supplemented very low state salaries with graft, kickbacks, and extortion, and those in the security and military services have been in a position to back these demands with force (Brooke 1992; Manguel 1992; Talbott 1992). In Peru, Venezuela, and Brazil, 1992 saw democratic reform leaders caught in the crossfire between military and state officials who challenged them for changes that went too far, too fast, and voters who challenged them for changes that did not go far enough, fast enough (Brooke 1992; Talbott 1992). By promising sweeping modernizations that they could not deliver, the Peruvian and Venezuelan leaders faced military coups. At the opposite extreme, the Brazilian leader faced being forced to resign for the very corruption and misappropriation of funds he had promised to clean up — the chief victim of his own success in raising voters' expectations for honest government (Brooke 1992; Talbott 1992). The Mexican president walked the tightrope between these two extremes by delivering rapid economic reform that led to high voter satisfaction, while making slow changes to government officials' power to profit illegally from their state appointments.

Since Salinas seemed skilled at carrying off this difficult balancing act, anti-NAFTA protest did not seem likely to have much effect. It did not even seem likely that the media would spread the message of those who saw a darker side to free trade and challenged government propaganda. In the rest of North America, journalists' attention and media coverage were major resources in social movements' calls for change (Oberschall 1977; Molotch 1979; Picard 1991). In Mexico, the government had tight control over media advertising budgets, newspaper distribution, and the major television station. This, plus its carrot-and-stick technique of using bribes to reward pro-government journalists, limited the media's role in dissent (Manguel 1992). Local anti-NAFTA activists feared that their serious questions about the pact's potential effects on the environment, worker health and safety, and increased strains on inadequate state services might never reach the Mexican public (Morley 1992). They were counting on the "embarrassment factor" created in the freer Canadian and American anti-NAFTA protest situation to put pressure on the Mexican government for change.

Overcoming the Obstacles to Mobilization

Currently, the most widespread approach to the study of social movements focuses on the ways discontented groups overcome the obstacles to mobilization. Discontent, frustration, and unfulfilled ideals are all considered too common to explain the appearance of a protest group, when so many other groups continue to suffer in silence. Making collective demands for social change requires a lot of resources, co-ordination, and persistence in the face of opposition. In this resource mobilization approach, social movements are considered most likely to emerge when the people facing a new problem already form a solidary group. The more a discontented group has solidary traits — pre-established leaders, shared outlooks, friendship networks, formal organizations, and other mechanisms for encouraging commitment to group ends — the more likely the individual members are to support collective solutions to their problems. Of course, discontented groups seldom have a perfect, pre-established solidary base. But there are often many distinct, well-organized groups within the larger collection of people who share a social problem. Movements frequently mobilize by recruiting the most central leaders and most active participants from these various organizations. Movements overcome high mobilization costs by building a coalition of the most solidary subgroups in the larger discontented group. These groups' already-assembled resources are then transferred to the new cause.

But building on solidarity is not the only solution movements can use to overcome their high organizational costs. Not all dissatisfied groups rely solely on their own members' donations to sustain the fight for social change. Some build social movements on the donations of outside sympathizers — better-off people or organizations that support the cause as a matter of conscience. In prosperous times, when many individuals and organizations have free time and money at their disposal, causes that defend important social ideals may attract considerable backing from outside allies. At times, movements receive enough outside financial support for leaders and organizers to make a full-time career of pursuing social

change (McCarthy and Zald 1973). Such movements, maintained by a small, full-time core of activists dependent on the financial backing of outside sympathizers, are called **professional social movements**. Pollution Probe is one example of a movement that has been highly subsidized by outside agencies. These movements can be built with very little support from the discontented base itself, thus avoiding heavy mobilization costs. However, professional social movements are vulnerable to changing economic conditions and to the shifting priorities of well-off sympathizers. A cause may be "in" one year and "out" the next, and the leaders' salaries disappear with the changing trendiness of social problems (see the box entitled "Environmentalists: An Endangered Species?").

A full-time leadership core is more likely to be sustained by "conscience money" when many well-off people are part of the dissatisfied group. In very affluent groups, a movement may be maintained by a small core of unpaid activists who donate their leadership resources out of ideological commitment to the cause (Fitzsimmons-LeCavalier 1983). People who have a high level of organizational skills, leisure time, and money are resource-full and, unlike resource-poor groups, can often afford to pursue their ideals. Still, highly committed people who work only for the pleasure of doing what they believe in tend to suffer burnout if the challenging action is too risky, time-consuming, or drawn out. Movements led by people getting only ideological rewards are also prone to split into warring ideological **factions** — splinter groups whose ideals of social change are incompatible. With everyone working for different ideological rewards, the movement disintegrates long before the battle for social change has been won.

Although there are many ways to mobilize for collective action, social movements built on a solidary organizational base are more likely to endure through the highs and lows of a major challenge for social change.

SUMMARY

1. Social movements are collective attempts to promote, maintain, or resist social change. The changes may be related to the material, social,

ideological, or political status of a dissatisfied group.

2. Change-seekers and change-resisters can only be considered to form a social movement when the individuals involved consciously support a shared cause. Social change brought about by a series of unrelated individual decisions does not constitute a social movement.

3. Social-movement action is essentially non-routine, noninstitutionalized action to promote interests that are not met through society's established institutions or conventions.

4. In the traditional collective behaviour approach, social movements are seen as part of a wide range of unconventional crowd behaviour that has an irrational base.

5. Current approaches treat social movements as normal outgrowths of conflicts of interest regarding the distribution of rewards in society.

6. In the resource mobilization approach — the currently dominant perspective — discontent, frustration, and unfulfilled ideals are all considered too common to explain directly the appearance of a social movement.

7. Making collective demands for social change requires lots of resources: time, money, leadership, co-ordination, and persistence in the face of opposition. Groups advocating social change have heavy mobilization costs, since they start with few established resources or means of influence but face opponents who have low-cost, institutionalized means of defending the status quo.

8. Dissatisfied groups are most likely to overcome the high costs of mobilizing a social movement if they have a longstanding shared identity, established leadership, friendship networks, and organizational links, as well as weak ties to opponents. Such a solidary organizational base offers built-in incentives for individuals to support group action.

9. Movements may also overcome the obstacles to mobilization by relying on well-off individuals and agencies to donate enough resources out of sympathy to the cause to sustain full-time leadership. Such movements are vulnerable to the shifting priorities of their well-off backers, however, and are not as likely as those built on a solidary institutional base to maintain a long-term challenge.

10. No matter what kind of organizational base it has, a social movement is not likely to push collective demands for social change if those demands provoke nothing but heavy losses. Social movements are sensitive to the opportunities for success and adapt their action according to the authorities' and their opponents' expected response.

GLOSSARY

Absolute deprivations. Structured disadvantages rooted in concrete inequalities of wealth, status, or power.

Bloc recruitment. Attraction of sets of supporters already linked by friendship or organizational ties.

Breakdown theory. Approach that attributes social-movement formation to the disorganization and disorientation caused by rapid social change.

Circular reaction. Process through which individuals in crowds directly copy one another's excited moods and actions, leading to disorderly, irrational behaviour.

Coercive tactics. Symbolic or actual disruption of institutional routines in order to attract support or exert pressure for movement demands.

Collective good. Benefit available to all members of a group, whether or not they contribute to the cost of gaining it.

Counter-movements. Collective attempts to resist or reverse change or the demands for change made by some other social movement.

Emergent norms. Norms generated in exceptional circumstances to guide and contain group behaviour.

Factions. Splinter organizations within a movement holding conflicting views on the degree, nature, or tactics of social change to be pursued.

Free riders. Individuals who benefit from a collective good without contributing to the costs of acquiring it.

Frustration–aggression approach. Approach that makes a direct link between the level of dissatisfaction and the intensity of rebellion it will provoke.

Movement success. Process of institutionalization through which the movement's goals become recognized and routinely enforced by society as rights.

Noninstitutionalized activity. Nonroutine action taken to promote interests that are not met by society's established institutions and conventions.

Professional social movements. Movements maintained by a small, full-time core of activists dependent on the financial donations of unrelated sympathizers or outside agencies.

Radical movement. A social movement that seeks to overturn and replace the established social order.

Reformist movement. A social movement that seeks some adjustment in society while maintaining the overall system.

Relative deprivation. Feeling of unfairness provoked by a gap between the rewards that people expect to receive and those they actually do receive.

Resource mobilization. Process of attracting, co-ordinating, and applying resources for a collective goal.

Safety in numbers. Factor, operative in large gatherings, whereby the larger the crowd the less the blame for disorder is likely to be attached to any one person, allowing a potentially rational base for disorder.

Selective incentives. Personal rewards available only to individuals who contribute to a collective cause, not to free riders.

Social incentives. Built-in rewards and penalties solitary groups have available to assure that individual members act in a group-oriented way.

Social movements. Collective attempts with varying degrees of formal organization to promote, maintain, or resist social change.

Social segmentation. Deep break between social groups, in which there are few co-operative ties to bind the groups and separate sets of social institutions to maintain the division between them.

FURTHER READING

Behiels, Michael D. (ed.). *The Meech Lake Primer: Conflicting Views of the 1987 Constitutional Accord.* Ottawa: University of Ottawa Press, 1989. This collection of readings offers a wide range of the conflicting views of governments, academics, and Canadian women's, Native, minority-language, and multicultural movements over the Meech Lake Accord and constitutional reform.

Clark, Sam, J. Paul Grayson, and L.M. Grayson (eds.). *Prophecy and Protest: Social Movements in Twentieth-Century Canada.* Toronto: Gage, 1975. A collection of articles covering a wide range of such Canadian social movements as the social gospel, CCF, union, and western protest movements in English Canada, as well as Quebec's nationalist and Social Credit movements.

Freeman, Jo (ed.). *Social Movements of the Sixties and Seventies.* New York: Longman, 1983. A reader presenting analyses of typical 1960s and 1970s movements, such as the women's, environmental, anti-war, civil rights, disabled, and counter-cultural movements from a resource mobilization perspective.

Gifford, C.G. *Canada's Fighting Seniors.* Toronto: James Lorimer, 1990. This book traces the rapid growth of the Canadian seniors' movement. It describes the wide range of Canadian seniors' organizations and tactics and compares them with their American and European counterparts.

Oberschall, Anthony. *Social Conflict and Social Movements.* Englewood Cliffs, NJ: Prentice-Hall, 1973. The first major theoretical outline of the resource mobilization perspective, this study documents the way in which prior social organization and the dynamics of

conflict with opponents affect the identity and course of social movements.

Pinard, Maurice. *The Rise of a Third Party.* Englewood Cliffs, NJ: Prentice-Hall, 1971. A study of the emergence of the Social Credit Party in Quebec. This work draws on a wide range of data to show how the grievances, available organizational base, and political opportunities came together to shape a specific movement.

Ponting, J. Rick (ed.). *Arduous Journey: Canadian Indians and Decolonization.* Toronto: McClelland and Stewart, 1986. A collection of readings offering much data on the situation and social movements among Canadian Native peoples and includes articles by social scientists, movement activists, and legislators.

Torrance, Judy M. *Public Violence in Canada.* Montreal: McGill-Queen's, 1986. A review of the major incidents of social-movement action that turned to violence in Canada; incorporates a wide range of collective behaviour as well as resource mobilization approaches.

CHAPTER 19

Current Issues and Theories in Sociology

ROBERT HAGEDORN

What is sociology? After reading most or all of this book, you should be in a better position to answer the question posed in Chapter 1, but you may still feel uncomfortable with your answer. In the preceding chapters, you discovered what sociologists study: virtually each chapter is an area of specialization. Yet you are aware that other social sciences also study the same phenomena — family, education, deviance, and so on — and so you may still be somewhat perplexed as you reflect on what is different in sociological explorations of these domains.

Again, in the previous chapters you have read about the following theories: modernization, disengagement, activity, psychoanalytic, demographic transition, open systems, human capital, dependency, and selection. Then there are the terms used to refer to theories or models including social breakdown, assimilation, amalgamation, pluralism, human relations, scientific management, family life course, feminist perspective, cultural convergence, modern man, postmodernist, relative deprivation, resource mobilization, concentric zone, multinuclei, and differential association. It is not difficult to decide whether each of these is a macro or micro perspective; however, to further categorize them under one of the four perspectives — consensus theory, conflict theory, symbolic interaction, and exchange theory — would be oversimplifying the work of the people who coined or use these terms. The problem each chapter's authors has faced has been to organize masses of data gathered by a variety of people who are trying to explain research problems in specific areas, such as deviance, socialization, industrialization, or urbanization. If there are twelve different theories to explain one area of specialization, then the likelihood of developing a single theory is remote. Consequently, a theory explaining the empirical findings in two or more areas is in the distant future. This is why advanced courses in sociology usually begin with an analysis of the theories in that specialty. The large number of theories within an area of specialization and the fact that there is little similarity in the theories across areas partially explain why the question "What is sociology?" is difficult to answer.

However, the situation is not hopeless — most of the information and explanations found in this book can be organized around the following two questions.

first, how much of our behaviour and values can be explained by "social facts" or social structure? Structure refers to things external to the individual, the "things out there" that affect or determine our behaviour, norms, or values. In this book, social structure refers to three types of phenomena:

1. Technology, industrialization, urbanization, demographic, and economic variables. For example, cultural convergence argues that industrialization will produce a common world culture.
2. Social positions, in which power, status, and prestige are attached to the position. Positions frequently referred to are age, gender, race–ethnicity, and positions in organizations.
3. A set of enduring social relations or patterns of interaction. The units of interaction can be individuals, such as members of a jury; positions, such as student–teacher; groups, such as Serbians and Muslims; organizations, such as governments and universities; or nations.

Regardless of the unit of analysis, if the explanation of the behaviour or values is external to the individual, whether it is in terms of technology, positions, or patterns of interaction, it is a structural explanation.

The second question is, how much of our behaviour is explained by our values, beliefs, and attitudes? In this view, we are systematically socialized into the values and norms of our society. In order to understand and predict behaviour, we must know the values, norms, beliefs, and atti-

tudes of the individuals. A very useful concept, used throughout this book, is that of role. A role is usually defined as a set of expectations — that is, the norms, values, and attitudes — associated with a particular status or position in a group or society. We learn the role or the appropriate behaviour associated with the status or positions we occupy — for example, that of a boy or a girl or a student or a professor.

These two questions account for almost all the theories and explanations in this book. The differences between specific theories are largely the result of employing different definitions of structure or differing emphases on values, norms, and roles. The specific variables used in a given study are related to the perspective and interest of the researcher. Keeping these two questions in mind will help you to simplify the various sociological approaches used in this book and perhaps give a somewhat clearer picture of what sociologists do. Nevertheless, a large number of sociologists will still be left out of the picture. To arrive at an even more accurate description of what sociology is, we must look at two additional questions.

The first question is, "Is sociology a science?" The second asks, "What are the current theories in sociology?"

A Problem That Won't Go Away

The question of whether sociology is a science has been with the discipline since its inception. You will recall that Durkheim, Weber, and Simmel answered yes to this question, but they meant different things. Those who answered no are still with us. Indeed, at least among current theorists, a majority would say that sociology is not a science. We will first discuss those who argue that sociology is a science and what they mean by this. Then we will look at the critics of this "positivist view."

Sociology Is a Science

According to Aristotelian physics, the motion of material objects was governed by motives and goals. Earthly matter sought the centre of the earth as its natural goal; and because heavenly bodies were alleged to be composed of a "quintessence," they were supposed to move only in circular orbits at a uniform speed. Such a theory led to conclusions that conflicted with observations of falling bodies and the motions of planets.

Slowly, through careful observation, more direct knowledge was gathered about the physical world, first about the stars and much later about human anatomy. Astronomy and physiology became *empirical* — based on observation. "Prove it" became "Show me." As an example, physicists used controlled experiments to observe balls rolling down inclined planes and objects falling under different conditions and, as a result, it was suggested that in a vacuum a feather would fall as fast as a rock. Physicists did not actually observe this because they could not then effect the necessary near-perfect vacuum. But using this assumption they could account, for instance, for the rate at which objects do fall under stated conditions, as well as why we do not fly off the earth. Much later, using the theory of relativity, they could predict where a rocket to the moon would land and be correct within one-third of a metre.

But the social world in Aristotle's time gave rise to very much the same sorts of questions that we ask today. Why are some people warlike? Why are some rich and others poor? Why are we civilized, while they are barbarians? Why do some people go crazy? Why do some men have many wives and some only one? The answers to these questions — like the answers to questions about the earth's surface, the sun, the functioning of the body, and madness — were based on authority, tradition, revelation, or intuition. All are ways of knowing. It was Auguste Comte who, in the early 1800s, first suggested that sociology should use the scientific method as its way of knowing.

Positivism

The positivist position of social science holds that the scientific method can be applied to the study of social behaviour and that, through the use of the scientific method, causal and law-like statements can be established in sociology. The positivist position is accepted by some members of each of the three main sociological perspectives

(consensus theory, conflict theory, and symbolic interaction), and by almost all exchange theorists.

In the positivist view, **science** is basically a method for collecting and explaining facts. The primary goal of this method when applied to sociology is to discover patterns of social behaviour and to explain these patterns by developing laws. A fact or relationship is explained if it can be subsumed under a **scientific law.** Scientific laws contain predictive statements that certain effects will occur given specified conditions. Scientific laws, then, are statements of relations between two or more variables. These relations have been supported repeatedly by **objective** tests. That we can walk on earth is explained by the law of gravity. If some of us were to go flying off the face of the earth, this law would have to be modified. Thus the law, in order to be a law, must predict correctly. If it does not — that is, if there are negative cases that do not conform to it — the law must be revised.

In order to make such predictive statements and establish laws, the assumption is made that there is order in the physical and social universes. It is assumed that systematic relations exist that can be observed and formulated into laws. The task for sociologists is to find the order in social phenomena and to express it by using the scientific method.

Characteristic of Science. The goal of the scientific method is to construct scientific laws. But how do we reach this goal? According to the positivist position, we reach it in three ways:

1. by verifiability;
2. by unbiased observation; and
3. by unbiased interpretation.

Verifiability. **Verifiability** means that an observation can be confirmed by independent observers. If we walk out of a movie and you say the heroine had red hair and I say she did not, we have two independent observations that contradict each other. Who is right? We ask twenty friends; nineteen say she had red hair and one says no. But on further questioning we determine that the one who said no is colour-blind and therefore not a competent observer. Then we agree that you are right. Your observation is verified because several other observers made the same observation;

we can now say that it is a fact that the heroine had red hair. We say something is a fact when several qualified observers, after careful observation, achieve the same results.

It should be clear that, for science, the final arbiter of knowledge is observation. Consequently, science can answer questions only about phenomena that can be directly or indirectly observed. It is important to recognize that observation can be indirect. In many instances, we form concepts about things that we are unable to observe at the time — molecules and atoms, for example. However, these concepts are then employed in science theoretically so that there is an observable outcome. If atoms behave as we think theoretically they do, then when we split them, the bomb should go off. If the bomb detonates as expected, we say that it is useful to accept the existence of atoms as fact. If the observable outcome predicted by our theory does not occur, then we conclude that the theory needs to be revised.

Thus it follows that, while science has proven to be a powerful way of viewing the world, it is restricted to those problems that deal with the observable world. In turn, it should be apparent that some very important problems and concerns cannot be resolved by the scientific method. Thou shalt not kill. We should obey the law. What is beauty? Is there a God? Such questions and statements do not permit an empirical approach. In other words, they cannot be resolved by observation. We may use logic, tradition, authority, common sense, revelation, faith, or intuition to answer these questions, but we cannot answer them by observation. With science restricted to the realm of the observable, scientists are limited to studying facts. The bomb goes off; crime rates increase; a higher proportion of women were in the labour force in 1990 than in 1970. Such statements are factual; they can be verified by observation. Factual statements are distinguished from statements or questions of preference or values. *Should* the bomb go off? A high crime rate is *bad*. Is it *good* that more women are working outside the home?

Science cannot help us answer such questions. Most Canadians, for example, want capital punishment for certain crimes. Sociologists cannot, as scientists, state that capital punishment is right or wrong. They *can* say that there is no clear relationship between capital punishment and a re-

duction in the crime rate. They can also state that a poll (Gallup 1981) showed that as many as 74 percent of the Canadians sampled favoured the return of capital punishment for certain crimes. Sociologists can study scientifically what people *do* want, but there is nothing in this method that enables them to tell individuals what they *should* want.

Science, then, is concerned with questions that have observable answers. The colour of the movie heroine's hair can be observed. The colour of a unicorn is not at this time observable and is thus outside the scope of science. It should be noted that the frequently mentioned conflicts between religion and science occur only over questions of fact — that is, questions that pertain to the world of observation. In this perspective, science is objective or unbiased: it is assumed that observations can be made that are unaffected by beliefs, values, or preferences.

Unbiased observation. It follows from the idea that science is based on verifiable knowledge that, if the observations are biased — if we see what we want to see, rather than what is — there can be no science. Unbiased observation, the second way we reach our goal of constructing laws, assumes that researchers' values can be controlled adequately in doing social research. For example, if you are a democratic socialist and I am a conservative, is it possible for us to conduct a survey poll without allowing our political biases to affect our results? Can an anti-abortionist conduct an objective (value-free) study of abortion?

Sociologists who accept the positivist position would say yes, it is possible to control bias. They would also say that the amount of bias can be determined by independent observers. If your poll has the New Democratic Party winning and mine has the Progressive Conservatives winning, we do not know who is right. It might be that, just by looking at how the polls were conducted, we could determine who is most likely correct. However, if several other pollsters support your findings, then the evidence suggests either that I did a bad job of polling or that my biases affected my observation.

Unbiased interpretation. Besides the problem of unbiased observation, there is also the problem of unbiased interpretation, the third way we reach our goal. If, for example, you do a study that finds higher levels of aggressiveness in salespeople as compared with people in several other occupations, how do you interpret this information? A sociologist with a social-action perspective, who sees motives as important, might argue that because being a salesperson requires a certain amount of aggressive behaviour, people who are aggressive to start out with are attracted to this type of occupation. A sociologist with a structuralist orientation, on the other hand, might suggest that salespeople become aggressive, whether or not they start out that way, because the occupation causes the behaviour and attitude. Most facts or relationships can, like this one, be interpreted in more than one way. Consequently, our biases frequently affect our interpretations.

The positivist offers a solution to this problem by requiring that interpretations be stated so that they are capable of being tested. In other words, the interpretation becomes a hypothesis, a testable statement asserting a relationship between two or more variables. If the structuralist is right, then a study of people before they become salespeople and of people who go into other occupations should show no difference in aggressiveness. A study showing that salespeople are initially more aggressive would support social action interpretation. Until a study has been conducted, either interpretation is plausible. Before beginning research, it is necessary to state the interpretation in such a way that observations can determine the truth or falsity of the statement. Some interpretations are by definition not testable. If I state that the plague was caused by God's wrath, there seems to be no way that I could test this to determine scientifically whether it is true or false.

One final example of the problems of interpreting facts is in the study of dreaming. The question of whether people dream is easily answered: we remember our dreams and can relate them. Other behaviour, such as rapid eye movement during sleep, indicates that people dream: it has been found that if we wake sleeping subjects every time we observe rapid eye movement, they will report that they were dreaming. But what if we want to know whether dogs dream? Most people would say yes. We see the dog asleep; we see the creature tremble and make noises; we infer from these observations that the dog is dreaming. But we cannot ask the dog. We have no way of deter-

mining, directly or indirectly, whether a dog truly dreams. Consequently, other interpretations of what we observe are possible: for instance, indigestion or some other physical cause. Because none of these interpretations is testable scientifically, we cannot know whether or not dogs dream. At this point you might say, "Science is a waste of time. I know dogs dream." But the knowledge you claim to have is based on intuition, authority, or common sense — something other than science.

The ability to test whether one interpretation or another is correct is a way of controlling for bias in interpreting observation. Another aid is the fact that science is public. There is nothing more sobering and conducive to careful analysis for sociologists than the knowledge that their colleagues will read carefully and criticize what they say. Once incorrect research results have been made public, sooner or later, someone will point out the problem. It may take time, and the reasons for the delay are not always clear; sometimes, for example, a given theory fits the biases of most people. So there may be a gap before the error is identified, because most people want to believe the inaccurate interpretation. Sometimes the scientist who makes the erroneous statement is very powerful or has a great deal of prestige in the discipline, and this hinders the discovery of errors in the scientist's work.

To summarize, the positivist position proposes that

1. there are invariant properties of the social universe;
2. sociologists can develop laws explaining these properties;
3. these laws can be tested — that is, hypotheses formulated on the basis of these laws can be verified or falsified by empirical observation;
4. there is a clear distinction between fact and value; and
5. science studies what is, not what ought to be.

Sociology Is Not a Science

In this view it is argued that sociology is not a science in the positivist sense that it can and should resemble natural science both in its procedures and in the character of its findings. Following are the main arguments against declaring sociology to be a science like the natural sciences. All of these arguments are at least 50 years old.

Historicism

Historicists argue that a society is the product of unique events, or that "social laws" are specific to historical epochs. They reject the notion of universal laws applicable to all times and places. Because events are explained by particular historical circumstances, generalizations are impossible. "We cannot hope to understand any single society without the use of historical material — any given society is to be understood in terms of the specific period in which it exists" (Mills 1959). Historicism views the major events and turning points of history as either infrequent or one-of-a-kind events that cannot be explained by general laws. If we cannot understand present-day Canada, Mexico, or the United States and their interactions without knowing their unique histories, we cannot establish general laws. A less sophisticated version of this argument is the "great man theory." If Napoleon or Hitler had not existed, would history be different? If the answer is yes, general laws are not possible.

Humans Are Different from Physical Objects

Sociologists study activities that are meaningful to the people who engage in them — people are active, feeling, emotional, and self-aware. The activities they engage in bring them joy and despair and make them laugh and cry. These are characteristics that are unique to humans and that make them different from physical objects. Because people are different from physical objects, it is argued that, first of all, humans know what is said about them and are capable of changing their behaviour. Consequently, if there is a "law" of human behaviour and if one is aware of it, one can behave contrary to the law. Therefore, it is impossible to have general laws of human behaviour. This is currently stated as "Knowing a sociological law reflexively overturns it." (This is similar to the argument of free will versus determinism.) A second way in which humans are different from physical objects is in the fact that they are active agents in the construction of society. Humans create society at the same time that they are created by it. One variation of this view is that the world is negotiated. In this view, you interpret my behaviour and react to it; I, in turn, interpret your reaction and respond to it, and so on. The outcome is an inherently unpredictable "negotiated" order. Third, in one way or another, the acceptance of the fact that people are different from physical objects has led sociologists from Weber to the present to stress that a different methodology is needed to understand subjective meanings, ideas, beliefs, motives. The absence of an objective structure "out there" means that all we can study are subjective meanings; these require a different method which precludes the positivistic methodology of the physical sciences. This methodology must enable one to "get at" the subjective meanings, to see the situation from the members' viewpoint, to interpret the situation.

The Value-Neutral Myth

There are two basic arguments concerning the relationship between values and sociology, both of which reject the positivist position. The first argument accepts the belief that sociology is a science but argues that sociologists should use their research findings and knowledge to improve the human condition. Values that sociologists have stated should be pursued include democracy (Lynd 1946), reason and freedom (Mills 1959), peace, and basic human rights (Neubeck 1986). Sociologists should use their knowledge and expertise to implement these values. What separates this view from the positivist position is the argument that sociologists should use their position as sociologists to promote their values. Contrast this view with the position that "What is really at issue is the intrinsically simple demand that the investigator and teacher should keep unconditionally separate the establishment of empirical facts — and his own practical evaluation, i.e., his evaluations of these facts as satisfactory or unsatisfactory" (Weber 1964, originally published in 1917).

The second and currently more widely held argument is that the scientific method is not value-neutral, that objectivity is a myth, and that sociology is not and cannot be a science. In this view, the sociologist's values enter into every stage of the research process. What is defined as a problem, how the problem is conceptualized, what is measured, how the data are gathered, and how the data are interpreted reflect the researchers' values and are therefore inherently biased. Depending on the specific critic, sociological research has supported the values of whites, males, and the bourgeoisie.

Sociologists who think they are doing science are in reality supporting the status quo. This includes the agencies funding the research, the organizations they work for, and their own self-interest. Rather than delude themselves, sociologists should recognize that science is but one value perspective on reality and therefore commit themselves to the pursuit of a more just and humane world. Furthermore, if social research is inherently biased, then such research can be evaluated on the basis of whether it produces knowledge that works toward those ends. The argument for evaluating research based on values is at odds with the positivist position but consistent with that of most feminist, Marxist, and neo-Marxist sociologists.

Like the previous two arguments concerning why sociology is not and cannot be a science, this argument has been around for a long time and has produced a very large number of articles, both for it and against it. Unlike the previous two, it has produced a great deal of bitterness.

Scientism

Scientism is the belief that *only* through the use of the scientific method can we understand or explain social reality. According to Mills (1959:16), positivists who accept this are "dogmatic ideologists" believing in a "false and pretentious Messiah" who tend to become "technicians operating Science Machines" (Mills 1959:16).

Critics of positivism say that its adherents have a "fascination" with quantification "which is entirely foreign to the spirit of a humanistic conception of science" (Tibbetts 1982:196). It is this "fascination" with quantification that is largely responsible for the label "scienticism." However, it is much more than simply being fascinated with statistics and measurement that accounts for the positivists' concern with quantification. Their concerns with testable hypotheses, reliability,

replication, empirical generalizations, and making comparisons over time and between units, such as nations, all lead to quantification.

Most positivists would give an understanding nod to Cohen's (1985:60) description of Galileo after he had observed the moon with his improved telescope in 1609: "Not only did Galileo describe the appearance of mountains on the moon; he also measured their height. It is characteristic of Galileo as a scientist of the modern school that as soon as he found any kind of phenomenon he wanted to measure it. ... How much more convincing, to be told that they are exactly four miles high" (Cohen 1985:60). Positivist sociologists show the same desire to measure phenomena, but their interest is in social phenomena — values, norms, industrialization, power, and so on. To all the nonpositivists this is at best a waste of time and at worst mindless scientism seeing all reality as that which is measured. Several university sociology departments have had bitter disputes over the qualitative–quantitative issue. It should be clear that this issue is part of the more general question of whether or not sociology is or can be a science or, for some sociologists, what kind of science sociology can or should be.

These four arguments about why sociology cannot be a science have existed almost as long as the claim by Comte that sociology is a science. These four arguments do not exhaust the list of reasons why sociology cannot be a science, but they do seem to be the most persistent and most common (for others, see Collins 1989:124–139; Tibbetts 1982:184–199).

Now, back to the question, "What is sociology?" There are two parts to this question. The first is, "How do we study the social world?" The second is, "What do we study?" To answer these questions, we need to look at the current "theories" in sociology.

Current Theories

There has been a growing split between theorist theory and researchers theory. Current sociological theory is a subspecialty divided among theoretical schools; thus, with a few exceptions, it has little or no relevance to sociological research. I reached this conclusion in doing research for this section: I discovered that most sociologists doing quantitative research have no idea what is being written by sociological theorists. I also reached the conclusion that "theory" is the most misused word in sociology. Theory is most frequently defined as a set of logically interrelated statements from which hypotheses are derived. By this definition, none of the "theories" discussed — except, possibly, exchange theory — are, in fact, theories. In almost all cases, "perspective" is a more accurate description. However, since most of them are called theories, I will refer to them as such.

To the extent that these theories specify the subject matter and the methods to be used, they offer an answer to the question of what sociology is. For a complete answer to this question, positivists would require rules of evidence — that is, determining how facts are to be established and some concept of what constitutes an explanation — at what point is a fact explained or understood?

In Chapter 1, you met four major sociological perspectives. In the rest of the book many "theories" were mentioned that fit loosely, if at all, with the four perspectives. The following descriptions of most of the current sociological theories will help you pull together information presented throughout this book. There is no attempt to evaluate the theories; it is hoped that you will use the references and suggested readings to evaluate them for yourself.

Functionalism

Thought to be a dead theory by many sociologists, functionalism as represented by Parsons is very much alive. There are two different views, both derived from Parsons. Lauman claims that, "In recent decades, only one attempt has been made to formulate a general theory of sufficient complexity": Parsons's theory of action. Luhmann also points out that Parsons has gained increasing attention in Europe, especially in Germany (Lauman 1990:255). In North America, the focus of attention is on "neofunctionalism" (Colomy 1989). Alexander and Colomy argue that the functionalist tradition can be the foundation of a successful theory: "Neofunctionalism can be distinguished from functionalism by its effort to reconstruct the core of the Parsonian tradition" (Alexander and Colomy 1990:46). The term "reconstruction" acknowledges the differences from Parsons's theory. The term "neofunctionalism" shows both a continuity with functionalism and an attempt to overcome the problems associated with it, including anti-individualism, lack of attention to change, and conservatism. Neofunctionalists are also attempting to explore connections with other theories and to link macro and micro concepts.

Conflict Perspective

Conflict theory has been used to refer either to theories of conflict or to sets of assumptions about the nature of society. As in Chapter 1, the latter definition is used here. It is a macro approach that focuses on how society is organized and how it changes.

The social-conflict perspective views the word as made up of individuals and groups — which includes organizations and nations which pursue their interests by controlling scarce or desirable but limited resources. Because the distribution of rewards and resources in a society or group is unequal, inequality is a fundamental concern of this perspective. Moreover because the resources are scarce and unequal, change is a necessary outcome of the conflict between individuals and groups trying to maintain or increase their resources and rewards. It also follows that power is a primary concern in the conflict over scarce resources.

What differentiates the current perspective on conflict is that it is oriented toward empirical research and that it is not directly concerned with promoting a particular set of values (Collins 1990: 68, 72). Because of its general concern with power, resources, and stratification and its general methodology, this perspective is found in almost all areas of sociology. Because important scarce resources are found everywhere, conflict is ubiquitous. Whether the concern is the relationship between old and young, husband and wife, parent and child, racial and ethnic groups, departments in an organization, one organization and another, or one nation and another, whether the resource is oil, land, money, or the use of the car, you are likely to find the conflict perspective being used.

Marxist Perspectives

Marxist sociology has shown a dramatic growth since the 1960s. With this growth, a number of different types of Marxist positions have emerged: structural Marxist, post-Marxist, scientific Marxist, rational-choice Marxist, orthodox Marxist, and critical theorist. All of these positions reflect different interpretations of, disagreement with, or divergence from some of the ideas of Marx and Engels while stressing other ideas. For example, some see the superstructure, especially the state, as relatively autonomous, as having a more determinate influence in shaping social development. Others replace the theory of surplus value with a broader theory that applies to socialism as well as capitalism. Still others take a different view of the class structure, seeing "contradictory class locations" — that is, as set out in Chapter 9, positions where individuals are exploiters and exploitees at the same time. And some argue that there is no necessary relation between emancipatory values and class location. Obviously there are serious differences between these various schools, but regardless of the differences, Marx and Engels remain a powerful source of ideas that have influenced a large number of people in the social sciences and humanities. Furthermore, despite the various schools, most Marxists are macro-oriented, prefer a historical materialist approach, and believe that theory and research should be evaluated on the basis of whether or not they work toward emancipatory values.

Network Theory and Social Structures

A social network is the interconnections or relations between units. Units can refer to individuals, groups, organizations, households, or nations. A network is made up of the relations between concrete social units. The particular network and the characteristics of the network are determined by the interest of the researcher.

For example, among college students, those whose networks included relatively large numbers of other college students were less likely to drop out of college than were students with "few" students in their network. In another study, after mothers were asked who their child interacted with during the day, the interactions were categorized as those with adults and those with children and were related to speech acquisition (Salziner et al. 1988). These two examples demonstrate that it is the relationship between the units that is important, not the characteristics of the units, their motives, or in these cases anything about the specific individuals, other than the general categories of adult versus children and students versus nonstudents.

Network analysis refers to the methods used to analyze relations. If the basic units of analysis are relationships, then other methods are required than the usual statistical and probability methods that require integrating units — correlating age with suicide rates, for example. Between 1988 and 1992, most of the articles in the journal *Social Networks* were methodological. Volume 14 (3 and 4, 1992) was devoted to "the location of power in exchange networks." This issue is instructive because the title alone shows that the network approach is highly concerned with integrating theory (in this case, theories of power), with research that is methodologically rigorous and focuses on the social structure. Power is seen as a property of networks, and the authors try to determine the conditions under which actors in the structure will exercise or use power. These articles also show emerging ties with exchange theory. While not explicit in the title of this special issue, there are also growing ties to conflict theory.

The heading of this section, "Network Theory and Social Structures," draws attention to a confusion in terminology. For some, it seems that the network is the social structure and that the main concern is to describe the various patterns of networks and their causes and consequences. For others, "structural analysis" is the analysis of "the ordered arrangements of relations that are contingent upon the exchange among members of social systems," and the analysis of networks is the "fundamental intellectual tool for the study of social structures" (Wellman and Berkowitz 1988: 3–4).

We can conclude that those concerned with networks focus on the relations between units, on how these pattern relationships affect member behaviour and attitudes and "develop" methods that are directly concerned with measuring relationships and networks of relationships.

Exchange Theory

In Chapter 1, the basic features of exchange theory were outlined. You will recall that exchange processes are ubiquitous and that social interaction is a process involving the exchange of valued resources over time. The primary unit of analysis is the social relations between actors. Rather than try to explain the nature of the relationship as the result of the qualities within the actors, exchange theorists explain the qualities of the actors by the nature of the relationship.

In Chapter 1, exchange theory was called a micro theory because it originally studied primarily dyads in experimental laboratory situations. However, recent trends include more field-work research, more emphasis on larger networks, and attempts to link exchange theory with "structural sociology." In the latter case, theorists look at the interconnections of various positions in an exchange network and at how these structures can change. For example, a given structure can change as a result of the addition or deletion of one or more exchange partners. "Partners" here refers to corporate actors, firms, markets, and nation states. Given these trends, it is difficult to label exchange theory as simply a micro theory. Whether the bridge between micro and macro theory can be built with exchange theory remains to be seen.

Symbolic Interactionism

Interactionists assume that meaning cannot be separated from the social-interaction situations in which meaning arises and that "these meanings are handled in and modified through an interpretive process used by the person in dealing with the things he encounters" (Blumer 1969:2).

Interactionism has had two main streams of research and theory (Fine 1990:119). One has been the study of the "self"; the other focuses on the situation. The current focus seems to be on the situations of everyday life. Current interactionism can also be seen as lively, indeed, if only by the number of types of interactionist — for example, Durkheimian, Simmelian, Weberian, postmodernist, phenomenological, radical feminist, semiotic, and Marxist interactionist (Fine 1990:121, 136). Some of the more recent trends include a growing concern with building general theory; the study

of emotions, suggesting that emotions constitute a symbolic transaction; and attempts to address macro-issues.

Ethnomethodology

When a jury decides whether a person is guilty or not guilty, or a coroner decides in debatable cases whether deaths are suicides, what procedures are used to reach the decision? Harold Garfinkel's research on this problem led him to coin the term "ethnomethodology" to refer to the methods people use in their everyday activities, the ways in which they carry out their routine activities, and how they use language to account for their actions in terms of a "local logic." It is important to recognize that people, usually referred to as "members" or "agents," are considered knowledgeable and usually rational. However, their logic is local or situational and can be understood only in terms of the detailed concrete particulars of their activities.

It follows that the scientific method is simply one kind of everyday method and, as such, has no claim to being superior to any other method. It also follows that sociologists are in no superior position to understand the social world. Science becomes a question of what scientists do, and the focus is on what scientists actually do when they do science. This emphasis on observable activity and its sequential arrangement demonstrates ethnomethodologists' distinctive concern with activities rather than with meanings.

Traditionally, when asked why we do what we do, sociologists have answered that we follow the norms or the rules. Ethnomethodologists reject this explanation. In their view, goals, norms, rules, and even "laws" are general, abstract statements that must be modified in specific situations. All norms, rules, and instructions are inherently vague and must be interpreted in every situation in which they are used. A particular person in a particular situation must know how to use the rules, including knowing when to break them. For example, it was found that ordinary words and very simple sentences did not elicit identical explanations when presented to different persons (Schegloff 1992:1295). In order to understand this, what is required is a detailed analysis of the mundane features of the everyday world.

If order does not come from internalized norms and values or from a social structure "out there" that determines what people do, where does it come from? "Order results from people doing what they do, right then and there under local conditions of knowledge, action, and material resources" (Boden 1990:189). "Structure is actualized in the interactional work of temporarily and spatially located activities whose meaning is *discovered* in the work of producing them" (Boden 1990:200).

Reflexivity is the idea that structure is produced and its meaning discovered in the process of producing it. Inherent in the term is the notion of reflexive sociology. Reflexivity refers to the belief that the social activities of members create and maintain the social world they are in at the same time that they are acting in it. Members of society continuously create and maintain the social world so that it continues to give the appearance of always being there, independent from themselves. Reflexive sociology argues that sociologists, by studying and gaining knowledge of the social world, inevitably change that world and are changed by it. The findings of sociologists become part of the world they study and change that world.

Ethnomethodology is not a new methodology but a theoretical perspective of a reflexive social world. The way to know this world is through the eyes of its members. This is achieved through the detailed study of the sequential arrangement of everyday activities. It is concerned with activities, not meanings or motives.

This description of ethnomethodology ignores the diversity of opinion within the school. Regardless of their diversity, as a relatively small but very prolific group, ethnomethodologists have made contributions to sociological theory and the empirical investigation of everyday life.

Feminist Sociological Theory

Most feminist sociologists would agree that our society is one in which males are dominant, women are systematically oppressed, and social research and theory have shown a clear male bias. Granted that sociology has been sexist — what next? Establishment sociologists tend to choose between two approaches: (1) to see sexism as a marginal problem and largely ignore it; or (2) to see it as a valid concern and attempt to resolve the problem by an "add-women-and-stir" approach. The latter response implies that sociological research must be designed to include women, particularly if the results are generalized to "all humankind," and that data analysis must use gender as a variable when appropriate. Sociologists must remove any perceived sexist bias before claiming objectivity. A third view argues that sexism is a central issue in the social sciences. They consider the first two approaches inadequate and pose the question "What next?"

So far, the major effort of feminist sociologists seems directed at exposing and correcting biases in language, concepts, questions, and interpretations. The demonstration of a consistent bias in sociological theories and research is in itself a major contribution to sociology. Beyond this, however, lies what has been called a "women-centred" approach, which includes "women's studies," "feminist studies," or "feminology": the world as experienced by women. Some feminist scholars suggest that specific methods are required, and strong disagreement persists among them over the issue of methodology.

One side in the methodology debate argues that quantitative methods are sexist (or, if not sexist, inappropriate) and that qualitative methods are preferable. Others have suggested specific methods such as "communal approach," simulation, nonhierarchical interviewing, or a historical dialectical method that takes into account the reproductive process. Still others maintain that methods are neutral and consider methodology a nonissue. Most of these arguments are not restricted to feminist social science but are typical of sociology in general.

Methodology in feminist research is analytically separate from the issue of perspective. Again, given that sociologists have yet to agree on any one perspective, it is hardly surprising to find several perspectives suggested. Some feminists take a Marxist approach. Others, frequently referred to as socialist feminists, take a Marxist perspective combined with the recognition of patriarchy as a separate, independent force. Opposed to these essentially structural Marxist theorists are feminists who stress a symbolic interaction perspective, or an ethnomethodological approach, favoured by Smith (1987). All these approaches are found to some degree in mainstream sociology. However, the approach referred to as the radical feminist perspective is not found in traditional discussions of sociological perspectives. It argues that patriarchy (male domination) is the base of sexist social relations: "Women suffer wherever male supremacy exists. It is male supremacy first and foremost, not capitalism, socialism, or industrialization, that exploits women" (French 1985). Or, as Lerner (1986) argues, "the sexual regulation of women underlies the formation of classes and is one of the foundations upon which the state rests."

So far, three general responses to sexism in social science have been described: ignore it, add-women-and-stir, and women-centred research. Eichler (1987) suggests a fourth and ultimate goal: "nonsexist" research — which, once it is achieved, "will cease to be feminist research and simply become good social science."

While feminist social theory is in its early formative stages and will undergo changes in coming years, following is one current statement concerning feminist sociologist theory:

Feminist theory is woman-centred in three ways. First, its major "object" for investigation, the starting point of all its investigation, is the situation (or the situations) and experiences of women in society. Second, it treats women as the central "subjects" in the investigative process; that is, it seeks to see the world from the distinctive vantage point (or vantage points) of women in the social world. Third, feminist theory is critical and activist on behalf of women, seeking to produce a better world for women — and thus, it argues, for humankind. (Lengermann and Niebrugge-Brantley 1993:308–357)

Central to their orientation is a rejection of objectivity and a rational, positivistic scientific procedure. There is also a preference, if not an insistence, on qualitative methods, in which the research subject is seen as another human being rather than an object of research. Like the Marxist and neo-Marxist, feminist social theory evaluates feminist research and theory along value lines — that is, the degree to which the research and theory help achieve the goals of eliminating domination and empowering the oppressed.

Whatever the final outcome of feminist sociological theory, it has been and will continue to be a very active area of research and theory.

Poststructuralism and Postmodernism

Poststructuralism and postmodernism are relatively new ideas that are, however, increasingly being written about and that are affecting sociology in a variety of ways. Since there is no unified social theory around either of these views, all that can be accomplished here is to give you a rough idea of what these terms mean and possibly arouse your curiosity.

To understand poststructuralism, it is first necessary to have some understanding of structuralism. Structuralism is a formal theory of the structure of language. It is the application of linguistic models to explain cultural and social phenomena. Language, or the analysis of the structure of language, is seen as the key to understanding the social world.

My introduction to poststructuralism and postmodernism was from an English professor whose primary concern was literary criticism. I was impressed with the importance he gave these new ideas; how esoteric they sounded, yet how similar they were to some of the discussion and writings in recent sociology. It was clear that poststructuralism and postmodernist thoughts blurred the lines between disciplines and that sociological theorists were using theories developed in the humanities and other social sciences.

Structuralism, poststructuralism, and postmodernism derive from French social theory, and while there are substantial disagreements between and among them, language is their central consideration. As Lemert concludes, "One way or another, everything in the three structuralisms comes back to language, or more accurately, to a specific commitment to the idea that language is now necessarily the central consideration in all attempts to know, act, and live." Also, all three structuralisms "intend to replace modernist principles of positive knowledge in the sciences, the social sciences, and philosophy with a new approach based on language" (Lemert 1990:234).

Postmodernism specifically refers to the shift away from rationality, science, and progress and sees a plurality of claims to knowledge. Knowledge, especially scientific knowledge, is a form of discourse; there is no one reason, only reasons. The rational "scientific" bases of knowledge are seen as unreliable. A key aspect of postmodernism is to subvert boundaries between disciplines. And a poststructuralist sociology would "move sociology away from its historic role as a discipline, a social science" (Lemert 1990:240).

I have no idea how influential poststructuralism and postmodernism will be among sociologists. These views seem very compatible with ethnomethodology. Their anti-positivist views will be readily acceptable to many of the theories discussed. The blurring of the boundaries between disciplines has had more acceptance among sociologists than I would have thought possible. With some sociologists quite willing to accept that the term sociology "is a convenient inconvenience," it does seem that the extreme anti-rationalist bias of those who argue that there is no objective basis for distinguishing between true and false beliefs is too nihilistic to be generally accepted. There is also no doubt that some theorists will strongly disagree with these ideas. Mouzelis in his book *Back to Sociological Theory* states, "Sociologists are at present so much absorbed, not to say overpowered, by developments in other disciplines (particularly in epistemology, moral philosophy, and linguistics) that they fail to translate the insight generated in such neighbouring fields into appropriate sociological concepts." They have "not managed to prove any systematically useful concepts for sociologists interested in theoretically oriented empirical work" (Mouzelis 1991:25). The positivist-oriented theorist will, of course, reject most of these views, as will most empirically oriented researchers.

Theorist Theory

"Theory" may be the most absurd word in sociology. With the possible exception of exchange theory, all of these "theories" are better described with the word "perspective." It also seems accurate to consider social theories as a subspecialty divided among theoretical schools.

The evaluation of these "theories" in large part depends on the position taken on the "problems that won't go away." The current trend among theorists is definitely "postpositivist." Only conflict theory, network theory, and exchange theory are consistent with a positivist approach, and this is a very small subset. For positivists, current theories are a source of pessimism: the glass is half empty (Turner 1990:338).

For the rest of the theorists, these are exciting times, and the pluralism is frequently seen as an advantage and a way to avoid dogma: the glass is half full. This is a time of drastic change, best served by a wide-open analysis of many points of view. Perhaps it is even a time like the industrial revolution, which produced Durkheim, Weber, Marx, and Simmel.

SUMMARY

1. Almost all of the "theories" discussed in this text can be classified as either macro- or microsociology. To classify all of these theories under the four perspectives mentioned in Chapter 1 strains credibility. Nevertheless, three themes are found throughout the theories: (1) social structure as an independent variable; (2) internalized norms and values as independent variables; and (3) society and the situation as being negotiated or created by individuals as they interact.

2. The large number of theories and models discussed in the preceding chapters result from attempts to explain specific problems within the areas of specialization. Theories about formal organizations are different from theories of deviance, and demographic theories are different from both. Also, within an area like deviance, theories of gangs are different from theories of suicide.

3. The positivist perspective believes that sociology can be a science like the natural sciences. This view is sometimes called the naturalist position or a naturalistic perspective. In this view, sociologists are concerned with verifiability, unbiased observation, and unbiased interpretation.

4. Another variety of sociologists argues that sociology is not a science, cannot be a science, and should not be a science. Many reasons are given to support this view, and four of them have been with sociology since its inception: (1) historicism; (2) people are different from the phenomena that the natural sciences study; (3) the value-neutral myth; and (4) scientism. I have tried to present these arguments from the viewpoint of those who agree with them, leaving the evaluation of the arguments up to you. (Note that the majority of

the authors of this book, including myself, believe that sociology can be a science.)

5. Currently sociological theory can be seen as being composed of separate areas of specialization. Many of these theories have little or no relevance for quantitative research, the concern of those interested in general laws or empirical generalizations. The clear exceptions to this are network theory, exchange theory, and conflict theory, excluding the Marxist theory. Feminist theorists range from those who believe that sociology without sexism will be a better science to those for whom sociology is not a science. The other current theories reject the belief that sociology is or can be a science, on the basis of one or more of the above arguments.

6. Functionalism, conflict theory, network theory, and most Marxist theories are macro theories. Symbolic interaction and ethnomethodology are micro theories. Exchange theory is showing a growing concern for macro problems. It is too early to tell what success exchange theory will have, but it is difficult to clearly label it a micro theory. The other theories cannot be clearly labelled as micro or macro at this time. If the poststructuralist and postmodernist prevail, sociological theory will be transformed into something else, and I have no idea where it will go.

7. For positivist theorists, pessimism probably prevails. For all of the other theorists (that is, most of them), these are exciting times. Sociologists oriented toward quantitative research aside from engaging in the occasional departmental battle, will probably continue with business as usual.

FURTHER READING

Gans, Herbert J. (ed.). *Sociology in America.* Newbury Park, NJ: Sage, 1990. Of special interest is the section on American sociology viewed from abroad.
Hawkesworth, Mary E. (1989). "Knowers, knowing and known: Feminist theory and claims of truth. *Signs* 14:533–557. Presents three models of feminist epistemology: feminist empiricism, feminist standpoint, and feminist postmodernism.
Jansen, Sue Currey. "Is science a man? New feminist epistemologies and reconstructions of knowledge: A review essay." *Theory and Society.* 19 (1990):235–246. Good summary of current thinking and problems, with a good introduction to the current literature.
Mouzelis, Nicos P. *Back to Sociological Theory: The Construction of Social Orders.* New York: 1991. St. Martin's Press. Chapter 1 is a clear statement of what the author thinks a sociological theory is, what is wrong with current theories, and his solution.
Ritzer, George (ed.). *Frontiers of Social Theory.* New York: Columbia University Press, 1990. The single best source, so far, for a discussion of all the theories mentioned in this chapter except network theory. Highly recommended.
Turner, Stephen Park, and Joanathan H. Turner. *The Impossible Science: An Institutional Analysis of American Sociology.* Newbury Park, NJ: Sage Publications, 1990. Explains the diversity and problems of American sociology in terms of the resources, or lack of them, available to sociologists. As the authors state, "Ideas are produced by people in organizations who require money, time, intellectual capital, colleagues, students, libraries, physical facilities, and other resources" (p. 9).

GLOSSARY

Objective. Capable of being observed and interpreted in such a way that subjective judgements and biases are eliminated.
Science. Systematic methods by which reliable, empirical knowledge is obtained. Also refers to the body of knowledge obtained by these methods.
Scientific law. A hypothesis that has been repeatedly supported by empirical tests.
Verifiability. Characteristic of a conclusion or factual statement by which it can be subjected to more than one observation or test.

Works Cited

Abercrombie, Nicholas, Stephen Hill, and Bryan S. Turner. 1980. *The Dominant Ideology Thesis*. London: George Allen and Unwin.

Aberle, D., and K. Naegele. 1952. "Middle-class fathers' occupational roles and attitudes towards children." *American Journal of Orthopsychiatry* 22:366–378.

Abu-Laban, Sharon McIrvin. 1980. "Social supports in older age: The need for new research directions." *Essence* 4:195–210.

Abu-Laban, Sharon McIrvin. 1981. "Woman and aging: A futurist perspective." *Psychology of Women Quarterly* 6(1):85–98.

Abu-Laban, Sharon McIrvin, and Abu-Laban, Baha. 1980. "Women and the aged as minority groups: A critique." In *Aging in Canada: Social Perspectives*. Victor W. Marshall, ed. Toronto: Fitzhenry and Whiteside.

Acheson, T.W. 1977. "The maritimes and Empire Canada." In *Canada and the Burden of Unity*. D.J. Bercuson, ed. Toronto: Macmillan.

Acker, Joan. 1992. "The future of women and work: Ending the twentieth century." *Sociological Perspectives* 35:53–68.

Acock, Alan C. 1984. "Parents and their children: The study of intergenerational influence." *Sociology and Social Research* 68:151–171.

Acosta-Belen, Edna, and Christine E. Bose. 1990. "From structural subordination to empowerment: Women and development in Third World contexts." *Gender and Society* 4:299–320.

Adams, Bert N. 1980. *The Family: A Sociological Interpretation*. 3rd edition. Chicago: Rand McNally.

Adams, O. 1990. "Life expectancy in Canada: An overview." *Health Reports*, 2:361–376.

Adams, O.B., and L.A. Lefevre. 1980. *Retirement and Mortality: An Examination of Mortality in a Group of Retired Canadians*. Ottawa: Statistics Canada, Health Division, catalogue no. 83-521e, occasional.

Adams, O.B., and D.N. Nagnur. 1988. *Marriage, Divorce and Mortality*. Ottawa: Statistics Canada, catalogue no. 84–536.

Adams, Robert M. 1960. "The origin of cities." *Scientific American* 203(Sept.):153–172.

Adamson, Nancy, Linda Briskin, and Margaret McPhail. 1988. *Feminist Organizing for Change: The Contemporary Women's Movement in Canada*. Toronto: Oxford University Press.

Ade-Rider, L., and T.H. Brubaker. 1983. "The quality of long-term marriages." In *Family Relationships in Later Life*. T.H. Brubaker, ed. Beverly Hills, CA: Sage.

Adler, Freda. 1975. *Sisters in Crime*. New York: McGraw-Hill.

Adler, Nancy. 1986 *International Dimensions of Organizational Behavior*. Boston: Kent.

Adler-Karlsson, G. 1970. *Reclaiming the Canadian Economy*. Toronto: Anansi.

Aird, John S. 1978. "Fertility decline and birth control in the People's Republic of China." *Population and Development Review* 4:225–253.

Alcock, J.E., D.W. Carment, and S.W. Sadava. 1988. *A Textbook of Social Psychology*. Scarborough, ON: Prentice-Hall.

Alder, Patricia A., Steven J. Kless, and Peter Adler. 1992. "Socialization to gender roles: Popularity among elementary school boys and girls." *Sociology of Education* 65:169–187.

Alexander, Jeffrey C. 1985. "Toward neo-functionalism" *Sociological Theory* 3:11–23.

Alexander, Jeffrey and Paul Colomy. 1990. "New-functionalism today. Reconstructing a theoretical tradition." In *Frontiers of Social Theory: The New Synthesis*. G. Ritzer (ed.). New York: Columbia Press. 33–67.

Alford, Robert R. 1963. *Party and Society: The Anglo-American Democracies*. Chicago: Rand McNally.

Al-Issa, Ihsan. 182. *Gender and Psychopathology*. New York: Academic.

Allen, Richard. 1971. *The Social Passion: Religion and Social Reform in Canada, 1914–28*. Toronto: University of Toronto Press.

Allport, Gordon W. 1954. *The Nature of Prejudice*. New York: Doubleday.

Alm, Richard. 1992. "Mexico Inc.: Old guard makes way for young turks but established families still rule the roost." *The Gazette* (Aug. 15):D1.

Almond, Gabriel, and James S. Coleman (eds.). 1960. *The Politics of Developing Areas*. Princeton, NJ: Princeton University Press.

Almy, Fredric. 1902. "Juvenile courts in Buffalo." *Annals of the American Academy of Political and Social Science* 20:279–285.

Ambert, Anne-Marie. 1976. *Sex Structure.* 2nd edition. Don Mills, ON: Longman Canada.

Ambert, Anne-Marie. 1985. "Custodial parents: Review and a longitudinal study." In *The One-Parent Family in the 1980s.* Benjamin Schlesinger, ed. Toronto: University of Toronto Press.

Ambert, Anne-Marie. 1990. "Marital dissolution: Structural and ideological changes." In *Families: Changing Trends in Canada.* M. Baker, ed. 2nd edition. Toronto: McGraw-Hill Ryerson.

Ambert, Anne-Marie. 1992. *The Effect on Children on Parents.* New York: Haworth Press.

Ambert, Ann-Marie, and Maureen Baker. 1984. "Marriage dissolution: Structural and ideological changes." In *The Family: Changing Trends in Canada.* Maureen Baker, ed. Toronto: McGraw-Hill Ryerson.

Amin, S. 1976. *Unequal Development. Sussex,* UK: Harvester Press.

Amirault, Ernest, and Maurice Archer. 1976. *Canadian Business Law.* Toronto: Methuen.

Andersen, M.L. 1991. "Feminism and the American family ideal." *Journal of Comparative Family Studies* 22:235–246.

Anderson, C.A. 1944. "Sociological elements in economic restrictionism." *American Sociological Review* 9(Aug.):345–358.

Anderson, Grace M., and J.M. Alleyne. 1979. "Ethnicity, food preferences and habits of consumptions as factors in social interaction." *Canadian Ethnic Studies* 11:83–87.

Anderson, Michael. 1971. *Family Structure in Nineteenth Century Lancashire.* Cambridge: Cambridge University Press.

Angus Reid Group. 1989. *Immigration to Canada: Aspects of Public Opinion.* Winnipeg: Angus Reid Group.

Anstett, Richardson, and Mark Stevenson. 1992. "The Myth of the Overpaid Executive" *Financial Times of Canada,* May 11–17, 1992, p. 4.

Anyon, J. 1979. "Workers, labor and economic history and textbook content." *Harvard Education Review* 49:361–386.

Apple, M. 1988. *Teachers and Texts.* New York: Routledge.

Archer, Dane, and Rosemary Gartner. 1984. *Violence and Crime in Cross-National Perspective.* New Haven: Yale University Press.

Archer, John. 1976. "Biological explanations of psychological sex differences." *Exploring Sex Differences.* Barbara Lloyd and John Archer, eds. New York: Academic.

Armstrong, D. 1970. *Education and Economic Achievement.* Ottawa: Information Canada.

Armstrong, Pat. 1987. "Women's work: Women's wages." In *Women and Men: Interdisciplinary Readings on Gender.* Greta Hofmann Nemiroff, ed. Toronto: Fitzhenry and Whiteside.

Armstrong, Pat, and Hugh Armstrong. 1978. *The Double Ghetto: Canadian Women and Their Segregated Work.* Toronto: McClelland and Stewart.

Armstrong, Pat, and Hugh Armstrong. 1983. *A Working Majority: What Women Must Do For Pay.* Ottawa: Canadian Advisory Council on the Status of Women.

Armstrong, Pat, and Hugh Armstrong. 1984a. *The Double Ghetto: Canadian Women and Their Segregated Work.* Revised edition. Toronto: McClelland and Stewart.

Armstrong, Pat, and Hugh Armstrong. 1984b. "The structure of women's labour force work: Everywhere and nowhere." In *Working Canadians: Readings in the Sociology of Work and Industry.* Graham S. Lowe and H.J. Krahn, eds. Toronto: Methuen.

Armstrong, Pat, and Hugh Armstrong. 1987. "The conflicting demands of 'work' and 'home.'" In *Family Matters: Sociology and Contemporary Canadian Families.* Karen L. Anderson et al., eds. Toronto: Methuen.

Armstrong, Pat, and Hugh Armstrong. 1990. *Theorizing Women's Work.* Toronto: Garamond Press.

Arnold, Bruce, and John Hagan. 1992. "Careers of misconduct: The structure of prosecuted professional deviance among lawyers." *American Sociological Review.* In press.

Aronoff, Joel, and William D. Crano. 1975. "A re-examination of the cross-cultural principles of task segregation and sex role differentiation in the family." *American Sociological Review* 40:12–20.

Aronson, Jane. 1985. "Family care of the elderly: Underlying assumptions and their consequences." *Canadian Journal on Aging* 4(3):115–125.

Aronson, Jane. 1990. "Old women's perceptions of needing care: Choice or compulsion?" *Canadian Journal on Aging* 9(3):234–247.

Aronson, Jane, Victor W. Marshall, and Joanne Sulman. 1987. "Patients awaiting discharge from hospital." In *Aging in Canada: Social Perspectives.* Victor W. Marshall, ed. 2nd edition. Toronto: Fitzhenry and Whiteside.

Ascah, Louis. 1984. "Recent pension reports in Canada: A survey." *Canadian Public Policy* 10(4):415–428.

Atchley, R.C. 1971. "Disengagement among professors." *Journal of Gerontology* 26(4):476–480.

Atchley, R.C. 1977. *The Social Forces in Later Life.* Belmont, CA: Wadsworth.

Atwood, Margaret. 1972. *Survival: A Thematic Guide to Canadian Literature.* Toronto: Anansi.

Auer, L. 1987. *Canadian Hospital Costs and Productivity.* Ottawa: Economic Council of Canada.

Axelrod, Paul. 1982. *Scholars and Dollars: Politics, Economics and the Universities of Ontario.* Toronto: University of Toronto Press.

Axelrod, P. 1990. *Making a Middle Class: Student Life in English Canada During the Thirties.* Montreal: McGill–Queen's University Press.

Bachrach, Peter. 1967. *Democratic Elitism.* Boston: Little, Brown.

Baer, Douglas E., and James E. Curtis. 1984. "French-Canadian–English-Canadian differences in values:

National survey findings." *Canadian Journal of Sociology* 10(4):405–427.

Baer, Douglas E., and James E. Curtis. 1988. "Differences in the achievement values of French Canadians and English Canadians." In *Social Inequality in Canada*. J.E. Curtis et al., eds. Scarborough, ON: Prentice-Hall.

Baer, Douglas E., E. Grabb, and W. Johnston. 1990. "The values of Canadians and Americans: A critical analysis and reassessment." *Social Forces* 68:693–713.

Baer, Douglas E., and Ronald D. Lambert. 1982. "Education and support for dominant ideology." *Canadian Review of Sociology and Anthropology* 19(2):173–195.

Bailey, M.B., B.W. Haberman, and H. Alksne. 1965. "The epidemiology of alcoholism in an urban residential area." *Quarterly Journal of Studies on Alcohol* 26:19–40.

Bain, Richard, and A. Lynn McMurray. 1984. *Toronto: An Urban Study*. 3rd edition. Toronto: Irwin.

Bainbridge, William Sims, and Rodney Stark. 1982. "Church and cult in Canada." *Canadian Journal of Sociology* 7:351–366.

Baker, Maureen. 1985. *"What Will Tomorrow Bring? ...": A Study of the Aspirations of Adolescent Women*. Ottawa: Canadian Advisory Council on the Status of Women.

Baker, Maureen, and J.I. Hans Bakker. 1980. "The double-bind of the middle-class male: Men's liberation and the male sex role." *Journal of Comparative Family Studies* 11:547–561.

Baker, Maureen, and Mary-Anne Robeson. 1986. "Trade union reactions to women workers and their concerns." In *Work in the Canadian Context*. Katherina L.P. Lundy and Barbara Warme, eds. 2nd edition. Toronto: Butterworths.

Balakrishnan, T.R. 1976. "Ethnic residential segregation in the metropolitan areas of Canada." *Canadian Journal of Sociology* 1(1):481–498.

Balakrishnan, T.R. 1979. "Changing patterns of residential segregation in the metropolitan areas of Canada." *Canadian Review of Sociology and Anthropology*.

Balakrishnan, T.R., and John Kralt. 1987. "Segregation of visible minorities in Montreal, Toronto, and Vancouver." In *Ethnic Canada: Identities and Inequalities*. Leo Driedger, ed. Toronto: Copp Clark Pitman.

Balakrishnan, T.R., K.J. Krotki, and E. Lapierre-Adamcyk. 1985. "Contraceptive use in Canada, 1984." *Family Planning Perspectives*, 17:209–215.

Balakrishnan, T.R., K. Vaninadha Rao, Evelyne Lapierre-Adamcyk, and Karol J. Krotki. 1987. "A hazard model analysis of the covariates of marriage dissolution in Canada." *Demography* 24(3):395–406.

Bandura, A. and R.H. Walters. 1963. *Social Learning and Personality Development*. New York: Holt, Rinehart and Winston.

Bank, Stephen P., and Michael D. Kahn. 1982. *The Sibling Bond*, New York: Basic.

Bardwick, Judith M., and Elizabeth Douvan. 1971. "Ambivalence: The socialization of women." In *Women in Sexist Society*. Vivian Gornick and Barbara K. Moran, eds. New York: Signet.

Barfield, Ashton. 1976. "Biological influences on sex differences in behaviour." In *Sex Differences: Social and Biological Perspectives*. Michael S. Teitelbaum, ed. Garden City, NY: Anchor.

Barnard, Chester. 1938. *The Functions of the Executive*. Cambridge, MA: Harvard University Press.

Barnes, Rosemary. 1985. "Women and self-injury." *International Journal of Women's Studies* 8:465–474.

Barrett, David B. (ed.). 1982. *World Christian Encyclopedia*. New York: Oxford University Press.

Barrett, Michele. 1980. *Women's Oppression Today*. London: Verso.

Barter, James T., George Mizner, and Paul Werme. 1970. "Patterns of drug use among college students: An epidemiological and demographic survey of student attitudes and practices." Department of Psychiatry, University of Colorado Medical School. Unpublished.

Basavarajappa, K.G. 1979. "Incidence of divorce and the relative importance of death and divorce in the dissolution of marriage in Canada, 1921–1976." Paper presented at the annual meeting of the Canadian Population Society.

Basow, Susan A. 1986. *Gender Stereotypes: Traditions and Alternatives*. 2nd edition. Monterey. CA: Brooks/Cole.

Basow, Susan A. 1992. *Gender stereotypes and roles*. 3rd edition. Pacific Grove, CA: Brooks/Cole.

Bater, James H. 1980. *The Soviet City*. London: Edward Arnold.

Bauch, Hubert. 1992. "The Equality Party: Divided, dispirited and in disarray." *The Gazette* (Aug. 15):B2.

Beasley, Maurine. 1989. "Newspapers: Is there a new majority defining the news?" In *Women in Mass Communication: Challenging Gender Values*. Pamela J. Creedon, ed. Newbury Park, CA: Sage Publications.

Beaujot, Roderic P. 1978. "Canada's population: Growth and dualism," *Population Bulletin* 33(2). Washington, DC: Population Reference Bureau.

Beaujot, Roderic P. 1982. "The family." In *Introduction to Sociology: A Canadian Focus*. James J. Teevan, ed. Scarborough, ON: Prentice-Hall.

Beaujot, Roderic P. 1990. "The family and demographic change in Canada: Economic and cultural interpretations and solutions." *Journal of Comparative Family Studies* 21:25–38.

Beaujot, Roderic P. 1991. *Population Change in Canada*. Toronto: McClelland and Stewart.

Beaujot, Roderic P., and E. Beaujot. 1991. "Social and economic effects of changing family patterns: The case of child care." Prepared for the *Review of Demography and Its Social and Economic Implications*. Ottawa: Health and Welfare Canada.

Beaujot, Roderic P., and Kevin McQuillan. 1982. *Growth and Dualism: The Demographic Development of Canadian Society*. Toronto: Gage.

Beck, R.W., and S.H. Beck. 1989. "The incidence of

extended households among middle-aged black and white women: Estimates from a 5-year panel study." *Journal of Family Issues* 10:147–168.

Becker, Howard. 1963. *Outsiders: Studies in the Sociology of Deviance.* New York: Free Press.

Becker, Howard. 1964. *The Other Side: Perspectives on Deviance.* New York: Free Press.

Becker, Howard, Blanche Greer, and Everett Hughes. 1960. *Making the Grade.* New York: Wiley.

Becker, Howard, and Leopold Von Wiese. 1950. *Systematic Sociology.* Gary, IN: Norman Paul Press.

Beckett, J.O., and A.D. Smith. 1981. "Work and family roles: Egalitarian marriage in black and white families." *Social Service Review* 55:314–326.

Beecher, T. 1989. *Academic Tribes and Territories: Intellectual Enquiry and the Culture of Disciplines.* Milton Keynes, UK: Open University Press.

Beetham, David. 1974. *Max Weber and the Theory of Modern Politics.* London: George Allen and Unwin.

Behiels, Michael D. (ed.). 1989a. *The Meech Lake Primer: Conflicting Views of the 1987 Constitutional Accord.* Ottawa: University of Ottawa Press.

Behiels, Michael D. 1989b. "Introduction: Aboriginal and northern rights: Integrating the First Peoples into the constitution." In *The Meech Lake Primer: Conflicting Views of the 1987 Constitutional Accord,* Michael D. Behiels, ed. Ottawa: University of Ottawa Press.

Béland, François. 1987. "Living arrangement preferences among elderly people." *Gerontologist* 10(6):797–803.

Béland, François. 1987. "Patterns of health and social services utilization." *Canadian Journal on Aging* 8(1):19–33.

Bell, Alan P., Martin S. Weinberg, and Sue K. Hammersmith. 1981. *Homosexualities: A Study of Diversity among Men and Women.* New York: Simon and Schuster.

Bell, Daniel. 1953. "Crime as an American way of life." *Antioch Review* 13:1–154.

Bell, Daniel. 1967. "The post-industrial society: A speculative view." In *Scientific Progress and Human Values.* Elizabeth Hutchings, ed. New York: Elsevier.

Bell, Daniel. 1973. *The Coming of Post-Industrial Society.* New York: Basic.

Bell, Daniel. 1977. "The return of the sacred: The argument on the future of religion." *British Journal of Sociology* 28:419–449.

Bell, D.V.J., and Lorne Tepperman. 1979. *The Roots of Disunity.* Toronto: McClelland and Stewart.

Bellah, Robert. 1967. "Civil religion in America." *Daedalus* 96:1–21.

Bellah, Robert, et al. 1985. *Habits of the Heart.* Berkeley: University of California Press.

Bellamy, L., and N. Guppy. 1992. "Opportunities and obstacles for women in Canadian higher education." In *Women and Education.* J. Gaskell and A. McLaren, eds. Calgary: Detselig.

Bem, Sandra L. 1976. "Probing the promise of androgyny." In *Beyond Sex-Role Stereotypes: Readings toward a Psychology of Androgyny.* Alexander G. Kaplan and Joan P. Bean, eds. Boston: Little, Brown.

Bem, Sandra L. 1981. "Gender Schema theory: A cognitive account of sex typing." *Psychological Review* 88:354–364.

Bem, Sandra L. 1983. "Gender schema theory and its implications for child development: Raising gender-aschematic children in a gender-schematic society." *Signs* 8:598–616.

Bem, Sandra, and Daryl J. Bem. 1971. "Training the woman to know her place: The power of a nonconscious ideology." In *Roles Women Play: Readings toward Women's Liberation.* Michele Hoffnung Garskof, ed. Belmont, CA: Brooks/Cole.

Bendix, Reinhard. 1962. *Max Weber: An Intellectual Portrait.* New York: Doubleday.

Bendix, Reinhard (ed.). 1968. *State and Society.* Boston: Little Brown.

Beneria, Lourdes, and Martha Roldan. 1987. *The Crossroads of Class and Gender: Industrial Homework, Subcontracting, and Household Dynamics in Mexico City.* Chicago: University of Chicago Press.

Bengtson, Vern L., and J.A. Kuypers. 1971. "Generational differences and the developmental stake." *Aging and Human Development* 2(4):249–260.

Benston, Margaret. 1969. "The political economy of women's liberation." *Monthly Review* 21:13–27.

Berardo, Felix M. 1970. "Survivorship and social isolation: The case of the aged widower." *Family Coordinator* 1(Jan.):11–25.

Berg, Bruce L. 1989. *Qualitative Research Methods for the Social Sciences.* Needham Heights, MA: Allyn and Bacon.

Berg, D.F. 1970. "The non-medical use of dangerous drugs in the United States: A comprehensive view." *International Journal of Addictions* 5(4):777–834.

Berg, Ivar. 1970. *Education and Jobs: The Great Training Robbery.* New York: Beacon.

Berg, Ivar. 1979. *Industrial Sociology.* Englewood Cliffs, NJ: Prentice-Hall.

Berger, Brigitte, and Peter L. Berger. 1984. *The War Over the Family: Capturing the Middle Ground.* Garden City, NY: Doubleday Anchor.

Berger, Carl. 1969. *Imperialism and Nationalism 1884–1914: A Conflict in Canadian Thought.* Toronto: Copp Clark.

Berger, Carl. 1970. *The Sense of Power: Studies in the Ideas of Canadian Imperialism, 1867–1914.* Toronto: University of Toronto Press.

Berger, Peter. 1961. *The Noise of Solemn Assemblies.* New York: Doubleday.

Berger, Thomas R. 1981. *Fragile Freedoms: Human Rights and Dissent in Canada.* Toronto: Clark, Irwin.

Berk, Richard. 1974. *Collective Behavior.* Dubuque, IA: Wm. C. Brown.

Berk, S.F. 1985. *The Gender Factory.* New York: Plenum.

Bernard, Jessie. 1971. "The paradox of the happy marriage." In *Women in Sexist Society.* Vivian Gornick and Barbara K. Moran, eds. New York: Mentor.

Bernard, Jessie. 1973a. *The Future of Marriage.* New York: Bantam.

Bernard, Jessie. 1973b. "My four revolutions: An

autobiographical history of the USA." *American Journal of Sociology* 78:773–791.

Bernard, Jessie. 1975. *Women, Wives, Mothers: Values and Options*. Chicago: Aldine.

Bernard, Jessie. 1981. *The Female World*. New York: Free Press.

Bernstein, Basil. 1970. "Education cannot compensate for society." *New Society* 26 (Feb.):345.

Bernstein, Basil. 1971. "On the classification and framing of educational knowledge." In *Knowledge and Control: New Directions for the Sociology of Education*. M. Young, ed. London: Collier-Macmillan.

Bernstein, Basil. 1973, 1974, 1976. *Class, Codes and Control*. (3 vols.). London: Routledge and Kegan Paul.

Bernstein, Basil. 1977. *Class, Codes and Control. Vol. 3: Toward a Theory of Educational Transmission*. 2nd edition. London: Routledge and Kegan Paul.

Berry, Albert. 1987. "Poverty and inequality in Latin America." *Latin American Research Review* 22:202–214.

Berry, John W., Rudolf Kalin, and Donald M. Taylor. 1977. *Multiculturalism and Ethnic Attitudes in Canada*. Ottawa: Supply and Services.

Best, Raphaela. 1983. *We've All Got Scars: What Boys and Girls Learn in Elementary School*. Bloomington, IN: Indiana University Press.

Beynon, Erdmann D. 1938. "The voodoo cult among Negro migrants to Detroit." *American Journal of Sociology* 43(May):894–907.

Bianchi, S.M. 1990. "America's children: Mixed prospects." *Population Bulletin* 45:(1). Washington, DC: Population Reference Bureau.

Bianchi, S.M., and D. Spain. 1986. *American Women in Transition*. New York: Russell Sage.

Bibby, Reginald W. 1976. "Project Canada: A story of deviance, diversity, and devotion in Canada." Codebook. Lethbridge, AB: University of Lethbridge.

Bibby, Reginald W. 1979. "Consequences of religious commitment: The Canadian case." Paper presented to the Society for the Scientific Study of Religion.

Bibby, Reginald W. 1980. "Sources of religious commitment: The Canadian case." Paper presented to the Society for the Scientific Study of Religion.

Bibby, Reginald W. 1983. "Religionless Christianity." *Social Indicators Research* 13:1–16.

Bibby, Reginald W. 1985. "Religious encasement in Canada: An argument for Protestant and Catholic entrenchment." *Social Compass*.

Bibby, Reginald W. 1987a. *Fragmented Gods: The Poverty and Potential of Religion in Canada*. Toronto: Irwin.

Bibby, Reginald W. 1987b. "Bilingualism and multiculturalism: A national reading." In *Ethnic Canada: Identities and Inequalities*. Leo Driedger, ed. Toronto: Copp Clark Pitman.

Bibby, Reginald W., and Merlin B. Brinkerhoff. 1973. "The circulation of the saints: A study of people who join conservative churches." *Journal for the Scientific Study of Religion* 12:273–283.

Bibby, Reginald W., and Merlin B. Brinkerhoff. 1983. "Circulation of the saints revisited: A longitudinal look at conservative church growth." *Journal for the Scientific Study of Religion* 22:253–262.

Bibby, Reginald W., and Merlin B. Brinkerhoff. 1992. "Circulation of the saints: 1966–1990: New data, new reflections." Presented at the annual meeting of the Society for the Scientific Study of Religion, Washington, November.

Bibby, Reginald W., and Armand Mauss. 1974. "Skidders and their servants: Variable goals and functions of the skid road rescue mission." *Journal for the Scientific Study of Religion* 13:421–436.

Bibby, Reginald W., and Donald C. Posterski. 1985. *The Emerging Generation: An Inside Look at Canada's Teenagers*. Toronto: Irwin.

Bibby, Reginald W., and Donald C. Posterski. 1992. *Teen Trends: A Nation in Motion*. Toronto: Stoddart.

Bibby, Reginald W., and Harold R. Weaver. 1985. "Cult consumption in Canada: A Critique of Stark and Bainbridge. *Sociological Analysis*.

Bienvenue, Rita M., and Betty Havens. 1986. "Structural inequalities, informal networks: A comparison of native and non-native elderly." *Canadian Journal on Aging* 5(4):241–248.

Biersteker, Thomas J. 1978. *Distortion or Development? Contending Perspectives on the Multinational Corporation*. Cambridge, MA: MIT Press.

Bird, Frederick, and Bill Reimer. 1982. "Participation rates in new religious movements and para-religious movements." *Journal for the Scientific Study of Religion* 21:1–14.

Black, Donald J., and Albert J. Reiss, Jr. 1970. "Police control of juveniles." *American Sociological Review* 35 (Feb.):63–77.

Blackwell, Judith. 1988. "An overview of Canadian illicit drug use epidemiology." In *Illicit Drugs in Canada: A Risky Business*. Judith Blackwell and Patricia Erickson, eds. Scarborough, ON: Nelson Canada.

Blandford, Audrey, and Neena L. Chappell. 1990. "Subjective well-being among Native and Non-native elderly persons: Do differences exist?" *Canadian Journal on Aging* 9(4):386–399.

Blau, Peter M., and O. Duncan. 1967. *The American Occupational Structure*. New York: John Wiley & Sons.

Blau, Peter M., and Richard A. Schoenherr. 1971. *The Structure of Organizations*. New York: Basic Books.

Blauner, Robert. 1964. *Alienation and Freedom*. Chicago, IL: University of Chicago Press.

Blishen, Bernard R. 1967. "A socio-economic index for occupations in Canada." *Canadian Review of Sociology and Anthropology* 4:41–53.

Block, J.H. 1979. *Socialization influences on personality development in males and females*. Invited address presented at the annual meeting of the American Psychological Association, New York.

Block, J.H., J. Block, D. Harrington. 1974. *The relationship of parental teaching strategies to ego-resiliency in pre-school children*. Paper presented at the annual meeting of the Western Psychological Association, San Francisco.

Blount, Roy, Jr. 1984. "Erma Bombeck gets the dirt out." *Esquire* 101 (June):208–210.

Blumberg, Abraham S. 1967. "The practice of law as a confidence game." *Law and Society Review* 1(Jan.):15–39.

Blumberg, Paul. 1968. *Industrial Democracy.* London: Constable.

Blumberg, Rae L. 1978. *Stratification: Socioeconomic and Sexual Inequality.* Dubuque, IA: Wm. C. Brown.

Blumer, Herbert. 1951. "Collective behavior." In *New Outline of the Principles of Sociology.* Alfred McLung Lee, ed. New York: Barnes and Noble.

Blumer, Herbert. 1962. "Society as symbolic interaction." In *Human Behavior and Social Processes: An Interactionist Approach.* Arnold Rose, ed. Boston: Houghton Mifflin.

Blumer, Herbert. 1969. *Symbolic Interactionism.* Englewood Cliffs, NJ: Prentice-Hall.

Bobo, Larry, 1992. "Los Angeles County social survey." *Los Angeles Times,* (Sept. 3):B-l, B-8.

Boden, Deirdre. 1990. "The world as it happens: Ethnomethodology and conversation analysis" in *Frontiers of Social Theory: The New Synthesis.* G. Ritzer (ed.). New York: Columbia University Press. 185–224.

Bogardus, Emory S. 1959. *Social Distance.* Los Angeles: Antioch.

Bogatz, G.A., and S. Ball. 1972. *The Second Year of Sesame Street: A Continuing Evaluation.* Princeton, NJ: Educational Testing Service.

Bogue, Donald J. 1969. *Principles of Demography.* New York: Wiley.

Boisen, B. 1939. "Economic distress and religious experience." *Psychiatry* (May).

Bolin, Anne. 1987. "Transsexualism and the limits of traditional analysis." *American Behavioral Scientist* 31: 41–65.

Bongaarts, John. 1988. "Modeling the demographic impact of AIDS in Africa." In *AIDS 1988.* R. Kulstad, ed. Washington, DC: American Association for the Advancement of Science.

Bongaarts, John, and R.G. Potter. 1983. *Fertility, Biology and Behaviour.* New York: Academic Press.

Bonger, Willem Adrian. 1916. *Criminality and Economic Conditions.* Boston: Little, Brown.

Bonnie, Richard J., and Charles H. Whitebread. 1974. *The Marihuana Connection.* Charlottesville, VA: University of Virginia Press.

Boocock, Sarane. 1972. *An Introduction to the Sociology of Learning.* Boston: Houghton Mifflin.

Booth, A., D.R. Johnson, L. White, and J.N. Edwards. 1984. "Women, outside employment, and marital instability." *American Journal of Sociology* 90:567–583.

Bottomore, T.B. 1964. *Karl Marx: Selected Writings in Sociology and Social Philosophy.* New York: McGraw-Hill.

Bottomore, T.B., and Maximilian Rubel (eds.). 1956. *Selected Writings in Sociology and Social Philosophy.* New York: McGraw-Hill.

Bottomore, T.B., and Maximilian Rubel. 1963. *Karl Marx.* Middlesex, UK: Pelican.

Boudon, R. 1973. *Education, Opportunity, and Social Inequality: Changing Prospects in Western Society.* New York: John Wiley & Sons.

Boulet, J.A., et al. 1983. *L'évolution des disparités linguistiques de revenue de travail au Canada de 1970 à 1980.*

Ottawa: Economic Council of Canada: Document no. 245.

Bouma, Gary D. 1970. "Assessing the impact of religion: A critical review." *Sociological Analysis* 31:172–179.

Bourbeau, R., and J. Legare. 1982. *Evolution de la mortalité au Canada et au Québec 1831–1931.* Montréal: Les presses de l'université de Montréal.

Bourdieu, P. 1974. "The school as a conservative force: Scholastic and cultural inequalities." In *Contemporary Research in the Sociology of Education.* J. Eggleston, ed. London: Methuen.

Bourdieu P., and J-C. Passeron. 1977. *Reproduction in Education, Society and Culture.* Beverly Hills, CA: Sage.

Bourne, L.S. 1975. *Urban Systems: Strategies for Regulation.* London: Oxford University Press.

Bourne, L.S. 1978. "Emergent realities of urbanization in Canada: Some parameters and implications of declining growth." Research paper 96. Toronto: University of Toronto, Centre for Urban and Community Studies.

Bowles, Samuel, and Herbert Gintis. 1976. *Schooling in Capitalist America: Educational Reform and the Contradictions of Economic Life.* New York: Basic.

Boyd, Monica. 1975. "English-Canadian and French-Canadian attitudes toward women: Results of the Canadian Gallup Polls." *Journal of Comparative Family Studies* 6:153–169.

Boyd, Monica. 1977. "The forgotten minority: The socioeconomic status of divorced and separated women." In *The Working Sexes.* Patricia Marchak, ed. Vancouver: University of British Columbia.

Boyd, Monica. 1984. *Canadian Attitudes Toward Women: Thirty Years of Change.* Ottawa: Women's Bureau, Labour Canada.

Boyd, Monica. 1985. "Immigration and occupational attainment in Canada." In *Ascription and Achievement.* M. Boyd et al., eds. Ottawa: Carleton University Press.

Boyd, Monica, et al. 1985a. *Ascription and Achievement: Studies in Mobility and Status Attainment in Canada.* Ottawa: Carleton University Press.

Boyd, Monica, et al. 1985b. "Summary and concluding comments." In *Ascription and Achievement.* M. Boyd et al., eds. Ottawa: Carleton University Press.

Boyd, Monica, and Edward T. Pryor. 1989. "The cluttered nest: The living arrangements of young Canadian adults." *Canadian Journal of Sociology* 14:463–479.

Brady, Diane. 1991. "Saving the boomers." *Maclean's* (June 3):50–51.

Braithwaite, John. 1981. "The myth of social class and criminality reconsidered." *American Sociological Review* 46:36–57.

Brancken, A. 1991. "Causes of death, 1989." *Health Reports,* 3:170–175.

Brannen, Julia, and Gail Wilson (eds.). 1987. *Give and Take in Families: Studies in Resource Distribution.* London: Allen & Unwin.

Brannon, Robert. 1971. "Organizational vulnerability in modern religious organizations." *Journal for the Scientific Study of Religion* 10:27–32.

Braverman, Harry. 1974. *Labor and Monopoly Capital: The Degradation of Work in the Twentieth Century.* New York: Monthly Review.

Breckenridge, Joan. "Canada Suffering Bad Case of Blues." *Globe and Mail*, October 1, 1992, p. 10A.

Breton, Raymond. 1964. "Institutional completeness of ethnic communities and personal relations to immigrants." *American Journal of Sociology* 70:193–205.

Breton, Raymond. 1972. *Social and Academic Factors in the Career Decisions of Canadian Youth.* Ottawa: Information Canada.

Breton, Raymond. 1978. "Stratification and conflict between ethnolinguistic communities with different social structures." *Canadian Review of Sociology and Anthropology* 15(2):148–157.

Breton, Raymond. 1991. *The Governance of Ethnic Communities: Political Structures and Processes in Canada.* New York: Greenwood.

Breton, Raymond, Wsevolod W. Isajiw, Warren E. Kalbach, and Jeffrey G. Reitz. 1990. *Ethnic Identity and Equality: Varieties of Experience in a Canadian City.* Toronto: University of Toronto Press.

Breton, Raymond, Jeffrey G. Reitz, and Victor Valentine. 1980. *Cultural Boundaries and the Cohesion of Canada.* Montreal: Institute for Research on Public Policy.

Breton, Raymond, and Pierre Savard (eds.). 1982. *The Quebec and Acadian Diaspora in North America.* Toronto: Multicultural History Society of Ontario.

Brill, A.A. (ed. and transl.). 1938. *The Basic Writings of Sigmund Freud.* New York: Modern Library.

Brim, Orville G., Jr. 1966. "Socialization through the life cycle." In O.G. Brim, Jr. and Staunton Wheeler, *Socialization After Childhood: Two Essays.* New York: Wiley.

Brim, Orville G., Jr., and Jerome Kagan. 1980. "Constancy and change: A view of the issues." In *Constancy and Change in Human Development.* O.G. Brim, Jr., and J. Kagan, eds. Cambridge, MA: Harvard University Press.

Brinkerhoff, Merlin B., and Eugene Lupri. 1978. "Theoretical and methodological issues in the use of decision-making as an indicator of conjugal power." *Canadian Journal of Sociology* 3(1):1–20.

Brinkerhoff, Merlin B., and Eugen Lupri. 1988. "Interspousal violence." *Canadian Journal of Sociology* 13: 407–434.

Brinkerhoff, Merlin B., and Marlene Mackie. 1985. "Religion and gender: A comparison of American and Canadian student attitudes." *Journal of Marriage and the Family.*

Britton, John N.H., and James M. Gilmour. 1978. *The Weakest Link: A Technological Perspective on Canadian Industrial Underdevelopment.* Background study 43. Ottawa: Science Council of Canada.

Brody, Elaine M. 1978. "The aging and the family." *Annals of the American Academy of Political and Social Science* 438:13–27.

Brody, Elaine M. 1981. "Women in the middle and family help to older people." *Gerontologist* 21(5):471–480.

Brodzinsky, David M., Karen Burnet, and John R. Aiello. 1981. "Sex of subject and gender identity as factors in humor appreciation." *Sex Roles* 7:561–573.

Broman, C.L. 1988. "Household work and family life satisfaction of blacks." *Journal of Marriage and the Family* 50:743–748.

Bronfenbrenner. U. 1961. Some familial antecedents of responsibility and leadership in adolescents. In L. Petrullo & B.M. Bass (eds.), *Leadership and interpersonal behavior* (pp. 239–271). New York: Holt, Rinehart & Winston.

Bronowski, J. 1973. *The Ascent of Man.* London: British Broadcasting Corporation.

Bronstein, Phyllis, "Differences in mothers' and fathers' behaviours toward children," *Developmental Psychology* 20(6) (1984):995–1003.

Brooke, James. 1992. "A radical idea sweeps Latin America: Honest government." *The New York Times* (Aug. 30): p. D5.

Brooke, N., J. Oxenham, and Little. 1978. *Qualifications and Employment in Mexico.* Brighton, UK: Institute of Development Studies.

Brophy, J.E., and T.L. Good. 1974. *Teacher-Student Relationship.* New York: Holt, Rinehart and Winston.

Broverman, I.K., et al. 1972. "Sex-role stereotypes: A current appraisal." *Journal of Social Issues* 28:59–78.

Brown, Claude. 1984. "Manchild in Harlem." *The New York Times Magazine* (Sept. 16):36–44, 54, 76–78.

Brown, L., and L. Brown. 1973. *An Unauthorized History of the R.C.M.P.* Toronto: Lewis and Samuel.

Brubaker, T.H. 1991. "Families in later life: A burgeoning research area." In *Contemporary Families: Looking Forward, Looking Back.* A. Booth, ed. Minneapolis: National Council on Family Relations.

Bruce, Christopher J. 1978. "The effect of young children on female labour force participation rates: An exploratory study." *Canadian Journal of Sociology* 3: 431–439.

Brunelle, Dorval, and Christian Deblock. 1992. "Economic blocs and the challenge of the North American free trade agreement." In *North America Without Borders? Integrating Canada, the United States, and Mexico.* Stephen J. Randall, ed. Calgary: University of Calgary Press.

Bryden, M.P. 1979. "Evidence of sex-related differences in cerebral organization." In *Sex-Related Differences in Cognitive Functioning: Developmental Issues.* M.A. Wittig and A.C. Peterson, eds. New York: Academic.

Brym, Robert J. 1978. "Regional social structure and agarian radicalism in Canada: Alberta, Saskatchewan and New Brunswick." *Canadian Review of Sociology and Anthropology* 15(3):339–351.

Brym, Robert J. 1986. "Trend report: Anglo-Canadian sociology." *Current Sociology* 34:1–152.

Bullock, Henry A. 1961. "Significance of the racial factor in the length of prison sentences." *Journal of Criminal Law, Criminology, and Police Science* 52:411–417.

Bumpass, L.L. 1984. "Children and marital disruption: A replication and update." *Demography* 21:93–116.

Bumpass, L.L. 1990. "What's happening to the family? Interactions between demographic and institutional change." *Demography* 27:483–498.

Bumpass, L.L., and J.A. Sweet. 1989. "National estimates of cohabitation." *Demography* 26:615–625.

Burch, Thomas K. 1985. *Family History Survey: Preliminary Findings*. Ottawa: Statistics Canada, catalogue no. 99–955.

Burgess, Ernest W. 1925. "The growth of the city." In *The City*. Robert E. Park, E.W. Burgess, and R.D. McKenzie, eds. Chicago: University of Chicago Press.

Burgess, Ernest W. 1960. "Aging in western culture." In *Aging in Western Societies*. E.W. Burgess, ed. Chicago: University of Chicago Press.

Burke, Gerald, and Runberger, Russell W. 1984. *The Future Impact of Technology on Work and Education*. London: Falmer Press.

Burke, Mary Anne. 1986. "The growth of part-time work." *Canadian Social Trends* Autumn:9–14.

Burnet, Jean. 1978. "The policy of multiculturalism within a bilingual framework: A stocktaking." *Canadian Ethnic Studies* 10:107–113.

Burns, Tom, and G.M. Stalker. 1961. *The Management of Innovation*. London: Tavistock Institute.

Burstein, M., et al. 1984. "Canadian work values." In *Working Canadians*. Graham S. Lowe and Harvey J. Krahn, eds. Toronto: Methuen.

Bush, Diane Mitsch, and Roberta G. Simmons. 1981. "Socialization processes over the life course." In *Social Psychology: Sociological Perspectives*. Morris Rosenberg and Ralph H. Turner, eds. New York: Basic.

***Business Week*. 1990.** "Mexico: A new economic era." *Business Week* (Nov. 12): 102–110.

Butterworth, D., and J.K. Chance. 1981. *Latin American Urbanization*. New York: Cambridge University Press.

Cahalan, Don. 1970. *Problem Drinkers*. San Francisco: Jossey-Bass.

Cahill, Spencer E. 1980. "Directions for an interactionist study of gender development." *Symbolic Interaction* 3:123–138.

Cahill, Spencer E. 1987. "Children and civility: Ceremonial deviance and the acquisition of ritual competence." *Social Psychology Quarterly* 50:312–321.

Cahill, Spencer E. 1989. "Fashioning males and females: Appearance management and the social reproduction of gender." *Symbolic Interaction* 12:281–298.

Cahill, Spencer E. 1990. "Childhood and public life: Reaffirming biographical divisions." *Social Problems* 37:390–402.

Cairns, Alan. 1977. "The governments and societies of Canadian federalism." *Canadian Journal of Political Science* 10(4):695–726.

Caldwell, J.C. 1976. "Toward a restatement of demographic transition theory." *Population and Development Review* 2:321–366.

Caldwell, J.C. 1980. "Mass education as a determinant of the timing of fertility decline." *Population and Development Review* 6:225–255.

Calzavara, Liviana. 1985. "Trends in the employment opportunities of women in Canada, 1930–1980." *Equality in Opportunity: A Royal Commission Report*. Rosalie Silberman Abella, ed. Ottawa: Supply and Services Canada.

Campbell, C., and G. Szablowski, 1979. *The Superbureaucrats*. Toronto: Macmillan.

Campbell, Ernest Q. 1975. *Socialization: Culture and Personality*. Dubuque, IA: Wm. C. Brown.

Canada Facts 1989: An International Business Comparison. 1989. Ottawa: Prospectus Investment and Trade Partners.

Canadian Radio-television and Telecommunications Commission. 1982. *Images of Women: Report of the Task Force on Sex-Role Stereotyping in the Broadcast Media*. Ottawa: Supply and Services.

Cantor, Muriel G. 1988. "Feminism and the media." *Society* 25:76–81.

Cape, Elizabeth. 1987. "Aging women in rural settings." In *Aging in Canada: Social Perspectives*. Victor W. Marshall, ed. 2nd edition. Toronto: Fitzhenry and Whiteside.

Cape, Ronald D.T., and Philip J. Henschke. 1980. "Perspective of health in old age." *Journal of the American Geriatrics Society* 28(7):295–299.

Caplow, Theodore. 1971. *Elementary Sociology*. Englewood Cliffs, NJ: Prentice-Hall.

Caplow, Theodore. 1991. *American Social Trends*. San Diego: Harcourt Brace Jovanovich.

Cardinal, Harold. 1969. *The Unjust Society: The Tragedy of Canada's Indians*. Edmonton: Hurtig.

Carnoy, Martin, and Henry M. Levin. 1976. *The Limits of Educational Reform*. New York: David McKay.

Carrigan, Tim, Bob Connell, and John Lee. 1985. "Towards a new sociology of masculinity." *Theory and Society* 14:551–604.

Carrigan, Tim, Bob Connell, and John Lee. 1987. "Hard and heavy: Toward a new sociology of masculinity." In *Beyond Patriarchy: Essays by Men on Pleasure, Power, and Change*. Michael Kaufman, ed. Toronto: Oxford University Press.

Carroll, Lewis. 1896. *Through the Looking-Glass*. New York: Random House.

Carroll, William K. 1986. *Corporate Power and Canadian Capitalism*. Vancouver: University of British Columbia Press.

Castells, Manuel. 1976. "Theory and ideology in urban sociology." In *Urban Sociology: Critical Essays*. C.G. Pickvance, ed. London: Tavistock.

Castells, Manuel. 1977. *The Urban Question*. London: Edward Arnold.

Castells, Manuel. 1983. *The City and the Grassroots: A Cross-Cultural Theory of Urban Social Movements*. Berkeley: University of California Press.

Caves, R.E., and G.L. Reuber. 1969. *Canadian Economic Policy and the Impact of International Monetary Flows*. Toronto: University of Toronto Press.

Celebrity, P.S. "Kiss." *Herald Sunday Magazine*, September 4, 1988, p. 15.

Chafetz, Janet Saltzman, and Anthony Gary Dworking. 1986. *Female Revolt: Women's Movements in World* *and Historical Perspective.* Totowa, NJ: Rowman and Allanheld.

Chaison, Gary N., and Joseph B. Rose. 1989. "Unions: Growth, structure, and internal dynamics." In *Union–Management Relations in Canada.* John C. Anderson, Morley Gunderson, and Allen Ponak, eds. 2nd edition. Don Mills, ON: Addison-Wesley.

Chalfant, Paul H., Robert E. Beckley, and C.E. Palmer. 1986. *Religion in Contemporary Society.* 2nd edition. Palo Alto, CA: Mayfield.

Chambliss, William, and Robert Seidman. 1971. *Law, Order and Power.* Reading, MA: Addison-Wesley.

Chappell, Neena L. 1983. "Informal support networks among the elderly." *Research on Aging* 5(1): 77–99.

Chappell, Neena L. 1992. *Social Support and Aging.* Toronto: Butterworths.

Chappell, Neena L., and Nina Lee Colwill. 1981. "Medical schools as agents of professional socialization." *Canadian Review of Sociology and Anthropology* 18:67–81.

Chappell, Neena L., and Betty Havens. 1980. "Old and female: Testing the double jeopardy hypothesis." *Sociological Quarterly* 21 (Spring):157–171.

Chappell, Neena L., Laurel A. Strain, and Audrey A. Blandford. 1986. *Aging and Health Care: A Social Perspective.* Toronto: Holt, Rinehart and Winston.

Charon, Joel M. 1979. *Symbolic Interactionism.* Englewood Cliffs, NJ: Prentice-Hall.

Chatters, L.M., R.J. Taylor and J.S. Jackson. 1989. "Size of informal helper network mobilized during a serious personal problem among black Americans." *Journal of Marriage and the Family* 51:667–676.

Chawla, R. 1991. "An aging society: Another Viewpoint." *Canadian Social Trends,* 20, 2–5.

Cheal, David J. 1983. "Intergenerational family transfers." *Journal of Marriage and the Family* 45(4):805–813.

Cheal, David J. 1991. *Family and the State of Theory.* Toronto: University of Toronto Press.

Cherlin, A.J., and F.F. Furstenberg, Jr. 1986. *The New American Grandparent: A Place in the Family, a Life Apart.* New York: Basic.

Cherlin, Andrew, and Pamela Barnhouse Walters. 1981. "Trends in United States men's and women's sex-role attitudes: 1972–1978." *American Sociological Review* 46:453–460.

Chesney-Lind, Meda, and Randall Shelden. 1992. *Girls, Delinquency and Juvenile Justice.* Pacific Grove, CA: Brooks/Cole.

Childe, J. Gordon. 1950. "The urban revolution." *Town Planning Reviews* 21:4–7.

Chinchilla, Norma Stoltz. 1991. "Marxism, feminism, and the struggle for democracy in Latin America." *Gender and Society* 5:291–310.

Chiricos, Theodore, and Gordon Waldo. 1975. "Socioeconomic status and criminal sentencing: An empirical assessment of a conflict proposition." *American Sociological Review* 40:753–772.

Chirikos, Thomas N., and Gilbert Nestel. 1981. "Impairment and labor market outcomes: A cross-sectional and longitudinal analysis." In *Work and*

Retirement. Herbert S. Parnes, ed. Cambridge, MA: MIT Press.

Chirot, D. 1985. "The rise of the west." *American Sociological Review* 50(2):181–195.

Chubb, J., and T. Moe. 1990. *Politics, Markets and America's Schools* Washington, DC: Brookings Institute.

Churchill, Linsey. "Ethnomethodology and measurement." *Social Forces,* 50 (1971):182–191.

Cicirelli, V.G. 1983. "Adult children and their elderly parents. In *Family Relations in Later Life.* T.H. Brubaker, ed. Beverly Hills, CA: Sage.

Clark, Burton R. 1956. *Adult Education in Transition.* Berkeley, CA: University of California Press.

Clark, Burton R. 1960. "The 'cooling-out' function in higher education." *American Journal of Sociology* 65(May):569–576.

Clark, Burton R. 1962. *Educating the Expert Society.* San Francisco: Chandler.

Clark, Lorenne, and Debra Lewis. 1977. *Rape: The Price of Coercive Sexuality.* Toronto: Canadian Women's Educational Press.

Clark, Matt, and David Gelman, with Mariana Gosnell, Mary Hager, and Barbara Schuler. 1987. "A user's guide to hormones." *Newsweek* (Jan. 12):50–59.

Clark, Samuel, J.P. Grayson, and L.M. Grayson, eds. 1975. *Prophecy and Protest: Social Movements in the Twentieth Century.* Toronto: Gage.

Clark, S.D. 1948. *Church and Sect in Canada.* Toronto: University of Toronto Press.

Clark, S.D. 1966. *The Suburban Society.* Toronto: University of Toronto Press.

Clark, S.D. 1968. *The Developing Canadian Community.* 2nd edition. Toronto: University of Toronto Press.

Clark, S.D. 1976. *Canadian Society in Historical Perspective.* Toronto: McGraw-Hill Ryerson.

Clark, S.D. 1978. *The New Urban Poor.* Toronto: McGraw-Hill Ryerson.

Clark, Susan, and Andrew S. Harvey. 1976. "The sexual division of labour. The use of time." *Atlantis* 2(1): 44–66.

Clark, Warren, Margaret Laing, and Edith Rechnitzer. 1986. *The Class of 82: Summary Report on the Findings of the 1984 National Survey of the Graduates of 1982.* Ottawa: Supply and Services.

Clausen, John A. 1968. "Perspectives on childhood socialization." In *Socialization and Society.* J.A. Clausen, ed. Boston: Little, Brown.

Clement, Wallace. 1975. *The Canadian Corporate Elite.* Toronto: McClelland and Stewart.

Clement, Wallace. 1977. *Continental Corporate Power.* Toronto: McClelland and Stewart.

Clifford, Diana. "Quizzes and Quantums. An Eclectic Grab Bag of the New North America." *Globe and Mail,* September 24, 1992, p. 10C.

Clio Collective. 1987. *Quebec Women: A History.* Toronto: Women's Press.

Cloward, Richard, and Lloyd Ohlin. 1960. *Delinquency and Opportunity: A Theory of Delinquent Gangs.* New York: Free Press.

Coale, Ansley. 1973. "The demographic transition reconsidered." *International Population Conference.* Liege,

Belgium: International Union for the Scientific Study of Population.

Coale, Ansley. 1974. "The history of the human population." *Scientific American* 231:41–51.

Coale, Ansley. 1986. "The decline of fertility in Europe since the eighteenth century as a chapter in human demographic history." In *The Decline of Fertility in Europe*. A.J. Coale and S.C. Watkins, eds. Princeton, NJ: Princeton University Press.

Coale, Ansley, and Edgar M. Hoover. 1958. *Population Growth and Economic Development in Low Income Countries*. Princeton, NJ: Princeton University Press.

Cogley, John. 1968. *Religion in a Secular Age*. New York: New American Library.

Cohen, Albert. 1955. *Delinquent Boys*. New York: Free Press.

Cohen, Andrew. 1991. *A Deal Undone: The Making and Breaking of the Meech Lake Accord*. Vancouver: Douglas and McIntyre.

Cohen, Bernard I. 1985. *The Birth of a New Physics*. (2nd ed.) New York: W.W. Norton & Co.

Cohen, Lawrence E., and Marcus Felson. 1979. "Social change and crime rate trends: A routine activities approach." *American Sociological Review* 44:588–607.

Coleman, J.A. 1966. *Equality of Educational Opportunity*. Washington, DC: U.S. Office of Education.

Collins, K. 1978. *Women and Pensions*. Ottawa: Canadian Council on Social Development.

Collins, Randall. 1968. "A comparative approach to political sociology." In *State and Society*. Reinhard Bendix, ed. Boston: Little, Brown.

Collins, Randall. 1971. "Functional and conflict theories of educational stratification." *American Sociological Review* 36(Dec.):1002–1019.

Collins, Randall. 1975. *Conflict Sociology*. New York: Academic.

Collins, Randall. 1979. *The Credential Society: An Historical Sociology of Education and Stratification*. New York: Academic.

Collins, Randall. 1985. *Three Sociological Traditions*. New York: Oxford University Press.

Collins, Randall. 1989. "Sociology: Proscience or antiscience?" *American Sociological Review* 54:124–139.

Collins, Randall. 1990. "Conflict theory" in *Frontiers of Sociological Theory: The New Synthesis*. G. Ritzer (ed.). New York: Columbia University Press, 67–87.

Collins, W. Andrew, and Megan Gunnar. 1990. "Social and personality development." *Annual Review of Psychology* 41:387–416.

Colomy, Paul. 1990. "Introduction: The neofunctionalist movement" in P. Colomy (ed.) *Neofunctionalist Sociology*. Brookfield, Vermont: Elgar Publishing.

Coltrane, Scott. 1989. "Household labor and the routine production of gender." *Social Problems* 36:473–490.

Colwill, Nina L. 1982. *The New Partnership: Women and Men in Organizations*. Palo Alto, CA: Mayfield Publishing.

Condry, John C., and Douglas Keith. 1983. "Educational and recreational uses of computer technology." *Youth and Society* 15:87–112.

Connell, R.W. 1987. *Gender and Power*. Stanford, CA: Stanford University Press.

Connelly, M. Patricia. 1978. *Last Hired, First Fired: Women and the Canadian Work Force*. Toronto: Women's Press.

Connelly, Patricia, and Linda Christiansen-Ruffman. 1977. "Women's problems: Private troubles or public issues? *Canadian Journal of Sociology* 2:167–178.

Connidis, Ingrid. 1982. "Women and retirement: The effect of multiple careers on retirement adjustment." *Canadian Journal on Aging* 1(3–4):17–27.

Connidis, Ingrid. 1983. "Living arrangement choices of older residents: Assessing quantitative results with qualitative data." *Canadian Journal of Sociology* 8(4):359–375.

Connidis, Ingrid. 1987. "Life in older age: The view from the top." In *Aging in Canada: Social Perspectives*. 2nd edition. Victor W. Marshall, ed. Toronto: Fitzhenry and Whiteside.

Connidis, Ingrid. 1989. "Contact between siblings in later life." *Canadian Journal of Sociology* 14:429–442.

Connidis, Ingrid. 1989. *Family Ties and Aging*. Toronto: Butterworths.

Connidis, Ingrid, and Judith Rempel. 1983. "The living arrangements of older residents: The role of gender, marital status, age, and family size." *Canadian Journal on Aging* 2(3):91–105.

Connor, W. 1979. *Socialism, Politics and Equality*. New York: Columbia University Press.

Cook, Karen S. et al. 1990. "Exchange theory: A blue print for structure and process" in *Frontiers of Social Theory: The New Synthesis*. G. Ritzer (ed.) New York: Columbia University Press. 158–181.

Cook, Shirley, 1969. "Canadian narcotics legislation, 1908–1923: A conflict model interpretation." *Canadian Review of Sociology and Anthropology* 6(1):36–46.

Cook, T.D., et al. 1975. *Sesame Street Revisited*. New York: Russell Sage.

Cooley, Charles H. 1902. *Human Nature and the Social Order*. New York: Scribner's.

Cordell, Arthur J. 1985. *The Uneasy Eighties: The Transition to an Information Society*. Ottawa: Science Council of Canada.

Corin, Ellen. 1987. "The relationship between formal and informal social support networks in rural and urban contexts." In *Aging in Canada: Social Perspectives*. Victor W. Marshall, ed. 2nd edition. Toronto: Fitzhenry and Whiteside.

Cornbleth, C. 1992. "Controlling curriculum knowledge: Multicultural politics and policymaking." Paper delivered at the meetings of the American Educational Research Association, San Francisco.

Corsaro, William A., and Donna Eder. 1990. "Children's peer cultures." *Annual Review of Sociology* 16:197–220.

Coser, Lewis. 1975. "Presidential address: Two methods in search of a substance." *American Sociological Review* 40:691–700.

Coser, Rose Laub. 1974. *The Family: Its Structure and Functions*. 2nd edition. New York: St. Martin's.

Coser, Rose Laub, and Gerald Rokoff. 1971. "Women in the occupational world: Social disruption and conflict." *Social Problems* 18:535–554.

Costa, Paul T., Jr., and Robert R. McCrae. 1989. In *The Adult Years: Continuity and Change.* Martha Storandt and Gary R. Vanden Bos, eds. Washington, D.C.: American Psychological Association.

Cousineau, D.F., and J.E. Veevers. 1972. "Juvenile justice: An analysis of the Canadian Young Offenders Act." In *Deviant Behaviour and Societal Reaction.* C. Boydell et al., eds. Toronto: Holt, Rinehart and Winston.

Cowan, Ruth Schwartz. 1986. "Twentieth century changes in household technology." In *Family in Transition.* A.S. Skolnick and J.H. Skolnick, eds. 5th edition. Boston: Little, Brown.

Cowgill, Donald O. 1986. *Aging Around the World.* Belmont, CA: Wadsworth.

Cowgill, Donald O., and Lowell D. Holmes. 1972. *Aging and Modernization.* New York: Appleton-Century-Crofts.

Coyne, D. 1988. "Corporate concentration and policy." In *Social Inequality in Canada.* J. Curtis et al., eds. Scarborough, ON: Prentice-Hall.

Crawford, Craig, and James E. Curtis. 1979. "English-Canadian–American differences in value orientations: Survey comparisons bearing on Lipset's thesis." *Studies in Comparative International Development* 14(Fall-Winter):23–44.

Crean, Susan M. 1976. *Who's Afraid of Canadian Culture?* Don Mills, ON: General Publishing.

Crean, Susan M., and Marcel Rioux. 1983. *Two Nations.* Toronto: James Lorimer.

Creighton, Donald. 1956. *The Commercial Empire of the St. Lawrence.* Toronto: Macmillan.

Cressey, Donald. 1971; 1953. *Other People's Money: A Study of the Social Psychology of Embezzlement.* Glencoe, IL: Free Press.

Crothers, Charles. 1979. "On the myth of rural tranquillity: Comment on Webb and Collette." *American Journal of Sociology* 84(6):1441–1445.

Crow, Ben, and Alan Thomas. 1983. *Third World Atlas.* Milton Keynes, UK: Open University Press.

Crysdale, Stewart. 1961. *The Industrial Struggle and Protestant Ethics in Canada.* Toronto: Ryerson Press.

Cuff, John Haslett, "Tipping teen-agers to consumerism." *The Globe and Mail.* February 6, 1993:C3.

Cumming, Elaine, and William H. Henry. 1961. *Growing Old: The Process of Disengagement.* New York: Basic.

Cummins, J., and M. Danesi. 1990. *Heritage Languages: The Development and Denial of Canada's Linguistic Resources.* Toronto: Ourschools/Ourselves.

Cuneo, Carl J., and James E. Curtis. 1974. "Quebec separatism: An analysis of determinants within social class levels." *Canadian Review of Sociology and Anthropology* 11(1):1–29.

Cuneo, Carl J., and James E. Curtis. 1975. "Social ascription in the educational and occupational status attainment of urban Canadians." *Canadian Review of Sociology and Anthropology* 12:6–24.

Currie, Ray, Rick Linden, and Leo Driedger. 1980. "Properties of norms as predictors of alcohol use among Mennonites." *Journal of Drug Issues* (Winter): 93–107.

Curtis, James E., E.G. Grabb, and Douglas E. Baer. 1992. "Voluntary association membership in fifteen countries: A comparative analysis." *American Sociological Review* 57:139–152.

Curtis, James E., and Ronald D. Lambert. 1975. "Status dissatisfaction and out-group rejection: Cross-cultural comparisons within Canada." *Canadian Review of Sociology and Anthropology* 12(2):178–192.

Curtis, James E., and Ronald D. Lambert. 1976. "Educational status and reactions to social and political heterogeneity." *Canadian Review of Sociology and Anthropology* 13(2):189–203.

Curtis, James E., Ronald D. Lambert, S. Brown, and B. Kay. 1989. "Affiliating with voluntary associations: Canadian–American comparisons." *Canadian Journal of Sociology* 14:143–161.

Cutler, Neal E. 1981. "Political characteristics of elderly cohorts in the twenty-first century." In *Aging: Social Change.* Sara B. Kiesler, James N. Morgan, and Valerie Kincade Oppenheimer, eds. New York: Academic.

Daciuk, Joanne, and Victor W. Marshall. 1990. "Health concerns as a deterrent to seasonal migration of elderly Canadians." *Social Indicators Research* 22: 181–197.

Dahl, Roald. 1961. *Who Governs?* New Haven: Yale University Press.

Dahrendorf, Rolf. 1959. *Class and Class Conflict in Industrial Society.* Palo Alto, CA: Stanford University Press.

Daniels, Arlene Kaplan. 1975. "Feminist perspective in sociological research." In *Another Voice: Feminist Perspectives on Social Life and Social Science.* Marcia Millman and Rosabeth Moss Kanter, eds. Garden City, NY: Doubleday Anchor.

Dannefer, Dale. 1984. "Adult development and social theory: A paradigmatic reappraisal." *American Sociological Review* 49(Feb.):100–116.

D'Arcy, Carl. 1980. "The manufacture and obsolescence of madness: Age, social policy and psychiatric morbidity in a prairie province." In *Aging in Canada: Social Perspectives.* V.W. Marshall, ed. 1st edition. Don Mills, ON: Fitzhenry and Whiteside.

Darroch, A. Gordon. 1979; 1980. "Another look at ethnicity, stratification and social mobility in Canada." *Canadian Journal of Sociology* 4:1–25; also in *Ethnicity and Ethnic Relations in Canada.* J. Goldstein and R. Bienvenue, eds. Toronto: Butterworths.

Dashefsky, Arnold. 1976. *Ethnic Identity in Society.* Chicago: Rand McNally.

David, Deborah S., and Robert Brannon. 1976. *The Forty-Nine Percent Majority: The Male Sex Role.* Reading, MA: Addison-Wesley.

Davies, James C. 1962. "Toward a theory of revolution." *American Sociological Review* 27:5–19.

Davies, Mark, and Denise B. Kandel. 1981. "Parental

and peer influences on adolescents' educational plans: Some further evidence." *American Journal of Sociology* 87:363–387.

Davis, A.K. 1971. "Canadian society and history as hinterland versus metropolis." In *Canadian Society: Pluralism, Change and Conflict*. R.J. Ossenberg, ed. Scarborough, ON: Prentice-Hall.

Davis, F. James, and Robert Hagedorn. 1954. "Testing the reliability of systematic field observations." *American Sociological Review* 19(3):345–348.

Davis, Kingsley. 1940. "Extreme social isolation of a child." *American Journal of Sociology* 45:544–564.

Davis, Kingsley. 1947. "Final note on a case of extreme isolation." *American Journal of Sociology* 52:432–437.

Davis, Kingsley. 1949. *Human Society*. New York: Macmillan.

Davis, Kingsley. 1955. "The origin and growth of urbanization in the world." *American Journal of Sociology* 60:429–437.

Davis, Kingsley. 1974. "The migration of human populations." *The Human Population*. San Francisco: W.H. Freeman.

Davis, Kingsley, and Wilbert E. Moore. 1945. "Some principles of stratification." *American Sociological Review* 10:242–249.

Davis, Kingsley, and Pietronella van den Oever. 1982. "Demographic foundations of new sex roles." *Population and Development Review* 8:495–511.

Day, Lincoln H. 1972. "The social consequences of a zero population growth rate in the United States." In *United States Commission on Population and the American Future: Demographic and Social Aspects of Population Growth*. Charles F. Westoff and Robert Parke, Jr., eds. Washington, DC: U.S. Government Printing Office.

Deaton, Richard Lee. 1989. *The Political Economy of Pensions. Power, Politics and Social Change in Canada, Britain and the United States*. Vancouver: University of British Columbia Press.

Deaux, Kay. 1984. "From individual differences to social categories: Analysis of a decade's research on gender." *American Psychologist* 39:105–116.

Deaux, Kay. 1985. "Sex and gender." *Annual Review of Psychology* 36:49–81.

Decore, John V. 1964. "Criminal sentencing: The role of the Canadian courts of appeal and the concept of uniformity." *Criminal Law Quarterly* 6(Feb.):324–380.

DeFleur, Melvin L., and Lois B. DeFleur. 1967. "The relative contribution of television as a learning source for children's occupational knowledge." *American Sociological Review* 32:777–789.

DeMaris, Alfred, and Gerald Leslie. 1984. "Cohabitation with the future spouse: Its influence upon marital satisfaction and communication." *Journal of Marriage and the Family* 46:77–84.

DeMaris, Alfred, and K.V. Rao. 1992. "Premarital cohabitation and subsequent marital stability in the United States: A reassessment." *Journal of Marriage and the Family* 54:178–190.

Demerath, N.J., III. 1965. *Social Class in American Protestantism*. Chicago: Rand McNally.

Demerath, N.J., III, and Phillip E. Hammond. 1969. *Religion in Social Context*. New York: Random House.

Demos, John. 1986. *Past, Present and Personal: The Family and Life Course in American History*. New York: Oxford University Press.

Denton, Frank T., Christine H. Feaver, and Byron G. Spencer. 1987. "The Canadian population and labour force: Retrospect and prospect." In *Aging in Canada: Social Perspectives*. Victor W. Marshall, ed. 2nd edition. Toronto: Fitzhenry and Whiteside.

Denton, Frank T., S. Neno Li, and Byron G. Spencer. 1987. "How will population aging affect the future costs of maintaining health-care standards?" In *Aging in Canada: Social Perspectives*. Victor W. Marshall, ed. 2nd edition. Toronto: Fitzhenry and Whiteside.

Denton, Margaret A., and Alfred A. Hunter. 1991. "Education and the child." In *The State of the Child in Ontario*. Richard Barnhorst and Laura C. Johnson, eds. Toronto: Oxford University Press.

deSilva, Arnold. 1992. *Earnings of Immigrants: A Comparative Analysis*. Ottawa: Economic Council of Canada.

Deutsch, Morton, and Robert M. Krauss. 1965. *Theories in Social Psychology*. New York: Basic.

de Vaus, David, and Ian McAllister. 1987. "Gender differences in religion: A test of the structural location theory." *American Sociological Review* 52:472–481.

Devereux, E.C., Shouval, R., Bronfenbrenner, U., Rogers, R.R., Kav-Venaki, S., & Kiely, E. 1974. Socialization practices of parents, teachers, and peers in Israel: The kibbutz versus the city. *Child Development*, 45, 269–281.

DeVos, S. 1989. "Leaving the parental home: Patterns in six Latin American countries." *Journal of Marriage and the Family* 51:615–626.

DeVos, S. 1991. "The one-person household in Latin America: A brief note." *Social Biology* 38:277–280.

deVries, John, and Frank G. Vallee. 1980. *Language Use in Canada*. Ottawa: Supply and Services.

Dickason, Olive Patricia. 1992. *Canada's First Nations: A History of Founding Peoples from Earliest Times*. Toronto: McClelland and Stewart.

di Leonardo, Micaela (ed.). 1991. *Gender at the Crossroads of Knowledge: Feminist Anthropology in the Postmodern Era*. Berkeley, CA: University of California Press.

Dill, William R. 1958. "Environment as an influence on managerial autonomy." *Administrative Science Quarterly* 2(Mar.):409–443.

Dion, K., and E. Berscheid. 1972. "Physical attractiveness and social perception of peers in preschool children." Mimeographed research report.

Disman, Milada. 1983. "Immigrants and other grieving people: Insights for counselling practices and policy issues." *Canadian Ethnic Studies* 15:106–118.

Dobash, R. Emerson, and Russell P. Dobash. 1979. *Violence Against Wives: A Case Against the Patriarchy*. New York: Free Press.

Doern, Bruce G., and Brian W. Tomlin. 1991. *Faith and Fear: The Free Trade Story.* Toronto: Stoddart.

Dohrenwend, Bruce P., and Barbara S. Dohrenwend. 1975. *Social Status and Psychological Disorder.* New York: John Wiley and Sons.

Dowd, James J. 1980. *Stratification among the Aged.* Monterey, CA: Brooks/Cole.

Dowd, James. 1986. "The old person as stranger." In *Later Life: The Social Psychology of Aging.* Victor W. Marshall, ed. Beverly Hills, CA: Sage.

Downs, A. 1957. *An Economic Theory of Democracy.* New York: Harper.

Doyle, James A. 1983. *The Male Experience.* Dubuque, IA: Wm C. Brown.

Doyle, James A. 1985. *Sex and Gender.* Dubuque, IA: Wm. C. Brown.

Doyle, James A. 1989. *The Male Experience.* 2nd edition. Dubuque, IA: Wm. C. Brown.

Drakich, Janice, and Connie Guberman. 1987. "Violence in the family." In *Family Matters: Sociology and Contemporary Canadian Families.* Karen L. Anderson et al., eds. Toronto: Methuen.

Dreeben, R. 1968. *On What Is Learned in School.* Boston: Addison Wesley.

Driedger, Leo. 1974. "Doctrinal belief: A major factor in the differential perception of social issues." *Sociological Quarterly* (Winter):66–80.

Driedger, Leo. 1975. "In search of cultural identity factors: A comparison of ethnic students." *Canadian Review of Sociology and Anthropology* 12:150–162.

Driedger, Leo. 1976. "Ethnic self-identity: A comparison of ingroup evaluations." *Sociology* 39:131–141.

Driedger, Leo. 1986. "Community conflict: The Eldorado invasion of Warman." *Canadian Review of Sociology and Anthropology* 23(2):247–269.

Driedger, Leo. 1989. *Ethnic Canada: Identities and Inequalities.* Toronto: Copp Clark Pitman.

Driedger, Leo, and Neena L. Chappell. 1987. *Aging and Ethnicity: Toward an Interface.* Toronto: Butterworths.

Driedger, Leo, and Glen Church. 1974. "Residential segregation and institutional completeness: A comparison of ethnic minorities." *Canadian Review of Sociology and Anthropology* 11:30–52.

Driedger, Leo, Raymond Currie, and Rick Linden. 1982. "Traditional and rational views of God and the world." *Review of Religious Research.*

Driedger, Leo, and Richard Mezoff. 1980. "Ethnic prejudice and discrimination in Winnipeg high schools." *Canadian Journal of Sociology* 6:1–17.

Dubin, Robert. 1968. "Workers." *International Encyclopedia of the Social Sciences.* New York: Macmillan and Free Press.

Dubin, Robert, R. Alan Hedley, and T.C. Taveggia. 1976. "Attachment to work." In *Handbook of Work, Organization, and Society.* R. Dubin, ed. Chicago: Rand McNally.

Duffy, Ann. 1986. "Reformulating power for women." *Canadian Review of Sociology and Anthropology* 23: 22–46.

Duffy, Ann Doris. 1988. "Struggling with power: Feminist critiques of family inequality." In *Constructing the Canadian Family: Feminist Perspectives.* Nancy Mandell and Ann Duffy (eds.). Toronto: Butterworths.

Duffy, Ann, Nancy Mandell, and Norene Pupo. 1989. *Few Choices: Women, Work and Family.* Toronto: Garamond Press.

Duffy, Ann, and Norene Pupo. 1992. *Part-time Paradox: Connecting Gender, Work, and Family.* Toronto: McClelland and Stewart.

Dufour, D., and Y. Peron. 1979. *Vingt ans de mortalité au Québec.* Montreal: Les presses de l'université de Montréal.

Dumas, Jean. 1987. *Current Demographic Analysis: Report on the Demographic Situation in Canada 1986.* Ottawa: Supply and Services.

Dumas, Jean. 1991. *Report on the Demographic Situation in Canada 1991.* Ottawa: Statistics Canada.

Duncan, Greg J., and Willard Rodgers. 1991. "Has children's poverty become more persistent?" *American Sociological Review* 56:538–550.

Duncan, Otis Dudley. 1959. "Human ecology and population studies." In *The Study of Population.* Philip M. Hauser and O.D. Duncan, eds. Chicago: University of Chicago Press.

Duncan, Otis Dudley, and Leo F. Schnore. 1959. "Cultural, behavioral, and ecological perspectives in the study of social organization." *American Journal of Sociology* 65:132–146.

Durdin-Smith, Jo, and Diane DeSimone. 1983. *Sex and the Brain.* New York: Arbor House.

Durkheim, Emile. 1938; 1895. *The Rules of Sociological Method.* Sarah A. Solway and John H. Mueller, transl. George E.G. Catlin, ed. Glencoe, IL: Free Press.

Durkheim, Emile. 1951; 1897. *Suicide.* John A. Spaulding and George Simpson, transl. Glencoe, IL: Free Press.

Durkheim, Emile. 1964. *The Rules of Sociological Method.* 8th edition. Trans. Sarah A. Soloway and John H. Muller. George E.G. Catlin (ed.) (p. 104). Glenco, IL.: Free Press.

Durkheim, Emile. 1964a; 1893. *The Division of Labor in Society.* George Simpson, transl. Glencoe, IL: Free Press.

Durkheim, Emile. 1964b; 1897. *Suicide.* John A. Spaulding and George Simpson, transl. Glencoe, IL: Free Press.

Durkheim, Emile. 1965; 1912. *The Elementary Forms of the Religious Life.* New York: Free Press.

Durkin, Kevin. 1986. "Sex roles in the mass media." In *The Psychology of Sex Roles.* David J. Hargreaves and Ann M. Colley, eds. New York: Harper and Row.

Duster, Troy. 1970. *The Legislation of Morality: Law, Drugs and Moral Judgment.* New York: Free Press.

Dutchin-Eglash, S. 1988. "Housework and the division of labor: 1987–88." Master's thesis, University of Wisconsin–Madison.

Eagly, Alice H. 1987. *Sex Differences in Social Behavior: A Social-Role Interpretation.* Hilldale, NJ: Lawrence Erlbaum.

Eagly, Alice H., and L.L. Carli. 1981. "Sex of researchers and sex-typed communications as determinants of sex differences in influenceability: A meta-analysis of social influence studies." *Psychological Bulletin* 90:1–20.

Eagly, Alice H., and Valerie J. Steffen. 1984. "Gender stereotypes stem from the distribution of women and men into social roles." *Journal of Personality and Social Psychology* 46:735–754.

Eakins, Barbara Westbrook, and R. Gene Eakins. 1978. *Sex Differences in Human Communication*. Boston: Houghton Mifflin.

Easterlin, R.A. 1987. *Birth and Fortune*. 2nd edition. Chicago: University of Chicago Press.

Economic Council of Canada. 1964. *First Annual Review*. Ottawa: Supply and Services.

Economic Council of Canada. 1965. *Second Annual Review*. Ottawa: Supply and Services.

Economic Council of Canada. 1986. *Changing Times: Twenty-Third Annual Review*. Ottawa: Supply and Services.

Economic Council of Canada. 1987. *Innovation and Jobs in Canada*. Ottawa: Supply and Services.

Economic Council of Canada. 1992. *A Lot to Learn: Education and Training in Canada*. Ottawa: Minister of Supply and Services.

Eden, Lorrain, and Maureen Appel Molot. 1992. "The view from the spokes: Canada and Mexico face the United States." In *North America Without Borders? Integrating Canada, the United States and Mexico*. Stephen J. Randall, ed. Calgary: University of Calgary Press.

Eder, Donna, and Maureen T. Hallinan. 1978. "Sex differences in children's friendships." *American Sociological Review* 43:237–250.

Editors of *Time*. 1993. "Megacities." *Time* 141(2):30–40.

Edwards, John N. 1969. "Families' behavior as social exchange." *Journal of Marriage and the Family* 31:518–526.

Eggebeen, David J., and Daniel T. Lichter. 1991. "Race, family structure, and changing poverty among American children." *American Sociological Review* 56:801–817.

Ehrlich, Paul. 1968. *The Population Bomb*. New York: Ballantine.

Ehrlich, Paul, and Anne Ehrlich. 1990. *The Population Explosion*. New York: Simon & Schuster.

Eichler, Margrit. 1978. "Women's unpaid labour." *Atlantis* 3(2):52–62.

Eichler, Margrit. 1980. *The Double Standard*. New York: St. Martin's.

Eichler, Margrit. 1981. "The inadequacy of the monolithic model of the family." *Canadian Journal of Sociology* 6:367–388.

Eichler, Margrit. 1983. *Families in Canada Today: Recent Changes and Their Policy Implications*. Toronto: Gage.

Eichler, Margrit. 1987. "Family change and social policies." In *Family Matters: Sociology and Contemporary Canadian Families*. Karen L. Anderson et al., eds. Toronto: Methuen.

Eichler, Margrit. 1987. "Sexist, non-sexist, women centered and feminist research in the social sciences," in *Women and Men: Interdisciplinary Readings on Gender*. Greta Hoffman Nemiroff (ed.) Montreal: Fitzhenry and Whiteside.

Ekeh, Peter. 1974. *Social Exchange Theory*. London: Heinemann.

Ekstedt, John W., and Curt T. Griffiths. 1984. *Corrections in Canada: Policy and Practice*. Toronto: Butterworths.

Elder, Glen H., Jr. 1974. *Children of the Great Depression*. Chicago: University of Chicago Press.

Elder, Glen H., Jr. 1985. *Life Course Dynamics: Trajectories and Transitions, 1968–1980*. Ithaca, NY: Cornell University Press.

Elder, Jules. 1992. "We all share the blame." *Maclean's* (May 18):32.

Elkin, Frederick. 1983. "Family, socialization, and ethnic identity." In *The Canadian Family*. K. Ishwaran, ed. Toronto: Gage.

Elliott, Jean Leonard, and Augie Fleras. 1992. *Unequal Relations: An Introduction to Race and Ethnic Dynamics in Canada*. Scarborough, ON: Prentice-Hall.

Ellis, Godfrey J. 1983. "Youth in the electronic environment: An introduction." *Youth and Society* 15:3–12.

Ellul, Jacques. 1981. *Perspectives on Our Age*. Toronto: Canadian Broadcasting Corporation.

Ellwood, D. 1988. *Poor Support*. New York: Basic.

Emerson, Richard M. 1981. "Social exchange theory." In *Social Psychology*. Morris Rosenberg and Ralph H. Turner, eds. New York: Basic.

Employment and Immigration Canada. 1984. *Background Paper on Future Immigration Levels*. Ottawa: Supply and Services.

Employment and Immigration Canada. 1991. *Immigration Statistics 1989*. Ottawa: Minister of Supply and Services.

Empson-Warner, Susan, and Harvey Krahn. 1992. "Unemployment and occupational aspirations: A panel study of high school graduates." *Canadian Review of Sociology and Anthropology* 29:38–54.

Engels, Friedrich. 1942; 1884. *The Origin of the Family, Private Property and the State*. New York: International Publishers.

England, Paula, and Irene Browne. 1992. "Trends in women's economic status." *Sociological Perspectives* 35:17–51.

Epstein, Cynthia Fuchs. 1988. *Deceptive Distinctions: Sex, Gender, and the Social Order*. New York: Russell Sage Foundation and Yale University Press.

Ericson, Richard V. 1982. *Reproducing Order: A Study of Police Patrol Work*. Toronto: University of Toronto Press.

Erikson, Erik. 1963. *Childhood and Society*. 2nd edition. New York: Norton.

Erikson, Erik. 1968. *Identity: Youth and Crisis*. New York: Norton.

Espenshade, Thomas J. 1978. "Zero population growth and the economies of developed nations." *Population and Development Review* 4:645–680.

Estes, Carroll L. 1979. *The Aging Enterprise.* San Francisco: Jossey-Bass.

Estes, Richard J. 1984. *The Social Progress of Nations.* New York: Praeger.

Estes, Richard J. 1988. *Trends in World Social Development: The Social Progress of Nations, 1970–1987.* New York: Praeger.

Ewen, Robert B. 1980. *An Introduction to Theories of Personality.* New York: Academic.

Eyre, Linda. 1991. "Gender relations in the classroom: A fresh look at coeducation." In *Women and Education.* J. Gaskell and A. McLaren, eds. Calgary: Detselig.

Fact Book on Aging. **1983.** Document prepared for the Second Canadian Conference on Aging. Ottawa: Supply and Services.

Falicov, C.J. 1982. "Mexican families." In *Ethnicity and Family Therapy.* M. Goldrick, J.K. Pierce, and J. Giordano, eds. New York: Guildford.

Fallding, Harold. 1978. "Mainline Protestantism in Canada and the United States: An overview." *Canadian Journal of Sociology* 2:141–160.

Fallo-Mitchell, Linda, and Carol D. Ryff. 1982. "Preferred timing of female life events: Cohort differences." *Research on Aging* 4(2):249–267.

Farley, R., and W.R. Allen. 1987. *The Color Line and the Quality of Life in America.* New York: Russell Sage.

Feagin, J.R., and H. Han. 1973. *Ghetto Revolts.* New York: Macmillan.

Federation of Women Teachers of Ontario. 1988. *The More Things Change ... The More They Stay the Same.* Toronto: Federation of Women Teachers of Ontario.

Felson, Marcus, and Lawrence E. Cohen. 1980. "Human ecology and crime: A routine activity approach." *Human Ecology* 8:389–406.

Felson Richard B., and Lisa Trudeau. 1991. "Gender differences in mathematics performance." *Social Psychology Quarterly* 34 (2) (June): 113–126.

Ferber, Marianne A. 1982. "Labor market participation of young married women: Causes and effects." *Journal of Marriage and the Family* 44:457–468.

Ferber, Marianne A., and H.M. Lowry. 1976. "The sex differential in earnings: A reappraisal." *Industrial and Labor Relations Review* 29(3):377–387.

Ferree, Myra Marx. 1984. "The view from below: Women's employment and gender equality in working class families." In *Women and the Family: Two Decades of Change.* B.B. Hess and M.B. Sussman, eds. New York: Haworth.

Ferree, Myra Marx, and Beth B. Hess. 1987. "Introduction." In *Analyzing Gender: A Handbook of Social Science Research.* Beth B. Hess and Myra Marx Ferree, eds. Newbury Park, CA: Sage.

Feschuk, Scott. 1992. "The ad world takes on free trade." *The Globe and Mail* (Aug. 22):B4.

Feuer, Lewis S. (ed.). 1959. *Marx and Engels: Basic Writings on Politics and Philosophy.* New York: Doubleday/Anchor.

Fidler, Richard (ed.). 1991. *Canada, Adieu? Quebec Debates Its Future.* Halifax: Institute for Research on Public Policy.

Fine, Gary Alan. 1986. "The dirty play of little boys." *Society* 24(Nov./Dec.):63–67.

Fine, Gary Alan. 1990. "Symbolic interactionism in the post-Blumerian age" in G. Ritzer (ed.), *Frontiers of Social Theory: The New Syntheses.* New York: Columbia University Press. 117–157.

Fink, Arlene, and Jacqueline Kosecoff. 1977. "Girls' and boys' changing attitudes toward school." *Psychology of Women Quarterly* 2:44–49.

Finke, Roger, and Rodney Stark. 1992. *The Churching of America, 1776–1990.* New Brunswick, NJ: Rutgers University Press.

Finkelhor, David. 1983. "Common features of family abuse." In *The Dark Side of Families: Current Family Violence Research.* David Finkelhor et al., eds. Beverly Hills, CA: Sage.

Firestone, Melvin M. 1978. "Socialization and interaction in a Newfoundland outport." *Urban Life* 7(Apr.): 19–110.

Fischer, Claude S. 1981. "The public and private worlds of city life." *American Sociological Review* 46(3): 306–316.

Fischer, Claude, S. 1984. *The Urban Experience.* 2nd edition. New York: Harcourt Brace Jovanovich.

Fitzsimmons-LeCavalier, Patricia. 1983. "Resourceful movements: The mobilization of citizens for neighbourhood planning control." Doctoral dissertion. Montreal: McGill University.

Fitzsimmons-LeCavalier, Patricia, and Guy LeCavalier. 1981. "Becoming a minority: Quebec's nonfrancophones and the sovereignty question." Paper presented to the American Sociological Association.

Fitzsimmons-LeCavalier, Patricia, and Guy LeCavalier. 1984. "Individual versus collective action: The minority response of Quebec's nonfrancophones." Paper presented to the Canadian Sociology and Anthropology Association.

Fitzsimmons-LeCavalier, Patricia, and Guy LeCavalier. 1989. "Fight, flight or accommodate? Quebec's nonfrancophones' response to language conflict." Paper presented at the annual meeting of the American Sociological Association in San Francisco.

Flacks, Richard. 1979. "Growing up confused." In *Socialization and the Life Cycle.* Peter I. Rose, ed. New York: St. Martin's.

Flanders, Allan. 1965. *Trade Unions.* London: Hutchinson University Library.

Fleming, W.G. 1974. *The Individualized System: Findings from Five Studies.* Toronto: Ontario Institute for Studies in Education.

Fleras, Augie, and Jean Leonard Elliott. 1992a. *The Challenge of Diversity: Multiculturalism in Canada.* Scarborough, ON: Nelson Canada.

Fleras, Augie, and Jean Leonard Elliott. 1992b. *The Nations Within: Aboriginal–State Relations in Canada, the United States, and New Zealand.* Toronto: Oxford University Press.

Flowers, Ronald. 1988. *Minorities and Crime.* Westport, CT: Greenwood.

Foner, Anne. 1974. "Age stratification and age conflict

in political life." *American Sociological Review* 39(Apr.): 187–196.

Foner, Anne, and David Kertzer. 1978. "Transitions over the life course: Lessons from age-set societies." *American Journal of Sociology* 83(5):1081–1104.

Foner, Anne, and Karen Schwab. 1981. *Aging and Retirement.* Monterey, CA: Brooks/Cole.

Foot, David K. 1982. *Canada's Population Outlook: Demographic Futures and Economic Challenges.* Toronto: James Lorimer.

Forbes, William F., Jennifer A. Jackson, and Arthur S. Kraus. 1987. *Institutionalization of the Elderly in Canada.* Toronto: Butterworths.

Forcese, D. 1980. *The Canadian Class Structure.* 2nd edition. Toronto: McGraw-Hill Ryerson.

Ford, Catherine. 1983. "Leave-me-alone group tunes out." *Calgary Herald* (July 23).

Form, William. 1979. "Comparative industrial sociology and the convergence hypothesis." *Annual Review of Sociology* 5:1–25.

Fouts, Gregory T. 1980. "Parents as censors of TV content for their children." *Journal of the Canadian Association for Young Children* 6:20–31.

Fox, Bonnie (ed.). 1982. *Hidden in the Household: Women's Domestic Labour Under Capitalism.* Toronto: Women's Press.

Franck, K.A. 1980. "Friends and strangers: The social experience of living in urban and non-urban settings." *Journal of Social Issues* 36(3):52–71.

Frank, André Gunder. 1969. *Capitalism and Underdevelopment in Latin America.* New York: Monthly Review.

Frank, J.A. 1984. "La dynamique des manifestations violentes." *Canadian Journal of Political Science* 17(2): 325–350.

Frank, J.A., and M. Kelly. 1979. "Street politics in Canada: An examination of mediating factors." *American Journal of Political Science* 23:593–614.

Frankel, B. Gail, W.E. Hewitt, and Richard M. Nixon. 1992. "Religion and well-being: A Canadian assessment." Unpublished paper, Department of Sociology, University of Western Ontario, London, Ontario.

Fraser, Sylvia. 1987. *My Father's House: A Memoir of Incest and of Healing.* Toronto: Doubleday.

Frazier, E. Franklin. 1964. *The Negro Church in America.* New York: Schocken Books.

Freeman, Jo. (ed.). 1983. *Social Movements of the Sixties and Seventies.* New York: Longman.

Freeman, Richard B. 1976. *The Overeducated American.* New York: Academic.

Freeman, Richard. 1991. "The relation of criminal activity to black youth employment." *Review of Black Political Economy* 16:99–107.

French, Marilyn. 1985. *Beyond Power, On Women, Men, and Morals.* New York: Summit Books.

Frenken, H. 1991. "The pension carrot: Incentives to early retirement." *Perspectives on Labour and Income* 3(3):18–27.

Freud, Sigmund. 1962; 1928. *The Future of an Illusion.* New York: Doubleday.

Frey, W.H. 1987. "Migration and depopulation of the metropolis: Regional restructuring or rural renaissance?" *American Sociological Review* 52(2):240–57.

Frideres, James S. 1974. *Canada's Indians: Contemporary Conflict.* Scarborough, ON: Prentice-Hall.

Friedan, Betty. 1963. *The Feminine Mystique.* Harmondsworth, UK: Penguin.

Friedl, Ernestine. 1975. *Women and Men: An Anthropologist's View.* New York: Holt, Rinehart and Winston.

Friedl, Ernestine. 1978. "Society and sex roles." *Human Nature* (Apr.):70.

Friedland, Martin. 1981. "Gun control in Canada: Politics and impact." Paper presented to Seminar on Canadian–U.S. Relations, Harvard Center for International Affairs, University Consortium for Research on North America.

Frieze, Irene H., et al. 1978. *Women and Sex Roles: A Social Psychological Perspective.* New York: W.W. Norton.

Fry, Christine L. 1976. "The ages of adulthood: A question of numbers." *Journal of Gerontology* 31(2): 170–177.

Fuguitt, Glen, and James Zuiches. 1975. "Residential preferences and population distribution." *Demography* 12(3):167–80.

Fukuyama, Francis. 1992. *The End of History and the Last Man.* New york: Free Press.

Fullan, Michael. 1970. "Industrial technology and worker integration in the organization." *American Sociological Review* 35(Dec.):1028–1039.

Fuller, Mary. 1978. "Sex-role stereotyping and social science." In *The Sex Role System: Psychological and Sociological Perspectives.* Jane Chetwynd and Oonagh Hartnett, eds. London: Routledge and Kegan Paul.

Furstenberg, F.F., Jr. 1988. "Good dads, bad dads: Two faces of fatherhood." In *The Changing American Family and Public Policy.* A.J. Cherlin, ed. Washington, DC: Urban Institute Press.

Gaffield, Chad M. 1979. "Canadian families in cultural context: Hypotheses from the mid-nineteenth century." *Historical Papers* Canadian Historical Association: 48–61.

Galt, Virginia. "Agencies Still Refer Whites Only." *Globe and Mail*, September 8, 1992, p. 8A.

Gamson, William. 1975. *The Strategy of Social Protest.* Homewood, IL: Dorsey.

Gans, Herbert. 1962a. "Urbanism and suburbanism as ways of life." In *Human Behavior and Social Processes.* Arnold M. Rose, ed. Boston: Houghton Mifflin.

Gans, Herbert. 1962b. *The Urban Villagers.* New York: Free Press.

Gans, Herbert. 1967. *The Levittowners: Way of Life and Politics in a New Suburban Community.* New York: Pantheon.

Gans, Herbert. 1972. "The positive functions of poverty." *American Journal of Sociology* 78:275–289.

Garfinkel, Harold. 1967. *Studies in Ethnomethodology.* Englewood Cliffs, NJ: Prentice Hall.

Garfinkel, I., and S. McLanahan. 1986. *Single Mothers*

and Their Children: A New American Dilemma. Washington, DC: Urban Institute Press.

Garn, Stanley M. 1966. "Body size and its implications." In *Review of Child Development Research* 2. Lois W. Hoffman and Martin L. Hoffman, eds. New York: Sage.

Garnets, Linda, and Joseph H. Pleck. 1979. "Sex role identity, androgyny, and sex role transcendence: A sex role strain analysis." *Psychology of Women Quarterly* 3:270–283.

Garreau, Joel. 1981. *The Nine Nations of North America.* New York: Avon.

Garreau, Joel. 1991. *Edge City: Life on the New Frontier.* New York: Doubleday.

Garrison, Howard H. 1979. "Gender differences in the career aspirations of recent cohorts of high school seniors." *Social Problems* 27:170–185.

Gaskell, J. 1992. *Gender Matters from School to Work.* Milton Keynes, UK: Open University Press.

Gecas, Viktor. 1976. "The socialization and child care roles." In *Role Structure and Analysis of the Family.* F. Ivan Nye, ed. Beverly Hills, CA: Sage.

Gecas, Viktor. 1981. "Contexts of socialization." In *Social Psychology: Sociological Perspectives.* Morris Rosenberg and Ralph H. Turner, eds. New York: Basic.

Gee, Ellen M. Thomas. 1980. "Female marriage patterns in Canada: Changes and differentials." *Journal of Comparative Family Studies* 11:457–473.

Gee, Ellen M. 1986. "The life course of Canadian women: An historical and demographic analysis." *Social Indicators Research* 18:263–283.

Gee, Ellen M. 1987. "Historical change in the family life course of men and women." In *Aging in Canada: Social Perspectives.* Victor W. Marshall, ed. 2nd edition. Toronto: Fitzhenry and Whiteside.

Gee, Ellen M. 1990. "Demographic change and intergenerational relations in Canadian families: Findings and social policy implications." *Canadian Public Policy* 16:191–199.

Gee, Ellen M. 1990. "Preferred timing of women's life events: A Canadian study." *International Journal of Aging and Human Development* 31:281–296.

Gee, Ellen M. 1991. "The transition to grandmotherhood: A quantitative study." *Canadian Journal on Aging* 10(3):254–270.

Gee, Ellen M., and Meredith M. Kimball. 1987. *Women and Aging.* Toronto: Butterworths.

Gee, Ellen M., and Susan A. McDaniel. 1991. "Pension politics and challenges: Retirement policy implications." *Canadian Public Policy* 17(4):456–472.

Gee, Ellen M., and Jean E. Veevers. 1990. "Religious involvement and life satisfaction in Canada." *Sociological Analysis* 51:387–394.

Geer, James, Julia Heiman, and Harold Leitenberg. 1984. *Human Sexuality.* Englewood Cliffs, NJ: Prentice-Hall.

Geertz, Clifford. 1968. "Religion as a cultural system." In *The Religious Situation.* Donald Cutler, ed. Boston: Beacon.

Gelles, R.J., and J.R. Conte. 1991. "Domestic violence and sexual abuse of children: A review of research in the eighties." In *Contemporary Families: Looking Forward, Looking Back.* A. Booth, ed. Minneapolis: National Council on Family Relations.

Gentleman, Judith. 1987. "Mexico after the oil boom: PRI management of the political impact of national disillusionment." In *Mexican Politics in Transition.* Judith Gentleman, ed. Boulder, CO: Westview.

Gerbner, George, and Larry Gross. 1976. "The scary world of TV's heavy viewer." *Psychology Today* 9(Apr.): 41–45, 89.

Gereffi, Gary. 1992. "Mexico's maquiladora industries and North American integration." In *North America Without Borders? Integrating Canada, the United States, and Mexico.* Stephen J. Randall, ed. Calgary: University of Calgary Press.

Gergen, K.J., and S. Worchel (eds.). 1980. *Social Exchange: Advances in Theory and Research.* New York: Plenum.

Gerlach, Luther P., and Virginia H. Hine. 1968. "Five factors crucial to the growth and spread of a modern religious movement." *Journal for the Scientific Study of Religion* 7:23–40.

Gerth, H., and C. Wright Mills (eds.). 1958. *From Max Weber: Essays in Sociology.* New York: Oxford University Press.

Ghorayshi, Parvin. 1989. "The indispensable nature of wives' work for the farm family enterprise." *Canadian Review of Sociology and Anthropology* 26:571–595.

Gibbins, Roger, J. Rick Ponting, and Gladys L. Symons. 1978. "Attitudes and ideology: Correlates of liberal attitudes towards the role of women." *Journal of Comparative Family Studies* 9:19–40.

Gibbs, Jack P., and Maynard Erickson. 1976. "Crime rates of American cities in an ecological context." *American Journal of Sociology* 82:605–620.

Gibson, Kevin J., and David K. Foot. 1993. "Population aging in the Canadian labour force: Changes and challenges." *Journal of Canadian Studies* 28(2): 59–74.

Gibson, R.C., and J.S. Jackson. 1987. "The health, physical functioning, and informal supports of the black elderly." *Milbank Quarterly* 65:421–454.

Giddens, A. 1973. *The Class Structure of the Advanced Societies.* London: Hutchinson.

Giddens, Anthony. 1980. *The Class Structure of the Advanced Societies.* 2nd edition. London: Hutchinson.

Giddens, Anthony. 1987. *Sociology.* 2nd edition. New York: Harcourt Brace Jovanovich.

Gidney, B., and W. Millar. 1990. *Inventing Secondary Education: The Rise of the High School in Nineteenth Century Ontario.* Kingston and Montreal: McGill–Queen's Press.

Giffen, P.J. 1966. "The revolving door: A functional interpretation." *Canadian Review of Sociology and Anthropology* 3(3):154–166.

Gillie, Oliver. 1979. "The great IQ fraud." *Atlas* (Feb.): 26–28.

Gilligan, Carol. 1982. *In a Different Voice.* Cambridge, MA: Harvard University Press.

Gillis, A.R. 1974. "Population density and social pathology: The case of building type, social allowance, and juvenile delinquency." *Social Forces* 53(2):306–314.

Gillis, A.R. 1977. "High-rise housing and psychological strain." *Journal of Health and Social Behavior* 18(4): 418–431.

Gillis, A.R. 1979a. "Coping with crowding: Television, patterns of activity, and adaptation to high-density environments." *Sociological Quarterly* 20:267–277.

Gillis, A.R. 1979b. "Household density and human crowding: Unravelling a non-linear relationship." *Journal of Population* 2(2):104–117.

Gillis, A.R. 1983. "Strangers next door: An analysis of density, diversity and scale in public housing projects." *Canadian Journal of Sociology* 8(1):1–20.

Gillis, A.R. 1984. "Violent crime, policing, and urbanization in nineteenth century France: An analysis of trends." Paper presented to the Social Science and History Association.

Gillis, A.R. 1985. "Domesticity, divorce, and deadly quarrels: A macro analysis." In *Critique and Explanation: Essays in Honor of Gwynne Nettler.* Timothy F. Hartnagel and Robert A. Silverman, eds. New Brunswick, NJ: Transaction.

Gillis, A.R. 1987a. "CMAs, submetro areas, and megalopolis: An examination of Montreal, Toronto, and Vancouver." Report submitted to Statistics Canada.

Gillis, A.R. 1987b. "Crime, punishment, and historical perspectives." *Sociological Forum* 2(3):602–609.

Gillis, A.R. 1989. "Crime and state surveillance in nineteenth-century France." *American Journal of Sociology* 95(2):259–278.

Gillis, A.R. 1994a. "Urbanization and crime, in historical context." In *Criminological Controversies.* J. Hagan, A.R. Gillis, and D. Brownfield, eds. Boulder: Westview.

Gillis, A.R. 1994b. "Repression, reaction, and policing." In *Criminological Controversies.* J. Hagan, A.R. Gillis, and D. Brownfield. Boulder: Westview.

Gillis, A.R. 1994c. "Literacy and the expression of violence in 19th-century France." (Journal submission.)

Gillis, A.R., and John Hagan. 1982. "Density, delinquency and design: Formal and informal control and the residential environment." *Criminology* 19(4): 514–529.

Gillis, A.R., and John Hagan. 1983. "Bystander apathy and the territorial imperative." *Sociological Inquiry* 53(4):448–460.

Gillis, A.R., and John Hagan. 1990. "Delinquent Samaritans: A study of group conflict, subcultural sentiment, and the willingness to intervene." *Journal of Research on Crime and Delinquency.*

Gillis, A.R., Madeline A. Richard, and John Hagan. 1986. "Ethnic susceptibility to crowding: An empirical analysis." *Environment and Behavior* 18(6):683–706.

Gillis, A.R., and Paul C. Whitehead. 1970. "The Halifax Jews: A community within a community." In *Minority Canadians: Immigrant Groups.* Jean Leonard Elliott, ed. Scarborough, ON: Prentice-Hall.

Ginzberg, Eli. 1982. "The mechanization of work." *Scientific American* 247(3):67–75.

Glaser, Barry G., and Anselm L. Strauss. 1971. *Status Passage.* Chicago: Aldine Atherton.

Glazer, Nathan, and Daniel P. Moynihan. 1963. *Beyond the Melting Pot.* Cambridge, MA: MIT Press.

Glazer, Nona. 1977. "Introduction to part two." In *Women in a Man-Made World.* N. Glazer and Helen Youngelson Waehrer, eds. 2nd edition. Chicago: Rand McNally.

Glenn, Evelyn Nakano. 1987. "Gender and the family." In *Analyzing Gender: A Handbook of Social Science Research.* Beth B. Hess and Myra Marx Ferree (eds.). Newbury Park, CA: Sage Publications.

Glick, P.C., and S.L. Lin. 1986. "More young adults are living with their parents: Who are they?" *Journal of Marriage and the Family* 48:107–112.

Glickman, Yaacov, and Alan Bardikoff. 1982. *The Treatment of the Holocaust in Canadian History and Social Science Textbooks.* Downsview, ON: B'nai Brith Canada.

Glock, Charles, Benjamin Ringer, and Earl Babbie. 1967. *To Comfort and to Challenge.* Berkeley, CA: University of California Press.

Glock, Charles, and Rodney Stark. 1965. *Religion and Society in Tension.* Chicago: Rand-McNally.

Godfrey, Stephen. "Artists Deserve a Hand." *Globe and Mail,* August 1, 1992, p. 1A.

Goetting, A. 1986. "The developmental tasks of siblingship over the life cycle." *Journal of Marriage and the Family* 48:703–714.

Goffman, Erving. 1959. *The Presentation of Self in Everyday Life.* Garden City, NY: Doubleday Anchor.

Goffman, Erving. 1963a. *Behavior in Public Places.* New York: Free Press.

Goffman, Erving. 1963b. *Stigma: Notes on the Management of Spoiled Identity.* Englewood Cliffs, NJ: Prentice-Hall.

Goffman, Erving. 1977. "The arrangement between the sexes." *Theory and Society* 4:301–331.

Gold, Deborah T. 1987. "Siblings in old age: Something special." *Canadian Journal on Aging* 6(3):199–215.

Gold, Gerald L. 1975. *St. Pascal.* Montreal: Holt, Rinehart and Winston.

Goldberg, Herb. 1976. *The Hazards of Being Male: Surviving the Myth of Masculine Privilege.* New York: Signet.

Goldberg, Michael A., and John Mercer. 1986. *The Myth of the North American City: Continentalism Challenged.* Vancouver: University of British Columbia Press.

Golden, Tim. 1992. "Mexicans dispute election as 5 other votes near." *The New York Times* (Aug. 2):A9.

Goldscheider, F.K., and L.J. Waite. 1991. *New Families, No Families? The Transformation of the American Home.* Berkeley: University of California Press.

Goldsen, Rose K. 1979. Book review of Marie Winn, *The Plug-in Drug: Television, Children and the Family.* In *American Journal of Sociology* 84:1054–1056.

Goldstein, Jay. 1981. "Has the popularity of Anglo-conformity waned?: A study of school naming events in Winnipeg, 1881–1979." *Canadian Ethnic Studies* 13: 52–60.

Goleman, Daniel. 1978. "Special abilities of the sexes: Do they begin in the brain?" *Psychology Today* (Nov.): 48–49, 51, 54–56, 58–59, 120.

Gomme, Ian. 1993. *The Shadow Line.* Toronto, ON: Harcourt Brace and Company Canada Inc.

Goode, William J. 1970 (3rd edition); 1963 (1st edition). *World Revolution and Family Patterns.* New York: Free Press.

Goodstadt, L. 1982. "China's one-child family: Policy and public response." *Population and Development Review,* 8:37–58.

Gordon, Milton M. 1964. *Assimilation in American Life.* New York: Oxford University Press.

Gordon, R.A. 1976. "Prevalence: The rare datum in delinquency measurement and its implications for the theory of delinquency." In *The Juvenile Justice System.* Malcolm Klein, ed. Beverly Hills, CA: Sage.

Gorsuch, Richard, and Daniel Aleshire. 1974. "Christian faith and ethnic prejudice: A review and interpretation of research." *Journal for the Scientific Study of Religion* 13:281–307.

Gould, Meredith, and Rochelle Kern-Daniels. 1977. "Toward a sociological theory of gender and sex." *American Sociologist* 12:182–189.

Gouldner, Alvin W. "The sociological as partisan: Sociology and the welfare state." *American Sociologist,* 3 (1963):103–117.

Gove, Walter R. 1973. "Sex, marital status, and mortality." *American Journal of Sociology* 79:45–67.

Gove, Walter R. 1975. "Labelling and mental illness: A critique." In *The Labelling of Deviance: Evaluating a Perspective.* Walter Gove, ed. New York: Halsted.

Gove, Walter R., Michael Hughes, and Omer R. Galle. 1979. "Overcrowding in the home: An empirical investigation of its possible consequences." *American Sociological Review* 44:59–80.

Gove, Walter R., and Jeanette Tudor. 1973. "Adult sex roles and mental illness." *American Journal of Sociology* 78:812–835.

Goyder, John C. 1983. "Ethnicity and class identity: The case of French- and English-speaking Canadians." *Ethnic and Racial Studies* 6:72–89.

Goyder, John C., and James E. Curtis. 1979. "Occupational mobility in Canada over four generations." In *Social Stratification: Canada.* J. Curtis and W. Scott, eds. 2nd edition. Scarborough, ON: Prentice-Hall.

Goyder, John C., and Peter C. Pineo. 1979. "Social class self-identification." In *Social Stratification: Canada.* J. Curtis and W. Scott, eds. 2nd edition. Scarborough, ON: Prentice-Hall.

Grabb, Edward G. 1992. "Social stratification." In *Introduction to Sociology: A Canadian Focus,* James J. Teevan, ed. 4th edition. Scarborough, ON: Prentice-Hall.

Graff, Harvey J. 1975. "Towards a meaning of literacy: Literacy and social structure in Hamilton, Ontario, 1861." In *Education and Social Change: Themes from Ontario's Past.* Michael B. Katz and Paul H. Mattingly, eds. New York: New York University Press.

Granato, Stephanie, and Aida Mostcoff. 1990. "The class structure of Mexico, 1895–1980." In *Society and Economy in Mexico.* J.W. Wilkes, ed. Los Angeles: UCLA Latin American Publications.

Granatstein, J.L., and K. McNaught (eds.). 1991. *"English Canada" Speaks Out.* Toronto: Doubleday.

Grauerholz, Elizabeth, and Bernice A. Pescosolido. 1989. "Gender representation in children's literature: 1900–1984." *Gender and Society* 3:113–125.

Gray Report. 1972. *Foreign Direct Investment in Canada.* Ottawa: Supply and Services.

Grayson, J.P., and L.M. Grayson. 1978. "The Canadian literary elite: A socio-historical perspective." *Canadian Journal of Sociology* 3(3):291–308.

Greeley, Andrew. 1972. *The Denominational Society.* Glenview, IL: Scott, Foresman.

Greeley, Andrew. 1989. *Religious Change in America.* Cambridge, MA: Harvard University Press.

Greeley, Andrew. 1991. "American exceptionalism: The religious phenomenon." In *Is America Different? A New Look at American Exceptionalism.* Byron E. Shafer, ed. Oxford: Clarendon Press.

Green, Edward. 1961. *Judicial Attitudes in Sentencing.* London: Macmillan.

Green, Richard. 1974. *Sexual Identity Conflict in Children and Adults.* Baltimore: Penguin.

Greenberg, David. 1981. *Crime and Capitalism.* Palo Alto, CA: Mayfield.

Greenfield, Patricia Marks. 1984. *Mind and Media: The Effects of Television, Video Games, and Computers.* Cambridge, MA: Harvard University Press.

Greenglass, Esther R. 1982. *A World of Difference: Gender Roles in Perspective.* Toronto: Wiley.

Greenglass, Esther R. 1985. "A social-psychological view of marriage for women." *International Journal of Women's Studies* 8:24–31.

Greenhalgh, S. 1986. "Shifts in China's population policy, 1984–1986." *Population and Development Review* 12:491–515.

Gregg, Allan, and Michael Posner. 1990. *The Big Picture.* Toronto: Macfarlane Walter & Ross.

Griffin, John Howard. 1961. *Black Like Me.* Boston: Houghton-Mifflin.

Grindstaff, Carl F. 1975. "The baby bust: Changes in fertility patterns in Canada." *Canadian Studies in Population* 2:15–22.

Grossman, Brian A. 1969. *The Prosecutor.* Toronto: University of Toronto Press.

Guberman, Connie, and Margie Wolfe (eds.). 1985. *No Safe Place: Violence Against Women and Children.* Toronto: Women's Press.

Guest, A. 1969. "The applicability of the Burgess Zonal Hypothesis to urban Canada." *Demography* 6: 271–277.

Guillemard, Anne-Marie. 1977. "The call to activity among the old: Rehabilitation or regimentation?" In *Canadian Gerontological Collection* (Vol. I). Blossom T. Wigdor, ed. Winnipeg: Canadian Association on Gerontology.

Guillemard, Anne-Marie. 1980. *La vieillesse et l'Etat.* Paris: Presses Universitaires de France.

Guindon, Hubert. 1975. "Social unrest, social class and Quebec's bureaucratic revolution." In *Prophecy and Protest*. S.D. Clark et al., eds. Toronto: Gage.

Gunderson, Morley. 1976. "Work patterns." In *Opportunity for Choice: A Goal for Women in Canada*. Gail C.A. Cook, ed. Ottawa: Information Canada.

Gunderson, Morley 1983. *Economics of Poverty and Income Distribution*. Toronto: Butterworths.

Guppy, Neil. 1984. "Access to higher education in Canada." *Canadian Journal of Higher Education* 14: 79–93.

Guppy, Neil, Doug Balson, and Susan Vellutini. 1987. "Women and higher education in Canadian society." In *Women and Education: A Canadian Perspective*. Jane Gaskell and Arlene McLaren, eds. Calgary: Detselig.

Guppy, Neil, Paulina D. Mikicich, and Ravi Pendakur. 1984. "Changing patterns of educational inequality in Canada." *Canadian Journal of Sociology* 9: 319–331.

Guppy, N., and K. Pendakur. 1989. "The effects of gender and parental education on participation within post-secondary education in the 1970's and 1980's. *Canadian Journal of Higher Education* 19(1):49–62.

Gurr, Ted. 1970. *Why Men Rebel*. Princeton: Princeton University Press.

Gurr, Ted Robert. 1981. "Historical trends in violent crime: A critical review of the evidence." In *Crime and Justice: An Annual Review of Research*. N. Morris and M. Tonry, eds. Chicago: University of Chicago Press.

Gusfield, Joseph R. 1963. *Symbolic Crusade: Status Politics and the American Temperance Movement*. Urbana, IL: University of Illinois Press.

Guterman, S.S. 1969. "In defence of Wirth." *American Journal of Sociology* 74(5):492–499.

Gutman, Gloria M. 1980. "The elderly at home and in retirement housing: A comparative study of health problems, functional difficulties, and support service needs." In *Aging in Canada: Social Perspectives*. Victor W. Marshall, ed. Toronto: Fitzhenry and Whiteside.

Haas, Jack, Victor Marshall, and William Shaffir. 1981. "Initiation into medicine: Neophyte uncertainty and the ritual ordeal of professionalization." In *Work in the Canadian Context*. Katherina L.P. Lundy and Barbara D. Warne, eds. Toronto: Butterworths.

Haas, Jack, and William Shaffir. 1992. "Socialization of medical students." *Everyday Life: A Reader*. Lorne Tepperman and James Curtis, eds. Toronto: McGraw-Hill Ryerson.

Hacker, Helen Mayer. 1951. "Women as a minority group." *Social Factors* 30:60–69.

Hadden, Jeffrey. 1969. *The Gathering Storm in the Churches*. Garden City, NJ: Rutgers University Press.

Hagan, John. 1974a. "Extra-legal attributes and criminal sentencing: An assessment of sociological viewpoints." *Law and Society Review* 8(3):357–383.

Hagan, John. 1974b. "Criminal justice and native people: A study of incarceration in a Canadian province." *Canadian Review of Sociology and Anthropology* (Aug): 220–236.

Hagan, John. 1975. "Parameters of criminal prosecution: An application of path analysis to a problem of criminal justice." *Journal of Criminal Law, Criminology, and Police Science* 65(4):536–544.

Hagan, John. 1977. "Finding discrimination: A question of meaning." *Ethnicity* 4:167–176.

Hagan, John. 1982. "The corporate advantage: The involvement of individual and organizational victims in the criminal justice process." *Social Forces* 60(4): 993–1022.

Hagan, John. 1984. *The Disreputable Pleasures: Crime and Deviance in Canada*. 2nd edition. Toronto: McGraw-Hill Ryerson.

Hagan, John. 1985. "Toward a structural theory of crime, race and gender: The Canadian case." *Crime and Delinquency* 31:129–146.

Hagan, John. 1991. "Destiny and drift: Subcultural preferences, status attainments and the risks and rewards of youth." *American Sociological Review* 56: 567–582.

Hagan, John, and Celesta Albonetti. 1982. "Race, class and the perception of criminal injustice in America." *American Journal of Sociology* 88:329–355.

Hagan, John, and Kirsten Bumiller. 1983. "Making sense of sentencing: A review and critique of sentencing research." In *Research on Sentencing: The Search for Reform*. Alfred Blumstein et al., eds. Washington, DC: National Academy Press.

Hagan, John, A.R. Gillis, and J. Chan. 1978. "Explaining official delinquency: A spatial study of class, conflict, and control." *Sociological Quarterly* 19:386–398.

Hagan, John, A.R. Gillis, and John Simpson. 1985. "The class structure of gender and delinquency: Toward a power-control theory of common delinquent behavior." *American Journal of Sociology* 90:1151–1178.

Hagan, John, A.R. Gillis, and John Simpson. 1987. "Class in the household: A power-control theory of gender and delinquency." *American Journal of Sociology* 92:788–816.

Hagan, John, and Jeffrey Leon. 1977. "Rediscovering delinquency: Social history, political ideology and the sociology of law." *American Sociological Review* 42:587.

Hagan, John, Ilene Nagel, and Celesta Albonetti. 1980. "The differential sentencing of white-collar offenders in ten federal district courts." *American Sociological Review* 45:802–820.

Hagan, John, and Alberto Palloni. 1990. "The social reproduction of a criminal class in working-class London, circa 1950–1980." *American Journal of Sociology* 96:265–299.

Hagan, John, and Patricia Parker. 1985. "White collar crime and punishment: The class structure and legal sanctioning of securities violations." *American Sociological Review* 50:302–316.

Hagestad, Gunhild O. 1982. "Life-phase analysis." In *Research Instruments in Social Gerontology: Clinical and Social Psychology* (Vol. 1). David J. Mangen and Warren A. Peterson, eds. Minneapolis: University of Minnesota Press.

Hagestad, Gunhild O., and Bernice L. Neugarten.

1985. "Age and the life course." In *Handbook of Aging and the Social Sciences*. Robert H. Binstock et al., eds. 2nd edition. New York: Van Nostrand Reinhold.

Hajnal, John. 1965. "European marriage patterns in historical perspective." In *Population in History: Essays in Historical Demography*. D.V. Glass and D.E.C. Eversley, eds. London: Edward Arnold.

Hall, Edward T. 1962. "Our silent language." *Americas* 14(Feb.):6.

Hall, Peter M. 1972. "A symbolic interactionist analysis of politics." In *Perspectives in Political Sociology*. Andrew Effrat, ed. Indianapolis, IN: Bobbs-Merrill.

Hall, Tony. 1989. "What are we? Chopped liver? Aboriginal affairs in the constitutional politics of Canada in the 1980s." In *The Meech Lake Primer*. Michael D. Behiels, ed. Ottawa: University of Ottawa Press.

Haller, A., and D. Bills. 1979. "Occupational prestige hierarchies: Theory and evidence." *Contemporary Sociology* 8:721–734.

Haller, Mark. 1970. "Urban crime and criminal justice: The Chicago case." *Journal of American History* 57:619–635.

Hamilton, Richard F. 1982. *Who Voted for Hitler?* Princeton, NJ: Princeton University Press.

Hammer, Muriel. 1963–64. "Influence of small social networks on factors of mental hospital admission." *Human Organization* 22(Winter):243–251.

Hardee-Cleaveland, K., and J. Banister. 1988. "Fertility policy and implementation in China, 1986–1988." *Population and Development Review* 14:245–286.

Hardin, Herschel. 1974. *A Nation Unaware: The Canadian Economic Culture*. Vancouver: J.J. Douglas.

Harding, Deborah, and Emily Nett. 1984. "Women and rock music." *Atlantis* 10:60–76.

Hardwick, W.G. 1971. "Vancouver: The emergence of a 'core-ring' urban pattern." In *Geographical Approaches to Canadian Problems*. R.L. Gentilcore, ed. Scarborough, ON: Prentice-Hall.

Hareven, Tamara K. 1978. *Transitions: The Family and the Life Course in Historical Perspective*. New York: Academic.

Hareven, Tamara K. 1987. "Family history at the crossroads." *Journal of Family History* 12:iv–xxiii.

Hargreaves, D.H. 1967. *Social Relations in a Secondary School*. London: Routledge and Kegan Paul.

Harlow, Harry F. 1959. "Love in infant monkeys." *Scientific American* 200(June):68–74.

Harlow, Harry F., and Margaret Harlow. 1962. "Social deprivation in monkeys." *Scientific American* 207 (Nov.):136–146.

Harrington, M. 1972. *Socialism*. New York: Saturday Review.

Harris, Chauncy D., and Edward L. Ullman. 1945. "The nature of cities." *Annals of the American Academy of Political and Social Science* 242(Nov.):7–17.

Harris, Louis, et al. 1975. *The Myth and Reality of Aging in America*. Washington, DC: National Council on the Aging.

Harris, Marvin. 1978. *Cannibals and Kings: The Origins of Cultures*. New York: Vintage Books.

Harris, Marvin. 1981. *America Now: Why Nothing Works*, New York: Simon and Schuster.

Harrison, Kathryn, and G. Hoberg. 1991. "Setting the environmental agenda in Canada and the United States: The case of dioxin and radon." *Canadian Journal of Political Science* 24(1):3–28.

Harrison, Paul. 1959. *Authority and Power in the Free Church Tradition: A Social Case Study of the American Baptist Convention*. Princeton, NJ: Princeton University Press.

Hartley, Ruth E. 1959. "Sex-role pressures in the socialization of the male child." *Psychological Reports* 5: 457–468.

Hartz, Louis. 1964. *The Founding of New Societies*. New York: Harcourt, Brace and World.

Harvey, David. 1975. "The political economy of urbanization in advanced capitalist societies: The case of the United States." In *The Social Economy of Cities*. Gary Geppert and Harold M. Rose, eds. Beverly Hills, CA: Sage.

Harvey, David. 1976. "Labor, capital, and class struggle around the built environment in advanced capitalist societies." *Politics and Society* 265–295.

Harvey, Edward. 1974. *Educational Systems and the Labour Market*. Toronto: Longman.

Harvey, Edward, and Jos. Lennards. 1973. *Key Issues in Higher Education*. Toronto: Ontario Institute for Studies in Education.

Hatchett, S.J., D.L. Cochran, and J.S. Jackson. 1991. "Family life." In *Life in Black America*. J.S. Jackson, ed. Newbury Park, CA: Sage.

Hawthorne, H.B., et al. 1967. *A Survey of Contemporary Indians of Canada* 1 & 2. Ottawa: Indian Affairs.

Hayford, Alison. 1987. "Outlines of the family." In *Family Matters: Sociology and Contemporary Canadian Families*. Karen L. Anderson et al., eds. Toronto: Methuen.

Heald, Tim. 1982. "A job well done." *Today* (Feb. 6): 7–11.

Health and Welfare Canada. 1990. *Background Paper on Women and Tobacco (1987) and Update (1990)*. Ottawa: Minister of Supply and Services.

Health and Welfare Canada 1992. *Smoking behaviour of Canadians: A National Alcohol and Other Drugs Survey (1989) Report*. Ottawa: Minister of Supply and Services.

Hedley, R. Alan. 1980. "Work values: A test of the conveyance and cultural diversity theses." *International Journal of Comparative Sociology* 21(1–2):100–109.

Hedley, R. Alan. 1982. "Work, life, and the pursuit of happiness: A study of Australian industrial workers." *Journal of Industrial Relations* 23(3):397–404.

Hedley, R. Alan. 1984. "Social generalizations: Biases and solutions." *International Journal of Comparative Sociology* 25:159–172.

Hedley, R. Alan. 1984a. "Work–nonwork contexts and orientations to work: A crucial test." *Work and Occupations* 11(3):353–376.

Hedley, R. Alan. 1992a. "Industrialization in less developed countries." In *Encyclopedia of Sociology*, Vol. 2.

Edgar F. and Marie L. Borgatta, eds. New York: Macmillan.

Hedley, R. Alan. 1992b. *Making a Living: Technology and Change.* New York: HarperCollins.

Hedley, R. Alan. 1992c. "Transnational corporations." In *Encyclopedia of Sociology*, Vol. 4. Edgar F. and Marie L. Borgatta, eds. New York: Macmillan.

Hedley, R. Alan, and Susan M. Adams. 1982. "Mom in the labour force — Verdict: not guilty!" *Perception* 6(1):28–29.

Hedley, R. Alan, R. Dubin, and T.C. Taveggia. 1980. "The quality of working life, gender, and occupational status: A cross-national comparison." In *The Quality of Life.* A. Szalai and F.M. Andrews, eds. Beverly Hills, CA: Sage.

Hemsworth, Wade. "Poverty rate climbing again." *The Globe and Mail.* December 1, 1992:A3.

Hendricks, Jon. 1981. "The elderly in society: Beyond modernization." Paper presented to the Gerontological Society of America and the Canadian Association on Gerontology.

Henley, Nancy M. 1975. "Power, sex, and nonverbal communication." In *Language and Sex: Difference and Dominance.* Barrie Thorne and N. Henley, eds. Rowley, MA: Newbury House.

Henry, F., and E. Ginzberg. 1988. "Racial discrimination in employment." In *Social Inequality in Canada.* J Curtis et al., eds. Scarborough, ON: Prentice-Hall.

Henry, Louis. 1961. "Some data on natural fertility." *Eugenics Quarterly* 8:81–91.

Henschel (Ambert), Anne-Marie. 1973. *Sex Structure.* Don Mills, ON: Longman.

Herberg, Edward N. 1988. *Ethnic Groups in Canada: Adaptations and Transitions.* Toronto: Nelson.

Herberg, Edward N. 1990. "The ethno-racial socioeconomic hierarchy in Canada: Theory and analysis of the new vertical mosaic." *International Journal of Comparative Sociology* 31:206–221.

Herberg, Will. 1955. *Protestant, Catholic, Jew.* New York: Doubleday.

Herberg, Will. 1960. *Protestant, Catholic, Jew.* Revised edition. New York: Doubleday.

Herskowitz, M. 1952. "Population size, economic surplus, and social leisure." In *Economic Anthropology.* Melville Herskowitz, ed. New York: Alfred A. Knopf.

Hetherington, E. Mavis, and Ross D. Parke. 1979. *Child Psychology: A Contemporary Viewpoint.* 2nd edition. New York: McGraw-Hill.

Hewitt, C. 1977. "The effect of political democracy on equality in industrial societies: A cross-national comparison." *American Sociological Review* 42:450–464.

Hewitt, W.E. 1992. "The social justice program of the Canadian Catholic church: An international case-comparative analysis." *Sociological Analysis* 53:141–158.

Hexham, Irving, Raymond Currie, and Joan Townsend. 1985. "The new religions." *New Canadian Encyclopedia.* Edmonton: Hurtig.

Hexham, Irving, Raymond Currie, and Joan Townsend. 1988. "The new religions." *The New Canadian Encyclopedia.* 2nd edition. Edmonton: Hurtig.

Hill, Clifford. 1971. "From church to sect: West Indian religious sect development in Britain." *Journal for the Scientific Study of Religion* 10:114–123.

Hill, W., and J. Scanzoni. 1982. "An approach for assessing marital decision-making processes." *Journal of Marriage and the Family* 44:927–942.

Hiller, Harry H. 1976. "The sociology of religion in the Canadian context." In *Introduction to Canadian Society.* G.N. Ramu and Stuart D. Johnson, eds. Toronto: Macmillan.

Hiller, Harry H. 1986. *Canadian Society.* Scarborough, ON: Prentice-Hall.

Hindelang, M.J. 1978. "Race and involvement in common law personal crimes." *American Sociological Review* 43:93–109.

Hindelang, M.J. 1979. "Sex differences in criminal activity." *Social Problems* 27(2):143–156.

Hindelang, Michael, Travis Hirschi, and Joseph Weis. 1981. *Measuring Delinquency.* Beverly Hills, CA: Sage.

Hirschi, Travis, 1969. *Causes of Delinquency.* Berkeley, CA: University of California Press.

Hobart, Charles. 1979. "Courtship process: Premarital sex." In *The Canadian Family.* G.N. Ramu, ed. Toronto: Holt, Rinehart and Winston.

Hobart, Charles. 1983. "Marriage or cohabitation." In *Marriage and Divorce in Canada.* K. Ishwaran, ed. Toronto: Methuen.

Hobart, Charles. 1988. "Relationships in remarried families." *Canadian Journal of Sociology* 13:261–282.

Hobart, C.W. 1989. "Premarital sexuality." In *Marriage and the Family in Canada Today.* G.N. Ramu, ed. Scarborough, ON: Prentice-Hall.

Hobart, Charles, and C. Brant. 1966. "Eskimo education Danish and Canadian: A comparison." *Canadian Review of Sociology and Anthropology* 3:47–66.

Hochschild, Arlie Russell. 1973. *The Unexpected Community.* Englewood Cliffs, NJ: Prentice-Hall.

Hochschild, Arlie Russell. 1975. "Disengagement theory: A critique and proposal." *American Sociological Review* 40(5):553–569.

Hochschild, Arlie. 1989. *The Second Shift: Working Parents and the Revolution at Home.* New York: Viking Penguin.

Hoffman, L.W. 1987. "The effects on children of maternal and paternal employment." In *Families and Work.* N. Gerstel and H. Gross, eds. Philadelphia: Temple University Press.

Hofstede, Geert. 1980. *Culture's Consequences: International Differences in Work-Related Values.* Beverly Hills, CA: Sage.

Hogan, Dennis P. 1981. *Transitions and Social Change: The Early Lives of American Men.* New York: Academic.

Hogarth, John. 1971. *Sentencing as a Human Process.* Toronto: University of Toronto Press.

Hoge, Dean. 1976. *Division in the Protestant House.* Philadelphia: Westminster Press.

Hoge, Dean, and David Roozen. 1979. "Some sociological conclusions about church trends." In *Understanding Church Growth and Decline: 1950–1978.* Dean

Hoge and David Roozen (eds.). New York: Pilgrim Press.

Holmes, Janelle, and Eliane Leslau Silverman. 1992. *We're Here, Listen to Us!: A Survey of Young Women in Canada.* Ottawa: Canadian Advisory Council on the Status of Women.

Holsti, Ole R. 1969. *Content Analysis for the Social Sciences and Humanities.* Reading, MA: Addison-Wesley.

Holt, John B. 1940. "Holiness religion: Cultural shock and social reorganization." *American Sociological Review* 5(Oct.):740–747.

hooks, bell. 1981. *Ain't I a Woman? Black Women and Feminism.* Boston: South End Press.

Hoppock, Robert. 1935. *Job Satisfaction.* New York: Harper and Brothers.

Horan, P. 1978. "Is status attainment research atheoretical?" *American Sociological Review* 43:534–540.

Hornung, Rick. 1991. *One Nation Under the Gun: Inside the Mohawk Civil War.* Toronto: Stoddart.

Horowitz, A. 1985. "Family caregiving to the frail elderly." In *Annual Review of Gerontology and Geriatrics.* (Vol. 4). C. Eisdorfer, ed. New York: Springer.

Horowitz, Gad. 1968. "Conservatism, liberalism, and socialism in Canada: An interpretation." In his *Canadian Labour in Politics.* Toronto: University of Toronto Press.

Horton, Paul B., and Chester L. Hunt. 1972. *Sociology.* 3rd edition. New York: McGraw-Hill.

Hostetler, John A., and Gertrude Enders Huntington. 1967. *The Hutterites in North America.* New York: Holt, Rinehart and Winston.

Houghland, James G., and James R. Wood. 1979. "Inner circles in local churches." *Sociological Analysis* 40:226–239.

House, J.D. 1985. "The Don Quixote of Canadian politics?: Power in and power over Newfoundland society." *Canadian Journal of Sociology* 10(2):171–188.

Houston, Barbara. 1987. "Should public education be gender-free?" In *Women and Men: Interdisciplinary Readings on Gender.* Greta Hofmann Nemiroff, ed. Toronto: Fitzhenry and Whiteside.

Howe, Florence. 1974. "Sexual stereotypes and the public schools." In *Women and Success: The Anatomy of Achievement.* Ruth B, Kundsin, ed. New York: William Morrow.

Hoyt, Homer. 1939. *The Structure and Growth of Residential Neighborhoods in American Cites.* Washington, DC: Federal Housing Authority.

Huber, Joan. 1976. "Toward a socio-technological theory of the women's movement." *Social Problems* 23:371–388.

Hughes, David R., and Evelyn Kallen. 1974. *The Anatomy of Racism: Canadian Dimensions.* Montreal: Harvest House.

Hughes, Everett C. 1943. *French Canada in Transition.* Chicago: University of Chicago Press.

Hughes, Everett C. 1971. *The Sociological Eye: Selected Papers.* Chicago: Aldine Atherton.

Hughes, Everett C., et al. (eds.). 1950. *Race and Culture: Vol. 1, The Collected Papers of Robert Ezra Park.* Glencoe, IL: Free Press.

Huizinga, Johan. 1924. *The Waning of the Middle Ages.* New York: St. Martin's.

Hunsberger, Bruce. 1980. "A reexamination of the antecedents of apostasy." *Review of Religious Research* 21:158–170.

Hunsberger, Bruce. 1984. "Religious socialization, apostasy, and the impact of family background." *Journal for the Scientific Study of Religion* 23:239–251.

Hunter, Alfred A. 1986. *Class Tells: On Social Inequality in Canada.* 2nd edition. Toronto: Butterworths.

Hunter, Alfred A. 1988. "Formal education and initial employment: Unravelling the relationships between schooling and skills over time." *American Sociological Review* 53:753–765.

Hunter, Alfred A. 1993. "The changing distribution of income." In *Social Inequality in Canada: Patterns, Problems, Policies.* James Curtis, Edward Grabb and Neil Guppy, eds. 2nd edition. Scarborough: Prentice-Hall.

Hunter, Alfred A., and Jean McKenzie Leiper. Forthcoming. "On formal education, skills and earnings: The role of educational certificates in earnings determination." *Canadian Journal of Sociology.*

Hyde, Janet. 1979. *Understanding Human Sexuality.* New York: McGraw-Hill.

Hyde, Janet Shibley. 1990. "Meta-analysis and the psychology of gender differences." *Signs* 16:55–73.

Iannaccone, Laurence R. 1990. "Religious practice: A human capital approach." *Journal for the Scientific Study of Religion* 29:297–314.

Inciardi, James. 1975. *Careers in Crime.* Chicago: Rand McNally.

Inglehart, Ronald. 1977. *The Silent Revolution: Changing Values and Political Styles Among Western Publics.* Princeton, NJ: Princeton University Press.

Inglehart, Ronald. 1981. "Post-materialism in an environment of insecurity." *American Political Science Review* 74(4):880–900.

Inglehart, Ronald. 1990. *Culture Shift in Advanced Industrial Society.* Princeton, NJ: Princeton University Press.

Inglehart, Ronald, et al. 1990. *World Values Survey, 1981–1983: Computer File and Codebook.* Ann Arbor: Inter-University Consortium for Political and Social Research, University of Michigan.

Inglis, J., and J. Lawson. 1981. "Sex differences in the effects of unilateral brain damage on intelligence." *Science* 212:693–695.

Ingoldsby, Bron B. 1991. "Latin American family: Familism vs. machismo." *Journal of Comparative Family Studies* 22:57–62.

Inkeles, A., and D.H. Smith. 1974. *Becoming Modern: Individual Change in Six Developing Countries.* Cambridge, MA: Harvard University Press.

Innis, Harold A. 1930. *The Fur Trade in Canada: An Introduction to Canadian Economic History.* Toronto: Oxford University Press.

Innis, Harold A. 1940. *The Cod Fisheries: The History of* *an International Economy.* New Haven, CT: Yale University Press.

Innis, Harold A. 1951. *The Bias of Communication.* Toronto: University of Toronto Press.

Irving, John. 1959. *The Social Credit Movement in Alberta.* Toronto: University of Toronto Press.

Ishwaran, K. (ed.). 1976. *The Canadian Family.* Revised edition. Toronto: Holt, Rinehart and Winston.

Ishwaran, K. (ed). 1980. *Canadian Families: Ethnic Variations.* Toronto: McGraw-Hill Ryerson.

Jackman, R. 1975. *Politics and Social Equality.* New York: Wiley.

Jackson, John D. 1975. *Community and Conflict: A Study of French–English Relations in Ontario.* Montreal: Holt, Rinehart and Winston.

Jacobs, Jane. 1961. *The Death and Life of Great American Cities.* New York: Random House.

Jacobs, Jane. 1980. *The Question of Separatism.* New York: Random House.

Jacobs, Jane. 1982. *Canadian Cities and Sovereignty Association.* Toronto: Canadian Broadcasting Corporation.

Jacot, Martine. 1992. "Les Latinos-américains réclament le retour des Yankees." *Le Devoir* (July 21): (originally published in *Le Monde*).

Jalée, P. 1968. *The Pillage of the Third World.* New York: Monthly Review.

James, P. 1979. *Population Malthus.* London: Routledge and Kegan Paul.

Jencks, C. 1972. *Inequality.* New York: Basic.

Jenkins, J. Craig. 1981. "Sociopolitical movements." In *The Handbook of Political Behavior.* Samuel L. Long, ed. New York: Plenum.

Jensen, G.F., J.H. Strauss, and V.W. Harris. 1977. "Crime, delinquency and the American Indian." *Human Organization* 36:252–257.

Johnson, Harry M. 1960. *Sociology: A Systematic Introduction.* New York: Harcourt, Brace and World.

Jones, Jack. 1992. *Let Me Take You Down: Inside the Mind of Mark David Chapman, the Man Who Killed John Lennon.* New York: Villiard.

Joseph, Alun E., and Anne Martin Matthews. 1993. "Growing old in aging communities." *Journal of Canadian Studies* 28(2):14–29.

Jourard, Sidney M. 1964. *The Transparent Self.* New York: Van Nostrand Reinhold.

Joy, Richard J. 1972. *Languages in Conflict.* Toronto: McClelland and Stewart.

Juteau, Danielle, and Louis Maheo. 1989. "Sociology and Sociologist in Francophone Quebec: Science and Politics." *The Canadian Review of Sociology and Anthropology,* 26:363–393.

Kagan, Jerome. 1984. *The Nature of the Child.* New York: Basic.

Kagan, J., Hosken, B., & Watson, S. 1961. Child's symbolic conceptualization of parents. *Child Development,* 32, 625–636.

Kahn, Robert L. 1975. "In search of the Hawthorne effect." In *Man and Work in Society.* E.L. Cass and F.G. Zimmer, eds. Toronto: Van Nostrand Reinhold.

Kalbach, Warren E. 1980. "Historical and generational perspectives of ethnic residential segregation in Toronto, Canada: 1851–1971." Research paper 118. Toronto: University of Toronto, Centre for Urban and Community Studies.

Kalbach, Warren E., and Wayne W. McVey. 1979. *The Demographic Bases of Canadian Society.* 2nd edition. Toronto: McGraw-Hill Ryerson.

Kalbach, Warren E., and M.A. Richard. 1991. *Cross-Cultural Variations in the Evolution of the Canadian Family.* Report prepared for the Review of Demography and Its Implications for Economic and Social Policy. Ottawa: Health and Welfare Canada.

Kalish, Richard A. 1982. *Late Adulthood: Perspectives on Human Development.* Monterey, CA: Brooks/Cole.

Kallen, Horace M. 1924. *Culture and Democracy in the United States.* New York: Liverright.

Kalmijn, M. 1991. "Shifting boundaries: Trends in religious and educational homogamy." *American Sociological Review* 56:786–800.

Kamieniecki, Sheldon. 1991. "Political mobilization, agenda building and international environmental policy." *Journal of International Affairs* 44(2):339–358.

Kandel, Denise B. 1978. "Homophily, selection, and socialization in adolescent friendships." *American Journal of Sociology* 84:427–436.

Karoly, Lynn A. 1992. "The trend in inequality among families, individuals, and workers in the United States." *In Uneven Tides: Rising Inequality in America.* Sheldon Danziger and Peter Gottschalk, eds. New York: Russell Sage.

Katz, Fred E. 1967. "Explaining informal work groups in complex organizations: The case for autonomy." In *Readings in Industrial Sociology.* W.A. Faunce, ed. New York: Appleton-Century-Crofts.

Katz, Jack. 1988. *Seductions of Crime: Moral and Sensual Attractions for Doing Evil.* New York: Basic.

Katz, M. 1975a. *Bureaucracy and Schools.* New York: Praeger.

Katz, Michael. 1975b. *The People of Hamilton West: Family and Class in a Mid-Nineteenth Century City.* Cambridge, MA: Harvard university Press.

Keating, Norah C., and Priscilla Cole. 1980. "What do I do with him 24 hours a day?: Changes in the housewife role after retirement." *Gerontologist* 20(1): 84–89.

Keating, Norah C., and Judith Marshall. 1980. "The process of retirement: The rural self employed." *Gerontologist* 20(4):437–443.

Keith, Jennie. 1982. *Old People as People.* Toronto: Little, Brown.

Kelly, Kevin, Otis Port, James Treece, Gail DeGeorge, and Zachary Schiller. 1992. "Learning from Japan." *Business Week* (Jan. 27):52–60.

Kelly, W., and N. Kelly. 1976. *Policing in Canada.* Toronto: Macmillan.

Kelner, M. 1970. "Ethnic penetration into Toronto's elite structure." *Canadian Review of Sociology and Anthropology* 7:128–137.

Kemper, Theodore David. 1974. "On the nature and

purpose of ascription." *American Sociological Review* 39:844–853.

Kendig, Hal L. 1986. "Intergenerational exchange." In *Ageing and Families: A Social Networks Perspective*. Hal L. Kendig, ed. Boston: Allen and Unwin.

Kennedy, Michael. 1986. "Measuring Canada's international competitiveness." *Quarterly Economic Review* (Dec.):37–45.

Kerckhoff, A. 1990. *Getting Started: Transition to Adulthood in Great Britain*. Boulder, CO: Westview.

Kernaghan, Kenneth. 1982. "Politics, administration, and Canada's aging population." *Canadian Public Policy* 8(1):66–79.

Kerr, Clark, et al. 1964; 1960. *Industrialism and Industrial Man*. Oxford: Basil Blackwell.

Kerr, Donald. 1968. "Metropolitan dominance in Canada." In *Canada: A Sociological Profile*. W.E. Mann, ed. Toronto: Copp Clark.

Kessler, Suzanne J., and Wendy McKenna. 1978. *Gender: An Ethnomethodological Approach*. New York: John Wiley.

Kesterton, Michael. "Social studies." *Globe and Mail*, July 22, 1992, p. 14A.

Kimmel, Michael S. (ed.). 1987. *Changing Men: New Directions in Research on Men and Masculinity*. Newbury Park, CA: Sage.

Kingston, Anne. 1989. "When marital status is a dubious asset." *Financial Times* (Feb. 13):35.

Kirkpatrick, Clifford. 1949. "Religion and humanitarianism: A study of institutional implications." *Psychological Monographs* 63, 9.

Kitschelt, Herbert. 1987. *The Logic of Party Formation: Ecological Politics in Belgium and West Germany*. Ithaca, NY: Cornell University Press.

Kliebard, H.M. 1986. *The Struggle for the American Curriculum 1893–1958*. Boston: Routledge and Kegan Paul.

Knipscheer, Kees, and Anton Bevers. 1985. "Older parents and their middle-aged children: Symmetry or asymmetry in their relationship." *Canadian Journal on Aging* 4(3):145–159.

Knodel, J., A. Chamratrithirong, and N. Debavalya. 1987. *Thailand's Reproductive Revolution*. Madison, WI: University of Wisconsin Press.

Knodel, J., and E. van de Walle. 1986. "Lessons from the past: Policy implications of historical fertility studies." In *The Decline of Fertility in Europe*. A.J. Coale and S.C. Watkins (eds.) Princeton, NJ: Princeton University Press.

Knotterus, J. 1987. "Status attainment research and its image of society." *American Sociological Review* 52:1.

Kohlberg, Lawrence. 1976. "Moral stages and moralization: The cognitive-developmental approach." In *Moral Development and Behavior*. T. Lickona, ed. New York: Holt, Rinehart and Winston.

Kohn, Melvin L. 1977. *Class and Conformity*. 2nd edition. Homewood, IL: Dorsey.

Komarovsky, Mirra. 1946. "Cultural contradictions and sex roles." *American Journal of Sociology* 52:184–189.

Kome, Penney. 1982. *Somebody Has To Do It: Whose Work Is Housework?* Toronto: McClelland and Stewart.

Kotelchuck, M. 1976. "The infant's relationship to the father: Experimental evidence." In M.E. Lamb (Ed.), *The Role of the Father in Child Development* (pp. 329–344), New York: Wiley.

Koyl, L.F. 1977. "The aging Canadian." In *Canadian Gerontological Collection* (Vol. I) Blossom T. Wigdon, ed. Winnipeg: Canadian Association on Gerontology.

Kozol, J. 1991. *Savage Inequalities: Children in America's Schools*. New York: Crown.

Kunkel, John H. 1977. "Sociobiology vs biosociology." *American Sociologist* 12:69–73.

Kurian, George. 1991. "Socialization of South Asian immigrant youth." In *Immigrants and Refugees in Canada*. S.P. Sharma, A.M. Ervin, and D. Meintel, eds. Saskatoon: University of Saskatchewan.

Kurian, George Thomas. 1991. *The New Book of World Rankings*. New York: Facts on File.

Kurz, Demie. 1989. "Social science perspectives on wife abuse: Current debates and future directions." *Gender and Society* 3:489–505.

Kuypers, Joseph A., and Vern L. Bengtson. 1973. "Competence and social breakdown: A social-psychological view of aging." *Human Development* 16(2): 37–49.

Labour Canada. 1986. *When I Grow Up: Career Expectations and Aspirations of Canadian Schoolchildren*. Ottawa: Women's Bureau.

Labour Canada. 1987. *Women in the Labour Force*. Ottawa: Supply and Services Canada.

Labour Canada. 1990. *Women in the Labour Force*. Ottawa: Supply and Services Canada.

LaFree, Gary. 1980. "The effect of sexual stratification by race on official reactions to rape." *American Sociological Review* 45:842–854.

Lai, David Chuenyan. 1988. *Chinatowns: Towns Within Cities in Canada*. Vancouver: University of British Columbia Press.

Lamb, M.E. 1977. "The development of mother-infant and father-infant attachment in the second year of life." *Development Psychology*, 13:637–648.

Lamb, M.E. 1977. The development of parental preferences in the first two years of life. *Sex Roles*, 3, 495–497.

Lamb, Michael (ed.). 1987. *The Father's Role: Cross-Cultural Perspectives*. Hillsdale, NJ: Lawrence Erlbaum.

Lamb, Theodore A. 1981. "Nonverbal and paraverbal control in dyads and triads: Sex or power differences?" *Social Psychology Quarterly* 44:49–53.

Lambert, Ronald D. 1971. *Sex Role Imagery in Children: Social Origins of Mind*. Study 6. Royal Commission on the Status of Women in Canada. Ottawa: Information Canada.

Lambert, Ronald D. 1981. *The Sociology of Contemporary Quebec Nationalism: An Annotated Bibliography and Review*. New York: Garland.

Lambert, Ronald D., and James E. Curtis. 1979. "Education, economic dissatisfaction, and nonconfidence in Canadian social institutions." *Canadian Review of Sociology and Anthropology* 16(1):47–59.

Lambert, Ronald D., and James E. Curtis. 1982. "The French- and English-Canadian language communities and multicultural attitudes." *Canadian Ethnic Studies* 14(2):43–58.

Lambert, Ronald D., and James E. Curtis. 1983. "Opposition to multiculturalism among Québécois and English-Canadians." *Canadian Review of Sociology and Anthropology* 20(2):193–207.

Lambert, Ronald, et al. 1986. "Effect of identification with governing parties on feelings of political trust and efficacy." *Canadian Journal of Political Science* 19(4): 705–728.

Lancaster, Jane Beckman. 1976. "Sex roles in primate societies." In *Sex Differences: Social and Biological Perspectives*. Michael S. Teitelbaum, ed. Garden City, NY: Doubleday Anchor.

Landes, Ronald G. 1983. The Canadian Polity: A Comparative Introduction. Scarborough, ON: Prentice-Hall.

Landis, David S. 1983. *Revolution in Time: Clocks and the Making of the Modern World.* Cambridge, MA: Harvard University Press (Belknap).

Landsberg, Michele. 1982. *Women and Children First.* Markham, ON: Penguin.

Lane, Roger. 1980. "Urban homicide in the nineteenth century: Some lessons for the twentieth." In *History and Crime: Implications for Criminal Justice Policy.* J. Inciardi and C. Faupel, eds. Beverly Hills, CA: Sage.

Langer, William. 1973. "The black death." In *Cities: Their Origin, Growth and Human Impact. (Scientific American.)* San Francisco: W.H. Freeman.

Langford, Tom, and J. Rick Ponting. 1992. "Canadians' responses to aboriginal issues: The role of prejudice, perceived group conflict and economic conservatism." *Canadian Review of Sociology and Anthropology* 29(2):140–166.

Lareau, A. 1991. *Home Advantage: Social Class and Parental Intervention in Elementary Education.* Philadelphia: Falmer.

Large, Mary-Jane. 1981. "Services for the elderly." *Ontario Medical Review* (Jan.):38–41.

LaRossa, Ralph, and Maureen Mulligan LaRossa. 1989. "Baby care: Fathers vs. mothers." In *Gender in Intimate Relationships: A Microstructural Approach.* Barbara J. Risman and Pepper Schwartz, eds. Belmont, CA: Wadsworth.

Larson, Reed, and Robert Kubey. 1983. "Television and music: Contrasting media in adolescent life." *Youth and Society* 15:13–31.

Lasch, Christopher. 1977. *Haven in a Heartless World: The Family Besieged.* New York: Basic.

Laslett, Barbara. 1972. "The family as a public and private institution: A historical perspective." *Journal of Marriage and the Family* 35:480–492.

Laslett, Peter. 1976. "Societal development and aging." In *Handbook of Aging and the Social Sciences.* Robert Binstock and Ethel Shanas, eds. New York: Van Nostrand Reinhold.

Laslett, Peter. 1977. "The history of aging and the aged." *Family Life and Illicit Love in Earlier Generations.* Cambridge: Cambridge University Press.

Laslett, Peter. 1983. *The World We Have Lost.* 3rd edition. New York: Scribner.

Laslett, Peter, and Richard Wall. 1972. *Household and Family in Past Time.* Cambridge: Cambridge University Press.

Laub, John H. 1983. "Urbanism, race, and crime." *Journal of Research on Crime and Delinquency* (July):183–198.

Lauer, Robert H., and Warren B. Handel. 1977. *Social Psychology: The Theory and Application of Symbolic Interactionism.* Boston: Houghton Mifflin.

Lautard, E. Hugh, and D.J. Loree. 1984. "Ethnic stratification in Canada, 1931–1971." *Canadian Journal of Sociology* 9(3):333–343.

Lawrence, Paul R., and Jay W. Lorsch. 1967. *Organization and Environment: Managing Differentiation and Integration.* Cambridge, MA: Harvard University Press.

Laws, Judith Long. 1979. *The Second X: Sex Role and Social Role.* New York: Elsevier, North Holland.

Laxer, Gordon. 1975. "American and British influences on metropolitan development in Canada, 1878–1913." Paper presented to the Canadian Sociology and Anthropology Association.

Laxer, Robert (ed.). 1973. *Canada Ltd.: The Political Economy of Dependency.* Toronto: McClelland and Stewart.

Lazarsfeld, P.F., and R.K. Merton. 1954. "Friendship as a social process." In *Freedom and Control in Modern Society.* M. Berger, T. Abel, and C.H. Page, eds. Princeton, NJ: Van Nostrand.

Lazerson, M., J. McLaughlin, B. McPherson, and S. Bailey. 1985. *An Education of Value.* Cambridge: Cambridge University Press.

Leacock, Eleanor B. 1982. *Myths of Male Dominance.* New York: Monthly Review.

LeBon, Gustave. 1960; 1895. *The Crowd.* New York: Viking.

Le Devoir. **1992.** "Avec le libre-échange, le Mexique rêve d'une économie à l'américaine." *Le Devoir* (July 25):A9.

Lee, Dennis. 1974. *Alligator Pie.* Toronto: Macmillan.

Lee, Gary, and Robert Clyde. 1974. "Religion, socioeconomic status and anomie." *Journal for the Scientific Study of Religion* 13:35–47.

Leighton, Alexander. 1959. *My Name is Legion.* New York: Basic.

LeMasters, E.E. 1977. *Parents in Modern America.* 3rd edition. Homewood, IL: Dorsey.

Lemert, Charles. 1990. "The uses of French structuralisms in sociology" in G. Ritzer (ed.) *Frontiers of Social Theory: The New Syntheses.* New York: Columbia University Press. 230–254.

Lemert, Edwin. 1967. *Human Deviance, Social Problems and Social Control.* Englewood Cliffs, NJ: Prentice-Hall.

Lemon, B.W., Vern L. Bengtson, and J.A. Peterson. 1972. "An exploration of the activity theory of aging: Activity types and life satisfaction among in-movers to a retirement community." *Journal of Gerontology* 27: 511–523.

Lengermann, Patricia M., and Jill Neibrugge-Brantley. 1990. "Feminist sociological theory: The near-future prospects" in *Frontiers of Social Theory: The New*

Synthesis. G. Ritzer (ed.) New York: Columbia University Press. 316–371.

Lenski, Gerhard. 1961. *The Religious Factor.* New York: Doubleday.

Lenski, Gerhard. 1966. *Power and Privilege.* New York: McGraw-Hill.

Lenski, Gerhard, and Jean Lenski. 1982. *Human Societies: An Introduction to Macrosociology.* 4th edition. New York: McGraw-Hill.

Lenski, Gerhard, Jean Lenski, and Patrick Nolan. 1991. *Human Societies: An Introduction to Macrosociology.* New York: McGraw-Hill.

Lenton, Rhonda L. 1990. "Techniques of child discipline and abuse by parents." *Canadian Review of Sociology and Anthropology* 27:157–185.

Lerner, Gerda. 1986. *The Creation of Patriarchy.* New York: Oxford University Press.

Lever, Janet. 1978. "Sex differences in the complexity of children's play." *American Sociological Review* 43: 471–483.

Levin, Jeffrey S., and Kyriakos S. Markides. 1986. "Religious attendance and subjective health." *Journal for the Scientific Study of Religion* 25:31–40.

Levine, Donald H., Ellwood B. Carter, and Eleanor Miller Gorman. 1976. "Simmel's influence on American sociology." *American Journal of Sociology* 81:813–845.

LeVine, Robert A., and Donald T. Campbell. 1972. *Ethnocentrism: Theories of Conflict, Ethnic Attitudes, Group Behavior.* New York: Wiley.

Levine, Saul V. 1979. "Role of psychiatry in the phenomenon of cults." *Canadian Journal of Psychiatry* 24: 593–603.

Levinson, Daniel J., et al. 1978. *The Seasons of a Man's Life.* New York: Knopf.

Levitt, Cyril. 1984. *Children of Privilege: Student Revolt in the Sixties.* Toronto: University of Toronto Press.

Levitt, K. 1970. *Silent Surrender.* Toronto: Macmillan.

Levy, J. 1976. "Cerebral lateralization and spatial ability." *Behavior Genetics* 6:71–78.

Levy, Marion J. 1965. "Aspects of the analysis of family structure." In *Aspects of the Analysis of Family Structure.* A.J. Coale et al., eds. Princeton, NJ: Princeton University Press.

Lewin, Kurt. 1948. *Resolving Social Conflicts.* New York: Harper.

Lewis, Michael. 1972. "Culture and gender roles: There's no unisex in the nursery." *Psychology Today* 5(May): 54–57.

Lewis, Oscar. 1961. *The Children of Sanchez.* New York: Random House.

Leyton, Elliott. 1986. *Hunting Humans: The Rise of the Modern Multiple Murderer.* Toronto: Seal Books.

Li, Peter S. (ed.) 1988. *Race and Ethnic Relations in Canada.* Toronto: Oxford University Press.

Li, Peter S., and B. Singh Bolaria (eds.). 1983. *Racial Minorities in Multicultural Canada.* Toronto: Garamond.

Lichter, D.T. 1988. "Racial differences in underemployment in American cities." *American Journal of Sociology* 93(4):771–792.

Lieberson, Stanley, and Mary C. Waters. 1990. *From Many Strands: Ethnic and Racial Groups in Contemporary America.* New York: Russell Sage Foundation.

Liebert, Robert M., and Joyce Sprafkin. 1988. *The Early Window: Effects of Television on Children and Youth.* 3rd edition. New York: Pergamon.

Liebert, Robert M., Joyce N. Sprafkin, and Emily S. Davidson. 1982. *The Early Window: Effects of Television on Children and Youth.* 2nd edition. New York: Pergamon.

Liebowitz, Lila. 1983. "Origins of the sexual division of labor." In *Woman's Nature: Rationalizations of Inequality.* Marian Lowe and Ruth Hubbard, eds. New York: Pergamon.

Lindblom, Charles E. 1977. *Politics and Markets.* New York: Basic.

Lindenthal, Jacob, et al. 1970. "Mental status and religious behavior." *Journal for the Scientific Study of Religion* 9:143–149.

Lindesmith, Alfred. 1947. *Opiate Addiction.* Bloomington, IN: Principia.

Lindesmith, Alfred R., Anselm L. Strauss, and Norman K. Denzin. 1977. *Social Psychology.* 5th edition. New York: Holt, Rinehart and Winston.

Lindsay, Colin, and Craig McKie. 1986. "Annual review of labour force trends." *Canadian Social Trends* Autumn:2–7.

Linteau, P., and J. Robert. 1977. "Land ownership and society in Montreal: An hypothesis." In *The Canadian City: Essays in Urban History.* Gilbert A. Stelter and Alan F.J. Artibise, eds. Toronto: McClelland and Stewart.

Lipman-Blumen, Jean. 1984. *Gender Roles and Power.* Englewood Cliffs, NJ: Prentice-Hall.

Lipman-Blumen, Jean, and Ann R. Tickamyer. 1975. "Sex roles in transition: A ten-year perspective." *Annual Review of Sociology* 1:297–337.

Lippmann, Walter. 1922. *Public Opinion.* New York: Harcourt and Brace.

Lips, Hilary M. 1991. *Women, Men, and Power.* Mountain View, CA: Mayfield.

Lipset, S.M. 1960. *Political Man.* Garden City, NY: Doubleday.

Lipset, S.M. 1961. "Introduction." In *Political Parties* (by Robert Michels). New York: Collier-Macmillan.

Lipset, Seymour Martin. 1963. *The First New Nation.* New York: Basic Books.

Lipset, Seymour Martin. 1965. "Revolution and counter-revolution: Canada and the United States." In *The Revolutionary Theme in Contemporary America.* Thomas Ford, ed. Lexington, KY: University of Kentucky Press.

Lipset, Seymour Martin. 1968. *Agrarian Socialism.* New York: Doubleday Anchor.

Lipset, Seymour Martin. 1985. "Canada and the United States: The cultural dimension." In *Canada and the United States.* Charles F. Doran and John H. Sigler, eds. Englewood Cliffs, NJ: Prentice-Hall.

Lipset, Seymour Martin. 1990. *The Continental Divide: The Values and Institutions of Canada and the United States.* New York: Routledge.

Lisée, Jean-François. 1992. "Le Canada dans la peau." *L'Actualité* (July):22–28.

Lithwick, N.H.G., and G. Paquet. 1968. "Urban growth and regional contagion." In *Urban Studies: A Canadian Perspective.* N.H.G. Lithwick and G. Paquet, eds. Toronto: Methuen.

Litwak, Eugene. 1965. "Extended kin relations in an industrial democratic society." In *Social Structure and the Family.* Ethel Shanas and Gordon F. Streib, eds. Englewood Cliffs, NJ: Prentice-Hall.

Livingstone, D.W., and Meg Luxton. 1989. "Gender consciousness at work: Modification of the male breadwinner norm among steelworkers and their spouses." *Canadian Review of Sociology and Anthropology* 26:240–275.

L.K. "Are the Reichmanns in trouble?" *Forbes,* July 20, 1992, p. 160.

Lodhi, A.Q., and Charles Tilly. 1973. "Urbanization, crime and collective violence in nineteenth century France." *American Journal of Sociology* 79(2):296–318.

Lofland, Lyn H. 1975. "The 'thereness' of women: A selective review of urban sociology." In *Another Voice: Feminist Perspectives on Social Life and Social Science.* Marcia Millman and Rosabeth Moss Kanter, eds. Garden City, NY: Doubleday Anchor.

Lomnitz, L.A., and M.P. Lizaur. 1978. "The history of a Mexican urban family." *Journal of Family History* 3: 392–409.

Lopata, Helena Z. 1979. *Women as Widows: Support Systems.* New York: Elsevier.

Lorimer, James. 1978. *The Developers.* Toronto: James Lorimer.

Lorinc, John. 1991. "Managing when there's no middle." *Canadian Business* (June):86–94.

Lott, Bernice. 1981. "A feminist critique of androgyny: Toward the elimination of gender attributions for learned behavior." In *Gender and Nonverbal Behavior.* Clara Mayo and Nancy M. Henley, eds. New York: Springer-Verlag.

Lowe, George D., and H. Eugene Hodges. 1972. "Race and treatment of alcoholism in a southern state." *Social Problems* (Fall):240–252.

Lowe, Graham S. 1980. "Women, work and the office: The feminization of clerical occupations in Canada, 1901–1931." *Canadian Journal of Sociology* 5:361–381.

Lowe, Graham. 1991. "Retirement attitudes, plans and behaviour." *Perspectives on Labour and Income* 3(3): 8–17.

Lowe, Graham S., and Harvey J. Krahn. 1984. "Working women: Editors' introduction." In *Working Canadians: Readings in the Sociology of Work and Industry.* Graham S. Lowe and Harvey J. Krahn, eds. Toronto: Methuen.

Lowe, Marian. 1983. "The dialectic of biology and culture." In *Woman's Nature: Rationalizations of Inequality.* Marian Lowe and Ruth Hubbard, eds. New York: Pergamon.

Lower, A.R.M. 1939. "Geographical determinants in Canadian history." In *Essays in Canadian History.* Ralf Flenley, ed. Toronto: Macmillan.

Lucas, Rex A. 1971. *Minetown, Milltown, Railtown: Life in Canadian Communities of Single Industry.* Toronto: University of Toronto Press.

Luckmann, Thomas. 1967. *The Invisible Religion.* New York: Macmillan.

Luhmann, Niklas. 1990. "General theory and American sociology." In *Sociology in America.* Herbert Gans (ed.). Newbury Park: Sage. 253–264.

Lupri, Eugen. 1990. *Reflections on Marriage and the Family in Canada: A Study in the Dialectics of Family and Work Roles.* Toronto: Holt, Rinehart and Winston.

Lupri, Eugen, and J. Frideres. 1981. "The quality of marriage and the passage of time: Marital satisfaction over the family life cycle." *Canadian Journal of Sociology* 6(3):283–305.

Lupri, Eugen, and Donald L. Mills. 1987. "The household division of labour in young dual-earner couples: The case of Canada." *International Review of Sociology* 23.

Lupri, Eugen, and Gladys L. Symons. 1982. "The emerging symmetrical family: Fact or fiction?" *International Journal of Comparative Sociology* 23:166–189.

Lupsha, P.A. 1976. "On theories of urban violence." In *Urbanism, Urbanization, and Change.* P. Meadows and E. Mizruchi, eds. 2nd edition. Reading, MA: Addison-Wesley.

Lusk, Mark W., Felipe Peralta, and Gerald W. Vest. 1989. "Street children of Juarez: A field study." *International Social Work* 32:289–302.

Luxton, Meg. 1980. *More Than a Labour of Love: Three Generations of Women's Work in the Home.* Toronto: Women's Press.

Luxton, Meg. 1981. "Taking on the double day." *Atlantis* 7(1):15–16.

Luxton, Meg. 1987. "Thinking about the future." In *Family Matters: Sociology and Contemporary Canadian Families.* Karen L. Anderson et al., eds. Toronto: Methuen.

Luxton, Meg, and Harriet Rosenberg. 1986. *Through the Kitchen Window.* Toronto: Garamond Press.

Lynd, Robert S. 1946. *Knowledge for What?* New Jersey: Princeton University.

Lynn, David B. 1959. "A note on sex differences in the development of masculine and feminine identification." *Psychological Review* 66:126–135.

Lynn, David B. 1969. *Parental and Sex-Role Identification: A Theoretical Formulation.* Berkeley, CA: McCutchan.

Maccoby, Eleanor Emmons. 1980. *Social Development: Psychological Growth and the Parent-Child Relationship.* New York: Harcourt Brace Jovanovich.

Maccoby, Eleanor Emmons, and Carol Nagy Jacklin. 1974. *The Psychology of Sex Differences.* Stanford, CA: Stanford University Press.

Maccoby, Eleanor Emmons, and Carol Nagy Jacklin. 1980. "Sex differences in aggression: A rejoinder and reprise." *Child Development* 51:964–980.

Macdonald Commission. 1985. See *Royal Commission on the Economic Union and Development Prospects for Canada.*

Mackie, Marlene. 1973. "Arriving at 'truth' by definition: The case of stereotype inaccuracy." *Social Problems* 20:431–447.

Mackie, Marlene. 1974. "Ethnic stereotypes and prejudice: Alberta Indians, Hutterites and Ukrainians." *Canadian Ethnic Studies* 6:39–52.

Mackie, Marlene. 1975. "Defection from Hutterite colonies." In *Socialization and Values in Canadian Society* (Vol. 2). Robert M. Pike and Elia Zureik, eds. Toronto: McClelland and Stewart.

Mackie, Marlene. 1987. *Constructing Women and Men: Gender Socialization*. Toronto: Holt, Rinehart and Winston.

Mackie, Marlene. 1990. "Who is laughing now? The role of humour in the social construction of gender." *Atlantis* 15:11–26.

Maclean's. 1992. "Anatomy of a riot." *Maclean's* (May 18):30–31.

Maclean's. 1992. "Partners in power." (Dalglish, Brenda 1992) *Maclean's* (Dec. 14): 28–39.

MacLeod, Linda. 1987. *Battered But Not Beaten: Preventing Wife Battering in Canada*. Ottawa: Canadian Advisory Council on the Status of Women.

MacLeod, R.C. 1976. *The North-West Mounted Police and Law Enforcement, 1873–1905*. Toronto: University of Toronto Press.

MacPherson, C.B. 1953. *Democracy in Alberta*. Toronto: University of Toronto Press.

Mac Rae, Hazel. 1990. "Old women and identity maintenance in later life." *Canadian Journal on Aging* 9(3):248–267.

Maddox, George L. 1970. "Themes and issues in sociological theories of human aging." *Human Development* 13:17–27.

Magnusson, Warren E. 1983. "The development of Canadian urban government." In *City Politics in Canada*. W.E. Magnusson and A. Sancton, eds. Toronto: University of Toronto Press.

Malthus, Thomas R. 1970; 1798. *An Essay on the Principle of Population*. Harmondsworth: Penguin Books.

Manguel, Alberto. 1992. "Shooting the messenger." *The Globe and Mail* (Nov. 30):D3.

Manheimer, Dean I., Glen D. Millinger, and Mitchell B. Balter. 1969. "Use of marijuana among the urban cross-section of adults." Unpublished manuscript.

Mann, Michael. 1970. "The social cohesion of liberal democracy." *American Sociological Review* 35(3): 423–439.

Mann, W.E. 1962. *Sect, Cult, and Church in Alberta*. Toronto: University of Toronto Press.

Mannheim, Karl. 1936. *Ideology and Utopia*. New York: Harcourt, Brace and World.

Mannheim, Karl. 1953; 1952. "The sociological problem of generations." In *Essays on the Sociology of Knowledge*. P. Kecskemeti, ed. London: Routledge and Kegan Paul/New York: Oxford University Press.

Mantoux, Paul. 1961; 1928. *The Industrial Revolution in the Eighteenth Century*. New York: Harper and Row.

Manzer, R. 1974. *Canada: A Socio-Political Report*. Toronto: McGraw-Hill Ryerson.

Marchak, Patricia. 1975. *Ideological Perspectives on Canada*. Toronto: McGraw-Hill Ryerson.

Marchak, Patricia. 1979. *Whose Interests: An Essay on Multinational Corporations in a Canadian Context*. Toronto: McClelland and Stewart.

Marcil–Gratton, Nicole, and Jacques Légaré. 1992. "Will reduced fertility lead to greater isolation in old age for tomorrow's elderly?" *Canadian Journal on Aging* 11(1):54–71.

Mare, R.D. 1991. "Five decades of assortive mating." *American Sociological Review* 56:15–32.

Mare, R.D., and C. Winship. 1991. "Socioeconomic change and the decline of marriage for blacks and whites." In *The Urban Underclass*. C. Jenks and P.E. Peterson, eds. Washington, DC: Brookings Institute.

Marglin, S.A. 1974. "What do bosses do? The origins and functions of hierarchy in capitalist production." *Review of Radical Political Economics* 6:33–60.

Marini, Margaret Mooney, and Ellen Greenberger. 1978. "Sex differences in occupational aspirations and expectations." *Sociology of Work and Occupations* 5:147–175.

Marsden, Lorna R., and Edward R. Harvey. 1979. *Fragile Federation: Social Change in Canada*. Toronto: McGraw-Hill Ryerson.

Marshall, Victor W. 1975a. "Socialization for impending death in a retirement village." *American Journal of Sociology* 80(5):1124–1144.

Marshall, Victor W. 1975b. "Organizational features of terminal status passage in residential facilities for the aged." *Urban Life* 4:349–358.

Marshall, Victor W. 1980a. *Last Chapters: A Sociology of Aging and Dying*. Monterey, CA: Brooks/Cole.

Marshall, Victor W. 1980b. "No exit: An interpretive perspective on aging." In *Aging in Canada: Social Perspectives*. Victor W. Marshall, ed. Toronto: Fitzhenry and Whiteside.

Marshall, Victor W. 1981. "State of the art lecture: The sociology of aging." In *Canadian Gerontological Collection* (Vol. III). John Crawford, ed. Winnipeg: Canadian Association on Gerontology.

Marshall, Victor W. 1983. "Generations, age groups and cohorts: Conceptual distinctions." *Canadian Journal on Aging* 2(2):51–61.

Marshall, Victor W. 1986a. "Dominant and emerging paradigms in the social psychology of aging." In *Later Life: The Social Psychology of Aging*. Victor W. Marshall, ed. Beverly Hills, CA: Sage.

Marshall, Victor W. 1986b. "A sociological perspective on aging and dying." In *Later Life: The Social Psychology of Aging*. Victor W. Marshall, ed. Beverly Hills, CA: Sage.

Marshall, Victor W. 1987a. "The health of very old people as a concern of their children." In *Aging in Canada: Social Perspectives*. Victor W. Marshall, ed. 2nd edition. Toronto: Fitzhenry and Whiteside.

Marshall, Victor W. 1987b. "Older patients in the acute hospital setting." In *Health in Aging: Sociological Issues and Policy Directions*. Russell Ward and Sheldon Tobin, eds. New York: Springer.

Marshall, Victor W. 1987c. "Social perspectives on aging: Theoretical notes." In *Aging in Canada: Social Perspectives.* Victor W. Marshall, ed. 2nd edition. Toronto: Fitzhenry and Whiteside.

Marshall, Victor W. 1993. "Health policy and aging." *Journal of Canadian Studies* 28(2):153–165.

Marshall, Victor W., and Vern L. Bengtson. 1983. "Generations: Cooperation and conflict." In *Gerontology in the Eighties: Highlights of the Twelfth International Conference on Gerontology.* M. Bergener et al., eds. New York: Springer.

Marshall, Victor W., Fay Lomax Cook, and Joanne Gard Marshall. 1993. "Conflict over inter-generational equity: Rhetoric and reality in a comparative context." In *The New Contract Between the Generations.* V.L. Bengtson and W.A. Achenbaum, eds. New York: Aldine DeGruyter.

Marshall, Victor W., Sarah H. Matthews, and Carolyn J. Rosenthal. 1992. "The elusiveness of family life: A challenge for the sociology of aging." *Annual Review of Geriatrics and Gerontology.* George Maddox and M. Powell Lawton, eds.

Marshall, Victor W., and Carolyn J. Rosenthal. 1982. "Parental death: A life course marker." *Generations* 7(2):30–39.

Marshall, Victor W., Carolyn J. Rosenthal, and Joanne Daciuk. 1987. "Older parents' expectations for filial support." *Social Justice Review* 1(4):405–425.

Marshall, Victor W., Carolyn J. Rosenthal, and Janet Synge. 1983. "Concerns about parental health." In *Women and Aging.* Elizabeth W. Markson, ed. Lexington, MA: Lexington.

Marshall, Victor W., and Richard D. Tucker. 1990. "Canadian seasonal migrants to the sunbelt: Boon or burden?" *Journal of Applied Gerontology* 9(4):420–432.

Marshall, Victor W., and Blossom T. Wigdor. In press. "Health and social services for the aged in Canada." In *International Handbook on Service for the Elderly.* Jordan Kosberg, ed. Westport, CT: Greenwood.

Marston, W.G., and A.G. Darrock. 1971. "The social class of ethnic residential segregation: The Canadian case." *American Journal of Sociology* 77(3):491–510.

Martel, Angeline, and Linda Peterat. 1984. "Naming the world: Consciousness in a patriarchal iceberg." In *Taking Sex into Account: The Policy Consequences of Sexist Research.* Jill McCalla Vickers (ed.). Ottawa: Carleton University Press.

Martin, M. Kay, and Barbara Voorhies. 1975. *Female of the Species.* Toronto: Methuen.

Martin, Wilfred B.W., and Allan J. Macdonell. 1978. *Canadian Education: A Sociological Analysis.* Scarborough, ON: Prentice-Hall.

Martin Matthews, Anne. 1982. "Canadian research on women as widows: A comparative analysis of the state of the art." *Resources for Feminist Research.* Toronto: Ontario Institute for Studies in Education.

Martin Matthews, Anne. 1987. "Widowhood as an expectable life event." In *Aging in Canada: Social Perspectives.* Victor W. Marshall, ed. 2nd edition. Don Mills, ON: Fitzhenry and Whiteside.

Martin Matthews, Anne. 1991. *Widowhood in Later Life.* Toronto: Butterworths.

Martin Matthews, Anne, and Ralph Matthews. 1986. "Infertility and involuntary childlessness: The transition to non-parenthood." *Journal of Marriage and the Family* 48:641–649.

Martin Matthews, Anne, et al. 1982. "A crisis assessment technique for the evaluation of life events." *Canadian Journal on Aging* 1(3–4):28–39.

Martyna, Wendy. 1980. "Beyond the 'he/man' approach: The case of nonsexist language." *Signs* 5:482–493.

Maruyama, G., and N. Miller. 1975. *Physical Attractiveness and Classroom Acceptance.* Social Science Research Institute Report 75-2. Los Angeles: University of Southern California.

Marx, Gary, and James L. Wood. 1975. "Strands of theory and research in collective behavior." *Annual Review of Sociology* 1:363–428.

Marx, Karl. 1906. *Capital: A Critique of Political Economy.* New York: The Modern Library.

Marx, Karl. 1965; 1867–1895. *Capital: A Critical Analysis of Capitalist Production* (Vol. 1) New York: International.

Marx, Karl. 1967. *Capital: A Critique of Political Economy.* Trans. from 3rd German ed. by Samuel Moore and Edward Aveling. Edited by Frederick Engels. New York: International Publishers.

Marx, Karl. 1970; 1843. *Critique of Hegel's 'Philosophy of Right.'* Annette Jolin and Joseph O'Malley, transl. Cambridge, MA: Harvard University Press.

Marx, Karl. 1974. *The First International and After.* David Fernbach, ed. New York: Random House.

Marx, Karl. 1978. *Karl Marx: Selected Writings.* D. McLellan, ed. Oxford: Oxford University Press.

Marx, Karl, and Friedrich Engels. 1959. *Basic Writings on Politics and Philosophy.* Lewis Feuer, ed. Garden City, NY: Anchor.

Marx, Karl, and Friedrich Engels. 1964. *On Religion.* New York: Schocken.

Maslow, Abraham A. 1963. *Toward a Psychology of Being.* Princeton, NJ: Van Nostrand.

Maslow, Abraham A. 1970. *Motivation and Personality.* 2nd edition. New York: Harper and Row.

Massey, D.S., and N.A. Denton. 1987. "Trends in the residential segregation of blacks, Hispanics, and Asians: 1970–1980." *American Sociological Review* 52(6): 802–825.

Massey Report. 1951. See *Royal Commission on National Development in the Arts, Letters and Sciences.*

Mathewson, S.B. 1931. *Restriction of Output among Unorganized Workers.* New York: Viking.

Matras, J. 1980. "Comparative Social Mobility." *Annual Review of Sociology* 6:401–431.

Matthews, Sarah H. 1979. *The Social World of Old Women: Management of Self-Identity.* Beverly Hills, CA: Sage.

Matthews, Sarah H. 1986. *Friendships Through the Life Course.* Beverly Hills, CA: Sage.

Matthews, Victor. 1972. *Social-Legal Statistics in Al-*

berta: A Review of Their Availability and Significance. Edmonton: Human Resources Research Council.

Mauss, Armand, and Milton Rokeach. 1977. "Pollsters as prophets." *Humanist* (May-June):48–51.

Maxim, Paul S., and Carl Keane. 1992. "Gender, age and the risk of violent death in Canada, 1950–1986." *Canadian Review of Sociology and Anthropology* 29:329–345.

Maynard, Rona. 1984. "Women and men: Is the difference brain-deep?" *Chatelaine* 57(Oct.):76, 86, 88, 90, 98.

Mayo, Elton. 1945. *The Social Problems of an Industrial Civilization.* Cambridge, MA: Harvard University Press.

McAdoo, H.P. 1988. *Black Families.* 2nd edition. Newbury Park, CA: Sage.

McCarthy, J.D., and M.N. Zald. 1973. *The Trends of Social Movements in America: Professionalization and Resource Mobilization.* Morristown, NJ: General Learning.

McDaniel, Susan A. 1986. *Canada's Aging Population.* Toronto: Butterworths.

McDaniel, Susan A. 1987. "Demographic aging as a guiding paradigm in Canada's welfare state." *Canadian Public Policy* 13(3):330–336.

McDaniel, Susan A. 1989. "A new stork rising? Women's roles and reproductive changes." *Society/Société* 13:6–14.

McDaniel, Susan A. 1991. "Feminist Scholarship in Sociology: Transformation from within?" *Canadian Journal of Society* 16:303–312.

McDavid, John W., and Herbert Harari. 1966. "Stereotyping of names and popularity in grade-school children." *Child Development* 37:453–460.

McDonald, L., and R.A. Wanner. 1982. "Work past age 65 in Canada: A socioeconomic analysis." *Aging and Work* 5:169–179.

McDonald, L., and R.A. Wanner. 1984. "Socioeconomic determinants of early retirement in Canada." *Canadian Journal on Aging* 3(3):105–116.

McDonald, Lynn P., and Richard A. Wanner. 1990. *Retirement in Canada.* Toronto: Butterworths.

McDonald, Neil. 1978. "Egerton Ryerson and the school as an agent of political socialization." In *Egerton Ryerson and His Times.* Neil McDonald and A. Chaiton, eds. Toronto: Macmillan.

McEvedy, Colin. 1988. "The bubonic plague." *Scientific American* 258(2):118–123.

McFarlane, A.H., et al. 1980. "A longitudinal study of influence of the psychosocial environment on health status: A preliminary report." *Journal of Health and Social Behavior* 21:124–133.

McGlone, Jeannette. 1980. "Sex differences in human brain asymmetry: A critical survey." *Behavioral and Brain Sciences* 3:215–227.

McGlone, J., and A. Kertesz. 1973. "Sex differences in cerebral processing of visual-spatial tasks." *Cortex* 9:313–320.

McInnes, Craig, and R. MacLeod. 1992. "Experts say climate was right for vandals." *The Globe and Mail* (May 7):A1–A2.

McKenna, Barrie. 1993. "Rough road ahead for unemployed youth." *The Globe and Mail,* January 14, 1993: B1.

McKenzie, Roderick D. 1968. *On Human Ecology.* Chicago: University of Chicago Press.

McKeown, Thomas. 1976. *The Modern Rise of Population.* New York: Academic.

McKie, D.C., B. Prentice, and P. Reed. 1983. *Divorce: Law and the Family in Canada.* Ottawa: Statistics Canada, Catalogue No. 89-502E.

McKitrick, Ross. 1989. *The Current Industrial Relations Scene in Canada 1989: The Economy and Labour Markets Reference Tables.* Kingston, ON: Industrial Relations Centre, Queen's University.

McLanahan, S., and K. Booth. 1991. "Mother-only families: Problems, prospects, and politics." In *Contemporary Families: Looking Forward, Looking Back.* A. Booth, ed. Minneapolis: National Council on Family Relations.

McLanahan, S., and L.L. Bumpass. 1988. "Intergenerational consequences of family disruption." *American Journal of Sociology* 94:130–152.

McLaren, Peter. 1980. *Cries From the Corridor: The New Suburban Ghetto.* Toronto: Methuen.

McLoyd, V.C. 1989. "Socialization and development in a changing economy." *American Psychologist* 44:293–302.

McNaught, Kenneth. 1975. "Political trials and the Canadian political tradition." In *Courts and Trials: A Multi-Discipline Approach.* M.L. Friedland, ed. Toronto: University of Toronto Press.

McNeil, Linda. 1986. *Contradictions of Control, School Structures and School Knowledge.* New York: Routledge.

McNeill, William H. 1976. *Plagues and Peoples.* Garden City, NY: Doubleday.

McPherson, Barry, and Neil Guppy. 1979. "Preretirement life-style and the degree of planning for retirement." *Journal of Gerontology* 34(2):254–263.

McQuillan, K. 1979. "Common themes in Catholic and Marxist thought on population and development." *Population and Development Review* 5:689–698.

McQuillan, K. 1980. "Economic factors and internal migration: The case of nineteenth-century England." *Social Science History* 4(4):479–499.

McQuillan, K. 1990. "Family change and family income in Ontario." In *Children, Families and Public Policy in the 90s.* L.C. Johnson and D. Barnhorst, eds. Toronto: Thompson Educational Publishing.

McRoberts, H. 1985. "Language and mobility: A comparison of three groups." In *Ascription and Achievement.* M. Boyd et al., eds. Ottawa: Carleton University Press.

McRoberts, Hugh A., et al. 1976. "Différences dans la mobilité professionnelle des francophones et des anglophones." *Sociologie et Sociétés* 8(2):61–79.

McRoberts, K., and D. Posgate. 1980. *Quebec: Social Change and Political Crisis.* Revised edition. Toronto: McCelland and Stewart.

McTavish, Donald G. 1982. "Perceptions of old people." In *Research Instruments in Social Gerontology* (Vol. 1): *Clinical and Social Psychology.* David J. Mangen and

Warren A. Peterson, eds. Minneapolis: University of Minnesota Press.

Mead, George H. 1934. *Mind, Self, and Society.* Chicago: University of Chicago Press.

Mead, Margaret. 1950; 1935. *Sex and Temperament in Three Primitive Societies.* New York: Mentor.

Medina, A., and C. Izquerdo. 1978. "Mexico." In *Education and Youth Employment in Less Developed Countries.* Berkeley, CA: Carnegie Council on Policy Studies in Higher Education.

Meisel, John. 1985. "The decline of party in Canada." pp. 98–114. In Hugh G. Thornburn (ed.) *Party Politics in Canada.* 5th ed. Scarborough, Ontario: Prentice-Hall Canada, Inc.

Meissner, Martin. 1971. "The long arm of the job: A study of work and leisure." *Industrial Relations* 10(3): 239–260.

Meissner, Martin, et al. 1975. "No exit for wives: Sexual division of labour and the cumulation of household demands." *Canadian Review of Sociology and Anthropology* 12(Part I):424–439.

Melbin, Murray. 1987. *Night as Frontier: Colonizing the World After Dark.* New York: Free Press.

Meltzer, Bernard N. 1978. "Mead's social psychology." In *Symbolic Interaction: A Reader in Social Psychology.* Jerome G. Manis and B.N. Meltzer, eds. 3rd edition. Boston: Allyn and Bacon.

Menaghan, E.G., and T.L. Parcel. 1991. "Parental employment and family life: Research in the 1980s." In *Contemporary Families; Looking Forward, Looking Back.* A. Booth, ed. Minneapolis: National Council on Family Relations.

Menzies, Heather. 1984. "Women and microtechnology." In *Working Canadians.* Graham S. Lowe and Harvey J. Krahn, eds. Toronto: Methuen.

Mertl, Steve. 1992. "Wilson begins selling the benefits of our new Mexican connection." *The Gazette* (Aug. 15):D1.

Merton, Robert. 1938. "Social structure and anomie." *American Sociological Review* 3(Oct.):672–682.

Merton, Robert. 1957. *Social Theory and Social Structure.* Glencoe, IL: Free Press.

Messinger, Hans, and Brian J. Powell. 1987. "The implications of Canada's aging society on social expenditures." In *Aging in Canada: Social Perspectives.* Victor W. Marshall, ed. 2nd edition. Toronto: Fitzhenry and Whiteside.

Metz, Donald. 1967. *New Congregations: Security and Mission in Conflict.* Philadelphia: Westminster.

Miall, Charlene. 1986. "Self-labelling and the stigma of involuntary childlessness." *Social Problems* 33(4): 268–282.

Michael, R.T. 1988. "Why did the U.S. divorce rate double within a decade?" In *Research in Population Economics.* Vol. 6. T.P. Schultz, ed. Greenwich, CN: JAI Press.

Michelson, William. 1976. *Man and His Urban Environment.* 2nd edition. Reading, MA: Addison-Wesley.

Michelson, William. 1977. *Environmental Choice, Human Behavior, and Residential Satisfaction.* New York: Oxford University Press.

Michelson, William. 1985a. *From Sun to Sun: Daily Obligations and Community Structure in the Lives of Employed Women and Their Families.* Totowa, NJ: Rowman and Allanheld.

Michelson, William. 1985b. "Divergent convergence: The daily routines of employed spouses as a public affairs agenda." *Public Affairs Report* 26(4):1–10.

Mikenna, Barrie. "Rough road ahead for unemployed youth." *The Globe and Mail,* January 14, 1993:B1.

Milgram, S. 1970. "The experience of living in cities." *Science* 167(3924):1461–1468.

Miliband, Ralph. 1973; 1969. *The State in Capitalist Society.* London: Quartet Books.

Miller, Casey, and Kate Swift. 1977. *Words and Women.* Garden City, NY: Doubleday Anchor.

Millman, Marcia, and Rosabeth Moss Kanter (eds.). 1975. *Anther Voice: Feminist Perspectives on Social Life and Social Science.* Garden City, NY: Doubleday Anchor.

Mills, C. Wright. 1951. *White Collar.* New York: Oxford University Press.

Mills, C. Wright. 1959. *The Sociological Imagination.* New York: Oxford University Press.

Miner, Horace. 1939. *St. Denis: A French-Canadian Parish.* Chicago: University of Chicago Press.

Ministry of Education, Ontario. 1975. *Education in the Primary and Junior Divisions.* Toronto: Queen's Printer.

Mitchell, Alanna. "Keeping house worth billions." *Gobe and Mail,* June 19, 1992, p. 1A.

Mitchell, Robert. 1966. Polity, church attractiveness, and ministers' careers." *Journal for the Scientific Study of Religion* 5:241–258.

Molotch, Harvey. 1979. "Media and movements." In *The Dynamics of Social Movements.* Mayer N. Zald and John D. McCarthy, eds. Cambridge, MA: Winthrop.

Mommsen, Max. 1974. *The Age of Bureaucracy.* New York: Harper and Row.

Money, John, and A.A. Ehrhardt. 1972. *Man and Woman, Boy and Girl: The Differentiation and Dimorphism of Gender Identity from Conception to Maturity.* Baltimore: Johns Hopkins University Press.

Money, John, and Patricia Tucker. 1975. *Sexual Signatures: On Being a Man or a Woman.* Boston: Little, Brown.

Moore, Barrington, Jr. 1966. *Social Origins of Dictatorship and Democracy.* Boston: Beacon.

Moore, K., D. Spain, and S.M. Bianchi. 1984. "The working wife and mother." *Marriage and Family Review* 7:77–98.

Moore, Maureen. 1987. "Women parenting alone." *Canadian Social Trends* Winter:31–36.

Moore, Maureen. 1990. "Women parenting alone." In *Canadian Social Trends.* Craig McKie and Keith Thompson, eds. Toronto: Thompson Educational Publishing.

Moore, Wilbert. 1966. "Aging and the social system." In *Aging and Social Policy.* John C. McKinney and Frank T. de Vyver, eds. New York: Appleton-Century-Crofts.

Morales-Gomez, D.A., and C.A. Torres. 1990. *The State, Corporatist Politics, and Educational Policy Making in Mexico.* New York: Praeger.

More, R.D. 1991. "Five decades of assortive mating." *American Sociological Review* 56:15–32.

Morely, David. 1992. "More hard times for Mexico's poor?" *The Globe and Mail* (Aug. 24):A21.

Morgan, W.R., and T.N. Clark. 1973. "The causes of racial disorders." *American Sociological Review* 38:611–624.

Morris, Cerise. 1980. "Determination and thoroughness: The movement for a royal commission on the status of women in Canada." *Atlantis* 5:1–21.

Morris, Raymond N., and C. Michael Lanphier. 1977. *Three Scales of Inequality: Perspectives on French–English Relations.* Don Mills, ON: Longman.

Mortimer, Jeylan T., and Roberta G. Simmons. 1978. "Adult socialization." *Annual Review of Sociology* 4: 421–454.

Morton, Peggy. 1972. "Women's work is never done." In *Women Unite!: An Anthology of the Canadian Women's Movement.* Toronto: Canadian Women's Educational Press.

Morton, William L. 1950. *The Progressive Party in Canada.* Toronto: University of Toronto Press.

Mouzelis, Nicos P. 1991. *Back to Sociological Theory: The Construction of Social Orders.* New York: St. Martin's Press.

Moynihan, D.P. 1965. *The Negro Family: A Case for National Action.* Washington, DC: U.S. Government Printing Office.

Müller, Georg P. 1988. *Comparative World Data: A Statistical Handbook for Social Science.* Baltimore: Johns Hopkins University Press.

Mumford, Lewis, 1961. *The City in History: Its Origin, Its Transformation, and Its Prospects.* New York: Harcourt, Brace and World.

Mumford, Lewis. 1963. *Technics and Civilization.* New York: Harcourt, Brace and World.

Mumford, Lewis. 1968. *The Urban Prospect.* New York: Harcourt, Brace and World.

Murdoch, Peter. 1957. "World ethnographic sample." *American Anthropologist* 59(4):664–687.

Murdoch, William W. 1980. *The Poverty of Nations.* Baltimore: Johns Hopkins University Press.

Murdock, G.P. 1931. "Ethnocentrism." In *Encyclopedia of the Social Sciences* 5. E.R.A. Seligman, ed. New York: Macmillan.

Murphy, Emily F. 1920. "The grave drug menace." *Macleans'* 33(3):1.

Murphy, Emily F. 1922. *The Black Candle.* Toronto: Thomas Allen.

Murphy, Raymond. 1981. "Teachers and the evolving structural context of economic and political attitudes in Quebec society." *Canadian Review of Sociology and Anthropology* 18:157–182.

Musto, David. 1973. *The American Disease: Origins of Narcotic Control.* New Haven, CT: Yale University Press.

Mutran, Elizabeth, and Donald C. Reitzes. 1984. "Intergenerational support activities and well-being among the elderly: A convergence of exchange and symbolic interaction perspectives." *American Sociological Review* 49:117–130.

Muuss, Rolf E. 1988. *Theories of Adolescence.* 5th edition. New York: Random House.

Myles, John F. 1980. "The aged, the state, and the structure of inequality." In *Structured Inequality in Canada.* John Harp and John Hofley, eds. Scarborough, ON: Prentice-Hall.

Myles, John F. 1984. *Old Age in the Welfare State: The Political Economy of Pensions.* Boston: Little, Brown.

Myles, John. 1988. "The expanding middle: Some Canadian evidence on the deskilling debate." *Canadian Review of Sociology and Anthropology* 25:335–364.

Myles, John, and Gail Fawcett. 1990. "Job skills and the service economy." Ottawa: Economic Council of Canada.

Myles, John F., and Les Teichrow. 1991. "The politics of dualism: Pension policy in Canada." In *States, Labor Markets, and the Future of Old-Age Policy.* J. Myles and J. Quadagno, eds. Philadelphia: Temple University Press.

(NACA) National Advisory Council on Aging. 1989. *Understanding Seniors' Independence. Report No. 1: The Barriers and Suggestions for Action.* Ottawa: Minister of Supply and Services, catalogue no. H71-3/11-1-1989E.

(NACA) National Advisory Council on Aging. 1991. *The Economic Situation of Canada's Seniors. A Fact Book.* Ottawa: Ministry of Supply and Services, catalogue no. H71-3/14-1991E.

Nagel, Stuart. 1969. *The Legal Process from a Behavioral Perspective.* Homewood, IL: Dorsey.

Nagnur, Dhruva, and Owen Adams. 1987. "Tying the knot: An overview of marriage rates in Canada." *Canadian Social Trends* Autumn:2–6.

Nasar, Sylvia. "The rich get richer, but never the same way twice." *New York Times*, August 16, 1992, p. 3E.

Nash, Dennison, and Peter L. Berger. 1962. "The child, the family, and the 'religious revival' in suburbia." *Journal for the Scientific Study of Religion* 2:85–93.

Nash, June. 1990. "Latin American women in the world capitalist crisis." *Gender and Society* 4:338–353.

Nash, June, and Helen Safa (eds.). 1986. *Women and Change in Latin America.* South Hadley, MA: Bergin & Garvey.

Nathanson, Constance. 1977. "Sex, illness and medical care: A review of data, theory and method." *Social Science and Medicine* 111:13–25.

National Center for Health Statistics. 1992. *Health, United States, 1991.* Hyattsville, MD: Public Health Service.

"National Report" *New York Times,* July 5, 1992, p. 12.

Nelsen, Hart M., and Raymond H. Potvin. 1980. "Toward disestablishment: New patterns of social class, denomination, and religiosity among youth?" *Review of Religious Research* 22:137–154.

Nelson, L.D., and Russell Dynes. 1976. "The impact of devotionalism and attendance on ordinary and emergency helping behavior." *Journal for the Scientific Study of Religion* 15:47–59.

Nett, Emily. 1981. "Canadian families in social-historical perspective. *Canadian Journal of Sociology* 6(3): 239–260.

Nettler, Gwynn. 1973. "Embezzlement without problems." *British Journal of Criminology* 14(1):L70–L77.

Nettler, Gwynn. 1978. *Explaining Crime.* New York: McGraw-Hill.

Nettler, Gwynn. 1982. *Killing One Another.* Cincinnati, OH: Anderson.

Neubeck, Kenneth J. 1986. *Social Problems: A Critical Approach.* New York: Random House.

Neugarten, Bernice L. 1970. "The old and the young in modern societies." *American Behavioral Scientist* 14(1):13–24.

Neugarten, Bernice L., W. Crotty, and S. Tobin. 1964. "Personality types in an aged population." In *Personality in Middle and Later Life: Empirical Studies.* New York: Atherton.

Nevitte, Neil, H. Bakvis and R. Gibbins. 1989. "The ideological contours of 'New Politics' in Canada: Policy mobilization and partisan support." *Canadian Journal of Political Science* 22(3):475–503.

Nevitte, Neil, Miguel Basañez, and Ronald Inglehart. 1992. "Directions of value change in North America." In *North America Without Borders? Integrating Canada, the United States, and Mexico.* Stephen J. Randall, ed., Calgary: University of Calgary Press.

Newcomb, Peter, and Jean Sherman Chatzky. "The top 40" *Forbes,* September 28, 1992, pp. 87–91.

Newman, Oscar. 1972. *Defensible Space.* New York: Macmillan.

Newman, P. 1982. *The Acquisitors: The Canadian Establishment* (Vol. 2). Toronto: McClelland and Stewart.

Newman, William M. 1973. *American Pluralism.* New York: Harper and Row.

Newsweek. **1992.** "The siege of L.A." *Newsweek* (May 11):30–38.

Ng, Edward. 1992. "Children and elderly people: Sharing public income resources." *Canadian Social Trends.* 25:12–15.

Ngor, Haing, and Roger Warner. 1988. *A Cambodian Odyssey.* New York: Macmillan.

Nicholson, John. 1984. *Men and Women: How Different Are They?* Oxford: Oxford University Press.

Niebuhr, H. Richard. 1929. *The Social Sources of Denominationalism.* New York: Holt.

Nielsen, Joyce McCarl. 1978. *Sex in Society: Perspectives on Stratification.* Belmont, CA: Wadsworth.

1987 World Population Data Sheet. 1987. Washington, DC: Population Reference Bureau.

Niosi, J. 1981. *Canadian Capitalism.* R. Chodos, transl. Toronto: Lorimer.

Nishio, Harry K., and Heather Lank. 1987. "Patterns of labour participation of older female workers." In *Aging in Canada: Social Perspectives.* Victor W. Marshall, ed. 2nd edition. Toronto: Fitzhenry and Whiteside.

Nock, David A. 1987. "Cult, sect and church in Canada: A re-examination of Stark and Bainbridge." *Canadian Review of Sociology and Anthropology* 24:514–525.

Norris, Joan E. 1980. "The social adjustment of single and widowed older women." *Essence: Issues in the Study of Aging, Dying and Death* 4(3):135–144.

Norris, Joan E. 1987. "Psychological processes in the development of late-life social identity." In *Aging in Canada: Social Perspectives.* Victor W. Marshall, ed. 2nd edition. Toronto: Fitzhenry and Whiteside.

Northcott, Herbert C. 1984. "Widowhood and remarriage trends in Canada 1956–1981." *Canadian Journal on Aging* 3(1):63–77.

Notestein, F.W. 1945. "Population: The long view." In *Food for the World.* T.W. Schultz, ed. Chicago: University of Chicago Press.

Nye, F. Ivan. 1982. *Family Relationships: Rewards and Costs.* Beverly Hills, CA: Sage.

Oberschall, Anthony. 1968. "The Los Angeles riot." *Social Problems* 15(Winter).

Oberschall, Anthony. 1973. *Social Conflict and Social Movements.* Englewood Cliffs, NJ: Prentice-Hall.

Oberschall, Anthony. 1977. "The decline of the 1960s social movements." In *Research in Social Movements, Conflict and Change.* L. Kriesberg, ed. Greenwich, CT: JAI.

OECD. 1975. *Education, Inequality and Life Chances* (2 vols.). Paris: OECD.

OECD. 1976. *Reviews of National Policies for Education: Canada.* Paris: OECD.

Ogburn, William F. 1922. *Social Change with Respect to Culture and Original Nature.* New York: B.W. Huebsch.

Ogburn, William F. 1933. "The family and its functions." In *Recent Social Trends in the U.S.* W.F. Ogburn, ed. New York: McGraw-Hill.

Ogburn, William F. 1964; 1956. "Technology as environment." In *William F. Ogburn on Culture and Social Change.* Otis D. Duncan, ed. Chicago: University of Chicago Press.

Ogburn, William F., and Meyer F. Nimkoff. 1964. "The social effects of innovation." In *Sociology.* W.F. Ogburn an M.F. Nimkoff, eds. 4th edition. Boston: Houghton Mifflin.

Ogmundson, R. 1975. "Party class images and the class vote in Canada." *American Sociological Review* 40: 505–512.

Ogmundson, R. 1976. "Mass-elite linkages and class issues in Canada." *Canadian Review of Sociology and Anthropology* 13(1):1–12.

Ogmundson, R. 1980a. "Toward study of the endangered species known as the Anglophone Canadian." *Canadian Journal of Sociology* 5:1–12.

Ogmundson, R. 1980b. Liberal ideology and the study of voting behaviour." *Canadian Review of Sociology and Anthropology* 17:45–54.

Ohmae, Kenichi. 1991. *The Borderless World: Power and Strategy in the Interlinked Economy.* London: Fontana.

Oja, G. 1987. *Changes in the Distribution of Wealth in Canada, 1970–84.* Ottawa: Minister of Supply and Services.

Okediji, Francis O. 1974. "Changes in individual reproductive behavior and cultural values." *Lecture Series on Population.* Bucharest, Romania: International Union for the Scientific Study of Population.

Olsen, Dennis. 1977. "The state elites." In *The Canadian State: Political Economy and Political Power.* Leo Panitch, ed. Toronto: University of Toronto Press.

Olsen, Dennis. 1980. *The State Elite.* Toronto: McClelland and Stewart.

Olsen, P., and P. Burns. 1983. "Politics, class and happenstance: French immersion in a Canadian context," *Interchange,* 14(1):1–17.

Olson, Manur. 1965. *The Logic of Collective Action.* Cambridge, MA: Harvard University Press.

Ontario Arts Council. 1991. *Occupation Artist.* Toronto: Ontario Arts Council.

Ontario Council of Health. 1978. *Health Care for the Aged.* Toronto: Ontario Council of Health.

Oppenheimer, Valerie K. 1973. "Demographic influence on female employment and the status of women." In *Changing Women in a Changing Society.* Joan Huber, ed. Chicago: University of Chicago Press.

Orbach, Harold L. 1981. "Mandatory retirement and the development of adequate retirement provisions for older persons." *Canadian Gerontological Collection* (Vol. II). George Gasek, ed. Winnipeg: Canadian Association on Gerontology.

Ortner, Sherry B., and Harriet Whitehead. 1981. *Sexual Meanings: The Cultural Construction of Gender and Sexuality.* Cambridge, UK: Cambridge University Press.

Osberg, L. 1981. *Economic Inequality in Canada.* Toronto: Butterworths.

Osborne, K. 1980. *"Hard Working, Temperate and Peaceable": The Portrayal of Workers in Canadian History Textbooks.* Winnipeg: University of Manitoba.

Ostry, Bernard. 1978. *The Cultural Connection.* Toronto: McClelland and Stewart.

Otero, G. 1992. Personal communication.

O'Toole, James. 1981. *Making America Work.* New York: Continuum.

Ouchi, William. 1981. *Theory Z.* Reading, MA: Addison-Wesley.

Overbeek, Johannes. 1974. *History of Population Theories.* Rotterdam, Netherlands: Rotterdam University Press.

Packer, H. 1964. "Two models of the criminal process." *University of Pennsylvania Law Review* 113:1–68.

Palen, John. 1987. *The Urban World.* 3rd edition. New York: McGraw-Hill.

Palloni, A. 1981. "Mortality in Latin America: Some emerging patterns." *Population and Development Review* 7:623–649.

Palloni, A., and M. Glicklich. 1991. "Review of approaches to modelling the demographic impact of the AIDS epidemic." In *The AIDS Epidemic and its Demographic Consequences.* New York: United Nations.

Palmore, Erdman. 1969. "Sociological aspects of aging." In *Behaviour and Adaptation in Late Life.* Ewald W. Busse and Eric Pfeiffer, eds. Boston: Little, Brown.

Palmore, Erdman, and Clark Luikart. 1972. "Health and social factors related to life satisfaction." *Journal of Health and Social Behavior* 13(Mar.):68–80.

Palmore, Erdman, and Kenneth Manton. 1974. "Modernization and status of the aged: International comparisons." *Journal of Gerontology* 29:205–210.

Pappert, Ann. 1983. "The one and only." *Quest* (Dec.): 38–42.

Parcel, Toby L. 1992. "Secondary data analysis and data archives." *Encyclopedia of Sociology,* (Vol. 4). Edgar F. and Marie L. Borgatta, eds. New York: Macmillan.

Park, Robert E., Ernest W. Burgess, and Roderick D. McKenzie. 1925. *The City.* Chicago: University of Chicago Press.

Parke, R.O., & O'Leary, S.E. 1976. "Father-mother-infant interaction in the newborn period: Some findings, some observations, and some unresolved issues." In K. Riegel & J. Meacham (Eds.), *The Developing Individual in a Changing World: Vol. 2. Social and Environmental Issues* (pp. 653–663). The Hague. The Netherlands: Mouton.

Parker, Graham. 1976. "The Juvenile Court Movement." *University of Toronto Law Journal* 26:140–172.

Parkes, C.M., B. Benjamin, and R.G. Fitzgerald. 1969. "Broken heart: A statistical study of increased mortality among widowers." *British Medical Journal* 1:740.

Parkin, F. 1979. *Marxism and Class Theory.* New York: Columbia University Press.

Parkin, Frank. 1972. *Class Inequality and Political Order.* London: Paladin.

Parlee, Mary Brown. 1973. "The premenstrual syndrome." *Psychological Bulletin* 80:454–465.

Parlee, Mary Brown. 1982. "Changes in moods and activation levels during the menstrual cycle in experimentally naive subjects." *Psychology of Women Quarterly* 7:119–131.

Parliament, Jo-Anne. 1990. "Increased life expectancy, 1921–1981." In *Canadian Social Trends.* Craig McKie and Keith Thompson (eds.). Toronto: Thompson Educational Publishing.

Parsons, H.M. 1974. "What happened at Hawthorne?" *Science* 8(Mar.):922–932.

Parsons, Talcott. 1942. "Age and sex in the social structure of the U.S." *American Sociological Review* 7: 604–612.

Parsons, Talcott. 1949. "The kinship system of the contemporary United States." *Essays in Sociological Theory: Pure and Applied.* Glencoe, IL: Free Press.

Parsons, Talcott. 1951. *The Social System.* New York: Free Press.

Parsons, Talcott. 1954. "The kinship system of the contemporary United States." In *Essays in Sociological Theory: Pure and Applied.* Revised edition. Glencoe, IL: Free Press.

Parsons, Talcott. 1955. "The American family: Its relation to personality and social structure." In *Family Socialization and Interaction Patterns.* T. Parsons and R.F. Bales, eds. New York: Free Press.

Parsons, Talcott. 1959. "The school as a social system." *Harvard Educational Review* 29:297–318.

Parsons, Talcott. 1960. *Structure and Process in Modern Societies.* New York: Free Press.

Parsons, Talcott. 1964. "Christianity and modern industrial society." In *Religion, Culture, and Society.* Louis Schneider, ed. New York: Wiley.

Parsons, Talcott, and Robert F. Bales (eds.). 1955. *Family Socialization and Interaction Process.* Glencoe, IL: Free Press.

Parsons, Talcott, and Neil Smelser. 1956. *Economy and Society.* London: Routledge and Kegan Paul.

Payne, Barbara J., and Laurel A. Strain. 1990. "Family social support in later life: Ethnic variations." *Canadian Ethnic Studies* 22(2):99–110.

Pearlin, Leonard I., and Melvin L. Kohn. 1966. "Social class, occupation, and parental values: A cross-national study." *American Sociological Review* 31(4): 466–479.

Peitchinis, Stephen G. 1989. *Women at Work: Discrimination and Response.* Toronto: McClelland and Stewart.

Penalosa, F. 1968. "Mexican family roles." *Journal of Marriage and the Family* 30:680–689.

Peplau, Letitia Anne, and Steven L. Gordon. 1985. "Women and men in love: Gender differences in close heterosexual relationships." In *Women, Gender, and Social Psychology.* Virginia E. O'Leary, Rhoda K. Unger, and Barbara S. Wallston, eds. Hillsdale, NJ: Lawrence Erlbaum Associates.

Perry, Robert L. 1971. *Galt, U.S.A.* Toronto: Maclean-Hunter.

Persons, Stow. 1987. *Ethnic Studies at Chicago 1905–45.* Urbana, IL: University of Illinois Press.

Pestieau, Caroline. 1976. "Women in Quebec." In *Women in the Canadian Mosaic.* Gwen Matheson (ed.). Peter Martin Associates.

Peter, Karl. 1988. Personal communication.

Peters, John. 1982. "Children as socialization agents through the parents' middle-years." Paper presented to the Canadian Sociology and Anthropology Association.

Peters, John. 1984. "Cultural variations in family structure." In *The Family: Changing Trends in Canada.* Maureen Baker, ed. Toronto: McGraw-Hill Ryerson.

Peters, John F. 1987. "Changing perspectives on divorce." In *Family Matters: Sociology and Contemporary Canadian Families.* Karen L. Anderson et al., eds. Toronto: Methuen.

Petersen, W. 1979. *Malthus.* Cambridge, MA: Harvard University Press.

Peterson, Gary W., and David F. Peters. 1983. "Adolescents' construction of social reality: The impact of television and peers." *Youth and Society* 15:67–85.

Peterson, Linda S. 1989. *Labor Force and Informal Employment in Mexico: Recent Characteristics and Trends.* Washington, DC: U.S. Bureau of the Census.

Peterson, Richard A. 1979. "Revitalizing the culture concept." *Annual Review of Sociology* 5.

Pfeffer, Naomi, and Anne Woollett. 1983. *The Experience of Infertility.* London: Virago.

Phillips, Andrew, and Cindy Barrett. 1988. "Defining identity." *Maclean's* (Jan.):44–45.

Phillips, Susan D. 1991. "Meaning and structure in social movements: Mapping the network of national Canadian women's organizations." *Canadian Journal of Political Science* 24(4):754–782.

Piaget, Jean. 1928. *Judgment and Reasoning in the Child.* New York: Harcourt.

Piaget, Jean. 1932. *The Moral Judgment of the Child.* New York: Harcourt.

Picard, Robert G. 1991. "The journalist's role in coverage of terrorist events." In *Media Coverage of Terrorism: Methods and Diffusion.* O. Odasuo Alali and Kenoye Kelvin Eke, eds. Newbury Park, CA: Sage.

Pike, Robert. 1981. "Sociological research on higher education in English Canada 1970–1980: A thematic review." *Canadian Journal of Higher Education* 11(2): 1–25.

Pike, Robert M. 1975. "Introduction and overview." In *Socialization and Values in Canadian Society* (Vol. 2). R.M. Pike and Elia Zureik, eds. Toronto: McClelland and Stewart.

Piliavin, Irving, and Scott Briar. 1964. "Police encounters with juveniles." *American Journal of Sociology* 70 (Sept.):206–214.

Pinard, Maurice. 1975; 1971. *The Rise of a Third Party.* Montreal and Kingston: McGill-Queen's University Press (enlarged edition)/Englewood Cliffs, NJ: Prentice-Hall.

Pinard, Maurice. 1992. "The dramatic reemergence of the Quebec independence movement." *Journal of International Affairs* 45(2):471–497.

Pinard, Maurice, and Richard Hamilton. 1984. "The class bases of the Quebec independence movement: Conjectures and evidence." *Ethnic and Racial Studies* 7(1):19–54.

Pincus, F. 1980. "The fake promises of community colleges: Class conflict and vocational education." In *Harvard Educational Review* 50:332–361.

Pineo, Peter C. 1971. "The extended family in a working-class area of Hamilton." In *Canadian Society.* Bernard Blishen, ed. Toronto: Macmillan.

Pineo, Peter C. 1976. "Social mobility in Canada: The current picture." *Sociological Focus* 9(2):120.

Pineo, Peter C. 1980. "The social standing of ethnic and racial groupings." In *Ethnicity and Ethnic Relations in Canada.* J. Goldstein and R. Bienvenu, eds. Toronto: Butterworths.

Pineo, Peter C. 1983. "Stratification and social class." In *An Introduction to Sociology.* M.M. Rosenberg et al., eds. Toronto: Methuen.

Pineo, Peter C., and Dianne Looker. 1983. "Class conformity in the Canadian setting." *Canadian Journal of Sociology.* 8:293–317.

Pineo, Peter C., and John Porter. 1967. "Occupational prestige in Canada." *Canadian Review of Sociology and Anthropology* 4:24–40.

Pineo, Peter C., et al. 1977. "The 1971 census and the socioeconomic classification of occupations." *Canadian Review of Sociology and Anthropology* 1:91–102.

Pirenne, Henri. 1939. *Medieval Cities.* Princeton, NJ: Princeton University Press.

Platt, Anthony M. 1969. *The Child Savers: The Invention of Delinquency.* Chicago: University of Chicago Press.

Pleck, J.H. 1985. *Working Wives/Working Husbands.* Beverly Hills, CA: Sage.

Pleck, Joseph. 1981. "Men's power with women, other men, and society: A men's movement analysis." In *Men in Difficult Times.* Robert A. Lewis, ed. Englewood Cliffs, NJ: Prentice-Hall.

Polanyi, Karl. 1957. In *Trade and Markets in the Early Empires.* C.M. Arsenberg and H.W. Pearson, eds. Glencoe, IL: Free Press.

Ponak, Allen, and Mark Thompson. 1989. "Public sector collective bargaining." In *Union-Management*

Relations in Canada. John C. Anderson, Morley Gunderson, and Allen Ponak, eds. 2nd edition. Don Mills, ON: Addison-Wesley.

Ponting, J. Rick. 1986. "Canadian gender-role attitudes." Unpublished manuscript. University of Calgary.

Ponting, J. Rick (ed.). 1986. *Arduous Journey: Canadian Indians and Decolonization.* Toronto: McClelland and Stewart.

Ponting, J. Rick, and Roger Gibbins. 1980. *Out of Irrelevance: A Socio-Political Introduction to Indian Affairs in Canada.* Toronto: Butterworths.

Ponting, J. Rick, and Roger Gibbins. 1981. "The reactions of English Canadians and French Québécois to native Indian protest." *Canadian Review of Sociology and Anthropology* 18(2):222–238.

Pope, Liston. 1942. *Millhands and Preachers.* New Haven, CT: Yale University Press.

Population Reference Bureau. 1991. *1991 World Population Data Sheet.* Washington, DC: Population Reference Bureau.

Population Reference Bureau. 1992. *World Population Data Sheet, 1992.* Washington, DC: Population Reference Bureau.

Porter, Elaine. 1987. "Conceptual frameworks for studying families." In *Family Matters: Sociology and Contemporary Canadian Families.* Karen L. Anderson et al., eds. Toronto: Methuen.

Porter, John. 1965. *The Vertical Mosaic: An Analysis of Social Class and Power in Canada.* Toronto: University of Toronto Press.

Porter, John. 1967. *Canadian Social Structure: A Statistical Profile.* Toronto: McClelland and Stewart.

Porter, John. 1970. "Research biography on a macrosociological study: *The Vertical Mosaic.*" In *Macrosociology: Research and Theory.* James S. Coleman, Amitai Etzioni, and John Porter, eds. Boston: Allyn and Bacon.

Porter, John. 1979. *The Measure of Canadian Society.* Toronto: Gage.

Porter, John, Marion Porter, and Bernard Blishen. 1982. *Stations and Callings: Making It Through the Ontario Schools.* Toronto: Methuen.

Porter, Marion, John Porter, and Bernard Blishen. 1973. *Does Money Matter?* Toronto: York University, Institute for Behavioural Research.

Posner, Judith. 1980. "Old and female: The double whammy." In *Aging in Canada: Social Perspectives.* Victor W. Marshall, ed. Toronto: Fitzhenry and Whiteside.

Posner, Judith. 1987. "The objectified male: The new male image in advertising." In *Women and Men: Interdisciplinary Readings on Gender.* Greta Hofmann Nemiroff, ed. Toronto: Fitzhenry and Whiteside.

Postman, Neil. 1982. *The Disappearance of Childhood.* New York: Penguin.

Poulantzas, N. 1973. *Political Power and Social Classes.* London: New Left.

Powell, Brian J., and James K. Martin. 1980. "Economic implications of Canada's aging society." In *Aging in Canada: Social Perspectives.* Victor W. Marshall, ed. Toronto: Fitzhenry and Whiteside.

Power, Margaret. 1975. "Women's work is never done — by men: A socioeconomic model of sex-typing in occupations." *Journal of Industrial Relations* 17:225–239.

Pratt, David. 1984. "Bias in textbooks: Progress and problems." In *Multiculturalism in Canada: Social and Educational Perspectives.* Ronald J. Samuda, John W. Berry, and Michel Laferrière, eds. Toronto: Allyn and Bacon.

Prentice, A. 1975. *The School Promoters: Education and Social Class, in Mid-Nineteenth Century Upper Canada.* Toronto: McClelland & Stewart.

Press, Andrea. 1985. "The differential effects of liberal feminism on working-class and middle-class women." Paper presented to the Pacific Sociological Association.

Presser, H.B. 1989. "Can we make time for children? The economy, work schedules, and child care." *Demography* 26:523–543.

Preston, S.H. 1984. "Children and the elderly: Divergent paths for America's dependents." *Demography* 21: 435–457.

Provenzo, Eugene F., Jr. 1991. *Video Kids: Making Sense of Nintendo.* Cambridge, MA: Harvard University Press.

Putnam, R. 1976. *The Comparative Study of Political Elites.* Englewood Cliffs, NJ: Prentice-Hall.

Pyke, S.W. 1975. "Children's literature: Conceptions of sex roles." In *Socialization and Values in Canadian Society* (Vol. 2). Robert M. Pike and Elia Zureik, eds. Toronto: McClelland and Stewart.

Quadagno, Jill S. 1980. "The modernization controversy: A socio-historical analysis of retirement in nineteenth century England." Paper presented to the American Sociological Association.

Quinney, Richard. 1970. *The Social Reality of Crime.* Boston: Little, Brown.

Rainwater, Lee. 1966. "Work and identity in the lower class." In *Planning for a Nation of Cities.* Sam Bass Warner, Jr., ed. Cambridge, MA: MIT Press.

Ram, B. 1990. *New Trends in the Family: Demographic Facts and Features.* Ottawa: Statistics Canada, catalogue no. 91-535E.

Ramcharan, Subhas. 1982. *Racism: Nonwhites in Canada.* Toronto: Butterworths.

Rank, M.R. 1982. "Determinants of conjugal influence in wives' decision making." *Journal of Marriage and the Family* 44:591–604.

Ravanera, Z.R., F. Rajulton, and T.K. Burch. 1992. *A Cohort Analysis of Home-Leaving in Canada, 1910–1975.* London, ON: University of Western Ontario, Population Studies Centre, Discussion Paper 92-3.

Ray, Arthur J. 1974. *Indians in the Fur Trade: Their Role as Hunters, Trappers and Middlemen in the Lands Southwest of Hudson Bay 1660–1870.* Toronto: University of Toronto Press.

Reasons, Charles. 1974. "The politics of drugs: An inquiry in the sociology of social problems." *Sociological Quarterly* 15(3):381–404.

Reavis, Dick J. 1990. *Conversations with Moctezuma: Ancient Shadows Over Modern Life in Mexico.* New York: Morrow.

Reevis, D.J. 1990. "Afterword." In *Conversations with Moctezuma.* Dick J. Reavis. New York: William Morrow.

Regnier, R. 1987. "Survival schools as emancipatory education." In *Canadian Journal of Native Education* 14(2):42–53.

Reichard, S., F. Livson, and P.G. Petersen. 1962. *Aging and Personality.* New York: Wiley.

Reiss, Albert J., Jr. 1959. "The sociological study of communities." *Rural Sociology* 24:118–130.

Reiss, Albert. 1971. *The Police and the Public.* New Haven, CT: Yale University Press.

Reiss, Albert, and Jeffrey Roth (eds.). 1993. *Understanding and Preventing Violence.* Washington, DC: National Academy.

Reskin, B.F., and S. Coverman. 1985. "Sex and race in the determinants of psychophysical distress: A reappraisal of the sex-role hypothesis." *Social Forces* 63: 1038–1059.

Rex, John. 1968. "The sociology of a zone of transition." In *Readings in Urban Sociology.* R.E. Pohl, ed. Oxford: Pergamon.

Reynolds, Lloyd G. 1959. *Labor Economics and Labor Relations.* Englewood Cliffs, NJ: Prentice-Hall.

Rheingold, Harriet L. 1966. "The development of social behavior in the human infant." In *Concept of Development: A Report on a Conference in Commemoration of the 40th Anniversary of the Institute of Child Development.* H.W. Stevenson, ed. Monographs of the Society for Research in Development 31 (5, whole no. 107). Minneapolis: University of Minnesota.

Rheingold, Harriet L. 1969. "The social and socializing infant." In *Handbook of Socialization Theory and Research.* David A. Goslin, ed. Chicago: Rand McNally.

Rich, H. 1976. "The vertical mosaic revisited." *Journal of Canadian Studies* 11(1):14–31.

Richardson, Laurel Walum. 1981. *The Dynamics of Sex and Gender.* 2nd edition. Boston: Houghton Mifflin.

Richardson, R.J. 1992. "Free trade: Why did it happen." *Canadian Review of Sociology and Anthropology* 29:307–328.

Richer, Stephen. 1979. "Sex-role socialization and early schooling." *Canadian Review of Sociology and Anthropology* 16:195–205.

Richer, Stephen. 1983. "Sex-role socialization: Agents, content, relationships, and outcomes." In *The Canadian Family.* K. Ishwaran, ed. Toronto: Gage.

Richer, Stephen. 1984. "Sexual inequality and children's play." *Canadian Review of Sociology and Anthropology* 21:166–180.

Richling, Barnett. 1985. "'You'd never starve here': Return migration to rural Newfoundland." *Canadian Review of Sociology and Anthropology* 22:236–249.

Richmond, Anthony H. 1972. *Ethnic Residential Segregation in Toronto.* Toronto: York University, Institute for Behavioural Research.

Richmond, Anthony H., and Warren E. Kalbach. 1980. *Factors in the Adjustment of Immigrants and Their Descendants.* Ottawa: Statistics Canada.

Richmond-Abbott, Marie. 1983. *Masculine and Feminine: Sex Roles over the Life Cycle.* Reading, MA: Addison-Wesley.

Riding, Alan. 1989. *Distant Neighbors: A Portrait of the Mexicans.* New York: Vintage.

Rifkin, Jeremy. 1987. *Time Wars: The Primary Conflict in Human History.* New York: Henry Holt.

Riley, Matilda White. 1976. "Age strata in social systems." In *Handbook of Aging and the Social Sciences.* Robert Binstock and Ethel Shanas, eds. New York: Van Nostrand Reinhold.

Riley, Matilda White. 1980. "Age and aging: From theory generation to theory testing." In *Sociological Theory and Research: A Critical Approach.* Hubert M. Blalock, Jr., ed. New York: Free Press.

Riley, Matilda White, Marilyn Johnson, and Anne Foner. 1972. *Aging and Society: Vol. 2 A Sociology of Age Stratification.* New York: Sage.

Riley, Matilda White, et al. 1969. "Socialization for the middle and later years." In *Handbook of Socialization Theory and Research.* David Goslin, ed. Chicago: Rand McNally.

Riley, Susan. 1985. "Anti-feminist group incensed over lack of funding." *Calgary Herald* (July 2).

Rindfuss, R.R., and A.M. Parnell. 1989. "The varying connection between marital status and childbearing in the United States." *Population and Development Review* 15:447–470.

Rinehart, James W. 1987. *The Tyranny of Work.* 2nd edition. Toronto: Harcourt Brace Jovanovich.

Rioux, Marcel. 1971. *Quebec in Question.* Toronto: James, Lewis, and Samuel.

Ritchie, Marguerite. 1975. "Alice through the statutes." *McGill Law Journal* 21:702.

Roberts, Donald F., and Nathan Maccoby. 1985. "Effects of mass communication." In *The Handbook of Social Psychology* (Vol. 2). Garner Lindzey and Elliot Aronson, eds. 3rd edition. New York: Random House.

Roberts, Keith A. 1984. *Religion in Sociological Perspective.* Homewood, IL: Dorsey.

Roberts, Sam. 1992. "No society rejoices at helping its poor." *The New York Times* (July 5):6.

Robertson, Ann. 1990. "The politics of Alzheimer's disease: A case study in apocalyptic demography" *International Journal of Health Services* 20(3):429–442.

Robertson, Ian. 1981. *Sociology.* 2nd edition. New York: Worth.

Robinson, Barrie W., and Wayne W. McVey, Jr. 1985. "The relative contributions of death and divorce to marital dissolution in Canada and the United States." *Journal of Comparative Family Studies* 16(1): 93–109.

Rock, Ronald, Marcus Jacobson, and Richard Janopaul. 1968. *Hospitalization and Discharge of the Mentally Ill.* Chicago: University of Chicago Press.

Roethlisberger, F.J., and W.J. Dickson. 1947. *Management and the Worker.* Cambridge, MA: Harvard University Press.

Rohner, Ronald P., and Evelyn C. Rohner. 1970. *The Kwakiutl: Indians of British Columbia.* New York: Holt, Rinehart and Winston.

Rohter, Larry. 1988a. "Mexican victor urges party to adapt to new challenge." *The New York Times* (July 15):A3.

Rohter, Larry. 1988b. "200,000 in Mexican capital protest vote count." *The New York Times* (July 17):A5.

Rohter, Larry. 1988c. "Mexican leader takes over today: Salinas dogged by charges of vote fraud, is pledged to transform system." *The New York Times* (Dec. 1):A5.

Rokeach, Milton. 1965. "Paradoxes of religious belief." *Information Service.* National Council of Churches (Feb. 13):1–2.

Rokeach, Milton, 1969. "Religious values and social compassion." *Review of Religious Research* 11:3–23.

Rokeach, Milton. 1974. "Some reflections about the place of values in Canadian social science." In *Perspectives on the Social Sciences in Canada.* T.N. Guinsberg and G.L. Reuber, eds. Toronto: University of Toronto Press.

Romanos, M.C. 1979. "Forsaken farms: The village-to-city movement in Europe." In *Western European Cities in Crisis.* M.C. Romanos, ed. Lexington, KY: Lexington Press.

Roniger, Luis. 1990. *Hierarchy and Trust in Modern Mexico and Brazil.* New York: Praeger.

Roof, Wade Clark, and Dean R. Hoge. 1980. "Church involvement in America: Social factors affecting membership and participation." *Review of Religious Research* 21:405–426.

Roof, Wade Clark, and William McKinney. 1987. *American Mainline Religion.* New Brunswick, NJ: Rutgers University Press.

Roozen, David A., William McKinney, and Wayne Thompson. 1990. "The 'big chill' generation warms to worship." *Review of Religious Research* 31:314–322.

Rosaldo, Michelle Zimbalist. 1974. "Woman, culture, and society: A theoretical overview." In *Woman, Culture and Society.* M.Z. Rosaldo and Louise Lamphere, eds. Stanford, CA: Stanford University Press.

Rosaldo, Michelle Zimbalist. 1980. "The use and abuse of anthropology: Reflections on feminism and cross-cultural understanding." *Signs* 5:389–417.

Rosaldo, Michelle Zimbalist, and Louise Lamphere, eds. 1974. *Woman, Culture and Society.* Stanford, CA: Stanford University Press.

Rose, Arnold L. 1965. "The subculture of aging: A framework of social gerontology." In *Old People and Their Social World.* Arnold M. Rose and Warren A. Peterson, eds. Philadelphia: F.A. Davis.

Rosen, B.C. 1965. *Adolescence and Religion.* Cambridge, MA: Schenkman.

Rosenberg, Miriam. 1976. "The biological basis for sex role stereotypes." In *Beyond Sex-Role Stereotypes: Readings toward a Psychology of Androgyny.* Alexandra G. Kaplan and Joan P. Bean, eds. Boston: Little, Brown.

Rosenberg, M. Michael, and Morton Weinfeld. 1983. "Ethnicity." In *An Introduction to Sociology.* M.M. Rosenberg et al., eds. Toronto: Methuen.

Rosenfeld, Rachel A. 1979. "Women's occupational careers: Individual and structural explanations." *Sociology of Work and Occupations* 6:283–311.

Rosenhan, D.L. 1973. "On being sane in insane places." *Science* 179(Jan. 19):250–258.

Rosenmayr, Leopold. 1977. "The family: A source of hope for the elderly." In *Family, Bureaucracy and the Elderly.* Ethel Shanas and marvin B. Sussman, eds. Durham, NC: Duke University Press.

Rosenthal, Carolyn J. 1982. "Family responsibilities and concerns: A perspective on the lives of middle-aged women." *Resources for Feminist Research* (Winter).

Rosenthal, Carolyn J. 1985. "Kinkeeping in the familial division of labor." *Journal of Marriage and the Family* 47(4):965–974.

Rosenthal, Carolyn J. 1986. "The differentiation of multigenerational households." *Canadian Journal on Aging* 5(1):27–42.

Rosenthal, Carolyn J. 1987a. "Aging and intergenerational relations in Canada." In *Aging in Canada: Social Perspectives.* Victor W. Marshall, ed. 2nd edition. Toronto: Fitzhenry and Whiteside.

Rosenthal, Carolyn J. 1987b. "Generational succession: The passing on of family headship." *Journal of Comparative Family Studies* 18:61–77.

Rosenthal, Carolyn J. 1987c. "The comforter: Providing personal advice and emotional support to generations in the family." *Canadian Journal on Aging* 6(3): 228–240.

Rosenthal, Carolyn J., and Victor W. Marshall. 1986. "The head of the family: Social meaning and structural variability." *Canadian Journal of Sociology* 11(2): 183–198.

Rosenthal, R., and L. Jacobson. 1968. *Pygmalion in the Classroom.* New York: Holt, Rinehart and Winston.

Rosow, Irving. 1967. *Social Integration of the Aged.* New York: Free Press.

Rosow, Irving. 1973. "The social context of the aging self." *Gerontologist* 13(Spring):82.

Rosow, Irving. 1974. *Socialization to Old Age.* Berkeley, CA: University of California Press.

Rosow, Irving. 1976. "Status and role change through the life span." In *Handbook of Aging and the Social Sciences.* Robert H. Binstock and Ethel Shanas, eds. New York: Van Nostrand Reinhold.

Ross, C.E. 1987. "The division of labor at home." *Social Forces* 65:816–833.

Ross, C.E., and J. Huber. 1985. "Hardship and depression." *Journal of Health and Social Behavior* 26:312–327.

Ross, E.E., and J. Mirowsky. 1988. "Child-care and emotional adjustment of wives' employment." *Journal of Health and Social Behavior* 29:127–138.

Ross, Michael W. 1986. "Causes of gender dysphoria: How does transsexualism develop and why?" In *Transsexualism and Sex Reassignment.* William A.W. Walters and Michael W. Ross (eds.). New York: Oxford University Press.

Rossi, Alice S. 1980. "Life-span theories and women's lives." *Signs* 6:4–32.

Rossi, Alice S. 1984. "Gender and parenthood." *American Sociological Review* 49:1–19.

Rossi, Alice S., and Peter H. Rossi. 1990. *Of Human Bonding: Parent–Child Relations Across the Life Course.* New York: Aldine de Gruyter.

Rowe, G., and M.J. Norris. 1985. *Mortality Projections of Registered Indians, 1982–1996.* Ottawa: Ministry of Indian Affairs and Northern Development.

Roy, Donald. 1952. "Quota restriction and goldbricking in a machine shop." *American Journal of Sociology* 57:427–442.

Roy, Donald. 1954. "Efficiency and 'the fix': Informal intergroup relations in a piecework machine shop." *American Journal of Sociology* 60:255–266.

Roy, Donald. 1959. "Banana time: Job satisfaction and informal interaction." *Human Organization* 18(4): 158–168.

Royal Commission on Bilingualism and Biculturalism. 1965. *Report.* Ottawa: Queen's Printer.

Royal Commission on the Economic Union and Development Prospects for Canada. (Macdonald Commission.) 1985. *Report* (Vols. 1–3). Ottawa: Supply and Services.

Royal Commission on National Development in the Arts, Letters and Sciences. (Massey Report.) 1951. Ottawa: Supply and Services.

Royal Commission on the Status of Women in Canada. 1970. *Report.* Ottawa: Information Canada.

Rubin, J.Z., F.J. Provenzano, and Z. Luria. 1974. "The eye of the beholder: Parents' views on sex of newborns." *American Journal of Orthopsychiatry* 44:512–519.

Rubin, Lillian B. 1979. *Women of a Certain Age: The Midlife Search for Self.* New York: Harper and Row.

Rudé, George. 1967. *The Crowd in the French Revolution.* New York: Oxford University Press.

Rudner, Richard S. 1966. *Philosophy of Social Science.* Englewood Cliffs, NJ: Prentice Hall.

Ruether, Rosemary R. (ed.). 1974. *Religion and Sexism: Images of Woman in the Jewish and Christian Traditions.* New York: Simon and Schuster.

Rusche, George, and Otto Kirchmeimer. 1939. *Punishment and Social Structure.* New York: Columbia University Press.

Rushby, William, and John Thrush. 1973. "Mennonites and social compassion." *Review of Religious Research* 15:16–28.

Russell, Peter. 1975. "The political role of the Supreme Court of Canada inn its first century." *Canadian Bar Review* 53(3):576–596.

Ryan, William. 1971. *Blaming the Victim.* New York: Pantheon.

Ryder, Norman B. 1965. "The cohort as a concept in the study of social change." *American Sociological Review* 30(6):834–861.

Ryff, Carol D. 1986. "The subjective construction of self and society: An agenda for life-span research." In *Later Life: The Social Psychology of Aging.* Victor W. Marshall, ed. Beverly Hills, CA: Sage.

Sacco, V.F. 1985. "City size and perceptions of crime." *Canadian Journal of Sociology* 10(3):277–293.

Sallot, Jeff. "Career pause expensive for wives." *Globe and Mail,* July 7, 1992, p. 6A.

Salziner, Susanne et al. (ed.) 1988. *Social Networks of Children, Adolescents, and College Students.* New Jersey: Lawrence Earlbaum Associates, Publishers.

Sanday, P.R. 1981. *Female Power and Male Dominance: On the Origins of Sexual Inequality.* Cambridge, UK: Cambridge University Press.

Sanders, T. 1979. *Education, Language and Culture Among the Contemporary Maya.* AUFS report No. 50. Hanover: New Hampshire.

Sardon, J-P. 1990. "Le remplacement des générations en Europe depuis le début du siècle." *Population* 45: 947–967.

Sarlo, Christopher. 1992. "Poverty line way too high author claims." *Hamilton Spectator,* in *Vancouver Sun,* July 15, 1992:p.1A.

Saunders, John, and D. Fagan. 1992. "Long war to follow NAFTA signing: No guarantee deal will be ratified." *The Globe and Mail* (Aug. 7):A1–A2.

Sayers, Janet. 1982. *Biological Politics: Feminist and Anti-feminist Perspectives* London: Tavistock.

Scanzoni, John. 1982. *Sexual Bargaining: Power Politics in the American Marriage.* 2nd edition. Chicago: University of Chicago Press.

Scanzoni, Letha Dawson, and John Scanzoni. 1981. *Men, Women, and Change: A Sociology of Marriage and Family.* New York: McGraw-Hill.

Scheff, Thomas. 1966. *Being Mentally Ill: A Sociological Theory.* Chicago: Aldine.

Schegloff, Emanuel A. 1992. "Repair after next turn: The last structural provided defense of intersubjectivity in conversation." *The American Journal of Sociology* 97:1295–1345.

Schellenberg, James A. 1974. *An Introduction to Social Psychology.* 2nd edition. New York: Random House.

Schellenberg, James A. 1978. *Masters of Social Psychology: Freud, Mead, Lewin, and Skinner.* New York: Oxford University Press.

Schelsky, K. 1961. "Family and school in modern society." In *Education, Economy, and Society.* A.H. Halsey et al., eds. Glencoe, IL: Free Press.

Schlesinger, Benjamin. 1978. *Remarriage in Canada.* Toronto: University of Toronto Press.

Schlesinger, Benjamin. 1983. "Living in one-parent families: The children's perspective." In *The Canadian Family.* K. Ishwaran, ed. Toronto: Gage.

Schlossman, Steven. 1977. *Love and the American Delinquent.* Chicago: University of Chicago Press.

Schmidt, Wolfgang, Reginald Smart, and Marie Moss. 1968. *Social Class and the Treatment of Alcoholism* Monograph No. 7. Toronto: University of Toronto/ Addiction Research Foundation.

Schnaiberg, Allan, and Shelley Goldenberg. 1986. "From empty nest to crowded nest: Some contradictions in the returning young-adult syndrome." Paper presented to the American Sociological Association.

Schneider, Frank W., and Larry M. Coutts. 1979. "Teacher orientations towards masculine and feminine: Role of sex of teacher and sex composition of school." *Canadian Journal of Behavioural Science* 11: 99–111.

Schnore, Leo F. 1958. "Social morphology and human ecology." *American Journal of Sociology* 63:620–634.

Schoen, R. 1992. "First unions and the stability of first marriages." *Journal of Marriage and the Family* 54:281–284.

Schreiber, E. 1980. "Class awareness and class voting in Canada." *Canadian Review of Sociology and Anthropology* 17:37–44.

Schulz, David A. 1984. *Human Sexuality.* 2nd edition. Englewood Cliffs, NJ: Prentice-Hall.

Schwenger, C.W., and M.J. Gross. 1980. "Institutional care and institutionalization of the elderly in Canada." In *Aging in Canada: Social Perspectives.* Victor W. Marshall, ed. Toronto: Fitzhenry and Whiteside.

Science Council of Canada. 1977. *Uncertain Prospects: Canadian Manufacturing Industry, 1971–1977.* Ottawa: Supply and Services Canada.

Science Council of Canada. 1984. *Canadian Industrial Development: Some Policy Directions.* Ottawa: Supply and Services Canada.

Scott, Joseph W., and M. El-Assal. 1969. "Multiuniversity, university size, university quality and student protest: An empirical study." *American Sociological Review* 34:702–709.

Scott, W. Richard. 1987. *Organizations.* 2nd edition. Englewood Cliffs, NJ: Prentice-Hall.

Scull, Andrew. 1977. *Decarceration: Community Treatment and the Deviant — A Radical View.* Englewood Cliffs, NJ: Prentice-Hall.

Seashore, Stanley E. 1954. *Group Cohesiveness in the Industrial Work Group.* Ann Arbor, MI: University of Michigan, Survey Research Center.

Seligson, Mitchell A. 1984. "The dual gaps: An overview of theory and research." In *The Gap Between Rich and Poor.* M.A. Seligson, ed. Boulder, CO: Westview.

Selznick, Philip. 1949. *TVA and the Grass Roots.* Berkeley, CA: University of California Press.

Seneker, Harold (ed.). 1992. "The world's billionaires." *Forbes,* July 20, 1992, pp. 158;160.

Seneker, Harold and Dolores Lataniotis (eds.). 1992. "The richest people in America." *Forbes,* October 19, 1992, p. 92.

Sennet, Richard. 1970. *The Uses of Disorder: Personal Identity and City Life.* New York: Vintage.

Shamai, Shmuel. 1992. "Ethnicity and educational achievement in Canada: 1941–1981." *Canadian Ethnic Studies* 24:43–57.

Shanas, Ethel, with the assistance of Gloria Heinemann. 1982. *National Survey of the Aged.* Publication No. OHDS 83–20425. Washington, DC: U.S. Department of Health and Human Services, Administration on Aging.

Shanas, Ethel, et al. 1968. *Old People in Three Industrial Societies.* New York: Atherton.

Shapiro, Evelyn, and N.P. Roos. 1987. "Predictors, patterns and consequences of nursing-home use in one Canadian province." In *Aging in Canada: Social Perspectives.* Victor W. Marshall, ed. 2nd edition. Toronto: Fitzhenry and Whiteside.

Sharer, Robert J., and David C. Grove (eds.). 1989. *Regional Perspectives on the Olmecs.* Cambridge: Cambridge University Press.

Shaw, Marvin E., and Philip R. Costanzo. 1970. *Theories of Social Psychology.* New York: McGraw-Hill.

Shaw, S.M. 1988. "Gender differences in the definition and perception of household labour." *Family Relations* 37:333–337.

Shea, Latarine. 1990. "Changes in women's occupation." Statistics Canada. *Canadian Social Trends.* Autumn, 1990, p. 23.

Sheehy, Gail. 1976; 1974. *Passages: Predictable Crises in Adult Life.* Toronto: Clarke Irwin/New York: Dutton.

Shepherd, J., and G. Vulliamy. 1983. "A comparative sociology of school knowledge." *British Journal of Sociology of Education* 4(1):3–18.

Shibutani, Tamotsu, and Kian M. Kwan. 1965. *Ethnic Stratification: A Comparative Approach.* New York: Macmillan.

Sigelman, Lee. 1977. "Multi-nation surveys of religious beliefs." *Journal for the Scientific Study of Religion* 16:289–294.

Silberman, Charles. 1970. *Crisis in the Classroom.* New York: Random House.

Simmel, Georg. 1950a. *The Sociology of Georg Simmel.* Kurt Wolff, ed. Glencoe, IL: Free Press.

Simmel, Georg. 1950b. "The metropolis and mental life." In *Neighborhood, City, and Metropolis.* Robert Gutman and David Popenoe, eds. New York: Random House.

Simon, Herbert A. 1987. "The steam engine and the computer: What makes technology revolutionary." *Computers and People* 36(11–12):7–11.

Simon, Julian L. 1981. *The Ultimate Resource.* Princeton, NJ: Princeton University Press.

Sinclair, Clayton. 1992. "Home-Price Index at 20-Year Low." *Financial Times of Canada,* August 10–16, p. 4.

Singer, Benjamin D. 1986. *Advertising and Society.* Don Mills, ON: Addison-Wesley.

Singer, J.L., and D.G. Singer. 1988. "Some hazards of growing up in a television environment: Children's aggression and restlessness." In *Television as a Social Issue.* Stuart Oskamp, ed. Newbury Park, CA: Sage.

Sjoberg, Gideon. 1960. *The Preindustrial City.* Glencoe, IL: Free Press.

Sjoberg, Gideon. 1973. "The origin and evolution of cities." In *Cities: Their Origin, Growth and Human Impact. (Scientific American.)* San Francisco: W.H. Freeman.

Skinner, B.F. 1953. *Science and Human Behavior.* New York: Macmillan.

Skogstad, Grace. 1980. "Agrarian protest in Alberta." *Canadian Review of Sociology and Anthropology* 17(1):55–73.

Smelser, Neil J. 1963. *Theory of Collective Behavior.* New York: Free Press.

Smith, Adam. 1937; 1776. *The Wealth of Nations.* New York: Modern Library.

Smith, C.W. 1985. "Uncle dad." *Esquire* 103(Mar.):73–85.

Smith, Denis. 1967. "Prairie revolt, federalism and the party system." In *Party Politics in Canada.* H.G. Thorburn, ed. Scarborough, ON: Prentice-Hall.

Smith, Dorothy E. 1974. "Women's perspective as a

radical critique of sociology." *Sociological Inquiry* 44: 7–13.

Smith, Dorothy E. 1975. "An analysis of ideological structures and how women are excluded: Considerations for academic women." *Canadian Review of Sociology and Anthropology* 12(1):353–369.

Smith, Dorothy E. 1977. *Feminism and Marxism: A Place to Begin, A Way to Go.* Vancouver: New Star.

Smith, Dorothy E. 1983. "Women, the family and the productive process." In *Introduction to Sociology.* J. Paul Grayson, ed. Toronto: Gage.

Smith, Dorothy. 1987. *The Everyday World as Problematic. A Feminist Sociology.* Toronto: University of Toronto Press.

Smith, Douglas. 1982. "Street level justice: Situational determinants of police arrest decisions." *Social Problems* 29:167–177.

Smith, Douglas, and Christy Visher. 1980. "Sex and involvement in deviance crime: A quantitative review of the empirical literature." *American Sociological Review* 45(4):691–701.

Smith, Drake S. 1985. "Wife employment and marital adjustment: A cumulation of results." *Family Relations* 34:483–490.

Smith, K.R., D.D. Zick, and G.J. Duncan. 1991. "Remarriage patterns among recent widows and widowers." *Demography* 28:361–374.

Smith, Kathleen, Muriel Pumphrey, and Julian Hall. 1963. "The 'last straw': The decisive incident resulting in the request for hospitalization in 100 schizophrenic patients." *American Journal of Psychiatry* 120(Sept.): 228–232.

Smith, Michael D. 1975. "The legitimation of violence: Hockey players' perceptions of their reference groups' sanctions for assault." *Canadian Review of Sociology and Anthropology* 12(1):72–80.

Smith, Michael D. 1979. "Towards an explanation of hockey violence: A reference other approach." *Canadian Journal of Sociology* 4:105–124.

Smith, Robert Paul. 1979. "Kids, clubs, and special places." In *Socialization and the Life Cycle.* Peter I. Rose, ed. New York: St. Martin's.

Smith, Vivian. 1990. "Women of the press." *The Globe and Mail* (Mar. 24):D1, D8.

Smucker, Joseph. 1980. *Industrialization in Canada.* Scarborough, ON: Prentice-Hall.

Smyth, J.E., and D.A. Soberman. 1976. *The Law and Business Administration.* Scarborough, ON: Prentice-Hall.

Snyder, David, and Charles Tilly. 1972. "Hardship and collective violence, 1830–1960." *American Sociological Review* 37:520–532.

Sorokin, Pitirim. 1927. *Social and Cultural Mobility.* New York: Free Press.

Sorokin, Pitirim, and C.C. Zimmerman. 1929. *Principles of Rural–Urban Sociology.* New York: Holt, Rinehart and Winston.

Southard, Samuel. 1961. *Pastoral Evangelism.* New York: Abingdon.

Spanier, Graham B., and Frank F. Furstenberg, Jr. 1987. "Remarriage and reconstituted families." In *Handbook of Marriage and the Family.* Marvin B. Sussman and Suzanne K. Steinmetz, eds. New York: Plenum.

Spelt, Jacob. 1955. *Urban Development in South-Central Ontario.* Toronto: Collier-Macmillan.

Spelt, Jacob. 1973. *Toronto.* Toronto: Collier-Macmillan.

Spender, Dale. 1985. *Man Made Language.* 2nd edition. London: Routledge and Kegan Paul.

Sperling, Susan. 1991. "Baboons with briefcases: Feminism, functionalism, and sociobiology in the evolution of primate gender." *Signs* 17:1–27.

Spilerman, Seymour. 1976. "Structural characteristics of cities and severity of racial disorders." *American Sociological Review* 41:771–793.

Spitzer, Steven. 1975. "Toward a Marxian theory of deviance." *Social Problems* 22:638–651.

Srole, Leo. 1956. "Social integration and certain corollaries." *American Sociological Review* 21:709–716.

Stack, S. 1980. "The political economy of income inequality: A comparative analysis." *Canadian Journal of Political Science* 13:273–286.

Stanley, George F.G. 1960. *The Birth of Western Canada: A History of the Riel Rebellion.* Toronto: University of Toronto Press.

Stark, Rodney. 1971. "Psychopathology and religious commitment." *Review of Religious Research* 12:165–176.

Stark, Rodney, and William Sims Bainbridge. 1985. *The Future of Religion.* Berkeley, CA: University of California Press.

Stark, Rodney, and Charles Glock. 1968. *American Piety.* Berkeley, CA: University of California Press.

Statistics Canada. 1973. *Education in Canada 1973: A Statistical Review for the Period 1960–1961 to 1970–1971.* Ottawa: Supply and Services.

Statistics Canada. 1975. *Vital Statistics: Births 1973.* Ottawa: Information Canada, catalogue no. 84–204.

Statistics Canada. 1978. *Historical Compendium of Education Statistics: Fro Confederation to 1975.* Ottawa: Supply and Services Canada.

Statistics Canada. 1981. *Education in Canada 1980.* Ottawa: Supply and services Canada.

Statistics Canada. 1983. *Vital Statistics: Births and Deaths 1980.* Ottawa: Minister of Supply and Services, catalogue no. 84–204.

Statistics Canada. 1984. *Labour Force Annual Averages, 19751983.* Ottawa: Supply and Services Canada.

Statistics Canada. 1985a. *Language in Canada.* Ottawa: Supply and Services Canada.

Statistics Canada. 1985b. *Women in Canada: A Statistical Report.* Ottawa: Statistics Canada, catalogue no. 64–202.

Statistics Canada. 1986. *Education in Canada 1985.* Ottawa: Supply and Services Canada.

Statistics Canada. 1987a. "Report on the demographic situation in Canada, 1986." *Current Demographic Analysis* (Vol. 2). Ottawa: Supply and Services Canada.

Statistics Canada. 1987b. *Health and Social Support, 1985.* Ottawa: Minister of Supply and Services, catalogue no. 11–612, no. 1.

Statistics Canada. 1989. *Mobility Status and Inter-*

provincial Migration. Ottawa: Minister of Supply and Services, catalogue no. 93–108.

Statistics Canada. 1990. *Women in Canada*. 2nd edition. Ottawa: Supply and Services.

Statistics Canada. 1990. "Mortality: Summary list of causes 1988." *Health Reports* 2(1):Supplement 12.

Statistics Canada. 1991. *Income Distributions in Canada, 1990*. Ottawa: Statistics Canada, catalogue no. 13-210.

Statistics Canada. 1991. "Births 1989." *Health Reports* 3(2):Supplement 14.

Statistics Canada. 1992. "Births 1990." *Health Reports* 3(2):Supplement 14 (catalogue no. 82-003514).

Statistics Canada. 1992. *The Nation*. Ottawa: Statistics Canada, catalogue no. 93–310.

Statistics Canada. 1993. *Fertility*. (catalogue no. 93-321).

Stebbins, Robert A. 1967. "A theory of the definition of the situation." *Canadian Review of Sociology and Anthropology* 4:148–164.

Steffensmeier, D. 1978. "Crime and the contemporary woman: An analysis of changing levels of female property crime, 1969–75." *Social Forces* 57:566–584.

Stephan, G.E. and D.R. McMullin. 1982. "Tolerance of sexual nonconformity: City size as a situational and early learning determinant." *American Sociological Review* 47:411–415.

Stephens, William. 1963. *The Family in Cross-Cultural Perspective*. New York: Holt, Rinehart and Winston.

Stephenson, Marylee (ed.). 1973. *Women in Canada*. Toronto: New Press.

Sternbach, Nancy Saporta, Marysa Navarro-Aranguren, Patricia Churchryk, and Sonia E. Alvarez. 1992. "Feminisms in Latin America: From Bogota to San Bernardo." *Signs* 17:393–434.

Stevens, Evelyn P. 1973. "Marianismo: The other face of machismo in Latin America." In *Female and Male in Latin America*. Ann Pescatello, ed. Pittsburgh: University of Pittsburgh Press.

Stines, Graham L., R.P. Quinn, and L.J. Shepard. 1976. "Trends in occupational sex discrimination: 1969–1973." *Industrial Relations* 15(1):88–98.

Stockhard, Jean, and Miriam M. Johnson. 1992. *Sex and Gender in Society*. 2nd edition. Englewood Cliffs, NJ: Prentice-Hall.

Stolnitz, George J. 1964. "The demographic transition: From high to low birth rates and death rates." In *Population: The Vital Revolution*. Ronald Freeman, ed. New York: Anchor.

Stone, Leroy O. 1967. *Urban Development in Canada*. Ottawa: Dominion Bureau of Statistics.

Stone, Leroy O., and Susan Fletcher. 1987. "The hypothesis of age patterns in living arrangement passages." In *Aging in Canada: Social Perspectives*. Victor W. Marshall, ed. 2nd edition. Toronto: Fitzhenry and Whiteside.

Storey, Robert. 1991. "Studying work in Canada." *Canadian Journal of Sociology* 16:241–264.

Storm, Christine, Thomas Storm, and Janet Strike-Schurman. 1985. "Obligations for care: Beliefs in a small Canadian town." *Canadian Journal on Aging* 4(2): 75–85.

Stout, C. 1991. "Common law: A growing alternative." *Canadian Social Trends*. 23. Ottawa: Statistics Canada, catalogue no. 11-008E.

Strain, Laurel A., and Barbara J. Payne. 1992. "Social networks and patterns of social interaction among ever-single and separated/divorced elderly Canadians." *Canadian Journal on Aging* 11(1):31–53.

Strong, D.F. 1991. "Some observations on demographic and energy trends as non-conventional security issues of the next century." Paper presented to the NPCSD Workshop on Non-conventional Security of the North Pacific Region, East–West Center, University of Hawaii.

Stryckman, Judith. 1981. "The decision to remarry: The choice and its outcomes." Paper presented to the Gerontological Society of America and the Canadian Association on Gerontology.

Stryckman, Judith. 1987. "Work sharing and the older worker in a unionized setting." In *Aging in Canada: Social Perspectives*. Victor w. Marshall, ed. 2nd edition. Toronto: Fitzhenry and Whiteside.

Suchman, Edward. 1968. "The hang-loose ethic and the spirit of drug use." *Journal of Health and Social Behavior* 9:146–155.

Sudman, Seymour. 1976. *Applied Sampling*. New York: Academic.

Sudnow, David. 1965. "Normal crimes: Sociological features of the penal code in a public defender office." *Social Problems* (Winter):255–276.

Suitor, J.J. 1991. "Marital quality and satisfaction with the division of household labor across the family lifecycle." *Journal of Marriage and the Family* 53:221–230.

Sullivan, Teresa A. 1983. "Family morality and family mortality: Speculation on the demographic transition." In *Families and Religions*. William. V. D'Antonio and Joan Aldous, eds. Beverly Hills, CA: Sage.

Sumner, William G. 1960; 1906. *Folkways*. New York: Ginn.

Supreme Court of Canada. 1981. *The Supreme Court Decisions on the Canadian Constitution*. Toronto: James Lorimer.

Surtees, R.J. 1969. "The development of an Indian reserve policy in Canada." *Ontario History* 61:87–98.

Sutherland, Edwin. 1924. *Criminology*. Philadelphia: J.B. Lippincott.

Sutherland, Edwin. 1949. *White Collar Crime*. New York: Dryden.

Swatos, William H., Jr. 1991. "Cultural-historical factors in religious economies." *Review of Religious Research* 33:60–75.

Swinamer, J.L. 1990. "The value of household work in Canada. In *Canadian Social Trends*. Craig McKie and Keith Thompson (eds.). Toronto: Thompson Educational Publishing.

Swinton, Katherine, and C.J. Rogerson (eds.). 1988. *Competing Constitutional Visions: The Meech Lake Accord*. Toronto: Carswell.

Sydie, R.A. 1987. *Natural Women Cultured Men: A Feminist Perspective on Sociological Theory*. Toronto: Methuen.

Sykes, Gresham, and David Matza. 1957. "Techniques of neutralization: A theory of delinquency." *American Sociological Review* 22:664–670.

Symons, G.L. 1986. "Careers and self-concepts: Managerial women in French and English Canada." In *Work in the Canadian Context*. Katherina L.P. Lundy and Barbara Warme, eds. 2nd edition. Toronto: Butterworths.

Synge, Janet. 1977. "The sex factor in social selection processes in Canadian education." In *Education, Change and Society*. Richard Carlton et al., eds. Toronto: Gage.

Synge, Janet. 1980. "Work and family support patterns of the aged in the early twentieth century." In *Aging in Canada: Social Perspectives*. Victor W. Marshall, ed. Toronto: Fitzhenry and Whiteside.

Szelenyi, Ivan. 1972. *Social Structure and the Housing System. (Tarsadalm: Struktura es Lakastrendszer.)* Budapest: Kandidatusi eretekezes.

Szelenyi, Ivan. 1981. "Structural changes and alternatives to capitalist development in the contemporary urban and regional system."

Talbott, Strobe. 1992. "Why the people cheer the bad guys in a coup." *Time* (May 4):45.

Tannenbaum, Frank. 1938. *Crime and the Community.* Boston: Ginn.

Tanner, Julian, and Harvey Krahn. 1991. "Part-time work and deviance among high-school seniors." *Canadian Journal of Sociology* 16:281–302.

Tasch, R.J. 1952. "The role of the father in the family." *Journal of Experimental Education*, 20, 319–361.

Tasch, R.J. 1955. "Interpersonal perceptions of fathers and mothers." *Journal of Genetic Psychology*, 87, 59–65.

Task Force on Canadian Unity. 1978. *Report.* Ottawa: Information Canada.

Tauber, M.A. 1979. "Sex differences in parent–child interaction styles during a free-play session." *Child Development*, 50, 981–988.

Tavris, Carol. 1988. "Beyond cartoon killings: Comments on two overlooked effects of television." In *Television as a Social Issue*. Stuart Oskamp, ed. Newbury Park, CA: Sage.

Tavris, Carol. 1992. *The Mismeasure of Women.* New York: Simon & Schuster.

Tavris, Carol, and Carole Wade. 1984. *The Longest War.* 2nd edition. San Diego, CA: Harcourt Brace Jovanovich.

Taylor, Frederick W. 1947; 1911. *Scientific Management.* New York: Harper and Row.

Taylor, Ian, Paul Walton, and Jock Young. 1973. *The New Criminology: For a Social Theory of Deviance.* London: Routledge and Kegan Paul.

Taylor, Ian, Paul Walton, and Jock Young (eds.). 1975. *Critical Criminology.* London: Routledge and Kegan Paul.

Taylor, Norman W. 1964. "The French-Canadian industrial entrepreneur and his social environment." In *French-Canadian Society* (Vol. 1) M. Rioux and Y. Martin, eds. Toronto: McClelland and Stewart.

Taylor, W. 1985. *Hormonal Manipulation: A New Era of Monstrous Athletes.* Jefferson, NC: McFarland.

Teitelbaum, M.S. 1975. "Relevance of demographic transition theory for developing countries." *Science* 188:420–425.

Tepperman, Lorne. 1975. *Social Mobility in Canada.* Toronto: McGraw-Hill Ryerson.

Terry, C., and M. Pellens. 1970. *The Opium Problem.* Montclair, NJ: Patterson Smith.

Theberge, Nancy. 1989. "Women's athletics and the myth of female frailty." In *Women: A Feminist Perspective*. Jo Freeman, ed. 4th edition. Mountain View, CA: Mayfield.

Thomas, Kauser, and Andrew Wister. 1984. "Living arrangements of older women: The ethnic dimension." *Journal of Marriage and the Family* 46:301–311.

Thomas, W.I. 1928. *The Child in America.* New York: Knopf.

Thomlinson, Ralph. 1965. *Population Dynamics: Causes and Consequences of World Demographic Change.* New York: Random House.

Thompson, Hunter. 1968. *Hell's Angels.* New York: Ballantine.

Thompson, James D. 1967. *Organization in Action.* New York: McGraw-Hill.

Thompson, Warren, and David Lewis. 1965. *Population Problems.* 5th edition. New York: McGraw-Hill.

Thorburn, Hugh G. (ed.). 1985. *Party Politics in Canada.* 5th ed. Scarborough, Ontario: Prentice-Hall Canada, Inc.

Thorndike, E.L. 1898. *Animal Intelligence.* New York: Macmillan.

Thorndike, E.L. 1913. *The Psychology of Learning.* New York: Columbia University.

Thorne, Barrie. 1983. "An analysis of gender and social groupings." In *Feminist Frontiers: Rethinking Sex, Gender, and Society*. Laurel Richardson and Verta Taylor, eds. Reading, MA: Addison-Wesley.

Thorne, Barrie, with Marilyn Yalom (eds.) 1982. *Rethinking the Family: Some Feminist Questions.* New York: Longman.

Thornton, A. 1989. "Changing attitudes about family issues in the United States." *Journal of Marriage and the Family* 51:873–895.

Thornton, Arland, Duane F. Alwin, and Donald Camburn. 1983. "Causes and consequences of sex-role attitudes and attitude change." *American Sociological Review* 48:211–227.

Thrasher, Frederic. 1927. *The Gang.* Chicago: University of Chicago Press.

Thurow, Lester. 1975. *Generating Inequality.* New York: Basic.

Tiano, Susan. 1987. "Gender, work, and world capitalism: Third World women's role in development." In *Analyzing Gender: A Handbook of Social Science Research*. Beth B. Hess and Myra Marx Ferree (eds.). Newbury Park, California: Sage Publications.

Tibbets, Paul. 1982. "The positivism–humanism debate in sociology: A reconstruction." *Sociological Inquiry* 52, 184–199.

Tienhaara, Nancy. 1974. *Canadian Views on Immigration and Population: An Analysis of Post-War Gallup Polls.* Ottawa: Manpower and Immigration.

Tierney, J. 1990. "Betting the planet." *New York Times Magazine* (Dec. 2):52.

Tillich, Paul. 1966. *On the Boundary.* New York: Scribner's.

Tilly, Charles. 1974. "Ecological triangle." In *An Urban World.* C. Tilly, ed. Boston: Little, Brown.

Tilly, Charles. 1976a. *Sociology, history and the origins of the European proletariat.* Working paper 148. Ann Arbor, MI: University of Michigan, Center for Research on Social Organization.

Tilly, Charles. 1976b. "A travers le chaos des vivantes cités." In *Urbanism, Urbanization and Change.* P. Meadows and E. Mizurchi, eds. 2nd edition. Reading, MA: Addison-Wesley.

Tilly, Charles. 1978. *From Mobilization to Revolution.* Reading, MA: Addison-Wesley.

Tilly, Charles. 1981. *The Urban Historian's Dilemma: Faceless Cities or Cities Without Hinterlands?* Working paper 248. Ann Arbor, MI: University of Michigan, Center for Research on Social Organization.

Tilquin, C., et al. 1980. "The physical, emotional, and social condition of an aged population in Quebec." In *Aging in Canada: Social Perspectives.* Victor W. Marshall, ed. Toronto: Fitzhenry and Whiteside.

Timberlake, James. 1963. *Prohibition and the Progressive Movement: 1900–1920.* Cambridge, MA: Harvard.

Time. 1992a. "The fire this time." *Time* (May 11):22–29.

Time. 1992b. "Lessons of Los Angeles." *Time* (May 18):34–35.

Tinbergen, Jan. 1976. *Reshaping the International Order.* New York: Dutton.

Tindale, Joseph A. 1980. "Identity maintenance processes of old poor men." In *Aging in Canada: Social Perspectives.* Victor W. Marshall, ed. Toronto: Fitzhenry and Whiteside.

Tindale, Joseph A. 1987. "Age, seniority, and class patterns of job strain." In *Aging in Canada: Social Perspectives.* Victor W. Marshall, ed. 2nd edition. Toronto: Fitzhenry and Whiteside.

Tindale, Joseph A., and Victor W. Marshall. 1980. "A general conflict perspective for gerontology." In *Aging in Canada: social Perspectives.* Victor W. Marshall, ed. Toronto: Fitzhenry and Whiteside.

Tittle, C.R., W.J. Villemez, and D. Smith. 1978. "The myth of social class and criminality: An empirical assessment of the empirical evidence." *American Sociological Review* 43:643–656.

Tittle, Charles R., and Robert F. Meier. 1990. "Specifying the SES delinquency relationship." *Criminology* 28:271–299.

Tobin, Sheldon S., and Regina Kulys. 1980. "The family and services." In *Annual Review of Gerontology and Geriatrics* (Vol. 1). Carl Eisdorfer, ed. New York: Springer.

Toby, Jackson. 1974. "The socialization and control of deviant motivation." In *Handbook of Criminology.* Daniel Glaser, ed. Chicago: Rand McNally.

Toffler, Alvin. 1970. *Future Shock.* New York: Random House.

Toffler, Alvin. 1982. *The Third Wave.* New York: Bantam.

Tomkins, G.S. 1986. *A Common Countenance: Stability and Change in the Canadian Curriculum.* Scarborough, ON: Prentice-Hall.

Toner, Robin. 1992. "New politics of welfare focuses on its flaws." *New York Times,* July 5, p. 16L.

Tönnies, Ferdinand. 1957; 1887. *Community and Society (Gemeinschaft und gesellschaft)* New York: Harper Torch.

Torrance, Judy M. 1986. *Public Violence in Canada, 1867–1982.* Kingston and Montreal: McGill-Queen's University Press.

Touraine, Alain. 1971. *The Post-Industrial Society: Tomorrow's Social History; Classes, Conflicts and Culture in the Programmed Society.* New York: Random House.

Treaster, Joseph B. 1989. "Arrest of oil union chief in Mexico sets off strike." *The New York Times* (Jan. 12): A1.

Treiman, Donald. 1977. *Occupational Prestige in Comparative Perspective.* New York: Academic.

Tresemer, Davis. 1975. "Assumptions made about gender roles." In *Another Voice: Feminist Perspectives on Social Life and Social Sciences.* Marcia Millman and Rosabeth Moss Kanter, eds. Garden City, NY: Doubleday Anchor.

Trigger, Bruce G. 1969. *The Huron: Farmers of the North.* New York: Holt, Rinehart and Winston.

Trist, E.L., and K.W. Bamforth. 1951. "Some social and psychological consequences of the Longwall method of coal getting." *Human Relations* 4:3–38.

Troeltsch, Ernest. 1931. *The Social Teaching of the Christian Churches* (2 vols.). New York: Macmillan.

Trow, Martin. 1961. "The second transformation of American secondary education." *International Journal of Comparative Sociology* 2:144–165.

Tsui, Amy Ong, and Donald J. Bogue. 1978. "Declining world fertility: Trends, causes, implications." *Population Bulletin* 33(4). Washington, DC: Population Reference Bureau.

Tuan, Yi-Fu. 1974. *Topophilia: A Study of Environmental Perception Attitudes and Values.* Englewood Cliffs, NJ: Prentice-Hall.

Tuchman, Gaye. 1978. "Introduction: The symbolic annihilation of women by the mass media." In *Hearth and Home: Images of Women in the Mass Media.* G. Tuchman, Arlene Kaplan Daniels, and James Benet, eds. New York: Oxford University Press.

Tuchman, Gaye. 1979. "Women's depiction in the mass media." *Signs* 4:528–542.

Tucker, M.B., and C. Mitchell-Kernan. 1990. "New trends in black American interracial marriage: The social structural context." *Journal of Marriage and the Family* 52:209–218.

Tucker, Richard D., Larry C. Mullins, François Béland, Charles F. Longino, Jr., and Victor W. Marshall. 1992. "Older Canadians in Florida: A comparison of anglophone and francophone seasonal migrants." *Canadian Journal on Aging* 11(3):281–297.

Tumin, M. 1967. *School Stratification: The Form and Functions of Inequality.* Englewood Cliffs, NJ: Prentice-Hall.

Turk, Austin. 1969. *Criminality and the Legal Order.* Chicago: Rand McNally.

Turner, Jonathan. 1990. "The past present and future of theory" in *American Sociology in Frontiers of Social Theory: The New Synthesis.* G. Ritzer (ed.) New York: Columbia University Press. 371–391.

Turner, Ralph H. 1961. "Modes of social ascent through education: Sponsored and contest mobility." In *Education, Economy, and Society.* A.H. Halsey, ed. Glencoe, IL: Free Press.

Turner, Ralph H. 1962. "Role-taking: Process versus conformity." In *Human Behavior and Social Processes: An Interactionist Approach.* Arnold M. Rose, ed. Boston: Houghton Mifflin.

Turner, Ralph H., and Lewis M. Killian. 1972. *Collective Behavior.* Englewood Cliffs, NJ: Prentice-Hall.

Turner, Stephen Park, and Johnathan H. Turner. 1990. *The Impossible Science: An Institutional Analysis of American Sociology.* Newbury Park: Sage Publications.

Turrittin, Anton H., Paul Anisef, and Neil J. MacKinnon. 1983. "Gender differences in educational achievement: A study of social inequality." *Canadian Journal of Sociology* 8:395–419.

Tyack, D. 1974. *One Best System.* Cambridge, MA: Harvard University Press.

Tyree, A., et al. 1979. "Gaps and glissandos: Inequality, economic development, and social mobility." *American Sociological Review* 44:410–424.

Uhlenberg, Peter. 1980. "Death and the family." *Journal of Family History* 5:313–320.

Ujimoto, K. Victor. 1987. "The ethnic dimension of aging in Canada." In *Aging in Canada: Social Perspectives.* Victor W. Marshall, ed. 2nd edition. Toronto: Fitzhenry and Whiteside.

Umberson, D. 1989. "Parenting and well-being." *Journal of Family Issues* 10:427–439.

Umberson, D., and W.R. Gove. 1989. "Parenthood and psychological well-being: Theory, measurement, and stage in the family life course." *Journal of Family Issues* 10:440–462.

UNDP (United Nations Development Program). 1991. *Human Development Report 1991.* New York: Oxford University Press.

United Nations. 1984. *The World Population Situation in 1983.* Population Studies No. 85. New York: U.N., Department of International Economic and Social Affairs.

United Nations. 1991. *The World's Women 1970–1990: Trends and Statistics.* New York: United Nations.

United Nations. 1992. *1990 Demographic Yearbook.* New York: United Nations.

United Nations Children's Fund. 1992. *The State of the World's Children.* New York: Oxford University Press.

U.S. Bureau of the Census. 1975. *Historical Statistics of the United States, Colonial Times to 1970.* (Part 1). Washington, DC: U.S. Government Printing Office.

U.S. Bureau of the Census. 1983. *Statistical Abstract of the United States 1984.* Washington, DC: U.S. Government Printing Office.

U.S. Bureau of the Census. 1991. *Statistical Abstract of the United States 1991.* Washington, DC: U.S. Government Printing Office.

Vachon, M.L.S. 1979. "Identity change over the first two years of bereavement: Social relationships and social supports." Doctoral dissertation. Toronto: York University, Department of Sociology.

Vachon, M.L.S., et al. 1976. "Stress reactions to bereavement." *Essence* 1(1):23–33.

Valentine, V. 1980. "Native peoples and Canadians: A profile of issues and trends." In *Cultural Boundaries and the Cohesion of Canada* (Part 2). R. Breton et al., eds. Montreal: Institute for Research on Public Policy.

Vallee, Frank G., and John deVries. 1975. *Data Book for the Conference on the Individual Language and Society.* Ottawa: Canada Council.

Vallieres, Marc. 1988. "Quebec." In *The Canadian Encyclopedia.* 2nd edition. Vol. 3. Edmonton: Hurtig.

Van den Berghe, Pierre. 1974. "Bringing beasts back in." *American Sociological Review* 39(6):777–788.

Van Stolk, Mary. 1983. "A harder look at the battered and abused child." In *The Canadian Family.* K. Ishwaran, ed. Toronto: Gage.

Vaz, E.W. 1965. "Middle-class adolescents: Self-reported delinquency and youth culture activities." *Canadian Review of Sociology and Anthropology* 2:52–70.

Veevers, Jean E. 1980. *Childless by Choice.* Toronto: Butterworths.

Verbrugge, L.M. 1985. "Gender and health: An update on hypotheses and evidence." *Journal of Health and Social Behavior* 26:156–182.

Verbrugge, Lois M. 1989. "The twin meet: Empirical explanations of sex differences in health and mortality." *Journal of Health and Social Behavior* 30:282–304.

Verdon, Michel. 1980. "The Quebec stem family revisited." In *Canadian Families: Ethnic Variations.* K. Ishwaran, ed. Toronto: McGraw-Hill Ryerson.

Vernick, Andrew. 1987. "From voyeur to narcissist: Imaging men in contemporary advertising." In *Beyond Patriarchy.* Michael Kaufman, ed. Toronto: Oxford University Press.

Von Eschen, Donald, J. Kirk, and Maurice Pinard. 1971. "The organizational substructure of disorderly politics." *Social Forces* 49:529–544.

Wadhera, S., and W.J. Miller. 1991. "Patterns and change in Canadian fertility: First births after age 30." *Health Reports* 3:149–162.

Wagley, Charles, and Marvin Harris. 1958. *Minorities in the New World.* New York: Columbia University Press.

Wakil, S. Parvez, C.M. Siddique, and F.A. Wakil. 1981. "Between two cultures: A study in socialization of children of immigrants." *Journal of Marriage and the Family* 43:929–940.

Wallace, Amy. 1992. "Riots changed few attitudes, poll finds." *Los Angeles Times* (Sept. 3):B-1, B-8.

Wallace, James, and Jim Erickson. 1992. *Hard Drive: Bill Gates and the Making of the Microsoft Empire.* New York: Wiley.

Waller, Irvin. 1974. *Men Released from Prison.* Toronto: University of Toronto Press.

Waller, Irvin, and Janet Chan. 1975. "Prison use: A Canadian and international comparison." *Criminal Law Quarterly* 47–71.

Wallerstein, Immanuel. 1974. *The Modern World System.* New York: Academic.

Wallis, Roy, and Steve Bruce. 1984. "The Stark-Bainbridge theory of religion: A critical analysis and counter proposals." *Sociological Analysis* 45:11–28.

Walter, E.V. 1988. *Placeways: A Theory of the Urban Environment.* Chapel Hill, NC: University of North Carolina Press.

Ward, Dawn, and Jack Balswick. 1978. "Strong men and virtuous women: A content analysis of sex role stereotypes." *Pacific Sociological Review* 21:45–53.

Waring, Joan. 1976. "Social replenishment and social change." In *Age in Society.* Ann Foner, ed. Beverly Hills, CA: Sage.

Warnock, John W. 1970. *Partner to Behemoth.* Toronto: New Press.

Warnock, John W. 1974. "Metropolis/hinterland: The lost theme in Canadian letters." *Canadian Dimension* 10(2):42–46.

Warren, Kay B., and Susan C. Bourque. 1991. "Women, technology, and international development ideologies." In *Gender at the Crossroads of Knowledge: Feminist Anthropology in the Postmodern Era.* Micaela di Leonardo (ed.). Berkeley, CA: University of California Press.

Waters, H.F. 1977. "What TV does to kids." *Newsweek* (Feb. 21):62–70.

Watkins, M. 1973. "The trade union movement in Canada." In *Canada Ltd.* R. Laxer, ed. Toronto: McClelland and Stewart.

Watkins, S.C. 1986. "Conclusions." In *The Decline of Fertility in Europe.* A.J. Coale & S.C. Watkins, eds. Princeton, NJ: Princeton University Press.

Weaver, Kent R. (ed.). 1992. *The Collapse of Canada?* Washington, DC: The Brookings Institute.

Webb, Eugene J., et al. 1981. *Nonreactive Measures in the Social Sciences.* Boston: Houghton Mifflin.

Webb, Stephen D., and John Collette. 1977. "Rural–urban differences in the use of stress-alleviative drugs." *American Journal of Sociology* 83:700–707.

Webb, Stephen D., and John Collette. 1979. "Rural–urban differences in the use of stress-alleviative drugs." *American Journal of Sociology* 84(6):446–452.

Webber, Melvin. 1963. "Order in diversity: Community without propinquity." In *Cities and Space: The Future Use of Urban Land.* L. Wingo, Jr., ed. Baltimore, MD: Johns Hopkins University Press.

Weber, Max. 1946. *From Max Weber: Essays in Sociology.* Hans H. Gerth and C. Wright Mills, eds. and trans. Glencoe, IL: Free Press.

Weber, Max. 1947. *The Theory of Social and Economic Organization.* A.M. Henderson and Talcott Parsons, transl. New York: Free Press.

Weber, Max. 1958a; 1921. *The City.* D. Martindale and G. Neuwirth, transl. New York: Free Press.

Weber, Max. 1958b; 1930. *The Protestant Ethnic and the Spirit of Capitalism.* New York: Scribner's.

Weber, Max. 1963. *Sociology of Religion.* Boston: Beacon.

Weber, Max. 1964. *The Methodology of the Social Sciences.* Trans. Edward A. Shills and Henry A. Finch (eds.) Glencoe, Ill.: Free Press.

Weber, Max. 1968. *Economy and Society.* 2 vols. Guenther Roth and Claus Wittich, eds. Berkeley, CA: University of California Press.

Weber, Max. 1969. "Class, status, party." In *Structured Social Inequality.* C. Heller, ed. New York: Macmillan.

Weil, T.E. 1975. *Area Handbook for Mexico.* Washington, DC: Foreign Area Studies of the American University.

Weinstein, Eugene A. 1969. "The development of interpersonal competence." In *Handbook of Socialization Theory and Research.* David A. Goslin, ed. Chicago: Rand McNally.

Weisstein, Naomi. 1971. "Psychology constructs the female, or the fantasy life of the male psychologist." In *Roles Women Play: Readings toward Women's Liberation.* Michele Hoffnung Garskof, ed. Belmont, CA: Brooks/Cole.

Wellman, Barry. 1979. "The community question: The intimate networks of East Yorkers." *American Journal of Sociology* 84(5):201–231.

Wellman, Barry and S.D. Berkowitz. (eds.) 1988. *Social Structures: A Network Approach.* Cambridge: Cambridge University Press.

Wellman, Barry, and Alan Hall. 1986. "Social networks and social support: Implications for later life." In *Aging in Canada: Social Perspectives.* Victor W. Marshall, ed. 2nd edition. Beverly Hills, CA: Sage.

Wernick, Andrew. 1987. "From voyeur to narcissist: Imaging men in contemporary advertising." In *Beyond Patriarchy.* Michael Kaufman, ed. Toronto: Oxford University Press.

Westhues, Kenneth. 1973. "The established church as an agent of change." *Sociological Analysis* 34:106–123.

Westhues, Kenneth. 1975. "Inter-generational conflict in the sixties." In *Prophecy and Protest.* Samuel D. Clark et al., eds. Toronto: Gage.

Westhues, Kenneth. 1978. "Stars and stripes, the maple leaf, and the papal coat of arms." *Canadian Journal of Sociology* 3:245–261.

Westley, Frances. 1978. "The cult of man: Durkeim's predictions and new religious movements." *Sociological Analysis* 2:135–145.

White, James M. 1987. "Premarital cohabitation and marital stability in Canada." *Journal of Marriage and the Family* 49:641–647.

White, L.K., and A. Booth. 1985a. "The quality and stability of remarriages: The role of stepchildren." *American Sociological Review* 59:689–698.

White, L.K., and A. Booth. 1985b. "Transition to parenthood and marital quality." *Journal of Family Issues* 6:435–45.

White, Morton, and Lucinda White. 1962. *The Intellectual versus the City.* Cambridge: Harvard University Press.

White, Terrence H. 1977. *Organization Size as a Factor*

Influencing Labour Relations. Ottawa: Royal Commission on Corporate Concentration.

White, Terrence H. 1978. *Power or Pawns: Boards of Directors in Canadian Corporations.* Toronto: Commerce Clearing House.

Whiteford, Michael B. 1978. "Women, migration and social change: A Colombian case study." *International Migration Review* 12:236–247.

Whitehurst, Robert N. 1984. "The future of marriage and the nuclear family." In *The Family: Changing Trends in Canada.* Maureen Baker, ed. Toronto: McGraw-Hill Ryerson.

Whyte, Donald. 1966. "Religion and the rural church." In *Rural Canada in Transition.* M.A. Tremblay and W.J. Anderson, eds. Ottawa: Agricultural Economics Research Council of Canada.

Whyte, William Foote. 1943. *Street-Corner Society: The Social Structure of an Italian Slum.* Chicago: University of Chicago Press.

Whyte, William Foote. 1982. "Social inventions for solving human problems." *American Sociological Review* 47(1):1–13.

Whyte, William H., Jr. 1956. *The Organization Man.* New York: Simon and Schuster.

Wiest, Raymond E. 1983. "Male migration machismo, and conjugal roles: Implications for fertility control in a Mexican municipio." *Journal of Comparative Family Studies* 14:167–181.

Wilensky, Harold L. 1960. "Work, careers, and social integration." *International Social Science Journal* 12: 543–560.

Wilensky, Harold L. 1961. "Orderly careers and social participation: The impact of work history on social integration in the middle class." *American Sociological Review* 26:521–539.

Wiley, N. 1967. "America's unique class politics: The interplay of the labor, credit, and commodity markets." *American Sociological Review* 32:529–541.

Wilkes, J.W., ed. 1990. *Society and Economy in Mexico.* Los Angeles: UCLA Latin American Centre Publications.

Wilkins, R., O. Adams, and A. Brancken. 1990. "Changes in mortality by income in urban Canada from 1971 to 1986." *Health Reports* 1:137–174.

Willhoite, F. 1976. "Primates and political authority." *American Political Science Review* 70(4):1110–1126.

Williams, John E., and Deborah L. Best. 1982. *Measuring Sex Stereotypes: A Thirty-Nation Study.* Beverly Hills, CA: Sage.

Williams, Juanita H. 1987. *Psychology of Women: Behavior in a Biosocial Context.* 3rd ed. New York: W.W. Norton.

Williams, Tannis MacBeth (ed.). 1986. *The Impact of Television: A Natural Experiment in Three Communities.* Orlando, FL: Academic.

Williams, Thomas Rhys. 1983. *Socialization.* Englewood Cliffs, NJ: Prentice-Hall.

Williamson, Nancy E. 1976. "Sex preferences, sex control, and the status of women." *Signs* 1:847–862.

Willie, C.V. 1991. *A New Look at Black Families.* 4th edition. Dix Hills, NY: General Hall.

Willis, P. 1977. *Learning to Labour.* Farnborough, UK: Saxon House.

Wilson, Alan B. 1959. "Residential segregation of social classes and aspirations of high school boys." *American Sociological Review* 24:836–845.

Wilson, Bryan. 1975. "The secularization debate." *Encounter* 45:77–83.

Wilson, James Q. 1968. "The police and the delinquent in two cities." In *Controlling Delinquents.* Stanton Wheeler, ed. New York: John Wiley.

Wilson, J.D., R. Stamp, and L-P. Audet (eds.). 1970. *Canadian Education: A History.* Scarborough, ON: Prentice-Hall.

Wilson, Robert A., and David A. Shulz. 1978. *Urban Sociology.* Englewood Cliffs, NJ: Prentice-Hall.

Wilson, T.C. 1985. "Urbanism and tolerance: A test of some hypotheses drawn from Wirth and Stouffer." *American Sociological Review* 50(1):117–123.

Wilson, William J. 1987. *The Truly Disadvantaged: The Inner City, The Underclass, and Public Policy.* Chicago: University of Chicago Press.

Wimberley, Ronald C. 1971. "Mobility in ministerial career patterns: Exploration." *Journal for the Scientific Study of Religion* 10:249–253.

Winn, C. 1988. "The socio-economic attainment of visible minorities: Facts and policy implications." In *Social Inequality in Canada.* J. Curtis et al., eds. Scarborough, ON: Prentice-Hall.

Winn, Marie. 1977. *The Plug-in Drug: Television, Children and the Family.* New York: Viking.

Winn, Marie. 1983. *Children without Childhood.* New York: Pantheon.

Winsor, Hugh. 1991. "Canadians cool to proposals for new constitution." *The Globe and Mail* (Nov. 4):A1, A6.

Wirth, Louis. 1938. "Urbanism as a way of life." *American Journal of Sociology* 44:3–24.

Wister, Andrew V. 1985. "Living arrangement choices among the elderly." *Canadian Journal on Aging* 4(3): 127–144.

Wister, Andrew V., and Laurel Strain. 1986. "Social support and well-being: A comparison of older widows and widowers." *Canadian Journal on Aging* 5(3): 205–220.

Wolf, E. 1969. *Peasant Wars of the Twentieth Century.* New York: Harper and Row.

Wolf, Wendy C., and Neil D. Eligstein. 1979. "Sex and authority in the workplace: The causes of sexual inequality." *American Sociological Review* 44:235–252.

Wolfgang, Marvin, and Marc Riedel. 1973. "Race, judicial discretion, and the death penalty." *Annals of the American Academy of Political and Social Science* 407 (May):119–133.

Wood, James L., and Maurice Jackson (eds.). 1982. *Social Movements: Development, Participation and Dynamics.* Belmont, CA: Wadsworth.

Wood, James R. 1981. *Leadership in Voluntary Organizations.* New Brunswick, NJ: Rutgers University Press.

Wood, Patricia. 1982. "The environmental movement: Its crystallization, development and impact." In *Social Movements: Development, Participation and Dynamics.* J.L. Wood and M. Jackson, eds. Belmont, CA: Wadsworth.

World Bank. 1991. *World Development Report 1991.* New York: Oxford University Press.
***World Bank Atlas 1991.* 1991.** Washington, DC: World Bank.
***The World in Figures.* 1987.** Boston: G.K. Hall.
Worklife Report. 1987. 5(5).
Wright, Erik Olin. 1978. *Class, Crisis and the State.* London: New Left.
Wright, Erik Olin. 1985. *Classes.* London: New Left Books.
Wright, James D., and Sonia R. Wright. 1976. "Social class and parental values for children: A partial replication and extension of the Kohn thesis." *American Sociological Review* 41:527–537.
Wrong, D.H. 1961. "The oversocialized concept of man in modern sociology." *American Sociological Review* 26(Apr.):183–193.
Wuthnow, Robert. 1973. "Religious commitment and conservatism: In search of an elusive relationship." In *Religion in Sociological Perspective.* Charles Glock, ed. Belmont, CA: Wadsworth.
Wynne, Derek, and Tim Hartnagel. 1975a. "Plea negotiation in Canada." *Canadian Journal of Criminology and Corrections* 17(1):45–56.
Wynne, Derek, and Tim Hartnagel. 1975b. "Race and plea negotiation: An analysis of some Canadian data." *Canadian Journal of Sociology* 1(2):147–155.
Yinger, J. Milton. 1971. *The Scientific Study of Religion.* New York: Macmillan.
Yoels, William C., and David A. Karp. 1978. "A social psychological critique of 'over-socialization': Dennis Wrong revisited." *Sociological Symposium* 24:27–39.
York, Geoffrey, and L. Pindera. 1991. *People of the Pines. The Warriors and the Legacy of Oka.* Toronto: Little, Brown.
Young, M., and P. Willmot. 1957. *Family and Kinship in East London.* London: Routledge and Kegan Paul.
Yussen, Steven R., and John W. Santrock. 1978. *Child Development.* Dubuque, IA: Wm. C. Brown.
Zelizer, Viviana A. 1989. "The social meaning of money: 'Special monies.'" *American Journal of Sociology* 95:342–377.
Zerubavel, Eviatar. 1977. "The French Republican calendar: A case study in the sociology of time." *American Sociological Review* 42(Dec. 6):870.
Zerubavel, Eviatar. 1981. *Hidden Rhythms: Schedules and Calendars in Social Life.* Chicago: University of Chicago Press.
Zetterberg, Hans L. 1966. *On Theory and Verification in Sociology.* Totowa, NJ: Bedminster.
Zick, C.D., and K.R. Smith. 1988. "Recent widowhood, remarriage, and changes in economic well-being." *Journal of Marriage and the Family* 50:233–244.
Zinn, Maxine Baca. 1990. "Family, feminism, and race in America." *Gender and Society* 4:68–82.
Zinn, M.B., and D.S. Eitzen. 1987. *Diversity in American Families.* New York: Harper & Row.
Zinsser, Hans. 1965; 1935. *Rats, Lice, and History.* New York: Bantam.
Zukin, Sharon. 1980. "A decade of the new urban sociology." *Theory and Society* 9:539–574.

Zureik, Elia T., and Robert M. Pike (eds.). 1975. *Socialization and Values in Canadian Society* (Vol. 1). Toronto: McClelland and Stewart.
Zusman, J. 1966. "Some explanations of the changing occurrence of psychotic patients: Antecedents of the social breakdown syndrome concept." *Milbank Memorial Fund Quarterly* 64(1):1–2.

Photo Credits

Glossary

Absolute deprivations. Structured disadvantages rooted in concrete inequalities of wealth, status, or power.

Absolute poverty. The inability to provide for the essential requirements of life.

Achieved status. A position in a status hierarchy attained by individual effort, such as educational or occupational attainment.

Activities of daily living (ADL). Everyday activities, such as rising and going to bed, personal hygiene, and shopping.

Activity theory. A theory that emphasizes that continuing activity through social roles is required in order to attain high life satisfaction in the later years.

Adult socialization. Socialization that takes place after childhood to prepare people for adult roles (for example, husband, mother, computer technician).

Age-specific birth rate. Incidence of births in a given year per 1000 women of a given age group. The rates are calculated for five-year age groups. For example, the age-specific birth rate for women aged 20 to 24 would be calculated as follows:

$$\text{Age-specific} \atop \text{birth rate} = \frac{\begin{array}{c}\text{Number of births to}\\\text{women aged 20 to 24}\\\text{in a given year}\end{array}}{\begin{array}{c}\text{Mid-year population of}\\\text{women aged 20 to 24}\end{array}} \times 1000$$

Age-specific death rates. Measures of mortality for specific age groups. They are computed by dividing the total number of deaths occurring to persons in a given age group by the total number of persons in that age group.

Age-specific fertility rates. Measures of the rate of child-bearing for specific age groups of women. They are computed by dividing the number of births occurring to women of a given age group by the total number of women in that group.

Age strata. Socially recognized divisions ordered over the life course, with which are associated rights, responsibilities, obligations, and access to rewards.

Age-stratification perspective. A theoretical approach that focuses on the progression of birth cohorts through the age strata of a society and, in addition, view the age-stratification system as changing in response to cohort characteristics and other social phenomena.

Age structure. When pertaining to population, the proportion of people in each age category.

Agricultural society. Society in which at least half the labour force is engaged in the primary sector.

Agricultural surplus. Quantity of food greater than that required to meet the needs of its producers.

Alienation. Individuals' feelings that, as workers, they are small, meaningless parts of an insensitive production system over which they have little control.

Allocation. Process of matching people to positions in the labour force on the basis of their schooling.

Altercasting. Casting the other person in a role we choose for him or her in order to manipulate the situation.

Amalgamation. Process by which groups are blended into a melting pot where none remains distinctive.

American Civil Religion. Tendency for nationalistic emphases in the United States to have many characteristics similar to religions; established Judeo-Christian tradition is drawn upon selectively.

Androgyny. Presence of both masculine and feminine characteristics within individuals of both sexes.

Anomie. Term originally used by Durkheim to refer to an absence of social regulation, or normlessness. Merton revived the concept to refer to the consequences of a faulty relationship between goals and the legitimate means of attaining them.

Anticipatory socialization. Role-learning that occurs in advance of the actual playing of roles.

Arbitration. Process whereby a third party intervenes between management and labour and passes binding judgement on the new collective agreement.

Arranged marriage. Marriage in which the spouses are chosen by parents or other family elders.

Ascribed status. A position in a status hierarchy into which an individual is born or assigned on the basis of inherited characteristics, such as sex or race.

Assimilation. Process by which a group becomes like the dominant group, and no longer remains distinctive. Also referred to in North America as "Anglo-conformity."

Association. Statistical relation between two or more variables. The most common measures of association are *gamma, tau, rho, lambda,* and *r*.

Authority. The ability of an individual or group to have their commands obeyed because they are perceived as legitimate.

Averages. Measures that reduce a set of data to one meaningful value: for example, **the mean**, the **median**, or **the mode**.

Biosociology. The branch of sociology that studies the interaction and mutual influences between the social order and the biological makeup of its members.

Blended family. Type of nuclear family that is based on remarriage and includes children from previous marriages; also known as a *reconstituted family*.

Bloc recruitment. The attraction of sets of supporters already linked by friendship or organizational ties.

Bourgeois democracy. The view held by Marxists that government policies in a capitalist society necessarily favour the bourgeoisie — that is, the capitalist class. This is so even in polities with universal voting rights.

Bourgeoisie. Karl Marx's term for people who own and control the means of production.

Breakdown theory. An approach that attributes social movement formation to disorganization and disorientation caused by rapid social change.

Bureaucracy. A formal organization based on the application of legal-rational principles.

Care orientation. Gilligan's feminine orientation to mortality, which emphasizes concern for and connectedness with others.

Case study. A type of research design in which one or a few individuals (cases) are studied intensively, usually over a long period of time.

Centralized structure. Structure of an organization in which authority and decision-making are concentrated in a few people at senior levels.

Charismatic authority. Authority that is based on the belief that the individual leader is special and possesses some exceptional ability or magic, which inspires loyalty in the followers.

Charter groups. The two original European migration groups (British and French) whose legalized claims for such historically established privileges as the perpetuation of their separate languages and cultures are enshrined in the Canadian Constitution.

Church–sect typology. Framework, dating back to Weber and historian Ernst Troeltsch (1931), that examines religious organizations in terms of ideal-type, church, and sect characteristics.

Circular reaction. A process through which individuals in crowds directly copy one another's excited moods and actions leading to disorderly, irrational behaviour.

City. Large concentration of people engaged in a wide range of specialized and interdependent occupations that, for the most part, do not involve the primary production of food.

Class. A set of individuals sharing similar economic conditions.

Class conflict. Antagonism between social classes, especially between the class that owns the means of production and the classes that do not.

Class consciousness. Categories of people sharing the same economic position who are aware of their common class position and identify with it.

Classical conditioning. Type of learning that involves the near-simultaneous presentation of an unconditioned stimulus (UCS) and a condition stimulus (CS) to an organism in a drive state (that is, a state during which needs such as hunger or thirst require satisfaction). After several trials, the previously neutral stimulus (CS) alone produces the response normally associated with the UCS.

Classical experimental design. Research design that involves the comparison of two equivalent groups at two points in time to determine the effects of an independent variable on a dependent variable.

Class, status, party. For Weber, class is economic, status is prestige, and party is political power. All three are measures of inequality and can vary independently.

Closed class-caste. A society characterized by maximum inequalities of opportunity. There is little or no upward mobility. Positions are assigned by ascription.

Closed system. Theoretical perspective of organizations as relatively self-contained units in which particular structural arrangements and individual behaviour patterns can be accounted for by factors internal to the organization.

Coding. Process of transforming answers in a questionnaire into usable data.

Coercive tactics. The symbolic or actual disruption of institutional routines in order to attract support or exert pressure for movement demands.

Cohesiveness. Conditions whereby individuals identify themselves as members of the group, members want the group to remain together, and group members have a high regard for each other.

Cohort. Group of people in a population sharing a common demographic event (for example, year of birth, or year of marriage).

Cohort (birth). A set of individuals born at approximately the same time, who move through the life course together.

Cohort measures. Measures of the frequency of a given event characteristic of a cohort.

Collective conscience. Durkheim's term for the awareness that the group is more than the sum of its individual members; norms, for example, appear to exist on a level beyond the consciences of individual group members.

Collective good. A benefit available to all members of a group, whether or not they contribute to the cost of gaining it.

Collective religiosity. Religious commitment as manifested in and through religious groups; key to the creation and sustenance of personal religiosity.

Commodity production. Goods and services created for exchange in the marketplace.

Community. Identifiable self-conscious group with shared common interests. Communities may or may not have a territorial base, and they vary in their level of self-sufficiency.

Competition. Action of two or more groups or activities that attempt to occupy the same area.

Concentric zone model. Model of the city in which economic and residential activity patterns and social groups are segregated in concentric zones, with economic activities located at the centre of the city and residential activities located toward the periphery.

Conciliation. Process whereby a third party intervenes between management and labour and makes recommendations regarding a new collective agreement.

Conflict crimes. Acts that are defined by law as criminal and are often severely punished, but are usually regarded as only marginally harmful; typically they are subjects of conflict and debate.

Conflict perspective. A macrosociological view emphasizing that conflict, power, and change are permanent features of society.

Conflict subculture. Illegal group activity that is prone to violence and is common in settings (for example, "disorganized slums") where legitimate and illegitimate spheres are not integrated.

Conflict theories of deviance. Theories that focus particularly on the way dominant societal groups impose their legal controls on members of subordinate societal groups.

Conjugal family. Type of nuclear family pattern characterized by an emphasis on the husband–wife tie and a relative de-emphasis on the wider kin network.

Consensus crimes. Acts defined by law as criminal that are widely regarded as extremely harmful, are severely punished, and are consensually identified as deviant.

Consensus perspective. A macrosociological perspective that stresses the integration of society through shared values and norms.

Conservative perspective on social inequality. Normative theory holding that inequality is necessary, inevitable, and basically just.

Content analysis. Any systematic procedure for examining the content of recorded information; usually applied to the mass media.

Contest mobility. Open competition for elite status.

Continuity theory. A loosely defined theoretical approach that argues that life satisfaction in the later years is enhanced by a continuation of lifelong patterns of activity and role involvement, whether high or low.

Control group. The comparison group that is denied the effects of the independent variable in the classical experimental design.

Convergence thesis. Thesis asserting that the process of industrialization produces a common world culture.

Corporate elite. Those who sit on the boards of directors of the largest corporations and financial institutions.

Corporation. Legal entity created for purposes of conducting business; it has an existence separate from that of its members while providing them with limited liability.

Counter-ideologies. Reformist and radical ideologies that call for changes in the status quo.

Counter-movements. Collective attempts to resist or reverse change or the demands for change made by some other social movement.

Craft union. Formal organization of workers based on their specialized skills. (Also called a trade union.)

Credentialing. Process of giving diplomas and other formal recognition of school achievement, which in turn makes candidates eligible for jobs.

Crime control model. Model of law enforcement that places heavy emphasis on the repression of criminal conduct, because ensuring order is seen as the only way to guarantee individual freedom.

Cross-sectional design. Research design in which two or more groups with varying degrees of an independent variable are measured at one point in time to determine how they compare with respect to a dependent variable.

Crude birth rate. A measure of fertility or child-bearing computed by dividing the total number of births in a given period of time by the total population.

Crude death rate. Measure of mortality computed by dividing the total number of deaths in a given period of time by the total population.

Crude rate. Frequency of an event per unit of the total population, usually 1000. Applied especially to deaths and births.

Cultural convergence. Thesis that advocates that the process of industrialization will produce a common world culture.

Cultural diffusion. The process whereby cultural elements are borrowed by one society from another (as opposed to independent development of these elements in each society).

Cultural infrastructure. Specialized groups with an interest, often economic, in the production and preservation of cultural symbols and the supporting ground rules.

Cultural lag. Failure of one aspect of a culture to keep pace with the changes in a related aspect, such as the failure of social institutions to keep pace with advances in science.

Cultural relativism. The view that all cultures are equally valid and valuable and that each culture must be judged by its own standards.

Cultural universals. Behaviour patterns found in many cultures.

Culture. Shared set of symbols and their definitions of meanings prevailing in a society.

Decentralized structure. Structure of an organization in which authority and decision-making are widely distributed among people at various levels.

Definition of the situation. Beliefs and norms about an interaction setting.

Delinquent subculture. Collective response of working-class adolescents to their failure to satisfy middle-class expectations; the result is an inversion of middle-class values.

Democratic citizenship training. Preparation for political participation in the affairs of a democratic society.

Democratic elitism. Idea that the most important function of mass participation in politics is the formation of a political elite, the members of which compete for the votes of a largely passive electorate.

Demographic momentum. Tendency for future population growth due to a concentration of people in the young ages.

Demographic transition theory. Description and explanation of the three-stage transition or "shift" from high birth and death rates to low birth and death rates as societies become industrialized and urbanized.

Demography. Scientific study of population.

Denominationalism. Tendency for a wide variety of Protestant religious groups to come into being, seemingly reflecting variations not only in theology but also — and perhaps primarily — in social characteristics.

Dependency ratio. Ratio of the economically dependent population (under 15, 65 and over) to the productive population (15 to 64). Calculated as follows:

$$\text{Dependency ratio} = \frac{\text{Population under 15 + Population aged 65 and over}}{\text{Population aged 15 to 64}} \times 100$$

Dependency theory. Theory that the economies of hinterland areas become so specialized in primary industries (such as farming, fishing, or the extraction of raw materials) that trade with metropolitan areas for manufactured goods and services is necessary for the hinterland population to maintain a given standard of living. This places the hinterland in a politically disadvantageous position.

Dependent variable. The variable that research attempts to explain according to how it is affected by some other variable(s).

Descriptive beliefs. Statements or claims about what is, was, or will be, including ideas about cause and effect.

Deurbanization. A decrease in the proportion of a given population inhabiting urban areas.

Deviance. Variation from a norm, made socially significant through the reaction of others.

Differential association. Process by which criminal behaviour is learned in conjunction with people who define such behaviour favourably and in isolation from those who define it unfavourably.

Dimensions of religiosity. Various facets of religious commitment; Glock and Stark, for example, identify four — belief, experience, practice, and knowledge.

Discrimination. Process by which a person is deprived of equal access to privileges and opportunities available to others.

Disengagement theory. A theory that argues that successful aging involves a mutual withdrawal of the aging individual and society. This is seen as functional for the society and beneficial for the individual. Such disengagement is viewed as normal and, ideally, voluntary on the part of the individual.

Dispersion. Statistics that describe the spread in the scores of distribution.

Distributive inequalities. Inequalities in privileges or possessions.

Division of labour. Process whereby general tasks and roles become increasingly specialized.

Dominant ideologies. Ruling ideologies that explain and justify the existing ways of doing things.

Doubling time. Number of years it would take for a population to double its present size, given the current rate of population growth. Calculated as follows:

$$\text{Doubling time} = \frac{693}{\text{Annual rate of growth}}$$

Due process model. Model of law enforcement that emphasizes procedural safeguards thought useful in protecting accused persons from unjust applications of criminal penalties.

Dynamic equilibrium. Parsons's term for the orderly change that constantly occurs among the interrelated parts of a social system.

Dysfunctional. Adjective applied to parts of a social system that disrupt or are harmful to the system.

Edge cities. Self-contained, new suburban cities located adjacent to older cities.

Education. Deliberate, organized transmission of values, knowledge, and skills.

Egalitarian families. Families in which the spouses share equally in power and authority.

Ego. The director of the Freudian personality. The Ego attempts to mediate among the demands of the Id, the Super-ego, and the external world. The Ego, which encompasses the cognitive functions and the defence mechanisms, is governed by the reality principle.

Elaborated language code. Form of communication that makes meanings explicit and universal.

Elite. A relatively small number of persons who occupy the key decision-making positions in an institutional sphere.

Elite preparatory. Stage of educational development in a society: the majority of students do not finish high school, and the function of the high school is restricted to preparing a select group of students for university education.

Emergent norms. Norms that are generated in exceptional circumstances to guide and contain group behaviour.

Empty box view of education. View that schools are passive transmitters for outside influences, with no life of their own.

Endogamy. Marriage rule stipulating that marriages must occur within a defined social group.

Entrance groups. Ethnic groups that are not founders of the country and whose members enter as immigrants after the national framework has been established.

Equality of access. Removal of external barriers to educational participation.

Equality of nurture. Removal or barriers to educational performance.

Equilibrium. In consensus theory, or structural functionalism, the overall balance that exists among the elements in a system.

Ethnic group. Group of individuals with a shared sense of peoplehood based on presumed shared sociocultural experiences and/or similar characteristics. They perceive themselves as alike by virtue of their common ancestry.

Ethnic identity. Attitude of being united in spirit, outlook, or principle with an ethnic heritage. An attachment and positive orientation toward a group with whom individuals believe they have a common ancestry and interest.

Ethnic stratification. Order in which ethnic groups form a hierarchy of dominance and socioeconomic status in a society.

Ethnocentrism. Tendency to use one's own group or culture as the only valid standard for evaluating other cultures, societies, and peoples.

Ethnomethodology. Sociological perspective concerned with the methods people use to carry out their everyday activities; language and meaning; and the implicit norms that govern behaviour.

Exchange theory. A view of social interaction as an exchange of rewards. Individuals are assumed to seek to maximize rewards and minimize costs.

Exogamy. Marriage rule stipulating that marriages must occur outside a defined social group. This rule may be seen as an extension of the incest taboo.

Expectation of life at birth. A measure derived from a life table that estimates the average length of life for persons exposed to a given set of age-specific death rates.

Experimental group. The comparison group that is subjected to the independent variable in the classical experimental design.

Extended family. Family type consisting of two or more nuclear families joined though blood ties — that is, through a parent/child relationship.

Factions. Splinter organizations within a movement holding conflicting views on the degree, nature, or tactics of social change to be pursued.

Family time. Changes that occur within a family as it develops over time.

Fecundity. Physiological capacity of a woman or group of women to produce children.

Federal system. Political system in which entrenched powers are divided between a central government and subcentral governments. In Canada, the latter are called provinces.

Fertility. Actual child-bearing performance of a woman or group of women; an important component of population change.

Folkways. Traditional rules about customary ways of behaving that are informally enforced and of mild concern to society members.

Forces of production. A Marxist term for the resources, both natural and human, and for the technology typical of a particular economic system.

Foreign direct investment. Financial investment, usually by a transnational corporation, in the assets of another country.

Formalization. Process by which the informality of relationships is gradually replaced by varying degrees of rules, codes of conduct, laws, and other means of regulation.

Formal organization. Relatively enduring or continuing social collectivity in which roles and resources are co-ordinated through a division of labour in the use of a technology to achieve a goal or goals. Co-ordination, control, and problem-solving are facilitated through communication, leadership, and varying degrees of written rules and procedures.

Free riders. Individuals who benefit from a collective good without contributing to the costs of acquiring it.

Free trade. Trade between two or more nations that is unrestricted by tariffs, quotas, or other protectionist policies.

Frustration–aggression approach. Approach that makes a direct link between the level of dissatisfaction and the intensity of rebellion it will provoke.

Functional. Adjective applied to parts of a social system that contribute to the overall stability of the system.

Gemeinschaft. Tönnies's term for relatively small organizations characterized by a commitment to tradition, informal social control, intimate interpersonal contact, a collective orientation, and group consciousness.

Gender. Societal definition of appropriate female and male traits and behaviours.

Gender assignment. Designation of a person as female or male.

Gender identity. Individual's conviction of being male or female.

Gender-role attitudes. People's beliefs about the status of the genders and appropriate gender division of labour in the home and workplace.

Gender scripts. Details of a society's ideas about masculinity and femininity contained, for example, in gender stereotypes and gender attitudes.

Gender socialization. Lifelong processes through which people learn to be feminine or masculine according to the expectations current in their society.

Gender transcendence. Ideal socialization goal in which masculinity and femininity are superseded as ways of labelling and experiencing psychological traits. Boy/girl and male/female would then refer exclusively to biological distinctions.

General fertility rate. The incidence of births in a given year per 1000 women between the ages of 15 and 49. Calculated as follows:

$$\text{GFR} = \frac{\text{Number of births in a year}}{\text{Mid-year population of women aged 15 to 49}} \times 1000$$

Generalized other. Mead's "organized community or social group [that] gives to the individual his unity of self." Although the equivalence of terms is not exact, "reference group" is the more modern way of referring to this notion of the organized attitudes of social groups.

Generation. When used in other than the kinship or family sense, the term refers to a cohort, large proportions of whose members have experienced significant socio-historical experiences. Such generational experiences frequently lead to the development of shared generational consciousness.

Gesellschaft. Tönnies's term for relatively large organizations characterized by formal social control, impersonal contact, an orientation to individualism, and little commitment to tradition.

Global economy. Increasing economic interdependence of and integration among all nations, resulting from technological innovations in transportation, communications, and information transfer.

Group marriage. The marriage of more than one man and more than one woman.

Growth rate. Number of people added to or subtracted from a population in a given period for every 100 or 1000 total population.

Hinterland. Rural or nonindustrialized region from which a city or metropolitan area extracts labour, food, and other raw materials.

Holistic model. Perspective asserting that there is no essential division between work and non-work.

Homogamy. Persons with similar characteristics choosing one another for marriage partners. Occurs along two dimensions: personal and social.

Human capital theory. Economic theory holding that the skill level of the labour force is the prime determinant of economic growth.

Human ecology. Application of such ecological principles as competition, invasion, and succession to the scientific study of human behaviour.

Human perspectives. Systems of meaning used to interpret the world without a supernatural referent (for example, communism, scientism).

Hypothesis. Prediction of what you expect to find as a result of research; a statement of the relation between two or more variables.

I. The dimension of Mead's notion of self that is active, spontaneous, creative, and unpredictable. The "I" is a component of a process, not a concrete entity.

Id. The reservoir of inborn, biological propensities in the Freudian personality structure. The selfish, impulsive Id operates according to the pleasure principle.

Ideologies. Emotionally charged sets of descriptive and normative beliefs and values that either explain and justify the status quo or, in the case of counter-ideologies, call for and justify alternative arrangements.

Incest taboo. Rule that prohibits close relatives from marrying and/or having intimate sexual relations.

Independent variables. Causal or explanatory variables.

Indicators. Empirical measures of variables.

Industrial capitalism. Economic system in which productive property (for example, factories) is privately owned and goods and services are produced for profit.

Industrialization. The movement of workers out of the primary sector into the secondary (manufacturing) sector.

Industrial revolution. A series of technological and organizational changes in the process of manufacturing that occurred in Britain during the latter part of the eighteenth century; essential features included machine production, the factory system of manufacturing, and mechanical motive power.

Industrial society. Society in which less than half the labour force is engaged in the primary sector.

Industrial union. Formal organization of non-craft workers based on the private-sector industry in which they work.

Industrial world-view. Outlook associated with industrialization and characterized by empiricism (the limiting of reality to what can be known through the senses) and materialism (the commitment of one's life to the pursuit of empirical reality).

Inequality of condition. Inequality in the overall distribution of rewards (for example, money or prestige) in a society.

Inequality of opportunity. Inequality in the chances available to various members of a society for obtaining resources such as money, prestige, or power.

Infant mortality rate. Incidence of death among children under the age of one in a population.

$$\text{IMR} = \frac{\text{Number of deaths of children under the age of 1 in a given year}}{\text{Number of live births in a given year}} \times 1000$$

Infecund. Term applied to people incapable of producing children.

Infrastructure. Social-services support structure of a society, including health, education, welfare, transportation and communication systems, and justice.

Interests. A basis for individual or group profit, benefit, or advancement.

International division of labour. Process engaged in by transnational corporations, wherein they conduct various operations and produce particular products throughout the world according to strategic corporate objectives.

Justice orientation. Gilligan's masculine orientation to morality, which emphasizes preserving rights and upholding principles.

Lateralization. Functional specialization of left and right hemispheres of the brain.

Laws. Norms that have been formally promulgated by

a legislative body and are enforced by an executive body of government.

Legal-rational authority. Authority based on belief in the legality of formally specified rules and relationships.

Life expectancy at birth. Statistic indicating the average number of years that newborn babies can expect to live.

Life table. Mathematical model used to estimate the average number of years that people of a given age and a given sex can expect to live.

Limiting factors. Variables that can prevent or inhibit change in other variables.

Lobbying. Activities by special interest groups aimed at influencing government legislation.

Longitudinal design. Research design in which either the same group or similar groups are measured on two or more occasions to determine the extent of change in a dependent variable.

Looking-glass self. Cooley's formulation of the self as the interpreted reflection of others' attitudes. It consists of "the imagination of our appearance to the other person, the imagination of his judgment of that appearance, and some sort of self-feeling, such as pride or mortification."

Machismo. A Latin American gender ideology that depicts men as strong, aggressive, physically powerful, arrogant, and devoted to the conquest of women.

Macromanipulation. Use by the dominant group of the major societal institutions — such as law, religion and the military — to regulate thinking and behaviour.

Macrosociology. Study of large-scale structures and processes of society.

Maquiladora program. Border industrialization program instituted by Mexico in which foreign-controlled factories import duty-free components that are assembled by low-wage Mexican workers for subsequent export.

Marianismo. A Latin American gender ideology that portrays women as spiritually and morally superior to men.

Marital power arrangements. Varying arrangements of power between the husband and wife in a marriage. These arrangements include *owner/property* (the husband is legally and in practice the owner of his wife); *head/complement* (the husband is the decision-maker); *senior-partner/junior-partner* (the husband and wife are unequal partners with the husband having more power); and *equal-partner/equal partner* (husband and wife contribute equally to income and tasks).

Marriage. A commitment or exchange, recognized either legally, contractually, or socially, in which reciprocal rights and obligations (both instrumental and expressive) are carried out.

Marxism. A conflict theory that emphasizes the economic basis of social inequality.

Mass terminal. Stage of educational development in a society: secondary education has become universal, but postsecondary education is pursued by a minority only.

Material culture. Physical artifacts or products of a society embodying cultural meanings.

Matriarchal families. Families in which power (authority) is vested in females.

Me. The dimension of Mead's notion of self that represents internalized societal attitudes and expectations. The "Me" is an aspect of a process, not a concrete entity.

Mean. Sum of all of the scores divided by the number of scores; the score each case would have if the variable were distributed equally.

Mechanical solidarity. Feeling of people in primitive societies that they are held together by kinship, neighbourliness, and friendliness.

Mechanistic management. Management style in which duties and responsibilities are precisely defined, communication is filtered upward through a formalized hierarchy of authority, and control is maintained at the top.

Median. Score that divides a distribution into two equal parts.

Megalopolis. Greek term for the most powerful of several cities in a given country or region. The term is now used to describe an unbroken urban region created when the borders of two or more metropolitan areas expand into one another (also known as *conurbation*).

Melting pot. Situation in which the amalgamation and blending of groups have left none distinctive.

Meritocracy. Society in which merit constitutes the basis for social stratification and in which all people have an equal chance to display their talents and to be evaluated fairly.

Metropolis. Relatively large urban area containing a city and its surrounding suburbs. The term has also been used to refer to an industrial region or society that transforms raw materials extracted from its hinterland.

Micromanipulation. Use by the less powerful of intelligence, interpersonal skill, charm, sexuality, deception, and so on to offset the control of the powerful.

Microsociology. Study of small-scale structures and processes of society.

Migration. Movement of people from one geographic locale to another; can be either internal or international.

Ministerial responsibility. Principle that cabinet ministers in a parliamentary system are held accountable for the actions of civil service officials in the departments over which the ministers preside.

Minority group. Ethnic group that is subordinate to another group.

Mode. Score that occurs most frequently in a distribution.

Modernization thesis. An argument that maintains that as societies modernize, aspects of modernization — such as industrialization, urbanization, increased emphasis on technology, and improved health and longevity — contribute to a decline in the social status of the aged.

Modified pluralism. Glazer's and Moynihan's modification of pluralism theory, describing a situation in which numerous groups maintain distinctly different cultures, ideologies, or interests; although they will be changed and modified somewhat, they will not be transformed entirely.

Monogamous marriage. The marriage of one man and one woman.

Moral autonomy. Piaget's later stage of moral thought, in which children over age eight judge wrongdoing in terms of intentions and extenuating circumstances, as well as consequences, and view rules as social conventions that can be changed.

Moral realism. Piaget's early stage of moral development, in which children from four to seven years old judge wrongdoing strictly in terms of its consequences, and believe all rules are immutable absolutes.

Morbidity. Occurrence of illness in a population.

Mores. Traditional rules about how the individual must or must not behave, invested with strong feelings and informally enforced.

Mortality. Occurrence of deaths in a population; an important component of population change.

Motivating factors. Variables that can produce an encourage changes in other variables.

Movement success. The process of institutionalization through which the movement's goals become recognized and routinely enforced by society as rights.

Multicultural. Relating to or designed for a combination of several distinct cultures.

Multiple-nuclei model. Model of a city as several specialized areas located along and connected by major traffic arteries, such as highways. Unlike the concentric zone and the sector models, the multiple-nuclei model does not suggest that zones radiate from the centre of the city.

Multistage random sample. Combination of random samples through several stages.

Multivariate assimilation. Gordon's modification of assimilation theory, which maintains that assimilation is not a single social process but a number of cultural, structural, marital, identificational, attitudinal, behavioural, and civic subprocesses.

Natural fertility. Fertility that is lower than the biological maximum level and results from behaviour not aimed deliberately at reducing child-bearing.

Natural increase. Excess of births over deaths in a population in a given time period.

Naturalist position. View that the scientific method, as used in the physical sciences, can be used to study social phenomena. Facts are established by reliable and verifiable observation.

Negative (inverse) relation. Relation in which two or more variables change in opposite directions; as one increases the other decreases.

Net migration. Difference between the number of immigrants and the number of out-migrants.

Neutralization techniques. Linguistic expression that, through a subtle process of justification, allow individuals to drift into deviant lifestyles.

"New left" movement. A largely student-centred movement in many Western societies in the 1960s and early 1970s that emphasized participatory democracy (in contrast to the state-centred views of what adherents called the "old left"). In both cases, a socialist society was the goal.

Newly industrializing country (NIC). Country that is industrialized with respect to some indicators but not others. Examples include Mexico, Brazil, Taiwan, South Korea, Hong Kong, and Singapore.

New urban sociology. This perspective, which is based on Marxian conflict theory and the dependency model, emphasizes the impact of industrial capitalism on the form of urban areas and the lives of the people they contain.

Noninstitutionalized activity. Nonroutine action taken to promote interests that are not met by society's established institutions and conventions.

Nonparticipant observation. Systematic, objective observation of social behaviour using explicit predefined categories.

Nonrandom samples. Samples in which the probability of elements within the population being chosen cannot be known; easier and less costly than random samples.

Normative beliefs. Ideas about what should or should not be, referring especially to goodness, virtuousness, or propriety.

Normative theory. Any theory concerned mainly with moral evaluation and the question of justice. Can be contrasted with scientific theory.

Norms. Formal or informal rules stating how categories of people are expected to act in particular situations, violations of which are subject to sanction.

Nuclear family. Family type consisting of a married couple and their unmarried children who live apart from other relatives.

Objective class analysis. Measuring social classes based on such factors as occupation, income, and education.

Objectivity. Ability to observe and interpret reality in such a way that subjective judgements and biases are eliminated.

Observational learning. No reinforcement or reward is required for the initial learning to occur. However, reinforcements do influence where and when learned responses that are in the individual's repertoire (for example, swearing) will be performed.

Occupational prestige. Rankings of occupations in terms of their social standing. Indicators of social standing include the power, privilege, income, education, authority, autonomy, and complexity associated with occupational roles.

Occupational segregation. The concentration of one sex in a relatively few occupations in which they greatly outnumber the other sex.

Occupational sex-typing. The societal view that certain occupations are more appropriate work for one sex than the other.

Occupational socialization. Preparation for entering the job market.

Open-class society. A society in which opportunities for social mobility are maximized.

Open system. Theoretical perspective or organizations whereby particular structural arrangements and individual behaviour patterns can be accounted for by a combination of factors internal to the organization and its external environment.

Operant conditioning. Type of learning whereby the organism gives a number of trial-and-error responses. Those responses followed by reward (positive reinforcement) tend to be repeated on future occasions. Those responses followed by negative reinforcement, or by no reinforcement, tend to be extinguished.

Operational definition. Precise set of instructions enabling a researcher to measure indicators that correspond to variables; operational definitions enable different researchers to get the same results when measuring the same phenomena.

Organic management. Management style in which decisions are based on knowledgeable suggestions, communication patterns tend to be lateral as well as horizontal, duties and responsibilities are not rigidly defined, and status differentials are of minor importance.

Organic solidarity. Dependencies among people in developed societies created as a result of a more specific division of labour.

Organization. A collectivity in which people and resources are co-ordinated through a division of labour in the use of a technology to achieve a goal. Co-ordination, control, and problem-solving are facilitated through communication and leadership.

Organizational structure. Patterns of relationships among organization statuses.

Panel study. A type of longitudinal research design in which individuals are identified such that it is possible to measure both individual and group change over time.

Participant observation. Situation in which the researchers take an active part, in varying degrees, in the situation they are directly observing.

Partnership. Joint business venture in which normally all partners experience unlimited liability equally.

Patriarchal families. Families in which power (authority) resides with males and is meted out autocratically.

Patriarchy. A society oriented toward and dominated by males.

Period measures. Measures of the frequency of a given event at one point in time.

Persistence argument. Assertion that religion will continue to have a significant place in the modern world, arguing either that it has never actually declined, or that people can absorb only so much rationality and materialism.

Personal religiosity. Religious commitment at the level of the individual.

Physical trace evidence. Observational data based on accretion or erosion.

Plural elites. Situation in which the elites in each of the major institutional spheres remain sufficiently autonomous to enable them to check each other's power and compete for additional power resources.

Pluralism. Social situation in which numerous ethnic, racial, religious, and/or social groups maintain distinctly different cultures, ideologies, or interests.

Polyandry. The marriage of one woman and two or more men.

Polygamous families. Occur when nuclear families are joined together through marriage ties.

Polygyny. The marriage of one man and two or more women.

Population. Largest number of individuals or units of interest to the researcher.

Population composition. The characteristics of people within a population, particularly age and sex. Also included are marital status, religion, ethnicity, and other characteristics.

Population distribution. The geographic location of people within a population.

Population pyramid. Graphic representation of the age and sex composition of a population.

Population size. The number of people in a given area.

Positive (direct) relation. Relation in which two or more variables change in the same direction; as one increases the other increases, or as one decreases the other decreases.

Postindustrial society. Society in which at least half the labour force is engaged in the tertiary sector.

Prejudice. A feeling (usually negative) toward a person, group, or thing prior to, or not based on, actual experience. Prejudging others without sufficient warrant.

Prestige. Social honour, reputation, or respect.

Primary deviance. Deviant behaviours that precede a societal or legal response and have little impact on the individual's self-concept.

Primary sector. Division of the occupational structure in which employment involves either harvesting or extraction of goods (e.g., agriculture, logging, mining, fishing, hunting, and trapping).

Primary socialization. Socialization that occurs during childhood.

Privatization. Parsons's term for people's alleged tendency to work out their own religious beliefs and associations in an individualistic, autonomous manner.

Production of use-values. Goods and services produced in the home.

Profane and the sacred. Two categories into which Durkheim claimed all things are classified by human beings; the sacred represents those things viewed as warranting profound respect, the profane encompasses everything else.

Professional social movements. Movements maintained by a small, full-time core of activists dependent on the financial donations of unrelated sympathizers or outside agencies.

Proportional representation. Electoral system in which each party is allotted seats according to the percentage of the popular vote it receives.

Protestant Ethic. Term (associated with Weber) that refers to the emphasis placed by Calvin, Luther, and other leaders of the Protestant Reformation on the importance of work performed well as an indication of living one's life "to the glory of God"; key characteristics include diligence, frugality, and rational use of time.

Protestant work ethic. Ideology that states (1) work is service to God; (2) one's duty is to work hard; and (3) success in work is measured by money and property.

Public-sector union. Formal organization of workers employed in some type of government enterprise.

Quota sample. Sample with the same proportion of certain characteristics as found in the population; the non-random equivalent of a stratified random sample.

Race. Arbitrary biological grouping of people on the basis of physical traits.

Radical movement. A social movement that seeks to overturn and replace the established social order.

Radical perspective on social inequality. Normative theory holding that inequality is unnecessary and unjust.

Random samples. Samples in which each element within the population has an equal chance of appearing; also called *probability samples*.

Rate of natural increase. A measure of population growth based on the difference between the birth rate and the death rate. The measure can be computed by subtracting the crude death rate from the crude birth rate.

Refined rate. Frequency of an event per unit of population, usually 1000, that are exposed to the risk of experiencing that event.

Reformist movement. A social movement that seeks some adjustment in society while maintaining the overall system.

Regional mosaic. Distinctive ethnic patterns formed by the various regions of a country that have different combinations of linguistic and cultural groups.

Relative deprivation. A feeling of unfairness provoked by a gap between the rewards that people expect to receive and those they actually do receive.

Relative poverty. The poor have fewer resources than others. Economic deprivation compared with other individuals or groups.

Reliability. Consistency of results over time or with several investigators.

Religions. Systems of meaning used to interpret the world that have a supernatural referent (for example, Christianity, Hinduism, astrology).

Replication. Systematic repeated measurement of a given relationship.

Research design. A plan for conducting research in order to reduce measurement error and eliminate competing alternative explanations.

Reserve army of labour. According to conflict theorists, women constitute a flexible labour supply, drawn into the labour market when needed, and sent home when the need is past.

Residual rule-breaking. Category conventionally called "mental illness" that includes forms of rule-breaking for which society has no specific labels.

Resocialization. Replacement of established attitudes and behaviour patterns.

Resource mobilization. The process of attracting, co-ordinating, and applying resources toward a collective goal.

Restricted language code. Form of communication that leaves meanings implicit.

Retreatist subculture. Group-supported forms of escapist behaviour, particularly drug abuse, that result from failure in both legitimate and illegitimate spheres of activity.

Role-taking. Process of imaginatively putting yourself in the role of another and seeing the world from that person's perspective.

Ruling class concept. Idea that the economically dominant class has the overriding influence on government policies; a central tenet of Marxist theory.

Safety in numbers. A factor, operative in large gatherings, whereby the larger the crowd, the less the blame for disorder is likely to be attached to any one person, allowing a potentially rational base for disorder.

Sample. Smaller representation of a population or universe; properties of the sample are studied to gain information about the whole.

Science. Systematic methods by which reliable, empirical knowledge is obtained. Also refers to the actual body of knowledge obtained by these methods. See also **naturalist position**.

Scientific beliefs. Thoughts about what actually exists (or could exist) that are felt to be consistent with what is known about empirical reality. Can be contrasted with value judgements and normative theories.

Scientific law. A hypothesis that has been repeatedly supported by empirical tests.

Scientific management. Taylor's term for achieving perfection in productivity by finding the one best way to do each and every task.

Secondary deviance. Deviant behaviours that follow a societal or legal response and involve a transformation of the individual's self-concept.

Secondary sector. Division of the occupational structure in which employment involves the transformation of raw materials into semifinished or finished manufactured goods. The secondary sector includes all manufacturing and construction industries.

Sector model. Model of a city as a series of wedge-shaped sectors radiating from the centre of the city, each containing different activities or land uses and separated from each other by major traffic arteries or natural boundaries.

Secularization argument. Assertion that religion as it has been traditionally known is declining continuously and irreversibly.

Segmental model. A perspective asserting that there is an essential division between work and non-work.

Segregation. Separation or isolation of a race, class, or ethnic group by forced or voluntary residence.

Selection theory. Viewpoint that relationships between the physical environment and behaviour reflect the migration or movement of people with particular characteristics to particular places.

Selective incentives. Personal rewards that are available only to individuals who contribute to a collective cause, not to free riders.

Self-report surveys. Paper-and-pencil questionnaires used with adolescents and adults to obtain first-person accounts of amounts and types of deviant behaviour.

Self-selected marriage. Marriage in which individuals choose for themselves whom they will marry.

Sensitization. Process by which subjects become aware that they are being studied.

Sex. The physiological differences between females and males.

Sex ratio. Number of males per 100 females in a population.

Significant other. The particular individuals whose standpoint the child adopts in responding to himself or herself during Mead's play stage.

Single-member plurality system. Electoral system in which the candidate with the most votes wins the seat in each constituency, and the number of seats won by each political party is determined on a constituency-by-constituency basis.

Social action. Occurs between two individuals when each person takes into account the other's actions.

Social clock. Socially shared expectations about the normal or appropriate timing and sequence of events over the life course. For example, people may see themselves as making slow or rapid career progress compared to general expectations, or they may see themselves as "delaying" marriage or parenthood.

Social democracy. Normative theory of inequality holding that ownership consists of a divisible bundle of rights and that satisfactory progress toward equality can be achieved through nonviolent, gradual reform within the political institutions of democratic capitalist societies.

Social deviations. Noncriminal variations from social norms that are nonetheless subject to frequent official control.

Social distance. In contrast to social nearness, Simmel defines social distance as ecological, emotional, and social detachment from others.

Social diversions. Variations of lifestyle, including fads and fashions of appearance and behaviour.

Social-exchange perspective. Set of propositions that relates people's interactions to the level of satisfying outcomes they experience and that specifies the consequences of these outcomes.

Social facts. Durkheim's term to indicate things that are external to, and constraining upon, the individual.

Social incentives. The built-in rewards and penalties solidary groups have available to assure that individual members act in a group-oriented way.

Social inequality. Situation in which various members of a society have unequal amounts of socially valued resources (for example, money or power) and unequal opportunities to obtain them.

Socialization. Complex learning process through which individuals develop selfhood and acquire the knowledge, skills, and motivations required to participate in social life.

Social mobility. Upward or downward movement of individuals or groups into different positions in the social hierarchy.

Social movements. Collective attempts with varying degrees of formal organization to promote, maintain, or resist social change.

Social perspective. Point of view about society and social behaviour that provides an overall orientation for examining sociological problems.

Social segmentation. A deep break between social groups, in which there are few co-operative ties to bind the groups and separate sets of social institutions to maintain the divisions between them.

Social structure. Factors that are persistent over time, are external to the individual, and are assumed to influence behaviour and thought.

Social system. Within the consensus, or structural-functionalist, perspective, a series of interrelated parts in a state of equilibrium, with each part contributing to the maintenance of other parts.

Social time. Changes occurring in the wider society that have an influence on the family life course.

Sociology. The description and explanation of social behaviour, social structures, and social interaction in terms of these social structures, and/or in terms of people's perceptions of the social environment.

Sole proprietorship. Simplest manner in which to establish a business; the sole owner experiences unlimited liability.

Solidary traits. Social arrangements that integrate individuals to cohesive groups; examples include a longstanding shared identity, friendship networks, and formal organizations.

Sponsored mobility. Competition for elite status on the basis of criteria set by the existing elite.

Spontaneous organization. Temporary co-ordination of individuals and resources that disbands when its task or mission has been completed.

Stable criminal subculture. Illegal group enterprises made more persistent by the protection they receive from persons in legitimate social roles (for example, politicians and police).

Standard deviation (SD). Measure of dispersion based on deviations from the mean.

Statistics. Actual numbers; and the theories and techniques used to manipulate data.

Status. Culturally defined position in society, consisting of ideas about rights and obligations.

Status attainment models. Models of the determinants of achievement in the labour force based on regression models, which include individual models such as social class, status, schooling, intelligence, aspirations, and achievement.

Status quo. The existing state of affairs.

Status socialization. Process of teaching people to accept their position in the social stratification system. Includes two components: *ambition regulation* and *legitimation*.

Stem family. A three-generational family in which one son, upon marriage, remains in the parental home, along with his wife and children.

Stereotype. Folk beliefs about the attributes characterizing a social category (the genders, ethnic groups) on which there is substantial agreement.

Stratified random sample. Series of random samples designed to represent some population characteristic.

Structural-functional perspective. A perspective that stresses what parts of the system do for the system. This perspective is usually classified with the consensus perspective.

Structural mobility. Social mobility that occurs as a result of occupational changes.

Subcultures. More or less distinctive beliefs, norms, symbols, values, and ideologies shared by groups within a larger population.

Subfecund. Term applied to people who are biologically able to produce children but, even without using birth-control measures, have difficulty doing so.

Subjective class analysis. Defining and measuring social class based on respondents' perceptions of their own position in the class hierarchy.

Suburbanization. Increase in the proportion of a given population living on the outer limits of a metropolitan area.

Super-ego. The Freudian conscience, or internalization of societal values and behavioural standards.

Symbol. Anything that can stand for or represent something else, such as a word or gesture.

Symbolic interaction. A microsociological perspective that emphasizes the interactions between people that take place through symbols, especially language.

Synthesis. A theoretical approach to the study of social inequality that attempts to use insight from both the radical and the conservative perspectives and attempts to be scientific in its methodology.

Systematic sample. Sample in which the first element from a population is selected at random followed by every succeeding *n*th element.

Task environment. Those elements in an organization's environment that are relevant or potentially relevant to setting goals and attaining them.

Technological functionalism. A perspective that sees rising educational requirements as a reflection of the increased complexity of the occupational structure.

Technology. Application of a body of knowledge through the use of tools and processes in the production of goods and/or services.

Tertiary sector. Division of the occupational structure in which employment involves the provision of services.

Third parties. In Canada, any party contesting an election other than one of the two major parties that have formed the government and the official opposition, changing places from time to time, since Confederation.

Totalitarian society. A one-party state that exercises control over all institutional spheres and mobilizes mass participation in the building of a new social order.

Total fertility rate. A measure of fertility that indicates the average number of children a group of women will have in their lifetime if they experience a particular set of age-specific fertility rates.

Traditional authority. Authority that is based on followers' belief that the monarch has a divine right to rule that is transferred down through eligible descendants.

Transnational corporation (TNC). Enterprise that undertakes foreign direct investment, or owns or controls income-gathering assets in more than one country, or produces goods or services outside its country of origin, or engages in international production.

Treaty status. Certain privileges and obligations passed on to Canada's Native peoples from their ancestors, who signed treaties with the Canadian government.

Urbanism. Set of attitudes, beliefs, and behaviours that are thought to be characteristic of city-dwellers.

Urbanization. An increase in the proportion of a given population inhabiting areas designated as urban.

Validity. Property of measurement whereby what is measured is what was intended to be measured.

Value-free sociology. The position, held by naturalists, that personal judgments and biases can and should be excluded from social observations and interpretations.

Value judgements. Moral or ethical opinions about what is right or wrong, good or bad, desirable or undesirable. Can be contrasted with scientific judgements about what actually exists or could exist.

Values. Cultural conceptions about what are desirable goals and what are appropriate standards for judging actions.

Variable. Factor that can differ or vary from one situation to another, or from one individual or group to another; a concept that has more than one value.

Verifiability. Characteristic of a conclusion or factual statement by which it can be subjected to more than one observation or test.

Verstehen. Weber's term for the subjective interpretation of social behaviour and intensions, usually based on empathy (in German, literally "to understand").

Weimar constitution. Document drawn up in Germany following World War I that abolished the monarchy and established in its place a republic with a popularly elected president and a two-chamber parliament.

Work. Activity that permits one a livelihood. Work includes conventional paid employment, illegal employment, and homemaking.

Index

NAME INDEX

SUBJECT INDEX

Page numbers in boldface refer to glossary terms.

READER REPLY CARD

We are interested in your reaction to *Sociology* by Robert Hagedorn. You can help us to improve this book in future editions by completing this questionnaire.

1. What was your reason for using this book?

   ❑ university course
   ❑ college course
   ❑ continuing education course
   ❑ professional development
   ❑ personal interest
   ❑ other _____

2. If you are a student, please identify your school and the course in which you used this book.

3. Which chapters or parts of this book did you use? Which did you omit?

4. What did you like best about this book? What did you like least?

5. Please identify any topics you think should be added to future editions.

6. Please add any comments or suggestions.

7. May we contact you for further information?

   Name: _____

   Address: _____

   Phone: _____

(fold here and tape shut)

MAIL ➤ POSTE

Canada Post Corporation / Société canadienne des postes

Postage paid
If mailed in Canada

Port payé
si posté au Canada

Business Reply

Réponse d'affaires

0116870399   01

0116870399-M8Z4X6-BR01

Heather McWhinney
Publisher, College Division
HARCOURT BRACE & COMPANY, CANADA
55 HORNER AVENUE
TORONTO, ONTARIO
M8Z 9Z9